FEMINISM IN LITERATURE

A Gale Critical Companion

FEMINISM IN LITERATURE

A Gale Critical Companion

Volume 6: 20th Century, Authors (H-Z)

Foreword by *Amy Hudock, Ph.D.*
University of South Carolina

Jessica Bomarito, Jeffrey W. Hunter, Project Editors

THOMSON
GALE

Detroit • New York • San Francisco • San Diego • New Haven, Conn. • Waterville, Maine • London • Munich

Feminism in Literature, Vol. 6

Project Editors
Jessica Bomarito, Jeffrey W. Hunter

Editorial
Tom Burns, Jenny Cromie, Kathy D. Darrow, Michelle Kazensky, Jelena O. Krstović, Michael L. LaBlanc, Julie Landelius, Michelle Lee, Allison McClintic Marion, Ellen McGeagh, Joseph Palmisano, Linda Pavlovski, James E. Person Jr., Thomas J. Schoenberg, Marie Toft, Lawrence J. Trudeau, Russel Whitaker

Indexing Services
Synapse, the Knowledge Link Corporation

Permissions
Emma Hull, Lori Hines, Shalice Shah-Caldwell

Imaging and Multimedia
Lezlie Light, Daniel Newell, Kelly A. Quin

Product Design
Michael Logusz, Pamela Galbreath

Composition and Electronic Capture
Carolyn Roney

Manufacturing
Rhonda Williams

Product Manager
Janet Witalec

LIBRARY OF CONGRESS CATALOGING-IN-PUBLICATION DATA

Feminism in literature : a Gale critical companion / foreword by Amy Hudock ; Jessica Bomarito, project editor, Jeffrey W. Hunter, project editor.
    p. cm. -- (Gale critical companion collection)
    Includes bibliographical references and index.
    ISBN 0-7876-7573-3 (set hardcover : alk. paper) -- ISBN 0-7876-7574-1 (vol 1) -- ISBN 0-7876-7575-X (vol 2) -- ISBN 0-7876-7576-8 (vol 3) -- ISBN 0-7876-9115-1 (vol 4) -- ISBN 0-7876-9116-X (vol 5) -- ISBN 0-7876-9065-1 (vol 6)
    1. Literature--Women authors--History and criticism. 2. Women authors--Biography. 3. Women--History. I. Bomarito, Jessica, 1975- II. Hunter, Jeffrey W., 1966- III. Series.
    PN471.F43 2005
    809'.89287--dc22
                                            2004017989

Printed in the United States of America
10 9 8 7 6 5 4 3 2

CONTENTS

VOLUME 2

VOLUME 3

VOLUME 4

VOLUME 5

Anna Akhmatova 1889-1966
  Russian poet, essayist, and translator

Isabel Allende 1942-
  Chilean novelist, essayist, journalist, short
  story writer, memoirist, playwright, and
  juvenile fiction writer

VOLUME 6

CONTENTS

When I was a girl, I would go to the library with my class, and all the girls would run to the Nancy Drew books, while the boys would head toward the Hardy Boys books—each group drawn to heroes that resembled themselves. Yet, when I entered formal literary studies in high school and college, I was told that I should not read so much in the girls' section any more, that the boys' section held books that were more literary, more universal, and more valuable. Teachers and professors told me this in such seemingly objective language that I never questioned it. At the time, the literary canon was built on a model of scarcity that claimed that only a few literary works could attain "greatness"—defined according to a supposed objective set of aesthetic criteria that more often than not excluded women authors. New Criticism, a way of reading texts that focuses on a poem, short story, or novel as an autonomous artistic production without connections to the historical and social conditions out of which it came, ruled my classrooms, making the author's gender ostensibly irrelevant. Masculine experience was coded as universal, while women's experience was particular. Overall, I had no reason to question the values I had been taught, until I encountered feminism.

Feminism, sometimes put in the plural *feminisms*, is a loose confederation of social, political, spiritual, and intellectual movements that places women and gender at the center of inquiry with the goal of social justice. When people in the United States speak of feminism, they are often referring to the mainstream liberal feminism that grew out of the relationship between grassroots civil rights movements of the 1960s and 1970s and these movements' entrance into the academy through the creation of Women's Studies as an interdisciplinary program of study in many colleges and universities. Mainstream liberal feminism helped many women achieve more equity in pay and access to a wider range of careers while it also transformed many academic disciplines to reflect women's achievements. However, liberal feminism quickly came under attack as largely a movement of white, heterosexual, university-educated, middle-class women who were simply trying to gain access to the same privileges that white, middle-class men enjoyed, and who assumed their experiences were the norm for a mythical universal "woman." Liberal feminists have also been critiqued for echoing the patriarchal devaluation of traditional women's nurturing work in their efforts to encourage women to pursue traditional men's work, for creating a false opposition between work and home, and for creating the superwoman stereotype that can cause women to believe they have failed if they do not achieve the perfect balance of work and home lives. Other feminisms developed representing other women and other modes of thought: Marxist, psychoanalytic, social/radical, lesbian, trans- and bi-sexual, black womanist, first nations, chicana, nonwestern, postcolonial, and approaches that even question the use of "woman" as a unifying signifier in the first place. As Women's Studies and these many feminims gained power and credibility in the academy, their presence forced the literary establishment to question its methodology, definitions, structures, philosophies, aesthetics, and visions as well at to alter the curriculum to reflect women's achievements.

Once I learned from Women's Studies that women mattered in the academy, I began exploring women in my own field of literary studies. Since male-authored texts were often the only works taught in my classes, I began to explore the images of women as constructed by male authors. Many other women writers also began their critique of women's place in society studying similar sites of representation. Mary Wollstonecraft's *A Vindication of the Rights of Women* (1792), Margaret Fuller's *Woman in the Nineteenth Century* (1845), Simone de Beauvoir's *The Second Sex* (1949), and Kate Millet's *Sexual Politics* (1969) explored how published images of women can serve as a means of social manipulation and control—a type of gender propaganda.

However, I began to find, as did others, that looking at women largely through male eyes did not do enough to reclaim women's voices and did not recognize women's agency in creating images of themselves. In *Sexual/Textual Politics* (1985), Toril Moi further questioned the limited natures of these early critical readings, even when including both male and female authors. She argued that reading literature for the accuracy of images of women led critics into assuming their own sense of reality as universal: "If the women in the book feel real to me, then the book is good." This kind of criticism never develops or changes, she argued, because it looks for the same elements repetitively, just in new texts. Also, she was disturbed by its focus on content rather than on how the text is written—the form, language, and literary elements. Moi and others argued for the development of new feminist critical methods.

However, examination of images of women over time has been fruitful. It has shown us that representation of women changes as historical forces change, that we must examine the historical influences on the creators of literary texts to understand the images they manufacture, and that we cannot assume that these images of women are universal and somehow separate from political and culture forces. These early explorations of woman as image also led to discussions of

femininity as image, not biologically but culturally defined, thus allowing analysis of the feminine ideal as separate from real women. This separation of biological sex and socially constructed gender laid the foundation for the later work of Judith Butler in *Gender Trouble: Feminism and the Subversion of Identity* (1990) and Marjorie Garber's *Vested Interests: Cross Dressing and Cultural Anxiety* (1992) in questioning what IS this thing we call "woman." These critics argued that gender is a social construct, a performance that can be learned by people who are biologically male, female, or transgendered, and therefore should not be used as the only essential connecting element in feminist studies. The study of woman and gender as image then has contributed much to feminist literary studies.

Tired of reading almost exclusively texts by men and a small emerging canon of women writers, I wanted to expand my understanding of writing by women. As a new Ph. D. student at the University of South Carolina in 1989, I walked up the stairs into the Women's Studies program and asked the first person I saw one question: were there any nineteenth-century American women writers who are worth reading? I had recently been told there were not, but I was no longer satisfied with this answer. And I found I was right to be skeptical. The woman I met at the top of those stairs handed me a thick book and said, "Go home and read this. Then you tell me if there were any nineteenth-century American women writers who are worth reading." So, I did. The book was the *Norton Anthology of Literature by Women* (1985), and once I had read it, I came back to the office at the top of the stairs and asked, "What more do you have?" My search for literary women began here, and this journey into new terrain parallels the development of the relationship between western feminism and literary studies.

In *A Room of Her Own* (1929), Virginia Woolf asks the same questions. She sits, looking at her bookshelves, thinking about the women writers who are there, and the ones who are not, and she calls for a reclaiming and celebrating of lost women artists. Other writers answered her call. Patricia Meyer Spacks's *The Female Imagination: A Literary and Psychological Investigation of Women's Writing* (1972), Ellen Moers's *Literary Women: The Great Writers* (1976), Elaine Showalter's *A Literature of Their Own: British Women Novelists from Brontë to Lessing* (1977), and Sandra Gilbert and Susan Gubar's *The Madwoman in the Attic* (1979) are a few of the early critical studies that explored the possibility of a tradition in women's literature.

While each of these influential and important books has different goals, methods, and theories, they share the attempt to establish a tradition in women's literature, a vital means through which marginalized groups establish a community identity and move from invisibility to visibility. These literary scholars and others worked to republish and reclaim women authors, expanding the number and types of women-authored texts available to readers, students, and scholars.

Yet, I began to notice that tradition formation presented some problems. As Marjorie Stone pointed out in her essay "The Search for a Lost Atlantis" (2003), the search for women's traditions in language and literature has been envisioned as the quest for a lost continent, a mythical motherland, similar to the lost but hopefully recoverable Atlantis. Such a quest tends to search for similarities among writers to attempt to prove the tradition existed, but this can sometimes obscure the differences among women writers. Looking to establish a tradition can also shape what is actually "found": only texts that fit that tradition. Traditions are defined by what is left in and what is left out, and the grand narratives of tradition formation as constructed in the early phases of feminist literary criticism inadvertently mirrored the exclusionary structures of the canon they were revising.

Some critics began discussing a women's tradition, a lost motherland of language, in not only what was written but also how it was written: in a female language or *ecriture feminine*. Feminist thinkers writing in France such as Hélène Cixous, Julia Kristeva, and Luce Irigaray argued that gender shapes language and that language shapes gender. Basing their ideas on those of psychoanalyst Jacques Lacan, they argued that pre-oedipal language—the original mother language—was lost when the law and language of the fathers asserted itself. While each of these writers explored this language differently, they all rewrote and revisioned how we might talk about literature, thus offering us new models for scholarship. However, as Alicia Ostriker argued in her essay, "Notes on 'Listen'" (2003), for the most part, women teach children language at home and at school. So, she questioned, is language really male and the "the language of the father," or is it the formal discourse of the academy that is male? Ostriker and others question the primacy of the father as the main social/language influence in these discussions. Other critics attacked what came to be known as "French Feminism" for its ahistorical, essentializing approach to finding a women's

tradition in language. Despite its problems, it offered much to the general understanding of gender and language and helped us imagine new possible forms for scholarship.

The idea that language might be gendered itself raised questions about how aesthetic judgement, defined in language, might also be gendered. Problems with how to judge what is "good" literature also arose, and feminist literary critics were accused of imposing a limited standard because much of what was being recovered looked the same in form as the traditional male canon, only written by women. Early recovered texts tended to highlight women in opposition to family, holding more modern liberal political views, and living nontraditional lives. If a text was "feminist" enough, it was included. Often times, this approach valued content over form, and the forms that were included did not differ much from the canon they were reacting against. These critics were still using the model of scarcity with a similar set of critical lens through which to judge texts worthy of inclusion. However, because later scholars started creating different critical lenses through which to view texts does not mean we need to perceive difference as inequality. Rather, texts that differ greatly began to be valued equally for different reasons. In order to do this, critics had to forfeit their tendency to place literary forms on a hierarchical model that allows only one at the apex. Instead, they exchanged the structure of value from one pyramid with a few writers at the apex for one with multiple high points, a model which celebrates a diversity of voices, styles, and forms. The model functioning in many past critical dialogues allowed for little diversity, privileging one type of literature—western, male, linear, logical, structured according to an accepted formula—over others—created by women and men who fail to fit the formula, and, thus, are judged not worthy. Creating hierarchies of value which privilege one discourse, predominantly Anglo male, over another, largely female, non-Anglo, and nonwestern undermines the supposed "impartiality" of critical standards. Breaking down the structure of canon formation that looks for the "great men" and "great women" of literature and instead studies what was actually written, then judging it on its own terms, has the potential for less bias. Challenging the existence of the canon itself allows more writers to be read and heard; perhaps we can base our understanding of literature not on a model of scarcity where only a few great ones are allowed at the top of the one peak, but where there are multiple peaks.

Another problem is that the tradition that was being recovered tended to look most like the critics who were establishing it. Barbara Smith's essay "Toward a Black Feminist Criticism" (1977) and bell hooks's *Ain't I a Woman? Black Women and Feminism* (1981) argued that academic feminism focused on the lives, conditions, histories, and texts of white, middle-class, educated women. Such writers revealed how the same methods of canon formation that excluded women were now being used by white feminists to exclude women of color. They also highlighted the silencing of black women by white women through the assumption that white womanhood was the norm. These writers and others changed the quest for one lost Atlantis to a quest for many lost continents as anthologies of African American, Chicana, Native American, Asian, Jewish, lesbian, mothers, and many more women writers grouped together by identity began to emerge. *This Bridge Called My Back: Writings by Radical Women of Color* (1981), edited by Ana Castillo and Cherríe Moraga, is one such collection. Yet, while these and other writers looked for new traditions of women's writing by the identity politics of the 1980s and 1990s, they were still imposing the same structures of tradition formation on new groups of women writers, still looking for the lost Atlantis.

Western feminist critics also began looking for the lost Atlantis on a global scale. Critiques from non-western critics and writers about their exclusion from feminist literary histories that claimed to represent world feminisms is bringing about the same pattern of starting with an exploration of image, moving to recovery of writers and traditions, then a questioning of recovery efforts that we have seen before. Now, however, all these stages are occurring at the once. For example, American feminist critics are still attempting to make global primary texts available in English so they can be studied and included at the same time they are being critiqued for doing so. Chandra Talpade Mohanty in "Under Western Eyes: Feminist Scholarship and Colonial Discourses" (1991) argues that systems of oppression do not affect us all equally, and to isolate gender as the primary source of oppression ignores the differing and complex webs of oppressions non-western women face. Western tendencies to view non-western women as suffering from a totalizing and undifferentiated oppression similar to their own "universal" female oppression cause feminist literary critics to impose structures of meaning onto non-western texts that fail to reflect the actual cultures and experiences of the writers. Therefore, to simply add the women from non-western literary traditions into existing western timelines, categories, and periodizations may not fully reflect the complexity of non-western writing. In fact, critics such as Gayatri Chakravorty Spivak, Ann DuCille, and Teresa Ebert argue post-colonial and transnational critics have created yet another master narrative that must be challenged. Yet, before the westernness of this new, transnational narrative can be addressed, critics need to be able read, discuss, and share the global texts that are now being translated and published before we can do anything else; therefore, this reclaiming and celebration of a global women's tradition is a necessary step in the process of transforming the very foundations of western feminist literary criticism. But it is only an early step in the continual speak, react, revise pattern of feminist scholarship.

Some critics argue that the ultimate goal of feminist literary history should be to move beyond using gender as the central, essential criteria—to give up looking for only a woman's isolated traditions and to examine gender as one of many elements. In that way, we could better examine female-authored texts in relationship with male-authored texts, and, thus, end the tendency to examine texts by women as either in opposition to the dominant discourse or as co-opted by it. As Kathryn R. King argues in her essay "Cowley Among the Women; or, Poetry in the Contact Zone" (2003), women writers, like male writers, did not write in a vacuum or only in relationship to other women writers. King argues for a more complex method of examining literary influence, and she holds up Mary Louise Pratt's discussion of the contact zone in *Imperial Eyes: Travel Writing and Transculturation* (1992) as a potential model for exploring the web of textual relationships that influence women writers. Pratt argues that the relationship between the colonized and the colonizer, though inflected by unequal power, often creates influence that works both ways (the contact zone). Using Pratt's idea of mutual influence and cultural hybridity allows, King argues, women's literary history to be better grounded in social, historical, philosophical, and religious traditions that influenced the texts of women writers.

So, what has feminism taught me about literary studies? That it is not "artistic value" or "universal themes" that keeps authors' works alive. Professors decide which authors and themes are going to "count" by teaching them, writing scholarly books and articles on them, and by making sure they appear in dictionaries of literary biography, bibliographies, and in the grand narratives of literary history. Reviewers decide who gets attention by reviewing them. Editors and publishers decide who gets read by keeping them in print. And librarians decide what books to buy and to keep on the shelves. Like the ancient storytellers who passed on the tribes' history from generation to generation, these groups keep our cultural memory. Therefore, we gatekeepers, who are biased humans living in and shaped by the intellectual, cultural, and aesthetic paradigms of an actual historical period must constantly reassess our methods, theories, and techniques, continually examining how our own ethnicities, classes, genders, nationalities, and sexualities mold our critical judgements.

What has literary studies taught me about feminism? That being gendered is a text that can be read, interpreted, manipulated, and altered. That feminisms themselves are texts written by real people in actual historical situations, and that feminists, too, must always recognize our own biases, and let others recognize them. That feminism is forever growing and changing and reinventing itself in a continual cycle of statement, reaction, and revision. As the definitions and goals of feminisms change before my eyes, I have learned that feminism is a process, its meaning constantly deferred.

—Amy Hudock, Ph.D.
University of South Carolina

The Gale Critical Companion Collection

In response to a growing demand for relevant criticism and interpretation of perennial topics and important literary movements throughout history, the Gale Critical Companion Collection (GCCC) was designed to meet the research needs of upper high school and undergraduate students. Each edition of GCCC focuses on a different literary movement or topic of broad interest to students of literature, history, multicultural studies, humanities, foreign language studies, and other subject areas. Topics covered are based on feedback from a standing advisory board consisting of reference librarians and subject specialists from public, academic, and school library systems.

The GCCC is designed to complement Gale's existing Literary Criticism Series (LCS) , which includes such award-winning and distinguished titles as *Nineteenth-Century Literature Criticism* (*NCLC*), *Twentieth-Century Literary Criticism* (*TCLC*), and *Contemporary Literary Criticism* (*CLC*). Like the LCS titles, the GCCC editions provide selected reprinted essays that offer an inclusive range of critical and scholarly response to authors and topics widely studied in high school and undergraduate classes; however, the GCCC also includes primary source documents, chronologies, sidebars, supplemental photographs, and other material not included in the LCS products. The graphic and supplemental material is designed to extend the usefulness of the critical essays and

provide students with historical and cultural context on a topic or author's work. GCCC titles will benefit larger institutions with ongoing subscriptions to Gale's LCS products as well as smaller libraries and school systems with less extensive reference collections. Each edition of the GCCC is created as a stand-alone set providing a wealth of information on the topic or movement. Importantly, the overlap between the GCCC and LCS titles is 15% or less, ensuring that LCS subscribers will not duplicate resources in their collection.

Editions within the GCCC are either single-volume or multi-volume sets, depending on the nature and scope of the topic being covered. Topic entries and author entries are treated separately, with entries on related topics appearing first, followed by author entries in an A-Z arrangement. Each volume is approximately 500 pages in length and includes approximately 50 images and sidebar graphics. These sidebars include summaries of important historical events, newspaper clippings, brief biographies of important figures, complete poems or passages of fiction written by the author, descriptions of events in the related arts (music, visual arts, and dance), and so on.

The reprinted essays in each GCCC edition explicate the major themes and literary techniques of the authors and literary works. It is important to note that approximately 85% of the essays reprinted in GCCC editions are full-text, meaning that they are reprinted in their entirety, including footnotes and lists of abbreviations. Essays are selected based on their coverage of the seminal works and themes of an author, and based on the importance of those essays to an appreciation of the author's contribution to the movement and to literature in general. Gale's editors select those essays of most value to upper high school and undergraduate students, avoiding narrow and highly pedantic interpretations of individual works or of an author's canon.

Scope of Feminism in Literature

Feminism in Literature, the third set in the Gale Critical Companion Collection, consists of six volumes. Each volume includes a detailed table of contents, a foreword on the subject of feminism in literature written by noted scholar Amy Hudock, and a descriptive chronology of key events throughout the history of women's writing. Volume 1 focuses on feminism in literature from antiquity through the 18th century. It consists of three topic entries, including Women and Women's Writings from Classical Antiquity through the Middle Ages, and seven author entries on such women writers from this time period as Christine de Pizan, Sappho, and Mary Wollstonecraft. Volumes 2 and 3 focus on the 19th century. Volume 2 includes such topic entries as United States Women's Suffrage Movement in the 19th Century, as well as author entries on Jane Austen, Charlotte Brontë, and Elizabeth Barrett Browning. Volume 3 contains additional author entries on figures of the 19th century, including such notables as Kate Chopin, Emily Dickinson, and Harriet Beecher Stowe. Volumes 4, 5, and 6 focus on the 20th century to the present day; volume 4 includes coverage of topics relevant to feminism in literature during the 20th century and early 21st century, including the Feminist Movement, and volumes 5 and 6 include author entries on such figures as Margaret Atwood, Charlotte Perkins Gilman, Sylvia Plath, and Virginia Woolf.

Organization of Feminism in Literature

A *Feminism in Literature* topic entry consists of the following elements:

- The **Introduction** defines the subject of the entry and provides social and historical information important to understanding the criticism.

- The list of **Representative Works** identifies writings and works by authors and figures associated with the subject. The list is divided into alphabetical sections by name; works listed under each name appear in chronologi-

cal order. The genre and publication date of each work is given. Unless otherwise indicated, dramas are dated by first performance, not first publication.

- Entries generally begin with a section of **Primary Sources**, which includes essays, speeches, social history, newspaper accounts and other materials that were produced during the time covered.

- Reprinted **Criticism** in topic entries is arranged thematically. Topic entries commonly begin with general surveys of the subject or essays providing historical or background information, followed by essays that develop particular aspects of the topic. Each section has a separate title heading and is identified with a page number in the table of contents. The critic's name and the date of composition or publication of the critical work are given at the beginning of each piece of criticism. Unsigned criticism is preceded by the title of the source in which it appeared. Footnotes are reprinted at the end of each essay or excerpt. In the case of excerpted criticism, only those footnotes that pertain to the excerpted texts are included.

- A complete **Bibliographical Citation** of the original essay or book precedes each piece of criticism.

- Critical essays are prefaced by brief **Annotations** explicating each piece. Unless the descriptor "excerpt" is used in the annotation, the essay is being reprinted in its entirety.

- An annotated bibliography of **Further Reading** appears at the end of each entry and suggests resources for additional study. In some cases, significant essays for which the editors could not obtain reprint rights are included here.

A *Feminism in Literature* author entry consists of the following elements:

- The **Author Heading** cites the name under which the author most commonly wrote, followed by birth and death dates. Also located here are any name variations under which an author wrote. If the author wrote consistently under a pseudonym, the pseudonym will be listed in the author heading and the author's actual name given in parentheses on the first line of the biographical and critical information. Uncertain birth or death dates are indicated by question marks.

- A **Portrait of the Author** is included when available.

- The **Introduction** contains background information that introduces the reader to the author that is the subject of the entry.

- The list of **Principal Works** is ordered chronologically by date of first publication and lists the most important works by the author. The genre and publication date of each work is given. Unless otherwise indicated, dramas are dated by first performance, not first publication.

- Author entries are arranged into three sections: **Primary Sources, General Commentary,** and **Title Commentary.** The Primary Sources section includes letters, poems, short stories, journal entries, novel excerpts, and essays written by the featured author. General Commentary includes overviews of the author's career and general studies; Title Commentary includes in-depth analyses of seminal works by the author. Within the Title Commentary section, the reprinted criticism is further organized by title, then by date of publication. The critic's name and the date of composition or publication of the critical work are given at the beginning of each piece of criticism. Unsigned criticism is preceded by the title of the source in which it appeared. All titles by the author featured in the text are printed in boldface type. However, not all boldfaced titles are included in the author and subject indexes; only substantial discussions of works are indexed. Footnotes are reprinted at the end of each essay or excerpt. In the case of excerpted criticism, only those footnotes that pertain to the excerpted texts are included.

- A complete **Bibliographical Citation** of the original essay or book precedes each piece of criticism.

- Critical essays are prefaced by brief **Annotations** explicating each piece. Unless the descriptor "excerpt" is used in the annotation, the essay is being reprinted in its entirety.

- An annotated bibliography of **Further Reading** appears at the end of each entry and suggests resources for additional study. In some cases, significant essays for which the editors could not obtain reprint rights are included here. A list of **Other Sources from Gale** follows the further reading section and provides references to other biographical and critical sources on the author in series published by Gale.

Indexes

The **Author Index** lists all of the authors featured in the *Feminism in Literature* set, with references to the main author entries in volumes 1, 2, 3, 5, and 6 as well as commentary on the featured author in other author entries and in the topic volumes. Page references to substantial discussions of the authors appear in boldface. The Author Index also includes birth and death dates and cross references between pseudonyms and actual names, and cross references to other Gale series in which the authors have appeared. A complete list of these sources is found facing the first page of the Author Index.

The **Title Index** alphabetically lists the titles of works written by the authors featured in volumes 1 through 6 and provides page numbers or page ranges where commentary on these titles can be found. Page references to substantial discussions of the titles appear in boldface. English translations of foreign titles and variations of titles are cross-referenced to the title under which a work was originally published. Titles of novels, dramas, nonfiction books, films, and poetry, short story, or essay collections are printed in italics, while individual poems, short stories, and essays are printed in roman type within quotation marks.

The **Subject Index** includes the authors and titles that appear in the Author Index and the Title Index as well as the names of other authors and figures that are discussed in the set, including those covered in sidebars. The Subject Index also lists hundreds of literary terms and topics covered in the criticism. The index provides page numbers or page ranges where subjects are discussed and is fully cross referenced.

Citing Feminism in Literature

When writing papers, students who quote directly from the *FL* set may use the following general format to footnote reprinted criticism. The first example pertains to material drawn from periodicals, the second to material reprinted from books.

Bloom, Harold. " Feminism as the Love of Reading," *Raritan* 14, no. 2 (fall 1994): 29-42; reprinted in *Feminism in Literature: A Gale Critical Companion*, vol. 6, eds. Jessica Bomarito and Jeffrey W. Hunter (Farmington Hills, Mich: Thomson Gale, 2004), 29-42.

Coole, Diana H. "The Origin of Western Thought and the Birth of Misogyny," in *Women in Political Theory: From Ancient Misogyny to Contemporary Feminism* (Brighton, Sussex: Wheatsheaf Books, 1988), 10-28; reprinted in *Feminism in Literature: A Gale Critical Companion*, vol. 1, eds. Jessica Bomarito and Jeffrey W. Hunter (Farmington Hills, Mich: Thomson Gale, 2004), 15-25.

Feminism in Literature *Advisory Board*

The members of the *Feminism in Literature* Advisory Board—reference librarians and subject specialists from public, academic, and school library systems—offered a variety of informed perspectives on both the presentation and content of the *Feminism in Literature* set. Advisory board members assessed and defined such quality issues as the relevance, currency, and usefulness of the author coverage, critical content, and topics included in our product; evaluated the layout, presentation, and general quality of our product; provided feedback on the criteria used for selecting authors and topics covered in our product; identified any gaps in our coverage of authors or topics, recommending authors or topics for inclusion; and analyzed the appropriateness of our content and presentation for various user audiences, such as high school students, undergraduates, graduate students, librarians, and educators.

We wish to thank the advisors for their advice during the development of *Feminism in Literature.*

Suggestions are Welcome

Readers who wish to suggest new features, topics, or authors to appear in future volumes of the Gale Critical Companion Collection, or who have other suggestions or comments are cordially invited to call, write, or fax the Product Manager.

Product Manager, Gale Critical Companion Collection
Thomson Gale
27500 Drake Road
Farmington Hills, MI 48331-3535
1-800-347-4253 (GALE)
Fax: 248-699-8054

The editors wish to thank the copyright holders of the excerpted criticism included in this volume and the permissions managers of many book and magazine publishing companies for assisting us in securing reproduction rights. We are also grateful to the staffs of the Detroit Public Library, the Library of Congress, the University of Detroit Mercy Library, Wayne State University Purdy/ Kresge Library Complex, and the University of Michigan Libraries for making their resources available to us. Following is a list of the copyright holders who have granted us permission to reproduce material in this edition of *Feminism in Literature*. Every effort has been made to trace copyright, but if omissions have been made, please let us know.

Copyrighted material in Feminism in Literature *was reproduced from the following periodicals:*

African American Review, v. 35, winter, 2001 for "'The Porch Couldn't Talk for Looking': Voice and Vision in *Their Eyes Were Watching God*" by Deborah Clarke; v. 36, 2002 for "Phillis Wheatley's Construction of Otherness and the Rhetoric of Performed Ideology" by Mary McAleer Balkun. Copyright © 2001, 2002 by the respective authors. Both reproduced by permission of the respective authors.—*Agora: An Online Graduate Journal,* v. 1, fall, 2002 for "Virgin Territory: Murasaki Shikibu's Ôigimi Resists the Male" by Valerie Henitiuk. Copyright © 2001-2002 Maximiliaan van Woudenberg. All rights reserved. Reproduced by permission of the author.—*American Literary History,* v. 1, winter, 1989 for "Bio-Political Resistance in Domestic Ideology and *Uncle Tom's Cabin*" by Lora Romero. Copyright © 1989 by Oxford University Press. Reproduced by permission of the publisher and the author.—*American Literature,* v. 53, January, 1982. Copyright © 1982, by Duke University Press. Reproduced by permission.—*The American Scholar,* v. 44, spring, 1975. Copyright © 1975 by the United Chapters of Phi Beta Kappa. Reproduced by permission of Curtis Brown Ltd.—*The Antioch Review,* v. 32, 1973. Copyright © 1973 by the Antioch Review Inc. Reproduced by permission of the Editors.—*Ariel: A Review of International English Literature,* v. 21, January, 1990 for "Female Sexuality in Willa Cather's *O Pioneers!* and the Era of Scientific Sexology: A Dialogue between Frontiers" by C. Susan Wiesenthal; v. 22, October, 1991 for "Margaret Atwood's *Cat's Eye*: Re-Viewing Women in a Postmodern World" by Earl G. Ingersoll. Copyright © 1990, 1991 The Board of Governors, The University of Calgary. Both reproduced by permission of the publisher and the author.—*Atlantis: A Women's Studies Journal,* v. 9, fall, 1983. Copyright © 1983 by *Atlantis*. Reproduced by permission.—*Black American Literature Forum,* v. 24, summer, 1990 for "Singing the Black Mother: Maya Angelou and Autobiographical Continuity" by Mary Jane Lupton. Copyright © 1990 by the author. Reproduced by permission of the author.—*The Book Collector,* v. 31, spring, 1982. Reproduced by permission.—*The CEA Critic,* v. 56, spring/summer, 1994 for "Feminism and Children's Literature: Fitting *Little Women* into the American Literary Canon" by Jill P. May. Copyright © 1994 by the College English Association, Inc. Reproduced by permission of the publisher and the author.—*The Centennial Review,* v. xxix, spring, 1985 for "'An Order of Constancy': Notes on Brooks and the Feminine" by Hortense J. Spillers. Michigan State University Press. Copyright © 1985 by *The Centennial Review.* Reproduced by permission of the publisher.—*Chaucer Review,* v. 37, 2003. Copyright © 2003 by The Pennsylvania State University. All rights reserved. Reproduced by permission.—*Christianity and Literature,* v. 51, spring, 2002. Copyright © 2002 by the Conference on Christianity and Literature. Reproduced by permission.—*CLA Journal,* v. XXXIX, March, 1996. Copyright © 1966 by The College Language Association. Used by permission of The College Language Association.—*Classical Quarterly,* v. 31, 1981 for "Spartan Wives: Liberation or Licence?" by Paul Cartledge. Copyright © 1981 The Classical Association. Reproduced by permission of Oxford University Press and the author.—*Colby Library Quarterly,* v. 21, March, 1986. Reproduced by permission.—*Colby Quarterly,* v. XXVI, September 1990; v. XXXIV, June, 1998. Both reproduced by permission.—*College English,* v. 36, March, 1975 for "Who Buried H. D.?: A Poet, Her Critics, and Her Place in 'The Literary Tradition'" by Susan Friedman. Copyright © 1975 by the National Council of Teachers of English. Reproduced by permission of the publisher and the author.—*Connotations,* v. 5, 1995-96. Copyright © Waxmann Verlag GmbH, Munster/New York 1996. Reproduced by permission.—*Contemporary Literature,* v. 34, winter, 1993. Copyright © 1993 by University of Wisconsin Press. Reproduced by permission.—*Critical Quarterly,* v. 14, autumn, 1972; v. 27, spring, 1985. Copyright © 1972, 1985 by Manchester University Press. Both reproduced by permission of Blackwell Publishers.—*Critical Survey,* v. 14, January, 2002. Copyright © 2002 Berghahn Books, Inc. Reproduced by permission.—*Critique: Studies in Modern Fiction,* v. XV, 1973. Copyright © by *Critique,* 1973. Copyright © 1973 by Helen Dwight Reid Educational Foundation. Reproduced with permission of the Helen Dwight Reid Educational Foundation, published by Heldref Publications, 1319 18th Street, NW, Washington, DC 20036-1802.—*Cultural Critique,* v. 32, winter, 1995-96. Copyright © 1996 by *Cultural Critique.* All rights reserved. Reproduced by permission.—*Denver Quarterly,* v. 18, winter, 1984 for "Becoming Anne Sexton" by Diane Middlebrook. Copyright © 1994 by Diane Middlebrook. Reproduced by permission of Georges Bou-chardt, Inc. for the author.—*Dissent,* summer, 1987. Copyright © 1987, by Dissent Publishing Corporation. Reproduced by permission.—*The Eighteenth Century,* v. 43, spring, 2002. Copyright © 2002 by Texas Tech University Press. Reproduced by permission.—*Eighteenth-Century Fiction,* v. 3, July, 1991. Copyright © McMaster University 1991. Reproduced by permission.—*Emily Dickinson Journal,* v. 10, 2000. Copyright © 2000 by The Johns Hopkins University Press for the Emily Dickinson International Society. All rights reserved. Reproduced by permission.—*The Emporia State Research Studies,* v. 24, winter, 1976. Reproduced by permission.—*Essays and Studies,* 2002. Copyright © 2002 Boydell & Brewer Inc. Reproduced by permission.—*Essays in Literature,* v. 12, fall, 1985. Copyright © 1985 Western Illinois University. Reproduced by permission.—*Feminist Studies,* v. 6, summer, 1980; v. 25, fall, 1999. Copyright © 1980, 1999 by *Feminist Studies.* Both reproduced by permission of Feminist Studies, Inc., Department of Women's Studies, University of Maryland, College Park, MD 20724.—*French Studies,* v. XLVIII, April, 1994; v. LII, April, 1998. Copyright © 1994, 1998 by The Society for French Studies. Reproduced by permission.—*Frontiers,* v. IX, 1987; v. XIV, 1994. Copyright © The University of Nebraska Press 1987, 1994. Both reproduced by permission.—*Glamour,* v. 88, November 1990 for "Only Daughter" by Sandra Cisneros. Copyright © 1996 by Wendy Martin. All rights reserved. Reproduced by permission of Susan Bergholz Literary Services, New York.—*Harper's Magazine,* for "Women's Work" by Louise Erdrich. Copyright © 1995 by *Harper's Magazine.* All rights reserved. Reproduced from the May edition by special permission.—*History Today,* v. 50, October, 2000; v. 51, November, 2001. Copyright © 2000, 2001 by The H. W. Wilson Company. All rights reserved. Reproduced by permission.—*The Hudson Review,* v. XXXVI, summer, 1983. Copyright © 1983 by The Hudson Review, Inc. Reproduced by permission.—*Hypatia,* v. 5, summer, 1990 for "Is There a Feminist Aesthetic?" by Marilyn French. Copyright by Marilyn French. Reproduced by permission.—*International Fiction Review,* v. 29, 2002. Copyright © 2002. International Fiction Association. Reproduced by permission.—*Irish Studies Review,* spring, 1996 from "History, Gender and the Colonial Movement: Castle Rackrent" by Colin Graham. Reproduced by permission of Taylor & Francis and the author.—*Journal of Evolutionary Psychology,* v. 7, August, 1986. Reproduced by permission.—*Journal of the Midwest Modern Language Association,* v. 35, 2002 for "The Gospel According to Jane Eyre: The Suttee and the Seraglio" by Maryanne C. Ward. Copyright © 2002 by The Midwest Modern Language Association. Reproduced by permission of the publisher and the author.—*Journal of the Short Story in English*, autumn, 2002. Copyright © Université d'Angers, 2002. Reproduced by permission.—*Keats-Shelley Journal*, v. XLVI, 1997. Reproduced by permission.—*Legacy*, v. 6, fall, 1989. Copyright © The University of Nebraska Press 1989. Reproduced by permission.—*The Massachusetts Review*, v. 27, summer, 1986. Reproduced from *The Massachusetts Review*, The Massachusetts Review, Inc. by permission.—*Meanjin*, v. 38, 1979 for "The Liberated Heroine: New Varieties of Defeat?" by Amanda Lohrey. Copyright © 1979 by *Meanjin*. Reproduced by permission of the author.—*MELUS*, v. 7, fall, 1980; v. 12, fall, 1985; v.18, fall, 1993. Copyright © MELUS: The Society for the Study of Multi-Ethnic Literature of the United States, 1980, 1985, 1993. Reproduced by permission.—*Modern Drama*, v. 21, September, 1978. Copyright © 1978 by the University of Toronto, Graduate Centre for Study of Drama. Reproduced by permission.—*Modern Language Studies*, v. 24, spring, 1994 for "Jewett's Unspeakable Unspoken: Retracing the Female Body Through *The Country of the Pointed Firs*" by George Smith. Copyright © Northeast Modern Language Association 1990. Reproduced by permission of the publisher and author.—*Mosaic*, v. 23, summer, 1990; v. 35, 2002. Copyright © 1990, 2002 by *Mosaic*. All rights reserved. Acknowledgment of previous publication is herewith made.—*Ms.*, v. II, July, 1973 for "Visionary Anger" by Erica Mann Jong; June 1988 for "Changing My Mind About Andrea Dworkin" by Erica Jong. Copyright © 1973, 1988. Both reproduced by permission of the author.—*New Directions for Women*, September-October, 1987 for "Dworkin Critiques Relations Between the Sexes" by Joanne Glasgow. Copyright © 1987 New Directions for Women, Inc., 25 West Fairview Ave., Dover, NJ 07801-3417. Reproduced by permission of the author.—*The New Yorker*, 1978 for "Girl" by Jamaica Kincaid. Copyright © 1979 by Jamaica Kinkaid. All rights reserved. Reproduced by permission of the Wylie Agency; v. 73, February 17, 1997 for "A Society of One: Zora Neal Hurston, American Contrarian" by Claudia Roth Pierpont. Copyright © 1997 by The New Yorker Magazine, Inc. All rights reserved. Reproduced by permission of the author.—*Nineteenth-Century Feminisms*, v. 2, spring-summer, 2000. Reproduced by permission.—*Nineteenth-Century French Studies*, v. 25, spring-summer, 1997. Copyright © 1977 by *Nineteenth-Century French Studies*. Reproduced by permission.—*Novel*, v. 34, spring, 2001. Copyright © NOVEL Corp. 2001. Reproduced with permission.—*Oxford Literary Review*, v. 13, 1991. Copyright © 1991 the *Oxford Literary Review*. All rights reserved. Reproduced by permission.—*P. N. Review*, v. 18, January/February, 1992. Reproduced by permission of Carcanet Press Ltd.—*Papers on Language & Literature*, v. 5, winter, 1969. Copyright © 1969 by The Board of Trustees, Southern Illinois University at Edwardsville. Reproduced by permission.—*Parnassus*, v. 12, fall-winter, 1985 for "Throwing the Scarecrows from the Garden" by Tess Gallagher; v. 12-13, 1985 for "Adrienne Rich and Lesbian/Feminist Poetry" by Catharine Stimpson. Copyright © 1985, 1986 by Poetry in Review Foundation. Both reproduced by permission of the publisher and the respective authors.—*Philological Papers*, v. 38, 1992. Copyright © 1992 by *Philological Papers*. Reproduced by permission.—*Philological Quarterly*, v. 79, winter, 2000. Copyright © 2001 by the University of Iowa. Reproduced by permission.—*Quadrant*, v. 46, November, 2002 for "The Mirror of Honour and Love: A Woman's View of Chivalry" by Sophie Masson. Copyright © 2002 Quadrant Magazine Company, Inc. Reproduced by permission of the publisher and the author.—*Raritan*, v. 14, fall, 1994. Copyright © 1994 by *Raritan: A Quarterly Review*. Reproduced by permission.—*Resources for American Literary Study*, v. 22, 1996. Copyright © 1996 by The Pennsylvania State University. Reproduced by permission of The Pennsylvania State University Press.—*Revista Hispánica Moderna*, v. 47, June, 1994. Copyright © 1994 by Hispanic Institute, Columbia University. Reproduced by permission.—*Rhetoric Society Quarterly*, v. 32, winter, 2002. Reproduced by permission of the publisher, conveyed through the Copyright Clearance Center.—*Romanic Review*, v. 79, 1988. Copyright © 1988 by The Trustees of Columbia University in the City of New York. Reproduced by permission.—*The Russian Review*, v. 57, April, 1998. Copyright © 1998 *The Russian Review*. Reproduced by permission of Blackwell Publishers.—*San Jose Studies*, v. VIII, spring, 1982 for "Dea, Awakening: A Reading of H. D.'s *Trilogy*" by Joyce Lorraine Beck. Copyright © 1982 by Trustees of the San Jose State University Foundation. Reproduced by permission of the publisher and the author.—*South Atlantic Review*, v. 66, winter, 2001. Copyright © 2001 by the South Atlantic Modern Language Association. Reproduced by permission.—*Southern Humanities Review*, v. xxii, summer, 1988. Copyright © 1988 by Auburn University. Reproduced by permission.—*The Southern Quarterly*, v. 35, spring, 1997; v. 37, spring-summer, 1999. Copyright © 1997, 1999 by the University of Southern Mississippi. Both reproduced by permission.—*Southern Review*, v. 18, for "Hilda in Egypt" by Albert Gelpi. Reproduced by permission of the author.—*Soviet Literature*, v. 6, June, 1989. Reproduced by permission of FTM Agency Ltd.—*Studies in American Fiction,* v. 9, autumn, 1981. Copyright © 1981 Northeastern University. Reproduced by permission.—*Studies in American Humor,* v. 3, 1994. Copyright © 1994 American Humor Studies Association. Reproduced by permission.—*Studies in the Humanities,* v. 19, December, 1992. Copyright © 1992 by Indiana University Press of Pennsylvania. Reproduced by permission.—*Studies in the Novel,* v. 31, fall 1999; v. 35, spring, 2003. Copyright © 1999, 2003 by North Texas State University. Reproduced by permission.—*Textual Practice,* v. 13, 1999 for "Speaking Un-likeness: The Double Text in Christina Rossetti's 'After Death' and 'Remember'" by Margaret Reynolds. Copyright © 1999 Routledge. Reproduced by permission of the publisher and the author.—*The Threepenny Review,* 1990 for "Mother Tongue" by Amy Tan. Reproduced by permission.—*Transactions of the American Philological Association,* v. 128, 1998. Copyright © 1998 American Philological Association. Reproduced by permission of The Johns Hopkins University Press.—*Tulsa Studies in Women's Literature,* v. 6, fall, 1987 for "Revolutionary Women" by Betsy Erkkila. Copyright © 1987, The University of Tulsa. All rights reserved. Reproduced by permission of the publisher and the author.—*The Victorian Newsletter,* v. 82, fall, 1992 for "Revisionist Mythmaking in Christina Rossetti's 'Goblin Market': Eve's Apple and Other Questions" by Sylvia Bailey Shurbutt; v. 92, fall, 1997 for "The Poet and the Bible: Christina Rossetti's Feminist Hermeneutics" by Lynda Palazzo; spring, 1998 for "'No Sorrow I Have Thought More About': The Tragic Failure of George Eliot's St. Theresa" by June Skye Szirotny. All reproduced by permission of The Victorian Newsletter and the author.—*Victorians Institute Journal,* v. 13, 1985. Copyright © Victorians Institute Journal 1985. Reproduced by permission.—*Women: A Cultural Review,* v. 10, winter, 1999 from "Consorting with Angels: Anne Sexton and the Art of Confession" by Deryn Rees-Jones. Copyright © 1999, by Taylor & Francis Ltd. Reproduced by permission of the publisher and the author. (http://www.tandf.co.uk/journals).—*Women and Language,* v. 13, March 31, 1995; v. 19, fall, 1996. Copyright © 1995, 1996 by Communication Department at George Mason University. Reproduced by permission of the publisher.—*Women's Studies: An Interdisciplinary Journal,* v. 3, 1975; v. 4, 1976; v. 17, 1990; v. 18, 1990; v. 23, September, 1994; v. 30, 2001. Copyright © 1975, 1976, 1990, 1994, 2001 Gordon and Breach Science Publishers S.A. Reproduced by permission.—*Women's Studies in Communication,* v. 24, spring, 2001. Reproduced by permission.—*Women's Writing,* v. 3, June, 1996. Reproduced

by permission of the publisher; v. 4, 1997 for "(Female) Philosophy in the Bedroom: Mary Wollstonecraft and Female Sexuality" by Gary Kelly. Copyright © Triangle Journals Ltd, 1997. All rights reserved. Reproduced by permission of the publisher and the author.—*World & I,* v. 18, March, 2003. Copyright © 2003 News World Communications, Inc. Reproduced by permission.—*World Literature Today,* v. 73, spring, 1999. Copyright © 1999 by the University of Oklahoma Press. Reprinted by permission of the publisher.—*World Literature Written in English,* v. 15, November, 1976 for "Doris Lessing's Feminist Plays" by Agate Nesaule Krouse. Copyright © 1976 by WLWE. Reproduced by permission of the publisher and the author.

Copyrighted material in Feminism in Literature *was reproduced from the following books:*

Acocella, Joan. From *Willa Cather and the Politics of Criticism.* University of Nebraska Press, 2000. Copyright © 2000, by Joan Acocella. All rights reserved. Reproduced by permission.—Aimone, Joseph. From "Millay's Big Book, or the Feminist Formalist as Modern," in *Unmanning Modernism: Gendered Re-Readings.* Edited by Elizabeth Jane Harrison and Shirley Peterson. University of Tennessee Press, 1997. Copyright © 1997 by The University of Tennessee Press. All rights reserved. Reproduced by permission of The University of Tennessee Press.—Allende, Isabel. From "Writing as an Act of Hope," in *Paths of Resistance: The Art and Craft of the Political Novel.* Edited by William Zinsser. Houghton Mifflin Company, 1989. Copyright © 1989 Isabel Allende. Reproduced by permission of the author.—Angelou, Maya. From *And Still I Rise.* Random House, 1978. Copyright © 1978 by Maya Angelou. Reproduced by permission of Random House, Inc. and Time Warner Books UK.—Arenal, Electa. From "The Convent as Catalyst for Autonomy: Two Hispanic Nuns of the Seventeenth Century," in *Women in Hispanic Literature.* Edited by Beth Kurti Miller. University of California Press, 1983. Copyright © 1983 by The Regents of the University of California. Reproduced by permission of the publisher and the author.—Arndt, Walter. From "Introduction: I The Akhmatova Phenomenon and II Rendering the Whole Poem," in *Anna Akhmatova: Selected Poems.* Edited and translated by Walter Arndt. Ardis, 1976. Reproduced by permission.—Atwood, Margaret. From *Second Words.* Anansi Press Limited, 1982. Copyright © 1982, by O. W. Toad Limited. All rights reserved. Reproduced by permission of the author.—Baker, Deborah Lesko. From "Memory, Love, and Inaccessibility in *Hiroshima mon amour,*" in *Marguerite*

Susan. From *In Our Time: Memoir of a Revolution.* The Dial Press, 1999. Copyright © 1999, by Susan Brownmiller. All rights reserved. Reproduced by permission of The Dial Press/Dell Publishing, a division of Random House, Inc.—Brügmann, Margret. From "Between the Lines: On the Essayistic Experiments of Hélène Cixous in 'The Laugh of the Medusa'," translated by Debbi Long in *The Politics of the Essay: Feminist Perspectives.* Edited by Ruth-Ellen Boetcher Joeres and Elizabeth Mittman. Indiana University Press, 1993. Copyright © 1993 by Indiana University Press. All rights reserved. Reproduced by permission.—Bunch, Charlotte. From "Women's Human Rights: The Challenges of Global Feminism and Diversity," in *Feminist Locations: Global and Local, Theory and Practice.* Edited by Marianne DeKoven. Rutgers University Press, 2001. Copyright © 2001 by Rutgers, the State University. All rights reserved. Reproduced by permission.—Burke, Sally. From *American Feminist Playwrights: A Critical History.* Twayne, 1996. Copyright © 1996 by Twayne Publishers. All rights reserved. Reproduced by permission of The Gale Group.—Butler-Evans, Elliott. From *Race, Gender, and Desire: Narrative Strategies in the Works of Toni Cade Bambara, Toni Morrison, and Alice Walker.* Temple University Press, 1989. Copyright © 1989, by Temple University. All rights reserved. Reproduced by permission.—Byerman, Keith. From "Gender and Justice: Alice Walker and the Sexual Politics of Civil Rights," in *The World is Our Home: Society and Culture in Contemporary Southern Writing.* Edited by Jeffrey J. Folks and Nancy Summers Folks. The University Press of Kentucky, 2000. Copyright © 2000 by The University Press of Kentucky. Reproduced by permission.—Callaghan, Dympna C. From "The Ideology of Romantic Love," in *The Weyward Sisters: Shakespeare and Feminist Politics.* Edited by Dympna C. Callaghan, Lorraine Helms, and Jyotsna Singh. Blackwell Publishers, 1994. Copyright © Dympna C. Callaghan, Lorraine Helms and Jyotsna Singh 1994. Reproduced by permission of Blackwell Publishers.—Carmody, Denise Lardner. From *Biblical Woman: Contemporary Reflections on Scriptural Texts.* Crossroad Publishing Company, 1988. Copyright © 1988 by Denise Lardner Carmody. All rights reserved. Reproduced by permission of the author.—Castro, Ginette. From *American Feminism: A Contemporary History.* Translated by Elizabeth Loverde-Bagwell. New York University Press, 1990. Copyright © Presses de la Foundation Nationale des Sciences Politiques, Paris, 1990. All rights reserved. Reproduced by permission of New Directions Publishing Corporation and in the UK by Pollinger Limited and the proprietor.—Chadwick, Whitney. From *Women, Art, and Society.* Thames and Hudson, 1990. Copyright © 1990 Thames and Hudson Ltd, London. All rights reserved. Reproduced by permission.—Chafe, William H. From "World War II as a Pivotal Experience for American Women," in *Women and War: The Changing Status of American Women from the 1930s to the 1940s.* Edited by Maria Diedrich and Dorothea Fischer-Horning. Berg, 1990. Copyright © 1990, by Maria Diedrich and Dorothea Fischer-Hornung. All rights reserved Reproduced by permission.—Chesler, Ellen. From *Woman of Valor: Margaret Sanger and the Birth Control Movement in America.* Anchor Books, 1992. Copyright © 1992 by Ellen Chesler. All rights reserved. Reproduced by permission of International Creative Management, Inc.—Cholmeley, Katherine. From *Margery Kempe, Genius and Mystic.* Longmans, Green and Co., 1947. Reproduced by permission.—Christian, Barbara T. From an introduction to *"Everyday Use": Alice Walker.* Edited by Barbara T. Christian. Rutgers University Press, 1994. Copyright © 1994 by Rutgers, The State University. Reproduced by permission of Rutgers, The State University.—Christine de Pizan. From *The Writings of Christine de Pizan.* Translated by Charity Cannon Willard. Persea Books, 1994. Copyright © 1994 by Persea Books, Inc. Reproduced by permission.—Cixous, Hélène. From "The Laugh of the Medusa," in *New French Feminisms: An Anthology.* Edited by Elaine Marks and Isabelle de Courtivron. Essay translated by Keith and Paula Cohen. *Signs,* 1975. All rights reserved. Reproduced by permission of University of Chicago Press and the author.—Conley, Verana Andermatt. From *Hélène Cixous: Writing the Feminine.* University of Nebraska Press, 1984. Copyright © 1984 by University of Nebraska Press. All rights reserved. Reproduced by permission.—Coole, Diana H. From *Women in Political Theory: From Ancient Misogyny to Contemporary Feminism.* Wheatsheaf Books Ltd, 1988. Copyright © Diana Coole, 1988. All rights reserved. Reproduced by permission of the author.—Cooper, Michaela Bruckner. From "Textual Wandering and Anxiety in Margaret Fuller's *Summer on the Lakes,*" in *Margaret Fuller's Cultural Critique: Her Age and Legacy.* Edited by Fritz Fleischmann. Peter Lang, 2000. Copyright © 2000 Peter Lang Publishing. All rights reserved. Reproduced by permission.—Cott, Nancy. From "Historical Perspectives: The Equal Rights Amendment Conflict in 1920s," in *Conflicts in Feminism.* Edited by Marianne Hirsch and Evelyn Fox Keller. Routledge, 1990. Copyright © 1990 by Routledge, Chapman and Hall, Inc. All rights reserved. Reproduced by permission of Routledge/Taylor & Francis Books and the author.—Cotton, Nancy. From "Women Playwrights in England," in *Read-*

ings in *Renaissance Women's Drama: Criticism, History, and Performance 1594-1998*. Edited by S. P. Cerasano and Marion Wynee-Davies. Bucknell University Press 1981. Reproduced by permission of Associated University Presses and the author.—Coultrap-McQuin, Susan. From *Doing Literary Business: American Women Writers in the Nineteenth Century*. The University of North Carolina Press, 1990. Copyright © 1990 Susan Coultrap-McQuin. All rights reserved. Used by permission of the University of North Carolina Press.—Daly, Brenda. From *Lavish Self-Divisions: The Novels of Joyce Carol Oates*. University Press of Mississippi, 1996. Copyright © 1996 by the University Press of Mississippi. All rights reserved. Reproduced by permission.—Davis, Cynthia J. "What 'Speaks in Us': Margaret Fuller, Woman's Rights, and Human Nature," in *Margaret Fuller's Cultural Critique: Her Age and Legacy*. Edited by Fritz Fleischmann. Peter Lang, 2000. Copyright © 2000 Peter Lang Publishing. All rights reserved. Reproduced by permission.—de Gouges, Olympe. From "The Rights of Women," in *Women in Revolutionary Paris 1789-1795: Selected Documents*. Edited and translated by Daline Gay Levy, Harriet Branson Applewhite, and Mary Durham Johnson. University of Illinois, 1979. Reproduced by permission.—Depla, Annette. From "Women in Ancient Egyptian Wisdom Literature," in *Women in Ancient Societies: An Illusion of the Night*. Edited by Léonie J. Archer, Susan Fischler, and Maria Wyke. Macmillan Press Ltd, 1994. Copyright © The Macmillan Press Ltd 1994. Reproduced with permission of Palgrave Macmillan and Routledge/Taylor & Francis Books, Inc.—Deutsch, Sarah Jane. From "From Ballots to Breadlines: 1920-1940," in *No Small Courage: A History of Women in the United States*. Edited by Nancy F. Cott. Oxford University Press, 2000. Copyright © 2000, by Sarah Jane Deutsch. All rights reserved. Used by permission of Oxford University Press.—Dever, Carolyn. From "Obstructive Behavior: Dykes in the Mainstream of Feminist Theory," in *Cross-Purposes: Lesbians, Feminists, and the Limits of Alliance*. Indiana University Press, 1997. Copyright © 1997, by Indiana University Press. All rights reserved. Reproduced by permission.—Donawerth, Jane. From "Women's Poetry and the Tudor-Stuart System of Gift Exchange," in *Women, Writing, and the Reproduction of Culture in Tudor and Stuart Britain*. Edited by Mary E. Burke, Jane Donawerth, Linda L. Dove, and Karen Nelson. Syracuse University Press, 2002. Reproduced by permission.—Doolittle, Hilda. From *HERmione*. New Directions Publishing, 1981. Copyright © 1981 by the Estate of Hilda Doolittle. Reproduced by permission of New Directions Publishing

Corp.—Douglas, Ann. From *The Feminization of American Culture*. Anchor Press/Doubleday, 1988. Copyright © 1977 by Ann Douglas. Used by permission of Alfred A. Knopf, a division of Random House, Inc.—Driver, Dorothy. From "Reconstructing the Past, Shaping the Future: Bessie Head and the Question of Feminism in a New South Africa," in *Black Women's Writings*. Edited by Gina Wisker. St. Martin's Press, 1993. Copyright © 1993, by Editorial Board, Lumière (Co-operative) Press Ltd. All rights reserved. Reprinted by permission of Palgrave Macmillan.—DuBois, Ellen Carol. From *Remembering Seneca Falls: Honoring the Women Who Paved the Way: An Essay*. Reproduced by permission of the author.—DuBois, Ellen Carol. From "Taking the Law Into Our Own Hands: Bradwell, Minor and Suffrage Militance in the 1870s," in *One Woman, One Vote: Rediscovering the Woman Suffrage Movement*. Edited by Marjorie Spruill Wheeler. NewSage Press, 1995. Copyright © 1995 by NewSage Press and Educational Film Company. All rights reserved. Reproduced by permission.—DuBois, Ellen Carol. From the introduction to *Feminism and Suffrage: The Emergence of An Independent Women's Movement in America*. Cornell University Press, 1978. Copyright © 1978 by Cornell University. All rights reserved. Used by permission of Cornell University Press.—DuBois, Ellen Carol. From "The Limitations of Sisterhood: Elizabeth Cady Stanton and the Division of the American Suffrage Movement, 1875-1902" in *Women and the Structure of Society*. Duke University Press, 1984. Copyright © 1984 by Duke University Press, Durham, NC. All rights reserved. Used by permission.—DuBois, Ellen Carol. From *Woman Suffrage and Women's Rights*. New York University Press, 1998. Copyright © 1998 by New York University. All rights reserved. Reproduced by permission of the publisher and the author.—DuBois, Ellen Carol. From "Woman Suffrage Around the World: Three Phases of Suffragist Internationalism," in *Suffrage and Beyond: International Feminist Perspectives*. Edited by Caroline Daley and Melanie Nolan. Auckland University Press, 1994. Copyright © by Auckland University Press 1994. All rights reserved. Reproduced by permission of the publisher and the author.—Ducrest, Stéphanie-Félicité. From "The Influence of Women on French Literature," in *Women Critics: 1660-1820: An Anthology*. Indiana University Press, 1995. Copyright © 1995 by Indiana University Press. All rights reserved. Reproduced by permission.—Dworkin, Andrea. From *Letters from a War Zone: Writings 1976-1989*. E. P. Dutton, 1988. Copyright © 1988 by Andrea Dworkin. Reproduced by permission of Elaine Markson Literary Agency.—Echols, Alice.

From *The Sixties: From Memory to History.* Edited by David R. Farber. University of North Carolina Press, 1994. Copyright © 1994 by the University of North Carolina Press. Used by permission of the Publisher.—Ehrenreich, Barbara and Deirdre English. From *For Her Own Good: 150 Years of the Experts' Advice to Women.* Anchor Books/Doubleday, 1978. Copyright © 1978 by Barbara Ehrenreich and Deirdre English. All rights reserved. Used by permission of Doubleday, a division of Random House.—Elbert, Sarah. From *A Hunger for Home: Louisa May Alcott and Little Women.* Temple University Press, 1984. Copyright © 1984 by Temple University. All rights reserved. Reproduced by permission of the author.—Emecheta, Buchi. From "Feminism with a Small 'f'!," in *Criticism and Ideology: Second African Writers' Conference.* Edited by Kirsten Holst Petersen. Scandinavian Institute of African Studies, 1988. Copyright © 1988 by Scandinavian Institute of African Studies. All rights reserved. Reproduced by permission of Nordic Africa Institute.—Ensler, Eve. From *The Vagina Monologues: The V-Day Edition.* Villard, 2001. Copyright © 1998, 2001 by Eve Ensler. All rights reserved. Reproduced by permission of Villard Books, a division of Random House, Inc.—Enstad, Nan. From *Ladies of Labor, Girls of Adventure: Working Women, Popular Culture, and Labor Politics at the Turn of the Twentieth Century.* Columbia University Press, 1999. Copyright © 1999 Columbia University Press, New York. All rights reserved. Republished with permission of the Columbia University Press, 61 W. 62nd St., New York, NY 10023.—Ezell, Margaret J. M. From "Women and Writing," in *A Companion to Early Modern Women's Writing.* Edited by Anita Pacheco. Blackwell Publishing Ltd, 2002. Copyright © 2002 by Blackwell Publishers Ltd. Reproduced by permission of Blackwell Publishers.—Fallaize, Elizabeth. From "Resisting Romance: Simone de Beauvoir, *The Woman Destroyed* and the Romance Script," in *Contemporary French Fiction by Women: Feminist Perspectives.* Edited by Margaret Atack and Phil Powrie. Manchester University Press, 1990. Reproduced by permission of the author.—Feng, Pin-chia. From *The Female Bildungsroman* by Toni Morrison and Maxine Hong Kingston: A Postmodern Reading. Peter Lang, 1998. Copyright © 1988 Peter Lang Publishing, Inc. All rights reserved. Reproduced by permission.—Ferree, Myra Marx and Beth B. Hess. From *Controversy and Coalition: The New Feminist Movement across Three Decades of Change.* Twayne Publishers, 1994. Copyright © 1994 by Twayne Publishers. All rights reserved. Reproduced by permission of The Gale Group.—Fishkin, Shelley Fisher. From an interview with Maxine Hong Kingston, in *Con-versations with Maxine Hong Kingston.* Edited by Paul Skenazy and Tera Martin. University Press of Mississippi, 1998. Copyright © 1998 by University Press of Mississippi. All rights reserved. Reproduced by permission of the author.—Fishkin, Shelley Fisher. From "Reading Gilman in the Twenty-First Century," in *The Mixed Legacy of Charlotte Perkins Gilman.* Edited by Catherine J. Golden and Joanna Schneider Zangrando. University of Delaware Press, 2000. Copyright © 2000 by Associated University Press. Reproduced by permission.—Fleischmann, Fritz. From "Margaret Fuller, the Eternal Feminine, and the 'Liberties of the Republic'," in *Women's Studies and Literature.* Edited by Fritz Fleischmann and Deborah Lucas Schneider. Palm & Enke, 1987. Reproduced by permission.—Foster, M. Marie Booth. From "Voice, Mind, Self: Mother-Daughter Relationships in Amy Tan's *The Joy Luck Club* and *The Kitchen God's Wife,*" in *Women of Color: Mother-Daughter Relationships in 20th-Century Literature.* Edited by Elizabeth Brown-Guillory. University of Texas Press, 1996. Copyright © 1996 by the University of Texas Press. All rights reserved. Reproduced by permission.—Fowler, Robert Booth. From *Carrie Catt: Feminist Politician.* Northeastern University Press, 1986. Copyright © 1986 by R. B. Fowler. All rights reserved. Reproduced by permission.—Fraiman, Susan. From "The Humiliation of Elizabeth Bennett," in *Refiguring the Father: New Feminist Readings of Patriarchy.* Edited by Patricia Yaeger and Beth Kowaleski-Wallace. Southern Illinois University Press, 1989. Copyright © 1989 by the Board of Trustees, Southern Illinois University. All rights reserved. Reproduced by permission.—Francis, Emma. From "Is Emily Brontë a Woman?: Femininity, Feminism, and the Paranoid Critical Subject," in *Subjectivity and Literature from the Romantics to the Present Day.* Edited by Philip Shaw and Peter Stockwell. Pinter, 1991. Copyright © Emma Francis. All rights reserved. Reproduced by permission of the author.—Freedman, Estelle B. and Erna Olafson Hellerstein. From an introduction to *Victorian Women: A Documentary Account of Women's Lives in Nineteenth-Century England, France, and the United States.* Edited by Erna Olafson Hellerstein, Leslie Parker Hume, and Karen M. Offen. Stanford University Press, 1981. Copyright © 1981 by the Board of Trustees of Leland Stanford Junior University. Reproduced with permission of Stanford University Press, www.sup.org.—Frenk, Susan. From "The Wandering Text: Situating the Narratives of Isabel Allende," in *Latin American Women's Writing: Feminist Readings in Theory and Crisis.* Edited by Anny Brooksbank Jones and Catherine Davies. Oxford at the Clarendon Press, 1996. Copyright © 1996 by Anny Brooksbank Jones and Catherine Davies. All rights reserved. Reproduced by permission of Oxford University Press.—From *Victorian Women: A Documentary Account of Women's Lives in Nineteenth-Century England, France, and the United States.* Edited by Erna Olafson Hellerstein, Leslie Parker Hume, and Karen M. Offen. Stanford University Press, 1981. Copyright © 1981 by the Board of Trustees of Leland Stanford Junior University. Reproduced with permission of Stanford University Press, www.sup.org.—Galvin, Mary E. From *Queer Poetics: Five Modernist Women Writers.* Praeger, 1999. Copyright © 1999 by Mary E. Galvin. All rights reserved. Reproduced by permission.—Garner, Shirley Nelson. From "Constructing the Mother: Contemporary Psychoanalytic Theorists and Women Autobiographers," in *Narrating Mother: Theorizing Maternal Subjectivities.* Edited by Brenda O. Daly and Maureen T. Reddy. University of Tennessee Press, 1991. Copyright © 1991 by The University of Tennessee Press. Reproduced by permission of the publisher.—Ghymn, Esther Mikyung. From an introduction to *Images of Asian American Women by Asian American Women Writers.* Peter Lang, 1995. Copyright © 1995, by Esther Mikyung Ghymn. All rights reserved. Reproduced by permission.—Gilbert, Sandra M. and Gubar, Susan. From "Charred Skirts and Deathmask: World War II and the Blitz on Women," in *No Man's Land: The Place of the Woman Writer in the Twentieth Century, Volume 3: Letters from the Front.* Yale University Press, 1994. Copyright © 1994, by Sandra M. Gilbert and Susan Gubar. All rights reserved. Reproduced by permission.—Gilbert, Sandra M. and Susan Gubar. From "The Battle of the Sexes: The Men's Case," in *No Man's Land: The Place of the Woman Writer in the Twentieth Century, Volume 1: The War of the Words.* Yale University Press, 1988. Copyright © 1988, by Yale University Press, All rights reserved. Reproduced by permission.—Gilbert, Sandra M., and Susan Gubar. From "The Second Coming of Aphrodite: Kate Chopin's Fantasy of Desire," in *No Man's Land: The Place of the Woman Writer in the Twentieth Century.* Yale University Press, 1989. Copyright © 1989 by Yale University. Copyright © 1984 by Sandra M. Gilbert and Susan Gubar. All rights reserved. Reproduced by permission.—Gilbert, Susan M., and Susan Gubar. From *The Madwoman in the Attic: The Woman Writer and the Nineteenth-Century Literary Imagination.* Yale University Press, 1979. Copyright © 1979 by Yale University. All rights reserved. Reproduced by permission.—Gleadle, Kathryn. From an introduction to *The Early Feminists: Radical Unitarians and the Emergence of The Women's Rights Movement, 1831-51.* Macmillan Press Ltd., 1995.

Copyright © Kathryn Gleadle 1995. All rights reserved. Reproduced by permission of Palgrave Macmillan.—Golden, Catherine. From "One Hundred Years of Reading 'The Yellow Wallpaper'," in *The Captive Imagination: A Casebook on "The Yellow Wallpaper."* Edited by Catherine Golden. The Feminist Press at the City University of New York, 1992. Copyright © 1992 by Catherine Golden. All rights reserved. Reproduced by permission.—Gorsky, Susan Rubinow. From *Femininity to Feminism: Women and Literature in the Nineteenth Century.* Twayne Publishers, 1992. Copyright © 1992 by Twayne Publishers. All rights reserved. Reproduced by permission of The Gale Group.—Greer, Germaine. From *The Madwoman's Underclothes: Essays and Occasional Writings.* The Atlantic Monthly Press, 1986. Copyright © 1970, 1986, by Germaine Greer. All rights reserved. Reproduced by permission.—Grewal, Gurleen. From *Circles of Sorrow, Lines of Struggle: The Novels of Toni Morrison.* Louisiana State University Press, 1998. Copyright © 1998 by Louisiana State University Press. All rights reserved. Reproduced by permission.—Griffin, Alice and Geraldine Thorsten. From *Understanding Lillian Hellman.* University of South Carolina Press, 1999. Copyright © 1999 University of South Carolina. Reproduced by permission.—Griffin, Susan E. From "Resistance and Reinvention in Sandra Cisneros' *Woman Hollering Creek*," in *Ethnicity and the American Short Story.* Edited by Julie Brown. Garland Publishing, Inc., 1997. Copyright © 1997 by Julie Brown. All rights reserved. Reproduced by permission of the publisher and the author.—Grogan, Susan K. From an introduction to *French Socialism and Sexual Difference: Women and the New Society, 1803-44.* St. Martin's Press, 1992. Copyright © Susan K. Grogan 1992. All rights reserved. Reprinted by permission of Palgrave Macmillan.—Grössinger, Christa. From *Picturing Women in Late Medieval and Renaissance Art.* Manchester University Press, 1997. Copyright © Christa Grössinger 1997. Reproduced by permission.—Grubbs, Judith Evans. From *Women and the Law in the Roman Empire: A Sourcebook on Marriage, Divorce and Widowhood.* Routledge, 2002. Reproduced by permission of the publisher.—Grundy, Isobel. From "(Re)discovering Women's Texts," in *Women and Literature in Britain 1700-1800.* Edited by Vivien Jones. Cambridge University Press, 2000. Copyright © 2000 by Cambridge University Press. Reproduced by permission of Cambridge University Press.—Gubar, Susan. From "Feminist Misogyny: Mary Wollstonecraft and the Paradox of 'It Takes One to Know One'," in *Feminism Beside Itself.* Edited by Diane Elam and Robyn Wiegman. Routledge, 1995. Copyright © 1995 by Routledge.

ACKNOWLEDGMENTS

All rights reserved. Reproduced by permission of Routledge/Taylor & Francis and the author.—Gubar, Susan. From "Sapphistries," in *Re-reading Sappho: Reception and Transmission*. Edited by Ellen Greene. University of California Press, 1996. Copyright © 1996 by The Regents of The University of California. Reproduced by permission of the publisher and the author.—Gunther-Canada, Wendy. From *Rebel Writer: Mary Wollstonecraft and Enlightenment Politics*. Northern Illinois University Press, 2001. Copyright © 2001 by Northern Illinois University Press. All rights reserved. Reproduced by permission.—Hagen, Lyman B. From *Heart of a Woman, Mind of a Writer, and Soul of a Poet: A Critical Analysis of the Writings of Maya Angelou*. University Press of America, 1997. Copyright © 1997 by University Press of America. All rights reserved. Reproduced by permission.—Hallett, Judith From "The Role of Women in Roman Elegy: Counter-Cultural Feminism," in *Women in the Ancient World: The Arethusa Papers*. Edited by John Peradotto and J. Sullivan. State University of New York Press, 1984. Reproduced by permission of the State University of New York Press.—Hansberry, Lorraine. From *A Raisin in the Sun*. Modern Library, 1995. Copyright © 1958, 1986 by Robert Nemiroff, as an unpublished work. Copyright © 1959, 1966, 1984, 1987, 1988 by Robert Nemiroff. All rights reserved. Reproduced by permission of Random House, Inc., Jewell Gresham-Nemiroff and Methuen Publishing Ltd.—Harris, Susan K. From "'But is it any good?' Evaluating Nineteenth-Century American Women's Fiction," in *The (Other) American Traditions: Nineteenth-Century Women Writers*. Edited by Joyce W. Warren. Rutgers University Press, 1993. Copyright © 1993 by Rutgers University Press. All rights reserved. Reproduced by permission of the author.—Head, Bessie. From "Despite Broken Bondage, Botswana Women Are Still Unloved," in *A Woman Alone: Autobiographical Writings*. Selected and edited by Craig MacKenzie. Heinemann, 1990. Copyright © 1990, by The Estate of Bessie Head. Reproduced by permission of Johnson & Alcock.—Head, Bessie. From "The Woman from America," in *A Woman Alone: Autobiographical Writings*. Selected and edited by Craig MacKenzie. Heinemann, 1990. Copyright © 1990, by The Estate of Bessie Head. Reproduced by permission of Johnson & Alcock.—Hellerstein, Erna, Leslie Parker Hume and Karen M. Offen from an introduction to *Victorian Women: A Documentary Account of Women's Lives in Nineteenth-Century England, France, and the United States*. Edited by Erna Olafson Hellerstein, Leslie Parker Hume, and Karen M. Offen. Stanford University Press, 1981. Copyright © 1981 by the Board of Trustees of the Leland Stanford Junior University. Reproduced with permission of Stanford University Press, www.sup.org.—Henderson, Bruce. From *Images of the Self as Female: The Achievement of Women Artists in Re-envisioning Feminine Identity*. Edited by Kathryn N. Benzel and Lauren Pringle De La Vars. The Edwin Mellen Press, 1992. Copyright © 1992 by Kathryn N. Benzel and Lauren Pringle De La Vars. All rights reserved. Reproduced by permission.—Hill, Mary A. From "Charlotte Perkins Gilman: A Feminist's Struggle with Womanhood," in *Charlotte Perkins Gilman: The Woman and Her Work*. Edited by Sheryl L. Meyering. UMI Research Press, 1989. Copyright © 1989 by Sheryl L. Meyering. All rights reserved. Reproduced by permission of Boydell & Brewer, Inc.—Hobby, Elaine. From *Virtue of Necessity: English Women's Writing 1649-88*. The University of Michigan Press, 1989. Copyright © 1988 by Elaine Hobby. All rights reserved. Reproduced by permission of the author.—Hoffert, Sylvia D. From an introduction to *When Hens Crow: The Woman's Rights Movement in Antebellum America*. Indiana University Press, 1995. Copyright © 1995 by Sylvia D. Hoffert. All rights reserved. Reproduced by permission.—Hurston, Zora Neale. From *Their Eyes Were Watching God*. Perennial Library, 1990. Copyright © 1937 by Harper & Row, Publishers, Inc. Renewed 1965 by John C. Hurston and Joel Hurston. Reproduced by permission of Time Warner Books UK. In North America by HarperCollins Publishers Inc.—James, Adeola. From "Bessie Head's Perspectives on Women," in *Black Women Writers across Cultures*. Edited by Valentine Udoh James, James S. Etim, Melanie Marshall James, and Ambe J. Njoh. International Scholars Publications, 2000. Copyright © 2000, by International Scholars Publications. All rights reserved. Reproduced by permission.—Jardine, Alice A. From an interview with Marguerite Duras, translated by Katherine Ann Jensen, in *Shifting Scenes: Interviews on Women, Writing, and Politics in Post-68 France*. Edited by Alice A. Jardine and Anne M. Menke. Columbia University Press, 1991. Copyright © 1991 Columbia University Press, New York. All rights reserved. Reprinted with the permission of the publisher.—Jelinek, Estelle C. From "The Paradox and Success of Elizabeth Cady Stanton," in *Women's Autobiography: Essays in Criticism*. Edited by Estelle C. Jelinek. Indiana University Press, 1980. Copyright © Estelle C. Jelinek. Reproduced by permission of the author.—Juhasz, Suzanne. From "Maxine Hong Kingston: Narrative Technique & Female Identity," in *Contemporary American Women Writers: Narrative Strategies*. Edited by Catherine Rainwater and William J. Scheik. The University Press of Kentucky, 1985. Copyright © 1985 by The University Press of

Kentucky. Reproduced by permission.—Kaminer, Wendy. From "Feminism's Identity Crisis," in *Public Women, Public Words: A Documentary History of American Feminism.* Edited by Dawn Keetley and John Pettegrew. First published in *The Atlantic.* Reproduced by permission of the author.—Kaplan, Cora. From "Pandora's Box: Subjectivity, Class and Sexuality in Socialist Feminist Criticism," in *Making a Difference: Feminist Literary Criticism.* Edited by Gayle Greene and Coppélia Kahn. Methuen & Co., 1985. Copyright © 1985 Gayle Greene and Coppélia Kahn. All rights reserved. Reproduced by permission of Routledge and the author.—Keetley, Dawn and John Pettegrew. From "Identities through Adversity," in *Public Women, Public Words: A Documentary History of American Feminism.* Edited by Dawn Keetley and John Pettegrew. Madison House Publishers, Inc., 1997. Copyright © 1997 by Madison House Publisher, Inc. All rights reserved. Reproduced by permission.—Kelly, Gary. From *Revolutionary Feminism: The Mind and Career of Mary Wollstonecraft.* St. Martin's Press, 1996. Copyright © 1996 by Gary Kelly. All rights reserved. Reproduced by permission of Palgrave Macmillan.—Kempe, Margery. From "Margery Kempe's Visit to Julian of Norwich," in *The Shewings of Julian Norwich.* Edited by Georgia Ronan Crampton. Medieval Publishing Institute, 1994. Reproduced by permission.—Kempe, Margery. From *The Book of Margery Kempe.* Translated by B. A. Windeatt. Penguin, 1985. Copyright © B. A. Windeatt, 1985. All rights reserved. Reproduced by permission.—Kirkham, Margaret. From *Jane Austen, Feminism, and Fiction.* Harvester Press Limited, 1983. Copyright © Margaret Kirkham, 1983. All rights reserved. Reproduced by permission.—Klemans, Patricia A. From "'Being Born a Woman': A New Look at Edna St. Vincent Millay," in *Critical Essays on Edna St. Vincent Millay.* Edited by William B. Thesing. G. K. Hall, 1993. Copyright © by 1993 by William B. Thesing. All rights reserved. Reproduced by permission of The Gale Group.—Knapp, Bettina L. From *Gertrude Stein.* Continuum, 1990. Copyright © 1990 by Bettina L. Knapp. All rights reserved. Reproduced by permission.—Kolodny, Annette. From "Dancing Through the Minefield: Some Observations on the Theory, Practice, and Politics of a Feminist Literary Criticism," originally published in *Feminist Studies,* 1980. Copyright © 1980 by Annette Kolodny. All rights reserved. Reproduced by permission of the author.—Kumin, Maxine. From "How It Was," in *The Complete Poems: Anne Sexton.* Houghton Mifflin Company, 1981. Copyright © 1981, by Maxine Kumin. All rights reserved. Reproduced by permission of Houghton Mifflin and The Anderson Literary Agency.—Lam-

onica, Drew. From *We Are Three Sisters: Self and Family in the Writing of the Brontës.* University of Missouri Press, 2003. Copyright © 2003 by The Curators of the University of Missouri. All rights reserved. Reproduced by permission.—Larsen, Jeanne. From "Lowell, Teasdale, Wylie, Millay, and Bogan," in *The Columbia History of American Poetry.* Edited by Jay Parini. Columbia University Press, 1993. Copyright © 1993 Columbia University Press, New York. All rights reserved. Reprinted with permission of the publisher.—Lascelles, Mary. From *Jane Austen and Her Art.* Oxford University Press, 1939. Reproduced by permission of Oxford University Press.—Lavezzo, Kathy. From "Sobs and Sighs Between Women: The Homoerotics of Compassion in *The Book of Margery Kempe,*" in *Premodern Sexualities.* Edited by Louise Fradenburg and Carla Freccero. Routledge, 1996. Copyright © 1996 by Routledge. All rights reserved. Reproduced by permission of Routledge/Taylor & Francis and the author.—Lessing, Doris. From a preface to *The Golden Notebook* in *A Small Personal Voice.* Edited by Paul Schleuter. Alfred A. Knopf, Inc., 1974. Copyright © 1974 by Doris Lessing. All rights reserved. Reproduced by permission of Jonathan Clowes, Ltd.—Levertov, Denise. From *Poems, 1960-67.* New Directions, 1966. Copyright © 1967, by Denise Levertov. All rights reserved. Reproduced by permission of New Directions Publishing Corporation and in the UK by Pollinger Limited and the proprietor.—Logan, Shirley Wilson. From *"We are Coming": The Persuasive Discourse of Nineteenth-Century Black Women.* Southern Illinois University Press, 1999. Copyright © 1999 by the Board of Trustees, Southern Illinois University. All rights reserved. Reproduced by permission of Southern Illinois University Press and the University of South Carolina Press.—Lorde, Audre. From *The Black Unicorn.* Norton, 1978. Copyright © 1978, by Audre Lorde. All rights reserved. Reproduced by permission of W. W. Norton & Company and Charlotte Sheedy Literary Agency.—Lumsden, Linda J. From *Rampant Women: Suffragists and the Right of Assembly.* The University of Tennessee Press, 1997. Copyright © 1997 by The University of Tennessee Press. Reproduced by permission of The University of Tennessee Press.—Lunardini, Christine A. *From Equal Suffrage to Equal Rights: Alice Paul and the National Women's Party, 1910-1928.* New York University Press, 1986. Copyright © 1986 by New York University. All rights reserved. Reproduced by permission of the author.—Madsen, Deborah L. From "Sandra Cisneros," in *Understanding Contemporary Chicana Literature.* Edited by Matthew J. Bruccoli. University of South Carolina Press, 2000. Copyright © 2000 by University of South Carolina. Reproduced by permission.—Marder, Herbert. From *Feminism & Art: A Study of Virginia Woolf.* University of Chicago Press, 1968. Copyright © 1968 by the University of Chicago. All rights reserved. Reproduced by permission of the publisher and the author.—Marilley, Suzanne M. From *Woman Suffrage and the Origins of Liberal Feminism in the United States.* Harvard University Press, 1996. Copyright © 1996 by the President and Fellows of Harvard College. All rights reserved. Reproduced by permission Harvard University Press.—Marsh-Lockett, Carol P. From "What Ever Happened to Jochebed? Motherhood as Marginality in Zora Neale Hurston's *Seraph on the Suwanee*," in *Southern Mothers: Facts and Fictions in Southern Women's Writing.* Edited by Nagueyalti Warren and Sally Wolff. Louisiana State University, 1999. Reproduced by permission.—Mason, Nicholas. From "Class, Gender, and Domesticity in Maria Edgeworth's *Belinda*," in *The Eighteenth-Century Novel,* Vol. 1. Edited by Susan Spencer. AMS Press, 2001. Reproduced by permission.—Massardier-Kenney, Françoise. From *Gender in the Fiction of George Sand.* Rodopi, 1985. Copyright © Editions Rodopi B. V. Reproduced by permission.—McCracken, Ellen. From "Sandra Cisneros' *The House on Mango Street*: Community-Oriented Introspection and the Demystification of Patriarchal Violence," in *Breaking Boundaries: Latina Writing and Critical Readings.* Edited by Asunción Horno-Delgado, Eliana Ortega, Nina M. Scott, and Nancy Saporta Sternbach. University of Massachusetts Press, 1989. Copyright © 1989 by The University of Massachusetts Press. All rights reserved. Reproduced by permission.—McNamara, Jo Ann. From "Women and Power through the Family Revisited," in *Gendering the Master Narrative: Women and Power in the Middle Ages.* Edited by Mary C. Erler and Maryanne Kowaleski. Cornell University Press, 2003. Copyright © 2003 by Cornell University Press. Used by permission of Cornell University Press.—Meisenhelder, Susan. From "Ethnic and Gender Identity in Zora Neale Hurston's *Their Eyes Were Watching God*," in *Teaching American Ethnic Literatures: Nineteen Essays.* Edited by John R. Maitino and David R. Peck. University of New Mexico Press, 1996. Copyright © 1996, by the University of New Mexico Press. All rights reserved. Reproduced by permission.—Mellor, Anne K. From "Possessing Nature: The Female in Frankenstein," in *Romanticism and Feminism.* Edited by Anne K. Mellor. Indiana University Press, 1988. Copyright © 1988 by Indiana University Press. All rights reserved. Reproduced by permission.—Mermin, Dorothy. From *Godiva's Ride: Women of Letters in England, 1830-1880.* Indiana University Press, 1993. Copyright © 1993 by Dorothy Mermin. All rights reserved. Repro-

duced by permission.—Millay, Edna St. Vincent. From "Sonnet III of Fatal Interview," in *Collected Sonnets of Edna St. Vincent Millay.* HarperCollins, 1952. Copyright © 1931, 1958 by Edna St. Vincent Millay and Norma Millay Ellis. All rights reserved. Reproduced by permission of Elizabeth Barnett, Literary Executor.—Millay, Edna St. Vincent. From "First Fig," in *Collected Poems of Edna St. Vincent Millay.* HarperCollins, 1952. Copyright © 1922, 1950 by Edna St. Vincent Millay. Reproduced by permission of Elizabeth Barnett, Literary Executor.—Millay, Edna St. Vincent. From "I, Being Born a Woman and Distressed," in *Collected Poems of Edna St. Vincent Millay.* HarperCollins, 1952. Copyright © 1923, 1951 by Edna St.Vincent Millay and Norma Millay Ellis. All rights reserved. Reproduced by permission of Elizabeth Barnett, Literary Executor.—Millett, Kate. From "How Many Lives Are Here...," in *The Feminist Memoir Project.* Edited by Rachel DuPlessis and Ann Snitow. Three Rivers Press, 1998. Copyright © 1998 by Rachel DuPlessis and Ann Snitow. All rights reserved. Used by permission of Crown Publishers, a division of Random House, Inc. and Sanford J. Greenburger Associates.—Moi, Toril. From "Who's Afraid of Virginia Woolf? Feminist Readings of Woolf," in *New Casebooks: 'Mrs. Dalloway' and 'To the Lighthouse.'* Edited by Su Reid. St. Martin's Press, 1993. Copyright © Su Reid 1993. All rights reserved. Reproduced by permission of Palgrave Macmillan.—Moore, Marianne. From *The Selected Letters of Marianne Moore.* Edited by Bonnie Costello. Alfred A. Knopf, 1997. Copyright © 1997 by the Estate of Marianne Moore. Introduction, annotations and additional editorial material copyright 1997 by Bonnie Costello. All rights reserved. Reproduced by permission of Alfred A. Knopf, Inc., a division of Random House, Inc.—Morgan, Winifred. From "Alice Walker: *The Color Purple* as Allegory," in *Southern Writers at Century's End.* Edited by Jeffrey J. Folks and James A. Perkins. The University Press of Kentucky, 1997. Copyright © 1997 by The University Press of Kentucky. All rights reserved. Reproduced by permission.—Morrison, Toni. From *Race-ing Justice, En-Gendering Power.* Pantheon Books, 1992. Copyright © 1992 by Toni Morrison. All rights reserved. Used by permission International Creative Management, Inc.—Morrison, Toni. From "What the Black Woman Thinks About Women's Lib," in *Public Women, Public Words: A Documentary History of American Feminism.* Edited by Dawn Keetley and John Pettegrew. Madison House, 1997. Copyright © 1997 by Toni Morrison. Reproduced by permission of International Creative Management, Inc.—Mortimer, Armine Kotin. From "Male and Female Plots in Staël's *Corinne*," in *Correspondences:*

Studies in Literature, History, and the Arts in Nineteenth-Century France: Selected Proceedings of the Sixteenth Colloquium in Nineteenth-Century French Studies, The University of Oklahoma-Norman, October 11th-13th, 1990. Edited by Keith Busby. Rodopi, 1992. Copyright © Editions Rodopi B. V. Reproduced by permission.—Motard-Noar, Martine. From "From Persephone to Demeter: A Feminist Experience in Cixous's Fiction," in *Images of Persephone: Feminist Readings in Western Literature.* Edited by Elizabeth T. Hayes. University Press of Florida, 1994. Copyright © 1994 by Board of Regents of the State of Florida. All rights reserved. Reproduced with the permission of the University Press of Florida.—Mukherjee, Bharati. From *The Middleman and Other Stories.* Viking, 1988. Copyright © 1988, by Bharati Mukherjee. All rights reserved. Reprinted by permission of Penguin Group Canada and the author.—Mumford, Marilyn R. From "A Feminist Prolegomenon for the Study of Hildegard of Bingen," in *Gender, Culture, and the Arts: Women, the Arts, and Society.* Edited by Ronald Dotterer and Susan Bowers. Associated University Presses, 1993. Copyright © 1993 by Associated University Presses.—Oates, Joyce Carol. From *Where I've Been, and Where I'm Going.* Plume, 1999. Copyright © The Ontario Review, 1999. All rights reserved. Reproduced by permission of Plume, an imprint of Penguin Putnam Inc. In the United Kingdom by John Hawkins & Associates, Inc.—Okely, Judith. From "Re-reading The Second Sex," in *Simone de Beauvoir: A Re-Reading.* Virago, 1986. Reproduced by permission of the author.—Ovid. From "Sappho to Phaon," in *The Sappho Companion.* Edited by Margaret Reynolds. Chatto and Windus, 2000. Copyright © Margaret Reynolds 2000. Reproduced by permission of the editor.—Pan Chao. From *Pan Chao: Foremost Woman Scholar of China.* Edited by Nancy Lee Swann. University of Michigan Center for Chinese Studies, 1932. Copyright © The East Asian Library and the Gest Collection, Princeton University. Reproduced by permission.—Parks, Sheri. From "In My Mother's House: Black Feminist Aesthetics, Television, and *A Raisin in the Sun,*" in *Theatre and Feminist Aesthetics.* Edited by Karen Laughlin and Catherine Schuler. Farleigh Dickinson University Press, 1995. Copyright © 1995 by Associated University Presses. All rights reserved. Reproduced by permission.—Paul, Alice. From *Party Papers: 1913-1974.* Microfilming Corporation of America, 1978. Reproduced by permission of Sewall-Belmont House and Museum.—Paz, Octavio. From "The Response," in *Sor Juana or, The Traps of Faith.* Translated by Margaret Sayers Peden. Cambridge, Mass.: The Belknap Press of Harvard University Press, 1988. Copyright © 1988 by the President and Fellows of Harvard College. All rights reserved. Reproduced by permission.—Perkins, Annie. From "The Poetry of Gwendolyn Brooks (1970s-1980s)," in *Women Making Art: Women in the Visual, Literary, and Performing Arts Since 1960.* Edited by Deborah Johnson and Wendy Oliver. Peter Lang, 2001. Copyright © 2001 Peter Lang Publishing, Inc., New York. Reproduced by permission.—Pierpont, Claudia Roth. From *Passionate Minds: Women Rewriting the World.* Alfred A. Knopf, 2000. Copyright © 2000 by Claudia Roth Piepont. All rights reserved. Reproduced by permission of Alfred A. Knopf, Inc., a division of Random House, Inc.—Plath, Sylvia. From *The Bell Jar.* Faber & Faber, 1966; Harper & Row, 1971. Copyright © 1971 by Harper & Row, Publishers, Inc. Reproduced by permission Faber & Faber Ltd. In the United States by HarperCollins Publishers Inc.—Pryse, Marjorie. From "Origins of American Literary Regionalism: Gender in Irving, Stowe, and Longstreet," in *Breaking Boundaries: New Perspectives on Women's Regional Writing.* Edited by Sherrie A. Inness and Diana Royer. University of Iowa Press, 1997. Copyright © 1997 by the University of Iowa Press. All rights reserved. Reproduced by permission.—Radice, Betty. From an introduction to *The Letters of Abelard and Heloise.* Translated by Betty Radice. Penguin Books, 1974. Copyright © Betty Radice, 1974. Reproduced by permission of Penguin Books, a division of Penguin Putnam Inc.—Rendall, Jane. From an introduction to *The Origins of Modern Feminism: Women in Britain, France and the United States 1780-1860.* Macmillan, 1985. Copyright © Jane Rendall 1985. All rights reserved. Reproduced by permission of Palgrave Macmillan.—Rich, Adrienne. From "Vesuvius at Home: The Power of Emily Dickinson," in *On Lies, Secrets, and Silence: Selected Prose 1966-1978.* W. W. Norton & Company, Inc., 1979. Copyright © 1979 by W. W. Norton & Company, Inc. Reproduced by permission of the author and W. W. Norton & Company, Inc.—Rich, Adrienne. From "When We Dead Awaken: Writing as Re-Vision," in *Arts of the Possible: Essays and Conversations.* W. W. Norton & Company, Inc., 2001. Copyright © 2001 by Adrienne Rich. Reproduced by permission of the publisher and the author.—Richmond, M. A. From *Bid the Vassal Soar: Essays on the Life and Poetry of Phillis Wheatley and George Moses Horton.* Howard University Press, 1974. All rights reserved. Copyright © 1974 by Merle A. Richmond. Reproduced by permission.—Risjord, Norman K. From *Representative Americans: The Colonists.* Second Edition. Rowman & Littlefield Publishers, Inc., 2001. Copyright © 2001 by Rowman & Littlefield Publishers, Inc. All rights reserved. Reproduced by permission.—Robbins,

Ruth. From *Transitions: Literary Feminisms*. St. Martin's Press, 2000. Reproduced with permission of Palgrave Macmillan.—Rohrbach, Erika. From H. D. and Sappho: 'A Precious Inch of Palimpsest'," in *Re-Reading Sappho: Reception and Transmission*. Edited by Ellen Greene. University of California Press, 1996. Copyright © 1996 by The Regents of the University of California. Reproduced by permission.—Rosenman, Ellen Bayuk. From *"A Room of One's Own": Women Writers and the Politics of Creativity*. Twayne, 1995. Copyright © 1995 by Twayne Publishers. All rights reserved. Reproduced by permission of The Gale Group.—Rosslyn, Wendy. From "Don Juan Feminised," in *Symbolism and After: Essays on Russian Poetry in Honour of Georgette Donchin*. Edited by Arnold McMillin. Bristol Classical Press, 1992. Copyright © 1992 by Gerald Duckworth & Co. Ltd. All rights reserved. Reproduced by permission of The School of Slavonic Studies in the University of London.—Sanders, Valerie. From "Women, Fiction and the Marketplace," in *Women and Literature in Britain: 1800-1900*. Edited by Joanne Shattock. Cambridge University Press, 2001. Copyright © Cambridge University Press 2001. Reproduced by permission of Cambridge University Press.—Sandler, Martin W. From *Against the Odds: Women Pioneers in the First Hundred Years of Photography*. Rizzoli International Publications, Inc., 2002. Copyright © 2002, by Martin W. Sandler. All rights reserved. Reproduced by permission of the author.—Saunders, Corinne. From *Rape and Ravishment in the Literature of Medieval England*. D. S. Brewer, 2001. Copyright © Corinne J. Saunders 2001. All rights reserved. Reproduced by permission.—Scheick, William J. From *Authority and Female Authorship in Colonial America*. The University Press of Kentucky, 1998. Copyright © 1998 by The University Press of Kentucky. Reproduced by permission of The University Press of Kentucky.—Schroeder, Patricia R. From "Remembering the Disremembered: Feminist Realists of the Harlem Renaissance," in *Realism and the American Dramatic Tradition*. Edited by William W. Demastes. University of Alabama Press, 1996. Copyright © 1996, by the University of Alabama Press. All rights reserved. Reproduced by permission.—Selous, Trista. From *The Other Woman: Feminism and Femininity in the Work of Marguerite Duras*. Yale University Press, 1988. Copyright © 1988 by Yale University. All rights reserved. Reproduced by permission.—Sexton, Anne. From "All God's Children Need Radios," in *No Evil Star: Selected Essays, Interviews, and Prose of Anne Sexton*. Edited by Steven E. Colburn. The University of Michigan Press, 1985. Copyright © Anne Sexton. Reproduced by permission of SLL/Sterling Lord Literistic.—Shaw,

Harry B. From "*Maud Martha*: The War with Beauty," in *A Life Distilled: Gwendolyn Brooks, Her Poetry and Fiction*. Edited by Maria K. Mootry and Gary Smith. University of Illinois Press, 1987. Copyright © 1987 by the Board of Trustees of the University of Illinois. Reproduced by permission.—Shiach, Morag. From an introduction to *Hélène Cixous: A Politics of Writing*. Routledge, 1991. Copyright © 1991 by Morag Shiach. All rights reserved. Reproduced by permission of the publisher and the author.—Showalter, Elaine. From *A Literature of Their Own: British Women Novelists from Brontë to Lessing*. Princeton University Press, 1977. Copyright © 1977 by Princeton University Press. Renewed 2005 Princeton University Press, 1999 exp. Paperback edition. Reproduced by permission of Princeton University Press.—Showalter, Elaine. From *Sister's Choice: Tradition and Change in American Women's Writing*. Oxford at the Clarendon Press, 1991. Copyright © 1991, by Elaine Showalter. All rights reserved. Reproduced by permission of Oxford University Press.—Sigerman, Harriet. From "Laborers for Liberty," in *No Small Courage: A History of Women in the United States*. Edited by Nancy F. Cott. Oxford University Press, 2000. Copyright © 2000 by Oxford University Press, Inc. Copyright © 1994, 2000 by Harriet Sigerman. All rights reserved. Used by permission of Oxford University Press.—Signori, Lisa F. From *The Feminization of Surrealism: The Road to Surreal Silence in Selected Works of Marguerite Duras*. Peter Lang, 2001. Copyright © 2001 Peter Lang Publishing, Inc., New York. All rights reserved. Reproduced by permission.—Silko, Leslie Marmon. From *Storyteller*. Seaver Books, 1981. Copyright © 1981, by Leslie Marmon Silko. All rights reserved. Reproduced by permission.—Simson, Rennie. From "Afro-American Poets of the Nineteenth Century," in *Nineteenth-Century Women Writers of the English-Speaking World*. Edited by Rhoda B. Nathan. Greenwood Press, 1986. Copyright © 1986 by Hofstra University. All rights reserved. Reproduced by permission of Greenwood Publishing Group, Inc., Westport, CT.—Sizer, Lyde Cullen. From *The Political Work of Northern Women Writers and the Civil War, 1850-1872*. The University of North Carolina Press, 2000. Copyright © 2000 The University of North Carolina Press. All rights reserved. Reproduced by permission.—Smith, Hilda L. From "Introduction: Women, Intellect, and Politics: Their Intersection in Seventeenth-Century England," in *Women Writers and the Early Modern British Political Tradition*. Edited by Hilda L. Smith. Cambridge University Press, 1998. Copyright © Cambridge University Press 1998. Reproduced with the permission of Cambridge University Press.—Smith,

Johanna M. From "'Cooped Up': Feminine Domesticity in *Frankenstein*," in *Case Studies in Contemporary Criticism: Mary Shelley's* **Frankenstein**. Edited by Johanna M. Smith. St. Martin's Press, 1992. Copyright © 1992 by Bedford Books of St. Martin's Press. All rights reserved. Reproduced by permission.—Smith, Sidonie. From "Resisting the Gaze of Embodiment: Women's Autobiography in the Nineteenth Century," in *American Women's Autobiography: Fea(s)ts of Memory*. Edited by Margo Culley. University of Wisconsin University Press, 1992. Copyright © 1992 The Board of Regents of the University of Wisconsin System. All rights reserved. Reproduced by permission.—Smith, Sidonie. From *Where I'm Bound: Patterns of Slavery and Freedom in Black American Autobiography*. Greenwood Press, 1974. Copyright © 1974 by Sidonie Smith. All rights reserved. Reproduced by permission of Greenwood Publishing Group, Inc., Westport, CT.—Snyder, Jane McIntosh. From *The Woman and the Lyre: Women Writers in Classical Greece and Rome*. Southern Illinois University Press, 1989. Copyright © 1989 by the Board of Trustees, Southern Illinois University. All rights reserved. Reproduced by permission.—Sor Juana Ines de la Cruz. From *The Answer = La respuesta*. Edited by Electa Arenal and Amanda Powell. The Feminist Press, 1994. Copyright © 1994 by Electa Arenal and Amanda Powell. All rights reserved. Reproduced by permission of The Feminist Press at the City University of New York. www.feministpress.org.—Spender, Dale. From "Introduction: A Vindication of the Writing Woman," in *Living by the Pen: Early British Women Writers*. Edited by Dale Spender. Teachers College Press, 1992. Copyright © 1992 by Teachers College. All rights reserved. Reproduced by permission.—Staley, Lynn. From *Margery Kempe's Dissenting Fictions*. Pennsylvania State University Press, 1994. Copyright © 1994 The Pennsylvania State University. All rights reserved. Reproduced by permission.—Stehle, Eva. From *Performance and Gender in Ancient Greece: Nondramatic Poetry in Its Setting*. Princeton University Press, 1997. Copyright © 1997 by Princeton University Press. All rights reserved. Reproduced by permission of Princeton University Press.—Stein, Gertrude. From "Degeneration in American Women," in *Sister Brother: Gertrude and Leo Stein*. Edited by Brenda Wineapple. G. Putnam's Sons, 1996. Copyright © 1996 by Brenda Wineapple. All rights reserved. Used by permission of G. Putnam's Sons, a division of Penguin Group (USA) Inc. and Bloomsbury Publishing Plc.—Stott, Rebecca. From *Elizabeth Barrett Browning*. Pearson Education Limited, 2003. Copyright © Pearson Educated Limited 2003. All rights reserved. Reproduced by permission.—Straub, Kristina. From *Divided Fic-*

tions: Fanny Burney and Feminine Strategy. University Press of Kentucky, 1987. Copyright © 1987 by the University Press of Kentucky. Reproduced by permission.—Swann, Nancy Lee. From *Pan Chao: Foremost Woman Scholar of China*. Russell & Russell, 1968. Copyright © The East Asian Library and the Gest Collection, Princeton University. Reproduced by permission.—Tanner, Laura E. From *Intimate Violence: Reading Rape and Torture in Twentieth-Century Fiction*. Indiana University Press, 1994. Copyright © 1994, by Laura E. Tanner. All rights reserved. Reproduced by permission.—Terborg-Penn, Rosalyn. From *African American Women in the Struggle for the Vote, 1850-1920*. Indiana University Press, 1998. Reproduced by permission.—Tharp, Julie. From "Women's Community and Survival in the Novels of Louise Erdrich," in *Communication and Women's Friendships: Parallels and Intersections in Literature and Life*. Edited by Janet Doubler Ward and JoAnna Stephens Mink. Bowling Green State University Popular Press, 1993. Copyright © 1993 by Bowling Green State University Popular Press. Reproduced by permission of the University of Wisconsin Press.—Trilling, Lionel. From "Emma and the Legend of Jane Austen," in *Beyond Culture: Essays on Literature and Learning*. Harcourt Brace Jovanovich, 1965. Copyright © 1965 by Lionel Trilling. All rights reserved. Reproduced by permission of the Wylie Agency, Inc.—Turner, Katherine S. H. From "From Classical to Imperial: Changing Visions of Turkey in the Eighteenth Century," in *Travel Writing and Empire: Postcolonial Theory in Transit*. Edited by Steve Clark. Zed Books, 1999. Copyright © Katherine S. H. Turner. Reproduced by permission.—Van Dyke, Annette. From "Of Vision Quests and Spirit Guardians: Female Power in the Novels of Louise Erdrich," in *The Chippewa Landscape of Louise Erdrich*. Edited by Allan Chavkin. The University of Alabama Press, 1999. Copyright © 1999, by The University of Alabama Press. Copyright © 1999. All rights reserved. Reproduced by permission.—Waelti-Waters, Jennifer and Steven C. Hause. From an introduction to *Feminisms of the Belle Époque: A Historical and Literary Anthology*. Edited by Jennifer Waelti-Waters and Steven C. Hause. University of Nebraska Press, 1994. Copyright © The University of Nebraska Press, 1994. All rights reserved. Reproduced by permission.—Wagner-Martin, Linda. From "Panoramic, Unpredictable, and Human: Joyce Carol Oates' Recent Novels," in *Traditions, Voices, and Dreams: The American Novel since the 1960s*. Edited by Melvin J. Friedman and Ben Siegel. University of Delaware Press, 1995. Copyright © 1995 by Associated University Presses, Inc. Reproduced by permission.—Wagner-Martin, Linda. From *Sylvia Plath: A Literary Life*.

St. Martin's Press, 1999. Copyright © 1999 by Linda Wagner-Martin. All rights reserved. Reproduced by permission of Palgrave Macmillan.—Walker, Alice. From *Revolutionary Petunias & Other Poems.* Harcourt Brace Jovanovich, 1971. Copyright © 1970, 1971, 1972, 1973, renewed 1998 by Alice Walker. All right reserved. Reproduced by permission of Harcourt Inc. In the British Commonwealth by David Higham Associates.—Watts, Linda S. From *Rapture Untold: Gender, Mysticism, and the 'Moment of Recognition' in Works by Gertrude Stein.* Peter Lang, 1996. Copyright © 1996 Peter Lang Publishing, Inc., New York. All rights reserved. Reproduced by permission.—Weatherford, Doris. From *A History of the American Suffragist Movement.* ABC-CLIO, 1998. Copyright © 1998 by The Moschovitis Group, Inc. Reproduced by permission of Moschovitis Group, Inc.—Weeton, Nellie. From "The Trials of an English Governess: Nelly Weeton Stock," originally published in *Miss Weeton: Journal of a Governess.* Edited by Edward Hall. Oxford University Press (London), H. Milford, 1936-39. Reproduced by permission of Oxford University Press.—Weston, Ruth D. From "Who Touches This Touches a Woman," in *Critical Essays on Alice Walker.* Edited by Ikenna Dieke. Greenwood Press 1999. Reproduced by permission of Greenwood Publishing Group, Inc., Westport, CT.—Wheeler, Marjorie Spruill. From an introduction to *One Woman, One Vote: Rediscovering the Woman Suffrage Movement.* Edited by Marjorie Spruill Wheeler. NewSage Press, 1995. Copyright © 1995 by NewSage Press and Educational Film Company. All rights reserved. Reproduced by permission.—Willard, Charity Cannon. From *Christine de Pizan: Her Life and Works.* Persea Books, 1984. Copyright © 1984 by Charity Cannon Willard. Reproduced by permission.—Willis, Sharon A. From "Staging Sexual Difference: Reading, Recitation, and Repetition in Duras' *Malady of Death,*" in *Feminine Focus: The New Women Playwrights.* Edited by Enoch Brater. Oxford University Press, 1989. Copyright © 1989 by Oxford University Press, Inc. Reproduced by permission of Oxford University Press.—Winter, Kate H. From *Marietta Holley: Life with "Josiah Allen's Wife."* Syracuse University Press, 1984. Copyright © 1984 by Syracuse University Press. All rights reserved. Reproduced by permission.—Woolf, Virginia. From "George Eliot," in *The Common Reader,* Harcourt, Brace & Company, 1925, L. & V. Woolf, 1925. Copyright 1925 by Harcourt Brace & Company. Renewed 1953 by Leonard Woolf. Reprinted by permission of Harcourt, Brace & Company and The Society of Authors.—Wynne-Davies, Marion. From an introduction to *Women Poets of the Renaissance.* Edited by Marion Wynne-Davies.

Routledge, 1999. Reprint. Copyright © 1998 by J. M. Dent. All rights reserved. Reproduced by permission of Routledge/Taylor & Francis and the author—Yalom, Marilyn. From "Toward a History of Female Adolescence: The Contribution of George Sand," in *George Sand: Collected Essays.* Edited by Janis Glasgow. The Whitson Publishing Company, 1985. Reproduced by permission of the author.—Yu Xuanji. From "Joining Somebody's Mourning and Three Beautiful Sisters, Orphaned Young," in *The Clouds Float North: The Complete Poems of Yu Xuanji.* Translated by David Young and Jiann I. Lin. Wesleyan University Press, 1998. Copyright © 1998 by David Young and Jiann I. Lin. All rights reserved. Reproduced by permission.

Photographs and Illustrations in Feminism in Literature *were received from the following sources:*

16th century men and women wearing fashionable clothing, ca. 1565 engraving. Hulton/Archive.—A lay sister preparing medicine as shown on the cover of *The Book of Margery Kempe,* photograph. MS. Royal 15 D 1, British Library, London.—Akhmatova, Anna, photograph. Archive Photos, Inc./Express Newspaper.—Alcott, Louisa May, drawing. The Granger Collection, New York.—Alcott, Louisa May, photograph. Archive Photos, Inc.—Allen, Joan, Joanne Camp, Anne Lange, and Cynthia Nixon, in a scene from the play "The Heidi Chronicles," photograph. Time Life Pictures/Getty Images.—Allende, Isabelle, photograph. Getty Images.—An estimated 5,000 people march outside the Minnesota Capitol Building in protest to the January 22, 1973 Supreme Court ruling on abortion as a result of the "Roe vs. Wade" case, photograph. AP/Wide World Photos.—Angelou, Maya, photograph. AP/Wide World Photos.—Anthony, Susan B., Frances Willard, and other members of the International Council of Women, photograph. Copyright © Corbis.—Atwood, Margaret, photograph by Jerry Bauer. Copyright © Jerry Bauer.—Autographed manuscript of Phillis Weatley's poem "To the University of Cambridge." The Granger Collection, New York.—Beller, Kathleen as Kate in the 1980 film version of Margaret Atwood's novel, *Surfacing,* photograph. Kobal Collection/Surfacing Film.—Blackshear, Thomas, illustrator. From a cover of *The Bluest Eye,* written by Toni Morrison. Plume, 1994. Reproduced by permission of Plume, a division of Penguin USA.—Broadside published by the National American Woman Suffrage Association, featuring "Why Women Want to Vote." The Library of Congress.—Brontë, Anne, Emily and Charlotte, painting by Patrick Branwell Brontë, located at the National Portrait Gallery,

1939, photograph. Copyright © Corbis-Bettmann.—Brontë, Charlotte, painting. Archive Photos.—Brooks, Gwendolyn, holding a copy of *The World of Gwendolyn Brooks,* photograph. AP/Wide World Photos.—Brown, John Mason (right) talking to National Book Award winners Marianne Moore, James Jones, and Rachel Carson, in New York City, NY, 1952, photograph. AP/Wide World Photos.—Brown, Rita Mae, photograph. AP/Wide World Photos.—Browning, Elizabeth Barret, 1848, illustration. Copyright © Corbis-Bettmann.—Burney, Fanny, engraving. Archive Photos, Inc.—Carter, Angela, photograph by Jerry Bauer. Copyright © Jerry Bauer.—Cather, Willa, photograph. AP/Wide World Photos.—Catherine the Great, illustration. Copyright © Archivo Iconografico, S.A./Corbis.—Catt, Carrie Chapman, photograph. The Library of Congress.—Cavendish, Margaret Lucas, engraving. Mary Evans Picture Library.—Child, Lydia Maria, photograph. The Library of Congress.—Childress, Alice, photograph by Jerry Bauer. Copyright © Jerry Bauer.—Chin, Tsai and Tamlyn Tomita in the 1993 film production of Amy Tan's *The Joy Luck Club.* Buena Vista/Hollywood/The Kobal Collection.—Chopin, Kate, photograph. The Library of Congress.—Cisneros, Sandra, 1991, photograph by Dana Tynan. AP/Wide World Photos.—Cixous, Hélène, photograph. Copyright © Bassouls Sophie/Corbis Sygma.—Class on a field trip to Library of Congress, photograph by Frances Benjamin Johnston. Copyright © Corbis.—Cleopatra VII, illustration. The Library of Congress.—Cyanotype by Frances Benjamin Johnson, ca. 1899, of girls and a teacher in a high school cooking class, photograph. Copyright © Corbis.—de la Cruz, Juana Inez, painting. Copyright © Philadelphia Museum of Art/Corbis-Bettmann.—de Pizan, Christine, writing in her study, photograph. MS. Harley 4431, f.4R. British Library, London.—Dickinson, Emily, photograph of a painting. The Library of Congress.—Doolittle, Hilda, 1949, photograph. AP/Wide World Photos.—Duras, Marguerite, photograph. AP/Wide World Photos.—Dworkin, Andrea, 1986, photograph. AP/Wide World Photos.—Edgeworth, Maria, engraving. The Library of Congress.—Eliot, George, photograph. Copyright © The Bettman Archive.—Emecheta, Buchi, photograph by Jerry Bauer. Copyright © Jerry Bauer.—Emily Dickinson Homestead in Amherst, Massachusetts, photograph. Copyright © James Marshall/Corbis.—Erdrich, Louise, photograph by Eric Miller. AP/Wide World Photos.—French, Marilyn, photograph by Jerry Bauer. Copyright © Jerry Bauer.—Friedan, Betty, president of the National Organization for Women, and other feminists march in New York City, photograph. Copyright © JP Laffont/Sygma/Corbis.—Friedan, Betty, with

Yoko Ono, photograph. Copyright © Bettmann/Corbis.—Frontpiece and title page from *Poems on Various Subjects, Religious and Moral,* written by Phillis Wheatley. Copyright © The Pierpont Morgan Library/Art Resource, NY.—Fuller, Margaret, painting by John Plumbe. The Library of Congress.—Gandhi, Indira, photograph. Copyright © Corbis-Bettmann.—Garrison, William Lloyd, (bottom right), with the Pennsylvania Abolition Society, photograph. National Portrait Gallery.—Gilman, Charlotte Perkins, cover photograph. Copyright © Corbis.—Gilman, Charlotte P., photograph. Copyright © Corbis-Bettmann.—Godwin, Mary Wollstonecraft, illustration. Copyright © Corbis-Bettmann.—Hansberry, Lorraine, photograph by David Attie. AP/Wide World Photos.—Head, Bessie, photograph. Reproduced by the kind permission of the Estate of Bessie Head.—"Head of Medusa," marble sculpture by Gianlorenzo Bernini. Copyright © Araldo de Luca/Corbis.—Hellman, Lillian, photograph. AP/Wide World Photos.—Hurston, Zora Neale looking at "American Stuff," at the *New York Times* book fair, photograph. The Library of Congress.—Hurston, Zora Neale, photograph by Carl Van Vechten. The Carl Van Vechten Trust.—Hypatia, conte crayon drawing. Copyright © Corbis-Bettmann.—Illustration depicting a woman's body being the subject of political and social conflict, photograph. Barbara Kruger/Mary Boone Gallery.—Jolie, Angelina (right), and unidentified person, in the film *Foxfire,* photograph by Jane O'Neal. The Kobal Collection/O'Neal, Jane.—Karloff, Boris, in movie *Frankenstein;* 1935, photograph. The Kobal Collection.—Kingston, Maxine Hong, photograph by Jerry Bauer. Copyright © Jerry Bauer.—"La Temptation," depicting Adam and Eve in the Garden of Paradise. The Library of Congress.—Lessing, Doris, photograph by Jerry Bauer. Copyright © Jerry Bauer.—Luce, Clare Booth, portrait. Copyright © UPI/Bettmann Archive.—Manuscript page from *The Book of Ladies,* by Christine de Pizan. Bibliotheque Nationale de France.—Manuscript page of *Vieyra Impugnado,* written by Sor Margarita Ignacia and translated to Spanish by Inigo Rosende. Madrid: Antonio Sanz, 1731. The Special Collections Library, University of Michigan.—Martineau, Harriet, engraving. The Library of Congress.—Migrant mother with child huddled on either shoulder, Nipomo, California, 1936, photograph by Dorothea Lange. The Library of Congress.—Millay, Edna St. Vincent, photograph. AP/Wide World Photos.—Montagu, Lady Mary Wortley, engraving. Archive Photos, Inc.—Moore, Marianne, photograph by Jerry Bauer. Copyright © Jerry Bauer.—Morrison, Toni, 1993, photograph. AP/Wide World Photos.—Murasaki, Lady, looking out from the veranda of a monastery, illustration

ACKNOWLEDGMENTS

from *Tale of Genji.* Copyright © Asian Art Archaeology, Inc./Corbis.—National League of Women Voters' Headquarters, photograph. Copyright © Corbis-Bettmann.—National Women's Suffrage Association (NWSA), during a political convention in Chicago, Illinois, photograph. Copyright © Bettmann/Corbis.—Naylor, Gloria, photograph. Marion Ettlinger/AP/Wide World Photos.—Oates, Joyce Carol, 1991, photograph. AP/Wide World Photos.—October 15, 1913 publication of the early feminist periodical, *The New Freewoman,* photograph. McFarlin Library, Department of Special Collections, The University of Tulsa.—Paul, Alice (second from right), standing with five other suffragettes, photograph. AP/Wide World Photos.—Pfeiffer, Michelle, and Daniel Day-Lewis, in the film *The Age of Innocence,* 1993, photograph by Phillip Caruso. The Kobal Collection.—Plath, Sylvia, photograph. AP/Wide World Photos.—Poster advertising *Uncle Tom's Cabin,* by Harriet Beecher Stowe, "The Greatest Book of the Age," photograph. Copyright © Bettmann/Corbis.—Rich, Adrienne, holding certificate of poetry award, Chicago, Illinois, 1986, photograph. AP/Wide World Photos.—Rossetti, Christina, 1863, photograph by Lewis Carroll. Copyright © UPI/Bettmann.—Russell, Rosalind and Joan Crawford in the 1939 movie *The Women,* written by Clare Boothe Luce, photograph. MGM/The Kobal Collection.—Salem Witch Trial, lithograph by George H. Walker. Copyright © Bettmann/Corbis.—Sand, George, illustration. Copyright © Leonard de Selva/Corbis.—Sand, George, photograph. The Library of Congress.—Sanger, Margaret, Miss Clara Louise Rowe, and Mrs. Anne Kennedy, arranging the first American Birth Control Conference, photograph. Copyright © Underwood and Underwood/Corbis.—Sappho, bronze sculpture. The Library of Congress.—Sappho, illustration. The Library of Congress.—Sappho performing outdoors, illustration. The Library of Congress.—"Sara in a Green Bonnet," painting by Mary Cassatt, c. 1901. National Museum of American Art, Smithsonian Institution, Washington, DC, U.S.A.—Scene from the film *Mill on the Floss,* by George Eliot, engraving. Hulton Archive/Getty Images.—Segwick, Catherine Maria, slide. Archive Photos, Inc.—Sexton, Anne, photograph. Copyright © Bettmann/Corbis.—Sexton, Anne, with her daughters Joy and Linda, photograph. Time Life Pictures/Getty Images.—Shelley, Mary Wollstonecraft, painting by Samuel John Stump. Copyright © Corbis-Bettmann.—Stael, Madame de, color lithograph. Archive Photos, Inc.—Stanton, Elizabeth Cady, illustration. Copyright © Bettmann/Corbis.—Stanton, Elizabeth Cady, photograph. AP/Wide World Photos.—Stein, Gertrude (left), arriving in New York aboard the S. S. Champlain with her secretary and companion Alice B. Toklas, photograph. AP/Wide World Photos.—Stein, Gertrude, photograph by Carl Van Vechten. The Estate of Carl Van Vechten.—Steinem, Gloria, photograph. AP/Wide World Photos.—Stowe, Harriet Beecher, photograph. Copyright © Bettmann/Corbis.—Suffrage parade in New York, New York, October 15, 1915, photograph. The Library of Congress.—Supporters of the Equal Rights Amendment carry a banner down Pennsylvania Avenue, Washington, DC, photograph. AP/Wide World Photos.—Sur la Falaise aux Petites Dalles, 1873. Painting by Berthe Morisot. Copyright © Francis G. Mayer/Corbis.—Tan, Amy, 1993, photograph. AP/Wide World Photos.—*Time,* cover of Kate Millett, from August 31, 1970. Time Life Pictures/Stringer/Getty Images.—Title page of *A Vindication of the Rights of Woman: With Strictures on Political and Moral Subjects,* written by Mary Wollstonecraft. William L. Clements Library, University of Michigan.—Title page of *Adam Bede,* written by George Eliot. Edinburgh & London: Blackwood, 1859, Volume 1, New York: Harper, 1859. The Graduate Library, University of Michigan.—Title page from *De L'influence des Passions sur le Bonheur des Individus et des Nations,* (A Treatise on the Influence of the Passions upon the Happiness of Individuals and of Nations), written by Stael de Holstein, photograph. The Special Collections Library, University of Michigan.—Title page from *Evelina,* written by Fanny Burney, photograph. The Special Collections Library, University of Michigan.—Title page from *Mansfield Park,* written by Jane Austen. The Special Collections Library, University of Michigan.—Title page of *Mary, A Fiction,* written by Mary Wollstonecraft.—Title page from *Youth and the Bright Medusa,* written by Willa Cather. New York, Alfred A Knopf. The Special Collections Library, University of Michigan.—Title page of *A New-England Tale,* written by Catharine Maria Sedgewick. New York: E. Bliss and E. White, 1822. The Special Collections Library, University of Michigan.—Title page of *Aurora Leigh,* written by Elizabeth Barrett Browning. New York, Boston: C. S. Francis and Co., 1857. The Special Collections Library, University of Michigan.—Title page of *Mrs. Dalloway,* written by Virginia Woolf. London: Hogarth Press, 1925. The Special Collections Library, University of Michigan.—Title page of *The Dial: A Magazine for Literature, Philosophy, and Religion.* Boston. Weeks, Jordan and Company (etc.); London, Wiley and Putnam (etc.). Volume 1. The Special Collections Library, University of Michigan.—Title page of *The House of Mirth,* written by Edith Wharton. New York: C. Scribner's Sons, 1905. The Special Collections Library, University of Michigan.—Title page of *The Little Review,*

March 1916. The Purdy/Kresge Library, Wayne State University.—Title page of *Woman in the Nineteenth Century,* written by Sarah Margaret Fuller. New York, Greeley and McElrath. 1845. The Special Collections Library, University of Michigan.—Title page of *Wuthering Heights,* written by Emily Brontë. New York: Harper and Brothers. 1848. The Special Collections Library, University of Michigan.—Truth, Sojourner, photograph. Archive Photos, Inc.—Tubman, Harriet, photograph. The Library of Congress.—Victoria, Queen of England, illustration. The Library of Congress.—Walker, Alice, 1989, photograph. AP/Wide World Photos.—Welles, Orson, as Edward Rochester, with Joan Fontaine as Jane Eyre, in the film *Jane Eyre,* photograph. The Kobal Collection.—Wharton, Edith, photograph. AP/Wide World Photos.—Wheatley, Phillis, photograph. Copyright © The Bettman Archive.—Winfrey, Oprah, as Celie and Danny Glover as Albert with baby in scene from the film *The Color Purple,* written by Alice Walker, directed by Steven Spielberg, photograph. The Kobal Collection.—Women in French Revolution, invade assembly, demanding death penalty for members of the aristocracy, Woodcut. Copyright © Bettmann/Corbis.—Women workers in a shoe factory in Lynn, Massachusetts, photograph. Copyright © Corbis.—Woodhull, Victoria, reading statement before House Committee, drawing. The Library of Congress.—Woolf, Virginia, photograph. AP/Wide World Photos.—Woolson, Constance Fenimore, engraving. Archive Photos.

● = historical event

■ = literary event

1570 B.C.

● Queen Ahmose Nefertari, sister and principal wife of King Ahmose, rules as "god's wife," in a new position created by a law enacted by the King.

C. 1490 B.C.

● Queen Hatshepsut rules as pharaoh, several years after the death of her husband, King Thutmose II.

C. 1360 B.C.

● Queen Nefertiti rules Egypt alongside her husband, pharaoh Akhenaten.

C. 620 B.C.

● Sappho is born on the Isle of Lesbos, Greece.

C. 600 B.C.

■ Sappho organizes and operates a *thiasos,* an academy for young, unmarried Greek women.

● Spartan women are the most independent women in the world, and are able to own property, pursue an education, and participate in athletics.

C. 550 B.C.

● Sappho dies on the Isle of Lesbos.

C. 100 B.C.

● Roman laws allow a husband: to kill his wife if she is found in the act of adultery, to determine the amount of money his wife is owed in the event of divorce, and to claim his children as property.

69 B.C.

● Cleopatra VII Philopator is born in Egypt.

36 B.C.

● Marriage of Antony and Cleopatra.

C. 30 B.C.

● Cleopatra VII Philopator commits suicide in Egypt.

18

● Emperor Augustus decrees the *Lex Julia,* which penalizes childless Roman citizens, adulterers, and those who marry outside of their social rank or status.

C. 370

● Hypatia is born in Alexandria, Egypt.

415

● Hypatia is murdered in Alexandria, Egypt.

C. 500

● Salians (Germanic Franks living in Gaul) issue a code of laws which prohibit women from inheriting land; the law is used for centuries to prevent women from ruling in France.

592

● Empress Suiko (554-628) becomes the first woman sovereign of Japan.

C. 690

● Wu Zetian (624-705) becomes the only female emperor of Imperial China.

C. 700

● Japanese legal code specifies that in law, ceremony, and practice, Japanese men can be polygamous—having first wives and an unlimited number of "second wives" or concubines—, but women cannot.

877

● Lady Ise, Japanese court lady, is born. She is considered one of the most accomplished poets of her time and her poems are widely anthologized.

935

● Hrotsvitha (also Hrotsvit or Roswitha), considered the first German woman poet, is born.

940

● Lady Ise dies.

950

■ Publication of the *Kagero Nikki* (*The Gossamer Years*), a diary written by an anonymous Japanese courtesan. The realism and confessional quality of the work influence the works of later court diarists.

C. 960

● Japanese poet Izumi Shikibu, known for her expression of erotic and Buddhist themes, is born. Her body of work includes more than 1,500 *waka* (31-syllable poems).

C. 1002

■ Sei Shonagon, Japanese court lady, writes *Makura no Soshi* (*The Pillow Book*), considered a classic of Japanese literature and the originator of the genre known as *zuihitsu* ("to follow the brush") that employs a stream-of-consciousness literary style.

C. 1008

■ Murasaki Shikibu writes *Genji Monogatari* (*The Tale of Genji*), considered a masterpiece of classical prose literature in Japan.

C. 1030

● Izumi Shikibu dies.

1098

● Hildegard von Bingen is born in Bermersheim, Germany.

C. 1100

■ Twenty women troubadours—aristocratic poet-composers who write songs dealing with love—write popular love songs in France. About twenty-four of their songs survive, including four written by the famous female troubadour known as the Countess of Dia, or Beatrix.

1122

● Eleanor of Aquitaine is born in Aquitaine, France. Her unconventional life is chronicled for centuries in books and dramatic works.

C. 1150

● Sometime in the twelfth century (some sources say 1122), Marie de France, the earliest known female French writer and author of *lais*, a collection of twelve verse tales written in octosyllabic rhyming couplets, flourished. She is thought to be the originator of the *lay* as a poetic form.

C. 1170

- Marie of Champagne (1145-1198), daughter of King Louis VII of France and Eleanor of Aquitaine, cosponsors "courts of love" to debate points on the proper conduct of knights toward their ladies. Marie encourages Chrétien de Troyes to write *Lancelot,* and Andreas Capellanus to write *The Art of Courtly Love.*

1179

- Hildegard von Bingen dies in Disibodenberg, Germany.

C. 1200

- Women shirabyoshi performances are a part of Japanese court and Buddhist temple festivities. In their songs and dances, women performers dress in white, male attire which includes fans, court caps, and swords. This form of traditional dance plays an important role in the development of classical Japanese noh drama.

1204

- Eleanor of Aquitaine dies on 1 April.

C. 1275

- Japanese poet and court lady Abutsu Ni (1222?-1283) writes her poetic travel diary, *Izayoi Nikki* (*Diary of the Waning Moon*) on the occasion of her travel to Kyoto to seek inheritance rights for herself and her children.

C. 1328

- The French cite the Salic Law, which was promulgated in the early medieval period and prohibits women from inheriting land, as the authority for denying the crown of France to anyone—man or woman—whose descent from a French king can be traced only through the female line.

1346

- Famous mystic St. Birgitta of Sweden (c.1303-1373) founds the Roman Catholic Order of St. Saviour, whose members are called the Brigittines. She authors *Revelations,* an account of her supernatural visions.

1347

- Caterina Benincasa (later St. Catherine of Siena) is born on 25 March in Siena, Italy.

C. 1365

- Christine de Pizan is born in Venice, Italy.

C. 1373

- Margery Kempe is born in King's Lynn (now known as Lynn), in Norfolk, England.

1380

- St. Catherine of Siena dies on 29 April in Rome, Italy.

C. 1393

- Julian of Norwich (1342?-1416?), the most famous of all the medieval recluses in England, writes *Revelations of Divine Love,* expounding on the idea of Christ as mother.

1399

- Christine de Pizan writes the long poem "Letter to the God of Love," which marks the beginning of the *querelle des femmes* (debate on women). This attack on misogyny in medieval literature triggers a lively exchange of letters among the foremost French scholars of the day, and the *querelle* is continued by various European literary scholars for centuries.

1429

- Joan of Arc (1412-1431)—in support of Charles I, who is prevented by the English from assuming his rightful place as King of France—leads liberation forces to victory in Orléans.

1431

- Joan of Arc is burned at the stake as a heretic by the English on 30 May. She is acquitted of heresy by another church court in 1456 and proclaimed a saint in 1920.

C. 1431

- Christine de Pizan dies in France.

C. 1440

● Margery Kempe dies in England.

1451

● Isabella of Castile, future Queen of Spain, is born. She succeeds her brother in 1474 and rules jointly with her husband, Ferdinand of Aragon, from 1479.

1465

● Cassandra Fedele, who becomes the most famous woman scholar in Italy, is born in Venice.

1469

● Laura Cereta, outspoken feminist and humanist scholar, is born in Brescia, Italy.

1485

● Veronica Gambara is born in Italy. Her court becomes an important center of the Italian Renaissance, and Gambara earns distinction as an author of Petrarchan sonnets as well as for her patronage of the artist Corregio.

1486

■ *Malleus Maleficarum* (*The Hammer of Witches*), an encyclopedia of contemporary knowledge about witches and methods of investigating the crime of witchcraft, is published in Europe. The volume details numerous justifications for women's greater susceptibility to evil, and contributes to the almost universal European persecution of women as witches that reaches its height between 1580 and 1660 and makes its way to Salem, Massachusetts in 1692.

1492

● Marguerite de Navarre is born on 11 April in France.

1499

● Laura Cereta dies in Brescia, Italy.

C. 1512

● Catherine Parr is born in England.

1515

● Teresa de Alhumadawas (later St. Teresa de Ávila) is born on 28 March in Gotarrendura, Spain.

1524

● Courtesan Gaspara Stampa, widely regarded as the greatest woman poet of the Renaissance, is born in Padua, Italy.

1533

● Queen Elizabeth I is born on 7 September in Greenwich, England, the daughter of King Henry VIII and his second wife, Anne Boleyn.

1536

● King Henry VIII of England beheads his second wife, Anne Boleyn, on 19 May. Boleyn is convicted of infidelity and treason after she fails to produce the desired male heir.

1538

■ Vittoria Colonna (1492-1547), an influential woman in Renaissance Italy, achieves distinction as a poet with the publication of her first book of poetry.

1548

● Catherine Parr dies in England.

1549

● Marguerite de Navarre dies in France.

1550

● Veronica Gambara dies in Italy.

1554

● Gaspara Stampa dies on 23 April in Venice, Italy.

1555

● Moderata Fonte (pseudonym of Modesta Pozzo) is born in Venice, Italy.

1558

● Elizabeth I assumes the throne of England and presides over a period of peace and prosperity known as the Elizabethan Age.

Cassadra Fedele dies in Venice. She is honored with a state funeral.

1559

Marguerite de Navarre completes her *L'Heptaméron des Nouvelles* (the *Heptameron*), a series of stories primarily concerned with the themes of love and spirituality.

1561

Mary Sidney, noted English literary patron, is born in England. She is the sister of poet Sir Philip Sidney, whose poems she edits and publishes after his death in 1586, and whose English translation of the Psalms she completes.

1565

French scholar Marie de Gournay is born on 6 October in Paris. Known as the French "Minerva" (a woman of great wisdom or learning), she is a financial success as a writer of treatises on various subjects, including *Equality of Men and Women* (1622) and *Complaint of Ladies* (1626), which demand better education for women.

1582

St. Teresa de Avila dies on 4 October in Alba.

1592

Moderata Fonte (pseudonym of Modesta Pozzo) dies in Venice, Italy.

C. 1600

Catherine de Vivonne (c. 1588-1665), Madame de Rambouillet, inaugurates and then presides over salon society in Paris, in which hostesses hold receptions in their salons or drawing rooms for the purpose of intellectual conversation. Salon society flourishes in the seventeenth and eighteenth centuries, and stimulates scholarly and literary development in France and England.

Geisha (female artists and entertainers) and prostitutes are licensed by the Japanese government to work in the pleasure quarters of major cities in Japan.

1603

Queen Elizabeth I dies on 24 March in Surrey, England.

Izumo no Okuni is believed to originate kabuki, the combination of dance, drama, and music which dominates Japanese theater throughout the Tokugawa period (1600-1868).

1607

Madeleine de Scudéry, one of the best-known and most influential writers of romance tales in seventeeth-century Europe, is born on 15 November in Le Havre, France.

C. 1612

American poet Anne Bradstreet is born in Northampton, England.

1614

Margaret Askew Fell, who helps establish the Society of Friends, or Quakers, and becomes known as the "mother of Quakerism," is born in Lancashire, England. Quakers give women unusual freedom in religious life. An impassioned advocate of the right of women to preach, Fell publishes the tract *Women's Speaking Justified, Proved and Allowed of by the Scriptures* in 1666.

1621

Mary Sidney dies in England.

C. 1623

Margaret Lucas Cavendish, later Duchess of Newcastle, is born in England. She authors fourteen volumes of works, including scientific treatises, poems, and plays, and her autobiography *The True Relation of My Birth, Breeding and Life* (1656).

1631

Katherine Phillips (1631-1664), who writes poetry under the pseudonym "Orinda," is born. She is the founder of a London literary salon called the Society of Friendship that includes such luminaries as Jeremy Taylor and Henry Vaughn.

C. 1640

● Aphra Behn is born.

C. 1645

● Deborah Moody (c. 1580-c. 1659) becomes the first woman to receive a land grant in colonial America when she is given the title to land in Kings County (now Brooklyn), New York. She is also the first colonial woman to vote.

C. 1646

● Glückel of Hameln, who records her life as a Jewish merchant in Germany in her memoirs, is born in Hamburg.

1651

● Juana Ramírez de Asbaje (later known as Sor Juana Inés de la Cruz) is born on 12 November on a small farm called San Miguel de Nepantla in New Spain (now Mexico).

1670

■ Aphra Behn becomes the first professional woman writer in England when her first play *The Forced Marriage; or, The Jealous Bridegroom,* is performed in London.

1672

● Anne Bradstreet dies on 16 September in Andover, Massachusetts.

C. 1673

■ Francois Poulain de la Barre publishes *The Equality of the Sexes,* in which he supports the idea that women have intellectual powers equal to those of men. His work stimulates the betterment of women's education in succeeding centuries.

1673

● Margaret Lucas Cavendish, Duchess of Newcastle, dies in England.

1676

■ After being captured and then released by Wampanaoag Indians, Puritan settler Mary White Rowlandson (1636-1678) writes what becomes a famous account of her captivity.

1689

● Mary Pierrpont (later Lady Mary Wortley Montagu) is born on 26 May in London, England.

● Aphra Behn dies on 16 April and is buried in the cloisters at Westminster Abbey.

1692

● The Salem, Massachusetts, witch hysteria begins in February, and eventually leads to the execution of eighteen women convicted of witchcraft in the infamous Salem Witchcraft Trials (1692-1693).

C. 1694

■ Mary Astell (1666-1731) publishes the treatise *A Serious Proposal to the Ladies* in two volumes (1694-1697). In the work, Astell calls for the establishment of private institutions where single women live together for a time and receive quality education.

1695

● Sor Juana Inés de la Cruz dies on 17 April at the Convent of St. Jerome in Mexico.

1701

● Madeleine de Scudéry dies on 2 June in Paris, France.

C. 1704

■ Sarah Kemble Knight (1666-1727), a Puritan author, records her arduous journey from Boston to New York to settle the estate of her cousin.

C. 1713

■ Anne Kingsmill Finch (1661-1720) writes many poems dealing with the injustices suffered by women of the aristocratic class to which she belonged. As Countess of Winchilsea, she becomes the center of a literary circle at her husband's estate in Eastwell, England.

1728

● Mercy Otis Warren is born on 14 September in Barnstable, Massachusetts.

1729

● Catherine the Great is born on 2 May in Germany as Sophia Friederica Augusta.

1744

● Abigail Adams is born Abigail Smith on 11 November in Weymouth, Massachusetts.

1748

● Olympe de Gouges, French Revolutionary feminist, is born Olympe Gouze in Montauban, France. She plays an active role in the French Revolution, demanding equal rights for women in the new French Republic.

1752

● Frances "Fanny" Burney is born on 13 June in England.

C. 1753

● Phillis Wheatley is born in Africa.

1759

● Mary Wollstonecraft is born on 27 April in England.

1762

● Lady Mary Wortley Montagu dies on 21 August in London, England.

● Catherine the Great becomes Empress of Russia.

1766

● Germaine Necker (later Madame de Staël) is born on 22 April in Paris, France.

1768

● Maria Edgeworth is born on 1 January at Black Bourton in Oxfordshire, England.

1774

▨ Clementina Rind (1740-1774) is appointed publisher of the *Virginia Gazette* by the House of Burgesses in Virginia.

1775

● Jane Austen is born on 16 December at Steventon Rectory, Hampshire, England.

1776

● Men and women who hold property worth over 50 pounds are granted suffrage in New Jersey.

C. 1780

▨ Madame Roland (1754-1793), formerly Marie Philppon, hosts an important salon where revolutionary politicians and thinkers debate during the French Revolution. An outspoken feminist, she presses for women's political and social rights.

1784

▨ Hannah Adams (1758-1831) becomes the first American woman author to support herself with money earned from writing, with the publication of her first book, *View of Religions* (later *Dictionary of Religions*).

● Phillis Wheatley dies on 5 December in Boston, Massachusetts.

1787

▨ Catherine Sawbridge Macaulay publishes *Letters on Education,* an appeal for better education of women.

▨ Mary Wollstonecraft's *Thoughts on the Education of Daughters: With Reflections on Female Conduct, in the More Important Duties of Life* is published by J. Johnson.

1789

● Catharine Maria Sedgwick is born on 28 December in Stockbridge, Massachusetts.

▨ Olympe de Gouges writes *The Declaration of the Rights of Women and Citizen,* a 17-point document demanding the recognition of women as political, civil, and legal equals of men, and including a sample marriage contract that emphasizes free will and equality in marriage.

1792

● Sarah Moore Grimké is born on 26 November in Charleston, South Carolina.

■ Mary Wollstonecraft's *A Vindication of the Rights of Woman, with Strictures on Political and Moral Subjects* is published by J. Johnson.

1793

● Lucretia Coffin Mott is born on 3 January in Nantucket, Massachusetts.

● Olympe de Gouges is executed by guillotine for treason on 3 November.

● Madame Roland is executed in November, ostensibly for treason, but actually because the Jacobins want to suppress feminist elements in the French Revolution.

1796

● Catherine the Great dies following a stroke on 6 November in Russia.

1797

● Mary Wollstonecraft Shelley is born on 30 August, in London, England.

● Mary Wollstonecraft dies on 10 September in London, England, from complications following childbirth.

● Sojourner Truth is born Isabella Bomefree in Ulster County, New York.

1799

■ Mary Wollstonecraft's *Maria; or, The Wrongs of Woman: A Posthumous Fragment* is published by James Carey.

1801

● Caroline M. (Stansbury) Kirkland is born on 11 January in New York City.

1802

● Lydia Maria Child is born on 11 February in Medford, Massachusetts.

1804

● George Sand (pseudonym of Armandine Aurore Lucille Dupin) is born on 1 July in Paris, France.

● The Napoleonic Code is established in France under Napoleon I, and makes women legally subordinate to men. The code requires women to be obedient to their husbands, bars women from voting, sitting on juries, serving as legal witnesses, or sitting on chambers of commerce or boards of trade.

1805

● Angelina Emily Grimké is born on 20 February in Charleston, South Carolina.

1806

● Elizabeth Barrett Browning is born on 6 March in Coxhoe Hall, Durham, England.

1807

■ Germaine de Staël's *Corinne, ou l'Italie (Corinne, or Italy)* is published by Nicolle.

● Suffrage in New Jersey is limited to "white male citizens."

1808

● Caroline Sheridan Norton is born on 22 March in England.

1810

● (Sarah) Margaret Fuller is born on 23 May in Cambridgeport, Massachusetts.

● Elizabeth Cleghorn Gaskell is born on 29 September in London, England.

1811

● Harriet Beecher Stowe is born on 14 June in Litchfield, Connecticut.

■ Jane Austen's *Sense and Sensibility* is published by T. Egerton.

1813

● Harriet A. Jacobs is born in North Carolina.

■ Jane Austen's *Pride and Prejudice* is published by T. Egerton.

1814

● Mercy Otis Warren dies on 19 October in Plymouth, Massachusetts.

1815

- Elizabeth Cady Stanton is born on 12 November in Johnstown, New York.

- King Louis XVIII of France outlaws divorce.

1816

- Charlotte Brontë is born on 21 April in Thornton, Yorkshire, England.

- Jane Austen's *Emma* is published by M. Carey.

1817

- Madame Germaine de Staël dies on 14 July in Paris, France.

- Jane Austen dies on 18 July in Winchester, Hampshire, England.

1818

- Emily Brontë is born on 30 July in Thornton, Yorkshire, England.

- Lucy Stone is born on 13 August near West Brookfield, Massachusetts.

- Abigail Adams dies on 28 October in Quincy, Massachusetts.

- Jane Austen's *Northanger Abbey and Persuasion* is published by John Murray.

- Educator Emma Hart Willard's *A Plan for Improving Female Education* is published by Middlebury College.

- Mary Wollstonecraft Shelley's *Frankenstein; or, The Modern Prometheus* is published by Lackington, Hughes, Harding, Mavor & Jones.

1819

- Julia Ward Howe is born on 27 May in New York City.

- George Eliot (pseudonym of Mary Ann Evans) is born on 22 November in Arbury, Warwickshire, England.

1820

- Susan B. Anthony is born on 15 February in Adams, Massachusetts.

1821

- Emma Hart Willard establishes the Troy Female Seminary in Troy, New York.

1822

- Frances Power Cobbe is born on 4 December in Dublin, Ireland.

1823

- Charlotte Yonge is born 11 August in Otterbourne, Hampshire, England.

1825

- Frances Ellen Watkins Harper is born on 24 September in Baltimore, Maryland.

1826

- Matilda Joslyn Gage is born on 24 March in Cicero, New York.

1830

- Christina Rossetti is born on 5 December in London, England.

- Emily Dickinson is born on 10 December in Amherst, Massachusetts.

- *Godey's Lady's Book*—the first American women's magazine—is founded by Louis Antoine Godey and edited by Sarah Josepha Hale (1788-1879).

1832

- Louisa May Alcott is born on 29 November in Germantown, Pennsylvania.

- George Sand's *Indiana* is published by Roret et Dupuy.

1833

- Oberlin Collegiate Institute—the first coeducational institution of higher learning— is established in Oberlin, Ohio.

1836

- Marietta Holley is born on 16 July near Adams, New York.

1837

- Mt. Holyoke College—the first college for women—is founded by Mary Lyon in South Hadley, Massachusetts.

Alexandria Victoria (1819-1901) becomes Queen Victoria at the age of eighteen. Her reign lasts for 63 years, the longest reign of any British monarch.

1838

Victoria Woodhull is born on 23 September in Homer, Ohio.

Sarah Moore Grimké's *Letters on the Equality of the Sexes, and the Condition of Woman* is published by I. Knapp.

1840

Frances "Fanny" Burney dies on 6 January in London, England.

Ernestine Rose (1810-1892) writes the petition for what will become the Married Woman's Property Law (1848).

C. 1844

Sarah Winnemucca is born on Paiute land near Humboldt Lake in what is now Nevada.

1845

Margaret Fuller's *Woman in the Nineteenth Century* is published by Greeley & McElrath.

1847

Charlotte Brontë's *Jane Eyre* is published by Smith, Elder.

Emily Brontë's *Wuthering Heights* is published by T. C. Newby.

1848

The first women's rights convention is called by Lucretia Coffin Mott and Elizabeth Cady Stanton on 19 July and is held in Seneca Falls, New York on 20 July.

Emily Brontë dies on 19 December in Haworth, Yorkshire, England.

New York State Legislature passes the Married Woman's Property Law, granting women the right to retain possession of property they owned prior to marriage.

1849

Maria Edgeworth dies on 22 May in Edgeworthstown, her family's estate in Ireland.

Sarah Orne Jewett is born on 3 September in South Berwick, Maine.

Amelia Bloomer publishes the first issue of her Seneca Falls newspaper *The Lily,* which provides a forum for both temperance and women's rights reformers.

The first state constitution of California extends property rights to women in their own name.

1850

Margaret Fuller drowns—along with her husband and son—on 19 July in a shipwreck off of Fire Island, New York.

The first National Woman's Rights Convention, planned by Lucy Stone and Lucretia Mott, is attended by over one thousand women on 23 and 24 October in Worcester, Massachusetts.

Elizabeth Barrett Browning's *Poems,* containing her *Sonnets from the Portuguese,* is published by Chapman & Hall.

The Narrative of Sojourner Truth, transcribed by Olive Gilbert, is published in the Boston periodical, the *Liberator.*

1851

Mary Wollstonecraft Shelley dies on 1 February in Bournemouth, England.

Kate Chopin is born on 8 February in St. Louis, Missouri.

Sojourner Truth delivers her "A'n't I a Woman?" speech at the Women's Rights Convention on 29 May in Akron, Ohio.

1852

Harriet Beecher Stowe's *Uncle Tom's Cabin; or, Life among the Lowly* is published by Jewett, Proctor & Worthington.

Susan B. Anthony founds The Women's Temperance Society, the first temperance organization in the United States.

1853

Charlotte Brontë's *Villette* is published by Smith, Elder.

Paulina Kellogg Wright Davis (1813-1876) edits and publishes *Una,* the first newspaper of the women's rights movement.

1854

- Margaret Oliphant's *A Brief Summary in Plain Language of the Most Important Laws Concerning Women,* a pamphlet explaining the unfair laws concerning women and exposing the need for reform, is published in London.

1855

- Charlotte Brontë dies on 31 March in Haworth, Yorkshire, England.

- Elizabeth Cady Stanton, speaking in favor of expanding the Married Woman's Property Law, becomes the first woman to appear before the New York State Legislature.

1856

- Harriot Eaton Stanton Blatch is born on 20 January in Seneca Falls, New York.

1857

- Elizabeth Barrett Browning's *Aurora Leigh* is published by Chapman & Hall.

1858

- Emmeline Pankhurst is born on 4 July in Manchester, England.

- Anna Julia Haywood Cooper is born on 10 August in Raleigh, North Carolina.

1859

- Carrie Chapman Catt is born on 9 January in Ripon, Wisconsin.

1860

- Charlotte Perkins Gilman is born on 3 July in Hartford, Connecticut.

- Jane Addams is born on 6 September in Cedarville, Illinois.

1861

- Victoria Earle Matthews is born on 27 May in Fort Valley, Georgia.

- Elizabeth Barrett Browning dies on 29 June in Florence, Italy.

- Harriet Jacobs's *Incidents in the Life of a Slave Girl, Written by Herself,* edited by Lydia Maria Child, is published in Boston.

1862

- Edith Wharton is born on 24 January in New York City.

- Ida B. Wells-Barnett is born on 16 July in Holly Springs, Mississippi.

- Julia Ward Howe's "The Battle Hymn of the Republic" is published in the *Atlantic Monthly.*

1864

- Caroline M. (Stansbury) Kirkland dies of a stroke on 6 April in New York City.

1865

- Elizabeth Cleghorn Gaskell dies on 12 November in Holybourne, Hampshire, England.

1866

- The American Equal Rights Association— dedicated to winning suffrage for African American men and for women of all colors—is founded by Susan B. Anthony and Elizabeth Cady Stanton on 1 May. Lucretia Coffin Mott is elected as the group's president.

- Elizabeth Cady Stanton runs for Congress as an independent; she receives 24 of 12,000 votes cast.

1867

- Catharine Maria Sedgwick dies on 31 July in Boston, Massachusetts.

1868

- Susan B. Anthony and Elizabeth Cady Stanton found the New York-based weekly newspaper, *The Revolution,* with the motto: "The true republic—men, their rights and nothing more; women, their rights and nothing less," in January.

- Julia Ward Howe founds the New England Woman Suffrage Association and the New England Women's Club.

- Louisa May Alcott's *Little Women; or, Meg, Jo, Beth, and Amy* (2 vols., 1868-69) is published by Roberts Brothers.

1869

- John Stuart Mill's treatise in support of women's suffrage, *The Subjection of Women,* is published in London.

Emma Goldman is born on 27 June in Kovno, Lithuania.

Louisa May Alcott's *Hospital Sketches and Camp and Fireside Stories* is published by Roberts Brothers.

Women are granted full and equal suffrage and are permitted to hold office within the territory of Wyoming.

The National Woman Suffrage Association is founded by Elizabeth Cady Stanton and Susan B. Anthony in May in New York City.

The American Woman Suffrage Association is founded by Lucy Stone, Julia Ward Howe, and others in November in Boston, Massachusetts.

1870

The Woman's Journal, edited by Lucy Stone, Henry Blackwell, and Mary Livermore, begins publication on 8 January.

Victoria Woodhull and Tennessee Claflin publish the first issue of their controversial New York weekly newspaper, *Woodhull and Claflin's Weekly.*

1871

Women are granted full and equal suffrage in the territory of Utah. Their rights are revoked in 1887 and restored in 1896.

Victoria Woodhull presents her views on women's rights in a passionate speech to the House Judiciary Committee, marking the first personal appearance before such a high congressional committee by a woman.

Wives of many prominent U. S. politicians, military officers, and businessmen found the Anti-Suffrage party to fight against women's suffrage.

1872

Victoria Woodhull, as a member of the Equal Rights Party (or National Radical Reform Party), becomes the first woman candidate for the office of U.S. President. Her running mate is Frederick Douglass.

Susan B. Anthony and 15 other women attempt to cast their votes in Rochester, New York, in the presidential election. Anthony is arrested and fined $100, which she refuses to pay.

Sojourner Truth attempts to cast her vote in Grand Rapids, Michigan in the presidential election but is denied a ballot.

1873

Colette is born on 28 January in Burgundy, France.

Maria Mitchell (1818-1889), astronomer and faculty member at Vassar College, establishes the Association of the Advancement of Women.

Willa Cather is born on 7 December in Back Creek Valley, Virginia.

Sarah Moore Grimké dies on 23 December in Hyde Park, Massachusetts.

Louisa May Alcott's *Work: A Story of Experience* is published by Roberts Brothers.

1874

Gertrude Stein is born on 3 February in Allegheny, Pennsylvania.

Amy Lowell is born on 9 February in Brookline, Massachusetts.

1876

George Sand dies on 9 June in Nohant, France.

Susan Glaspell is born on 1 July (some sources say 1882) in Davenport, Iowa.

1877

Caroline Sheridan Norton dies on 15 June in England.

1878

Passage of the Matrimonial Causes Act in England enables abused wives to obtain separation orders to keep their husbands away from them.

The "Susan B. Anthony Amendment," which will extend suffrage to women in the United States, is first proposed in Congress by Senator A. A. Sargent.

1879

Margaret Sanger is born on 14 September in Corning, New York.

Angelina Emily Grimké dies on 26 October in Hyde Park, Massachusetts.

1880

- Christabel Pankhurst is born on 22 September in Manchester, England.

- Lydia Maria Child dies on 20 October in Wayland, Massachusetts.

- Lucretia Coffin Mott dies on 11 November in Philadelphia, Pennsylvania.

- George Eliot (pseudonym of Mary Ann Evans) dies on 22 December in London, England.

1881

- Hubertine Auclert founds *La Citoyenne* (*The Citizen*), a newspaper dedicated to female suffrage.

- The first volume of *A History of Woman Suffrage* (Vols. 1-3, 1881-1888; Vol. 4, 1903), edited and compiled by Susan B. Anthony, Elizabeth Cady Stanton, Ida Harper Husted, and Matilda Joslyn Gage, is published by Fowler & Welles.

1882

- Virginia Woolf is born on 25 January in London, England.

- Sylvia Pankhurst is born on 5 May in Manchester, England.

- Aletta Jacobs (1854-1929), the first woman doctor in Holland, opens the first birth control clinic in Europe.

1883

- Sojourner Truth dies on 26 November in Battle Creek, Michigan.

- Olive Schreiner's *The Story of an African Farm* is published by Chapman & Hall.

1884

- Eleanor Roosevelt is born on 11 October in New York City.

1885

- Alice Paul is born on 11 January in Moorestown, New Jersey.

- Isak Dinesen is born Karen Christentze Dinesen on 17 April in Rungsted, Denmark.

1886

- Emily Dickinson dies on 15 May in Amherst, Massachusetts.

- H. D. (Hilda Doolittle) is born on 10 September in Bethlehem, Pennsylvania.

1887

- Marianne Moore is born on 15 November in Kirkwood, Missouri.

- Article five of the Peace Preservation Law in Japan prohibits women and minors from joining political organizations and attending meetings where political speeches are given, and from engaging in academic studies of political subjects.

1888

- Louisa May Alcott dies on 6 March in Boston, Massachusetts, and is buried in Sleepy Hollow Cemetery in Concord, Massachusetts.

- Susan B. Anthony organizes the International Council of Women with representatives from 48 countries.

- Louisa Lawson (1848-1920) founds Australia's first feminist newspaper, *The Dawn*.

- The National Council of Women in the United States is formed to promote the advancement of women in society. The group also serves as a clearinghouse for various women's organizations.

1889

- Anna Akhmatova is born Anna Adreyevna Gorenko on 23 June in Bolshoy Fontan, Russia.

1890

- The National American Woman Suffrage Association (NAWSA) is formed by the merging of the American Woman Suffrage Assocation and the National Woman Suffrage Association. Elizabeth Cady Stanton is the NAWSA's first president; she is succeeded by Susan B. Anthony in 1892.

1891

- Zora Neale Hurston is born on 15 (some sources say 7) January in Nostasulga, Alabama. (Some sources cite birth year as c. 1901 or 1903, and birth place as Eatonville, Florida).

Sarah Winnemucca dies on 16 October in Monida, Montana.

1892

Edna St. Vincent Millay is born on 22 February in Rockland, Maine.

Djuna Barnes is born on 12 June in Cornwall on Hudson, New York.

Rebecca West (pseudonym of Cicily Isabel Fairfield) is born on 21 December in County Kerry, Ireland.

Charlotte Perkins Gilman's *The Yellow Wallpaper* is published in *New England Magazine*.

Frances E. W. Harper's *Iola Leroy; or, Shadows Uplifted* is published by Garrigues Bros.

Olympia Brown (1835-1926), first woman ordained minister in the United States, founds the Federal Suffrage Association to campaign for women's suffrage.

Ida Wells-Barnett's *Southern Horrors. Lynch Law in All its Phases* is published by Donohue and Henneberry.

1893

Lucy Stone dies on 18 October in Dorchester, Massachusetts.

The National Council of Women of Canada is founded by Lady Aberdeen.

Suffrage is granted to women in Colorado.

New Zealand becomes the first nation to grant women the vote.

1894

Christina Rossetti dies on 29 December in London, England.

1895

The first volume of Elizabeth Cady Stanton's *The Woman's Bible* (3 vols., 1895-1898) is published by European Publishing Company.

1896

Harriet Beecher Stowe dies on 1 July in Hartford, Connecticut.

Idaho grants women the right to vote.

The National Assocation of Colored Women's Clubs is founded in Washington, D.C.

1897

Harriet A. Jacobs dies on 7 March in Cambridge, Massachusetts.

1898

Matilda Joslyn Gage dies on 18 March in Chicago, Illinois.

Charlotte Perkins Gilman's *Women and Economics* is published by Small Maynard.

The Meiji Civil Law Code, the law of the Japanese nation state, makes the patriarchal family, rather than the individual, the legally recognized entity.

1899

Elizabeth Bowen is born on 7 June in Dublin, Ireland.

Kate Chopin's *The Awakening* is published by Herbert S. Stone.

1900

Colette's *Claudine a l'ecole* (*Claudine at School*, 1930) is published by Ollendorf.

Carrie Chapman Catt succeeds Susan B. Anthony as president of the NAWSA.

1901

Charlotte Yonge dies of bronchitis and pneumonia on 24 March in Elderfield, England.

1902

Elizabeth Cady Stanton dies on 26 October in New York City.

Women of European descent gain suffrage in Australia.

1903

The Women's Social and Political Union, led by suffragists Emmeline and Christabel Pankhurst, stage demonstrations in Hyde Park in London, England.

1904

Frances Power Cobbe dies on 5 April.

Kate Chopin dies following a cerebral hemorrhage on 22 August in St. Louis, Missouri.

- Susan B. Anthony establishes the International Woman Suffrage Alliance in Berlin, Germany.

C. 1905

- Lillian Hellman is born on 20 June in New Orleans, Louisiana.

1905

- Austrian activist and novelist Bertha von Suttner (1843-1914) receives the Nobel Peace Prize.

1906

- Susan B. Anthony dies on 13 March in Rochester, New York.

- Finnish women gain suffrage and the right to be elected to public office.

1907

- Victoria Earle Matthews dies of tuberculosis on 10 March in New York City.

- Mary Edwards Walker, M.D.'s pamphlet on women's suffrage, "Crowning Constitutional Argument," is published.

- Harriot Stanton Blatch founds the Equality League of Self-Supporting Women, later called the Women's Political Union.

1908

- Simone de Beauvoir is born on 9 January in Paris, France.

- Julia Ward Howe becomes the first woman to be elected to the American Academy of Arts and Letters.

1909

- Sarah Orne Jewett dies on 24 June in South Berwick, Maine.

- Swedish author Selma Lagerlöf (1858-1940) becomes the first woman to receive the Nobel Prize for Literature.

- "The Uprising of the 20,000" grows from one local to a general strike against several shirtwaist factories in New York City. Over 700 women and girls are arrested, and 19 receive

workhouse sentences. The strike is called off on 15 February 1910. Over 300 shops settle with the union, and workers achieve the terms demanded.

- Jeanne-Elisabeth Archer Schmahl (1846-1915) founds the French Union for Woman Suffrage.

1910

- Julia Ward Howe dies of pneumonia on 17 October in Newport, Rhode Island.

- The Women' Political Union holds the first large suffrage parade in New York City.

- Suffrage is granted to women in Washington State.

- Jane Addams's *Twenty Years at Hull House* is published by Macmillan.

1911

- Frances Ellen Watkins Harper dies on 22 February in Philadelphia, Pennsylvania.

- A fire at the Triangle Shirtwaist Factory in New York City on 25 March claims the lives of 146 factory workers, 133 of them women. Public outrage over the fire leads to reforms in labor laws and improvement in working conditions.

- Suffrage is granted to women in California.

- Edith Wharton's *Ethan Frome* is published by Scribner.

1912

- Suffrage is granted to women in Arizona, Kansas, and Oregon.

- A parade in support of women's suffrage is held in New York City and draws 20,000 participants and half a million onlookers.

1913

- Muriel Rukeyser is born on 15 December in New York City.

- Willa Cather's *O Pioneers!* is published by Houghton.

- Ida Wells-Barnett founds the Alpha Suffrage Club in Chicago.

- Suffrage is granted to women in Alaska.

- The Congressional Union is founded by Alice Paul and Lucy Burns.

1914

- Marguerite Duras is born on 4 April in Gia Dinh, Indochina (now Vietnam).

- The National Federation of Women's Clubs, which includes over two million white women and women of color, formally endorses the campaign for women's suffrage.

- Suffrage is granted to women in Montana and Nevada.

- Margaret Sanger begins publication of her controversial monthly newsletter *The Woman Rebel,* which is banned as obscene literature.

1915

- Charlotte Perkins Gilman's *Herland* is published in the journal *Forerunner.*

- *Woman's Work in Municipalities,* by American suffragist and historian Mary Ritter Beard (1876-1958), is published by Appleton.

- Icelandic women who are age 40 or older gain suffrage.

- Members of the NAWSA from across the United States hold a large parade in New York city.

- Most Danish women over age 25 gain suffrage.

1916

- Ardent suffragist and pacifist Jeannette Pickering Rankin (1880-1973) of Montana becomes the first woman elected to the U. S. House of Representatives. She later votes against U. S. involvement in both World Wars.

- The Congressional Union becomes the National Women's Party, led by Alice Paul and Lucy Burns.

- NAWSA president Carrie Chapman Catt unveils her "Winning Plan" for American women's suffrage at a convention held in Atlantic City, New Jersey.

- Suffrage is granted to women in Alberta, Manitoba, and Saskatchewan, Canada.

- Margaret Sanger opens the first U. S. birth-control clinic in Brooklyn, New York. The clinic is shut down 10 days after it opens and Sanger is arrested.

- Margaret Sanger's *What Every Mother Should Know; or, How Six Little Children were Taught the Truth* is published by M. N. Maisel.

1917

- Gwendolyn Brooks is born on 7 June in Topeka, Kansas.

- The National Women's Party becomes the first group in U.S. history to picket in front of the White House. Picketers are arrested and incarcerated; during their incarceration, Alice Paul leads them in a hunger strike. Many of the imprisoned suffragists are brutally force-fed, including Paul. The suffragettes' mistreatment is published in newspapers, the White House bows to public pressure, and they are released.

- White women in Arkansas are granted partial suffrage; they are able to vote in primary, but not general, elections.

- Suffrage is granted to women in New York.

- Suffrage is granted to women in Estonia, Latvia, and Lithuania.

- Women in Ontario and British Columbia, Canada, gain suffrage.

- Suffragists and members of the NAWSA, led by president Carrie Chapman Catt, march in a parade in New York City.

- Margaret Sanger founds and edits *The Birth Control Review,* the first scientific journal devoted to the subject of birth control.

1918

- Willa Cather's *My Antonia* is published by Houghton.

- Suffrage is granted to women in Michigan, Oklahoma, and South Dakota; women in Texas gain suffrage for primary elections only.

- President Woodrow Wilson issues a statement in support of a federal constitutional amendment granting full suffrage to American women.

- A resolution to amend the U.S. constitution to ensure that the voting rights of U.S. citizens cannot "be denied or abridged by the United States or any state on account of sex" passes in the House of Representatives.

- President Wilson urges the Senate to support the 19th amendment, but fails to win the two-thirds majority necessary for passage.

- Women in the United Kingdom who are married, own property, or are college graduates over the age of 30, are granted suffrage.

- Women in Austria, Czechoslovakia, Germany, Luxembourg, and Poland gain suffrage.

- Women in New Brunswick and Nova Scotia, Canada, gain suffrage. Canadian women of British or French heritage gain voting rights in Federal elections.

- Marie Stopes's *Married Love* and *Wise Parenthood* are published by A. C. Fifield.

- Harriot Stanton Blatch's *Mobilizing Woman-Power*, with a foreword by Theodore Roosevelt, is published by The Womans Press.

1919

- Women in the Netherlands, Rhodesia, and Sweden gain suffrage.

- Doris Lessing is born on 22 October in Kermanshah, Persia (now Iran).

- The "Susan B. Anthony Amendment," also known as the 19th Amendment to the U. S. Constitution, after it is defeated twice in the Senate, passes in both houses of Congress. The amendment is sent to states for ratification.

1920

- The 19th Amendment to the U.S. Constitution is ratified by the necessary two-thirds of states and American women are guaranteed suffrage on 26 August when Secretary of State Bainbridge Colby signs the amendment into law.

- The NAWSA is reorganized as the National League of Women Voters and elects Maud Wood Park as its first president.

- Bella Abzug is born on 24 July in New York City.

- Icelandic women gain full suffrage.

- Edith Wharton's *The Age of Innocence* is published by Meredith.

- Colette's *Cheri* is published by Fayard.

1921

- Betty Friedan is born on 4 February in Peoria, Illinois.

- Edith Wharton receives the Pulitzer Prize for fiction for *The Age of Innocence*.

- Margaret Sanger organizes the first American Conference on Birth Control in New York City.

1922

- Irish women gain full suffrage.

- Grace Paley is born on 11 December in New York City.

- Edna St. Vincent Millay's *The Ballad of the Harp-Weaver* is published by F. Shay.

1923

- Edna St. Vincent Millay receives the Pulitzer Prize for Poetry for *The Ballad of the Harp-Weaver*.

- Margaret Sanger opens the Birth Control Clinical Research Bureau in New York to dispense contraceptives to women under the supervision of a licensed physician and to study the effect of contraception upon women's health.

- Margaret Sanger founds the American Birth Control League.

- The Equal Rights Amendment (ERA), written by Alice Paul, is introduced in Congress for the first time in December.

1924

- Phyllis Schlafly is born on 15 August in St. Louis, Missouri.

- Shirley Chisolm is born on 30 November in Brooklyn, New York.

1925

- Amy Lowell dies on 12 May in Brookline, Massachusetts.

- *Collected Poems of H.D.* is published by Boni & Liveright.

- Virginia Woolf's *Mrs. Dalloway* is published by Harcourt.

1926

- Marietta Holley dies on 1 March near Adams, New York.

- Marianne Moore becomes the first woman editor of *The Dial* in New York City, a post she holds until 1929.

- Carrie Chapman Catt and Nettie Rogers Schuler's *Woman Suffrage and Politics; the Inner Story of the Suffrage Movement* is published by Charles Scribner's Sons.

- Grazia Deledda receives the Nobel Prize in Literature.

1927

- Victoria Woodhull dies on 10 June in Norton Park, England.

- Virginia Woolf's *To the Lighthouse* is published by Harcourt.

1928

- Maya Angelou is born Marguerite Johnson on 4 April in St. Louis, Missouri.

- Emmeline Pankhurst dies on 14 June in London, England.

- Anne Sexton is born on 9 November in Newton, Massachusetts.

- Virginia Woolf's *Orlando* is published by Crosby Gaige.

- Women are granted full suffrage in Great Britain.

- Gertrude Stein's *Useful Knowledge* is published by Payson & Clarke.

- Sigrid Undset receives the Nobel Prize in Literature.

1929

- Adrienne Rich is born on 16 May in Baltimore, Maryland.

- Marilyn French is born on 21 November in New York City.

- While Arthur M. Schlesinger Sr. reads her speech for her, Margaret Sanger appears in a gag on a stage in Boston where she has been prevented from speaking.

- Virginia Woolf's *A Room of One's Own* is published by Harcourt.

1930

- Lorraine Hansberry is born on 19 May in Chicago, Illinois.

- Cairine Wilson is appointed the first woman senator in Canada.

1931

- Jane Addams receives the Nobel Peace Prize.

- Toni Morrison is born Chloe Anthony Wofford on 18 February in Lorain, Ohio.

- Ida B. Wells-Barnett dies on 25 March in Chicago, Illinois.

1932

- Sylvia Plath is born on 27 October in Boston, Massachusetts.

1933

- Gertrude Stein's *The Autobiography of Alice B. Toklas* is published by Harcourt.

- Frances Perkins (1882-1965) is appointed Secretary of Labor by President Franklin D. Roosevelt, and becomes the first female cabinet member in the United States.

1934

- Gloria Steinem is born on 25 March in Toledo, Ohio.

- Kate Millett is born on 14 September in St. Paul, Minnesota.

- Lillian Hellman's *The Children's Hour* debuts on 20 November at Maxine Elliot's Theatre in New York City.

1935

- Jane Addams dies of cancer on 21 May in Chicago, Illinois.

- Charlotte Perkins Gilman commits suicide on 17 August in Pasadena, California.

- The National Council of Negro Women is founded by Mary McLeod Bethune (1875-1955).

1936

- First lady Eleanor Roosevelt begins writing a daily syndicated newspaper column, "My Day."

- Margaret Mitchell's *Gone with the Wind* is published by Macmillan.

1937

- Hélène Cixous is born on 5 June in Oran, Algeria.

- Bessie Head is born on 6 July in Pietermaritzburg, South Africa.

- Edith Wharton dies on 11 August in St. Brice-sous-Foret, France.

- Zora Neale Hurston's *Their Eyes Were Watching God* is published by Lippincott.

- Margaret Mitchell (1900-1949) receives the Pulitzer Prize in Letters & Drama for novel for *Gone with the Wind*.

- Anne O'Hare McCormick becomes the first woman to receive the Pulitzer Prize in Journalism, which she is given for distinguished correspondence for her international reporting on the rise of Italian Fascism in the *New York Times*.

1938

- Joyce Carol Oates is born on 16 June in Lockport, New York.

- Pearl Buck receives the Nobel Prize in Literature.

1939

- Germaine Greer is born on 29 January near Melbourne, Australia.

- Lillian Hellman's *The Little Foxes* debuts on 15 February at National Theatre in New York City.

- Margaret Atwood is born on 18 November in Ottawa, Ontario, Canada.

- Paula Gunn Allen is born in Cubero, New Mexico.

- French physician Madeleine Pelletier (1874-1939) is arrested for performing abortions in Paris, France; she dies later the same year. Throughout her medical career, Pelletier advocated women's rights to birth control and abortion, and founded her own journal, *La Suffragist*.

1940

- Emma Goldman dies on 14 May in Toronto, Ontario, Canada.

- Maxine Hong Kingston is born on 27 October in Stockton, California.

- Harriot Eaton Stanton Blatch dies on 20 November in Greenwich, Connecticut.

1941

- Virginia Woolf commits suicide on 28 March in Lewes, Sussex, England.

1942

- Erica Jong is born on 26 March in New York City.

- Isabel Allende is born on 2 August in Lima, Peru.

- Ellen Glasgow (1873-1945) receives the Pulitzer Prize for her novel *In This Our Life*.

- Margaret Walker (1915-1998) becomes the first African American to receive the Yale Series of Young Poets Award for her collection *For My People*.

1944

- Alice Walker is born on 9 February in Eatonton, Georgia.

- Martha Gellhorn (1908-1998) is the only woman journalist to go ashore with Allied troops during the D-Day invasion of Normandy, France in June.

- Buchi Emecheta is born on 21 July in Yaba, Lagos, Nigeria.

- Rita Mae Brown is born on 28 November in Hanover, Pennsylvania.

- Women are granted suffrage in France and Jamaica.

1945

- Eleanor Roosevelt becomes the first person to represent the U. S. at the United Nations. She serves until 1951, is reappointed in 1961, and serves until her death in 1962.

- Gabriela Mistral receives the Nobel Prize in Literature.

- Louise Bogan is named U. S. Poet Laureate.

1946

- Gertrude Stein dies of cancer on 27 July in Neuilly-sur-Seine, France.

- Andrea Dworkin is born on 26 September in Camden, New Jersey.

- Mary Ritter Beard's *Woman as a Force in History: A Study in Traditions and Realities* is published by Macmillan.

- Eleanor Roosevelt becomes chair of the United Nations Human Rights Commission. She remains chair until 1951.

1947

- Carrie Chapman Catt dies on 9 March in New Rochelle, New York.

- Willa Cather dies on 24 April in New York City.
- Dorothy Fuldheim, a newscaster in Cleveland, Ohio, becomes the first female television news anchor at WEWS-TV.

1948

- Susan Glaspell dies on 27 July in Provincetown, Massachusetts.
- Ntozake Shange is born Paulette Linda Williams on 18 October in Trenton, New Jersey.
- Leonie Adams is named U. S. Poet Laureate.

1949

- Simone de Beauvoir's *Le deuxième sexe* (*The Second Sex*, H. M. Parshley, translator: Knopf, 1953) is published by Gallimard.
- Elizabeth Bishop is named U. S. Poet Laureate.
- Gwendolyn Brooks's *Annie Allen* is published by Harper.

1950

- Gloria Naylor is born on 25 January in New York City.
- Edna St. Vincent Millay dies of a heart attack on 19 October at Steepletop, Austerlitz, New York.
- Gwendolyn Brooks receives the Pulitzer Prize for poetry for *Annie Allen*.

1951

- Marianne Moore's *Collected Poems* is published by Macmillan.
- Marguerite Higgins (1920-1960) receives the Pulitzer Prize for Journalism in overseas reporting for her account of the battle at Inchon, Korea in September, 1950.

1952

- Amy Tan is born on 19 February in Oakland, California.
- Rita Dove is born on 28 August in Akron, Ohio.
- bell hooks is born Gloria Jean Watkins on 25 September in Hopkinsville, Kentucky.
- Marianne Moore receives the National Book Critics Circle award for poetry and the Pulitzer Prize for poetry for *Collected Poems*.

1953

- *A Writer's Diary: Being Extracts from the Diary of Virigina Woolf,* edited by Leonard Woolf, is published by Hogarth.
- The International Planned Parenthood Federation is founded by Margaret Sanger, who serves as the organization's first president.
- Women are granted suffrage in Mexico.

1954

- Louise Erdrich is born on 7 June in Little Falls, Minnesota.
- Colette dies on 3 August in Paris, France.
- Sandra Cisneros is born on 20 December in Chicago, Illinois.

1955

- On 1 December American civil rights activist Rosa Parks (1913-) refuses to move from her seat for a white passenger on a Montgomery, Alabama bus and is arrested.

1956

- The Anti-Prostitution Act, written and campaigned for by Kamichika Ichiko, makes prostitution illegal in Japan.

1958

- Christabel Pankhurst dies on 13 February in Los Angeles, California.

1959

- Susan Faludi is born on 18 April in New York City.
- Lorraine Hansberry's *A Raisin in the Sun* debuts in March at the Ethel Barrymore Theatre in New York City.
- Lorraine Hansberry becomes the youngest woman and first black artist to receive a New York Drama Critics Circle Award for best American play for *A Raisin in the Sun*.

1960

- Zora Neale Hurston dies on 28 January in Fort Pierce, Florida.
- Sylvia Pankhurst dies on 27 September in Addis Ababa, Ethiopia.

The U.S. Food and Drug Administration approves the first oral contraceptive for distribution to consumers in May.

Harper Lee's *To Kill a Mockingbird* is published by Lippincott.

1961

H. D. (Hilda Doolittle) dies on 27 September in Zurich, Switzerland.

Harper Lee receives the Pulitzer Prize for the novel for *To Kill a Mockingbird.*

President John F. Kennedy establishes the President's Commission on the Status of Women on 14 December and appoints Eleanor Roosevelt as head of the commission.

1962

Isak Dinesen dies on 7 September in Rungsted Kyst, Denmark.

Eleanor Roosevelt dies on 7 November in New York City.

Naomi Wolf is born on 12 November in San Francisco, California.

Doris Lessing's *The Golden Notebook* is published by Simon & Schuster.

1963

Betty Friedan's *The Feminine Mystique* is published by Norton and becomes a bestseller.

Sylvia Plath's *The Bell Jar* is published under the pseudonym Victoria Lucas by Heinemann.

Sylvia Plath commits suicide on 11 February in London, England.

Barbara Wertheim Tuchman (1912-1989) becomes the first woman to receive the Pulitzer Prize for general nonfiction for *The Guns of August.*

The Equal Pay Act is passed by the U.S. Congress on 28 May. It is the first federal law requiring equal compensation for men and women in federal jobs.

Entitled *American Women,* the report issued by the President's Commission on the Status of Women documents sex discrimination in nearly all corners of American society, and urges the U.S. Supreme Court to clarify legal status of women under the U.S. Constitution.

1964

Anna Julia Haywood Cooper dies on 27 February in Washington, DC.

1965

Lorraine Hansberry dies of cancer on 12 January in New York City.

Women are granted suffrage in Afghanistan.

1966

Anna Akhmatova dies on 6 March in Russia.

Margaret Sanger dies on 6 September in Tucson, Arizona.

National Organization for Women (NOW) is founded on 29 June by Betty Friedan and 27 other founding members. NOW is dedicated to promoting full participation in society for women and advocates for adequate child care for working mothers, reproductive rights, and the Equal Rights Amendment to the U.S. Constitution.

Anne Sexton's *Live or Die* is published by Houghton.

Nelly Sachs (1891-1970) receives the Nobel Prize in Literature, which she shares with Shmuel Yosef Agnon.

1967

Anne Sexton receives the Pulitzer Prize for poetry for *Live or Die.*

Senator Eugene McCarthy, with 37 cosponsors, introduces the Equal Rights Amendment in the U.S. Senate.

1968

Audre Lorde's *The First Cities* is published by Poets Press.

1969

Joyce Carol Oates's *them* is published by Vanguard Press.

Shirley Chisolm becomes the first African American woman elected to Congress when she takes her seat in the U.S. House of Representatives on 3 January.

Golda Meir (1898-1978) becomes the fourth Prime Minister of Israel on 17 March.

- California adopts the nation's first "no fault" divorce law, allowing divorce by mutual consent.

1970

- Toni Morrison's *The Bluest Eye* is published by Holt.

- Germaine Greer's *The Female Eunuch* is published by MacGibbon & Kee.

- Maya Angelou's *I Know Why the Caged Bird Sings* is published by Random House.

- Kate Millett's *Sexual Politics* is published by Doubleday and becomes a bestseller.

- Joyce Carol Oates receives the National Book Award for fiction for *them.*

- The Equal Rights Amendment passes in the U.S. House of Representatives by a vote of 350 to 15 on 10 August.

- Bella Abzug is elected to the U.S. House of Representatives on 3 November.

- The Feminist Press is founded at the City University of New York.

- *Off Our Backs: A Women's News Journal* is founded in Washington, D.C.

- *The Women's Rights Law Reporter* is founded in Newark, New Jersey.

1971

- Josephine Jacobsen is named U. S. Poet Laureate.

1972

- Marianne Moore dies on 5 February in New York City.

- *Ms.* magazine is founded; Gloria Steinem serves as editor of *Ms.* until 1987. The 300,000 copy print run of the first issue of *Ms.* magazine sells out within a week of its release in January.

- Shirley Chisolm becomes the first African American woman to seek the presidential nomination of a major political party, although her bid for the Democratic Party nomination is unsuccessful.

- The Equal Rights Amendment is passed by both houses of the U.S. Congress and is signed by President Richard M. Nixon. The amendment expires in 1982, without being ratified by the required two-thirds of the states; it is three states short of full ratification.

- President Nixon signs into law Title IX of the Higher Education Act banning sex bias in athletics and other activities at all educational institutions receiving federal assistance.

- Women's Press is established in Canada.

1973

- The U.S. Supreme Court, in their decision handed down on 21 January in *Roe v. Wade,* decides that in the first trimester of pregnancy women have the right to choose an abortion.

- Elizabeth Bowen dies of lung cancer on 22 February in London, England.

- Rita Mae Brown's *Rubyfruit Jungle* is published by Daughters, Inc.

- Erica Jong's *Fear of Flying* is published by Holt and becomes a bestseller.

- Alice Walker's *In Love and Trouble: Stories of Black Women* is published by Harcourt.

- The Boston Women's Health Book Collective's *Our Bodies, Ourselves: A Book By and For Women* is published by Simon and Schuster.

1974

- Andrea Dworkin's *Women Hating* is published by Dutton.

- Adrienne Rich receives the National Book Award for *Diving into the Wreck: Poems, 1971-1972.*

- Anne Sexton commits suicide on 4 October in Weston, Massachusetts.

- Katharine Graham (1917-2001), publisher of the *Washington Post,* becomes the first woman member of the board of the Associated Press.

1975

- Paula Gunn Allen' essay "The Sacred Hoop: A Contemporary Indian Perspective on American Indian Literature" appears in *Literature of the American Indian: Views and Interpretations,* edited by Abraham Chapman and published by New American Library.

- Hélène Cixous and Catherine Clement's *La Jeune nee (The Newly Born Woman,* University of Minnesota Press, 1986) is published by Union Generale.

- Margaret Thatcher is elected leader of the Conservative Party and becomes the first woman to head a major party in Great Britain.

- Susan Brownmiller's *Against our Will: Men, Women, and Rape* is published by Simon and Schuster.

1976

- Andrea Dworkin's *Our Blood: Prophecies and Discourses on Sexual Politics* is published by Harper.

- Maxine Hong Kingston's *The Woman Warrior: Memoirs of a Girlhood among Ghosts* is published by Knopf.

- Maxine Hong Kingston's receives the National Book Critics Circle award for general nonfiction for *The Woman Warrior.*

- Barbara Walters (1931-) becomes the first female network television news anchorwoman when she joins Harry Reasoner as coanchor of the *ABC Evening News.*

- Shere Hite's *The Hite Report: A Nationwide Study of Female Sexuality* is published by Macmillan.

1977

- Alice Paul dies on 9 July in Moorestown, New Jersey.

- Marilyn French's *The Women's Room* is published by Summit.

- Toni Morrison's *Song of Solomon* is published by Knopf.

- Toni Morrison receives the National Book Critics Circle Award for fiction for *Song of Solomon.*

- Labor organizer Barbara Mayer Wertheimer's *We Were There: The Story of Working Women in America* is published by Pantheon.

- Women's Press is established in Great Britain.

1978

- The Pregnancy Discrimination Act bans employment discrimination against pregnant women.

- Tillie Olsen's *Silences* is published by Delcorte Press/Seymour Lawrence.

1979

- Margaret Thatcher becomes the first woman prime minister of Great Britain. She serves until her resignation in 1990, marking the longest term of any twentieth-century prime minister.

- Barbara Wertheim Tuchman becomes the first woman elected president of the American Academy and Institute of Arts and Letters.

- Mother Teresa (1910-1997) receives the Nobel Peace Prize.

- Sandra M. Gilbert and Susan Gubar's *The Madwoman in the Attic: The Woman Writer and the Nineteenth-Century Imagination* is published by Yale University Press.

1980

- Muriel Rukeyser dies on 12 February in New York City.

- Adrienne Rich's essay "Compulsory Heterosexuality and Lesbian Experience" is published in *Signs: Journal of Women in Culture and Society.*

1981

- bell hooks's *Ain't I a Woman: Black Women and Feminism* is published by South End Press.

- Sylvia Plath's *Collected Poems,* edited by Ted Hughes, is published by Harper.

- Sandra Day O'Connor (1930-) becomes the first woman Justice of the U.S. Supreme Court, after being nominated by President Ronald Reagan and sworn in on 25 September.

- Women of Color Press is founded in Albany, New York by Barbara Smith.

- Cleis Press is established in Pittsburgh, Pennsylvania, and San Francisco, California.

- *This Bridge Called My Back: Writings by Radical Women of Color,* edited by Cherríe Moraga and Gloria Anzaldúa, is published by Persephone Press.

- Maxine Kumin is named U. S. Poet Laureate.

1982

- Djuna Barnes dies on 19 June in New York City.

- Sylvia Plath is posthumously awarded the Pulitzer Prize in poetry for *Collected Poems.*

- Alice Walker's *The Color Purple* is published by Harcourt.

- Carol Gilligan's *In a Different Voice: Psychological Theory and Women's Development* is published by Harvard University Press.

1983

● Rebecca West dies on 15 March in London, England.

■ Gloria Steinem's *Outrageous Acts and Everyday Rebellions* is published by Holt.

1984

■ Sandra Cisneros's *The House on Mango Street* is published by Arte Publico.

● Lillian Hellman dies on 30 June in Martha's Vineyard, Massachusetts.

● Geraldine Ferraro (1935-) becomes the first woman to win the Vice-Presidential nomination and runs unsuccessfully for office with Democratic Presidential candidate Walter Mondale.

■ Firebrand Books, publisher of feminist and lesbian literature, is established in Ann Arbor, Michigan.

■ bell hooks's *Feminist Theory: From Margin to Center* is published by South End Press.

1985

■ Margaret Atwood's *The Handmaid's Tale* is published by McClelland & Stewart.

● Wilma P. Mankiller is sworn in as the first woman tribal chief of the Cherokee nation. She serves until 1994.

■ Gwendolyn Brooks is named U. S. Poet Laureate.

1986

● Simone de Beauvoir dies on 14 April in Paris, France.

● Bessie Head dies on 17 April in Botswana.

■ Rita Dove's *Thomas and Beulah* is published by Carnegie-Mellon University Press.

■ Sylvia Ann Hewlett's *A Lesser Life: The Myth of Women's Liberation in America* is published by Morrow.

1987

■ Toni Morrison's *Beloved* is published by Knopf.

■ Rita Dove receives the Pulitzer Prize for poetry for *Thomas and Beulah*.

1988

■ Toni Morrison receives the Pulitzer Prize for fiction for *Beloved*.

■ *The War of the Words,* Volume 1 of Sandra M. Gilbert and Susan Gubar's *No Man's Land: The Place of the Woman Writer in the Twentieth Century,* is published by Yale University Press.

1989

■ Amy Tan's *The Joy Luck Club* is published by Putnam.

1990

■ Naomi Wolf's *The Beauty Myth: How Images of Beauty Are Used against Women* is published by Chatto & Windus.

● The Norplant contraceptive is approved by the FDA on 10 December.

■ Camille Paglia's *Sexual Personae: Art and Decadence from Nefertiti to Emily Dickinson* is published by Yale University Press.

■ Wendy Kaminer's *A Fearful Freedom: Women's Flight from Equality* is published by Addison-Wesley.

■ Laurel Thatcher Ulrich's *A Midwife's Tale: The Life of Martha Ballard, Based on Her Diary, 1785-1812* is published by Knopf.

■ Judith Butler's *Gender Trouble: Feminism and the Subversion of Identity* is published by Routledge.

1991

■ Susan Faludi's *Backlash: The Undeclared War Against American Women* is published by Crown.

● Antonia Novello (1944-) is appointed by President George H.W. Bush and becomes the first woman and first person of Hispanic descent to serve as U. S. Surgeon General.

● Bernadine Healy, M.D. (1944-) is appointed by President George H.W. Bush and becomes the first woman to head the National Institutes of Health.

■ Suzanne Gordon's *Prisoners of Men's Dreams: Striking Out for a New Feminine Future* is published by Little, Brown.

■ Laurel Thatcher Ulrich receives the Pulitzer Prize for history for *A Midwife's Tale: The Life of Martha Ballard, Based on Her Diary, 1785-1812.*

1992

- Carol Elizabeth Moseley Braun (1947-) becomes the first African American woman elected to the U. S. Senate on 3 November.

- Carolyne Larrington's *The Feminist Companion to Mythology* is published by Pandora.

- Marilyn French's *The War against Women* is published by Summit.

- Clarissa Pinkola Estes's *Women Who Run with the Wolves: Myths and Stories of the Wild Woman Archetype* is published by Ballantine.

- Naomi Wolf's *Fire with Fire: The New Female Power and How It Will Change the Twenty-first Century* is published by Random House.

- Mona Van Duyn is named U. S. Poet Laureate.

1993

- Appointed by President Bill Clinton, Janet Reno (1938-) becomes the first woman U.S. Attorney General when she is sworn in on 12 March.

- Toni Morrison receives the Nobel Prize in Literature.

- Toni Morrison receives the Elizabeth Cady Stanton Award from the National Organization for Women.

- Canada's Progressive Conservative party votes on 13 June to make Defense Minister Kim Campbell the nation's first woman prime minister. Canadian voters oust the Conservative party in elections on 25 October as recession continues; Liberal leader Jean Chrétien becomes prime minister.

- On 1 October Rita Dove becomes the youngest person and the first African American to be named U. S. Poet Laureate.

- Faye Myenne Ng's *Bone* is published by Hyperion.

1994

- The Violence Against Women Act tightens federal penalties for sex offenders, funds services for victims of rape and domestic violence, and provides funds for special training for police officers in domestic violence and rape cases.

- Mary Pipher's *Reviving Ophelia: Saving the Selves of Adolescent Girls* is published by Putnam.

1995

- Ireland's electorate votes by a narrow margin in November to end the nation's ban on divorce (no other European country has such a ban), but only after 4 years' legal separation.

1996

- Marguerite Duras dies on 3 March in Paris, France.

- Hillary Rodham Clinton's *It Takes a Village, and Other Lessons Children Teach Us* is published by Simon and Schuster.

1998

- Bella Abzug dies on 31 March in New York City.

- Drucilla Cornell's *At the Heart of Freedom: Feminism, Sex, and Equality* is published by Princeton University Press.

1999

- Susan Brownmiller's *In Our Time: Memoir of a Revolution* is published by Dial Press.

- Gwendolyn Mink's *Welfare's End* is published by Cornell University Press.

- Martha C. Nussbaum's *Sex and Social Justice* is published by Oxford University Press.

2000

- Gwendolyn Brooks dies on 3 December in Chicago, Illinois.

- Patricia Hill Collins's *Black Feminist Thought: Knowledge, Consciousness, and the Politics of Empowerment* is published by Routledge.

- Jennifer Baumgardner and Amy Richards's *Manifesta: Young Women, Feminism, and the Future* is published by Farrar, Straus, and Giroux.

2002

- Estelle B. Freedman's *No Turning Back: The History of Feminism and the Future of Women* is published by Ballantine.

- *Colonize This! Young Women of Color on Today's Feminism*, edited by Daisy Hernandez and Bushra Rehman, is published by Seal Press.

2003

- Iranian feminist and human rights activist Shirin Ebadi (1947-) receives the Nobel Peace Prize.

- Louise Glück is named U. S. Poet Laureate.

- *Catching a Wave: Reclaiming Feminism for the 21st Century,* edited by Rory Cooke Dicker and Alison Piepmeier, is published by Northeastern University Press.

2004

- The FDA approves the contraceptive mifepristone, following a 16-year struggle by reproductive rights activists to have the abortion drug approved. Opponents made repeated efforts to prevent approval and distribution of mifepristone.

- *The Fire This Time: Young Activists and the New Feminism,* edited by Vivien Labaton and Dawn Lundy Martin, is published by Anchor Books.

- *The Future of Women's Rights: Global Visions and Strategies,* edited by Joanna Kerr, Ellen Sprenger, and Alison Symington, is published by ZED Books and Palgrave Macmillan.

LORRAINE HANSBERRY

(1930 - 1965)

(Full name Lorraine Vivian Hansberry) American playwright and essayist.

The first African American and the youngest woman to win the New York Drama Critics Circle Award, Hansberry is best known for her play *A Raisin in the Sun* (1959). The story of a black working-class family and their decision to move into a white neighborhood, the play helped pioneer the acceptance of black drama by Broadway producers and audiences. Although dismissed by some militant blacks as assimilationist, *A Raisin in the Sun* nevertheless garnered praise for its sensitive and revealing portrait of a black family in America. It has also attracted attention for its depiction of strong African American female characters who strive against a male-dominated society.

BIOGRAPHICAL INFORMATION

Hansberry was born into a middle-class family on Chicago's south side in 1930. Around the age of seven, Hansberry and her family moved into a restricted white neighborhood, deliberately violating the city's "covenant laws" that legally sanctioned housing discrimination. When ordered to abide by the law, Hansberry's family, with the help of the NAACP, took their case to the Illinois Supreme Court, which struck down the legislation as unconstitutional. During litigation, white neighbors continually harassed the Hansberry family; in one incident, a brick thrown through their living room window barely missed Hansberry's head.

In high school, Hansberry became interested in theater. She attended the University of Wisconsin, where she became further acquainted with the works of such distinguished playwrights as August Strindberg, Henrik Ibsen, and Sean O'Casey. She studied painting in Chicago and abroad for a time but moved to New York City in 1950 to begin her career as a writer. Politically active in New York, Hansberry wrote for Paul Robeson's *Freedom* magazine and participated in various liberal crusades, particularly the civil rights and women's movements.

During a protest at New York University, she met Robert Nemiroff, a white writer and himself a pursuer of liberal politics. A romance developed, and in 1953 they married. Nemiroff encouraged Hansberry in her writing efforts, going so far as to salvage her discarded pages from the wastebasket. One night in 1957, while the couple was entertaining a group of friends, they read a scene from Hansberry's play in progress, *A Raisin in the Sun*. The impact left by the reading prompted Hansberry, Nemiroff, and friends to push for the completion, financing, and production of the drama within the next several months.

A Raisin in the Sun made its New York debut in March 1959 at the Ethel Barrymore Theatre. It was the first play written by a black woman to be produced on Broadway and the first to be directed by a black director in more than fifty years. When *A Raisin in the Sun* won the New York Drama Critics Circle Award, Hansberry became the youngest writer and the first black artist ever to receive the honor, competing that year with such theater luminaries as Tennessee Williams, Eugene O'Neill, and Archibald MacLeish. In June 1959 Hansberry was named the "most promising playwright" of the season by *Variety*'s poll of New York drama critics. *A Raisin in the Sun* ran for 530 performances. Shortly thereafter, in 1961, a film version of the drama was released, starring Sidney Poitier and Claudia McNeil. Hansberry won a special award at the Cannes Film Festival and was nominated for a Screen Writers Guild award for her screenplay.

Hansberry then began work on a play about a Jewish intellectual who vacillates between social commitment and paralyzing disillusionment. Entitled *The Sign in Sidney Brustein's Window* (1964), the play ran on Broadway for 101 performances despite mixed reviews and poor sales. The play closed on January 12, 1965, the day Hansberry died of cancer at the age of thirty-four.

MAJOR WORKS

Hansberry originally named her best-known play *The Crystal Stair* after a line in the Langston Hughes poem "Mother to Son," but she later changed its title to *A Raisin in the Sun,* an image taken from another Hughes piece, "A Dream Deferred." Set in a modest apartment in south Chicago after World War II, *A Raisin in the Sun* focuses on the Younger family: Lena, the matriarch; her son Walter Lee, a chauffeur; her daughter Beneatha, a college student; Walter Lee's wife, Ruth; and their son, Travis. In the opening scene, Ruth rouses her family on an early Friday morning. Ruth is described by Hansberry as "a settled woman" whose disappointment in life clearly shows in her demeanor. Walter, conversely, is a lean, intense man whose voice always contains "a quality of indictment." His second question of the morning—"Check come today?"—immediately reveals the central conflict of the play. Walter's father has died, leaving a ten-thousand-dollar insurance policy to Lena. Walter plans to persuade his mother to give him the money so that he, along with two other men, can invest it in a liquor store. Lena, however, uses part of the money as a

down payment on a house in another neighborhood. Yet when a white representative from the neighborhood to which the family plans to move offers to buy back their home, Walter refuses. He submerges his materialistic aspirations—for a time, at least—and rallies to support the family's dream. The play ends as the Youngers close the door to their apartment and head for their new home.

Although Hansberry and her husband divorced in 1964, Nemiroff remained dedicated to the playwright and her work. Appointed her literary executor, he collected Hansberry's writings after her death in the informal biography *To Be Young, Gifted, and Black: Lorraine Hansberry in Her Own Words* (1969). The work presents a collection of portions of her letters, poetry, speeches, essays, and dramatic scenes, accompanied by drawings and sketches. Nemiroff also edited and published her last three plays. *Les Blancs,* produced in 1970, is a psychological and social drama about a European-educated African who returns home to protest colonialism, the eponymous title piece in *Les Blancs: The Collected Last Plays of Lorraine Hansberry* (1972). This collection includes two other plays, *The Drinking Gourd,* a black woman's story of slavery and emancipation, and *What Use Are Flowers?* a fable about an aging hermit who, in a ravaged world, tries to impart to children his remembrances of a past civilization.

CRITICAL RECEPTION

Hansberry is best known for her play *A Raisin in the Sun,* which is ranked with Arthur Miller's *Death of a Salesman,* Tennessee Williams's *Glass Menagerie,* and Eugene O'Neill's *Long Day's Journey into Night* as a classic in American theater. Recently the play has attracted a new generation of admirers. In 1984 Nemiroff published an expanded, twenty-fifth anniversary edition of the play. With the restoration of scenes and text originally removed from the first production, *A Raisin in the Sun* was also adapted for television in 1989, starring Danny Glover, Esther Rolle, and Kim Yancey. Feminist critics have applauded Hansberry's portrayal of strong female characters in the play, women who challenge stereotypes of African American women at that time. Moreover, feminist commentators have noted Hansberry's recurring concern with the role of women in theater and society and her activism concerning equal rights for women during her lifetime. Overall, Hansberry has been acknowledged as a gifted playwright and an articulate and strong supporter of the civil rights and women's movements.

PRINCIPAL WORKS

A Raisin in the Sun (play) 1959; expanded edition, 1984

A Raisin in the Sun (screenplay) 1960

The Sign in Sidney Brustein's Window (play) 1964

Lorraine Hansberry's "Les Blancs" (play) 1966

To Be Young, Gifted, and Black: A Portrait of Lorraine Hansberry in Her Own Words (letters and sketches) [edited by Robert Nemiroff] 1969

Les Blancs [edited by Robert Nemiroff] (play) 1970

*Les Blancs: The Collected Plays of Lorraine Hansberry (plays) [edited by Robert Nemiroff] 1972

* This collection includes *Les Blancs*, produced for the stage in 1970, and published by Hart Stenographic Bureau in 1966 as *Lorraine Hansberry's "Les Blancs."* The volume also includes two other plays, *The Drinking Gourd* and *What Use Are Flowers?*

PRIMARY SOURCES

LORRAINE HANSBERRY (PLAY DATE 1959)

SOURCE: Hansberry, Lorraine. *A Raisin in the Sun.* 1959. Reprint, pp. 7-20. New York: Random House, Modern Library Edition, 1995.

In the following excerpt from the opening scene of Hansberry's play A Raisin in the Sun, *Walter and Ruth discuss their positions in life, Walter's opinions about black women, and the aspirations of Beneatha, Walter's sister, to become a doctor.*

The YOUNGER living room would be a comfortable and well-ordered room if it were not for a number of indestructible contradictions to this state of being. It's furnishings are typical and undistinguished and their primary feature now is that they have clearly had to accommodate the living of too many people for too many years—and they are tired. Still, we can see that at some time, a time probably no longer remembered by the family (except perhaps for MAMA), the furnishings of this room were actually selected with care and love and even hope—and brought to this apartment and arranged with taste and pride.

That was a long time ago. Now the once loved pattern of the couch upholstery has to fight to show itself from under acres of crocheted doilies and couch covers which have themselves finally come to be more important than the upholstery. And here a table or a chair has been moved to disguise the worn places in the carpet; but the carpet has fought back by showing its weariness, with depressing uniformity, elsewhere on its surface.

Weariness has, in fact, won in this room. Everything has been polished, washed, sat on, used, scrubbed too often. All pretenses but living itself have long since vanished from the very atmosphere of this room.

Moreover, a section of this room, for it is not really a room unto itself, though the landlord's lease would make it seem so, slopes backward to provide a small kitchen area, where the family prepares the meals that are eaten in the living room proper, which must also serve as dining room. The single window that has been provided for these "two" rooms is located in this kitchen area. The sole natural light the family may enjoy in the course of a day is only that which fights its way through this little window.

At Left, a door leads to a bedroom which is shared by MAMA and her daughter, BENEATHA. At Right, opposite, is a second room (which in the beginning of the life of this apartment was probably a breakfast room) which serves as a bedroom for WALTER and his wife, RUTH.

TIME:

Sometime between World War II and the present.

PLACE:

Chicago's Southside.

AT RISE:

It is morning dark in the living room. TRAVIS is asleep on the make-down bed at Center. An ALARM CLOCK sounds from within the bedroom at Right, and presently RUTH enters from that room and closes the door behind her. She crosses sleepily toward the window. As she passes her sleeping son she reaches down and shakes him a little. At the window she raises the shade and a dusky Southside morning light comes in feebly. She fills a pot with water and puts it on to boil. She calls to the boy, between yawns, in a slightly muffled voice.

RUTH is about thirty. We can see that she was a pretty girl, even exceptionally so, but now it is apparent that life has been little that she expected, and disappointment has already begun to hang in her face. In a few years, before thirty-five even, she will be known among her people as a "settled woman."

She crosses to her son and gives him a good, final, rousing shake.

RUTH: Come on now, boy, it's seven thirty!
(*Her son sits up at last, in a stupor of sleepiness.*)
I say hurry up, Travis! You ain't the only person in the world got to use a bathroom.

(The child, a sturdy, handsome little boy of ten or eleven, drags himself out of the bed and almost blindly takes his towels and "today's clothes" from drawers and a closet and goes out to the bathroom, which is in an outside hall and which is shared by another family or families on the same floor.)

(RUTH crosses to the bedroom door at Right and opens it and calls in to her husband.) Walter Lee! . . . It's after seven thirty! Lemme see you do some waking up in there now! *(She waits.)* You better get up from there, man! It's after seven thirty I tell you. *(She waits again.)* All right, you just go ahead and lay there and next thing you know Travis be finished and Mr. Johnson'll be in there and you'll be fussing and cussing around here like a mad man! And be late too! *(She waits, at the end of patience.)* Walter Lee—it's time for you to get up! *(She waits another second and then starts to go into the bedroom, but is apparently satisfied that her husband has begun to get up. She stops, pulls the door to, and returns to the kitchen area. She wipes her face with a moist cloth and runs her fingers through her sleep-disheveled hair in a vain effort and ties an apron around her housecoat.)*

(The bedroom door at Right opens and her husband stands in the doorway in his pajamas, which are rumpled and mismated. He is a lean, intense young man in his middle thirties, inclined to quick nervous movements and erratic speech habits—and always in his voice there is a quality of indictment.)

WALTER: Is he out yet?

RUTH: What you mean *out?* He ain't hardly got in there good yet.

WALTER: *(Wandering in, still more oriented to sleep than to a new day.)* Well, what was you doing all that yelling for if I can't even get in there yet? *(Stopping and thinking.)* Check coming today?

RUTH: They *said* Saturday and this is just Friday and I hopes to God you ain't going to get up here first thing this morning and start talking to me 'bout no money—'cause I 'bout don't want to hear it.

WALTER: Something the matter with you this morning?

RUTH: No—I'm just sleepy as the devil. What kind of eggs you want?

WALTER: Not scrambled.

(RUTH starts to scramble eggs.)
Paper come?

(RUTH points impatiently to the rolled-up Tribune on the table, and he gets it and spreads it out and vaguely reads the front page.)
Set off another bomb yesterday.

RUTH: *(Maximum indifference.)* Did they?

WALTER: *(Looking up.)* What's the matter with you?

RUTH: Ain't nothing the matter with me. And don't keep asking me that this morning.

WALTER: Ain't nobody bothering you. *(Reading the news of the day absently again.)* Say Colonel McCormick is sick.

RUTH: *(Affecting tea-party interest.)* Is he now? Poor thing.

WALTER: *(Sighing and looking at his watch.)* Oh, me. *(He waits.)* Now what is that boy doing in that bathroom all this time? He just going to have to start getting up earlier. I can't be being late to work on account of him fooling around in there.

RUTH: *(Turning on him.)* Oh, no he ain't going to be getting up no earlier no such thing! It ain't his fault that he can't get to bed no earlier nights 'cause he got a bunch of crazy good-for-nothing clowns sitting up running their mouths in what is supposed to be his bedroom after ten o'clock at night. . . .

WALTER: That's what you mad about, ain't it? The things I want to talk about with my friends just couldn't be important in your mind, could they? *(He rises and finds a cigarette in her handbag on the table and crosses to the little window and looks out, smoking and deeply enjoying this first one.)*

RUTH: *(Almost matter of factly, a complaint too automatic to deserve emphasis.)* Why you always got to smoke before you eat in the morning?

WALTER: *(At the window.)* Just look at 'em down there . . . running and racing to work . . . *(He turns and faces his wife and watches her a moment at the stove, and then, suddenly.)* You look young this morning, baby.

RUTH: *(Indifferently.)* Yeah?

WALTER: Just a second—stirring them eggs. It's gone now—just for a second it was—you looked real young again. *(Then, drily.)* It's gone now—you look like yourself again.

RUTH: Man, if you don't shut up and leave me alone.

WALTER: *(Looking out to the street again.)* First thing a man ought to learn in life is not to make love to no colored woman first thing in the morning. You all some evil people at eight o'clock in the morning.

(TRAVIS appears in the hall doorway, almost fully dressed and quite wide awake

now, his towels and pajamas across his shoulders. He opens the door and signals for his father to make the bathroom in a hurry.)

TRAVIS: *(Watching the bathroom.)* Daddy, come on!

(WALTER gets his bathroom utensils and flies out to the bathroom.)

RUTH: Sit down and have your breakfast, Travis.

TRAVIS: Mama, this is Friday. *(Gleefully.)* Check coming tomorrow, huh?

RUTH: You get your mind off money and eat your breakfast.

TRAVIS: *(Eating.)* This is the morning we supposed to bring the fifty cents to school.

RUTH: Well, I ain't got no fifty cents this morning.

TRAVIS: Teacher say we have to.

RUTH: I don't care what teacher say. I ain't got it. Eat your breakfast, Travis.

TRAVIS: I *am* eating.

RUTH: Hush up now and just eat!

(The boy gives her an exasperated look for her lack of understanding, and eats grudgingly.)

TRAVIS: You think Grandmama would have it?

RUTH: No! And I want you to stop asking your grandmother for money, you hear me?

TRAVIS: *(Outraged.)* Gaaaleee! I don't ask her, she just gimme it sometimes!

RUTH: Travis Willard Younger—I got too much on me this morning to be—

TRAVIS: Maybe Daddy—

RUTH: TRAVIS!

(The boy hushes abruptly. They are both quiet and tense for several seconds.)

TRAVIS: *(Presently.)* Could I maybe go carry some groceries in front of the supermarket for a little while after school then?

RUTH: Just hush, I said.

(TRAVIS jabs his spoon into his cereal bowl viciously, and rests his head in anger upon his fists.)

If you through eating, you can get over there and make up your bed.

(The boy obeys stiffly and crosses the room, almost mechanically, to the bed and more or less carefully folds the covering. He carries the bedding into his mother's room and returns with his books and cap.)

TRAVIS: *(Sulking and standing apart from her unnaturally.)* I'm gone.

RUTH: *(Looking up from the stove to inspect him automatically.)* Come here. *(He crosses to her and she studies his head.)* If you don't take this comb and fix this here head, you better!

(TRAVIS puts down his books with a great sigh of oppression, and crosses to the mirror. His mother mutters under her breath about his "slubbornness.")

'Bout to march out of here with that head looking just like chickens slept in

it! I just don't know where you get your slubborn ways. . . . And get your jacket, too. Looks chilly out this morning.

TRAVIS: *(With conspicuously brushed hair and jacket.)* I'm gone.

RUTH: Get carfare and milk money—*(Waving one finger.)*—and not a single penny for no caps, you hear me?

TRAVIS: *(With sullen politeness.)* Yes'm. *(He turns in outrage to leave.)*

(His mother watches after him as in his frustration he approaches the door almost comically. When she speaks to him, her voice has become a very gentle tease.)

RUTH: *(Mocking; as she thinks he would say it.)* Oh, Mama makes me so mad sometimes, I don't know what to do! *(She waits and continues to his back as he stands stock still in front of the door.)* I wouldn't kiss that woman good-bye for nothing in this world this morning!

(The boy finally turns around and rolls his eyes at her, knowing the mood has changed and he is vindicated; he does not, however, move toward her yet.)

Not for nothing in this world! *(She finally laughs aloud at him and holds out her arms to him and we see that it is a way between them, very old and practiced.) (He crosses to her and allows her to embrace him warmly but keeps his face fixed with masculine rigidity. She holds him back from her presently and looks at him and runs her fingers over the features of his face.)*

(With utter gentleness.) Now—whose little old angry man are you?

TRAVIS: *(The masculinity and gruffness start to fade at last.)* Aw gaalee—Mama . . .

RUTH: *(Mimicking.)* Aw—gaaaaallee-eee, Mama! *(She pushes him, with the rough playfulness and finality, toward the door.)* Get on out of here or you going to be late.

TRAVIS: *(In the face of love, new aggressiveness.)* Mama, could I *please* go carry groceries?

RUTH: Honey, it's starting to get so cold evenings.

WALTER: *(Coming in from the bathroom and drawing a make-believe gun from a make-believe holster and shooting at his son.)* What is it he wants to do?

RUTH: Go carry groceries after school at the supermarket.

WALTER: Well, let him go. . . .

TRAVIS: *(Quickly, to the ally.)* I have to—she won't gimme the fifty cents. . . .

WALTER: *(To his wife only.)* Why not?

RUTH: *(Simply, and with flavor.)* 'Cause we don't have it.

WALTER: *(To RUTH only.)* What you tell the boy things like that for? *(Reaching down into his pants with a rather important gesture.)*

Here, son—*(He hands the boy the coin, but his eyes are directed to his wife's.)*
(TRAVIS Takes the money happily.)

TRAVIS: Thanks, Daddy. *(He starts out.)*
(RUTH watches both of them with murder in her eyes. WALTER stands and stares back at her with defiance, and suddenly reaches into his pocket again on an after-thought.)

WALTER: *(Without even looking at his son, still staring hard at his wife.)* In fact, here's another fifty cents. . . . Buy yourself some fruit today—or take a taxicab to school or something!

TRAVIS: Whoopee—*(He leaps up and clasps his father around the middle with his legs, and they face each other in mutual appreciation.)*
(Slowly WALTER LEE peaks around the boy to catch the violent rays from his wife's eyes and draws his head back as if shot.)

WALTER: You better get down now—and get to school, man.

TRAVIS: *(At the door.)* O.K. Good-bye. *(He exits.)*

WALTER: *(After him, pointing with pride.)* That's *my* boy.
(She looks at him in disgust and turns back to her work.)
You know what I was thinking 'bout in the bathroom this morning?

RUTH: No.

WALTER: How come you always try to be so pleasant!

RUTH: What is there to be pleasant 'bout!

WALTER: You want to know what I was thinking 'bout in the bathroom or not!

RUTH: I know what you thinking 'bout.

WALTER: *(Ignoring her.)* 'Bout what me and Willy Harris was talking about last night.

RUTH: *(Immediately—a refrain.)* Willy Harris is a good-for-nothing loud mouth.

WALTER: Anybody who talks to me has got to be a good-for-nothing loud mouth, ain't he? And what you know about who is just a good-for-nothing loud mouth? Charlie Atkins was just a "good-for-nothing loud mouth" too, wasn't he! When he wanted me to go in the dry-cleaning business with him. And now—he's grossing a hundred thousand a year. A hundred thousand dollars a year! You still call *him* a loud mouth!

RUTH: *(Bitterly.)* Oh, Walter Lee. . . . *(She folds her head on her arms over the table.)*

WALTER: *(Rising and coming to her and standing over her.)* You tired, ain't you? Tired of everything. Me, the boy, the way we live—this beat-up hole—everything. Ain't you?
(She doesn't look up, doesn't answer.)
So tired—moaning and groaning all the time, but you wouldn't do nothing to help, would you? You couldn't be on my side that long for nothing, could you?

RUTH: Walter, please leave me alone.

WALTER: A man needs for a woman to back him up . . .

RUTH: Walter—

WALTER: Mama would listen to you. You know she listen to you more than she do me and Bennie. She think more of you. All you have to do is just sit down with her when you drinking your coffee one morning and talking 'bout things like you do and—*(He sits down beside her and demonstrates graphically what he thinks her methods and tone should be.)*—you just sip your coffee, see, and say easy like that you been thinking 'bout that deal Walter Lee is so interested in, 'bout the store and all, and sip some more coffee, like what you saying ain't really that important to you—and the next thing you know, she be listening good and asking you questions and when I come home—I can tell her the details. This ain't no fly-by-night proposition, baby. I mean we figured it out, me and Willy and Bobo.

RUTH: *(With a frown.)* Bobo?

WALTER: Yeah. You see, this little liquor store we got in mind cost seventy-five thousand and we figured the initial investment on the place be 'bout thirty thousand, see. That be ten thousand each. Course, there's a couple of hundred you go to pay so's you don't spend your life just waiting for them clowns to let your license get approved—

RUTH: You mean graft?

WALTER: *(Frowning impatiently.)* Don't call it that. See there, that just goes to show you what women understand about the world. Baby, don't *nothing* happen for you in this world 'less you pay *somebody* off!

RUTH: Walter, leave me alone! *(She raises her head and stares at him vigorously—then says, more quietly.)* Eat your eggs, they gonna be cold.

WALTER: *(Straightening up from her and looking off.)* That's it. There you are. Man say to his woman: I got me a dream. His woman say: Eat your eggs. *(Sadly, but gaining in power.)* Man say: I got to take hold of this here world, baby! And a woman will say: Eat your eggs and go to work. *(Passionately now.)* Man say: I got to change my life, I'm choking to death, baby! And his woman say—*(In utter anguish as he brings his fists down on his thighs.)*—Your eggs is getting cold!

RUTH: *(Softly.)* Walter, that ain't none of our money.

WALTER: *(Not listening at all or even looking at her.)* This morning, I was lookin' in the mirror and thinking about it . . . I'm thirty-five years old; I been married eleven years and I got a boy who sleeps in the living room—*(Very, very quietly.)*—and all

*I got to give him is stories about how rich
white people live. . . .*

RUTH: Eat your eggs, Walter.

WALTER: DAMN MY EGGS . . . DAMN ALL THE
EGGS THAT EVER WAS!

RUTH: Then go to work.

WALTER: *(Looking up at her.)* See—I'm trying to talk
to you 'bout myself—*(Shaking his head
with the repetition.)*—and all you can say
is eat them eggs and go to work.

RUTH: *(Wearily.)* Honey, you never say nothing new.
I listen to you every day, every night and
every morning, and you never say nothing new. *(Shrugging.)* So you would rather
be Mr. Arnold than be his chauffeur.
So—I would *rather* be living in Bucking-
ham Palace.

WALTER: That is just what is wrong with the colored
woman in this world . . . don't understand about building their men up making 'em feel like they somebody. Like
they can do something.

RUTH: *(Drily, but to hurt.)* There are colored men
who do things.

WALTER: No thanks to the colored woman.

RUTH: Well, being a colored woman, I guess I can't
help myself none. *(She rises and gets the
ironing board and sets it up and attacks a
huge pile of rough-dried clothes, sprinkling
them in preparation for the ironing and then
rolling them into tight fat balls).*

WALTER: *(Mumbling.)* We one group of men tied to a
race of women with small minds.

GENERAL COMMENTARY

STEVEN R. CARTER (ESSAY DATE FALL 1980)

SOURCE: Carter, Steven R. "Commitment amid Complexity: Lorraine Hansberry's Life in Action." *MELUS* 7,
no. 3 (fall 1980): 39-53.

*In the following essay, Carter provides a chronology of
Hansberry's life and career and describes her dedication
to the women's rights movement.*

I. Thirty-four Years

It may seem odd to precede an article with a
chronology, but it is odder still that to date no
chronology has been published on Lorraine Hansberry. This failure in scholarship is symptomatic
of the continuing critical and scholarly neglect of
important black artists and especially of Hansberry. During the fifteen years since her death, the
only attempt at a formally structured, "lengthy"
biography was Catherine Scheader's *They Found a
Way: Lorraine Hansberry,* a recently published

seventy-eight page book which (though informative and accurate) was intended for children.
Moreover, Robert Nemiroff's informal biography,
To Be Young, Gifted and Black (a juxtaposition of
Hansberry's autobiographical writings with portions of her essays, speeches, poetry and dramatic
scenes), was ignored by critics, receiving no review
in the *New York Times* or any of the major news
magazines and scholarly journals. Similarly, few
books on American or twentieth-century drama
mention Hansberry, and these cite only her
pioneering role in black drama with *A Raisin in
the Sun.* The time is long past due to give her the
treatment accorded to other major twentieth-
century dramatists.

An accurate Hansberry chronology is needed,
in part, to correct the enormous amount of
misinformation about her. She did not, for example, meet her husband, Robert Nemiroff, while
working as a waitress in a restaurant owned by his
family, as implied in *Current Biography 1959*;
neither did she own slum property, as Harold
Cruse maliciously asserted in *The Crisis of the Negro
Intellectual.* In addition, even a rudimentary
chronology should help to clear away the general
ignorance of her many radical activities which has
permitted critics and students—on too many occasions—to succumb to the myth that Hansberry
was an "establishment artist," less interested in
changing the system than in getting a home in
suburbia, a television, and two cars. An examination of her funeral, by itself, would preclude a
facile acceptance of this myth since representatives from all sides of the black struggle paid
tribute to her; the integrationist Martin Luther
King sent a message praising "her commitment of
spirit" and "her profound grasp of the deep social
issues confronting the world today." The Marxist
Paul Robeson and SNCC Executive Secretary James
Foreman delivered eulogies, and the Black Nationalist Malcolm X sat among the mourners.

The main reason for including a chronology
in an article on Hansberry, however, is to indicate
the close relationship between her life and her
ideas. Taken together, they demonstrate that the
thread uniting the many sides of her personality
and beliefs was her commitment to social change.
Introduced to fear at any early age by a howling
white mob which attacked her home, Hansberry
dedicated her life to fighting such forces in our
society. This will to struggle focused all her energies and enabled her to remain whole in the face

of social pressures that have warped and destroyed countless other human beings. Her extraordinary example of completeness amid the crush of modern life, her model of commitment amid complexity, should make it impossible for future generations to forget her, or for future scholars to ignore her.

Scholarship may finally be ready to deal justly with Hansberry. A special issue of *Freedomways* (vol. 19, no. 4, 1979) is devoted exclusively to as the most comprehensive bibliography of works by and about her. The chronology presented here is, in effect, a joint effort by the editors of *Freedomways*, Robert Nemiroff, and myself, but the final responsibility is mine; like everything else on Hansberry, it should be regarded as a preliminary work.

> 1930 Born in Chicago, Illinois, on May 19, to Nannie Perry Hansberry and Carl A. Hansberry
>
> 1930-40 Hansberry home is a center of black cultural, political, and economic life. Lorraine's uncle, William Leo Hansberry, a distinguished Africanist at Howard University, visits the home, as do African students and exiles and such celebrated figures as Paul Robeson, Duke Ellington, Walter White, Joe Louis, Jesse Owens. Carl Hansberry is a realtor and is active in the NAACP, Urban League, civic, and business affairs. He runs for Congress as a Republican. Nannie Hansberry, formerly a schoolteacher, is a leader in the black community and a ward committeewoman. Lorraine visits her mother's birthplace in Tennessee, where she also hears tales from her grandmother that will figure in her play, *The Drinking Gourd*.
>
> 1938 Carl Hansberry moves his family into a "restricted" area near the University of Chicago to test real estate covenants barring blacks. Mobs demonstrate, throw bricks and concrete slabs through the family's windows. After losing suit and appeals in Illinois courts challenging legality of covenants, family is evicted from home. This incident will form part of the background for Lorraine's most famous play, *A Raisin in the Sun*, the first draft of which concludes with the black family sitting in the dark, armed, awaiting an attack by hostile whites.
>
> 1940 Hansberry and NAACP legal team win U.S. Supreme Court decision (*Hansberry vs. Lee*) against restrictive covenants on November 12, but in practice covenants continue.
>
> 1944 Lorraine graduates from Betsy Ross Elementary School.
>
> 1946 Carl Hansberry dies in Mexico, March 17. He had taken refuge there from U.S. racism and was in the midst of planning family's relocation at time of death.
>
> 1947 Lorraine elected president of debating society at Englewood High School. Racial tension erupts in riot at school. She is moved by the way that

> poorer blacks from nearby Wendell Phillips High fight back against their oppressors.
>
> 1948-50 Attends University of Wisconsin, studying art, literature, drama, and stage design.
>
> 1949 *Summer:* Studies painting at University of Guadalajara extension in Ajijic, Mexico, and Mexican Art Workshop.
>
> 1950 *Summer:* Studies art at Roosevelt University. *August:* Arrives in New York City—"to seek an education of a different kind." Lives on Lower East Side. Takes courses: jewelry-making, photography, short story writing for "about two erratic months" at New School for Social Research. Starts work for *Freedom*, radical black monthly published by Paul Robeson. Gets involved in peace and freedom movements.
>
> 1951 Moves to Harlem. Member of delegation of women who present Governor of Mississippi with petition of almost one million signatures gathered around the world in support of Willie McGee, under death sentence for alleged rape. McGee is executed.
>
> 1952 Represents Paul Robeson, who has been denied passport by State Department, at Intercontinental Peace Congress in Montevideo, Uruguay. (Congress deals with disarmament, social and economic liberation of the Americas.) Also visits Buenos Aires, Rio de Janeiro, and Trinidad. Becomes associate editor of *Freedom*.
>
> 1953 Marries Robert Nemiroff on June 20. He is an aspiring writer and graduate student in English and history at New York University; she had become acquainted with him in a picket line protesting discrimination. They settle in Greenwich Village, which will become setting for her play, *The Sign in Sidney Brustein's Window*. Studies African history and culture under W. E. B. DuBois at Jefferson School for Social Science. Resigns from full-time work at *Freedom* to concentrate on writing.
>
> 1953-56 Three plays in progress. Has series of jobs—in fur shop, as typist, as production assistant in theatrical firm, on staff of *Sing Out* magazine, as recreation leader at Federation for the Handicapped. (Husband works part-time as typist, copywriter; after graduation, becomes promotions director, Avon Books.)
>
> 1956 Success of hit song by husband and Burt D'Lugoff, "Cindy, Oh, Cindy," enables Hansberry to write full time. Nemiroff goes to work running music publishing firm for their friend, Philip Rose.
>
> 1957 Reads completed play, *A Raisin in the Sun*, to friends D'Lugoff and Rose. Rose decides to produce it, signs Sidney Poitier and Broadway's first black director, Lloyd Richards.
>
> 1959 Denied Broadway theatre, Rose gambles on out-of-town try-outs in New Haven and Philadelphia. *Raisin in the Sun* does well out-of-town, moves to Chicago while awaiting Broadway theatre. *March 11: A Raisin in the Sun*, first play by a black woman to be produced on Broadway, opens at Ethel Barrymore Theatre. Wins New York Drama

Critics Circle Award as "Best Play of the Year" over Tennessee Williams's *Sweet Bird of Youth*, Archibald MacLeish's *JB*, Eugene O'Neill's *A Touch of the Poet*. She is youngest American, first woman, first black to win this award. *Raisin* sold to the movies.

1960 Writes two screenplays of *A Raisin in the Sun* that expand on play's themes. Columbia Pictures rejects both as too racially controversial in favor of third draft closer to stageplay. Commissioned to write slavery drama for NBC as first of a series of five TV specials by major theatre dramatists to commemorate Civil War centennial. Writes *The Drinking Gourd*, which is considered "superb" but "too controversial," and the entire series is dropped. Begins research for opera called *Toussaint* and play about Mary Wollstonecraft, the famous 18th century feminist. Works on *The Sign in Jenny Reed's Window* (title later changed), *Les Blancs*, and other projects.

1961 Moves to Croton-on-Hudson, New York. Film version of *A Raisin in the Sun* nominated "Best Screenplay of the Year" by Screen Writers Guild; wins special award at Cannes Film Festival.

1962 Continues work on plays, while mobilizing support for Student Non-Violent Coordinating Committee (SNCC) in its struggle against Southern segregation. Speaks out against House Un-American Activities Committee and Cuban "missile crisis." Writes *What Use Are Flowers?*

1963 Hospitalized for tests; results suggest cancer. Scene from *Les Blancs* staged at Actors Studio Writers Workshop with Arthur Hill, Roscoe Lee Browne, Rosemary Murphy, Pearl Primus; directed by Arthur Penn. *May 24:* Joins James Baldwin, other prominent blacks, and a few whites at widely publicized meeting with Attorney General Robert Kennedy on racial crisis. *June 19:* Chairs meeting in Croton-on-Hudson to raise money for SNCC (proceeds bought station wagon from which Cheney, Schwerner and Goodman were kidnapped). *June 24:* Operated on unsuccessfully in New York. *August 2:* Second operation in Boston. For a time, recovers strength.

1964 *The Movement: Documentary of a Struggle for Equality* is published, a photo-book prepared by SNCC with text by Hansberry. All proceeds go to SNCC. *March 10:* Marriage to Robert Nemiroff ends in divorce, but creative collaboration continues. Because of her illness, they tell only closest friends about divorce and see each other daily until her death. From April to October, is in and out of hospital for radiation treatments, chemotherapy, while continuing work on *Brustein, Les Blancs*, research for *Wollstonecraft*, and other projects. *May 1:* Released from hospital for afternoon to deliver **"To Be Young, Gifted and Black"** speech to winners of United Negro College Fund writing contest. *June 15:* Leaves sickbed to participate in Town Hall debate between militant black artists Amiri Baraka, John Killens, Paule Marshall, Ossie Davis and Ruby Dee, and white liberals Charles Silberman, James Wechsler, David Susskind on "The Black Revolution and the White Backlash." *October:* Moves to Hotel Victoria to be near rehearsals of *The Sign in Sidney Brustein's Window*, produced by Nemiroff and D'Lugoff, with Gabriel Dell, Rita Moreno, Alice Ghostley in cast. *October 15:* Attends opening of *Brustein* at Longacre Theatre. Play receives mixed reviews. Stage and screen actors collaborate to keep it running in tribute to gravely ill playwright and her work.

1965 Dies of cancer on January 12, at age 34.

II. Political and Social Concerns

At the time Lorraine Hansberry began creating her dramas, many writers pictured the modern world as overly complex, baffling, and overwhelming. They showed human beings groping endlessly for meaning in a world that contained no god, no absolute values, no certainties of any kind, a multitude of frivolous and pointless activities, and little reason to hope for any improvement. This attitude was epitomized in the Theatre of the Absurd, a form of drama which mingled clowning and despair, large issues and trivia, a drop of clarity and a bucketful of nonsense. In a typical absurdist drama, one might find a pair of bums who resembled Laurel and Hardy crying alternately about nuclear fallout and their untied shoelaces or a woman in a laundry hamper making a speech that combined the Gettysburg address with a Euclidean equation and an underarm deodorant commercial. In short, one was usually presented with a dramatic jigsaw puzzle in which the pieces—by intention—never fit together, a crazy quilt pattern which theoretically demonstrated the lack of coherence in everyone's life.

Hansberry's response to the Theatre of the Absurd was considerable. Large portions of *The Sign in Sidney Brustein's Window*, for example, contain a continuing argument between the protagonist, Sidney Brustein, and the absurdist playwright, David Ragin, over the significance of political activity, the meaning of life, and the proper form of artistic expression. David in each instance presents the absurdist view which Sidney counters with Hansberry's brand of humanism. The climactic scene occurs when, disillusioned by the breakdown of his marriage and the defeat of his hopes for political reform, Sidney abandons his humanism and social commitment and turns his life into a drama of absurdist despair. At this point, the form of Hansberry's play shifts from realism to that of the Theatre of the Absurd. After that, Sidney returns to a strengthened belief in the virtues of humanism and the struggle for social change, and the form of the play returns to realism. Another Hansberry play that serves as a response to the Theatre of the Absurd is *What*

Use Are Flowers?. According to Robert Nemiroff, "Its inspiration was not *The Lord of the Flies* . . . but Samuel Beckett's *Waiting for Godot*."[1] Hansberry was so moved by Beckett's important absurdist drama that she also wrote a parody of it entitled "The Arrival of Mr. Todog." This unpublished parody is only eleven pages long, but it clearly reflects her feeling that absurdist drama was itself absurd. In addition to these plays, Hansberry also wrote many articles and letters expressing her views on the Theatre of the Absurd.

Hansberry agreed with the absurdists that there were no gods and no values extrinsic to human beings, but she argued that humans could "do what the apes never will—impose the reason for life on life."[2] She refused to see life as absurd and futile, even in the face of the Cuban Missile Crisis or her personal crisis with cancer, and thought that no matter how complex things seemed to be, one could still find clear issues about which one should take a stand. In an unpublished letter discussing *After the Fall,* Arthur Miller's play about his former wife Marilyn Monroe and about the universal guilt of humanity, Hansberry asserted:

> Things are very, very complicated. . . . But—they aren't *that* complicated either. The English [colonialists] are wrong, the [rebelling subject] Kikuyu are right; we are wrong, Castro is right; the Viet Namese people (there doesn't appear to be any difference between the Viet Namese people and the "Viet Cong" any more by our own account) are right and we are wrong!; the Negro people are right and the shameful dawdling of Federal authority [in securing their civil rights] is wrong; the concept of "woman" which fashioned, warped and destroyed a human being such as Marilyn Monroe (or "Audrey Smith" . . . or "Lucy Jones"—daily) IS HIDEOUSLY WRONG—and she, *in her repudiation of it,* in trying tragically to RISE ABOVE it by killing herself is (in the Shakespearean sense)—right.[3]

Like her protagonist Sidney Brustein, Hansberry considered the metaphysical debate about why we are here on earth to be only "an intrigue for adolescents" and preferred to concentrate on the social question of how we should live. She felt that the metaphysical debate could not be resolved on the basis of our present knowledge and thus became a game played in a fog, an amusement for absurdists; however, the social question could receive many distinct answers and "should command the living."[4]

One of her least noted but most profound commitments was to women's rights. In a radio interview with Studs Terkel in 1959, Hansberry observed "that obviously the most oppressed group of any oppressed group will be its women" and when they are "twice oppressed" they often become "twice militant."[5] She expressed her respect for such militancy unequivocally in her ironically titled essay "In Defense of the Equality of Men": "In deed and oratory, in their recognition of direct political action as the true key to social transformation, American Feminist leaders, in particular, set a path that a grateful society will undoubtedly, in time, celebrate." Noting the efforts that women's groups have made toward enlarging "the Constitutional promises of the American Republic to include the largest numbers of its people of both sexes," she further contended that "we might well long for the day when the knowledge of the debt all society owes to organized womanhood in bringing the human race closer together, not pushing it farther apart, will still the laughter in the throat of the uninformed."[6] Although she once established her devotion to the cause of women's equality by resigning from a job as a production secretary for a theatrical producer because her primary duty was to serve coffee, the best demonstration of her militancy lies in her many yet unpublished feminist essays and the feminist implications of her published works.

Actually, of course, Hansberry's whole way of life was a repudiation of the limitations that society has tried to place on women. Instead of seeking fulfillment in the traditional limiting roles of homemaker, mother, pillar of the church, and sexual toy, she sought it in the same areas men did—in artistic creation, in intellectual speculation, in political struggle, in public speaking, and in the pursuit of knowledge about all aspects of life. She peopled her dramas with many powerful female characters whose strength was like that of their creator, but others of her characters were lamed by their efforts to accept the socially-dictated roles.

Hansberry's bitterness over the subject status of women was tempered, however, by her belief that some remarkable men would always spring to defend the rights of others. In an unpublished essay entitled "Simone de Beauvoir and *The Second Sex:* An American Commentary," she observed that "in times past, woman, ignorant, inarticulate, has often found her most effective and telling champion among great men" and argued "that if by some miracle women should not ever utter a single protest against their condition there would still exist among men those who could not endure in peace until her liberation had been achieved." Moreover, she believed that "to the extent that the Feminist leaders pronounced *man* rather than ideology as enemy they deserved correction."[7]

Her foremost commitment, of course, was to the liberation of her fellow blacks in America, and here too she noted the human capacity of self-transcendence. During a 1964 Town Hall debate between several militant black artists and three white liberals on "The Black Revolution and the White Backlash," she noted that "we have a very great tradition of white radicalism in the United States" and that she had "never heard Negroes boo the name of John Brown."[8] Later in the debate she observed that "white kids on the firing line in Mississippi" displayed a commitment worth respect.[9] Given the charged atmosphere of the debate in which the blacks, including Imamu Baraka, John O. Killens, and Hansberry herself, strongly attacked the ways in which white liberals had dominated and inhibited the black liberation movement, these were courageous and significant statements. She further contended that "some of the first people who have died so far in this struggle have been white men" and that she "would be prepared to accept the leadership of the person who gives that much devotion as against someone who would exhibit the traitorous character of, say, a Moise Tshombe [black puppet ruler of the African province of Katenga]."[10] The problem with whites, as she saw it, was how "to encourage the white liberal to stop being a liberal and become an American radical."[11]

She considered radicalism necessary because she felt that "the basic fabric of our society . . . after all, is the thing which must be changed to really solve the problem," that "the basic organization of American society is the thing that has Negroes in the situation that they are in."[12] Her complex vision of mankind enabled her to perceive the humanity of even the most rabid white racist, but she asserted that this humanity could never reach its full development in contemporary American society. In her view, the social framework of America encouraged whites to betray their humanity daily by treating blacks (and other "inferior" races) with arrogance, contemptuousness, economic and sexual exploitativeness, callousness toward manifest suffering, and frequently atrocious, bestial, totally unjustifiable cruelty. For this reason, she was convinced that the social framework had to be altered for the sake of both the victimized minorities and the victimizing white supremacists. Her television play, *The Drinking Gourd*, although set in the period immediately preceding the Civil War, may be interpreted as speaking in some ways for Hansberry's

America with its rich whites "forced" by decreasing profits to compel already overworked blacks to perform additional tasks, its poor whites "forced" by their need for economic security to aid the rich in their degradation of blacks, and its victims and honorable men "forced" by circumstance and conscience to fight against the destructive system which had "already cost us, as a nation, too much of our soul."[13]

Hansberry's commitment to gaining justice for blacks was first displayed when she joined the staff of the radical black newspaper *Freedom,* of which Paul Robeson became the "symbolic leader" in 1951.

> His fame as a radical cultural personality drew such Harlem writers as John Oliver Killens, twenty-year-old Lorraine Hansberry, and Julian R. Mayfield to the *Freedom* orbit, with an editorial board that included noted leftists, writer Shirley Graham DuBois (the wife of W. E. B. DuBois), the intellectual Louis E. Burnham, editor ["He taught me that *everything* is political," Hansberry said], and George B. Murphy, Jr., general manager. *Freedom* contained occasional reportorial pieces about Harlem schools and housing, but in the main, its writers hammered away at national and international issues—poll taxes, the Fair Employment Practices Commission, the antilynch bill, China, British Guiana, the war in Korea, Africa.[14]

Hansberry wrote such articles as **"Child Labor Is Society's Crime against Youth," "Church Always Led Freedom's Struggles," "Negroes Cast in Same Old Roles in TV Shows," "No More Hiroshimas," "Gold Coast's Rulers Go: Ghana Moves to Freedom,"** and **"Kenya's Kikuyus: a Peaceful People Wage Struggle against British."** In addition, she reviewed books and the small amount of drama by blacks that was produced in that time.

While working at *Freedom,* Hansberry also demonstrated her dedication to the cause by marching on picketlines, by speaking on street corners in Harlem, and by helping to move the furniture of evicted black tenants back into their apartments. Later, in the wake of the huge success of her play, *A Raisin in the Sun,* she utilized her new fame to gain attention for her ideas about black social, political, and economic equality. She spoke about the needs of her people on television, in lecture halls, at fund-raising programs for Civil Rights groups, in debates with other celebrities, and, on one memorable occasion, in an emotion-charged small group meeting with Attorney General Robert Kennedy. Even while she lay deathly sick, she considered going to the embattled and perilous South to test the continuing strength of her black revolutionary convictions.

However, immensely powerful though it was, Hansberry's sympathy for blacks was never limited to those in America; she was certain that the fate of all people of African descent was bound up together. Her Pan-Africanism was based not only on her profound respect for her racial background and for African culture, but also on her recognition that changes in the situation of African blacks could promote changes in the situation of American blacks and vice versa. As African blacks began to throw off the tyrannical, thieving grip of white colonizers and to establish independent countries courted by the communists, they found that they could pressure the American government into making more efforts on behalf of American blacks. Similarly, as American blacks gained some small voice in their country's affairs, they could, as Andrew Young did recently, exert this influence in favor of African blacks both in the independent countries and in those still subject to colonial rule.

The emergence of black-ruled countries in Africa filled Hansberry with optimism about the future. She frequently scoffed at white intellectuals who despaired over the future and talked about the "decline of the West" because she suspected that what really upset them was the loss of empire, the defeat of colonialism. She contended that the sense of desolation affecting many Western intellectuals, such as Albert Camus, should therefore have no appeal for American or African blacks who were starting to gain independence and power. In an essay entitled "**Images and Essences: 1961 Dialogue with an Uncolored Egghead**," she stated that:

> the gloom and doom of so much of Western art and thought . . . leaves me cold. Africa and Asia and American Negroes, in their own comparatively decrepit way, are in anything but states of collapse or decay. On the contrary they are in their most insurgent mood in modern history.[15]

Although her major commitments were to those of her own gender and race, she had an abiding concern for all victims of oppression and injustice. Like the great men and women she admired, such as Paul Robeson, Albert Einstein, and Mary Wollstonecraft (about whom she planned to write a play), she transcended narrow group interests and struggled for the right of others who had little in common with her. For example, on the night before her wedding, she and her future husband took part in a demonstration protesting the execution of the Rosenbergs, the white Jewish American couple who were convicted of treason amid the hysteria of the anticommunist witch-hunt in the early nineteen fifties. Similarly, although she grew up in a "rich" family (rich by black standards, upper middleclass by white ones), she strongly championed the poor, including the poor whites in the South. Hansberry asserted that "there's a fine and important distinction between that kind of material base of life which simply provides what people need to live a decent life and the middle-class preoccupation with acquisition, with affluence, with those things that they can demonstrate to their neighbors to show that they are keeping up with the fashions."[16] She advocated only the former type of materialism and was infuriated that many people could still starve and be subjected to rickets in this country while others grew fat on the most expensive gourmet meals.

Having been alarmed and outraged during her youth by the second World War and the dropping of the atom bomb on Hiroshima, she also became committed to the cause of world peace. Once, when an interviewer inquired about her dreams for the future, Hansberry responded:

> I would like very much to live in a world where some of the more monumental problems could at least be solved. I'm thinking, of course, of peace. That's part of my dream, that we don't fight. Nobody fights. We get rid of all the little bombs—and the big bombs.[17]

However, unlike many of her contemporaries, including Arthur Miller in *After the Fall*, Hansberry did not feel a special sense of "destructiveness hanging over this age." In her letter about Miller's play, she asked, "What in the name of God was hanging over the age of the War of Roses? Or the Crusades? Or the Byzantine conquests; the Civil War?" She then chided Miller—and the absurdists—by proclaiming:

> The ages of man have been hell. But the difference [between our age and the Renaissance] was that [Elizabethan] artists assumed the hell of it and went on to create figures *in battle with it* rather than overwhelmed with it and apologizing and "explaining" their frailty.[18]

In spite of her considerable efforts on behalf of world peace through articles, lectures, interviews, and the post-atomic war play *What Use Are Flowers?*, Hansberry was not totally opposed to violence. She believed firmly in the justice of some wars—in the right and necessity of revolution at moments in history, of wars of national liberation, and of self-defense of the people against their oppressors, as in the armed struggle against fascism. Correspondingly, she asserted that "it is no longer acceptable to allow racists to define Negro manhood—and it will have to come to pass that they can no longer define his weaponry." She argued that blacks "must concern themselves with every single means of struggle: legal, illegal, passive, active, violent and non-violent. . . . They must harass, debate, petition, give money to court struggles, sit-in, lie-down, strike, boycott, sing hymns, pray on steps—and shoot from their windows when the racists come cruising through their communities."[19] In a television interview made in 1959 when the Kikuyu were still fighting against British rule, Hansberry commented that she believed "most of all in humanism" and was "not interested in having white babies murdered any more than [she could] countenance the murder of Kikuyu babies in Kenya"; she hated "all of that kind of thing." However, she contended that one should not "equalize the oppressed with the oppressor." She was convinced that the oppressed were reacting to "intolerable conditions" which were imposed by the oppressor and that therefore the primary guilt for injustice lay with the oppressors.[20] On many occasions, she warned white racists not to rely on the supposed passivity, endurance, and infinite forbearing of black people; she knew that her fellow blacks could act inhumanely too, that they could respond to viciousness with viciousness, and that the whites would then have themselves to blame for their own suffering and that of their children.

All of these commitments were involved in Hansberry's dedication to the growth of socialism. In her tribute to the black intellectual giant, W. E. B. DuBois, she observed "that certainly DuBois' legacy teaches us to look forward and work for a socialist organization of society as the next great and dearly won universal condition of mankind."[21] She thought that socialism was the best way to organize society, the means which held the greatest possibility of providing the basic necessities for a decent life for all, and a potentially more democratic form of government with no individual or group having too much power. She argued that such a sharing of power might at least keep contending social groups (including contending races) from slitting each other's throats; she never expected everyone to love each other. Socialism could hopefully be a form of government which would encourage creativity and which would teach people to appreciate and even applaud individual and cultural differences; she did not want a socialism which would impose a homogeneous culture and a party line.

Hansberry's advocacy of power-sharing and diversity may be illustrated by her character Lena Younger's decisions in *A Raisin in the Sun.* As

sole parent and a woman of considerable strength. Lena Younger wields enormous power over her children. In the beginning, she assumes the role of a benevolent dictator. When she feels that her family is falling apart, she decides without consulting any other member of the family to use the insurance money from her husband's death to buy a house (unfortunately located in the all white neighborhood of Clyborne Park) in order to keep her family together. Also, she refuses to tolerate dissent concerning her most fundamental beliefs. She views her daughter Beneatha's atheism as a threat and forces her to say that in her "mother's house, there is still God."[22] However, when she realizes that her decisions have damaged and alienated her children, she begins to relinquish control. Believing that her dismissal of her son Walter Lee's plans for the insurance money may have been demeaning and destructive, she puts the remaining money in his hands and, in effect, grants him his independence coupled with a large responsibility. She is then forced to take the further step of deciding to stand by him after he loses the money, thus injuring his sister and the rest of the family, because she now understands that the only genuine freedom includes the freedom to make mistakes. At the end, she confirms that she has learned her lesson about granting independence by listening respectfully to Beneatha's dismissal of George Murchison (a suitor whom Lena had considered a desirable match for her daughter) and by delighting in the final argument between Walter and Beneatha over what is important in life. It is, therefore, appropriate that she, who has been taught the necessity of independence to growth, should join with her children in struggling against an outside threat to independence. Her family with its hard earned respect for differences contrasts strongly with the Clyborne Park people who want to keep their neighborhood homogeneous and conformist. The pattern set by Lena Younger and her family implies that unity in a struggle against oppression need not involve uniformity in either viewpoint or behavior and that any attempt to impose such uniformity would involve another form of oppression. The paradox is that Lena can only hold her family together by granting them the freedom to disagree with her and with each other.

Above all her commitments, Hansberry was devoted to the struggle for the progress of the human race. However, she recognized that this struggle had to be made according to the specific terms dictated by the time and country in which one lived. Her actions and writings left little doubt

FROM THE AUTHOR

HANSBERRY ON EARLY CRITICAL REACTION TO *A RAISIN IN THE SUN*

My colleagues and I were reduced to mirth and tears by that gentleman writing his review of [*A Raisin in the Sun*] in a Connecticut paper who remarked of his pleasure at seeing how "our dusky brethren" could "come up with a song and hum their troubles away." It did not disturb the writer in the least that there is no such implication in the entire three acts. He did not need it in the play; he had it in his head.

Hansberry, Lorraine. Excerpt from "Willy Loman, Walter Younger, and He Who Must Live," in *Village Voice* 4, no. 42 (12 August 1959): 7-8.

about what kinds of stands she wanted her fellow humans to take in America in her day.

Although some of the positions that Hansberry took so vigorously have since become fashionable, they were not so during her lifetime. Powerful forces, such as the McCarthy anticommunists, the Congressional House Committee on UnAmerican Activities, the official Cold War policies of the Truman, Eisenhower, and Kennedy administrations, the FBI, and entrenched white racism—always—in both the South and the North, destroyed the careers and lives of many people, among them close friends and associates, who held views similar to hers. However, she was willing to face such a high risk of destruction from these forces by continuing to express her views because she regarded knowledge of the truth as a necessity for group survival. She knew that, when the truth about a situation can't be spoken, the situation will probably become unmanageable—and explosive.

The best summary of Hansberry's position on the need for commitment in a complex world is contained in a fable which she invented for **Les Blancs,** her play about colonialism in Africa. In the fable, a hyena named Modingo ("One Who Thinks Carefully Before He Acts") refuses to take sides in a dispute over the land between elephants and hyenas because he considered himself a friend to both groups. He sympathizes with the el-

ephants' claim that "they needed more space because of their size" and with the hyenas' claim that "they had been *first* in that part of the jungle and were accustomed to running free."[23] However, while he explains his inability to take a stand to his fellow hyenas, the elephants take advantage of this opportunity to seize the land. The moral is clear and is not spelled out in the final version of the play. But it is stated explicitly in an unpublished early draft: "It is a good thing to discover that the elephant has a point of view, but it is a crime to forget that the hyena most has justice on his side."[24] The most remarkable qualities of Lorraine Hansberry were that she made great efforts to understand all sides of a conflict and that she felt compassion for everyone involved while firmly deciding where justice lay—and acting on that decision.

Notes

See also, Steven R. Carter, "The John Brown Theatre: Lorraine Hansberry's Cultural Views and Dramatic Goals," *Freedomways*, Vol. 19, No. 4, 186-91.

All unpublished material cited in the text comes from the collection of Robert Nemiroff, Hansberry's literary executor, and is copyrighted by Robert Nemiroff and may not be reproduced without permission.

1. Robert Nemiroff, ed., *Les Blancs: The Collected Last Plays of Lorraine Hansberry* (New York: Random House, 1972), p. 318.

2. Lorraine Hansberry, *To Be Young, Gifted and Black* (Englewood Cliffs, N.J.: Prentice Hall, 1969), p. 100.

3. Unpublished letter about Arthur Miller's *After the Fall*, dated "Tuesday" (year unstated but probably 1963), recipient unspecified.

4. Lorraine Hansberry, *A Raisin in the Sun/The Sign in Sidney Brustein's Window* (New York: New American Library, 1966), pp. 261-62.

5. From "An Interview with Lorraine Hansberry by Studs Terkel," May 12, 1959, recorded at 1145 Hyde Park Boulevard, Chicago. Unpublished.

6. Unpublished manuscript titled "In Defense of the Equality of Men."

7. Unpublished manuscript titled "Simone de Beauvoir and *The Second Sex*: An American Commentary, 1957."

8. "Black Revolution and White Backlash," *National Guardian* (July 4, 1964), p. 8. This is a nearly complete transcript of the Town Hall debate.

9. *National Guardian*, p. 9.

10. *National Guardian*, p. 8.

11. *National Guardian*, p. 7.

12. John O. Killens, James Wechsler, and Lorraine Hansberry, "The Black Revolution and the White Backlash," in *Black Protest: History, Documents and Analyses, 1619 to the Present*, ed. Joanne Grant (New York: Fawcett World Library, 1968), p. 447.

13. *Les Blancs*, p. 310.

14. Dorothy Butler Graham, *Paul Robeson: All-American* (Washington: The New Republic Book Co., 1978), p. 160.

15. *The Urbanite*, I, 3 (May 1961), 11.

16. Unpublished transcript of an interview with Eleanor Fisher for CBC on June 7, 1961.

17. *Young, Gifted and Black*, pp. 253-54.

18. Unpublished letter about *After the Fall.*

19. *Young, Gifted and Black*, pp. 213-14.

20. Lorraine Hansberry, "The Beauty of Things Black— Towards Total Liberation: An Interview with Mike Wallace, May 8, 1959," *Lorraine Hansberry Speaks Out: Art and the Black Revolution*, Caedmon, TC 1352, 1972.

21. Lorraine Hansberry, "Tribute," in *Black Titan: W. E. B. DuBois, an Anthology by the Editors of* Freedomways, ed. John Henrik Clarke, Esther Jackson, Ernest Kaiser, and J. H. O'Dell (Boston: Beacon Press, 1970), p. 17.

22. *Raisin/Brustein*, p. 39.

23. *Les Blancs*, p. 126.

24. Speech by Peter in an unpublished early draft of *Les Blancs*.

TITLE COMMENTARY

A Raisin in the Sun

SHERI PARKS (ESSAY DATE 1995)

SOURCE: Parks, Sheri. "In My Mother's House: Black Feminist Aesthetics, Television, and *A Raisin in the Sun.*" In *Theatre and Feminist Aesthetics*, edited by Karen Laughlin and Catherine Schuler, pp. 200-28. Madison, N.J.: Fairleigh Dickinson University Press, 1995.

In the following essay, Parks contends that the 1989 PBS television production of A Raisin in the Sun *effectively underscores Hansberry's central feminist themes.*

The Public Broadcasting Station's television production of Lorraine Hansberry's **A Raisin in the Sun** was first aired in 1989 to mark the thirtieth anniversary of the play's Broadway opening. The television production, currently available on videotape, was an ambitious one, particularly by public television standards, and tested the network's ability to deliver demanding material to a large audience. The PBS presentation was also truer to Hansberry's original message, marking the first time that a professional production of the uncut script was made available to an audience. By closely following Hansberry's directions and reinserting information that was considered too controversial for American audiences in 1959, the directors placed the play back into the center of black women's concerns for the continuity of the culture and survival of self and family. By presenting the play to a mass audience, PBS recaptured Hansberry's original aim of art designed for large-scale social utility. The issues of black traditional female power that Hansberry presented in 1959 remain central to the lives of black women, perhaps providing evidence of the historical significance and intrinsic nature of those issues. The production also suggests that the medium has an ability to convey black feminist theatre to millions more viewers than can even the most successful stage production. A television production of the play provides a discussion of the lives of black women in a form that is aesthetically attractive and available to black women, many of whom do not have regular access to the more elite form of live stage theatre.

Culture and Consciousness

A Raisin in the Sun is a play already put to many cultural uses by both black and white audiences. Originally produced in 1959, it showed white American audiences the intimacies of black life and validated the daily existences of its black audiences. The play also heralded the arrival of the Black Arts Movement as well as the civil rights movement as a part of the national agenda but later, black male critics would use its fame to lambaste "integrationist" works. Meanwhile, the play was popular enough to warrant a film version, which won an award at Cannes, and a Broadway musical version, which won a Tony. Buried beneath all the racially related criticism was the fact that the author was a black feminist and the play bespoke a particular brand of feminism, that practiced by women within the family in traditional black culture. Hansberry biographer Anne Cheney writes that Hansberry was a feminist only in the most general sense,[1] but if the play is put in the context of its time and place, Hansberry appears to be a feminist in a most specific sense, that of black women coping simultaneously with issues of race, caste, and gender.

Hansberry's cultural message was heavily influenced by the person and the works of W. E. B. Du Bois. He was a frequent visitor to the Hansberry family home, and Lorraine later studied African culture and philosophy under him. Hansberry's husband, Robert Nemiroff, told Cheney that Lorraine was particularly influenced by Du Bois's *The Souls of Black Folk*, originally published in 1903. The influence of Du Bois is most evident in **Raisin** in the concepts of double and merged consciousness. Du Bois wrote that the consciousnesses of imprisoned people might take one of three main forms: a state of rebellion and revenge; a state of double consciousness, in which one tries to adopt the consciousness of the ruling people; and merged consciousness, in which one successfully mixes one's cultural history and one's present situation to achieve self-realization.[2] Double consciousness is a result of trying to re-contextualize oneself, to lose one's own history, which is impossible, and to adopt, wholecloth, someone else's history and culture without any opportunity for complete entry and privilege in that culture. It is, in a sense, cultural limbo:

> It is a peculiar sensation, this double consciousness, this sense of always looking at one's self through the eyes of others. . . . One ever feels his twoness,—an American, a Negro; two souls, two thoughts, two unreconciled strivings; two warring ideals in one dark body, whose dogged strength alone keeps it from being torn asunder.[3]

Merged consciousness allows the person to reach a new equilibrium, bringing the past into one's journey through the present; it is described by Du Bois as a tool for an imprisoned people:

> The history of the American Negro is the history of this strife,—this longing . . . to merge his double self into a better and truer self. In this merging he wishes neither of the older selves to be lost. He would not Africanize America. . . . He would not bleach his Negro soul in a flood of white Americanism . . . He simply wishes to make it possible for a man to be both a Negro and an American.[4]

Culture is an important element of the black feminist message. Black women have always been concerned with the multidimensional character of their disenfranchisement. Angela Davis, historian Paula Giddings, and others provide evidence that black women have been hesitant to address issues of gender apart from issues of race. Giddings argues that if either had to come first for political reasons, race consistently emerged as the definitive issue. As a result, much of what might be considered prefeminist or feminist has been defined as black rather than feminist. A common theme in the writings of black women and, more recently, in black feminist criticism is that of cultural duality and double racial consciousness. Gwendolyn Brooks and Toni Morrison, among others, have written about black women in cultural limbo. Maude Martha, Brooks's protagonist in her autobiographical novel of the same name, sees herself through a white culture's gaze and proclaims herself ugly and worthless. Toni Morrison's *The Bluest Eye* is the story of a black woman in cultural limbo. Morrison is also concerned with

maintaining Afro-American heritage once relationships to the black rural South have been stretched thin over distance and time. Michael Awkward, Barbara Christian, Mary Helen Washington, and Susan Willis have all examined various aspects of double racial consciousness in the works of black women writers.[5]

Hansberry took the concept of double consciousness and feminized it to reflect the multifaceted roles of black women by expanding the concept into two other spheres of double consciousness. While various characters move from holding dichotomous and paradoxical conceptualizations of race, they also move from the dichotomy of individual identity versus group identity to the merged position of individual within a family group, and from the gender dichotomy of male versus female to the merged role of an adult. Hansberry's women encounter or experience all three forms of double consciousness: race, family, and gender.

Reconciliation of double consciousness is portrayed in form as well as content. In *Raisin,* Hansberry appears to use blues music as a background sound of merged consciousness. The blues are a culturally merged aesthetic form, an amalgam of African descendent, rural Southern black sound transported to the urban North to give voice to urban problems. The music evokes the emotionality of the black micro-experience, and the Youngers listen to it almost constantly. When one character temporarily rejects Hansberry's symbol of merged state, Hansberry makes clear in her notes that we are not to regard blues in the same way that Beneatha does. "(*She promenades to the radio and, with an arrogant flourish, turns off the good loud blues that is playing.*) Beneatha says, 'Enough of this assimilationist junk!'"[6]

Group identity with the culture and the family are historically significant tools of survival for black people. While assimilation is a cornerstone of American society, African Americans have never been allowed full access to mainstream institutions and remain largely alienated from the dominant culture. The adoption of mainstream American consciousness is emotional orphanage for a black American. However, failure to adapt somehow to current living conditions is to endanger one's physical survival. The reconciliation of cultural dichotomy is itself a tool of survival. *Raisin* is a story of family members in different stages of racial double consciousness moving toward cultural reconciliation. At the beginning of the play, Mama and Walter form the endpoints of a racial consciousness continuum. Walter, played by

Danny Glover, exhibits the most extreme manifestations of double consciousness. He overvalues a capitalistic American dream of power and wealth, and his dream of money has led to his attempt to break with the cultural group and the history that he blames for his difficulties. He is bitter with frustration, seeing himself as trapped with "the world's most backward race of people" (26). Mama, played by Ester Rolle, recognizes Walter's ahistorical perspective:

> You something new, boy. In my time we was worried about not being lynched and getting to the North if we could and how to stay alive and still have a pinch of dignity too. . . . You ain't satisfied or proud of nothing we done. I mean that you had a home; that we kept you out of trouble till you was grown; that you don't have to ride to work on the back of nobody's streetcar—You my children but how different we done become.
>
> (61)

Mama's emotional survival is based upon culturally contextualized and reconciled strategies: religion and a sense of historical interrelatedness. Her spirituality is so strong as to be visible. "She has, we can see, wit and faith of a kind that keeps her eyes lit and full of interest and expectancy. She is in a word, a beautiful woman" (27). Her spirituality, while heavily laced with Christianity, also has a strong Afrocentric element of cultural and familial ancestry. The mother as link to cultural history is quickly established. "Her bearing is perhaps most like the women of the Hereros of Southwest Africa—rather as if she imagines that as she walks she still bears a basket or a vessel upon her head" (27). Mama remembers a cultural and familial past that the others do not. As she speaks of the early family history, she is "seeing back to times that only she can see," when furnishings "were selected with care and love and even hope—and brought to this apartment and arranged with taste and pride. That was a long time ago" (33). A significant part of Mama's memory of the past is her memory of Big Walter, her dead husband. Big Walter is still very present in the family. He and Mama shared the dream of a better home, and he literally worked himself to death for a house of the sort that the family is about to acquire. The television production makes Big Walter's spiritual presence very visible. There is a large, framed photograph of him, positioned strategically in the living room so that he is present for family discussions and events. Often characters are placed so that, just for a moment, Big Walter's face is actually between them. Mama is not dependent upon Big Walter or his memory; rather, his memory is one part of her past and a

source of her strength. Hansberry was a student of African history and philosophy and probably was familiar with prominent cross-tribal conceptualizations of the past as part of the present and future and of the spiritual presence of dead ancestors.[7]

Her link to a pastoral Southern history is also a central spiritual theme for Mama. She has "a feeble little plant, growing doggedly in a small pot on the window sill." She worries that it does not get enough sun in the almost sunless apartment (27-28) as she remembers lusher gardens "down home" (41). Mama's plant expresses both her personality (191) and her dream of a place to garden, and her children give her gardening tools and a gardening hat before the family moves to the new house (11). The historical role of flower gardening in black women's creativity and spiritual survival has been deeply explored in Alice Walker's *In Search of Our Mothers' Gardens,* in which Walker remembers her own mother's gardens.[8]

Mama's particular merging of Christianity with Afrocentric and pastoral spirituality depicts the spiritual reconciliation common in black America. James Evans suggests that in black culture, there is a lack of division between the secular and sacred in black life.[9] God is politicized as the God of spiritual empowerment and of the liberation of the poor and disenfranchised. The God of black people is not a distant, angry God, but is a friendly, immediate source of strength. In black folktales, God smokes cigars, sits in a rocking chair, and often resembles one or several of the traditional African deities.[10] In black traditional culture, spiritual life is an amalgam of Christianity and folk belief that is practiced in a less ritualized and fractionalized manner than "church" religion often is. God and spirituality have been popularized and reconstructed to meet the spiritual needs of black people, and so it is common to hear religious references on the street corner and in popular secular black music. Mama Younger's spirituality reflects a black merged religious experience.

Beneatha and Ruth are at different places on the continuum. Ruth's behavior suggests a double consciousness that is less extreme than Walter's. She is less concerned with cultural continuity than is either Mama or Beneatha and affects the polite distance of white, bourgeois manners with George Murchison and Karl Lindner. Beneatha is just beginning to have a merged consciousness, with a few traces of double consciousness remaining. She is an educated black woman with more access to the dominant cultural institutions than her mother, but she retains some cultural traits.

> Her speech is a mixture of many things; it is different from the rest of the family's insofar as education has permeated her sense of English—and perhaps the Midwest rather than the South has finally—at last—won out in her inflection; but not altogether, because over all of it is a soft slurring and transformed use of vowels which is the decided influence of the Southside.
>
> (23)

The potential poles of Beneatha's consciousness are represented by the men she dates. George Murchison is the son of a wealthy black businessman and is heavily invested in the consciousness of the white upper class. He believes that Beneatha's (and his) cultural heritage is best forgotten. He tells her, "Let's face it, baby, your heritage is nothing but a bunch of raggedy-assed spirituals and some grass huts" (68). She resists him, telling her family, "The only people in the world who are more snobbish than rich white people are rich colored people" (37).

In contrast to Mama, who is deeply invested in the recent cultural past, Beneatha is relearning her African past from another, more favored man. Asagai, a Yoruba from Nigeria, is deeply invested in his own culture. He brings Beneatha gifts of Yoruba music and robes. He teases her about looking for her identity and encourages her to make decisions and learn her own heart (50). Then, he presents her with the robes of a Nigerian woman, his sister (47), and questions the texture of her straightened hair. "Assimilationism is so popular in your country," he says, telling her that she really more closely resembles a queen of the Nile than a Hollywood queen (49). At first, Beneatha responds to the robes in a manner closer to romanticized Western feminine images than to actual African women. When she wears them for the first time, "She is coquettishly fanning herself with an ornate oriental fan, mistakenly more like Butterfly than any Nigerian that ever was" but she quickly "remembers" (63). In the robes, listening to the music, "a lovely Nigerian melody, she listens, enraptured, her eyes far away—'back to the past'" (64). In the 1989 television production, Beneatha sees the aesthetic inconsistency of her hair and the robes and has her hair cut into an Afro. When she eventually takes off the robes, the hairstyle remains and she appears as a merged, African American woman. When Mama meets Asagai, the African American past confronts and becomes comfortable with the African present. He is respectful of an elder. Mama smiles, repeats what Beneatha has told her about Africa and begins to mother him. Asagai is moved (51-52).

It is left to Beneatha to merge her own past with the present, but she has to confront and become comfortable with her personal past as well. Beneatha's education has cost her. She is having trouble finding her bearings, for she has come to distrust the spiritual anchors so useful to her mother. Beneatha thinks Ideas are Life, that life is simply a question of which ideas to incorporate, a spiritual betrayal which leads to a pivotal confrontation. Beneatha says she is "sick of hearing about God. . . . What has He got to do with anything? Does he pay tuition?" Mama warns her off. Ruth agrees that Beneatha has overstepped her limits, but Beneatha insists:

> Mama, you don't understand. It's all a matter of ideas, and God is just one idea I don't accept. It's not important. I am not going out and be immoral or even think about it. It's just that I get tired of Him getting credit for all the things the human race achieves though its own stubborn effort. There simply is no blasted God—there is only man and it is he who makes miracles!
>
> (39)

The conflict between Mama's spiritualism and Beneatha's humanism had been foreshadowed early in the play when Beneatha and her mother argue over her reciting scripture "in vain" (34). With this more serious transgression, Mama moves swiftly to reestablish her dominance of person and ideas.

> (Mama *absorbs this speech, studies her daughter and rises slowly and crosses to* Beneatha *and slaps her powerfully across the face. After, there is only silence and the daughter drops her eyes from her mother's face, and* Mama *is very tall before her.)* Mama. Now—you say after me, in my mother's house there is still God. (*There is a long pause and* Beneatha *stares at the floor wordlessly.* Mama *repeats the phrase with precision and cool emotion.*) In my mother's house there is still God.
>
> Beneatha. In my mother's house there is still God (*A long pause.*) [In the television production, Beneatha is looking into her mother's eyes with a mixture of hurt and respect as she says the words.]
>
> Mama. (*Walking away from* Beneatha, *too disturbed for triumphant posture. Stopping and turning back to her daughter.*) There are some ideas we ain't going to have in this house. Not long as I am the head of this family.
>
> Beneatha. Yes ma'am. (*Mama walks out of the room.*)
>
> (39)

Beneatha appears to her mother to be tossing aside the tools of her emotional survival. Beneatha is experimenting with many ideas, and her "flitting" from idea to idea has heretofore been tolerated by her family. This time she has, perhaps, ventured too far into European relativism, and her mother must act to curb the potentially dangerous wandering. Given Hansberry's extensive knowledge of African life and philosophy, the importance of this scene may go well beyond Christianity and childish rebellion. Hansberry was fond of puns and there are several different interpretations of "In my mother's house there is still God." Mama did not say, "God is alive," or "There is a God." She said that in her house there is God. In African spiritualism, the gods are literally with you, in your house, and for them to leave is a very unusual and dangerous thing. The spirits of the dead are also with you; a person is not really dead as long as somebody remembers him or her. God could be the abstracted Christian God, the African deities, or the soul of Big Walter. The line may be interpreted in one of the several ways or, in keeping with reconciliation of culture, in a mixture of the three.

Differences of caste and race force a wide gap between the concerns of black women and those of elite, white feminism. I use the term *caste* rather than *class* to capture the permanence of blacks' marginalization in the United States. Class membership is perceived as relatively fluid and subject to individual initiative. Class mobility is at the heart of American mythology. All of the Youngers are trying to change their class status. However, for blacks, caste membership is assigned at birth and does not change in the face of class mobility. Although Hansberry was raised in affluence, she realized that affluence does not change caste membership, that her family's relative wealth did not bring privilege or protection. She was born in a ghetto because of racial housing covenants and soon learned that her race made her more vulnerable to sexual harassment by white men. She wrote in the autobiographical play **To Be Young, Gifted and Black,** "The white boys in the streets, they look at me and think of sex. . . . Baby, you could be Jesus in drag—but if you're brown they're sure you're selling."[11]

Raisin is set "somewhere between World War II and the present," a relatively affluent period in U.S. history, but it is immediately established that the Youngers have not shared in the nation's affluence (11). Their home is a poor one, showing the ravages of "too many people for too many years" (11). A previously deleted bit of material reemphasizes the amalgam of race, caste, and gender issues that are of concern to black women. The original stage production, which deemphasized the issue of the Youngers' poverty, excluded a short speech by Travis in which he describes seeing a rat as large as a small dog in the street. Witnessing this small but graphic detail of daily urban poverty lends new urgency to the family's move to a healthier neighborhood and adds new context to statements such as Beneatha's "We've all got acute ghettoitis" (47).

Previous productions also downplayed the danger of the move and the warnings of the potential for white racial violence in the new white neighborhood. Another previously deleted scene makes it clear that the Youngers (and the audience) know the chance they are taking. Mrs. Johnson, a neighbor with whom the Youngers are on cordial, but not intimate terms, warns of racial violence by showing them a black newspaper account of violence directed toward another black family who moved into a white neighborhood. The Younger family had not known of the violence, which adds further concern regarding their own move. The reintroduction of the speech changes the ending of the play, in which the family happily moves to their new home, to an emotionally charged and ambiguous one. Staying with the original script, the television production did not include additions written by Hansberry for the 1961 movie, which added a safe arrival at the new home and so diffused some of the original dramatic tension of the play.

While **Raisin** was not autobiographical, Hansberry did draw from figures and events in her own life. The wealth of Hansberry's father, Carl, was accrued through real estate investments, and the family lived in several predominantly white neighborhoods where she and her family experienced racial violence in the forms of vandalism and physical threat. When Carl Hansberry purchased a house in a particularly hostile neighborhood, an angry crowd gathered outside the home and someone threw a brick, narrowly missing eight-year-old Lorraine's head. Racially restrictive covenants kept them out of some neighborhoods altogether, but Carl Hansberry fought and eventually won a celebrated United States Supreme Court case against covenants.

Hansberry seemed aware that class mobility was a precarious step for members of a lower caste, who might never gain full membership into the dominant society. Mrs. Johnson, the Youngers' neighbor, also warns of the dangers of class mobility and education, of leaving that which one knows for an uncertain future. "Education has spoiled many a good plowhand," she quotes, and she attributes the line to Booker T. Washington. Hansberry's intellectual mentor W. E. B. Du Bois was an intellectual and political adversary of Washington and wrote that "Mr. Washington represents in Negro thought the old attitude of adjustment and submission."[12] Mama Younger responds to Mrs. Johnson by calling Washington a fool. It is significant that Mama, a lover of the pastoral past and so, one might think, a potential admirer of Washington, should call him a fool, but Mama is particularly interested in education and upward mobility for her children.

The Younger family has invested its collective dreams of upward mobility in the daughter rather than the son, a dramatic portrayal which has a certain verisimilitude. Education, rather than commerce, has historically been a common class mobility strategy for blacks. It has also been historically common for families to give priority to educating their girls, since boys could earn as much money through skilled labor as they might have through college related job fields. Black families have traditionally sent more women than men to college and continue to do so.[13] Mama Younger is determined that nothing will stand in the way of Beneatha's education (32), while nothing is said about the elder male child's education. Education, however, does not bring about a change in family members' status. Although Mama is uneducated, she retains her status as head of the family and will act to reinforce her status if necessary.

Traditional Black Female Power and Family Consciousness

Mama Younger is a Black Mother, an example of a prominent traditional black feminist role. A very strong and pervasive female culture has survived within black communities, but its role has been disguised by negative "matriarchy" arguments of white and black men. While black, middle-class, male critics continue to decry the "mammy" as a negative black stereotype, the Black Mother continues to be a strong, historically based symbol of black feminism for working-class black women. The Black Mother situates black feminism in the place where it is ordinarily and traditionally practiced by black women, in the home. While part of the mainstream, academic feminist agenda has deemphasized mothering as an important part of women's lives, to do so with black women would be to dismiss a traditional locus of black female power. The two older Younger women are the backbone of the family, as interested in the long-term emotional survival of their family as they are in its short-term physical survival. Their caretaking as well as their

income enable the Younger family to survive. As a result of their position vis-à-vis men and the family, black women shoulder much responsibility for day-to-day family life. The black-traditional definition of the family means that children, and often extended family, are of primary concern to black women. Having a child in the black community is a rite of passage to womanhood; it connotes status that a permanent relationship to a man does not. The definition of motherhood and the black mother's relationship to her children are black feminist issues.

The Younger women cannot depend upon Walter to keep the family intact. While Walter has dreams that are consistent with American capitalism, the women make him go to work so they can pay the rent. The women work to keep the family alive. Because the structural relationships between African American men and women are fundamentally different from those intergender relationships in the dominant culture, any feminism that professes to represent black women must confront those differences. Black men have never been in a position to completely disenfranchise black women; theirs is an equality of powerlessness in relation to the dominant culture.

Black women often assume or share primary responsibility for their own survival and that of their families regardless of class. A reconstruction of the role of women in the black community may find that the artificially easy dichotomy between male and female is even more problematic here than it is in the dominant culture. A dominant historical and theoretical theme in mainstream American feminism is the modern dichotomization of private and public life. The privatization of the American home marks the point at which the popular feminine ideal became that of a nonproductive consumer whose daily work produced no capital and came to be undervalued. It is also at this point that a poignant difference between black women and white women emerged. All American homes were not privatized. Like Mama and Ruth Younger, the vast majority of black women never stopped producing capital. Although the same is true of poor women of all races, black women in the middle class continued to work and still do. Many black households also have "side hustles," the postmodern equivalent of Ruth's laundry service, operated out of the home. The home as a locus of capital production has continued to be an economic reality for black America. The black home and the black community are not easily dichotomized for other social reasons; like Mrs. Johnson, community members who are not blood kin are likely to be somewhat more active in black homes than in white homes.

The entire play occurs in the domestic arena, so that all of the interaction is under the leadership of Mama. Domestic stories are prevalent among black female writers, perhaps as a commentary upon the centrality of black mothers. More than a blind following of tradition, domestic story lines are a commentary upon the importance of family to the political orientation of black women since outside events are filtered through their effect upon the family. So it is with the Youngers. Information about racial violence, of interest to the larger black community, is filtered through its immediate meaning for the family. The information is delivered to the home in a way that dictates this application; a relationship with a neighbor woman, based upon the borrowing of domestic supplies and the serving of pie and coffee, becomes the entry point of the politically charged information and reframes it as information pertinent to the survival of the family. The "women's room" in this family is the kitchen; it is literally the source of the light, a small, determined light: "The sole natural light the family may enjoy in the course of a day is only that which fights its way though this little window" (12). The women wage war on the ravages of poverty but "weariness, has in fact, won in this room. Everything has been polished, washed, sat on, used scrubbed too often" (11-12). The fight to stay in touch with the hopeful past has been a feminine one—cleaning is mentioned more often than use, indicating the sheer energy needed for survival. The audience sees only the women participating in domestic labor. Hansberry captured the symbolic importance of cleanliness in poor black homes, where women have fought the ravages of poverty and stereotypes by cleaning. Hansberry wrote in *To Be Young, Gifted and Black*:

> I think you could find the tempo of my people on their back porches. The honesty of their living is there in the shabbiness. Scrubbed porches that sag and look their danger. Dirty gray wood steps. And always a line of white and pink clothes scrubbed so well, waving in the dirty wind of the city. My people are poor. And they are tired. And they are determined to live.[14]

(National marketers have already traced related consumer trends and identified black women as a ripe market for cleaning products—they tend to use more cleaning products per household than do white families.)[15]

The women work hard in this family and they know that it is for their family that they work. Mama tells Walter that although he has never understood it, she "ain't got nothing, don't own nothing, ain't never really wanted nothing that wasn't for you" (86). When Mama tells Walter about Ruth's planned abortion, Walter objects that Ruth would not have an abortion. Mama instructs him, "When the world gets ugly enough—a woman will do anything for her family. *The part that's already living*" (Hansberry's emphasis, 61-62). Illegal abortion becomes an act of family survival perpetuated by women for women; the fact that the doctor is a "she" makes Mama "immediately suspicious."

The Youngers are a whole family and Mama is the head of it. Despite all the current discussion of the crisis in the black family, black people, particularly working-class black people, have long considered a female-headed home to be a family. Niara Sudarkasa has produced a body of anthropological work which presents the female-centered household as the Afrocentrically traditional form.[16] The physical absence of a black father does not mean that the family has been destroyed. Given the arrival of the insurance money, Mama must be a fairly recent widow, yet there is no sense of this. She does not seem the helpless widow new to heading her family. Despite the cries of middle-class black men and well-meaning but culturally ignorant whites, the traditional form of black family is female oriented. Clearly then, the gender-based definition of the black family and of black family leadership are feminist issues.

The cultural message is that the children are more central to the definition of the woman than is the traditional husband. Children are the focus of the Younger family. Ruth's pregnancy and possible abortion sparks a running theme of the value of children. The dialogue is arranged so that the audience hears Mama remember the death of one of her infant children before Ruth actually says she is pregnant. Ruth says, in sympathy for Mama and perhaps for herself, "Ain't nothin' can tear at you like losing your baby" (33). Despite the obvious emotional and financial difficulties, Mama expresses "grandmotherly enthusiasm" at the news of Ruth's pregnancy, hoping for a girl, because Travis needs a sister (45). Indeed, Ruth must fight Mama to be Travis's primary mother (28, 76). Mama includes Ruth when she refers to "my children" (31), often calling her "child." Ruth in turn often calls the older Mrs. Younger "Mama." The primacy of Ruth as the biological mother is asserted by Ruth but not always allowed by Mama.

Mama nurtures everybody and keeps tabs on most of the activity in the apartment, even that of Travis, who has another mother, and the resistant Beneatha and Walter. She has a habit of "listening vigorously" to others' conversations. (44). Mama is the economic and ideological head of the family, and she controls the ideas and the actions within it. Her children deviate from her teaching only with her benign permission and risk her anger if they stray too far; twice she strikes her children when she thinks they are pursuing courses that endanger their own or the family's physical or emotional survival. Yet Mama's strength and the power which it garners within her family are usually carried with gentleness. "Her speech . . . is as careless as her carriage is precise—she is inclined to slur everything—but her voice is perhaps not as much quiet as simply soft" (27). This is not a romantic caricature of the old black mammy with her little black brood. Both biological children are trying desperately, each in his or her own way, to break away from Mama and the familial-cultural collective history that she represents even as each acknowledges his or her continuing dependency. Mama compares them to the little plant in the kitchen window; neither has had enough sunshine or anything else—they have spirit but are twisted.

The power held by black women in the family makes the domestic role fundamentally different from the more passive, ideal mother-wife in mainstream American society, whose life is consumed by a family in which she has little power. The responsibility that black women traditionally hold in the family suggests that the family is a traditional locus of black female power which demands a particular leadership style. Rather than a traditional leader, what Antonio Gramsci calls an inorganic leader who assumes power through heredity, wealth, or military might, black mothers are organic leaders who naturally emerge to facilitate group survival and gain power though responsibility and history. An organic leader knows and cares for the concerns of the group.[17]

Through the characterizations of the Youngers, Hansberry demonstrates levels of family group consciousness that are analogous to Du Bois's states of racial consciousness. One state, demonstrated by Walter and Beneatha, is that of individual consciousness, in which a person is concerned only with him or herself to the detriment of the group. The second state, demonstrated by Ruth, is that of total family consciousness, in which one is focused upon the concerns of the group to the detriment of the self. The third state,

that of the individual with group consciousness, is a reconciliation of the first two states and facilitates survival of the self and the family. The third state is best demonstrated by Mama. Although the racial messages of the play took precedence in earlier interpretations of the work, the timing and emphasis of the television play allow as much attention to be paid to the lives of the black women who are central to the Younger family and to the black feminist ideas contained within the work itself. Mama Younger is the family's and the play's central character. As if to make her more regal, she is introduced last. Her presence provides a stark contrast to the unrest of the adult children. Although Ruth bears the closest resemblance to Mama, Ruth shows that biological motherhood alone does not make a viable Black Mother. While much older than Ruth, Mama has none of Ruth's weariness of spirit. Loosely based upon Hansberry's own mother, she is "full bodied and strong. She is one of those women of a certain grace and beauty who wear it so unobtrusively that it takes a while to notice. . . . Being a woman who has adjusted to many things in life and overcome many more, her face is full of strength" (27). In a more general sense she is based upon the archetypical Black Mother, whom Hansberry, quoting Langston Hughes's poem "Washerwoman," described as the "the black matriarch incarnate . . . who scrubs floors of a nation in order to create black diplomats and university professors."[18]

Her children help to define Mama and she considers distance from one's family to be the luxury of others. Ruth suggests that Mama travel alone, not worrying about her family, like rich white women do. In the television production, Mama laughs at this suggestion before she says, "Something always told me I wasn't no rich white woman" (32). Mama's dreams as well as her actions are all oriented to a better life for her children. She does not buy a new house in a white suburb for artificially politicized reasons, but to get the best house for her family for the money she has. Houses in areas for blacks are further out and much more expensive (78). Mama is also interested in her own survival and in growth for her sake and for her family's sake. In the face of widespread poverty and disenfranchisement, survival of the body and spirit are central individual concerns for black women. Although the emotional support of one's family is central to the individual's emotional survival, the black woman's role in the physical survival of her family dictates that she find multiple ways to stay physically and emotionally functional in the face of adversity. She must find her personal strength if she and her family are to survive. A lack of strength can be devastating to the woman and, eventually, to the family.

Ruth, the "good" and long-suffering wife who is not as strong or as spiritually supported as Mama, most closely approximates the role of the completely family oriented wife-mother who tries to get through life without a sense of self. About thirty, she "was a pretty girl, even exceptionally so. . . . Now disappointment has already begun to hang in her face" (12). Hansberry notes that in a few years she will be a "settled woman," which on its surface, simply means a married, middle-aged woman. But here marriage and middle age also carry a weariness and disappointment that comes with settling for less than one had hoped. Ruth is so tired of this life that she wakes up sleepy. Hansberry's notes direct the actress to play the role of Ruth with a strong undertone of weariness. She speaks "like someone disinterested and old" (25). While Hansberry describes Ruth's weariness, she also immediately shows her dogged determination and pained energy with her son and her anger at her husband as she tries to jump-start them for the day.

Ruth constantly thinks in terms of family. What is Ruth's personal dream? Where does *her* rage go? We never know. She seems to live for her family and, unlike Mama, *through* her family. (Mama does not fear Walter's disapproval or change her actions to the point that all her plans are lost.) Although Ruth has a job, she is the only character who seems to almost never leave home, the exception being her preliminary visit to the abortionist. Her only creations are two children, and she almost loses both. Travis is quickly gaining a life of his own and is testing the limits of his autonomy, and she comes close to aborting the baby, despite her own wishes. Involvement without power or personal strength is an emotionally draining experience. Although Ruth is capable of gentleness and motherly humor with Travis and with Walter, her moods also change rapidly, from humor to brusqueness, perhaps because she is struggling to maintain the appearance of emotional equilibrium without the supports that are useful to her mother-in-law (18). She speaks of her life as a burdensome one, "I got too much on me this morning" (16).

When Mama remembers her life in the South with its gardens and different life, she asks Ruth to sing "No Ways Tired." Ruth collapses (41). The title and lyrics of the spiritual which Ruth never gets to sing and are not included in the script would not be lost on a black audience:

> I don't feel no ways tired.
> I've come too far from where I started from.
> No body tole me that the road would be easy.
> I don't believe he brought me this far to leave
> me.

The lyrics speak of surviving an arduous journey by the ability to draw strength from religious belief. Mama has the ability and is the stronger for it. Ruth does not and suffers for it.

Beneatha, Mama's daughter, is based upon a younger Lorraine Hansberry; the name is a pun, for there was a time in Hansberry's life when she felt superior to all things.[19] Nevertheless, Hansberry describes Beneatha as less beautiful than Ruth or Mama, perhaps because of her youth and lack of wisdom. Beneatha is really a woman-child, and the name may actually be a double pun—she is beneath her mother. Although twenty years old, she is seen by the other women as a "fresh" child (34), as a little girl (36), and as childish (40). She is self-centered, more individualistic than the other women, and an unreliable source of strength.

Walter, Mama's son and Ruth's husband, is still a man-child, a "lean, intense young man," as opposed to Ruth, who is actually younger but seems older and more tired (13). He behaves in almost stereotypically shifty ways, "inclined to quick nervous movements and erratic speech habits" (13). Walter loves to pontificate in a distracted philosophical style, giving vent to long romantic speeches, full of "hysterical promise" (89). He is childish and lacks group survival skills. Ruth's humor is motherly; Walter's is boyish (27). Since he is played by Danny Glover in the television version, this Walter is in striking contrast to Sidney Poitier's characterization in the original stage production and film. While Poitier was lean and skittish so that the childishness was almost fitting, Glover is big and powerful so that the childishness is an aberration.

Because he is the male lead, directors may have assumed that Walter is the central character of the play, that it is his dream deferred that had dried up, but there are many dreams in this play and they are all at one point deferred or dead. Walter is an artificial center of attention in a female-headed household. Like a child, he commands an enormous amount of attention with his louder-than-life actions and temper tantrums that other family members try to rein in, but his "acting out" is destructive to the family and himself. Walter actually adds little to the family. He appears to be a drain—emotionally and, after he stops going to work and gets conned by a close associate, financially. If he were gone, the family would be calmer and steadier.

Walter is childish because he is selfish. Mama and Ruth are still trying to raise him, emotionally, morally, financially, and familially. Ruth is trying to teach him to spend money wisely, to go to work, to stop drinking so much, to stop trusting conmen, to get off the furniture, to be polite to guests. Mama tries to teach him how to handle large sums of money, to set up his own bank account (with Mama's money), and to stop yelling at his wife. Walter's selfishness and lack of group identification manifests itself in an extreme lack of cooperation with, or sympathy for, family members. He is alone and blames everyone else—the family, the race, the family as race—for his life situation; "always in his voice there is a quality of indictment" (13). He gives only to those who give to him, joins only those who join him first. When Ruth asks him, "Oh, Walter—ain't you with nobody!" Walter answers "violently," "No! 'Cause ain't nobody with me! Not even my own mother!" (71). (It is important to note here that he expects the greatest amount of support from his mother while in a mainstream American play, the wife would have been the expected selfless supporter.) As part of the "raising" process, Mama and Ruth continually try to encourage Walter's family participation but he, just as constantly, resists. Walter's hunger for money causes him to dream in ways that are inappropriate and dangerous to his family. They cannot afford to lose big, but Walter declares, "I mean think big, like he does. *Big*. Invest big, gamble big, hell lose *big* if you have to" (Hansberry's emphasis, 70).

Although Walter wants what his mother and wife cannot give him, he does not accept that which they can give him. He asks Ruth, "Why you always trying to give me something to eat?" Ruth "(*Standing and looking at him helplessly*)" responds, "What else can I give you, Walter Lee Younger?" (74). Even when Walter speaks of family concerns, he sees them from an idiosyncratic point of view. *He* thinks that only he suffers when the women have to work to provide for the family; he complains, "Everytime we need a new pair of curtains and I have to watch you go out and work in somebody's kitchen" (58). More often, his selfishness leads him away from family relationships. He has left the family, betraying the group dream in his "quest." He sees no benefit in his relationship with Ruth since it brings him no financial reward. When Mama warns Walter about his treatment of Ruth, he asks, "Why—what she

do for me?" Mama answers, "She loves you." Walter responds by leaving the house to be alone, but not before Mama suggests that it is dangerous for a man to go outside his home to look for peace (59-60).

Gender Consciousness

Concern for family is an intercultural commonality among women, and Hansberry initially posits group consciousness with women. Concern for the group is also held to be a traditionally desirable trait for blacks, regardless of gender. While a Eurocentric reading might define Walter in terms of his quest for manhood through materialistic gain and masculine assumption of inorganic power, in an Afrocentric reading he would become a good man by reconciling the group's needs with his own. Walter is not a good man fighting against racist forces for the good of the group. Racist forces have already literally turned him inside out. Before Walter can reach adulthood in his cultural context, he will have to take on a stereotypically feminine trait and merge it with his masculinity. Hansberry has taken the concept of double consciousness and applied it also to gender, so that the characters are struggling with gender double consciousness.

For Walter, male adulthood is defined in outside, extracultural terms, in the taking over and running the world, in the bossing of secretaries, and he is frustrated that he cannot have the sort of power which he assumes will guarantee his manhood (70, 89). A black man's adoption of the mainstream culture's traditional gender dichotomy is depicted by George Murchison who, assuming women to be best seen and not heard, instructs Beneatha to "drop the atmosphere" since she is "a good looking girl . . . all over" and that men will "go for what they see" (82). As the son of a wealthy businessman, George has adopted many mainstream attitudes and because of his relative privilege, he may play at that game for a while. Walter does not have the luxury of the game. Although he values an externally powerful "man's" life, he is still largely dependent upon the mother figures in the family, and he hates them for it. His double racial consciousness interacts with his gender consciousness when he projects the perceived faults of his self-despised race upon the black women upon whom he is dependent—the black race becomes feminized for Walter. When he complains of "the world's most backward race of people," he is referring to the black women in his family (26). He despises the very pragmatism that keeps the rent paid and groceries on the table.

Walter's argument is shot full of contradiction and irony. Extradomestic "manhood" would be obtained in the extradomestic world, but Walter thinks that if the black woman would only spend her efforts supporting her man, he would also become a man in the eyes of the outside world. He suggests that women of other races know how to do that, "That is just what is wrong with the colored woman in this world. . . . Don't understand about building their men up and making 'em feel like they somebody. Like they can do something. . . . We a group of men tied to a race of women with small minds" (22-23). Meanwhile Ruth shows the irony of his speech as she begins to iron a "huge pile" of laundry. It is unclear whether the laundry belongs to the family or whether she is taking in laundry but, either way, she is working for her family's benefit while Walter complains.

Walter wants Ruth to be on his side, to use her relationship with Mama toward his end: "A man needs a woman to back him up. Mama would listen to you. You know she listen to you more than she do me and Bennie. She think more of you" (20). If the ideal of manhood is something that is assumed or taken, if the main arena is the nondomestic world, it is a contradiction of the European masculine ideal when black men demand that black women help them to be men. Walter's viewpoint is an illogical collision of two cultures: one assuming that his manhood rests on the support of women even at the expense of the family and the other that in order to be a man in the extracultural world, black women must move over, give up their position of family power, and dedicate precious family resources to his ascension into power.

Although Walter has his own ideas, it is Mama who is ultimately in a position powerful enough to define Younger manhood; according to her, a good man is a man who loves his children and makes them central to his own life. Mama's definition of a good man is much like her definition of a good woman: an individual who holds responsibility and concern for the group. It is a merged position. Big Walter is the standard with whom Walter is compared, but Big Walter was a good father rather than a good husband. He was "hard-headed, mean, kind of wild with women—plenty wrong with him. But he sure loved his children," (33) and Mama loves him for that. Big Walter's dreams of a better place to live and education for

his children were family oriented in nature but he "couldn't catch up with his dreams" (34). "He sure loved his children and wanted them to have something—be something. . . . Big Walter used to say, he'd get right wet in the eyes sometimes, lean his head back with the water standing in his eyes and say, 'Seem like God didn't see fit to give the black man nothing but dreams—but He did give us children to make them dreams worth while'" (33). Walter Lee's dream is a skewed version of his father's dream, gone rotten and illegitimate with selfishness and greed. His is a quick and dirty scheme rather than the kind one works hard and long to achieve, like Mama's and Big Walter's house or Beneatha's medical degree. Big Walter's love for his children indirectly killed him through overwork; it is the resultant insurance money, "made of his flesh," that is finally making the larger family dream come true. The memory of Big Walter and his dream-legacy become a presence in the Younger family interaction, particularly so in the PBS production, in which Big Walter's portrait is a silent character.

Walter achieves his adulthood in very domestic terms through the family issues of financial crisis and abortion. The type of adult he becomes is in keeping with the kind Mama and Ruth value—cooperative, sensitive to the effects of his actions upon the family, and aware of his historical context. The instruments of his transformation are twofold. One is the threatened logical extreme of a family with a diseased member, that of the desperate drama of his wife willing to risk a back alley abortion to insure the family's survival in the face of an irresponsible, terminally angry husband. The other is the temporary and artificial patriarchal restructuring of the family through which he is shown that the dominant culture's traditional patriarchal system and extrafamilial orientation will not work in this family—because of the type of man, the type of women, and the world in which they and all African Americans live. Mama tells Walter to persuade Ruth to keep the baby that Ruth would abort so the rest of the family might survive more easily. Mama invokes the memory of the past and of Walter's father and of Walter's position as her son. She is waiting for him to be a strong adult, like his father and mother, and begins to instruct him in manhood.

Mama. I'm waiting to hear how you be your father's son. Be the man he was. . . . (*Pause.*) Your wife say she is going to destroy your child. And I'm waiting to hear you talk like him and say we a people who give children life, not who destroys them—(*She rises.*) I'm waiting to see you stand up and look like your daddy and say we done give up one baby to poverty and that we ain't going to give up nary another one. . . . I'm waiting. . . . If you a son of mine, tell her! (*Walter turns, looks at her and can say nothing. She continues, bitterly.*) You . . . you are a disgrace to your father's memory. Somebody get me my hat.

(62)

He fails and she is disgusted. He may never be the adult that his mother is or that his father was. His father was more of a man precisely because he loved and valued children. It is clear that if Walter becomes a man, he will be initiated into it by a superior woman. The conflict flares when Mama buys the house despite Walter's wishes. The conflict is between Walter's world view, which is consistent with the European male world view, or Mama's, Ruth's, and by this time, Beneatha's, which is consistent with traditional black feminism. He claims that Mama "butchered up a dream of mine," but his dreams are dependent upon her money (80). Mama wants Walter to see she did the right thing by buying the family a house, but what he thinks will not change the doing of it and he knows it. Walter declares what has already been made clear, "What you need me to say you done right for? *You* the head of this family" (80, Hansberry's emphasis).

Mama recognizes the conflict and, like Ruth, is willing to sacrifice to save her family. She fights for her family by doing a very unwarlike thing, by appearing to capitulate. She says that although he never understood that she "ain't got nothing, don't own nothing, ain't never really wanted nothing that wasn't for you," that perhaps she has also "been doing to him what the rest of the world has done to him" (86-87). Although she appears to be relinquishing power, her power is still there. She gives him sixty-five hundred dollars and the responsibility to deposit Beneatha's college money into an account, taking the risk that he will keep the money safe over the weekend. However, she gives him explicit instructions and tells him to be the head of the family. When she says, "I'm telling you to be the head of this family from now on like you supposed to be," (87) she is voicing the contradiction. In Walter's version of manhood, a man takes control, but here he has to be given it by a woman, and instructed what to do with it. Superficially, Mama's move seems to work because Walter becomes a pleasant person who speaks "sweetly, more sweetly than we have ever known him." He begins to treat Ruth better, taking her to the movies, holding hands and dancing. When Mr. Linder, a representative of a thinly veiled effort to keep the Youngers out of a white neighborhood, attempts to buy out their mort-

gage, Walter kicks the white man out of "his" house (a very "manly" thing to do), forsaking the money that he previously valued so much and will come to value again (99). He takes on a new, important role and the attitude that comes with it, that of "Man of the House," which seems almost a pun—HouseMan—an artificial man who is a man nowhere else but where the women make him so (89). But we know enough about Walter and Mama to know that he is not really the head nor, even in 1959, are we to assume that he is the natural head of this household. It is of little surprise when he very shortly exhibits gross lack of responsibility by trusting the untrustworthy and losing the family money to con men.

When Bob, Walter's "business partner," comes to tell him that Willy has absconded with the family's money, Ruth senses that something is amiss before Walter does (105). (Big Walter's picture is very prominent here.) When Mama hears, she hits Walter and Walter accepts it. (In one of the television production's few deviations from the playscript, which calls for Mama to beat Walter in the face, Mama hits Walter's back as he has fallen on the floor.) Beneatha stops her (109), but when Beneatha voices her own disgust for Walter by saying there was nothing left to love, Mama delivers a speech which could summarize the black woman's relation to the black man, even in the 1990s.

> There is always something left to love. And if you ain't learned that, you ain't learned nothing. (*Looking at her.*) Have you cried for that boy today? I don't mean for yourself and for the family 'cause we lost the money. I mean for him; what he been through and what it done to him. Child, when do you think is the time to love somebody the most; when they done good and made things easy for everybody? Well then, you ain't through learning—because that ain't the time at all. It's when he's at his lowest and can't believe in his-self 'cause the world done whipped him so. When you starts measuring somebody, measure him right, child, measure him right. Make sure you done taken into account what hills and valleys he come through before he got to wherever he is.
>
> (125)

Walter's brief exercise in Eurocentric manhood is over; Mama calls him a boy now and he has even less status than before. He has endangered their brief economic stability and their dreams, including Beneatha's education and the new house. Mama assumes that it is now impossible to move to the new house. Ironically, the threat of losing the new house awakens the dream in Ruth, who originally had no dream of her own. It is she who now fights to go forward to the new house, simultaneously taking on some concern for herself and bucking Mama's authority for a better life for the family. Once she came to visualize one, she will not let it go. Walter commits one last "mannish" act. He takes it upon himself to speak for the family and to offer what is left of the family dignity, but here lies his true rite of passage in adulthood. (The portrait of Big Walter is prominently featured and very much a character here.) When Mama challenges him to take the money from Mr. Linder in front of Travis, Walter finds his strength. He stands up to Mr. Linder and says the family will move into the white neighborhood despite the danger. He even manages to express that the family is very proud of Beneatha and her plans to become a doctor.

Despite Walter's passage into adulthood, it is clear that the family is not restructured because of it. Mama has to validate his words to Mr. Lindner (128). As an adult he will share power with Mama, Ruth, and Beneatha and is positioned, not as a would-be-patriarch, but as one adult among several in the family. His double gender consciousness is resolved. Mama and Ruth share a proud moment, for his "coming into his manhood" (130). His double racial consciousness is also resolved: he becomes a person-with-history. He has looked back to the past, both culturally and familially, and has contextualized himself. His consciousness of race, group, and gender is reconciled. In the PBS production, the audience last sees Walter as he proudly takes Big Walter's portrait from the wall to move it to the new home. One of the last shots of the play is the wallpaper where Big Walter's portrait hung.

Black Feminism and Television

The potential of television as a beneficial black feminist forum is particularly significant since the form can reach women who are the backbone of a traditional, popularist black feminism that operates in the black family and community, away from the more privileged centers of feminism. Many of the most successful feminist works are fine art—museum and stage art—forms that are less accessible and perhaps less attractive to the larger potential audience for black feminist works. The majority of black women in this country are not like middle-class, college-educated white women, and there is little reason to assume that their concerns or the forms and arenas of their discourse would be similar. Black women are still rare within the academy and the halls of "fine" art. The form of any black feminism that is to be accepted by the majority of black women is not

that of the academy. Black culture is not a print-based culture; the majority of African Americans consume most of their mass mediated information from inside and outside the culture through electronic media, in accordance with the tradition of an oral culture. Black feminism must use the forms which black women use.

The television production of **Raisin** makes use of the audience's familiarity with electronic media actors and their personae. Ester Rolle is most familiar as the strong mother of the television show *Good Times* (1974-1979). Danny Glover was the brutal husband in *The Color Purple* (1985). Helen Martin, who played the gossipy neighbor, Mrs. Johnson, played a similar role in the black-cast television show *227* (1984-1989), and Joseph C. Phillips, who played George Murchison, has portrayed middle-class "nerd" types in a series of movies and television shows, including a regular character during the later years of *The Cosby Show* (1984-1992).

The adaptation of this play for television emphasizes the potential of the play and of television as mediums of a black feminist aesthetic. Two aesthetic formal features of television, closeness and sound reproduction, are shown to their best advantage in **Raisin**. Subtle, nonverbal expression is important both to Hansberry in particular and to female and black communication in general.[20] Hansberry's stage directions give information about the expression in a character's eyes, shared glances, and physical twitches that give the audience interpretive cues. While some of the information could be communicated by an excellent stage actor, the form of television, with its inherent ability for extreme close-ups, can transmit the most subtle nuances of feeling. Hansberry writes stage directions as if for television or film, with subtle cues that are best conveyed through close-ups, rather than the distance of live stage theatre, and the television production was able to be consistent with her intentions. Sound reproductive qualities of television also become useful. Blues songs are an important element of the cultural message of the play, and Hansberry uses music to convey emotional tone; but despite her extensive stage notes, Hansberry rarely prescribes which blues songs are to be used. Since the sound reproduction of television is superior to all but the most acoustically sophisticated theatre houses, the presence of blues lyrics as well as a particular sound can be easily heard and the aural message made more explicit.

Hansberry intended that her play provide a microcosm of the issues facing black women in one discrete, aesthetically attractive piece; she contended that all art does and should serve propagandistic purposes. In 1959 she told the First Conference of Negro Writers that "All art is ultimately social."[21] She felt that black writers needed to be particularly aware of the potential for aesthetic propaganda, and she worked to make use of her play's propagandistic potential. The communication strategy for propaganda is as important as the content, and television may provide a particularly effective medium for black women. The television production of *A Raisin in the Sun,* as well as other works such as *The Women of Brewster Place* and the television premiere of *The Color Purple,* demands that television presentation of black feminist pieces be carefully examined and considered.

In order to be effective, the aesthetic form must be present in the social reality of the audience. Television, unlike the stage play, is already present in the social reality of black women. Television is an ordinary medium that plays a huge part in the aesthetic lives of ordinary people. I am using "ordinary" in the sense of "most frequently occurring." The usage is not intended to be derogatory, indeed, I hope to promote the reevaluation of elitist feminist aesthetics that undervalues the aesthetic lives of the vast majority of people in this country, white or black. Only 12 percent of the U.S. population over eighteen years old saw a nonmusical play in 1985, the last year for which statistics are available, and only 17 percent saw a musical play once. College graduates make up the majority of audiences in both categories.[22] Unlike live stage theatre, which even members of the middle class rarely attend, television is part of the daily lives of most American families. Ninety-nine percent of American families own at least one television, and the average household has the set on seven hours a day.[23] The messages of television are the primary aesthetically cased messages of Americans and this is particularly so for black Americans, who consume more television and embrace the meaning more than do their white counterparts.[24] Black feminism, in particular, cannot ignore popularist media. Black feminist discourse that will reach ordinary black women must use the mediums that black women use. (A similar argument may be made for Hispanic women or poor white women, who also watch large amounts of television.)[25]

Popularly accepted aesthetic forms can become powerful vehicles for emotional survival and political change. Herbert Marcuse writes that it is the attractiveness of the aesthetic form and the safety that comes from the inherent abstraction of art that allows it to be a useful ideological tool, especially in the face of lessened direct control over one's physical and social environment. Art provides a counterconsciousness, a socially safe place to examine and discuss the social situation and to arrive at coping mechanisms or, at a higher level of social enlightenment, social solutions to the problem. The attractiveness of art, meanwhile provides an affirmative environment, an alternative and emotionally pleasant haven to escape to, to rest in, that helps to insure emotional survival within the social reality. Art becomes a hospital for the wounded soul.[26]

Hans Robert Jauss further develops the argument of aesthetic form as mechanism of emotional survival and social change. The same distance that allows aesthetic enjoyment also allows the audience member to examine his or her social situation, perhaps even enjoying a portrayal that would be painful or dangerous in reality. Life is dressed in art. Art becomes a safe place to discuss what could not otherwise be discussed as lightly, if at all. The better vantage point encourages the discovery of otherwise unconsidered characteristics present in the social reality as well as the potential for change. Jauss argues that the realistic popular media are particularly effective in doing this.[27]

The concept of television as medium of a feminist aesthetics has not been popular with academic feminists, on the assumption that the medium is antifeminist. While many studies have shown that commercial, network television programming has not been kind to feminist perspectives,[28] there may be nothing inherently antifeminist in the *form* of television. Cable television programming can be many things to many people, and the opportunity for feminist programming can begin to open up now that a majority of the population is cabled.[29] Public television programmers have already shown a willingness to address feminist issues. Although public television content is not always aesthetically appealing to black women across class, it is accessible. The appeal of television to black women, however, suggests the medium bears examination as a potential vehicle for feminist communication. The PBS production of *A Raisin in the Sun* lends more evidence that the form of television has the potential to communicate successfully the themes, issues, and communication strategies which Hansberry originally wrote into her script and to deliver them into the homes of ordinary black women.

Lorraine Hansberry would have approved.

Notes

1. Anne Cheney, *Lorraine Hansberry* (Boston: Twayne, 1984), 17.

2. W. E. B. Du Bois, *Souls of Black Folk* (Millwood, N.Y.: Kraus-Thomson, 1973), 1-2.

3. Ibid., 3.

4. Ibid., 4.

5. See Michael Awkward, *Inspiriting Influences: Tradition, Revision and Afro-American Women's Novels* (New York: Columbia University Press, 1989); Barbara Christian, *Black Feminist Criticism: Perspectives on Black Women Writers* (New York: Pergamon, 1985); Mary Helen Washington, "Taming All That Anger Down: Rage and Silence in Gwendolyn Brooks's *Maud Martha*," in *Black Literature and Literary Theory*, ed. Henry Louis Gates (New York: Methuen, 1984), 249-62; Susan Willis, "Eruptions of Funk: Historicizing Toni Morrison," in *Black Literature and Literary Theory*, 263-322.

6. Lorraine Hansberry, *A Raisin in the Sun* (New York: Signet, 1966), 63. All subsequent quotations are cited parenthetically within the text.

7. See John Mbiti, *African Religions and Philosophy* (Garden City, N.Y.: Anchor, 1970).

8. See Alice Walker, *In Search of Our Mothers' Gardens: Womanist Prose* (San Diego: Harcourt Brace Jovanovich, 1983).

9. See James H. Evans, *Spiritual Empowerment in Afro-American Literature* (Lewiston, N.Y.: Edwin Mellen, 1987).

10. Julius Lester, "How God Made Butterflies," in *Black Folktales* (New York: Grove, 1978), 15-20.

11. Lorraine Hansberry, *To Be Young, Gifted, and Black: Lorraine Hansberry in Her Own Words,* ed. Robert Nemiroff (New York: New American Library, 1970), 78.

12. Du Bois, *Souls*, 50.

13. See Bart Landry, *The New Black Middle Class* (Berkeley: University of California Press, 1987).

14. Hansberry, *Young, Gifted, and Black,* 17.

15. Simmons Market Research Bureau, *Study of Media Markets: Household Cleaners, Room Deodorizers, Pest Control and Pet Food* (New York: Simmons Market Research Bureau, 1989), 0002, 0030, 0068, 0088, 0108, 0104.

16. See Niara Sudarkasa, "African and Afro-American Family Structure: A Comparison," *The Black Scholar* 11.8 (November-December 1980): 37-60.

17. Antonio Gramsci, *Prison Notebooks,* trans. Joseph A. Buttigieg and Antonio Callari, ed. Joseph A. Buttigieg (New York: Columbia University Press, 1992), 133.

18. Cheney, *Lorraine Hansberry,* 60-61.

19. Ibid., 60.

20. See Thomas Kochman, *Black and White Styles in Conflict* (Chicago: University of Chicago Press, 1981); Judy Pearson, *Gender and Communication* (Dubuque, Iowa: William C. Brown, 1985); Geneva Smitherman, *Talking and Testifyin': The Language of Black America* (Detroit: Wayne State University Press, 1986).

21. Lorraine Hansberry, quoted in Anne Cheney, "The Negro Writer and His Roots: Towards a New Romanticism," *Black Scholar* 12.2 (March-April 1981), 136.

22. U.S. Bureau of the Census, *Statistical Abstract of the United States* (Washington, D.C.: Government Printing Office, 1989), 231.

23. Census, 544.

24. George Comstock, Steven Chaffee, Nathan Katzman, Maxwell McCombs, and Donald Roberts, *Television and Human Behavior* (New York: Columbia University Press, 1978), 295.

25. See Ronald W. Lopez and Darryl D. Enos, "The Role and Functions of Spanish-language-only Television in Los Angeles," *Aztlan* 4.2 (1973), 283-313; T. C. O'Guinn, T. P. Meyer and R. J. Faber, "Ethnic Segmentation and Spanish-language Television," *Journal of Advertising* 14.3 (1985), 63-66; Comstock, 296.

26. Herbert Marcuse, *The Aesthetic Dimension: Toward a Critique of Marxist Aesthetics* (Boston: Beacon, 1978).

27. Hans Robert Jauss, *Toward an Aesthetic of Reception,* trans. Timothy Bahti (Minneapolis: University of Minnesota Press, 1982).

28. F. L. Geis, V. Brown, and J. Jennings, "Sex vs. Status in Sex-associated Stereotypes," *Sex Roles* 11 (1984), 711-85; Gaye Tuchman, "Women's Depiction by the Mass Media: Review Essay," *Signs: Journal of Women in Culture and Society* 4 (1979), 528-42.

29. Census, 444.

FURTHER READING

Criticism

Cheney, Anne. *Lorraine Hansberry.* Boston: Twayne Publishers, 1984, 174 p.

Full-length critical study.

Freedomways 19, no. 4 (1979).

Special issue devoted to Hansberry, including essays by James Baldwin, Nikki Giovanni, and Alex Haley.

hooks, bell. "*Raisin* in a New Light." *Christianity and Crisis* 49, no. 1 (6 February 1989): 21-3.

Asserts that A Raisin in the Sun challenges stereotypical images of African American women.

Olauson, Judith. "1950-1960." In *The American Playwright: A View of Criticism and Characterization,* pp. 77-99. Troy: The Whitston Company, 1981.

Analysis of A Raisin in the Sun, focusing on characterization.

Peerman, Dean. "*A Raisin in the Sun*: The Uncut Version." *The Christian Century* (25 January 1989): 71-3.

Discusses material excised from the original production of A Raisin in the Sun.

Sharadha, Y. S. *Black Women's Writing: Quest for Identity in the Plays of Lorraine Hansberry and Ntozake Shange.* New Delhi: Prestige Books, 1998, 144 p.

Examines the search for identity in the plays of Hansberry and Ntozake Shange.

Shyma, O. P. "Women in Lorraine Hansberry's Plays." In *Indian Views on American Literature*, pp. 107-11. New Delhi: Prestige, 1998.

Focuses on Hansberry's treatment of women in her plays.

Wilkerson, Margaret B. "The Sighted Eyes and Feeling Heart of Lorraine Hansberry." *Black American Literature Forum* 17, no. 1 (spring 1983): 8-13.

Overview of Hansberry's work, touching on the feminist themes of her plays.

OTHER SOURCES FROM GALE:

Additional coverage of Hansberry's life and career is contained in the following sources published by the Gale Group: *African American Writers*, Eds. 1, 2; *American Writers Supplement*, Vol. 4; *Authors and Artists for Young Adults*, Vol. 25; *Black Literature Criticism; Black Writers*, Eds. 1, 3; *Concise Dictionary of American Literary Biography*, 1941-1968; *Contemporary American Dramatists; Contemporary Authors*, Vols. 25-28R, 109; *Contemporary Authors Bibliographical Series*, Vol. 3; *Contemporary Authors New Revision Series*, Vol. 58; *Contemporary Literary Criticism*, Vols. 17, 62; *Contemporary Women Dramatists; Dictionary of Literary Biography*, Vols. 7, 38; *DISCovering Authors; DISCovering Authors: British Edition; DISCovering Authors: Canadian Edition; DISCovering Authors Modules: Dramatists, Most-studied* and *Multicultural; DISCovering Authors 3.0; Drama Criticism*, Vol. 2; *Drama for Students*, Vol. 2; *Encyclopedia of World Literature in the 20th Century*, Ed. 3; *Feminist Writers; Literature and Its Times*, Vol. 4; *Literature Resource Center; Major 20th-Century Writers*, Eds. 1, 2; *Reference Guide to American Literature*, Ed. 4; and *Twayne's United States Authors.*

BESSIE HEAD

(1937 - 1986)

South African novelist, short story writer, and historian.

Head is known for her writings exploring the sources of racial and sexual inequalities in southern Africa. A mixed-race South African who spent most of her life as an exile in her adopted land of Botswana, Head wrote from the perspective of an outsider attempting to understand her environment and her social position. In her works, Head addresses problems of sexual and racial discrimination in Africa by emphasizing the similarities among all forms of prejudice, stressing such themes as the disintegration of rural traditions, the corruption of authority, and the equally powerful forces of good and evil.

BIOGRAPHICAL INFORMATION

Head was the daughter of an upper-class white woman and a black stablehand in South Africa. When her mother, Bessie Emery, was found to be pregnant with the child of a black South African, she was institutionalized by her parents and labeled insane. Head was born in the asylum but was quickly sent off to live with white foster parents, who later became ashamed of Head's dark skin color and sent her to live with Catholic missionaries. When Head was about thirteen, her mother, still institutionalized, committed suicide.

Head was trained as at teacher and taught elementary school children for several years in South Africa. In 1961 she married a journalist but divorced shortly thereafter. When she was twenty-seven Head left for Botswana with her young son because, according to her, she could no longer tolerate apartheid in South Africa. For the next fifteen years she lived in poverty as a refugee at the Bamangwato Development Farm. Despite the harsh living conditions, Head found in her village a sense of community she had hitherto not experienced, and she did eventually gain Botswanan citizenship. After suffering a psychological breakdown, which became the focus of her novel *A Question of Power* (1973), Head dedicated herself to writing and maintaining a seedling nursery for vegetables. She later represented Botswana at writers' conferences in the United States, Canada, Europe, and Australia. She died of hepatitis in 1986.

MAJOR WORKS

Throughout her career, Head emphasized the need for Africans to abandon power struggles. She stated that until she moved to Botswana in 1964, she "had never encountered human ambition and greed before in a black form." In South Africa her experiences with domination had been primarily with the white system of apartheid; in Botswana, she found that similar structures of oppression toward women and other social groups existed in tribal communities. Head's first novel, *When Rain Clouds Gather* (1968), was an attempt to suggest an alternative to the desire for power. This book focuses on Makhaya, a young South African who leaves his country only to become an outcast in Golema Mmidi, a refugee community in Botswana. Many of the stories in Head's later book of short stories, *The Collector of Treasures* (1977), reiterate the futility of power struggles.

In her later works Head identified oppression and discrimination as major tools for those in power. In her novel *Maru* (1971) two village leaders fall in love with a young Masarwa schoolteacher, Margaret, who admits her association with the Masarwa, who have traditionally been considered inferior to other black Botswanans. As both men vie for her affections, they begin to understand the plight of the Masarwa people, and a union is ultimately created between the two groups through Margaret's marriage to one of the village leaders. Head called her autobiographical novel *A Question of Power* "a private journey to the sources of evil." Elizabeth, the protagonist, is a South African refugee in Botswana who experiences temporary insanity. In dreams and fantasies she encounters both local and mythical figures representing the nature of her femininity and Africanness. This psychological work explores the roots of female oppression and questions the existence of God.

In addition to her fiction, Head wrote two studies on Botswana, both of which combine local folklore with historical information. *Serowe: Village of the Rain Wind* (1981) recounts tales of the Bamangwato nation from the nineteenth and twentieth centuries, and *A Bewitched Crossroad: An African Saga* (1984) focuses on African tribal wars in the early nineteenth century.

CRITICAL RECEPTION

Although critics have tried to identify Head as a "feminist" or "African" writer, Head herself resisted these labels, seeing her works instead as individually crafted pieces that did not fall into ideological categories. Critics have noted that Head respected but did not idealize African history and tradition. Rather, she worked for substantial change in customs, envisioning equality for citizens of Africa. Scholars have identified themes of exile and oppression in her works, and commented on the universal relevance of Head's social observations. Commentators have also noted feminist themes in Head's short stories and novels such as *A Question of Power*, focusing discussion on the topics of sexuality, male images of authority, and the subjugation of women that are presented in these works.

PRINCIPAL WORKS

When Rain Clouds Gather (novel) 1968

Maru (novel) 1971

A Question of Power (novel) 1973

The Collector of Treasures and Other Botswana Village Tales (short stories) 1977

Serowe: Village of the Rain Wind (history) 1981

A Bewitched Crossroad: An African Saga (history) 1984

Tales of Tenderness and Power (short stories) 1989

A Woman Alone: Autobiographical Writings (essays) 1990

A Gesture of Belonging: Letters from Bessie Head, 1965-1979 (letters) 1991

PRIMARY SOURCES

BESSIE HEAD (ESSAY DATE 1966)

SOURCE: Head, Bessie. "The Woman from America." In *A Woman Alone: Autobiographical Writings*, selected and edited by Craig MacKenzie, pp. 31-36. Nairobi, Kenya: Heinemann, 1990.

In the following essay, originally published in 1966, Head describes her friendship with an American woman who had married a Botswanan and moved to Head's village.

This woman from America married a man of our village and left her country to come and live with him here. She descended on us like an avalanche. People are divided into two camps. Those who feel a fascinated love and those who fear a new thing. The terrible thing is that those who fear are always in the majority. This woman and her husband and children have to be sufficient to themselves because everything they do is not the way people here do it. Most terrible of all is the fact that they really love each other and the husband effortlessly and naturally keeps his eyes on his wife alone. In this achievement he is seventy years ahead of all the men here.

We are such a lot of queer people in the Southern part of Africa. We have felt all forms of suppression and are subdued. We lack the vitality, the push, the devil-may-care temperament of the people of the north of Africa. Life has to seep down to us from there and that pattern is already establishing itself. They do things first, then we. We are always going to be confederators and not initiators. We are very materialistically minded and I think this adds to our fear. People who hoard little bits of things cannot throw out and expand, and, in doing so, keep in circulation a flowing current of wealth. Basically, we are mean, selfish. We eat each other all the time and God help poor Botswana at the bottom.

Then, into this narrow, constricted world came the woman from America like an avalanche upon us. Some people keep hoping she will go away one day, but already her big strong stride has worn the pathways of the village flat. She is everywhere about because she is a woman, resolved and unshakeable in herself. To make matters worse or more disturbing she comes from the West side of America, somewhere near California. I gather from her conversation that people from the West are stranger than most people, and California is a place where odd and weird cults spring up every day. For instance, she once told me about the Church-of-the-Headless-Chicken! It seems an old woman bought a chicken but the place where she bought it was very haphazard about killing and plucking fowls. They did not sever the head properly and when the old woman brought the chicken home and placed it on the kitchen table, it sprang up out of the newspaper and began walking about with no head and no feathers—quite naked. It seems then that the old woman saw a vision, grabbed the chicken and ran next door to a neighbour who had been bed-ridden for many years, and, in great excitement, told him the strange happening. The poor old bed-ridden neighbour leapt from the bed, healed of his ailment and a miracle had been performed. The story spread like wild-fire and in a matter of hours money was collected, a congregation formed and the Church-of-the-Headless-Chicken was born. The chicken was interviewed by many newspapers and kept alive for some months on soluble food mixture dropped into its open gullet!

Then, another thing too. People of the West of America must be the most oddly beautiful people in the world; at least this woman from the West is the most oddly beautiful person I have ever seen. Every cross current of the earth seems to have stopped in her and blended into an amazing harmony. She has a big dash of Africa, a dash of Germany, some Cherokee and heaven knows what else. Her feet are big and her body is as tall and straight and strong as a mountain tree. Her neck curves up high and her thick black hair cascades down her back like a wild and tormented stream. I cannot understand her eyes though, except that they are big, black and startled like those of a wild free buck racing against the wind. Often they cloud over with a deep, intense brooding look.

It took a great deal of courage to become friends with a woman like that. Like everyone here I am timid and subdued. Authority, everything can subdue me; not because I like it that way but because authority carries the weight of an age pressing down on life. It is terrible then to associate with a person who can shout authority down. Her shouting matches with authority is the terror and sensation of the village. It has come down to this. Either the woman is unreasonable or authority is unreasonable, and everyone in his heart would like to admit that authority is unreasonable. In reality, the rule is: If authority does not like you then you are the outcast and humanity associates with you at their peril. So, try always to be on the right side of authority, for the sake of peace, and please avoid the outcast. I do not say it will be like this forever. The whole world is crashing and inter-changing itself and even remote bush villages in Africa are not to be left out!

It was inevitable though that this woman and I should be friends. I have an overwhelming curiosity that I cannot keep within bounds. I passed by the house for almost a month, but one cannot crash in on people. Then one day, a dog they have had puppies and my small son chased one of the puppies into the yard and I chased after him. Then one of the puppies became his and there had to be discussions about the puppy, the desert heat and the state of the world, and as a result of curiosity an avalanche of wealth has descended on my life. My small hut-house is full of short notes written in a wide sprawling hand. I have kept them all because they are a statement of human generosity and the wide care-free laugh of a woman who is as busy as women the world over about things women always entangle themselves in—a man, children, a home . . . Like this . . .

'Have you an onion to spare? It's very quiet here this morning and I'm all fagged out from sweeping and cleaning the yard, shaking blankets, cooking, fetching water, bathing children, and there's still the floor inside to sweep, and dishes to wash and myself to bathe—it's endless!'

Or again . . .

'Have you an extra onion to give me until tomorrow? If so, I'd appreciate it. I'm trying to do something with these awful beans and I've run out of all of my seasonings and spices. A neighbour brought us some spinach last night so we're in the green. I've got dirty clothes galore to wash and iron today.'

Or . . .

'I'm sending the kids over to get 10 minutes' peace in which to restore my equilibrium. It looks as if rain is threatening. Please send them back immediately so they won't get caught out in it. Any fiction at your house? I could use some light diversion.'

Or . . .

'I am only returning this tin in order to get these young folk out of my hair long enough pour faire my toilette. I've still cleaning up to do and I'm trying to collect my thoughts in preparation for the day's work. It looks like we face another scorcher today!'

And, very typical . . .

'This has been a very hectic morning! First, I was rushing to finish a few letters to send to you to post for me. Then it began to sprinkle slightly and I remembered you have no raincoat, so I decided to dash over there myself with the letters and the post key. At the very moment I was stepping out of the door, in stepped someone and that solved the letter posting problem, but I still don't know whether there is any mail for me. I've lost my P.O. Box key! Did the children perhaps drop it out of that purse when they were playing with it at your house yesterday?'

Or my son keeps getting every kind of chest ailment and I prefer to decide it's the worst . . .

'What's this about whooping cough! Who diagnosed it? Didn't you say he had all his shots and vaccinations? The D.P.T. doesn't require a booster until after he's five years old. Diphtheria— Pertussis (Whooping cough)—Tetanus is one of the most reliable vaccinations. This sounds incredible! You know all three of mine and I have had hoarse, dry coughs but certainly it wasn't whooping cough. Here's Dr Spock to reassure you!'

Sometimes too, conversations get all tangled up and the African night creeps all about and the candles are not lit and the conversation gets more entangled, intense; and the children fall asleep on the floor dazed by it all. The next day I get a book flung at me with vigorous exasperation . . .

'Here's C. P. Snow. Read him, dammit!! And dispel a bit of that fog in thy cranium. The chapters on Intellectuals and the Scientific Revolution are stimulating. Read it, dammit!!'

I am dazed too by Mr C. P. Snow. Where do I begin to understand the industrial use of electronics, atomic energy, automation in a world of mud huts? What is a machine tool? he asks. What are the Two Cultures and the Scientific Revolution? The argument could be quaint to one who hasn't even one leg of culture to stand on. But it isn't really, because even a bush village in Africa begins to feel the tug and pull of the spider-web of life. Would Mr Snow or someone please write me an explanation of what a machine tool is? I'd like to know. My address is: Serowe, Botswana, Africa.

The trouble with the woman from America is that people would rather hold off, sensing her world to be shockingly apart from theirs. But she is a new kind of American or even maybe will be a new kind of African. There isn't anyone here who does not admire her. To come from a world of chicken, hamburgers, T.V., escalators and what not to a village mud hut and a life so tough, where the most you can afford to eat is ground millet and boiled meat? Sometimes you cannot afford to eat at all. Always you have to trudge miles for a bucket of water and carry it home on your head. And to do all this with loud, ringing, sprawling laughter?

Black people in America care about Africa and she has come here on her own as an expression of that love and concern. Through her too, one is filled with wonder for a country that breeds individuals about whom, without and within, rushes the wind of freedom. I have to make myself clear, though. She is a different person who has taken by force what America will not give black people. We had some here a while ago, sent out by the State Department. They were very jolly and sociable, but for the most innocent questions they kept saying: 'We can't talk about the government. That's politics. We can't talk politics.' Why did they come here if they were so afraid of what the American government thinks about what they might think or say in Africa? Why were they so afraid? Africa is not alive for them. It seems a waste of State Department's money. It seems so strange a thing to send people on goodwill projects and at the same time those people are so afraid that they jump at the slightest shadow. Why are they so afraid of the government of America which is a government of freedom and democracy? Here we are all afraid of authority and we never pretend anything else. Black people who are sent here by the State Department are tied up in some deep and shameful hypocrisy. It is a terrible pity because such things are destructive to them and hurtful to us.

The woman from America loves both Africa and America, independently. She can take what she wants from both and say: 'Dammit'. It is a most strenuous and difficult thing to do.

BESSIE HEAD (ESSAY DATE 1975)

SOURCE: Head, Bessie. "Despite Broken Bondage, Botswana Women Are Still Unloved." In *A Woman Alone: Autobiographical Writings,* selected and edited by Craig MacKenzie, pp. 54-57. Nairobi, Kenya: Heinemann, 1990.

In the following essay, originally published in 1975, Head discusses the treatment of Botswanan women as chattel in spite of changes in their legal status.

In the old days a woman was regarded as sacred only if she knew her place, which was in her yard with her mother-in-law and children. A number of oppressive traditions, however, completely obliterated her as a thinking, feeling human being and she was exploited in all sorts of ways. So heavy is the toll of the centuries on the women of Botswana, that even with present-day political independence for the country, one finds that the few highly literate women of the country talk in uncertain terms of their lives and fear to assert themselves.

In strongly traditional societies there is a long thread of continuity between the past and the present and one often looks back to the past to explain the social maladies of the present. One of the earliest and surprisingly accurate views of Botswana society was recorded in 1805 by a German traveller,[1] Dr W. H. C. Lichtenstein. Many an old man of the tribe will confirm Dr Lichtenstein's observations. About the position of women in the society, he recorded:

. . . The husband secures a livelihood by hunting, tending the cattle and milking the cows. When at home he only prepares hides and makes skin coats and cloth for himself and his wife. About the children he hardly cares . . . the gentler sex plays a very inferior part in the life of the tribe . . . It must not be overlooked that this servitude of women is not a consequence of tyranny by men, but due to certain causes, which ameliorate the lot of a Bechuana woman, although it might not be desirable according to our standards. The number of men is relatively small and they have to hunt and go to war, so naturally all the peaceful duties and occupations are done by women. Only such work as can suddenly be dropped and can be interrupted for some length of time, such

as sewing of clothes, is done by men. All other work which has to be done continuously such as building, tilling of the soil, the making of pots, baskets, ropes and other household utensils is done by women. Two-thirds of the nation are women and even without any wars they would have to belong to the working class . . .

It has also been said that a true man in this world did not listen to the opinion of women; under polygamy women shared a husband with one or several other women and the custom of *bogadi* or the offering of a gift of cattle by her husband's family to her own family at the time of marriage, had overtones of complete bondage to a husband and his family and undertones of a sales bargain. But in spite of all this, women have experienced considerable emancipation in Botswana. Their emancipation has never been an applied or intellectual movement; it centres around a number of historical factors, not the least being the complicated and dominant role Christianity played in the political history of the country.

All the tribes in Botswana have a shared history so that it is possible to discuss changes that took place in broad terms. Unlike South Africa, Botswana had a benign form of colonial rule and invasion under the old British Bechuanaland Protectorate established in 1885. Colonial rule was benign for an odd reason—the country was grim and unproductive, subject to recurrent cycles of drought. The British had no interest in it, except as a safe passageway to the interior. British interest was focused on Mashonaland (now Rhodesia), which, they erroneously believed, held huge deposits of gold. Due to this, Botswana remained independent in a way; its customs and traditions were left intact and people's traditional rulers had a large say in governing their people. Thus, the real Southern African dialogues took place in Botswana. Christianity was a dialogue here, as was black people's ownership of the land and the retention of the ancient African land tenure system, as was trade.

It was about 1890 that the iron hand-plough was introduced into the country and this implement played a major role in lightening woman's burden as an all-round food producer. Formerly, women scratched at the earth with a hoe. When the iron plough was introduced it created a small social problem that could only be solved by the men. It was forbidden in custom for women to handle cattle so men were needed to inspan the oxen and pull the plough. Agriculture then became a joint task shared by a man and his family. The peaceful establishment of trade brought a new form of clothing into the country, 'European clothes', which was universally adopted.

Christianity then presented itself as a doctrine above all traditions and mores; a moral choice freely available to both men and women and it is in this sphere that all major social reforms took place. Attention has to be shifted briefly at this point to an area of the country where Christianity and all it implied became the major dialogue. It was in the Bamangwato area of the country, over the years 1866-1875 where a young chief, later known as Khama, The Great, suffered religious persecution from his father, Chief Sekgoma I, for making a complete and absolute conversion to Christian doctrine. This brought Khama into conflict with traditional African custom, which was upheld by his father. The act of suffering persecution for a belief eventually made Khama the victor in the struggle and the leading social reformer of the country. It could also be said of Khama that he was a compassionate man by inclination because some of his reforms, which must have been extremely difficult to initiate, appear to have been motivated entirely by compassion and this is no more evident than in his abolition of *bogadi* or the bride price.

It is significant that of the five major tribes of the country, only the Bomangwato and Batawana completely abolished *bogadi*. All the other tribes still adhere to the custom. People vehemently deny that *bogadi* is the 'purchase of women' and yet central to its functioning is human greed and the acquisition of wealth through cattle. Under *bogadi* marriages are so arranged as to retain cattle wealth within kinship groups, so that young girls were usually married to close relatives, a cousin, a father's brother's son.

Many poignant dramas were played out against this background. Marriage was superficially secure. *Bogadi* made a woman a silent slave and chattel in the home of her in-laws; if she was ill-treated by her mother-in-law or husband, she could not complain. Her parents were always anxious that she do nothing to destroy the marriage in case they lose the *bogadi* cattle offered at the time of marriage. *Bogadi* also bonded over to a woman's husband's family all the children she could bear in her lifetime. As frequently happened, her first husband died and should she acquire children from another man, those children too were claimed by her deceased husband's family. *Bogadi* was eventually abolished in Bamangwato country on these compassionate grounds: that each man ought to be the father of his own children. When Khama abolished *bogadi*, he also,

for the first time, allowed women to lodge complaints against their husbands on their own and not through a male sponsor, as was required by custom.

Change and progress has always been of a gentle and subtle nature—the widespread adoption of Christianity gradually eliminated polygamous marriages. At independence in 1966, women were given the right to vote alongside men. They did not have to fight for it. But strangely, this very subtlety makes it difficult to account for the present social crisis. The country is experiencing an almost complete breakdown of family life and a high rate of illegitimate births among the children. No one can account for it. It just happened somewhere along the line. A woman's place is no longer in her yard with her mother-in-law but she finds herself as unloved outside the restrictions of custom, as she was, within it. When I first arrived in Botswana in 1964, women confided to me as follows: 'Botswana men are not nice. When you take up with a man he sleeps with you for two weeks, then he passes you on to his friend, who passes you on to his friend. That is how we live . . .'

Possibly two thirds of the nation are still women and about children procreated under such circumstances, the men hardly care.

Note

1. W. H. C. Lichtenstein. *Foundation Of The Cape & About The Bechuanas.* A. A. Balkema: Cape Town, 1973.

GENERAL COMMENTARY

ADEOLA JAMES (ESSAY DATE 2000)

SOURCE: James, Adeola. "Bessie Head's Perspectives on Women." In *Black Women Writers across Cultures: An Analysis of Their Contributions,* edited by Valentine Udoh James, James S. Etim, Melanie Marshall James, and Ambe J. Njoh, pp. 13-38. Lanham, Md.: International Scholars Publications, 2000.

In the following essay, James discusses Head's analysis and interpretation of contemporary feminism in South Africa in her novels.

Background

Bessie Head, who died prematurely in 1986 at the age of forty-eight years, is recognized today as one of Africa's leading writers. At the time of her death she had published three novels, a collection of short stories, a book based on oral traditions, and an historical book.[1] Since her death, there have been further evidence of her fecund mind;

another collection of short stories, a selection of her letters, and a full biography have been published.[2] There are researches being done all over the world which will, eventually appraise us of the full stature of this dedicated, but enigmatic mind.

In studying Head's works, one thing that is most striking is her concern about the position of women under an oppressed traditional as well as the political system of colonization. The colonial period, though [it] gave power to the Africans, the experience of women did not change much. Head, in giving voice to the experiences of women, invokes a feminist criticism of her work, though she herself might have resisted this definition. Her objection, like that of many even today, would derive from the incorrect negativism attached to the term "feminist." A clear definition of my premise will make my purpose clear.

> Feminists [are those who] believe that women have been locked off in a condition of lesser reality by the dominant attitudes and customs of our culture. We find these attitudes and customs reified in the institutions of literature and literary criticism.[3]

From the above definition we can understand that feminist criticism can be described as a mode of negation seen within a fundamental dialectic. The fundamental dialectic being the radical transformation of consciousness taking place at this time in history, almost everywhere in the world including Africa. What is generally referred to as "the women question" is the recognition of the necessity of restoring women to their place in history, recognizing that they have always been around though, ignored and denied voice. The feminist approach, when applied to the critique of Head's works, yields a rewarding result as I intend to prove in this chapter.

Chinua Achebe is one of the earliest writers in post-colonial Africa to give voice to the exploitation of Africa through colonialism and the ensuing tragic results of that experience. Indeed most of the first generation writers like Soyinka, Okot p. Bitek, Ngugi wa Thiong'o, Okigbo and J. P. Clark, to name a few, attained renown through their powerful dramatization of the inescapable conflicts within African societies following the colonial encounter.

Literature should enlarge one's vision of life but for the first two decades of writing in Africa, literature has neglected the representation of men and women. Women were made invisible and voiceless or, at best, they were presented in stereotypical images. Women writers reversed the

FROM THE AUTHOR

HEAD ON HER RESPONSE TO THE PRESENCE OF EVIL

If all my living experience could be summarised I would call it knowledge of evil, knowledge of its sources, of its true face and the misery and suffering it inflicts on human life. I have always tended to work with great force and authority; all my conclusions are sweeping ones based on learning and experience. Certain insights I had gained into the nature of evil were initially social ones, based entirely on my South African experience. I welcomed any social order or individual who represented broad and unselfish planning for everyone. I later worked deeper than that, bringing the problem of evil closer to my own life. I found myself in a situation where there was no guarantee against the possibility that I could be evil too. I found that one earns only a slight guarantee against the possibility of inflicting harm on others through an experience which completely destroys one's own ego or sense of self-esteem. This can be so devastating that one is not likely to survive it. I had tended to leave my work at that stage with rough outlines of good and evil, which either I or someone else might fill in at a later stage. What has driven me is a feeling that human destiny ought not to proceed along tragic lines, with every effort and every new-born civilisation throttling itself in destruction with wrong ideas and wrong ways of living.

Head, Bessie. Excerpt from "Some Notes on Novel Writing." In *A Woman Alone: Autobiographical Writings*, p. 63. Nairobi, Kenya: Heinemann, 1990.

invisibility and voicelessness of women in literature and, in a general way, fought against the culture of silence in which African women were traditionally drowned. Most importantly, through their writing we begin to understand women's position on important issues about the African world view, history, politics, heritage, the Diaspora, love, bonding, and relationship.

The fundamental contribution of the African women writers is the location of the conflicts and the ultimate tragedy of Africa in the exploitation and deprivation of her women folk by men folk. Bessie Head, Ama Ata Aidoo, Buchi Emecheta, and Zulu Sofola have written boldly about this in the hope that they can add their voices to the recipe for change. Women writers have dramatized the double burden of their women folk. They are oppressed and exploited by the inhuman exertions of the twin mode of capitalism and colonialism. Underlying this, however, is the position of weakness to which women are traditionally relegated. Bessie Head clearly and unequivocally states:

> The ancestors made so many errors and one of the most bitter-making things was that they relegated to men a superior position in the tribe, while women were regarded, in a congenital sense, as being an inferior form of human life. To this day women still suffer from all the calamities that befall an inferior form of life.
>
> (p. 92)[4]

The personal is the political. The women writers have brought the female world into the public view in a way that men either have deliberately or inadvertently failed to do. Our women writers represent female experience from the woman's perspective and create complex and credible images of women as they come to terms with their lives as modern women in a continent that has been traumatized by slavery and colonialism, but is undergoing promising transformation.

Summary

> Long ago, when the land was only cattle tracks and footpaths, the people lived together like a deep river, which was unruffled by conflict. . . .
>
> (p. 1)[5]

> What could be done? Nothing could sort out the world. It would always be a painful muddle.
>
> (p. 109)[6]

These quotations are the opening and closing statements found in *The Collector of Treasures*. In a way they sum up the history of Africa, capturing succinctly what has happened to us over these last few centuries, the transformation from an "unruffled" life to "a painful muddle." Head's mature vision and painful personal experiences enabled her to analyze what is our tragedy. I believe she succeeds in taking us beyond the great statement of this tragedy dramatized in *Things Fall Apart*. Head takes us beyond colonial injustices, locating the problem of Africa in the sufferings and injustices endured by her women throughout the ages.

The first statement is from a story which celebrates the great love between two young people. Sebembele was willing to renounce his kingdom for the sake of a woman who loved him. It was acknowledged by all that Rankana was "a beautiful woman . . . she was gentle and kind and loving . . ." When Sebembele refused to bow to the machinations of his brothers and stood firmly by Rankana and his son, he won the respect of his people who "saw that they had a ruler who talked with deeds rather than words" (p. 5).

The second statement above is Thato's observation on the incredible muddle people make of their lives each day: she has just finished briefing her husband on happenings in the village and what a list of woes!

> There's trouble again between Felicia and her husband . . . Rapula had taken up with a she been queen and arrived home dead drunk every other night and beat his wife because she complained and scolded. . . .

Reddock defines feminism as

> the awareness of the oppression, exploitation and/or subordination of women within society and the conscious action to change and transform this situation.

Head was interested in changing the oppressive situation of women as she observed and experienced it in Africa. Before she could do this, her first step was to make us aware of the exploitation and subordination of the women. Hence, life for women, in all its ramifications, is her primary theme. Her analysis in novel after novel is detailed, clear and incisive as we will observe as I examine each work.

The Tragedy of Male Ego

"The Collector of Treasures," appropriately, the story that gives that collection of short stories its title, contains the most moving portraiture of a tragic, dignified, and most admirable woman. In analyzing her fate, the narrator gives us the most profound analysis of the tragedy of the African man, from which that of the woman cannot be divorced. As a central statement in Head's writing, one which is germane to the perspectives she presents on women, it deserves to be quoted in full. The author-narrator asserts that "there were really only two kinds of men in the society. The one kind created such misery and chaos that he could be broadly damned as evil." Having likened his behaviour to that of "the village dogs chasing a bitch on heat" describing graphically the repulsive excesses of the winner, she says "like the dogs and bulls and donkeys, he also accepted no responsibility for the young he procreated and like the dogs and bulls and donkeys, he also made females abort." She continues, "since that kind of man was in the majority in the society" and since, "he was responsible for the complete breakdown of family life," he could be analyzed over three time spans. What follows is a most gripping analysis of the tragic destruction of the African male ego, his attempt to recapture his sense of manliness by subjugating his female counterpart. This results in the chaos that we are familiar with. In explaining the present situation, Head takes us through the history of Africa seen in three different eras—the time of the ancestors, the colonial period and independence. She writes,

> In the old days, before the colonial invasion of Africa, he was a man who lived by the traditions and taboos outlined for all the people by the forefathers of the tribe. He had little individual freedom to assess whether these traditions were compassionate or not—they demanded that he comply and obey the rules, without thought. But when the laws of the ancestors are examined, they appear on the whole to have been vast, external disciplines for the good of the society as a whole with little attention given to individual preferences and needs.

Of course, the rules of the ancestors are not faultless and one of the major errors they made is "that they relegated to men a superior position in the tribe, while women were regarded, in a congenital sense, as being an inferior form of human life."

The male ego was further destroyed in the colonial era, the period of migratory mining labour. Worse still, this form of labour destroyed family life—"it broke the old, traditional form of family life and for long periods a man was separated from his wife and children while he worked for a pittance in another land in order to raise the money to pay British Colonial polltax." The African man lost his self respect because he became "the boy of the white man."

Independence brought very little relief to his pain and the destiny of his people. Head writes:

> African independence seemed merely one more affliction on top of the afflictions that had visited this man's life.

The thrust of Head's penetrating analysis is to seek the meaning of our history while showing how women have survived the massive onslaught on their beings. Whether it was during the time of the ancestors, the colonial period, or the independence period the male whose sense of self-worth has been destroyed always "turns to the woman in a dizzy kind of death dance of wild destruction and dissipation." As a result of this exploration Head's fictional world is peopled by women who have not only survived but have assisted the regeneration of their menfolk, paving the way for a new harmonious existence.

The Search for Spiritual and Physical Emancipation

When Rain Clouds Gather dramatizes emancipatory yearnings, the search for both physical and spiritual emancipation. For Makhaya, who leaves his mother in South Africa "in a state of complete collapse" to travel somewhere because "he could not marry and have children in a country, where Black men were called 'boy' and 'kaffir,' his search for liberation from political oppression is actively connected with greater spiritual enlightenment which he experiences in the course of his moral development living and working in Botswana. Another male, Gilbert, an Englishman, disengages himself from the country of 'nice, orderly queues' where everybody lines up for a place and position in the world (p. 28)." Like Makhaya, he is in search of fulfillment and a more meaningful existence. In the village of Golema Mmidi where he devotes himself to assisting 'in agricultural development and improved techniques of food production,' he finds a richer life. Both Makhaya's and Gibert's moral and spiritual development are linked with the lives of three women who become the focus of our attention in the novel, namely Mma-Millipede, Maria, and Pauline.

Mma-Millipede is the mother of the village, she recalls the West Indian mother (the mainstay of family life since slavery), and the traditional African grandmother who used to regulate the affairs of everyone. Mma-Millipede is described as "one of those rare individuals with a distinct personality at birth . . . she was able to grasp the religion of the missionaries and use its message to adorn and enrich her own originality of thought and expand the natural kindness of her heart (p. 63)." When Dinorego becomes acquainted with Makhaya's problems, the old man advises the younger one "you must approach my friend Mma-Millipede . . . she may help you to find the woman you seek, as she knows the heart of everyone (p. 91)." The unintrusive voice of the narrator makes an important observation about Mma-Millipede. She

> had traced two distinct relationships women had with men in her country. The one was a purely

physical relationship. It caused no mental break-down and was free and casual each woman having 'six or seven lovers, including a husband as well. The other was more serious and more rare. It could lead to mental breakdown and suicide on the part of the woman.'[7]

She prefers the other one, reasoning that

it was far better to have a country of promiscuous women than a country of dead women.

(p. 91-2)

With such a pragmatic attitude she looks after the interest of all who come within her orbit of activities. She senses Maria's interest better than her father and through her intervention both Gilbert and Maria are able to achieve fulfillment.

Similarly, she guides Makhaya through bitterness, hatred, and despair to accept all men as his brothers. He observes that "the old woman had a fire inside her that radiated outward and he could feel it and it warmed him. . . . He liked this direct people-caring and this warm fire in an old woman (p. 121)." In this enriching exchange, Makhaya begins to assume "new mental outlooks." Once he is spiritually opened up he is able to say to Paulina "perhaps, I'll find out what love is as we go along together (p. 147)." His voyage towards self-discovery, personal and spiritual regeneration, is complete in his union with Paulina and he observes:

All his life he had wanted some kind of Utopia, and he had rejected in his mind and heart a world full of ailments and faults. He had run and run away from it all . . . loving one woman had brought him to this realization: that it was only people who could bring the real rewards of living: that it was only people who give love and happiness.

(p. 152)[8]

Gilbert's life is less agonizing because of his belonging to a race that is on the giving end of oppression and therefore, immuned to it. Nevertheless, if he were to experience the new dispensation of spiritual awakening he too had to leave his accustomed comfort. For when life is too selfishly smooth, it could kill with its boredom and monotony. Mma-Millipede adores Gilbert "as she identified him with her own love of mankind."

It is Mma-Millipede's task to direct the young to develop a creative attitude that nurtures life. She does this with a loving heart and genuine generosity.

Maria is regarded by her father as "a difficult daughter." Old Dinorego had led Makhaya into the village in the hope that he might prove to be a suitable suitor for his daughter.

Maria appears in the novel on very few occasions. She is of significance only in relation to the fulfilling relationship that emerges between herself and Gilbert. Through his friend Makhaya, Gilbert affirms that life might have something more to offer than "running away from it." He confesses that ninety per cent of the time he doesn't want a woman. "Then also there's that ten percent when I'm lonely, but I don't know of any woman who'd go for the ten percent. (p. 29)." Maria "was one of those women who had a life of her own" she is "a preoccupied self-absorbed woman," with "an almighty air of neatness and orderliness about her . . . her small black eyes never seemed to gaze outward, but inward." She is a woman of few words. Such a woman is able to transform "the ten percent" of life that a very busy man like Gilbert could share [with] her. Maria is presented as the typical housewife who is industrious. Apart from keeping her home she joins in the agricultural projects organized by her husband and Makhaya. She discharges her responsibility towards her community; at the cattle post, she takes on the responsibility of cooking for the men, and for Paulina's household as well. Her reaction on the occasion of the tragic death of Paulina's son is the only positive one. She observes:

. . . death was like trying to clutch the air, and you had to let it be and slowly let it pass aside, without fuss and indignity. Instead, you had to concentrate the mind on all that was still alive and treat it as the most precious treasure you had ever been given.

(p. 153)

She is a woman of action rather than words. Her affirmation of life is contained in her reply to her husband who informs her during the terrible drought that "even the trees were dying, from the roots upwards." Maria said

No, you may see no rivers on the ground but we keep the rivers inside us. That is why all good things and all good people are called rain. Sometimes we see the rain clouds gather even though not a cloud appears in the sky. It is all in our heart.

(p. 157)

Maria encapsulates women's spiritual strength and deep hope that life will last in spite of temporary setbacks.

Paulina bridges the age gap between Mma-Millipede and Maria and forms the last in Head's images of well-grounded women, portrayed with positive and life-enhancing spirits. Paulina is industrious, in addition "she was daring and different" which make all the other women follow her leadership. What sets her apart most significantly is her ability to think and analyze. Paulina, unlike the other women has no permanent lover or husband. The women come to admit that the reason why Paulina dominated them all was because she was the kind of woman who could not lie to men (p. 86). She fears "the untrustworthiness of men with no strength or moral values." Intuitively she feels something is wrong with a whole society which "had connived at producing a race of degenerate men by stressing their superiority in the law and overlooking how it affected them as individuals (p. 86)."

Paulina, the narrator says:

> Was not like the women of Golema Mmidi, although she had been born into their kind of world and fed on the same diet of their maize porridge by a meek, repressed, dull-eyed mother.
>
> (p. 18)

She is distinguished by a superior education and by retaining since childhood a "fresh, lively curiosity." What we remember most about this dignified woman is her natural ability to lead. Gilbert's request that she should get one hundred women organized into a tobacco-growing co-operative receives a "generous smile from her. Later it is largely through her effort that this project, which transformed the lives of the village women who have never worked for money, succeeded. What are most memorable about her are her controlled and courageous stance in time of tragedy, when her son dies alone at the cattlepost; most importantly, her ability to question radically old and popularly accepted practices in the man/woman relationship.

She was aware of her physical need but she would not yield to having lovers because of a "blind and intense desire" to own and possess a man to herself. "But in a society like this" she asks "which man cared to be owned and possessed when there were so many women freely available?" She objected to "the excessive love-making" which was purposeless and aimless, "just like tipping everything into an awful cess-pit where no one really cared to take a second look. Paulina "was too proud a woman" to be treated like a "cess-pit" she wanted "a man who wasn't a free for-all."

Following this line of thoughts to its conclusion she adds,

> No doubt, the other women longed for this too because intense bloody battles often raged between women and women over men, and yet, perversely, they always set themselves up for sale

to the first bidder who already had so many different materials in his shop that he was simply bored to death by the display.

> (p. 104)

> Botswana men no longer cared. In fact a love affair resulting in pregnancy was one sure way of driving a man away and it was a country of fatherless children now.
>
> (p. 111)

Wisdom then lies in self control and certain understanding among the women to prevent the exploitation the men are permitted because of their weakness and disunity.

Paulina's concern is not for herself alone. Her own experience enables her to empathize with the suffering of women in a society in which

> Every protection for women was breaking down and being replaced by nothing. And there was something so deeply wrong in the way a woman had to live, holding herself together with her backbone, because, no matter to which side a woman might turn, there was this trap of loneliness. Most women had come to take it for granted, entertaining themselves with casual lovers. Most women with fatherless children thought nothing of sending a small boy out to a lonely cattle post to herd cattle to add to the family income. But then, such women expected life to give them nothing. And if you felt the strain of such a life, all the way down your spine surely it meant that you were just holding on until such time as a miracle occurred? And how many miracles an ordinary woman needed these days. Paulina sighed bitterly and deeply. . . .
>
> (p. 111)

In the creation of Paulina, Head presents one of her most touching and profoundest characters. The circumstances of her life, her inter-relationships with others, are real ones that any reader can identify with, so compelling and truthful are they. In her creation, Head further shows that feminism is not a creation of the misguided western-educated African woman. You don't have to read too much to learn where your shoes are hurting.

There are certain areas of Paulina's attitude that need changing as well. She forbids Makhaya to help her in preparing the meal saying "Don't touch the fire. 'It's woman's work'." Most African men and women will agree with this sentiment. However, in their journey together towards enlightenment Makhaya teaches Paulina the new way. He says to her, "It's time you learned that men live on this earth too. If I want to make tea, I'll make it, and if I want to sweep the floor, I'll sweep it (p. 130)."

Makhaya was thankful for Paulina's love which "was like a warm sun on all the shadows of his life." At the same time he notes that "a woman's life was a clutter of small everyday things—of babies, gossip, pots, food, fires, cups, and plates (p. 142)." Is Makhaya suggesting that the African woman too deserves a better life? The love that developed between Paulina and Makhaya gives the reader an opportunity to see an enlightened, symbiotic relationship in action. At the end Makhaya is able to affirm that "loving one woman had brought him to this realization, that it was only people who could bring the real rewards of living, that it was only people who give love and happiness (p. 152)."

Paulina is Head's presentation of ideal womanhood, the maturing influence of suffering and an unflagging ability to look life straight in the face without giving up the struggle to change it.

In the presentation of these three female characters—Mma-Millipede, Maria, and Paulina—Head portrays women as life-givers, life-preservers and life-transformers. The authorial voice paying homage to the women for transforming village-life by their work in the tobacco cooperative comments,

> No men ever worked harder than Botswana women, for the whole burden of providing food for big families rested with them. It was their sticks that threshed the corn at harvesting time and their winnowing baskets that filled the air for miles and miles around with the dust of husks, and they often, in addition to broadcasting the seed when the early rains fell, took over the tasks of the men and also ploughed the land with oxen.
>
> (p. 97)

Their successful elimination of the retrograde chief Matenge "a Solomon stalking the land in his golden Chevrolet" (p. 173) is an indication of the miracle that could happen when women are united. In a male-dominated world, Head is pointing to the channels of change.

Maru

In *Maru,* her second novel, Head presents a woman's version of racial problem in Africa. She tells an interviewer that "*Maru* was a thesis against racialism. . . . It is an examination of racial prejudices but I used black against black instead of white against black." The novel describes the experience of a Masarwa, an untouchable who was found and raised by a white missionary. In dramatizing this story, Head exposes the senseless prejudices that separate us. Though Head's stated focus is on racial prejudice, the novel offers some clear perspectives on the position of women in Africa. Women are the sufferers but in their suffering they find the grace to become the agent of change. Margaret, the protagonist, highlights this in her own statement when she remarks "There was no word to explain the torture of those days, but out of it she had learned" (p. 102).[9] The woman may be a victim of prejudice, yet it is through her positive attitude that she leads her people through the process of reexamination and ultimate change. This meaning is enclosed in Margaret's painting. Commenting on Margaret's work, in one of the central passages of the book, Maru remarks:

> She chose her themes from the ordinary, common happenings in the village as though those themes were the best expression of her own vitality. The women carried water buckets up and down the hill but the eye was thrown, almost by force, towards the powerful curve of a leg muscle, *resilience* in the back and neck, and the *animated* expressions and gestures of the water-carriers as they stopped to gossip . . . Look! Don't you see! We are the people who have the strength to build a new world!
>
> (p. 107-108) [Italics are supplied]

This is not Maru's voice *per se,* but that of the omniscient narrator paying tribute to the African woman as she emerges through suffering, endurance and struggle into the dawn of a new world.

A Question of Power

It is Head's conviction that the new world cannot be created without excruciating suffering. This is the conviction dramatized in *A Question of Power,* the most powerful of Head's writing at the same time the most enigmatic. *A Question of Power,* is Head's version of "life-writing in the feminine," where her protagonist, Elizabeth struggles to define herself as a subject through figuring out her life story in different versions. It is in this novel that we encounter Head's most sustained effort to put the African experience in the context of her own world view. She writes:

> In my novel, *A Question of Power,* I was extremely bothered to define evil. I was looking for answers all along to questions of exploitation. And I was looking for balances; that is, if we have to live with good and evil we ought to present them as they really are.[10]

It is not without significance that Head focuses her exploration of evil on the life of one woman. It is through Elizabeth that the fundamental question of exploitation and suffering is fleshed out. Head combines the physical with the psychic in dramatizing through Elizabeth's life, the Biblical verse "For we wrestle not against flesh and blood, but against principalities, against powers, against the rulers of the darkness of this world, against spiritual wickedness in high places" (Ephesians 6:12). In this statement, Paul might have been directing his warnings at men; in Head's view, however, it seems that women, particularly Black women, are the ones who face this devastating apocalyptic struggle.

There are four unforgettable women in *A Question of Power,* Elizabeth, Kenosi, Birgette, and Camilla. All four serve as counterpoints to one another revealing the author's views on the experiences of women.

It is Elizabeth's story for we encounter the other characters in relation to her need of them or in her reaction to them. The plot of the novel is the evolution of Elizabeth's soul. This is gathered from the opening paragraphs of the book. Sello wonders

> how often was a learner dependent on his society for his soul-evolution? . . . It had always been like this, for him—a hunger after the things of the soul, in which other preoccupations were submerged. . . . To him love was freedom of heart.
>
> (p. 11)

The narrator informs us that

> A woman in the village of Motabeng paralleled his [Sello's] inner development. Most of what applied to Sello applied to her, because they were twin souls with closely-linked destinies and the same capacity to submerge other preoccupations in a pursuit after the things of the soul.
>
> (p. 11)

Sello and Dan were the two sides of Elizabeth. Her spiritual struggle with these evil powers made her suffer mental breakdown twice. Recurrent in her subconscious Sello and Dan become hallucinatory symbols turning her life into a nightmare. "Dan" she says "understood the mechanics of power. From his gestures, he clearly thought he had a wilting puppet in his hands." (p. 13) Sello is her guardian angel, he tells her "love isn't like that; Love is two people mutually feeding each other" (p. 14). This thought or idea is to occur again and again guiding Elizabeth throughout her soul-journey until she is able to make that ultimate "sharp, short leap to freedom."[11]

Elizabeth narrates how she became a pawn in the hands of Sello, Dan, and Medusa. She was born in South Africa. It was at a mission school where she was placed in her childhood that the inauspicious circumstances surrounding her birth were callously revealed to [. . .] her

> Your mother was insane. If you're not careful you'll get insane just like your mother. Your mother was a white woman. They had to lock her up, as she was having a child by the stable boy, who was a native.
>
> (p. 16)

This was her first rude awakening to "the details of life and oppression in South Africa."

For a few years she quietly lived on the edge of South Africa's life. She spent some time living with Asian families, where she learnt about India and its philosophies, and some time with a German woman from "whom she learnt about Hitler and Jesus and the Second World War." A year before her marriage she tentatively joined a political party. It was banned two days later and in the state of emergency which was declared she was searched and briefly arrested.

Elizabeth married "a gangster just out of jail," who said he had thought deeply about life while in prison. But soon women were complaining of being molested by him. After a year, Elizabeth picked up her small boy and walked out of the home. Through a newspaper advertisement she got a teaching post in Botswana and she took "an exit permit, which like her marriage, held the never return clause." The above are the necessary data Elizabeth herself provides for the reader to understand her circumstances. The source of her nightmarish existence are the circumstances of her birth in an oppressive racist society, where being Black tantamounts to a congenital sickness, and a disastrous marriage that barely lasted a year. Both spell out her double yoke. Elizabeth learns to defend herself by resorting to madness. She suffered periodic mental breakdowns.

Elizabeth says that it was in Botswan "where, mentally, the normal and the abnormal blended completely" in her mind. "It was barely three months after her arrival in the village of Motabeng when her life began to pitch over from an even keel, and it remained from then onwards at a pitchedover angle." (p. 21). The bulk of the narrative is about Elizabeth's agony, her baptism by fire which prepared her for the knowledge of the truth. Her dream images include Egyptian, Greek, Roman, and Oriental gods—Medusa, Osiris, Buddha, and "the brotherhood of man." In her clear moments she makes revealing statements about her experiences. For example, she welcomes her suffering in this thought:

> It seemed to her as though all suffering gave people and nations a powerful voice for the future and a common meeting-ground . . . the Gods

turned out on observation to be ordinary, practical, sane people, seemingly their only distinction being that they had consciously concentrated on spiritual earnings.

(p. 31)

Sometimes she resented the agony. For example looking at her son she thought:

> Journeys into the soul are not for women with children, not all that dark heaving turmoil. They are for men, and the toughest of them took off into the solitude of the forests and fought out their battles with hell in deep seclusion. No wonder they hid from view. *The inner life is ugly.*
> (p. 50) (Italics are mine)

Elizabeth survived to become a strong, powerful spiritual being, well grounded in the things of the spirit. She, like Tutuola's Palm-wine drunkard, has been to the land of the dead and is back armed not only with insight but with a remedy for triumphant living. Lawrence's famous poem[12] provides the words to express that triumphant feeling welling up in her soul:

> Not I, but the wind that blows through me! A fine wind is blowing the new direction of time. If only I let it bear me . . . if only, most lovely of all, I yield myself and am borrowed by the wind that takes its course through the chaos of the world . . . Oh, for the wonder that bubbles into my soul.
> (p. 205)

Elizabeth tells us how she survives her ordeal:

> It wasn't any kind of physical stamina that keep her going, but a vague, instinctive pattern of normal human decencies combined with the work she did, the people she met each day and the unfolding of a project with exciting inventive.
> (p. 146)

Elizabeth's survival was aided by three other women encountered in *A Question of Power*. Through their interaction with Elizabeth we learn a lot about female bonding,[13] a central concept in feminist ideology. One woman alone cannot survive the onslaught of exploitation and abuse often meted out to women, but with the aid of other women, healing, and self affirmation are realized.

We encounter two Danish ladies in the novel. Camilla is evil whilst Brigette, on the other hand, counteracts her as a benevolent force. Both act as foils for Elizabeth. Camilla who is working as an Agricultural Officer in Botswana, is a negative influence on Elizabeth. She reminds her of the hypocrisy and arrogance of whites in South Africa. She recoils from her who she refers to as "the half-mad Camilla woman" and "Rattle-tongue." In her portrayal Bessie Head presents the image of a frustrated and insensitive woman who needs to acquire humility. Through the openness of Elizabeth and Brigette, she is redeemed.

Brigette is the opposite of Camilla. Elizabeth finds in her a twin soul, a kindred spirit with whom she could relate. Their brief contact is a symbiotic experience of spiritual growth. Talking to Elizabeth Brigette says "Life is such a gentle, treasured thing. I learn about it every minute. I think about it so deeply." (p. 81) She agrees with Elizabeth's comments on suffering in South Africa that "the faces of the oppressed people are not ugly" even though the torturers become more hideous day by day. "Who is the greater man—the man who cries, broken by anguish, or his scoffing, mocking, jeering oppressor?" (p. 84) Elizabeth asks rhetorically. Birgette agreeing says to Elizabeth

> You say everything I have in my own heart. . . . But I cannot express myself so well because I have never suffered. I see suffering. It hurts me.

She is not renewing her contract because the suffering she sees around her affects her emotionally.

Birgette is a correction of the impression one gets from Camilla. It is not true that one only becomes sensitive to suffering for having suffered. What is necessary is an openness and sympathetic attitude towards life. Of course, the society nourishes this, hence the major difference Elizabeth identifies between herself and Birgette is not race but the fact that one belongs to a progressive society whilst the other belongs to a morally decadent one. She surmises:

> The human soul is alone in the battle of life. It is helped . . . by profoundly moral social orders, such as Moses established for the Jews. . . . The questions of tenderness, love, appeal, compassion, truth, still lie within.
> (p. 86)

While Birgette enables Elizabeth to work out answers to some fundamental questions that have bothered her Kenosi was an agent of life and regeneration. Her simple outlook on life is nourished by the humaneness of the society in which she was raised. That society exalts life above all things.

Kenosi came into Elizabeth's life at a time when she was approaching a mental breakdown and she was concerned about her son's well being in the event of her illness. Kenosi, who was about Elizabeth's age had no difficulty loving the little boy. "It was a way of village life. . . . Children were caressed and attended to, their conversations were listened to with affectionate absorption" (p. 88). Elizabeth was to look back at Kenosi's sudden appearance as "one of the miracles or accidents that saved her life" (p. 89). Observing her closely Elizabeth remarks:

> Her movements were extraordinarily quiet, soft, intensely controlled. . . . She was really an exceedingly beautiful woman in strength and depth of facial expression, in knowingness and grasp of life; its joys, its expected disillusionment. She was really the super-wife, the kind who would keep a neat, ordered house and adore in a quiet, undemonstrative way both the husband and children.

Perhaps Kenosi's statement about herself is a clue to her beautifully coordinated life—"I work with my hands," she said, proudly. "I have always worked. I do any kind of work." Kenosi and Elizabeth became business partners, working miracles in the production of all kinds of fresh vegetables, even growing "Cape Gooseberries" in Botswana and gradually introducing the peasant women there to profit oriented economy.

After one of Elizabeth's crises, when "her head exploded into a thousand fragments of fiery darkness"' and she lay in bed for two days barely conscious, Kenosi came around. She sat down on a chair beside the bed. "She was silent, self-contained alertly practical." She was concerned about the rain storm which caused water to over-run the beds of tomatoes. She later said to Elizabeth, "you must never leave the garden . . . I cannot work without you." This quiet expression of affection and need for her jolted Elizabeth out of her mental stupor. She thought "the way this woman brought her back to life and reality!"

Elizabeth indirectly pays full tribute to Kenosi in attributing to her both her full recovery, mental sanity as well as a new vision of life. She says, at sunset when work with Kenosi at the garden was over and everything was peaceful it was then she began to jot down the fragmentary notes "such as a ship-wrecked sailor might make on a warm sandy beach as he stared back at the stormy sea that had nearly taken his life." It is at this point that she sings her "Magnificent" referred to earlier "Not I, but the wind that blows through me!" Her song glorifies bonding between women which enables them to survive.

Elizabeth's presentation in *A Question of Power* is Bessie Head's most sustained and complete dramatization of her philosophy of "sanctifying affliction" and her conviction about women's strength.

The Collector of Treasures

Bessie Head's final fictional work is a collection of short stories entitled *The Collector of Treasures*. The short story is a flexible form which allows the writer a quick and focused treatment of chosen themes. A number of memorable female characters emerge in *The Collector of Treasures* which is a collection of thirteen moving short stories. Together the stories become a drawing together of all the various images of women that we have encountered in Head's fictional world. There is Dikeledi whose pride, independence, and appetite for living act as a catalyst for others. There is Life whose rebellious spirit leads her to challenge the social order of the patriarchal and racist community in which she lives. We have women of all ages, traditional women who under the burden of custom, have learnt to survive and take care of their needs. But we also encounter the beer drinkers who find marriage boring and enslaving. Through this group the writer explores the negative tendency among modern women and the degenerating influence of prostitution.

The men come off badly as the ones who help to destroy homes. In the most moving story which gives the collection its title, Dikeledi is the beautiful soul who collects treasures. She suffers but never looses hold of her dignity, her warmth, friendship, and eagerness to share draw people towards her. Her imprisonment is a symbol of physical and psychological imprisonment of women, their emasculation by the inimical systems. Head, however, portrays through Dikeledi that even in prison, in an anti-heroic situation, a woman can still achieve heroic proportion. This is very important because it is the first time we encounter an anti-heroic heroine in African Literature. Achebe and most of our writers, present Aristotelian heroes but Head's anti-hero is made heroic.

Conclusion

The three identified preoccupation's that direct as well as empower Head's fictional world are the dehumanizing of Black people in South Africa, the experiences of women under oppression and the individual's struggle for self-liberation. All three impinge on one another, for Head has identified the cause of African men's inhuman treatment of their women to be due to the frustration of history.[14] Disadvantages of history, however, are not sufficient excuse for the continuity of decadence. Like Paul Thebolo, the men must seek within themselves "the power to create themselves anew." Each of the novels has dramatized a spiritual journey towards liberation. In some of them this spiritual journey involves a man, however, his agent of vision leading him towards self fulfillment is a woman. The highest compliment paid to womanhood in her works is the creation of Elizabeth. Through her sufferings she emerges as the visionary of a new world. The challenge to continue to affirm human goodness in spite of everything. Like Dikeledi our lives must be filled "with treasures of kindness and love" gathered in our inter-action with one another.

The message that comes through her fictions is that living is a spiritual journey towards liberation and greater enlightenment: that suffering sanctifies the oppressed whilst it disfigures the oppressor. But the great leap to personal freedom is not reserved for one race alone. It is what makes one really human. These are not new themes, in fact, they are the most popular themes of literature from its very beginning in Oral Traditions and the great European and oriental literary tradition through to the most significant and revolutionary literature of our time being produced in the Third World. What is significant about Bessie Head's work is that she focuses on women, whereas the protagonists of the great novels that come to mind—*Don Quixote, Robinson Crusoe,* and *A Hundred Years of Solitude*—are men. Head's treatment of her theme, the formal precision and assuredness with which her novels are executed make them compulsory reading.

We are impressed by her narrative strategies such as the use of symbols[15] the orality of the language of her ordinary people recreating the real life speech style in the African villages: the lively dialogue and the unintrusive voice of the omniscient narrator which directs our response rather than interfere with the narrative process. All these blend together making for the resonance of the main message which echoes throughout all her works. Her main message is that

> . . . all suffering gave people and nations a powerful voice for the future and a common meeting-ground.[16]

In all her writing women's sufferings leave their imprint on our consciousness. At the same time they are portrayed as the ones "who have the strength to build a new world." Head allows us to experience the difficulties and struggles of her female characters, eventually to enable us to celebrate their victories as women who surmount their oppressed situations.

Head's work proves conclusively the statement that:

Individual awareness and consciousness of their subordinate position has always existed among individuals or groups of women. It is only when this becomes evident through collective action by large numbers of women that it can be said that a feminist movement exists.[17]

Do I dare to suggest that women writers like Bessie Head have paved the way for the emergence of strong feminist movements in our continent that will transform our lives.

Notes

1. *When Rain Clouds Gather.* 1968. Penguin Books Ltd.: U.K.

   Maru, 1971. Heinemann: London.

   A Question of Power. 1974. Heinemann: London.

   The Collector of Treasures and Other Botswana Village Tales. 1977. Heinemann: London.

   Serowe Village of the Rain Wind. 1991. Heinemann: London.

   A Bewitched Crossroads. 1984. A. D. Donker Ltd.: Cape Town, South Africa.

2. Eilersen, Gillian Stead ed. 1989. *Tales of Tenderness and Power.* A. D. Donker: Cape Town, South Africa.

   Mackenzie, Craig. ed. 1990. *A Woman Alone: Autobiographical Writings.* Heinemann: Oxford.

   Vigne, Randolph ed. 1991. *A Gesture of Belonging.* Heinemann: London.

   1993. *The Cardinals, with Meditations and Short Stories.* M. J. Daymond: Cape Town.

   Eilersen, Gillian Stead. 1995. *Bessie Head: Thunder Behind Her Ears.* David Philip Publishers Ltd.: South Africa.

3. Donvan, J. 1989. *Feminist Literary Criticism.* University of Kentucky Press. p. 74.

4. 1977. *The Collector of Treasures.* All page references are to the Heinemann ed.

5. Ibid.

6. Ibid.

7. Rhoda Reddock. 1988. "Feminism and Feminist Thought: An Historical Overview" in *Gender in Caribbean Development.* P. Mohamed and C. Shepherd (ed.). UWI.

8. Nichols, Lee (ed.). 1981. *Conversations with African Writers.* Voice of America: Washington D.C.

9. 1971. All page references are to *Maru.* Heinemann: London.

10. Nichols, Lee (ed.) *Op. cit.*

11. 1974. All page references are to *A Question of Power.* Heinemann: London.

12. Lawerence, D. H. 1960. "Not I, Not I, But the Wind That blows Through Me!" in *The Faber Book of Modern Verse* ed. Michael Roberts: London.

13. Bonding among women is a familiar theme in the writings of African Americans. It is found in Alice Walker's *The Color Purple,* Toni Morrison's *Beloved,* and Paule Marshall's *Praise Song For the Widow.* It occurs in Ama Ata Aidoo's *Changes* as well. Bonding is related to the theme of healing which is the essential difference between Western feminist literature and the womanist alternative adopted by Black writers.

14. *The Collector of Treasures.* pp. 91-93.

15. In *Maru* as in *To The Light House* by Virginia Woolf, Margaret Cadmore's painting is the most eloquent representation of her thought and helps to clarify the message of that novel. In *A Question of Power,* the womb, the images of Buddha, Medusa are some of the significant symbols.

16. *A Question of Power.* p. 31.

17. Rhoda Reddock, *Op. cit.*

TITLE COMMENTARY

The Collector of Treasures

DOROTHY DRIVER (ESSAY DATE 1993)

SOURCE: Driver, Dorothy. "Reconstructing the Past, Shaping the Future: Bessie Head and the Question of Feminism in a New South Africa." In *Black Women's Writings,* edited by Gina Wisker, pp. 160-87. New York: St. Martin's Press, 1993.

In the following essay, Driver discusses Head's treatment of the "new" woman in South Africa in her short stories in The Collector of Treasures.

Black women have long operated at a disadvantage. Now you as the storyteller are going to shape the future.

Bessie Head[1]

Given Bessie Head's vehement feminist claim in *The Collector of Treasures* (1977) that in Botswanan society women are 'of no account' or are treated like 'dogs',[2] her story **'Snapshots of a Wedding'** seems surprisingly muted. Its subject is the marriage between a young man and a school-educated woman, called Neo for 'new'. After an idyllic opening—the wedding takes place at the 'haunting, magical hour of early dawn' (p. 76)—the story begins to establish the specific voices which make up the community. 'This is going to be a modern wedding' (p. 76), says one of the relatives of the groom. One of the bride's relatives responds: 'Oh, we all have our own ways. . . . If the times are changing, we keep up with them' (pp. 76-7). Uneasy about the marriage, the female members of the community instruct Neo in her duties: 'Daughter, you must carry water for your husband. Beware, that at all times, he is the owner

of the house and must be obeyed. Do not mind if he stops now and then and talks to other ladies. Let him feel free to come and go as he likes' (p. 79).

At such a point, the story may seem to be less about the community's desire to 'keep up with' women like Neo than about forms of control. Even though she will be keeping her job as a secretary, rather than being 'the kind of wife who went to the lands to plough' (p. 80), Neo adjusts in other ways to community demands, becoming less aloof and more engaged in the life of the village. The community despises Neo for her 'conceit and pride' (p. 77) and appreciates the 'natural' Mathata, who is 'smiling and happy' (p. 78) despite her impregnation and abandonment by the man whom Neo is going to marry. This opposition—whereby the educated woman is conceited and the uneducated woman content—is one of the givens of the story.

There *are* suggestions of an ironic stance being taken in the text towards this rural community's construction of a dutiful wife: the phrase 'we all have our ways' may seem sinister to some readers, and so may the manner in which the relatives 'nod their heads in that fatal way, with predictions that one day life would bring [Neo] down' (p. 77). The reference to the sacrificial ox—'unaware of his sudden and impending end as meat for the wedding feast' (p. 76)—offers itself as a veiled allusion to the bride about to be sacrificed, and the fact that the marriage takes place at the police camp adds to the coercive undertones.

But these hints of the sinister or coercive can in the end only be part of the repressed of the text. The community of women exhort Neo to obedience in terms of the idyllic, which is in itself a marker of authorial sympathy—even yearning—in Head's writing: 'The hoe, the mat, the shawl, the kerchief, the beautiful flute-like ululating of the women seemed in itself a blessing on the marriage' (p. 80). Moreover, the final command 'Be a good wife! Be a good wife!' (p. 80), given by the aunt, is placed in the context of ritual and habitual gesture which form so important a part of Head's presented world. The aunt pounds the ground in a gesture symbolic of the act of pounding the newly-laid floor of the young couple's dwelling and, just before this, an old woman dashes towards Neo and chops at the ground with a hoe, symbolising the agricultural work which traditionally falls to women. Such acts—pounding floors, smearing walls, thatching roofs—contribute throughout Head's collection of stories to a harmonious village atmosphere, for they belong to a life made up of group activities and the sharing of tasks. The very congruence in this story between the aunt's gestures of pounding, the old woman's gestures of hoeing and the words themselves might add to the atmosphere of coercion lurking in the story's subtext. However, in the story's smooth return to the opening atmosphere of idyll, the village women deny the possibility of the existence of 'new' women who are other than 'good' wives.

Head expressed her attitude to the subjection of women in strong terms:

> In the old days a woman was regarded as sacred only if she knew her place, which was in her yard with her mother-in-law and children. A number of oppressive traditions, however, completely obliterated her as a thinking, feeling, human being and she was exploited in all sort of ways. So heavy is the toll of centuries on the women of Botswana, that even with present-day political independence for the country, one finds that the few highly literate women of the country talk in uncertain terms of their lives and fear to assert themselves.[3]

This would seem to invite an ironic reading of 'Snapshots of a Wedding', with the narrator characterised as a 'village narrator', as Sara Chetin suggests, morally quite distinct from the writer herself.[4] There are no formal indications, however, that the third-person narrator is intradiegetic, and the very covertness of the narrative position suggests 'reliability'.[5] The motive behind an ironic reading is presumably the need to account for the sharp reference on the part of the primary narrator to Neo's 'conceit and pride'. In my own reading, however, the narrative voice is intricately structured around the writer's personal and political anxieties and desires.

The 'new' woman appears in expanded form under the name Life, in the short story of that name. The way she is depicted will help clarify Head's relation to modern women and the community, as well as to feminism. Life, who returns to her village from Johannesburg after an absence of many years, represents the world of urban capitalism, its commercial ethic particularly evident in the contamination of sex by money. In the rural world, sex flows freely ('People's attitude to sex was broad and generous'—[p. 39]); in the world introduced by Life, money flows freely and sex becomes unfree—paid for by the men, and then paid for, in a different way, by Life. When she marries Lesego, he demands fidelity, and kills her when she disobeys.

This might have been a story about a 'new' woman coming into a world which is character-

ised by male ownership of the female body, and trying to insist—within a tradition of feminism—that her body is her own. But this is not, quite, the story Head writes, although in one important respect a feminist judgement *is* being made: the brief prison sentence Lesego is given for killing an unfaithful wife stands in obvious and sharp contrast to the death sentence delivered on Dikeledi in 'The Collector of Treasures' for killing the husband who abuses her and leaves her to feed, clothe and rear their children alone. Life is associated with the beer-brewers, 'a gay and lovable crowd who had emancipated themselves some time ago' (p. 39). The term 'emancipated' puts them in their place: it is offered with as much sharp disfavour as the term 'hysterical' (p. 42), used in relation to Life's behaviour. Life exhibits 'the bold, free joy of a woman who had broken all the social taboos' (p. 40); the gaiety of the beer-brewing women is similarly out of bounds. They may have emancipated themselves from the commands 'Do this! Do that!' (which echo the commands under which Neo has been told to live) but this leaves them with 'a language all their own' (p. 39), divorced from the codes, gestures and rituals by which a culture knows itself.

Thus 'Life', like 'Snapshots', seems to become a vehicle for the rejection of all that Head takes women's emancipation to be. Yet both stories are more complex than this, for in their refusal of contemporary models of emancipation (as Head chooses to represent them) another possibility is opened up.

In 'Snapshots of a Wedding' the 'new' woman is drawn back into a community by means of a series of gestures which make up the community's way of constructing a world. The exhortation to hoeing is 'only a formality' (p. 79) (the women know that Neo already has a secretarial job, and do not expect her to hoe). This reference to 'formality' suggests that the words 'Be a good wife! Be a good wife!' themselves be placed in the context of what Head called, elsewhere, the 'courtesies' of community life.[6]

In 'Life' the direction of Head's thinking in this regard becomes clearer. The villagers recall a world of communality—the task-sharing marks a barter economy—but they are also caught in a world of barely flourishing peripheral capitalism, whose figure is the set of anaemic calves owned by Lesego. Even before Life's arrival 'the men hung around, lived on the resources of the women' (p. 39). The farmers and housewives, a group of women set apart from the beer-brewers, and called 'the intensely conservative hard-core of village life' (p. 39), admire Life's independence, for they live in a world where only men 'built up their own, individual reputations' (p. 41). But they turn away from her when she becomes a prostitute, in a moment important in the story as a whole, not least because it prefigures one of the story's closing moments. This is a comment made to Lesego by Sianana: 'Why did you kill that fuck-about? You had legs to walk away' (p. 46). Like Sianana, the 'conservative' women are marginal to the plot, whose focus falls on a drama enacted between the 'new' woman and characters not fully representative of rural society, as Head sees it—Life as against Lesego, not Sianana; in accord with the beer-brewers, not the farmers and housewives. But their response, as we shall see, is crucial.

The final word on the drama between Life and Lesego takes the form of a drunken song sung by the beer-brewing women about two worlds colliding. The worlds they refer to are the worlds we have seen in conflict: contemporary South Africa (Life) and contemporary Botswana (Lesego). The words they sing come from a song sung by Jim Reeves, a cowboy-type, like Lesego, as well as a voice from a corrupt world. There is no consolation to be drawn from either world; neither can offer the writer the future she wants. Her solution is to go [into] the world represented by the marginal characters, which functions as a sign of the past. It becomes the writer's business to reconstruct this past, and to depict it more fully, in subsequent stories. **'Snapshots of a Wedding'** also alludes to this project, pointing to the way the 'past' tries to *contain* the educated woman. The complexity of the concept of *containment,* suggesting incorporation and expansion as well as limitation and control, precisely reflects the precariousness of Head's literary-political project.

Head is under no illusion regarding the position of women in pre-industrial, pre-colonial Southern Africa. Any nostalgic indication of a conservative past is not intended to revive an old world where women were systematically marginalised, but to reject a new world—'Johannesburg', in this story—where individualism flourishes, but where neither men nor women can rely on having importance as individuals, where a section of the population lives a privileged existence, but where whole groups of people can be consigned to a life of material and psychological wretchedness, and where Life's apparently carefree slogan— 'live fast, die young, and have a good-looking corpse' (p. 40)—is both in itself the sign of entrapment in a world fundamentally hostile to women, and the heritage of a capitalist consumer culture,

FROM THE AUTHOR

HEAD ON GENDER AND WRITING
Writing is not a male/female occupation. My femaleness was never a problem to me, not now, not in our age. More than a century ago, a few pioneer women writers, writing fearfully under male pseudonyms, established that women writers were brilliant thinkers too, on a par with men. I do not have to be a feminist. The world of the intellect is impersonal, sexless. The young struggle with questions of literacy, nationalism in Africa. It is constructive to outline to the young the road one has travelled, the themes one has worked on in one's private workshop and the way in which life conspired to make one a writer. I have worked outside all political and other ideologies, bowing to life here and there and absorbing all that I felt to be relevant, but always fighting for space and air. I needed this freedom and independence, in order that I retain a clarity of thought, in order that my sympathies remain fluent and responsive to any given situation in life.

Head, Bessie. Excerpt from "Writing Out of Southern Africa." In *A Woman Alone: Autobiographical Writings*, p. 95. Nairobi, Kenya: Heinemann, 1990.

'glaring paltry trash'.[7] **'Life'** may be read, then, as a justification of Head's refusal to accept models of emancipation from the modern world. She wants not to see choice in terms of what is offered by two versions of the present, but to cut another route, taking the past as point of departure.

It is of course true that the text's use of the term 'hysterical' itself recalls the hysterical anxiety on the part of patriarchal culture towards women who have managed to break free of its rule; the congruence set up in the text between emancipation and sexual immorality or prostitution also betrays this hysterical response. Moreover, the conflation of 'feminism' and 'Johannesburg' or the world dominated by 'white' South Africa has its own political dangers: rebellious Black South African women are often slapped down as 'white'.[8] Nevertheless, it is worth taking seriously Head's desire to circumvent the package offered by the present, not only because the particular ways in which her writing returns to the past reveal a version of feminism other than that represented by the 'new' woman, not only because it is true that European models have often been hostile to Africa, but also because the route through the past corresponds, *mutatis mutandis,* to the direction being taken by other contemporary South African writers. Ellen Kuzwayo, for instance, has said that Black thinking on women would have developed differently were it not for the stultifying effect of laws entrenching 'ethnicity', many of which artificially elevate male authority over women: in this regard she constructs a certain version of the past in order to *inform,* like Head, the present and the future.[9]

Head's particular strategy is also symptomatic of the 'double allegiance' of African women writers to liberation from neo-colonialism on the one hand and to a feminist consciousness on the other.[10] One kind of reading may simply insist that this 'double allegiance' manifests itself in ambivalence and contradiction, but another kind of reading may see an altogether different shape emerging, finding its own precarious balance in a way which refuses the false polarity of national struggle and feminist struggle. Looking at some of the choices Head made through her writing career, and focusing particularly on the construction of the relation between women and community in some of the stories in *The Collector of Treasures,* her last published fiction, I intend in this essay to point to a certain feminism which, albeit by another name, is in the process of being forged in Black Southern Africa.

Community, Orality and the Question of Women

Speaking of her early life in apartheid South Africa, Head says:

> Twenty-seven years of my life was lived in South Africa but I have been unable to record this experience in any direct way, as a writer. . . . It is as though, with all those divisions and signs, you end up with no people at all. The environment completely defeated me, as a writer. I just want people to be people, so I had no way of welding all the people together into a cohesive whole.[11]

Using writing as 'some kind of shrine to go to—some means of spiritual survival',[12] Head made a home for herself out of what she saw as Botswana's potential to be a 'cohesive whole'. Her ideal community is characterised above all by continuity: temporal continuity, where the past is recalled in the present, with the sense of a continuing and secure future; continuity between people, where neighbours are truly neighbours and not identified and thus separated in terms of class and race; and continuity between economic existence and natural surroundings, or, in Marxist terms, between the individual and the mode of production. The need to idealise certain aspects of the Botswanan community is a personal *and* political need which does not prevent her from recognising that real-life Botswana falls short of this ideal, but does lead her to optimistic conclusions in the novels that precede *The Collector of Treasures.*

Her first novel, **When Rain Clouds Gather** (1969),[13] finds its main fictional dynamic in an abuse of chiefly power, and its resolution in rural resilience and co-operation on the part of the people. The next novel, **Maru** (1971),[14] presents the racist attitudes in Setswana society towards the Basarwa (the San, once called 'Bushmen' in white South African discourse) whom the text identifies as 'the slaves and downtrodden dogs of the Batswana' (p. 18). Resolution is provided through romantic love—the chief offers an example to his people by marrying Margaret, a Masarwa—and the implication that a new community is in the making. The marriage gives hope to the Basarwa: 'a door silently opened on the small, dark airless room in which their souls had been shut for a long time. The wind of freedom . . . turned and flowed into the room' (p. 126).

In Head's first two novels the main focus is on feudal class relations in the first novel and tribal or race relations in the second: the question of gender is subordinated to the question of relations between chiefly authority, community leaders, and people. However, **When Rain Clouds Gather** does allude to problems regarding the patriarchal objectification and marginalisation of women, and offers as a model a particular male/female relationship which is not marked by neglect or abuse. It is worth looking at this novel and the next in some detail, as they reveal crucial problems and issues in Head's specifically feminist concerns.

The question of gender in **When Rain Clouds Gather** is addressed in the context of the breakdown of family structure under the system of migrant labour, with the text suggesting that the development of family feeling in men, and specifically romantic love, might help reinstate family life. This proposition is buttressed by the possibility of material improvement: the agricultural work that the women perform (under male direction) will eventually restore fertility to an overgrazed land and thus relieve the country of poverty. Head sees the need for men to develop feeling towards both family and community: the harmony of the second depends on the harmony of the first. Interestingly, only part of the necessary consciousness is rooted in the past (old tribal customs forced Makhaya 'to care about children'—p. 119) and so it needs to combine with a newer strain, the capacity for romantic, monogamous attachment: 'In this way Makhaya differed from all African men' (p. 172). Makhaya is also uncharacteristic in treating women as his equals, and in his non-tribalism. He is a man of the future, who has made a specific break with the past: 'It was only once his father died that he was able to come forward with his own strange Makhaya smiles and originality of mind' (p. 124).

At one point in the text, after a comment about women who are 'dead' because of their habitual abjection, the narrator suggests that 'even if a door opened somewhere' most women would not be able to grasp their freedom (p. 126). Only Paulina offers the hint of an exception; Maria, a woman composed of two selves, subordinates her feminist self to a self 'soft', 'meditative' and obedient (pp. 101, 103). In *Maru* a door is opened, but not on the question of gender. This is to say that the 'wind of freedom' which blows through the door is directed only at the Basarwa. The wind that Margaret feels, as woman, is a 'strong wind' (p. 103) blowing, as it were, in the opposite direction: towards a vision of romantic love which materialises in a marriage which promises to be the site of domestic subjection.

This signals, of course, a subtextual interest in gender. Yet, in a fascinating textual and ideological complication, Margaret's (like Dikeledi's) subordination within the ideology of romantic love cannot be addressed for fear of disturbing the function romantic love plays in the novel. Romantic love sets the world in motion in *Maru*, on both the realistic and allegorical planes of the story: Moleka is urged into monogamy, which heralds a new existence for women, and Maru is given an occasion for solving racism. Love also sets in motion the power of creativity which surges through the text in various forms: in the creation myth with its neo-Lawrentian sun/moon/earth symbolism, and (to speak of compassion rather than romantic love) in the artistic vision of Margaret Cadmore II, which differs from the coldly scientific vision of the first Margaret Cadmore. It is true that the women characters in *Maru* escape the deathly docility of oppressed women referred to in the earlier novel: they are both teachers, Margaret is also an artist, and in certain respects

they know how to speak and think for themselves. Yet, even with the particular status given Dikeledi and Margaret within the framework of romantic love and monogamous marriage, which means that they are not consigned to 'some back room' (*When Rain Clouds Gather,* p. 124), the novel cannot help but give a sense of their subordination: Margaret because of the shift from financial and psychological independence, and Dikeledi because of the pain of loving more than she is loved. While this inequality is in an interesting way balanced by Margaret's ability to look away from Maru, for she also loves Moleka, the text keeps such meanings submerged, along with the whole question of gender. Some of them emerge in *A Question of Power* (1974),[15] Head's third novel, where humiliation, dependence and pain become the major topic. This makes all the more imperative the careful definition of romantic love that will take place in *The Collector of Treasures* if Head's social vision of family and community is to be possible.

But the particular anguish of *A Question of Power* goes deeper than this, for it records what Head has pointed to as a growing and finally devastating recognition that cruelty and lack of compassion could exist as readily in Botswana as in South Africa, and could, equally, be a part of her own psyche: 'there is a line that forms the title of the book—if the things of the soul are really a question of power then anyone in possession of the power of the spirit could be Lucifer'.[16] The particular forms taken by the 'madness' of the narrative self in this novel dramatise the artificial divisions or splits at war in the racist, sexist social order. The text's affirmative ending—which reads more like an act of will than an organically conceived resolution—is again constructed around the sense of community, which (appropriately to Head's general project) is emphatically placed as vision rather than reality: '[falling asleep, Margaret] placed one soft hand over her land. It was a gesture of belonging.'[17]

After this novel of personal breakdown, Head moved away for a while from fiction, with its particular inward-turning, and began to collect oral tradition, as if needing by this means to bring community and communality once again to the foreground. She collected and transcribed the set of oral accounts that would make up *Serowe: Village of the Rain Wind* (1981);[18] some of these would later provide the germs for the short stories in *The Collector of Treasures*.[19] (Though published later, *Serowe* precedes *The Collector of Treasures*.)

Despite these close links, the books differ from each other in two major ways, both of them of import for the argument being developed in this essay. One difference is the writer's insertion of women into the presented world. With the exception of the anecdote that produces **'Heaven is not Closed'**, the oral accounts give virtually no sense of women's presence. The other difference concerns the question of orality. Even as the record of oral accounts, *Serowe* retains little connection with orality, since the performative element is missing: the gestures, expressions and movements of the oral tale-teller are silenced in the literal transcription. In *The Collector of Treasures,* however, Head strives, as writer, to recreate that sense of performance. We need to look at this process first, before we turn to the textual incorporation of women.

As part of their artistic reconstruction of the oral tradition, Head's texts incorporate into the ontology of the presented world both storyteller and audience, setting up one or more subordinate narrators—distinct from the authorial narrator—as well as a group of listeners. Through these devices the reader is invited to adopt a spatio-temporal perspective within that world, becoming part of the community. This is a common device in regional literature which intends to seduce the outside metropolitan reader into its world, and is employed by writers as diverse as William Faulkner and Ama Ata Aidoo. Head's stories often reconstruct the gestures around the act of storytelling, referring to the postures, positions and physical responses of both storyteller and audience, and thus continue to reinforce the sense of a community gathering together to tell and to hear a tale.

In a slightly different way, Head's writing recalls the oral tradition by incorporating into the collection: (a) genealogy, or epic history; (b) proverbs and sayings; and (c) gossip and community responses to events and people. These three devices draw attention to the continuing presence and contemporary reconstruction of community voice and community values, reminding the reader that in a culture with no written history, no codified legal system, no written text books, it is word-of-mouth accounts, passed from generation to generation, in a process of frequent debate, which provide history, entertainment, education and law. For the first story in the collection the narrator draws on community memory in order to present the genealogy of the Taloate people, who broke away from the Monamapee people, thus placing the written text within the

oral tradition, that 'ancient stream of holiness' (*Collector of Treasures*, p. 11) referred to in her story **'Heaven is not Closed'**.

Head also sometimes incorporates proverbs and sayings into her narrative, in a way comparable to, although considerably less often and less explicitly than, Chinua Achebe in *Things Fall Apart,* where the male speakers deploy the proverb in order to reach back to traditional wisdom for their authority. In **'Jacob: the Story of a Faith-Healing Priest'**, Head has a woman speaker reach back for her authority. Johannah needs to justify herself in the face of accusations from her relatives about having entered a number of sexual relationships: 'At last Johannah was allowed to speak. She raised her hand proudly and quoted an old proverb: "I agree with all that has been said about me. . . . But I am a real woman and as the saying goes the children of a real woman do not get lean or die"' (p. 30). And she later repeats: 'the children of a real woman cannot fall into the fire' (p. 31).[20]

Probably the most noticeable example of orality in Head's texts is the constant use of 'they said', 'they exclaimed' and so on, which give the impression of everyone talking, having their say: a community of volubility. The standard trajectory of Head's stories is to open with a wide-angle focus on the community, to close in on individuals within that community, and to end with a focus on community again, so that the individual voice typically emerges from and then slips back into communality. The voice of the (impersonal, virtually invisible) authorial narrator is generally taken over by one or more voices within the community, or what I call here a community voice. Only in two stories is the primary narrator placed explicitly apart from the community; but in **'The Special One'** she is represented as a visitor being drawn into the village community, despite her initial remoteness and confusion, and in **'Jacob: the Story of a Faith-Healing Priest'** as the one gathering together the voices that will make up the full (written) story.

The implicit disjunction between literary and oral voice notwithstanding, there is as little reminder as possible in the stories generally of the literary as opposed to the oral, for Head's representation of the storyteller and storytelling involves a refusal both of the authorial authority and the authorial creative function that typically mark the literary text (I refer to the general realist tradition, within which Head writes). The shift is of course not to a modernist disappearance of the author and her replacement by the individual subject, but to an impression of communal creativity and communal response. In this regard there is a marked similarity between Head and other Black South African writers, although the particular strategies are very different: Noni Jabavu, for instance, whose project in *The Ochre People*[21] is virtually to repress the individual by means of the communal, and Ellen Kuzwayo, whose *Call Me Woman*[22] flips back and forth between the voice of the autobiographical subject and the voices, or lives, of other South African women.

One consequence of the authorial limitation of authority and the focus on community response is an invitation to the reader to share in the dramatic conflict around which the story pivots. Michael Thorpe, who also looks at Head's constructed kinship with the village storyteller of the oral tradition, attempts to come to terms with the various contradictions in Head's stories by arguing that 'the [authorial] narrator seems often to be telling the story as an exploration, as a way to develop or even question her own understanding'.[23] It is hard to say whether she *is* developing her own understanding by dramatising community responses, but certainly through this dramatisation Head reveals a desire not to construct the stories as an expression of moral judgement, and thus, I suggest, refuse to cast herself as outsider, as part of the world of missionaries, colonial legislators and judges and what she on one occasion calls the 'lily-white artist'.[24]

But even if Head as author of the literary text disappears behind the voice of the community and its varying and often uncertain intellectual and emotional responses, this does not mean that we do not periodically hear an authorial attitude at odds with the patriarchal communal voice. The opening story of the collection, **'The Deep River'**, heralds the concern with gender evident in many of the stories. Tracing the emergence of individual desire from the single 'face' (p. 1) of the people, the story represents the individual as specifically anti-patriarchal: young Sebembele falls in love with the woman possessed but not loved by his father. This picks up the father-son difference referred to earlier in relation to **When Rain Clouds Gather**, confirms that the concept of community has all too easily referred to a *patriarchal* community whose idea of cohesiveness depends on the subjection of women, and suggests that the idea of community will be differently defined.

Often the authorial attitude is explicit. Some of the critical statements regarding the community's treatment of women were mentioned at the start of the essay. **'The Collector of Treasures'**,

the title story, provides the most extended feminist statement, commenting on both pre-colonial and post-colonial times. Correspondingly, then, in view of her overall project, we shall see Head taking particular pains in this story to close the distance between feminist writer and oral community. In the collection as a whole she takes pains to represent the voices of women, and often 'hears' in these voices the origins of her own feminist voice.

The Voices of Women: Reconstructing Community

The feminist intervention in **'The Collector of Treasures'** reads as follows. In the pre-colonial African world women were regarded 'in a congenital sense, as being an inferior form of human life' (p. 92). By diminishing customary paternal authority, colonialism has also neutralised paternal responsibility, and in the process has helped entrench anti-female behaviour:

> The colonial era and the period of migratory mining labour to South Africa was a further affliction. . . . It broke the hold of the ancestors. It broke the old, traditional form of family life. . . . [The man] became 'the boy' of the white man. . . . Men and women, in order to survive, had to turn inwards to their own resources. It was the man who arrived at this turning point, a broken wreck with no inner resources at all. . . . [I]n an effort to flee his own inner emptiness, he spun away from himself in a dizzy kind of death dance of wild destruction and dissipation.
>
> (p. 92)

In general, Head's solution to the problems posed for women in such a community is to reconstruct patriarchalism by inserting or reinserting women into oral tradition, and thus both giving women a central moral place in communal life and creating a different kind of community. This process of reconstruction will also involve, as we shall see towards the end of this chapter, the creation of a different kind of male figure, who modifies the nature of the patriarchal community.

'The Wind and a Boy' concerns itself, particularly poignantly, with the idea of a woman trying to take charge of a story. The grandmother artfully incorporates into her storytelling that British novel which marks the start of the novelistic tradition, for she tells a wonderful story about Robinson Crusoe as a hunter who serves the community by killing an elephant. The grandmother, Sejosenye, is the Black and female Daniel Defoe; her grandson's name Friedman marks him as an emancipated version of the enslaved Friday. However, Friedman is killed within the ambit of an altogether uglier story: by 'progress' (p. 75) in the form of a 'small green truck' (p. 74) driven by a man with 'neither brakes on his car nor a driving licence' (p. 75): 'And thus progress, development, and a pre-occupation with status and living-standards first announced themselves to the village. It looked like being an ugly story with many decapitated bodies on the main road' (p. 75). When she learns of his death Sejosenye says, 'Can't you return those words back?' (p. 74), and spends the rest of her life feverishly singing and talking to herself, as if still desperately hoping to substitute her own story for someone else's version of progress.

In 'Kgotla' the focus is on people having their say, with the woman's moral authority voiced at the end of the story. Women were traditionally not allowed into the *kgotla,* the seat of tribal administration or council where court activities traditionally take place and, after the establishment of colonial rule with its magistrate's court, the 'people's place' (p. 62), where 'people could make their anguish and disputes heard' (ibid.). Under the leadership of Khama (Kgama III: 1875-1923) women were allowed for the first time to come to court to lodge a complaint personally rather than through a male sponsor.[25] Head observed that Khama gave women a 'feeling . . . that they could talk for themselves'.[26] Women are still excluded from being judges, but since, as the male judges admit, 'we can never settle cases at kgotla' (p. 68), it is noteworthy that the woman called Rose, who has had an unfair informal judgment passed on her by the community, is now in a formal setting able to produce her own words of generosity and commitment to the well-being of the community, thus providing a settlement accessible neither to the male judges nor her extended family nor the 'bureaucratic world' (p. 62) bequeathed by British rule, which had 'no time to listen' (p. 61).

In 'The Deep River' the oral account produced by the old men at the end of the story characterises the whole story as a piece of genealogy, or epic history. As the Africanist historian Basil Davidson notes, 'There is scarcely a modern African people without a more or less vivid tradition that speaks of movement from another place. Younger sons of paramount chief would hive off with their followers, and become paramount themselves in a new land.'[27] Epic history such as this is typically narrated by men.[28] Head, as woman writer, thus takes over the epic, inserting

women into a tradition which has excluded them. (Head later added *A Bewitched Crossroad*[29] to her historical *oeuvre.*)

What difference does the woman's voice make? At the very least, its presence invites one to take a critical perspective on patriarchalism. Within the general community the different values given to 'woman' become the sign of the community's internal differences: the new community is defined as one in which women are valued for more than their reproductive capacities. Nevertheless, the fact that difference speaks itself in the following way—some say 'A man who is influenced by a woman is no ruler. He is like one who listens to the advice of a child' (p. 3), others say 'Let him keep her' (ibid.), as if women were in some sense still like dogs—betrays the marks of *the same:* the romantic resolution continues to place woman as object rather than subject.

The ending of the story offers comment on the romantic resolution. Echoing Moleka's insistence in *Maru* that '[attractive] women like you are the cause of all the trouble in the world' (p. 83), this story ends:

> The old men there keep on giving confused and contradictory accounts of their origins, but they say they lost their place of birth over a woman. They shake their heads and say that women have always caused a lot of trouble in the world.
>
> (p. 6)

As the men see it, the story is thus one of loss rather than reparation, and the 'account' with which women are now credited is simply one of *blame,* the inverse of the romantic idealisation of women (in both moves they are the objects against which men define themselves and towards which they yearn). In this way 'The Deep River' puts under scrutiny its own romantic ending as well as, by implication, those of the earlier novels to which it indirectly alludes.

The resolution of the plot is provided by the marriage and the establishment of a new community, with the closure of the story represented as a patriarchal account. This juxtaposition (again) casts doubt on whether attitudes to women in the new community differ at all from the old. But, as I have suggested, only in one sense *is* this the story's last word: the story is ultimately *written* not by the old men but by the writer, a woman, who presides over all the tale-telling in the text, gathering, shaping, invisibly narrating, occasionally commenting, and taking to print. A gap thus opens up in 'The Collector of Treasures' between the oral account, defined here as a patriarchal account, and the written account which questions it, with the act of representation—the representation of women, and of romantic love—posing itself as an issue straddling that gap.

The writer's interest in elevating the voices of women, which she does in many of the subsequent stories, is in part an interest in reconstructing a male-dominated community. In this way Head heralds the current interest in South African literary and political life in hearing the voices of women. But the problem of the relation between men and women remains, even if women become more vocal, if the representation of women does not change: if, in other words, women still define women in terms of the patriarchal symbolic system, thus confirming themselves as the signs of the feminine as it is patriarchally conceived, however much the presence of women's voices seems otherwise to contradict such conceptions. The pressure on women in terms of the liberation struggle has been and still is enormous: men have spoken out publicly about the need for women to 're-encourage' them rather than to deflate or 'castrate' them, as if continuing the damage done by white racist rule.[30] Head's contribution in the face of this difficulty *is* to define masculinity in different terms, but at the same time to find the roots for this new masculinity in the past itself, as discussion of her 'new man', generally called her 'great man', will show.

The 'Great Man'/The 'New Man'

The period of reading and research in between writing *A Question of Power* and *The Collector of Treasures,* a period during which Head makes a turn from personal to community focus and also attends more carefully and explicitly to the position of women in the community, is also marked by Head's developing respect for Khama the Great, in whom she found qualities which cohered with what she had already been dreaming of in a figure like Makhaya. In a lengthy interview Head gave in 1983, there are fascinating links to be detected between what Head sees as the contribution of Khama the Great and the processes of her own creativity. Most obviously, Head's strong response to what she called Khama's 'balancing act'[31] offers itself as a model for her own literary project as it unfolds in *The Collector of Treasures.* In her view, Khama adopted a number of new practices from the 'West' without disrupting the continuity of traditional life, and managed to resist what Cecil Rhodes was planning for Botswana, thus saving the country 'from what happened to South Africa'.[32] More subtly, Khama functions as the god-like figure who replaces the 'Lucifer' referred to in relation to *A Question of Power,* affirming Head's vision of god-on-earth, and turning the author's potentiality for destructiveness on to the path of creativity and good.[33]

The great man, for Head, is one who is able to reform custom and tradition without losing the customary 'courtesies'. By this Head means more than ritual or social gesture; 'courtesies' refers above all to a consciousness of the community which expresses itself in community service and personal responsibility to family as well. The observance of such 'courtesies' helps forge in people an awareness of their own continuity, which involves an awareness of history, accessible through Botswana rather than South Africa, where the history is primarily one of 'land-grabbing wars and diamond- and gold-rushes', with 'whole breaks' instead of a 'beautiful pattern' of human coexistence.[34]

Besides being primarily concerned with the welfare and dignity of others, men and women alike, Head's great man has a 'broader view of life' which is the gift of the literary artist, too, who has 'the biggest view possible';[35] this view enables both man and writer to stand against racism, she says, and against sexism, as her fiction implies. Interestingly, Head suggests that this 'broader view' is developed from influences outside Botswana, even from South Africa, which 'with all its horrors, creates international sorts of people. They identify with the problems of mankind in general, rather than their own.'[36] She also says, 'It's not so much a question of being black as of having got control of life's learning.' All this, in her view, accounts for her literary contribution: the 'broader view' brought in from outside, along with her own freedom from particular customs and traditions, given the specific dislocations of her childhood as well as her foreignness in Botswana: 'I shape the future with this cool stance.'[37]

What Head means by 'life's learning' is not explicitly clarified, but—in view of her literary and other references—I conclude that it implies an interest in ideas, what she once called a 'life of the mind',[38] as well as book-learning of a particular kind: the agricultural knowledge that Gilbert brings to Botswana is the obvious example here. Head's alignment with the figure of the 'great man' who can solve Botswana's social problems is evident in her first novel, in the figure of Makhaya, a man from South Africa, de-tribalised and in search of a better world. Some contribution is made through his links with the communal past, to which he can make certain crucial adjustments of his own, given his 'broader [external] view'; other contributions are made through his absorption of Gilbert's university education and agricultural research.

But if Head is herself her own 'great man', she is also his creator. She makes clear that when these great men do not exist in reality they must be produced. Speaking of *Maru* she says: 'A Botswana chief is not going to marry a Masarwa and publicly make it a huge thing like that. But he was created to do it. . . . We don't walk around with gods in our heart. We have to have a character like that to solve racialism.' And speaking of the anecdote from which she wrote '**The Collector of Treasures**', she says, 'that's why the basic plot I borrowed from life. Now, when I actually wrote that story I mentioned all these things. I borrowed it exactly more or less as it happened, but there's a huge, majestic man that moves into the story—now he's going to solve all the problems.' The writer clearly distinguishes between the collected story and the invented story, the original taken from the reality that the oral tradition offers (a story from the community), with her version adding what reality fails to provide: 'you've got to solve a problem. . . . [Paul Thebolo] is juxtaposed against a man who has low animal tendencies—but the problem is it is all too much of a reality in the society, and the story wasn't entirely invented in my own head.'[39]

The language here bears out the terms with which *Maru* was discussed, Head in both cases distinguishing between reality and literary invention. Perhaps fancifully, but in tune I think with the unconscious logic of Head's thinking, my imagination has been caught by the use of her own surname in the phrase 'in my own head', whose juxtaposition against 'all too much of a reality' emphasises—her projected image as a writer who invents what is not provided by the oral and experienced material offered her in her village community, and who is engaged in the detached judgement that the word 'shaping' must imply. At the same time Head is anxious not to be seen as the 'lily-white artist' removed from communal life and its oral tradition. The 'writing of books', Head claimed, is like 'baking bread and peeling potatoes'.[40] Thus adjusting at least some of her references to 'life's learning', her stories take pains to reintegrate writing into such everyday acts, to make the figure of the artist a part of communal action and communal expression, and thus to make her fictional resolutions seem organic to the community rather than brought out of the 'head' of a remote outsider.

This is one of the contributions of *The Collector of Treasures*, offered, I think, as a kind of propitiation for her outsider status, and her learning, and—in the title story of the collection—as a screen for the radical way in which she rewrites the community.

'The Collector of Treasures'

'The Collector of Treasures' focuses on the work done by women's hands: Dikeledi, for instance, is good at knitting, sewing, weaving baskets and thatching. Then the text focuses, too, on the hands themselves, the beautiful hands of this creative woman: 'she had soft, caressing, almost boneless, hands of strange power—work of a beautiful design grew from those hands' (p. 90). With these hands, she says, she 'fed and reared [her] children' (p. 90). And with these hands, 'with the precision and skill of her hard-working hands' (p. 103) Dikeledi castrates her husband.

Given the implicit connections between creativity and the work that hands do, castration here signifies the creative and constructive rather than the destructive act. Dikeledi has another skill: 'she had always found gold amidst the ash, deep loves that had joined her heart to the hearts of others. . . . She was the collector of such treasures' (p. 91). That '**The Collector of Treasures**' is the title for the collection as a whole extends the referent of that phrase, even as it is used in this story, to the figure of the author herself: also a 'collector of treasures', whose heart has been 'joined' through her writing to the 'hearts of others', and who has also found gold amidst the ash. If Dikeledi is admired for 'the pattern she had invented in her own head' (p. 90), so now is the writer.

The connection between writer and creative character makes its conscious or semi-conscious emergence when Head speaks about first hearing the anecdote that provides the source for the story: 'it was so shocking to me, it was actually the first time I had ever heard of a man dying like that. When the relative told me, the first thing that I felt was the knife going through me. I even put my hand out.'[41] Initially, her response suggests an identification with the corrupted male figure who is being destroyed, himself destroyer of family life. But she also says that she puts her hand out, as if to take hold of that knife, which suggests an identification with Dikeledi. And, in fact, character and writer are linked, for the writer's characterisation of Paul Thebolo carries hints of metaphorical castration. Just after Garesego has been literally castrated, Thebolo steps 'out of the dark' (p. 103), with 'a tortured expression' (ibid.) on his face, and for a moment words fail him. Of course in the full metaphorical meaning of the term he is not 'castrated': the writer associates him throughout the story with power, in the positive sense, and even specifically with the power of virility (he is man enough for two women, the text tells us, but also man enough not to have to prove himself in that way). But, given the representation of Thebolo as kind, gentle and compassionate, a man who is not afraid to bind himself romantically to a single woman and who does not define his masculinity in a way that leaves mothering to women, Thebolo functions in the story as a 'feminised' hero, something like Makhaya in **When Rain Clouds Gather.**

Dikeledi stands as a figure for the author, then, and the castrating act is to be seen here as an equivalent of the writerly act. Or, to put it another way, the writerly act camouflages itself as a community act, as just one of the expressive acts women perform in a world that comes to the writer through the oral tradition. Having represented herself as the male god-like figure associated in her mind with Khama the Great, as I suggested earlier, Head takes this link further: 'what was beautiful about the man was that he would slice any harmful . . . eliminate . . . but keep'. The lexical choices here recall and extend the word 'slice' used for Garesego's genitals; the horror of that act still remains, as the hesitancy of expression suggests (the ellipses mark the hiatuses in Head's original speech).[42]

Why am I labouring this connection between Head and Dikeledi, and Head and the 'great man' curative figure, the social healer who comes in with elements from an imagined world which are the products to some extent of the Botswanan past and to some extent of an outsider's experience and detachment? There are two reasons: one to do with understanding the precariousness of Head's literary project as a 'balancing act', and the other to do with the question of feminism in South Africa today; the route that it tends to take through the African past, rather than the corrupted present; the oblique, courteous manner in which it takes up its feminist voice; the merging of the individual voice with the voice of the community; and the continual elevation of communality. Like **'Life'** and **'Snapshots of a Wedding'**, **'The Collector of Treasures'** is a tale about the modern world which has lost the values of the communal world. But here the modern world is represented not by 'conceited' or 'hysterical' women, but by the way Dikeledi's life has been ruined by Garesego. Moreover, in this world, neighbours shun Dikeledi, which means that (apart from her idyllic relations with Thebolo and Kenalepe) she does not live in communality.

Then it is also about an ideal world, which the writer has constructed as a vision of the (reconstructed) past. The relationship between Dikeledi, Kenalepe and Paul is built on barter, neighbourliness and task-sharing, with paternal responsibility and romantic love put forward as the two major components of Head's feminist vision. We even almost shift back into a world of polygyny, for Kenalepe suggests that Dikeledi become Thebolo's unofficial second wife, taking over the conjugal duties that Kenalepe, pregnant, does not wish to perform, and experiencing a sexual pleasure Dikeledi's husband was too brutish to make possible. Kenalepe *offers* her husband to Dikeledi, proposing (in small) a kinship system where women are the negotiators rather than the objects of exchange. Nevertheless, this textual direction into the (idealised and redirected) polygynous past is deflected, and the nuclear family, bound by monogamous romantic love and paternal responsibility, is maintained as one of the elements of Head's idyll.

Within these two tales there are two acts: literal castration and feminisation. The act of castration is the solution of a group of women *in the world*. Given to Head through the oral tradition, it may thus be placed in a communal world; moreover, all the women in the prison have killed their husbands. But it keeps them imprisoned: if they form a happy community of women within the wider community, they are also set apart, kept in a space characterised by high walls and an anxious male warder who insists that the women stand with their hands at their sides: 'He does not mind anything but that. He is mad about that' (p. 90). The act of feminisation is the solution offered by the literary artist, pointing to a new world premised on what Head sees as the best of the old (task-sharing, barter, communal cohesion) and the best of the new (romantic love, nuclear family, monogamy, greater value and voice for women, men stripped of their phallic egos). Although the act of writing is not referred to, it becomes associated, through the association of feminisation with castration, with the other creative acts I have mentioned, and thus characterised as a communal act, where writing is linked to thatching and knitting and weaving, the acts women perform in their construction of home and community. Thus the writer defines herself not as a *writer* who stands outside the community, but as a figure within. However much the act of writing may look like an extraneous act—for it produces what is not produced by a rural, predominantly pre-literate community—it becomes, in this story, part of the oral/communal act. And so it is that the writer places herself within a community, reconstructed in terms of a feminism whose origins are now not outside, but inside.

In 'The Special One' the first-person narrator makes its only extended appearance,[43] and in certain ways the device functions to blur the separation made in this essay, largely on the basis of Head's own statements, between the literary, individual and feminist voice and the oral, communal and patriarchal voice. It is not, at first, the narrator but one of the rural characters who says 'women are just dogs in this society' (p. 81). Marked as an outsider to the community, the peripheral narrator comes to take that belief as her own, as if she has been educated by this woman's story. In this way Head establishes a feminist voice as organic to the community, which is now—in general terms—largely defined by the voices and judgements of women.

The question of representation is raised, as I have said, in 'The Deep River'. Women are viewed by one section of the male population in terms of their reproductive functions, and then by another section as the objects of romantic love, which simply leads to their being finally placed in the patriarchal shuttle between praise and blame. Head's incorporation of women's voices and women's views means that women can no longer be considered 'of no account'. Conservative her project certainly remains, for although it expands and adjusts the nature of community and family to make a more hospitable space for women, it also calls upon the feminine in its conventional idealised associations: in 'Kgotla', for instance, Rose is valued for her self-sacrifice to the larger good of the extended family, and in 'Jacob' the proverb Johanna brings forward from the past defines her as 'real woman' precisely through her motherhood.

Yet such moments of representation need to be seen in the context of Head's careful redefinition of masculinity in precisely the terms accorded the feminine: generosity, compassion, self-sacrifice and motherliness. These are the community 'courtesies' being demanded of both men and women. Head's new men in *The Collector of Treasures* eschew greed and power, and are characterised by generosity and humility, like Tholo in 'Hunting' and Thebolo in 'The Collector of

Treasures' in their realised forms, and like Sianana in 'Life' and Friedman in 'The Wind and a Boy' in their potential. For specific textual indications that Head's characterisation of such men is to be read as a feminising act, beyond the subtle metaphor set up in 'The Collector of Treasures', we may go to the story 'Hunting', where one of the villagers says of Tholo: 'I don't know whether he is a girl or what' (p. 105). And, reversing the conventional literary situation where men are the poets and women the poems, Thebolo in 'The Collector of Treasures' is 'a poem of tenderness' (p. 93).

Thinking again of the construction of community in 'Snapshots of a Wedding', any authorial correction that might await this community would involve Neo's husband, in the terms offered by 'The Collector of Treasures' and 'Hunting'. Neo herself has been defined as 'good wife', and the story makes clear that this function is to be seen in communal rather than simply familial terms. Life, in 'Life', cannot be contained by the community in this way, for she lacks—like Head's damaged modern men—the resources to see village life as anything but a 'big, gaping yawn' (p. 43). Head's feminism directs itself away from any tendency in middle-class feminist practice to take male access to power and independence as its model; individualism is defined as 'conceit', unacceptable in both women and men. Given Head's *de facto* relation with the Botswanan community, this approach must involve repressing—or containing—certain aspects of herself.

Noni Jabavu, also writing about the problem posed to the community by modern manners in men and women (in the Eastern Cape rather than Botswana) refers to the 'chasms [that] yawned before you' if your 'personal inclinations and habits' of privacy 'tended against the principle' of sociability, which she glosses as an 'exposure to the public gaze'.[44] The topic is slightly different, and the points of departure and destination are too, for throughout *The Ochre People* Jabavu represents herself as obedient to patriarchal rules about women. Yet what binds Head and Jabavu, and Kuzwayo as well, is their recognition of the risk people take when they separate themselves from the demands made in the name of community, for this leaves them without a social structure by which to know themselves. Although Head and Jabavu accept the cost of this communal incorporation, the word 'yawn' in both cases betrays a semi-conscious resistance, and briefly points to the gap that necessarily exists between modern, cosmopolitan, highly educated writer and rural, conservative, pre-literate community.

To what extent are Head's women freed from the grip of patriarchal ideology? Even in **'The Collector of Treasures'**, within the idealised world created between Dikeledi, Kenalepe and Paul, Dikeledi and Kenalepe still sit 'on the edge' (p. 95) of male political debate about colonialism and independence, listening but never participating, although they go over the discussions themselves the next day. Perhaps at this moment, despite the idealised representation in other respects, Head feels herself limited by social reality. As Miriam Tlali has explained regarding her own writing, her women characters play a supportive role to their husbands not because she thinks women ought to, but because in reality they are not allowed to come to the forefront.[45] However much Head's women characters *are* brought to the forefront, their voices preside over rural communal and familial concerns, and do not extend into the politics of modern life.

The main project of this essay has been to *listen* to the contribution being made by Head to the question of feminism, and to recognise some aspects of the personal and political desire that lies behind some of her textual decisions and strategies. But it must also be said that an ideological gap keeps opening up between Head as writer (that is, the position formulated in her texts) and myself as (white, urban, post-Lacanian) critic, precisely over the representation of women as mothers and wives, over the ideological place of family and community, and over the definition of feminism itself, to say nothing of the difficulty of translating Head's vision into an urban environment and making it speak in the face of contemporary political realities, however, much I yearn, like her, to find a place in Africa no longer marked by 'all those divisions and signs'.

Notes

1. 'Bessie Head: Interviewed by Michelle Adler, Susan Gardner, Tobeka Mda and Patricia Sandler', in C. MacKenzie and C. Clayton (eds), *Between the Lines* (Grahamstown, S. Africa: National English Literary Museum, 1989) p. 11.

2. Bessie Head, *The Collector of Treasures and Other Botswanan Village Tales* (London: Heinemann Educational, 1977) pp. 3, 83.

3. Bessie Head, 'Despite Broken Bondage, Botswana Women are Still Unloved', *The Times,* 13 August 1975, p. 5.

4. While Chetin's analysis of *The Collector of Treasures* is interesting and useful, her desire to read Head's narrator as a 'village narrator' and her general focus on myth ('around which all our lives are constructed') mean that she is not engaged with the specificities of the writer's relation with the village community, which I need to look at as part of a political debate. Another difference between Chetin's approach and mine is that she is interested in the 'distinctly ambiguous, unresolved tone' in Head's writing, whereas my interest lies in tonal precariousness, which again involves political intentions (S. Chetin, 'Myth, Exile and the Female Condition: Bessie Head's *The Collector of Treasures', Journal of Commonwealth Literature,* Vol. 24, no. 1 (1989) pp. 132, 115, 114).

5. S. Rimmon-Kenan, *Narrative Fiction: Contemporary Poetics* (London: Methuen, 1983) p. 103.

6. 'There were so many things in African custom and tradition that were good. You had to offer life certain courtesies' (MacKenzie and Clayton (eds), *Between the Lines,* p. 16).

7. 'The cheap, glaring paltry trash of a people who are living it up for themselves alone dominates everything' (Bessie Head, 'African Story', *Listener,* vol. 88, no. 2279 (1972) p. 736).

8. Kirsten Holt Peterson quotes a South African woman speaking as follows:

> In South Africa the question of Western feminism, encroaching into the minds of the African women is a very, very sensitive question, particularly for the African man. Anytime you ask him to do something, to go and fetch the child today, or something like that he says: 'Look, you are already a feminist. You are a white woman and a feminist.' It is thrown into your face in the same way in which Communist is thrown into the face of the blacks in South Africa.
>
> K. H. Peterson (ed.), *Criticism and Ideology: Second African Writers' Conference, Stockholm 1986* (Uppsala: Scandinavian Institute of African Studies, 1988) p. 185

> Like most other South African (and African) women writers, Head did not call herself a feminist. But this was not for fear of being called 'white': 'I do not have to be a feminist. The world of the intellect is impersonal, sexless. . . . I have worked outside all political and other ideologies, bowing to life here and there and absorbing all that I felt to be relevant, but always fighting for space and air. I needed this freedom and independence, in order that my sympathies remain fluent and responsive to any given situation in life'.
> ('Writing out of Southern Africa', *New Statesman,* 16 August 1985, p. 22)

9. Ellen Kuzwayo has spoken of the way the South African government has capitalised on the traditions and customs of Black South Africans in an interview with Beata Lipman (B. Lipman, *We Make Freedom* (London: Pandora Press, 1984) p. 18). For further discussion of Kuzwayo's feminism, in relation to Black Consciousness, see D. Driver, 'M'a-Ngoana O Tsoare Thipa ka Bohaleng—The Child's Mother Grabs the Sharp End of the Knife: Women as Mothers, Women as Writers', in M. Trump (ed.), *Rendering Things Visible: Essays on South African Literary Culture* (Johannesburg: Ravan Press, 1990) pp. 225-55.

10. See C. B. Davies, 'Introduction: Feminist Consciousness and African Literary Criticism', in C. B. Davies and A. A. Graves (eds), *Ngambika: Studies of Women in African Literature* (Trenton, N. J.: Africa World Press, 1986) p. 1.

11. B. Head, 'Some Notes on Novel Writing', *New Classic*, vol. 5 (1978) p. 30.

12. Quoted in J. Marquard, 'Bessie Head: Exile and Community in Southern Africa', *London Magazine*, vol. 18, nos. 9 and 10 (1978) p. 54.

13. B. Head, *When Rain Clouds Gather* (London: Heinemann Educational Books, 1987). Page references to this novel are given in the essay itself.

14. B. Head, *Maru* (London: Heinemann Educational Books, 1972). Page references to this novel are given in the essay itself.

15. B. Head, *A Question of Power* (London: Heinemann Educational Books, 1974).

16. Quoted in Marquard, 'Bessie Head', p. 53. In 'Some Notes on Novel Writing', Head says 'I found myself in a situation where there was no guarantee against the possibility that I could be evil too' (p. 31).

17. Head, *A Question of Power*, p. 206. Head noted that she balanced the 'inward turning' of the book by incorporating 'an everyday world where a little village gets on with its everyday affairs and is interested in progress and development' ('Bessie Head', in L. Nichols (ed.), *Conversations with African Writers* (Washington, D.C.: Voice of America, 1981) p. 54).

18. B. Head, *Serowe: Village of the Rain Wind* (London: Heinemann Educational Books, 1981).

19. See Craig MacKenzie, 'Short Fiction in the Making: the Case of Bessie Head', *English in Africa* (Grahamstown), vol. 15, no. 1 (1988) pp. 17-28.

20. Bessie Head gives formal acknowledgement to C. L. S. Nyembezi, *Zulu Proverbs* (Johannesburg: Witwatersrand University Press, 1954), which draws attention to the frequent incorporation of proverbs in her writing, but I am referring here to the self-conscious use of proverbs by characters in dialogue. In 'Life' Head presents a saying in the making: 'I'm not like Lesego with money in the bank' (*Collector of Treasures*, p. 41).

21. N. Jabavu, *The Ochre People* (London: John Murray, 1963).

22. E. Kuzwayo, *Call Me Woman* (Johannesburg: Raven Press, 1985).

23. M. Thorpe et al., *Essays in African Literature* (Mysore, India: Center for Commonwealth Literature and Research, University of Mysore, 1978) p. 414.

24. MacKenzie and Clayton (eds), *Between the Lines*, p. 24.

25. For a discussion of Khama's revisions regarding the *kgotla* see I. Schapera, *Tribal Innovators: Tswana Chiefs and Social Change, 1795-1940* (London: University of London, The Athlone Press, 1970) p. 93. Schapera also discusses Khama's abolition of *bogadi* (p. 93) and his revision of the laws of inheritance for women (pp. 144-5). Head refers to these changes in 'Bessie Head', in MacKenzie and Clayton (eds), *Between the Lines*, p. 16. Schapera is probably her source.

26. MacKenzie and Clayton (eds), *Between the Lines*, p. 16.

27. Quoted in Thorpe, p. 416, n. 71.

28. Research by Harold Scheub and A. C. Jordan shows a gender division in the oral tradition: epic history is typically narrated by men, generally as part of public performance, whereas the narrative fictional tale is the domain of women, and told in a domestic setting. See A. C. Jordan, *Tales from Southern Africa* (Berkeley, Cal.: California University Press, 1973) pp. 1-2; H. Scheub, *The Xhosa Ntsomi* (London: Oxford University Press, 1975) pp. 5-6, 12. The division is not rigid, except in the obviously significant case of public performance. Elizabeth Gunner confirms that although women do participate in the genre of the praise poem, closely linked to the epic, their recital-performances are conducted in the company of women. See E. Gunner, 'Songs of Innocence and Experience: Women as Composers and Performers of *Izibongo*, Zulu Praise Poetry', in C. Clayton (ed.), *Women and Writing in South Africa: A Critical Anthology* (Johannesburg: Heinemann, 1989) pp. 13, 16.

29. B. Head, *A Bewitched Crossroad* (New York: Paragon House, 1986).

30. The term 're-encourage' comes from V. February in conference discussion, November 1986: 'South African Literature: Liberation and the Art of Writing' Special Issue of *Dokumente Texte und Tendenzen*, vol. 7 (1987) p. 79. A similar point has been made by the psychologist N. C. Manganyi, *Being-Black-in-the-World* (Johannesburg: Spro-cas/Ravan, 1973) pp. 10-11. This desire for support is what lies behind the accusations of 'white-ism' referred to earlier.

31. MacKenzie and Clayton (eds), *Between the Lines*, p. 16.

32. B. Fradkin, 'Conversation with Bessie', *World Literature Written in English* (WLWE), vol. 17, no. 2 (1987) p. 432.

33. Bessie Head wrote:

> I have used the word God in a practical way in my books. I cannot find a substitute word for all that is most holy but I have tried to deflect people's attention into offering to each other what they offer to an Unseen Being in the sky. When people are holy to each other, war will end, human suffering will end. . . . I would propose that mankind will one day be ruled by men who are God and not greedy, power-hungry politicians.
>
> ('Writing out of Southern Africa', p. 23)

34. MacKenzie and Clayton (eds), *Between the Lines*, p. 11.

35. Ibid., p. 13.

36. Fradkin, 'Conversations with Bessie', p. 429.

37. MacKenzie and Clayton (eds), *Between the Lines*, p. 13.

38. Quoted in Marquard, 'Bessie Head', p. 51. At various times in interviews and essays Head refers to reading Russian novelists and Indian philosophers, as well as historians and anthropologists of Southern Africa. Among the writers she singles out for mention and/or quotes from are Bertolt Brecht, Chinua Achebe, D. H. Lawrence, Gabriel Garcia Marquez and Olive Schreiner. *When Rain Clouds Gather* shows her own keen interest in agricultural research.

39. See MacKenzie and Clayton (eds), *Between the Lines*, pp. 19, 14, 13. However, I have quoted from the original transcript of the taped interview, held at the

National English Literary Museum (NELM), Grahamstown, since this is a slightly fuller and more faithful version. See pp. 17, 11, 10 of typescript held at NELM. In 'Writing out of Southern Africa' Head says, 'I would propose that mankind will one day be ruled by men who are God and not greedy, power-hungry politicians. . . . Only then can the resources of the earth be cared for and shared in an equitable way among all mankind' (p. 23).

40. Ibid., p. 24.

41. Ibid., p. 14.

42. I have again quoted from the original transcript of the taped interview (p. 13; See note 39 above). The published version edits the original to read, 'So he would eliminate, but keep' MacKenzie and Clayton (eds), p. 16.

43. It is one of the contentions of this essay that the first-person point of view lies behind the authorial narrative situation of all the stories in the particular sense that Head as writer has collected and shaped these tales. What I mean here is made clear in 'Jacob: the Story of a Faith-Healing Priest', although instead of using the first-person pronoun the text uses the word 'you', in order to camouflage the first-person relation with the story: 'There is a point in the story when you begin to doubt . . .'; 'you lean forward eagerly . . . [and] ask . . .'; 'So you say, almost violently . . .' (p. 25).

44. Jabavu, *The Ochre People,* p. 132.

45. 'Miriam Tlali: Interviewed by Cecily Lockett', in MacKenzie and Clayton (eds), *Between the Lines,* p. 75.

FURTHER READING

Biographies

Abrahams, Cecil, ed. *Tragic Life: Bessie Head and Literature in Southern Africa.* Trenton, N.J.: Africa World Press, 1990, 131 p.

Collection of essays that explore Head's personal life, politics, and spirituality.

Eilersen, Gillian Stead. *Bessie Head: Thunder behind Her Ears: Her Life and Writing.* Portsmouth, N.H.: Heinemann, 1995, 312 p.

Covers Head's life and development as a writer, with information on her travels abroad.

Criticism

Bazin, Nancy Topping. "Venturing into Feminist Consciousness: Two Protagonists from the Fiction of Buchi Emecheta and Bessie Head." *SAGE: A Scholarly Journal on Black Women* 2, no. 1 (spring 1985): 32-36.

Analyzes budding African feminist concerns in novels by Buchi Emecheta and Head.

Flockemann, Miki. "Breakdown and Breakthrough? The Madness of Resistance in *Wide Sargasso Sea* and *A Question of Power." MaComère* 2 (1999): 65-79.

Explores the relation of living in exile to the search for identity and, ultimately, to madness in Wide Sargasso Sea *and* A Question of Power.

Ibrahim, Huma. *Bessie Head: Subversive Identities in Exile.* Charlottesville: University of Virginia Press, 1996, 252 p.

Posits that women of third-world countries are inherently subversive, examining Head's works in this context.

————, ed. *Emerging Perspectives on Bessie Head.* Trenton, N.J.: Africa World Press, 2003, 326 p.

Collection of essays representing the most recent scholarship on Head.

MacKenzie, Craig. *Bessie Head.* New York: Twayne Publishers, 1999, 140 p.

Thematic analysis of each of Head's works, including those published posthumously.

Matsikidze, Isabella P. "Toward a Redemptive Political Philosophy: Bessie Head's *Maru." World Literature Written in English* 30, no. 2 (autumn 1990): 105-109.

Explores Maru *to find evidence of Head's political philosophy as it appears in her fiction.*

Ola, Virginia U. "Women's Role in Bessie Head's Ideal World." *Ariel* 17, no. 4 (October 1986): 39-47.

Examines Head's celebration of the life of the individual woman in her novels.

Osei-Nyame Jr., Kwadwo. "Writing between 'Self' and 'Nation': Nationalism, (Wo)manhood, and Modernity in Bessie Head's *The Collector of Treasures and Other Botswana Village Tales." Journal of the Short Story in English,* no. 39 (autumn 2002): 91-107.

Argues that Head, despite her unusual parentage and lack of family history, was not constrained in her writing by her sense of "otherness" in male-dominated black African society.

Taylor, Carole Anne. "Tragedy Reborn(e): *A Question of Power* and the Soul-Journeys of Bessie Head." *Genre* 26, nos. 2-3 (summer-fall 1993): 331-51.

Explores Head's use of the genre of tragedy in A Question of Power, *specifically as it relates to African women's suffering.*

OTHER SOURCES FROM GALE:

Additional coverage of Head's life and career is contained in the following sources published by the Gale Group: *African Writers; Black Literature Criticism; Black Writers,* Eds. 2, 3; *Concise Dictionary of World Literary Biography,* Vol. 3; *Contemporary Authors,* Vols. 29-32R, 119; *Contemporary Authors New Revision Series,* Vols. 25-82; *Contemporary Literary Criticism,* Vols. 25, 67; *Dictionary of Literary Biography,* Vols. 117, 225; *DISCovering Authors Modules: Multicultural; DISCovering Authors 3.0; Encyclopedia of World Literature in the 20th Century,* Ed. 3; *Exploring Short Stories; Feminist Writers; Literature Resource Center; Major 20th-Century Writers,* Eds. 1, 2; *Reference Guide to Short Fiction,* Ed. 2; *Short Stories for Students,* Vols. 5, 13; *Short Story Criticism,* Vol. 52; *World Literature and Its Times,* Vol. 2; and *World Writers in English,* Vol. 1.

LILLIAN HELLMAN

(c. 1905 - 1984)

American playwright, scriptwriter, memoirist, short story writer, director, critic, and editor.

Hellman was a critically and popularly acclaimed playwright. Her work was occasionally political and often controversial, and the events of her personal life garnered as much publicity as her writing. She is best known for her plays *The Children's Hour* (1934) and *The Little Foxes* (1939), and her memoir of the McCarthy era, *Scoundrel Time* (1976).

BIOGRAPHICAL INFORMATION

An only child, Hellman was born in New Orleans on June 20 in either 1905 or 1906, to Max Hellman and Julia Newhouse Hellman. Although both parents were descended from German Jewish families who came to the United States in the 1840s, Hellman's maternal relatives were far more successful in America than her father's family. Her father started a shoe company with the money he acquired through marriage, but the business failed and the family moved to New York City, where the Newhouses had relocated. Starting at the age of six, Hellman divided her time between her two vastly different extended families, spending summers in the well-appointed Newhouse quarters on the upper west side of Manhattan and winters in

the New Orleans boardinghouse run by her father's sisters. Her education suffered as a result of the frequent moves and the necessity of adjusting to different home environments and school districts. Hellman attended New York University from 1921 to 1924 and Columbia University in 1924 but dropped out of college in 1925 before finishing her degree. She worked briefly as a manuscript reader, and in December 1925 she married Arthur Kober, a publicist. She began doing publicity for plays and writing book reviews, publishing her first piece in the *New York Herald Tribune* in 1925.

The following year, Kober became editor of the literary journal *Paris Comet,* and the couple moved to France. Hellman began traveling around Europe and writing short stories, some of which were published in her husband's magazine. In 1929 the Kobers briefly returned to New York, where Hellman worked as a reader for Broadway plays, but a year later they moved to Hollywood, where Hellman took a position at Metro-Goldwyn-Mayer. There she met Dashiell Hammett, a well-known detective novelist, and the two began a relationship—both personal and professional—that lasted for thirty-one years, until Hammett's death in 1961. Hellman and Kober divorced amicably in 1932.

In 1934, having returned to New York with Hammett, Hellman produced her first play, the well-received but controversial *The Children's Hour,* which was nominated for a Pulitzer Prize. Her next effort, *Days to Come* (1936), was far less successful and closed after just a few performances. However, three years later she produced her most famous play, *The Little Foxes.* Hellman continued writing plays and screenplays throughout the 1940s, 1950s, and early 1960s. She retired from the theatre in 1963 and began writing her memoirs.

Hellman's politics, meanwhile, had embroiled her in further controversy. Frequently associated with liberal and radical causes, Hellman produced an editorial in the Screen Writers' Guild magazine critical of the Congressional House Committee on Un-American Activities. She was never actually charged with being a Communist, but she was blacklisted nonetheless and called to testify before the Committee in 1952. Refusing to name fellow writers and other Hollywood figures who might be Communists, Hellman wrote the Committee a letter that has often been reprinted as evidence of her personal principles. "I cannot and will not cut my conscience to fit this year's fashions," she informed the Committee, "even though I long ago came to the conclusion that I was not a political person and could have no comfortable place in any political group."

In 1969, however, she again became involved in politics, this time in opposition to the war in Vietnam. She remained active in the movement for many years. Throughout the 1970s she served as visiting lecturer at a variety of prestigious universities, among them Harvard, Yale, and Berkeley, until her declining health forced her to give up her strenuous schedule. A lifelong smoker, Hellman suffered from emphysema and died June 30, 1984, in Martha's Vineyard.

MAJOR WORKS

Hellman's first produced play, *The Children's Hour,* deals with a young girl who falsely accuses her school headmistresses of involvement in a lesbian relationship. The resulting scandal causes many parents to remove their daughters from the school, and although the lie is exposed in the end, one of the headmistresses has by this time committed suicide. A commercial and critical success, the play was nonetheless banned in Boston, London, and Chicago, and its failure to win the Pulitzer Prize was widely attributed to its controversial subject matter.

Hellman's next major work was *The Little Foxes,* a carefully-researched drama set in 1900 in an Alabama town. The ruthless members of the Hubbard family—characters inspired by Hellman's maternal relatives—vie for control of the family business in a plot involving larceny, blackmail, and murder. The moral center of the play is Addie, who is modeled on Hellman's childhood nurse, Sophronia Mason, the only figure from Hellman's early life to receive positive treatment in her plays.

Hellman turned to contemporary politics for her next play, *Watch on the Rhine* (1941), a tale of international intrigue set in Washington, D.C., but very much involved with the events in 1940 Nazi Germany. Aimed at inspiring Americans to abandon neutrality, the play was a success both critically and commercially; it won the Drama Critics Circle Award, and ran for 378 performances. In 1944 Hellman's most political work, *The Searching Wind,* opened in New York, and once again the playwright used a domestic setting to explore issues of fascism abroad.

After the war, Hellman returned to family matters with *Another Part of the Forest* (1946) and *The Autumn Garden* (1951). *Another Part of the Forest* is a prequel to *The Little Foxes,* while *The Autumn Garden* offers a considerable departure from Hellman's earlier style and is often regarded as her most mature dramatic work. *Toys in the Attic* (1960) was Hellman's last original play. Set in New Orleans, the plot involves interracial relationships, the hint of incestuous desire, and the dangers of living in the past.

Hellman's most famous non-dramatic works include her three memoirs: *An Unfinished Woman* (1969), *Pentimento: A Book of Portraits* (1973), and *Scoundrel Time* (1976). A chapter from *Pentimento,* which describes Hellman's 1937 mission to aid a childhood friend by smuggling currency to an anti-fascist group in Germany, became the basis for the motion picture *Julia* (1977). The story, along with Hellman's account of her role in the McCarthy hearings in *Scoundrel Time,* were both controversial; critics charged that both works were self-serving and riddled with untruths.

CRITICAL RECEPTION

Hellman's major works were well received by both critics and audiences. Two of her plays, *Watch on the Rhine* and *Toys in the Attic,* received the New York Drama Critics Circle Award, and many productions of her work enjoyed long, successful theatrical runs. Because of the political nature of her dramas and her treatment of American capitalism, Hellman's plays attracted the attention of Marxist critics long after her death. More recently her work has been examined by feminist scholars, many of whom contend that Hellman was a feminist despite her statements to the contrary. Sally Burke (see Further Reading) includes Hellman in her study of feminist playwrights, despite the common critical contention that Hellman aspired to be "one of the boys" and Hellman's own contention that she encountered no discrimination as a woman in the theatre. Burke insists that the playwright "gave voice to feminist themes while publicly eschewing the title of feminist." Citing *The Little Foxes* as an example, Burke maintains that the play deals with "woman's status as chattel to be disposed of at the discretion of the patriarchy, and the convergence of race and class as well as gender in determining one's destiny." Judith E. Barlow also concludes that *The Little Foxes,* "with its attention to gendered role playing," meets the criteria associated with feminist drama. For Barlow, the play challenges the stereotypical domestic role for women and confronts "the hypocrisy of excluding the women from direct participation in business negotiations." Mary Lynn Broe suggests that Hellman's use of passivity in her dramas was at odds with the usual stereotypical association of women with passivity. According to Broe, the words and actions of Hellman's female characters "suggest not only new possibilities for moral being, a new range of expression for female behavior, but also a new approach to reevaluating Lillian Hellman's play-writing skills."

PRINCIPAL WORKS

The Children's Hour (play) 1934

Days to Come (play) 1936

The Little Foxes (play) 1939

Watch on the Rhine (play) 1941

The Searching Wind (play) 1944

Another Part of the Forest (play) 1946

Montserrat [adapted from the play by Emmanuel Roblès] (play) 1949

The Autumn Garden (play) 1951

The Lark [adapted from the play by Jean Anouilh] (play) 1955

Candide [adapted from the novel by François Marie Arouet de Voltaire] (play) 1956

Toys in the Attic (play) 1960

My Mother, My Father, and Me [adapted from the novel *How Much?* by Burt Blechman] (play) 1963

An Unfinished Woman: A Memoir (memoir) 1969

The Collected Plays (plays) 1972

Pentimento: A Book of Portraits (memoir) 1973

Scoundrel Time (memoir) 1976

Maybe: A Story (memoir) 1980

Eating Together: Recipes and Recollections [with Peter Feibleman] (nonfiction) 1984

Conversations with Lillian Hellman (interviews) 1986

PRIMARY SOURCES

LILLIAN HELLMAN (LETTER DATE 19 MAY 1952)

SOURCE: Hellman, Lillian. "Letter to the House Committee on Un-American Activities." In *Letters of the Century: America 1900-1999,* edited by Lisa Grunwald and Stephen J. Adler, pp. 376-77. New York: Dial Press, 1999.

In the following letter, written in 1952, Hellman states her position on testifying against friends and acquaintances before the House Committee on Un-American Activities.

May 19, 1952

Honorable John S. Wood, Chairman House Committee on Un-American Activities Room 226 Old House Office Building, Washington 25, D.C.

Dear Mr. Wood:

As you know, I am under subpoena to appear before your Committee on May 21, 1952.

I am most willing to answer all questions about myself. I have nothing to hide from your Committee and there is nothing in my life of which I am ashamed. I have been advised by counsel that under the Fifth Amendment I have a constitutional privilege to decline to answer any questions about my political opinions, activities and associations, on the grounds of self-incrimination. I do not wish to claim this privilege. I am ready and willing to testify before the representatives of our Government as to my own opinions and my own actions, regardless of any risks or consequences to myself.

But I am advised by counsel that if I answer the Committee's questions about myself, I must also answer questions about other people and that if I refuse to do so, I can be cited for contempt. My counsel tells me that if I answer questions about myself, I will have waived my rights under the Fifth Amendment and could be forced legally to answer questions about others. This is very difficult for a layman to understand. But there is one principle that I do understand: I am not willing, now or in the future, to bring bad trouble to people who, in my past association with them, were completely innocent of any talk, or any action that was disloyal or subversive. I do not like subversion or disloyalty in any form and if I had ever seen any I would have considered it my duty to have reported it to the proper authorities. But to hurt innocent people whom I knew many years ago in order to save myself is, to me, inhuman and indecent and dishonorable. I cannot and will not cut my conscience to fit this year's fashions, even though I long ago came to the conclusion that I was not a political person and could have no comfortable place in any political group.

I was raised in an old-fashioned American tradition and there were certain homely things that were taught to me: to try to tell the truth, not to bear false witness, not to harm my neighbor, to be loyal to my country, and so on. In general, I respected these ideals of Christian honor and did as well with them as I knew how. It is my belief that you will agree with these simple rules of human decency and will not expect me to violate the good American tradition from which they spring. I would, therefore, like to come before you and speak of myself.

I am prepared to waive the privilege against self-incrimination and to tell you anything you wish to know about my views or actions if your Committee will agree to refrain from asking me to name other people. If the Committee is unwilling to give me this assurance, I will be forced to plead the privilege of the Fifth Amendment at the hearing.

A reply to this letter would be appreciated.

Sincerely yours, Lillian Hellman

GENERAL COMMENTARY

MARY LYNN BROE (ESSAY DATE 1981)

SOURCE: Broe, Mary Lynn. "Bohemia Bumps into Calvin: The Deception of Passivity in Lillian Hellman's Drama." In *Critical Essays on Lillian Hellman*, edited by Mark W. Estrin, pp. 78-90. Boston: G. K. Hall, 1989.

In the following essay, originally published in 1981, Broe examines Hellman's use of passivity in her plays, *maintaining that its use often ran counter to the social stereotype associated with female characters.*

Her face like a thousand year old siennese mask sheds time in runnels, etched with the vivacity of a life lived passionately and well. Undaunted, she has visited battle fronts during bombings, foraged bayou country for wild duck, scarfed jambalaya and raccoon stew, whisked contraband in a hatbox across the German border. She is as much at home decapitating snapping turtles as she is captivating the world of high fashion clad in a Balmain dress or a Blackgama coat. Her "spit-in-the-eye" rebelliousness can change mercurially from rampaging anger to demure deference.[1]

Although at every turn "Bohemia bumps into Calvin" in her character, Lillian Hellman is seldom linked with the concept of passivity. In both the political and literary establishments, she has become one of the foremost authorities on decisive action and pure forcefulness. According to one critic, "Miss Hellman dreams of living successfully by masculine standards: honor, courage, aggression."[2] Yet in *An Unfinished Woman* she admits: "I feel at my best when somebody else drives the car, gives the orders, knows me well enough to see through the manner that . . . was thought up early to hide the indecision, the vagueness." In *An Unfinished Woman* and *Pentimento,* both autobiographical works, the apparent powerlessness that begins as a consistent social pose is a paradoxical one: in incident after incident, the social posture quickly becomes the means to her most penetrating insights. Passivity—both a triumph and a compensation wrested from years of female victimhood—functions as an artistic means to spiritual-moral development in Hellman's writing. "If you are willing to take the punishment, you are halfway through the battle," she announces, recalling herself as a child who, having run away from home, understands the advantageous manipulative power of absence. And later, "I was ashamed that I caused myself to lose so often," she remarks to Hammett, who, when rebuked by her, grinds a burning cigarette into *his* cheek. From characters such as her childhood maid Sophronia, Dash Hammett, Horace Liveright, Dorothy Parker and friend Julia, she learns the vital function of being morally free to be socially passive. Whether she leaves the judgment of others inconclusive, or "refuses to preside over violations against herself," Lillian Hellman employs passivity in the autobiographies as a vehicle for powerful action, compassion, and finally, moral authority.[3]

So, too, in her major plays.[4] Any reevaluation of her drama requires our acknowledgment of her use of passivity in its variegated forms as a catalyst for truth-telling, deception, and most importantly, self-deception: all recurrent themes in her plays.

Lillian Hellman's plays redeem the impediment of a social role of passivity as a calculated artistic choice in a curious, perhaps unlikely, way. It is less Hellman's theme of passivity than her structural *reworking* of the quality within each drama that reclaims these plays from labels of infectious villainy or triumphant duplicity. For it is no longer illuminating to see her characters in the simple categories of initiators of evil, the "despoilers" who execute their destructive aims on the one hand, or the "by-standers" who, because of naiveté or lack of self-knowledge, suggest evil as the "negative failure of good."[5] Rather, passivity redefined to include aspects of deception and moral disguise is both thematically and structurally crucial to any reevaluation of Hellman as a significant contemporary playwright. As Addie in **The Little Foxes** (1939) says: "Well, there are people who eat the earth and eat all the people on it like in the Bible with the locusts. And other people who stand around and watch them eat it. Sometimes I think it ain't right to stand and watch them eat it" (p. 182). The socially negligible female characters, the ones who "stand around and watch them [the locusts] eat," actually control the more brutishly powerful, but often in indirect, unobtrusive ways. As General Griggs (**The Autumn Garden** [1951]) might say of their passive behavior, it is simply a way "to remain in training while you wait" for the big moments, the turning points in life. The minor female characters—Lavinia, Birdie Hubbard, Sophie, Lily Prine and Lily Mortar—candidly, if unwittingly, reveal dramatic "truth" in certain situations. By their revelations they catalyze the outcome of dramatic action. Thus the socially negligible become the dramatically invaluable.

Of course, passivity is not a foreign concept to female authors and characters of the nineteenth or twentieth centuries. Victorian literature is replete with its Mrs. Gamps (professional servants of deaths and entrances), Maggie Tullivers and Edna Pontelliers, whose place is more to suffer than to do. From Thea Elvstead's blond snivellings in *Hedda Gabler* to Blanche Dubois' begging the gallantry of a gentleman caller, to Sylvia Plath's bedding down in a "cupboard of rubbish," at home in "turnipy chambers" among roots, husks and owl pellets, the passive role has become a pejorative image of a lot of hand-wringers, retiring mealy-mouths, or women playing Galatea to some man's Pygmalion. These female lives seem to guarantee that the meek are not so blessed after all, but simply cursed with social insignificance. No wonder then that one critic has described the circumstance of so many passive women characters as a sentimentally disinvolved torpidity, never deliberate, but always lending a strong impression of sluggish flies hatching indoors in early winter.[6]

But fortunately a number of contemporary thinkers have redefined passivity, retrieving it from the convention of social role to the authority of moral virtue, from a limited stereotype to a limitless capacity for real feeling, intelligence and choice. Mary Ellmann has likened the workings of the stereotype to the dynamics of Negro apathy: once the social restriction is placed on the group, the characteristic inactivity is found and then called innate, not social.[7] And in studying Victorian women, Patricia Meyer Spacks suggests that the lack of social opportunity is less an impediment than a chance for moral and emotional fulfillment. Assuming an unfashionable pose, Spacks defies the old saw that a limited social status necessarily creates a limited personality.[8] Mahatma Gandhi, moreover, elevated passivity beyond either politics or stereotype to a creed of personal ethics that emphasized integrity as a form of struggle. According to Gandhi, one could gain a moral authority worthy of *The Sermon on the Mount* or the *Bhagavad-Gita* by "Satyagraha," an act of the mind and will. If we bear in mind this brief history as we look at five Hellman plays, we see that an apparent social disadvantage actually allows a distinct capacity for being as a *moral* individual, or catalyzes action that permits such moral truth to be recognized.

In **The Children's Hour** (1934), Hellman dismantles the social stereotype of passivity in Aunt Lily Mortar and her parodic distortion, Mary Tilford. Early in the play, the decaying ex-actress Lily Mortar is overheard calling the relationship of the headmistresses of a New England girl's school "just as unnatural as it can be." Her words, repeated to and distorted by Mary Tilford, bring about the suicide of one of the women, who actually does acknowledge so-called unnatural feeling for the other. By shrewdly calculating the cliché of social passivity (the demure silence of an abused child), Mary blackmails and manipulates both her grandmother and a fellow student into the character assassination of Karen and Martha, the headmistresses. She engineers her "great, awful lie" into acceptable truth by exaggerating a social stereotype.

In the course of the play, Aunt Lily Mortar makes a career out of absence, omission, and inadvertence. Living in the days of steamer trunks and roadshows, Lily has made theatrics her domain, chatter her trademark. For Lily the natural thing is the socially customary, courtesy a mere matter of breeding, passivity an unconscious and uncritical way of life. In the play's opening scene, Lily and the schoolgirls are involved in a "great show of doing nothing," their theatrical passivity itself a lie for gainful learning. Here the beaux arts of womanhood become useless, truncated labors, images of incompletion. Hair is being cut as irregularly as Latin verbs are conjugated. Haphazard sewing and basting complement the fake social graces. Theatrics replaces the candor of labor. Unwittingly, Lily herself points out the deception, calling their labors simply women's "tricks."

Perhaps the most critical meta-theatrical moment in this opening scene is Lily's hammy reading of Portia's "mercy" speech from Shakespeare's *The Merchant of Venice*.[9] On Lily Mortar's lips, these celebrated lines dwindle to a mere elocutionary exercise just as the truth she utters central to the outcome of action is but an overheard perception. Portia's moral and verbal disguise contrasts with Lily's inadvertent catastasis of the play's end. (Hellman at once sneers and laughs at the element of "pretend" that infects the stage: as she says the playwright's "tricking up the scene" is the only fitting response.) But ironically, it is the three lines Lily *omits* that seem to anticipate the outcome of the dramatic action in *The Children's Hour*: "Therefore, Jew / Though justice be thy plea, consider this / That in the course of justice none of us / Should see salvation."

No one *does* see salvation in the girl's school where universal deception is rampant. Although Mary Tilford is exposed for her malignant manipulations, and Mrs. Tilford, her rich granny, recants her character slander, both events occur too late to save either Martha's life or the headmistresses' careers. Moreover, Lily's verbal omissions in the first scene foreshadow her crucial absence when Karen and Martha need her witness for their trial. Muttered asides and throwaway lines, Lily's words emerge only indirectly as canny truths about the other characters: "I love you that way—maybe the way they said" (p. 62), Martha admits to Karen following Lily's charge of "unnaturalness"; or Lily's comment that "one master passion in the breast . . . swallows all the rest" (p. 9) accurately describes Mary's maliciousness, Mrs. Tilford's righteousness, as well as Martha's love for Karen before the play ends. In one of Hellman's best deceptions of the intractable theater audience, Lily Mortar has the force of a daft Cassandra.

Mary Tilford is the theatrical caricature and complement to Lily Mortar's genuine social weakness. Mary feigns homesickness, fainting, even a heart attack in a Grand Guignol representation of weakness. Even though this whiner has her facts wrong in the play's Inquisition scene (there is no keyhole in the headmistress's bedroom door, as Mary claims, nor is the other headmistress's room near enough for the girl to overhear anything), Mary turns her calculated passive behavior into a triumph over authority and maturity, as once again moral disguise and meta-theatrics are closely linked. She is coyly frail, consciously retiring in scenes with Mrs. Mortar, her grandmother, and Dr. Cardin. She blackmails Rosalie, her chum, and then defers to Rosalie's facts. As an innocent bystander who sees and hears only inadvertently, she never once utters an incriminating word of her own. But in the end of the play, her mummery of passivity does her in, does not triumph.

Just as meta-theatrics permits moral disguise in Lily's incomplete Portia and Mary's failed Inquisition, so too does it become a metaphor for other forms of playing in *The Children's Hour.* Even structurally, the play proves deceptive. All the truth-revealing scenes are interrupted so that the continuous action of dramatic unravelling and revelation are missing from the play. By such sleight of structure, Hellman shifts the focus from blackmail, extortion, and lesbianism (more melodramatic topics) to the quiet business of redefining a moral capacity. The headmistresses' tense, oblique exchange of feelings about Karen's impending marriage is interrupted by Joe, Karen's fiance, with his talk of the black bulls "breeding in the hills." Eavesdropping girls behind the door halt Lily Mortar's discussion of Martha's "unnatural" sentiments for Karen. And as Mrs. Tilford begins to elaborate that "something horrible" is wrong with Karen, the young woman herself arrives to ask, "Is it a joke, Joe?" mistaking villainy for comedy. Hellman suggests complex new moral possibilities for passivity by giving a dramatically central role to the indirect revelations of Lily Mortar. At the same time, she mocks the theatrics of social passivity by linking it with moral disguise in both Lily and Mary Tilford. She will elaborate these possibilities throughout her playwriting career.

Hellman's general theme of duplicity is more specifically focused on two women characters and their portraits of passivity in *The Little Foxes.* Regina Hubbard Giddens feigns the role of the inept and demure Southern belle in a character study that is, in words Hellman once used to describe Dorothy Parker, a combination of Little Nell and Lady Macbeth. "I don't know about these things," Regina postures. "I shouldn't like to be too definite," she demurs about the family's business bargaining terms (p. 149). But Regina knows both terms and money. She has been systematically juggling her family's lives and fortunes for a long time. She puts her own daughter up for forty percent collateral in a deal, using her also as bait to get an invalid husband home. When told that her husband is dying, Regina can't understand "why people have to talk about this kind of thing" (p. 168). She uses her husband's reticence about committing money and finally even his death as bargaining tools that she wields sharply against her brothers. Outwitting the thieving Hubbards, she gets seventy-five percent of the money for herself, in an actively malignant parody of passivity. Once again, moral dissembling, social passivity, and meta-theatrics are linked in the character of Regina.

The dramatic complement to Regina's feigned passivity is the battered Aunt Birdie. Though Birdie is repeatedly belittled by her family, who claims she'll get a headache if she babbles too much truth—"that's a lie they tell for me," she knows (p. 183)—Birdie reveals the play's central and ironic truth. Flighty and high on elderberry wine, felled by a case of the hiccups, she nevertheless sets the shadowy standard for moral judgment in *The Little Foxes*. Early on, she begins telling more truth than the Hubbards care to hear: she recognizes ethical values. Although her father gave his life as a soldier in the war, she sees through the senseless "killing just for killing." She supports Horace's wishes when he is being pawned by the family's expediency and laments, "If only we could go back to Lionnet." But Birdie's values and her words are not so much nostalgia for an aristocratic past than desire for sources of information and power whereby Horace and Alexandra are able to check Regina's financial and personal manipulations. Birdie, the magpie chatterer who seems financially dominated and personally insignificant, utters the central, empowering moral judgment in the play. What she tells is that Oscar has "made their money charging awful interest to ignorant niggers and cheating them on what they bought" (p. 182). Her emotions are candid and unconventional, even if she does deliver them as pathetic memories and throwaway lines. She hates her own son Leo, warns her niece Alexandra against family dependency ("Don't love

me. Because in twenty years you'll just be like me"), and debunks the myth of romantic love between herself and her husband: "Ask why *he* married *me* . . . My family was good and the cotton on Lionnet's field was better. Ben Hubbard wanted the cotton and Oscar Hubbard married it for him" (p. 182).

In the opening scene, Birdie criticizes the unethical behavior practiced by the new Southern industrialists and hints at what will become of the Hubbards in their ruthless use of one another. The information and influence she provides Alexandra and her allegiance to Horace prompt the younger woman's final refusal. Birdie's words give her "the courage to fight" instead of being "one of the people who stand around and watch." While good may not be rewarded or evil sufficiently punished in *The Little Foxes*, Hellman does expand and explore the character of those "little foxes whose vines have tender grapes" through the figure of Aunt Birdie. In Birdie's intoxicated asides, truth is given ultimate, though unlikely, power over apparently active evil. If not redeemed, the passive are victims redefined.

In *The Children's Hour* and *The Little Foxes* both Mary's pose as a battered child and Regina's feigned Southern belle routine set the stage for a very different sort of passivity. These two self-conscious dramas contrast with Birdie's intoxicated asides that narrate the Hubbard history, and Lily's erratic Portia and words whispered on the staircase—both of which create the circumstances on which the dramatic outcome of each play depends. The real moral quality of passivity (which Birdie in particular represents) triumphs over feigned artifice as it exists in Mary and Regina's meta-theatrics.

In *Another Part of the Forest* (1947), Lavinia claims to have a good memory. And indeed she has. Keeping her all night vigils, wandering about "colored" churches clutching her Bible, Lavinia is easily dismissed as a babbling, mad hanky-wringer. She even lives in silence for a decade on Marcus's promises that "next year they will talk." Like Ghandi, Lavinia literally and morally clings to the truth with an act of mind and will that proves her personal integrity. Unlike the old aristocratic Bagtrys, whose backward nostalgia "got in the way of history," Lavinia's throwaway comments make a curious kind of sense. "It's not easy to send your own husband into a hanging rope," she admits. For despite her dismissal as a crazy pipedreamer, Lavinia knows the truth about the viper's tangle of Hubbard family history. "Imagine taking money for other people's misery," she mutters about Marcus's rise to fortune. Years before, privy to her husband's cheating and lying—now a family trademark—she has recorded events in her Bible. Her facts prove that Marcus has run a blockade to scalp salt to the poor and dying during the war. She also knows that by his action he had been responsible for the Union massacre of twenty-seven Confederate boys in training camp.

Stifled now by a corrupt family, Lavinia tries repeatedly to air her secret, but fails. Instead, she develops an escape fantasy of teaching poor black children "the word" she has never uttered, only clutched. Unlike Mary Tilford's or Regina's postures, Lavinia's pretending functions as an imaginative moral restitution for the deceptive silence she has kept for over sixteen years. "There's got to be one little thing you do that you want to do, all by yourself you want to do it" (p. 332), she insists.

Once again in the Hellman canon, meta-theatrics—now in the form of Lavinia's pipedream of escape—becomes the vehicle for moral disguise. The hand-wringing, babbling Lavinia is really lucidly oversane. She is immune to bribery and nostalgic myths, just as she knows the difference between sacred vows and a bad marriage. Throughout the play, her asides reveal information about the suspicion cast on the family by Marcus's actions, about the "hot tar and clubs and ropes that night" (p. 377). But the truth she finally utters in act 3 allows her son Ben to check Marcus's power as well as his words, which, as Lavinia reminds them, do *not* match his actions. Supremely guileless, Lavinia toys with that gap between language and reality that has supported Marcus's fictive life: "Why Marcus," she reminds her husband about the incriminating information the prostitute Laurette has just volunteered, "The girl only told the truth. Salt is just a word, it's in the Bible quite a lot. And that other matter, why, death is also just a word" (p. 372).

Lavinia borrows words from her Bible, if not to prompt justice in the play, at least to offer a more lucid understanding of the nature of "truth" on which the dramatic action turns. "I only have what I have," she announces. Truth is neither brute power nor written facts, but "whatever people want to believe," Lavinia knows, "I'm not going to have any Bibles in my school. That surprise you all? It's the only book in the world but it's just for grown people, after you know it don't mean what it says" (p. 391). The chicanery of nearly every member of the family backfires, as Lavinia finally "tells the truth to everybody," clutching her Bible. She deals various members of the family symbolic gifts at the end of the play,

proving not only the restoration of her memory, but her degree of moral sense that is not shared by even the shrewd Regina or the greedy Ben. Lavinia, perhaps even more than Mrs. Mortar or Birdie, deceives by redefining a social role of passivity as a capacity for moral understanding, fulfillment, even nuance.

With *The Autumn Garden* (1951), Hellman moves from crass entrepreneurs and claptrap confrontations to the muted haze of middle-life. In a world subtly Chekhovian—and in a play Hellman reluctantly admits is her best—she makes nostalgia a form of consciousness. Pity and compassion are the only bonding possible among weak, aging characters. Under the cabbage roses of the once grand Tuckerman boardinghouse, each character seems stalled in a particular version of the past—unfinished paintings, mothy romances, worn family legacies. Each is sunken into an after-dinner doze of self-deception: "I think as one grows older it is more and more necessary to reach out your hand for the sturdy old vines you knew when you were young and let them lead you back to the roots of things that matter" (p. 483). But it is precisely this waste that Hellman warns against in *Autumn Garden* through the action of two negligible women characters.

The dramatic situation develops when Nick Denerey, artist manqué with cosmopolitan pretensions, returns to the "summer mansion" of his childhood in order to grab onto those "sturdy old vines" just as they were twenty years before. His memories have never matured, however, only inflated his enormous capacity for myth, philandering, flirting, and do-gooder meddling. One night, on a drunken "rampage of good-will," he compromises the maid Sophie, who is Frederick's affianced. Servants and friends in the provincial town quickly learn the scandal of the boardinghouse. Ironically, the publication of the news combined with Sophie's ingenuity serves to rescue this indentured Cinderella from a miserable future life with Frederick Ellis and his mother. The outcome of the dilemma depends upon a few pungent perceptions of an old dismissible grandmother, Mrs. Ellis, who warns Sophie about the consequences of the gossip and saves her from a disastrous marriage of convenience with the son.

By virtue of their outcast status or age, both Sophie and old Mrs. Ellis are late examples of Hellman's artistically tooled "passives" who reclaim a social label as a dramatic strength. Both Sophie and Mrs. Ellis join the gallery of Lavinias, Lily Mortars and Birdies, catalysts for action who capitalize on a formerly narrow social quality, dramatically retrieving it. Amidst all the ruin of wasted lives, both of these characters manage to act realistically, not to doze or deceive. They stand in contrast to Rose, the "Army manual wife," who with fluttering eyelids and heart staves off the divorce that her husband the General so desperately wants. Like the faded buttercup Rose, or Ned Crossman, the boarder who makes his valedictories to a bottle of brandy, most of the other characters beg reality never to correct the "indefinite pronouns" of their Southern gentility.

Bored with this passel of self-deceivers, Mrs. Ellis has a strong grasp of the real issues of life—power, sensuality, money: "I say to myself, one should have power, or give it over. But if one keeps it, it might as well be used, with as little mealy-mouthness as possible" (p. 503). Like Granny in Albee's *American Dream,* who debunks myths by turning them back on the family, Mrs. Ellis is a straight shooter with a razor-sharp tongue who has built a solid financial empire for herself. She uses her power and her overheard words to create the situation that saves Sophie. Walter Kerr has compared her to "the goddess Athena in a snap-brim fedora," delivering her haymakers with aplomb.[10] She knows that it's easy to afford the luxury of morality when somebody else "clips the coupons." She readily admits that the happiest years of her life are those she has spent in solitude since her husband's death. She chides Nick for inflicting his bear hugs, friendly pats, and tiny bursts of passion: "One should have sensuality whole or not at all." Mocking him as one of the "touchers and leaners," she asks if he doesn't find "pecking at it ungratifying." When Frederick discovers that his writer-friend Payson's real attraction to him is money, Mrs. Ellis orders him to "Take next week to be sad. A week's long enough to be sad in" (p. 509). She knows well the system of patronage in which people like Fred, a professional proofreader and simp, must pay for the interest of people like Payson with their literary coteries. Like Lily Mortar's words, Mrs. Ellis's non sequiturs (such as her speech that "nobody in the South has tapeworm anymore") describe candidly the parasitic relationships that surround her—Frederick and Carrie, Nick and Nina, Constance and Nick, Payson and Fred, Rose and the General.

Sophie, another minor female character, has a central dramatic role. She is the impoverished European niece, "indentured" to the family for her cultural and social status. Like Mrs. Ellis, she is far too pragmatic to be arrested in self-deceptions. In the words of General Griggs at the end of the play, Sophie spends her life "in training" for the big moment of her escape. Perceptually, verbally, and morally, she piles up a lot of little moments to stand on. Seemingly tongue-tied and retiring when she first appears, in the course of the play Sophie manages wry words for, and rare understanding of, the others' pretenses. She knows that decisions are made "only in order to speak about changing them." Quite matter of factly she says: "You know it is most difficult in another language. Everything in English sounds important. I get a headache from the strain of listening" (pp. 473-74). And to Constance: "I think perhaps you worry sometimes in order that you should not think" (p. 520). Sophie sees the social facade of Constance's romantic malingering: "Such a long, long time to stay nervous. Great love in tender natures. . . . It always happens that way with ladies. For them it is once and not again: it is their good breeding that makes it so" (p. 480). Sophie admits the bargain she is striking with Frederick (the exchange of social position for sexual cover); knows the prevalent social code for women ("little is made into very much here"); and knows also that "somehow sex and money are simpler in French" (pp. 536-37) than in the indirect metaphors and oblique rhetoric employed by the Ellises and Denerys.

Sophie is shrewd about the female ploys she uses to threaten Nina Denery with exposure of her husband's seduction: her word is ominous, but, held in reserve, carries the power of Lavinia's clutched Bible. "We will call it a loan, come by through blackmail" (p. 537), she says of the five thousand dollars she extorts as escape money with which she will return to Europe. She realistically turns Nick's playful charm-seduction-disposal game back on him by demanding the exact commission he was to receive for doing a portrait of Rose Griggs's homely niece. Most significantly, the trade value of her bargain, that is, her role as marriage counselor, is not lost on Sophie: "How would you and Mr. Denery go on living without such incidents as me? I have been able to give you a second, or a twentieth, honeymoon" (p. 538).

Linked in a socially negligible partnership, but oracular in their throwaway lines, Sophie and old Mrs. Ellis support one another both in dramatic action and verbal power. Now we see the collaboration of the passive, dismissible characters, extremes (impoverished youth to wry old age) on the continuum of life. With realistic savvy about money as power, they use the meta-theatrics of their social roles not for moral disguise, as do Re-

ABOUT THE AUTHOR

PATRAKA COMMENTS ON THE "JULIA" EPISODE OF HELLMAN'S MEMOIR *PENTIMENTO*

Heroism itself is no longer the province of males, of fathers and sons vested with familial authority, when Hellman relocates acts of courage within a matrix of female friendships. The story marks the way Julia depends on this friendship to seduce Hellman via letters to come to Europe, recognize the gravity of what was happening, and risk carrying money across the border to Germany to secure the release of those interned in concentration camps. Even the props of this resistance work—fur hat and candy box—portray the paraphernalia of femininity as a strategy to defeat fascists instead of as a trivialized comic device. In its focus on female friendship, "Julia" historicizes the role of emotion and personal feeling outside the family and marriage in relation to politics.

Patraka, Vivian M. Excerpt from "Lillian Hellman's *Watch on the Rhine*: Realism, Gender, and Historical Crisis." *Modern Drama* 32, no. 1 (March 1989).

gina and Mary Tilford, but as means to physical escape or greater self-awareness. Through their final camaraderie, we realize that **Autumn Garden** issues a stern warning reminiscent of F. Scott Fitzgerald's early stories: life is a valuable and precious trust whose capital must be invested early and wisely, set in a committed direction and tended energetically *before* mid-life, or its returns will never be reaped. If it is squandered, the Sophies of the world will deceive themselves into becoming Rose Griggses.

In **Toys in the Attic** (1960) the demented child-bride Lily Prine wanders about in her slip or with a nightgown over her dress, desperately trying to babble the truth of her suspicions about her roué husband, Julian Berniers. But the world of the Berniers sisters does not promote either candor or truthfulness: they dote on their pasts, on their renegade gambler brother, and on the colognes and candied oranges they trade with each other every week. As Carrie Berniers remarks

to her sister, "Funny how you can live so close and long and not know things, isn't it?" (p. 687).

Like flighty Birdie Hubbard or muted Lavinia, Lily has knowledge but not audience, awareness but not articulation. She knows her husband talks every evening at six with "the not such a young lady with the sad face" (p. 701), the same woman seen with him on an Audubon Park bench. Lily cannot quite connect Julian's loss of the Chicago shoe factory with his current wealth that takes him away for so much of the day and permits him to buy ball gowns, pianos, and flaming red mantillas. When she guilelessly asks her questions, whispers her vagaries about the "*not* happenings of the night before," and mutters hallucinatory non-sequiturs, Lily is stifled by her husband Julian. He sends her to her room, locks her in a hotel, or reprimands her that "That's not the way to be married" (p. 702). As Lavinia clutches "the word" in the Bible, Lily Prine totes with her the "sacred knife of truth" (for which she traded her wedding ring in a morphine den), waiting for the moment when she might wield it.

The moment comes when Lily can tolerate no more of her husband's suspected infidelity. She phones Cyrus Warkins, the husband of the elusive other woman. In a babble of typical non-sequiturs, baby talk, and illogical words, she begs him for "just one more year with Julian," thereby revealing the liaison with Warkins's wife. But Lily's action—that slice of the "sacred knife of truth"—cuts grossly, mangles the truth.

The real stakes are far more dangerous than Julian's fictitious adultery. Julian's actual venture is a shady but lucrative business deal based on a tip about a couple of acres of swampland precious to Warkins. Warkins's wife, a sentimental old flame of Julian, has put him onto the scheme to rob her brutal husband of his fortune. Because of Lily's call, Charlotte Warkins is slashed up, Julian robbed and mugged by hired thugs.

Although Lily slices deeply with her knife of truth, she mismanages truth, which seems to have its own aesthetic momentum. She is not the catalyst for the dramatic outcome so crucial to the lives of the Berniers sisters. Curiously, her action returns Julian to a state of passivity, impotence, and dependency on his maiden sisters, who with their cloying affections, paltry fictions, and meagre savings, require his need for their very survival. As Anna says to Carrie after a painful confession scene: "I loved you and so whatever I knew didn't matter. You wanted to see yourself a way you never were. Maybe that's a game you let people play when you love them. Well, we had made something together, and the words would have stayed where they belonged as we waited for our brother to need us again. But our brother doesn't need us anymore, and so the poor house came down" (pp. 745-46).

Like so many Hellman characters, the negligible Lily has the oblique lucidity of the mad, as well as the practical savvy that is, literally, too direct for the Berniers' attic world of mismanaged truth: "I spoke to Mr. Warkins and told him to ask her to wait for Julian for one more year. After that, if Julian doesn't want me—Where would I ever go, who would ever want me? I'm trouble, we all know that. I wouldn't have anywhere to go" (p. 748). Just as the crusty, bohemian Albertine Prine steps in and returns Lily's knife of truth to the gypsy den, fetching back her wedding ring, so, too, does she return her daughter to her husband, counseling her in life-saving deceptions. Like Carrie, whose incestuous feelings for Julian have surfaced through Lily's action, Albertine Prine realizes that "you take your chances on being hated by speaking out the truth." She says to Lily, "Go in and sit by him. Just sit by him and shut up. . . . Can you have enough pity for him not to kill him with truth?" (p. 750).

Lillian Hellman plays passivity in her minor female characters the way a jazz musician ranges over musical notes. She improvises variations on a chordal progression that vibrates from Lily Mortar to Lily Prine; from inadvertent truth-telling to conscious moral restitution and shrewd self-awareness; from moral disguise (Lily in *The Children's Hour*) to physical escape (Sophie in *The Autumn Garden*). Close examination of the negligible women in each of the five plays suggests that Hellman is a consummate trickster both in characterization and in theme—a role for this contemporary dramatist only broached by current criticism. She never appears to be the drum banging melodramatist that critics of her work have insisted. As if to defy what she calls the "pretence of representation" in the theatre, its claptrap as well as its "tight, unbending, unfluid, meagre" form, Hellman cleverly tailors a socially assigned role—passivity—into variegated moral and dramatic authority. And the artistic as well as the moral clout of passive characters has grown increasingly complex as Hellman's playwriting has matured over a quarter of a century. Sophie is surely a more wry, sophisticated blackmailer than Mary Tilford; Mrs. Ellis, more consciously skilled than Lavinia in reversing family events; Lily Prine, a more thorough "undoer" than Lily Mortar. And

in the case of Regina's wiles or Mary Tilford's theatrics, Hellman tricks up a counterpoint to the authentic truth-tellers, those who clutch their own word with stubborn personal integrity.

By a painful arithmetic of craft, Lillian Hellman reexamines language, theatrical convention, and the calculated effects of acting and staging, as well as passivity. Shunning "labels and isms," she formally realizes the hazards of moral, verbal, and theatrical absolutes in the effect of these minor characters on the dramatic outcome. Her "spit-in-the-eye" rebelliousness proclaims that the just and the worthy are never adequately credited by social labels, no more than her dismissible women are justly summed up by the inelastic social appearance of passivity. The writer's skill prevails, Hellman insists, not society's foibles: "The manuscript, the words on the page, was what you started with and what you have left . . . the pages are the only wall against which to throw the future or measure the past."[11] Hellman's words—but especially the words and actions of the passive women in five major plays—suggest not only new possibilities for moral being, a new range of expression for female behavior, but also a new approach to reevaluating Lillian Hellman's playwriting skills.

Notes

1. Surely one of the best recent portraits of Hellman as a spunky, rebellious life force is John Hersey's essay, "Lillian Hellman," *New Republic*, 18 Sept. 1976, pp. 25-27. Hersey speaks of her *outside* the formal politics with which she is often associated: "She cuts through all ideologies to their taproot: To the decency their adherents universally profess but almost never deliver" (p. 27). The phrase "Bohemia bumps into Calvin" is Hersey's.

2. Patricia Meyer Spacks, *The Female Imagination* (1975; reprint, New York: Avon, 1976), p. 381.

3. *An Unfinished Woman* (1969; rpt., New York: Bantam, 1970), pp. 164, 23, 167; *Pentimento* (1973; rpt., New York: New American Library-Signet, 1973).

4. Citations are to *The Collected Plays* (Boston: Little Brown and Co., 1972). Page numbers appear in the text.

5. Doris Falk, *Lillian Hellman* (New York: Frederick Ungar Publishing Co., 1978), pp. 29-34.

6. See Mary Ellmann, *Thinking About Women* (1968; reprint, New York: Harvest Books, 1968), pp. 78-82. Ellmann bases her discussion on Samuel Beckett's *Malloy*.

7. Ellmann, pp. 81-82.

8. Spacks, chapter 2, "Power and Passivity," in *The Female Imagination*.

9. Meta-theatre departs from tragedy or psychological realism to produce, instead, the calculated effects of acting and stage design. In something "meta-

theatrical," we are convinced not of reality, but of the reality of the dramatic imagination *before* the playwright has begun to exercise his/her own. In brief, meta-theatre or meta-theatrics suggests the inherent theatricality of life or an event. See Lionel Abel, *Metatheatre* (New York: Hill and Wang, 1963).

10. Walter Kerr, "A Nearly Perfect 'Autumn Garden,'" *New York Times,* 28 November 1976, sec. D, p. 42, col. 4.

11. *Pentimento*, p. 151.

TITLE COMMENTARY

The Little Foxes

JUDITH E. BARLOW (ESSAY DATE 1996)

SOURCE: Barlow, Judith E. "Into the Foxhole: Feminism, Realism, and Lillian Hellman." In *Realism and the American Dramatic Tradition,* edited by William W. Demastes, pp. 156-71. Tuscaloosa, Ala.: University of Alabama Press, 1996.

In the following essay, Barlow discusses The Little Foxes, *refuting feminist criticism that dismisses Hellman's work because of its realism.*

Realism has been under attack almost since it became the dominant mode of playwriting around the turn of the century—whether from Eugene O'Neill, who claimed that "most of the so-called realistic plays deal only with the appearance of things,"[1] or Thornton Wilder, who complained that realism robs drama of its magic by binding it to a particular "time and place."[2] But realism has come under perhaps its greatest assault in recent years from materialist feminist critics who, following a variety of postmodern theories, question the nature and value of both representation and narrative. Sue-Ellen Case has presented the point perhaps most strongly: "Cast the realism aside—its consequences for women are deadly."[3]

This attack would seem to sound the death knell for Lillian Hellman's work; in fact, at one point Jill Dolan refers to the "realist, Hellmanesque model of" Jane Chambers's early plays, thus making "Hellmanism" virtually a synonym for realism.[4] Elin Diamond sums up the anti-realist argument when she writes that "realism, more than any other form of theater representation, mystifies the process of theatrical signification. Because it naturalizes the relation between character and actor, setting and world, realism operates in concert with ideology. And because it depends on, insists on a *stability* of reference, an objective world that is the source and guarantor of knowl-

edge, realism surreptitiously reinforces (even if it argues with) the arrangements of that world."[5] From this perspective, realism can never be used as a tool for social criticism because its very methods undermine the goals of such criticism.

If the assault on realism sounds an ominously prescriptive and elitist note for present and future women dramatists (and their audiences) by defining how women should or should not write,[6] it is even more problematic for writers of the past. Realism was the preeminent theatrical mode in this country for the first half of the twentieth century, and a wholesale rejection of realism means the dismissal of three generations of women dramatists—from Rachel Crothers to Lorraine Hansberry—as well as of the audiences to which they appealed. Hellman's work, realism with a strain of melodrama, stands squarely in this now despised tradition.

Without denying that realistic drama has sometimes—inadvertently as well as intentionally—served to reify the very society it would indict, I would like to suggest that many of the criticisms of the realistic mode underestimate author, text, and audience. Realism invokes a far more complex worldview than its detractors acknowledge, and its usefulness as an instrument for societal change is much greater than they recognize. Hellman's most famous play, **The Little Foxes,** and especially its protagonist Regina Giddens, offer a provocative test case for examining the contemporary critique of realism.

It may be well to begin with Demastes's warning that "the term 'realism' is one that many claim to understand but few have been able to define, a fact that has played into the critical hands of its opponents and often hurt its advocates" (p. 1). In her study of realism on the American stage, Brenda Murphy explores the conflicting definitions of realism that abounded even in its earliest days, when William Dean Howells and Henry James offered substantially different interpretations of this new theatrical trend.[7] The final definition of stage realism at which Murphy arrives is useful:

a representation of the playwright's conception of some aspect of human experience in a given milieu, within the fourth-wall illusion and in the low mimetic style. It should have characters who were individuals as well as social types, a setting that aimed at producing the illusion of the milieu as fully as possible rather than simply importing "real" objects onto the stage, thought that expressed the social issues of the milieu and the psychological conflicts of the characters in dialogue they would naturally speak, a form that was derived from the human experience being depicted, and a structure designed to produce the fullest illusion for the audience that the action onstage was taking place in reality.

(p. 49)

Even so extensive a definition, however, leaves vast room for interpretation. (How much detail makes a character an "individual," for example?) We must also acknowledge that all critical labels force artificial groupings among diverse works that will inevitably fail to fit comfortably into the categories in which we attempt to entrap them. Perhaps most important, we must be aware when a term—*realism, expressionism, melodrama,* whatever—is being used as a device to illuminate the characteristics of literary works and when it is being used primarily as a stick to beat them.

As a first step in exploring the current critique of realism, it is useful to acknowledge that realism in theory and what actually happens in the theatre often do not coincide. Realism may aim to "naturalize the relation between character and actor"—that is, ask the audience to believe that character and actor are one—but few if any spectators fail to distinguish between player and role, between Bette Davis's interpretation of Regina Giddens and Tallulah Bankhead's. The 1981 revival of *The Little Foxes* enjoyed among the biggest advance sales in history because prospective viewers knew exactly who would be *playing* the part of Regina: Elizabeth Taylor.[8] In a paper given at the ATHE (Association for Theatre in Higher Education) conference in 1991, Lynda Hart aptly referred to realism as "the most naive of illusions." Why then are we so willing to believe that audiences are naive enough to succumb to that illusion, to believe that what they are watching onstage is an unclouded mirror of some coherent world outside the theatre—or actually is that world? Jacob H. Adler may claim that Hellman's plays include "real people speaking real language and carrying out real actions in a real world,"[9] but audiences know that the Hubbards are fictional characters whose razor-sharp repartee is carefully constructed stage dialogue distinctly *un*like what they hear over their breakfast coffee.

While realism does not suppose spectators as innocent as Royall Tyler's Jonathan, who thought he was looking "right into the next neighbour's house"[10] as he sat in the playhouse gallery, Elin Diamond is correct in observing that "mimesis, from its earliest and varied enunciations, posits a *truthful* relation between world and word, model and copy, nature and image or, in semiotic terms, referent and sign" (p. 58). Hellman herself saw

FROM THE AUTHOR

plays like *The Little Foxes* as deriving their force from that very mimesis, from the viewer's ability to identify—and identify with—the characters on the stage. Writing in **Pentimento**, she insists, "I had meant the audience to recognize some part of themselves in the money-dominated Hubbards; I had not meant people to think of them as villains to whom they had no connection."[11] What critics of realism often fail to acknowledge, however, is not only how complex the relationship between referent and sign is in the theatre but that neither the referent nor the sign is itself simple or stable. Martin Esslin makes this point when he argues that "reality itself, even the most mundane, everyday reality, has its own symbolic component. The postman who brings me the telegram which announces the death of a friend is also, in a sense, a messenger of death, an Angel of Death. . . . What the stage gives us is an enhanced reality that itself becomes a sign, a metaphor, a dramatic symbol."[12] Teresa L. Ebert adds still more elements to the equation when she observes that the "features, effects, and uses" of mimesis vary among historical periods "and are determined by class, gender, and race. . . . Thus what is realistic—commonly assumed to be faithful to everyday experiences and consciousness—to one group may seem quite unrealistic to another."[13] Simply put, no two groups' (or individuals') "realities" are ever identical.

The relationship between model and copy is further problematized when the copy—the play—offers us a fragmented mirror-world characterized by lying, chicanery, and masquerade. In *The Little Foxes,* "truth" is the province of the best liar and every character—from the most pitiable to the most loathsome—is practiced at fabricating stories. Birdie lies about her twisted ankle and headaches, Leo about opening the safe deposit box; Ben and Oscar lie about stealing Horace's bonds, while Horace willingly agrees to play along with their ruse. Indeed, deception is so clearly the lingua franca here that audience members—like the characters—are stunned by Birdie's impropriety in honestly telling Horace how ill he looks.

Moreover, chicanery in *The Little Foxes* is clearly set in the context of theatricality: the medium is the subject. The long first scene is a play-within-a-play carefully directed to impress Mr. Marshall, the visiting capitalist; Birdie and Leo even have to be "cued" when they misplay the roles assigned to them. Katherine Lederer points out that both Regina and her brother Ben are consummate actors,[14] and the battle for supremacy between the two offers a powerful subtext about gender roles that necessarily draws audience attention to all the levels of role playing inside the theatre and out. Once again this self-reflexivity foregrounds the complexity of the relationship among actor, character, and some referent outside the text. Ben repeatedly prompts his sister in her social role as a woman, invoking tradition and their mother as arbiter and ideal. "For how many years have I told you a good-looking woman gets more by being soft and appealing?" he asks; "Mama used to tell you that."[15] Regina, however, needs no coaching. Taking the part of both actor and playwright, Regina wins the competition by threatening a bravura performance of poor helpless female ("You couldn't find a jury that wouldn't weep for a woman whose

brothers steal from her") and adding "what's necessary" to fabricate a convincing narrative for her auditors (p. 196). As in Brecht's *The Good Woman of Setzuan,* a Shen Te metamorphoses into a Shui Ta and back again with amazing grace and speed, and nothing is certain except pretense. And if this slippery world of games and changing scripts is a "copy" of some "model" outside the play, it would appear that neither model nor copy has quite the coherence or stability that critics claim they have.

With its attention to gendered role playing, *The Little Foxes* seems to answer Janelle Reinelt's demand that feminist drama include "active and engaged struggle with gender inscription [which] must accompany the recognition that gender opposition is a false construct."[16] Yet the presentation of sex roles is at the heart of still another materialist feminist accusation against realism, one that categorically denies the possibility that realism can critique these very roles. In her indispensable book *Feminism and Theatre,* Sue-Ellen Case charges: "Realism, in its focus on the domestic sphere and the family unit, reifies the male as sexual subject and the female as the sexual 'Other.' The portrayal of female characters within the family unit—with their confinement to the domestic setting, their dependence on the husband, their often defeatist, determinist view of the opportunities for change—make realism a 'prison-house of art' for women."[17] While it is absolutely true that realism and domesticity have historically been linked—the realistic domestic drama is the quintessential American play—the two are not necessarily joined; the bond between form and content in this case is descriptive, not prescriptive. Even more important, to demand that women playwrights eschew the domestic setting is to place a severe constraint on any female dramatist who would expose societal ills, many of which are rooted in that site. Ironically, the materialist feminist attack on realism and its bond with domesticity echoes a complaint lodged in 1937 by Joseph Mersand in his condescending essay "When Ladies Write Plays." Deploring "women dramatists for their emphasis on realism,"[18] he complains that "they know how to reconstruct for us on the stage our own little houses, and our own little, petty lives, with our worries and cares, and few moments of laughter" (p. 28). Mersand too confuses the subject (domestic life) with the form (realism) to the detriment of women dramatists; since women's concerns are by definition "little" and "petty," any reenactment of them onstage merits wholesale dismissal. Mersand sweeps aside three decades of plays by Rachel Crothers—concerning issues like the double standard, marital infidelity, and unequal career opportunities for men and women—as "Much ado about nothing" (p. 8). Blanket attacks on realistic presentations of the domestic sphere, when they fail to discriminate among the widely divergent forms such presentations take, come uncomfortably close to replicating Mersand's condescension, however different the reasoning behind those attacks may be.

When we turn to **The Little Foxes,** we see how Lillian Hellman's "portrayal of female characters" actually interrogates conventional notions of women's domestic roles—onstage and off. While the alcoholic Birdie has clearly given up hope of escaping from the tyranny of her husband and son, has there ever been a literary character less defeatist or determinist than Regina, who declares: "There are people who can never go back, who must finish what they start. I am one of those people"?[19] Sharon Friedman rightly notes that the Giddens home "is the setting for business negotiations" in **Foxes.**[20] By locating **Foxes** in the home, Hellman demystifies the relationship between the domestic on the one hand and the economic and political on the other. The hypocrisy of excluding the women from direct participation in business negotiations is foregrounded as Birdie, Alexandra, and Regina are bought, sold, or traded in this domicile of capitalism.[21] Even the befuddled Birdie is aware that marrying her was the "price" Oscar paid to obtain Lionnet, and she vows to prevent her niece from being a pawn in a similar transaction. Hellman's commentary on the gender relationships spawned by capitalism, in sum, virtually necessitates the play's location in the domestic sphere, a sphere inseparable from economic and political realms.

Still another objection to realism is lodged by Catherine Belsey in her influential essay "Constructing the Subject: Deconstructing the Text." Belsey argues that "the classic realist text moves inevitably and irreversibly to an end, to the conclusion of an ordered series of events." Classic realism, she contends, involves "the dissolution of enigma through the re-establishment of order, recognizable as a reinstatement or a development of the order which is understood to have preceded the events of the story itself."[22] On one level, of course, all drama reaches closure: the curtain (if there is one) comes down, the lights come up, the audience leaves. Closure in the sense of the reinstatement of an ordered world, however—a "correction" of the problem presented in the play—is precisely what most modern drama, realistic or otherwise, *lacks.* As Katherine Lederer observes, "Hellman ends her plays on an indeterminate note" (p. 44).[23] Renaissance authors and audiences could believe in such a return to "normality," whether political stability in tragedy or marriage in comedy, but most serious twentieth-century dramatists cannot even conceive of what terms such a reestablishment would take. Alexandra Giddens is no Fortinbras, and she has no army to reestablish stability in the disordered state of the turn-of-the-century South.

The last moments of **Foxes** owe more to the agitprop theater of the 1920s and 1930s in the United States than to the well-made play, and may even be—as Timothy J. Wiles suggests—closer still "to Brecht's dramaturgy."[24] Without breaking the frame of realism, Hellman turns the play outward to the audience for a resolution of the problems exposed during the previous three hours. Alexandra stands up to her mother and the greed and deceit she represents, vowing, "I'm not going to stand around and watch you do it. I'll be fighting as hard as he [Ben]'ll be fighting . . . someplace else" (p. 199).[25] She will not, however, be fighting to reestablish the Old South, a world that lives on only in Birdie's alcoholic imagination. This conclusion points not toward the reinscription of some previous social structure but to the hope of creating a new order—still undefined—based on sharply different values.

The scene is further complicated by the fact that the challenge to capitalist hegemony is uttered by a very young character whose strength has barely been tested, and by the chronological gap between play and audience: the action is set in 1900, thirty-nine years before opening night. Reeling from a decade of economic depression, audience members knew perfectly well that Zan had lost the fight to the Hubbards, and they knew what the consequences of that loss spelled in terms of human misery. Jeanie Forte complains that realistic plays yield "the illusion of change without really changing anything."[26] On the contrary, it is clear that little was altered when power passed from Ben to Regina—a reversal that may be temporary, as Ben's threat suggests, if he can gain the evidence to blackmail his sister as she is blackmailing him. More importantly, Hellman makes explicit that the responsibility for genuine change is lodged squarely with the audience. It is they who must conceive a way to fight the cupidity symbolized by the Hubbard clan. As we have already seen, the role of that audience looms large in critiques of realism. Catherine Belsey takes the issue still one step further: "Classic realism . . . performs . . . the work of ideology, not only in its representation of a world of consistent subjects who are the origin of meaning, knowledge and action, but also in offering the reader, as the position from which the text is most readily intelligible, the position of subject as the origin both of understanding and of action in accordance with that understanding" (pp. 51-52).[27] Belsey's contention is that the realist text—fiction or drama—creates *one* vantage point from which the text makes coherent sense, that the author coerces the spectator into believing that she has reached this position on her own when in fact she has been "written" into her role as spectator by the author, whose singular point of view the spectator is forced to share. I would counter, however, that all plays have designs upon the viewer, are acts of coercion attempting to gain our agreement with the author's "truth" even if that "truth" is that there is no truth at all. In Terry Eagleton's words, "every literary text intimates by its very conventions the way it is to be consumed, encodes within itself its own ideology of how, by whom and for whom it was produced."[28]

Moreover, any work of literature is open not to one but to a myriad of "truthful" readings. How do we account, to take one example, for the fact that critics have dubbed Regina Giddens everything from "a kind of single-handed Lady Macbeth"[29] to a "hateful woman [who] has to be respected for the keenness of her mind and the force of her character"[30] to the logical product of a sexist, capitalist system who "could compete in a male-controlled society only by pursuing her own self-interest, and by being more manipulative than the men around her"?[31] The subject position of the audience member is not infinitely elastic, to be sure, but neither is it quite so narrow as some theorists would suggest. It also clearly varies over time—as recent, more sympathetic views of Regina suggest. Are all but one reading somehow subversive because they are not the interpretation encoded by the author in the work and inscribed in the subject position we imagine we occupy? Belsey's notion of encoding seems to imply that the writer has complete control over the meanings of her text, an assertion most creative writers would challenge. In an interview, Hellman claimed to have been "extremely surprised that anybody thought" **The Little Foxes** was a critique of the industrialization of the South and of the spread of capitalism, but she conceded that "I don't think that what writers intend makes very much difference. It's what comes out."[32] Hell-

man is certainly being coy here, and her appropriate warning against the intentional fallacy must be balanced against a notion of authorial responsibility. Still, the attack on the way realism "performs . . . the work of ideology" tends unfairly to chastise the realistic text for what all texts do, at the same time as it underestimates the complexity of the composition process and the multiplicity of audience positions from which the characters and events onstage may be rendered comprehensible. Theatrical performance—the intricate interaction of director, actor, designer, and so forth—yet further complicates the question of just who is controlling audience response to a given play at a given moment.

We must also wonder whether readers and spectators are really unable to recognize and criticize the realist author's designs on them. Do all realist playwrights try to hide their presence in the text, as Jill Dolan suggests when she writes that realism "masks the ideology of the author, whose position is mystified by the seemingly transparent text"?[33] It may well be that the melodramatic elements Hellman builds into her text—the elaborate business about protecting Horace's medicine bottle, Regina's verbalized hopes that her husband will meet an early death—are Hellman's way of reminding us that there is a designer at work here manipulating not only plot but audience as well. Yet even without these melodramatic trappings, Hellman's ideology is scarcely masked in her presentation of such characters as the wily Ben, the physically and morally crippled Horace, or the speeches about "people who eat the earth . . . [and] other people who stand around and watch them eat it" that echo through the last act. Finally, Hellman's decision to set her play in "a small town in the South" at the dawn of the new century is still one more attempt to show that **Foxes** is not, as Thornton Wilder would complain, about "one time and place." The year 1900 symbolizes nearly forty years to come, and what we witness is the South turning into the North, trading its tradition for a promise of prosperity. The double lens of history through which Hellman views a turn-of-the-century story in the moral and social terms of the late 1930s is still one more distancing device (one Hellman shares with Bertolt Brecht, among others) that reminds us of the deliberate artifice at work in the not entirely "transparent" medium of realistic drama.[34]

Without question there are limitations—sometimes dangerous ones—in the traditional realistic forms favored by women dramatists early in this century (as well as by many writing now), and we have an obligation to identify and acknowledge these. Materialist feminist theorists have done an important job of locating and articulating these limitations. To return to Catherine Belsey: "In its attempt to create a coherent and internally consistent fictive world the [realistic] text, in spite of itself, exposes incoherences, omissions, absences and transgressions which in turn reveal the inability of the language of ideology to create coherence" (p. 56). In *The Little Foxes* the most crucial "absence," to use Belsey's terminology, is the character of Addie. The realistic framework of the drama does indeed mask the fact that while Addie may be the moral center of the work—the one who points out the dangers of both active villainy and passive complicity—she is the only major character denied a story. It may be a comforting thought for white liberals that the black women who work for them are devoted solely to their white "families," have no ties to their own families or African-American communities, but it is a dishonest fiction grounded in a racist worldview—something Hellman herself implicitly acknowledged many years later in *An Unfinished Woman.*[35] Although realism as a theatrical style certainly does not *demand* that Hellman ignore the anger a character like Addie, born into slavery, would likely have felt toward whites like Horace Giddens who still control her life, it may well facilitate such gaps. At the very least, it fails to call attention to them.

Moreover, as Vivian Patraka convincingly argues, Hellman can use and has used realism to reinforce the status quo, to reify the most "traditional model of gender relations, including female subservience wedded to conjugal bliss and family devotion."[36] In *Watch on the Rhine*, Patraka points out, Hellman uses the realistic mode to chastise American complacency and naivete in the face of fascism, at the same time defining fascism in the most patriarchal terms: "an evil based on its opposition to the nuclear family" (p. 139). This does not, however, negate the very forceful questioning of gender roles that appears in similarly realistic works like *The Little Foxes* and *Another Part of the Forest,*[37] as well as *The Children's Hour, The Autumn Garden,* and even *Toys in the Attic.*

Jeanie Forte proposes that "the challenge for feminist dramatic criticism is one of empowerment, for women writers, performers and reader/spectators" (p. 125). Forte is not naively asking that feminist critics and theorists become cheerleaders for any and all works by women, but rather that we find and acknowledge the strengths and successes, as well as the limitations and failures, in our dramatic legacy. We have an obligation to women playwrights of the past—Rachel Crothers, Zona Gale, Lillian Hellman, Georgia Douglas Johnson, May Miller, Rose Franken, Maxine Wood, Alice Childress, Lorraine Hansberry, to name just a few who mined the ore of realism—to understand the value and power of their work as art and as protest against a society marked by racism, sexism, poverty, greed, and war. In her introduction to *Strike While the Iron is Hot,* Michelene Wandor argues that "historically, artistic movements which seek to represent the experiences of oppressed groups reach initially for a realistic and immediately recognisable clarity."[38] Building on Wandor's comments, Patricia Schroeder adds that "perhaps this appropriation of the devices of realism will turn out to be only a small step in the history of feminist drama, but it is a step that should not be overlooked or undervalued. Depicting what is can help create what should be."[39]

The works of Georgis Douglas Johnson, Shirley Graham, Mary P. Burrill, May Miller, Alice Childress, and Lorraine Hansberry—written from the doubly oppressed position of women of color—are obvious cases in point. Interestingly, some of the very same scholars who attack realism in theory still praise realistic plays by women of color. Sue-Ellen Case, for example, admires Childress's *Trouble in Mind* (p. 101)—a drama that, like virtually all of Childress's works, is clearly cast in the realist mold. *Trouble in Mind,* indeed, is *about* realism, about a black actress's refusal to play a dramatic role that falsifies how "real" black women would feel and act. If female playwrights are writing against the societal notion that women have no story—no lives of their own separate from the lives of the men they serve—denying them the use of narrative threatens to undermine the very project of affirming women's existence. This battle for a story and voice of one's own is a central issue in *The Little Foxes,* where Birdie is literally silenced by her husband. "Miss Birdie has changed her mind," Oscar announces in the opening scene, blithely canceling her order to a servant (p. 136). When simple contradiction does not suffice, he uses physical violence to keep her from talking. Regina, in contrast, spends much of the play shouting. However questionable her goals, Regina is determined to be heard, to write her own story, to shape a narrative for herself beyond the boundaries set by her husband, brothers, and the patriarchal society in which she lives. Regina, in many ways, is a realist playwright.

We may finally speculate that realism is the ideal mode for a writer who is more interested in what one does than in why one does it, and who believes that there is no such thing as an innocent bystander. Hellman's primary concern is neither with personal psychology nor with action for its own sake (as some who label her works "melo-drama" imply) but with individuals' behavior: no excuse, no fear for the safety of loved ones, can justify Alex Hazen's attempts to appease the Nazis in **The Searching Wind**, Mrs. Tilford's destruction of two women's lives in **The Children's Hour,** or Horace Giddens's past dealings with the Hubbards in **The Little Foxes.** In perhaps her last words on the subject of moral inertia, the conclusion to the 1979 revision of **Scoundrel Time,** Hellman writes: "I never want to live again to watch people turn into liars and cowards and others into frightened, silent collaborators. And to hell with the fancy reasons they give for what they did."[40] While Hell-man is recalling the McCarthy witch-hunts here, the lines sum up the philosophy that undergirds all her work: she uses realistic stagecraft to show not only what people do but the consequences of their actions. As Doris V. Falk observes, "realism assumes that there is a certain logical connection between events; that all actions have conse-quences."[41] Hellman biographer Carl Rollyson puts it another way: "She required a realistic and unambiguous form in order to attack the appease-ment of iniquity" (p. 12).

Like many of her female colleagues in the theatre in the first half of this century, Hellman used realism as a tool to explore and expose a capitalist society with narrowly inscribed gender roles, and to counter the demeaning portraits of women typically proffered by male playwrights. Materialist feminist theorists have done an impor-tant job of showing the pitfalls in this theatrical mode, the ways in which it may undermine the very criticism of society that it attempts to promul-gate. But to dismiss utterly the usefulness of real-ism to women as an instrument of social com-mentary and change is to erase a large part of our theatrical heritage and to deny future women playwrights still one more valuable weapon in their dramatic arsenal.

Notes

1. Qtd. in Barbara and Arthur Gelb, *O'Neill* (New York: Harper & Row, 1962), p. 520. O'Neill made this state-ment in the early 1920s. The great plays he wrote in his last years are, ironically, fundamentally realistic works.

2. Thornton Wilder, "Preface" to *Three Plays by Thornton Wilder* (New York: Bantam, 1958), p. x. See also Wil-liam W. Demastes, *Beyond Naturalism: A New Realism in American Theatre* (Westport, Conn.: Greenwood Press, 1988). Demastes identifies "a critical thread that has historically reviled realism as a form whose dominance in the late 19th and 20th centuries has limited theatre (and other literary fields as well) to restrictive and reductive presentations of complex thought and feeling" (pp. 1-2). Subsequent references to Demastes are cited in the text.

3. Sue-Ellen Case, "Toward a Butch-Femme Aesthetic," in *Making a Spectacle: Feminist Essays on Contemporary Women's Theatre,* ed. Lynda Hart (Ann Arbor: U of 'Michigan P, 1989), p. 297.

4. Jill Dolan, "'Lesbian' Subjectivity in Realism: Dragging at the Margins of Structure and Ideology," in *Perform-ing Feminisms: Feminist Critical Theory and Theatre,* ed. Sue-Ellen Case (Baltimore: Johns Hopkins UP, 1990), p. 52.

5. Elin Diamond, "Mimesis, Mimicry, and the 'True-Real,'" *Modern Drama* 32.1 (March 1989): 58-72, at 60-61. Subsequent references are cited in the text.

6. Sue-Ellen Case, in the Introduction to *Performing Femi-nisms,* p. 9, acknowledges that the charge of elitism might be leveled against those who repudiate represen-tation.

7. Brenda Murphy, *American Realism and American Drama, 1880-1940* (Cambridge: Cambridge UP, 1987). See especially chap. 2, "Realistic Dramatic Theory." Subsequent references are cited in the text.

8. Gerald Clarke, "The Long Way to Broadway," *Time* (March 30, 1981): 76.

9. Jacob H. Adler, *Lillian Hellman* (Austin: Steck-Vaughn Co., 1969), p. 7.

10. Royall Tyler, *The Contrast,* in *Dramas from the American Theatre, 1762-1909,* ed. Richard Moody (Boston: Houghton Mifflin, 1966), p. 47.

11. Lillian Hellman, *Pentimento,* in *Three: An Unfinished Woman, Pentimento, Scoundrel Time* (Boston: Little Brown, 1979), p. 482.

12. Martin Esslin, qtd. in Demastes, *Beyond Naturalism.* Demastes quotes the passage to make the point that certain "reductive assessments of realism by its op-ponents [are] unfortunate and misleading" (p. 2).

13. Teresa L. Ebert, "Gender and the Everyday: Toward a Postmodern Materialist Feminist Theory of Mimesis," in *"Turning the Century": Feminist Theory in the 1990s,* ed. Glynis Carr (Lewisburg: Bucknell UP, 1992), p. 104.

14. Katherine Lederer, *Lillian Hellman* (Boston: Twayne Publishers, 1979), p. 41. Subsequent references are cited in the text.

15. Hellman, *The Little Foxes,* in *Lillian Hellman: The Col-lected Plays* (Boston: Little, Brown, 1972), p. 195. Subsequent references are cited in the text.

16. Janelle Reinelt, "Feminist Theory and the Problem of Performance," *Modern Drama,* 32.1 (March 1989): 52.

17. Sue-Ellen Case, *Feminism and Theatre* (New York: Meth-uen, 1988), p. 124. Subsequent references are cited in the text.

18. Joseph Mersand, "When Ladies Write Plays: An Evaluation of Woman's Contribution to American Drama," *Players Magazine* 13 (Sept.-Oct. 1937): 26. Subsequent references are cited in the text.

19. Hellman deleted these lines—originally near the end of Act III—when she edited *The Little Foxes* for *The Collected Plays*, but they are an apt summary of Regina. Presumably Hellman cut the lines because they are too obviously apt, hence unnecessary.

20. Sharon Friedman, "Feminism as Theme in Twentieth-Century American Women's Drama," *American Studies* 25.1 (1984): 82.

21. Gayle Austin discusses the similar use of women as commodities in Hellman's *Another Part of the Forest*. See Austin's *Feminist Theories for Dramatic Criticism* (Ann Arbor: U of Michigan P, 1990), pp. 51-55.

22. Catherine Belsey, "Constructing the Subject: Deconstructing the Text," in *Feminist Criticism and Social Change*, ed. Judith Newton and Deborah Rosenfelt, pp. 45-64 (New York: Methuen, 1985), pp. 55, 53. Subsequent references are cited in the text.

23. Lederer notes that, by contrast, the movies made from Hellman's films tend toward closure. Hollywood is apparently less comfortable with open-endedness than Broadway is.

24. Timothy J. Wiles, "Lillian Hellman's American Political Theater: The Thirties and Beyond," in *Critical Essays on Lillian Hellman*, ed. Mark W. Estrin (Boston: G. K. Hall, 1989), p. 102. Wiles concurs that the concluding moments of *Foxes* transfer "the solution to this play's problem to the audience," and finds a similar refusal of closure in *Days to Come*.

25. This line was revised for the 1972 *Collected Plays*. In the original (1939) version, Alexandra's line is slightly longer but only marginally less vague. In the earlier rendering she vows "I'll be fighting as hard as he'll be fighting . . . some place where people don't just stand around and watch."

26. Jeanie Forte, "Realism, Narrative, and the Feminist Playwright—A Problem of Reception," *Modern Drama* 32.1 (March 1989): 115-27, at 117. Subsequent references are cited in the text. The specific play to which Forte here refers is Marsha Norman's *'night, Mother*, but she is making a general point about realistic drama. Perhaps we need to talk about "realists" and to distinguish precisely what the dramatic equivalent of Belsey's "classic realism" might be. Most materialist feminist theorists working with drama, however, seem to use *realism* as a monolithic term. Sue-Ellen Case makes a similar complaint about the "closure of . . . realistic narratives" in "Toward a Butch-Femme Aesthetic," p. 297.

27. Belsey concedes that "this process is not inevitable, in the sense that texts do not determine like fate the ways in which they must be read. I am concerned at this stage primarily with ways in which they are conventionally read" (p. 53). My argument is that even the "conventional" reader's or viewer's position is more flexible than Belsey acknowledges.

28. Terry Eagleton, quoted in Michele Barrett, "Ideology and the Cultural Production of Gender," in Newton and Rosenfelt, eds., *Feminist Criticism and Social Change*, p. 77.

29. Otis Ferguson, "A Play, A Picture," *New Republic* (April 12, 1939): 279.

30. Brooks Atkinson, "Miss Bankhead Has a Play," *New York Times* (Feb. 26, 1939) sec. 9, p. 1. Writing several decades after Atkinson, Hellman biographer William Wright gives a very similar interpretation of Regina. He is, however, disturbed by the ambiguity of the character, by the fact that audiences "can applaud" a woman who allows her husband to die. Not only have critical interpretations of the character and the play varied widely, but what one critic sees as a strength another may see as a flaw (*Lillian Hellman: The Image, the Woman* [New York: Simon and Schuster, 1986], p. 153).

31. Mel Gussow, "Women Playwrights: New Voices in the Theater," *New York Times Magazine* (May 1, 1983): 30.

32. *Playwrights Talk About Writing: 12 Interviews with Lewis Funke* (Chicago: Dramatic Publishing Co., 1975), p. 105. In the famous *Paris Review* interview, Hellman also admits her "great surprise" that audiences saw the play's conclusion as "a statement of faith in Alexandra, in her denial of her family. I never meant it that way. She did have courage enough to leave, but she would never have the force or vigor of her mother's family." Here again, however, Hellman adds a crucial qualification: "That's what I meant. Or maybe I made it up afterward" (John Phillips and Anne Hollander, "Lillian Hellman: An Interview"; rpt. in Estrin, ed., *Critical Essays on Lillian Hellman*, p. 232).

33. Jill Dolan, *The Feminist Spectator as Critic* (Ann Arbor: UMI Research Press, 1988), p. 84.

34. In her later years—long after writing *The Little Foxes*—Hellman became an admirer of Brecht's work. For a discussion of similarities between Hellman's plays and Brecht's, see Wiles, "Lillian Hellman's American Political Theater," pp. 90-112 passim.

35. Hellman, in her portrait of Helen, an African-American woman who worked for her, acknowledges "the hate and contempt" as well as the "old, real-pretend love" for white people that Helen had brought with her from the South. See *An Unfinished Woman* in *Three*, p. 251. Interestingly, in early drafts of *The Little Foxes*, Addie apparently played a larger role and had at least one family member, a daughter named Charlotte. In the final version, however, her concern and devotion are wholly directed toward Alexandra, and she seems to have no reservations about leaving her home in order to shepherd her young white charge. For discussions of these early drafts, see Richard Moody, *Lillian Hellman, Playwright* (New York: Bobbs-Merrill, 1972), pp. 105-8, and Carl Rollyson, *Lillian Hellman: Her Legend and Her Legacy* (New York: St. Martin's Press, 1988), pp. 128-29. Subsequent references to Rollyson are cited in the text.

36. Vivian M. Patraka, "Lillian Hellman's *Watch on the Rhine*: Realism, Gender, and Historical Crisis," *Modern Drama* 32.1 (March 1989): 130.

37. For a thoughtful, sympathetic reading of *Another Part of the Forest*, see Gayle Austin, *Feminist Theories for Dramatic Criticism*, pp. 51-55.

38. Michelene Wandor, "Introduction" to *Strike While the Iron is Hot: Three Plays on Sexual Politics* (London: Journeyman Press, 1980), p. 11.

39. Patricia R. Schroeder, "Locked Behind the Proscenium: Feminist Strategies in *Getting Out* and *My Sister in This House*," *Modern Drama* 32.1 (March 1989): 112. Subsequent references are cited in the text.

40. Hellman, *Scoundrel Time*, in *Three*, p. 726.

41. Doris V. Falk, *Lillian Hellman* (New York: Frederick Ungar, 1978), p. 32.

The Children's Hour

ALICE GRIFFIN AND GERALDINE THORSTEN (ESSAY DATE 1999)

SOURCE: Griffin, Alice, and Geraldine Thorsten. "*The Children's Hour.*" In *Understanding Lillian Hellman,* pp. 27-38. Columbia, S.C.: University of South Carolina Press, 1999.

In the following essay, Griffin and Thorsten discuss the moral implications of The Children's Hour.

"This is not really a play about lesbianism, but about a lie," said Lillian Hellman, describing *The Children's Hour* to a reporter. "The bigger the lie, the better, as always."[1] Opening on Broadway on 20 November 1934, the play centers upon two young women who open a school for girls and are destroyed when a malicious student charges them with lesbianism. By emphasizing the characters of Karen Wright and Martha Dobie and developing action that is as believable as it is theatrical, Hellman drove home her serious theme and achieved, at the age of twenty-nine, an immediate hit that would run for 691 performances.

Because lesbianism was a taboo subject in 1934, the play was banned in Boston, Chicago, and London. Despite its critical and public success in New York and France, it failed to earn the Pulitzer Prize for drama in 1935 because of its subject matter. New York theater critics protested by forming the Drama Critics' Circle, which has been presenting its own awards ever since.

Although *The Children's Hour* was a shocking, controversial play that took courage to write and to produce, it contained certain safeguards that made it morally acceptable. The charge that Karen Wright and Martha Dobie are in a lesbian relationship is untrue, for it is the fabrication of teenager Mary Tilford, a prototypical "bad seed." Karen is in love with and engaged to Dr. Joe Cardin. Martha, who begins to suspect toward the end of the play that she may be a lesbian, commits suicide immediately after sharing that revelation with Karen. In compliance with the 1930s view of homosexuality, she pays with her life for her "crime," an action to satisfy the most conservative audience.

While the sensationalism of the subject had to account in some part for the play's success, Hellman, who considered herself primarily "a moral writer," is concerned here with the harm done by so-called "good people," who do not challenge evil. It is the theme of Hellman's best-known play, *The Little Foxes,* and was to recur in her writing and her life from 1934 on. The character who accepts Mary's lie at face value is her wealthy grandmother, Amelia Tilford, a patron of the school.

Hellman found her plot, at the suggestion of Dashiell Hammett, in a chapter about an Edinburgh lawsuit called "Closed Doors; or, the Great Drumsheugh Case," in *Bad Companions,* a book written by law historian William Roughead. She retained such elements of the original account as the fourteen-year-old student's false charge; her resolute, patrician grandmother; the difficult, interfering aunt of one of the women; and the close relationship between the two teachers—one nervous and high-strung and the other stable and placid. Hellman added a fiancé for Karen (to clarify at the onset the fact that the charge is a lie), developed all of the characters, and carried the action forward with ever-increasing tension. The amazing final scene combines the characters' self-revelation and discovery with the kind of theatrical punch that would mark Hellman's plays in the future.

As women are central to Hellman's plays and memoirs, they reflect women's position in society at the time of writing. Karen and Martha are women who earn their own money and achieve the power and independence this brings. Unlike Regina in *The Little Foxes,* set in 1900, who without money is dependent on what she is given by or can manipulate from men, these women in their late twenties have the teaching and administrative skills that have made the school a success.

Joe, who is more egalitarian than most men were at that time, supports Karen's desire to continue her career after their marriage and respects the women's dedication to the school. In the second scene of act 2, after Mrs. Tilford has summarily withdrawn Mary from the school and warned others to do the same, he champions the women to his aunt: "They've worked eight long years to save enough money to buy that farm, to start that school. They did without everything that young people ought to have . . . That school meant things to them: self-respect, and bread and butter, and honest work."

Young Mary Tilford is so appalling yet mesmerizing a creation that audiences mistook her for the central character and could not understand why she was absent from act 3. Even critics were baffled and faulted Hellman's structuring of the play, but Hellman never intended her as the main character or planned for her to be "the utterly malignant creature which playgoers see in her." Hellman explains that "on the stage a person is twice as villainous as, say, in a novel."[2] The fact that Mary's lie is of a sexual nature intensifies its impact. In the thirties, children, especially girls, were shielded from sexual information and were believed to be uninterested in sex until late puberty. Mary's lie succeeds because adults in her community find it inconceivable that she should know about a lesbian relationship unless she had seen actual evidence of it, and Mary is clever enough to disguise how much she has learned from reading illicit French novels. In telling her story to her grandmother, she gives a convincing portrayal of young innocence unaware of the import of what she is saying. Another reason Mary still has the power to horrify is that Hellman anchors her behavior in reality, drawing upon memories of her own childhood bullying and lying to get her way.[3]

Because Karen is a teacher who believes in being fair and treating the granddaughter of a patron the same as the other students, Mary cannot wheedle her way out when Karen catches her in a lie about picking flowers for Mrs. Mortar, a bouquet she actually found in an ashcan. That Mary will not retreat from so trivial a lie, despite Karen's sympathetic appeals, foreshadows Mary's obduracy in act 2 in defense of her far greater lie. Her blackmailing and bullying of schoolmates in order to run away from the school are also the same techniques she will use in the second act to maintain the lie that allows her the freedom of life with her permissive grandmother.

Mary's grandmother, Amelia Tilford, is a type who will appear regularly in Hellman's plays: the wealthy widow who has been content to be provided for handsomely first by her father and then by her husband. Whether Hellman's portrayal is positive, as it is of Fanny Farrelly in **Watch on the Rhine**, or less sympathetic, as here with Mrs. Tilford, the character is a woman who does not think for herself but has inherited her views, principles, and status from the men in her life. Because her principles are hers only superficially, Mrs. Tilford deserts them when she is confronted with a crisis. One would expect her to investigate Mary's story and to confront Karen and Martha first with what she has heard. However, the lie Mary tells so challenges Mrs. Tilford's concept of the right order of things that after only the most cursory questioning of its truth, she is stampeded

into acting. Mrs. Tilford also is led astray by self-righteousness, another failing of which Hellman is critical in the plays. Not only does Amelia Tilford believe her opinions are infallible, but so does the community: when she accepts Mary's lie as truth and alerts the parents, they immediately withdraw their children from the school.

Karen Wright and Martha Dobie command attention and interest almost equally until the end of the play. Although both are competent, intelligent, and committed to their work, they differ in the degree to which they are independent. Martha is less so by virtue of her situation and her temperament. It is Karen's small capital they use to start their venture, a financial disparity that means Martha is not on an equal footing. It is Karen who is more determined to be self-sufficient: she objects when Martha suggests that Karen's fiancé discuss Mary's behavior with his aunt, Mrs. Tilford: "That would be admitting we can't do the job ourselves." On the subject of their retaining Martha's aunt, the incompetent Lily Mortar, Karen can act more firmly. In act 1 she asks Martha outright: "Couldn't we get rid of her soon, Martha? I hate to make it hard on you but she really ought not to be here."

At the close of this conversation, Martha, learning that Karen and Joe plan to marry at the end of the term, is stunned: "You haven't talked of marriage for a long time," as if she had lulled herself into believing that the marriage would never become a reality. Karen's response, "I've talked of it with Joe," again points up the difference between them. Karen has both her close friendship with Martha and an intimate relationship with Joe, another claim on her loyalty and love. Martha has only her friendship with Karen, and is understandably fearful of losing the one relationship that has emotional resonance for her. Their earlier discussion of vacation plans highlights Martha's greater need for Karen and Karen's somewhat unrealistic attitude about the impact her marriage will have on their lives. Martha has envisioned a vacation for just the two of them, like one they had during their college years; Karen's vision is similar, except it is just the three of them. Whether or not Karen is willing to admit it, her marriage *will* make a difference, and Martha's outcry is the anguish of the one who stands to lose the most from the changes it will bring.

To balance Martha's dependency, Hellman endows her with a sharp sense of humor. This is not a play rife with humor; the issues it deals with are too somber for that. But the occasional wit that enlivens the otherwise serious dialogue is usually Martha's. When Joe semijokingly boasts in act 1 that the Tilfords are "a proud old breed," Martha retorts, "The Jukes were an old family, too."

Conversations with Aunt Lily Mortar suggest why Martha is "nervous and highstrung," tense, with low self-esteem. While Amelia Tilford will gain, at enormous cost, understanding and integrity, Mrs. Mortar undergoes no such transformation. Vain and self-centered, a mediocre actress who no longer can find work, she has been hired as an elocution teacher because Martha feels indebted for her upbringing, despite a childhood with Aunt Lily that was neither happy nor comfortable. Seeing herself as a victim in order to put others in the wrong, Lily twists Martha's offer of a pension, if she will leave: "You're turning me out? At my age! Nice grateful girl you are." She does not leave soon enough, for it is her malicious remarks to Martha, overheard by Evelyn and Peggy, that provide the basis for Mary's lie.

Lily Mortar accuses Martha outright of being jealous of Joe and "unnatural" in her affection for Karen, and compounds this by claiming that Martha was "always like that even as a child." Aunt Lily concludes with, "Well, you'd better get a beau of your own now—a woman of your age," an admonition guaranteed to stir anxiety in virtually any woman's heart in those days. Inspired by mere pique, her malice is an assault on Martha's inmost self, and gains unfairly in strength from her role as Martha's surrogate mother, the person, presumably, who has known her best. Her remarks serve to cast Martha's sexuality in an ambiguous light in act 1 and to make Martha's self-revelation and subsequent action in act 3 believable, although nonetheless shocking.

The tragic events Mary's lie sets in motion affect Karen profoundly, but they are external to her. Her essential self remains intact. Philip M. Armato believes Karen lacks compassion for Mrs. Mortar and Mary Tilford and that these characters treat her as she has treated them. He claims Karen's punishment of Mary is unduly harsh and that Mary is justified in feeling persecuted.[4] A careful reading of this scene fails to support this view. Karen is both reasonable and compassionate toward Mary; she also is committed to making a success of her business. Her compassion, therefore, is exercised within the larger context of the school, of ensuring that it is a wholesome environment, with standards of discipline maintained by all students.

Karen's discipline of Mary demonstrates her courage. Given their dependence on Mrs. Tilford's goodwill and financial backing, it would have been easy for Karen to let Mary off with only a token punishment, but she does not. Neither does she shrink from confronting Mrs. Tilford in act 2 to demand an explanation for her abrupt withdrawal of support. Nor in act 3 does she avoid the painful reality that her relationship with Joe is no longer tenable and, with compassion for his anguish, releases him from their engagement.

It is also Karen who has the courage to broach the subject of lesbianism, saying, "But this isn't a new sin they tell us we've done. Other people aren't destroyed by it." But Karen speaks as one for whom the charge is external, imposed on them by the outside world. Martha, on the other hand, internalizes that charge and sees herself through the lens society holds up to her. Underlying the tension characteristic of Martha's personality is a brittleness, at once fragile and rigid, born of her conviction that there is and always has been something radically "wrong" with her. Mary Tilford's lie seems to offer a plausible explanation of the truth about herself.

Despite Martha's wit, her efforts at independence, and her battle against her aunt's attacks, she has achieved neither full self-awareness nor true independence of mind. Hellman explains that "suspecting herself of lesbian desires, not lesbian acts, but lesbian desires, and thus feeling that the charge made against her had some moral truth, although no actual truth," Martha convicts herself of a thought crime and summarily executes herself.[5] The evidence she cites—that she has never felt an intense attachment to anybody but Karen and has "never loved a man"—could be construed as indicating a lesbian cast to her sexuality. Neither the audiences nor critics had any difficulty accepting her judgment at face value. Martha feels she is to blame for the disaster that has befallen them, and yet her claims to that guilt are framed in "I don't know" and "maybe." In one short speech, for example, she repeats the word "maybe" four times, giving the scene a disturbing ambiguity. Judith Olauson observes that the "allegations are believed first by the town, then by friends, and finally by the two women themselves."[6] Martha may be mistaken about herself, for one of the awful powers of such a lie is to convince its victims to believe the image of themselves devised by their oppressors.

Critics saw Hellman as influenced by Ibsen in her careful plotting, social realism, and use of violence. Jacob Adler cites Martha's suicide, Mary's extortion of money from Peggy, and her blackmail of Rosalie as reminiscent of Ibsen's technique.[7] Hellman had a flair for dramatic ways to capture and hold audience attention, but the devices she uses are not for theatricality alone; they are logical extensions of character or situation. In *The Children's Hour,* Mary Lynn Broe observes, "all the truth-revealing scenes are interrupted so that the continuous action of dramatic unraveling and revelation are missing from the play. By such sleight of structure, Hellman shifts the focus from blackmail, extortion, and lesbianism (more melodramatic topics) to the quiet business of redefining a moral capacity."[8] By limiting to the first two acts Mary's presence in the play as the agent of destruction, Hellman in act 3 shifts the audience's attention from the means Mary uses to the wreckage that has resulted from her lie.

With an excellent ear for American speech, Hellman employs language and rhythm to convey character. Her preliminary notes describe Karen as the "voice of reason, straight, clear, dull but educated, balanced, unemotionally awakened."[9] This contrasts with Martha's more fiery, nervous qualities and tension. Their respective dialogue reveals that Karen's speeches are smooth, stable, verging on brisk, and containing no surprises, whereas Martha's are choppy, fragmented, and wry, with unexpected turns. Hellman's use of language to support and underscore action is evident in the final act, for which her notes indicate that "after the suicide, no one must talk with the same words or rhythms as they have before."[10] Through such dislocations of speech, the emotional impact of the tragedy is conveyed, although there is little discussion of the suicide.

The wintry desolation of act 3 is in stark contrast to the hopeful, springtime bustle of act 1, alive with schoolgirls, teachers, and fiancé. A significant drop in energy in act 3 accords with the hopelessness of Karen and Martha, who are the picture of defeat as the act opens, with Karen in an armchair and Martha lying on the sofa. A long two to three minutes of silence indicates to the audience how barren their lives have become. The act proceeds with a further stripping away: first Lily Mortar, then Joe, and finally Martha, so that when Mrs. Tilford arrives to say she has discovered Mary was lying and now wants to make reparations, the irony is complete. Karen's pallid inquiry, "Is it nice out?" hints at the return of hope, and the action comes to a close with commonplaces about the weather signaling the return of normal life.

Not everyone was satisfied with this ending, including Hellman, but she would allow no one else to tinker with her plot. In the course of time, she became convinced that the play should have ended with Martha's suicide. However, for the 1952 revival, she says, "I worked for weeks and weeks trying to take out the last eight or ten minutes of the play, which sounds very easy, as if I could have done it, but I couldn't do it. It had been built into the play . . . so far back, that I finally decided that a mistake was as much a part of you as a non-mistake, and that I had better leave it alone before I ended up with nothing."[11]

The success of *The Children's Hour* opened the door to Hollywood for Hellman as a screenwriter. She adapted the play for the screen as *These Three,* in which she converted the slander to infidelity to satisfy the Hayes Office's strict moral code. In 1962 *The Children's Hour,* with a script by John Michael Hayes from an outline by Hellman, was one of the first movies to be made under the liberalized production codes that replaced the Hayes regulations. In addition to its stagings through the years in the professional and nonprofessional theater, two major revivals were to have an impact. The first was in 1952 during the McCarthy era, with the production and its implications about "the big lie" causing a good deal of controversy, being praised or maligned according to one's political inclinations. In 1995 an acclaimed production by the Royal National Theatre in London testified to the endurance of "one of the most compelling works to emerge from the serious American theatre before Blanche DuBois and Willy Loman arrived on Broadway in the late 1940s."[12]

Notes

1. Harry Gilroy, "The Bigger the Lie," in *The Children's Hour: Acting Edition* (New York: Dramatists Play Service, 1953), 3.

2. Ibid.

3. Margaret Case Harriman, "Miss Lily of New Orleans: Lillian Hellman," in *Take Them up Tenderly* (New York: Knopf, 1944), 102.

4. Philip M. Armato, "'Good and Evil' in Lillian Hellman's *The Children's Hour,* in *Critical Essays on Lillian Hellman,* ed. Mark W. Estrin (Boston: G. K. Hall, 1989), 73-78.

5. Fred Gardner, "An Interview with Lillian Hellman" (1968), in *Conversations with Lillian Hellman,* ed. Jackson R. Bryer (Jackson: University Press of Mississippi, 1986), 110.

6. Judith Olauson, *The American Woman Playwright: A View of Criticism and Characterization* (Troy, N.Y.: Whitston, 1981), 34.

7. Jacob Adler, "The Dramaturgy of Blackmail in the Ibsenite Hellman," in *Critical Essays on Lillian Hellman,* ed. Mark W. Estrin (Boston: G. K. Hall, 1989), 34.

8. Mary Lynn Broe, "Bohemia Bumps into Calvin: The Deception of Passivity in Lillian Hellman's Drama," in *Critical Essays on Lillian Hellman,* ed. Mark W. Estrin (Boston: G. K. Hall, 1989), 82.

9. Carl Rollyson, *Lillian Hellman: Her Legend and Her Legacy* (New York: St. Martin's, 1988), 66.

10. Manfred Triesch, *The Lillian Hellman Collection at the University of Texas* (Austin: University of Texas Press, 1966), 104.

11. Gardner, "Interview," 111.

12. Mark W. Estrin, "Introduction," in *Critical Essays on Lillian Hellman,* ed. Mark W. Estrin (Boston: G. K. Hall, 1989), 2.

FURTHER READING

Bibliographies

Estrin, Mark W. *Lillian Hellman: Plays, Films, Memoirs.* Boston: G. K. Hall, 1980, 378 p.

Complete record of essays, reviews, and news articles about Hellman's work from 1934 to 1979.

Horn, Barbara Lee. *Lillian Hellman: A Research and Production Sourcebook.* Westport, Conn.: Greenwood Press, 1998, 170 p.

Comprehensive sourcebook containing play synopses, critical overviews, and annotated bibliographies of both primary and secondary sources.

Triesch, Manfred. *The Lillian Hellman Collection at the University of Texas,* compiled by Manfred Triesch. Austin: University of Texas, 1966, 167 p.

Bibliography of the manuscripts, letters, and papers in the Hellman Collection.

Biographies

Dick, Bernard F. *Hellman in Hollywood.* Rutherford, N.J.: Fairleigh Dickinson University Press, 1982, 183 p.

Coverage of Hellman's life and career as a Hollywood screenwriter.

Moody, Richard. *Lillian Hellman: Playwright.* New York: Pegasus, 1972, 372 p.

Comprehensive study of Hellman's life as a playwright.

Criticism

Austenfeld, Thomas Carl. "The Moral Act: Lillian Hellman Fights Fascists in the Parlor." In *American Women Writers and the Nazis: Ethics and Politics in Boyle, Porter, Stafford, and Hellman,* pp. 85-106. Charlottesville, Va.: University Press of Virginia, 2001.

Maintains that in Watch on the Rhine *and* The Searching Wind *Hellman was attempting to draw America into the war against fascism.*

Austin, Gayle. "The Exchange of Women and Male Homosocial Desire in Arthur Miller's *Death of a Salesman* and Lillian Hellman's *Another Part of the Forest.*" In *Feminist Rereadings of Modern American Drama,* edited by June Schlueter, pp. 59-66. Rutherford, N.J.: Fairleigh Dickinson University Press, 1989.

Employs Gayle Rubin's feminist essay "The Traffic in Women" to analyze plays by Miller and Hellman.

Burke, Sally. "Anticipating the Second Wave." In *American Feminist Playwrights: A Critical History,* pp. 100-38. New York: Twayne, 1996.

Examines Hellman as a feminist playwright.

Erhart, Julia. "'She Could Hardly Invent Them!' From Epistemological Uncertainty to Discursive Production: Lesbianism in *The Children's Hour.*" *Camera Obscura: Feminism, Culture, and Media Studies* 35 (May 1995): 87-105.

Discusses the issue of lesbianism in The Children's Hour.

Falk, Doris V. *Lillian Hellman.* New York: Frederick Ungar, 1978, 180 p.

Collection of critical essays on Hellman's plays and memoirs.

Friedman, Sharon. "Feminism as Theme in Twentieth-Century American Women's Drama." *American Studies* 25, no. 1 (spring 1984): 69-89.

Explores the theme of feminism in several American plays, including Hellman's The Little Foxes *and Another Part of the Forest.*

Lederer, Katherine. *Lillian Hellman.* Boston: Twayne, 1979, 159 p.

Critical essays on Hellman's life and major works.

Mooney, Theresa R. "These Four: Hellman's Roots Are Showing." In *Southern Women Playwrights,* edited by Robert L. McDonald and Linda Rohrer Paige, pp. 27-41. Tuscaloosa, Ala.: University of Alabama Press, 2002.

Examines the representation of the South in four of Hellman's plays.

Reaves, Gerri. "Lillian Hellman's *Scoundrel Time* and the Ownership of Memory." In *Mapping the Private Geography: Autobiography, Identity, and America,* pp. 51-82, 135-58. Jefferson, N.C.: McFarland & Company, Inc., 2001.

Examination of Hellman's unorthodox manner of rendering personal memories in Scoundrel Time.

Sauer, David Kennedy. "*Oleanna* and *The Children's Hour*: Misreading Sexuality on the Post/Modern Realistic Stage." *Modern Drama* 43, no. 3 (fall 2000): 421-41.

Compares the treatment of sexuality in plays by Hellman and by David Mamet.

Tuhkanen, Mikko. "Breeding (and) Reading: Lesbian Knowledge, Eugenic Discipline, and *The Children's Hour.*" *Modern Fiction Studies* 48, no. 4 (2002): 1001-1040.

Explores the racial subtext of The Children's Hour.

OTHER SOURCES FROM GALE:

Additional coverage of Hellman's life and career is contained in the following sources published by the Gale Group: *American Writers Supplement,* Vol. 1; *Authors and Artists for Young Adults,* Vol. 47; *Authors in the News,* Vols. 1, 2; *Contemporary American Dramatists; Contemporary Authors,* Vols. 13-16R, 112; *Contemporary Authors New Revision Series,*

Vol. 33; *Contemporary Literary Criticism*, Vols. 2, 4, 8, 14, 18, 34, 44, 52; *Contemporary Women Dramatists*; *Dictionary of Literary Biography*, Vols. 7, 228; *Dictionary of Literary Biography Yearbook, 1984*; *DISCovering Authors Modules: Dramatists*; *DISCovering Authors 3.0*; *Drama Criticism*, Vol. 1; *Drama for Students*, Vols. 1, 3, 14; *Encyclopedia of World Literature in the 20th Century*, Ed. 3; *Feminist Writers*; *Literature and Its Times*, Vol. 3; *Literature Resource Center*; *Major 20th-Century Writers*, Eds. 1, 2; *Modern American Women Writers*; *Reference Guide to American Literature*, Ed. 4; *Twayne's United States Authors*; and *Twentieth-Century Literary Criticism*, Vol. 119.

ZORA NEALE HURSTON

(1891 - 1960)

American novelist, folklorist, essayist, short story writer, playwright, anthropologist, and autobiographer.

Hurston is widely considered one of the foremost writers of the Harlem Renaissance, a period of great achievement in African American art and literature during the 1920s and 1930s. Her fiction, which depicts relationships among black residents in her native southern Florida, was largely unconcerned with racial injustices. While not well known during her lifetime, Hurston's works have undergone a substantial re-evaluation, particularly since the advent of the black protest novel and the elevation in literary status of authors Richard Wright, Ralph Ellison, and James Baldwin during the post-World War II era. Hurston's present reputation and popularity are evidenced by the reprinting of several of her works in the late 1980s, including *Their Eyes Were Watching God* (1937). This book has been read as a feminist manifesto for its unconventional female protagonist, Janie Crawford, who is considered by many as a representation of the author herself. Hurston's novel has become a staple in women's studies programs and has inspired many female authors to create nonstereotypical black female characters.

BIOGRAPHICAL INFORMATION

Hurston was born January 15, 1891, in Notasulga, Alabama, to John, a Baptist preacher, and Lula (called Lucy), a seamstress. When she was still a young child her family moved to Eatonville, Florida, the first incorporated black township in the United States and the setting for most of her fiction. In 1904 her mother died, which devastated Hurston. Her father married a much younger woman with whom Hurston did not get along, and Hurston was sent to school in Jacksonville and then to live with relatives. At the age of fourteen, Hurston left home to work as a maid with a traveling Gilbert and Sullivan theatrical troupe.

For a short time in 1917 Hurston studied at Morgan State University in Baltimore, and in 1918 she entered Howard University in Washington, D.C. While at Howard, Hurston published short stories in *Stylus,* the university literary magazine, and attracted the attention of noted sociologist Charles S. Johnson. With Johnson's encouragement, Hurston moved to New York City in 1925 and subsequently secured a scholarship to Barnard College with the assistance of Annie Nathan Meyer, a white philanthropist and well-known supporter of Harlem Renaissance artists. While at Barnard, Hurston studied anthropology under Franz Boas, one of the most renowned anthropologists of the era. After her graduation in 1928, she continued her work with Boas as a graduate student at Columbia University.

With the aid of fellowships and a private grant from Charlotte Osgood Mason, a New York socialite interested in "primitive Negro art," Hurston returned to the South to collect folklore. She traveled to Alabama, Louisiana, and Florida, living among sharecroppers and workers lodged in labor camps whose primary form of entertainment consisted of telling tall tales, or "lies." In 1935 Hurston compiled *Mules and Men* (1935), a collection of African American folktales that expanded upon her academic studies and anthropological field work. Through the next decade Hurston continued to travel for her anthropological research and continued to write fiction.

In 1945 Hurston was accused of sexual corruption of a minor. The charges were dismissed, but the controversy damaged Hurston's reputation. She continued to write but did not find much interest from publishers. After trying to support herself with odd jobs, Hurston became ill and moved into the county welfare home in Fort Pierce, Florida, where she died in 1960.

MAJOR WORKS

In addition to tales and descriptions of voodoo practices and beliefs, *Mules and Men* includes work songs, legends, rhymes, and lies, all of which contained hidden social and philosophical messages considered essential to survival in a racist society. African American folklore forms a basis for all of Hurston's writing, including what critics refer to as her greatest novel, *Their Eyes Were Watching God*. Thought to be essentially autobiographical, *Their Eyes Were Watching God* focuses on a woman's search for self-definition in the sexist society of the early 1900s. Janie Crawford is a beautiful, light-skinned African American woman unable to discover her true self until she begins to take charge of her life. The oral narrative employed to relate Janie's quest implies that her strength and identity grow as she becomes more attuned to her black heritage; the telling of tales is as integral a part of black culture as the tales themselves. Similarly, Janie's account is a story within a story, told in a flashback to her good friend Pheoby Watson.

Hurston's autobiography *Dust Tracks on a Road* (1942) reveals more about Hurston's writing style and her opinions on many of the issues of the day than about her early life. Hurston discusses very little about her birth, her early family life,

relationships, and her involvement in the Harlem Renaissance. In *Seraph on the Suwanee* (1948) Hurston used white protagonists for the first time in her work. Arvay Henson comes from a poor, white "cracker" family and believes she has found her salvation in Jim Meserve, a man who raped her and whom she subsequently married. However, Arvay finds herself stifled by her sexist husband and consistently feels inadequate in meeting his expectations.

CRITICAL RECEPTION

Critics have generally praised Hurston's narrative recreation of southern black rural dialect; however, several critics have reacted negatively to Hurston's use of the same dialect with her white characters in *Seraph on the Suwanee*. From the initial publication of *Their Eyes Were Watching God*, critics have debated Hurston's ostensible disregard of the issue of racism. Many of Hurston's black contemporaries considered her an opportunist who catered to white benefactors, and early reviewers believed her book to be an attempt at escapism. However, other commentators have noted that Janie's dilemmas are not centered on issues of racism, but sexism, a concern for all women during the 1920s. Most contemporary critics have argued that Hurston concentrates on strength and affirmation within the black community, and not the denial and anger racism often evokes.

There has also been disagreement among critics regarding Hurston's relationship to feminism. Some commentators have asserted that Hurston's life and work make her a model feminist: as a woman who refused to conform to other's expectations and who did not rely on a man for support, she practiced several feminist traits. Some reviewers have viewed Janie Crawford as a feminist icon, but others have been troubled by the way she relies upon a man to help her and by how long it takes for her to find her voice. Another issue of intense feminist debate amongst scholars concerning *Their Eyes Were Watching God*, is the death of Tea Cake—Janie's companion after her husband's death. Most commentators have agreed it is essential to Janie's quest that she return to Eatonville alone, but many question whether it is necessary for Tea Cake to be sacrificed for Janie to obtain her sense of identity. The novel's ironic ending is generally considered representative of Hurston's beliefs regarding her writing and her life—in both she challenged conventional norms.

PRINCIPAL WORKS

Color Struck (play) 1926

The First One: A Play, in Ebony and Topaz (play) 1927

The Great Day (play) 1932

The Gilded Six-Bits (folklore) 1933

Jonah's Gourd Vine (novel) 1934

Mules and Men (folklore) 1935

Their Eyes Were Watching God (novel) 1937

Tell My Horse (folklore) 1938; also published as *Voodoo Gods: An Inquiry into Native Myths and Magic in Jamaica and Haiti* 1939

Moses, Man of the Mountain (novel) 1939; also published as *The Man of the Mountain* 1941

Dust Tracks on a Road (autobiography) 1942

Polk County: A Comedy of Negro Life on a Sawmill Camp [with Dorothy Waring] (play) 1944

Seraph on the Suwanee (novel) 1948

I Love Myself When I Am Laughing . . . and Then Again When I Am Looking Mean and Impressive: A Zore Neale Hurston Reader (fiction and nonfiction) 1979

The Sanctified Church (novel) 1981

Spunk: The Selected Stories of Zora Neale Hurston (short stories) 1985

The Complete Stories (short stories) 1994

Folklore, Memoirs, and Other Writings (nonfiction) 1995

Novels and Stories (novels and short stories) 1995

Collected Essays (essays) 1998

Every Tongue Got to Confess: Negro Folk Tales from the Gulf States (folklore) 2001

Zora Neale Hurston: A Life in Letters [edited by Carla Kaplan] (letters) 2002

PRIMARY SOURCES

ZORA NEALE HURSTON (NOVEL DATE 1937)

SOURCE: Hurston, Zora Neale. "Chapter 12." In *Their Eyes Were Watching God*, 1937. Reprint, pp. 105-10. New York: Harper and Row, Perennial Library, 1990.

In the following excerpt from Their Eyes Were Watching God, *Hurston relates the consternation of the townspeople with the growing relationship between Tea Cake and Mrs. Janie Starks. Janie's husband, Joe Starks, has recently died.*

It was after the picnic that the town began to notice things and got mad. Tea Cake and Mrs. Mayor Starks! All the men that she could get, and fooling with somebody like Tea Cake! Another thing, Joe Starks hadn't been dead but nine months and here she goes sashaying off to a picnic in pink linen. Done quit attending church, like she used to. Gone off to Sanford in a car with Tea Cake and her all dressed in blue! It was a shame. Done took to high heel slippers and a ten dollar hat! Looking like some young girl, always in blue because Tea Cake told her to wear it. Poor Joe Starks. Bet he turns over in his grave every day. Tea Cake and Janie gone hunting. Tea Cake and Janie gone fishing. Tea Cake and Janie gone to Orlando to the movies. Tea Cake and Janie gone to a dance. Tea Cake making flower beds in Janie's yard and seeding the garden for her. Chopping down that tree she never did like by the dining room window. All those signs of possession. Tea Cake in a borrowed car teaching Janie to drive. Tea Cake and Janie playing checkers; playing coon-can; playing Florida flip on the store porch all afternoon as if nobody else was there. Day after day and week after week.

"Pheoby," Sam Watson said one night as he got in the bed, "Ah b'lieve yo' buddy is all tied up with dat Tea Cake shonough. Didn't b'lieve it at first."

"Aw she don't mean nothin' by it. Ah think she's sort of stuck on dat undertaker up at Sanford."

"It's somebody 'cause she looks might good dese days. New dresses and her hair combed a different way nearly every day. You got to have something to comb hair over. When you see uh woman doin' so much rakin' in her head, she's combin' at some man or 'nother."

"'Course she kin do as she please, but dat's uh good chance she got up at Sanford. De man's wife died and he got uh lovely place tuh take her to—already furnished. Better'n her house Joe left her."

"You better sense her intuh things then 'cause Tea Cake can't do nothin' but help her spend whut she got. Ah reckon dat's whut he's after. Throwin' away whut Joe Starks worked hard tuh git tuhgether."

"Dat's de way it looks. Still and all, she's her own woman. She oughta know by now whut she wants tuh do."

"De men wuz talkin' 'bout it in de grove tuhday and givin' her and Tea Cake both de devil. Dey figger he's spendin' on her now in order tuh make her spend on him later."

"Umph! Umph! Umph!"

"Oh dey got it all figgered out. Maybe it ain't as bad as they say, but they talk it and make it sound real bad on her part."

"Dat's jealousy and malice. Some uh dem very mens wants tuh do whut dey claim deys skeered Tea Cake is doin'."

"De Pastor claim Tea Cake don't 'low her tuh come tuh church only once in awhile 'cause he want dat change tuh buy gas wid. Just draggin' de woman away from church. But any-how, she's yo' bosom friend, so you better go see 'bout her. Drop uh lil hint here and dere and if Tea Cake is tryin' tuh rob her she kin see and know. Ah laks de woman and Ah sho would hate tuh see her come up lak Mis' Tyler."

"Aw mah God, naw! Reckon Ah better step over dere tomorrow and have some chat wid Janie. She jus' ain't thinkin' whut she doin' dat's all."

The next morning Pheoby picked her way over to Janie's house like a hen to a neighbor's garden. Stopped and talked a little with everyone she met, turned aside momentarily to pause at a porch or two—going straight by walking crooked. So her firm intention looked like an accident and she didn't have to give her opinion to folks along the way.

Janie acted glad to see her and after a while Pheoby broached her with, "Janie, everybody's talkin' 'bout how dat Tea Cake is draggin' you round tuh places you ain't used tuh. Baseball games and huntin' and fishin'. He don't know you'se useter uh more high time crowd than dat. You always did class off."

"Jody classed me off. Ah didn't. Naw, Pheoby, Tea Cake ain't draggin' me off nowhere Ah don't want tuh go. Ah always did want tuh git round uh whole heap, but Jody wouldn't 'low me tuh. When Ah wasn't in de store he wanted me tuh jes sit wid folded hands and sit dere. And Ah'd sit dere wid de walls creepin' up on me and squeezin' all de life outa me. Pheoby, dese educated women got uh heap of things to sit down and consider. Somebody done tole 'em what to set down for. Nobody ain't told poor me, so sittin' still worries me. Ah wants tuh utilize mahself all over."

"But, Janie, Tea Cake, whilst he ain't no jail-bird, he ain't got uh dime tuh cry. Ain't you skeered he's jes after yo' money—him bein' younger than you?"

"He ain't never ast de first penny from me yet, and if he love property he ain't no different from all de rest of us. All dese ole men dat's settin' round me is after de same thing. They's three mo' widder women in town, how come dey don't break dey neck after dem? 'Cause dey ain't got nothin', dat's why."

"Folks seen you out in colors dey thinks you ain't payin' de right amount uh respect tuh yo' dead husband."

"Ah ain't grievin' so why do Ah hafta mourn? Tea Cake love me in blue, so Ah wears it. Jody ain't never in his life picked out no color for me. De world picked out black and white for mournin', Joe didn't. So Ah wasn't wearin' it for him. Ah was wearin' it for de rest of y'all."

"But anyhow, watch yo'self, Janie, and don't be took advantage of. You know how dese young men is wid older women. Most of de time dey's after whut dey kin git, then dey's gone lak uh turkey through de corn."

"Tea Cake don't talk dat way. He's aimin' tuh make hisself permanent wid me. We done made up our mind tuh marry."

"Janie, you'se yo' own woman, and Ah hope you know whut you doin'. Ah sho hope you ain't lak uh possum—de older you gits, de less sense yuh got. Ah'd feel uh whole heap better 'bout yuh if you wuz marryin' dat man up dere in Sanford. He got somethin' tuh put long side uh whut you got and dat make it more better. He's endurable."

"Still and all Ah'd ruther be wid Tea Cake."

"Well, if yo' mind is already made up, 'tain't nothing' nobody kin do. But you'se takin' uh awful chance."

"No mo' than Ah took befo' and no mo' than anybody else takes when dey gits married. It always changes folks, and sometimes it brings out dirt and meanness dat even de person didn't know they had in 'em theyselves. You know dat. Maybe Tea Cake might turn out lak dat. Maybe not. Anyhow Ah'm ready and willin' tuh try 'im."

"Well, when you aim tuh step?"

"Dat we don't know. De store is got tuh be sold and then we'se goin' off somewhere tuh git married."

"How come you sellin' out de store?"

"'Cause Tea Cake ain't no Jody Starks, and if he tried tuh be, it would be uh complete flom-muck. But de minute Ah marries 'im everybody is gointuh be makin' comparisons. So us is goin' off somewhere and start all over in Tea Cake's way. Dis ain't no business proposition, and no race after property and titles. Dis is uh love game. Ah done lived Grandma's way. Now Ah means tuh live mine."

"What you mean by dat, Janie?"

"She was borned in slavery time when folks, dat is black folks, didn't sit down anytime dey felt lak it. So sittin' on porches lak de white madam looked lak uh mighty fine thing tuh her. Dat's whut she wanted for me—don't keer whut it cost. Git up on uh high chair and sit dere. She didn't have time tuh think whut tuh do after you got up on de stool uh do nothin'. De object wuz tuh git dere. So Ah got up on de high stool lak she told me, but Pheoby, Ah done nearly languished tuh death up dere. Ah felt like de world wuz cryin' extry and Ah ain't read de common news yet."

"Maybe so, Janie. Still and all Ah'd love tuh experience it for just one year. It look lak heben tuh me from where Ah'm at."

"Ah reckon so."

"But anyhow, Janie, you be keerful 'bout dis sellin' out and goin' off wid strange men. Look whut happened tuh Annie Tyler. Took whut little she had and went off tuh Tampa wid dat boy dey call Who Flung. It's somethin' tuh think about."

"It sho is. Still Ah ain't Mis' Tyler and Tea Cake ain't no Who Flung, and he ain't no stranger tuh me. We'se just as good as married already. But Ah ain't puttin' it in de street. Ah'm tellin' *you*."

"Ah jus lak uh chicken. Chicken drink water, but he don't pee-pee."

"Oh, Ah know you don't talk. We ain't shame faced. We jus' ain't ready tuh make no big ker-flommuck as yet."

"You doin' right not tuh talk it, but Janie, you'se takin' uh mighty big chance."

"'Tain't so big uh chance as it seem lak, Pheoby. Ah'm older than Tea Cake, yes. But he done showed me where it's de thought dat makes de difference in ages. If people thinks de same they can make it all right. So in the beginnin' new thoughts had tuh be thought and new words said. After Ah got used tuh dat, we gits 'long jus' fine. He done taught me de maiden language all over. Wait till you see de new blue satin Tea Cake done picked out for me tuh stand up wid him in. High heel slippers, necklace, earrings, *everything* he wants tuh see me in. Some of dese mornin's and it won't be long, you gointuh wake up callin' me and Ah'll be gone."

CLAUDIA ROTH PIERPONT (ESSAY DATE 17 FEBRUARY 1997)

SOURCE: Pierpont, Claudia Roth. "A Society of One: Zora Neale Hurston, American Contrarian." *New Yorker* 73, no. 1 (17 February 1997): 80-91.

In the following essay, Pierpont provides an overview of Hurston's career and the public's response to it, and asserts that it is impossible to categorize Hurston's writing.

In the spring of 1938, Zora Neale Hurston informed readers of the *Saturday Review of Literature* that Mr. Richard Wright's first published book, *Uncle Tom's Children,* was made up of four novellas set in a Dismal Swamp of race hatred, in which not a single act of understanding or sympathy occurred, and in which the white man was generally shot dead. "There is lavish killing here," she wrote, "perhaps enough to satisfy all male black readers." Hurston, who had swept onto the Harlem scene a decade before, was one of the very few black women in a position to write for the pallidly conventional *Saturday Review*. Wright, the troubling newcomer, had already challenged her authority to speak for their race. Reviewing Hurston's novel **Their Eyes Were Watching God** in the *New Masses* the previous fall, he had dismissed her prose for its "facile sensuality"—a problem in Negro writing that he traced to the first black American female to earn literary fame, the slave Phillis Wheatley. Worse, he accused Hurston of cynically perpetuating a minstrel tradition meant to make white audiences laugh. It says something about the social complexity of the next few years that it was Wright who became a Book-of-the-Month Club favorite, while Hurston's work went out of print and she nearly starved. For the first time in America, a substantial white audience preferred to be shot at.

Black anger had come out of hiding, out of the ruins of the Harlem Renaissance and its splendid illusions of justice willingly offered up to art. That famed outpouring of novels and poems and plays of the twenties, anxiously demonstrating the Negro's humanity and cultural citizenship, counted for nothing against the bludgeoning facts of the Depression, the Scottsboro trials, and the first-ever riot in Harlem itself, in 1935. The advent of Richard Wright was a political event as much as a literary one. In American fiction, after all, there was nothing new in the image of the black man as an inarticulate savage for whom rape and murder were a nearly inevitable means of expression. Southern literature was filled with Negro portraits not so different from that of Bigger

Thomas, the hero of Wright's 1940 bombshell, *Native Son*. In the making of a revolution, all that had shifted was the author's color and the blame.

As for Hurston, the most brazenly impious of the Harlem literary avant-garde—she called them "the niggerati"—she had never fit happily within any political group. And she still doesn't. In this respect, she was the unlikeliest possible candidate for canonization by the black- and women's-studies departments. Nevertheless, since Alice Walker's "In Search of Zora Neale Hurston" appeared in *Ms.* in 1975, interest in this neglected ancestress has developed a seemingly unstoppable momentum. All her major work has been republished (most recently by the Library of America), she is the subject of conferences and doctoral dissertations, and the movie rights to *Their Eyes Were Watching God*—which has sold more than a million copies since 1990—have been bought by Oprah Winfrey and Quincy Jones. Yet, despite the almost sanctified status she has achieved, Hurston's social views are as obstreperous today as they were sixty years ago. For anyone who looks at her difficult life and extraordinary legacy straight on, it is nearly impossible to get this disarming conjure artist to represent any cause except the freedom to write what she wanted.

Hurston was at the height of her powers in 1937, when she first fell seriously out of step with the times. She had written a love story—*Their Eyes Were Watching God*—and become a counter-revolutionary. Against the tide of racial anger, she wrote about sex and talk and work and music and life's unpoisoned pleasures, suggesting that these things existed even for people of color, even in America; and she was judged superficial. By implication, merely feminine. In Wright's account, her novel contained "no theme, no message, no thought." By depicting a Southern small-town world in which blacks enjoyed their own rich cultural traditions, and were able to assume responsibility for their own lives, Hurston appeared a blithely reassuring supporter of the status quo.

The "minstrel" charge was finally aimed less at Hurston's subjects, however, than at her language. Black dialect was at the heart of her work, and that was a dangerous business. Disowned by the founders of the Harlem Renaissance for its association with the shambling, watermelon-eating mockeries of American stage convention, dialect remained an irresistible if highly self-conscious resource for writers, from Langston Hughes and Sterling Brown to Wright himself (whose use of the idiom Hurston gleefully dismissed as tone

deaf). But the feat of rescuing the dignity of the speakers from decades of humiliation required a rare and potentially treacherous combination of gifts: a delicate ear and a generous sympathy, a hellbent humor and a determined imperviousness to shame. All this Hurston brought to *Their Eyes Were Watching God*—a book that, despite its slender, private grace, aspires to the force of a national epic, akin to works by Mark Twain or Alessandro Manzoni, offering a people their own language freshly caught on paper and raised to the heights of poetry.

"It's sort of duskin' down dark," observes the otherwise unexceptional Mrs. Sumpkins, checking the sky and issuing the local evening variant of rosy-fingered dawn. "He's uh whirlwind among breezes," one front-porch sage notes of the town's mayor; another adds, "He's got uh throne in de seat of his pants." The simplest men and women of all-black Eatonville have this wealth of images easy at their lips. This is dialect not as a broken attempt at higher correctness but as an extravagant game of image and sound. It is a record of the unique explosion that occurred when African people with an intensely musical and oral culture came up hard against the King James Bible and the sweet-talking American South, under conditions that denied them all outlet for their visions and gifts except the transformation of the English language into song.

Hurston was born to a family of sharecroppers in tiny Notasulga, Alabama, in 1891—about ten years before any date she ever admitted to. Both her biographer, Robert E. Hemenway, and her admirer Alice Walker, who put up a tombstone in 1973 to mark Hurston's Florida grave (inscribed "'A Genius of the South' 1901-1960 Novelist, Folklorist, Anthropologist"), got this basic fact as wrong as their honored subject would have wished. Hurston was a woman used to getting away with things: her second marriage license lists her date of birth as 1910. Still, the ruse stemmed not from ordinary feminine vanity but from her desire for an education and her shame at how long it took her to get it. The lie apparently began when she entered high school, in 1917, at twenty-six.

She had been very young when the family moved to Eatonville, Florida, the first incorporated black town in America (by 1914 there would be some thirty of them throughout the South), in search of the jobs and the relief from racism that such a place promised. In many ways, they found precisely what they wanted: John Hurston became a preacher at the Zion Hope Baptist Church and served three terms as mayor. His daughter's depictions of this self-ruled colored Eden have become legend, and in recent years have seemed to hold out a ruefully tempting alternative to the ordeals of integration. The benefits of the self-segregated life have been attested to by the fact that Eatonville produced Hurston herself: a black writer uniquely whole-souled and self-possessed and imbued with (in Alice Walker's phrase) "racial health."

Her mother taught her to read before she started school, and encouraged her to "jump at de sun." Her father routinely smacked her back down and warned her not to act white; the child he adored was her docile older sister. One must go to Hurston's autobiographical novel, *Jonah's Gourd Vine,* for a portrait of this highly charismatic but morally weak man, whose compulsive philandering eventually destroyed all he'd built. The death of Zora's mother, in 1904, began a period she would later seek to obliterate from the record of her life. Although her actual autobiography, *Dust Tracks on a Road,* is infamously evasive and sketchy (burying a decade does not encourage specificity), it does acknowledge her having been shunted among her brothers' families with the lure of school ever giving way to cleaning house and minding children. And all the while, she recalls, "I had a way of life inside me and I wanted it with a want that was twisting me."

Working at every kind of job—maid, waitress, manicurist—she managed to finish high school by June, 1918, and went on to Howard University, where she published her first story, in the literary-club magazine, in 1921. Harlem was just then on the verge of vogue, and the Howard club was headed by Alain Locke, founding prince of the Renaissance, a black aristocrat out of Harvard on the lookout for writers with a sense of the "folk." It was what everybody would soon be looking for. The first date that Hurston offers in the story of her life is January, 1925, when she arrived in New York City with no job, no friends, and a dollar and fifty cents in her pocket—a somewhat melodramatic account meant to lower the lights behind her rising glory.

One story had already been accepted by *Opportunity,* the premier magazine of "New Negro" writing. That May, at the first *Opportunity* banquet, she received two awards—one for fiction and one for drama—from such judges as Fannie Hurst, a best-selling, four-handkerchief novelist, and Eugene O'Neill. Hurston's flamboyant entrance at a party following the ceremonies, sailing a scarf over her shoulder and crying out the title of her play—"*Color Struck!*"—made a greater impression than her work would do for years. This was the new, public Zora, all bravado and laughter, happily startling her audience with the truth of its own preoccupations.

That night, she attached herself to Fannie Hurst, for whom she was soon working as a secretary and then, when it turned out that she couldn't type or keep anything in order, as a kind of rental exotic, complete with outlandish stories and a turban. (Her new boss once tried to pass her off in a segregated restaurant as an African princess.) Hurston's Harlem circle was loudly scornful of the part she was willing to play. For her, though, it was experience: it was not washing floors, it was going somewhere. And the somewhere still hadn't changed. At the banquet she had also met Annie Nathan Meyer, a founder of Barnard College. In the fall of 1925, this ever-masquerading, newly glamorous Scott-within-Zelda of Lenox Avenue enrolled in school again—she had completed less than two years at Howard, and had finagled a scholarship out of Meyer—and discovered anthropology.

Hurston dived headlong into this new field of intellectual possibility, which had been conceived principally by her teacher, Franz Boas, a German-Jewish immigrant who'd founded the department at Columbia. (Like all his students, Hurston called him Papa Franz, and he teased that of course she was his daughter, "just one of my missteps.") The bedrock of Boas's frankly political theorizing was the adaptability and mutability of the races. Believing that culture and learning have as much influence on human development as heredity, he set out to prove how close the members of the family of man might really be. Probably no one except her mother influenced Hurston more.

Boas's fervent belief in the historic importance of African cultures had already had tremendous impact on W. E. B. Du Bois, and Hurston was similarly inspired by the sense of importance that Boas gave to Southern black culture, not just as a source of entertaining stories but as the transmitted legacy of Africa—and as an independent cultural achievement, in need of preservation and study. Boas literally turned Hurston around: he sent her back down South to put on paper the things that she'd always taken for granted. Furthermore, his sanction gave her confidence in the value of those things—the old familiar talk and byways—which was crucial to the sense of "racial health" and "easy self-acceptance" that so many relish in her work today. It seems safe to say that no black woman in America was ever simply allotted such strengths, no matter how strong she was or how uniformly black her home town. They had to be won, and every victory was precarious.

As a child, Hurston informs us in her autobiography, she was confused by the talk of Negro equality and Negro superiority which she heard in the town all around her: "If it was so honorable and glorious to be black, why was it the yellow-skinned people among us had so much prestige?" Even in first grade, she saw the disparity: "The light-skinned children were always the angels, fairies and queens of school plays." She was not a light-skinned child, although her racial heritage was mixed. If the peculiarities of a segregated childhood spared her the harshest brunt of white racism, the crippling consciousness of color in the black community and in the black soul was a subject she knew well and could not leave alone.

Such color-consciousness has a long history in African-American writing, starting with the first novel written by a black American, William Wells Brown's 1853 *Clotel* (a fantasy about Thomas Jefferson's gorgeous mulatto daughter), which takes color prejudice "among the negroes themselves" as its premise. By 1929, the heroine of Wallace Thurman's bitterly funny novel *The Blacker the Berry* . . . was drenching her face with peroxide before going off to dance in Harlem's Renaissance Casino. But there is no more disconcertingly morbid document of this phenomenon than Hurston's prize-winning **Color Struck**. This brief, almost surreal play tracks a talented and very dark-skinned woman's decline into self-destructive madness, a result of her inability to believe that any man could love a woman so black. Although the intended lesson of **Color Struck** seems clear in the retelling, the play's fevered, hallucinatory vehemence suggests a far more complex response to color than Hurston's champions today can comfortably allow—a response not entirely under the author's control.

It would be wrong to say that whites did not figure prominently in Hurston's early life, despite their scarcity. It was precisely because of that scarcity that she took hold of racism not at its source but as it reverberated through the black community. Whites around Eatonville were not the murderous tyrants of Richard Wright's Deep South childhood, but they exerted, perhaps, an equally powerful force—as tantalizing, world-withholding gods, and as a higher court (however unlikely) of personal justice.

There is a fairy-tale aspect to the whites who pass through her autobiography: The "white man

of many acres and things" who chanced upon her birth and cut her umbilical cord with his knife; the strangers who would drive past her house and give her rides out toward the horizon. (She had to walk back, and was invariably punished for her boldness.) Most important was a pair of white ladies who visited her school and were so impressed by her reading aloud—it was the myth of Persephone, crossing between realms of dark and light, which, she recalls, she read exceptionally well because it "exalted" her—that they made her a present of a hundred new pennies and the first real books she ever owned.

Hurston's autobiography won an award for race relations, in 1943, and put her on the cover of the *Saturday Review*. The book has since been reviled by the very people who rescued her fiction from oblivion, and for the same reason that the fiction was once consigned there: a sense that she was putting on a song and dance for whites. In fact, there is nothing in **Dust Tracks on a Road** that is inconsistent with the romantic images of white judges and jurors and plantation owners which form a fundamental part of Hurston's most deeply admired work. The heroine of **Their Eyes Were Watching God** ends up on trial for the murder—in self-defense—of the man she loved. (Having been infected by a rabid dog, he lost his senses and came at her with a gun.) The black folks who knew the couple have sided against her at the trial, hoping to see her hanged. It is the whites—the judge and jury and a group of women gathered for curiosity's sake—who see into the anguished depths of a black woman's love, and acknowledge her dignity and her innocence.

Does this reflect honest human complexity or racial confusion? In what world, if any, was Hurston ever at home? While at Barnard, she apparently told the anthropologist Melville Herskovits that, as he put it, she was "more white than Negro in her ancestry." On her first trip back South to gather evidence of her native culture she could not be understood because of her Barnard intonations. She couldn't gain people's confidence; the locals claimed to have no idea what she wanted. When Hurston returned to New York, she and Boas agreed that a white person could have discovered as much.

So she learned, in effect, to pass for black. In the fall of 1927, in need of a patron, she offered her services to Mrs. R. Osgood Mason, a wealthy white widow bent on saving Western culture from rigor mortis through her support of Negro artistic primitivism. For more than three years, Mrs. Mason paid for Hurston to make forays to the

South to collect Negro folk material. Hurston's findings were not always as splendidly invigorating nor her attitude as positive as they later appeared. "I have changed my mind about the place," she wrote despairingly from Eatonville, in an unpublished letter of 1932. "They steal everything here, even greens out of a garden." But she became increasingly accomplished at ferreting out what she had been hired to find, and the results (if not always objectively reliable) have proved invaluable. Alan Lomax, who worked with Hurston on a seminal 1935 Library of Congress folk-music-recording expedition, wrote of her unique ability to win over the locals, since she "talks their language and can out-nigger any of them."

The fruits of her field work appeared in various forms throughout the early thirties: stories, plays, musical revues, academic articles. Her research is almost as evident in the 1934 novel *Jonah's Gourd Vine* as in her book of folklore, *Mules and Men,* which appeared the following year. Now routinely saluted as the first history of black American folklore by a black author, *Mules and Men* was faulted by black critics of its own time for its adamant exclusion of certain elements of the Southern Negro experience: exploitation, terror, misery, and bitterness.

By this time, however, Hurston had won enough recognition to go off on a Guggenheim grant to study voodoo practices in the Caribbean. It was not a happy trip. The anecdotal study she produced—*Tell My Horse,* published in 1938—is tetchy and belligerent, its author disgusted by the virulent racism of light-skinned mulattoes toward blacks in Jamaica, and as distinctly put out by the unreliability and habitual lying she experienced among the Haitians. In any case, this particular trip had been prompted less by an interest in research than by a need to escape from New York, where she'd left the man she thought of as the love of her life—a still mysterious figure who belongs less to her biography than to her art. In a period of seven weeks, in Haiti, in the fall of 1936, she wrote *Their Eyes Were Watching God,* a novel meant to "embalm all the tenderness of my passion for him."

In her autobiography, Hurston quickly dismisses her first marriage and entirely neglects to mention her second; each lasted only a matter of months. She wed her longtime Howard University boyfriend in May, 1927, and bailed out that August. (Apparently unruffled, Hurston wrote her friends that her husband had been an obstacle, and had held her back.) In 1939, her marriage to a twenty-three-year-old W.P.A. playground worker

dissolved with her claims that he drank and his claims that she'd failed to pay for his college education and had threatened him with voodoo. "The great difficulty lies in trying to transpose last night's moment to a day which has no knowledge of it," she writes in *Dust Tracks on a Road.* She concludes, "I have come to know by experience that work is the nearest thing to happiness that I can find."

Those admirers who wish Hurston to be a model feminist as well as a racial symbol have seized on the issue of a woman's historic choice between love and work, and have claimed that Hurston instinctively took the less travelled path. On the basis of Hurston's public insouciance, Alice Walker describes, with delicious offhand aplomb, "the way she tended to marry or not marry men, but enjoyed them anyway, while never missing a beat in her work." No sweat, no tears—one for the girls. It is true that Hurston was never financially supported by a man—or by anyone except Mrs. Mason. Hemenway, her biographer, writes that it was precisely because of her desire to avoid "such encroachment" on her freedom that her marriages failed.

Without doubt, Hurston was a woman of strong character, and she went through life mostly alone. She burned sorrow and fear like fuel, to keep herself going. She made a point of not needing what she could not have: whites who avoided her company suffered their own loss; she claimed not to have "ever really wanted" her father's affection. Other needs were just as unwelcome. About love, she knew the way it could make a woman take "second place in her own life." Repeatedly, she fought the pull.

There is little insouciance in the way Hurston writes of the man she calls P.M.P. in *Dust Tracks on a Road.* He was "tall, dark brown, magnificently built," with "a fine mind and that intrigued me. . . . He stood on his own feet so firmly that he reared back." In fact, he was her "perfect" love—although he was only twenty-five or so to her forty, and he resented her career. It is hard to know whether his youth or his resentment or his perfection was the central problem. Resolved to "fight myself free from my obsession," she took little experimental trips away from him to see if she could stand it. When she found she couldn't, she left him for good.

Her diligent biographer, who located the man decades later, reports that he had never known exactly what had happened. She'd simply packed her bags and gone off to the Caribbean. Once there, of course, she wrote a book in which a woman who has spent her life searching for passion finally finds it, lets herself go within its embrace, and learns that her lover is honest and true, and that she is not being played for a fool—despite the familiar fact that he is only twenty-five or so and she is forty. (He tells her, "God made it so you spent yo' ole age first wid somebody else, and saved up yo' young girl days to spend wid me.") And then, in the midst of love's perfection, the woman is forced—not out of anger or betrayal but by a hurricane and a mad dog and a higher fate—to shoot him dead, and return to a state of enlightened solitude.

Their Eyes Were Watching God brought a heartbeat and breath to all Hurston's years of research. Raising a folk culture to the heights of art, it fulfilled the Harlem Renaissance dream just a few years after it had been abandoned; Alain Locke himself complained that the novel failed to come to grips with the challenges of "social document fiction." The recent incarnation of Hurston's lyric drama as a black feminist textbook is touched with many ironies, not the least of which is the need to consider it as a social document. The paramount ironies, however, are two: the heroine is not quite black, and becomes even less black as the story goes on; and the author offers perhaps the most serious Lawrentian vision ever penned by a woman of sexual love as the fundamental spring and power of life itself.

The heroine of *Eyes*, Janie Crawford, is raised by her grandmother, who grew up in "slavery time," and who looks on in horror as black women give up their precious freedom for chains they forge themselves. "Dis love! Dat's just whut's got us uh pullin' and uh haulin' and sweatin' and doin' from can't see in de mornin' till can't see at night." But no one can give a woman what she will not claim. Nanny's immovable goal to see Janie "school out" meets its match in the teenager's bursting sexuality. Apprehensive, Nanny marries her off to a man with a house and sixty acres and a pone of fat on the back of his neck. "But Nanny, Ah wants to want him sometimes. Ah don't want him to do all de wantin'," Janie complains, and she walks off one day down the road, tossing her apron onto a bush.

It isn't exactly Nora slamming the door. There's another man in a buggy waiting for Janie, and another unhappy marriage—this time to a bully who won't let her join in the dazzling talk, the wildly spiralling stories, the earnest games of an Eatonville that Hurston raises up now like a darktown Camelot. After his death, a full twenty

years later, she is rather enjoying the first freedom of widowhood when a tall, laughing man enters the general store and asks her to play checkers: "She looked him over and got little thrills from every one of his good points. Those full, lazy eyes with the lashes curling sharply away like drawn scimitars. The lean, overpadded shoulders and narrow waist. Even nice!"

It's the checkers almost as much as the sex. After Nanny, this man, who is called Tea Cake ("Tea Cake! So you sweet as all dat?"), is the staunchest feminist in the novel. He pushes Janie to play the games, talk the talk, "have de nerve tuh say whut you mean." They get married and set off together to work in the Everglades, picking beans side by side all day and rolling dice and dancing to piano blues at night. Hurston isn't unaware of the harsh background to these lives—trucks come chugging through the mud carrying migrant workers, "people ugly from ignorance and broken from being poor"—but she's willing to leave further study to the Wrights and the Steinbecks. Her concern is with the flame that won't go out, the making of laughter out of nothing, the rhythm, the intensity of feeling that transcends it all.

During the nineteen-seventies, when ***Their Eyes Were Watching God*** was being rediscovered with high excitement, Janie Crawford was granted the status of "earliest . . . heroic black woman in the Afro-American literary tradition." But many impatient questions have since been asked about this new icon. Why doesn't Janie speak up sooner? Why can't she go off alone? Why is she always waiting for some man to show her the way? Apologies have been made for the difficulties of giving power and daring to a female character in 1936, but then Scarlett O'Hara didn't fare too badly with the general public that year. The fact is that Janie was not made to suit independent-minded female specifications of any era. She is not a stand-in for her author but a creation meant to live out other possibilities, which are permitted her in large part because—unlike her author—she has no ambition except to live, and because she is beautiful.

"I got an overwhelming complex about my looks before I was grown," Hurston wrote her friend and editor Burroughs Mitchell in 1947, but went on to declare that she had triumphed over it. "I don't care how homely I am now. I know that it doesn't really matter, and so my relations with others are easier." Despite the possible exaggerations of a moment, this vibrantly attractive woman was well acquainted with what might be called the aesthetic burdens of race ("as ugly as Cinderella's sisters" is a phrase meaning Negro, Hurston reported to Mrs. Mason), and she spared her romantic heroine every one of them.

Janie recalls of an early photograph, "Ah couldn't recognize dat dark chile as me," and by the middle of the book neither can we. By then, we've heard a good deal about her breasts and buttocks and so extraordinarily much about her "great rope of black hair"—a standard feature of the gorgeous literary mulatto—that one critic wrote that it seemed to be a separate character. But it is only when Janie and Tea Cake get to the Everglades and confront the singularly racist Mrs. Turner, eager to "class off" with other white-featured blacks ("Ah ain't got no flat nose and liver lips. Ah'm uh featured woman"), that we hear of Janie's "coffee-and-cream complexion" and "Caucasian characteristics." The transformation is both touching and embarrassing—something like George Eliot's suddenly making Dorothea sublimely beautiful in the Roman-museum scene of *Middlemarch*. It's as though the author could no longer withhold from her beloved creation the ultimate reward: Dorothea starts to look like a Madonna, and Janie starts to look white.

With Hurston, though, pride always rushes back in after a fall. These alternating emotional axes are what make her so unclassifiable, so easily susceptible to widely different readings, all of which she may intend. For Janie never acts white, or even seems to care whether she looks that way. She is sincerely mystified by Mrs. Turner's tirades. "We'se uh mingled people," she responds, seeming to rebuke her author's own reflexive notions of beauty, too. "How come you so against black?"

Although Janie spends much of the book struggling to gain the right to speak her mind, she is not particularly notable for her eloquence. There is, however, a great deal of poetry of observation running through her head, which we hear not as her thoughts, precisely, but in the way the story is told. Those who analyze "narrative strategies" have pulped small forests trying to define Hurston's way of slipping in and out of a storytelling voice that sometimes belongs to Janie and sometimes doesn't and, by design, isn't always clear. (As in "Mrs. Dalloway," the effect is of a woman's sensual dispersal through the world.) Janie's panting teen-age sexuality is rendered in a self-consciously hyper-adolescent prose of kissing bees and creaming blossoms—prose that Wright seized on for its "facile sensuality" and that Hurston's admirers now quote with dismaying regularity as

an example of her literary art. But Hurston at her best is simple, light, lucid, nearly offhand, or else just as simply, Biblically passionate. Janie wakes to see the sun rise: "He peeped up over the door sill of the world and made a little foolishness with red." (There is an archaic sense of power in Hurston's sexing of all things: "Havoc was there with her mouth wide open.") As for Tea Cake, even as Janie tries to push his image away he "seemed to be crushing scent out of the world with his footsteps," Hurston writes. "Crushing aromatic herbs with every step he took. Spices hung about him. He was a glance from God."

This is a sermon from the woman's church of Eros. And, like the sermons in which Hurston was schooled—like her entire book, as it winds in and out of this realization of sexual grace—her message lives in its music. At her truest as a writer, Hurston was a musician. The delightfully quotable sayings that she "discovered" on her field trips (many of which recur as plucked examples in **Mules and Men** and her other books) are embedded in this single volume like folk tunes in Dvořák or Chopin: seamlessly, with beauties of invention often indistinguishable from beauties of discovery. The rhythms of talk in her poetry and the substance of poetry in her talk fuse into a radiant suspension. "He done taught me de maiden language all over," Janie says of Tea Cake, and there may be some truth to the tribute: Hurston had never written this way before, and she never rose to it again. It seems likely that without the intensity of her feelings for "P.M.P." this famously independent woman would not have written the novel that is her highest achievement and her lasting legacy. It perhaps complicates the issue of a woman's life and work that the love she tore herself away from so that she could be free, and free to write, turned out to have been the Muse.

Hurston's ability to write fiction seems to have dried up after the commercial failure of **Their Eyes Were Watching God**, which sank without a trace soon after publication. Her next novel, **Moses, Man of the Mountain**, published in 1939, seems a failed reprise of the Bible-based all-Negro Broadway hit *Green Pastures*, with the story of Exodus as its blackface subject. ("Oh, er—Moses, did you ask about them Hebrews while you was knocking around in Egypt?") Gone is the miraculous ear. Gone, too, are her great humor and heart. **Moses** is a weary book, heavy with accumulated resentments. Hurston's disillusionment is fully evident in her mordant, angry journalism of the nineteen-forties, in which she witheringly commends the

Southern custom of whites favoring their own "pet Negroes" (and their eager pets returning the favor) as a functioning racial system, and rails against the substandard Negro colleges she calls "begging joints." The title of one article—**"Negroes Without Self-Pity"**—speaks for itself.

This was her life's theme, and she sounded it all the louder as two new novels were rejected, her poverty went from bohemian to chronic, and her health gave way. She bought a houseboat and spent much of the mid-forties sailing Florida rivers: individualism, her refuge from racism, had lapsed into nearly total isolation. She returned to New York in 1946, looking for work, and wound up in the campaign office of the Republican congressional candidate running against Adam Clayton Powell. When her side lost, she was stranded for a terrible winter in a room on 124th Street, in a different sort of isolation. She didn't ask for help, and she didn't get any. She felt herself slipping, surrounded by racists and haters, the whole city "a basement to Hell."

It was just after this that she wrote her last published novel, *Seraph on the Suwanee.* The story of a white Southern woman and her family, it contains no prominent black characters. Among Hurston's supporters, Alice Walker has called it "reactionary, static, shockingly misguided and timid," and Mary Helen Washington has called it "vacuous as a soap opera." Everyone agrees that Hurston had fallen into the common trap of believing that a real writer must be "universal"—that is to say, must write about whites—and that she had simply strayed too far from the sources that fed her. In fact the book is poisonously fascinating, and suggests, rather, that she came too close.

The story of beautiful, golden-haired Arvay Henson, who believes herself ugly and unworthy of love, contains many echoes of Hurston's earlier work, but its most striking counterpart is the long-ago play *Color Struck.* The works set a beginning and an end to years of struggle with their shared essential theme—the destructive power of fear and bitterness in a woman's tortured psyche. Arvay is born to a poor-white "cracker" family; in a refraction of Hurston's own history, a preference for her older sister "had done something to Arvay's soul across the years." She falls in love with a magnificent fallen aristocrat, who rapes her—for Arvay this is an act of ecstatic, binding possession—and marries her. Tormented by her failure to live up to his perfection, she comes to hate him almost as much as she hates herself.

The book is a choking mixture of cynicism and compulsion. Hurston was desperate for a success, and hoped for a movie sale—hence, no doubt, the formulaic rape and the book's mawkish ending, in which Arvay learns to sing happily in her marital chains. But to reach this peace Arvay must admit, after years of pretense, that she is not really proud of her own miserably poor and uneducated family, that poverty and ignorance lend them neither moral superiority nor charm, and that she is, in fact, shamed and disgusted by them. Arvay's last attempt to go home to her own people results in her burning down the house in which she was raised.

The book was sharply criticized because Hurston's white Southerners speak no differently from the Eatonville blacks of her earlier work. The inflections, the rhythms, the actual expressions that had been declared examples of a distinctive black culture were all now simply transferred to white mouths. The incongruous effects, as in her *Moses* book, point to a failure of technique, an aural exhaustion. But in a letter to her editor Hurston gave an even more dispiriting explanation for what she'd done. "I think that it should be pointed out that what is known as Negro dialect in the South is no such thing," she wrote, in a repudiation nearly as sweeping as Arvay's, at once laying waste to her professional past and her extraordinary personal achievement. The qualities of Southern speech—black and white alike, she claimed—were a relic of the Elizabethan past preserved by Southern whites in their own closed and static society. "They did *not* get it from the Negroes. The Africans coming to America got it from them."

The novel's publication, in the fall of 1948, was swallowed up in a court case that tested all Hurston's capacity for resisting bitterness. That September, in New York, an emotionally disturbed ten-year-old boy accused her of sexual molestation. The Children's Society filed charges, and Hurston was arrested and indicted. Although the case was eventually thrown out, a court employee spilled the news to one of the city's black newspapers—the white papers were presumably not interested—and the lurid story made headlines. Hurston contemplated suicide, but slowly came back to herself on a long sailing trip.

She never returned to New York. For the rest of her life, she lived in Florida, on scant money and whatever dignity she was able to salvage. In Miami, she worked as a maid. Later, she moved to a cabin up the coast that rented for five dollars a week, where she grew much of her own food. She labored over several books, none considered publishable. Her radical independence was more than ever reflected in her politics: fervently anti-Communist, officially Republican, resisting anything that smacked of special pleading. When Brown v. Board of Education was decided, in 1954, she was furious—and wrote furiously—over the implication that blacks could learn only when seated next to whites, or that anyone white should be forced to sit beside anyone black. It was plain "insulting." Although there was some hard wisdom in her conclusion—"the next ten years would be better spent in appointing truant officers and looking after conditions in the homes from which the children come"—her defiant segregationist position was happily taken up by whites of the same persuasion. Her reputation as a traitor to her people overshadowed and outlasted her reasoning, her works, and her life.

Hurston died in January, 1960, in the Saint Lucie County welfare home, in Fort Pierce, Florida, four days before the first sit-in took place, at a Woolworth lunch counter in Greensboro, North Carolina. She was buried in an unmarked grave in a segregated cemetery in Fort Pierce. All her books were out of print. In 1971, in one of the first important reconsiderations of writers of the Harlem Renaissance, the critic Darwin Turner wrote that Hurston's relative anonymity was understandable, for, despite her skills, she had never been more than a "wandering minstrel." He went on to say that it was "eccentric but perhaps appropriate"—one must pause over the choice of words—for her "to return to Florida to take a job as a cook and maid for a white family and to die in poverty." There was a certain justice in these actions, he declared, in that "she had returned to the level of life which she proposed for her people."

The gleaming two-volume Library of America edition of Hurston's *Novels and Stories* and *Folklore, Memoirs, and Other Writings* makes for a different kind of justice. These books bring Hurston a long way from the smudged photocopies that used to circulate, like samizdat, at academic conventions, and usher her into the national literary canon in highly respectable hardback. She is the fourth African-American to be published in this august series, and the fifth woman, and the first writer who happens to be both. Although the Hurston revival may have been driven in part by her official double-victim status—a possibility that many will take as a sign that her literary status has been inflated—*Their Eyes Were Watching God* can stand unsupported in any company. Harold

Bloom has written of Hurston as continuing in the line of the Wife of Bath and Falstaff and Whitman, as a figure of outrageous vitality, fulfilling the Nietzschean charge that we try to live as though it were always morning.

Outside of fiction, this kind of strength is mainly a matter of determination. For many who have embodied it in literature—Nietzsche, Whitman, Lawrence, Hurston—it is a passionate dream of health (dreamed while the simply healthy are sound asleep) which stirs a rare insistence and bravado. "Sometimes, I feel discriminated against, but it does not make me angry," Hurston wrote in 1928. "It merely astonishes me. How *can* any deny themselves the pleasure of my company!" In the venerable African-American game of "the dozens," the players hurl monstrous insults back and forth as they try to rip each other apart with words. (Hurston and Wright both call up the game, and quote the same now rather quaint chant of abuse: "Yo' mama don't wear no DRAWS, Ah seen her when she took 'em OFF"). The near-Darwinian purpose was to get so strong that, no matter what you heard about whomever you loved, you would not let on that you cared to do anything but laugh. It's a game that Richard Wright must have lost every time. But Zora Neale Hurston was the champ.

It is important not to blink at what she had to face and how it made her feel. Envy, fury, confusion, desire to escape: there is no wonder in it. We know too well the world she came from. It is the world she rebuilt out of words and the extraordinary song of the words themselves—about love and picking beans and fighting through hurricanes—that have given us something entirely new. And who is to say that this is not a political achievement? Early in *Their Eyes Were Watching God* Hurston describes a gathering of the folks of Eatonville on their porches at sundown: "It was the time to hear things and talk. These sitters had been tongueless, earless, eyeless conveniences all day long. Mules and other brutes had occupied their skins. But now, the sun and the bossman were gone, so the skins felt powerful and human. They became lords of sounds and lesser things. They passed notions through their mouths. They sat in judgment."

The powerless become lords of sounds, the dispossessed rule all creation with their tongues. Language is not a small victory. It was out of this last, irreducible possession that the Jews made a counter-world of words, the Irish vanquished England, and Russian poetry bloomed thick over Stalin's burial grounds. And in a single book one woman managed to suggest what another such heroic tradition, rising out of American slavery, might have been—a literature as profound and original as the spirituals. There is the sense of a long, ghostly procession behind Hurston: what might have existed if only more of the words and stories had been written down decades earlier, if only Phillis Wheatley had not tried to write like Alexander Pope, if only literate slaves and their generations of children had not felt pressed to prove their claim to the sworn civilities. She had to try to make up for all of this, and more. If out of broken bits of talk and memory she pieced together something that may once have existed, out of will and desire she added what never was. Hurston created a myth that has been gratefully mistaken for history, and in which she herself plays a mythic role—a myth about a time and place fair enough, funny enough, unbitter enough, glad enough to have produced a woman black and truly free.

TITLE COMMENTARY

Their Eyes Were Watching God

SUSAN MEISENHELDER (ESSAY DATE 1996)

SOURCE: Meisenhelder, Susan. "Ethnic and Gender Identity in Zora Neale Hurston's *Their Eyes Were Watching God*." In *Teaching American Ethnic Literatures: Nineteen Essays*, pp. 105-17. Albuquerque: University of New Mexico Press, 1996.

In the following essay, Meisenhelder addresses how Janie, the protagonist of Hurston's Their Eyes Were Watching God, *struggles with her identity as a black woman.*

A. Analysis of Themes and Forms

In [Zora Neale Hurston's *Their Eyes Were Watching God,* the] story of a black woman's search for identity, the main character, Janie, suffers through two unfulfilling marriages to oppressive, materialistic men, who "squinch" her spirit until she meets Tea Cake, a carefree, fun-loving bluesman who encourages her independence and self-expression. Janie leaves behind her "respectable," economically secure life to go with Tea Cake to the Everglades where they enjoy life to the fullest until a hurricane strikes. After this disaster, Janie returns home, comforted by her memories and sustained by the spirit of affirmation with which, despite tragic events, she faces life.

A major theme Hurston develops in the novel (and one characteristic of much of her work) is a celebration of black folklife. In the section of the novel that takes place in the Everglades (on the "Muck"), she depicts a kind of black Eden—a world of equality, exuberance, and vitality drawn in sharp contrast to the materialism and dehumanization many black writers have seen in the dominant, white world. In this respect, the novel is written in the spirit of black cultural affirmation characterizing the Harlem Renaissance of the 1920s and early 1930s. Like such writers as Langston Hughes and Claude McKay, Hurston was often critical of middle-class blacks (who, she felt, imitated whites) and much more interested in the life of the black person "farthest down." In the lives of rural, uneducated blacks Hurston found not only a rich cultural tradition of folklore and music, but a set of values opposed to (and in her mind, superior to) those of the dominant culture. Responding to Hurston's treatment of this theme, Alice Walker has praised the novel for its "racial health; [the] sense of black people as complete, complex, undiminished human beings" (85).

While earlier readers of Hurston's work focused on racial and cultural issues, contemporary critics have investigated the importance of gender in the novel. Janie's search for identity, in fact, involves struggling with her place as black and female. Hurston highlights the racial component of Janie's quest, for instance, by detailing the negative effects that growing up in the backyard of whites has had on Janie's sense of self. She has been given so many names by others that she is finally called Alphabet (9), an indication of her fragmented identity reinforced by the fact that she does not see herself as black and cannot even recognize herself in a photograph. As Janie grows into young womanhood, however, the issue of identity—what it means to be black and a woman—becomes even more complex.

Janie's grandmother (a more sympathetic character for the reader perhaps than for Janie) offers her one vision of the black female self. Nanny's belief that "'de white man is de ruler of everything'" leads her to think of society as a multilayered hierarchy involving both race and sex: "'. . . de white man throw down de load and tell de nigger man tuh pick it up. He pick it up because he have to, but he don't tote it. He hand it to his women-folks. De nigger woman is de mule de world as fur as I can see'" (14). Drawing this model of black female identity from her own experience with the harshest forms of racial and sexual oppression (slavery and rape), Nanny dreams of marriage and economic security for Janie. Fearing that Janie may be a mule or a "spit-cup" for men, she seeks protection for her by marrying her off to a well-to-do older man. As that marriage graphically demonstrates, the price is high, for Janie is forced to sacrifice love. In more complex ways, Janie's first two marriages highlight the limitations of Nanny's analysis by revealing the ways in which women can be spit-cups and mules with male protection.

Janie has another vision of female possibility, imaged in her experience under the pear tree (10-11). On one level an obvious metaphor for sexual relationships, the passage is a powerful contrast to Nanny's spit-cup and mule metaphors with their suggestions of rape and female dehumanization. This metaphor for sexuality, on the contrary, is one free of domination and divisions into active and passive: there is no suggestion of rapacious violence on the part of the (male) bee or of passive victimization on the part of the "sister-calyxes [who] arch to meet the love embrace." The relationship imaged here, one between active equals, is not only one of delight, but as the metaphor of pollination implies, one of creativity. This passage is a key one in the novel: not only will Janie, in the search for a "bee for her blossom," measure her relationships against this ideal; but Hurston will associate nearly every black character in the novel with tree imagery to suggest their psychic wholeness or mutilation. Ultimately, the image becomes the novel's ideal for human interaction (sexual, interpersonal, or more broadly social), a model of relationships without hierarchy or domination.

Joe Starks is clearly no "bee" in his relationship with Janie or with the black community. While his role as oppressor is often obvious, much more subtle is Hurston's analysis of the source of his identity. Numerous details, from his white house (an imitation plantation one) to his fancy spittoon, suggest that he draws his model from a white world. He interacts with the townspeople like a slaveowner, talking like a "section foreman" (33) with "bow-down command" (44) in his face. Starks recreates power dynamics of the most oppressive sort in the town, a fact recognized by the residents themselves, who, when forced by Starks to dig ditches, "murmured hotly about slavery being over" (44). He sees himself as God (his most frequent exclamation is, in fact, "I god") and acts the part, even bringing light to the community in a parody of Genesis when he installs the first light-post.

Despite his superficially solicitous behavior, Starks's treatment of Janie is equally oppressive. He puts Janie on a pedestal, above other black

ABOUT THE AUTHOR

SUSAN MEISENHELDER ON HURSTON'S VOICE IN *DUST TRACKS ON A ROAD*

The published version of *Dust Tracks on a Road* is a discomfiting book because Hurston rarely expresses her defiance directly. Often "hitting a straight lick with a crooked stick" instead, she repeatedly emphasizes the necessity of this skill for a black woman to survive in a world that conspires to "squinch [her] spirit" and silence her voice. Documenting numerous instances in which her own iconoclastic voice had been silenced during her childhood, Hurston indicates that this problem was no less serious in her adult writing career. Although the "psychic bond" (175) between Hurston and Mrs. Charlotte Osgood Mason may have been real, Hurston must have felt equally real the psychic violence in her "lacerat[ing]" rebuke, "'Keep silent. Does a child in the womb speak?'" (176), and her control (including legal ownership) of Hurston's words. At times the silencing is more subtle but no less real in effect. When Hurston describes the writing of *Jonah's Gourd Vine*, she emphasizes the difficulty of writing a story that "was not what was expected" (206) by publishers and readers. Because her story "seemed off-key" (206), "I was afraid to tell a story the way I wanted, or rather the way the story told itself to me" (206).

Meisenhelder, Susan. An excerpt from "'With a Harp and a Sword in My Hand': Black Female Identity in *Dust Tracks on a Road*." In *Hitting a Straight Lick with a Crooked Stick: Race and Gender in the work of Zora Neale Hurston*, p. 147. Tuscaloosa: University of Alabama, 1999.

women in the community but decidedly beneath himself. This marriage graphically demonstrates the limitations of Nanny's mule metaphor: merely removing white faces from the social hierarchy changes nothing for Janie, for she is still oppressed by the man above her. Ironically, Janie lives a life with Joe that Nanny worked so hard to avoid for her, enduring what Nanny feared despite having attained the economic circumstances she desired. Hurston emphasizes this shortcoming of Nanny's strategy for black women by having Janie symbolically associated with the situations that Nanny most feared. Race and gender intersect in complex ways, for instance, when Joe demands that Janie bind her hair in a "head-rag" (86), an artifact of the slavery period. Despite her husband's wealth, Janie becomes a spiritual slave in this marriage, a sexual object owned and controlled by her master.

In terms of both racial and gender identity, Tea Cake is portrayed as Starks's antithesis. His feminized nickname promises a "sweeter," gentler kind of masculinity than that suggested by Starks's name. Unlike Starks, who draws his models from a white world, Tea Cake is emphatically black, a man who not only revels in his own cultural traditions but also rejects the hierarchy and crass materialism characterizing Starks's whitewashed world. Also rejecting hierarchy based on sex, he becomes "a bee to Janie's blossom," encouraging Janie to express herself and to experience life more fully. Janie must step down from her pedestal to enter a relationship with Tea Cake, but she steps into one built on reciprocity rather than hierarchy. In teaching Janie to play checkers, to shoot, and to drive, and in inviting her to work alongside of him, Tea Cake breaks down the rigid gender definitions that Joe sought to impose.

In the section on the Muck, Hurston projects this model of ideal relationships onto a larger plane. With the status differences and white values that Starks sought to reinforce absent on the Muck, artificial hierarchical divisions evaporate: Janie is just another person rather than Mrs. Mayor, and the West Indians, instead of being ostracized, are accepted as equals in the community. The hierarchies of Nanny's metaphor are also foreign to this community. With no white man present to toss his load to the black man, black men do not toss theirs on to black women. When Janie goes to work in the fields with Tea Cake, it is not because Tea Cake sees her as a mule but because he wants to be with her. Freely chosen, work for Janie becomes an expression of her equality and vitality rather than her oppression. She and Tea Cake "partake with everything," sharing in both paid labor and domestic work. With Janie and Tea Cake as the Adam and Eve at the center of this garden, the spirit of their relationship is mirrored in the community. The center of this world is not the commercial enterprise of Joe's store, but Janie and Tea Cake's house, the cultural heart of the community where everyone enjoys the guitar-playing and storytelling. Janie is not merely an outside observer, as she had been with Joe, but an active participant and speaker (127-28). In this section, Janie develops both a rich ethnic identity and a vigorous female one.

The exception to the racial health in the community (in fact, the serpent in this Eden) is Mrs. Turner, a woman who, as suggested in her name, rejects her own blackness. Like Starks, she wants to "class off" (135), to elevate herself above other blacks. Cut off from the rich cultural life of the community in her desire to be white, she is depicted as racially and sexually insipid, a pale contrast to the vital people around her.

From this point, critics adopt two different interpretations of the novel. For some, Tea Cake's death is a tragic end to this love story; these critics argue that the last few pages of the novel, filled with Janie's memories of Tea Cake, confirm him as an ideal. Other critics see important changes in Tea Cake while he and Janie are on the Muck and, often, a quite different significance in his death.

Critical to this latter view of Tea Cake is the beating he gives Janie as a result of his unfounded fear that she will be attracted to Mrs. Turner's brother. Clearly, it is not the violence of Tea Cake's act that Hurston pinpoints as problematic, but his motives. Hurston emphasizes this fact in the contrast between Tea Cake's beating of Janie and their earlier fight over Nunkie. When Janie feels jealous of Nunkie, she is more than ready to tackle Tea Cake in an honest expression of her passion: "Janie never thought at all. She just acted on feelings" (131). Tea Cake's violence toward Janie has both a very different motivation and a very different effect. His action is not a spontaneous expression of strong feeling, but a premeditated "brainstorm" (140). Fundamentally manipulative and coercive, the beating is calculated to assert domination over Janie, to demonstrate it to Mrs. Turner and to other men. In subtle ways, Tea Cake's behavior toward Janie changes from this point on, echoing the falsely solicitous actions of Starks. To assert the power of his masculinity by reassuring himself of Janie's passive femininity, he "would not let her go with him to the field. He wanted her to get her rest" (146). When the storm strikes, he not only ignores Janie's warnings but expresses a disconcerting acceptance of white superiority and the racial denigration of Indians (148).

Some critics see Tea Cake's illness as symbolic of changes in his attitude toward Janie. While his behavior is obviously explainable as the result of his disease, careful examination of details shows a sharp contrast to his earlier behavior toward Janie.

He begins, for instance, to speak to her as Starks had, even complaining about her housework (166-67). Some critics argue that Tea Cake now poses such a threat to Janie's new-found female identity (symbolized in his delirious attempt to kill her) that Janie's act must be viewed as spiritual, as well as physical, self-defense. Alice Walker, who was perhaps the first to see Janie's shooting of Tea Cake as a blow for her freedom, argues that Tea Cake's beating of Janie is "the reason Hurston permits Janie to kill Tea Cake" (305). Even critics who see problems with Tea Cake's character toward the end of the novel split on the question of whether Janie achieves complete liberation: some say yes, viewing Janie's attitudes at the end of the novel as evidence of a positive identity (whatever Tea Cake's faults); some offer a more qualified view, suggesting that Janie's dream of Tea Cake at the end demonstrates a denial of reality, but her own spiritual strength nonetheless; and some say no, analyzing the god and idol imagery running throughout the novel to conclude that Janie has created yet another false idol in her memory of Tea Cake, just as she had with Jody.

B. Teaching the Work

I think it's important to begin class discussion of this novel with some biographical material on Hurston's life. Hemenway's biography and Hurston's own *Dust Tracks on a Road* are helpful here. (Even though critics tend to agree that Hurston is, in many ways, an unreliable narrator in her autobiography, it at least provides insight into the persona that Hurston wanted to present to her contemporaries.) Born into the security of an all-black town in Florida as the daughter of a minister father and a spunky mother who urged her to "jump at the sun," Hurston found herself alone and unsupported when her mother died while Zora was still a child. By her own account, she was only able to continue her education through a combination of sheer willpower and help from assorted (often white) benefactors and patrons. She was able to finish college and to study anthropology under the direction of Franz Boas. Despite the fact that she never earned a Ph.D., Hurston did extensive fieldwork in anthropology, both in the South and in the Caribbean, publishing two book-length studies of black folk-ways, *Mules and Men* and *Tell My Horse*. In addition to *Their Eyes Were Watching God,* she published several other novels, *Jonah's Gourd Vine, Moses, Man of the Mountain,* and *Seraph on the Suwanee,* as well as an autobiography and numerous stories and articles. While she was well known during the Harlem Renaissance period, she was never able to make a decent living from her writing and died in obscurity and poverty in 1960. Alice Walker has been a major force in bringing Hurston back into popularity (see bibliography), and Hurston is now recognized by many contemporary black women writers as an important foremother.

Even though Hurston highlights both race and gender in *Their Eyes Were Watching God,* students (especially white students, but not exclusively) tend to highlight gender. They will quickly notice, for instance, that Starks is a chauvinist and Tea Cake is not, but they will need more prodding to see the complicated way in which Hurston comments on the racial identity as well as the masculine identity of both men. With the character of Starks, for instance, instructors may need to direct students to Hurston's many symbolic references to Starks's "whiteness." My students also sometimes overlook the way in which Hurston draws parallels between his oppression of Janie and of the town. While students often accept Starks's view of himself as a "leader" and "developer" of the community, Hurston repeatedly suggests a more sinister motive for his actions, namely a desire to control the town as he has seen white men do elsewhere. For him, the development of the community is not a cultural endeavor, but merely a commercial venture, one from which he will reap the profits. As one resident's bitter comment—"'All he got he done made it offa de rest of us'" (46)—suggests, Starks exploits the community as fully as he does Janie.

Another issue that often arises in discussing Starks is the manner in which Janie frees herself from him. After having been humiliated by him, she (in uncharacteristically blunt language) responds: "'You big-bellies round her and put out a lot of brag, but 'tain't nothin' to it but yo' big voice. Humph! Talkin' 'bout me looking old! When you pull down yo' britches, you look lak de change uh life'" (75). Some students (and at least one critic) feel that Janie's emasculating comment here is unnecessarily cruel; in discussing this section, it helps to point out that Joe has humiliated Janie in a similarly sexual and explicit way (74).

The issue of how to evaluate Tea Cake's character always engenders some of the most animated (and heated) discussions of any book I've taught. After reading the novel, some students come to class feeling he's a total fraud and others that he's a romantic ideal. Often these reactions stem from students' beliefs about popular contemporary controversies ("male-bashing" and black women "trashing" black men are, for instance, often alluded to when I begin a discussion by asking students for their reactions to the book). To foster more fruitful discussion grounded in the text, it is helpful to have students meet in small groups with others who view Tea Cake similarly in order to develop a case for their point of view. In addition to having them marshal evidence from the text for their interpretations, I also ask them to develop questions for "the other side" to answer. Asking and answering such questions ("If you believe Tea Cake is so wonderful, then how do you explain his beating of Janie?" or "If you think Tea Cake is so awful, then why does Hurston end the book with such beautiful images to describe him?") is an important part of this exercise because students will tend to leave out evidence that weakens their case. Even though I'm convinced that Hurston meant to suggest flaws in Tea Cake's character, the novel is ambiguous and complex enough in its treatment of issues to bear a number of divergent but plausible interpretations. I've heard admirers of Tea Cake develop quite respectable explanations for the beating episode: "Perhaps," some have argued, "Hurston wanted to highlight the power of sexism by making even a nearly perfect character like Tea Cake momentarily succumb to it. Hurston is writing realism, not romantic fairytale. Even Janie has dandruff, after all."

If students are having difficulty generating specifics, I sometimes turn their attention to particular passages that need to be addressed. I ask students enamored with Tea Cake, for instance, to examine closely the language Hurston uses to describe the beating and its aftermath, especially his statement that "'Janie is wherever *Ah* wants tuh be'" (141). I ask students critical of Tea Cake to examine the imagery of the last part of the book: If Tea Cake is a villain, why does Hurston associate him with seed imagery, so suggestive of rebirth and the powerful pear tree scene. If discussion is going well, I sometimes push students to think about the ambiguity of earlier passages, such as the money-stealing episode that occurs in Jacksonville right after Janie and Tea Cake are married. Although, on the one hand, the threat implicit in that event seems diffused (Tea Cake, at least, spends the money in a very unStarksian fashion by throwing a party and only excludes Janie because he fears her disapproval), he does admit to motivations at odds with the characteristics we most value in him: he throws the party

not just for fun, but to let people "know who he was" and "to see how it felt to be a millionaire" (117).

One issue that often comes up in this discussion of Tea Cake's character and his relationship with Janie is the nature of oppression. The reaction of some students—Janie is not oppressed by Tea Cake because she doesn't feel that she is—has often led to interesting discussions in my class about what constitutes oppression. (For students to at least consider the possibility that oppression does not have to be defined in terms of awareness seems crucial to their understanding of many ethnic and women writers.) Students respond even more energetically to more specific discussion of the treatment of romantic love in the novel. More than one critic has suggested that Janie's blindness to Tea Cake's faults is precisely the result of an idealizing love for him. In discussion of this very sensitive issue, Nanny's comments on love always elicit student reaction: love, she argues, is "de prong all us black women gits hung on. Dis love! Dat's just whut's got us uh pullin' and uh haulin' and sweatin' and doin' from can't see in de mornin' till can't see at night" (22). Hurston's own account of the major love affair of her life (the one, in fact, that served as the rough model for **Their Eyes Were Watching God**) also sparks discussion. In the account narrated in **Dust Tracks on a Road,** Hurston not only stresses her adoration of her lover, but the subtle ways in which he became the "master kind" (257) and she "his slave" (258).

One question students nearly always raise about the novel is the function of the "mule talk" section (Chapter 6). Just as critics have, students see it as anomalous, seemingly unrelated to events preceding it and conflicting with the novel's realism when the buzzards speak to one another after the funeral. Given Hurston's emphasis on the black woman as "the mule of the world," however, students can draw some interesting parallels between the mule and Janie. Like the yellow mule who is the superficial focus of the men's concern, the light-skinned Janie, while seemingly pampered by her husband, is elevated for his own aggrandizement. At the mule's funeral, he "stands on [its] distended belly . . . for a platform" (57), just as his status in the community requires him to elevate himself above Janie. Almost as if she senses her affinities with the mule (she is the only person to pity it and speak up for it), Janie soon frees herself from Starks after this episode.

After discussing *Their Eyes Were Watching God,* students benefit from returning to some discussion of Hurston's struggles as a writer. I like to end my study of the novel by drawing on Alice Walker's version (*In Search of Our Mother's Gardens*) of Hurston's life and on her own "discovery" of Hurston's work (all of it out of print when Walker was in college). Students are invariably moved by her comments on the plight of Hurston and other black women writers and by Walker's account of her search for Hurston's unmarked grave.

With its focus on gender, race, and class, *Their Eyes Were Watching God* works extremely well in the classroom in a unit on how writers of different backgrounds view these issues. Richard Wright's *Uncle Tom's Children,* for instance, with a different conception of blackness, offers interesting contrasts to Hurston's treatment of race and also fosters good discussion of the role gender plays in ethnic literature. The reviews each author wrote on the other's book can supplement discussion. In his review, "Between Laughter and Tears," published in the October 1937 issue of *New Masses,* Wright had this to say about *Their Eyes Were Watching God*:

> Miss Hurston *voluntarily* continues in her novel the tradition which was forced upon the Negro in the theater, that is, the minstrel technique that makes the 'white folks' laugh. Her characters eat and laugh and cry and work and kill; they swing like a pendulum eternally in that safe and narrow orbit in which America likes to see the Negro live: between laughter and tears.

His searing comments were matched by Hurston's equally caustic ones in her review of *Uncle Tom's Children,* "**Stories of Conflict**," published in *Saturday Review,* April 2, 1938: "There is lavish killing here, perhaps enough to satisfy all male black readers" (32).

Three novels that foster discussion highlighting race differences in gender identity are Hurston's *Seraph on the Suwanee* (which echoes many aspects of *Their Eyes Were Watching God* in a treatment of white southern life that emphasizes differences in female oppression in black and white communities); Kate Chopin's *The Awakening* (which, with its notion of selfhood defined in individualistic terms, contrasts with Hurston's communal one); and Tillie Olsen's *Yonnondio* (which offers many possibilities for comparing Maisie and Janie and for analyzing different views of the effect that class has on gender identity).

I have also found several novels by other black women to be fruitful companions to *Their Eyes Were Watching God.* Gloria Naylor's *Mama Day,* a contemporary treatment of a black woman's identity by a writer clearly indebted to Hurston, can be used as another view of how race and sex interact in the lives of black women. The novel also offers rich possibilities for comparing Janie and Tea Cake with the main protagonists in Naylor's novel, Cocoa and George. Nella Larsen's *Quicksand,* written by one of Hurston's contemporaries, provides a sharp contrast both in its emphasis on black female identity in the middle class and its seeming pessimism about the possibilities for black women generally. Finally, *Nervous Conditions,* a novel by a Zimbabwean woman writer, Tsitsi Dangaremgba, also examines the relationship between race and gender through an exploration of the effects of colonialism on black female and male identity.

DEBORAH CLARKE (ESSAY DATE WINTER 2001)

SOURCE: Clarke, Deborah. "'The Porch Couldn't Talk for Looking': Voice and Vision in *Their Eyes Were Watching God.*" *African American Review* 35, no. 4 (winter 2001): 599-613.

In the following essay, Clarke asserts that in Hurston's novel Their Eyes Were Watching God, *"her concern goes beyond presenting an individual woman's journey to self-awareness" and contends that Hurston's accomplishment is a redefining of African American rhetoric.*

> "So 'tain't no use in me telling you somethin' unless Ah give you de understandin' to go 'long wid it. Unless you see de fur, a mink skin ain't no different from a coon hide."
>
> (Hurston, *Their Eyes* 7)

When Janie [in Zora Neale Hurston's *Their Eyes Were Watching God*] explains to her friend Pheoby the reason that simply telling her story will not suffice, why she needs to provide the "'understandin' to go 'long wid it,'" she employs a metaphor of vision: Unless you *see* the fur, you can't tell a mink from a coon. Stripped of their defining visual characteristics, the hides collapse into sameness. Recognizing visual difference, Hurston suggests, is crucial to understanding how identity is constructed: by skin and color. With this claim, she invokes new avenues into an African American tradition that has privileged voice as its empowering trope. From Phillis Wheatley's demonstration that an African can have a poetic voice, to Frederick Douglass's realization that freedom is measured by words and the ability to address a white audience, to Charles Chesnutt's presentation of the triumph of black storytelling in *The Conjure Woman,* voice has prevailed as the primary medium through which African American writers have asserted identity and humanity. Voice announced that visual difference was only skin deep, that black bodies housed souls that were, in essence, no different from those residing in white bodies. ***Their Eyes Were Watching God*** is very much a part of this tradition, and has inspired many fine studies on the ways that its protagonist finds a voice and a self.[1] Yet, as others have pointed out, Janie's voice is by no means unequivocally established by the end of the book. Robert Stepto was among the first to express dissatisfaction with the narrative structure and its third-person narrator; for him, the use of the narrator implies that "Janie has not really won her voice and self after all" (166). More recently, Michael Awkward has pointed out that Janie is not interested in telling the community her story upon her return (6), and Mary Helen Washington argues that Janie is silenced at crucial spots in the narrative. Carla Kaplan, reviewing the discussions of voice that the novel has inspired, examines the ways that voice is both celebrated and undermined, noting that "Hurston privileges dialogue and storytelling at the same time as she represents and applauds Janie's *refusal* to speak" (121). Clearly, Janie's achievement of a voice is critical to her journey to self-awareness, but the highly ambivalent presentation of voice in the novel indicates that voice alone is not enough. As Maria Tai Wolff notes, "For telling to be successful, it must become a presentation of sights with words. The best talkers are 'big picture talkers'" (226). For Hurston, then, the construction of African American identity requires a voice that can make you see, a voice that celebrates the visible presence of black bodies.

I would suggest that, with its privileging of "mind pictures" over words, ***Their Eyes Were Watching God*** goes beyond a narrative authority based solely on voice, for, as Janie tells Pheoby, "'Talkin' don't amount tuh uh hill uh beans when yuh can't do nothin' else'" (183). In contrast to Joe Starks, who seeks to be a "big voice" only to have his wish become humiliatingly true when Janie informs him that he "'big-bellies round here and put out a lot of brag, but 'tain't nothin' to it but yo' big voice'" (75), Janie seeks for a voice which can picture, which can make you see. The ability to use voice visually provides a literary space for African American women to relate their experiences in a world where, as Nanny says, "'We don't know nothin' but what we see'" (14). Thus,

to expand "what we see" increases what we know. Throughout the novel, Hurston's use of visual imagery challenges dominant theories about the power hierarchies embedded in sight, long associated with white control, with Plato's rationality and logic, and, from a Freudian perspective, with male sexual dominance. She recasts the visual to affirm the beauty and power of color and to provide a vehicle for female agency.

In so doing, Hurston opens up different ways of conceptualizing the African American experience. Responding to the long history of blacks as spectacle—from slavery to minstrelsy to colonized object—she offers the possibility of reclaiming the visual as a means of black expression and black power. Controlling vision means controlling what we see, how we define the world. Visual power, then, brings political power, since those who determine what is seen determine what exists.[2]

In recent times, the Rodney King beating trial highlighted the significance of this power, when white interpretation sought to reverse the apparent vision presented by the video of the assault. Commenting on the trial, Judith Butler writes that the "visual field is not neutral to the question of race; it is itself a racial formation, an episteme, hegemonic and forceful" (17). Zora Neale Hurston recognized this, anticipating what Houston Baker terms the "'scening' of the African presence" as a means of silencing that presence (42). As opposed to the King jurors, who learned not to see what was presented, Hurston's Janie makes readers "see" her story, and thus takes control of both the visual field and its interpretation. Visual control is not, obviously, the answer to racist oppression: Had the jurors "seen" what happened to Rodney King, it would not have undone his beating, and Hurston fully realized that black bodies bear the material evidence of racial violence (indeed, Janie's perceived beauty—her long hair and light skin—results from an interracial rape). But by taking visual control, Hurston looks back, challenges white dominance, and documents its material abuse of African Americans.

She thus manages to present a material self that can withstand the power of the gaze, transforming it into a source of strength. In establishing a rhetoric of sight, Hurston ensures that black bodies remain powerfully visible throughout the novel, particularly the bodies of black women.[3] As Audre Lorde has noted, visibility is the cornerstone of black female identity, "without which we cannot truly live":

> Within this country where racial difference creates a constant, if unspoken, distortion of vision,

Black women have on one hand always been highly visible, and so, on the other hand, have been rendered invisible through the depersonalization of racism. Even within the women's movement, we have had to fight, and still do, for that very visibility which also renders us most vulnerable, our Blackness. . . . And that visibility which makes us most vulnerable is that which also is the source of our greatest strength.

(Lorde 42)

In attempting to reclaim visibility, Hurston focuses not just on rendering black bodies visible, but also on redeeming the "distortion of vision" of which Lorde speaks. Neither is an easy task, for Janie's visible beauty makes her vulnerable to both adoration and abuse, and the ability to see does not come readily. As the title of the novel indicates, Hurston is interested in far more than the development of one woman's journey to self-knowledge; she seeks to find a discourse that celebrates both the voices and the bodies of African Americans. By emphasizing "watching God," she foregrounds sight.

The existing theoretical work on vision is both useful and limiting for one seeking to understand Hurston's use of visual language. While various feminist theorists such as Braidotti, Haraway, and Keller have contributed greatly to our understanding of the topic, joining film theorists Mulvey, Doane, and Silverman, their work does not always take race sufficiently into account, though Jane Gaines reminds us of the racial privilege inherent in the gaze: "Some groups," she remarks, "have historically had the license to 'look' openly while other groups have 'looked' illicitly" (25). Some African American theorists such as Fanon, Wallace, and hooks do engage issues of visibility, but it is surprisingly underexamined in African American literary and film theory despite the fact that the visual is critical to black female identity, the source, Lorde insists, of black women's vulnerability and strength. Michelle Wallace has noted that "black women are more often visualized in mainstream American culture . . . than they are allowed to speak their own words or speak about their condition as women of color" (*Invisibility* 3). Hurston takes this visualization and turns it into a source of strength and a kind of language, thus redeeming visibility and establishing voice. While vision has long been associated with objectivity, this objective position has been assumed to be raceless (white) and sexless (male). Hurston exposes these dynamics, and in so doing lays the groundwork for a kind of vision that embodies blackness as both body and voice. The visible presence of Janie's material body reflects the complex

historical and cultural forces which have created her and offers her a unique, individual identity. The visual, then, allows for a negotiation between the post-structuralist argument that identity is largely a construction and the concerns, particularly by nonwhites, that such a position erases individual identity and presence just as non-white peoples are beginning to lay claim to them. Awareness of the visible brings together the "politics of positioning," of who can look, with a recognition of the political and psychological significance of the gaze and with the "real" presence of a material body and individual self (Braidotti 73).

Hurston's insistence on the importance of visual expression, of course, stems largely from racism's disregard for African American individuality. In **"What White Publishers Won't Print,"** Hurston explains the American attitude toward blacks as "THE AMERICAN MUSEUM OF UN-NATURAL HISTORY. This is an intangible built on folk belief. It is assumed that all non-Anglo-Saxons are uncomplicated stereotypes. Everybody knows all about them. They are lay figures mounted in the museum where all may take them in at a glance" (170).[4] By characterizing the white American perspective as that of museum-goers, Hurston suggests that the non-white population becomes mere spectacle, "lay figures" to be taken in "at a glance" by white eyes. We generally see this power dynamic in operation when black bodies are displayed. In minstrel shows, as Eric Lott points out, "'Black' figures were there to be looked at, shaped to the demands of desire; they were screens on which audience fantasy could rest, and while this purpose might have had a host of different effects, its fundamental outcome was to secure the position of white spectators as superior, controlling figures" (140-41).

The dynamic still exists. Steven Speilberg's 1997 film *Amistad,* for example, opens with an extended display of naked black bodies and offers its black cast few words, inviting the public to view blackness rather than listen to it.[5] One is defined by how one is seen. For African Americans, this leads to a condition of "hypervisibility," in which "the very publicness of black people as a social fact works to undermine the possibility of actually seeing black specificity" (Lubiano 187). We need only look to Frantz Fanon for confirmation: ". . . already I am being dissected under white eyes, the only real eyes. I am *fixed.* . . . I feel, I see in those white faces that it is not a new man who has come in, but a new kind of man, a new genus. Why, it's a Negro!" (116). The racist power of visibility thus seems daunting, but Hurston not only takes on the challenge of reclaiming the visual as racially affirmative, she does so in response to a masculinist tradition in which visual power so often objectifies women. Her fiction reveals that, even in the context of a black community, the ability to see "black specificity" may be impaired, particularly when the specific individual is a woman. Hurston, a student of Franz Boas, who pioneered the participant-observer model of anthropological study, recognized the need for looking closely and carefully.[6]

Their Eyes opens with almost an anthropological tone, presenting us with a group of people who have been "tongueless, earless, eyeless conveniences all day long" (1). After spending their days erased by white eyes as a specific presence, they become talkers and lookers. In order to regain human identity after "mules and other brutes had occupied their skins," they need to speak, listen, and see. It is important to note that Hurston equates all three sensory apparati; she does not privilege the verbal over the visual. Just as Pheoby's "hungry listening" helps Janie tell her story, so Janie's keen vision provides her with a story to tell. This vision is far different from one which "glances" at objects in a museum; such a way of seeing merely replicates white erasure of everything but skin color. Hurston seeks a uniquely African American vision, a way of seeing that both recognizes color and sees beyond it. But being black does not automatically confer, for Hurston, visual ability. In fact, visual language is predominantly associated with women in her work. As Michelle Wallace has observed, "Gender is as important as 'race' to understanding how 'invisibility' has worked historically in all fields of visual production" ("Race" 258). Initially, the "big picture talkers" are male in this novel, and much of the talk centers on impressing and evaluating women. Janie's first appearance in Eatonville causes Hicks to proclaim his plans to get a woman just like her "'Wid mah talk'" (34). Hurston's challenge is to redeploy the language of the visual in ways that do not simply reevoke the objectification of women of any color by situating them as objects of the male gaze.

In a culture that has so long defined black people as spectacle and black women as sexualized bodies, one needs to transform and redeem the potential of vision. While the visual certainly holds the threat of objectification, it can also serve as action—both personal and political. bell hooks argues that, for blacks, looking can be viewed as an act of resistance. She asserts that "all attempts to repress our / black peoples' right to gaze . . .

produced in us an overwhelming longing to look, a rebellious desire, an oppositional gaze." With this gaze African Americans declared, "Not only will I stare. I want my look to change reality" (116). Looking becomes an act charged with political resistance, a way to reconfigure the world and its power dynamics.[7] One must look, then, at African American writing as a means of challenging the power of the white gaze. We need to employ what Mae Hendersen terms a new "angle of vision" (161), a means of looking back, of seeing without objectifying. To analyze Hurston's "angle of vision," I would argue, necessitates bringing together a wide range of theoretical perspectives, for seeing and being seen are highly complex acts in her fiction, acts which place individuals within an intricate web of personal and historical forces.

In Hurston's work, looking is more than a confrontational challenge. Her fiction is replete with examples of women's need to look, see, understand, and use language visually. In **"Drenched in Light,"** an autobiographical story which recalls Hurston's descriptions of her childhood days, Isis, "a visual minded child," "pictur[es] herself gazing over the edge of the world into the abyss" (942). She escapes punishment for her many mischievous actions by impressing a white lady as being "drenched in light" (946); her strong visual force marks her as a child destined for creative accomplishment. Delia, the protagonist of **"Sweat,"** prefigures Janie in her use of visual metaphors to re-evaluate her marriage. "She lay awake, gazing upon the debris that cluttered their matrimonial trail. Not an image left standing along the way" (957). This visual realization grants Delia the strength to defy her abusive husband. **"The Gilded Six-Bits"** presents the story of Missie May, unable to see through the shining currency to recognize its meager value; this missight leads her to an affair with the man who owns the false coins, nearly ruining her marriage. Interestingly, her husband Joe finally forgives her when her son is born and turns out to be "'de spittin image'" (995) of Joe himself. Only visual proof of paternity can erase his anger.

Jonah's Gourd Vine, in many ways a pre-text for *Their Eyes*, examines many of the same issues of voice and identity with a male protagonist. But though John Pearson, like Janie Crawford, struggles to establish a self, he does not employ her rhetoric of sight. In fact, his white boss specifically associates him with blindness as an explanation for John's lack of foresight:

Of course you did not know. Because God has given to all men the gift of blindness. That is to say that He has cursed but few with vision. Ever hear tell of a happy prophet? This old world wouldn't roll on the way He started it if men could see. Ha! In fact, I think God Himself was looking off when you went and got yourself born.

(86)

Not only is John a result of God's blindness, but John consistently fails to see his way, particularly in failing to pick up on Hattie's use of conjure tricks to entrap him into a second marriage. The vision in the novel belongs to his first wife, Lucy. She is the one whose "large bright eyes looked thru and beyond him and saw too much" (112). Lucy, far more self-aware and perceptive than John, harnesses the power of vision so successfully that her visions live on after her death. Interestingly, when John finally does attain a degree of vision, it proves highly ambiguous and problematic, leading to his death when he drives his car into a railroad crossing: "He drove on but half-seeing the railroad from looking inward" (167). Lacking Lucy's ability to put her visual power to practical use, John fatally blinds himself to his surroundings and pays the ultimate price for his inability to see. Here Hurston sets up her paradigm: Vision must be embodied, one must see outwardly as well as inwardly.

Hurston establishes the full power of the visual in *Their Eyes Were Watching God*. Initially subjected to the defining and objectifying power of a communal gaze, Janie, unlike John Pearson, learns to employ vision in ways that are self-affirming rather than self-sacrificing. Returning to Eatonville at the novel's start, Janie finds herself in a position very familiar to her: the object that all eyes are upon. When she approaches, the people are full of hostile questions to which they "hoped the answers were cruel and strange" (4). But when she keeps on walking, refusing to stop and acquiesce to their voyeuristic desires, talk becomes specularization: "The porch couldn't talk for looking." The men notice her "firm buttocks like she had grape fruits in her hip pockets; the great rope of black hair swinging to her waist and unraveling in the wind like a plume; then her pugnacious breasts trying to bore holes in her shirt." The women focus on the "faded shirt and muddy overalls." Looking at her body, the men see her as sexed; for the women, gazing on her apparel, she is gendered. In both cases, it seems, Janie vanishes. The men define her as female body parts and the women deny her feminine identity. While the female resentment of her attire may seem less intrusive than the male x-ray vision,

both looks constitute "mass cruelty" (2). Yet having set up Janie as spectacle, Hurston then illuminates the positive potential of vision in the ensuing interchange with Pheoby. Here, the visual takes on a different tone. Just as voice, according to Kaplan, becomes a kind of double-edged sword, so can vision—particularly when shared between friends—both specularize and affirm. Pheoby tells Janie, "'Gal you sho looks *good*. . . . Even wid dem overhalls on, you shows yo' womanhood'" (4). What she sees is presence, not absence. To look like a woman is to look good, a way of visualizing which does not fixate on sexual anatomy but which allows for materiality. She *shows* her womanhood, a far different sight than that gazed upon by the men, who see not Janie's presence but their own desire, desire which her body is expected to satisfy.

The materiality of Janie's body as an object of desire has, of course, determined much of her history. Her first husband, Logan Killicks, presumably wants to marry her based on what he sees, though her own eyes tell her something very different: "'He look like some old skullhead in de grave yard'" (13). But her vision lacks authority; despite what her eyes tell her, she is married off to him, defeated by Nanny's powerful story of her own oppression which seems to give her the right to impose her will upon Janie. Having "'save[d] de text,'" Nanny uses language to desecrate Janie's vision of the pear tree (16). Joe Starks, Janie's next husband, is likewise attracted to her beauty: "He stopped and looked hard, and then he asked her for a cool drink of water." This time, Janie does not submit passively to this specularization, and tries to look back, to return the gaze, pumping the water "until she got a good look at the man" (26). But her look still lacks the controlling power of the male gaze, what hooks calls the ability to "change reality." At this point, Janie has difficulty even seeing reality, as is evidenced by her inability to see through Joe Starks. She takes "a lot of looks at him and she was proud of what she saw. Kind of portly, like rich white folks" (32). What Janie sees is whiteness, and her valuation of this sets her on a path that will take twenty years to reverse. Looking at Joe's silk shirt, she overlooks his language of hierarchy, his desire to be a big voice. She has privileged the wrong kind of sight, a vision that fails to see into blackness and thus fails to see through language.

Still, Janie is not entirely fooled. Joe does "not represent sun-up and pollen and blooming trees, but he spoke for far horizon. He spoke for change and chance" (28). Janie thus gives up a vision she has seen—that of the pear tree—in favor of one she can only imagine: horizons, chance, and change. In allowing herself to be swayed by his language, she fails to notice that his rhetoric is that of speech, not vision. Joe only speaks; he does not see. Consequently, Janie's own vision deteriorates even further. Having initially recognized that Joe does not represent "sun-up and pollen," she later manages to convince herself that he does: "From now on until death she was going to have flower dust and springtime sprinkled over everything. A bee for her bloom" (31). Stubbornly, she tries to force Joe into her vision, possibly to justify running off with him. Convincing herself to see what is not there leads Janie into an unequal marriage in which she is expected to sit on a "high chair" (58), an infantilizing position where she can overlook the world and yet also be subjected to its envious eyes.

But Joe has a problem, for while he wants to put Janie on display in order to reap the benefit of reflected glory as her owner, this is precisely the position which is threatened by the eyes of other men. He wants her to be both present and absent, both visible and invisible, a task he attempts to accomplish by insisting that she keep her hair tied up in a head rag because he sees the other men not just "figuratively wallowing in it" (51) but literally touching it, and she "was there in the store for *him* to look at, not those others" (52). Joe wants to engage privately in scopophilia within a public forum, without subjecting Janie herself to this public gaze. Once she is fixed by gazes other than his own, he loses his exclusive ownership of her body. As Lorde notes, while visibility entails vulnerability, it can also be a source of great strength, a characteristic Joe certainly does not want to see in Janie. But the situation reflects more than Joe's concern about Janie's gaining cultural power; Janie's visibility also invokes a classic Freudian scenario. Laura Mulvey, in her groundbreaking psychoanalytic study "Visual Pleasure and Narrative Cinema," notes that the female figure, beyond providing pleasure for the looker, also implies a certain threat: "her lack of a penis, implying a threat of castration and hence unpleasure. . . . Thus the woman as icon, displayed for the gaze and enjoyment of the men, the active controllers of the look, always threatens to evoke the anxiety it originally signified" (21). Indeed, Joe's greatest anxiety is not focused on Janie's body but on his own. He wants to have the dominant position, but without being visually objectified by the viewers. "The more his back

ached and his muscle dissolved into fat and the fat melted off his bones the more fractious he became with Janie. Especially in the store. The more people in there the more ridicule he poured over her body to point attention away from his own" (73-74).

But the racial situation problematizes this notion of woman as icon, which presumes looking to be a masculine act. The cultural permutations of the significance of the gaze within the African American community challenge a strictly Freudian reading. If looking is an act of political defiance, it cannot be exclusively associated with black masculinity, particularly given the long history of black female activism and resistance. When Janie challenges Joe, she does so not just to defend her female identity—"'Ah'm uh woman every inch of me'" (75)—but also to protest against Joe's almost constant oppression. Joe, with his prosperity and seemingly white values, fails to realize that his mouth is not all powerful, that, despite his favorite expression, "I god," he is not divine. His centrality as mayor and store owner renders him even more vulnerable to specularization than Janie, and he falls prey to a kind of reversed Freudian schema of the gaze which entails serious repercussions for his political power.

Having set up the dynamics of the body as visualized object, Joe becomes its victim, as Janie linguistically performs the castration of which she is the visual reminder. As she tells him publicly, "'When you pull down yo' britches, you look lak de change uh life,'" her pictorial language renders it impossible for him to deny the vision she creates. He tries to erase the image by questioning her speech. "'Whawhut's dat you said?'" It doesn't work, however, for Walter taunts him, "'You heard her, you ain't blind.'" This comment highlights the interconnection between hearing and seeing; to hear is to see. And yet, given the words of her insult, Joe might as well be blind, for Janie has, in fact, revealed his lack of visual difference. By not using a visual metaphor in this case, she emphasizes that there is nothing there to see. She bares his body to the communal gaze, not only denying his masculinity but displaying his lack to other men: "She had cast down his empty armor before men and they had laughed, would keep on laughing" (75). Feminized by the visual dynamics that he has established, Joe dies, unable to withstand the gaze which erases his masculinity and identifies him as empty armor. Not only is it impossible for him to continue as mayor under these circumstances, it is impossible for him to continue. Joe has no life once denied both sexual and political power.

Though Hurston uses the visual to expose the vulnerability of a phallocentrism which abuses women, she also recognizes its empowering potential. In transforming the visual into a tool of female power, Hurston reclaims the power of the visual as a vehicle for examining African American women's experiences. After all, if one erases vision, one erases race, which is culturally visualized by the physical body, the sign of visual difference. As Michelle Wallace notes, "How one is seen (as black) and, therefore, what one sees (in a white world) is always already crucial to one's existence as an Afro-American. The very markers that reveal you to the rest of the world, your dark skin and your kinky/curly hair, are visual" ("Modernism" 40). Racial visibility as a marker of difference allows black women to "show" their womanhood.

Yet, as Joe's experience makes clear, this must be a particular kind of vision, a way of seeing which expands rather than limits understanding. Despite Joe's entrapment in his own gaze, the novel is replete with examples of the affirmative quality of the visual. Janie's attempts to define a self originate with the act of looking. Her "conscious life" begins with her vision of the pear tree, leading to her sexual awakening. Having felt called to "gaze on a mystery" (10), she beholds a "revelation" in the bees and flowers. She seeks her own place in the picture, searching for "confirmation of the voice and vision." Looking down the road, she sees a "glorious being" whom, in her "former blindness," she had known as "shiftless Johnny Taylor." But the "golden dust of pollen" which "beglamored his rags and her eyes" changes her perspective (11). Johnny Taylor's kiss, espied by Nanny, sets Janie's course in motion. Whether or not Johnny Taylor represents a better possibility is both impossible to determine and irrelevant; what matters is Janie's realization that her fate is linked to her vision, though the recognition will lead her astray until she learns effectively to interpret what she sees.

This vision, after her mistake in mis-seeing Joe Starks, is finally fulfilled when she meets Tea Cake, a man who is willing to display himself rather than subject others to his defining gaze. When Janie says, "'Look lak Ah seen you somewhere,'" he replies, "'Ah'm easy tuh see on Church Street most any day or night'" (90-91). By denying any anxiety in thus being viewed, Tea Cake transforms sight from a controlling, defining gaze into a personal introduction, demystifying himself by inviting inspection. In fact, Tea Cake cautions her about the importance of looking closely in the ensuing checkers game, challenging her claim that he has no right to jump her king because "'Ah wuz lookin' off when you went and stuck yo' men right up next tuh mine. No fair!'" Tea Cake answers, "'You ain't supposed tuh look off, Mis' Starks. It's de biggest part uh de game tuh watch out!'" (92). His response underscores the importance of watching, of using one's vision not to fix and specularize but to see and think, to understand. Consequently, Janie realizes that he "could be a bee to a blossom—a pear tree blossom in the spring" (101), a man who can confirm her initial vision. She defines him with visual metaphors: "He was a glance from God." This metaphor highlights Tea Cake's connection to the visual; he recognizes the need to combine voice with understanding, remarking that Janie needs "'tellin' and showin'" (102) to believe in love.

But Janie does not need simply to find a man capable of assimilating voice and vision, she needs to learn for herself how to formulate a self which is not predicated upon oppression. She finds the task particularly challenging because her racial identity is founded upon invisibility, upon her inability to see herself. The photograph which reveals her color, her difference, divides her from her previous notion of the identity of sameness: "'Before Ah seen de picture Ah thought Ah wuz just like de rest.'" To be black is to be not just different but absent, for Janie looks at the photograph asking, "'Where is me? Ah don't see me'" (9). Both blackness and femininity are culturally predicated upon lack; thus Janie needs to learn to show her womanhood and to find visible presence in blackness. Priscilla Wald has suggested that Janie's problem with seeing herself stems from her "white eyes": "The white eyes with which Janie looks see the black self as absent, that is, do not see the black self at all" (83). This is a particularly important point, for it indicates that Janie needs not just vision, but black vision—black eyes. Vision, which initially divides her from herself, must then provide the means for re-inventing a self, one in which racial identity adds wholeness rather than division. To deny either her blackness or her whiteness is to deny the specificity of her being, for her body is the site of the physical evidence of white oppression and a partially white origin. The answer is not to retreat into colorlessness but to reconstitute the definition of the self into something that acknowledges the conditions of her physical being: the visible evidence of her white-ness and her blackness, the heritage of slavery and sexual abuse.

Janie takes the first step toward acquiring this visual sense of self in response to Joe's oppression. "Then one day she sat and watched the shadow of herself going about tending store and prostrat-ing itself before Jody, while all the time she herself sat under a shady tree with the wind blowing through her hair and clothes." (73). She sees the self that prostrates itself before Jody as her shadow, and this realization acts on her "like a drug," of-fering an escape from an oppressive life. In order to move from passive spectator to active doer, however, she needs to take that vision further. The act of seeing must become active and affirmative before she can re-integrate the disparate parts of her identity into one unified whole. As Andrew Lakritz has written, "Some of the most powerful moments in Zora Neale Hurston's writings occur when a figure in the narrative is represented as watching events unfold, when such acts of look-ing become constitutive of the entire question of identity" (17). But looking itself does not auto-matically constitute identity; one must learn how to do it. Barbara Johnson's much cited analysis of Janie's recognition of her division into inside and outside also can be viewed as an experience in learning to use the visual. Johnson identifies Jan-ie's realization that the spirit of the marriage has left the bedroom and moved into the parlor as an "externalization of the inner, a metaphorically grounded metonymy," while the following para-graph where Janie sees her image of Jody tumble off a shelf "presents an internalization of the outer, or a metonymically grounded metaphor." This moment leads Janie to a voice which "grows not out of her identity but out of her division into inside and outside. Knowing how not to mix them is knowing that articulate language requires the co-presence of two distinct poles, not their col-lapse into oneness" (Johnson 212). If, indeed, the moment leads her to voice, it does not lead to a voice of self-assertion, as Janie remains silent under Joe's oppressive control for several more years.

I would suggest that the moment does not engender Janie's voice so much as it moves her toward a way of visualizing her experience which will, in time, lead her toward a picturing voice. In imagining her marriage as living in the parlor, she creates, as Johnson notes, a metonymy. But her metaphor of Joe as statue is also a metaphor infused with vision:

She stood there until something fell off the shelf inside her. Then she went inside there to see what it was. It was her image of Jody tumbled down and shattered. But looking at it she saw that it never was the flesh and blood figure of her dreams. Just something she had grabbed up to drape her dreams over. In a way she turned her back upon the image where it lay and looked further. She had no more blossom openings dusting pollen over her man, neither any glistening young fruit where the petals used to be. . . . She had an inside and an outside now and suddenly she knew how not to mix them.

(67-68)

The significance of this moment lies not just in Janie's recognition of the division between inside and outside but also in the ability to turn her back on the image and "look further." No longer content with surface vision, Janie is learn-ing to "look further," a necessary precondition for finding an expressive voice.

Joe's death offers her further opportunity to use this knowledge as she fixes her gaze upon herself. Janie goes to the mirror and looks "hard at her skin and features. The young girl was gone, but a handsome woman had taken her place" (83). This scene illustrates why vision is so crucial to Hurston's work. Recalling Butler's comment that the "visual field" is a "racial formation," one sees Hurston establishing precisely that. In looking hard at her "skin and features," Janie looks hard at her interracial body, seeing it now not as differ-ent but as handsome. She uses her own vision to find beauty and value in her visually inscribed racial identity. She then burns her head rags, symbol of Joe's attempts to deny her beauty and to hide her from the communal gaze while sub-jecting her to his own. Displaying her abundant hair, presumably another indication of her racially mixed heritage, brings her still closer to an af-firmation of her visual self, a self that celebrates rather than denying the mark of race—of both races. Kaja Silverman asserts that the "eye can confer the active gift of love upon bodies which have long been accustomed to neglect and dis-dain. It can also put what is alien or inconsequen-tial into contact with what is most personal and psychically significant" (227). Even before Janie gains the aid of Tea Cake's loving eye, her own eyes confer love upon her body as she begins to assimilate what has often seemed an alien world into her own psyche.

Janie transforms her understanding of color so that the sting of her original recognition of her photograph, "'Aw! aw! Ah'm colored!'" (9), can be alleviated and reversed by recognizing the visual beauty of color. The evening she meets Tea Cake, she watches the moon rise, "its amber fluid . . . drenching the earth" (95). This scene reveals the darkness of night to be full of color, transcending the stark blackness of the sky and whiteness of the moon. Hurston thus presents color as a full range of variation and beauty. Janie starts wearing blue because Tea Cake likes to see her in it, telling Pheoby not only that visual mourning should not last longer than grief, but that "'de world picked out black and white for mournin'" (107-08). By specifically associating mourning with black and white, Hurston subtly suggests that going beyond the color binary moves one from grief to happiness, from mourning and loss to fulfillment. She further challenges the black-white binary with the episode after the storm in the Everglades, when Tea Cake is forcibly conscripted into burying bodies. The white overseers insist that the workers "'examine every last one of 'em and find out if they's white or black'" (162). This ridiculous and horrific command inspires Tea Cake to comment, "'Look lak dey think God don't know nothin 'bout de Jim Crow law'" (163). The suggestion that God needs the aid of coffins to "see" racial difference again highlights the absurdity of seeing the world only in terms of black and white. By tying vision so intricately to race, Hurston offers a way out of the oppositional hierarchy of both.[8]

Thus Hurston destabilizes the visual racial binary, and Janie learns a new respect for color and for her own image. She restores the image that was desecrated by the photograph, when Tea Cake tells her to look in the mirror so she can take pleasure from her looks. "Fortunately," says Silverman, "no look ever takes place once and for all" (223). As Hurston well understands, looking is not a static activity. To "transform the value," as Silverman puts it, of what is seen, one needs to use one's life-experience in order to see it better. Having stood up to her husband, survived the gossip implicating her in his death, taken over the business, and dared to consider a lover, Janie learns to transform her gaze into one that accepts and values her own image.

After learning to use her vision to value herself, Janie is ready to take the next step: using vision to find God. The title episode of the novel reveals the full importance of the power of sight and of being an active looker; watching God is an active rather than a passive enterprise.

> They sat in company with others in other shanties, their eyes straining against crude walls and their souls asking if He meant to measure their puny might against His. They seemed to be staring at the dark, but their eyes were watching God.
> (151)

Like Alice Walker in *The Color Purple,* Hurston re-visions the old white man with a long beard. Instead, one approaches God not just in darkness but by looking *through* darkness, to see God where others see blackness. In so doing, she enables a kind of vision that deifies darkness, replacing the emptiness with presence, presence in blackness. At the height of the storm, Janie tells Tea Cake, "'If you kin see de light at daybreak, you don't keer if you die at dusk'" (151). Since she can "see" the light in darkness, neither it nor death holds any fear for her. By having her characters watch God in darkness, Hurston redefines rationalist and masculine control of the gaze, transforming scopophilia into spirituality. Her enabled gaze does not make women specularizable, for it takes place in darkness; rather, it makes God viewable and blackness visible. Similarly, in Toni Morrison's *Paradise,* the midwife Lone, trying to find out what the men plan to do to the women at the convent, sits in the dark to read the signs: "Playing blind was to avoid the language God spoke in. He did not thunder instructions or whisper messages into ears. Oh, no. He was a liberating God. A teacher who taught you how to learn, to see for yourself" (273). Learning how to see—particularly, learning how to see in darkness—takes on special meaning for African American women. One comes to God not through light but through the ability to see in the dark.

But Hurston's world is not solely visual; material bodies exist tactilely as well as visually, and color is not always beautiful, as the historical forces of slavery and oppression can be read on Janie's body. She is the product of two generations of rape, one of them interracial. She suffers physically for her interracial body when Tea Cake beats her to display his ownership in the face of Mrs. Turner's theories of Janie's superiority due to her light skin. The bruises, of course, are clearly evident precisely because of that light skin, as Sop-de-Bottom enviously remarks, "'Uh person can see every place you hit her'" (140). These marks inscribe both visually and physically the full implications of her racial identity as well as the violence that brought it into being. Just as black women cannot ignore the visual, neither can they escape the tactile, a physical language which highlights the material racist and sexist abuse of the body.[9] As Sharon Davie argues, Hurston's bodily metaphors "acknowledge the tactile, the physical, which Western culture devalues" (454). But Hurston does more than acknowledge the tactile; she *reveals* it. In Hurston's world, the mark of violence is seen, making the tactile visual.

Though she celebrates the power of vision, she has no illusions that it can erase or replace the discourse of violence and racism. Rather, it documents, for all to see, the effects of brutality.

Janie's act of killing is an act of physical self-defense to protect the body that Tea Cake has restored to her. Yet even this highly tactile response has a visual component. She waits for a sign from the sky, a visual indication that God will relent and spare Tea Cake's life, but "the sky stayed hard looking and quiet" (169). I find it telling that this is a daytime supplication, as Janie seeks to find a message "beyond blue ether's bosom," waiting for a "star in the daytime, maybe, or the sun to shout." This daylight sky appears much less accessible to her searching eyes than the blackness of the storm. The God sought in darkness evokes a reaffirmation of love, but this light (skinned?) God forces murder. Lack of visual contact spells doom, and Tea Cake's vision consequently suffers to the point where the "fiend in him must kill and Janie was the only thing living he saw" (175). Thus Tea Cake's death both saves Janie's physical body and erases his false vision.

Her final test involves learning to integrate voice and vision in a different form of self-defense. The trial scene reconstitutes Janie as speaker rather than object. The spectators are there not to watch but to listen. Janie's verbal defense succeeds because she "makes them see," a phrase repeated three times in six sentences:

> She had to go way back to let them know how she and Tea Cake had been with one another so they could *see* she could never shoot Tea Cake out of malice.
>
> She tried to make them *see* how terrible it was that things were fixed so that Tea Cake couldn't come back to himself until he had got rid of that mad dog that was in him. . . . She made them *see* how she couldn't ever want to be rid of him.
>
> (178; emphasis added)

Despite critical concern with the narrator replacing Janie's voice at this crucial moment, we must recognize that Janie has made them see, as she has already made the reader see, that voice at this moment is subordinate to the ability to visualize, an effect that may be heightened by Hurston's deflection of Janie's story. We don't need to hear her, since we can see her story. She manages to refute the implications of the black male spectators, that "'dem white mens wuzn't goin tuh do nothin' tuh no woman dat look lak her'" (179), and they turn their anger against Mrs. Turner's brother who puts "himself where men's wives could look at him" (181). But Janie's looks have not been directed at him; she has been too busy learning to visualize to waste time specularizing.

Consequently, she returns home to discover "'dis house ain't so absent of things lak it used tuh be befo' Tea Cake come along'" (182). Having learned to make presence out of absence, she can now not only re-visualize Tea Cake, whose "memory made pictures of love and light against the wall," but can also call "in her soul to come and see" (184). In thus successfully employing a visualized voice, Janie becomes both spectator and participant in her own life. To speak the body, for an African American woman, means to recognize its visual racial difference as well as affirming its sexual identity. Hurston's mind-pictures and seeing-voices reclaim the physical world of pear trees and the beauty of the visible presence of blackness. As Hurston herself noted, pictorial language is of primary importance in black discourse, where everything is "illustrated. So we can say that the white man thinks in a written language and the Negro thinks in hieroglyphics" ("Characteristics" 24). By filling Janie "full of that oldest human longing—self revelation" (*Their Eyes* 6), Hurston presents a text of "revelation"—with all of its visual implications. Her hieroglyphics reflect a community of people whose world is their canvas and whose lives and bodies are pictured in living color.

She thus provides a model for reconciling voice and vision, for transforming black bodies from museum pieces or ethnographic objects into embodied voices, by recasting spectacle as visual, a move away from passive sensationalism to active participation. Hortense Spillers notes of the Du Boisian double-consciousness that "it is also noteworthy that his provocative claims . . . crosses [sic] their wires with the specular and spectacular: the sensation of looking at oneself and of imagining being seen through the eyes of another is precisely performative in what it demands of a participant on the other end of the gaze" (143). In Hurston's hands, looking is indeed a performative act. In fact, it becomes a linguistic performance which affirms bodily presence, reversing Fanon's claim that, in the white world, "consciousness of the body is solely a negating activity" (110). Hurston, as Priscilla Wald so aptly puts it, "redesignates 'color' as performance in a process that draws her readers into the dynamics of 'coloration'" (87). Through the use of hieroglyphics, she reconstitutes women as active and colored performers. Vision, so often a means of fixing and silencing African Americans, can also provide the means to foreground the body without surrendering the voice. As the title of Hurston's novel indicates, her concern goes beyond presenting an individual woman's journey to self-awareness; her accomplishment is nothing less than redefining African American rhetoric, rendering it verbal and visual.

Notes

1. Along with several studies cited within the text of my article, the following represent only a few of the many fine analyses of various aspects of voice and language in *Their Eyes*: Bond; Brigham; Callahan; Gates, "Zora"; Holloway; Kubitschek; McKay; Racine; Wall.

2. For more on the political power of the visual, see Rosi Braidotti, especially 73.

3. In this, Hurston differs markedly from Ralph Ellison, who focuses not so much on attaining vision as on the implications of invisibility. Whereas Ellison documents in intricate detail the confines of being invisible, Hurston examines the process of learning to see and be seen.

4. Indeed, in film theory, as Miriam Hansen points out, "an aesthetics of the glance is replacing the aesthetics of the gaze" (135). This reflects a move from the intensity of a gaze to the glance, "momentary and casual" (50), according to John Ellis, who notes that, with a glance, "no extraordinary effort is being invested in the activity of looking" (137). While this may result in a less controlling and hegemonic situation, it can also, as Hurston indicates, illustrate a lack of deep perception.

5. Film, both popular and documentary, has long specularized black bodies. According to Fatimah Tobing Rony, early-twentieth-century ethnographic films "incessantly visualized race" (267).

6. I am indebted to Lori Jirousek's 1999 Penn State dissertation "Immigrant Ethnographers: Critical Observations in Turn-of-the-Century America" for better understanding the significance of Boas to Hurston's fiction.

7. Indeed, vision can offer a challenge to the links which Homi Bhabha has traced between the scopic drive and colonial surveillance (28-29).

8. As Donna Haraway has suggested, "Vision can be good for avoiding binary oppositions" (188).

9. Again, we see further evidence in Morrison's work in *Beloved*'s scar and Sethe's "tree"; like Hurston, Morrison demands that one read the body visually.

Works Cited

Awkward, Michael. *Inspiring Influences: Tradition, Revision, and Afro-American Women's Novels.* New York: Columbia UP, 1989.

Baker, Houston A. "Scene . . . Not Heard." Gooding-Williams 38-48.

Bhabha, Homi K. "The Other Question.: The Stereotype and Colonial Discourse." *Screen* 24.6 (1983): 18-36.

Bond, Cynthia. "Language, Speech, and Difference in *Their Eyes Were Watching God.*" Gates and Appiah 204-17.

Braidotti, Rosi. *Nomadic Subjects: Embodiment and Sexual Difference in Contemporary Feminist Theory.* New York: Columbia UP, 1994.

Brigham, Cathy. "The Talking Frame of Zora Neale Hurston's Talking Book: Storytelling as Dialectic in *Their Eyes Were Watching God.*" *CLA Journal* 37.4 (1994): 402-19.

Butler, Judith. "Endangered/Endangering: Schematic Racism and White Paranoia." Gooding—Williams 15-22.

Callahan, John F. *In the African-American Grain: The Pursuit of Voice in Twentieth-Century Black Fiction.* Urbana: U of Illinois P, 1988.

Davie, Sharon. "Free Mules, Talking Buzzards, and Cracked Plates: The Politics of Dislocation in *Their Eyes Were Watching God.*" *PMLA* 108 (1993): 446-59.

Doane, Marianne. *The Desire to Desire: The Woman's Film of the 1940s.* Bloomington: Indiana UP, 1987.

Ellis, John. *Visible Fictions: Cinema, Television, Video.* Boston: Routledge & Kegan Paul, 1982.

Fanon, Frantz. *Black Skin, White Masks: The Experiences of a Black Man in a White World.* Trans. Charles Lam Markmann. New York: Grove P, 1967.

Gaines, Jane. "White Privileging and Looking Relations: Race and Gender in Feminist Film Theory." *Screen* 29.4 (1988): 12-27.

Gates, Henry Louis, Jr. "Zora Neale Hurston and the Speakerly Text." *Southern Literature and Literary Theory.* Ed. Jefferson Humphries. Athens: U of Georgia P, 1990. 142-69.

Gates, Henry Louis, Jr., and K. A. Appiah, eds. *Zora Neale Hurston: Critical Perspectives Past and Present.* New York: Armistad P, 1993.

Gooding-Williams, Robert, ed. *Reading Rodney King, Reading Urban Uprising.* New York: Routledge, 1993.

Hansen, Miriam. "Early Cinema, Late Cinema: Transformations of the Public Sphere." *Viewing Positions: Ways of Seeing Film.* Ed. Linda Williams. New Brunswick: Rutgers UP, 1995. 134-52.

Haraway, Donna. "Situated Knowledges: The Science Question in Feminism and the Privilege of Partial Perspective." *Simians, Cyborgs, and Women: The Reinvention of Nature.* London: Free Association Books, 1991. 183-201.

Henderson, Mae G. "Response" to Houston A. Baker, Jr.'s "There Is No More Beautiful Way: Theory and the Poetics of Afro-American Women's Writing." *Afro-American Literary Study in the 1990s.* Ed. Houston A. Baker, Jr., and Patricia Redmond. Chicago: U of Chicago P, 1989. 155-63.

Holloway, Karla F. C. *The Character of the Word: The Texts of Zora Neale Hurston.* Westport: Greenwood P, 1987.

hooks, bell. *Black Looks: Race and Representation.* Boston: South End P, 1992.

Hurston, Zora Neale. "Characteristics of Negro Expression." 1934. *Negro: An Anthology.* Ed. Nancy Cunard. Ed. and abridged by Hugh Ford. New York: Frederick Ungar, 1970. 39-46.

———. "Drenched in Light." 1924. Zora 940-48.

——. "The Gilded Six-Bits." 1933. Zora 985-96.

——. *Jonah's Gourd Vine.* 1934. Zora 1-171.

——. "Sweat." 1926. Zora 955-67.

——. *Their Eyes Were Watching God.* 1937. New York: Harper, 1990.

——. "What White Publishers Won't Print." 1950.

——. *I Love Myself When I Am Laughing . . . And Then Again When I Am Looking Mean and Impressive.* Ed. Alice Walker. Old Westbury: Feminist P, 1979. 169-73.

——. *Zora Neale Hurston: Novels and Stories.* New York: Library of America, 1995.

Johnson, Barbara. "Metaphor, Metonymy and Voice in *Their Eyes Were Watching God.*" *Black Literature and Literary Theory.* Ed. Henry Louis Gates, Jr. New York: Methuen, 1984. 205-19.

Kaplan, Carla. "The Erotics of Talk: 'That Oldest Human Longing' in *Their Eyes Were Watching God.*" *American Literature* 67.1 (1995): 115-42.

Kubitschek, Missy Dehn. "'Tuh de Horizon and Back': The Female Quest in *Their Eyes Were Watching God.*" *Black American Literature Forum* 17 (1983): 109-15.

Lakritz, Andrew. "Identification and Difference: Structures of Privilege in Cultural Criticism." *Who Can Speak?: Authority and Critical Identity.* Ed. Judith Roof and Robyn Wiegman. Urbana: U of Illinois P, 1995. 3-29.

Lords, Audre. *Sister Outsider.* Trumansburg, NY: Crossing P, 1984.

Loft, Eric. *Love and Theft: Blackface Minstrelsy and the American Working Class.* New York: Oxford UP, 1993.

Lubiano, Wahneema. "Don't Talk with Your Eyes Closed: Caught in the Hollywood Gun Sights." *Borders, Boundaries, and Frames: Cultural Criticism and Cultural Studies.* Ed. Mae Henderson. New York: Routledge, 1995. 185-201.

McKay, Nellie. "'Crayon Enlargements of Life': Zora Neale Hurston's *Their Eyes Were Watching God.*" *New Essays on "Their Eyes Were Watching God."* Ed. Michael Awkward. Cambridge: Cambridge UP, 1990.

Morrison, Toni. *Paradise.* New York: Knopf, 1998.

Mulvey, Laura. *Visual and Other Pleasures.* Bloomington: Indiana UP, 1989.

Racine, Maria J. "Voice and Inferiority in Zora Neale Hurston's *Their Eyes Were Watching God.*" *African American Review* 28 (1994): 283-92.

Rony, Fatimah Tobing. "Those Who Squat and Those Who Sit: The Iconography of Race in the 1895 Films of Felix-Louis Regnault." *Camera Obscura* 28 (Jan. 1992): 263-89.

Silverman, Kaja. *The Threshold of the Visible World.* New York: Routledge, 1996.

Spillers, Hortense J. "'All the Things You Could Be by Now, If Sigmund Freud's Wife Was Your Mother': Psychoanalysis and Race." *Female Subjects in Black and White: Race, Psychoanalysis, Feminism.* Ed. Elizabeth Abel, Barbara Christian, and Helene Moglen. Berkeley: U of California P, 1997. 135-58.

Stepto, Robert. *From Behind the Veil.* Urbana: U of Illinois P, 1979.

Wald, Priscilla. "Becoming 'Colored': The Self-Authorized Language of Difference in Zora Neale Hurston." *American Literary History* 2.1 (1990): 79-100.

Wall, Cheryl. "Zora Neale Hurston: Changing Her Own Words." *American Novelists Revisited: Essays in Feminist Criticism.* Ed. Fritz Fleischmann. Boston: Hall, 1982. 371-93.

Wallace, Michelle. *Invisibility Blues: From Pop to Theory.* New York: Verso P, 1990.

——. "Modernism, Postmodernism and the Problem of the Visual in Afro-American Culture." *Out There: Marginalization and Contemporary Cultures.* Ed. Russell Ferguson, Martha Gever, Trinh T. Minhha, and Comet West. Cambridge: MIT P, 1990. 39-50.

——. "Race, Gender, and Psychoanalysis in Forties Films: Lost Boundaries, Home of the Brave, and The Quiet One." *Black American Cinema.* Ed. Manthia Diawara. New York: Routledge, 1993. 257-71.

Washington, Mary Helen. "'I Love the Way Janie Crawford Left Her Husbands': Emergent Female Hero." Gates and Appiah 98-110.

Wolff, Maria Tai. "Listening and Living: Reading and Experience in *Their Eyes Were Watching God.*" Gates and Appiah 218-29.

Young, Lola. *Fear of the Dark: "Race," Gender and Sexuality in the Cinema.* New York: Routledge, 1996.

Seraph on the Suwanee

CAROL P. MARSH-LOCKETT (ESSAY DATE 1999)

SOURCE: Marsh-Lockett, Carol P. "What Ever Happened to Jochebed? Motherhood as Marginality in Zora Neale Hurston's *Seraph on the Suwanee.*" In *Southern Mothers: Facts and Fictions in Southern Women's Writing,* edited by Nagueyalti Warren and Sally Wolff, pp. 100-10. Baton Rouge: Louisiana State University Press, 1999.

In the following essay, Marsh-Lockett explores Hurston's portrayal of motherhood in Seraph on the Suwanee.

So, what ever happened to Jochebed? I raise this question in the context of Zora Neale Hurston's fiction not as an examination of Hurston's use of an Old Testament character but as a way of addressing a void in Hurston scholarship: the treatment of motherhood in her fiction. Study of her novels reveals that motherhood is a presence therein but that it exists in a marginalized, politically powerless form, the mothers themselves lacking communities of women and rarely finding their own voices except to uphold a patriarchal superstructure. In short, while motherhood is not an explicit theme and is not central to Hurston's writing, it is a problematic stretch in the fabric of her fiction. For the purposes of this essay, while I shall mention *Their Eyes Were Watching God,*

Zora Neale Hurston attends the *New York Times* book fair in November, 1973.

Jonah's Gourd Vine, and *Moses, Man of the Mountain,* I shall focus on the relatively untreated *Seraph on the Suwanee,* which appeared in 1948 during a controversial period of Hurston's life.[1]

In his comments on *Seraph on the Suwanee,* Hurston literary biographer Robert Hemenway concludes, "The book itself is not nearly so interesting as the authorial emotions that coalesced in the creating of it."[2] In his discussion, Hemenway suggests the necessity of extratextual evidence for a full understanding of the novel and its meaning. He also suggests, moreover, that the piece is given to certain failures because Hurston had abandoned black life and culture as a primary source of artistic inspiration. Indeed, Hurston was especially sensitive to the sanctions American society placed on black literary imagination and to the accompanying politics of the literary marketplace. To read and dismiss this text in terms of its failure to portray black life and culture, however, is to miss the salient portrayal of the sexual politics which renders it as relevant to gender issues at the end of the twentieth century as it was in 1948.

Seraph on the Suwanee, Hurston's last published work, openly explores sexism in family life and relates, more clearly than any other Hurston novel, a mother's story. The text contains a fully developed portrait of a mother, Arvay Henson Meserve, whose very mothering is a function of patriarchy and whose story is so psychologically violent that she cannot narrate it herself. Only twice in the novel does Arvay find her own maternal voice, both occasions in the context of great emotional turmoil and maternal loss resulting first from the death of a child and later from her other children's passage into adulthood. Most of her story is rendered through her consciousness from the limited omniscient point of view, and it is significant that in the novel she never achieves self-actualization or affirmation in her status as a mother. Like *Their Eyes Were Watching God, Seraph on the Suwanee* can be read as a feminist text. In *The Politics of Reproduction,* however, Mary O'Brien writes that in traditional or first wave feminist discourse, motherhood has been "despised, derided, and neglected." Interestingly, such treatment is actually patriarchal and hostile to women, since the virtues necessary for successful mothering require great control, discipline, and resourcefulness. In the world of **Seraph on the Suwanee,** motherhood is not dismissed so harshly. While—as opposed to many feminists— Hurston does not denigrate motherhood and portray it as an impediment to a woman's development and empowerment, she nonetheless allows motherhood to be marginalized and to survive only according to the dictates of a capitalist, patriarchal ethic.[3]

Set in the first quarter of the twentieth century, the novel centers upon Arvay Henson, an impoverished young white woman from Sawley, Florida, who spends most of her life nursing externally imposed insecurities about her attractiveness and desirability and harboring a distorted perception of the world as a menacing place. In her teens, in response to her sister's marrying a man whom Arvay, herself, loves, she embraces religion and seeks to become a foreign missionary. Eventually, she marries Jim Meserve, even though he pours turpentine in her eyes and later rapes her during their engagement. Meserve is an ambitious northerner who removes her from her impoverished "cracker" life and installs her in a solidly middle class existence. In light of the courtship and engagement, the marriage is unsurprisingly sexually and emotionally tense. Arvay's oppression in this new middle class existence is underscored by the symbolic surname (Me-serve) which she assumes upon marriage to Jim, for events in the marriage indicate that Arvay is to serve herself only through acquiescence and service to Jim. Although throughout the novel Arvay becomes increasingly privileged and quietly celebrates her escape from poverty, she never achieves true personal empowerment. Ultimately, the marriage experiences a fracture when Arvay asserts herself by withdrawing from Jim in response to his tyrannical and arbitrary behavior, and he leaves her. Reconciliation comes at the end of the novel when as a middle-aged woman, after more than twenty years as a victim of patriarchy, she now consciously conspires in her own oppression when she concludes peacefully that she must love Jim like a "mother"—which, in this context means self-effacing, unconditional capitulation to sexist dogma and failure to expect any growth on the part of her partner.

From a maternal feminist perspective—one which celebrates, embraces, and finds empowerment in motherhood—the portrayal of motherhood here is troubling. Miriam Johnson speaks to the issue at hand: "Feminists who do not separate motherhood from its male dominated context are likely to interpret a positive evaluation of motherhood as conservative."[4] Indeed, nowhere in Hurston's fiction is there a positive evaluation of motherhood. In **Their Eyes Were Watching God,** Hurston raises feminist arguments, but does not develop a maternal forum. In **Jonah's Gourd Vine,** Amy Crittenden and Lucy Pearson subsume maternal to marital concerns. And in **Moses, Man of the Mountain,** while Jochebed's very act of giving birth and subsequently guaranteeing Moses's existence transforms the mother from a traditionally passive observer and victim to an active revolutionary, Hurston does not develop the possibilities of the maternal voice, instead retaining the Old Testament focus on the story of Moses. We note, also, that Moses's mother-in-law is not given a name but remains "Jethro's Wife," and Jochebed cannot publicly admit to rearing her own child. Within the tales themselves, a woman's status as a mother is likely to be subordinated to her position as any other functionary (that is, wife, lover, daughter, sister). Moreover, within these fictive worlds, women remain subordinates of a patriarchal superstructure which ultimately determines their very movements through space and time. The problem with this is that there is no advancement of the maternal cause; in all of her fiction, Hurston theoretically perpetrates the disenfranchisement of an entire class of women.

This marginalization of motherhood is not new. O'Brien notes that as early as the *Timaeus,* Plato used the motif of motherhood, which he makes passive and abstract while ascribing to male creativity the qualities of potency and regeneration. The notion that Woman is little more than a womb, which has historically pervaded much of western thinking, is manifest in Jim Meserve's perception of women: "Women folks don't have no mind to make up nohow. They wasn't made for that. Lady folks were just made to act loving and kind and have a man to do for them all he's able, and have him as many boy children as he figgers he'd like to have, and make him so happy that he's willing to work and fetch every dad— blamed thing that his wife thinks she would like to have. That's what women are made for." In another instance, Jim says to Brock Henson, Arvay's father: "A woman knows who her master is, and she answers to his commands. We'll make out good enough." And later, he refers to Arvay as his "damn property."[5] In these statements lies the articulation of the patriarchal view of Woman as Other, clearly objectified, subordinate, and inferior to men. Such a notion, as has been widely documented, is essential to capitalism, in which motherhood and patriarchy form a curious but necessary union. Simply put, women constitute, when needed, a part of the labor force; more importantly, as mothers they facilitate the acquisition of private property in a system where children (ideally male) belong to the father. In this environment, beyond the functions of birth and nurturance, mothers serve no serious purpose.

Against this backdrop, then, we find Arvay. Mothers in her world are powerless. Worse yet, their very ability to bond with or mentor their children, especially daughters, who are potential mothers themselves, is interrupted at patriarchal will. In short, in this novel, there is no possibility for the development of a positive female identity because of the marginalization of motherhood within the world of the text.

The need for a healthy female identity, and the centrality of a healthy mother-daughter relationship to that identity, has been explored by feminist theorists. Nancy Chodorow and Carol Gilligan note that as opposed to male identity which develops through early separation from the mother, female identity develops through early continued connection with the mother. Thus the female identity is grounded in relationship with another. Emphasizing the importance of connection and affiliation in a woman's existence, Chodorow explains: "Because of their mothering by women, girls come to experience themselves as less separate than boys, as having more permeable boundaries. Girls come to define themselves more in relation to others." Gilligan goes further and addresses the area of moral development. She postulates a female ethic of relationship and concern for others; "[female] identity is defined in a context of relationship and judged by a standard of responsibility and care."[6] In the world of *Seraph on the Suwanee*, however, the intrusive nature of patriarchy and male chauvinism sabotage both the mother-daughter and mother-son relationships, with the result that the mother is forced to operate autonomously without the respect and consistent support of her husband and without the loyalty of her children. In addition, mothers frequently find themselves powerless to protect and assist their children at critical times. Throughout the novel, then, maternal impotence, which renders the maternal influence marginal at best, is evident.

Close reading of the novel reveals Arvay in a series of failed relationships, initially with her own mother and subsequently with her own children. Arvay's relationship with her mother, Maria Henson, is never characterized by the bonding essential to the development of an autonomous self. The relationship is apparently peripheral to Arvay's existence just as Hurston's portrayal of it is peripheral to the text. We see Arvay's interaction with Maria in the first three and the final three chapters of the novel, but as a mere extension of Arvay's father, Brock Henson, Maria has no autonomy and no originality of thought. Her loyalty to Arvay, then, is circumscribed by her husband's notions of social conventions and expectations. When she shepherds Arvay into marrying Jim Meserve, she merely mirrors Brock's sentiments:

"Call yourself trying to cold shoulder Jim Meserve, I take it. If you had the sense that God give a June bug you'd feel glad that he feels to scorch you to and from. Ain't you never going to have sense enough to get yourself a husband? You intend to lay round here on me for the rest of your days and moan and pray?"

"I help you to say," Maria Henson agreed. "Arvay ain't acting with no sense at all. Here all these girls around here 'bout to bust they guts trying to git to him, and Arvay, that seems like she got the preference with him, trying to cut the tom fool."[7]

While Brock's remarks are directed to Arvay, Maria's are directed away from her and function only to reinforce the father's disregard for his daughter. In another instance, when Brock embarrasses Arvay in front of Jim at the dinner table, Maria uses the gravy in the kitchen as an excuse not to support Arvay. Brock therefore sets the tone of the relationship between Maria and Arvay and consequently controls the extent to which Maria is able to mentor Arvay and influence her sense of connectedness.

The physical contact between Maria and Arvay is interrupted by Arvay's marriage, but resumes in the final chapter of the novel on the occasion of Maria's illness and death. As in earlier encounters, Maria is still powerless in her capacity to mother, but this time Arvay and Maria do achieve mutual affirmation. Impoverished and weak at the end of her life, Maria looks to Arvay for assurance of a decent burial, and finds comfort in Arvay's success as a mother. Ironically, however, Maria measures this success by the quality of material attention Arvay's children have paid her, all of which is a result of Jim's patriarchal and economic achievement.

Perhaps the most disconcerting feature of the relationship between Maria and Arvay, however, is that male influence continues to intrude negatively in Maria's death, even as it did in her life. That death and burial, Arvay's satisfaction with the closure of the relationship, and her successful completion of her responsibilities as a daughter all contribute to aid the political ambitions of Bradford Cary, a leading Sawley citizen. His subsequent gubernatorial success is linked in part to the exploitation of Arvay when he helps to bury her mother. The mother-child relationship, particularly because it involves two women, is no less vulnerable now to manipulation from outside the family circle and in the larger political arena than it was in Maria's lifetime.

Maria's ineffective mothering of Arvay both foreshadows and frames Arvay's relationship with her own children. Given that effective mothering is a choice based not only on biology but also on the decision to care for one's children, and given that effective mothering is characterized by a woman's total commitment to and strong will to act on behalf of her children's welfare, the maternal styles of Maria and Arvay are strikingly passive. Arvay is no more successful than Maria as a mother. Like the Henson household, the Meserve household still embraces patriarchal attitudes, and Arvay's maternal influence is clearly subordinate to Jim's will. Ultimately, Arvay's relationship with each of her children fails because Jim dictates the nature and development of the parent-child relationship in the household.

Arvay's relationship with Earl, her first born, effectively illustrates how mothers can be powerless to guarantee the physical well-being—and even the very lives—of their children. Born with an unnamed form of retardation, Earl requires special care and vigilance from birth. He elicits from Arvay a heightened sense of duty that Jim does not share. Moreover, early in the child's life, the marriage loses vitality. Mothering Earl, albeit halfheartedly, and fabricating delightful anecdotes about him compensate for the marital emptiness Arvay experiences.

Nevertheless, Arvay is basically powerless with regard to Earl's welfare, a fact evident in Jim's indifference to his son's special state and his role in Earl's destruction. When, for example, Arvay voices apprehension about Earl's safety around a tract of swamp land that Jim has purchased, Jim sneers at her fears. Later, when it is obvious that Earl is abnormally attracted to the Corregios, Jim suggests that Earl be institutionalized. When, as a result, Arvay becomes frantic—even accusing Jim of racial disloyalty—he dissociates from her pain, exerting his superiority over her and her family. Jim blames Arvay's parental lineage for Earl's condition and refuses to identify with her maternal anguish. When Earl attacks Lucy Ann, a lynch mob hunts him down and kills him with Jim's sanction. Arvay's essential right to mother is denied by her husband's violence, and here it is obvious that mothers cannot guarantee the physical existence of their children. Arvay is helpless to prevent Earl's death because Jim sanctions the violence. Worse yet, exhibiting unspeakable callousness, while Arvay mourns the death of the child, Jim insists on having sex. Jim discounts her grief by asserting sexual domination over her and further nullifies her maternal role.

Arvay's effectiveness as a mother to Angeline, her second child, is similarly compromised. Because of Earl's abnormality, Arvay's second pregnancy is a source of fear and insecurity. Her chief concern is that Jim will leave her should the baby not meet his expectations. With this pregnancy and the subsequent events of the child's life, we are again able to recognize the diminished correlation between motherhood and personhood as the woman's role as a womb emerges in the patriarchal schema of the novel. Angeline is born in physically comfortable but emotionally uncertain circumstances. Arvay is happy only after the baby seems normal, thus securing Jim's approval. Significantly, this birth is attended by a male doctor as opposed to a midwife, and rather than being woman centered, the birth event becomes a bastion of patriarchy in which the woman does not experience fulfillment as a principle player but participates, instead, to gratify the male ego by bearing a normal, healthy child.

That traditional patriarchy is a major contributor to the failure of Arvay's relationship with Angeline is evident from Angeline's infancy, when Jim makes himself central to both mother and child, and undermining an effective bond between them. Recording Angeline's birth in the family Bible, Jim in the act of writing her name marks Angeline's existence with his own imprimatur, and in so doing, he symbolically precludes further maternal involvement. By bonding himself to the baby, he perpetuates mother-daughter rivalry. He instructs Arvay in disciplining the child to such an extent that Arvay feels that Angeline has jurisdiction over her. Thus the reader is again aware that, as with Earl, maternal authority is not a serious factor. Jim also fuels Arvay's insecurities about her status with him and maintains his centrality with his assertion that he loves mother and daughter through each other.

As Angeline grows up, Jim continues to exercise his authoritarian will and maintain Arvay's position on the periphery of Angeline's development. His forceful presence makes Arvay reluctant to observe Angeline's maturity, and she does not involve herself in her daughter's psychological and social concerns, such as personal ambitions, awareness of men, and dating. Thus it is Jim who effectively shepherds Angeline into womanhood and marriage. When Arvay worries about Angeline's possible sexual involvement with Hatton Howland, whom she subsequently marries, Jim laughingly dismisses the mother's concerns and so emerges as the voice of reason in the matter. Jim assesses Hatton Howland's suitability for marriage to the underage Angeline and then excludes Arvay from the marriage, which he alone witnesses and informs Arvay of much later; Arvay's involvement is limited to her preparation, upon Jim's instruction, for the bride and groom's return. Jim has again undermined the maternal presence, and Angeline, through her silence, colludes in her mother's marginalization. And, finally, the economic success of the marriage and the couple's upward social mobility result both from Jim's instructions and from their own willingness to subscribe to a patriarchal, capitalist ethic that prevents Arvay from having any input into their welfare.

Arvay's relationship with third child Kenny, while not as dramatic, is as unsuccessful as her relationships with Earl and Angeline, thus underscoring the role of male privilege and authority in the polarization of mothers and children. The third pregnancy is a time of torment for the mother as Jim viciously teases her, demanding that the baby she is carrying be a son. Jim's chauvinism has rendered Arvay so insecure that eventually, doubting his ability to love and protect her, she retreats into religion, identifying with the biblical Hannah and Hagar as well as other "sorrowful women." Arvay's drawing on Old Testament stories, which reflect what is loosely referred to as the era of patriarchs, symbolizes her subscription to a value system that reduces the totality of womanhood to a woman's ability to bear sons. Like the women of the Old Testament, she articulates fears about events over which she has no control: "Be nice, honey. Be nice now, and come here a boy-child for your Mama. You see the fix I'm in. Jim is liable to leave me if you ain't a boy. Me with my three little hungry mouths to feed and to do for."[8] Here again there is no affirmation for Arvay in pregnancy and motherhood—only concern that she be able to satisfy Jim's patriarchal dictates, at the root of which lie his unconscionable ego demands. It is therefore not surprising that while Kenny demonstrates a normal developmental gender separation from Arvay as he ma-

tures, no significant bond develops between them, since Jim seizes control of Kenny's social, emotional, and professional growth. With the third of her children, then, Arvay is once again marginalized and her maternal authority trivialized and sabotaged.

Nowhere in the world of *Seraph on the Suwanee,* in either the marital or the parent-child relationship, is motherhood separated from its male-defined and male-dominated context. Therein lies the plight of Jochebed, the mother whose narrative encompasses manipulation of the text and reader expectations that allow no forum for the political empowerment of motherhood. In *Seraph on the Suwanee,* Hurston has subsumed Arvay's story as a mother to the narrator's story of Arvay as a wife. Thus while the novel was ahead of its time in raising strong feminist questions, especially regarding the institution of marriage, it also fails—as much of feminism has failed—to empower mothers, to lift the maternal voice, and to move mothers from the periphery to the center of social concerns and expectations. When Hurston allows Arvay in her maternal role to remain static—consistently weak, insecure, and irrational in her mothering—the novel reinforces the notion, popular with first-wave feminists, that motherhood is without credibility or respectability and that it undermines women. Writers and critics have recently begun to address this weakness in feminism. Marianne Hirsch, for example, in her examination of women's fiction, claims, "Feminist writing, continuing in large part to adopt a daughterly perspective, could be said to collude with patriarchy in placing the mother in a position of object and thereby keeping mothering outside of representation and maternal discourse a theoretical impossibility."[9] And so it is with Arvay's story.

One can only speculate why Hurston failed to capitalize artistically on this significant aspect of the female experience. We can perhaps conjecture that the death of her biological mother when Hurston was a young child, her tempestuous and hostile relationship with her stepmother, her own childlessness as an adult, and the pernicious, latent effects of patriarchy contributed to placing the issue of motherhood beyond her literary imagination. In any event, *Seraph on the Suwanee,* like the rest of her work, fails to make a full contribution to the strength of women which Adrienne Rich terms "the bloodstream of [women's] inheritance."[10] Thus the novel renders the important undertaking of mothering, in which much of the world's adult population engages and without which humanity would cease to exist, marginal and useless.

Notes

1. Zora Neale Hurston, *Their Eyes Were Watching God* (Philadelphia: J. B. Lippincott, 1937); Hurston, *Jonah's Gourd Vine* (Philadelphia: J. B. Lippincott, 1934); Hurston, *Moses, Man of the Mountain* (Philadelphia: J. B. Lippincott, 1937); Hurston, *Seraph on the Suwanee* (New York: Charles Scribner's Sons, 1948; reprint, Harper & Row, 1991).

2. *Zora Neale Hurston: A Literary Biography* (Urbana: University of Illinois Press, 1978), 314.

3. Mary O'Brien, *The Politics of Reproduction* (Boston: Routledge & Kegan Paul, 1983), 8. For useful insight into male privilege and dominance, see Miriam Johnson's discussion of women and family life in *Strong Mothers, Weak Wives: The Search for Gender Equality* (Berkeley and Los Angeles: University of California Press, 1988), 25-37.

4. Johnson, *Strong Mothers*, 30.

5. O'Brien, *Politics of Reproduction*, 125; Hurston, *Seraph on the Suwanee*, 25, 33, 216.

6. Nancy Chodorow, *The Reproduction of Mothering: Psychoanalysis and the Sociology of Gender* (Berkeley and Los Angeles: University of California Press, 1978), 93; Carol Gilligan, *In a Different Voice* (Cambridge: Harvard University Press, 1982), 160. Gilligan's observations would appear to mean only the matrix of white society. History suggests that the composition of viewing audiences at lynchings, for example, indicates that white women do not uniformly extend this concern to people of color. More specifically, in the novel, Arvay shows no concern for Belinda, the child of the black Kelsey family, when Kenny has obviously exploited her.

7. Hurston, *Seraph on the Suwanee*, 13-4.

8. Ibid., 99.

9. Marianne Hirsch, "Maternal Narratives: Cruel Enough to Stop the Blood," *Reading Black, Reading Feminist: A Critical Anthology*, ed. Henry Louis Gates (New York: Meridian Press, 1990), 415.

10. Adrienne Rich, *Of Woman Born: Motherhood as Experience and Institution* (New York: Bantam Books, 1977), 216.

FURTHER READING

Bibliographies

Cairney, Paul. "Writings about Zora Neale Hurston's *Their Eyes Were Watching God*: 1987-1993." *Bulletin of Bibliography* 52, no. 2 (June 1995): 121-32.

Provides a listing of material about Hurston's Their Eyes Were Watching God.

Dance, Daryl C. "Zora Neale Hurston." In *American Women Writers: Bibliographical Essays,* edited by Maurice Duke, Jackson R. Bryer, and M. Thomas Inge, pp. 321-51. Westport, Conn.: Greenwood, 1983.

A bibliography about Hurston and her life and work.

Davis, Rose Parkman. *Zora Neale Hurston: An Annotated Bibliography and Reference Guide.* Westport, Conn.: Greenwood, 1997, 224 p.

A listing of critical commentary and books about Hurston.

Glasrud, Bruce A., and Laurie Champion. "Zora Neale Hurston (1891-1960)." In *American Women Writers, 1900-1945: A Bio-Biographical Critical Sourcebook,* edited by Laurie Champion and Emmanuel S. Nelson, pp. 162-72. Westport, Conn.: Greenwood, 2000.

Details sources on Hurston's life and work.

Biographies

Boyd, Valerie. *Wrapped in Rainbows: The Life of Zora Neale Hurston.* New York: Scribner, 2003, 527 p.

A highly regarded biography focusing on details about both Hurston's life and writing, examining her politics and love interests in the context of the Harlem Renaissance, the Great Depression, and World War II.

Hemenway, Robert E. *Zora Neale Hurston: A Literary Biography.* Urbana: University of Illinois Press, 1980, 371 p.

Traces Hurston's life and work and addresses conflicting or inaccurate information from her autobiography.

Criticism

Anokye, Akua Duku. "Private Thoughts, Public Voices: Letters from Zora Neale Hurston." *Women: A Cultural Review* 7, no. 2 (autumn 1996): 150-59.

Provides a new perspective on Hurston's relationship with her white patrons by looking at some of Hurston's correspondence.

Awkward, Michael. *New Essays on "Their Eyes Were Watching God."* Cambridge: Cambridge University Press, 1990, 129 p.

Contains critical commentary about Hurston's Their Eyes Were Watching God.

Benesch, Klaus. "Oral Narrative and Literary Text: Afro-American Folklore in *Their Eyes Were Watching God.*" *Callaloo* 11 (1988): 627-35.

Assesses the relationship between Hurston's Their Eyes Were Watching God *and African American folklore.*

Bethel, Lorraine. "'This Infinity of Conscious Pain': Zora Neale Hurston and the Black Female Literary Tradition." In *All the Women Are White, All the Blacks Are Men, But Some of Us Are Brave: Black Women's Studies,* edited by Gloria T. Hull, Patricia Bell-Scott, and Barbara Scott, pp. 176-88. Old Westbury, N.Y.: Feminist Press, 1982.

Discusses Hurston's place in the canon of African American female literary tradition.

Bloom, Harold. *Zora Neale Hurston: Modern Critical Views,* edited by Harold Bloom. New York: Chelsea, 1986, 222 p.

Offers a variety of critical perspectives on Hurston's work.

——. *Zora Neale Hurston's "Their Eyes Were Watching God,"* edited by Harold Bloom. New York: Chelsea, 1987, 231 p.

Presents critical commentary about Hurston's Their Eyes Were Watching God.

Bordelon, Pam. "New Tracks on *Dust Tracks*: Toward a Reassessment of the Life of Zora Neale Hurston." *African American Review* 35, no. 5 (1997): 5-21.

Provides a close reading of Hurston's autobiography Dust Tracks on a Road.

Boxwell, D. A. "'Sis Cat' as Ethnographer: Self-Presentation and Self-Inscription in Zora Neale Hurston's *Mules and Men*." *African American Review* 26 (1992): 605-15.

Analyzes Hurston's Mules and Men.

Byrd, James W. "Zora Neale Hurston: A Novel Folklorist." *Tennessee Folklore Bulletin* 21 (1955): 37-41.

Discusses the importance of folklore in Hurston's work.

Caron, Timothy P. "'Tell Ole Pharoah to Let My People Go': Communal Deliverance in Zora Neale Hurston's *Moses, Man of the Mountain*." *Southern Quarterly* 36, no. 3 (1998): 47-60.

Examines Hurston's Moses, Man of the Mountain.

Cooper, Ian. "Zora Neale Hurston Was Always a Southerner Too." In *The Female Tradition in Southern Literature*, edited by Carol S. Manning, pp. 57-69. Urbana: University of Illinois Press, 1993.

Explores Hurston's work as part of the tradition of southern literature.

Crabtree, Claire. "The Confluence of Folklore, Feminism, and Black Self-Determination in Zora Neale Hurston's *Their Eyes Were Watching God*." *Southern Literary Journal* 17, no. 2 (1985): 54-66.

Evaluates Hurston's Their Eyes Were Watching God, *focusing on such issues as folklore, feminism, and black identity.*

Gates Jr., Henry Louis. "Zora Neale Hurston and the Speakerly Text." In *The Signifying Monkey: A Theory of Afro-American Literary Criticism*, pp. 170-216. New York: Oxford University Press, 1988.

Analyzes Hurston's writing style.

Jordan, Jennifer. "Feminist Fantasies: Zora Neale Hurston's *Their Eyes Were Watching God*." *Tulsa Studies in Women's Literature* 7 (1988): 105-17.

Offers a feminist reading of Hurston's Their Eyes Were Watching God.

Krasner, James N. "The Life of Women: Zora Neale Hurston and Female Autobiography." *Black American Literature Forum* 23 (1989): 113-26.

Discusses Hurston's autobiography Dust Tracks on a Road.

Lurie, Susan. "Antiracist Rhetorics and the Female Subject: The Trials of Zora Neale Hurston." In *Unsettled Subjects: Restoring Feminist Politics to Poststructuralist Critique*, pp. 44-77. Durham, N.C.: Duke University Press, 1997.

Analyzes Hurston's relationship to black feminist politics and her attempt to create an antiracist discourse that does not undermine black feminism.

Menefee, Samuel Pyeatt. "Zora Neale Hurston 1891-1960." In *Women and Tradition: A Neglected Group of Folklorists*, edited by Carmen Blacker and Hilda Ellis Davidson, pp. 159-72. Durham, N.C.: Carolina Academic Press, 2000.

Addresses Hurston's relationship with folklore throughout her life and career.

Meisenhelder, Susan. "False Gods and Black Goddesses in Naylor's *Mama Day* and Hurston's *Their Eyes Were Watching God*." *Callaloo* 23, no. 4 (fall 2000): 1440-48.

Asserts that Gloria Naylor drew on Hurston's Their Eyes Were Watching God *in her novel* Mama Day, *and delineates the similarities between the two texts.*

———. *Hitting a Straight Lick with a Crooked Stick: Race and Gender in the Work of Zora Neale Hurston.* Tuscaloosa: University of Alabama Press, 1999, 253 p.

Explores issues of race and gender in Hurston's work.

Oxindine, Annette. "Pear Trees beyond Eden: Women's Knowing Reconfigured in Woolf's *To the Lighthouse* and Hurston's *Their Eyes Were Watching God*." In *Approaches to Teaching Woolf's "To the Lighthouse,"* edited by Beth Rigel Daugherty and Mary Beth Pringle, pp. 163-68. New York: The Modern Language Association of America, 2001.

Compares Virginia Woolf's To the Lighthouse *to Hurston's* Their Eyes Were Watching God *to show how both authors use the sensual inner lives of their female protagonists to subvert the patriarchal order of the male characters.*

Plant, Deborah. *Every Tub Must Sit on Its Own Bottom: The Philosophy and Politics of Zora Neale Hurston.* Urbana: University of Illinois Press, 1995, 214 p.

Contains essays tracing Hurston's beliefs through her work.

Powers, Peter Kerry. "Gods of Physical Violence, Stopping at Nothing: Masculinity, Religion, and Art in the Work of Zora Neale Hurston." *Religion and American Culture: A Journal of Interpretation* 12, no. 2 (summer 2002): 229-47.

Examines Hurston's contribution, as a major writer of the Harlem Renaissance, to the discourse on gender, race, and religion.

Wall, Cheryl A. "*Mules and Men* and Women: Zora Neale Hurston's Strategies of Narration and Visions of Female Empowerment." *Black American Literature Forum* 23 (1989): 661-80.

Discusses Hurston's treatment of women in Mules and Men.

Walters, Keith. "'He Can Read My Writing but He Sho' Can't Read My Mind': Zora Neale Hurston's Revenge in *Mules and Men*." *Journal of American Folklore* 112, no. 445 (summer 1999): 343-71.

Traces the history of Mules and Men *and provides a close analysis of the book's opening and closing tales.*

OTHER SOURCES FROM GALE:

Additional coverage of Hurston's life and career is contained in the following sources published by the Gale Group: *African American Writers*, Eds. 1, 2; *American Writers Supplement*, Vol. 6; *Authors and Artists for Young Adults*, Vol. 15; *Beacham's Guide to Literature for Young Adults*, Vol. 12; *Black Literature Criticism*; *Black Writers*, Eds. 1, 3; *Concise Dictionary of American Literary Biography Supplement*; *Contemporary Authors*, Vols. 85-88; *Contemporary Authors New Revision Series*, Vol. 61; *Contemporary Literary Criticism*, Vols. 7, 30, 61; *Dictionary of Literary Biography*, Vols. 51, 86; *DISCovering Authors*; *DISCovering Authors: Canadian Edition*; *DISCovering Authors Modules: Most-studied Authors, Multicultural,* and *Novelists*; *DISCovering Authors 3.0*; *Drama Criticism*, Vol. 12; *Drama for Students*, Vol. 6; *Encyclopedia of World Literature in the 20th Century,* Ed. 3; *Exploring Novels; Exploring Short Stories; Feminist Writers; Harlem Renaissance: A Gale Critical Companion; Literary Movements for Students,* Vol. 2; *Literature and Its Times,* Vol. 3; *Literature and Its Times Supplement,* Ed. 1; *Literature Resource Center; Major 20th-Century Writers,* Eds. 1, 2; *Modern American Women Writers; Novels for Students,* Vol. 3; *Reference Guide to American Literature,* Ed. 4; *Reference Guide to Short Fiction,* Ed. 2; *St. James Guide to Young Adult Writers; Short Stories for Students,* Vols. 1, 6, 11; *Short Story Criticism,* Vol. 4; *Twayne's United States Authors; Twentieth-Century Literary Criticism,* Vols. 121, 131; and *World Literature Criticism Supplement.*

MAXINE HONG KINGSTON

(1940 -)

(Born Maxine Ting Ting Hong) American memoirist, nonfiction writer, novelist, essayist, and poet.

A highly acclaimed memoirist, Kingston integrates autobiographical elements with Asian legend and fictionalized history to delineate cultural conflicts confronting Americans of Chinese descent, particularly issues of female identity. Frequently studied in a variety of academic disciplines, her works bridge two civilizations in their examination of social and familial bonds from ancient China to contemporary California. Kingston often focuses on issues of cultural and institutional sexism and misogyny as well as female autonomy and identity. Writers such as Amy Tan, David Henry Hwang, Gish Jen, and Fae Myenne Ng have been strongly influenced by Kingston's portrayal of the history of Chinese American women.

BIOGRAPHICAL INFORMATION

Born in Stockton, California, to parents who were Chinese immigrants, Kingston experienced first-hand the often painful results of clashes between American and Chinese cultures. Her mother, who was a strong influence on Kingston, wanted her to remain essentially Chinese and instilled in her the beliefs, traditions, and customs of her native country. As a young woman, Kingston struggled academically, primarily because she refused to talk in class. Scholastically, her performance improved to the point where she was awarded a scholarship to the University of California, Berkeley. In 1965, she received her teaching certificate. She taught English and mathematics at the high school level in California and Hawaii for several years. The tension between her Chinese background and her immersion in American culture became a recurring theme in her later work. In 1976, her first book, *The Woman Warrior,* was published to critical and popular acclaim. She was appointed professor at the University of California, Berkeley in 1990. She has received several awards for her work, including two National Book Awards, for *The Woman Warrior* and *China Men* (1980), and other national and local recognitions for her writing. In 1992, she was inducted into the American Academy of Arts and Sciences. She and her husband live in Oakland, California.

MAJOR WORKS

As an American-born daughter of stern immigrant parents, Kingston explores in her work the anxiety that often results from clashes between radically different cultural sensibilities. Her exotic, myth-laden narratives are informed by several sources: the ordeals of immigrant forebears who endured brutal exploitation as they labored on American railroads and cane plantations; the "talk-stories," or cautionary tales of ancient heroes and family secrets told by her mother; and her own experiences as a first-generation American with confused cultural allegiances. From these foundations, Kingston forms epic chronicles of the Chinese immigrant experience that are esteemed for their accurate and disturbing illumination of such social patterns as Asian cultural misogyny and American institutional racism. Her first autobiographical volume, *The Woman Warrior,* has been deemed an innovative and important feminist work. It is viewed as a personal, unconventional memoir that seeks to reconcile Eastern and Western conceptions of female identity. Kingston eschews chronological plot and standard nonfiction techniques in her memoir, synthesizing ancient myth and imaginative biography to present a kaleidoscopic vision of female character. The narrative begins with Kingston's mother's brief caveat concerning No Name Woman, young Maxine's paternal aunt, whose disrepute has rendered her unmentionable. Left in their village by her émigré husband, No Name Woman became pregnant—perhaps by rape—and was forced by the villagers to drown herself and her baby. Affirming traditional attitudes, Maxine's mother, Brave Orchid, describes such practices as foot-binding and the sale of girls as slaves, and she threatens Maxine with servitude and an arranged marriage to a retarded neighborhood boy. Subsequent chapters, however, provide sharp contrast to these bleak visions, for Brave Orchid also recites the colorful legend of Fa Mu Lan, the woman who wielded a sword to defend her hamlet. Kingston then describes Brave Orchid's own incongruent character; independent enough to become one of rural China's few female doctors, she returned to her customary submissive role upon joining her husband in America. In *China Men* Kingston examines the lives and experiences of her mythological father, grandfather, great-grandfather, uncles, and brothers. In these narratives, BaBa serves as the father figure, Ah Goong as grandfather, and Bak Goong as great-grandfather. The concept of the father embodies a significant theme of the book: the importance of personal history as a means to self-awareness and self-confidence. Ah Goong works for the railroads planting dynamite charges in mountains and hillsides and digging holes for bridge supports. Several critics have noted that Ah Goong's coarse description of his onanistic acts functions as a way of feminizing the land and describing it in terms

of possession, elements typical of much Western writing. In this respect, Ah Goong's language raises questions about universal masculine responses to the environment while at the same time highlighting a search for female identity in the male-dominated Chinese-American myth of westward expansion.

Tripmaster Monkey (1989) is an experimental novel narrated by Kuan Yin, the Chinese goddess of mercy, and is loosely based on the "monkey tales" of Chinese folklore which feature a trickster hero who is also an artist and a magician. The protagonist is Wittman Ah Sing, a young Chinese playwright in San Francisco who reaches maturity during the hippie era of the late 1960s. Wittman, an Asian American wanting to become an important American playwright, is not only a monkey figure, or someone who must rely upon cunning and metaphorical sleight-of-hand to reach his goals, but also a jazz musician: he must improvise his life, attitudes, and behavior from moment to moment if he is to survive in the urban wilderness. *To Be the Poet* (2002) is a collection of prose and poetry based on Kingston's 2000 William E. Massey lectures at Harvard. The book provides readers with a glimpse of a poet at work during the creative process. *The Fifth Book of Peace* (2003) is a complex, stream of consciousness memoir that relates the destruction of a novel-in-progress that occurred when Kingston's Oakland, California, home burned to the ground in 1991. *The Fifth Book of Peace* incorporates a retelling of the narrative of the destroyed novel combined with several other elements: Kingston's memories about her attempts to rescue the manuscript from her burning house, her quest to understand myths surrounding the Chinese Three Lost Books of Peace, and her plea to veterans of all wars to help her proclaim a message of peace.

CRITICAL RECEPTION

Critics view Kingston as one of the most prominent and influential Asian American authors of the twentieth century. *The Woman Warrior* is considered her best-known work. Since its first printing, it has been translated into more than three dozen languages and has become an extremely popular university text, widely read in courses in education, sociology, psychology, anthropology, women's studies, Asian studies, and American literature. Feminist critics applaud the memoir for its insightful and poignant exploration of female identity. A few reviewers, however, have asserted that the emphasis on female character development has come at the expense of the male characters in the book. Some critics have viewed *The Woman Warrior* as a distortion of Asian mythology and culture. Asian American male writers, particularly Frank Chin, have accused Kingston of selling out by misrepresenting Chinese mythology and culture and utilizing a Western literary form—the memoir—to pander to Western audiences. Kingston, along with other critics and writers, has responded by asserting that her creative reworkings and personalization of Chinese mythology is a legitimate postmodern strategy. Moreover, Kingston contends that she will not allow her work to be influenced by narrow and questionable definitions of Asian American literature. Some allege that negative criticisms of Kingston's work—particularly of *The Woman Warrior*—are based on the male chauvinism and ethnocentrism of the critics themselves. With this ongoing debate, as well as her considerable literary accomplishments, Kingston is viewed as a controversial and vital American author.

PRINCIPAL WORKS

The Woman Warrior: Memoirs of a Girlhood among Ghosts (memoir) 1976

China Men (nonfiction) 1980

Hawai'i One Summer (essays) 1987

Tripmaster Monkey: His Fake Book (novel) 1989

To Be the Poet (prose and poetry) 2002

The Fifth Book of Peace (nonfiction) 2003

PRIMARY SOURCES

MAXINE HONG KINGSTON WITH SHELLEY FISHER FISHKIN (INTERVIEW DATE 1990)

SOURCE: Kingston, Maxine Hong with Shelley Fisher Fishkin. "Interview with Maxine Hong Kingston." In *Conversations with Maxine Hong Kingston*, edited by Paul Skenazy and Tera Martin, pp. 159-67. Jackson: University Press of Mississippi, 1998.

In the following interview, taped in 1990 and originally published in American Literary History in 1991, Kingston discusses gender stereotypes, the role of feminist writers, and the major influences on her writing.

[Fishkin]: *In a recent article you wrote in the magazine* Mother Jones *called "The Novel's Next Step," you explore what the novel of the future might look like—perhaps a sequel to* **Tripmaster Monkey**. *Among other things, you note that your hero's wife, Taña, will have to "use the freedom the feminists have won. These struggles have got to result in happy endings for all, and the readers must learn not to worship tragedy as the highest art any more." Are you suggesting that feminist writers need to write out of power and pride rather than anger and rage in the future? How can they build on "the freedom that's been won"?*

[Kingston]: I think that feminist writers *have* been writing with power and pride, but I am suggesting that we have to invent new images and ways of power. So far the world thinks of power as violence, that power comes from a gun. We must create a new kind of drama in which there *is* drama, but it's nonviolent. And this has barely been thought of. I'm saying that women especially have a duty to work in this direction. I felt really appalled when Miss U.S.A. said women ought to have every right to go into combat. I see that as women trying for power by being as good as men are in violent ways.

In **The Woman Warrior** *you counter the stereotype of the silent and confident Woman Warrior, and in* **Tripmaster Monkey** *you counter the stereotype of the Chinese man who came to make money—a story you explore in* **China Men**—*with the image of a Chinese man who came to play. In fact, one of your characters says, "What if we came for the fun of it?" Do you think that these wonderful new images of confident women and playful men can help shape a new reality?*

Yes. I hope when artists write new characters, we invent new archetypes and they are visions of ways that we can be.

So the stories we tell about who we are can shape who we become?

Yes. What we need to do is to be able to *imagine* the possibility of a playful, peaceful, nurturing, mothering man, and we need to imagine the possibilities of a powerful, nonviolent woman and the possibilities of harmonious communities—and if we can just *imagine* them, that would be the first step toward building them and becoming them.

You've occasionally alluded to the power of the imagination to create reality, to embody truth, to make something exist that may not have existed before—not just in a psychological sense, but in an almost tangible, real sense. You describe, for example, the whistling arrow that you saw in a museum that was exactly like one you had imagined in your book, and you wrote, "I felt I had created it. I wrote it, and therefore it appeared." Do you think that your imaginative vision can generate reality and can generate truth?

Yes. It was wonderful that I saw this whistling arrow in the museum, but the point of my story was that this heroine took the arrows and turned them into flutes, and then she composed songs for these flutes. My idea was that we can turn weapons into musical instruments. It's sort of like plowshares from swords, and, again, I'm saying that the first step is to have that kind of conscious-ness that can create the world and save it. We have to change human consciousness and that's a step towards changing the material world.

I was thrilled to find out that the main character in your novel was named Wittman Ah Sing, because ever since I read **The Woman Warrior** *I was convinced that Whitman had to be close by lurking somewhere in the shadows—Walt Whitman—*

Oh really? Walt Whitman? After reading **Woman Warrior**? Oh, that's wonderful! Am I glad! I'm touched!

It showed. Everywhere. I wondered if he's been an empowering influence for you?

Oh, yes, yes, yes. I like the freedom that Walt Whitman was using to play with and shape the American language. Especially in writing **Tripmas-ter Monkey**—I just lifted lines from *Leaves of Grass*. You would think they were modern Sixties' slang—"Trippers and Askers" and "Linguists and Contenders Surround Me"—all of that—"Song of the Open Road," "Song of Occupations"—I just took those for title headings for my book. I like the rhythm of his language and the freedom and the wildness of it. It's so American. And also his vision of a new kind of human being that was go-ing to be formed in this country—although he never specifically said Chinese—ethnic Chinese also—I'd like to think he meant all kinds of people. And also I *love* that throughout *Leaves of Grass* he always says "men and women," "male and female." He's so different from other writers of his time, and even of this time. Even a hundred years ago he always included women and he always used [those phrases], "men and women," "male and female."

What other writers have helped inspire and empower you to come up with your voice as an American writer and as a feminist writer?

I found that whenever I come to a low point in my life or in my work, when I read Virginia Woolf's *Orlando*, that always seems to get my life

force moving again. I just love the way she can make one character live for four hundred years, and that Orlando can be a man, Orlando can be a woman. Virginia Woolf broke through constraints of time, of gender, of culture. I think an American writer who does that same thing is William Carlos Williams. I love *In the American Grain* because it does that same thing. Abraham Lincoln is a "mother" of our country. He talks about this wonderful woman walking through the battle-fields with her beard and shawl. I find that so free-ing, that we don't have to be constrained to being just one ethnic group or one gender—both those writers make me feel that I can now write as a man, I can write as a black person, as a white person; I don't have to be restricted by time and physicality.

At one point the narrator of **The Woman Warrior** *who is totally exasperated with her mother's stories, complains, "You won't tell me a story and then say 'this is a true story,' or 'this is just a story.' I can't tell the difference. I can't tell what's real and what you make up." How do you respond to questions like that about your work?*

You mean when the audiences ask me, "Is it real?"—when students ask that? I think people ask me those things because I put the question in their minds. The people give me back the ques-tion I give them. I know why they do it. I meant to give people those questions so that they can wrestle with them in their own lives. You know, I can answer those questions, but then that means I just answer it for me. And what I want is to give people questions (which I think are very creative things)—and then when people wrestle with them and struggle with them in their own minds and in their own lives, all kinds of exciting things hap-pen to them. I don't want people to throw the responsibility back to me.

GENERAL COMMENTARY

SUZANNE JUHASZ (ESSAY DATE 1985)

SOURCE: Juhasz, Suzanne. "Narrative Technique & Female Identity." In *Contemporary American Women Writers: Narrative Strategies,* edited by Catherine Rainwa-ter and William J. Scheik, pp. 173-89. Lexington: University Press of Kentucky, 1985.

In the following essay, Juhasz maintains that The Woman Warrior *and* China Men *"compose a woman's autobiography, describing a self formed at the source by gender experience."*

Maxine Hong Kingston's two-volume autobiography, *The Woman Warrior* and *China Men,* embodies the search for identity in the narrative act. The first text places the daughter in relation to her mother, the second places her in relation to her father; they demonstrate how finding each parent is a part of finding oneself. For Kingston, finding her mother and father is to name them, to tell their stories. Language is the means with which she arrives at identity, first at home, and then in the world. But because a daughter's relation to her mother is psychologically and linguistically different from her relation to her father, so is the telling of these stories different.[1]

Although the two texts are superficially similar, they are generated from different narrative patterns. In *The Woman Warrior* alternating movements toward and away from the mother take place within a textual field in which a linear progression, defining first the mother, then the daughter, takes place. In *China Men* narrative movement goes in one direction only, toward the father. But because this impulse in the latter book is continually diffused into generalization and idealization, it begins over, again and again. Such narrative structures suggest the evolution of female identity, which is formed in relation to the mother through the achievement of individuation in the context of connection, in relation to the father through the understanding of separation, the creation of substitutes for connection. Taken together, *The Woman Warrior* and *China Men* compose a woman's autobiography, describing a self formed at the source by gender experience.

To say this is neither to ignore nor to minimize the question of national identity everywhere present in Kingston's writing. Born in the United States to Chinese immigrant parents, her search for self necessarily involves a definition of home. Is it America, China, or some place in between? For Kingston the question of national identity complicates the search for self. Yet it is possible to understand how gender identity and national identity can be versions of one another, how home is embodied in the mother and father who together stand for the primary source of the self. For Kingston, in fact, who has never been there, China is not so much a physical place as it is a construct used by her parents to define their own identities. America too, especially for her parents, is a psychological state as much as it is a place. My own focus here on sexual identity is therefore not meant to negate the other dimension of the problem, but rather to reveal sexual and national

identities as parts of one another. For it is as a Chinese-American woman that Kingston seeks to define herself.

The narrator's search for home in both books is for a place and a self. That search involves rejections of source as well as connections to it, even as the achievement of identity is a combination of individuation and attachment: "Whenever my parents said 'home,' they suspended America. They suspended enjoyment, but I did not want to go to China. In China my parents would sell my sisters and me. My father would marry two or three more wives, who would spatter cooking oil on our bare toes and lie that we were crying for naughtiness. They would give food to their own children and rocks to us. I did not want to go where the ghosts took shapes nothing like our own."[2]

The movement of both texts is toward her own definition of home as a place to which she *can* return. "The simple explanation makes it less scary to go home after yelling at your father and mother. It drives the fear away and makes it possible someday to visit China, where I now know they don't sell girls or kill each other for no reason" (*WW* [*Woman Warrior*], 238). The explanation is the writing of the book, telling stories of home—of China and America in general, but of mothers and fathers in particular. "I want to hear the stories about the rest of your life," the narrator of *China Men* says to her father: "the Chinese stories." Her purpose is thereby to know *him:* "I want to know what makes you scream and curse, and what you're thinking when you say nothing; and why when you do talk, you talk differently from mother."[3] In the first chapter of *The Woman Warrior,* telling the forbidden story—told to her, nevertheless, by her mother—of an aunt who committed suicide, the narrator explains, "Unless I see her life branching into mine, she gives me no ancestral help" (*WW,* 10). Telling her aunt's story is a way to bring their two lives together, to discover commonality. At the same time, however, it reveals their differences as well. Telling their stories, in fact, both frees her from them and binds her to them, which is the process of finding home. "Thank you, Mother, thank you, Father," says the narrator in her fantasy of herself as a woman warrior: "They had carved their names and addresses on me, and I would come back" (*WW,* 44).

The Chinese phrase for story telling is "talking-story," and it defines the narration of both books. It is as well the subject of both books, because finding words, telling stories, is in Kingston's writing the other major metaphor, along with home, for the process of achieving identity. Chinese into English, silence into speech: when they appear in her books, these themes are subject and technique. The narrator of *The Woman Warrior,* who literally could not speak in public as a child, later cries to another silent Chinese-American girl, "If you don't talk, you can't have a personality. You'll have no personality and no hair" (*WW,* 210). The narrator's fantasy of the powerful woman, the woman warrior of the title, involves a female avenger with words actually carved on her back: "The ideographs for *revenge* are 'report a crime' and 'report to five families.' The reporting is the vengeance—not the beheading, not the gutting, but the words. And I have so many words—'chink' words and 'gook' words too—that they do not fit on my skin" (*WW,* 63). That power, equated with the ability to talk-story, is specifically associated with her mother: "I saw that I too had been in the presence of great power, my mother talking-story" (*WW,* 24).

Talking-story, discourse itself, is central to the difference between the two books, representative in turn of the difference in the relationships between daughters and mothers, daughters and fathers. The narrator's mother talks to her; her father does not. "Whenever she had to warn us about life, my mother told stories . . . a story to grow up on" (*WW,* 5). *The Woman Warrior* begins and ends with the narrator's mother talking-story. By the end of the book, the daughter's independent identity can be understood through her connection to her mother; talking-story is indicative of both parts of the mother-daughter relationship: "Here is a story my mother told me, not when I was young but recently, when I told her I also talk-story. The beginning is hers, the ending mine" (*WW,* 240). Her father, in contrast, does not talk. Screams and curses define his speech, but more important yet is his silence: "You kept up a silence for weeks and months" (*CM* [*China Men*], 8).

At the core of the relationship between daughter and mother is identification. The mother-child bond has always been the primary one, and girls never have to break it in the way boys do, by understanding that they are of different sexes. Through her stories, the narrator's mother passes on her version of reality to her daughter: "She tested our strength to establish realities," explains the narrator as *The Woman Warrior* begins. The matter is complicated, however, by the fact that the mother often tells lies. In *China Men* the narrator specifically contrasts men's stories with "the fairy tales and ghost stories told by women" (*CM,*

37). "No, no," says the narrator's mother to her in *The Woman Warrior,* "there aren't any flags like that. They're just talking-story. You're always believing talk-story" (*WW,* 213). To find her own identity the daughter needs to ascertain the difference between herself and her mother. Discovering a separate identity for her mother is one way to help her find her own self. Discerning the relation between her mother's "truths" and "lies" is representative of this process.

With her father the narrator needs not to loosen a connection but to make one. His discourse, and especially the lack of it, is indicative of the fundamental separateness between daughter and father, a separateness that arises because the father is neither a daughter's primary love nor is he of the same sex. The narrator's father screams or curses at her, "Wordless male screams that jolted the house upright and staring in the middle of the night" (*CM,* 8). His curses defile women: "Your mother's cunt. Your mother's smelly cunt" (*CM,* 8). Worse are his long silences, whereby he "punished us by not talking . . . rendered us invisible, gone" (*CM,* 8). To believe that her father does not mean *her* with his curses, to find out who he really is, the daughter has to invent him: "I'll tell you what I suppose from your silences and few words, and you can tell me that I'm mistaken. You'll just have to speak up with the real stories if I've got you wrong" (*CM,* 10). In the face of silence, invention is her only possible recourse. Yet it cannot be trusted in the same way that the narrator of *The Woman Warrior* trusts her imaginings about the lives of women relatives. Furthermore, it would be better, in the end, if he would tell her himself.

Therefore, although the two texts are conceived of by their author as "one big book [, she] was writing them more or less simultaneously," and although their surface stylistic features are similar, there is a profound difference between them. Whereas she "thought there would be a big difference between the men and the women," Kingston does not in fact "find them that different."[4] On the surface, the texts do look and sound alike. Both tell stories of relatives, stories interspersed with memories of the narrator's own childhood, in a matter-of-fact tone and declarative sentences that permit the speaker a fluid interchange between fact and fantasy, reportage and poetry. Yet the results are different, indicating more profound differences in narrative structure. Kingston herself points to their different sources. "In a way," she says, "*The Woman Warrior* was a selfish book. I was always imposing my viewpoint on the stories. In *China Men* the person who 'talks-story' is not so intrusive. I bring myself in and out of the stories, but in effect, I'm more distant. The more I was able to understand my characters, the more I was able to write from their point of view and the less interested I was in relating how I felt about them."[5] "More distant": This distance is, I think, a necessary result of the difference in finding a father rather than a mother, and it produces a text that creates not a universal or an androgynous but a female understanding of masculine experience. The essential separation between daughter and father is bridged by fantasy that, while it may do its work with intelligence and love, is never empathetic and is always idealized. For all its attention to detail, the text it produces is curiously—or not so curiously—abstract. *The Woman Warrior* is a messier book, but for me it is more satisfying than *China Men.* Yet, taken together as they are meant to be, they offer valuable insights into the nature of female identity, as it is created in relation not simply to women, not simply to men, but to both sexes, both parents.

The Woman Warrior is "messy" insofar as its narrative patterns are several and intertwined. *Complex* is really a better word for the various kinds of narrative movements that taken together reflect the dynamics of the mother-daughter relationship. The move to individuate and the move to connect both arise from the essential attachment between daughter and mother; the need for separation thus exists in the context of connection. In consequence, the identity that the text establishes for its narrator is achieved through a process involving both individuation and attachment.

The largest narrative pattern has a linear direction. The first three stories move toward defining the mother, thereby distinguishing her from the daughter; the two final stories go on to define the daughter, distinguishing her from the mother. But within each of the stories other movements occur in alternating patterns, maintaining the necessary tension between separation and connection. The text as a whole, for example, can be seen as an alternation between the stories the mother tells and the stories the daughter tells. Each teller's stories, in turn, alternate between true stories and stories that are not true.

The mother creates her relationship with her daughter through the kinds of story she tells her, stories whose purpose is sometimes to keep the two women alike and sometimes to make them different, as when, for example, the mother tries

to offer her daughter a life other than her own. Seeking to know her mother, the daughter begins by thinking that what she has to understand is the difference between her mother's "truths" and "lies." Ultimately, however, she comes to discover not so much which ones are lies but why they are lies, and it is this kind of awareness that helps her to see her mother as another person.

At the same time, the daughter's own narrative style also alternates between "truths" and "lies." Her truths are her actual memories of her own past; but to write her history beyond herself, she invents or imagines stories—of her dead aunt in China, of her mother's young womanhood, of the woman warrior. This process of imaginative empathy should be understood not as prevarication but as fiction. It is, however, not the literal truth, and it establishes both connection with her subject, by means of empathy, and separation as well—the story is, after all, her own creation.

In each of the stories, these alternating rhythms create the double movement of individuation in the context of connection that enables the narrator to establish identity. In the first story, "No Name Woman," for example, the mother's telling of the aunt's story gives rise to her daughter's version of it, yet the daughter's version is revisionary. The daughter's story, in turn, both deepens her connection to her female heritage and creates some separation from it and thereby control over it.

The daughter begins her search for identity in *The Woman Warrior* by looking, not at her mother, but at another female relative, an aunt who took her own life in China, a woman whose own identity has been denied because the family never speaks of her. It is perhaps less frightening to approach her mother and the issue of female identity in this way at the outset of the book. Nevertheless, her mother's words begin and end the story, and it is her mother who has told her of the aunt's existence. "'You must not tell anyone,' my mother said, 'what I am about to tell you. In China your father had a sister who killed herself. She jumped into the family well. We say that your father has all brothers because it is as if she had never been born'" (*WW*, 3). The conclusion of her mother's story points specifically to connection with her own sex: "'Now that you have started to menstruate, what happened to her could happen to you.' . . . Whenever she had to warn us about life, my mother told stories that ran like this one, a story to grow up on" (*WW*, 5).

But the daughter is not satisfied with her mother's account. "My mother has told me once and for all the useful parts. She will add nothing unless powered by Necessity, a riverbank that guides her life" (*WW*, 6). The daughter wants to know, for example, what kind of clothes her aunt wore, "whether flashy or ordinary." She wants, in other words, access to the motivation, the feelings, the personality of this female ancestor, to "see her life branching into mine"; she wants "ancestral help." And she senses in the very abbreviation of her mother's version a duplicity: "The emigrants confuse the gods by diverting their curses, misleading them with crooked streets and false names. They must try to confuse their offspring as well, who, I suppose, threaten them in similar ways—always trying to get things straight, always trying to name the unspeakable. The Chinese I know hide their names; sojourners take new names when their lives change, and they guard their real names with silence" (*WW*, 6).

To name what her mother has left out the narrator employs imaginative empathy, making up her aunt's story and in that way coming to know her, to connect with her. Because she conceives of this aunt as like herself, rebelling against tradition, she identifies with her: "my aunt, my forerunner," who, "caught in a slow life, let dreams grow and fade and after some months or years went towards what persisted" (*WW*, 9). To "get it straight, to name the unspeakable," the narrator must use her own imagination, not her mother's.

It takes the narrator three chapters to apply this technique directly to her mother. This third chapter, "Shaman," stands at the center and heart of the text. What precedes it is "White Tigers," the story of the woman warrior, the fabulous Fa Mu Lan, the girl who took her father's place in battle, the girl with whom the narrator identifies and into whom she turns herself, the girl who comes at last to stand for the woman writer.

Once again, impetus for the narrator's imaginative reconstruction of the story of the woman warrior is given by her mother's version. Now the daughter begins to have some intimation that her mother's duplicity has a function other than to confuse or conceal. Chinese culture, as the narrator has described it in "No Name Woman," is strongly repressive of women. Yet, as she says in the opening lines of "White Tigers," "when we Chinese girls listened to adults talk-story, we learned that we failed if we grew up to be but wives or slaves. We could be heroines, swordswomen. Even if she had to rage across all China, a swordswoman got even with anybody who hurt her family. Perhaps women were once so dangerous they had to have their feet bound" (*WW*, 23). In telling her daughter stories of female heroism that directly contradict many of her other messages about the position of women, the mother shows her daughter another possibility for women that is not revealed in her equally strong desire for her daughter's conformity and thus safety in a patriarchal system. Which, then, is the "true" story?

In "White Tigers," too, the narrator replaces her mother's story with her own, yet at the same time she understands her mother's connection with her own version of the woman warrior, who is also an image of herself:

> Night after night my mother would talk-story until we fell asleep. I couldn't tell where the stories left off and the dreams began, her voice the voice of the heroines in my sleep. . . .
>
> At last I saw that I too had been in the presence of great power, my mother talking-story. After I grew up, I heard the chant of Fa Mu Lan, the girl who took her father's place in battle. Instantly I remembered that as a child I had followed my mother about the house, the two of us singing about how Fa Mu Lan fought gloriously and returned alive from war to settle in the village. I had forgotten this chant that was once mine, given me by my mother, who may not have known its power to remind. She said I would grow up a wife and a slave, but she taught me the song of the warrior woman, Fa Mu Lan. I would have to grow up a warrior woman.
>
> [*WW*, 24]

Not only is the mother's connection to her daughter acknowledged here but her female power as well, a power specifically associated with her ability to talk-story. In the telling of her own story—with herself as the woman warrior, a hero possessing most of all the power of imagination—a story which is then contrasted to her actual childhood memories of repression and misogyny, the narrator concludes by identifying language as the means by which she can become a woman warrior. The association with her own mother, the woman story teller, cannot be ignored: "The swordswoman and I are not so dissimilar. May my people understand the resemblance soon so that I can return to them. What we have in common are the words at our backs" (*WW*, 63).

In "Shaman" the narrator looks directly at Brave Orchid, the mother whose presence has infused and helped to create the stories that precede it. She tells not one but two stories, however—or tells the story twice: the "truth"— her actual memories of her mother, a laundress in

America—and the "fiction"—the story of her mother who in China became a doctor. The fiction includes her own postulation of thoughts and feelings, added to the facts she has been given to create the character of Brave Orchid. But of course both kinds of story, the mother as ordinary woman and the mother as hero, are necessary, both kinds of knowledge, truth and fiction—each a corrective for the other, each a part of the reality of character.

Brave Orchid's heroism, as her daughter tells it, identifies her with the woman warrior, because her success, like the woman warrior's, is based on powers of the imagination. "I learned to make my mind large," writes the narrator, as the woman warrior, in "White Tigers," "as the universe is large, so that there is room for paradoxes. Pearls are bone marrow; pearls come from oysters. The dragon lives in the sky, ocean, marshes, and mountains; and the mountains are also its cranium. Its voice thunders and jingles like copper pans. It breathes fire and water; and sometimes the dragon is one, sometimes many. . . . When I could point at the sky and make a sword appear, a silver bolt in the sunlight, and control its slashing with my mind, the old people said I was ready to leave" (*WW*, 35, 39). She describes Brave Orchid in similar fashion:

> My mother may have been afraid, but she would become a dragoness. . . . She could make herself not weak. During danger she fanned out her dragon claws and riffled her red sequin scales and unfolded her coiling green stripes. Danger was a good time for showing off. . . .
>
> My mother was wide awake again. She became sharply herself—bone, wire, antenna—but she was not afraid. She had been pared down like this before, when she had travelled up the mountains into rare snow—alone in the white not unlike being alone in the black.
>
> [*WW*, 79, 80]

In China, Brave Orchid is best at vanquishing ghosts, this power symbolic of her becoming a "new woman," a woman doctor. But in America, with its taxi ghosts, police ghosts, meter-reading ghosts, and five-and-dime ghosts, she is mystified, no longer in control. Although she remains brave in the face of these dangers, in her daughter's memory she is no hero but a very ordinary woman.

The factual and fantastic tales of Brave Orchid combine to make of her a complete person in her daughter's eyes, a person with a separate identity both to be proud of and of necessity to reject, to move beyond. The story ends, however, with a more recent memory, one which reminds the reader that it is the connection itself, both uncomfortable and satisfying, that endures, even after the daughter has gone on to her own life.

"'Aiaa,' sighs Brave Orchid to her daughter, now a grown woman: 'how can I bear to have you leave me again?'" (*WW*, 118). "Her eyes are big, inconsolable. A spider headache spreads out in fine branches over my skull. She is etching spider legs into the icy bone. She pries open my head and my fists and crams into them responsibility for time, responsibility for intervening oceans" (*WW*, 126). Yet even as the daughter pulls away from the connection and its corresponding need, she also, on the very next page, finds satisfaction, encouragement, and, yes, a sense of identity in it:

> She yawned. "It's better, then, for you to stay away. The weather in California must not agree with you. You can come for visits." She got up and turned off the light. "Of course you must go, Little Dog."
>
> A weight lifted from me. The quilts must be filling with air. The world is somehow lighter. She has not called me that endearment for years—a name to fool the gods. I am really a Dragon, as she is a Dragon, both of us born in dragon years. I am practically a first daughter of a first daughter.
>
> [*WW*, 127]

The next stage of the book moves onward, however, even if the stories themselves demonstrate that the process in life is not schematic. The next stage of the journey is to leave home, to define the self, or, Kingston says here, to speak for oneself. In the two final stories the narrator learns to talk.

"At the Western Palace" offers the story of female relatives, once again, as the prelude or first step. The association of women with madness is shown as the alternative to their achievement of self-identity. Moon Orchid, Brave Orchid's sister who cannot change Chinese reality into American reality, goes mad. "'The difference between mad people and sane people,' Brave Orchid explained to her children, 'is that sane people have variety when they talk-story. Mad people have only one story that they talk over and over'" (*WW*, 184). The story of Moon Orchid is expanded upon in the final chapter, "Song for a Barbarian Reed Pipe": "I thought talking and not talking made the difference between sanity and insanity. Insane people were the ones who couldn't explain themselves. There were many crazy girls and women. . . . I thought every house had to have its crazy woman or crazy girl, every village its idiot. Who would be it at our house? Probably me (*WW*, 216, 220).

The narrator's own childhood silence—"a dumbness, a shame"—comes from the conflict between her Chinese upbringing and the ways of an American school, but in the story she represents it as symbolically caused by her mother (China), who seems to have cut her tongue, slicing the frenum, when she was a child. "'It's your fault I talk weird,'" accuses the daughter, later, to a mother who however has explained, "'I cut it so that you would not be tongue-tied. Your tongue would be able to move in any language. . . . I cut it to make you talk more, not less, you dummy'" (*WW,* 234, 190).

Moving beyond this terrible shyness and silence demands the thing that happens at last, when the daughter starts to talk back. "I had grown inside me a list of over two hundred things that I had to tell my mother so that she would know the true things about me and to stop the pain in my throat" (*WW,* 229). In a fierce tirade against her mother she asserts her own American sense of independence and attacks, specifically, her mother's talk-stories: "And I don't want to listen to any more of your stories; they have no logic. They scramble me up. You lie with stories. You won't tell me a story and then say, 'This is a true story,' or, 'This is just a story.' I can't tell the difference. I don't even know what your real names are. I can't tell what's real and what you make up. Ha! You can't stop me from talking. You tried to cut off my tongue, but it didn't work" (*WW,* 235).

Establishing herself as a talker in opposition to her mother—as American instead of Chinese, a truth teller instead of a liar—makes it possible for her to define herself as separate from her mother. Leaving home at this stage means leaving China, and her mother's Chinese way of talking ("We like to say the opposite"), in order to understand difference: "I had to leave home in order to see the world logically, logic the new way of seeing. I learned to think that mysteries are for explanation. I enjoy the simplicity. Concrete pours out of my mouth to cover the forests with freeways and sidewalks. Give me plastics, periodical tables, TV dinners with vegetables no more complex than peas mixed with diced carrots. Shine floodlights into dark corners; no ghosts" (*WW,* 237).

Yet this way of seeing and talking, this complete sense of separation from her mother, from China, is not the whole truth either, the truth of her identity, and this fact the text itself has revealed. For the text is more complex and fuller

of insight than any particular moment of understanding within it. Poised against the linearity of the narrator's progress is the recurrent alternation of movement toward and tugs against connection that takes place within the narrative field, as it were, in which the forward progress occurs. Thus, when the narrator discovers her independence from her mother, that fact is indeed a part of her process toward identity but is not its fulfillment. Independence must be understood in order that connection can occur again, but a connection, finally, between two different people rather than between two people who together make one identity.

The Woman Warrior ends with its narrator's perception of this achievement, with the story of the Chinese woman poet Ts'ai Yen, with a celebration of the woman who is powerful because she can speak, can write. The story is begun by her mother, finished by the daughter. "It translates well" (*WW,* 243). In this way we see how the connection between mother and daughter, both storytellers, both women warriors, has been reestablished, but on terms that now both allow for separation and admit attachment.

China Men is less complicated textually than *The Woman Warrior*. As Kingston says, "the person who 'talks-story' is not so intrusive." Although here, too, the fact of memory is juxtaposed against the fiction of imaginative recreation, the memories are much fewer, and the imagining—the stories of male relatives, of grandfathers, father, uncles, and brother—is no longer urgent, no longer empathetic. These stories, lines thrown out across the chasm of separation, are more idealistic than realistic, more conceptual than kinetic, more parallel than developmental. The richness and tension created by the search for difference in the context of sameness—the mother-daughter relationship—is replaced by the clarity that distance offers, a lucidity that is at the same time monotonal. Only one person, after all, is talking here; narrative movement is in only one direction, not the tug toward and away from the mother but the yearning toward the father that goes so far but no farther, proceeding from anger and ignorance toward knowledge and admiration. The father need not be left, only loved:

> What I want from you is for you to tell me that those curses are only common Chinese sayings. That you did not mean to make me sicken at be-

ing female. "Those were only sayings," I want you to say to me, "I didn't mean you or your mother. I didn't mean your sisters or grandmothers or women in general."

I want to be able to rely on you, who inked each piece of our own laundry with the word *Center*, to find out how we landed in a country where we are eccentric people.

[*CM*, 9]

Her father's screams, curses, and, especially, his silence produce a profound ignorance that the narrator, whose love for her father is at war with her anger, longs to destroy. The fact of this ignorance is offered as an introduction to the book in a one-page piece entitled "On Fathers." Here the narrator and her brothers and sisters, waiting at the gate for their father to come home, see a man coming around the corner. They think he is their father. "But I'm not your father," he tells them: "Looking closely, we saw that he probably was not. We went back inside the yard, and this man continued his walk down our street, from the back certainly looking like our father, one hand in his pocket. Tall and thin, he was wearing our father's two-hundred-dollar suit that fit him just right. He was walking fast in his good leather shoes with the wingtips" (*CM*, 3).

The parable shows not only the children's lack of familiarity with their father but also the kind of evidence upon which they have based their false sense of knowledge: clothes, shoes, shape of the body. They recognize him from the outside only, from the back, the point being that this is not genuine knowledge. The purpose of the text as a whole is to gain that knowledge by imaginatively entering the father's interiority—something denied to the daughter by actual experience—by replacing opacity and abstractness with concrete particularities, a technique that served the narrator well in *The Woman Warrior* to establish the identity of her mother.

Yet in using this technique the narrator is self-conscious in a way she is not in *The Woman Warrior*. "I think this is the journey you don't tell me," she says as she introduces one version of her father's passage to America, to be followed later by "of course my father could not have come that way. He came a legal way, something like this" (*CM*, 50). Whereas in *The Woman Warrior* the transitions between "fact" and "fiction" occur almost seamlessly, *China Men* bases its structure on the artifice of these transitions and of their very creation. This format helps to make us aware

of the "distance" of which Kingston speaks, a distance necessitated by the nature of the father-daughter relationship, which begins in separation and difference, rather than in connection or sameness.

To tell the story of fathers is to tell the story of China's coming to America. Both the mother and the father represent China to the American-born narrator, but there is a difference in their experience and therefore in the aspect of the homeland they embody. While the women were left behind in China, coming afterward to join their husbands, the men were the sojourners who came to America to discover the "Gold Mountain" there. In seeking to know her father the narrator looks as well for the experience of active appropriation, however painful, even humiliating some of its aspects may be, that has been denied to women, who find their power in the imagination, as *The Woman Warrior* shows, not in the public world. *China Men* confronts that public world, as grandfathers and fathers wrestle with nature and society from Hawaii to Alaska, from New York to California.

Yet there is in *China Men* a generality, an abstractness to all this experience that seems to bespeak the impossibility of the narrator's ever claiming male experience as an integral part of her heritage. Each character in the book has his own name, his own adventures, but all are referred to more frequently as "the father," "the grandfather," "the brother," a mode of appellation that is itself indicative of the generic character of the men, their normative function. In reading, it is difficult to keep them separate. They merge into the common maleness, a concept that the prose creates. The following passage can serve as example:

> He sucked in deep breaths of the Sandalwood Mountain air, and let it fly out in a song, which reached up to the rims of volcanoes and down to the edge of the water. His song lifted and fell with the air, which seemed to breathe warmly through his body and through the rocks. The clouds and frigate birds made the currents visible, and the leaves were loud. If he did not walk heavy seated and heavy thighed like a warrior, he would float away, snuggle into the wind, and let it slide him down to the ocean, let it make a kite, a frigate bird, a butterfly of him. He would dive head first off the mountain, glide into the airstreams thick with smells, and curve into the ocean. From this mountaintop, ocean before him and behind him, he saw the size of the island. He sang like the heroes in stories about wanderers and exiles, poets

and monks and monkeys, and princes and kings out for walks. His arias unfurled and rose in wide, wide arcs.

[*CM*, 95]

What is most significant here is the combination of specific detail with a generalization of consciousness; the combination not only depersonalizes the individual man—in this instance it is Bak Gook, "The Grandfather of the Sandalwood Mountains"—so that he becomes akin to all the other male consciousnesses in the book, but also allows him, regardless of his immigrant status—he is a frequently brutalized sugarcane worker—to become heroic. All the Chinamen are capable of this kind of poetry, the result, I think, of an idealization of masculine experience representative of the daughter's approach to her father. Although the author seeks the humanizing middle ground between the father's generalized curses about the women and the daughter's idealized flights of poetic heroism, she creates such moments infrequently, despite many physical details, and these moments occur more often in actual memories than in imaginings.

These memories, which begin the book and reappear occasionally as the narrative continues, remind us that the search for the father is occasioned by both yearning and fear or anger. "The American Father" begins with memories of "father places": "He also had the power of going places where nobody else went, and making places belong to him. . . . When I explored his closet and desk, I thought, This is a father place; a father belongs here" (*CM*, 236-37). The father goes places nobody else went, made places belong to him, places that bespeak the Gold Mountain itself as well as the cellars, attics, and gambling hall of this particular father. The passage shows the daughter's yearning for the power of appropriation, heightened, perhaps, by its very inaccessibility.

After her father has lost his job at the gambling hall and becomes despondent, his children respond to his silence with a confusion—"I invented a plan to test my theories that males feel no pain; males don't feel" (*CM*, 251)—that finally turns to anger:

> We children became so wild that we broke Baba loose from his chair. We goaded him, irked him—*gikked* him—and the gravity suddenly let him go. He chased my sister, who locked herself in a bedroom. "Come out," he shouted. But of course, she wouldn't, he having a coat hanger in hand and angry. I watched him kick the door; the round mirror fell off the wall and crashed. The door

> broke open, and he beat her. Only my sister remembers that it was she who watched my father's shoe against the door and the mirror outside fall, and I who was beaten.

[*CM*, 252]

Such experiences, informed as they are by powerful unmediated responses to the father's separateness, can be contrasted to the imagined experiences of the men themselves, sympathetic but lacking this intensity, experiences narrated through the creation of a masculine consciousness. Sympathy is not empathy, and the very distance between them seems to influence the nature of the knowledge that is available to the narrator.

China Men demonstrates that finding the father, for the daughter, means finding what one has always known: that distance. Fear and anger may be transformed into love, but it is a love based on knowledge laced with idealization. Over and over in *China Men,* in each of its stories, the daughter begins in ignorance, with silence, and fills the gap or void with the fruits of her own imagination to gain—just that—her own creation. Never having been able to encounter the true interiority of the father, she has, finally, only the stories she has told about him. She finds her identity as a storyteller, a writer, here as in *The Woman Warrior,* but here there is a suggestion that the imagination is less the embodiment of life itself than an alternative to it.

Consequently, the two processes—finding the mother, finding the father—seem less than parallel for the daughter. Regardless of its author's intentions, *China Men* is more of a postscript to *The Woman Warrior* than a complement to it. Because the mother is not only of the same sex but, by virtue of the familial arrangements of society, the infant's first and primary love, she remains at the center of the daughter's search for identity. The familial arrangements of society ask as well that the female be understood in relation to the male—as the word *female* itself suggests—so that Kingston is correct in seeing *The Woman Warrior* as a partial text, an incomplete autobiography. Finding the father may be understood as synonymous with ascertaining the woman's relation to the external world, or the other. Difference and distance, which produce ignorance, fear, and idealization, create boundaries that can be bridged imaginatively but cannot really be destroyed. The yearning to destroy them, perhaps the most important feature of the search, in both its intensity and its frustrations or displacement, propels the text of **China Men** but is also diffused by it. Kingston sees that text as an achievement for herself as a writer—not so "selfish," not so "intrusive." Perhaps she is right. Perhaps this is the success daughters can have with fathers—to displace the yearning for him with the creation of something in his place, to understand that her love must be informed by the knowledge of separateness.

Taken together, the search for the mother and the search for the father allow a person to find home, a place both inside and outside the self, in the way that, for a woman, the mother is always inside, the father always outside. Finding home gives a sense of such boundaries, of understanding not only what is eternally beyond the self but what is eternally within the self. The woman, as in **The Woman Warrior** and **China Men,** establishes her individual identity in this context. Recognizing this context, this meaning for *home,* she can leave it, go on into her life, while she recognizes that home can never be left but only understood.

Telling is the way to understand, so finally both volumes of Kingston's autobiography are about becoming a writer. Taken together, the two texts demonstrate the special power of telling and, especially, of the imagination for women. Traditionally denied access to the outer world by literal appropriation, women can nevertheless follow a different route. Language is symbolic action, and it becomes, in this autobiography, the route and embodiment of female psychological development.

Notes

1. The understanding of female development that I bring to my reading of literature comes from recent studies in feminist psychology, such as Nancy Chodorow's *Reproduction of Mothering: Psychoanalysis and the Sociology of Gender* (Berkeley and Los Angeles: Univ. of California Press, 1978) and Carol Gilligan's *In a Different Voice: Psychological Theory and Women's Development:* (Cambridge: Harvard Univ. Press, 1982). I make no attempt here to correlate specific ideas of the psychologists with specific literary interpretations, for my point is neither to "prove" the psychological theories with the literary texts nor vice versa, but rather to show how literature as well as psychology is based in and seeks to articulate such ideas about human experience.

2. *The Woman Warrior* (New York: Alfred A. Knopf, 1976), 116; hereafter cited in the text as *WW.*

3. *China Men* (New York: Knopf, 1980), p. 10; hereafter cited in the text as *CM.*

4. Timothy Pfaff, "Talk with Mrs. Kingston," *New York Times Book Review,* 15 June 1980, 25-26.

5. Ibid., 26.

TITLE COMMENTARY

The Woman Warrior

LINDA HUNT (ESSAY DATE FALL 1985)

SOURCE: Hunt, Linda. "'I Could Not Figure out What Was My Village': Gender v. Ethnicity in Maxine Hong Kingston's *The Woman Warrior.*" MELUS 12, no. 3 (fall 1985): 5-12.

In the following essay, Hunt examines the relationship between gender and ethnicity in The Woman Warrior.

Feminist theorists have argued about the extent to which women share a common culture. In *Three Guineas* Virginia Woolf has a character assert, "as a woman I have no country. . . . As a woman my country is the whole world."[1] This has a fine ring to it, but if the sentiment were wholly true we would not find in women's lives so much pain, confusion, and conflict. Temma Kaplan explains the complexity of the subject: "It is impossible to speak of 'women's culture' without understanding its variation by class and ethnic group. Women's culture, like popular or working class culture, must appear in the context of dominant cultures."[2]

The truth of Kaplan's statement is borne out by reading fiction and autobiography written by women from different backgrounds. Such books not only show the great cultural diversity women experience but also evoke the incompatible definitions of femininity and the irreconcilable demands a woman is likely to encounter as she attempts to live in more than one cultural world at the same time.

Women's worlds may vary widely depending on ethnic background and social class, but in the societies from which we have written literature, male dominance is a common denominator.[3] Maxine Hong Kingston's autobiographical **The Woman Warrior** suggests that we need to pay attention to the contradictions male dominance creates for women who are at one and the same time subordinated by a culture, and yet, embroiled in its interstices; such women may be painfully at odds with themselves. A woman like Kingston,

FROM THE AUTHOR

KINGSTON COUNTERS ATTACKS THAT HER WRITING EMASCULATES ASIAN AMERICAN MEN

A lot of Asian American history is masculine history, because the women didn't come until very recently. For 100 years Chinatown was masculine—men founded and lived in Chinatown, and all the work that was here was done by men. It's only been in the last 40 or 50 years that we've had any feminine history in this country. Okay, so what happens when all our writers are women? The men critics say, "You have feminized our history, and you emasculate us when you do that."

Kingston, Maxine Hong, with Paul Skenazy. Excerpt from *Conversations with Maxine Hong Kingston.* Edited by Paul Skenazy and Tera Martin. University Press of Mississippi, 1998, p. 145.

who is doubly marginal (i.e. not a member of the dominant race or class) is likely to feel this conflict with particular acuteness because an affiliation with a minority culture tends to be particularly strong.[4]

Explaining to the reader one of the many contradictions which are part of the legacy of her Chinese-American girlhood, Kingston comments bitterly, "Even now China wraps double binds around my feet."[5] The most difficult double-bind has been the need to reconcile her loyalty to her Chinese-American heritage, a background which devalues and even insults women, with her own sense of dignity as a female.

This paper is about Kingston's attempt to resolve the war within herself, a struggle that is exacerbated by the tremendous emphasis Chinese culture puts on social cohesion. She has been raised to experience and require a powerful identification with family and community, and yet, as a woman, she cannot simply accept a place in a culture which calls people of her sex "maggots," "broom and dustpan," "slave."

Maxine Hong Kingston's personal struggle is fought—and resolved at least partially—on the battlefield of language. The words used against her sting, and, unable to find the right words and

the right voice to express her own point of view, and indeed, unsure of that point of view, she is rendered nearly voiceless for much of her youth. She speaks inaudibly or in a quack, and once physically assaults another Chinese girl whose silence reminds her of her own. The core of the problem is that by being simultaneously insider (a person who identifies strongly with her cultural group) and outsider (deviant and rebel against that tradition), she cannot figure out from which perspective to speak. It is only through mastery of literary form and technique—through creating this autobiography out of family stories, Chinese myths, and her own memories—that she is able to articulate her own ambivalence and hereby find an authentic voice.

Kingston begins with an aunt back in China whose name the family tried to forget, telling her story in such a way that she artfully shifts point of view and sympathy in order to convey her divided loyalties. The aunt became an outsider to her village by getting pregnant while her husband was in America. The enraged villagers, terrified by her behavior, drove her to suicide: any lust not socially-sanctioned was seen as disruptive of the social order.

The author identifies with the rebellious aunt, whom she calls "my forerunner," creating from her imagination various detailed scenarios, first of rape and then of romantic attraction, alternative versions of what might have happened, which are narrated in the omniscient third person. Kingston hypothesizes that her female relative might have succumbed to her impulses as relief from the burden of being "expected . . . alone to keep the traditional ways, which her brother now among the barbarians in America could fumble without detection" (p. 9). She expands on her theme, beginning to imagine in sensuous detail the pull that an attractive man might have had on this aunt "caught up in a slow life."

But Kingston's allegiance is abruptly withdrawn. Interrupting her sensuous description of the imagined lover, the narrator exclaims, "She offered *us* up for a charm that vanished with tiredness, a pigtail that didn't toss when the wind died" (p. 9, emphasis mine). The word "us" is startling because Kingston has abruptly shifted from third person to first person plural and from identification with the aunt, the outsider, to being one of the villagers, an insider.

The aunt's story is resumed in a more objective vein, and we are given an explanation of the motives of the avengers of the social code:

The frightened villagers, who depend on one another to maintain the real, went for my aunt to show her a personal, physical representation of the break she had made in the "roundness." . . . The villagers punished her for acting as if she could have a private life secret and apart from them.

(p. 14)

While the remainder of the tale emphasizes the events which befell the persecuted woman, her thoughts and feelings, the narrative remains riddled with ambivalence. Kingston's recounting of her aunt's story has been a defiant act of recompense towards the forgotten relative, a desire not to participate in her punishment. Yet, one more twist occurs in the last sentence of the chapter:

My aunt haunts me. . . . I alone devote pages of paper to her. . . . I do not think she always means me well. I am telling on her, and she was a spite suicide, drowning herself in drinking water.

(p. 19)

Suddenly the aunt is seen as an enemy, and Kingston's own act in writing her story appears in a different light.

Kingston's profound conflict about where her loyalty lies regarding the experience of this aunt she has never met serves to convey her own agonized indecision about what stance to take towards her own Chinese-American upbringing. If she identifies with the community, she must accept and even endorse her own humiliation at their hands; if she allows herself to fully experience the depths of her alienation, she is in danger of being cut off from her cultural roots. Thus she juxtaposes an exploration of the legend of Fa Mu Lan, a tale her story-telling mother used to chant, against the story of the outlaw aunt. The purpose is to test whether her culture's myth about a heroic woman who defends her village will provide a way for Kingston to transcend the degrading female social role, and yet, be loyal to the community.

Kingston retells the story, casting herself as the swordswoman who through magic and self-discipline is trained to bring about social justice while at the same time fulfilling her domestic obligations. Significantly, a good part of her training involves exercises which teach her how to create with her body the ideographs for various words: in Kingston's universe it is through mastery of language that a warrior is created. Language is again important in that before Fa Mu Lan sets out, dressed as a man, to lead her male army against the enemies of her people, the family carves on her back the words which suggest their endless list of grievances.

When the narrator, Kingston's fantasy of herself as Fa Mu Lan, returns home the villagers "make a legend about her perfect filiality" (p. 54). This myth, combining heroism and social duty as it does, is explored to see if winning the approval and admiration of the Chinese or Chinese-American community can provide so much gratification that Kingston will be persuaded to repress her injuries at the hands of the community. However, she subverts her own attempt by embedding within her tales of the female avenger certain elements which bring forth once again the theme of the injustices women suffer as a sex and the issue of female anger.

Hunting down the baron who had drafted her brother, she presents herself as defender of the village as a whole: "I want your life in payment for your crimes against the villagers." But the baron tries to appeal to her "man to man," lightly acknowledging his crimes against women in a misguided attempt at male-bonding:

Oh, come now. Everyone takes the girls when he can. The families are glad to get rid of them. "Girls are maggots in the rice. It is more profitable to raise geese than daughters." He quoted to me the sayings I hated.

(p. 51)

Since this version of the swordswoman's story is Kingston's own creation, she is surely introducing the baron's sexism at this juncture to show the reader that, try as she does, she *cannot* simply overlook the patriarchal biases of Chinese culture. The enemy of her village seeks to create an alliance with the defender of family and community on the common ground of misogyny. No wonder Kingston exclaims just after the swordswoman's tale is finished, "I could not figure out what was my village" (p. 54).

Even more subversively, in the process of spinning out her tale of the dutiful defender of the village, Kingston briefly indulges in a digression about a different kind of warrior woman. She has herself (the swordswoman) released from a locked room in the baron's castle a group of "cowering, whimpering women." These females who make "insect noises" and "blink weakly . . . like pheasants that have been raised in the dark for soft meat" are utterly degraded:

The servant who walked the ladies had abandoned them, and they could not escape on their little bound feet. Some crawled away from me, using their elbows to pull themselves along. These women would not be good for anything. I called the villagers to come identify any daughters they wanted to take home, but no one claimed any.

(p. 53)

As creator, Kingston allows herself to respond with hostility to her own fantasy of the ultimate in female humiliation by turning these pathetic creatures into "witch amazons" who "killed men and boys." Unlike Fa Mu Lan, who is impelled to be a warrior by idealism and disguises herself as a man, these women are mercenaries (i.e. *self*-interested), ride dressed as women (i.e. *female*-identified), and buy up girl babies from poor families; slave girls and daughters-in-law also run away to them. Kingston reveals her intense discomfort with this anti-social story she has used to deconstruct the socially-acceptable swordswoman myth by distancing herself from it. She falls into the conditional: "it would be said," "people would say," and concludes, "I myself never encountered such women and could not vouch for their reality" (p. 53).

Despite such subterfuges, the reader has not been allowed to forget that any Chinese woman who seeks to identify exclusively with the injustices experienced by the entire "village" at the hands of outsiders will be denying the damage she herself and others of her sex have suffered at the hands of outsiders and insiders alike. The term "female avenger" becomes ambiguous: can Kingston be satisfied with being an avenger who is a female or does she need to be the avenger of females?

Not ready to answer this question, Kingston uses the third and fourth chapters of *The Woman Warrior* to probe even further the implications of her culture's sanctioned way for a woman to be strong. Brave Orchid, Kingston's mother, has lived a life that conforms quite closely, within the limits of realistic possibility, to the woman warrior model. Left behind in China when her husband went off to America to improve the family's fortunes, she entered medical school and became a doctor. Through rigorous self-discipline she triumphed not only over her studies but over a "sitting ghost" who serves as the symbolic embodiment of the fear and loneliness she must have experienced. "You have no power over a strong woman," Brave Orchid asserts to the ghost.

After completing her studies Kingston's mother returned home to serve her people as a practitioner of medicine. For some years she braved the terror of the dark woods as she went from village to village on her rounds as a physi-

cian. Like the swordswoman of the legend who returns from public life to do farmwork, housework, and produce sons, Brave Orchid accepted the next, more mundane, phase of her life without complaint; when summoned by her husband to the United States she became his partner in a laundry and had six children (including the author) after the age of forty-five.

Kingston is being as fair as possible. Her mother's story shows that the warrior woman model could work for some women. Proud of her past achievements, Brave Orchid has turned them into materials to draw on when she "talk-stories." Yet Kingston follows the narrative of Brave Orchid with the experience of Moon Orchid, Brave Orchid's sister, whose emigration to the United States leads to her madness and death. This aunt is not a strong person—and it is important that Kingston remind us that not all women have access to the remarkable reserves of strength and inflexible will that have served her mother. Also, Brave Orchid is responsible for her sister's breakdown in that she insists that Moon Orchid aggressively pursue her Americanized and bigamously remarried husband. She assumes her sister's husband and his second wife will accept their obligation to Moon Orchid since she is "Big Wife" (first wife), and bolsters Moon Orchid's faith by reminding her of family stories from China in which the first wife had no difficulty reclaiming her position in the family after a lapse of time. Brave Orchid's advice is dangerous because she is holding onto a myth of reality structured around laws and traditions that regulated marital interaction in China and offered some protection to women but which is useless in America. Thus Kingston reminds us that new situations require new myths. The warrior woman legend may have been the best Chinese society could offer her mother, but if she herself is to use it, fundamental modification will be necessary.

It is in the final chapter, "A Song For A Barbarian Reed Pipe," that Kingston articulates most explicitly both her fury at her Chinese heritage and the strategies she has found for making peace with that heritage and salvaging from it what she can. She tells of how as a teenager she stored up in her mind a list of over two hundred truths about herself, bad thoughts and deeds to confess to her mother. When she tried to tell one item a day only to find Brave Orchid simply wasn't interested, she "felt something alive tearing at [her] throat."

Finally, one night when the family was having dinner at the laundry, her "throat burst open."

Instead of confessing her own disloyalty to family and Chinese tradition, Kingston found herself bitterly cataloguing her own numerous grievances:

> When I said them out loud I saw that some of the items were ten years old already, and I had outgrown them. But they kept pouring out anyway in the voice of Chinese opera. I could hear the drums and the cymbals and the gongs and brass horns.
>
> (p. 236)

The transmutation of sins into grievances is significant: the fact that Kingston conceptualized these items first one way and then the other reveals again the ambivalence about whether she is insider or outsider which caused her muteness. This outburst is an important breakthrough in that she is impelled to make a choice, and choosing to identify as injured outsider frees her to speak. At this stage what she articulates with that newfound voice is the need to get away from the Chinese-American community: "I won't let you turn me into a slave or a wife. I'm getting out of here. I can't stand living here anymore" (p. 234).

At the same time, Kingston's list of grievances is certainly an echo of the grievances the legendary swordswoman had had carved on her back, the difference being that Fa Mu Lan's list was not personal. Kingston's autobiography becomes her way of being a woman warrior on her own behalf and perhaps on behalf of other Chinese girls and women. She had found a way to exact revenge against her background (one idiom for revenge being to "report a crime") and yet to honor it. In crying out to the world about her culture's mistreatment of women, she has in a sense taken on the warrior role her culture recommended to those of its women most capable of heroism. In finding a literary form and techniques which allow her to give voice to the conflicts and contradictions which almost silenced her, Maxine Hong Kingston is paying tribute to the importance her family and culture have always placed on the verbal imagination.

Kingston's autobiographical masterpiece, with its theme of diverse cultural realities, reminds us to be careful about embracing a universal notion of what it means to be a woman. At the same time, however, the book raises the possibility that an important link not for all but for many women is the *disjunction* between female identity and the other aspects of cultural heritage. Agonizing contradictions between allegiance to gender and fidelity to some other dimension of one's cultural background—and this might be race or class instead of or as well as ethnicity—may be a commonplace of the female experience. From an artistic point of view the result may be an anxiety of *identity* that is at least as debilitating as the "anxiety of authorship" that Susan Gubar and Sandra Gilbert argue takes away women's sense of legitimacy as writers.[6] Maxine Hong Kingston found a way to break out of the silence created by this anxiety, but the alienation which stems from such a rupture at the very center of their beings may be one of the most profound obstacles women face in finding their voices.

Notes

1. Virginia Woolf, *Three Guineas* (New York: Harcourt, Brace and Company, 1938), p. 166.

2. Temma Kaplan, "Politics and Culture in Women's History: A Symposium," *Feminist Studies*, 6 (Spring, 1980), 44.

3. It is interesting to note that several anthropologists have made a convincing case for the existence of sexually egalitarian *pre-literate* societies. See, for example, Peggy Reeves Sanders, *Female Power and Male Dominance: On the Origins of Sexual Equality* (Cambridge: Cambridge University Press, 1981) and Eleanor Leacock, "Ideologies of Male Dominance As Divide and Rule Politics: An Anthropologist's View," in *Woman's Nature*, eds. Marian Lowe and Ruth Hubbard (New York: Pergamon Press, 1983).

4. See Margaret Homens, "Her Very Own Howl: The Ambiguities of Representation in Recent Women's Fiction," *Signs*, Winter, 1984, for an interesting discussion of the significance of women's double-marginality.

5. Maxine Hong Kingston, *The Woman Warrior* (New York: Random House, 1977), p. 57. (All further page references will be cited within the text and will be to this edition.)

6. Sandra Gilbert and Susan Gubar, *The Madwoman in the Attic* (New Haven and London: Yale University Press, 1979).

LINDA MORANTE (ESSAY DATE 1987)

SOURCE: Morante, Linda. "From Silence to Song: The Triumph of Maxine Hong Kingston." *Frontiers* 9, no. 2 (1987): 78-82.

In the following essay, Morante contends that The Woman Warrior *"narrates Kingston's own journey from silence and selflessness to song and selfhood."*

Maxine Hong Kingston begins **The Woman Warrior** with the tale of her nameless aunt, a woman engulfed by defeating silence. She concludes her memoir with the legend of Ts'ai Yen, a female poet who triumphs in song. An American heiress confounded by a legacy of Chinese language and culture, Kingston records her own struggle for self-expression. The mute schoolgirl who smeared paper with opaque black paint, the incommunicative adolescent who could not voice her sorrow to her mother, the inarticulate young adult who could only peep in protest to her racist employers eventually becomes the adult artist who "talks-story" in a "high and clear" voice.[1]

In *The Woman Warrior* Kingston inextricably knots this pursuit of words with the process of self-creation and survival. Silence obliterates identity. It blots the self from Kingston's child-hood paintings as it effaces her aunt's name, hence her being, from posterity's memory. Word-lessness is paired with insanity, the disintegration of the coherent self: "Insane people were the ones who couldn't explain themselves," Kingston's nar-rator decides (p. 216). Deranged women, all of them inarticulate, haunt the text's nightmarish landscape.[2] Kingston's neighbor, now chattering, now speechless, is eventually shut up in an insane asylum. Laughing, snarling, crazy Mary points at the invisible and lunges out of darkness. Pee-a-nah, the village idiot, wordlessly pursues children through slough and street. Moon Orchid, King-ston's transplanted aunt, her soft voice dissipating into whispered lunacies, ultimately finds others who "speak the same language" only in a mental hospital (p. 185). These nonspeakers torment young Kingston who believes "talking and not talking made the difference between sanity and insanity" (p. 216). She worries that she will join the mad sorority; she too is unable to speak to others; she too visits with the people inside her head.

Conversely, articulation creates selfhood. Kingston, unlike the lunatic women who plague her, in the end does not succumb to the silence that imperils her childhood and adolescence. As an adult, as the writer of her autobiography, she eventually discovers her voice and the courage to employ it. *The Woman Warrior* narrates King-ston's own journey from silence and selflessness to song and selfhood. This triumphant telling, the act of writing, engenders and preserves the iden-tity of its creator.[3]

Kingston depicts her childhood and adoles-cence as an unending, yieldless labor for words to express and beget her identity. Her taunt at another mute schoolgirl—"If you don't talk, you can't have a personality"—is actually the self-directed warning of a child frightened by a deso-late expanse of widening silence (p. 210). This early silence is, in part, a legacy from a people who believe that "a ready tongue is an evil."[4] The Chinese keep secrets, they conceal their real names, they withhold speech. The hovering threats of deportation directed toward Chinese immigrants in America deepen this taciturnity.[5] Even as a child Kingston realizes the cultural roots of her reticence: "The other Chinese girls did not talk either, so I knew the silence had to do with being a Chinese girl" (p. 193).

Her speechlessness has to do also with cultural dislocation: being a Chinese girl in an American school, a daughter of China exiled in an alien country.[6] She must disentangle the traditions and language, the legacies of her dual homelands: "Those of us in the first American generations have had to figure out how the invisible world the emigrants built around our childhoods fits in solid America" (p. 6). Her inability to enunciate or comprehend the American pronoun "I" suggests this cultural confusion amidst which her speech and identity falter:

> I could not understand "I." The Chinese "I" has seven strokes, intricacies. How could the American "I," assuredly wearing a hat like the Chinese, have only three strokes, the middle so straight? Was it out of politeness that this writer left off strokes the way a Chinese has to write her own name small and crooked? No, it was not politeness; "I" is a capital and "you" is lower-case. I stared at the middle line and waited so long for its black center to resolve into tight strokes and dots that I forgot to pronounce it.
>
> (p. 193)

The bold, simple, "straight" strokes of the gen-derless English pronoun radiate the imposing Individualism of the self in American culture. But the "small and crooked" feminine Chinese pro-noun figures the dwarfing of the female self in a culture that practiced "girl slavery and girl infanti-cide" (p. 222). Language is the vessel of culture; "There is a Chinese word for the female I which is a 'slave'" (p. 56). The two contradictory cultural concepts of the female self baffle and silence King-ston's younger self.[7]

She stutters not only over the pronoun "I." Her silence is "thickest-total" during her early schooling (p. 192). American kindergarten is "the first silent year": "When I went to kindergarten and had to speak English for the first time, I became silent" (p. 191). In first grade, when she is called upon to read out loud, "squeaks come out of [her] throat" (p. 193). In second grade her "too soft or nonexistent" voice excludes her from the class play (p. 194). Even in her Chinese school her voice rasps like a "crippled animal running on broken legs" (p. 196).

In sixth grade Kingston's effort for voice and selfhood crests when she tortures her Doppel-gänger, another wordless and insecure Chinese classmate.[8] Their lack of athletic skill yokes Kingston and her other self, hallmarking their shared passivity:

> We were similar in sports. We held the bat on our shoulders until we walked to first base. (You got a strike only when you actually struck at the ball.) Sometimes the pitcher wouldn't bother to throw to us. "Automatic walks," the other children would call, sending us on our way.
>
> (pp. 200-01)

Defeat in the all-American sports arena signals failure in the arena of American social life. Too unaggressive to strike at the ball, the last chosen for their teams, the girls are timid benchwarmers virtually excluded from their social group.

When she attacks her alter ego Kingston tries to destroy what she despises and fears in herself, the reticence and servility of the Chinese feminine self that hinder her becoming the confident, well-liked American "I." Aching for a "stout neck," "hard brown skin," and the daring to "hit the ball," she berates her shadow self for her "flower-stem neck," "baby-soft" skin, and inability to "swing at the ball" (pp. 201, 204-05, 208). Her unintentionally reflexive jeers unmask her own aspirations to become all-American: "Do you want to be like this, dumb . . . your whole life? Don't you ever want to be a cheerleader? Or a pompon girl? What are you going to do for a living?" (p. 210). It is not without irony that Kingston looks back on her younger self who applauds the American-feminine role model of cheerleader. Though it is better to be a cheerleader than a slave, American girls, instead of starring on the field, occupy the sidelines.[9]

Still, the satire of American sex roles, evident in this passage and throughout the work, is overshadowed by blatant Chinese misogyny. Kingston stresses the fact that it is her American teachers who foster her sense of self-worth, independence, and achievement. Moreover, the derision of the retrospective adult does not undercut the earnest intertwining of speech and selfhood in this passage. To become a cheerleader, the symbol of American schoolgirl "rah-rah" popularity, one must be able to shout. At heart, it is the voicelessness of her double, herself, the way "she would whisper read," the way that only "wheezes . . . came out of her plastic flute," that makes the young Kingston shudder (pp. 201, 202).

Thus, when she pinches and tears the soft flesh of her mute China Doll mirror self, she tries to slay the fabulous, monstrous concept of female worthlessness that extinguishes her speech. But the expunging of an inculcated psychological

"dragon" by excoriating its physical objectification is an impossible feat.[10] She fails utterly. Her descent into the underworld of the self, appropriately set in the sex-segregated, mazy hell of a basement lavatory, does not yield self-knowledge or voice. Rather, her own cries, pleas, and shrieks echo the "sobs, chokes, noises" of her double and bind them more inextricably (p. 207). Neither achieves meaningful speech. In the end, Kingston, self-annihilated, wraps herself in the silence of a sickbed. When she rises after a year and a half and returns to school, she "ha[s] to figure out again how to talk" (p. 212).

From childhood through adolescence, Kingston continues her quest for self-expression. As a teenager she is familiar with the English language and American culture, but her voice still squeals with ugly "duck"-like insecurity (p. 232). Reluctant incommunicativeness still isolates her. She seeks a pathway out of this aloneness by unbosoming her secret sins, dreams, and afflictions to her mother, Brave Orchid:

> I had grown inside me a list of over two hundred things that I had to tell my mother so that she would know the true things about me and to stop the pain in my throat . . . how I had prayed for a white horse of my own. . . . How I wanted the horse to start the movies in my mind coming true. How I had picked on a girl and made her cry. How I had stolen from the cash register. . . . If only I could let my mother know the list, she—and the world—would become more like me, and I would never be alone again.
>
> (pp. 229-30)

It is the wish of the adolescent for the magical telling that would transform her separation into connection, that would make her loneliness disappear. But her wish is unfulfilled. Even when she relays her least significant confidences, her mother's punctuating response, "m'm, m'm," intensifies Kingston's aloneness (pp. 232, 233). And when she divulges her longing for the imaginary steed that will carry her into the never-never land of adventure, her mother silences her: "I can't stand this whispering. . . . Senseless gabblings every night. I wish you would stop. . . . Whispering, whispering, making no sense. Madness. I don't feel like hearing your craziness. . . . Leave me alone" (p. 233). The real Brave Orchid is too distant from the fairy-tale land of communication: "So I had to stop. . . . I shut my mouth, but I felt something alive tearing at my throat. . . . Soon there would be three hundred things, and [it would be] too late to get them out before my mother grew old and died" (p. 233).

Just as Brave Orchid now silences young Kingston's confession, so has she interfered with her speech throughout her girlhood. Kingston recalls how as a child she believed her mother actually severed her frenum:

> I used to curl up my tongue in front of the mirror and tauten my frenum into a white line. . . . I saw no scars in my mouth. I thought perhaps I had had two frena, and she had cut one. . . . At . . . times I was terrified—the first thing my mother did when she saw me was to cut my tongue.
>
> (p. 190)

This recurrent memory embodies figurative truth: Brave Orchid has tampered with her daughter's speech. Kingston opens her memoir, suggestively, with her mother's command for silence: "You must not tell anyone . . . what I am about to tell you" (p. 4). As China's spokeswoman the mother instills in her daughter a sense of the literally "unspeakable" (pp. 6, 215). But her prohibition of speech wells from a more private source of paranoia. Like the other Chinese immigrants she is nervous about her precarious status. She distrusts even her own children, threatened by their foreignness.[11] When Kingston questions Brave Orchid about the shadowy issues of immigration and citizenship, she is shrilly warned: "Don't tell . . . Never tell . . . Don't tell" (pp. 213-15). Brave Orchid believes that if her daughter dares to speak out, they will be sent out, back to China.

Worried that the family will be deported if they stand out in any way, Brave Orchid orders her daughter to bury her identity and protests under a protective veil of quiet:

> "Don't tell," . . . Lie to Americans. Tell them you were born during the San Francisco earthquake. Tell them your birth certificate and your parents were burned up in the fire. Don't report crimes; tell them we have no crimes and no poverty. Give a new name every time you get arrested.
>
> (pp. 214-15)

Deny your birth, name, and ancestry, Brave Orchid cautions: swallow your protest. She demands the silence that is self-obliteration.

When Kingston fears that her parents have arranged her marriage to a retarded boy who has been loitering around inside her family's laundromat, her "throat bursts open" in a climactic confrontation with her mother. The adolescent begins to cross the threshold into selfhood (p. 233). Assuming that her parents have chosen a hideous half-wit for her mate—a "monster" altogether unfit to mount with her upon her white charger—she blurts out her most precious secrets:

> Do you know what the Teacher Ghosts say about me? They tell me I'm smart, and I can win scholarships. I can get into colleges. I'm smart. . . . I know how to get A's, and they say I could be a scientist or a mathematician if I want. I can make a living and take care of myself. . . . Not everybody thinks I'm nothing. I am not going to be a slave or a wife. . . . I am going to get scholarships, and I'm going away. . . . So get that ape out of here. . . . And I'm not going to Chinese school anymore. I'm going to run for office at American school, and I'm going to join clubs. I'm going to get enough offices and clubs on my record to get into college. . . . Ha! You can't stop me from talking. You tried to cut off my tongue, but it didn't work. So I told the hardest ten or twelve things on my list all in one outburst.
>
> (pp. 227, 234-35)

The monologue reiterates her taunts at her schoolgirl double. Now, when she refuses to become a slave or a wife or to attend Chinese school, she again rejects the traditional Chinese devaluation of women. Now, when she resolves to become a club officer and to attend college, she again determines to become the esteemed, self-reliant westerner. Appropriately, her voice, no longer whispering, no longer duck-like, is "like Chinese opera. I could hear the drums and the cymbals and the gongs and brass horns" (p. 236). Though the passage rings with the exaggeration of the mock epic, it describes a turning point in young Kingston's life. Her declaration of independence frees her and temporarily soothes her throat pain.[12] She leaves home "to see the world" (p. 237). She sets forth to discover "places in this country that are ghost free," where she can "belong" (p. 127).[13] Kingston's narrator is coming of age.

It is as an adult that Kingston tells her own story in *The Woman Warrior.* It is a story told both in spite of and because of the mother who silenced her and yet taught her to sing. A reproach and a tribute. Young Kingston justifiably accuses her mother of trying "to cut off [her] tongue" to stop her speech; Brave Orchid rightfully claims that she severed her daughter's frenum so that she "would not be tongue-tied" (pp. 235, 190).

Brave Orchid's paradoxical effects upon her daughter's speech emerge from the duality of her own character, a discordant marriage of feminism and misogyny. As a young woman she had courageously journeyed alone across China to medical school where she subdued ghosts and learned to conquer disease. Even in America her strength and spirit prevail over the drudgery of the family laundromat. Ironically, while living in China this paradigm of female power had gone to market and—after examining and bargaining like a shrewd farmer buying livestock—had purchased an adolescent girl to serve as her slave. In America, though she owns no slave girl, she has a daughter whose self-respect she batters with misogynist doctrine. Brave Orchid embodies the selfhood that she insists women can never possess.[14]

Kingston identifies this confounding contradiction in her mother-as-teacher: "She said I would grow up a wife and a slave, but she taught me the song of the warrior woman, Fa Mu Lan" (p. 24). While predicting her daughter's selflessness, Brave Orchid makes her cognizant of the Song of the Self; while demanding her wordlessness, she instructs her in the art of "talking-story."[15]

In fact, though Kingston reproaches her mother for impeding her speech, the structural design of the individual chapters of *The Woman Warrior* pays tribute to Brave Orchid and the "great power" of "talking-story" that she passes down to her daughter (p. 24). As Kingston constructs each of her chapters—either directly or indirectly—upon one of Brave Orchid's talk-stories, it is as if she is inheriting her mother's bequest of words again and again.[16] In "No Name Woman," for example, Brave Orchid's barely told tale of her sister-in-law's sexual violation and its consequences, the birth and death of the illegitimate baby, the punishment and suicide of the mother, is the germ of Kingston's lavish retelling of the same story. In the beginning of "White Tigers," the second chapter, Kingston recollects how as a girl she had trailed her mother around the house, "the two of us singing about how Fa Mu Lan fought gloriously and returned alive from war to settle in the village" (p. 24). Brave Orchid has "taught" her young daughter the "song" that stimulates the grown artist's elaborate fantasy of another young girl's becoming a victorious female avenger of crimes against her village (p. 24). As Brave Orchid has once again "given" Kingston the subject of her art, the design reappears (p. 24). "Shaman" describes the China her mother had "funneled . . . into [her] ears" (p. 89). This chapter, which narrates Brave Orchid's adventures as a medical student and doctor in China, is Kingston's imaginative flight to a time before her birth and to a land she has visited only in her mother's storytelling. Brave Orchid's tales allow her daughter to "return to China" where she has "never been" (p. 90). Kingston's own talk-story of the encounter between her mother and aunt with her bigamist uncle, "At the Western Palace," is thrice-removed from one of Brave Orchid's narratives.

Her account of her aunt's futile attempt to reclaim the husband who three decades before had left her in China and set out to discover a new life—and wife—in America is based upon the story passed from her mother to her brother to her sister to her. It is clearly fanciful, "twisted into designs" (p. 190). In "A Song for a Barbarian Reed Pipe," the final chapter of *The Woman Warrior*, she acknowledges her artistic debt to her mother: "Here is a story my mother told me . . . when I told her I also talk-story. The beginning is hers, the ending, mine" (p. 240). Kingston, in essence, has described the process and design of her autobiography. Brave Orchid is the womb from which her daughter's art is born.

Kingston christens her autobiography *The Woman Warrior* because in the legend of the female avenger she discovered an avatar of selfhood, an ideal that celebrated the union of femininity and verbal as well as physical power. Fa Mu Lan, Ts'ai Yen, the swordswoman of the "White Tigers" fantasy, and Brave Orchid—the women warriors real and make-believe who rage across the text—all possess the power of speech. The imaginary avenger of "White Tigers" sings to her troops "glorious songs that came out of the sky . . . when [she] opened [her] mouth, the songs poured out and were loud enough for the whole encampment to hear" (p. 44). Brave Orchid, the aptly named modern incarnation of the female warrior, is a "champion talker" whose voice never fails (p. 235).

Kingston likens herself to one of the woman warriors suggested by the title of her memoir, particularly the swordswoman of the "White Tigers" fantasy: "The swordswoman and I are not so dissimilar. . . . What we have in common are the words at our backs" (p. 62). Kingston has learned that these scarred grievances, the crimes against women and minorities, must be uttered in spite of the fearful mothers and racist executives determined to silence her. Unlike the spluttering adolescent who timidly objects to the bigotry of her employers, Kingston now shouts out against prejudice and stereotyping.[17] She protests loudly (and not too much) the sexist Chinese axioms that hammered upon her sense of self-worth: "Girls are maggots in the rice"; "It is more profitable to raise geese than daughters"; "Feeding girls is feeding cowbirds"; "When fishing for treasures in the flood, be careful not to pull in girls" (pp. 51, 54, 62). She denounces the Sins of the Fathers against the female self. Her words blast sexism and racism. While the imaginary swordswoman decapitates her enemies, Kingston surpasses this "childish myth"[18] because she wields deadlier arms:

> The idioms for *revenge* are "report a crime" and "report to five families." The reporting is the vengeance—not the beheading, not the gutting, but the words. And I have so many words— "chink" words and "gook" words too—that they do not fit on my skin.
>
> (p. 63)

But words, the weapons of destruction and aggression, paradoxically create and preserve. The act of writing—or telling—engenders selfhood. Suggestively, the first and last characters to serve as focal points of the book, the voiceless aunt and the victorious poet, mirror Kingston's own progress from the silence that is selflessness to the song that is selfhood.

As Kingston has fathomed, no-name aunt's real punishment for her sexual violation and pregnancy is not the suicidal drowning of her body in the well but the drowning of her name—or identity—in silence. The culture that venerates ancestors and eternalizes them by means of an oral tradition damns her to anonymity, to the underworld of the unmentionable. "You must not tell anyone . . . what I am about to tell you"; "Don't let your father know that I told you." Thus Brave Orchid encloses her skeletal version of her sister-in-law's story in warnings to her daughter (pp. 3, 5). And Kingston, though eager for the particulars of her aunt's life, "cannot ask" her mother further questions about "Father's-drowned-in-the-well sister" (p. 6).

Instead she directs her inquiry to her own imagination. With the power of fantasy she conjures her aunt's long-silent, invisible ghost and delivers her from oblivion by fleshing her out in generous detail. If she cannot baptize her with a name, she can at least sculpt her into a possible shape—as a romantic living in a culture condemning her to conforming sexlessness, as a slave cowering before male command.[19] Certainly the aunt was a woman defeated by silence, who labored "in eternal cold and silence," who, never pronouncing her impregnator's name, gave "silent birth" to a baby whose cry was quickly drowned, together with her own sobs, in the family well (pp. 16, 10). Even now her ghost "waits silently" to pull another down to oblivion (p. 19).

But in relating this story of wordless failure, Kingston not only rescues her aunt's memory, she overcomes the silence thwarting the final establishment of her own identity. Warned, on the day she began to menstruate, of her aunt's sexual transgression, she now tells the tale and thereby heralds her own crossing of the threshold into selfhood. The initial chapter demonstrates the triumph of speech in the entire work. As she finds the courage to speak when ordered to be silent, so does she discover "words so strong" that they can secure her identity (p. 18). The adult articulates for the child and adolescent once hushed by insecurity. The artifact creates and saves the artist.

Kingston concludes her memoir with the parable of Ts'ai Yen. In recounting the life story of this ancient woman warrior whose battle for self-expression culminated in songful victory, she retells her own story. She sings of her double; she celebrates herself. The child who shuddered at the strangled wheezes of the flute of her one-time alter ego is now the adult proclaiming the flute-like voice of another double self.[20] This triumphant song of becoming a woman and a warrior is the climax, the "high note" of the entire piece (p. 243).

Twenty-year-old Ts'ai Yen, at the portal of adulthood, is abducted to a barbarian land where no one understands her language. Like her legendary ancestress, Kingston has struggled to grow up among the uncomprehending "ghosts" of an alien land. Both women transform—this time the telling does work its magic—the desperate loneliness of their cultural dislocation into art. Ts'ai Yen, upon hearing the high-pitched music of flutes, longs for and then achieves voice to echo this sound; she sings "a song so high and clear, it matched the flutes" (p. 243). Her lyrics of her distant home and family articulate her "sadness and anger" to the barbarians (p. 243). The poet Ts'ai Yen has discovered a voice and language that "translated well" (p. 243). Her songs have descended to Kingston, the deserving heiress of this legacy. Like Ts'ai Yen, Kingston has yearned for voice and has learned to vocalize. She too has "translated" the wordless "anger and sadness" of her life "among ghosts" into an autobiography or a self that speaks eloquently to us. She too has become a woman and a warrior.

Notes

To my mother, Maria DeRobertis Morante, I dedicate this article with love because she taught me her own version of the woman warrior's song when I was a child. To my two daughters, Kristin and Marissa Morante Tester, I dedicate this article with hope that I can in turn teach them this song of womanly strength and dignity.

1. Maxine Hong Kingston, *The Woman Warrior: Memoirs of a Girlhood Among Ghosts* (New York: Random House, 1977), p. 243. All further references to this edition appear in the text.

2. Although there is one mentally retarded, also incoherent Chinese boy, madness is consistently associated with women in *WW*. See also Shirley Nelson Garner, "Breaking Silences: *The Woman Warrior*," *Hurricane Alice*, 1, No. 2 (Fall/Winter 1983/84), 5-6.

3. Suzanne Juhasz, in her essay "Towards a Theory of Form in Feminist Autobiography," in *Women's Autobiography: Essays in Criticism*, ed. Estelle C. Jelinek (Bloomington: Indiana Univ. Press, 1980), p. 236, observes, "It is through words—through finding them, forming them, saying them aloud, *in public*—that Kingston reaches selfhood." See also Robert Rolf, "On Maxine Hong Kingston and *The Woman Warrior*," *Kyushu American Literature* (May 1982), p. 5; Margaret Miller, "Threads of Identity in Maxine Hong Kingston's *Woman Warrior*," *Biography*, 6, No. 1 (Winter 1983), 27-28; Garner, p. 5.

4. Kingston, p. 190. See also p. 13: "Every word that falls from the mouth is a coin lost."

5. See Kingston, p. 213.

6. See Kingston, pp. 196-99, where she describes another incident underlining her cultural dislocation. See also Woon-Ping Chin Holaday, "From Ezra Pound to Maxine Hong Kingston: Expressions of Chinese Thought in American Literature," *MELUS*, 5, No. 2 (1978), 18, who maintains, "The biography it [*WW*] presents is that of someone belonging to a marginal group, the Asian-American, coping with its ethnic origins in American society"; and Juhasz, p. 233.

7. See Kingston, pp. 12, 200, where she describes how, when trying to modulate the "Chinese-feminine" voice into the softer tones of "American-feminine," she whispers inaudibly.

8. Deborah Homsher, "*The Woman Warrior* by Maxine Hong Kingston: The Bridging of Autobiography and Fiction," *Iowa Review*, 10, No. 4 (1979), 95. See also Miller, p. 21, and Garner, p. 6.

9. Rolf, p. 8, notes that in this passage Kingston mocks "the superficial trappings of traditional American femininity." Still, he maintains that both the American and Chinese "types of female are viewed with irony, neither is presented as clearly superior to the other."

10. Stephanie A. Demetrakopoulos, "The Metaphysics of Matrilinearism in Women's Autobiography: Studies of Mead's *Blackberry Winter*, Hellman's *Pentimento*, Angelou's *I Know Why the Caged Bird Sings*, and Kingston's *The Woman Warrior*," in *Women's Autobiography*, p. 200.

11. See Kingston, p. 213.

12. Rolf, p. 6, describes this scene as a "furious declaration of her independence." Garner, p. 6, notes the freeing power of this speech.

13. See Kingston, pp. 116-27, where she records a dialogue with her mother that takes place years after she has left home.

14. Several critics discuss Brave Orchid's contradictory nature. See Homsher, p. 96; Demetrakopoulos, pp. 201-02; Miller, p. 23.

15. Miller, p. 24, describes Brave Orchid as a woman warrior "diminished by the American reality." She contends that "there is only one power she has left to bequeath her daughter: the power to 'talk-story.'"

16. See Carol Mitchell, "'Talking-Story' in *The Woman Warrior*: An Analysis of the Use of Folklore," *Kentucky Folklore Record*, 27 (January-June 1981), pp. 6-7. Mitchell analyzes Kingston's use of oral stories to structure the autobiography. See also Homsher, p. 95, and Miller, p. 26.

17. See Kingston, pp. 57-58, where she describes the failure of her voice in confrontations with her racist employers.

18. Kingston, in "Cultural Mis-readings by American Reviewers," in *Asian and Western Writers in Dialogue: New Cultural Identities*, ed. Guy Amirthanayagam (London: Macmillan, 1982), p. 57, contends that the "White Tigers" chapter is a "childish myth . . . not the climax we reach for."

19. Note that Kingston also postulates, then rejects an identity of a scarlet woman for her aunt. See Juhasz, p. 232; Homsher, p. 94.

20. Several critics note likenesses between Kingston and Ts'ai Yen. See Holaday, p. 22; Patricia Lin Blinde, "The Icicle in the Desert: Perspective and Form in the Works of Two Chinese-American Women Writers," *MELUS*, 6, No. 3 (1979), 52; Rolf, p. 9.

FURTHER READING

Bibliography

Huang, Guiyou. "Maxine Hong Kingston (1940-)." In *Asian American Novelists: A Bio-Bibliograpical Critical Sourcebook*, edited by Emmanuel S. Nelson, pp. 138-55. Westport, Conn.: Greenwood Press, 2000.

Extensive bibliography of secondary sources which includes articles and reviews from both scholarly and popular journals and books.

Biographies

Sabine, Maureen. *Maxine Hong Kingston's Broken Book of Life: An Intertextual Study of the* Woman Warrior *and* China Men. Honolulu: University of Hawaii Press, 2004, 229 p.

Bio-critical examination of Kingston's life and works.

Wang, Jennie. "Maxine Hong Kingston." In *A Reader's Companion to the Short Story in English*, edited by Erin Fallon, R. C. Feddersen, James Kurtzleben, Maurice A. Lee, and Susan Rochette-Crawley, pp. 234-40. Westport, Conn.: Greenwood Press, 2001.

Short biographical introduction to Kingston's life and work.

Wong, Sau-ling Cynthia, ed. *Maxine Hong Kingston's* The Woman Warrior : A Casebook. New York: Oxford University Press, 1999, 193 p.

Biography of Kingston that also provides a critical review of The Woman Warrior.

Criticism

Chin, Frank. "This Is Not an Autobiography," *Genre* 18, no. 2 (1985): 109-30.

Argues that autobiography is not a Chinese genre, and that Kingston effectively "sells out" in her writing.

Feng, Pin-chia. *The Female Bildungsroman by Toni Morrison and Maxine Hong Kingston: A Postmodern Reading.* New York: Peter Lang, 1998, 193 p.

Examines the role of the bildungsroman in Morrison and Kingston.

Ho, Wendy. "Mother/Daughter Writing and the Politics of Race and Sex in Maxine Hong Kingston's *The Woman Warrior.*" In *Asian Americans: Comparative and Global Perspectives,* edited by Shirley Hune, Hyung-chan Kim, Stephen S. Fugita, and Amy Ling, pp. 225-38. Pullman: Washington State University Press, 1991.

Examines the mother-daughter relationship in The Woman Warrior.

Huntley, E. D. *Maxine Hong Kingston: A Critical Companion.* Westport, Conn.: Greenwood Press, 2001, 204 p.

Critical appraisal of Kingston with bibliographical resources.

Kramer, Jane. "The Woman Warrior." *The New York Times Book Review* (7 November 1976): 1, 18, 20.

Favorable review of The Woman Warrior.

Madsen, Deborah L. *Maxine Hong Kingston.* Detroit: Gale Group, 2000, 156 p.

Explores thematic and stylistic aspects of Kingston's work.

Rabine, Leslie W. "No Lost Paradise: Social Gender and Symbolic Gender in the Writings of Maxine Hong Kingston." *Signs* 12, no. 3 (spring 1987): 471-92.

Aims to "reconcile insights of symbolic and social feminism" in Kingston's work.

Schueller, Malini. "Questioning Race and Gender Definitions: Dialogic Subversion in *The Woman Warrior.*" *Criticism* 31, no. 4 (fall 1989): 421-37.

Considers gender and ethnic identity in The Woman Warrior.

Simmons, Diane. *Maxine Hong Kingston.* New York: Twayne Publishers, 1999, 184 p.

Full-length critical study, prefaced by an insightful 50-page biographical introduction to Kingston's life.

Skandera-Trombley, Laura E., ed. *Critical Essays on Maxine Hong Kingston.* New York: G. K. Hall, 1999, 359 p.

Collection of numerous critical essays, fairly evenly divided in coverage of The Woman Warrior, China Men, *and* Tripmaster Monkey.

Wogowitsch, Margit. *Narrative Strategies and Multicultural Identity: Maxine Hong Kingston in Context.* Wien: Braumüller, 1995, 179 p.

Comprehensive examination of Kingston with lengthy bibliography.

OTHER SOURCES FROM GALE:

Additional coverage of Kingston's life and career is contained in the following sources published by the Gale Group: *American Writers Supplement,* Vol. 5; *Asian American Literature; Authors and Artists for Young Adults,* Vols. 8, 55; *Beacham's Encyclopedia of Popular Fiction: Biography and Resources,* Vol. 2; *Concise Dictionary of American Literary Biography Supplement; Contemporary Authors,* Vols. 69-72; *Contemporary Authors New Revision Series,* Vols. 13, 38, 74, 87; *Contemporary Literary Criticism,* Vols. 12, 19, 58, 121; *Contemporary Novelists,* Ed. 7; *Dictionary of Literary Biography,* Vols. 173, 212; *Dictionary of Literary Biography Yearbook, 1980; DISCovering Authors Modules: Multicultural* and *Novelists; DISCovering Authors 3.0; Encyclopedia of World Literature in the 20th Century,* Ed. 3; *Feminist Writers; Literature and Its Times,* Vol. 5; *Literature Resource Center; Major 20th-Century Writers,* Eds. 1, 2; *Modern American Women Writers; Novels for Students,* Vol. 6; *Reference Guide to American Literature,* Ed. 4; *Short Stories for Students,* Vol. 3; *Something about the Author,* Vol. 53; and *World Literature Criticism Supplement.*

DORIS LESSING

(1919 -)

(Born Doris May Taylor; has also written under the pseudonym Jane Somers) Persian-born English novelist, short story writer, essayist, playwright, poet, nonfiction writer, autobiographer, and travel writer.

Considered a significant writer of the post-World War II generation, Lessing has explored many of the most significant ideologies and social issues of the twentieth century. Her prolific body of work displays many interests and concerns, ranging from racism, Communism, and feminism, to psychology and mysticism. Lessing began her career in the 1950s, writing realist fiction that focused on themes of racial injustice and colonialism. As her writing developed, Lessing began to compose fiction that anticipated many major feminist concerns of the late 1960s and 1970s. Her strong-willed, independent heroines often suffer emotional crises in male-dominated societies and must struggle with dominant sociopolitical constructs to reach higher levels of identity and liberation. A consistent theme cultivated throughout her work is the need for individuals to confront their fundamental assumptions about life in order to transcend preconceived belief systems and acquire self-awareness.

BIOGRAPHICAL INFORMATION

Lessing was born in Persia (now Iran) to English parents who moved their family to Rhodesia (now Zimbabwe) in the hopes of successful farming. She was educated in a convent school and later a government-run all-girls school, but her formal education ended at the age of thirteen. A voracious reader, Lessing had excelled in school and continued her education by reading the wealth of books her mother ordered from London. By the age of eighteen, Lessing had written two drafts for novels and was selling stories to South African magazines, although she would not publish her first novel, *The Grass Is Singing,* until 1950. In 1939 she married Frank Wisdom, a much older man with whom she had two children. The marriage, which lasted four years, inspired *A Proper Marriage* (1954), considered one of her most acutely autobiographical novels. Lessing joined the Communist Party in the early 1940s and also met and married Gottfried Lessing, a Jewish German with whom she had a son, Peter. In 1949 the couple separated, and Lessing and Peter moved to England. In London, Lessing established herself as a fiction writer, critic, journalist, and political activist. Though she severed her ties to the Communist party in the mid-fifties, in 1956 she was banned from returning to Rhodesia, presumably for anti-apartheid sentiments expressed in her writings. Although details of Lessing's personal life are limited, critics agree that her fiction draws significantly from her own experiences. Lessing continues to live in England.

MAJOR WORKS

The Grass Is Singing introduces two of Lessing's major recurring themes: the causes and effects of racism ("the colour bar") and the myriad ways that history and politics can determine the course of a person's life. The novel focuses on a white couple's impoverished, isolated life on a Rhodesian farm and the wife's reaction to her social and political condition. Lessing's highly acclaimed *Children of Violence* series is a *bildungsroman* that traces the intellectual and emotional development of Martha Quest. Like Lessing, Martha is a "child of violence" born at the end of World War I and raised in a bleak post-war era of social struggle, who must later face the tragedies of World War II. Over the course of the series, Martha moves away from personal, self-centered concerns to a broader awareness of others and the world around her. Imbedded in this process, though, is a keen exploration of feminine identity, creativity, and sexuality within a male-dominated space. In *Martha Quest,* (1952) Martha attempts to escape her restricted upbringing and her domineering mother. *A Proper Marriage* and *A Ripple from the Storm* (1958) recount Martha's two unsuccessful marriages to politically ambitious men and her involvement in left-wing, anti-apartheid, Communist activities. *Landlocked* (1965)—considered by many as an abrupt departure from the preceding concerns of the *Children of Violence* series—reflects Lessing's emerging interest in telepathy, extrasensory perception, and Sufism, the mystical branch of Islam. The novel follows Martha as she travels to England where she experiences an apocalyptic vision. Britain—and later the entire world—are destroyed in *The Four-Gated City* (1969), a novel in which Martha comes to realize the limitations of rational thought and seeks to understand and embrace the collective consciousness and the higher truth of her own intuition.

The Golden Notebook (1962) centers on novelist Anna Freeman Wulf, whose life is represented by four "notebooks." Characterized by a symbolic color and narrated from different perspectives, each notebook incorporates aspects of Wulf's latest novel in narratives that assume multiple levels of significance. The title of the novel refers to Anna's desperate attempt to integrate her fragmented experiences in order to achieve wholeness through art. Similarly, *The Summer Before the Dark* (1973) focuses on a middle-aged woman who has a brief affair with a younger man as a means to rediscover a sense of identity. Lessing's "space fiction" series—"Canopus in Argos: Archives"—concerns three competing galactic empires: the benign Canopeans, the self-centered Sirians, and the evil Shammat. The series continues Lessing's interest in Sufism, stressing the interconnectedness of one's own fate and well-being to that of others. Manipulating events on Earth to retain a gene pool for their own immortality, these empires continue to affect human history through the intervention of immortal beings. Lessing's series of novels written under the pseudonym "Jane Somers"—*The Diary of a Good Neighbour* (1983) and *If the Old Could . . .* (1984)—feature the diaries of a woman named Janna who struggles with her mistakes and an acceptance of herself. In *The Good Terrorist* (1985) a middle-class woman's extreme liberal idealism leads her to organize a group of would-be revolutionaries who commit an act of terrorism. The rhetoric of contemporary political slogans plays a key role in the novel. *The Fifth Child* (1988) concerns a violent, antisocial child named Ben who wreaks havoc on his family and society. Its sequel, *Ben, in the World* (2000), follows Ben as he enters adulthood. In 2001 Lessing published *The Sweetest Dream,* a novel that examines the lasting effects of war through the relationship of Frances Lennox—a self-described "earth mother" living in the 1960s—and a group of post-war children that she takes into her home. In *The Grandmothers* (2004), Lessing continues to probe the human condition and questions about love, identity, and race.

CRITICAL RECEPTION

Lessing has been recognized as one of the most accomplished writers of the twentieth century. Critics have praised the tension and immediacy in Lessing's work that is generated by her use of realistic descriptions, symbolism, and detailed imagery. Lessing's distinct, unapologetic rendering of marriage and motherhood, her anti-apartheid stance, and her experimentation with genre and form have made Lessing an exciting—and often controversial—literary figure. Initially criticized by some commentators for her "unfeminine" depictions of female anger and discontent, Lessing is now often commended for her candid portrayals of female characters who struggle with their roles and the division between their emotional and intellectual needs. According to Ellen W. Brooks, Lessing's appeal in her fiction "rests largely on her treatment of woman in modern life, the most thorough and accurate of any in literature. Her achievement is all the more significant in that so few writers have presented women with whom one can identify—complex, intelligent, questioning women who are not content with the status quo, who rebel against the established order."

PRINCIPAL WORKS

The Grass Is Singing (novel) 1950

*Martha Quest (novel) 1952

This Was the Old Chief's Country (short stories) 1952

Before the Deluge (drama) 1953

Five: Short Novels (novellas) 1953

*A Proper Marriage (novel) 1954

A Retreat to Innocence (novel) 1956

Going Home (essays) 1957

The Habit of Loving (short stories) 1957

Each His Own Wilderness (drama) 1958

Mr. Dollinger (drama) 1958

*A Ripple from the Storm (novel) 1958

Fourteen Poems (poetry) 1959

In Pursuit of the English: A Documentary (documentary) 1960

The Golden Notebook (novel) 1962

Play with a Tiger (drama) 1962

A Man and Two Women (short stories) 1963

African Stories (short stories) 1964

*Landlocked (novel) 1965

The Storm [adaptor; from a drama by Alexander Ostrovsky] (drama) 1966

Winter in July (short stories) 1966

Particularly Cats (autobiographical essay) 1967

Nine African Stories 1968

The Four-Gated City (novel) 1969

Briefing for a Descent into Hell (novel) 1971

The Story of a Non-Marrying Man and Other Stories [also published as *The Temptation of Jack Orkney and Other Stories*] (short stories) 1972

The Singing Door (drama) 1973

The Summer Before the Dark (novel) 1973

The Memoirs of a Survivor (novel) 1974

A Small Personal Voice: Essays, Reviews, and Interviews (essays, reviews, and interviews) 1974

Collected Stories. 2 vols. [also published as *Stories*] (short stories) 1978

†*Shikasta* (novel) 1979

†*The Marriages between Zones Three, Four, and Five* (novel) 1980

†*The Sirian Experiments* (novel) 1981

†*The Making of the Representative for Planet 8* (novel) 1982

The Diary of a Good Neighbour [as Jane Somers] (novel) 1983

†*Documents Relating to the Sentimental Agents in the Volyen Empire* (novel) 1983

‡*The Diaries of Jane Somers* (novel) 1984

If the Old Could . . . [as Jane Somers] (novel) 1984

The Good Terrorist (novel) 1985

Prisons We Choose To Live Inside (essays) 1987

The Wind Blows Away Our Words (nonfiction) 1987

The Fifth Child (novel) 1988

African Laughter: Four Visits to Zimbabwe (nonfiction) 1992

The Real Thing (short stories and sketches) 1992

Under My Skin: Volume One of My Autobiography, to 1949 (autobiography) 1994

Playing the Game (graphic novel) 1995

Love, Again (novel) 1996

Walking in the Shade: Volume Two of My Autobiography, 1949-1962 (autobiography) 1997

Mara and Dann: An Adventure (novel) 1999

Ben, in the World: The Sequel to The Fifth Child (novel) 2000

The Sweetest Dream (novel) 2001

The Grandmothers: Four Short Novels (novellas) 2004

*   These novels are collectively referred to as the *Children of Violence* series and the "Martha Quest" novels.

†   These novels are collectively referred to as the "Canopus in Argos: Archives" series.

‡   The work comprises two earlier novels, *The Diary of a Good Neighbour* and *If the Old Could,* that Lessing published under the pseudonym Jane Somers.

PRIMARY SOURCES

DORIS LESSING (ESSAY DATE 1974)

SOURCE: Lessing, Doris. "Preface to *The Golden Notebook.*" In *A Small Personal Voice,* edited by Paul Schlueter, pp. 23-43. New York: Alfred A. Knopf, 1974.

In the following excerpt from the preface to The Golden Notebook, *Lessing discusses the mixed reaction of women to the novel, the novel's original intent and central themes, and her support for the women's rights movement.*

The shape of this novel is as follows:

There is a skeleton, or frame, called *Free Women,* which is a conventional short novel, about 60,000 words long, and which could stand by itself. But it is divided into five sections and separated by stages of the four Notebooks, Black, Red, Yellow, and Blue. The Notebooks are kept by Anna Wulf, a central character of *Free Women.* She keeps four and not one because, as she recognises, she has to separate things off from each other, out of fear of chaos, of formlessness—of breakdown. Pressures, inner and outer, end the Notebooks; a heavy black line is drawn across the page of one after another. But now that they are finished, from their fragments can come something new, **The Golden Notebook.**

Throughout the Notebooks people have discussed, theorised, dogmatised, labelled, compartmented—sometimes in voices so general and representative of the time that they are anonymous, you could put names to them like those in the old Morality Plays, Mr. Dogma and Mr. I-Am-Free-Because-I-Belong-Nowhere, Miss I-Must-Have-Love-and-Happiness and Mrs. I-Have-to-Be-Good-at-Everything-I-Do, Mr. Where-Is-a-Real-Woman? and Miss Where-Is-a-Real-Man?, Mr. I'm-Mad-Because-They-Say-I-Am, and Miss Life-Through-Experiencing-Everything, Mr. I-Make-Revolution-and-Therefore-I-Am, and Mr. and Mrs. If-We-Deal-Very-Well-with-This-Small-Problem-Then-Perhaps-We-Can-Forget- We-Daren't-Look-at-the-Big-Ones. But they have also reflected each other, been aspects of each other, given birth to each other's thoughts and behaviour—*are* each other, form wholes. In the inner Golden Notebook, things have come together, the divisions have broken down, there is formlessness with the end of fragmentation—the triumph of the second theme, which is that of unity. Anna and Saul Green the American "break down." They are crazy, lunatic, mad—what you will. They "break down" into each other, into other people, break through the false patterns they have made of their pasts, the patterns and formulas they have made to shore up themselves and each other, dissolve. They hear each other's thoughts, recognise each other in themselves. Saul Green, the man who has been envious and destructive of Anna, now supports her, advises her, gives her the theme for her next book, *Free Women*—an ironical title, which begins: "The two women were alone in the London flat." And Anna, who has been jealous of

Saul to the point of insanity, possessive and demanding, gives Saul the pretty new notebook, *The Golden Notebook,* which she has previously refused to do, gives him the theme for his next book, writing in it the first sentence: "On a dry hillside in Algeria a soldier watched the moonlight glinting on his rifle." In the inner Golden Notebook, which is written by both of them, you can no longer distinguish between what is Saul and what is Anna, and between them and the other people in the book.

This theme of "breakdown," that sometimes when people "crack up" it is a way of self-healing, of the inner self's dismissing false dichotomies and divisions, has of course been written about by other people, as well as by me, since then. But this is where, apart from the odd short story, I first wrote about it. Here it is rougher, more close to experience, before experience has shaped itself into thought and pattern—more valuable perhaps because it is rawer material.

But nobody so much as noticed this central theme, because the book was instantly belittled, by friendly reviewers as well as by hostile ones, as being about the sex war, or was claimed by women as a useful weapon in the sex war.

I have been in a false position ever since, for the last thing I have wanted to do was to refuse to support women.

To get the subject of Women's Liberation over with—I support it, of course, because women are second-class citizens, as they are saying energetically and competently in many countries. It can be said that they are succeeding, if only to the extent they are being seriously listened to. All kinds of people previously hostile or indifferent say: "I support their aims but I don't like their shrill voices and their nasty ill-mannered ways." This is an inevitable and easily recognisable stage in every revolutionary movement: reformers must expect to be disowned by those who are only too happy to enjoy what has been won for them. I don't think that Women's Liberation will change much, though—not because there is anything wrong with their aims but because it is already clear that the whole world is being shaken into a new pattern by the cataclysms we are living through; probably by the time we are through, if we do get through at all, the aims of Women's Liberation will look very small and quaint.

But this novel was not a trumpet for Women's Liberation. It described many female emotions of aggression, hostility, resentment. It put them into print. Apparently what many women were thinking, feeling, experiencing, came as a great surprise. Instantly a lot of very ancient weapons were unleashed, the main ones, as usual, being on the theme of "She is unfeminine," "She is a man-hater." This particular reflex seems indestructible. Men—and many women—said that the suffragettes were defeminised, masculine, brutalised. There is no record I have read of any society anywhere when women demanded more than nature offers them that does not also describe this reaction from men—and some women. A lot of women were angry about *The Golden Notebook.* What women will say to other women, grumbling in their kitchens and complaining and gossiping or what they make clear in their masochism, is often the last thing they will say aloud—a man may overhear. Women are the cowards they are because they have been semi-slaves for so long. The number of women prepared to stand up for what they really think, feel, experience with a man they are in love with is still small. Most women will still run like little dogs with stones thrown at them when a man says: You are unfeminine, aggressive, you are unmanning me. It is my belief that any woman who marries or takes seriously in any way at all, a man who uses this threat, deserves everything she gets. For such a man is a bully, does not know anything about the world he lives in, or about its history—men and women have taken infinite numbers of roles in the past, and do now, in different societies. So he is ignorant, or fearful about being out of step—a coward. . . . I write all these remarks with exactly the same feeling as if I were writing a letter to post into the distant past: I am so sure that everything we now take for granted is going to be utterly swept away in the next decade.

(So why write novels? Indeed, why! I suppose we have to go on living *as if.* . . .)

Some books are not read in the right way because they have skipped a stage of opinion, assume a crystallisation of information in society which has not yet taken place. This book was written as if the attitudes that have been created by the Women's Liberation movements already existed. It came out first ten years ago, in 1962. If it were coming out now for the first time it might be read, and not merely reacted to: things have changed very fast. Certain hypocrisies have gone. For instance, ten, or even five years ago—it has been a sexually contumacious time—novels and plays were being plentifully written by men furiously critical of women—particularly from the States but also in this country—portrayed as bullies and betrayers, but particularly as underminers

and sappers. But these attitudes in male writers were taken for granted, accepted as sound philosophical bases, as quite normal, certainly not as woman-hating, aggressive, or neurotic. It still goes on, of course, but things are better, there is no doubt of it.

I was so immersed in writing this book that I didn't think about how it might be received. I was involved not merely because it was hard to write—keeping the plan of it in my head I wrote it from start to end, consecutively, and it was difficult—but because of what I was learning as I wrote. Perhaps giving oneself a tight structure, making limitations for oneself, squeezes out new substance where you least expect it. All sorts of ideas and experiences I didn't recognise as mine emerged when writing. The actual time of writing, then, and not only the experiences that had gone into the writing, was really traumatic: it changed me. Emerging from this crystallising process, handing the manuscript to publisher and friends, I learned that I had written a tract about the sex war, and fast discovered that nothing I said then could change that diagnosis.

Yet the essence of the book, the organisation of it, everything in it, says implicitly and explicitly, that we must not divide things off, must not compartmentalise.

"Bound. Free. Good. Bad. Yes. No. Capitalism. Socialism. Sex. Love. . . ." says Anna, in *Free Women,* stating a theme—shouting it, announcing a motif with drums and fanfares . . . or so I imagined. Just as I believed that in a book called *The Golden Notebook* the inner section called the Golden Notebook might be presumed to be a central point, to carry the weight of the thing, to make a statement.

But no.

Other themes went into the making of this book, which was a crucial time for me: thoughts and themes I had been holding in my mind for years came together.

One was that it was not possible to find a novel which described the intellectual and moral climate of a hundred years ago, in the middle of the last century, in Britain, in the way Tolstoy did it for Russia, Stendhal for France. (At this point it is necessary to make the obligatory disclaimers.) To read *The Red and the Black* and *Lucien Leuwen* is to know that France as if one were living there, to read *Anna Karenina* is to know that Russia. But a very useful Victorian novel never got itself written. Hardy tells us what it was like to be poor, to have an imagination larger than the possibilities of a very narrow time, to be a victim. George Eliot is good as far as she goes. But I think the penalty she paid for being a Victorian woman was that she had to be shown to be a good woman even when she wasn't according to the hypocrisies of the time—there is a great deal she does not understand because she is moral. Meredith, that astonishingly underrated writer, is perhaps nearest. Trollope tried the subject but lacked the scope. There isn't one novel that has the vigour and conflict of ideas in action that is in a good biography of William Morris.

Of course this attempt on my part assumed that that filter which is a woman's way of looking at life has the same validity as the filter which is a man's way. Setting that problem aside, or rather, not even considering it, I decided that to give the ideological "feel" of our mid-century, it would have to be set among socialists and marxists, because it has been inside the various chapters of socialism that the great debates of our time have gone on; the movements, the wars, the revolutions, have been seen by their participants as movements of various kinds of socialism, or Marxism, in advance, containment, or retreat. (I think we should at least concede the possibility that people looking back on our time may see it not at all as we do—just as we, looking back on the English, the French, or even the Russian Revolutions see them differently from the people living then.) But "Marxism" and its various offshoots, has fermented ideas everywhere, and so fast and energetically that, once "way out" it has already been absorbed, has become part of ordinary thinking. Ideas that were confined to the far left thirty or forty years ago had pervaded the left generally twenty years ago, and have provided the commonplaces of conventional social thought from right to left for the last ten years. Something so thoroughly absorbed is finished as a force—but it was dominant, and in a novel of the sort I was trying to do had to be central.

GENERAL COMMENTARY

ELAYNE ANTLER RAPPING (ESSAY DATE 1975)

SOURCE: Rapping, Elayne Antler. "Unfree Women: Feminism in Doris Lessing's Novels." *Women's Studies* 3, no. 1 (1975): 29-44.

In the following essay, Rapping explores how Lessing's female protagonists shape feminine identity and experience, especially within the context of a male-dominated society, in The Golden Notebook *and* Children of Violence.

The men that we call great are those who . . . have taken the weight of the world upon their shoulders; they have done better or worse, they have succeeded in re-creating it or they have gone down; but first they have assumed that enormous burden. This is what no woman has ever done, what none has ever been *able* to do. To regard the universe as one's own, to consider oneself to blame for its faults and to glory in its progress, one must belong to the caste of the privileged; it is for those alone who are in command to justify the universe by changing it, by thinking about it, by revealing it; they alone can recognize themselves in it and endeavor to make their mark upon it. . . .

—Simone de Beauvoir

The difference between the "male" approach to art and the "female," is not, as some like to think, simply a difference of "style" in treating the same subject matter . . . but the very subject matter itself. The sex role system divides human experience; men and women live in these different halves of reality; and culture reflects this.

—Shulamith Firestone

One can hardly think of Doris Lessing without thinking of the issue of feminine art raised in these two statements. For no other novelist has explored so deeply or charted so fully the conflicts and paradoxes of feminine creativity in a male-defined and dominated culture. Indeed, Lessing's two major works epitomize the two conflicting tendencies or demands which women have had to confront and resolve or choose between in their art. On the one hand *The Golden Notebook,* with its innovative use of diary entries to project the reality of the heroine's subjective inner life, is a nearly pure expression of feminine consciousness, of the need to create a fictional world which honestly reflects the truths of feminine experience as they differ in substance and quality from the male. And on the other hand *Children of Violence,* modeled after the nineteenth-century epic novels which portrayed the life of a hero against a background of social and historical change, expresses the need to move beyond the limits of subjective feminine consciousness to a perspective which includes and speaks meaningfully to all of human knowledge and experience.

That a single author should, in a single decade, produce two such different works is itself indicative of the ambiguities and conflicts besetting every woman who takes seriously both her art and her feminity. For to create fiction is to be true to one's vision, one's senses, one's experiences; but to be a woman is to be given a very special set of experiences, and thus, a very special kind of vision. It has been the goal of Lessing's career to overcome this paradox, to write seriously about the world of empires and revolutions without denying or compromising her femininity; to incorporate the feminine perspective into the mainstream of literary tradition; to find a place for feminine power and creativity in a world which at best ignores and at worst forbids them.

In pursuing this goal Lessing has considered herself a "humanist" rather than "feminist" writer, in the tradition of the nineteenth-century novel which, for her, marks "the highest point of literature";[1] and it was only insofar as she found it impossible, as a woman in the twentieth-century, to preserve and contribute to that tradition that she turned, after completing three volumes of **Children of Violence,** to the more narrowly feminist and experimental **Golden Notebook,** in an effort, as she put it, "to express my sense of despair about writing a conventional novel."[2] In recognizing and exploring fictionally the roots of her failure, however, she seems to have arrived at a solution to her problem. For **The Four-Gated City,** the final and most important volume of **Children of Violence,** is in fact a synthesis of humanism and feminism, convention and experimentation, unlike anything previously written by a man or woman; and the seeds of its brilliance and originality lie in the very flaws which led Lessing temporarily to abandon the series.

To understand this, one need only read through **Children of Violence** and note the increasingly dramatic conflict between the range and scope of Lessing's political vision and the limitations of her female protagonist. For as Martha Quest moves further from the private world of childhood and adolescence into the public world of politics and society she seems to dwindle before our very eyes, becoming smaller and less significant with each succeeding volume as the forces of history grow larger, more complex and more menacing, until at last she is stripped of her autonomy, her powers of rational action, her very status as a heroine, proving once and for all that there can be no female heroes in a male world, at least not in the conventional sense of heroism.

Lessing triumphs over this conflict not by resolving it but by yielding to it, for it is just this traditional sense of individual heroism which she finally and ingeniously abandons in **The Four-Gated City,** but only after thoroughly exploring the implications of Martha's failure to be a heroine in an anti-novel about an anti-heroine. For if **Children of Violence** was to have been "a study of the individual conscience in its relations with the collective,"[3] a feminine contribution to the great tradition of nineteenth-century humanism, **The**

Golden Notebook is a nightmare version of the same theme, a self-mocking caricature of the individual conscience trapped within itself in which the very concept of "the collective" is either meaningless or terrifying. Anna Wulf, the antiheroine, is a former political activist and novelist now paralyzed by a sense of impotence and futility. Like her creator, she "suffers torments of dissatisfaction and incompletion" because she is "incapable of writing . . . a book powered with an intellectual or moral passion strong enough to create order, to create a new way of looking at life."[4] ("I'm tormented by the inadequacy of the imagination . . . the conflict between my life as a writer and the terrors of our time," said Lessing recently, but although "I feel the writer is obligated to dramatize the political conflicts of the time . . . I am unable to embody my political vision in a novel."[5]) Psychologically blocked, politically disillusioned, abandoned by her lover, Anna retreats into the privacy of the four personal diaries which symbolize her life, and the four walls which she covers with news clippings to symbolize the world outside herself as perceived and interpreted through an isolated feminine intelligence. She approaches the brink of madness but returns, in the end, to care for her child, take a job as a social worker and complete the novel she had abandoned when she began her notebooks.

The conflicts in the novel and in Anna's life are thus resolved, but the resolution is anticlimactic. For the fruits of Anna's (and Lessing's) heroic quest into the unexplored depths of feminine existence remain trapped in the privacy of the diaries, cannot be expressed in the public form of the novel. This ironic truth is at the heart of the structure of *The Golden Notebook* which is based on a constant interplay between the diary entries, which are the bulk of the text, and the novel-within-a-novel, ironically entitled "Free Women," which Anna finally produces out of the material of the diaries, and which serves as a structural framework enclosing and integrating the various notebook sections.

There are, then, two novels in *The Golden Notebook,* two models or images of reality, which remain separate and distinct. On the one hand the diaries, full of details and daydreams, chaotic patches of thought and feeling, shifting roles and relationships, great and small things thrown willy-nilly together, insights which connect to nothing, fantasies and rages which find no outlet or expression; and on the other hand "Free Women," the slight, shallow narrative of acts and events which progresses from beginning to end, from conflict to resolution, flattening and distorting all the rest into a predictably if superficially comforting pattern.

To those for whom *The Golden Notebook* has been an important personal and literary experience there can be no doubt of the significance of those disconnected bits and pieces of feminine existence which comprise Anna's diaries. But for Lessing, primarily committed to traditional fiction, the problem still remains: how to integrate the world of the diaries into that other world of the novel. *The Golden Notebook* failed to solve the problem because it was too much a statement of it. In focusing so intensely on the heroine's personal failures it revealed the complex web of psychological, cultural and historical forces which trap and isolate us, and the inadequacies of conventional fiction which necessarily falsifies and omits so much of life. But because it stopped there, because the richness of Anna's inner life was balanced by nothing in the public life she finally accepted or the public work she finally accomplished, it was an ultimately frustrating and even misleading work. Personal relationships, Lessing seemed to be saying, are indeed false and mutually destructive, yet one must get on with the painful job of raising children; meaningful work is indeed nonexistent, yet one must plod on hypocritically at some pointless or even harmful job; novels are indeed lies, yet one must trudge on with the impossible job of saying what cannot be said in a form which simplifies to a point of absurdity. Why must one? Why not go the more interesting routes of violence or madness, destroying the world or escaping from it into private fantasy?

The problem, thus posed, is a false one, for it assumes what Lessing has never assumed: the primacy of the individual life, of personal fulfillment and happiness. It is this implicit focus on personal problems and solutions which Lessing regrets, for she has no patience with modern writers who project themselves into the center of the universe, making of the artist, with his heightened self-awareness and sensibility, a contemporary hero. "Ever since I started writing I've wondered why the artist himself has become a mirror of society . . . (why) now almost every novelist writes about himself," she said in a recent interview. And of her own career: "Since writing *The Golden Notebook* I've become less personal. I've floated away from the personal."[6]

This process of "floating away from the personal" could describe the development of the entire *Children of Violence* series. But where, in the early volumes, the effect was negative, leaving a vacuum where the noble heroes and powerful deeds should have been, in the volumes written after *The Golden Notebook,* and particularly *The Four-Gated City,* the opposite is true. For in plunging so far into the personal mode Lessing discovered a way to get beyond it to the kind of collective social novel written by her nineteenth-century idols, without giving up the twentieth-century truths, revealed in *The Golden Notebook,* which rendered their particular forms obsolete.

And even more interesting, although less apparent, she has managed, in giving up the personal focus of *The Golden Notebook,* to preserve and even heighten the feminist consciousness which

158

so enriched and illuminated it. For although Martha Quest, by this fifth volume, is bereft of all personal ambition and autonomy and reduced to a mere appendage of the household of Mark Coldridge, in relation to whom she functions in the most traditionally feminine and subservient roles; if we take our cue from Lessing and "float away from the personal" to a more general, historical perspective, we find in Martha a startlingly original image of feminine heroism, which goes beyond the exceptional woman usually found in books dealing with history, whether fiction or non-fiction, to include all the women who have anonymously contributed to the progress and civilization of the race. For if women have not often been among the powerful and famous of history, the reason, as a recent study of feminine history points out, is that:

> the prevailing notion of what makes things historically noteworthy excludes women *by definition*. To put it another way, the things that have usually been considered to constitute feminity, and which women have pressed so hard to conform to, are precisely those things that remove women from the political arena. Although the image of feminity has changed significantly in some ways, in one dimension it has remained the same: what is feminine is almost antithetical to what is powerful. Yet history is made, after all, by the powerful. Since women have had neither political nor economic nor military power, obviously they did not make history and obviously they are not in history books.[7]

And yet, collectively, women have had an enormous, if indirect influence on history and have at the very least contributed their labors and services to making male enterprises possible. For this reason women have a right to ask, as they are beginning to, "Where were the women when this was going on?" This is precisely the question Lessing asks in **The Four-Gated City,** and the answers she gives are more than informative.

At the beginning of the novel, when Martha, newly arrived in London, drifts from street to street preserving her anonymity and rejecting the various limiting and defining roles offered her, she has the following thought:

> Iris, Joe's mother, had lived in this street since she was born. Put her brain together with the other million brains, women's brains, that recorded in such tiny loving detail the histories of windowsills, skins of paint, replaced curtains and salvaged baulks of timber, there would be a recording instrument, a sort of six-dimensional map which included the histories and lives and loves of people, London—a section map in depth. This is where London exists, in the minds of people who have lived in such and such a street since they were born, and passing a baulk of timber remember, smiling, how it came rolling up out of the Thames on that Thursday afternoon it was raining, to lie on a pavement until it became the spine of a stairway—and then the bomb fell.[8]

And the rest of the book, from the point when Martha drifts as if inevitably into the Coldridge household and takes a position which eventually includes the entire spectrum of feminine roles and responsibilities, is the working out of this idea. For Lessing takes the stuff of male history, the public world of deeds and events, and over a period of more than half a century filters them through the veil of feminine sensibility, producing a multi-dimensional vision, or perhaps revision, of history in which women emerge as collective heroines, molding, preserving and interpreting the forms of life which make history possible.

Lessing's technique in accomplishing this is particularly interesting and daring, for from the moment Martha enters the house she is almost entirely imprisoned within it. Years and decades go by as she fulfills her household duties, thickening and graying with age and inertia as the world goes by her heavily draped windows, venturing outside to see the sky, the water, the rapidly and ominously changing landscape of advanced technological society only on the rarest and most routinely feminine occasions: to shop, attend a party, consult a doctor. And yet all of the social and technological changes taking place outside are reflected in the life of the house, and experienced and interpreted by Martha as she copes with their concrete, often dramatic effects on the personal lives of those she cares for. In this way the major events and eras of the late twentieth-century are filtered through and reconstructed by a feminine awareness of the details, the trivia of day-to-day life. What did the fifties feel like to people? What was the quality of life as lived then? Martha tells us first with sensory details: the look and smell of rooms; the shabby ornateness of "good" restaurants; the timid tastefulness of "the black dress worn with pearls"; the sweet gummy "nursery puddings" called by French names; all of this is recorded. And as the fifties drift into the sixties and toward the seventies, the sweep of history is made concrete and vivid in the changing shapes, colors, and textures of clothing, food, hairstyles. Rosy cheeks disappear under masks of ghostlike pallor; plump, dowdy women become fashionably angular and wraithlike; thick sauces give way to delicate wines; pale cashmeres and dark tweeds, to startling silks and satins draped and gathered into desperate, half-mad mimicries of a romantically imagined past.

And it is not only the trivia of fashion and atmosphere which Martha captures and records. The Coldridge house also absorbs and reflects the political upheavals of the times. The fear and hysteria of the cold war are objectified in the grim pathos of an abandoned child's birthday party rather than the headline event of which it is a minor by-product: the defection of a famous, wellborn scientist, Colin Coldridge, to Soviet Russia. Throughout this traumatic period Martha remains inside the besieged house, playing the role of housekeeper and surrogate mother, guarding the kitchen door against voracious newsmen grabbing after any bits of privacy which may be deemed worthy of elevation to the public domain.

There is some truth in one reviewer's claim that the style of this novel:

> is like that of an unskilled letter writer who feels he has to report everything: this happened and then that; Lynda came home from the hospital but had to go back and we had a big party and that night Colin defected to Russia so Sally killed herself and then we spent hours and hours arguing about Communism.

But although "the only ordering principle," is, as she says, "chronological, and even chronology gets swamped in the helter-skelter rush of large and small events," this is not the result of Lessing's "failure to select and focus."[9] On the contrary, she has selected very carefully, for each small event and each minor detail foreshadow and forewarn of more general, often devastating ramifications. The small boy abandoned by his parents in the fifties becomes one of an army of young men and women whose attitudes and actions define and mold the sixties and seventies. One could, as Martha suggests, "do" the great peace marches of the sixties by "talking to people under twenty-one," and finding out "that there was no person there whose conception, babyhood, childhood or youth had not been 'disturbed',"[10] by the last war. Thus the seeds of massive change are discovered in seemingly insignificant events apparent only to those, like Martha, who attend to details, preparing meals, making up guest rooms, tending to those nondescript souls whose presence no one else seems to notice. In this way women emerge as the guardians and interpreters of the common life, the maintainers of its order, pattern and meaning; for it is women who provide the glue of compassion and continuity without which men could not function and children could not replace them.

In *Landlocked*, the previous volume of *Children of Violence*, Martha had a recurrent dream of a house:

> with half a dozen different rooms in it, and she, Martha, (the person who held things together, who watched, who must preserve wholeness through a time of dryness and disintegration) moved from one room to the next, on guard . . . her role in life, for this period, was to walk like a housekeeper in and out of rooms, but the people in the rooms could not meet each other or understand each other and Martha must not expect them to.[11]

And this image becomes the controlling metaphor for *The Four-Gated City* as the symbolic house of Martha's dreams is transformed into the reality of the Coldridge house with its many storeys, each the setting for a unique area of experience and activity; its many rooms, each enclosing the private life of a unique and separate person. Martha plays the multi-faceted archetypal female role women always play in the privacy of such houses: she holds things together when they threaten to disintegrate; keeps things apart when they threaten to destroy each other; adds to things which are inadequate or incomplete; absorbs or disposes of things which have become excessive. When the house becomes shabby she orders repairs; when Mark's work bogs down she contributes her knowledge and experience to his projects; when children are incompatible she arranges a vacation or change of school; when someone approaches violence or madness she holds on to them, sharing and absorbing some of their destructive energy.

The house thus becomes a microcosm of the larger society in which the polarization of sexes, generations, classes creates a perpetual state of tension and warfare within and between people. But the tension and warfare of family life produce different effects on different characters, and because these differences are determined to a great extent by sex, Martha, a woman as well as the custodian of the common life, relates to and participates in the world of female experience and activity somewhat differently from the male. This is not apparent or even true in the early sections of the novel, for although Martha fulfills a classically feminine role as Mark's secretary, she is occupied for the most part with his literary and political projects, and since she is clearly more experienced and sophisticated than he in both areas, he seems, to the reader if not himself, to be totally dependent upon her. But as time passes and the characters grow older, Martha shifts her interests and activities first to the world of the children, and then, as they grow up and leave home, to the woman's world of Mark's wife, Lynda, and her friends. And in the course of this process the profound differences between the conditions and experiences of adults and children, and more importantly, men and women, are gradually revealed. All are trapped; all are children of violence brought up and molded in an atmosphere of physical and psychic brutality and conflict; all have made more or less crippling adjustments, devised more or less successful strategies for survival; and all entertain fantasies of escape; but only the men have been able to transform their fantasies into concrete public projects for which they are rewarded. Mark's political concerns are translated first into novels, and later into an international network of rescue projects modeled after his lifelong fantasy of an early, idyllic England. Martha's friend Jack, who retreats into a private world of sexual preoccupation, transforms his self-indulgence into a thriving business, recruiting and training young women to act out his fantasies in dreamlike settings designed and built by him; and even the strangely one-dimensional scientist, Jimmy Wood, who seems to have no grasp on human reality, finds outlets for his madly dehumanized fantasies, first in the machines he invents, and later in the science fiction novels he creates. Politics, art, business, all are available to men, and as society loses its bearings and plunges toward self-annihilation, the general madness is reflected more and more in the madness, perversion and violence expressed and perpetrated by men of power and genius.

But for women, with rare exceptions, there is only the home, the finite set of walls, doors and windows in which they are caged. They too long for escape but for them the only free space is inner space, mental space, and for this reason many, like Lynda, who will not or cannot function as wives, mothers and housekeepers, retreat into a private world of dreams and fantasies and are labelled clinically insane. Most of the women in the book go through periods of insanity, suffer "breakdowns," are treated by psychiatrists; most of the men do not. And the reasons are connected with the very different roles and settings into which men and women are placed.[12] For women are not only locked into rooms and houses, deprived of publicly valued work and denied space in which to create and produce for their own satisfaction; they are also the receptacles of all the psychic and emotional tension which the male world creates but will not acknowledge or deal with. Thus the very concept of madness with all

its embarrassing paraphernalia: voices, visions, hysteria, delusion, is connected with and grows logically out of the feminine condition. Lynda, threatened by and therefore highly attuned to the unspoken tensions between her parents, and later between her father, his fiancée and herself, begins to hear their voices, to pick up their thoughts. And Martha herself, caring for the troubled, often fearful Coldridge children, similarly begins to pick up thoughts, receiving emotional vibrations from those around her. Going "up the stairs, through a house separated with the people who inhabited it, into areas or climates, each with its own feel, or sense of individuality," Martha thinks:

> what an extraordinary business it is, being a middle-aged person in a family; like being a kind of special instrument sensitised to mood and need and state. For, approaching Paul, one needed this degree of attention; approaching Francis, that one; and for Lynda and for Mark quite different switches or gauges set themselves going, but automatically.

And simultaneously, as she thinks this, she notes the fraying carpet, the poorly varnished banister, and reflecting on her many roles and responsibilities, she sees a connection between the physical condition of the house, its emotional climate, and, by extension, the climate of the entire society. She sees herself "a mass of fragments, or facets, or bits of mirror reflecting qualities embodied in other people," and standing in the central stairway, surrounded by the many closed rooms, she feels "no centre in the house, nothing to hold it together." It too is "a mass of small separate things, surfaces, shapes, all needing different attention. . . . This was the real truth of what went on not only here but everywhere: everything declined, and frayed and came to pieces in one's hand. . . ." And she, a woman, is the "deputy in the centre of the house, the person who runs things, keeps things going, conducts a holding operation, in a perpetual battle with details."[13]

One could say that Martha and Lynda, sharing a house, supporting and learning from each other, are both aspects of Anna Wulf, at once drawn to madness and driven by responsibility, forced to choose or alternate between internal and external reality, a private or a shared life. But in **The Four-Gated City** Lessing gets beyond the either/or aspect of the problem by placing the themes and images of the earlier work in a broader fictional framework, expanding the boundaries of space, time and even human perception so all become aspects and units of a continuous collective experience. Images of isolation and fragmentation—notebooks, diaries, newspaper clippings tacked on walls, lists, maps, bare rooms enclosing and isolating individual souls—all are as abundant and important in *The Four-Gated City* as *The Golden Notebook,* but they are less frightening, less confining because they are not metaphors for individual situations requiring individual, immediate solutions. Anna, for example, could only escape her self-imposed exile into an inner world of notebooks and clippings through a personal, sexual relationship which drew her outside herself and catalyzed her into writing the fifth, liberating "golden notebook" which synthesized and transcended the other four. But the key to Mark Coldridge's escape from *his* four private clipping-covered walls is less personal and more cosmic; instead of a fifth notebook he creates, with the help of the others in the house, a "fifth wall" covered with clippings and reports of apparently mysterious technological and administrative accidents which "represented Factor X; that absolutely obvious, out-in-the-open, there-for-everybody-to-see fact which nobody was seeing yet,"[14] and a symbol of a growing collective awareness of and effort to interpret and control the destructive patterns and forces of contemporary history before they reach their inevitable apocalyptic conclusion. And Mark's room, unlike Anna's, is only one of many such rooms kept by similarly minded people throughout the world and over the years, slowly evolving and changing to fit the changes in world affairs and the development of human insight.

There is, then, an ultimate sense of things fitting together here, given time and collective effort, both of which were noticeably lacking in *The Golden Notebook,* and this movement toward connection and integration is most fully symbolized in the images of houses which absorb and replace the isolated rooms of the earlier work. For although the Coldridge house and Martha's role within it replace Anna's single room as the metaphorical center of *The Four-Gated City,* neither it nor she are as essential to its structure. The house represents open rather than closed space, and when it crumbles and Martha herself dies, the process of holding together, of connection and expansion of relationships and experiences continues. For both Martha and the house embody impersonal, timeless qualities in people and the structures they build to contain their lives.

Martha, and indeed all the women in the novel, are thus part of a collective feminine identity which transcends individual personalities and time periods, as it progresses from room to room, from house to house, from generation to generation; and it is one of Martha's functions, as observer and interpreter of life, to notice and comment upon this fact. The hostility she feels toward Patty, for example, a Communist Party official with whom Mark has an affair during his "political phase," is resolved when Martha realizes in a dream that Patty represents one of her own former selves; and even her long-despised mother is acknowledged and integrated into Martha's self-image as she finds herself helplessly drawn into the maternal role of antagonist and enemy by Phoebe Coldridge's adolescent daughters. This sense of a common identity among increasingly numerous and diverse characters permeates the book so that at last there are no unique personalities, only personality traits common to many people in a particular historical and biological situation; and no personally generated thoughts, acts or creations, only collectively engendered and expressed ideas and projects. ("Now, when I start writing," says Lessing, "I ask, who is thinking the same thought? Where are the other people who are like me? I don't believe anymore that I have a thought. There is a thought around.")[15]

Roles and relationships shift and change as the characters move through their various phases and levels of experience and insight, and these shifting human relationships are analogous to the physical process of change, growth and evolution described by Rachel Carson in the passage which heads the first section of the book. Carson speaks of:

> a continuing change now actually in progress . . . brought about by the life processes of living things. . . . Under the bridge a green mangrove seedling floats, long and slender, one end already beginning to show the development of roots. . . . Over the years the mangroves bridge the water gaps between the islands; they extend the mainland; they create new islands. And the currents that stream under the bridge, carrying mangrove seedlings, are one with the currents that carry plankton to the coral animals building the offshore reef, creating a wall of rocklike solidity, a wall that one day may be added to the mainland.[16]

And in the same way Lessing's characters represent a process of evolving change taking place in human history which cannot be discovered through an individualistic perspective, but can only emerge from a perspective of detachment and distance from personal, immediate facts. Nor can the nature of this evolutionary process be understood in the context of traditional western thought (which is *de facto* male thought). For the revolutionary development Lessing prophesies (and she has called *The Four-Gated City* a "prophetic novel"), is more than merely physical, historical, technological; it is most profoundly a revolution in consciousness, in sensibility, and it is fitting that she should choose the metaphors and images to express it, first, from the scientific works of a woman whose poetically expressed theories have never been fully accepted by the orthodox scientific establishment; and second, from the literature of mysticism, a tradition even less respected and respectable, even more associated in the western mind with things feminine: that is to say, irrational, insignificant, romantic, poetic, queer. For the world of religious cults, of mysticism and astrology, is a feminine world peopled by the most outcast, lonely, alienated of women; by those whose mental desperation Anna Wulf recognized but didn't quite share; by women like Lynda who, left out of the serious traditions and projects of western society, form a subculture coming together in mental hospitals, at seances, at horoscope readings, to share the secret knowledge and intuition for which they are branded mad. This is the subculture into which Martha finally moves, learning from Lynda and her friends the deep symbolic truths and connecting links available to those who give up the privileges of sanity to believe in and follow their inner voices and visions.

Lessing sums up this startling philosophical turnabout, whereby the mad become sane and the sane suicidally mad, in the passage from the mystical tales of the Sufis which heads the final apocalyptic section of the novel:

> Sufis believe that, expressed in one way, humanity is evolving towards a certain destiny. We are all taking part in that evolution. Organs come into being as a result of a need for specific organs. The human being's organism is producing a new complex of organs in response to such a need. In this age of the transcending of time and space, the complex of organs is concerned with the transcending of time and space. What ordinary people regard as sporadic and occasional bursts of telepathic and prophetic power are seen by the Sufi as nothing less than the first stirrings of these same organs. The difference between all evolution up to date and the present need for evolution is that for the past ten thousand years or so we have been given the possibility of a conscious evolution. So essential is this more ratified evolution that our future depends on it.[17]

What is implied in this passage, and there is no mistake about it, is that western civilization as we have known it has been a half-crazed nightmare dreamed up by blind and one-eyed leaders and wise men who, having "rationally" and scientifically done away with most human values, are about to blow us all to smithereens unless we wake up and recognize our salvation in the rantings and ravings of the mad; of those despised, wretched, irrational souls who, having no investment in things as they are, can reject the conventions of "reality" and open themselves to a radically new consciousness. It is Lynda of course who symbolizes this new kind of savior, this prophet without honor, as she quite literally makes possible the survival of the human race by foreseeing, in one of her mad visions, the bleak and frozen English landscape in the aftermath of the technological holocaust destined to erupt in the civilized world; and convincing first Martha and then her son Francis in time to insure the escape and survival of colonies of human exiles.

At this point, as may be (perhaps alarmingly) apparent, the novel drifts off into what can only be described as science fiction. Lessing's interest in and incorporation of the themes and techniques of science fiction as a way of renewing the possibility of narrative fiction, of the creation of novels in which the human past, present and imagined future fit coherently and plausibly together, is a subject for another and probably longer essay. For now it is sufficient to say that Lessing has done this, that she has integrated the visions of Jimmy Wood, clinically sane and by worldly standards successful as a scientist and science fiction writer, but in a deeper sense quite deranged; and Lynda Coldridge, clinically mad and by worldly standards wholly incompetent, but in the deepest sense rational, insightful, endowed with visionary wisdom and knowledge; and merged them, producing a work as vast and sweeping as any of Tolstoy's or Stendhal's, in which the heroes are women, common women, madwomen, women doing what women have always done, and at last being named and credited for it.

Notes

1. "A small personal voice," *Declaration*, Tom Maschler (Ed.), (New York, 1958), 188.

2. Florence Howe, "Talk with Doris Lessing," *Nation,* 204 (March 6, 1967), 311.

3. "A small personal voice," 196.

4. *The Golden Notebook* (New York, 1962), 59.

5. Jonah Raskin, "Doris Lessing at Stony Brook: An interview," *New American Review,* 8 (January, 1970), 174.

6. Ibid., 173.

7. Linda Gordon, "Sexism in American Historiography" (Unpublished paper presented to the American Historical Association, December, 1971. Mimeographed), 31.

8. *The Four-Gated City* (New York, 1969), 10.

9. Elizabeth Dalton, Review of *The Four-Gated City, Commentary,* 44 (January, 1970), 86.

10. *The Four-Gated City,* 395.

11. *Landlocked* (New York, 1965), 15.

12. Lessing's most recent novel, *Briefing for a Descent into Hell* (New York, 1970), does in fact portray a male protagonist in the role of visionary madman, but this simply emphasizes Lessing's primary commitment to a "humanist" rather than "feminist" point of view, her determination to give universal meaning to her insights (many of which, as *The Four-Gated City* makes clear, grew out of her experiences as a woman) into the nature of contemporary madness. She succeeds at the expense of all sexual and cultural implication, however, creating, I think, a far weaker, less compelling work than any of her earlier ones.

13. *The Four-Gated City,* 335-337.

14. Ibid., 414.

15. Raskin, 173.

16. *The Four-Gated City,* 2.

17. Ibid., 426.

AGATE NESAULE KROUSE (ESSAY DATE NOVEMBER 1976)

SOURCE: Krouse, Agate Nesaule. "Doris Lessing's Feminist Plays." *World Literature Written in English* 15, no. 2 (November 1976): 305-22.

In the following essay, Krouse asserts that Lessing's plays Each His Own Wilderness *and* Play with a Tiger *are "essential to understanding precisely the feminism of Doris Lessing."*

I

Critics of Doris Lessing's work have concentrated primarily on her fiction. Her novels, especially *The Golden Notebook* and the *Children of Violence* series, have received careful attention. Her numerous short stories have been discussed less frequently.[1] Even in the absence of a vast body of critical material explicating every aspect of her fiction, however, it is nevertheless widely read, taught, and discussed. With a few minor exceptions, all of Lessing's fiction is easily available in the United States.[2]

Her plays, however, remain unknown to many admirers of her work, largely because of realities of publication. Two have been discussed only briefly by specialists in contemporary theater, but have never been published and probably will not be since Lessing considers them "dead ducks" and "dated."[3] *Each His Own Wilderness* and *Play with a Tiger,* however, were published in England about the time of their first performances.[4] While first editions may be difficult to obtain, both plays are currently available in paperback anthologies.[5]

Each His Own Wilderness and *Play with a Tiger* have important parallels to Lessing's fiction, even as they underline her versatility. Both are essential to understanding precisely the feminism of Doris Lessing, who has expressed disappointment that her work has been considered in the context of Women's Liberation.[6] Both raise significant feminist issues, but differ markedly in their ways of doing so. While *Play with a Tiger* is occasionally strident and narrow, it can enlarge our appreciation of Lessing's other work, particularly *The Golden Notebook. Each His Own Wilderness,* on the other hand, presents a radical and convincing view of the oppression and liberation of women. It is, in fact, Lessing's *A Doll's House.* Both plays are interesting examples of literary feminism, and they also speak powerfully to Lessing's common reader, ". . . the Marthas of this world [who] read and search with the craving thought, What does this say about my life?"[7]

II

Play with a Tiger, first produced in 1962, shows one evening in the life of Anna Freeman, an Australian-born widowed writer living in London. In the course of the play, she breaks off her engagement to Tom Lattimer, who is on the point of conforming to middle class values; she talks to Harry, a friend strikingly similar to other philanderers created by Lessing such as Graham Spence in "One Off the Short List" and Richard Portmain in *The Golden Notebook;* she receives a visit from Janet Stevens, a naive young American woman, pregnant by Dave Miller; she talks intensely and intimately with Dave himself, a rootless American, and she recognizes that although she loves him and although they both understand each other and contemporary society, Dave is nevertheless walking out of her life and into marriage with Janet Stevens.

Play with a Tiger has a direct relationship to the Anna/Saul sections of *The Golden Notebook.* Anna Freeman, the name of the protagonist in the play, is also the "maiden" name of Anna Wulf, the protagonist in the novel. Dave and Saul, political and disillusioned Americans, have similarities too numerous to list, including a driving indiscriminate sexuality they discuss in slightly off-key American slang. In both works, Anna describes a dream about a tiger in almost identical terms.[8] Lessing herself has explicitly indicated the closeness of the play and the novel. After Anna in *The Golden Notebook* has the dream about the tiger, she thinks to herself, "I must write a play about Anna and Saul and the tiger."[9] And so we have a play by Doris Lessing about Anna and Dave and the tiger. Although Lessing has been justifiably annoyed by commentators who have regarded *The Golden Notebook* as primarily autobiographical, the very existence of *Play with a Tiger* suggests an especially close relationship between the sensibilities of author and character in the novel.

Play with a Tiger develops some of the same themes and situations as *The Golden Notebook*, though more simply and briefly because of dramatic requirements. One of the major themes in *The Golden Notebook* is that modern experience is chaotic, fragmentary and painful, yet acceptance of this truth can lead to new strength and creativity. The dialogue and staging of *Play with a Tiger* stress the value and necessity of openness to all kinds of experience. Dave insists that Anna leave the window open, that she not shut herself up against anything, no matter how painful or squalid.[10] Although deeply disappointed in himself, Dave isolates the value of living the way he and Anna have: they have always been ready for "anything new in the world anywhere, any new thought, or new way of living, . . . ready to hear the first whisper of it" (II.60-61). The unrealistic staging also emphasizes their openness; it underlines that they are very much part of the world that surrounds them rather than protected by slogans or self-created isolation. "The lights are out. The walls seem to have vanished, so that the room seems part of the street" (II.37).

The central symbol in the play, the tiger, stresses the power of imagination and the value of openness to experience as well. Both Dave and Anna despair because of their inability to imagine something better than themselves "to grow into" (II.61). Only once has Anna had a vision of something other than herself, an "enormous, glossy padding tiger" who "purred so loud that the sound drowned the noise of the traffic" (II.61-62). The tiger lashed out at Anna, so that she was covered with blood," . . . he stared and he glared, and then he was off. . . . Then I heard the keepers shouting after him and wheeling along a great cage. . . . That was the best I could do. I tried hard, but that was the best—a tiger. And I'm covered with scars" (II.62).

The tiger of Anna's imagination has some obvious literary parallels: as a representative of awesome power he is reminiscent of the tiger in Blake's poem; as a portent of a terrifying future, he is similar to the "vast image out of *Spiritus Mundi*," the "shape with lion body and the head

of a man" of "The Second Coming." He represents both the power and the limitations of the human imagination. On the one hand, he is beautiful and powerful and he purrs loud enough to drown out the traffic; he represents an escape from the ugliness and loneliness of everyday existence, not by excluding all experience but by admitting it on a different level of one's mind. On the other hand, he is vicious without provocation: in *The Golden Notebook*, the scars he gives in the dream are impermanent since Anna sees her arm is either not hurt at all or has already healed; in *Play with a Tiger*, however, Anna is "covered with scars" from her encounter with him. The tiger is also only momentarily free and wild before the keepers shut him in a cage. He is really no improvement over the human race: he is neither morally better nor existentially freer. He differs from "the golden spotted beast" who appears "as if . . . in a country where hostility or dislike had not yet been born" in Lessing's *Briefing for a Descent into Hell*.[11] The tiger is, finally, a symbol of the male, who maims and hurts, but whose beauty and momentary freedom are desirable nevertheless. Even more specifically, he is Dave Miller.

Considered as a companion piece to *The Golden Notebook*, *Play with a Tiger* underlines the richness of the novel. *The Golden Notebook* is an important treatment of the experience of modern women largely because it fully and specifically deals not only with their personal, but also their political, intellectual, and artistic commitments and problems. Necessarily narrower in scope, *Play with a Tiger* concentrates on the personal instead. Furthermore, *Play with a Tiger* indirectly underscores how crucial is Anna's and Saul's mutual descent into madness in *The Golden Notebook*, how the crackup restores sanity and creativity. Lessing has written that, ". . . nobody so much as noticed this central theme, because the book was instantly belittled . . . as being about the sex war, or was claimed by women as a useful weapon in the sex war."[12] *Play with a Tiger*, however, *is* about the sex war, and it dramatizes fully the blows struck in it.

But the sex war as presented by Lessing in *Play with a Tiger* is not entirely convincing, partly because dramatic form demands simplicity and partly because she relies excessively on stereotypes she uses with greater tact elsewhere. The monogamous female, the victim of male faithlessness or unfairness, appears in much that Lessing has written. So does the philandering male. He knows he causes women pain, but he refuses to change. He is usually dishonest, unfaithful, hypocritical, sentimental, unjust, or even all of these things. Contrasted to the women in the same work, he is a rat.[13] While the view that women are morally better than men has been held by some feminists, it does violence to individuals, it is the basis of the double standard, and it can also limit the power of literature.

In *Play with a Tiger,* as in much of Lessing's work, marriage and other arrangements with men hold disadvantages for women. A repeatedly made, bitter criticism of female-male relationships here is that men successfully use clichés about women to evade their human responsibilities. Although his wife is "cracking up" as a result of his current affair, Harry has the "much used formula" that she likes weak men, that he can't help himself, and that she doesn't really mind his affair (I.19-20). Dave Miller, in spite of his contempt for slogans, holds the trite but comfortable belief that women are tougher than men (III.69-70) and that they don't need to take men seriously if they have children (III.70).

There are no exceptions to the rule that men are unfair to women in their behavior and assumptions. In this way *Play with a Tiger* differs from *Each His Own Wilderness* where at least one male character, Mike, is a good human being. Anna accuses both Tom and Dave of an unfairness similar to Harry's, and there is no evidence she is wrong. Tom has made callous use of women [sexually] (I.23). Anna predicts that Dave when married will behave exactly like Harry: when his wife turns into a boring housewife with no choice but to stay married, he will have a succession of affairs, confess them to his wife, and even use her forgiveness as an added attraction to other women (I.20-21). Dave dishonestly uses one woman to keep free of others. Like the other men he expects his infidelity to be accepted as a matter of course. He aggressively asserts his independence: he is not going to be "any woman's pet" and he is not going to live "according to the rules laid down by the incorporated mothers of the universe" (I.32-33). He also cheerfully accepts the fact women have to suffer: he tells Anna mockingly, "Women always have to pay—and may it long remain that way" (I.35).

Faced with dishonesty and philandering—two characteristics all males in the play possess—a woman just can't win. Marriage, by its very nature, makes women dull, which in turn causes male unfaithfulness and the end of meaningful choice for women. It does not matter what kind of individual a woman is—she is likely to suffer at the hands of men. The philandering males cause pain to their housewifely wives, but they are even more destructive to women who have independence, intelligence, and integrity. Bored by stupid and dull women, they nevertheless are also unfaithful to women who could understand them and with whom they could have real intimacy. Janet Stevens, the pregnant young American woman who is so severely limited in insight she can only talk in awkward slogans, rather than Anna, gets Dave. Janet's values are much inferior to Anna's, who passionately wants an honest relationship with a man, and if she cannot have that, would rather be alone than compromise and accept the kind of self-deception and bitterness her parents had. Janet's values are also different from and inferior to the values of openness and sensitivity held by Dave and explicitly endorsed by the play as a whole.

The bitterest irony is that although men may verbally subscribe to advanced ideas about women, they nevertheless choose the limited and stupid ones. Dave recognizes Janet's limitations perfectly, and he has also repeatedly lectured to Anna that women should be independent; yet he concedes that "some of the time" he can't take women who live without "dishonest female ruses" (III.78-79). Anna is bitterly aware that although she and Dave share the same ethical concerns, he will choose Janet. Women, on the other hand, have more integrity in making their choices. As Anna remarks early in the play, "Perhaps she [Mary] prefers to be sex-starved than to [sic] marry an idiot. Which is more than can be said about most men" (I.23). Anna herself does not get what she wants: "Any man I have stays with me, voluntarily, because he wants to, without ties" (II.48). She suffers, but she does retain her integrity.

Dave, however, in spite of his bitter and convincing understanding of the shortcomings of conventional life generally and Janet specifically, does the most conventional of things: he does right by the girl he has gotten pregnant. While one could expect predictable reactions from Tom and Harry (i.e., every Tom, Dick, and Harry) Dave is clearly meant to be exceptional. All the values of this play and all of Dave's angry insights are violated by his decision to marry Janet. Furthermore, this decision makes *Play with a Tiger* extremely one-sided. In it, males use clichés or accept stereotypes about women when it is to their advantage to do so, even though their preconceptions are clearly wrong. On the other hand, although women, too, believe a number of trite things about men, these beliefs do not wound men, in spite of the fact that the structure of the play establishes that the female views are an accurate way of seeing reality.

Lessing's excessive reliance on the stereotype of men as dishonest and faithless makes the play disunified and limited. The first and simplest problem is the discrepancy in Dave's characterization, which is related to the question of how one is to regard the thematic values endorsed in the play. Dave's decision to marry Janet is unbelievable on a realistic level. He has slept with women and left them before. He has not reflected, as Anna insists that he should, what happens to those women and what his responsibility is. He has been unquestionably courageous politically. He is aware of the meaninglessness of conventional life and of marriage to a stupid woman. Such a man, realistically, would not suddenly marry a silly young pregnant woman from Philadelphia just because she happens to cry on the phone—especially since he has not had other powerful forces of society marshalled against him. No rich daddy has appeared with threats or bribes, no dispassionate advocate has convinced him that responsibility to an individual woman is part of responsibility to the whole human race or that his failure to do his duty would make his statements about society hypocritical. His abrupt decision is totally unmotivated.

That in itself would not matter so much, if it did not raise a more serious problem. Are we to regard Dave as a hypocrite, a label that fits perfectly the other two men who behave like him? That implied answer provides an easy way out of the discrepancy in characterization, yet it does not work. Dave so obviously means it when he says society stinks and that he doesn't want to be part of it. He has not been spouting advanced social ideas while secretly longing for the safety of marriage. But how seriously can one take his ideas, or his tormented longing for personal goodness, if the only real decision he has to make shows that he behaves according to the fact that he is male—in Lessing's definition here—rather than human? In other words, she has developed a character who is interesting from an aesthetic, philosophical, and sociological point of view, but the resolution of the play either oversimplifies him or undercuts the concepts he represents. It also trivializes the symbol of the tiger. Dave, like the tiger, is caught, and like him he is responsible for Anna's being covered with scars. But one would hope to see the keepers of the cage. The resolution of the play suggests that they are nothing more than a young woman from Philadelphia.

Lessing herself has sensed the one-sidedness of the play, but has blamed it on mistaken casting and unfair cutting of lines. In a postscript written in 1972, she has noted that "some Women's Liberation groups" have cast Dave "as a fool, a stud, or a nothing man, making it 'a woman's play' . . . a self-righteous aria for the female voice."[14] She goes on to observe that unless Dave is "cast and acted so that he has every bit as much weight as Anna, then the play goes to pieces."[15] But even without indiscriminate cutting, the resolution of the play makes its vision of female-male relationships one-sided.

Other problems in the play can also be seen by reference to the stereotype of the dishonest philandering male. A recurring theme is that the conventional beliefs of society are ridiculous and narrow. Both Anna and Dave are satiric toward them. And yet, Anna holds a highly traditional view of male sexuality and is shown to be right in holding it. The belief that men need more sexual outlets than one woman is not so different from the belief that society needs stable marriages. Both of these views are the basis of the double standard. But the men in the play, somewhat boringly, enact a cliché. Anna's and Lessing's irony does not extend to an examination of *all* assumptions of society. Instead, the irony is directed only against male beliefs and behavior. It is not all-encompassing.

The play is also narrow in its human sympathies. It is Anna's play: what hurts her is treated seriously, while parallel situations are dismissed, forgotten, or handled satirically. For example, Anna's suffering is real and terrible when she loses Dave. On the other hand, Tom Lattimer, who loves her and whom she rejects, is shown to be pompous, hypocritical, and cruel. That he could suffer equally as a victim of the sex war is not a consideration. In the same way, Harry's actions are shown to cause his wife pain, but his own anguish about the marriage of his mistress is not treated seriously. He dramatizes his problems, and he selfishly demands sympathy and sexual satisfaction. Unlike Anna, he is not covered with scars and never will be.

The most interesting case of a character whose suffering is not taken seriously and whose situation is not related to a thematic motif is Janet Stevens. Pregnant, young, desperate, and uninteresting, she is about to marry Dave. She is clearly getting no prize. While she is not likely to suffer as intensely as Anna, she will suffer long, consistently, and fully according to her capacity. Harry's wife, mentioned early in the play, probably foreshadows Janet's future. Dave will not be responsible for turning Janet into "just another boring housewife"—she already is that—but he is likely to be a terrible husband. Yet this connection is never made. Anna is sorry that it's not her baby and she sarcastically says that she wasn't as intelligent as Janet. But Janet is so stupid as to be almost a comic figure. The sympathy for all women as victims, which would follow logically from the assumption of male unfairness, is forgotten. Anna only, not Janet, is to be regarded as an object of sympathy. The kind of elementary sisterhood, so well treated by Lessing elsewhere, is not developed. Men are harder on intelligent women, but at least the housewifely women get the men. And, the play implies, that is a victory of sorts rather than the victimization that other motifs would lead one to expect. Anna keeps her integrity and suffers. She is superior to other women and all the men, but it is hard to accept her as an ideal in feelings or insights. She just happens to be right about female-male relationships because of abrupt elements in the plot and in spite of the fact that her view does not include all the complex situations touched on in the play.

And yet, *Play with a Tiger* cannot and should not be dismissed because of its flaws. Its value lies not only in its relationship to *The Golden Notebook,* but also in its anger. Lessing dramatizes the problems, not the victories of an intelligent and independent woman, and it is as unfair to expect calm impartiality from a play produced in 1962 as it is today. Certainly, a generation that elevated the idiosyncratic Jimmy Porter of *Look Back in Anger* into a profound critic of society, needs to consider Anna Freeman as seriously.[16] Probably more so.

III

Each His Own Wilderness has been warmly though not widely praised. T. C. Worsley called it "the most exciting new play to turn up in London since *Look Back in Anger,*" and discussed its relationship to the Angry Young Men.[17] "Tony is yet another specimen of the furiously articulate young men of today. And a very brilliant specimen Miss Lessing has made him. For the first time, too, since the specimen was exhibited to us, we get some understanding of what has caused the fury" (p. 405). According to Worsley, the cause of the young man's fury and the major theme of the play is "do-gooding." Myra, his mother, has sold the house he loves. "All she meant, poor woman, was to do him good; all she did was to destroy his world."[18]

However, Worsley himself is a bit uneasy with his analysis of the theme of *Each His Own Wilderness,* although he attributes the fault to Lessing. "I think Miss Lessing's play would have been clearer if she had got on to this theme earlier, 'prepared' it a little more thoroughly and brought it more into the centre. As it is, the play suffers slightly from a plethora of events and people, which there is not time or space to develop."[19]

George Wellwarth also discusses *Each His Own Wilderness* in the context of the Angry Young Men. He finds Lessing "more objective and realistic than Osborne," and praises her for creating a hero far more typical than Osborne's.[20] Like Worsley, he sees Tony as the protagonist and the most interesting character: Tony is "the real representative of the younger generation . . . the anti-angry young man—the angry young cocoon. . . . His only anger is directed against those who would draw him out of his cocoon of safe conventionality" (pp. 289-90).

Because both critics were concerned with the concept of the Angry Young Men and with showing that Doris Lessing is a better man than many, they assumed that Tony was the main character and missed a way of seeing the play that is equally or even more valid. Instead of Tony, Myra Bolton is the protagonist. Her appearances are certainly more flamboyant and more "dramatic" than Tony's. Lessing has also listed her first in the "Characters of the Play," even though Tony is the first to appear on the stage. More importantly, all other characters have a direct relationship to Myra, but only indirectly to Tony. Worsley's difficulty with the "plethora of events and people" obscuring the theme disappears if one accepts Myra as the protagonist rather than only a cause for Tony's fury. In addition, Myra has roughly the same number of lines and scenes as Tony. The final, forceful long speech is Myra's, and the values espoused in it are not undercut by irony or humor.

Each His Own Wilderness presents about twenty-four hours in the life of Myra Bolton. During this time, her son Tony returns from the army to find Myra busy with anti-war activities. Sandy, the son of Myra's close friend Milly, is living with Myra and helping with her political activities. Philip, the man whom Myra has loved, brings his young fiancée Rosemary to stay with Myra so he can get out of marrying her. Milly, Myra's friend, returns from a women's delegation to China. Myra finds it difficult to get along with Tony, but she is sure she has been right in selling the house they live in so that Tony can have money to be free. Various complications develop. Myra breaks off her affair with Milly's son, Sandy; she promises to marry her old friend Mike, but changes her mind; she breaks off her long friendship with Philip. Meanwhile, Milly has slept with Myra's son Tony, and the relationship between Philip and his fiancée Rosemary has broken up. At the end of the play, Myra finally tells Tony she has sold the house, only to discover the house is the only thing Tony has wanted and that he finds her disgusting. She leaves Tony and Rosemary to comfort each other and sets off for a new life.

If we consider Myra Bolton as the protagonist, *Each His Own Wilderness* becomes a contemporary *A Doll's House:* a play about the oppression and liberation of women. As such, it is much more interesting and radical than Clare Booth Luce's conscious attempt to update Ibsen in *A Doll's House, 1970.* Lessing's play, too, has some obvious parallels to Ibsen's, which does not mean, however, that Lessing necessarily had Ibsen in mind. Both plays are written in a realistic style, both employ a central metaphor of a house which represents the heroine's illusions about her relationship to others, both show the loss of those illusions, and both end by the heroine leaving her house and her previous life in order to find a new, more honest existence. In order to be a valuable human being capable of bringing up children, Nora in *A Doll's House* left her husband and the confining hypocrisies of marriage. *Each His Own Wilderness* exposes some similar hypocrisies in affairs rather than marriage. However, it goes a great deal further than Ibsen's play: it examines and rejects the final tyranny over modern women—the tyranny of the children they have brought up by themselves in the modern, post-stable-marriage era. Instead of leaving her husband as Nora did, Myra leaves her son Tony.

In this play, as in several other works by Lessing, there are paired complementary characters who function to suggest that the experiences presented have a wide rather than only unique significance and who make the thesis of the work convincing. Myra's son Tony and her ex-lover's fiancée Rosemary are paired: they are similar in appearance and opinions; they are the grown children whose values are rejected in the play. Myra, too, has a complementary character: her friend Milly. The two women have been friends for years, have lived without the protection and comfort of husbands, and have sons whom they have brought up by themselves but who have not turned out the way they have wished. The two women understand each other perfectly. The presence of Milly shows that Myra's experiences are

not unique; at the same time, it helps to establish the validity of Myra's rebellion.

Both Myra and Milly are free in a sense Nora never envisioned. They have chosen to live without the respectability and hypocrisy of marriage, and they are prepared to accept the consequences. Freedom here as elsewhere in Lessing's work is not treated sentimentally. It involves plenty of suffering and injustice. Most strikingly, Myra and Milly are free sexually to a point that would shock Nora and her contemporaries. Not only do they discuss affairs with men of their own generation, but each of them also has a sexual involvement with the other's son. Since the two women are almost like sisters, these sexual encounters with each other's children may seem vaguely incestuous. However, probably the prejudice that there is something predatory and unnatural about a woman sleeping with a considerably younger man (but not about a man sleeping with a younger woman) is partially responsible for seeing both Myra and Milly as liberated sexually.

As an implicitly feminist work, *Each His Own Wilderness* develops two major ideas. In dealing with the relationships of women and men, the play demonstrates that men are often shockingly dishonest to women, while women understand and regard these dishonesties with irony. In this respect, as well as some others, women are better than men. The second idea, which is both more original and more modern, is that children interfere with women's freedom and integrity. Since both Myra and Milly are mothers of sons, the two types of relationships examined—that is, between women and men, and women and children—are closely related.

The dishonesty of men towards women is so obvious and prevalent in the play that only a few examples will suffice. Philip has been and still is dishonest to Myra. In the past, he has put her into such a position that she has had to break off with him while he ironically has maintained the sentimental fiction he was the rejected one. He proposes and pretends to be rejected in the course of the play as well. He has also used his wife and uses Myra to protect himself from marriage. Philip's behavior is ironically mirrored by Milly's son, Sandy. When Myra tells him she is finished with him, he says he is sure *he* has done the right thing in breaking off the affair.

Even when not trying to get rid of women, men are dishonest. Milly details the hypocritical and obtuse concern for appearances which has caused her to walk out on the man she was about to marry (II.i.133-34). Myra recognizes Milly's experience as something that might have happened to herself, as a pattern that is perfectly normal in male behavior. In this scene, as elsewhere in the play, the agreement and understanding of the paired complementary characters help to establish an individual experience as common or universal. Dishonesty is almost a condition of being male in the world of the play.

Women are far more honest than men. Both Milly and Myra choose integrity rather than love. Women are also better than men in other ways. While Myra is often careless and tactless, she is also generous, warm, kind, and sympathetic. She is never vindictive, jealous, or petty. Without Myra's impulsiveness, Milly is perhaps an even better person. Both women also differ from almost all the male characters by their unselfish concern for humankind. They unquestioningly sacrifice time and personal safety for political causes, and they expect no personal recognition. They are clearly not radicals with ego problems, nor are they naively unaware of past horrors and present injustices, yet they continue political action.

The dishonesty and selfishness of men as contrasted to women is closely related to a second and more important theme, the exposure and rejection of the tyranny of children. Both mothers are disappointed in their sons, in part because they are from a generation which refuses unselfish political involvement. In this lack of social conscience, Rosemary (the young fiancée of Myra's ex-lover Philip) shares as well, which helps to establish the thesis that such selfishness is typical of the younger generation.

It is interesting, however, that the children of Myra and Milly are sons rather than daughters. That fact unifies the two themes. The sons are as dishonest and unfair as other men to their mothers. This common male dishonesty is all the more striking since the two sons are completely different from each other. Ambitious, aggressive, and opportunistic, Sandy holds his mother accountable for his less admirable traits and uses her to impress his posh friends. Apathetic, insecure, and self-pitying, Tony does not analyze his dislike of his mother's messiness, political activism, and sociability.

In several of Tony's objections to Myra a strong undercurrent of sexual jealousy can be discerned: he is bitterly ironic about Philip and the other "uncles" he has had; he is angry Sandy is staying in his room; he is sickened by sexual activity which includes his mother. That some of

Tony's objections are based on a female-male conflict is underlined in two ways. There is a strong ironic parallel between Tony's and Philip's objections to Myra's openness to people. Even similar language is used by both to state their objections. Second, Tony does not like women anyway. Like drinking and smoking, they bore him (I.i.101). He tells Milly, "I simply don't like women" (II.ii.149). Furthermore, Tony frequently lumps Myra and Milly together as a particular type of woman he can't stand: the "dilettante daughters of the revolution" (I.i.101) and "women who haven't succeeded in getting or staying married" (I.i.105). He feels overpowered by them: "It's their utterly appalling vitality. They exhaust me" (I.i.107).

Myra is also occasionally antagonistic to Tony because he is male and once includes him in a blanket condemnation of all men (I.ii.115). But she has a score of more emphatic objections to Tony. She is disappointed the young are leaving political action to her generation. She is irritated by his snobbishness, neatness, and lack of humor. She is hurt by his unkindness. She cannot accept his values of quiet and security. She is puzzled by his failure to live as she considers normal: she feels a young man should want to be free and rebel against parents rather than docilely stay with them.

The play raises the most basic question about the relationship of mothers and children. Myra asks this question explicitly: "Aren't our children our fault?" (II.ii.135). Several answers are suggested. Milly tells Myra she should consider the basic integrity of their whole lives before making harsh judgements, that the way their children have turned out cannot be viewed in isolation: ". . . we've neither of us given in to anything. . . . What's the use of living the way we have, what's the use of us never settling for any of the little cosy corners or the little cages or the second-rate men if we simply get tired now?" (II.ii.135). In other words, their lives have included far more than motherhood.

Another answer is also implied by Milly: "We've committed the basic and unforgivable crime of giving you birth—but we had no choice, after all . . ." (II.ii.150). A third answer is also implied when Milly sarcastically accepts responsibility for Sandy's tactless actions: "Of course, it's my fault. I'm your mother—that's what I'm for" (II.ii.157). Indirectly the whole question of responsibility is briefly reduced to absurdity. If children so clearly refuse responsibility for their actions, the facile assigning of blame to mothers is fallacious as well.

But the most emphatic answer to the question of responsibility is provided by the structure of the play: the complementary characters of the mothers and the obvious contrasts but basic similarities between the two sons. Taken together, these clearly establish that there is no causal relationship between the characters of mothers and children and that the whole question of responsibility is irrelevant. Unselfish Milly and Myra have almost identical values which have not carried over to their sons. Sandy and Tony are selfish opposites of their mothers. Myra sums up the differences perfectly: "My God, the irony of it— that *we* should have given birth to a generation of little office boys and clerks and . . . little people who count their pensions before they're out of school . . . little petty bourgeois" (II.ii.166).

The resolution of the conflict between Myra and Tony also answers the question of responsibility. Myra's attitudes are diametrically opposed to Tony's, but they are also the attitudes endorsed by the play. Myra's final speech, neither answered nor balanced by Tony's, reaffirms her values as the values of the play. It proposes a woman's individual freedom is the highest good and that this freedom surpasses the responsibility toward children which is a problematical value anyway. After Myra tells Tony she has sold the house and he has said he can't stand her, she announces she is leaving. In a powerful and vivid scene too long to quote here, Myra announces she is free for the first time in twenty-two years: previously her life has been governed by Tony's needs. She tentatively accepts the possibility a mother may be defined by her success in bringing up a child, but she asserts such a failure does not need to encompass her life and it need not control her forever. She may have failed with Tony since neither in her own nor society's terms is he a tangible justification for the way she has lived. However, she is still alive and ready for varied and meaningful experience. Her speech is basically an affirmation of life in opposition to the rigid, limiting, and sterile notions of responsibility, respectability, and dignity. It is also a rejection of the sentimental and cruel notion that a woman's whole life has to be or can be defined through her children.

Myra's values are clearly the values of the play. In fairness to her characters, Lessing has included earlier a long speech by Tony in which he explains the horror he felt when his father was killed and he and his mother were buried under rubble dur-ing a bombing attack. In this speech, the reasons for Tony's wish for quiet and security are made clear. Significantly, he has been molded more by large impersonal forces such as war than by his mother's influence. However, while we may understand Tony, judged by an absolute standard, his values are childish. Compared to Myra, who has also experienced the horrors of war, Tony seems petulant, self-pitying, and childish. While Lessing has made him quite understandable, she has not made him admirable.

Finally, Myra's values are shown to be valid by the structure of the play itself. Myra's speech is neither answered nor negated by Tony, yet that speech condemns everything he is or wants. After Myra has left, the triviality, uncertainty, and pathos of Tony and Rosemary contrast with Myra's strength and courage:

> TONY: Rosemary, do you know that not one word of what she said made any sense to me at all . . . slogans, slogans, slogans. . . .
> ROSEMARY: What's the matter with being safe—and ordinary? What's wrong with being ordinary—and safe?
> TONY: Rosemary, listen—never in the whole history of the world have people made a battlecry out of being ordinary. Never. Supposing we all said to the politicians—we refuse to be heroic. We refuse to be brave. We are bored with all the noble gestures—what then, Rosemary?
> ROSEMARY: Yes, Ordinary and safe.
> TONY: Leave us alone, we'll say. Leave us alone to live. Just leave us alone . . .
>
> (II.ii.166-67).

Tony's insistence that Myra has been speaking in senseless slogans is undercut. Her speech makes sense to the reader, so that Tony's assertion constitutes dramatic irony. Her similes are homely and far removed from the style of political slogans, but they judge Tony and Rosemary nevertheless (e.g., "I don't propose to keep my life clutched in my hand like small change," and "I don't have to shelter under a heap of old bricks—like a frightened mouse," II.ii.166). Furthermore, while Myra's speech is positive, Tony and Rosemary can only question and repeat. And the answers to their questions have been developed previously. Throughout the play it is made abundantly clear that it is impossible for human beings to be "ordinary and safe": wars come, love affairs end, people hurt each other. A play which opens with the sounds of an H-bomb explosion and machine-gun fire on a tape recorder and in which the second act starts with Tony "making machine-gun noises like a small boy" (p. 127) does not allow the reader or viewer to see Tony's wish to be left "alone to live" as a viable alternative. Likewise, the references to political horrors show Tony's wistful supposition about telling the politicians how they feel to be painfully naive.

Thus, **Each His Own Wilderness** as a whole endorses Myra's values and her wish for freedom. It exposes the unjustifiable demands of children. It suggests, though does not absolutely insist on, the superiority of women by showing men—with the exception of Mike—as basically dishonest and unfair. It questions several clichés about women: in this play women are not selfishly concerned with their families while the minds of men are on more significant issues; they are not defined as creatures whose primary duty is to their children; they are not useless, troublesome, possessive, and pathetic once their child-raising years are over. **Each His Own Wilderness** insists on the right of women to live as they wish. Their freedom is an individual necessity, but also a hope for mankind. Like **Play with a Tiger** it raises feminist issues but does so in a totally convincing and powerful way. Lessing's complementary characters, Myra and Milly, are interesting in their own right, parallel the common female pairs in her fiction, and tell us what middle-aged women are and should be. **Each His Own Wilderness**, like much that Lessing has written, can give us insight and inspiration in the crises of our own life.

Notes

1. While no critical study or article has been entirely devoted to Lessing's short stories, interesting references to them may be found in other contexts. For example, see Dorothy Brewster, *Doris Lessing* (N. Y.: Twayne Publishers, Inc., 1965) or Selma R. Burkom, "'Only Connect': Form and Content in the Works of Doris Lessing," *Critique*, 11, No. 1 (1969), 51-68.

2. With the exception of "The Other Woman," contained in Lessing's *Five: Short Novels* (London: Michael Joseph, 1953), all of her fiction has been available either in hardback or in paperback reprints. For a listing of her fiction, see Agate Nesaule Krouse, "A Doris Lessing Checklist," *Contemporary Literature*, 14, No. 4 (Fall 1973), 592-93.

3. For a brief discussion of "Mr. Dolinger," see John Russell Taylor, *The Angry Theater: New British Drama*, rev. ed. (N. Y.: Hill & Wang, 1969), p. 145. See also Myron Matlaw, *Modern World Drama: An Encyclopedia* (N. Y.: E. P. Dutton & Co., Inc., 1972), p. 456. For "The Truth About Billy Newton," see review by A. Alvarez, *New Statesman*, 59 (23 January 1960), 100-01. Also see Allardyce Nicoll, "Somewhat in a New Dimension," in Stratford-Upon-Avon-Studies 4, *Contemporary Theater* (London: Edward Arnold Publishers Ltd., 1968), pp. 82-83, 92. Ms. Lessing's entire comment is, "As regards 'Mr. Dolinger' and 'The Truth About Billy Newton,'

are both, as far as I am concerned, dead ducks. They are dated, and when plays are that, in my view they should simply be forgotten" (letter to Agate N. Krouse, 27 July 1974).

4. *Each His Own Wilderness* was first performed at the Royal Court Theatre, London, on 23 March 1958. It was published in *New English Dramatists: Three Plays*, ed. Elliot M. Browne (Harmondsworth, Middlesex: Penguin Books, 1959), pp. 11-95. *Play with a Tiger* was first performed at the Comedy Theater, London, on 22 March 1962. It was published as *Play with a Tiger: A Play in Three Acts* (London: Michael Joseph, 1962). Subsequent page references to the play are to this edition.

5. *Each His Own Wilderness* is included in Willis Hall, *The Long and the Short and The Tall, et. al.* (Harmondsworth, Middlesex: Penguin Books, 1962). The cover title is *Three Plays*. All subsequent page references are to this edition. *Play with a Tiger* is included in *Plays of the Sixties*, Vol. I, ed. J. M. Charlton (London: Pan Books Ltd., 1966). This edition includes a postscript by Lessing, added in 1972, p. [296]. *Play with a Tiger* is also included in *Plays By and About Women*, eds. Victoria Sullivan and James Hatch (Vintage Books of Random House, c. 1973), pp. 201-73.

6. See, for example, "A Talk with Doris Lessing," interview by Florence Howe, *The Nation*, 204 (6 March 1967), p. 312. Also, Doris Lessing, "Introduction" *The Golden Notebook* (1962; rpt. N. Y.: Bantam Books, Inc., 1973), pp. viii-ix. Subsequent page references are to this edition.

7. Doris Lessing, *A Proper Marriage, Children of Violence*, II (N. Y.: Simon and Schuster, 1964), 322.

8. *The Golden Notebook*, pp. 614-16; *Play with a Tiger*, pp. 61-62.

9. *The Golden Notebook*, p. 616.

10. *Play with a Tiger*, I, p. 35.

11. (N. Y.: Alfred A. Knopf, 1971), pp. 42-43.

12. "Introduction," *The Golden Notebook*, p. viii.

13. For a full discussion of Lessing's use of stereotypes, see my dissertation, "The Feminism of Doris Lessing," Univ. of Wisc., 1972.

14. *Plays of the Sixties*, I, [296].

15. Ibid.

16. For a convincing argument Jimmy Porter is an unusual and unrepresentative young man, see George Wellwarth, "John Osborne: 'Angry Young Man?,'" *The Theater of Protest and Paradox: Development in the Avant Garde Drama*, rev. ed. (N. Y. U. Press, 1971), pp. 254-69.

17. "The Do-Gooders," *New Statesman*, 55 (29 March 1958), 405.

18. Ibid.

19. Ibid.

20. *The Theater of Protest and Paradox*, p. 289.

TITLE COMMENTARY

The Golden Notebook

ELLEN W. BROOKS (ESSAY DATE 1973)

SOURCE: Brooks, Ellen W. "The Image of Woman in Lessing's *The Golden Notebook*." *Critique* 15, no. 1 (1973): 101-09.

In the following essay, Brooks studies Anna, the protagonist of The Golden Notebook, *as she struggles to transcend her divided self and archetypal female roles in order to emerge as a more aware, liberated woman.*

Doris Lessing is one of the most wide-ranging and comprehensive of contemporary novelists. Her strong, straightforward prose has embraced a number of modern social, political, and psychological questions. However, the immense appeal of Lessing's fiction rests largely on her treatment of woman in modern life, the most thorough and accurate of any in literature. Her achievement is all the more significant in that so few writers have presented women with whom one can identify—complex, intelligent, questioning women who are not content with the status quo, who rebel against the established order.

The female protagonists in Lessing's major work are complex human beings, their personalities the embodiment of that fragmentation and chaos which the novelist sees as a fundamental feature of modern life. Profound biological and emotional needs, as well as established conventions and attitudes, mold the woman into patterns of behavior which her intellect and desire for self-determination reject. A sense of an implacable destiny as a woman runs counter to a longing for bold self-assertion as an individual. Her women frequently appear as helpless onlookers, sensitive to conditions around them, longing to act, to take control, yet compelled by their dependent natures and narrowly defined social roles to remain passive observers. Their dilemma may fill them with rage and resentment, stoic resignation, or coldness and apathy. Compromises and adjustments are frequently made, always with a sense of loss. The drive to overcome inner divisions may lead them to madness, to withdrawal, or toward greater involvement with life through intense personal relations, artistic or political activity, or deep self-analysis. The strongest of Lessing's women move toward integration through fully experiencing their psychic divisions, achieving "breakthrough" through "breakdown."[1]

The supreme example of the divided woman—fragmented between her emotional needs and her intellect—is Anna Wulf, the protagonist of Lessing's most psychologically complex novel, **The Golden Notebook.** Highly intelligent and sensitive, she is deeply involved with the modern world and very responsive to its atmosphere of violence and personal betrayals. She is in her thirties, divorced, living in the London of the early 1950's with her young daughter, Janet. A former Communist and a writer with one successful novel to her credit, she is attempting to overcome a "writer's block," stemming from her ethical objections to spreading her disgust with the world. Having been discarded by a man with whom she was deeply in love, she conceals her pain beneath a jaunty, tightly controlled, slightly sardonic social mask.

The intricately structured novel moves into the past to explore the events which lead to Anna's psychic impasse, through the medium of four notebooks, a paradigm of her divided self, in which she records her experiences and outlines the plots of stories based on those problems too harrowing for her to confront directly. The action also moves forward in the present, to chart the working out of her psychological deadlock through the breakdown of her tight mental defenses, symbolized by her fusing all of her experience in one notebook, a golden one. Through being discarded by one man, Michael, she recognizes the extent of her vulnerability and weakness as a woman; her relationship with another man, Saul Green, enables her to overcome her inner divisions and regain a degree of strength and independence.

Although Anna calls herself a "free" woman, her freedom is more of an aspiration than a reality. She allows herself considerable sexual independence, yet she is bound by a deep emotional need for "being with one man, love, all that,"[2] which she attributes to her generalized condition as woman. During the course of her sessions with a Jungian therapist, nicknamed "Mother Sugar," Anna has learned to distinguish that part of herself which she shares with other women, her collective aspects. Identifying her "woman's emotions" as impersonal, as separate from her unique, individual self, she thus robs them of the power to overwhelm her.

Anna realizes that "women's emotions are still fitted for a kind of society that no longer exists," for a woman's deep need for love cannot be satisfied in the "careful, non-committal affairs" of

ON THE SUBJECT OF...

modern life (314). Her frustration generates feelings of betrayal, of resentment against men:

> For there is no doubt of the new note women strike, the note of being betrayed. It's in the books they write, in how they speak, everywhere, all the time. It is a solemn, self-pitying organ note. It is in me, Anna betrayed, Anna unloved, Anna whose happiness is denied, and who says, not: Why do you deny me, but why do you deny life?
>
> (596)

She recognizes such emotion as "the disease of women in our time . . . resentment against injustice, an impersonal one" (333).

Anna is deeply divided by the split between two distinct aspects of her personality: these collective, non-personal elements, and her intelligence, her will to independence and freedom. She knows that many of these "woman's emotions" are both anachronistic and irrational, and she fights to avoid self-pity or resentment, knowing how easily she could fall into the trap of the "man-hating spinster." Her struggles to overcome these emotions, to break out of her embittered role as "Anna betrayed," form the dynamics of the novel. The conflict between the various aspects of her fragmented personality drives her deeper into the chaotic underworld of her inner self. Her restless, probing, analyzing spirit gradually brings her to an awareness of the inner

equivalent of outer violence. Not until she gives vent to these dormant, repressed parts of her self, the various manifestations of the woman's emotion, in her relationship with Saul Green is she able to gain a sense of control, of ability to direct her life.

However, Anna recognizes that her generalized nature as a woman, generating a cold hostility, a fierce anger that cuts her off from life and robs her of her potential, has also a positive aspect, enabling her to empathize with others, particularly women, whose problems affect her immediately and deeply, for they are her own. The "woman's emotion" is linked with the creative imagination, giving Anna a faith in growth and change that enables her to see life in terms of phases, certain stages lived through and then transcended.

Anna's receptivity, her openness to the prevailing moods of society, is part of the vulnerability of her generalized condition as woman. Observing that she is cold and detached with men who are also cold and detached, she realizes: "Of course it's him, not me. For men create these things. They create us," although her characteristic desire to transcend her limitations makes her wonder "Why should this be true?" (501). The fact that "the man's desire creates a woman's desire" (456) implies emotional dependency, a curtailing of personal freedom, lack of initiative. In general, the "woman's emotion" warps the relationship between the sexes, putting women into placating, mothering, essentially submissive roles to "build up a man as a man" (484), an expression of compassion but also of masochism, inviting rejection from men and robbing women of their will:

> No, what terrifies me is my willingness. It is what Mother Sugar would call the "negative side" of the woman's need to placate, to submit. Now I am not Anna. I have no will, I can't move out of a situation once it has started, I just go along with it.
>
> (484)

Although Anna is gifted with a keen analytic mind and independent judgment, her non-rational self is directed by her relations with men, rather than by her intellect. She recognizes that her happiness is centered in a man: "The truth is I don't care a damn about politics or philosophy or anything else, all I care about is that Michael should turn in the dark and put his face against my breasts" (229).

The breakup with Michael drastically alters her life. She realizes that "being rejected by Michael . . . had changed . . . my whole personality" (476). Deprived of his support, her assurance and immunity to outside pressure collapse—her fears threaten to engulf her. A hostile, critical defensiveness develops in her manner. However, Anna expresses the softer aspects of her collective self as woman in her writing, in their embodiment in Ella, the heroine of a sketch for a novel. She is a gentler, less devastating version of the "woman in love" that Anna becomes in her relationship with Saul Green. Thus, Anna transmutes her suffering in the act of creation. In her writing she expresses "an intuition of some kind; a kind of intelligence . . . that is much too painful to use in ordinary life" (572). In fact, Anna admits that "my changing everything into fiction is simply a means of concealing something from myself" (229).

Ella lives out Anna's feelings, suffering the extremes of emotion while Anna remains her "thin, spiky self," the facade rarely cracking to show the turbulence beneath. While Ella experiences the elation of falling in love and the despair of being discarded, Anna is seeking treatment for the inability to feel: "I've had experiences which should have touched me and they haven't" (232). Through Ella's experience with Paul Tanner, Anna anticipates the end of her love affair with Michael, preparing herself for it unconsciously.

In the sketch for a novel, Ella is instantly attracted to Paul, "her real self open to him" (182). Trusting him, she makes love to him. Yet, after their lovemaking, he treats her with malice and suspicion, becoming for a time a hostile stranger. She calls this side of his nature his "negative personality" and chooses to ignore it. In order to respond fully to him, she must submit totally, suppressing the "knowing, doubting, sophisticated" self that would have shielded her against his "negative personality."

After writing this sketch, Anna recognizes her own naivete with Michael, an aspect of herself she does not acknowledge until she sees it in the full scope of her novel about Ella. Both Anna and Ella, her creation, exhibit a fragmented consciousness in their ignoring those traits of their respective lovers that do not fit into their vision of perfection, and thus each woman submits to an almost inevitable pattern of victimization.

By sacrificing her independent judgment and will in her love for a man, the woman becomes radically transformed, losing her sense of identity as a single individual and depending on him as a sole source of happiness and security. The irony is that what is most important to her, her love, becomes ultimately destructive, involving her in a web of self-deception and robbing her of emotional strength. However, a life without love is untenable. Not only does Anna feel worthless without love, but her idea of love is tied up with a sense of meaning and value in life, a bulwark against the underlying threat of nothingness, the dead end of not caring whether one is mad or sane.

In Lessing's view, men and women do not really confront each other, for they define each other according to vastly different needs, shaping reality to fit the pattern of their desires. Women, depending on men for happiness, deny their men's deficiencies. Men, in contrast, do not spare their women, using them as sexual scapegoats and viewing them as threatening, dominating mother figures, separating them into categories of conventional wife or sexual playmate, playing one off against the other. The "free" woman is an escape from the "dull tied wife," limited by her confinement to domestic routine. The high level of intelligence demonstrated by the men in *The Golden Notebook* is sharply at odds with their emotional insecurity, their need to enforce submission, their aggressive cruelty in the face of frustration. Frequently, they perceive women not as particular individuals, but as types of generalized woman. Some are capable of great sensitivity toward women, but at times their rationality vanishes under the force of a need to abuse and destroy, a kind of unmotivated spite, the "joy in malice" that Anna senses at the root of life. In short, both men and women share in the violence of the modern world by playing their opposing roles of oppressor and oppressed.

The ultimate expression of these archetypal roles is the relationship between Anna and Saul Green, the ex-Communist who moves in with her for several weeks, whose personality is even more dislocated and divided than her own. The relationship is the culmination of all the previous patterns of Anna's life—the desperate reaching out for love met by the cold evasiveness of the man, the pleasure of giving and receiving pain, the rapid shifting in and out of roles. She, attracted to the magnetic field of conflict, is galvanized by Saul, almost helplessly thrust into opposing roles. Their complementary needs bind them tightly in a parasitic relationship, a revolving cycle of aggression and cruelty arousing jealousy and guilt, giving way to tenderness and passion. As Anna begins to understand the process, the inevitable sequence of behavior, she senses that "something has to be played out, some pattern has to be worked through" (583).

Initially, both are trapped in the mechanisms of roles which serve as an outlet for their rage at an unsatisfactory world, she as the "woman betrayed," he as the "sardonic rake," a callous womanizer. Her deep need for happiness with a man renders her vulnerable and helpless; upon being rejected, she converts her pain into bitterness and resentment. He has fastened on women as "the jailors, the consciences, the voice of society" (630), authority figures whom he must outwit. Yet, he is caught in the process—he must first charm them and win them over, so that he can lash back at them for attempting to claim him.

By releasing her pent-up emotions, her long repressed destructive urges, Anna lets go of her tight mental control. No longer questioning and criticizing her hostile feelings, she releases her suppressed anger as the "woman betrayed," feeling jealousy drive "through every vein of my body like poison" (586). Through participating in Saul's many shifts of identity and mood, she recognizes the full potential of her being, her capacity to experience a whole spectrum of emotions and selves. She does not block off parts of her awareness, expressing her intuitions through a fictional surrogate, as she had in her previous affair. Although she again becomes helplessly submerged in another's personality—the rhythm of her moods dependent on his, she is able to simultaneously stand aloof from her experience and analyze it. She plays a dual role as observer and observed, watching herself as though she were a character in a novel.

The interaction of both aspects of her self, a synthesis of opposites, provides the forward thrust, the movement into deeper levels of self-knowledge. Gradually, Anna becomes less personally pained and disturbed by Saul and more deeply involved with him, using his madness as a catalyst for her own inward journey. Thus, she comes to acknowledge her part in shaping her life and is able to transcend the role of victim, freeing herself from the sense of "doom, fate, inevitability" that has oppressed her. Viewing her experience with a degree of objectivity and holding on to her belief in growth and change, she is released from the tight grip of the present and views herself from the perspective of the future. Her awareness that she is in the middle of a "period," she realizes, will move her on to a new stage of development.

In resisting the "betrayal" of pity for Saul and ultimately refusing to play the "mother role," in breaking out of the clinging dependency of the "woman's emotion," Anna "twists" the pattern of her life. She is able to let him go, because she realizes their ultimate fusion. Together they have stretched themselves to the limit, testing the belief that "anything is possible" (566). Playing "every man-woman role imaginable," they overcome the isolation of the fragmented consciousness. They transcend the man-woman dichotomy, realizing their human bi-sexuality. Hurling themselves into the experience, they feel the extremes of terror and happiness, living out Anna's belief: "Better anything than the shrewd, the calculated, the non-committal, the refusal of giving for fear of the consequence" (546).

Ultimately, the "woman's emotion"—empathy and concern for another, firmly guided by a strong intelligence—enables Anna to extend the limits of her being. Thus, the man-woman relationship in Doris Lessing's fiction, although destructive in its conventional forms, can serve as a vehicle for self-knowledge, for overcoming one's divisions, and enabling one to live as fully as possible. Paradoxically, Anna, through becoming tightly bound to another, becomes liberated. Her expanded consciousness, however, is achieved only by moving beyond the established values, roles, and institutions, for these are the means by which humanity is fragmented and separated. Considerable courage is required, involving great risk—the chance of total disintegration through experiencing the full extent of one's inner chaos and that of another.

Notes

1. R. D. Laing, *The Politics of Experience* (New York: Ballantine Books, 1968), p. 133.

2. Doris Lessing, *The Golden Notebook* (New York: Ballantine Books, 1968), p. 625. Subsequent references are to this edition.

FURTHER READING

Bibliography

Seligman, Dee. *Doris Lessing: An Annotated Bibliography of Criticism*. Westport, Conn.: Greenwood Press, 1981, 139 p.

Comprehensive bibliography of criticism on Lessing's canon through 1978.

Biographies

Brewster, Dorothy. *Doris Lessing*. New York: Twayne Publishers, 1965, 173 p.

Biography that traces major plots and themes in Lessing's early fiction.

Klein, Carol. *Doris Lessing: A Biography*. London: Duckworth, 2000, 283 p.

Provides a biography of Lessing.

Criticism

Fishburn, Katherine. "The Nightmare Repetition: The Mother-Daughter Conflict in Doris Lessing's *Children of Violence*." In *The Lost Tradition: Mothers and Daughters in Literature,* edited by Cathy N. Davidson and E. M. Broner, pp. 207-16. New York: Frederick Ungar Publishing Co., 1980.

Examines the mother-daughter relationship in Lessing's Children of Violence *series.*

Gardiner, Judith Kegan. "Gender, Values and Lessing's Cats." In *Feminist Issues in Literary Scholarship,* edited by Shari Benstock, pp. 110-23. Bloomington: Indiana University Press, 1987.

Explores Lessing's contradictory attitude toward motherhood through a survey of her fiction that features cats.

Greene, Gayle. *Doris Lessing: The Poetics of Change.* Ann Arbor: University of Michigan Press, 1994, 295 p.

Full-length critical study of Lessing's work.

Kaplan, Carey and Ellen Cronan Rose, eds. *Doris Lessing: The Alchemy of Survival.* Athens: Ohio University Press, 1988, 187 p.

Collection of critical essays by Elizabeth Abel, Victoria Middleton, Eve Bertelsen, and others.

Labovitz, Esther Kleinbord. "Doris Lessing: *Children of Violence.*" In *The Myth of the Heroine: The Female Bildungsroman in the Twentieth Century: Dorothy Richardson, Simone de Beauvoir, Doris Lessing, Christa Wolf,* pp. 145-200. New York: Peter Lang, 1986.

Contends that "the five volumes of Children of Violence *through which Doris Lessing follows the growth process of a single protagonist is a rich source for the evolution of the twentieth-century female* Bildungsroman.*"*

Libby, Marion Vlastos. "Sex and the New Woman in *The Golden Notebook.*" *The Iowa Review* 5, no. 4 (fall 1974): 106-20.

Considers Lessing's portrayal of sexuality and sexual relations within the sociopolitical context in The Golden Notebook.

Miller, Jane. "Doris Lessing and the Millennium." *Raritan* 18, no. 1 (summer 1998): 133-45.

Examines the autobiographies Under My Skin *and* Walking in the Shade *within the framework of Lessing's life and writings.*

Perrakis, Phyllis Sternberg, ed. *Spiritual Exploration in the Works of Doris Lessing.* Westport, Conn.: Greenwood Press, 1999, 150 p.

Examines the fiction of Lessing and provides a bibliographic index.

Rowe, Margaret Moan. *Doris Lessing.* New York: St. Martin's Press, 1994, 137 p.

Elucidates the major themes of Lessing's oeuvre, highlighting the feminist concerns of her fiction.

Spencer, Sharon. "'Femininity' and the Woman Writer: Doris Lessing's *The Golden Notebook* and the *Diary* of Anais Nin." *Women's Studies* 1, no. 3 (1973): 247-58.

Explores parallels between The Golden Notebook *and Anais Nin's* Diary.

Sprague, Claire and Virginia Tiger, eds. *Critical Essays on Doris Lessing.* Boston: G. K. Hall & Co., 1986, 237 p.

Collection of critical essays on aspects of Lessing's work, including several that focus on her feminist themes.

Waxman, Barbara Frey. "Beginning the Journey to Selfhood in Middle Age." In *From the Hearth to the Open Road: A Feminist Study of Aging in Contemporary Literature,* pp. 45-74. New York: Greenwood Press, 1990.

Discusses the middle-aged heroines in The Summer before Dark *and* The Diaries of Jane Somers.

OTHER SOURCES FROM GALE:

Additional coverage of Lessing's life and career is contained in the following sources published by the Gale Group: *African Writers; British Writers Supplement, Vol. 1; Concise Dictionary of British Literary Biography, 1960 to Present; Contemporary Authors, Vols. 9-12R; Contemporary Authors Autobiography Series, Vol. 14; Contemporary Authors New Revision Series, Vols. 33, 54, 76, 122; Contemporary British Dramatists; Contemporary Dramatists, Ed. 5; Contemporary Literary Criticism, Vols. 1, 2, 3, 6, 10, 15, 22, 40, 94, 170; Contemporary Novelists, Ed. 7; Contemporary Women Dramatists; Dictionary of Literary Biography, Vols. 15, 139; Dictionary of Literary Biography Yearbook, 1985; DISCovering Authors; DISCovering Authors: British Edition; DISCovering Authors: Canadian Edition; DISCovering Authors Modules: Most-studied Authors and Novelists; DISCovering Authors 3.0; Encyclopedia of World Literature in the 20th Century, Ed. 3; Exploring Short Stories; Feminist Writers; Literature and Its Times, Vol. 4; Literature Resource Center; Major 20th-Century Writers, Eds. 1, 2; Reference Guide to English Literature, Ed. 2; Reference Guide to Short Fiction, Ed. 2; St. James Guide to Science Fiction Writers, Ed. 4; Short Stories for Students, Vols. 1, 12; Short Story Criticism, Vols. 6, 61; Twayne's English Authors; World Literature and Its Times, Vols. 2, 4; World Literature Criticism Supplement.*

EDNA ST. VINCENT MILLAY

(1892 - 1950)

(Also wrote under the pseudonym Nancy Boyd)
American poet, playwright, short story writer, essayist, librettist, and translator.

Best known for her poetic chronicles of the Jazz Age of the 1920s, Millay's work opened a range of new subject matter to women authors. Her writings also helped popularize a new, more liberated way of life for women in the 1920s and 1930s. Though Millay's content was considered radical for its time, the style of most of her poetry is formal, employing traditional meter and rhyme schemes. She has frequently been deemed one of the most accomplished sonneteers of the twentieth century. Several critics have asserted that Millay's devotion to traditional forms, combined with her move to more philosophical and political subjects in her later verse prompted her work to fall from favor in the mid-twentieth century, but increasing attention has been focused on her poetry in recent decades, particularly by feminist critics.

BIOGRAPHICAL INFORMATION

Millay was born in Rockland, Maine. At the age of eight, her parents divorced. Millay and her two sisters remained with their mother who encouraged Millay's artistic inclinations. Millay began composing verse during her childhood, and several of her poems appeared in the children's magazine *St. Nicholas*. She was first noted as a poet at age twenty when her poem "Renascence" was published in the anthology *The Lyric Year*. With a scholarship obtained partly through the notoriety she gained from the poem, Millay attended Vassar College, where she studied literature and theater and created a stir by rebelling against the school's code of conduct. During the late 1910s and early 1920s, Millay lived in Greenwich Village, where she continued to write and worked as an actress. During this period, she gained a reputation as a free-spirited and rebellious social figure whose poetry reflected her celebration of love and life. Her image and verse proved extremely popular, and by the early 1920s she was among the best-known female poets in the world.

In 1923, following a psychological collapse and a two-year sojourn in Europe, Millay published *The Harp-Weaver and Other Poems* for which she was awarded the Pulitzer Prize in poetry. That same year she married Eugen Boissevain, and the couple bought a farmstead in Austerlitz, New York, where they lived the rest of their lives. Beginning in the late 1920s, Millay became increasingly involved in political issues, initially campaigning against social injustices and later warning of the growing militarism of Nazi Germany, both of which were addressed in her poetry. In 1944 Millay suffered a second psychological breakdown, and stopped writing for several years. Her final volume, *Mine the Harvest,* was completed shortly prior to her death following a fall down the stairs at her home in 1950. The work was published posthumously in 1954.

MAJOR WORKS

Millay's first entrance into the literary world occurred in 1912 with the poem "Renascence," an exploration of spirituality as revealed in nature. The poem's tetrameter couplets signaled Millay's devotion to traditional poetic forms, which she maintained throughout most of her career. With *A Few Figs from Thistles* (1920) and *Second April* (1921), both published in the wake of World War I, Millay emerged as the poetic spokesperson of the Jazz Age. Her brash, flippant, and witty poems from this period evoke women who live and love freely, valuing passion and adventure over long-term relationships. *The Harp-Weaver and Other Poems,* published in 1923, continued to focus on similar themes. One of the most noted is the untitled sonnet that begins "I, being born a woman and distressed," wherein the female speaker dismisses her lover after an impromptu coupling. The volume also considers other topics, such as the sequence "Sonnets from an Ungrafted Tree" which features the story of a woman who returns to care for her estranged husband before he dies.

With *The Buck in the Snow, and Other Poems,* published in 1928, Millay began addressing political issues in her poetry. The volume includes "Justice Denied in Massachusetts"—her consideration of the infamous Sacco-Vanzetti case in which two Italian immigrants were convicted of murder during the Red Scare of the 1920s—a conviction that has been controversial over the years. Millay's sonnet sequence "Epitaph for the Race of Man" contains a similar historical and political focus, tracing human history and warning of impending disaster. In two collections published during the 1930s, *Fatal Interview* (1931) and *Conversation at Midnight* (1937), Millay undertook additional new innovations in her poetic voice. *Fatal Interview,* a collection of fifty-two sonnets, drew on the traditions of love poetry and classical myth but used them to present a narrative of a love affair from the female point of view. *Conversation at Midnight* took another approach, and is voiced by a group of male characters who discuss a range of contemporary issues at a late-night gathering.

CRITICAL RECEPTION

Critical reaction to Millay's works has widely varied. During the late 1910s and early 1920s, her poetry was generally praised for its lyricism, wit, and engaging representation of the postwar period. By the 1930s, however, her literary stature had begun to decline. Some critics denounced her allegiance to traditional poetic forms, finding them outdated in comparison with the more experimental approaches of modernist poets. Another criticism leveled at Millay's work was that her earlier, popular writings failed to address serious issues. Critics who faulted her later poetry that focuses on political, social, and philosophical topics believed her personal works more emotionally moving and appealing. Some commentators have averred that collections such as *The Buck in the Snow* (1940), are less successful than Millay's earlier personal verse, and the latter works have been viewed by some as an indication of her declining talents. World War II-era works such as *Make Bright the Arrows* (1940) were commonly criticized as being propaganda more than poetry. In the decades following her death, Millay was often relegated to the role of a minor lyric poet studied for her Jazz Age lifestyle rather than the artistic works she produced.

More recently, however, Millay's work has received critical accolades, especially from feminist critics. Her poetic redefinition of women's roles has elicited praise. Some of this attention has been directed at her early portraits of liberated women, and *Fatal Interview* has been lauded as a revolutionary reconfiguration of lyric love poetry to include a female perspective. The charge that Millay's verse is intellectually superficial has also been challenged. Some critics have suggested that even the poet's more exuberant works include images of vulnerability, suffering, and victimization. Some commentators have claimed that Millay was a victim of sexual and political bias on the part of mid-century critics who dismissed her work in favor of modern poets who were male and relatively apolitical. Though Millay's poetry has yet to reclaim the widespread acceptance it once enjoyed, her writings are assuming a larger role in debates involving the literary canon.

PRINCIPAL WORKS

"Renascence" (poem) 1912; published in *The Lyric Year*

Renascence, and Other Poems (poetry) 1917

A Few Figs from Thistles (poetry) 1920; enlarged edition, 1922

*Aria da Capo (play) 1921

**The Lamp and the Bell* (play) 1921

Second April (poetry) 1921

**Two Slatterns and a King* (play) 1921

The Ballad of the Harp-Weaver (poetry) 1922

The Harp-Weaver and Other Poems (poetry) 1923

Distressing Dialogues [as Nancy Boyd] (fiction) 1924

Fear (essay) 1927

The King's Henchman (libretto) 1927

The Buck in the Snow, and Other Poems (poetry) 1928

Fatal Interview (poetry) 1931

Wine from These Grapes (poetry) 1934

Conversation at Midnight (poetry) 1937

Huntsman, What Quarry? (poetry) 1939

Make Bright the Arrows: 1940 Notebook (poetry) 1940

Collected Sonnets (poetry) 1941

The Murder of Lidice (ballad) 1942

Collected Lyrics (poetry) 1943

Letters of Edna St. Vincent Millay (letters) 1952

Mine the Harvest (poetry) 1954

Collected Poems (poetry) 1956

Edna St. Vincent Millay: Selected Poems (poetry) 1991

Early Poems (poetry) 1998

*   Published in *Three Plays* in 1926.

PRIMARY SOURCES

EDNA ST. VINCENT MILLAY (POEM DATE 1920)

SOURCE: Millay, Edna St. Vincent. "First Fig." In *Collected Poems of Edna St. Vincent Millay*, p. 127. New York: HarperCollins, 1952.

The following poem was originally published in A Few Figs from Thistles *in 1920.*

"FIRST FIG"

My candle burns at both ends;
    It will not last the night;
But ah, my foes, and oh, my friends—
    It gives a lovely light!

EDNA ST. VINCENT MILLAY (POEM DATE 1923)

SOURCE: Millay, Edna St. Vincent. "I, being born a woman and distressed." In *Collected Poems of Edna St. Vincent Millay*, pp. 601. New York: HarperCollins, 1952.

Originally published in 1923, the following untitled sonnet is one of Millay's best-known portraits of a free-loving woman.

I, being born a woman and distressed
By all the needs and notions of my kind,
Am urged by your propinquity to find
Your person fair, and feel a certain zest
To bear your body's weight upon my breast:
So subtly is the fume of life designed,
To clarify the pulse and cloud the mind,
And leave me once again undone, possessed.
Think not for this, however, the poor treason
Of my stout blood against my staggering brain,
I shall remember you with love, or season
My scorn with pity,—let me make it plain:
I find this frenzy insufficient reason
For conversation when we meet again.

EDNA ST. VINCENT MILLAY (POEM DATE 1931)

SOURCE: Millay, Edna St. Vincent. "Sonnet III of *Fatal Interview*." In *Collected Sonnets of Edna St. Vincent Millay*, pp. 632. New York: HarperCollins, 1952.

The following poem is part of Millay's sonnet sequence Fatal Interview, *originally published in 1931.*

"III"

No lack of counsel from the shrewd and wise
How love may be acquired and how conserved
Warrants this laying bare before your eyes
My needle to your north abruptly swerved;
If I would hold you, I must hide my fears
Lest you be wanton, lead you to believe
My compass to another quarter veers,
Little surrender, lavishly receive.
But being like my mother the brown earth
Fervent and full of gifts and free from guile,
Liefer would I you loved me for my worth,
Though you should love me but a little while,
Than for a philtre any doll can brew,—
Though thus I bound you as I long to do.

GENERAL COMMENTARY

COLIN FALCK (ESSAY DATE JANUARY/FEBRUARY 1992)

SOURCE: Falck, Colin. "The Occulting of Edna Millay." *P. N. Review* 18, no. 3 (January/February 1992): 21-3.

In the following essay, Falck defends Millay's poetic reputation, identifying her as a skilled lyric-ironist whose work addresses the conflict between societal roles and a woman's spiritual independence. Falck also contends that Millay has fared poorly with critics because her verse is straightforward and well-executed, prompting little need for interpretation.

As the centenary—1992—of her birth approaches, thoughtful admirers of Edna St Vincent Millay's poetry are going to have to ask themselves how it can be that the poet who was once the most widely known living poet in human history should now be so resoundingly neglected in official literary circles only four decades after her death. How is it that her whole unusually varied output can be represented by the same predictable two or three poems in the 'serious' anthologies, or that her name is a name you will perhaps occasionally encounter in certain secondary school English classes but will also inescapably leave behind there along with many other childish things? Is it—they will perhaps ask—a fear of the directness and simplicity of Millay's poetry, and of the challenge it poses to us to experience life with something of the intensity with which earlier and less *ironic* generations experienced it, that mainly lies behind her disappearance from view? Theories may be put forward, but if 1992 sees any discussion of Millay at all it will already mark a turn-around in her reputation, since as things currently stand she is almost wholly the captive of her least poetically-educated readers (for the most part self-confessedly ageing, sentimental and backward-looking) and is discussed by almost no one.

One of the most striking things about Millay's sensibility is that irony was always a deep need of her nature—and yet that she never at any time succumbed to the temptation to allow it to become the deepest need of all. Her satirical intelligence was as sharp as that of poets like E. A. Robinson or Frost or Eliot, and her wit—as in her letters or in her Greenwich Village-period writings for such journals as *Vanity Fair*—often as mercurial as Wilde's; yet her deepest instinct was always to pass through and beyond such left-handed engagements with the times she lived in and to address herself to the more essential, and essentially tragic, truths of human existence. Transcending life's ironies rather than taking her stand in them, she reached towards what Blake might have seen as a radical innocence on the far side of the 20th century we know.

A world-embracing intensity and a world-repudiating scorn were co-present in Millay's vision from the start, and the precocious nineteen-year-old schoolgirl from Camden, Maine who made her name with her two-hundred-line tetrameter poem 'Renascence' and the style-conscious Greenwich Village ironist of only a few years later were one and the same individual.

There is no incompatibility, and scarcely a very dramatic transition, between the final lines of 'Renascence'—

> But East and West will pinch the heart
> That can not keep them pushed apart;
> And he whose soul is flat—the sky
> Will cave in on him by and by

—and the advice which Millay (under her pseudonym Nancy Boyd) gave to an imaginary Greenwich Village correspondent worried about her inability to attract a sufficient number of aspiring artists to her apartment:

> The trouble is with the ashtrays; remove them. Get into the habit when alone of crushing out your cigarette against the wall-paper, or dropping it on the floor and carelessly grinding it into the rug, or tossing it in the general direction of the fire-place, if you have one, being very sure never to look anxiously after it to see where it lands. This easy manner on your part will do more than anything else to put your guests at ease. Soon they will be using your studio as if it were their own, going to sleep with their feet in the coffee-tray, wiping paint from their hair and elbows upon the sofa-pillows, making sketches on the walls of unclothed people with small heads and over-developed muscles, and dropping ashes just everywhere.

What links these very different kinds of exhortation together is poetic passion and a fierce contempt for all the prevailing forms of inauthentic living. Millay is less well understood as a backward-looking sentimentalist than as a lyric-ironist in a tradition which (as well as Blake and Emily Dickinson) includes the later French Symbolists, Wilde, Hardy, Housman and the younger Eliot, as well as many of the existentialist prose writers of the later 19th and earlier 20th centuries.

The existential fierceness with which Millay rejected—on behalf of herself, of all women, of all people—society's offered roles is expressed in poem after poem and is a central preoccupation of her earlier work. She could give such wildness a brilliant and disturbing comic turn, as in her famous 'My candle burns at both ends,' or in its less famous companion-epigram—

> Safe upon the solid rock the ugly houses stand:
> Come and see my shining palace built upon the
> sand!

—but the twentiesish precariousness of such spiritual integrity is never entirely distinguishable from nervous desperation or exhaustion. Wisdom was not her concern (although she later came to express a good deal of it); instead, she gives us an unworldly fervor and a refusal to compromise with the available worldly interpretations of life's meanings. In this, she has more in common with writers like Dostoevsky or Kafka than with the American women poets with whom she has usually been routinely compared. In the more serious and less epigrammatical of her early poems there is no fulfilment to be found in the world of ordinarily-breathing human passion:

Tiresome heart, forever living and dying,
House without air, I leave you and lock your
    door.
Wild swans, come over the town, come over
The town again, trailing your legs and crying!

A mysterious, once-heard voice can haunt us to the very end of what we think of as our lives:

Earth now
On the busy brow.
And where is the voice that I heard crying?

Trains can beguile us from our sleep and from our daily commitments—'there isn't a train I wouldn't take, / No matter where it's going'—and the sea continually calls to us with messages both of liberation and of extinction. All of these are the powerful and unsettling apprehensions of a poet for whom life's normal options are little more than options in claustrophobia: a poet who is ultimately homeless.

Millay's refusal to accept the actualities of life as they normally come to us can extend to an almost-philosophical arraignment of the physical body itself. Sometimes she commits herself to a notion (it is a philosophical illusion, in fact) of the essential separateness of mind and body, and makes a resigned and scornful poetry out of it. At other times, and more penetratingly, she recognizes that the war between body and soul that afflicts her is really not a metaphysical necessity but a war between a woman's spiritual independence and the roles that society, and especially men, have insisted on casting her in. Many of her poems explore this theme with great intelligence, and what may look superficially like the celebration or indulgence of flightiness (a notion of Millay and of her work which has dogged her reputation for half a century) is invariably some form of repudiation of the conventionally institutionalized subjection of women. Women *may* at times be witless, but there are reasons why they have come to be so, and there are other reasons why they may choose to go on acting so. In a sonnet like '**I think I should have loved you presently**' Millay both embraces, and also goes beyond, the classic feminist analyses of writers such as Wollstonecraft and Mill (and it is no surprise that she was willing to stand up and be counted as a militantly political feminist at many

points throughout her life). She goes beyond them, because she was unwilling ever to repudiate or to down-value the power and intensity of heterosexual love. She tried instead to write about the realities of such love; and what may sometimes come across to us as yet more poetry in the tradition of 'No love endures' is very often a poetry that goes as deeply as poetry itself ever can into the question of *why* no love endures. Here Millay's preoccupations come close to those of D. H. Lawrence, and her insights are no less perceptive or persuasive than his. What sets Millay apart from—and above—much present-day feminist theorizing and the more aggressive kinds of feminist poetry is that she is able to experience and to present love, both in its initial impulse and in its essential nature, as a passionate surrender. The question is where, in a better world, such a surrender might take us to.

In her later volumes Millay emerges as a truly philosophical poet, and her preoccupations with nature, with death, and with the nobilities and shortcomings of human aspirations are expressed in a range of intellectually substantial and technically widely varying poems. In her reflections on death, Millay is unable to attain to any state which might be seen as one of renunciation or resignation (and is hardly very unusual in this, even among poets), but she comes close to it on a few occasions, as in '**From a Train Window**':

Precious
In the early light, reassuring
Is the grave-scarred hillside
As if after all, the earth might know what it is
    about.

More often, her vision is stoic and Hardyish, and she acknowledges the reality of death both for herself and for others, but without acceptance: 'I shall die, but that is all that I shall do for Death'; 'I am not resigned.'

As we judge her now, we must judge Millay essentially as a lyricist. But we can also perhaps now see that she is a lyricist who is capable of incorporating a wide-ranging, sophisticated, and philosophically respectable kind of thought into her emotional apprehensions. Her superb intelligence was always more effectively expressed through the lyricist's flash of insight than through any kind of weightier lucubration. Where she uses a form as intellectually pointed as the Shakespearian sonnet (and some of her Shakespearian sonnets, such as '**Pity me not because the light of day,**' or '**Now by the path I climbed, I journey back,**' are surely among the best poems in this form in the language), it is usually the imagery in the earlier part of the poem that does most of the work, to make way for a quietly inevitable conclusion. Many of Millay's most powerful lines, and several of her most powerful poems, achieve their effect in a way that leaves very little for the reader or critic to gain by means of detailed interpretation. Consider, for example, the atmospherically-charged final lines of '**Winter Night**':

> The day has gone in hewing and felling,
> Sawing and drawing wood to the dwelling
> For the night of talk and story-telling.
>
> . . . . .
> Here are question and reply,
> And the fire reflected in the thinking eye.
> So peace, and let the bob-cat cry.

Much could be said about this 'thinking eye' and this 'bob-cat,' but we are surely here dealing with a case where there are unlimitedly many 'reasons' which (as William Empson long ago put it) 'combine to give the line [s their] beauty,' and where the meaning is 'hardly in reach of the analyst at all'. This is Millay's method over and over, and it may account for the fact that perhaps more than any other modern poet she has remained popular among such people as still read poetry while continuing to elude systematic analysis and most of those who practise it.

As well as exhibiting all these very modern poetic qualities Millay was also a brilliantly innovative verse technician—an aspect of her distinctively 20th-century poetic nature which has been wholly obscured by her reputation as a sonneteer and a purveyor of imitatively Housmanish quatrains. To the Whitmanian heritage of cadenced free verse she brings the greater reflective tightness of Robinson Jeffers (among the few icons in Millay's personal library was a framed photograph of Jeffers, her near-contemporary) and—still working with long lines—the kind of rhyming and sound-patterning which had so far only rarely been used in free verse (as for example by Pound and Eliot—who were, however, usually more interested in end- than in internal rhyming). The result is a formidable combination, and uniquely Millay's. The closing lines of '**New England Spring, 1942**' are one of its best exemplifications:

> But Spring is wise. Pale and with gentle eyes, one
> day
>   somewhat she advances;
> The next, with a flurry of snow into flake-filled
>   skies retreats
>   before the heat in our eyes, and the thing
>   designed
> By the sick and longing mind in its lonely fan-
>   cies—
> The sally which would force her and take her.
> And Spring is kind.

> Should she come running headlong in a wind-
>   whipped acre
> Of daffodil skirts down the mountain into this
>   dark valley we
>   would go blind.

Nothing like this exists anywhere else in English-language poetry, unless it be in others of Millay's later poems: the meaning of the lines is carried more by the rhythmic hesitations, the subtly insistent internal-rhyme structure and the skilfully-judged punctuation than by the usual poetic devices which are familiar to us in explicatory analysis. This is perhaps a still-unclosed chapter in modern versification.

Millay is a poet who has been buried twice over: once by the generation that needed to get modernism established, and a second time by the academically-inclined critics who have interested themselves only in poetry which presents verbal and intellectual complexities that can be discussed in professional articles or in the seminar room. Millay is to an almost embarrassing degree—but we should ask who it is that ought to be embarrassed—not that kind of poet. But she has also been badly misrepresented by those critics who have gone to the trouble of finding reasons for rejecting her work. Her use of traditional forms, for example, is often deceptive: for all the poems where she seems to fall into pastiche (as in some of her sonnets, or some of her early pieces of Housmanish irony) there are others where she is engaged in something rather more subtle. The interplay between the grand manner and the artless-conversational is essential to much of her work (it first shows itself in '**Renascence**'), and it enables her, as it also did later poets like Auden or Philip Larkin, to give the traditional forms a new lease of credibility. Sometimes her use of the grand manner seems almost designed to subvert itself: the sonnet '**Whereas at morning in a jeweled crown**,' about a turbulent contemporary relationship, could seem almost 'post-modernist' in the way it clears the air of the very poetic devices it uses:

> Whereas at morning in a jeweled crown
> I bit my fingers and was hard to please,
> Having shook disaster till the fruit fell down
> I feel tonight more happy and at ease:
> Feet running in the corridors, men quick-
> Buckling their sword-belts bumping down the
>   stair,
> Challenge, and rattling bridge-chain, and the
>   click
> Of hooves on pavement—this will clear the air.

There will perhaps always be those who see Millay's poetry as too simple, too sensuous, too passionate, too old-fashioned, too New England, too un-urban, too un-intellectual, too narrow-ranged, too light-weight, or just too straightforwardly comprehensible, but this can hardly justify the depths of neglect into which her work has been allowed to fall during the past forty years or so. The occulting of Millay's reputation has been one of the literary scandals of the 20th century, and it is time we found a proper place for this intense, thoughtful, and magnificently literate poet.

JOSEPH AIMONE (ESSAY DATE 1997)

SOURCE: Aimone, Joseph. "Millay's Big Book, or the Feminist Formalist as Modern." In *Unmanning Modernism: Gendered Re-Readings,* edited by Elizabeth Jane Harrison and Shirley Peterson, pp. 1-13. Knoxville: University of Tennessee Press, 1997.

In the following essay, Aimone takes issue with critics who have dismissed Millay's work for lacking the aesthetics of modernism, noting that Millay does, at times, employ free verse and other modern techniques and that her writing can be viewed as a reaction against male-dominated literary forms, both traditional and modern.

At best form gives concinnity, precision,
paring of words and widening of vision,
play for the mind, focus that is self-critical.
Poets, and poems, are not apolitical.
Women and other radicals who choose
venerable vessels for subversive use
affirm what Sophomore Survey often fails
to note: God and Anonymous are not white
      males.
"We always crafted language just as they did.
We have the use, and we reclaim the credit"
      —Marilyn Hacker, *Taking Notice,* 1980

Few contemporary feminist poets (though perhaps a growing share) are as sanguine as Marilyn Hacker about the use of traditional forms. "Such forms remind us too much of Edna St. Vincent Millay," one can almost hear them say. Even feminist critics with their hearts set on some kind of recuperation of Millay concede first the hurdles her reputation puts between them and their goal, foremost often her formalism. Debra Fried, closest to my own views, introduces a scrupulous study of the complex insinuations of Millay's sonneteering by noting, "In a critical climate in which we are rediscovering the powerful experiments of American women poets in the modernist era, the tidy verses of Edna St. Vincent Millay have remained something of an embarrassment" (229). In *Masks Outrageous and Austere,* the second volume of her landmark historical study of American women poets, Cheryl Walker, equally embarrassed, identifies Millay as one of the last of the

"nightingale" poets. Walker laments that "in truth, Millay was not really subversive" (164). In *Sentimental Modernism: Women Writers and the Revolution of the Word* Suzanne Clark situates her limited recuperation of Millay in a broader effort to recapture the sentimental, which Clark identifies as the repressed now returning to haunt the modernist and postmodernist text in the form of feminism (provided other feminists grasp her point and agree). But this recognition does not reelevate Millay to speaking with authority, especially regarding verse technique: "For her (passive?) repetition of conventional literary forms, the former gestures of power, is somehow feminine, slavish" (Clark 67). Even parenthetic doubts, while they hit on the crucial point of Millay's strategy of appropriation of male-dominated tradition, cannot undo Clark's clear vote of condemnation for Millay's "repetition."[1]

Such critics are not alone. In 1992 Amy Clampitt, a redoubtable contemporary poet, in a *New Republic* review of the recent Centenary Edition of Edna St. Vincent Millay's **Selected Poems,** sums up a common view of Millay: "Whatever else may be said of it, the poetry of Edna St. Vincent Millay is not modern" (44). I disagree with Clampitt, both about Millay and about the critical assumptions that underlie such a dismissive assessment. Millay was arguably an exemplary modern poet and an exemplary feminist poet.

Clampitt's reasons for her conclusion begin with oblique insinuation: She notes that Millay had harsh if casual words for the Armory show (which she attended) and for Duchamp (on a postcard). She faults Millay that she "failed to seek [Pound] out the year or two they were both in Paris" (44). Millay was by far the more widely published and often-read poet—but it seems she didn't know her proper place at the feet of the Master. Clampitt holds youthful fondness for poetry and Shakespeare in particular against Millay, explaining Millay's carefree use of archaic and literary locutions as a product of an overly bookish childhood, "[growing] up with book words and literaryisms" (Clampitt 45). Clampitt casually reproduces modernist prejudice against formal verse, claiming that "the effects produced by it are limited," and that "the bewilderments clutched at and grappled with by [William Carlos] Williams are beyond the ordering of anything so brittle" (Clampitt 45). This aesthetic of toughness, strength, and effectiveness sounds vaguely political or perhaps commercial, the preferred characteristics of a good district attorney in an era of rising

ABOUT THE AUTHOR

MILLAY'S MARRIAGE

When Edna St. Vincent Millay finally did marry, it was to Eugen Jan Boissevain, who was an unusual husband for an unusual marriage. Eugen, a Dutchman by birth, had previously been married to Inez Milholland, a suffragette leader and graduate of Vassar. In this marriage, Eugen and Inez had, according to Max Eastman [in *Enjoyment of Living,* 1948]; taken vows of unpossessive love, which meant complete freedom for both partners, and had maintained their love without possessiveness until Inez's untimely death. This same freedom apparently also characterized the marriage of Eugen and Edna. . . .

Eugen did everything he could to free Millay from the tasks of normal living in order that she could devote herself to writing poetry. He was not only a husband to her, but a kind of father, mother and nursemaid—an arrangement that both of them seemed to accept. They accepted, too, childless marriage at Steepletop, their farm in Austerlitz, perhaps because, as Janet Gassman suggests [in *Colby Library Quarterly* 9, no. 305 (June, 1971)], she considered poetry more important and enduring than any human relationships.

Despite their mutual acceptance of this unconventional marriage and despite their mutual devotion to Millay's poetic achievements, the couple's retreat to pastoral bliss did not remain happy. After the early 1930's, Millay's poetry declined sharply in quality as she began to write about social and political issues unsuited to her lyric gifts. Her health, both physical and emotional, led her to a kind of perpetual nervous exhaustion, probably intensified by excessive drinking. . . . Although she did manage to write some good poetry again, which is to be found in the posthumous *Mine the Harvest,* she lived only a bit more than a year after Eugen's death in 1949.

Minot, Walter S. Excerpt from "Millay's 'Ungrafted Tree': The Problem of the Artist as Woman." *New England Quarterly* 48, no. 2 (June 1975): 266-68.

crime or of a household cleaning utensil that gets the job done without breaking or requiring extra work. (One wonders if poetry really ought to be tough, strong, and effective, or at least whether that trio of utilitarian virtues are the most important values good poetry has.) But the killing blow is accusing Millay of a shallowness of intellect somehow directly a result of her formalism: "There is hardly any room for ambiguity of thought or feeling—for anything that critical analysis might take hold of or take apart" (Clampitt 45). Even Clampitt's praise of Millay (for she likes her as much as she can) suggests that what is right about Millay's best work is nothing Millay tried to achieve consciously: "a sensuous freshness that slips in and out of her work as regularly as the tide, inundating the formal music . . . with a vigor and a specificity from beyond itself" (Clampitt 45). In sum, Clampitt holds Millay too comfortable with conventionally elevated poetic diction, disrespectful of male modernists, too formal (and consequently limited, barred from serious thought), and at best the helpless vessel of an oceanic passion that only partly redeems her.

This attitude recapitulates in salient respects the dismissal John Crowe Ransom offered in "The Poet As Woman" in 1937. While Ransom would not so hastily equate form with incapacity for serious modern matter, his characterization of Millay as unintellectual and best when "sensuous freshness" is at hand anticipates Clampitt. It is only that Ransom's attitude toward women, his assumption that certain characteristics of her writing are essentially feminine, that might trouble a reader bred on contemporary poetry and ready to sympathize with Clampitt's jaundiced view of Millay. Conceding that Millay is an artist, he says, "She is also a woman. No poet ever registered herself more deliberately in that light. She therefore fascinates the male reviewer but at the same time horrifies him a little too. He will probably swing between attachment and antipathy, which may be the very attitudes provoked in him by generic woman in the flesh" (Ransom 76-77). The stereotype of feminine character that accompanies this gender anxiety translates into something very similar to Clampitt's assessment of Millay's writerly virtues and flaws. Here is Ransom's expatiation on the mental stance of women: "A woman lives for love, if we will but project that term to cover all her tender fixations upon natural objects of sense, some of them more innocent and far less reciprocal than men" (77). He concludes with backhanded praise: "man, at best is an intellectualized woman . . . [woman] is indifferent to intellectuality" (Ransom 77).

The resemblance between Ransom's patently masculinist attitude toward Millay and the conscientiously "contemporary poetic" ethos of Clampitt's review perhaps implies that sexism has gone underground and now appears as an ideology of modernism, at least in the criticism of poetry. Sandra Gilbert and Susan Gubar have suggested that male modernism in certain important respects is a reflection of male anxieties provoked by the emergence of women as potent political powers and literary progenitors, "words and works which continually sought to come to terms with, and find terms for, an ongoing battle of the sexes that was set in motion by the late nineteenth-century rise of feminism and the fall of Victorian concepts of 'femininity'" (Gilbert and Gubar, *No Man's Land* I:xii). Denuded of explicitly anti-female ideas, the aesthetic of male modernism in its recent incarnations continues to propagate the taint of hostility that brought it into existence, ironically even in the mouths of women poets, for example, Clampitt. But if the objections raised against Millay were true, we have now entered a period of reconsideration of literary judgment that wants to rethink the modernist aesthetic (in whatever New Critical or more recent guise) as something other than a perfect culmination of or an obviously unquestionable improvement on all previous or possible future ways of thinking. We might find something has been missed in Millay's poetry that deserves attention and approbation.

Ironically, the objections brought under the aegis of the supposed modernist consensus against Millay are not even true. She is an intellectual writer, complex and ironic, a carefully modern stylist, with a clear sense of the contemporary and the cleanly elegant. And she is a postmodern eclectic user of verse forms archaic and recent, unbenighted by simpleminded wholesale rejections of traditional form.

Millay regarded herself as a modern poet, though she was a formalist. She collaborated with George Dillon on volume of translations from Charles Baudelaire's *Fleurs du Mal*. In the preface she authored for it she holds up Baudelaire as the inaugural modern poet. She diagnoses his appeal for modern readers as a matter of a certain "quality of mind" (Dillon xxx). She describes him in terms that make clear the value she places on intellectuality: "This was a poet of the intellect, a lover of order, of perfection in form, deploring superstition, sentimentality and romanticism"

(Dillon xxxi). Her discussion of translation recognizes both the difficulties and the limited possibilities of success, with regard to sheer differences in vocabulary as much as differences in canons of versification between French and English. Amid this discussion she lays out her own attitude toward form: "To translate poetry into prose, no matter how faithfully and even subtly the words are reproduced, is to betray the poem. To translate formal stanzas into free verse, free verse into rhymed couplets, is to fail the foreign poet in a very important way" (Dillon vii). The grounds on which she accuses such betrayal is a concept of appropriate and necessary form:

> With most poets, the shape of the poem is not an extraneous attribute of it: the poem could not conceivably have been written in any other form. When the image of the poem first rises before the suddenly quieted and intensely agitated person who is to write it, its shadowy bulk is already dimly outlined; it is rhymed or unrhymed; it is trimeter, tetrameter, or pentameter; it is free verse, a sonnet, an epic, an ode, a five-act play. To many poets, the physical character of the poem, its rhythm, its rhyme, its music, the way it looks on the page, is quite as important as the thing they wish to say; to some it is vitally more important. To translate the poetry of E. E. Cummings into the rhymed alexandrines of Molière, would be to do Mr. Cummings no service.
>
> (Dillon vii)

Clearly Millay conceives of poetry as an intrinsically formal art. She accepts the possibility and even emphasizes the necessity of free verse. She is not a stylistic reactionary, but neither does she share the casual dismissal of traditional form as something "brittle," whose "effects . . . are limited." Free verse is for her one of a variety of technical choices rather than a kind of breakthrough into a bigger world. And given her insistence on the unity of intellectuality and formal perfectionism in the work of Baudelaire, it seems unlikely that she would accept an assumption (such as Clampitt's) that a traditional verse form, such as the sonnet, say, would have "hardly any room for ambiguity of thought or feeling—for anything that critical analysis might take hold of or take apart" (Clampitt 45). A cursory sample of her poetry will, in fact, show just the opposite.

It is customary to begin an examination of Millay's poetics with a look at **"Renascence,"** since its tetrameter rhyming, its easy optimism, and its straining idealism exemplify the stereotyped thoroughly unmodern Millay. A better example of Millay's modernism is **"Spring"** from *Second April*:

To what purpose, April, do you return again?
Beauty is not enough.
You can no longer quiet me with the redness
Of little leaves opening stickily.
I know what I know.
The sun is hot on my neck as I observe
The spikes of the crocus.
The smell of the earth is good.
It is apparent that there is no death.
But what does that signify?
Not only under ground are the brains of men
Eaten by maggots.
Life in itself
Is nothing,
An empty cup, a flight of uncarpeted stairs.
It is not enough that yearly, down this hill,
April
Comes like an idiot, babbling and strewing flow-
    ers.

        (Millay, **Collected Poems** 53)

This is free verse: freer than most free verse. The variations from regularity of line length are extreme. The line breaks emphasize or retard syntactic flow. The sentences are severely simple, for the most part. A grammatical break takes place in the first sentence, but the interrogatory appositive nomination of April forces emphasis on the preceding word, "purpose." The only inversion in the poem serves well the sarcastic irony it expresses, with "Not only under the ground are the brains of men / Eaten by maggots." The other images are also flatly unsentimental: the sun hot on the neck, the spikes of the crocus, the word "stickily" pulling the little red leaves out of their sentimental expectation, the mysteriously uncarpeted stairs, and finally, a babbling idiot tossing flowers. (One wonders if he drools!) And the poem is a kind of recognition of the irony of natural beauty for the disaffected subject and of the intellectually unsatisfying condition of human life. Yet this dark recognition is tempered by a hinted temptation simply to enjoy the sheer exuberance of April, a temptation that must be felt even if inevitably foregone by the uninnocent subject.

Even Millay's most simple verses, her most obviously traditional in form and diction, take on interesting resonance against the background of the wars of the sexes posited by Gilbert and Gubar. Consider **"The Witch Wife"**:

She is neither pink nor pale
    And she never will be all mine;
She learned her hands in a fairy-tale,
    And her mouth on a valentine.

She has more hair than she needs;
    In the sun 'tis a woe to me!
And her voice is a string of coloured beads,
    Or steps leading into the sea.

She loves me all that she can,
    And her ways to my ways resign;
But she was not made for any man,
    And she never will be all mine.

The meter is a loose, folky, anapestic stanza, rhythmically identical to the limerick, but marked with different rhyming positions:

She is neither pink nor pale,
    And she never will be all mine;
She learned her hands in a fairy tale,
    And her mouth on a valentine.

The singsong rhythm creates a progressively more compelling cadence, as each stanza puts forth first a pair of lines between which we pause, then a pair without pause—the relentless beat slams on in the third line right into the fourth, skipping and galloping through iambs and anapests.

This chanting seems as unmodern as possible, with modernism's studied insistence on maturity. (Stephen Dedalus may remain stuck in a lifelong adolescent crisis, but he does not return to his nursery). And the archaisms, such as "'tis," belong in a nursery rhyme as easily as in the nineteenth century, not in a poem made after Pound's gospel. The odd formulations hardly reflect a modern purity of expression: How does one learn one's hands and mouth? How can a voice be a string of colored beads or steps to the sea? These seem more like infelicities than salubrious difficulties.

One might try to write off this poem as a bit of juvenile-oriented Gothicism. Only the word "resign" comes out of an unchildish lexicon. But all this "childishness" has a point: the speaker is male, and he is speaking of the intractability of woman. The nursery rhyme thinking is masculine thinking, bewailing the female's nonconformity to his desires, designs, and purposes. He objects that she is "neither pink nor pale," neither an unworldly and protected indoor thing nor weak or fearful. She has acquired power, "learned her hands," in the imagination, "a fairy-tale." And she has acquired both blatantly sexual beauty and the ability to speak, her mouth "on a valentine," which pattern of acquisition suggests the transformation of her objectification in the discourse of romantic love into a position of power to speak.

That she has "more hair than she needs" identifies her as excessive in the male economy—he thinks he knows what she needs, and he knows she has more than he thinks she ought to, the fact that it is only hair notwithstanding. Further, it troubles him that her sign of excess be seen "in the sun." The double significance of the female mouth, as beauty object and as threatening power, recurs in the third and fourth lines of the second stanza, as her voice becomes first "a string of coloured beads" and then the way to oblivion as "steps leading into the sea."

The speaker explains in the last stanza that she loves him "all that she can," a limited affection which he translates into her submission as "her ways to my ways resign." It is notable that he erases her agency, recording no resignation by her, only by her "ways." And he admits the incompatibility of his desire with her, but attributes the incompatibility to her nature rather than her choice, saying "she was not made for any man." He concludes with a frustration that reveals the full measure of domination his quasi-infantile masculine desire demands: "And she never will be all mine."

This ironic use of a childish formalism to make a feminist riposte to masculinist sexual politics does not exhaust Millay's modes of exploiting traditional forms. She is best known as a sonneteer. A glance at one of them will make obvious the degree to which her poetry's virtues are confined to what Clampitt calls "sensuous freshness that slips in and out of her work as regularly as the tide, inundating the formal music . . . with a vigor and a specificity from beyond itself" (45). Consider this untitled sonnet from *The Harp Weaver*:

> I, being born a woman and distressed
> By all the needs and notions of my kind,
> Am urged by your propinquity to find
> Your person fair, and feel a certain zest
> To bear your body's weight upon my breast:
> So subtly is the fume of life designed,
> To clarify the pulse and cloud the mind,
> And leave me once again undone, possessed.
> Think not for this, however, the poor treason
> Of my stout blood against my staggering brain,
> I shall remember you with love, or season
> My scorn with pity,—let me make it plain:
> I find this frenzy insufficient reason
> For conversation when we meet again.
>
> (*Collected Poems* 601)

The orientation is intellectual, detached if not passionless. And the graces of this poem are in its intellectuality and wit. Sexual attraction becomes, coolly, "a certain zest." The alliterative pairings of "needs and notions," "stout blood" and "staggering brain," "clarify" and "cloud" lay on a thickly ironic "literaryism." Millay's speaker sarcastically reduces sexual passion to "frenzy" and "frenzy" to "insufficient reason" in a blunt refusal to talk to a former lover. The reversal of the form's generic expectations is complete: A male voice, speaking to and of a female object with transcendent pas-

sion and lasting if unhappy devotion, has become a female voice, speaking to and of a male object with untranscendent passion and blithely temporary interest. Here is the patriarchal Petrarchan's nightmare come true, the unfaithful woman who casually uses and loses her lover like a toy, while maintaining an at once appealing and threatening self-possession, with as cerebral a rationale as any male modernist womanizer could boast of.

Now this biting "lightness" may tempt the male modernist (in flight already) to disparage Millay for lack of sobriety if not for lack of intellect. But the volume containing this sonnet also contains the narrative series "**Sonnets from an Ungrafted Tree**," which gives the story of a woman returning to manage the passing of her former lover. The nature of the original separation is unclear, but he is now unloved by her, and the tale holds a mood of Hardyian gloom and disillusion. In the final sonnet of the sequence, the female protagonist experiences her distance from her previous engagement with him:

> Gazing upon him now, severe and dead,
> It seemed a curious thing that she had lain
> Beside him many a night in that cold bed,
> And that had been which would not be again.
> From his desirous body the great heat
> Was gone at last, it seemed, and the taut nerves
> Loosened forever. Formally the sheet
> Set forth for her today those heavy curves
> And lengths familiar as the bedroom door.
> She was as one who enters, sly and proud,
> To where her husband speaks before a crowd,
> And sees a man she never saw before—
> The man who eats his victuals at her side,
> Small, and absurd, and hers: for once, not hers,
> unclassified.
>
> (622)

Note the Frostian simplicity of "that had been which would not be again." And the simile in the sestet, likening the woman's state at the funeral to that of a woman watching her husband speak publicly and recognizing her alienation from him, subtly inflects the separation imposed by his death with relief. Metrical devices aid this effect, as the accent of the foot hammers on "once" in "for once, not hers" and the delayed completion of the rhyme (the line is seven iambs long) with "unclassified" produces a sense of long-awaited resolution, loading the dry, Latinate word with excruciating emotion.

Millay uses free verse, nursery rhyme, and the sonnet with equal freedom and with a subtle intelligence in working out the gendered politics of the modern. Millay's dramatic writing also argues for her seriousness as a modern writer, beginning with *Aria da Capo*, her first mature dramatic text.

Aria da Capo was written for and performed by the Provincetown Players and became an immediate success, with many other productions elsewhere soon after, as Millay explains in the author's note in the original Harper edition. It is a blank-verse masque, an expressionist tragic farce, replete with intellectual resonance, even anticipating in its black humor, logical impasses, and plot recursions perhaps Beckett's tramps or Stoppard's (or Pirandello's) caricatures. Two plots interweave in a complex metatheatrical interchange, both deceptively simple: Pierrot and Columbine banter blithely together, love-teasing and social commentary. Pierrot sets himself up first as a lover, then as a student who will "search into all things," then as a modern artist:

PIERROT:
    . . . I am become
A painter, suddenly,—and you impress me—
Ah, yes!—six orange bull's eyes, four green
    pinwheels,
And one magenta jelly-roll, m—the title
As follows: Woman Taking in Cheese from
    Fire-Escape.

(Millay, *Aria da Capo* 3)

Subsequently he takes up music "On a new scale. . . . Without tonality." He becomes a socialist: "I love / Humanity; but I hate people" (4). Columbine offers him a persimmon, which he refuses:

I am become a critic; there is nothing
I can enjoy. . . . However, set it aside;
I'll eat it between meals.

(7)

The happy repartee is interrupted by Cothurnus, called Masque of Tragedy in the dramatis personae, who runs Pierrot and Columbine off stage. When Pierrot, judging from appearances, says that Cothurnus is sleepwalking, Cothurnus replies with black irony, "I never sleep" (8). Cothurnus coaches two new characters, Thrysis and Corydon, through a rehearsal that slips in and out of its dramatic illusion, periodically prompted by Cothurnus from the playbook he holds, and occasionally interrupted by ejaculations from Pierrot and Columbine offstage. Thyrsis and Corydon initially resist Cothurnus's direction, complaining (as had Pierrot and Columbine) that this scene should come later in the play. They raise other objections, saying that they cannot build the wall their scene requires with only the tissue paper available on stage (though that is exactly what they will do). Thyrsis sums up unwittingly the project of the play as a whole when he says, "We cannot act / A tragedy with comic properties!" (10)

Thereafter unfolds a tragedy with comic properties, both in the sense that this tragedy has comic properties in general and in the specific sense of comic stage-properties: the aforementioned tissue, a bowl of confetti, and so on. In this tragedy, Thyrsis and Corydon are two shepherds meditatively tending their common flock. In proper bucolic fashion Corydon suggests they compose a song together. The subject of the song he proposes is "a lamb that thought himself a shepherd" (12). The hubris of the lamb will turn out to be the hubris of Thyrsis and Corydon. Thyrsis forgets his line and Cothurnus prompts him with "I know a game worth two of that" (12). Thyrsis picks up the thread of the script and suggests they build a wall instead of composing a song. They build a wall of tissue, separating the sheep of one from the sheep of the other. Each grows jealous of his own "property" as defined by the wall and envious of the other's. They mistrust each other, prompted by Cothurnus, who supplies at several junctures the forgotten line, "How do I know it isn't a trick?" (14) Thyrsis will not allow Corydon's sheep to drink the water which is only on Thyrsis's side of the wall. They both want to stop mistrusting each other but cannot. Corydon discovers jewels on his side of the wall, and Thyrsis offers to trade water for the sheep for jewels, but Corydon refuses. He claims to have given up his life as shepherd in favor of that of a merchant. And he becomes ambitious: "And if I set my mind to it / I dare say I could be an emperor" (21). Corydon contemplates the luxuries and fame that his great wealth can bring him, ignoring Thyrsis's warning that his sheep will die. Now, Thyrsis discovers a poisonous-rooted plant on his side of the wall, and when Corydon finally becomes thirsty, Thyrsis agrees to trade water for a necklace of Corydon's jewels. Thyrsis poisons Corydon with a bowl of offered water; Corydon in turn strangles Thyrsis to death as he dies himself of the poisoned water.

Cothurnus hides the bodies under the table at which Pierrot and Columbine had sat and calls them back on stage to do their scene again. Pierrot protests that the audience will not stand for the bodies to be left on stage while the farce is played. Cothurnus assures him that the audience will forget, though the bodies remain in plain sight. Pierrot and Columbine take up their exchange exactly where they had begun it, wondering what day it is, as if nothing had happened—or as if this state was implicit in the empty stage at the beginning of the play. The various postures of artist, socialist, critic, and so on, adopted by Pierrot as he verbally abuses Columbine, seem now to have been predicated on the tragedy of Thyrsis and Corydon having always already) happened. Their gendered byplay cohabits with the primal violence of equals entangled in deadly hostilities the origin of which they cannot remember, but which evolve out of a substitution of "a game worth two of that" for the collaborative production of a song. The song, were it possible to produce it, would be an admonitory one about a lamb that thinks it is a shepherd. Such a lamb among lambs is an equal with a delusion of superiority; and this same delusion is doubly present in the fatal competition of Thyrsis and Corydon.

It is hard to misread the intellectual complexity of this little play in light of later absurdist, existential, and minimalist drama in this century. The rest of Millay's dramatic writing may deserve a fuller examination on its own merits. But Millay also exploits the possibilities of dramatic polyvocality in works not intended for the stage. In 1937, the year John Crowe Ransom was damning her with faint praise for the feminine unintellectuality of her poetry, she published *Conversation at Midnight.* It is a closet drama of drawing-room conversation, the conversants exclusively male and educated but otherwise diverse enough: a stock-broker, a painter, a writer of short stories, a communist poet, a Catholic priest, a wealthy and liberal Euro-American aristocrat, an ad man, and a butler and chauffeur. The play explores the sometimes intractable differences of opinion between atheist and believer, communist and conservative, communist and liberal, and so on, spiced with discussions of "masculine" pursuits like hunting quail or women. The irony is thick.

The exclusion of women from the dramatis personae, plausible though it may be for the play's pretext, demands some explanation as the work of Millay, otherwise so committed to including a woman's view. I believe that one of Millay's untitled sonnets sums up nicely her sense of the literary politics of gender in a way that can shed some light on this exclusion:

> Oh, oh, you will be sorry for that word!
> Give back my book and take my kiss instead.
> Was it my enemy or my friend I heard,
> "What a big book for such a little head!"
> Come, I will show you now my newest hat,
> And you may watch me purse my mouth and
>   prink!
> Oh, I shall love you still, and all of that.
> I never again shall tell you what I think.
> I shall be sweet and crafty, soft and sly;
> You will not catch me reading any more;

> I shall be called a wife to pattern by;
> And some day when you knock and push the
>   door,
> Some sane day, not too bright and not too
>   stormy,
> I shall be gone, and you may whistle for me.
> <div align="right">(<i>Collected Poems</i> 591)</div>

The simple plot allegorizes the relationship of the woman writer to a male-dominated literary tradition as a marriage of woman and man. Her voice threatens revenge. She demands the return of her book, for which we may read something like control of the poetic imaginary. She offers him her kiss in exchange, knowing his presuppositions about her function as object of his desire. She questions, half-seriously it seems, whether he is her enemy or her friend, allowing that his answer may not be the same as hers. She reveals the events leading up to his theft of the book: he insulted her intelligence, presuming that her "little head" (read "small intelligence") and the "big book" (read, perhaps, "writing-in-general," the category of the literary itself) ill-matched. She offers to pose for him and show off what he might consider a more appropriate concern for her "little head," her latest item of millinery. She reassures him of her love casually, as if the assurance were unimportant as well as almost unneeded, "and all of that." Having lulled him, she becomes sarcastic, though we expect he may not catch her tone as she announces a campaign of deception, in which she will be "sweet and crafty" in concealing her interest in the "big book" from him. Finally, perhaps once she has that book in her possession, she will disappear from his domain, presumably into her own.

Reading this poem as a microcosm of Millay's attitudes about the situation of woman with respect to man and to the literary, this poem explains how she could want to write a serious bit of social commentary in verse and voice it entirely in male characters. In conforming to controlling expectations of the male-dominated literary tradition—that only men take up subjects like communism and liberalism, let alone quail hunting—Millay inscribes the female presence in its very absence: she doesn't let him see her reading.

Millay's campaign of deception may explain her broadly eclectic formalism also. [*Conversation at Midnight*], like Millay's work as a whole, makes evenhanded use of both traditional (even archaic) versification and free verse. Since both the tradition and the modernist "revolution" in verse technique are (or at least were for her) patently male-dominated affairs, her willingness to write in either formal or free-verse mode, her refusal to take sides, may betray a covert motive to get control of the "big book" rather than be read to by a self-important male who decides what she can understand with her "little head."

"Oh, oh, you will be sorry for that word" also allegorizes the relationship between Millay and her recent critical readers, theorists and poet alike. One way or another they treat her as somehow defective, citing as flaws her very strategies of deceptively occupying the expected positions in masculine poetics. They think she is out of her league up against contemporary feminists and canonical poets. They patronize her and take her book away. She offers, and they don't understand why, her flamboyantly feminized kiss and her thoughtful silence. Once we recognize her as a resourcefully ingenious and independent-minded poet, she has possession of the "big book," and they can go whistle.

Note

1. Jane Stanbrough, in perhaps the earliest of the feminist critical "recuperations" of Millay, characterizes Millay's entire poetics as inhabited by a congenital stance of tragic female vulnerability. In fact, I would not want to disagree with Stanbrough that Millay's "profound insight into her self's inevitable capitulation . . . makes Millay ultimately so vulnerable and her poetry so meaningful" (199), though I can imagine how this view might be seen as ultimately itself a capitulation to John Crowe Ransom's ill-taken dismissal of Millay as "the poet as Woman." As capitulation and recapitulation may be rusing signs of defeat, I can't help finding a bit more to Millay's acquisition of the dominant masculine poetics. (Even vulnerability, if it were all she were about, and it isn't, can be a weapon.) The most recent reassessment, in the third volume of Gilbert and Gubar's *No Man's Land, Letters from the Front*, traces the historic rewriting of Millay by a masculinist critical tradition with much more sense of Millay's power.

Works Cited

Clampitt, Amy. "Two Cheers for Prettiness: Edna St. Vincent Millay, **Selected Poems: The Centenary Edition**, Edited and with an Introduction by Colin Falck." *New Republic* 6 Jan., 13 Jan. 1992.

Clark, Suzanne. *Sentimental Modernism: Women Writers and the Revolution of the Word.* Bloomington: Indiana UP, 1991.

Dillon, George, and Edna St. Vincent Millay, trans. **Flowers of Evil: From the French of Charles Baudelaire with the Original Texts and a Preface by Miss Millay.** New York: Harper & Brothers, 1936.

Fried, Debra. "Andromeda Unbound: Gender and Genre in Millay's Sonnets." *Critical Essays on Edna St. Vincent Millay.* Ed. William B. Thesing. New York: G. K. Hall, 1993.

Gilbert, Sandra M., and Susan Gubar. *No Man's Land: The Place of the Woman Writer in the Twentieth Century.* Vol. 1, *The War of the Words.* New Haven: Yale UP, 1988.

———. *No Man's Land: The Place of the Woman Writer in the Twentieth Century.* Vol. 3, *Letters from the Front.* New Haven: Yale UP, 1994.

———. *Shakespeare's Sisters: Feminist Essays on Women Poets.* Bloomington: Indiana UP, 1979.

Hacker, Marilyn. *Collected Poems.* New York: Harper & Row, 1956.

———. *Taking Notice.* New York: Knopf, 1980.

Millay, Edna St. Vincent. **Aria da Capo: A Play in One Act.** New York: Harper, 1920.

———. **Collected Poems.** Evanston, IL: Harper & Row, 1956.

———. **Conversation at Midnight.** New York: Harper & Row, 1937.

Ransom, John Crowe. *The World's Body.* New York: Scribner's, 1938.

Stanbrough, Jane. "Edna St. Vincent Millay and the Language of Vulnerability." In Gilbert and Gubar, *Shakespeare's Sisters.* 183-99.

Walker, Cheryl. *Masks Outrageous and Austere: Culture, Psyche, and Persona in Modern Women Poets.* Bloomington: Indiana UP, 1991.

TITLE COMMENTARY

Fatal Interview

PATRICIA A. KLEMANS (ESSAY DATE 1979)

SOURCE: Klemans, Patricia A. "'Being Born a Woman': A New Look at Edna St. Vincent Millay." In *Critical Essays on Edna St. Vincent Millay*, edited by William B. Thesing, pp. 200-12. New York: G. K. Hall, 1993.

In the following essay, originally published in 1979, Klemans argues that Fatal Interview *is important and innovative because it presents a new type of female poetic personality while utilizing the form of traditional love poetry—a genre previously dominated by male poets.*

I, being born a woman and distressed
By all the needs and notions of my kind,
Am urged by your propinquity to find
Your person fair, and feel a certain zest
To bear your body's weight upon my breast:
So subtly is the fume of life designed,
To clarify the pulse and cloud the mind,
And leave me once again undone, possessed.
Think not for this, however, the poor treason
Of my stout blood against my staggering brain,
I shall remember you with love, or season
My scorn with pity,—let me make it plain:
I find this frenzy insufficient reason
For conversation when we meet again.[1]

This sonnet, written by Edna St. Vincent Millay, was first published in **The Harp-Weaver** *and Other Poems* in 1923. It is an excellent place to begin in looking at Millay as not only an important poet but also as a poet with contemporary appeal.

The subject matter obviously proclaims a feminist philosophy. While a passionate woman might be ruled at times by her natural sexual impulses, she has not necessarily lost her reason or powers of discrimination. Men have been proclaiming this philosophy—and practicing it—for centuries, but it was news when a woman said it. The terse conclusion, "I find this frenzy insufficient reason / For conversation when we meet again," characterizes a woman who refuses to conform to society's dictates. Millay, like the persona of her sonnet, was an independent spirit. Whether she was resisting a new style in poetry or philosophy, or insisting on her own life-style, she remained an individualist until she died.

Edna St. Vincent Millay shocked many people with the sexual honesty in her poetry and in her personal life. By 1923, when this poem appeared, she was one of the best known literary personalities in America. She had made a name for herself at the age of twenty when her first serious work, "Renascence," was published in *The Lyric Year,* to great critical acclaim. The attention precipitated by the poem led to a scholarship to Vassar as well as many contacts with the literary leaders of the time. After graduating from college she headed for Greenwich Village where, becoming involved in acting as well as writing, she became an influential member of the contemporary art scene. With the publication of *A Few Figs from Thistles,* Millay became a sensation. The verse from that collection,

> My candle burns at both ends;
> It will not last the night;
> But ah, my foes and oh, my friends—
> It gives a lovely light!

seemed to epitomize the sexual defiance of the post-war generation. Millay's poetry suggested that she was a hedonist and her life-style seemed to confirm this view. Because of her many love affairs and avoidance of marriage, as well as her physical attractiveness and dramatic abilities, she was a subject of great interest and criticism. Her fans loved her and couldn't wait for her next volume of poems; her critics dismissed her as being frivolous, narrow, and tradition bound in her poetic forms.

In 1923, after returning from a year in Europe and publishing *The Harp-Weaver,* Millay became the first woman to win the Pulitzer prize and she married Eugen Boissevain, the widower of the suffrage leader, Inez Milholland. The poet of "**I, being born a woman**" was not only a woman of perception, as all poets must be, but also of experience. She had, by the age of thirty-one, led a life of personal and sexual freedom generally reserved only for men in our society. Her poetry presents this new viewpoint to literature—the liberated woman's view. In the nineteenth century we have the idealization of Elizabeth Barrett and Christina Rossetti and the obliqueness of Emily Dickinson to explore a woman's emotional life. In Millay we get a different view of "the needs and notions of my kind."

The work which best illustrates this unique contribution to literature is *Fatal Interview,* a sequence of fifty-two Shakespearean sonnets. The title is taken from John Donne's "Elegy 16": "By our first strange and fatal interview, / By all desires which thereof did ensue."[2] Published in 1931, Donne's tercentenary year, *Fatal Interview* not only relies a great deal on Donne's love poetry for its imagery and philosophy, but more importantly, presents a persona which is the first female counterpart to Donne's sophisticated lover. Millay's speaker is a realist; she is a woman of experience who presents her observations honestly, devoid of romanticizing or rationalizing. Unlike the 1923 sonnet, which describes a passionate but casual sexual encounter, *Fatal Interview* is concerned with the all-important love in a woman's life—a love that not everyone experiences personally, but one that everyone can relate to vicariously through reading this superb group of poems.

The critical response to *Fatal Interview* at its publication was generally favorable. Although Millay's popularity had ebbed somewhat since its high point in the early Twenties, a new book by her was still greeted with great interest. Harriet Monroe in *Poetry* began her review with these words: "This book is the record of emotional experience, done in terms of precise and measured beauty. It would be impossible to over-praise the consummate art with which Miss Millay has taken over the much-practiced form of the Shakespearean sonnet and made it her own as no other poet has, perhaps, since Shakespeare himself."[3] Allen Tate said in the *New Republic:*

> It is doubtful if all of Miss Millay's previous work put together is worth the thin volume of these fifty-two sonnets. At no previous time has she given us so sustained a performance. Half of the sonnets, perhaps all but about fifteen, lack distinction of emotional quality. None is deficient in an almost final technique. From first to last every sonnet has its special rhythm and sharply defined imagery; they move like a smooth machine, but

ABOUT THE AUTHOR

MAX EASTMAN ON MILLAY'S WORLD WAR II-ERA POETRY.

She was tremendously sincere—sincere enough, had it occurred to her, to go to work in a munitions factory, or wrap packages, or knit socks for the soldiers. That would have been a better gift to the war effort than bad poetry. But it would not have been the sacrifice of self that New England's rigid moralism demands. Edna may have imagined her name to be so renowned that her poetry, diluted to newspaper copy, would be an important help in "rousing the country," but I find this hard to believe. Her statement, "I have one thing to give in the service of my country, my reputation as a poet," strikes me as one of the most aberrant products of the modern brain-disease of propaganda. It was righteousness on the rampage, the sense of duty gone mad. And it ended, naturally, in a nervous breakdown.

"For five years," she wrote, explaining her illness to Edmund Wilson, "I had been writing almost nothing but propaganda. And I can tell you from my own experience that there is nothing on this earth which can so much get on the nerves of a good poet as the writing of bad poetry."

In sending us her beautifully titled book, *Make Bright the Arrows*, she wrote on the fly-leaf an inscription that was painful to read: "To Max and Eliena, who will not like the many bad lines contained in this book, but who will like the thing it wants so much to help to do, and who will like the reaffirmation of my constant affection and love. . . ." Many American writers—most of them—have at times diluted the purity of their art in order to make money; Edna's sin, we can say at least, was of a nobler-seeming kind. But it was a sin no less. She acknowledged later that this debauch of self-sacrifice had been a mistake, and regretted it sadly. But then it was too late. She never recaptured her lost self. She never wrote a great poem after that. . . .

Eastman, Max. Excerpt from "My Friendship with Edna Millay." In *Critical Essays on Edna St. Vincent Millay*, edited by William B. Thesing, pp. 164-65. New York: G. K. Hall, 1993.

not machine-like, under the hand of a masterly technician. The best sonnets would adorn any of the great English sequences. There is some interesting analysis to be made of Miss Millay's skillful use of the Shakespearean form, whose difficult final couplet she has mastered, and perhaps is alone in having mastered since Shakespeare.[4]

And finally, Genevieve Taggard ends her review in the *New York Herald Tribune Books* by saying: "We remember always a poet's best, his high water mark—his poorest vanishes like mortal speech. Her best is in the world of Shakespeare's sonnets, and, in her own field—she cannot be excelled. Immortality here is defined, served and achieved."[5]

Although all three of these critics agree without reservations that Millay is a master of the Shakespearean sonnet form, they do not all agree on the total worth of this collection. Miss Monroe's review is the most glowing in its praise of *Fatal Interview.* She calls it "one of the finest love-sequences in the language" but also makes the following comment:

> Because we have, in Miss Millay, a poet of very unusual scope and power—moreover, a woman poet of an epoch which no longer verifies Byron's line, "Man's love is of man's life a thing apart, / 'Tis woman's whole existence—" because of these facts which make a demand upon her, we have a right to feel in *Fatal Interview* her scope has narrowed from the broad ranges of her youth; and her power, however intense, however creative of perfection, accepts lower ground for its exercise.[6]

This criticism by a woman of a woman is very revealing. Monroe's choice of Byron's line suggests that she wants a woman poet of her "epoch" to deal with topics which are worldly, philosophical, "masculine." By Millay's choosing to write a book about love, a traditionally "feminine" preoccupation, the poet had, in Monroe's estimation, betrayed her early promise. One of the most frequent comments made about **"Renascence"** was that it was unbelievable that it was written by a young woman. Its subject, a poet's vision of the world's grief and her reconcilement with the universe, as well as its great poetic proficiency, seemed beyond the range of a twenty year old girl from a small town in Maine. Monroe sees, therefore, *Fatal Interview* as a narrowing, an acceptance of "lower ground." Unfortunately, Monroe was unable to recognize how truly innovative the work was in presenting a feminine view of a subject for which the ground rules had been set by men. Instead she has reservations about how important a woman's love affair might be to the rest of the world.

Allen Tate makes it clear how important he feels it to be—not very. He damns Millay with faint praise, then compares her unfavorably with T. S. Eliot who he believes "penetrated to the fundamental structure of the nineteenth century mind and shows its breakdown." He continues, "Miss Millay assumed no such profound alteration of the intelligence because, I suppose, not being an intellect but a sensibility, she was not aware of it."[7] Tate's review is primarily an essay about his poetic tastes rather than an analysis of *Fatal Interview.* He spends more time discussing Eliot and Yeats than Millay, who is of course in his eyes a "sensibility" rather than an "intellect," whatever that means.

Genevieve Taggard's review, on the other hand, focuses on Millay and her poems but it too makes some ambiguous statements. After praising her for her skill as a sonnet writer, Taggard criticizes Millay for the very reasons that she has said she was effective. She says:

> It seems to me that Miss Millay worships only one thing—perfection. Such a worship throws difficulties in the path of human love, but it suits the ardors of the sonnet-writer and the lover of beauty alike. She does not value uniqueness, she has no patience with rebel esthetics, new forms, naturalism which loves irregularity, which everywhere opposes logic and the almost machinelike perfection of detached art. Odd insights are awkward to her. Her preferences are for those elegiac and harmonious gestures of the greatest Greek sculptures. I should even dare to push the statement further and say that Miss Millay is interested in perfection, not people, in art, not in life—her courage and self scorn testify to her own self-rejection for the sake of her first principle. Is it not natural then that Miss Millay should choose the sonnet form which demands in the very act of writing, this attitude?[8]

Taggard undoubtedly got carried away with her own rhetoric. Given the known facts of Millay's life, her many and varied experiences, her close personal relationships with her family and friends, as well as the very personal and moving quality which characterizes *Fatal Interview,* it was certainly inaccurate and unfair to accuse her of being uninterested in life and in people. One wonders if Taggard would have charged Petrarch, Spenser, or Shakespeare with this attitude. Or is it the woman who Millay characterizes in her poems that bothers this critic? A woman of pride and principle; a woman of courage and arrogance; a woman some would find difficult to sympathize with. Millay's speaker rejects the games that lovers play and in doing so undoubtedly antagonizes some, including women.

In looking at the reviews of these contemporaries of Millay we can see reflected the tastes of the time. Millay was writing perfect love sonnets at a time when love seemed trite and the sonnet was "out." In 1923 Millay won the Pulitzer prize for *Second April* and Eliot won the Dial prize for *The Waste Land.* The great difference in these two books marks the great parting of the ways for Millay and Eliot. In 1920, both poets were expressing a philosophy of despair and were greatly attracted to the Elizabethans, especially Donne and Webster, for their ironic, worldly view. By 1923, however, Eliot had turned to nihilism as a philosophy, and symbolism and fragmentation as a technique. Millay took a different road. Her view of the world was not more optimistic than Eliot's. She too saw the disintegrating forces of her times but unlike him, she turned to nature and the past to form a defense against them. Instead of reflecting the disintegration in her poetry, her object was to "put Chaos into fourteen lines / And keep him there."

In *Fatal Interview* she puts the chaos of a love affair into fifty-two tightly constructed, interwoven sonnets; she also illustrates her personal poetic philosophy. She believed that her poetry, like herself, must be honest and intelligible. In "Sonnet CLXV" from *Mine the Harvest,* published in 1954, four years after her death, she expresses her views on contemporary poetry:

> It is the fashion now to wave aside
> As tedious, obvious, vacuous, trivial, trite,
> All things which do not tickle, tease, excite
> To some subversion, or in verbiage hide
> Intent, or mock, or with hot sauce provide
> A dish to prick the thickened appetite;
> Straightforwardness is wrong, evasion right;
> It is correct, *de rigueur,* to deride.
> What fumy wits these modern wags expose,
> For all their versatility: Voltaire,
> Who wore to bed a night-cap, and would close,
> In fear of drafts, all windows, could declare
> In antique stuffiness, a phrase that blows
> Still through men's smoky minds, and clears the
>   air.

During her lifetime, poetic taste swung toward Eliot and experimentation and away from Millay and tradition. These three reviewers reflect this swing in their granting her skill yet being blind to the truly innovative aspects of the poems contained in *Fatal Interview.*

The sequence tells a moving story. The speaker, who first appears in Sonnet II, finds herself in the grips of a passion which she foresees from the very beginning as being ultimately disastrous. Although unable to free herself from her obsession, she refuses to conform to the expected behavior patterns associated with the woman's role in a love affair. She refuses to use guile to capture her lover and says in **"Sonnet III"**:

> Liefer would I you loved me for my worth,
> Though you should love me but a little while,
> Than for a philtre any doll can brew,—
> Though thus I bound you as I long to do.

And, in "Sonnet VI," the speaker becomes very assertive when she chides her lover for finding it safer to love the women of literature, Cressid, Elaine, and Isolt, than to respond to her in whom passion pounds all day long. Here, and throughout the sequence, the woman is an initiator, honest and fearless. No coy mistress she; it is the man who seems to require the urging. In "Sonnet XI" she insists that the lover's relationship will be honest and direct, "Love in the open hand, no thing but that, / Ungemmed, unhidden, wishing not to hurt."

The affair runs a passionate and tumultuous course with the speaker's emotions alternating between ecstasy and despair. Even at the risk of losing her lover she will not compromise her principles. She says in **"Sonnet XXIII"**:

> I know the face of Falsehood and her tongue
> Honeyed with unction, plausible with guile,
> Are dear to men, whom count me not among,
> That owe their daily credit to her smile;

This woman Millay characterizes is a new personality in love poetry. She is no innocent virgin, religious zealot, shrinking violet, or scheming man-hunter. She is direct and forthright with a personal morality she will not compromise. When the inevitable break between the lovers comes, in **"Sonnet XXXIX,"** she again offers her lover her hand, but this time it is to say farewell. She internalizes her pain and accepts the inevitable.

The final poems trace the process the speaker must go through to regain the self-esteem she has temporarily lost in her abandonment to love. In **"Sonnet XL"** she says:

> You loved me not at all, but let it go;
> I loved you more than life, but let it be.
> As the more injured party, this being so,
> The hour's amenities are all to me—

The suffering is long and intense but she is a survivor. In **"Sonnet L"** she reflects that it has been a half year since her heart "broke in two; / The world's forgotten well, if the world knew."

This account of a love affair from a passionate woman's point of view creates a rich and illuminating experience for the reader. Each poem

of the sequence leads logically into the next while being itself a lyric expressing a particular theme. Read independently, each poem is a complete experience; read in context, it is part of a complex design. *Fatal Interview* offers something new expressed in the framework and terms of the old. It presents love from a woman's point of view, yet it treats love as an ageless and natural experience. The poems are extremely personal, yet not private. Millay accomplishes this universality by interweaving the woman's experience with classical myth, traditional love literature, and nature.

The framework of the sequence is the legend of Selene and Endymion. The first and final sonnets have as their speaker the moon goddess who fell hopelessly in love with a shepherd. Unable to have him for her own, Selene enchanted him with eternal sleep and suffered the pain and anguish of mortal love forever. There are direct references as well as echoes of the tale throughout the work. Other characters from mythology are also present. In the poem celebrating the consummation of passion, **"Sonnet XII,"** the lover is likened to Jove when the speaker says:

> Olympian gods, mark now my bedside lamp
> Blown out; and be advised too late that he
> Whom you call sire is stolen into the camp
> Of warring Earth, and lies abed with me.

This passage is also reminiscent of the story of Cupid and Psyche in which Psyche is not allowed to see her lover and must extinguish her lamp when Cupid comes to her bed. Cupid and his mother, Venus, are directly referred to in **"Sonnet XV"** when the speaker says, "My worship from this hour the Sparrow-Drawn / Alone will cherish, and her arrowy child." This sonnet uses myth to emphasize the desperate plight of one who has abandoned herself to love. She says of Venus and Cupid:

> How have I stripped me of immortal aid
> Save theirs alone,—who could endure to see
> Forsworn Aeneas with conspiring blade
> Sever the ship from shore (alas for me)
> And make no sign; who saw, and did not speak,
> The brooch of Troilus pinned upon the Greek.

The effectiveness of this passage depends on the reader's knowledge of the stories of Aeneas and Dido and Troilus and Cressida. Millay assumes that her reader will know two of the greatest love stories of our culture and so she uses this comparison to emphasize the agelessness of her plight as well as the indifference of the universe.

Structuring her sequence on myth gives it a pagan base. The afterlife in Millay's sonnets only appears in a dream of the Elysian fields where the speaker meets the women who have been raped by Jove. The Gods which the speaker invokes are those of Greek mythology. Millay's world is pre-Christian and the Gods she acknowledges are indifferent to the plight of mankind. Her speaker does not have a personal deity who cares for her or promises her eternal life. She has no such consolation and so is as isolated from religious comfort as early pagans or twentieth century atheists.

There is a link in the poems with Christianity, of course, because that too is part of tradition. Millay alludes directly or indirectly to the literature of all ages but there is a particularly heavy emphasis on Donne and other metaphysical poets for the philosophy and imagery of the poems. It is not necessary that the reader of **Fatal Interview** be familiar with seventeenth century love poetry, but it adds a fascinating dimension to the sequence if one has such knowledge. The metaphysical poets are characterized by their wit—an ingenuity in literary invention, an ability to discover clever, surprising, or paradoxical figures. Millay is witty in that she uses the images of these early poets to create her own unique view of the subject. In "Sonnet III" she employs the compass image that Donne had made famous as a symbol of the perfect relationship between lovers. In "A Valediction Forbidding Mourning" he had likened himself and his love to a compass: "Thy soule the fixt foot, makes no show / To move, but doth, if the other doe." The woman is the fixed foot which only moves to follow the bent of the man.

Millay's compass is of a different variety and the woman is doing the moving. The speaker says:

> My needle to your north abruptly swerved;
> If I would hold you, I must hide my fears
> Lest you be wanton, lead you to believe
> My compass to another quarter veers,
> Little surrender, lavishly receive.

Here, instead of using the compass as the symbol of true love, Millay dramatizes man's propensity for wanting what is hard to get. The entire concept of the woman's character is changed from one of fidelity and dependency to one of experience and independence. Donne's compass encloses space; Millay's determines directions.

In "Sonnet XI," Millay seems to be conversing with Donne. In "The Token" he had asked his lover to "Send me some token, that my hope may live" and concludes, "Send me not this, nor that, t'increase my store, / But swear thou thinkst I love thee, and no more." Millay's sonnet seems to be a reply to Donne's poem. She denies this request,

deprecating his wish for a pledge of any sort. She offers, "Love in the open hand, no thing but that."

To the literary minded, Millay's sonnets abound with allusions to the immortals. Echoes of Chaucer, Virgil, Ovid, and the seventeenth century dramatists abound. Reading Millay's sonnets can, therefore, become a kind of game for literary buffs—just the kind of game that intrigued the seventeenth century mind but one which few modern readers have the background to participate in.

It is not necessary, however, for the reader of **Fatal Interview** to be familiar with myth or literary history to enjoy and to feel empathy with Millay's moving love sonnets. The poems are firmly connected and supported by a body of references common to all, that of nature. The fifty-two sonnets parallel the fifty-two weeks of the year during which time there is for all things, a season. It is autumn when the speaker first sees her lover; the consummation of the affair occurs in winter. The love blooms in spring, smolders through the summer, and is touched by frost in early fall. As the love affair ends the speaker longs for winter. She says:

> Freeze up the year; with sleet these branches
>   bend
> Though rasps the locust in the fields around.
> Now darken, sky! Now shrieking blizzard,
>   blow!—
> Farewell, sweet bank; be blotted out with snow.

The speaker, throughout the sequence, refers to herself as being close to nature. She knows from the very beginning of the affair that nothing can remain the same. In "Sonnet XLVI" she says:

> Even at the moment of our earliest kiss,
> When sighed the straitened bud into flower,
> Sat the dry seed of most unwelcome this;
> And that I knew, though not the day and hour.
> Too season-wise am I, being country-bred,
> To tilt at autumn or defy the frost:
> Snuffing the chill even as my fathers did,
> I say with them, "What's out tonight is lost."

This acceptance of the order of things, this resignation, is her way of maintaining her sanity. In her desolation she remembers the "island women" of Matinicus who stood alone in autumn "In gardens stripped and scattered peering north, / With dahlia tubers dripping from the hand" "Sonnet XXXVI". She finds some consolation in the thought that she has shared these common experiences. Like the women, she must accept change. Having experienced great joy, she must now endure the suffering—that is the balance of her world.

Gardens appear in many of the poems. When the affair is over, the speaker's garden is ruined, and the once still marigolds and sturdy zinnias are but "pale and oozy stalks." These details are Millay's observations of her immediate world. She grew up on the coast of Maine and lived on a farm in upper New York state after her marriage. These are rugged areas with early frosts and short summers. The gardens in Millay's world are strong and colorful but short-lived, like the brief but tumultuous love affair she describes.

The sea is even more important and pervasive in this sequence than the garden. The water imagery creates much of the sensuality of the poetry, as in **"Sonnet VII"** when she combines two of her favorite metaphors, the sea and night:

> Night is my sister, and how deep in love,
> How drowned in love and weedily washed
>   ashore,
> There to be fretted by the drag and shove
> At the tide's edge, I lie—these things and more:
> Whose arm alone between me and the sand,
> Whose voice alone, whose pitiful breath brought
>   near,
> Could thaw these nostrils and unlock this hand,
> She could advise you, should you care to hear.
> Small chance, however, in a storm so black,
> A man will leave his friendly fire and snug
> For a drowned woman's sake, and bring her back
> To drip and scatter shells upon the rug.
> No one but Night, with tears on her dark face,
> Watches beside me in this windy place.

In this poem, while using nature imagery to describe an emotional state, Millay creates in her female persona a bond with another female, Night. She carries this idea through the sonnets with her many references to women. The only ones who can understand the speaker's love are Selene, Leda, Danae, and Europa; the women of the Irish and Trojan coasts; the women of Matinicus; and perhaps the women reading this poetry. This affinity with women is unusual in any literature but very rare in love poetry where women are usually portrayed as rivals.

The lover in **Fatal Interview** does not leave the speaker for another woman; he leaves because he cannot love with an intensity and constancy equal to hers. The speaker says in this poem, "Small chance, however, in a storm so black, / A man will leave his friendly fire and snug / For a drowned woman's sake." She suggests that men are not capable of the depth of emotion which women are but are more concerned with comfort and security. This difference between the male and female lover is epitomized in the Selene-Endymion legend. Unlike the Keats poem which pities Endymion, Millay's sympathies are with Selene. The

Goddess is devastated and wanders over the sky, distraught over losing her love; the Mortal sleeps, oblivious to all the pain and anguish he has caused.

Still, Millay is not suggesting that only women can love completely and passionately. She refers to Troilus who broke his heart when Cressida gave his love token away. In this legend it is the man who loved too well. In addition, the close parallels to Donne's love poems in many of these sonnets suggest that Millay considered Donne a soulmate, despite their different points of view. They are certainly in agreement on the effect of a tragic love affair. Donne wrote in "The broken heart":

> And now as broken glasses show
> A hundred lesser faces, so
> My ragges of heart can like, wish, and adore,
> But after one such love, can love no more.

Millay says much the same in **"Sonnet L"**: "The heart once broken is a heart no more, / And is absolved from all a heart must be."

Obviously, love is an emotional experience common to both men and women. Most of the great love poetry, however, has been written by men and not until Millay do we have the experience of seeing a personal examination of an affair from a woman's point of view. This view was not easily accepted by some. The following poem by L. Robert Lind, published in 1935 in the *Sewanee Review,* is an interesting reaction:

Ad Feminam Tristem, Sed Poetam

> (After Reading Edna St. Vincent Millay's *Fatal
>   Interview*)
> O come away at last from this lorn love
> That will not hear, however sad you speak;
> O brood no more for him, you hurt wild
>   dove,
> Seeking the lost that comes not though you
>   seek.
> Were man so to be longed for and in truth
> The inmost object of your grave desire,
> And more than merely puppet in the booth
> Of sonnet-music, moved by a singing wire,
> You could not so your sorrow still rehearse
> And ring the changes in one mournful
>   measure,
> Exhaust the resolutions of your verse,
> Or find in repetition such wry pleasure:
> You could but, woman-like, grieve without a
>   word;
> Yet, being poet, your mourning must be
>   heard.[9]

Granting that Mr. Lind's main purpose in writing this poem was to exhibit his wit rather than to offer any serious critical insights, it does reveal an attitude that is not uncommon in men's reactions to women's work. He makes the writing of poetry by a woman, at least love poetry, a sort of "Catch-22" situation. If she were really sincere, he says, she would grieve "woman-like" and not write at all. Since she persists in writing, then she cannot be sincere. This attitude supports Millay's speaker who believes that a man is incapable of understanding the passion of a woman.

No one disputes that *Fatal Interview* contains perfectly written sonnets. Many, however, have failed to perceive that the poems are unique and innovative in their presentation of a feminine viewpoint on love. Millay reversed the masculine-feminine traditional stances while working within the traditional forms. Today we have many women poets who are speaking frankly about a woman's nature. In 1931, we had Edna St. Vincent Millay. The unfortunate fact is that many have overlooked the message while appreciating the medium. A Millay poem looks traditional—in form it is. But her characterization of a woman who is initiator, aggressor, and controller as well as victim, sufferer, and survivor is unique. The woman of the poems contains within herself the knowledge and experience of the ages. In this sense she is Mother Earth. But she is also a human being with an intellect. Through experience and introspection, she comes to terms with life, finding her truths in nature and its order.

The time has certainly come for a second look at Millay's work, which is both impressive and varied. *Fatal Interview* is only one of the many beautiful and meaningful collections of poetry which speaks particularly to a woman's experience. Millay belonged to the generation which saw women finally get the right to vote, a time of feminine idealism which lionized Amelia Earhart for crossing the Atlantic Ocean by plane. Millay spoke for a generation of young women who responded to her standards of sexual independence and feminine heroism. Pushed to the back shelves for so many years, Millay's books deserve a new reading. Millay can speak to the women and men of today as well as to those of the Twenties and Thirties, because her poetry is written with consummate skill and her message of feminine individuality is ageless.

Notes

1. Edna St. Vincent Millay, *Collected Poems* (New York: Harper & Row, 1956), p. 601. All subsequent quotations from Millay's poetry are taken from this edition. The poems are copyright 1923, 1931, 1951, 1954, 1958 by Edna St. Vincent Millay and Norma Millay (Ellis), and are reprinted by permission of Norma Millay (Ellis).

2. *Donne: Poetical Works*, ed. Herbert J. C. Grierson (New York: Oxford Univ. Press, 1971), p. 99. All subsequent quotations from Donne's poetry are taken from this edition.

3. "Advance or Retreat?," *Poetry*, XXXVIII (July 1931), p. 216.

4. "Miss Millay's Sonnets," *New Republic*, XLVI (May 6, 1931), p. 336.

5. "A Woman's Anatomy of Love," *New York Herald Tribune, Review of Books*, April 19, 1931.

6. "Advance or Retreat?," p. 219.

7. "Miss Millay's Sonnets," p. 335.

8. "A Woman's Anatomy of Love."

9. Vol. XLIII (Jan.-Mar. 1935), p. 104. Reprinted by permission of the editor.

FURTHER READING

Biography

Milford, Nancy. *Savage Beauty: The Life of Edna St. Vincent Millay*, New York: Random House, 2001, 550 p.

An account of Millay's life and times.

Criticism

Fairley, Irene R. "Edna St. Vincent Millay's Gendered Language and Form: 'Sonnets from an Ungrafted Tree'." *Style* 29, no. 1 (spring 1995): 58-75.

Assesses Millay's sonnet sequence as a reflective expression of a woman's emerging self-knowledge.

Frank, Elizabeth Perlmutter. "A Doll's Heart: The Girl in the Poetry of Edna St. Vincent Millay and Louise Bogan." In *Critical Essays on Edna St. Vincent Millay*, edited by William B. Thesing, pp. 179-99. New York: G. K. Hall, 1993.

Compares the two poet's presentation of female personae and their approaches to the past traditions of lyric poetry.

Fried, Debra. "Andromeda Unbound: Gender and Genre in Millay's Sonnets." *Twentieth Century Literature: A Scholarly and Critical Journal* 32, no. 1 (spring 1986): 1-22.

Explores Millay's sonnets and contends that she utilized the form to overcome the genre's history of silencing women's voices.

Gilmore, Susan. "'Posies of Sophistry': Impersonation and Authority in Millay's *Conversation at Midnight*." In *Millay at 100: A Critical Reappraisal*, edited by Diane P. Freedman, pp. 182-97. Carbondale: Southern Illinois University Press, 1995.

Analyzes Conversation at Midnight *and its chorus of male speakers as Millay's attempt to expose the masculine tendency to use discursive representations of femininity.*

Jones, Phyllis M. "Amatory Sonnet Sequences and the Female Perspective of Elinor Wylie and Edna St. Vincent Millay." *Women's Studies* 10 (1983): 41-61.

Discusses Millay's Fatal Interview *and Elinor Wylie's sonnet sequence* One Person, *concentrating on the ways in which the poets transform traditional poetic forms to present female-oriented love poetry.*

Newcomb, John Timberman. "The Woman as Political Poet: Edna St. Vincent Millay and the Mid-Century Canon." *Criticism: A Quarterly for Literature and the Arts* 37, no. 2 (spring 1995): 261-79.

Champions Millay's politically-oriented work and opposes critics John Crowe Ransom and John Ciardi, who denigrated Millay's poetry, suggesting that there was a strong sexual and aesthetic bias to their opinions.

Peppe, Holly. "Rewriting the Myth of the Woman in Love: Millay's *Fatal Interview*." In *Millay at 100: A Critical Reappraisal*, edited by Diane P. Freedman, pp. 52-65. Carbondale: Southern Illinois University Press, 1995.

Considers Millay's use of mythical material in Fatal Interview *and asserts that the speaker of the poems is ultimately strengthened by the conclusion of her love affair.*

Stanbrough, Jane. "Edna St. Vincent Millay and the Language of Vulnerability." In *Shakespeare's Sisters: Feminist Essays on Women Poets*, edited by Sandra M. Gilbert and Susan Gubar, pp. 183-89. Bloomington, Ind.: Indiana University Press, 1979.

Argues that despite the popular conception of Millay as liberated and self-assured, her poetry repeatedly presents vulnerable female characters victimized by exterior forces.

Walker, Cheryl. "The Female Body as Icon: Edna Millay Wears a Plaid Dress." In *Millay at 100: A Critical Reappraisal*, edited by Diane P. Freedman, pp. 85-99. Carbondale: Southern Illinois University Press, 1995.

Discusses Millay as a media icon and considers her self-critique of that position in the collection Huntsman, What Quarry?

——. "Antimodern, Modern, and Postmodern Millay: Contexts and Revaluation." In *Gendered Modernisms: American Women Poets and Their Readers*, edited by Margaret Dickie and Thomas Travisano, pp. 170-88. Philadelphia: University of Philadelphia Press, 1996.

Investigates how Millay's reputation among critics has varied over time in accordance with changing literary fashions.

OTHER SOURCES FROM GALE:

Additional coverage of Millay's life and career is contained in the following sources published by the Gale Group: *American Writers; Concise Dictionary of American Literary Biography, 1917-1929; Dictionary of Literary Biography,* Vols. 45, 249; *DISCovering Authors; DISCovering Authors: British Edition; DISCovering Authors: Canadian Edition; DISCovering Authors Modules: Most-studied Authors* and *Poets; DISCovering Authors 3.0; Encyclopedia of World Literature in the 20th Century,* Ed. 3; *Exploring Poetry; Literature Resource Center; Modern American Women Writers; Poetry Criticism,* Vol. 6; *Poetry for Students,* Vols. 3, 17; *Poets: American and British; Reference Guide to American Literature,* Ed. 4; *Twayne's United States Authors; Twentieth-Century Literary Criticism,* Vols. 4, 49; *World Literature Criticism Supplement;* and *World Poets.*

MARIANNE MOORE

(1887 - 1972)

(Full name Marianne Craig Moore) American poet, essayist, translator, short story writer, editor, playwright, and author of children's books.

One of America's foremost literary figures, Moore has been considered by feminist critics to be a singular and important female poetic voice. She is known for creating verse characterized by loose rhythms, carefully chosen words, close attention to descriptive detail, and acute observation of human character. Her poems often reflect her preoccupation with the relationships between the common and the uncommon; advocate discipline in both art and life; and espouse virtues of restraint, modesty, and humor. She frequently used animals as a central image to emphasize themes of independence, honesty, and the integration of art and nature. Although some critics consider much of her poetry overly affected and her subject matter inconsequential, Moore has been praised as an important poetic voice by such outstanding literary figures as T. S. Eliot, William Carlos Williams, Hilda Doolittle, and Ezra Pound.

BIOGRAPHICAL INFORMATION

Moore was born November 15, 1887, in Kirkwood, Missouri. She attended Bryn Mawr College, where she published her early poetry in the campus literary magazine, and received a degree in biology and histology in 1909. At Bryn Mawr, Moore established an enduring friendship with Doolittle as well as with Williams, Pound, and Eliot, to whom her work would later be compared. From 1911 to 1915 Moore taught stenography at the U.S. Indian School in Carlisle, Pennsylvania. In 1915 her poems began to appear in such respected literary periodicals as the *Egoist, Others,* and *Poetry*; her first volume, *Poems* (1921), includes many of these early pieces. Moore moved with her mother to Greenwich Village in New York City in 1918, and worked as an assistant at the New York Public Library branch in Hudson from 1921 to 1925. In 1925 she became editor of the *Dial,* a position she retained until the magazine ceased publication in 1929. Her experiences with the *Dial* brought her into contact with many of the noted literati of the time and helped advance her international reputation. In 1951 her *Collected Poems* (1951) was awarded both the Pulitzer Prize in poetry and a National Book Award, awards which brought her more widespread recognition outside the literary world. Moore died February 5, 1972.

MAJOR WORKS

Much of Moore's early verse is marked by stylistic originality, unique subject matter, and unconventional humor. Such poems as "Critics and Connoisseurs" and "Poetry" reflect Moore's concerns with literature and art. One of Moore's best-known pieces, "Marriage," is a long experimental work written in free verse that features collage-like assemblages of quotations and fragments. In this poem, Moore employs wit and satire to comment on the tensions of marital coexistence. Critics have noted the distant, often sexless perspective not only of "Marriage," but of all Moore's work.

The content of Moore's first book, *Poems,* was arranged by Doolittle and others; however, Moore chose the poems in her second volume, *Observations* (1924), to represent the variety of her themes and forms. *Observations* includes a scrupulously described exploration of the flora and fauna of Washington state's Mount Rainier in the poem "An Octopus." The poem derived its name from the shape of the glacier that surrounds the mountain peak, and it is often regarded as one of the twentieth century's great odes to nature.

Among Moore's other volumes are *The Pangolin and Other Verse* (1936), which reflects her interest in animals as subjects for art; *What Are Years* (1941), which combines poems from *The Pangolin* with several previously uncollected works; and *Nevertheless* (1944), which captures Moore at perhaps her most impassioned. One of her later poems, "In Distrust of Merits," details Moore's condemnation of the atrocities of war. This poem was singled out by W. H. Auden as the best poem to emerge in reaction to World War II, and the poem remains highly regarded and widely discussed. Publication of *The Complete Poems of Marianne Moore* (1967) prompted poet John Ashbery to predict that Moore's work would "continue to be read as poetry when much of the major poetry of our time has become part of the history of literature."

CRITICAL RECEPTION

Moore has been the subject of much feminist criticism. Some critics regard her work as an example of a strong female voice, as demonstrated by specific elements of her poetry in addition to her prominence in literary society. A few critics have contended that Moore emerged as an important poet because she denied femininity and sexuality in her work. Other critics fault Moore for this denial, claiming that her disregard for such central subjects as gender and sexuality reinforces the limitations society places on women. In the latter part of her life, Moore's literary contribu-

tions were recognized with a host of awards and honors, including the Poetry Society of America's Gold Medal for Distinguished Development, the National Medal for Literature, and an honorary doctorate from Harvard University. In the twenty-first century, noted poets and commentators continue to praise Moore's verse, hailing the poet as one of the most important in modern literature.

PRINCIPAL WORKS

Poems (poetry) 1921

Observations (poetry) 1924

Selected Poems (poetry) 1935

The Pangolin and Other Verse (poetry) 1936

What Are Years (poetry) 1941

Nevertheless (poetry) 1944

Collected Poems (poetry) 1951

The Fables of La Fontaine (translation) 1954

Predilections (essays and criticism) 1955

Like a Bulwark (poetry) 1956

O to Be a Dragon (poetry) 1959

A Marianne Moore Reader (poems and prose) 1961

The Absentee (play) 1962

The Arctic Ox (poetry) 1964

Tell Me, Tell Me: Granite, Steel, and Other Topics (poetry and prose) 1966

The Complete Poems of Marianne Moore (poetry) 1967; also published as *The Complete Poems of Marianne Moore* [revised edition], 1981

The Complete Prose of Marianne Moore (prose) 1986

The Selected Letters of Marianne Moore [edited by Bonnie Costello] (letters) 1997

Becoming Marianne Moore: The Early Poems, 1907-1924 (poetry) 2002

The Poems of Marianne Moore [edited by Grace Shulman] (poetry) 2004

PRIMARY SOURCES

MARIANNE MOORE (LETTER DATES 14 FEBRUARY 1909 AND 31 AUGUST 1921)

SOURCE: Moore, Marianne. *The Selected Letters of Marianne Moore,* edited by Bonnie Costello, pp. 63-6, 175-79. New York: Alfred A. Knopf, 1997.

In the following letters, written in 1909 and 1921, Moore discusses her thoughts on the suffragist movement and the institution of marriage.

To Mary Warner Moore and John Warner Moore

FEB[RUARY] 14, 1909

Dear Family,

I hate to think of your taking so hard, my anxieties. To think I could ever come so near the ragged brink though and miss it, makes me squirm. I find I did *not* have to get Merit in Philosophy. I merely had to get half 15 hours, but of course with persistent drawing of Passeds, it's very pleasant to have 10 hours. Mary Allen has 2 too few and Hilda S.-S. failed Philosophy (pretty badly), so there has been a general slaughter. Hilda will get her degree of course, for she can take the exam. at Easter.

Elsie failed English Comp.—(technically. Her critical papers are passed)—so she feels very sore but she got H.C. in one Mathematics and in Latin Comp.—and is so "proud of her High Credits," I feel they should salve her pain. She says not infrequently, "I'm pretty proud of my High Credits. Wouldn't you be?" I said I think I would and that I think I'll go in for one in Philosophy in June, ([J. M.] Barrie like).

I have a verse of not very high character which is coming out in *The Lantern*. I gave it to *Tip*. But Ruth George wrested it away to my ineffable joy.

> Ennui I call it—
> *He often expressed*
> *A curious wish*
> *To be interchangeably*
> *Man and fish*
> *To nibble the bait*
> *Off the hook said he*
> *And then slip away*
> *Like a ghost in the sea.*

I am not proud of it, but I like the rhythm and I intend to try, till I do write something. (I intend to try too for H.C. in Philosophy and in Daddy.)[1]

These sporadic poems I don't work over, (though my stories I do), so I smile, (as if I had found a penny) when people tell me how they like them and talk about writing poetry and so on as if it were gymnastics or piano practice.

Miss Shaw spoke last night on the Modern Democratic ideal. I couldn't say how she delighted me. No decent, half-kind, creature could possibly think of fighting suffrage if he or it had heard her arguments. They hold water so that they stand repeating, too. Elsie didn't go, so I gave her an extract today, (we went walking)—and she is "on the fence." (Flourish of trumpets.) I said when Elsie said for the 12th time she didn't see what

difference voting would make in "making people better," I said, if you want to oppose women's voting I said, you merely say you are willing to tramp over people's bodies to get all these luxuries you take so calmly. I said, "if women are going to support children and perhaps unproductive adults they ought to have as much pay as men and ought to work eight hours if men work eight hours, and not work ten." I delivered a cruel flow on the score of men. I said the *men* are all that keep you respectable. Just because they don't *choose* to grind women down more than women *are* ground down, is not the fault of the women. I said, (Educated!) women say, men give us every thing we want why try to get the ballot. I said, "the men give you what you want because they are a high grade of animal. The clothes of every woman in N.Y. a few years ago, belonged to her husband, no widow could legally be buried in the state—a widow inherited $\frac{2}{3}$ of her husband's property—(during her life). The cemetery lot came in the property, so the woman had $\frac{2}{3}$ of the cemetery lot during her lifetime and to get any use out of it would have to be buried before she was dead." Elsie laughed quizzically. I said also that the eight hour day was all a question of the ballot. Elsie said she didn't see how it could be. I said, "well, in Colorado, the men had an eight hour day, the women, a ten hour day, the women got an eight hour day because they put a bill in as voters (for state legislature). In N.Y. they did not." The philanthropy argument I think was Miss Shaw's best. But I think Elsie "tried not to pay attention"—and didn't see what I was talking about—the idea that if you prevent *all* babies from drinking infected milk, you do more good than if you solicit money and supply 200 with Pasteurized milk. Miss Shaw said, people were bringing up the argument that women would neglect charity (Dr. Lyman Abbott)[2] the idea of the ballot being to obviate the necessity of charity. She quashed the unladylike argument and the time argument. She said the ladies of Colorado get a bill through in one year and the ladies of N.Y. take a trip up the Hudson every year for *seven* years and don't get a bill passed *then*. She said the legislative measures were often more ethical than partisan and that feminine women oughtn't to feel too ignorant to *care* what happened. The point about the industrial school I thought squashing but Elsie did not. That you can't tell girls to stay at home when the girls who are fit to stay at home are a million in three and the girls that need to stay at home or get positions as housemaids have run on the streets all their lives and don't know what clean beds are or what cooking utensils look like. I wasn't as rabid as I sound here, but I was pretty bulldoggy. I said "of course woman suffrage doesn't mean much to you, because you're petted and have money lavished on you and you wouldn't think what a slum looks like and wouldn't think of touching an infected horse-hide or dangerous machinery for anything, but a lot of girls that haven't quite your chances could see why it might help some." Elsie said, "Did you see that bunch of flowers Glady Spry had on?" and I could have beat her with a book. But my words sank in, as someone asked Elsie in my presence later what she thought of woman suffrage and she said, "I can't decide."

Pres. Thomas had us at the Deanery after the lecture (the Suffrage Society) and I was struck dumb, the place is so beautiful. It's more educational than an art course. It rambles a little and there is a narrow passage I don't like, but the whole, is an Elysian garden. The reception hall, is a big square place with a tiled floor and gold (burlap!) on the walls and a hammered brass ceiling of which little shows for heavy brown beams go across—and sparsely filled with antique, capacious chairs, inlaid with gilded legs. The bedrooms upstairs are indescribable. The one I left my wraps in had a punctured bed, square, Indian brass (square posts and low head and foot boards) with a pale silk spread (embroidered flat) across it. The bathroom adjoining is a square room, size of my college room, mosaic floor, white tiled walls. All the ceilings through the house are stenciled, the lamps—Favrile glass—and the woodwork the color of the walls. In Pres. T's study the walls are blue and the window frames blue and the chandelier a bunch of (five) pale pepper shaped, conical lobes, greenish yellow. The Dean came in as we were looking at it, (standing in the doorway, Sh. Warner and Mabel Ashley and some Freshman and I) and said, "I think we shall have it done and have the curtains up, by the time of the Senior reception— the first after Easter." This room was adjacent to the "salon" so it was suitable we should be there, (we were encouraged moreover to circulate). I did the talking about the stone in the gymnasium, the stain on the wood, the gargoyles in the cloister and dozens of kindred topics. The Dean was more charming than I've ever known her. The way she has worked too for the gym. excites my admiration. Hours she worked every day in the hottest part of the summer, on the plans, Miss Lawther says. She said finally, "Now, won't you have some lemonade, nuts, cakes (in the *dining*-room). See how you like our grape-juice lemonade." The

grape-juice lemonade, nuts, cakes and candy were fine, a tinge of Deanery luxury. The old pieces of furniture decorated with brass and the electric lamps and the windows and rugs and the piano— and red patterned East Indian cover made me gasp. My suffrage experiences in New York hearing Mr. Zueblin stood me in good stead—(he is very well known and apparently universally liked) as I first shook hands, for I feel the ice thin at any party when I have to bow and grin and go and haven't time to get into a mellow conversation.

In the middle narrow passage I speak of there are low dark bookcases on which were various pieces of rainbow peacock glass. In the middle room (centre) from which opened the salon, and the office and the narrow hall was a table (low) but square with all the periodicals neatly arranged in columns and here and there on other tables, upstairs were odd modern books, Nonsense verses etc. The servants were masters—at their tasks— neat, very tall, very sagacious—the maids obsequious and busy, (upstairs). I smiled with satisfaction at the whole affair.

Today I went to church—took a walk with Elsie (after dinner) went to the Musseys', (with Elsie) and am now going to bed—10:15. Elsie is provoked with me because I didn't introduce her round, at the Musseys'. But I introduced her to Mrs. Mussey and after the spiel made a dart for the man to ask him a question which right Elsie had also as none of us knew him. Dr. de Laguna was there and I nosed out a seat near him on the sofa, (next to him) and of course left him to speak to Mr. Meeker afterward so I don't think Elsie has really a *casus belli*. Besides she had 3 years in which to make his acquaintance. Mr. Meeker was very delightful, had a drawl and a shy very humorous way of saying things. But I think Dr. Mussey beats them all. He is sound as a bell. He is crude occasionally, he is so much in earnest, but his clean way of looking at things and his energetic openminded broad-minded face is enough to set you housecleaning yourself. He looks like an inspired fieldhand very square and homespun with respect to ties and shoes. He is the finest type of social evangelism I've seen. He told a funny story (informally). He said a boy was telling about his brothers who had learned to play musical instruments of some kind and he said, "Maurice can play alone but Charles can only play when he plays with the band."

With love, Fangs

I have a story, **"The Blue Moth"** which I think will do for ye *Tip* this month or next. Shirley said she liked it, most of it, and gave it to Grace Branham to read. It elates me very much for it is like my poem, (what Dr. D. would call a "tentative" story).

Friday afternoon I went painting to Miss Garber's studio by Miss Baldwin's, she invited me, and did 2 bottles a green one and a brown one, very ugly I thought but I had to do what the others were doing. I hope however refined my taste may become, I shall not be perverted into calling cold gingerale-bottle-green "stunning" as Miss G. called it. I appreciated the invitation however and am going again. I expect to do things bigger, too. Small scale studies are very injurious to one's hand.

Don't forget Mrs. Landberton (the address). . . .

To Bryher

AUGUST 31, 1921

Dear Bryher:

I had already posted you *Adventure* when your letter came, saying to keep it till you decided what had best be done about it; I am so sorry. I shall review *Hymen* if Hilda approves; I am most anxious to see her stories. I should think there would be no trouble about placing them and shall do with them just as she directs.

I have not read [Oswald] Spengler's *Der Untergang des Abendlandes*. I shall try to see *Die Weissen Gotter*; I am especially interested in the Incas though I know nothing about them and I know nothing about Mexico. I have always thought of Cortez as an iron clad monster of the largest variety; picturesque of course on a large scale, too. I am most impatient to read Flaubert's correspondence. I have wanted to read it for some time.

I am highly in favour of a Bat-ears—later, for I should think as you say, that Berlin would interfere. We had one as a neighbor when we were in New Jersey and nothing could exceed his pansy-like attractiveness of feature and his general vigour, mental and other. When he had been in a fight with a large bulldog and was still so weak that he had to lie down as soon as he had got to the other side of the street, he limped over to attack another dog.

Robert's picture is very like him I think and I am delighted to have it.

We are just back from a delightful visit to a friend, in the mountains near Carlisle, our old home. I took pictures of nearly everything—a pine tree, two dogs in many positions—an airedale and a collie, an earthenware tea set, a winding path to the house—of logs sunk in the earth and two, out of five fringed gilled newts that I caught in a spring. I even allowed a stinging fly to settle on me and select a place to bite me rather than risk losing one of these lizards in a good position. I had them in a square dish of water belonging to the dogs—on a white cloth. I took a copperhead at our doorstep and the shed skin of another copperhead and caught a grasshopper of the kind I had been looking for—a large fawncoloured one with barred legs but had no more films; I also had to relinquish an immense iron crowfoot about two feet long, belonging to one of the carpenters. A live snake is worth feeling, or perhaps I should say a freshly killed one; it feels like a piece of old fashioned bead work made of infinitesimally small beads or a fine gold mesh bag with nothing in it and is silky like a poppy petal—dry and warm. The one I took was dead so it had not the remarkable bevel that a live copperhead has; the way the muscles of one of these snakes with a bevel, are connected with the spine is wonderful I think, like the complicated orderly appearance of the ropes by which a ship's sails are tethered to the mast. If the prints are good, I shall send you some. I saw a falling star which looked like a sheet of paper on fire and a bat so close that I could see light through its wings—a kind of amber—and could make out the veins and scallops. The most beautiful feature of this ledge in the mountains is a group of immense pines; the ends of the branches look like black fox tails against the dark blue of the sky at night and the stars, the times when I was out, glittered like cut silver.

I don't hate Lloyd George but I loathe Lord Northcliffe.[3]

I don't see in what way T. S. Eliot is not "with you." It strikes me that he has created a good deal of carnage and I certainly feel that in comparison, I am not a very large rock to heave at the stupidity of the public.

As for dressing down Mr. Latham, temerarious pterodactyl, maybe he will answer back like the echo in [Lucius] Osgood's *Second Reader*, "Foo-o-lish fel-low."

A great many trashy old time novels are being written today, there is no doubt of that and the form annoys one along with the content and I think with you, that in the case of anyone who can write, the idea will completely burst the bottle but I am sure that the play writing expedients of creating suspense and making people feel by the time they have got to the end—that something has happened—strengthen a presentation and we do not want to be in Dostoevsky's plight of attempting to carry milk without putting it in a jar. He belches out life as a smoke stack belches smoke and George Moore is justified in saying, "His farrago is wonderful but I am not won." We haven't his faults but we have our own, tending to exposit astuteness and sensibility without perspective and people are likely to say, "Very charming but not enough horse power." *Robinson Crusoe* is to my mind, the perfect novel both in detail and in conception. Apropos of Antar, I don't misunderstand what you say about disliking sentimentality but it recalls to me something I have thought for some time—that it is normal for young people to have a sentimental attitude to love and that it is abnormal for them to be aware of the sexual aspect of their relations.[4] In beating the drum of sex continually, the psychoanalytical wing of modern thought surely misses the mark; it is as if someone were to say to one of us, in accepting an invitation to tea, "I haven't any illusions about your intellect; my stomach is in good working order and I am here to prove it." Your poor Libyan probably shares my Baucis-Philemon[5] notion of marriage yet I can't but smile at her view of your corruptness. I don't like divorce and marriage is difficult but marriage is our attempt to solve a problem and I can't think of anything better. I think if people have a feeling for being married, they ought to be married and if they have made a mistake, or if one of them is not on a marriage level, there may have to be a separation. An intentional matrimonial grand right and left has no point whatever so far as I can see; in Turkey, monogamy is gaining as it is everywhere else and there is confusion of thought I think in advocating anything different in a plan where there is any kind of civil contract. If we do away with the marriage contract, the case is different but nobody seems to wish to do that since if we do, we get back to cave life. The canker in the whole situation I think, is that people who have no respect for marriage, insist on the respectability of a marriage contract. When one is at one's wits' end for a solution, I do believe that there is nothing to do but let the elements involved work out slowly.

The net result of my experiences at Bryn Mawr was to make me feel that intellectual wealth can't be superimposed, that it is to be appropriated; my experience there gave me security in my determination to have what I want. I can't very well illustrate, it would take too long, the more since you and Hilda and I are at the antipodes from

each other in our notions of education. In an article on the advantage to a musician of university training, a journalist quotes a friend of mine who is a musician as saying that her college experience gave her "a sense of repose and conscious strength" and "developed good taste and the power to think problems through," "breadth of style and a more strongly defined colour sense." At Bryn Mawr the students are allowed to develop with as little interference as is compatible with any kind of academic order and the more I see of other women's colleges, the more I feel that Bryn Mawr was peculiarly adapted to my special requirements.

Master Mouse and the narcissus and the manuscript have arrived. The narcissus, looking as if it had come right from the garden, is hanging on me on an old, old chain which I have never worn for lack of a suitable pendant and I am entranced with Master Musculus Mouse "from the tooth of an elephant." The polish ivory takes is almost incredible. Last year, I lost a white mouse up my sleeve; he bit me and came out at the far side of my collar and involved in mischief by me as he was, I cannot but contrast with him Sir Musculus Mouse, ten thousand times charming. As for that giraffe, he would have made me unspeakably poor. Do you remember the eight cornered tent that Nero insisted on having made, "a wonderful object both for its beauty and costliness" and how Seneca said, "You have now shown yourself to be poor for if you should lose this, you will not be able to procure such another" and how it happened that it actually was lost, in a shipwreck? I paid no duty.

I am delighted with the prints of you and Robert; I do wish that I could get scientific results.

As I told you, Mother drove me to Miss [Alice] Boughton's in June. The proofs were not good but Miss Boughton said she will try again as soon as it is cooler; your friends will be refreshed I am sure, when I am passed around.

I have not read the new version of *Adventure* as it has just come, but what I should like to do is to take it back to Macmillan. I am convinced that their reason for declining it was not commercial but because they misunderstood the Antar part in the way that I misunderstood it myself; my choice of publishers is as follows: Macmillan, Doran, Knopf, Huebsch. As for commission, no compensation would induce me to take the manuscript anywhere if I did not wish to take it and if I took ten manuscripts a month about for you, I should not feel that you were under any obligation to me; do you recall the ten dollars that you sent for postage; I don't remember the postage on anything I have mailed but I know that I could mail things all winter and not exhaust in postage, those ten dollars.

I am sorry that you decided not to answer Mr. Thayer's letter; it was not businesslike to ignore it. When friendship is balanced with pride, the result is never even and those least responsible bear the deficit. You feel that Mr. Thayer is not a gentleman but a ruffian does not allow his victim any leeway and Mr. Thayer tried to consult you so, although you can take him to task for his attitude to your marriage and for wishing to discuss it, it is not possible I think, to lay on him the whole responsibility of the article.

Don't think I have given up hope of coming over; you say everyone is quitting England for Berlin and I only wish I could fill their places as air fills a newly made vacuum.

I have no poems just now as I am under promise to *Broom* to submit something as quickly as I can get it ready. I have no idea what *Broom* will be but as I told you, I am friendly to Alfred Kreymborg and if you and Hilda are willing to go outside the established magazines, I think you might not regret submitting some things. I have been held up because I wanted to revise some poems taken by *The Dial* last spring—three, which resisted the most pertinacious attack.

In regard to Amy Lowell, don't think that I have any less friendly feeling for her than you have but that doesn't say that I admire her work.

I have for some time been watching for an opportunity to write to Robert.

When your dress is made, won't you send me a scrap and do send me a picture of your stand-up page curls; they sound very pleasing.

Mother sends her love to you, every one and would love to see Perdita in her rose and wonders if she was plane-sick.

Your affectionate albino-dactyl

Notes

1. MM and her friends referred to physiology professor Joseph Warren as Daddy.

2. Congregational clergyman (1835-1922), who edited *Outlook*; author of *The Life and Literature of the Ancient Hebrews*.

3. David Lloyd George (1863-1945), British statesman of Welsh extraction who was considered eloquent but unscrupulous and opportunistic. Lord Northcliffe (1865-1922), Irish-born British journalist whose newspaper campaigns during World War I were determining factors in England's conduct of the war and whose support of Lloyd George in 1916 was instrumental in bringing about the downfall of the Asquith government.

4. MM refers here to some of Bryher's remarks in *Adventure*.

5. Baucis and Philemon, an aged couple who received a visit from Zeus and Hermes, and whose house was then transformed by the gods in return for their hospitality.

GENERAL COMMENTARY

TESS GALLAGHER (ESSAY DATE 1985)

SOURCE: Gallagher, Tess. "Throwing the Scarecrows from the Garden." *Parnassus* 12, no. 2 (1985): 45-60.

In the following essay, Gallagher outlines and counters the negative critical reaction—particularly from feminist commentators—to Moore's poetry.

In 1970 when I began to read Marianne Moore in a class with the poet Jean Garrigue, I was determined not to like Moore's poems. But they were on the menu and I allowed my nose to be pressed into the plate—not by Ms. Garrigue, who was the gentlest of teachers, but by the poems themselves. I resented what I took to be their holier-than-thou, near Olympian chill, the lack of visible emotion, the magpie clutter, the pert glint in the bird's eye that said I was too dull-witted to ever catch her meaning without a sojourn in the moat. Luckily, this was not to be the lasting impression Moore made on me.

I happened upon George Eliot's insistence that "Women have not to prove that they can be emotional and rhapsodic, and spiritualistic; everyone believes that already. They have to prove that they are capable of accurate thought, severe study, and continuous self-command."[1] It was a call for women to "rebut the generalizations which had encouraged their onesidedness."[2] Seen in this light, I quickly began to revise my attitude toward Moore's poetry, and developed a hard-earned advocacy by the end of the course.

I begin here with my failure toward her work because I believe it to be the rule with readers, having by now taught her to classes myself—classes populated with recalcitrant Moore-haters, some of whom are never converted. One aspect of general reluctance toward her work arises from a too-narrow definition of passion, which young people especially yearn for in poetry. Being so

ON THE SUBJECT OF...

MOORE'S VERSE, ACCORDING TO W. H. AUDEN

Miss Moore's poems are an example of a kind of art which is not as common as it should be; they delight, not only because they are intelligent, sensitive and beautifully written, but also because they convince the reader that they have been written by someone who is personally good.

Auden, W. H. An excerpt from "Marianne Moore." In *The Dyer's Hand and Other Essays.* New York: Random House, Inc., 1962.

birch-trees,
  ferns, and lily-pads,
avalanche lilies, Indian paint-brushes,
bear's ears and kittentails,
and miniature cavalcades of chlorophylless fungi

With the "relentless accuracy" which is the passion of the naturalist and the scientist and of this artist, she observes the mountain and also what the mountain is not. It is not where some of these animals have their dens; they come there for things they need, just as the reader visits the worlds writers provide in order to experience joys and hardships of habitats other than those to which they have become accustomed. Moore's tertiary movement in the poem allows her to intend a direction and then turn back on it; or, she will embellish a minor movement until it takes on noteworthy proportions and has to be considered a legitimate digression relevant to some compelling inner sense of appropriateness Moore feels toward the subject. What emerges is a dialogue concerning interiors and surfaces. At first, one begins to feel that the mountain *is* what is *on* it. But as the poem nears its conclusion we are brought to understand that the ultimate forces of the mountain, as with Moore's writing, are unseen, "creeping slowly as with mediated stealth." It is not the surface which has the last say here, but the interiors which have been "planed by ice and polished by wind," and which have the power to send avalanches "with a sound like the crack of a rifle."

Juhasz seems unaware that the definition of passion also admits "appetite" and is synonymous with fervor, enthusiasm, zeal, and ardor; all "denoting strong feeling, either sustained or passing, for or about something or somebody."[6] Enthusiasm as it relates to passion "reflects excitement and responsiveness to more specific or concrete things."[7] It is in her enthusiasm and responsiveness that we must locate Moore's passion, and if she loves "in a mild distant, sisterly way"[8] it is still loving, and a variety of loving perhaps much underrated when opposed to the Latin sense of self-abandonment which argues for an authenticity based on surrender of the will. It is Moore's insistence on maintaining the means and terms of her loving, her responsiveness, that we should admire as something progressive in the literature of women.

To get closer to Moore's sense of passion, one must read her essay on Pavlova in which Moore notes that the Russian dancer was "self-controlled rather than a prison to what she prized,"[9] that "she did not project as valuable the personality

vested in bodily notions in our first understanding of the word passion, we neglect what Louise Bogan called "a passion wholly of the mind." It is here that Moore's poetry is situated.

Such misunderstanding of Moore is not restricted to the young or the uninitiated. In her book *Naked and Fiery Forms: Modern American Poetry by Women: A New Tradition,*[3] the critic Suzanne Juhasz continues a tradition of using Emily Dickinson to beat Moore over the head, Moore being "without Emily Dickinson's range and passion."[4]

If passion is the capacity to show evidence of burning, of being carried by one's enthusiasms and frustrations, then Moore has it. Time and time again we see her expertly adrift on her own tides, especially in the long poems such as **"An Octopus"** and **"Marriage."** When Moore gives us "the roar of ice" in **"An Octopus"**[5] I find myself thinking that this is indeed the cumulative effect of this poem which begins in the seeming desolation "of ice. Deceptively reserved, and flat," and ends "in a curtain of powdered snow launched like a waterfall." Her intensity is analogous to "the unegoistic action of the glaciers." Line by line Moore populates the mountain like Noah's ark turned upside down. On it are "bears, elk, deer, wolves, goats and ducks" as well as a water ouzel and a marmot. She is attentive also to the flora of the mountain:

from which she could not escape," and finally, the observation that "that which is able to change the heart proves itself."[10] Each of these insights may be valuably applied to Moore's own attitudes toward her art.

One cannot miss Moore's love for what this woman communicated of the human spirit by way of what Moore saw as the most naked of the arts—dance. The connection to Pavlova is so deep that Moore cannot resist retelling the circumstances of Pavlova's death in the chronology she provides at the end, so that the piece ends with Moore's own sense of the loss of this beautiful, passionate presence:

> In January 1931 she died in Holland, of pleurisy. While enroute to the Hague via the Riviera, to begin a tour, after a sleepless night in a train that had stood on a siding all night, she caught cold—recorded thus reverently by Mr. Beaumont: "Hardly settled in the Hotel des Indes, she fell ill; the flame that was her life flickered, burnt low, and half an hour after midnight, on Friday, January 23rd, went out."
>
> (p. 160, **Predilections**)

Moore did not need to supply this ending in such detail. The first line of this passage would have sufficed. The loss of the flame, the very metaphor Moore chooses to repeat in Mr. Beaumont's description, was necessary to what Moore needed to communicate of her own sense of Pavlova's intensity—her fire. One can't be a bystander to passion when it arrives so artfully given. Yet Moore appreciated in Pavlova the way in which her passion separated her even from those with whom she danced: "for in her dancing with persons, remoteness marked her every attitude." (p. 160, **Predilections**) This might also be applied to the remoteness of Moore's own tone in her poems at times.

I smile to think of Moore "sitting in" on Louise Bogan's 1956 class at the YW-YMHA and being advised with the rest of the class to "keep your abstract thought for the prose, your emotions for the poetry,"[11] and to remember that "emotion should remain direct and uncomplicated . . . issuing from the heart, not the 'ego.'" Moore was only partially obedient, ignoring the edict on abstractions and adopting directness in tone, while preferring to complicate her stance by recessing emotion or exchanging it for industry and insight. Emotion with her was itself form. And, of course, she must have decided all this long before her encounter with Bogan. It is this lack of visible emotion, what in speaking of Dryden and later of Auden has been called "the middle way" of writing, which has obscured Moore's particular brand of passion, for she reinterpreted the "middle" style to mean "the circumspectly audacious."[12] We are unused to meeting passion unattended by displays of emotion, except perhaps in its sharper forms as with Swift or Pope.

The charge that Moore sacrificed emotion in order to be "one of the boys" is one I find particularly obtuse. But Juhasz adopts it and seems to imply some Uncle Tom-ism as regards an essential element of the feminine: that women are emotional beings and that this has to be in the work of women writers we admire as such. Oh hogwash! And give that woman a bucket of newts. This is exactly the kind of non-thinking that cripples our response to what is truly individual in the best writing of women. Feminist scripts, like all scripts, are anathema. I daresay that had Moore begun writing at the time I did, in the late Sixties, she would have secured her poetry against the Belfast of feminist ideology in favor of some less compulsory relationship to feminist attitudes and its legitimate urgencies.

All one needs is a month-long stay in Northern Ireland to understand that all defections are not simply cowardice, as Juhasz implies when she notes that Moore abjures emotion. Good sense is often involved. Like Seamus Heaney leaving his birthplace in Derry for Black Rock in the Republic of Ireland, Moore was capable of a stringent vigilance toward her gift. Since hers was a gift vested in the desire to deliver us from our biases rather than confirm us in them, she was especially wary of responses dominated primarily by the emotions. Her brand of morality was marked by its utter lack of evangelism. Perhaps this continues to delay her reception by some readers.

Another complaint of feminist critics seems to be that Moore is too obsequious, always sitting in the corner eating humble pie. In a time when women writers want to be seen as having fully assumed the powers of their craft through the authority of their own skills, Moore's insistence on humility at every turn must strike them as a reprimand and also as an obsolete pretense meant to throw the hounds off the scent of what they assume to be her self-satisfied withdrawal from responsible connection to her creations. This, however, is not at all her circumstance, but one conferred on her by our times.

For Moore, humility was connected to a genuine sense of Grace, of being allowed knowledge in the face of odds, of being allowed her very art which had sources other than the audacity of her will. Or as Auden put it, "suffering plays a greater part than knowledge" in our acts of the will and "one must not discount Grace."[13] Like Pavlova, Moore would have considered genius as a trust, "concerning which vanity would be impossible."[14] Humility was a form of honesty with Moore, an honesty which, Donald Hall has been shrewd enough to point out, was not in the least self-effacing. It is not a concession when one considers oneself to be a beneficiary, especially for an intellect like Moore's which, as she well knew, was fully prepared for what Grace would deliver. She did her share of the work and took requisite pride in that.

Reticence is another detraction Juhasz enlists against Moore. It is true Moore is often reticent, but in all the skillful, interesting ways. Take, for instance, Moore's agility at chain-linking quotations one with another from borrowed sources, and coupling them with her own observations until she could project them into a quite unanticipated structure having its own integrity:

> But someone in New
> England has known to say
> that the student is patience personified,
>   a variety
> of hero, "patient
>   of neglect and of reproach,"—who can "hold
>   by
> himself." You can't beat hens to
> make them lay. Wolf's wool is the best wool,
> but it cannot be sheared, because
> the wolf will not comply. With knowledge as
>   with wolves' surliness,
> the student studies
>   voluntarily, refusing to be less
> than individual. He
> "gives his opinion and then rests upon it;"
>   (from **"The Student,"** p. 101-102)

Or in **"The Monkey Puzzle"**:

> this "Paduan cat with lizard," this tiger in a
>   bamboo thicket,
> "An interwoven somewhat," it will not come
>   out.
>   . . . . .
> It knows that if a nomad may have dignity,
> Gibraltar has had more—
> that "it is better to be lonely than unhappy."

Juhasz takes Moore's constant quoting of others as the sign of her unwillingness to accept responsibility for her own assertions. I prefer to see quotation as proof of Moore's ambition not to write simply in the isolation of the ego, but to write as if she were a team, or an orchestra:

> When three players on a side play three positions
> and modify conditions,
>   the massive run need not be everything.
>   ("**Baseball and Writing**")

She was willing to take responsibility to a new, enlarged arena then, to present and credit views other than her own, and to provide a context for hearing a concert of voices. She was, of course, the ever present conductor. She chose the score, was enigmatically "galvanized against inertia,"[15] delivered her baton strokes beginning "far back of the beat, so that you don't see when the beat comes. To have started such a long distance ahead makes it possible to be exact. Whereas you can't be exact by being restrained."[16] She preferred the responsibility of conversation to the responsibility of the orator. Her allegiance was to community and individual at once, no small commitment, and she ironically recognized the ways in which one compromised the other in the ending to "**Marriage**" when she puts a quote within a quote, and writes "'Liberty and union / now and forever'; / the Book on the writing-table; / the hand in the breastpocket."[17]

Moore's homage to her sources, what she called her "borrowed" and "hybrid method of composition," was proof, I believe, of a generosity of spirit that admitted that the work of the artist is often the result of "gifting" from others, as much as it is a matter of being gifted. It is an innovation not even Whitman, with all his pride of inclusion, thought to design.

One has only to read Moore's notes to the poems to be reminded of how rich non-literary sources can be for a writer. Moore knocked down the fence around literature. She let in the writers of books about tigers, books on physiography and anthropology. The list includes *The Harvard Journal of Asiatic Studies, The New York Times, The I-Ching,* a tour book guide to Italy, a progress report from research on cancer, an article on "Plastic Sponge Implants in Surgery," the dictionary, the *Christian Science Monitor,* and even a letter from a curator of reptiles and amphibians.

Reading Moore in 1970, I was impressed with the voracity of her interests. Reading her again fifteen years later, I feel that somehow a large amount of curiosity and attention toward the diversity and particularity of the history, the geography, the flora and fauna, the creatures of the earth and its inhabitants has been regrettably neglected by today's poets. It is refreshing to read a poet who has bothered to find out about more than her own traumas.

It is the lack of the contemporary central and exposed "I" which allows Moore to generalize and to extend both the range of her subject matter and the moral import of her explorations. There seems to be something in the very nature of her moralist's approach which prohibits confession. Probably this comes from the need to speak from a position of relative immunity. Auden managed it with the public "we." Recently Frank Bidart in his dramatic narrative, *The War of Vaslav Nijinsky,* calls on Nijinsky to fight the battles of his moral questionings. The dismay as to how to classify Bidart's work is not unlike that accorded Moore's poems when they first appeared: should we call this poetry? Donald Hall has responded in Bidart's favor by enlisting Moore's reliance on "the genuine": "Bidart is not a confessional poet; he is dramatic and universal, a moral observer of humanity. . . . When I read poems that are 'not poetry,' and yet 'wholly genuine,' I know that I am in the presence of something new."[18]

While Bidart's newness rests in his dramatic stance, his mixing of prose passages with lyrical bursts and dialogue, Moore's newness in technical matters comes from her incorporation of actual bits of prose into the bloodstream of her lines. In this she presaged Ashbery's experiments with prose elements in diction and gesture, as well as perhaps the current borrowing from prose characterized by a preference for methods of accumulating energy through narratives that comment upon one another such as Robert Hass's "Pascal Lamb."[19]

No one, however, has shown signs of developing a moral equivalent to Moore's content. Her poems "have a sense of civilization about them"[20] that seems outside the grasp of contemporary American practitioners. Just as America now buys its cars, blenders, galoshes, and pharmaceutical supplies abroad, it also seems to be looking to the Irish, the Polish, the Turkish, and the Russians of Akhmatova's generation for spiritual and moral qualities. Here also deficits accrue, and only intermittently, firefly style, do single accomplished poems with a moral approach hint at the general lack of Made-In-America resourcefulness Moore so much exemplified in this respect. Moore's conclusion to her essay on Louise Bogan allows one to see the lack of illusion with which she faced such issues: "we are told, if we do wrong that grace may abound, it does not abound. We need not be told that life is never going to be free from trouble and that there are no substitutes for the dead; but it is a fact as well as a mystery that handicap is proficiency, weakness is power, that the scar is a credential, that indignation is no adversary for gratitude or heroism for joy. These are medicines."[21] She had, in other words, no miracle cures, and would have agreed with the anthro-

pologist studying tribal healing who said "spells are not communiques: they are gestures."[22]

Still, the mania for solutions is a pressure the artist is usually aware of, and must with agility renounce. Doris Lessing on a recent tour in Australia remarked in a newspaper interview that she was appalled by the number of people in her audiences who asked her for answers to a set of wide-ranging problems that ran the gamut from personal to political to ideological and religious. What frightened her was the feeling that these people were hungry for answers, not hungry for ways of thinking toward the problems. They wanted to be told what to do, and this, as she realized, is very dangerous because it signals that people's resources and patience for self-generated action and for defining alternatives are lamentably low. Dangerous also because it invites someone of perhaps not altogether unimpeachable motives to do just what is asked, to tell them what to do. And therein lies an end to freedom.

A similar trend plagues us in the public moralism of the Reagan era which operates without (yes, surprise!) morality. It seeks to substitute dogma and ad-man hype for authentic action and discovery. Moore's aesthetic scorns such remedies, although the rather Confucian style of the wisdom she often provided at the ends of her poems would at first seem to indicate the opposite. But cut your teeth on advice like:

It was enough; it is enough
if present faith mend partial proof[23]

The application is in no one's hands but the reader's. Or, take the ending of **"Elephants"** in which Moore tells us that

as Socrates,
prudently testing the suspicious thing, knew
the wisest is he who's not sure that he knows.
Who rides on a tiger can never dismount;[24]

Here Moore has it both ways, says wisdom depends on a certain unsureness toward "the suspicious thing," and yet presents what seems a verity, that he "who rides on a tiger can never dismount." I mean, I wouldn't. It is this mixture of fable with aphoristic surety added to "conversities" that cause one not to know from moment to moment on which side the gavel is going to come down. Conversities is a word Moore invented to indicate that her meaning might work positively and negatively without canceling out either possibility. I can remember a wonderful afternoon in a cafe in my hometown during which Michael Burkard and I took a close look at **"Critics and Connoisseurs."** Whose side is she on? we kept asking. The ledger would strangely balance itself at moments when we seemed about to identify a victim. I don't think we ever did settle it. This "conscientious inconsistency," as she termed memory in **"The Mind Is An Enchanted Thing,"** is active throughout her poetry as a guarantee against rigidity of vision and narrow mandates. As Moore said when speaking of Williams, "the truth of poetry is not dogma, but a cry of a whole soul."[25] This does not mean Moore is reticent about what she values or the need for values. In **"Values in Use"** she makes clear that values should not overwhelm the use we make of them: "Certainly the means must not defeat the end."[26]

The tyranny of prescribed morality I spoke of earlier strikes me as not far removed from the feminist critic's practice of composing hit lists in which a poet's work is ransacked for poems useful to the cause, and if the tally is insubstantial, the writer is sent to the purgatory of "unrecommended reading." Juhasz, for instance, found that **"Marriage"** was the only poem of Moore's that could be counted as clearly having feminine experience as a central subject. Evidently, lines such as "Marriage, tobacco, and slavery, / initiated liberty"[27] were inadmissible. Nor did she note the application of sexual identity to a hedgehog in **"His Shield"** which directs it somewhat pointedly, as with others of Moore's animal poems in which the animal is assigned a sex.

> In his
> unconquerable country of unpompous
> gusto,
> gold was so common none considered it;
> greed
> and flattery were unknown.

In presenting the hedgehog as masculine here, Moore seems to highlight the pomposity men have for exactly these negative capabilities. Juhasz failed to surmise that Moore's femininity is most active in her tendency toward dualism, odd partnerships, and hairline distinctions between neighboring qualities or properties. Here I'm thinking of poems like **"Granite and Steel"** and **"Voracities and Verities Sometimes Are Interacting,"** although there are many other poems I might have chosen to mention. Oppositions of themselves invite "our metaphorical thinking to make one the masculine and one the feminine counterpart."[28] But surely we needn't go to these extremes to accept the gifts of one who is our own.

If pressed, however, I would recommend that **"Love in America"** with its "benign dementia,"

its "a Midas of tenderness; nothing else," and its hiss of yeses at the end be added to the stockpile of poems of particular interest to women. I would also single out **"He Wrote the History Book"** for how it reminds us of the *male* signature over all history writing and the "you" of the feminine contribution "to your father's / legibility" . . . which causes women to appear "sufficiently / synthetic." She ends the poem with a real karate chop disguised as a bouquet: "Thank you for showing me / your father's autograph." Some of her animal poems also allow us humor toward feminine predicaments, sexual and not—my favorite of these being **"The Lion In Love,"** with its: "Lions or such as were attracted / to young girls, sought an alliance,"[29] and "Love, ah Love, when your slipknot's drawn, / One can but say, 'Farewell, good sense.'"[30]

What is one to make of Juhasz' charge that in Moore's work "woman" and "poet" were "separated as the most effective means of achieving professional success"?[31] Or that Moore concentrated upon "technical brilliance coupled with a marked exclusion of feminine experience from art"?[32] Reading this makes me feel I've been caught in a strange time warp in which it is suddenly revealed that Bach is inferior because he doesn't seem to know anything about Reggae.

What is Moore writing about, then, if she is intent on neglecting feminine experience in order to make a success of herself? She is writing about aesthetic choices of all kinds, about being human in a world also inhabited by animals and insects whose world we have largely colonized, which in the worst sense of colonial, as Moore points out, has never been synonymous with mercy. She veritably puts the human family back on Noah's ark, where we have to lie down with each other while the waters rise. Indeed, her focus is on our very *beingness* itself. The questions she's asking are every bit as important to me as what I might be interested in writing with a view to women's issues, although that does interest me. Some of these questions are: What relation does the past have to the present? How do beauty and sensibility coexist when faced with an uncompromising power? How do we value, and why, and what? Is there such a thing as "progress" when we consider military endeavors ("fighting fighting fighting that where / there was death there may / be life")?[33] What is liberty? Union? How does one preserve judgment in a world of hucksters and "snake-charming controversialists?"[34] What is a critic's job? What is poetry and why should we value it? What endures? How do we choose? What is transcendence? Consolation? Envy? Charity? Justice? ("And so, as you are weak or are invincible / the court says white is black or that black crimes are white.")[35] How should one deal with an enemy? ("Choose wisdom, even in an enemy.")[36] What is freedom? ("The power of relinquishing what one would keep")[37].

If this reads like Topic Time at the back of a high school civics text, Moore's handling of these questions is always more an approach than a tourniquet. She is a poet who needs the constellation *and* the morning star, though she might object to their being yoked by that despised connective "and."

Moore, it seems likely, as with so many extraordinary women of her time, never assumed accepted sexual exclusions within the artistic, social, or political sphere; and so, in many ways never had to confront such issues in the way contemporary women have had to, sexual imperatives having defined our intellectual, social, and psychological battlefields for the past fifteen to twenty years.

I confess to being weary of feminist honor rolls in which Moore is addressed condescendingly as if she were merely the crumpled first step toward the Acropolis of Plath. Moore is no carriage-drawn supplicant at the mercy of General Motors. She was an originator, not simply an entrepreneur. And if she was a spare-parts wizard, she knew how to make things work, and did. She was also no pussycat, as many like to infer from her "mousing pose."[38] As she observed, "an animal with claws should have opportunity to use them,"[39] and she took several. How would you like, for instance, to have been the one for whom **"The Steam Roller"** was intended? Or told that you "lack half-wit"? Or that you are one of those "self-wrought Midases of brains / whose fourteen-carat ignorance aspires to rise in value"?[40] Nonetheless, Moore is closer to Molière than to Swift. She recognized Molière as a relative, I think, and paid homage to him in **"To the Peacock of France,"** seemingly enjoying kinship in his lack of popularity in certain quarters. Like Molière, she was concerned with manners, with those discrepancies between civility and brutality, action and word, intention and outcome that make us smile and wonder at human nature, make us take up our cudgels or our shields. She was a true archaeologist of the spirit, curious and exacting before the remnant of some variegated attitude, or "the

deft white-stockinged dance in thick-soled shoes!",[41] the "mantle lined with stars."[42]

One last scarecrow I would like to fling from Moore's imaginary garden is the idea that because she was a spinster her poetry is marred by the limitations of that social role, as Roy Harvey Pearce has implied.[43] Juhasz goes even further by accusing Moore of "opting for nonsexuality"[44] and thereby escaping "those feminine characteristics that threaten."[45] Juhasz is ready to assign Moore to a museum by virtue of her chastity. "Chastity is non-engagement; it leaves one in a position of safety."[46] Chastity was not "a position of safety" then, nor do I suspect it to be now, and the correctness of chastity as metaphor must, I think, bear witness to the act in order to support itself. Moore, as she put it best herself, simply "was not matrimonially ambitious."[47] She was nobody's fool and must, like Emily Dickinson, have understood that to take a husband in those times was tantamount to signing one's artistic death warrant. Adrienne Rich has retrieved Emily Dickinson from the myth of the madwoman in the attic by pointing out that Dickinson had reasons for choosing solitude—she was at work! Moore chose the companionship and nurturing of her mother for not dissimilar reasons, I think. Certainly, had she been "inclined," she could have managed to marry. All this is beside the point. I'm interested in Moore precisely for her difference. If one has access to the ultimate in virgin thought, one ought to prize it, pay attention, not pronounce it remedial. Give me a smart woman any day, whatever her gynecological qualifications.

There are so many things Moore has given me as a writer and human being over the years that I feel I ought to have acknowledged them long before now. I've needed her distrust of easy answers, her wonderful humor—"Humor saves a few steps, it saves years."[48] Her team spirit appeals to me, though I don't know much about baseball and I'd make a rotten cheerleader. But, I agree that some things have to be done together and that each person in that "together" has an important contribution. Still, I don't want to march or hear the national anthem played three times a day. And neither does Moore. I prize Moore's cinematic eye, the way she uses the close-up metaphor so you can forget what you saw and keep seeing: "the lion's ferocious chrysanthemum head," "the swan's maple leaflike feet." Her poems operate the way our sight does on objects at a distance, requiring us to guess what we're seeing before we can confirm it. There she is, like the retina, collecting until the image identifies itself as something seen for the first time. I enjoy how Moore often delays confirmation syntactically so that conclusiveness itself is mocked.

Moore's propensity for miniature self-portraits is rather like those childhood visual puzzles where one attempts to see how many faces are camouflaged in the seemingly unpopulated landscape of the drawing. She is always there in multiples, "porcupine-quilled":[49] in her "complicated starkness"[50] or as "that spectacular and nimble animal the fish, / whose scales turn aside the sun's sword by their polish"[51] or "an obedient chameleon in fifty shades of mauve and amethyst,"[52] or "like electricity, / depopulating areas that boast of their remoteness."[53]

There was the trick of writing messages invisibly in lemon juice which I used once or twice as a child. The scarcity of matches made it impractical. But when you could manage to scorch the paper just right, it was a thrill to see the words appear on the page as if out of nowhere. This somehow describes the way Moore's poems affect me. If she tells me "Titles are chaff,"[54] I get out my matches to see what else might be on the page. Sure enough, the meaning-after-the-meaning ripples across the brain. I see she meant more than that titles are to be discarded. It's the chaff, after all, that protects the germ of the wheat until it's matured toward harvest. I blow out the match.

Some final advice to those about to encounter the newest wave of resistance to Moore's poetry: to drink from a waterfall you have to get wet, but don't stand under it.

On my first visit to New York City in the summer of 1971, Jean Garrigue had invited me to meet Marianne Moore. The car I was driving across the country from Washington State had a sieve for a radiator, and I did not arrive in time. In the meanwhile, Moore had become very ill. That February she died. I was grateful, in a way, not to have met her at that time. How do you say goodbye to a waterfall?

Notes

1. George Eliot, "Women in France: Madame de Sable," in *Essays of George Eliot,* ed. Thomas Pinney (Routledge, 1963), p. 53.

2. Lynne Sukenick, "On Woman and Fiction," *The Authority of Experience: Essays in Feminist Criticism,* ed. Arlyn Diamond and Lee R. Edwards (U. of Mass., 1977), p. 33.

3. Suzanne Juhasz, *Naked and Fiery Forms: Modern American Poetry by Women: A New Tradition* (Harper, 1976).

4. *Ibid.,* p. 40, quoting Roy Harvey Pearce.

5. Marianne Moore, "The Octopus," *The Complete Poems of Marianne Moore* (Macmillan, 1982), pp. 71-76.

6. *The American Heritage Dictionary,* Second Edition (Houghton Mifflin, 1982).

7. *Ibid.*

8. Louise Bogan writing to Morton Zabel about her affection for T. S. Eliot whom she had just met. Elizabeth Frank, *Louise Bogan: A Portrait* (Knopf, 1985) p. 343.

9. Marianne Moore, "Anna Pavlova," *Predilections* (Viking Press, 1955), pp. 147-160.

10. *Ibid.,* p. 159.

11. Elizabeth Frank, *Louise Bogan* (Knopf, 1985), p. 346.

12. *Ibid.,* p. 85.

13. Marianne Moore, "W. H. Auden," *Predilections,* p. 87.

14. Marianne Moore, "Anna Pavlova," *Predilections,* p. 153.

15. Marianne Moore, *Predilections.*

16. Marianne Moore, "Feeling and Precision," Predilections, p. 5.

17. Marianne Moore, "Marriage," *The Complete Poems,* p. 70.

18. Donald Hall on the jacket of *The Sacrifice,* by Frank Bidart (Random House, 1983).

19. Robert Hass, *New Poets of the 80's,* ed. Jack Myers and Roger Weingarten (Wampeter Press, 1984), p. 124.

20. Roethke talking about Louise Bogan in *Louise Bogan,* by Elizabeth Frank, p. 364.

21. Marianne Moore, "Compactness Compacted," *Predilections,* p. 133.

22. Jonathan Miller, *The Body In Question* (Vintage, 1978), p. 85.

23. Marianne Moore, "Enough," *The Complete Poems,* p. 187.

24. *Ibid.,* "The Elephants," p. 130.

25. Marianne Moore, *Predilections.*

26. Marianne Moore, "Values in Use," *The Complete Poems,* p. 181.

27. *Ibid.,* "Enough," p. 186.

28. Lynn Sukenick, *On Women and Fiction,* p. 32.

29. Marianne Moore, "The Lion In Love," *The Complete Poems,* p. 246.

30. *Ibid.,* p. 247.

31. Suzanne Juhasz, *Naked and Fiery Forms,* p. 35.

32. *Ibid.,* p. 35.

33. Marianne Moore, "In Distrust of Merits," *The Complete Poems,* p. 137.

34. *Ibid.,* "The Labors of Hercules," p. 53.

35. Moore, but I don't know which poem. I'm quoting from memory.

36. Marianne Moore, "The Bear And the Garden-Lover," *The Complete Poems*, p. 257.

37. *Ibid.*, "His Shield," p. 144.

38. *Ibid.*, "Style," p. 169.

39. *Ibid.*, "Peter," p. 44.

40. *Ibid.*, "The Labors of Hercules," p. 53.

41. *Ibid.*, "A Carriage From Sweden," p. 132.

42. *Ibid.*, "Spenser's Ireland," p. 112.

43. Roy Harvey Pearce, *The Continuity of American Poetry* (Princeton University Press, 1961), p. 366.

44. Suzanne Juhasz, *Naked and Fiery Forms*, p. 39.

45. *Ibid.*, p. 39.

46. *Ibid.*, p. 39.

47. *A Marianne Moore Reader*, "Idiosyncrasy and Technique," (Viking, 1965), p. 170.

48. Marianne Moore, "The Pangolin," *The Complete Poems*, p. 119.

49. *Ibid.*, "The Monkey Puzzle," p. 80.

50. *Ibid.*, "The Monkey Puzzle," p. 80.

51. *Ibid.*, "An Egyptian Pulled Glass Bottle In the Shape of A Fish," p. 83.

52. *Ibid.*, "Peoples Surroundings," p. 56.

53. *Ibid.*, "The Labors of Hercules," p. 53.

54. *Ibid.*, "He Wrote the History Book," p. 89.

CHARLES ALTIERI (ESSAY DATE SUMMER 1988)

SOURCE: Altieri, Charles. "The Powers of Genuine Place: Moore's Feminist Modernism." *Southern Humanities Review* 22, no. 3 (summer 1988): 205-22.

In the following essay, Altieri explores the ways in which Moore's gender influenced her modernist verse.

Perhaps nothing captures the fundamental values projected by Modernist American poetry better than William Carlos Williams's image of the "artist figure of / the farmer—composing / —antagonist" who

in deep thought
is pacing through the rain
among his blank fields, with
hands in pockets,
in his head
the harvest already planted.
                ("Spring and All," in *Imaginations*, 98-99.)

This is Constructivism's lonely and sublime sense of the responsibilities of artistic intelligence faced with the daunting task of transposing the uncontaminated latent energies of that landscape into structures giving order and significance to cultural life. Any less blank sense of the field would risk losing the mystery of the radical contrast between hands and head that warranted rejecting both the symbolic and subjective models of expression cultivated by nineteenth century art. Each in its own way made too many demands on art's concern for mimetic content to allow the full tension between composer and antagonist roles to emerge. Romantic symbolic readings of the field would try to read as immanent within nature what Williams projects as dependent on the artist's compositional activity, while subjective models of expression simply locate all the relevant properties of the field in the psyche of the observer and the private (albeit potentially representative) history that shaped the associations. Thus in order for the full force of that antagonistic intelligence to be manifest and for the composing self fully to challenge and ground its own willfulness, Williams tries to make his artist figure capable of meeting two basic demands. He must be able to treat his work as a mode of objective expression that continues Romantic ideals of art as not copying the real but disclosing elemental forces within the artist's engaging it, and he must make that process of disclosure define the expressive subject in terms of objective or impersonal energies that it puts in literal motion. Poetry must have the same literal, testimonial force that Mondrian creates by having his paintings force the observer to participate self-reflexively within the dynamic balances which the work articulates.

I need not tell this audience that a good part of that farmer's exemplary status depends on his gender. But I do need to be able to tell myself what literary criticism can gain by insisting on that observation: what blindnesses derive from that gendering of the Modern, and, more important, what struggles or projects become possible within general Modernist ideals once that gendering is foregrounded? One can answer the first question without considering the second. But that seems to me to make it impossible to distinguish between the limits of Modernism and the limits of male imaginations, thus denying feminism the resources of Modernism and the challenge to confront its own tendencies to return to forms of self-assertion that rely on the modes of expression which Modernism saw as imaginatively bankrupt for the twentieth century. I propose instead that we ask ourselves how someone who accepted Modernist values could go on to criticize male versions of them and propose alternatives still faithful to constructivist commitments.

Williams provides a convenient beginning. It hardly takes someone of Moore's intelligence and stubbornness to grow a bit queasy at versions of constructivism so enamored of this role of "composing-antagonist" which confers the right to impose one's orders on the bland fields horizontal before a looming erect presence. Resisting such fantasies would not depend simply on abstract moral imperatives. To be a woman in Marianne Moore's society meant to be at times a victim of those wills; and, more important, woman's place afforded an imaginative position where other forms of imaginative power became available. If one replaced the composing will by a more flexible imaginative playfulness, it might be possible to show how the will itself could be understood in terms of new dispositions of the psyche which this constructivist art had the capacity to articulate. For example, Modernist abstraction from Mallarmé to Mondrian and Eliot had shown how resistance to the narcissistic fascinations of the synthetic image made available new transpersonal modes of consciousness. In this work it became possible to imagine replacing the willful assertion of the ego's images on experience by so bracketing the composing "I" that the force of the work came to depend on the ways in which the audience could complete it—the "I" of Eliot's "Preludes" becomes anyone who reconstitutes through the poem what it means to be an "infinitely suffering, infinitely gentle thing." And these possibilities in turn made it plausible to think that it would be precisely those whose place in the social order keeps them suspicious of all hegemonic images who must fully explore the powers latent in this new imaginative dispensation.

Moore had a variety of terms for those powers. She spoke of "sincerity," "genuineness," and "authenticity" as the qualities that best distinguished her ambitions.[1] These terms, however, seem to me at best simple indices of the kind of presence that concerns her: they so clearly bear the marks of her fear of staging and displacing the distinctive trait of her imaginative activity that they defer as much as they reveal. Therefore, rather than stay with her terms, I propose our reading some of her best poems in the light of a remark that she made on the poster-artist E. MacKnight Kauffer, attributing to him "an objectified logic of sensibility as inescapable as the colors refracted from a prism" (quoted in Costello, 190). That remark shows a remarkable awareness of both the way in which abstraction makes available new versions of the powers poets mediate and the possible objective means art could develop in order to testify to the claims such powers have within extra-textual experience. Thus where most

readings of Moore's work celebrate the ways that her mobile intelligence comes to possess objects, we shall try instead to locate the distinctive powers that she defines by showing how the content of the poems becomes inseparable from the leaps and projections that it invites its audience to see itself making as collaborators in the compositional activity. So the lady then manages to preserve her strangeness, yet also achieves the power to forge in her own terms imaginary trophies with real and abiding desires in them.

Moore never insists that these powers are distinctively those of a lady, so it is plausible to read most of her work as truly impersonal or directly transpersonal. However, two reasons lead me to proceed on the assumption that she wants us to read most of her poems in the light of those that emphasize the female situations that foster their distinctive powers. First, there is a good rationale for her refusing to have more of her poems insist on gender identifications. For the more art could distance the immediate urgencies of such identifications, the more it freed intelligence to a more flexible and complex set of interventions in the world. Yet the pure transumption of such identifications would severely limit a crucial aspect of Moore's own imaginative strengths because that would deny the ways in which her work promised an alternative to the male fantasies of the poet as Promethean forger of new cultural identities. So Moore had to experiment with establishing an aura of gender as a property not of the content of experience but of its formal structure within the reflective space of the poem. Instead of propounding a specific image of "female" experience, Moore would try to make the powers available to a gendered stance become part of the virtual presence that the work composed for its readers. As they flesh out the world the poem composes, they find themselves re-enacting powers that the mimetic level of the poem or its context in its volume signs as the specific orientation of an imagination consigned by history or biology to the cultural position deemed to be woman's place.

My second reason consists of the exemplary role Moore's Modernist project can play for a contemporary criticism highly suspicious of Modernist ideals. The dominant ideology in feminist discussions of Modernist poetry emphasizes the limitations in the cult of impersonality, celebrating in its stead those poets who manage to find or steal a voice and a language that can express the distinguishing features of their individual experiences.[2] That view, however, confuses the limits of Modernism with the limits of male imaginations and posits an alternative that must rely on the notoriously slippery notion of expressing the truth of one's experiences. When one takes that perspective on experience, one relies on an essentially empty concept that becomes whatever one wants—what is not "experience"? And, perhaps more disturbingly, what claims about experience do not eventually invite ironic laments about the source being alienated from the means of representation available? Caught in such empty pursuits it becomes all too easy to lose sight of the full range of resources which the history of poetry provides, so that there is little more driving the poetry than female versions of the narcissism that leaves male poets impotently prancing before the mirrors they make monuments to their own sensibilities. Such dangers are precisely what led Modernists like Moore to resist models of subjective expression which make poetry an analogue for the delusions Moore pilloried in her **"Marriage"**:

> The fact forgot
> that "some have merely rights
> while some have obligations,"
> he loves himself so much
> he can permit himself
> no rival in that love.
> She loves herself so much,
> she cannot see herself enough—
> (***The Complete Poems of Marianne Moore***, 68)

Therefore it seems to me crucial that feminism try to align itself provisionally with a critical spirit that links suspiciousness of the scenic self with a fierce commitment to individualism. For Moore those desires led to Modernist constructivism because the stances that it cultivated seemed to her the only ones that could isolate the full power of idiosyncrasy from the prevailing cultural codes which provide the script for more expressivist models of personal identity. Modernist concerns for the exemplary roles form might play may make it possible to envision a poetics that is best suited to female experience not because of what it talks about—and thereby stages as specular reflections for our imaginary senses of our own sensitivities—but because of what it shows poetry can do as a virtual force that negotiates a wide range of experiences without ever itself taking the kind of substance that leads even Williams to his fantasized identifications. Thus Moore felt that once a few poems demonstrated the ways in which her distinctive female "polish" could sustain elaborate structures of care, she could make the working out of those structures as impersonal as possible. Only on those terms could the work fully test how

qualities that derive from gendered situations make values available that can modify the life of anyone willing to participate fully in the transpersonal imaginative activity that reading promises.[3]

The first step in defining the qualities Moore establishes for her authorial energies is to turn to **"An Egyptian Pulled Glass Bottle in the Shape of a Fish,"** the poem that most clearly differentiates her model of composition from Williams's "composing-antagonist":

> Here we have thirst
> and patience, from the first,
>   and art, as in a wave held up for us to see
>   in its essential perpendicularity;
> not brittle but
> intense—the spectrum, that
>   spectacular and nimble animal the fish,
>   whose scales turn aside the sun's sword by
>   their polish.
> (***Complete Poems***, 83)

This is no Romantic plea for unity with nature; it is as insistent as Williams on the willfulness or resistance to the given which is necessary for the site art composes. Moore, however, is very careful not to turn such resistance into a self-sufficient "masked ball / attitude" that might impose on the quest for personal identity "a hollowness / that beauty's light momentum can't redeem" (86). There are hollownesses or gaps which are necessary to beauty, and to redemption, but one must be careful not to fill them in too quickly with one's own self-image. Rather than turn back on a representable will, Moore makes the movement of the poem itself the only possible definition of a willfulness which can be kept in public circulation, available for any consciousness willing to recapitulate the control giving this work its polish.

The result is a polish that extends beyond any social connotations to the most intricate and intimate relations between life and art. Notice first the two nouns which initially define the poem's "here," and thereby establish some of the qualities which give art an "essential perpendicularity" not translatable into any simpler, more naturalistic terms. What other site could so combine the physical and psychological properties of thirst and patience? "Here" we see the bottle's shape and function; we see the thirst it should alleviate strangely connected to the fish it represents; and we observe the traces of craft which ultimately align patience with another mode of thirst that only this play of forces might satisfy. No wonder that these appearances so quickly transpose what we see from physical object to the more abstract state of defining the art itself as a wave we can envision cutting against the planes that pure perception must occupy.

All that the wave implies immediately takes psychological form in the second pair of adjectives syntactically linking the two stanzas. "Brittle" describes the glass, but in conjunction with "intense" (and after the oxymorons of the first stanza) the adjectives expand to refer also to the activity (and thirst) of both the artist and the viewer. Yet the temptation to turn all this into mere metaphor, into what the farmer might keep in his head, is denied by the fact that the poem is also speaking about the spectrum of light growing inseparable from the movements of the fish. Now the fish begins actually to swim, although in an element that the artist has composed for it. And that light then becomes something very different from the sun's sword, something whose polish does transform that sword into the perpendicularities of its own prismatic waves. Language makes us see a new object. In fact the movement of this language so fuses the abstract and the concrete that it becomes an actual example of that polish which in the visual object literally gives the fish a different medium.

Moore's celebration of art then brilliantly combines the presentational forces of the two media, glass sculpture and language, showing how each transforms a world of thirsts into a world where the dynamic properties of the artistic acts compose a perpendicularity considerably more satisfying than any physical shape. Moore reveals no hidden symbolic forces and works out no deep psychological conflicts. She does, though, define modes of activity where it may be possible not to have to live in the sets of oppositions that are generated by those conflicts. "Egyptian Glass Bottle" suspends the claims of realism in order to create the effect of liberating the self and language into an awareness of how the world can be contained by what our arts can make of our care and attention. There is no denying Williams's insistence on the artist's will as antagonist to the sun's sword, but such intricate objective displays of what language can do make it unnecessary to turn that will into a specular icon of itself—whose imaginary structure then creates a thirst which no mode of polished play will be able to satisfy.

Moore can propose an alternative to that specular self because she envisions the artist not as the subject of the poem but as the perpendicular force which keeps the work of art in taut opposition to the realm of natural energies. That does not mean denying their claims. Rather it becomes the imperative to set polish against less self-reflexive modes of thirst. In fact, that ideal contains in itself precisely the playful resistance to the given which Moore proclaims. Her model of polish evokes standard cultural expectations about cultivated women, only to reappropriate them in a finer tone. Like Derrida on Nietzsche on the stylus, Moore plays her own artifice against what finishing schools were expected to produce, while crossing that irony with a sly reference to the kinds of attention one develops as one tries to keep one's mind alive while doing household chores. Irony, however, does not suffice. The intricacies of polish characterize the mode that establishes perpendicularity, but they do not adequately account for the full set of concerns that they bring to bear. For that, for a fully human sense of what formal activity makes available as content, Moore turns to a version of Mondrian's self-reflexive virtuality. By making perpendicularity a site where the artist can free the self from the theatrical ego, she can also call attention to the forms of care and identification which then become actual within the mode of agency that the poem establishes.

No Modernist poem makes fuller use of the resources of virtuality than Moore's final version of "Poetry":

I, too dislike it.
    Reading it, however, with a perfect contempt for it, one dis-
                                covers in
    it, after all, a place for the genuine
                            (*Complete Poems*, 36)

This is not Shelley. Indeed it is not much of anything until we find ways of locating where its poetry lies. But once we adapt the basic strategy necessary for non-iconic art, once we see that much of the force of the work depends on its refusing to be something else, we can begin to understand what its exclusions make present. First we must ask why the poem refers to poetry only as "it." What other options are there, and how does this choice martial the possibility of gaining authority for specific claims about the genuine that the poem wants to make? Suppose there is something about the ontological status of art, its tilt perhaps, that demands the indefinite pronoun, as in Dante's reference to Bertrand de Born, who faces him with his head in his hands. Perhaps the most important feature of any definition of poetry is its ability to acknowledge the ontological strangeness stressed in Crocean theorizing about the impossibility of holding poetry to any categorical constraints. Perhaps it is only by treating poetry as so indefinite a category that one can see how its content depends on the specific processes of disclosure set in motion by a linguistic intricacy that puts relation in the place of substance.

These hypotheses are not wrong, but they are severely limited by the Romantic framework in which they are cast. Moore pushes against those limits by refusing to be content with the moment of negation setting perpendicularity against reference. The very force of the perpendicular must make possible a strange yet evocative positive characterization of that site. In this case the basic vehicle for fleshing out the content of the "genuine" is her note on the poem that shows us what she cut from previous versions. For then we have a contrast to the "it" which motivates its strategic indefiniteness. Indeed we have a complex set of virtual forces leading both back into Moore's past and forward into a more dynamic sense of how contempt and genuineness may be closely linked, mutually reinforcing states. Once we feel the pressure of all these images that rush in to provide names for poetry but actually displace it, we begin to understand how those indefinite pronouns both reflect extremely intelligent choices and orient us toward the kind of negotiations necessary if poetry is to provide alternatives to those images. So long as one needs these supplemental metaphors to define poetry, one is condemned to the distance of attempting to explain the fully genuine—the site of perpendicularity and polish—in terms of merely illustrative materials, which are thus necessarily only partial realizations of what they attempt to instantiate. Such images turn the positive into positivity, preparing metaphors for the dump that so fascinated Moore's friend Stevens. But as we realize the failure of images, we also get a glimpse of the deepest efforts of poetry—to find within the transient a sense of the genuine that is abstract enough to allow for a range of contents and fluid enough to merge into the state of grace achieved by individual poems.

If we were to make generalizations about this sense of discovery we would have to say that the point of the poem is to show how we must conceive the genuine in poetry in terms of forces rather than of things or images. Poetry must be abstract in order to focus attention on the genuine concreteness of its processes that tend to be subsumed under the narcissistic substitutes that we impose upon them as we create scenic contexts and thematic interpretations. But as we make even that generalization, the deeper point of Moore's poem begins to become clear. Generalization itself must take the role of indefinite pronoun. Rather than explaining anything, it too becomes a means of tracking this sense of the genuine, which resides less in anything we say about the poem than in what we do as we try to cut through the images to what underlies them.

Moore's poem, in other words, is not about the genuine so much as it is the literal action of attempting to locate "it" in the only way that the "it" can be given significant content. Rather than proliferating names for the pronoun, we must let it lead us to reflecting on the forces that it actually gathers within the poem. These comprise what can be genuine about poetry. At one pole the poem shifts from images to the force the authorial process embodies as it works out what is involved in Moore's epigraph, "Omissions are not accidents." Omissions are, or can be, an author's means of asserting control over the complex energies of negation which we have been observing at work. Omissions are not accidents because they are perhaps the only way of negotiating between the accidental and the essential. Thus they lead us to the complex framework of memories, needs, and cares which provides the background that poetry must rely on and bring into focus. The poet's powers of negation are her richest means of showing what motivates her quest and abides within it to prepare for the satisfactions that poetry's perpendicular presences afford. Then all these powers call attention to the other pole of readerly activity. The virtual background that the negations evoke is ultimately not abstract at all since it takes specific form in the reader's own efforts to transform an initial befuddlement not unlike contempt into a momentary realization of all that the "it" comes to embody. Reading this poem engages us in precisely the process that the poem describes: puzzled by the "it," we must recover what the early drafts offered, understand why that fails to define poetry, and put in its place the realization that the genuine consists in this dialectical process that establishes a "place" (in all the senses of that term) where all readers can see what is shared in the effort to find something mediating between the "it" and its substitutes. To see what that entails is to demonstrate the power to achieve it.

This play of virtual forces and identifications is obviously not given a specific gendered context. Yet it does serve the crucial role of indicating how thoroughly certain active forces constitute the dynamic texture of Moore's poems, forces that can be made to resonate in conjunction with qualities that some situations can mark as gendered. So now we must turn to some ways in which Moore focuses attention on those properties. The quickest and most general means of doing that is to shift from what Moore shares with non-iconic painterly strategies to her departures from their characteristic concerns. Where the painters concentrate on rendering certain dynamic and irreducible balances that take form as essentially independent structures with which consciousness tries to align, Moore's virtual forces are irreducibly psychological and willful. The negation in **"Poetry"** is not a way of getting beyond the personal so much as a way of getting within it, getting to forces of an individual will too wise to theatricalize the terms of its caring, but freed by that wisdom to relish the more general form of that care as something approaching an absolute power. And if poetry is the will to care uncontaminated by the theatrics that the culture imposes on those impulses it hopes to ennoble, we begin to see how Moore's abstraction can employ its freedom to define that particular mode of caring as essentially female, as capable of thriving in a world where its only theatricalizing must take place in subtle winks and shifts of imaginative position—in polish wrought to its uttermost. And then what Williams, Stevens, and Burke all praised in Moore as liberating energies can be given concrete form in the forms of power realized as the lady of "Sea Unicorns and Land Unicorns," reduced to reading about heroic male deeds, nonetheless creates an order of "agreeing difference" that male demands for possession can neither imitate nor appreciate (77-79). This female writerly presence establishes a remarkably active form of passivity enabling her to domesticate a beast whose freedom and rarity can only be glimpsed in reading and whose rebellious capacity to escape all who remain its hunters can be "tamed only by a lady, inoffensive like itself—as curiously wild and gentle." The lady, in other words, literally exemplifies the "genuine place" of poetry, possessing the power to engage in hunts that need not destroy what they discover. Having insisted that the male dream of pushing back the limits of the known to map wild adventures has been replaced by a social order in which mapping is a science and the romance will has been victimized by its own will to power, Moore makes her actual processes of imagination evidence for a wile and patience that may be the only plausible way to extend the human world to the site where the unicorn's "mild wild head" might rest.

Moore wants this model of freedom to *appear* passive and simple. For understatement hones the irony that is the modern hunter's strongest weapon. What Douglas Collins calls being always already embarrassed becomes the imagination's best protection against setting up specular theaters where it spends the rest of its time watching itself rather than exploring the positive forces released by its capacity to withdraw into virtual space. But Moore also wants us to "have a record of" the philosophical weight made possible by these fluid forms of care enabling the imagination to contain what it thereby brings to life. Thus her **"The Plumet Basilisk"** puts the process of searching for the genuine to the specific task of locating psychological correlates for what in previous cultures had assumed mythic images. Here all of Pound's and Yeats's nostalgias about the old gods give way to a polish witty enough to compose a space where gods can still show themselves, made vital by the absences that they define.

The poem is a typical Moore journey, with books as her maps and the imagination her principle for exploring the various locales. After voyaging from lizards to dragons to stories of the gods, attention focuses once again on the basilisk:

> he is alive there
>   in his basilisk cocoon beneath
> the one of living green; his quicksilver ferocity
>   quenched in the rustle of his fall into the
>   sheath
> which is the shattering sudden splash that marks
>   his temporary loss.
>
> (**Complete Poems**, 24)

Here the immediacy of her poetic play captures not only the activity of the basilisk but also the ways in which that activity helps explain why such figures make the mind think of gods. For what engages us in what we see also provides confidence that what we cannot see will return. We are led to experience loss in such a way that it calls up virtual powers of renewal—in the mind as well as in what it observes and transforms. With "temporary" so fully captured as itself an aspect of a larger temporality, the poem concludes by calling upon the implications of all the allusive liberations which throughout the poem have given the lizard a place in our affections. Thus loss becomes a way of recognizing the significance and force of those affections. They testify to virtual relations between attention and temporality that warrant feelings that the gods are there in their loss—perhaps findable precisely because of the way in which that loss forces us to reconsider our own powers.

The principle of containment as release is a marvelous poetic ideal. But how far does it carry poetry into life? Or to put the question in gender terms, how well does it avoid complicity in certain cultural visions that would impose the burden of care on women in order to "free" men for more worldly pursuits while confining women's cleverness to the poetic imagination? Both questions are far too complex to answer here, partially because there are enormous differences between identifying certain concerns as characteristically female in our culture and deciding that they should or should not be cultivated by specific groups. Similarly Moore's own conservative individualism is content to propose certain imaginative possibilities which readers are then free to use or ignore, so it lacks any terms for adjudicating the actual political implications of such choices. Therefore I shall dodge the general issues by adapting what I think would be her strategy: there is no possibility of or need for defending every aspect of any poet's vision—what matters is being clear on what a poet makes available to those who may need it. There remains, however, one crucial particularizing move of Moore's that does address the question of social implications and that therefore must be considered as an index of her own sense of how the powers she explores have practical consequences. That move occurs in the poem **"Silence,"** which concludes her 1935 **Selected Poems** and thus raises the possibility that everything in the book contributes to and is modified by this dialectical assertion of her female strength:

> My father used to say,
> "Superior people never make long visits,
> have to be shown Longfellow's grave
> or the glass flowers at Harvard.
> Self-reliant like the cat—
> that takes its prey to privacy,
> the mouse's limp tail hanging like a shoelace
>   from its mouth—
> they sometimes enjoy solitude,
> and can be robbed of speech
> by speech which has delighted them.
> The deepest feeling always shows itself in silence;
> not in silence, but restraint."
> Nor was he insincere in saying, "Make my house
>   your inn."
> Inns are not residences.

(***Complete Poems***, 91)

That "nor was he insincere" marvelously fixes a prevailing tone defining the emotional burdens which I think demand a daughter's Modernist refusal of all the old representational securities. Facing a father so willfully manipulating the powers that language confers, the daughter's primary task is to appropriate those powers to her own mode of restraint that must grapple with the task of fixing him and freeing herself. Such needs, however, also bring extreme risks. Should she either overestimate her power or underestimate the task, she is likely to trap herself in poses of hatred and obsessive resistance that only confirm his victory. Ironically that is why the father's advice is so compelling. One in her situation must refrain from any self-staging—either as self-pity or as Plathian fantasies of revenge. Instead virtuality becomes a vital weapon, and Modernist formal strategies establish a possible psychology. All the care that attracts the unicorn or preserves traces of the basilisk here goes into investing herself in the father's basic sources of strength without having to fixate on either his deeds or any single fantasy of her own projected response. This empathic distance becomes formidable power as she replaces melodramatic rhetoric with a withering precision whose formulated phrases capture in the simple double negative of "nor was he insincere" the essential inhumanity of his reticence. Moore is by no means immune to the power of his control over language, but this "nor" superbly positions her attraction against the background of a deeper unspeakable negative which casts his self-control as bordering on the margin of a terrifying monstrosity. It is no wonder, then, that once the daughter's imagination is released by an extended simile it dwells on the morbid scenario of the mouse in the cat's mouth, an objective correlative for life with father.

For Moore, though, and for her **Selected Poems,** that terror must not be allowed to prevail or to generate a counter-violence sustaining a similar self-absorption. The first thing necessary to resist his authority is to do him justice by acknowledging the style and insight that make his idiosyncratic ways come to exemplify values she seeks in her own poetry. But then one must test what one has made from those beginnings by exploring both the poet's and the daughter's ability to transform the basic strengths of her internalized father figure into a precursor for her own sense of individual power. In order to understand, she must identify with him by continuing to quote his characteristic utterances, but in order to conquer she must be so supple in her identifications that she maintains her own difference, her own perpendicularity, without having to project it into the terms such fathers love to deconstruct. What better way to do that than to use her metamorphic abilities to appropriate the phrase most characteristic of her father's strengths and her fears, "Inns are not residences"?

An emblem which she continues to hold in this strange mix of awe and fear becomes through the testimony of this volume also the expression that best characterizes her own capacity to make language a provisional and fluid mode of dwelling. There remains the risk that even this degree of accepting the father's formulation will make playing at differences only an evasion of remaining at heart the dutiful daughter. But for Moore that risk becomes part of the implicit background, part of the contrast that reminds us of how thinking in such global categories either misses or denies precisely what gives Moore her claims to independence. Were one to avoid that risk, one would have to reject the entire culture shaped by such fathers. By quoting that authority, on the other hand, Moore can create a very complex site where we observe language playing out a drama of affiliation and difference that is basic to life within a culture. Yes, this is dependent on his formulation. But that dependency is a beginning, not a final state. It resounds as an implicit contrastive context testing her own ability to make language precise and fluid enough to appropriate what it echoes. As Pound would try to do on a much more theatrical scale, Moore uses her mobile shifts simultaneously to confirm her banishment to a life of inns and to make that instability a residence in its own right—a home won by the power to control virtual identifications with such grace that they need never be tied to forms that invite either the mirror or the dump.

By having to win a style against such a father (or such fathers, if we allow this concluding poem its full figural scope), Moore gave Modernism two distinctive and important ways of using foregrounded syntactic effects for semantic, extraformal purposes ignored by the grand ambitions of Williams and Eliot and Pound and Stevens—allies at least in their blindness. First, her model of virtual forces gives poetry a model for subjective interests that makes those formal activities an actual process of soul-making: the energies which allow personal idiosyncrasy to establish a perpendicular to the pressure of reality can be continually tested for the qualities of care that they make available as they are forced to muster intensity outside the traditional self-staging modes of lyrical expression. Second, by locating self within those energies, the poetry can generate sufficient mobility for the writing that it is free to define that care in the most concrete and discursive of ways. Once the lyrical energy need not depend on either melodrama or conceptual structures afforded by myth or politics, the poet need ground it only as a mode of care, a way of manifesting what it is about certain objects and states which can warrant the delight which, as poetry, ties the

subject to the world. As Auden and Ashbery would later realize, such a voice is free to make the most overt discursive statements, secure that its own intricacy and precision preserve the mobility of imagination. Inns, in effect, can fully suffice as residences. Then, taken as corollary principles, the two ways show how imaginative energy can refuse both the absoluteness of identification that cramps identity and the resoluteness of fact that represses the site of virtual play, putting in their place the power to replace the father's authority by the turning and twisting of a daughter's volition and consciousness where

> In the short-legged, fit-
> ful advance, the gurgling and all the
>   minutiae—we have the
>   classic
> multitude of feet. To what purpose! Truth is no
>   Apollo
>   Belvedere, no formal thing. The wave may go
>   over it if it likes.
> Know that it will be there when it says,
>   "I shall be there when the wave has gone by"
>   (*Complete Poems*, 41-42)

This way of surviving, however, is not without serious limitations which would emerge in Moore's later poetry. For there are some modes of care which require more stable residences, some pressures of reality which demand more overt and defined values than any sense of mobile virtuality can sustain. This Moore, like Stevens, learned in the late thirties as problems of social justice then of international order came to seem the inescapable burden of the poet. When confronted with these issues idiosyncrasy does not appear to generate sufficient public roles for the self, and the habit of making a constructive sensibility replace more abstract and rhetorical forms of self-assertion simply will not produce sufficiently discursive or actionable ways of referring to experience. I am not sure that any modern poetry can meet that challenge, or that it should even try, since there will always be a considerable private residue created by public issues. But it is hard not to attempt making the form of language that one most trusts address the problems that one finds most compelling.

This is obviously not the place for an extended discussion of Moore's later poetry. But I raise the issue in part to define the limits of her version of Modernism and in part to show how those limits are already present in a second crucial poem about place, **"The Steeple-Jack,"** which Eliot realized had to serve as the volume's opening balance to the freedoms that **"Silence"** wins from the father. Both poems insist that freedom makes sense only in relation to a sense of place or ground that frees it from having to stage an abstract self as its source and end. But as soon as that ground grows at all abstract in its own right it tempts one to relax one's vigilance and, more important, to begin thinking that, simply by submitting, one will receive something in return that comes as a gift and does not require the labors of constructive intelligence. In confronting those issues the poem's opening stanzas create a site as subtle and complex as anything in Modern poetry. An abstracting, synthetic style links a sea scene with Dürer's visions and then with the multiple relations which make of the whole "an elegance of which the source is not bravado," and hence a "fit-haven" for living. But here Moore seems to feel compelled to find an abstract reason why this elegance is significant, so she tries to go beyond the exemplary qualities which the constructive sensibility exemplifies to more thematic and symbolic ways of projecting significance for the details. This entails populating the place with symbolic surrogates which show how those powers pertain to society. But they also displace those powers—into rather simple roles, and into modes of activity and belief that have very little to do with what the poem can exhibit and test. Where the virtual powers of poetry had been able to carry a force which no image could quite capture as it shifted between presence and absence, the seen and what might be inferred by transpersonal features of the psyche, now the need to make those powers present demands embodying them in figures that must be able to stand as quasi-allegorical signifiers. These, ironically, become as legible and as pathetically ineffectual as the steeple-jack's sign.

Here poetry adapts its perpendiculars to concerns that would soon be even more overtly focused on the large moral and psychological questions pervading American life. But to do that means supplementing one's concerns for the virtual space that makes one free by positing ideas and images which that freedom could use to direct its interests. Freedom had to be acculturated, to claim a real residence. However, real residences are not very hospitable to the virtual, individualizing energies which actually gave Moore's poems means for fluidly negotiating the demands of the social world. The move from negotiating that world to become a spokesperson for it was not one she could have her poetry make without losing more than she could gain. Virtuality falls into its images and the non-assertive poet ends up confirming the assertions trumpeted by far less

refined minds. Late Moore dramatizes the failures of constructivist aesthetics to develop a practical cultural model which could extend their principles beyond individualism while demonstrating the need for a poetry that could handle the assertive will without theatricalizing that most theatrical of forces. We see why an Adrienne Rich would have to reject her early interest in Moore's virtuality for the risky path of trying to make "genuine" an adjective that could apply to will as well as to place.

Notes

1. Both John M. Slatin and Bonnie Costello begin their excellent books on Moore with the question of how questions of defining poetry in conjunction with models of identity are central to her enterprise. But where Slatin emphasizes the contexts that Moore manipulates, Costello focuses on matters of building a poetic ethos. Thus her *Imaginary Possessions* argues that the range of terms that Moore uses for poetry attempts to combine "moral and aesthetic or intentional and expressive categories: feeling and precision, idiosyncracy and technique" (2). Then she does a superb job of showing how Moore's mobile intelligence gathers and disperses energies as it resists making imagistic effigies of itself, and she adds a very informative and intelligent chapter on Moore's relation to the visual arts of her time. But while she is very clear on how Moore's use of her medium is Modernist, she seems to me to stay essentially within a realizational aesthetic that cannot take account of either the powers or the sense of mystery that Moore tries to evoke for the conditions of agency that her poems establish. For example, Moore is simply too abstract for this formulation: "Moore's poems are not, finally, representations of things or statements of opinions. They are imaginative acts, efforts to reconstruct the world in language, and thus in relation to the self, to render the world harmless and to give the self objectivity" (65). If I am right, it is not so easy to talk about self, or even about objectivity—not because these are not concerns of Moore's reconstructions, but because she succeeds at times all too well to allow so traditional a recuperative language. And without an adequate model of the forms of agency that Moore does compose one cannot adequately handle the degree to which agency becomes gendered within Moore's imaginative universe. Therefore, we need to take a critical tack that will emphasize the actual forces that Moore's compositional activity establishes. For that the best analogues are those painterly models which eschew realization entirely to focus attention on relational powers. In relying on those analogues I need not deny that the visual Modernism most interesting to Moore consisted mostly in Cubist works. I claim only that she learned from them much the same lessons learned by Mondrian and Malevich, both of whom continually cite Cézanne and Picasso, so that it is those painters who most clearly capture what she makes even of that Cubist work like Picasso's collages most dependent on virtuality. As a good test case for the differences I am trying to indicate, compare my treatment below of the last version of "Poetry" and Costello's. As in Slatin's fine reading of the poem's various stages, she sees all the intricacy of the pronouns, but then she concludes that "reducing the poem to three lines may

be Moore's attempt to uncover the genuine, but a short poem is no more genuine than an expansive one" (26). True enough, but *this* short poem's negation of the image introduces a quite different poetic theater. Pound sharply caught the differences involved in this way of reading when he compared Moore to Williams: "Williams is simple by comparison—not so thoughtful. It has a larger audience because of its apparent simplicity. It is the lyric of an aptitude. Aptitude, not attitude" (*Selected Prose* 399).

2. The best way to see the prevalence of the problem is to observe the many studies like Alicia Ostriker's *Stealing the Language* which celebrate the expressive ego's efforts to steal and remake a patriarchal language. I cannot quarrel with the ideal of remaking the language, but I worry about a critical framework that can praise such obviously mediocre poetry because it manages to express that mediocrity as a full definition of one's subjectivity. So long as it stays in this vein, new feminism is but old late romanticism writ large, and both the critical force and imaginative resources of Modernism simply get relegated to ancient history. For a good critique of those tendencies, as well as of the attendant language of victimage that would have appalled Moore, see Susan Howe, *My Emily Dickinson*. I should add that I support the remarks of my next sentence as implicitly critical of the concept of "experience" in my *Diacritics* review, "Reach Without a Grasp: Review of Paul Fry, *The Reach of Criticism: Method and Perception in Literary Theory*."

3. Moore's use of abstract testimonial principles and her blend of the personal and the impersonal also make it possible to claim that very little is lost even if I am wrong or if the specifically gendered poems that I deal with do not prove sufficiently representative. The central point is how she insists on making her authorial energies sustain a poetical character defining a fully ethical presence able to understand what its loves make possible. I think there is sufficient evidence to treat that ethos as gendered and sufficient cause to make that consideration. But even those who suspect that argument should see from the arguments it elicits how thoroughly Moore's experiments in constructivist ideals of virtuality and transpersonality distinguish her work from the more painterly and perceptual versions of abstraction pursued by Williams and Stevens, especially during the decade after the first World War when she was clearly embarked on a more radical rethinking of language than they were.

Works Cited

Altieri, Charles. "Reach Without a Grasp: Review of Paul Fry, *The Reach of Criticism: Method and Perception in Literary Theory*." *Diacritics*, 14, No. 4 (1984), 58-66.

William Cookson, ed., *Selected Prose 1909-1965: Ezra Pound*, New Directions, 1973.

Costello, Bonnie. *Marianne Moore: Imaginary Possessions.* Cambridge, MA: Harvard University Press, 1981.

Howe, Susan. *My Emily Dickinson.* Berkeley, CA: North Atlantic Books, 1985.

Moore, Marianne. *The Complete Poems of Marianne Moore.* New York: Viking, 1981.

———. *Selected Poems.* New York: Macmillan, 1935.

Ostriker, Alicia. *Stealing the Language: The Emergence of Women's Poetry in America.* Boston: Beacon Press, 1986.

Webster Schott, ed., *Imaginations*. New York: New Directions, 1970.

Slatin, John M. *The Savage's Romance: The Poetry of Marianne Moore.* University Park: Pennsylvania State University Press, 1986.

TITLE COMMENTARY

"Marriage"

BRUCE HENDERSON (ESSAY DATE 1992)

SOURCE: Henderson, Bruce. "The 'Eternal Eve' and 'The Newly Born Woman': Voices, Performance, and Marianne Moore's 'Marriage'." In *Images of the Self as Female: The Achievement of Women Artists in Re-envisioning Feminine Identity*, edited by Kathryn N. Benzel and Lauren Pringle De La Vars, pp. 119-33. Lewiston, N.Y.: The Edwin Mellen Press, 1992.

In the following essay, Henderson considers "Marriage" to be "the most complicated treatment by Moore of issues typically associated with the lives of women as women."

1987 marked the centenary of the birth of Marianne Moore, a poet more discussed than read, more often alluded to than analyzed: happily, with her centenary there seems to be a resurgence of interest in both the life and art of this idiosyncratic, yet often profoundly eloquent poet. Feminist critics and readers in particular have begun to revise earlier estimates of Moore, seeing, where once they found too much reserve and distance, a rigorous and imaginative authenticity of voice and perception. Moore's refusal to be autobiographical or confessional in the sense of revealing elements of her romantic or erotic life was once viewed as an unwillingness to deal with aspects of women's experience in a direct way; today, many critics prefer to see this as a very real and individualistic version of feminism: a refusal to write a certain kind of poetry (i.e., the love poems of Millay or Dorothy Parker) simply because it was deemed "proper" for feminine writers. It is not that Moore was unwilling to take a stand or reveal feeling in her poems about steamrollers and steeplejacks: rather, her path to the discourse of self was directed more outwardly than those of some of her peers. In terms of style, Moore is one of the least impersonal poets. Certainly it is next to impossible to read a poem by Marianne Moore and not know its author: the voice is unmistakable.

Elizabeth Bishop, herself a fine poet and a protegee of Moore, called for a reassessment of Moore's poetry vis-à-vis contemporary feminist criteria:

Marianne Moore (left) receives a National Book Award for *Collected Poems,* in New York City, 1952.

Lately I have seen several references critical of her poetry by feminist writers, one of whom described her as a 'poet who controlled panic by presenting it as whimsy.' Whimsy is there, of course, and so is humor (a gift these critics sadly seem to lack). Surely there is an element of mortal panic and fear underlying all works of art? Even so, one wonders how much of Marianne's poetry the feminist critics have read. Have they really read "**Marriage**," a poem that says everything they are saying and everything Virginia Woolf has said?

(143-144)

"**Marriage**" is the most complicated treatment by Moore of issues typically associated with the lives of women as women. Moore wrote it near the end of the first major period in her poetry. It is, with "**An Octopus**," one of her few poems sustained beyond the one- or two-page lyric.

"**Marriage**," the poem of a young woman in her mid-thirties, is an extended "observation" (one of Moore's favorite words, and the title of her first American volume) of this "institution." Unmarried, she took no individual part in the institution, but it surrounded her in rather involved ways. There are many speculations as to

what gave immediate rise to the poem, some connected to Moore's own life, some to those of her friends.[1]

Moore herself grew up in a family in which marriage was a painful subject: her mother left her father, who was at one time institutionalized for a nervous breakdown. About the time she wrote "**Marriage**" Moore joined the society of bohemian New York, the artists and writers who inhabited Greenwich Village: the often flexible interpretation of the marriage vow by some of her closest friends must have provoked her puzzlement or criticism or both. Certainly there is reason to believe that Moore herself was offered marriage, though whether she ever seriously considered it must remain a biographical mystery that may never be solved.

The poem is itself a brilliant example of how Moore "makes it new" (to borrow Ezra Pound's famous phrase). In "**Marriage**," Moore retells the story of Adam and Eve, casting the myth both diachronically and synchronically. Moore is selective in her refashioning of the story, focusing

ON THE SUBJECT OF...

MOORE'S "MARRIAGE," ACCORDING TO ROSEANNE WASSERMAN

Among the corpus of Marianne Moore's difficult poetry, the piece "Marriage" is particularly complex, well armored in gorgeous abstractions and dazzling transitions. Its structure depends upon a quest for definition of marriage. But clues as to the nature of this definition are buried under Moore's ornate decoration, crazy-quilt quotations, and her protean ironic tone. To follow Moore's meaning, the reader must attend to lexis: not only to the familiar rhetorics of transition and addition that hold her borrowings in proximity, but to the weight of repetition and synonymity as ironic overtones develop; not only to the eccentric vocabulary, contributing gusto, but also to the smaller, ambiguously simple words that shift and change through pressure of position. The poem is in itself a difficult marriage, its elements united through the linear process of reading and the structure of making sense of what is read, but always suffering disjunction due to the complexity and multiplicity of detail.

Wasserman, Roseanne. An excerpt from "Marianne Moore's 'Marriage': Lexis and Structure." In *New Interpretations of American Literature*, edited by Richard Fleming and Michael Payne, pp. 156-63. Lewisburg, N.J.: Bucknell University Press, 1988.

exclusively on the marital relationship: Adam and Eve as everycouple, not Adam and Eve as everyparents. Though there is some sense of temporal progression in the poem, this first marriage seems to exist contemporaneously with all marriages, almost in that lyric sense in which any historical moment may be contemplated in poetic time: the structure is not wholly unlike the "web" Estella Lauter describes in her introduction to this volume. Instead of using a straightforward, Aristotelian plot, Moore chooses to move between familiar incidents and images (such as the "colubrine" serpent) and an imagined, eternal dialogue between the "he" and "she" who are descendents of the archetypal Adam and Eve.

Adam and Eve, in this poem, are not in any simple sense the scriptural, quasi-historical personages familiar to all readers of the poem, nor even the more fully-dramatized characters in Milton's epic or in later treatments by writers like Twain or Arthur Miller. They are, at least on some level, these two people (and Moore names them as such); yet they are also what Mikhail Bakhtin might call "person-ideas," conflations of beings and represented ideologies.[2] What Moore has created is less a dramatic poem than a verbal performance, in the sense of the writer as an actor, a performer moving between a number of roles, as well as a discursive narrator, presenting her own consciousness simultaneously with those of her named speakers. Moore does not ask us to believe in the reality of her Adam and Eve as wholly separate from her own voice in the same way Frost or Browning do in their dramatic monologues: illusion does not seem to be a particularly desired condition of "**Marriage.**" Also contributing to this sense of the poem as a polyphonic performance is Moore's interweaving of a complex sub-structure of languages into the text, from various kinds of imitated speech situations to written sources as stylistically and philosophically diverse as Puritan Richard Baxter's *The Saints' Everlasting Rest* to a contemporary article in *Scientific American* to an inscription on a statue in Central Park. Clearly, there is more than one kind of "marriage" in this poem: linguistic couplings as well as social and erotic ones.

"**Marriage**" is a poem that can withstand and deserves considerably more extensive and detailed treatment than the scope of this essay permits. Using the notion of the poem as performance as my basis, I would like to focus on two aspects of the poem that relate the question of voice and language to issues of gender. First, I will examine Moore's use of different kinds of communicative and performance situations in the poem as they affect the evolving sense of contrast between male and female discourse. Second, I will consider the ways in which Moore's interpolation of quotations from other writers creates a many-layered textuality, one that may speak to feminism more significantly than previously thought.

In the first sentence of "**Marriage,**" Marianne Moore describes this "enterprise" as "requiring public promises / of one's intention / to fulfill a private obligation" (**Complete Poems** 62). Her wording immediately suggests at least an element of criticism of the verbal performances associated with the wedding ceremony: the contrast between public and private acts, traceable throughout her writings, is one the poet herself felt keenly. This is not merely a contrast between negative and positive qualities; rather, Moore seems more concerned with determining the ethical appropriateness of a situation. The public act of promising, she seems to be saying, is finally neither a guarantee that either party will fulfill the private obligation, nor is it the most authentic or sincere forum for such a statement of commitment.

The lines also suggest a second set of contrasts, and again these are neither hard and fast nor purely definitive: the typical gender associations of public performances versus private ones. In "Marriage," Adam is more often than not cast as the orator, the public speaker, while Eve is more at home in the world of conversation, a witty, sometimes artificial (in both the most and least pejorative senses of that word) conversation, not unlike that of an Enlightenment salon. Although, as we will see, both characters venture into other realms of spoken discourse, Moore fairly consistently schematizes them.

In this linkage of masculine to public speaking and feminine to "interpersonal" or "poetic" communication, Moore looks ahead to contemporary French feminist theories associated with the psychoanalytic theories of Lacan and the deconstructive sorties of Derrida. Hélène Cixous, who in some ways represents the interests of both these major thinkers, differentiates between typical masculine and feminine responses to the acts of speaking and writing. Here she refers to women's resistance to oratory:

> Every woman has known the torture of beginning to speak aloud, heart beating as if to break, occasionally falling into loss of language . . . because for woman speaking—even just opening her mouth—in public is something rash, a transgression. . . . We are not culturally accustomed to speaking . . . employing the suitable rhetoric. . . . The orator is asked to unwind a small thread, dry and taut. We like uneasiness, questioning.
>
> (92-93)

Contemporary specialists in gender and communication theory might take issue with some of Cixous' generalizations, but it is true that the history of women has more often than not kept them out of the traditional public forums for rhetoric, and "relegated" (from a patriarchal point of view) them to the more informal (that is, invisible) worlds of kitchen and schoolroom. This is also often true in the representation of women in literature. A St. Joan is such a *rara avis,* both historically and dramatically, because she is a public speaker.

Eve is the first speaker introduced in the poem (that is, after the narrator, who is either female, in keeping with the implied lyric association of the poet and her poem, or neuter), and she is praised for her linguistic ability:

> able to write simultaneously
> in three languages—
> English, German, and French—
> and talk in the meantime.
>
> (*Complete Poems* 62)

Eve is the writer in the poem (perhaps she is also the writer of the poem?), but her talents extend beyond the mere ability to compose sentences. She is also a polyglot (whereas Adam appears only to speak English, and the King's English at that), and a modern one, schooled in the three primary languages of twentieth-century scholarship: indeed, she might bypass many a contemporary Ph.D. in the humanities in this respect.

Not only this, but Eve is able to "talk in the meantime," suggesting both a superior mind and the traditional female dilemma of having to do more than one thing at a time: the image of the wife or mother who must tend house and do her "own" work of the mind simultaneously. Her first words are telling: "I should like to be alone." These are not the words of the rhetorician, but the blunt, declarative statement of the woman demanding a "room of one's own." Though Eve participates in rhetorical discourse throughout the poem, it is clear that language fulfills two principal functions for her: it is either a way of ordering her own experience of the world (a primarily poetic function) or a way of stating her needs and desires (here an essentially expressive function). Language and its enactment in performance are not, for Eve, strategies for persuasion; rather they allow her to maintain that sense of "unease" and "questioning" Cixous sees as the core of what she and other theorists call *l'écriture féminine* translated variously as "feminine writing" or "discourse of women."

Eve holds her own in the more traditionally rhetorical performances in the poem. Much of the last third of the poem consists of an exchange between Adam and Eve, an exchange that is somewhere between formal debate and heated discussion, initiated by Adam's critique of Eve's body, specifically her hair—"What monarch would not blush / to have a wife / with hair like a shaving-brush?" (*Complete Poems* 67). Her stylistically balanced but fierce responses to Adam's witty and wounding remarks are frequently composed of lists, rather than of arguments *per se,* and the objects in the lists are often connected through poetic inference, metaphoric and metonymic qualities, such as "Men are monopolists / of 'stars, garters, buttons / and other shining baubles.'" Similarly, in her response to Adam's definition of a "wife" as a "coffin" (these lines quoted, by the way, from Ezra Pound, one of Moore's closest friends and most respected peers), Eve questions, both rhetorically and existentially,

> . . . This butterfly,
> this waterfly, this nomad
> that has 'proposed
> to settle on my hand for life'—
> What can one do with it?

(Complete Poems 68)

Eve moves progressively from one species of fragile insect to another to the final and damning "nomad" in her need to name the creature who is both her lover and enemy. The question she asks is perhaps in part a rhetorical one, not requiring a specific, uttered response, but it is also a real and serious dilemma for Eve: where and how to fit man into her lexicon and into her life?

Adam's language is situationally and stylistically closer to the traditions of oratory. His first words to Eve are a response to her request for solitude: he says, "'I should like to be alone; / why not be alone together'" (Complete Poems 62-63). Adam's first verbal performance is a highly complex rhetorical act: he begins by echoing the words of his "opponent," thus effectively appropriating them. The repetition diminishes the individuality of Eve's statement of desire, as if to say "we all need to be alone—what makes woman so special?" He then paradoxically turns the very meaning of the critical word "alone": how can "alone" and "together" coexist? Yet perhaps this is the point, both mythically and psychologically. In the tradition of the Old Testament, only Adam (man) ever existed alone (Moore uses this notion as the basis of her poem "**In the Days of Prismatic Color**"), leading to the psychological inevitability of woman never having the opportunity to be "alone by herself": Eve—and thus all women—can only be "alone together," in the presence of at least the knowledge of man's existence. Given the inability of Adam and Eve ever to resolve their separate selves into a unity in the poem, "alone together" is both a description of the condition of being human (and, more specifically, female) and also a comment on the quality of this marriage (and perhaps by extension, the very state of being married).

More often than not Adam speaks in the voice of the rhetor. He advises an unspecified audience on the proper age for marriage; he takes the of-fensive in the debate, and, perhaps the most maddeningly for Eve, reminds her: "I am yours to command" (Complete Poems 69). The very granting of permission to "command" is itself a paradoxical statement, undermining any conventional sense of power suggested by "command." The distance Moore as narrator maintains from Adam underscores the ambiguity of such a statement: is Adam being purposely perverse, or is he unaware of his own irony?

This is not to suggest that Adam never displays moments of vulnerability or emotion: he does, and, interestingly enough, is most moving and human when at his least articulate. Reminding us of Keats' somewhat different response, Adam is "plagued" and "unnerved" by the nightingale "in the new leaves," evoking the early morning of creation. He is haunted not so much by the song of the bird, but by its "silence": "not its silence, but silences" (Complete Poems 64). This recognition of the variety of silences created by the nightingale seems analogous to Lacan's notion of Woman and the Real, as described by Alice Jardine: "The Real designates that which is categorically unrepresentable, non-human, at the limits of the known; it is emptiness, the scream, the 'zero-point' of death, the proximity of feminine *jouissance*" (567). The nightingale's song—and, more importantly, its silences, in some ways richer, by their very lack of single, finite meaning (like Isak Dinesen's "The Blank Page" and Tillie Olsen's history of women's *Silences*)—captivate him beyond his control, and he responds, at his most authentic moment of personal expression, "It clothes me with a shirt of fire" (Complete Poems 65). Moore maintains the neutrality of "it" in referring to the nightingale, but Adam's relationship to the nightingale evokes what Moore sees as the unbridgeable dimension of relations between men and women:

> He dares not clap his hands
> to make it go on
> lest it should fly off;
> if he does nothing, it will sleep;
> if he cries out, it will not
> "understand".

(Complete Poems 65)

Adam's traditional rhetoric fails him: not only is language ineffective to help him achieve his desires, he is unable to use language to establish for himself what those desires would lead to. He does not seem to know what he wants of this nightingale—song or silence, presence or absence, or, in Wallace Stevens' terms, "inflections" or "innuendoes." It is surely not coincidental that, "unnerved by the nightingale / and dazzled by the apple," Adam must next invent ("stumble over") Marriage, as a way of taming the emotions he cannot rein in by language he already possesses.

Although I used the word "schematize" earlier in this essay to describe Moore's presentation of Adam and Eve as verbal performers, it is clear that she does not wish to reduce either figure to a flat representation of "Male" and "Female." Rather, the complexity of their own relationships to language, to themselves, and to each other is the point of Moore's use of such distinctions. That they must resort to the over-formal language of a Restoration comedy or Augustan or Victorian parliamentary debate suggests that language serves both to create unity and maintain distance. Both Adam and Eve prove themselves consummate performers, in both public and private spheres, sometimes to creative effect (for what artist, what human being does not, to some degree, create his or her own "character"?), yet sometimes at the peril of becoming distanced from self, other, and world in the comforting script of the player.

In defining Woman, Adam says, "turn to the letter M / and you will find / that a 'wife is a coffin' . . ." (*Complete Poems* 67). Ezra Pound's phrase 'a wife is a coffin' is credited in the poem's notes, thus making Adam history's first intertextualist. A hallmark of Moore's poetry, particularly that of the middle periods, is its proliferation of quoted material. In many poems, Moore quotes a few phrases from sources directly relevant to the poem's subject (for instance, she quotes Sheldon Jackson in **"Rigorists"** and John Roebling in **"Granite and Steel"**). In other poems Moore lifts material out of its original context and uses it to her own purposes. Moore seems to have been searching for just the right combination of words for a given moment or description. It is doubtful that, as some contemporary theorists suggest, to her meaning was so self-reflexive and unstable as to make the original context irrelevant. She was too traditional an ethicist for that. Indeed, the almost painstaking quality of her notes to the poems attests to an authorial sense of obligation to the original sources; she went T. S. Eliot (in *The Waste Land*) one better by using quotation marks to indicate the words of others: these quotation marks have proven an endless source of discussion for Moore's critics. Are they to be read as indications of spoken dialogue (not always, apparently) or the idiosyncratic formality of a writer who viewed documentation of source material in poetry no differently than she would have in a scholarly article or library catalogue (more the case)?

What results is a sometimes dizzying arachnid stitching, in which the reader must adopt a number of different stances towards the text in order to get as full an experience as possible of a poem by Moore. The information offered by the notes is indispensable: to simply read the "poem" without delving into the accompanying notes is to miss not only half the fun, but also half the dialogue between poet, reader, and language.

This is perhaps nowhere more true than in **"Marriage."** Moore herself sheds some light on the relevance of the intertextual material in a comment she made in lecturing on the poem, and which became part of her Foreword to *A Marianne Moore Reader*. Warning readers and audiences against either too autobiographical or polemical an interpretation of the poem, she suggested that **"Marriage"** was:

> no philosophic precipitate; nor does it veil anything personal in the way of triumphs, entrapments, or dangerous colloquies. It is a little anthology of statements that took my fancy—phrasings that I liked.
>
> (*Reader*, xv)

At the beginning of the notes to **"Marriage"** in *Complete Poems*, she calls these intertextualities "Statements that took my fancy which I tried to arrange plausibly" (271). Interestingly, this is the only headnote in the volume offering a critical perspective on a poem or on its source material, as if Moore were once more trying to ensure that readers would not jump to either biographical speculation or ideological explication. While we may not simply accept Moore's statement of intention as a satisfactory account of the developing sense of dialogue of the sexes that emerges from the poem, her comment does help focus our attention less on decoding a predictable strategy for her intertextual choices, and more on the variety of effects created by some of the juxtapositions.

Most interestingly, Moore does not work towards any kind of one-to-one correspondence between gender of dramatic speaker (i.e., Adam and Eve) and that of the original writer or speaker quoted. For example, one of Adam's most insulting remarks, referring to Eve's "shaving-brush" hair, is from a parody of Pope's *Rape of the Lock*, written by Mary Frances Nearing "with suggestions by M. Moore" (272). In terms of gender, Moore has here created a twice-turning set of ironies: Adam's words were originally written by two women; the two women were writing a parody of a mock-epic, itself something of a parody of relations between the sexes, glorifying woman in a most ambivalent way. Is Moore's Eve a cousin to (ancestor to? descendent of?) Pope's Belinda?

Another quotation that seems to comment on the gender themes of the poem occurs in the quoted passage above in which Adam admits impotence in the presence of the nightingale. The immediate source for the nightingale reference is a poem by Hagop Boghossian, including the words, "It clothes me with a shirt of fire." The lines that follow, which describe in third person Adam's inability to take action, are credited (at least in part) to Edward Thomas, specifically to his 1910 book of criticism, *Feminine Influence on the Poets* (271): again, careful not to attribute definite intention here, we can enjoy the irony in the title of the book that provided the poem with its description of male fascination with, perhaps even fear of, the natural singer. Is this sense of discomfort and doubt, yearning and fear, the "feminine influence on the poets"?

It would be valuable to explore each one of the relationships between "**Marriage**" and the other texts cited in Moore's notes; it is certainly worth noting some of the other sources alluded to. The text Moore quotes most frequently is Richard Baxter's *The Saints' Everlasting Rest,* a Puritan religious tract, and a favorite of Moore's. The sentences and phrases taken from Baxter seem selected less for their theological content than for their stylistic balance: both Adam and Eve speak some of Baxter's words, so it is unlikely that Moore was attempting consistency of gender and voice in this instance. Other sources underscore Moore's Bryn Mawr education, both in the number of quotations taken from eighteenth- and nineteenth-century prose works and writers (such as Trollope, Godwin, Charles Reade, and Edmund Burke), as well as a passage highly critical of men's authority over women, placed in Eve's voice and attributed by Moore to "Miss M. Carey Thomas," the legendary president of Bryn Mawr during Moore's years as an undergraduate there. A few quotations come from French texts, including one from La Fontaine, prefiguring Moore's later association with that writer (though the specific lines used in "Marriage" are not Moore's translation, as she did not begin that work for another two decades). Still other sources include the Bible and Shakespeare, though fewer from these sacred and secular scriptures than might have been expected, and from contemporary journals and advertisements. All in all, the notes suggest a writer who was quite a wide reader herself—for whom every text, as contemporary theory suggests, was an "inter-text," bridging various aspects of her intellectual, spiritual, and aesthetic education and experience. This, itself, is a feminist testimony to the ability of the woman writer to integrate any number of traditions of the mind into her work, not limiting herself to "women's words" (not as in contemporary theories of language, but as stereotypically conceived in that period).

Moore's approach to intertextuality has a number of implications for this poem and, perhaps, for women's writing in general. First, her eclecticism and her seemingly random use of sources are designed not for strictly monistic ideological ends, but for the most appropriate stylistic effect, and for the creative playfulness of the act of weaving such a web of language: by spinning her thread in the pattern of the story of Adam and Eve, Moore allows herself to place the words in the voices of recognizable and somewhat archetypal figures; at the same time, her extensive use of the words of others and the accompanying notes also allows her to achieve a more resonantly polyphonic series of effects. Surely there is meaning in this "**Marriage**," but it is neither singular nor simple.

The eclecticism of texts used in the poem also distinguishes Moore from some traditional conceptions of intertextuality, particularly Harold Bloom's, whose "influence" roughly corresponds to the more deconstructive "intertextuality."[3] Bloom's celebrated "anxiety of influence" focuses on "literary paternity" (to use Gubar and Gilbert's phrase), with a high degree of Freudian oedipalism. Moore's intertextuality does not seem founded in any of the typical set of anxieties Bloom identifies in the post-Miltonic poets. Rather, Moore embraces language itself and the various galaxies of discourse she encounters in her reading and living. Moore's poetry seems fairly free of any feminine equivalent of Bloom's male-centered anxiety for women writers: there is a generosity and gratitude in her celebration of voices—her own and others (both female and male)—woven into this poem. The poem is critical of "**Marriage**," the "institution," the "enterprise," but it is supportive of the people who continue to try to make it work. The last image, derived from a statue of Daniel Webster in Central Park, captures Moore's own sense of affirming ambivalence:

'Liberty and union
now and forever';

the Book on the writing-table;
the hand in the breast-pocket.

(Complete Poems 70)

Thus, "**Marriage**" ends with both of the major traditions of communication, held in an eternal frieze, like the ever-pursuing lovers on the Grecian urn: the Book, the Biblical Word, for Moore the central written text from which all others derive, and the "hand in the breast-pocket," the speaker arguing with eloquence and integrity. A particularly masculine image, this is also an image of marriage: a marriage of writing and speech, of creative inspiration and logical rhetoric. It is the integration of these two traditions of verbal performance which Moore celebrates and criticizes in "**Marriage**"; it is also these two traditions in which Moore herself participates in the poem and participated in throughout her career. As a final note, it is interesting to observe that Moore frequently performed "**Marriage**" at her public readings. In the leather-bound notebook in which she kept notes and outlines for public performances, Marianne Moore wrote next to the title "**Marriage**," the phrase, "(but not all of it)." Though the natural interpretation of this statement is that the poem was too long to be spoken in its entirety as part of an evening's program, it is also a statement of limitations: "**Marriage**" is about that institution, and also, on some less direct levels, about other kinds of marriages (textual and linguistic, to name only two), but, as Moore said, it is "not all of it": perhaps that is why Moore could write about it with such eloquence, fascination, and passionate questioning.

Notes

1. For one interesting account of the possible origins of "Marriage," see Laurence Stapleton, *Marianne Moore: The Poet's Advance* (Princeton: Princeton University Press, 1978).

2. Bakhtin's theories of dialogism and particularly the relationship between characters and ideologies are found in a number of his works, perhaps most notably in *The Dialogic Imagination* (Austin: University of Texas Press, 1981) and *Problems of Dostoyevsky's Poetics* (Minneapolis: University of Minnesota Press, 1984).

3. I am using "intertextuality" in the relatively broad sense of the ways in which a text interacts with another text or set of texts, not in the more specialized usages of either Barthes or Derrida, two of the term's principal champions. I prefer it to "influence," which carries associations of a pervading impact of one or a number of authors or texts on a writer: as I argue, Moore seems less "influenced," in the current usage of that word in literary theory, than to have been delighted or moved by a turn of phrase or a writer's style, and to have picked up the language of the original source. "Allusion," another feasible term, suggests that the reader might be expected to bring a wider knowledge of the work quoted than I believe either Moore or her poem intend. "Intertextuality" retains the sense of openness of relationship between writer, text, and "intertexts" that characterizes Moore's use in "Marriage" and elsewhere of the words of others.

Works Cited

Bishop, Elizabeth. "Efforts of Affection: A Memoir of Marianne Moore." *The Collected Prose.* Ed. Robert Giroux. New York: Farrar, Straus, and Giroux, 1984.

Cixous, Hélène, and Catherine Clement. *The Newly Born Woman.* Trans. Betsy Wing. Minneapolis: University of Minnesota Press, 1986.

Jardine, Alice. "Gynesis." *Critical Theory Since 1965.* Ed. Hazard Adams and Leroy Searle. Tallahassee: Florida State University Press, 1986.

Moore, Marianne. *The Complete Poems.* New York: Macmillan/Viking, 1980.

———. *A Marianne Moore Reader.* New York: Viking, 1961.

———. Notes for Readings & Lectures. Marianne Moore Collection. Rosenbach Museum & Library.

FURTHER READING

Bibliographies

Abbott, Craig S. *Marianne Moore: A Descriptive Bibliography,* Pittsburgh: University of Pittsburgh Press, 1977, 265 p.

Lists primary and secondary material on Moore through 1975.

Willis, Patricia, ed.. *Marianne Moore, Woman and Poet.* Orono, Maine: National Poetry Foundation, University of Maine, 1990, 636 p.

Extensive bibliography of Moore with critical essays included.

Biography

Molesworth, Charles. *Marianne Moore: A Literary Life.* New York: Atheneum, 1990, 472 p.

Comprehensive biography and survey of Moore's literary career.

Criticism

Berger, Charles. "Who Writes the History Book?: Moore's Revisionary Poetics." *Western Humanities Review* 53, no. 3 (fall 1999): 274-86.

Provides a feminist perspective on several of Moore's poems.

Bishop, Elizabeth. "As We Like It: Miss Moore and the Delight of Imitation." *Quarterly Review of Literature* 4, no. 2 (1948): 129-35.

Notes Moore's descriptive prowess, offers a comparison of Moore and Edgar Allan Poe, and briefly discusses the animal imagery in Moore's work.

Bloom, Harold, ed. *Marianne Moore.* New York: Chelsea House, 1986, 184 p.

A collection of critical essays on Moore's verse.

Brownstein, Marilyn N. "The Archaic Mother and Mother and Mother: The Postmodern Poetry of Marianne Moore." *Contemporary Literature* 30, no. 1 (spring 1989): 13-32.

Views Moore as "the model for the feminine postmodern."

Engel, Bernard F. *Marianne Moore.* Boston: Twayne Publishers, 1989, 160 p.

Biographical and critical study of Moore and her works.

Gregory, Elizabeth, ed. *The Critical Response to Marianne Moore.* Westport, Conn.: Praeger Publishers, 2004, 320 p.

Presents seminal reviews and essays on Moore and her work from several prominent critics.

Hadas, Pamela White. *Marianne Moore: Poet of Affection.* Syracuse, N.Y.: Syracuse University Press, 1977, 243 p.

Elucidates thematic and stylistic aspects of Moore's verse.

Heuving, Jeanne. *Omissions Are Not Accidents: Gender in the Art of Marianne Moore.* Detroit: Wayne State University Press, 1992, 195 p.

Examines Moore's work from a feminist perspective.

Keller, Lynn. "'For Inferior Who is Free?': Liberating the Woman Writer in Marianne Moore's 'Marriage'." In *Influence and Intertextuality in Literary History*, edited by Jay Clayton and Eric Rothstein, pp. 219-44. Madison: The University of Wisconsin Press, 1991.

Examines Moore's poem "Marriage" and the various ways it can be interpreted by critics and readers.

Leithauser, Brad. "Digesting Hard Iron." *New York Times Book Review* 109, no. 1 (4 January 2004): 7.

Provides discussion of Moore's poetry in a new collection edited by her friend, Grace Shulman, commenting on the selection of poems in this volume that were cut from others, and noting the chronological rather than thematic organization of the verse.

Martin, Taffy. *Marianne Moore: Subversive Modernist.* Austin: University of Texas Press, 1986, 151 p.

Discusses Moore as a modernist poet.

Miller, Cristanne. *Marianne Moore: Question of Authority.* Cambridge: Harvard University Press, 1995, 303 p.

Critical analysis of Moore's work.

Ostriker, Alicia. "What Do Women (Poets) Want?: H. D. and Marianne Moore as Poetic Ancestresses." *Contemporary Literature* 27, no. 4 (winter 1986): 475-92.

Cites Moore and H. D. as inspirations for future generations of female poets and critics.

Parisi, Joseph. *Marianne Moore: The Art of a Modernist.* Ann Arbor: UMI Research Press, 1990, 182 p.

Collection of critical essays.

Sagetrieb: Marianne Moore Special Issue 6, no. 3 (winter 1987): 201 p.

Features essays on various aspects of Moore's work by several respected Moore scholars, including Bonnie Costello, Charles Molesworth, and Alan Nadel.

Schulman, Grace. *Marianne Moore: The Poetry of Engagement.* Urbana: University of Illinois Press, 1986, 137 p.

Assesses Moore's imagery, observations, and rhythmic methods.

Stapleton, Laurence. *Marianne Moore: The Poet's Advance.* Princeton, N.J.: Princeton University Press, 1978, 282 p.

Biographical and critical study.

Steinman, Lisa M. "'So As to Be One Having Some Way of Being One Having Some Way of Working': Marianne Moore and Literary Tradition." In *Gendered Modernisms: American Women Poets and Their Readers*, edited by Margaret Dickie and Thomas Travisano, pp. 97-116. Philadelphia: University of Pennsylvania Press, 1996.

Delineates Moore's attitude toward literary tradition and traces her development as a poet.

Tomlinson, Charles, ed. *Marianne Moore: A Collection of Critical Essays.* Englewood Cliffs, N.J.: Prentice-Hall, 1970, 185 p.

Contains essays by many of Moore's most highly regarded critics and fellow poets, including Ezra Pound, T. S. Eliot, William Carlos Williams, Wallace Stevens, Hugh Kenner, and Randall Jarrell.

Zona, Kirsten Hotelling. *Marianne Moore, Elizabeth Bishop, and May Swenson: The Feminist Poetics of Self-Restraint.* Ann Arbor: University of Michigan Press, 2002, 187 p.

Feminist interpretation of the poetry of Moore, Elizabeth Bishop, and May Swenson.

OTHER SOURCES FROM GALE:

Additional coverage of Moore's life and career is contained in the following sources published by the Gale Group: *American Writers; Concise Dictionary of Literary Biography,* Vols. 1929-1941; *Contemporary Authors,* Vols. 1-4R, 33-36R; *Contemporary Authors New Revision Series,* Vols. 3, 61; *Contemporary Literary Criticism,* Vols. 1, 2, 4, 8, 10, 13, 19, 47; *Dictionary of Literary Biography,* Vol. 45; *Dictionary of Literary Biography Documentary Series,* Vol. 7; *DISCovering Authors; DISCovering Authors: British Edition; DISCovering Authors: Canadian Edition; DISCovering Authors Modules: Most-studied* and *Poets; DISCovering Authors 3.0; Encyclopedia of World Literature in the 20th Century,* Ed. 3; *Exploring Poetry; Literature Resource Center; Major 20th-Century Writers,* Eds. 1, 2; *Modern American Women Writers; Poetry Criticism,* Vols. 4, 49; *Poetry for Students,* Vols. 14, 17; *Poets: American and British; Reference Guide to American Literature,* Ed. 4; *Something About the Author,* Vol. 20; *Twayne's United States Authors; World Literature Criticism Supplement;* and *World Poets.*

TONI MORRISON

(1931 -)

American novelist, essayist, editor, and playwright.

In 1993, Morrison became the first African American to be awarded the Nobel Prize for Literature. Her fiction was noted for its "epic power" and "unerring ear for dialogue and richly expressive depictions of black America" by the Swedish Academy, while exploring the difficulties of maintaining a sense of black cultural identity in a white world. Especially through her female protagonists, her works consider the debilitating effects of racism and sexism and incorporate elements of supernatural lore and mythology. Many of Morrison's novels—particularly *The Bluest Eye* (1970) and *Beloved* (1987)—have become firmly established within the American literary canon, while simultaneously working to redefine and expand it.

BIOGRAPHICAL INFORMATION

Morrison was born Chloe Ardelia Wofford on February 18, 1931, in Lorain, Ohio, to Ramah Willis and George Wofford. She was the second of four children. Her father was originally from Georgia, and her mother's parents had moved to Lorain after losing their land in Alabama and working briefly in Kentucky. Morrison's father worked in a variety of trades, often holding more than one job at a time in order to support his family. To send money to Morrison during her school years, her mother also took a series of hard, often demeaning positions. Music and storytelling—including tales of the supernatural—were a valued part of family life, and children as well as adults were expected to participate. Morrison became an avid reader at a young age, consuming a wide range of literature, including Russian, French, and English novels.

Morrison graduated from Howard University in 1953. She went on to earn a master's degree in English from Cornell University in 1955, and spent two years teaching at Texas Southern University in Houston. From 1957 to 1964 she served as an instructor at Howard. In 1958 she married Harold Morrison, a Jamaican architect, with whom she had two sons, Harold Ford and Slade Kevin. The marriage ended in divorce in 1964, and Morrison and her children returned briefly to her parents' home in Ohio. During this period she began to write, producing the story that would eventually become her first novel, *The Bluest Eye*. In 1966 she moved to Syracuse, New York, and took a job as an editor for a textbook subsidiary of Random House. She relocated again in 1968, this time to New York City, where she continued editing for Random House. She oversaw the publication of works by prominent black fiction writers such as Gayl Jones and Toni Cade Bambara, as well as the autobiographies of influential African

Americans, including Angela Davis and Muhammad Ali. In 1987, Morrison left Random House to return to teaching and to concentrate on her writing. She has taught at numerous colleges and universities, among them the State University of New York, Bard College, Yale University, Harvard University, and Trinity College, Cambridge. Morrison currently serves on the faculty at Princeton University.

MAJOR WORKS

Among her best known novels, *The Bluest Eye* recounts the tragic story of Pecola Breedlove, a poverty-stricken black child who longs for the blue eyes and blond hair that are prized by the society in which she lives. Evidenced by the superiority exhibited by light-skinned black characters in the novel—as well as the self-loathing of those, like Pecola, whose dark skin and African features mark them as unattractive and unlovable—the work explores black acceptance of white standards of female beauty. In 1973, Morrison published *Sula,* a novel chronicling the lives of two women. One woman assumes a traditional role in the community; the other leaves her hometown, returning only to resist established female roles and to assert her own standards and free will. *Song of Solomon* (1977) juxtaposes the pressures experienced by black families that feel forced to assimilate into mainstream culture with their unwillingness to abandon a distinctive African American heritage. More so than in her earlier novels, Morrison incorporates mythical and supernatural elements into the novel's narrative as a way for characters to transcend their everyday lives. *Tar Baby,* published in 1981 and set in the Caribbean, again uses myth and ghostly presences to mitigate the harshness of lives in which all relationships are adversarial—particularly in cultures where blacks are opposed to whites and women are opposed to men. In 1987 Morrison published *Beloved,* a novel based on the true story of a slave who murdered her child to spare it from a life of slavery; the book won the Pulitzer Prize. *Jazz* (1992) features dual narratives: one set during Reconstruction, the other during the Jazz Age. The novel explores the lasting effects of slavery and oppression on successive generations of African Americans. Morrison's most recent novels are *Paradise* (1998), featuring the lives of nine black families who settle a tiny farming community in Oklahoma in the 1940s,

and *Love* (2003), a story that portrays the owner of a once-popular East Coast seaside resort for African Americans.

In addition to her novels, Morrison has written a play, *Dreaming Emmett* (1986), a collection of literary criticism, *Playing in the Dark: Whiteness and the Literary Imagination* (1992), and several books for young readers in collaboration with her son Slade. Her children's works include *The Big Box* (1999), *The Book of Mean People* (2002), and *Who's Got Game?: The Ant or the Grasshopper?* (2003).

CRITICAL RECEPTION

Although some critics expressed reservations about the book's literary merits, *The Bluest Eye* received an impressive amount of attention for a first novel, garnering reviews by many prestigious publications. *Sula* met with more popular success, was serialized in *Redbook* magazine, and was nominated for the 1975 National Book Award. By the time *Song of Solomon* appeared, Morrison occupied a secure place as one of America's top novelists. Morrison's reputation was further enhanced by receipt of the Pulitzer Prize in 1988 for *Beloved* and the Nobel Prize for Literature in 1993.

Morrison is frequently faulted for her representations of a matriarchal culture that features poor, uneducated black females, with few positive black male characters and almost no white characters. Jacqueline Trace contends that this is partly attributable to Morrison's attempt to create a theology that is specifically black and specifically feminist.

Several critics have discussed Morrison's work—particularly *The Bluest Eye*—as a critique not only of the standards of female beauty prescribed by the dominant white culture, but of acceptance of those standards by blacks themselves. Pin-chia Feng discusses the development of the two young girls in the novel, concluding that "Claudia survives to tell the story by resisting social and racial conformity. Pecola fails the test precisely because of her unconditional internalization of the dominant ideology." Vanessa D. Dickerson (see Further Reading) contrasts Morrison's treatment of the black female body with its historical construction "as the ugly end of a wearisome Western dialectic: not sacred but profane, not angelic but demonic, not fair lady but ugly darky." Morrison, however, reappropriates black female representation within her fiction, particularly in *The Bluest Eye, Sula,* and *Beloved.* "In each of these novels," Dickerson asserts, "Morrison summons us to the validation of the black female body."

PRINCIPAL WORKS

The Bluest Eye (novel) 1970

Sula (novel) 1973

The Black Book [editor] (nonfiction) 1974

Song of Solomon (novel) 1977

Tar Baby (novel) 1981

Dreaming Emmett (play) 1986

Beloved (novel) 1987

Jazz (novel) 1992

Playing in the Dark: Whiteness and the Literary Imagination (criticism) 1992

Race-ing Justice, En-gendering Power: Essays on Anita Hill, Clarence Thomas, and the Construction of Social Reality [editor and author of introduction] (essays) 1992

Lecture and Speech of Acceptance Upon the Award of the Nobel Prize for Literature (speech) 1994

The Dancing Mind: Speech Upon Acceptance of the National Book Foundation Medal for Distinguished Contribution to American Letters (speech) 1996

Paradise (novel) 1998

The Big Box [with Slade Morrison] (juvenilia) 1999

I See You, I See Myself: The Young Life of Jacob Lawrence [with Deba Foxley Leach, Suzanne Wright, and Deborah J. Leach] (juvenilia) 2001

The Book of Mean People [with Slade Morrison] (juvenilia) 2002

Love (novel) 2003

Who's Got Game?: The Ant or the Grasshopper? [with Slade Morrison] (juvenilia) 2003

PRIMARY SOURCES

TONI MORRISON (INTRODUCTION DATE 1992)

SOURCE: Morrison, Toni. "Introduction: Friday on the Potomac." In *Race-ing Justice, En-gendering Power: Essays on Anita Hill, Clarence Thomas, and the Construction of*

Social Reality, edited by Toni Morrison, pp. vii-xxx. New York: Pantheon Books, 1992.

In the following introduction, Morrison evaluates the racial, sexual, and gender implications of Clarence Thomas's Supreme Court nomination and the greater sociopolitical significance of the event.

I have never asked to be nominated. . . . Mr. Chairman, I am a victim of this process.
— Clarence Thomas, Friday, October 11, 1991

It would have been more comfortable to remain silent. . . . I took no initiative to inform anyone. . . . I could not keep silent.
— Anita Hill, Friday, October 11, 1991

At last he lays his head flat upon the ground, close to my foot, and sets my other foot upon his head, as he had done before; and after this, made all the signs to me of subjugation, servitude, and submission imaginable, to let me know how he would serve me as long as he lived.
— Daniel Defoe, *Robinson Crusoe*

Clusters of black people pray in front of the White House for the Lord not to abandon them, to intervene and crush the forces that would prevent a black nominee to the Supreme Court from assuming the seat felt by them to be reserved for a member of the race. Other groups of blacks stare at the television set, revolted by the president's nomination of the one candidate they believed obviously unfit to adjudicate legal and policy matters concerning them. Everyone interested in the outcome of this nomination, regardless of race, class, gender, religion, or profession, turns to as many forms of media as are available. They read the *Washington Post* for verification of their dread or their hope, read the *New York Times* as though it were *Pravda,* searching between the lines of the official story for one that most nearly approximates what might really be happening. They read local papers to see if the reaction among their neighbors is similar to their own, or they try to figure out on what information their own response should be based. They have listened to newscasters and anchor people for the bits and bites that pointed to, or deflected attention from, the machinery of campaigns to reject or accept the nominee. They have watched television screens that seem to watch back, that dismiss viewers or call upon them for flavor, reinforcement, or routine dissent. Polls assure and shock, gratify and discredit those who took them into serious account.

But most of all, people talked to one another. There are passionate, sometimes acrimonious discussions between mothers and daughters, fathers and sons, husbands and wives, siblings, friends, acquaintances, colleagues with whom, now, there is reason to embrace or to expel from their close circle. Sophisticated legal debates merge with locker-room guffaws; poised exchanges about the ethics and moral responsibilities of governance are debased by cold indifference to individual claims and private vulnerabilities. Organizations and individuals call senators and urge friends to do the same—providing opinions and information, threatening, cajoling, explaining positions, or simply saying, Confirm! Reject! Vote yes. Vote no.

These were some of the scenes stirred up by the debates leading to the confirmation of Clarence Thomas, the revelations and evasions within the testimony, and by the irrevocable mark placed on those hearings by Anita Hill's accusations against the nominee. The points of the vector were all the plateaus of power and powerlessness: white men, black men, black women, white women, interracial couples; those with a traditionally conservative agenda, and those representing neoconservative conversions; citizens with radical and progressive programs; the full specter of the "pro" antagonists ("choice" and "life"); there were the publicly elected, the self-elected, the racial supremacists, the racial egalitarians, and nationalists of every stripe.

The intensity as well as the volume of these responses to the hearings were caused by more than the volatile content of the proceedings. The emptiness, the unforthcoming truths that lay at the center of the state's performance contributed much to the frenzy as people grappled for meaning, for substance unavailable through ordinary channels. Michael Rustin has described race as "both an empty category and one of the most destructive and powerful forms of social categorization." This paradox of a powerfully destructive emptiness can be used to illustrate the source of the confusion, the murk, the sense of helpless rage that accompanied the confirmation process.

It became clear, finally, what took place: a black male nominee to the Supreme Court was confirmed amid a controversy that raised and buried issues of profound social significance.

What is less clear is what happened, how it happened, why it happened; what implications may be drawn, what consequences may follow. For what was at stake during these hearings was history. In addition to what was taking place, something was happening. And as is almost always the case, the site of the exorcism of critical national issues was situated in the miasma of black life and inscribed on the bodies of black people.

It was to evaluate and analyze various aspects of what was and is happening that this collection suggested itself. The urgency of this project, an urgency that was overwhelming in November of 1991 when it began, is no less so now in 1992. For a number of reasons the consequences of *not* gathering the thoughts, the insights, the analyses of academics in a variety of disciplines would be too dire. The events surrounding the confirmation could be closed, left to the disappearing act that frequently follows the summing-up process typical of visual and print media. The seismic reactions of women and men in the workplace, in organizations and institutions, could be calmed and a return to "business as usual" made effortless. While the public, deeply concerned with the issues raised by the confirmation, waited for the ultimate historical account or some other text representing the "last word," there might not be available to it a more immediate aid to the reflective sorting out that subsequent and recent events would demand. Furthermore, the advancing siege upon American universities, launched by fears of "relevance" and change, has fostered an impression and atmosphere of scholarly paralysis, censorship, and intimidation. Yet residing in the academic institutions of the country are not only some of the most knowledgeable citizens, but also those most able to respond quickly with contextualized and intellectually focused insights. And insight—from a range of views and disciplines—seemed to us in low supply.

For insight into the complicated and complicating events that the confirmation of Clarence Thomas became, one needs perspective, not attitudes; context, not anecdotes; analyses, not postures. For any kind of lasting illumination the focus must be on the history routinely ignored or played down or unknown. For the kind of insight that invites reflection, language must be critiqued. Frustrating language, devious calls to arms, and ancient inflammatory codes deployed to do their weary work of obfuscation, short circuiting, evasion, and distortion. The timeless and timely narratives upon which expressive language rests, narratives so ingrained and pervasive they seem inextricable from "reality," require identification. To begin to comprehend exactly what happened, it is important to distinguish between the veneer of interrogatory discourse and its substance; to remain skeptical of topics (such as whether the "system" is "working") which pretend that the restoration of order lies in the question; to be wary of narrow discussions on the effectiveness or defect of the "process" because content, volatile and uncontextualized, cannot be approached, let alone adequately discussed, in sixteen minutes or five hundred words or less. To inaugurate any discovery of what happened is to be conscious of the smooth syruplike and glistening oil poured daily to keep the machine of state from screeching too loudly or breaking down entirely as it turns the earth of its own rut, digging itself deeper and deeper into the foundation of private life, burying itself for invisibility, for protection, for secrecy. To know what took place summary is enough. To learn what happened requires multiple points of address and analysis.

Nowhere, remarked an historian, nowhere in the debate before and during the confirmation hearings was there any mention, or even the implied idea, of the public good. How could there be, when the word "public" had itself become bankrupt, suffering guilt by association with the word "special," as the confusion of "public interest" with "special interest" proved. How could the notion of union, nation, or state surface when race, gender, and class, separately, paired, matched, and mismatched, collapsed in a heap or swinging a divisive sword, dominated every moment and word of the confirmation process?

For example, the nominee—chosen, the president said, without regard to race—was introduced by his sponsor with a reference to the nominee's laugh. It was, said Senator Danforth, second in his list of "the most fundamental points" about Clarence Thomas. "He is his own person. That is my first point. Second, he laughs. [Laughter] To some, this may seem a trivial matter. To me, it's important because laughter is the antidote to that dread disease, federalitis. The obvious strategy of interest groups trying to defeat a Supreme Court nominee is to suggest that there is something weird about the individual. I concede that there is something weird about Clarence Thomas. It's his laugh. It is the loudest laugh I have ever heard. It comes from deep inside, and it shakes his body. And here is something at least as weird in this most up-tight of cities: the object of his laughter is most often himself."

Weird? Not at all. Neither the laugh nor Danforth's reference to it. Every black person who heard those words understood. How necessary, how reassuring were both the grin and its being summoned for display. It is the laughter, the chuckle, that invites and precedes any discussion of association with a black person. For whites who require it, it is the gesture of accommodation and obedience needed to open discussion with a black person and certainly to continue it. The ethnic

joke is one formulation—the obligatory recognition of race and possible equanimity in the face of it. But in the more polite halls of the Senate, the laugh will do, the willingness to laugh; its power as a sign takes the place of the high sign of perfect understanding. It is difficult to imagine a sponsor introducing Robert Bork or William Gates (or that happy exception, Thurgood Marshall) with a call to this most clearly understood metonym for racial accommodation. Not simply because they may or may not have had a loud, infectious laugh, but because it would have been inappropriate, irrelevant, puzzling to do so.

But what was inappropriate, even startlingly salacious in other circumstances became the habitual text with this candidate. The *New York Times* found it interesting to include in that paper's initial story on the president's nominee a curious spotlight on his body. Weight lifting was among his accomplishments, said the *Times*, presciently, perhaps, since later on the candidate's body came violently into view. Of course, this may be simply a news account that aims to present an attractive image of a man about to step onto a national stage, yet a reference to a black person's body is de rigueur in white discourse. Like the unswerving focus on the female body (whether the woman is a judge, an actress, a scholar, or a waitress), the black man's body is voluptuously dwelled upon in biographies about them, journalism on them, remarks about them. "I wanted to find out," said Senator Pete Domenici, "as best I could what his life—from outhouse to the White House . . . has been like." With vulgar remarks like that in print, why wouldn't the public's initial view of this black nominee have an otherwise puzzling, even silly, reference to body-building? Other erstwhile oddities rippled through the media, glancing and stroking black flesh. President Bush probably felt he was being friendly, charmingly informal, when he invited this black man into his bedroom for the interview. "That is where Mr. Bush made the final offer and Judge Thomas accepted." To make Thomas feel at home was more important than to respect him, apparently, and the *Times* agreed, selecting this tidbit to report in an article that ended with a second tantalizing, not so veiled reference to the nominee's body. When asked by reporters whether he expected to play golf, "one of Mr. Bush's favorite sports," Thomas replied, "No. The ball's too small." Thomas's answer is familiar repartee; but the nuanced emphasis gained by the remark's position in the piece is familiar too. What would have been extraordinary would have been to ignore Thomas's body, for in ignoring it, the articles would have had to discuss in some detail that aspect of him more difficult to appraise—his mind.

In a society with a history of trying to accommodate both slavery and freedom, and a present that wishes both to exploit and deny the pervasiveness of racism, black people are rarely individualized. Even when his supporters were extolling the fierce independence and the "his own man" line about Clarence Thomas, their block and blocked thinking of racial stereotype prevailed. Without individuation, without nonracial perception, black people, as a group, are used to signify the polar opposites of love and repulsion. On the one hand, they signify benevolence, harmless and servile guardianship, and endless love. On the other hand, they have come to represent insanity, illicit sexuality, and chaos. In the confirmation hearings the two fictions were at war and on display. They are interchangeable fictions from a utilitarian menu and can be mixed and matched to suit any racial palette. Furthermore, they do not need logical transition from one set of associations to another. Like Captain Delano in *Benito Cereno*, the racist thinker can jump from the view of the slave, Babo, as "naturally docile, made for servitude" to "savage cannibal" without any gesture toward what may lie in between the two conclusions, or any explanation of the jump from puppy to monster, so the truth of Babo's situation—that he is leading a surreptitious rebellion aboard the slave ship, that he is a clever man who wants to be free—never enters the equation. The confirmation hearings, as it turned out, had two black persons to use to nourish these fictions. Thus, the candidate was cloaked in the garments of loyalty, guardianship, and (remember the laugh) limitless love. Love of God via his Catholic school, of servitude via a patriarchal disciplinarian grandfather, of loyalty to party via his accumulated speeches and the trophies of "America" on his office walls. The interrogator, therefore, the accusing witness Anita Hill, was dressed in the oppositional costume of madness, anarchic sexuality, and explosive verbal violence. There seemed to be no other explanation for her testimony. Even Clarence Thomas was at a loss to explain not her charges but why she would make them. All he could come up with is speculation on Professor Hill's dislike of "lighter-complexioned" women—meaning, one gathers, his marriage to a white woman. No other narrative context could be found for her charges, no motive except fantasy, wanton and destructive, or a jealousy that destabilized her. Since neither the press nor the Senate

Judiciary Committee would entertain seriously or exhaustively the truth of her accusations, she could be called any number or pair of discrediting terms and the contradictions would never be called into question, because, as a black woman, she was contradiction itself, irrationality in the flesh. She was portrayed as a lesbian who hated men *and* a vamp who could be ensnared and painfully rejected by them. She was a mixture heretofore not recognized in the glossary of racial tropes: an *intellectual* daughter of black *farmers*; a *black female* taking *offense*; a black *lady* repeating *dirty words*. Anita Hill's description of Thomas's behavior toward her did not ignite a careful search for the truth; her testimony simply produced an exchange of racial tropes. Now it was he, the nominee, who was in danger of moving from "natural servant" to "savage demon," and the force of the balance of the confirmation process was to reorder these signifying fictions. Is he lying or is she? Is he the benevolent one and she the insane one? Or is he the date raper, sexual assaulter, the illicit sexual signal, and she the docile, loyal servant? Those two major fictions, either/or, were blasted and tilted by a factual thing masquerading as a true thing: lynching. Being a fact of both white history and black life, lynching is also the metaphor of itself. While the mythologies about black personae debauched the confirmation process for all time, the history of black life was appropriated to elevate it.

An accusation of such weight as sexual misconduct would probably have disqualified a white candidate on its face. Rather than any need for "proof," the slightest possibility that it was publicly verifiable would have nullified the candidacy, forced the committee members to insist on another nominee rather than entertain the necessity for public debate on so loathsome a charge. But in a racialized and race-conscious society, standards are changed, facts marginalized, repressed, and the willingness to air such charges, actually to debate them, outweighed the seemliness of a substantive hearing because the actors were black. Rather than claiming how certain feminist interests forced the confrontation, rather than editorializing about how reluctant the committee members were to investigate Anita Hill's charges publicly and how humiliated they were in doing so, it seems blazingly clear that with this unprecedented opportunity to hover over and to cluck at, to meditate and ponder the limits and excesses of black bodies, no other strategies were going to be entertained. There would be no recommendation of withdrawal by sponsor, president, senators, or anybody. No request for or insistence that the executive branch propose another name so that such volatile issues could be taken up in a forum more suitable to their airing, and possibly receive an open and just decision. No. The participants were black, so what could it matter? The participants were black and therefore "known," serviceable, expendable in the interests of limning out one or the other of two mutually antagonistic fabulations. Under the pressure of voyeuristic desire, fueled by mythologies that render blacks publicly serviceable instruments of private dread and longing, extraordinary behavior on the part of the state could take place. Anita Hill's witnesses, credible and persuasive as they were, could be dismissed, as one "reporter" said, apparently without shame, because they were too intellectual to be believed(!). Under the pressure of racist mythologies, loyal staff (all female) had more weight than disinterested observers or publicly available documentation. Under such pressure the chairman of the committee could apply criminal court procedure to a confirmation hearing and assure the candidate that the assumption of innocence lay with the nominee. As though innocence—rather than malfeasance or ethical character or fitness to serve—was the charge against which they struggled to judge the judge. As though a rhetorical "I am not a crook" had anything at all to do with the heavy responsibility the committee was under.

Would such accusations have elicited such outsize defense mechanisms if the candidate had been white? Would the committee and many interest groups have considered the suitability of a white candidate untainted by these accusations? Hardly, but with a black candidate, already stained by the figurations of blackness as sexual aggressiveness or rapaciousness or impotence, the stain need only be proved reasonably doubted, which is to say, if he is black, how can you tell if that really is a stain? Which is also to say, blackness is itself a stain, and therefore unstainable. Which is also to say, if he is black and about to ascend to the Supreme Court bench, if the bench is to become stain-free, this newest judge must be bleached, race-free, as his speeches and opinions illustrated. Allegations of sexual misconduct re-raced him, which, in this administration, meant, restained him, dirtied him. Therefore the "dirt" that clung to him following those allegations, "dirt" he spoke of repeatedly, must be shown to have originated elsewhere. In this case the search for the racial stain turned on Anita Hill. Her character. Her motives. Not his.

Clarence Thomas has gone through the nomination process before, and in that connection has been investigated by the FBI before. Nothing is not known about him. And the senators know that nothing about him is not known. But what is known and what is useful to be distributed as knowledge are different things. In these hearings data, not to mention knowledge, had no place. The deliberations became a contest and the point was to win. At stake always was a court: stacked or balanced; irreproachable in its ethical and judicial standards or malleable and compliant in its political agenda; alert to and mindful of the real lives most of us live, as these lives are measured by the good of the republic, or a court that is aloof, delusional, indifferent to any mandate, popular or unpopular, if it is not first vetted by the executive branch.

As in virtually all of this nation's great debates, nonwhites and women figure powerfully, although their presence may be disguised, denied, or obliterated. So it is perhaps predictable that this instance—where serious issues of male prerogative and sexual assault, the issues of racial justice and racial redress, the problematics of governing and controlling women's bodies, the alterations of work space into (sexually) domesticated space—be subsumed into the debate over the candidacy for the Supreme Court. That these issues be worked out, on, and inscribed upon the canvas/flesh of black people should come as no surprise to anyone.

The contempt emanating from the White House was palpable—it was not necessary for the candidate to be a first-rate legal scholar (as it had not been necessary for other candidates). Nor was it necessary that he have demonstrated a particular sensitivity to the issues and concerns of a race he belonged to but which "had no bearing" on his selection to fill a seat vacated by the single Supreme Court Justice who both belonged to and did represent the interests of that race. The "race" that "had no bearing" on the president's choice could nevertheless be counted on to support the nominee, since "skin voting" would overwhelm every other consideration. This riskless gamble held almost perfect sway. Many blacks were struck mute by the embarrassing position of agreeing with Klansmen and their sympathizers; others leaped to the defense of the candidate on the grounds that he was "no worse than X," or that any white candidate would be a throwback, or that "who knows what he might do or become in those hallowed halls?" Who knows? Well, his nominators did know, and they were correct, as even the earliest action Clarence Thomas has taken in the cases coming before the court confirms.

Appropriate also was the small, secret swearing-in ceremony once the candidate was confirmed. For secrecy had operated from the beginning. Not only the dismissed and suppressed charges against the candidate, but also deeper, more ancient secrets of males bonding and the demonizing of females who contradict them.

In addition to race, class surfaced in both predictable and unexpected ways. Predictably, the nominee was required to shuck: to convince white men in power that operating a trucking business was lowly work in a Georgia where most blacks would have blessed dirt for such work. It wasn't a hard shuck. Because race and class—that is, black equals poor—is an equation that functions usefully if unexamined, it is possible to advance exclusionary and elitist programs by the careful use of race *as* class. It is still possible to cash in on black victimhood (the pain of being a poor innocent black boy), to claim victim status (Thomas called himself a victim of a process he of all people knew was designed to examine a candidate's worth), and to deplore the practice in others all at the same time. It is still possible to say "My father was a doorman" (meaning servant, meaning poor) and get the sympathy of whites who cannot or will not do the arithmetic needed to know the difference between the earnings of a Washington, D.C., doorman and those of a clerk at the census bureau.

In addition to class transformations, there was on display race transcendence. The nominee could be understood as having realized his yearning for and commitment to "racelessness" by having a white spouse at his side. At least their love, we are encouraged to conclude, had transcended race, and this matrimonial love had been more than ecstasy and companionship—it had been for Virginia Thomas an important education on how to feel and think about black people. The *People* magazine lead story, taken with a straight face, proved their devotion, their racelessness, which we already recognized because he shook her hand in public on three occasions. And it was envy of this racially ideal union that was one of the reasons Thomas came up with in trying to explain Anita Hill's charges. Professor Hill, he seemed to be suggesting, harbored reactionary, race-bound opinions about interracial love which, as everybody knows, can drive a black woman insane and cause her to say wild, incredible things. Expectedly, the nominee called for a transcendence of

race, remarked repeatedly on its divisive nature, its costliness, its undeniable degradation of principles of freedom. Unexpectedly, however, race surfaced on the very site of its interment. And it was hard not to murmur "Freddy's back" as the specter of this living corpse broke free of its hastily dug grave. But this resurrection was buoyed and winged by the fact of its gender component. If the forward face of the not-dead was racism, its backward face was sexism. The confirmation procedure held my attention partly because the shape it took, in an effort to hold its explosive contents, was unique—the twists and turns of the public debate and its manipulation, the responses of the senators on the committee. Yet what riveted my attention most during the hearings was not its strangeness but rather its familiarity. The sense that underneath the acrylic in which the political discourse was painted were the outlines of figures so old and so stable as to appear natural, not drawn or man-made at all.

It was trying to penetrate the brilliant, distracting color in which the political argument was painted in order to locate the outlines that informed the argument that led me to focus on the day of the week that both Anita Hill's testimony and Clarence Thomas's response to that testimony were aired. And to select out of all that each said on that day the themes that to me appeared salient: Anita Hill's inability to remain silent; Clarence Thomas's claims to being victimized. Silence and victimization. Broken silence and built victimization. Speech and bondage. Disobedient speech and the chosen association of bondage. On, and . . . Friday.

On a Friday, Anita Hill graphically articulated points in her accusation of sexual misconduct. On the same Friday Clarence Thomas answered, in a manner of speaking, those charges. And it was on a Friday in 1709 when Alexander Selkirk found an "almost drowned Indian" on the shore of an island upon which he had been shipwrecked. Ten years later Selkirk's story would be immortalized by Daniel Defoe in *Robinson Crusoe*. There the Indian becomes a "savage cannibal"—black, barbarous, stupid, servile, adoring—and although nothing is reported of his sexual behavior, he has an acquired taste for the flesh of his own species. Crusoe's narrative is a success story, one in which a socially, culturally, and biologically handicapped black man is civilized and Christianized—taught, in other words, to be like a white one. From Friday's point of view it is a success story as well. Not only is he alive; he is greatly enabled by his association with his savior. And it should not go unremarked that Crusoe is also greatly enabled—including having his own life saved—by Friday. Yet like all successes, what is earned is mitigated by what one has lost.

If we look at the story from Friday's point of view rather than Crusoe's, it becomes clear that Friday had a very complex problem. By sheer luck he had escaped death, annihilation, anonymity, and engulfment by enemies within his own culture. By great and astonishing good fortune he had been rescued. The gift of his own life was so unexpected, so welcome, he felt he could regulate the debt only by offering that life to his rescuer, by making the gift exchange literal. But he had a problem.

Before he appeared on the shore, his rescuer, Crusoe, had heard no other voice except a parrot's trained to say his owner's name—Robin, for short. Crusoe wanted to hear it again. For over twenty years he had had only himself for company, and although he has conquered nature and marked time, no human calls his name, acknowledges his presence or his authority. Lucky for him he discovers a refugee escaping certain slaughter. Once rescue has been effected, Crusoe is in a position to have more than unopposed dominion; now he is able to acquire status, to demonstrate and confirm his superiority. So important is status in Crusoe's self-regard he does not ask the refugee what his name is; instead, Crusoe names him. Nor does he tell the refugee his own name; instead, he teaches him the three words that for months will do just fine: "master," "yes," and "no."

Friday's real problem, however, was not to learn the language of repetition, easily, like the parrot, but to learn to internalize it. For longer than necessary the first words he is taught, first "master," then "yes" or "no," remain all he is permitted to say. During the time in which he knows no other English, one has to assume he thinks in his own language, cogitates in it, explains stimuli and phenomena in the language he was born to. But Crusoe's account suggests otherwise, suggests that before his rescue Friday had no language, and even if he did, there was nothing to say in it. After a year Friday is taught some English vocabulary and the grammar to hold it. "This was the pleasantest year of all the life I led in this place; Friday began to talk pretty well, and understand the names of almost everything I had occasion to call for, and of every place I had to send him to, and talked a great deal to me. . . ."

Had he expected that the life he offered Crusoe would include not just his services, his loyalty, his devotion, but also his language as well? Did he ever wonder why Crusoe did not want to learn *his* language? Or why he could never speak his master's name? In the absence of his master's desire to speak his tongue, did Friday forget completely the language he dreamed in? Think no more of the home he fled before the weapons of those who had conquered and occupied it? On the two or three occasions when Crusoe is curious enough to ask Friday a question about the black man's feelings, the answers are surprising. Yes, he longs for his home. Yes, it is beautiful on his island. Yes, he will refrain from eating human flesh. Yes, if he has the opportunity, he will teach his tribe to eat bread, cattle, and milk instead. (If Crusoe's assumption that Friday's people eat only each other were true, the practice would have decimated them long ago, but no matter—the white man teaches food habits; the black man learns them.) But no, he will not return to his home alone; he will go only if Crusoe accompanies him. So far, Friday can be understood to engage in dialogue with his master, however limited. Eventually, he learns more: he moves from speaking *with* to thinking *as* Crusoe.

The problem of internalizing the master's tongue is the problem of the rescued. Unlike the problems of survivors who may be lucky, fated, etc., the rescued have the problem of debt. If the rescuer gives you back your life, he shares in that life. But, as in Friday's case, if the rescuer saves your life by taking you away from the dangers, the complications, the confusion of home, he may very well expect the debt to be paid in full. Not "Go your own way and sin no more." Not "Here, take this boat and find your own adventure, in or out of your own tribe." But full payment, forever. Because the rescuer wants to hear his name, not mimicked but adored. This is a serious problem for Friday and gets more complicated the more one thinks about it.

Friday has left and been rescued from not only the culture that threatened him, that wants to kill and engulf him, but also from the culture that loves him. That too he has left behind forever.

Even when he discovers his own father, half dead, in precisely the danger he himself had been in when Crusoe saved his life, his joy is not so reckless as to quarrel with the menial labor he and his father are directed to do, while an also-rescued Spaniard, who has lived among Friday's tribe for years, is given supervisory responsibilities. Nor is his joy so great that he speaks to his father in their mutual tongue for both their delight. Instead, he translates for Crusoe what his father says.

This loss of the mother tongue seems not to disturb Friday, even though he never completely learns the master's. He negotiates a space somewhere in between. He develops a serviceable grammar that will never be eloquent; he learns to shout warnings of advancing, also black, enemies, but he can never dare speak *to* these enemies as his master does. Without a mother tongue, without the language of his original culture, all he can do is recognize his old enemies and, when ordered, kill them. Finally, Friday no longer negotiates space between his own language and Crusoe's. Finally, the *uses* of Crusoe's language, if not its grammar, become his own. The internalization is complete.

In one of the incidents that occur on the island, a band of Spanish mutineers come ashore, holding their captain prisoner. Crusoe and Friday liberate the captain and consider how to dispose of the criminals. Some of the mutineers are singled out by their captain as villains; others are identified as being forced into mutiny. So some are spared, others slaughtered. This discrimination is never applied to Friday's people. With one exception, an old man tied and bound for execution, all of the blacks Friday and Crusoe see are killed or wounded (most of whom, in Crusoe's tallying of the dead, Friday kills). The exception, who turns out to be Friday's father, is not given a name nor, as with his son Friday, is one solicited from him. He becomes part of Crusoe's team, called upon and relied on for all kinds of service. He is sent back to his island on an errand with the Spaniard. The Spaniard returns, Friday's father does not, but most curiously, once his services are no longer needed, there is no mention of him again—by the master or the son. While he was among them, and after he has gone, he is called by Robinson Crusoe "the old savage." We still do not know his name.

Voluntary entrance into another culture, voluntary sharing of more than one culture, has certain satisfactions to mitigate the problems that may ensue. But being rescued into an adversarial culture can carry a huge debt. The debt one feels one owes to the rescuer can be paid, simply, honorably, in lifetime service. But if in that transaction the rescued loses his idiom, the language of his culture, there may be other debts outstanding. Leon Higginbotham has charted the debt Clarence Thomas owes the culture that fought for and protected him before he arrived out of a turbulent social sea onto the shore of political patronage. In that sea Thomas was teased and humiliated by his own people, called ABC, American's Blackest Child. He was chastened for

wanting an education superior to theirs. He was also loved and nurtured by them. As in any and everybody's background, family, culture, race, and region, there are persecutors and providers, kindness and loathing. No culture ever quite measures up to our expectations of it without a generous dose of romanticism, self-delusion, or simple compassion. Sometimes it seems easier, emotionally and professionally, to deny it, ignore it, erase it, even destroy it. And if the language of one's culture is lost or surrendered, one may be forced to describe that culture in the language of the rescuing one. In that way one could feel compelled to dismiss African-American culture by substituting the phrase "culture of the victim" for the critique and redress of systemic racism. Minus one's own idiom it is possible to cry and decry victimization, loathing it when it appears in the discourses of one's own people, but summoning it up for one's expediently deracialized self. It becomes easy to confuse the metaphors embedded in the blood language of one's own culture with the objects they stand for and to call patronizing, coddling, undemanding, rescuing, complicitous white racists a lynch mob. Under such circumstances it is not just easy to speak the master's language, it is necessary. One is obliged to cooperate in the misuse of figurative language, in the reinforcement of cliché, the erasure of difference, the jargon of justice, the evasion of logic, the denial of history, the crowning of patriarchy, the inscription of hegemony; to be complicit in the vandalizing, sentimentalizing, and trivialization of the torture black people have suffered. Such rhetorical strategies become necessary because, without one's own idiom, there is no other language to speak.

Both Friday and Clarence Thomas accompany their rescuers into the world of power and salvation. But the problem of rescue still exists: both men, black but unrecognizable at home or away, are condemned first to mimic, then to internalize and adore, but never to utter one single sentence understood to be beneficial to their original culture, whether the people of their culture are those who wanted to hurt them or those who loved them to death.

Clarence Thomas once quoted someone who said that dwelling on the horrors of racism invited one of two choices: vengeance or prosperity. He argued for a third choice: "to appeal to that which is good." He did not elaborate on which he had chosen, finally, but the language he speaks, the actions he takes, the Supreme Court decisions he has made or aligned himself with, the foot, as it were, that he has picked up and placed on his head, give us some indication of what his choice has been. The footprint in the sand that so worried Crusoe's nights, that compelled him to build a fortress, and then another to protect his new world order, disappears from his nightmares once Friday embraces, then internalizes, his master's voice and can follow the master's agenda with passion.

It is hard not to think of these events in any way but as unfortunate. And it is difficult to convince anybody that what happened is over—without serious consequences. For those who looked forward eagerly to Thomas's confirmation, the expectation of a reliably conservative court may be reassuring. Time will have the most to say about that. For those who believe the future of the nation as a democracy is imperiled by this most recent addition to the bench, again, time will speak rather definitively. Yet regardless of political alliances, something positive and liberating has already surfaced. In matters of race and gender, it is now possible and necessary, as it seemed never to have been before, to speak about these matters without the barriers, the silences, the embarrassing gaps in discourse. It is clear to the most reductionist intellect that black people think differently from one another; it is also clear that the time for undiscriminating racial unity has passed. A conversation, a serious exchange between black men and women, has begun in a new arena, and the contestants defy the mold. Nor is it as easy as it used to be to split along racial lines, as the alliances and coalitions between white and black women, and the conflicts among black women, and among black men, during the intense debates regarding Anita Hill's testimony against Clarence Thomas's appointment prove.

This volume is one of the several beginnings of these new conversations in which issues and arguments are taken as seriously as they are. Only through thoughtful, incisive, and far-ranging dialogue will all of us be able to appraise and benefit from Friday's dilemma.

GENERAL COMMENTARY

GURLEEN GREWAL (ESSAY DATE 1998)

SOURCE: Grewal, Gurleen. Introduction to *Circles of Sorrow, Lines of Struggle: The Novels of Toni Morrison*, pp. 1-19. Baton Rouge: Louisiana State University Press, 1998.

In the following essay, Grewal examines how Morrison's novels contribute to a decolonizing black literature and how her acutely individual, interior characters operate within specific historical and social confines.

Freeing yourself was one thing, claiming ownership of that freed self was another.

—Toni Morrison

Social relations are not only received; they are also made and can be transformed.

—Raymond Williams

Toni Morrison is part of a long black—and American—literary tradition that finds its full and complicated bloom in her art. Her novels are multivoiced, multilayered, writerly and speakerly, both popular and literary highbrow. In her writing the confluence of two streams of narrative tradition is made visible and audible: one the oral tradition of storytelling passed down over generations in her own family and community, custodians of a history far removed from the world of the bourgeois novel, whose narrative tradition is the other Morrison appropriates. At Cornell Morrison studied the stylists of modernist memory, Virginia Woolf and William Faulkner, both of whom had cracked open the novel to observe more intimately the secular processes of fragmentation and madness. After them, Morrison takes the novel home to the intimate address of the rural and urban African American tradition from which she came, back to the blues with its longstanding tradition of voicing pain, registering complaint and comfort. The unrelenting lyrical pressure of her prose aims to unsettle as well as to heal. It charges us with nothing less than the charge of history; her characters, though seldom in powerful social positions, command their desires in an outlawed agency that puts into crisis the law of the land and the judgment of the witnessing jury of readers.

A powerful catalyst for Morrison's work—one so ubiquitous it can escape notice—is what Howard Winant calls the "pervasive crisis of race" facing the contemporary United States: "a crisis no less severe than those of the past. The origins of the crisis are not particularly obscure: the cultural and political meaning of race, its significance in shaping the social structure, and its experiential or existential dimensions all remain profoundly unresolved as the United States approaches the end of the twentieth century. As a result, the society as a whole and the population as individuals suffer from confusion and anxiety about the issue (or complex of issues) we call race." Morrison has increasingly committed herself to addressing issues of race outside her own fiction. Her unpublished drama ***Dreaming Emmett***, produced in 1985 to "commemorate the first celebration of the Rev. Dr. Martin Luther King Jr.'s birthday as a national holiday," was written in response to the 1955 racist killing in Mississippi of a fourteen-year-old black boy named Emmett Till; the play was "intended to symbolize the plight of contemporary black urban youth—their disproportionately high rate of death by violence." In *Playing in the Dark: Whiteness and the Literary Imagination,* a work of literary criticism, Toni Morrison undertakes the task of showing that "Africanism is inextricable from the definition of Americanness—from its origins on through its integrated or disintegrated twentieth-century self." In the national canonical literature, Morrison discovers "a sometimes allegorical, sometimes metaphorical, but always choked representation of an Africanist presence." *Playing in the Dark* thus brings to light the various roles played by "the thunderous, theatrical presence of black surrogacy" in the construction of whiteness in the nation's literary imagination.[1]

In assessing the phenomenon of Toni Morrison, we need to keep in mind "the pressures and limits of the social relationships on which as a producer, the author depends"—what Raymond Williams calls "the political economy of writing." We need to take into account the demand for and the reception of writings by black women following the civil rights movement. The contemporary literary renaissance started in 1965 with Margaret Walker's *Jubilee* and Paule Marshall's *The Chosen Place, The Timeless People* and took off in 1970 with Toni Morrison's *The Bluest Eye,* Toni Cade's edition of *The Black Woman,* Alice Walker's *The Third Life of Grange Copeland,* and Maya Angelou's *I Know Why the Caged Bird Sings.* Since the 1970s, we have witnessed a remarkable efflorescence. Toni Morrison herself has played an active role in promoting black voices. As editor at Random House, she ensured that black writers would find a receptive space in publishing, that the integrity of their voices would not be compromised by the imposition of alien standards. A host of important black publications (by authors such as Mohammed Ali, Toni Cade Bambara, Angela Davis, and Gayl Jones) have received Morrison's encouragement. It is important to note that this profusion of creative expression has been aided by a "community of cultural workers" that includes black feminist critics and teachers of literature whose receptive work shows, in Hortense Spillers' words, that "traditions are not born. They are made." A tradition "arises not only because there are writers there to make it, but also because there is a strategic audience of heightened consciousness prepared to read and interpret the work as such." Unlike their literary foremothers, writers like Toni Morrison and Alice Walker had sturdy black bridges already made for them. Their works paralleled the energy generated by the black cultural and political mobilization of the 1960s and 1970s and the black feminist resurgence of the 1980s. In what is now a landmark essay, "Toward a Black Feminist Criticism," Barbara Smith writes, "A viable, autonomous black feminist movement in this country would open up the space needed for the exploration of black women's lives and the creation of consciously black woman-identified art."[2]

Toni Morrison's feminism partakes of the black cultural resistance to liberal white feminism. In **"What the Black Woman Thinks about Women's Lib,"** she notes that the different histories, and therefore agendas, of white and black women are made apparent in bathroom signs designating "White Ladies" and "Colored Women." Morrison refers to the conflictual power relationship between the white *lady* and the colored *woman* in several of her works: in the relationship between Pauline Breedlove and Mrs. Fisher in *The Bluest Eye;* First Corinthians and her poet-mistress Michael Mary Graham in *Song of Solomon;* Ondine and her young mistress Margaret in *Tar Baby;* Sethe and her owner, Mrs. Garner, in *Beloved;* Vera Louise and True Belle in *Jazz.* Alice Walker joins Morrison in disclaiming bourgeois white feminism by claiming under the name *womanist* a feminism appropriate to the historical experience and needs of black women.[3] While a black feminist point of view is clearly evident in Toni Morrison's work, it is always contextual and relational, articulated with respect to issues of class and community. While the white-identified individualism of her male and female bourgeois characters is historicized and located within social relations of power and desire, narrative affect is usually on the side of those who are subordinated to bourgeois power.

Historically, the novel is an art form pertaining to the interests and values of the middle class. Morrison says her writing "bears witness" for a middle-class black audience: "I agree with John Berger that peasants don't write novels because they don't need them. They have a portrait of themselves from gossip, tales, music, and some celebrations. That is enough. . . . Now my people, we 'peasants,' have come to the city, that is to say, we live with its values. There is a confrontation between old values of the tribes and new urban values. It's confusing." In another interview Morrison returns to this theme: "when the peasant class, or lower class, or what have you, confronts the middle class, the city, or the upper classes, they are thrown a little bit into disarray." Toni Morrison's novels tend the gap between emergent middle-class black America and its subaltern origins: she has called her work "peasant literature for *my* people." Susan Willis situates black women's writing, Morrison's included, in the historical transition from an agrarian to an urban society. She makes the important point that "migration to the North signifies more than a confrontation with (and contamination by) the white world. It implies a transition in social class." Morrison is a writer with a firm grasp of the lived dynamics of class experience, a subject that has received less critical attention by feminist scholars than the issue of gender. Drawing on experiences as varied as those of her grandparents' southern rural life to her parents' small-town existence in the Midwest to her own life, which includes the cosmopolitan ethos of New York City, Morrison is able to command in her fiction a century's experience of change affecting African Americans. Wilfred Sheed's observation of Morrison's range of understanding is apt: "Most black writers are privy, like the rest of us, to bits and pieces of the secret, the dark side of their group experience, but Toni Morrison uniquely seems to have all the keys on her chain, like a house detective. . . . She [has] the run of the whole place, from ghetto to small town to ramshackle farmhouse, to bring back a panorama of black myth and reality that [dazzles] the senses."[4]

Morrison's novels may be read as anti-*Bildung* projects that subvert dominant middle-class ideology. *The Bluest Eye*, an indictment of racism, is also a stinging critique of an educated class of blacks who, in order to avail themselves of the bourgeois privileges of a capitalist economy, have made "individuals" of themselves. The three uneducated whores shunned by the town's respectable folk are presented more favorably than the educated Geraldine and Soaphead Church, whose complicity earns authorial contempt even as it requires our understanding. In *Sula,* the middle-class, color-conscious Helene Wright is treated with much less affection than the lesser-privileged Eva and Hannah Peace. *Song of Solomon*'s Milkman Dead, an individualist raised and trapped in the self-centered, bourgeois world of the middle-class nuclear family, has to be rescued from under the myopic vision of his genteel mother and petit-bourgeois father. The rescue is effected by his Aunt Pilate, a peasant woman who even in her isolation and marginality is endowed with formidable strength arising from her nonbourgeois identity. *Tar Baby* inscribes a greater sympathy for the vagabond son of the soil, Son Green, than for the upper-middle-class individualist, Jadine Childs. In an interview in 1981, Morrison shed light on the authorial resentment of Jadine: "There is a new, capitalistic, modern American black which is what everybody thought was the ultimate in integration. To produce Jadine, that's what it was for. I think there is some danger in the result of that production."[5] In *Jazz,* Joe Trace is not the New Negro of Alain Locke and the talented tenth of the Harlem Renaissance. The New Negro is the migrant peasant who died so many times he could not help being made new.

Thus an identity claimed by the privileged few—the educated cosmopolitan elite—is problematized and revised from the perspective of those who had no access to the bourgeois modes of self-making.

In an interview Morrison said that "black people have always been used as a buffer in this country between powers to prevent class war, to prevent other kinds of real conflagrations":

> If there were no black people here in this country, it would have been Balkanized. The immigrants would have torn each other's throats out, as they have done everywhere else. But in becoming an American, from Europe, what one has in common with that other immigrant is contempt for *me*—it's nothing less but color. Wherever they were from, they would stand together. They could all say, "I am not *that*." So in that sense, becoming an American is based upon an attitude: an exclusion of me. . . . It wasn't negative to them—it was unifying. When they got off the boat, the second word they learned was "nigger." . . . Every immigrant knew he would not come at the very bottom. He had to come above at least one group—and that was us.

However, the idea that others have constructed their unity through being nonblack does not imply that being black, in turn, promotes unity. In fact, the colonial policy of racialization (in which color lines organized class hierarchy) did not facilitate the formation of a collectivity. The very idea of collectivity is something that must be imagined or created, the divisions historicized and understood; it must be narrated or performed. As Benedict Anderson observed, this collective self-composition is the creative project of nationalism. In the case of Afro-America, where nationalism has literally no *ground* of its own, the project of nationalism or counternationalism becomes of necessity a cultural one. As Wahneema Lubiano notes, the question of black nationhood implies "the activation of a narrative of identity and interest" against the history of the U. S. state;

it is a discourse that "functions as a defense against cultural imperialism."[6]

Internationally, Toni Morrison is part of a growing body of contemporary writers who are responding to imperatives of cultural critique, reclamation, and redefinition—imperatives broadly termed *postcolonial*. Helen Tiffin defines the "dis/mantling, de/mystification and unmasking of European authority" along with the endeavour to "define a denied or outlawed self" as one of the main decolonizing endeavors of postcolonial literatures. N'gugi defines decolonization as a "quest for relevance" wherein the emphasis is interior, directed toward postcolonial society rather than outwardly toward the colonizer. Morrison's creative project has an affinity with the work of decolonization undertaken by Nigerian novelist Chinua Achebe. Although they are very different writers, note what Achebe considers "an adequate revolution for [him] to espouse" in his writing: "to help my society regain belief in itself and put away the complexes of the years of denigration and self-abasement. And it is essentially a question of education, in the best sense of the world. Here, I think my aims and the deepest aspirations of my society meet. For no thinking African can escape the pain of the wound in our soul."[7]

In her essay "Subaltern Studies in a U. S. Frame," Eva Cherniavsky notes that "a postcolonial approach to U. S. history and culture would speak to the contradictions of a naturalized/nationalized colonial domination," one that "systematically displaces both indigenous peoples and nonwhite labor from the social and symbolic territory of the consensual Euro-American state."[8] Just as the wealth and labor of the colonies consolidated the identity of Western Europe, so the colonized land of Native Americans and the colonized labor of African Americans provided the early cohesion of the nation of *immigrants,* a term that is itself part of an obfuscating nationalist vocabulary.

The term *domestic* (or *internal*) *colonialism* was developed by black historians in the 1960s and early 1970s to refer to the experience of black people in America. The theory of internal colonialism situates the African slave trade within the expansionist demands of Euro-American capitalism. According to Robert Allen, "the most profound conclusion to be drawn from a survey of the black experience in America [is] to consider Black America as a semi-colony." Social critic Harold Cruse explains it thus: "The only factor which differentiates the Negro's status from that

of a pure colonial status is that his position is maintained in the 'home' country in close proximity to the dominant racial group." Black feminist scholars such as Hazel Carby, Patricia Hill Collins, and Angela Davis have documented the various ways in which black women served the model of white womanhood by filling the role of the "self-consolidating Other" (Gayatri Spivak's succinct phrase). In a similar vein, Toni Morrison's **Playing in the Dark** examines the national shadow play wherein an unacknowledged blackness inheres in and constitutes white identity and unity, and spurs the anxiety that underlies the accomplished national persona of a *"new white man"* in the writings of Hawthorne, Melville, Twain, Poe, and others.[9] In the tradition of postcolonial writing and criticism, Morrison rewrites the nation from a perspective committed to what has been excised. Her novels mean to revise dominant historiography, reconsidering the scene of colonial violation from the inside, from subaltern perspectives hitherto ignored.

Morrison's literary project involves confronting the national chasms of race, class, and gender as they are lived by individuals. A cursory glance at some of the epigraphs of her novels clarifies the nature of the problems Morrison tackles in her work. The epigraph of **Song of Solomon** pursues the subject of liberating a suppressed identity: "The fathers may soar / And the children may know their names," and that of **Tar Baby** acknowledges the difficulty of a postcolonial solidarity: "For it hath been declared / unto me of you, my brethren . . . that there are contentions among you." Solidarity can best be established on the collective ground of past oppression, as evident in both the dedication of **Beloved,** for "Sixty Million / and more," and its epigraph, "I will call them my people, / which were not my people; / and her beloved, / which was not beloved." As the epigraph to **Jazz** indicates, Morrison's novels may be read as a designation of divisions and a prodigious attempt to historicize them. Satya Mohanty's comment about **Beloved** illuminates what is at stake in a postcolonial return to the archives: "[**Beloved**] is one of the most challenging of postcolonial texts because it indicates the extent to which the search for a genuinely noncolonial moral and cultural identity depends on a revisionary historiography. We cannot really claim ourselves morally or politically until we have reconstructed our collective identity, reexamined our dead and our disremembered. The project is not simply one of adding to one's ancestral line, for . . . it involves fundamental discoveries about

FROM THE AUTHOR

TONI MORRISON ON BLACK FEMINISM

I think black women are in a very special position regarding black feminism, an advantageous one. White women generally define black women's role as the most repressed because they are both black and female, and these two categories invite a kind of repression that is pernicious. But in an interesting way, black women are much more suited to aggressiveness in the mode that feminists are recommending, because they have always been both mother and laborer, mother and worker, and the history of black women in the States is an extremely painful and unattractive one, but there are parts of that history that were conducive to doing more, rather than less, in the days of slavery. We think of slave women as women in the house, but they were not, most of them worked in the fields along with the men. They were required to do physical labor in competition with them, so that their relations with each other turned out to be more comradeship than male dominance/female subordination. When they were in the field plowing or collecting cotton or doing whatever, the owner of the slaves didn't care whether they were women or men—the punishment may have varied: they could beat both, and rape one, so that women could receive dual punishment, but the requirements were the same, the physical work requirements. So I have noticed among a certain generation of black men and women—older black men and women—the relationship is more one of comradeship than the you-do-this-and-I-do-this; and it's not very separate. In addition, even after slavery, all of us knew in my generation, that we always had to work, whether we were married or not. We anticipated it, so we did not have the luxury that I see certain middle class white women have, of whether to work OR to have a house. Work was always going to be part of it. When we feel that work and the house are mutually exclusive, then we have serious emotional or psychological problems, and we feel oppressed. But if we regard it as just one more thing you do, it's an enhancement. Black women are both ship and safe harbor.

Lester, Rosemarie K. Excerpt from "An Interview with Toni Morrison, Hessian Radio Network, Frankfurt West Germany" (1983) in *Critical Essays on Toni Morrison*, edited by Nellie Y. McKay. Boston: G. K. Hall and Co., 1988, pp. 47-54.

---

what ancestry is, what continuity consists in, how cultural meanings do not just sustain themselves through history but are in fact materially embodied and fought for." *Beloved* allows us to see that a revisionary postcolonial historiography must also be feminist. As Kumkum Sangari and Sudesh Vaid have insisted, it must "acknowledg[e] that each aspect of reality is gendered," and that it "may be feminist without being, exclusively, women's history."[10]

For Morrison, language implies agency—"an act with consequences." The first sentence of Morrison's Nobel speech addressed to the members of the Swedish academy is, "Ladies and Gentlemen: Narrative has never been merely entertainment for me."[11] Given the context of cultural and political domination, we can appreciate why storytelling assumes such a critical function in both African American and Native American literature, why in Leslie Marmon Silko's novel *Ceremony* we are told:

[Stories] aren't just entertainment.
Don't be fooled.

. . . . .

You don't have anything
if you don't have the stories.

As Raymond Williams argues, literature is part of "a whole social process, which, as it is lived, is not only process but is an active history, made up of the realities of formation and of struggle."[12] Toni Morrison's contemporary fiction self-consciously takes its place in the continuum of sociopolitical struggle that has historically characterized African American experience.

In their discussion of Kafka's writing, Gilles Deleuze and Felix Guattari coin the term *minor literature* to denote "that which a minority constructs out of a major language." Far from denoting a diminutive function, it is "the glory" of minor literature "to be the revolutionary force for all literature." In its salient features they see the conditions of all revolutionary literature: "the de territorialization of language, the connection of the individual to a political immediacy, and the collective assemblage of enunciation."[13] Deleuze and Guattari's assertions invite testing in relation to the works of Toni Morrison, who constructs her African American literary worlds out of the major language of English, just as Kafka, a Czech Jew, deterritorialized high German.

Morrison certainly deterritorializes the English language. Entering the bourgeois aesthetic field of the Anglo-American novel, Morrison appropriates classical and biblical myths and the canonical writings of high modernism and places them in the matrix of black culture. In this she is supported by the long vernacular tradition of work songs, spirituals, and blues that had already appropriated the Bible and renamed the Israelites as the people chosen from Africa. Morrison's own practice of naming not only deterritorializes Anglo-European usage, it signifies on its history—consider the biblical names in *Song of Solomon*, or *Jazz* with its southern towns of Wordsworth, Troy, Vienna, and Rome. What makes this appropriation so impressive is the claim made on the unyielding land by African American desire—the force that breaks through the liminality of a history of suffering, enlarging the space of marginality until it opens out into the entire field of history on its own terms.

A second characteristic that marks minor literatures is that "everything in them is political. In major literatures, in contrast, the individual concern (familial, marital, and so on) joins with other no less individual concerns, the social milieu serving as a mere environment or a background. . . . Minor literature is completely different; its cramped space forces each individual intrigue to connect immediately to politics. The individual concern thus becomes all the more necessary, indispensable, because a whole other story is vibrating within it."[14] Minor literature, in other words, constructs a different discourse, whose burden is to challenge dominant ideologies and representations by claiming an alternative epistemological and ethical space. The social milieu cannot serve as a mere background—and it never does in Morrison's work—because what is at stake in minor literature is precisely the reconstitution of an untenable social milieu; it aims to reorient the reader's relationship to an existing reality by foregrounding the environment.

A third feature Deleuze and Guattari observe in minor literatures is that "everything takes on a collective value." Because collective consciousness is not operant "in external life," or "the condi-

tions of a collective enunciation" are absent, "literature finds itself positively charged with the role and function of collective, and even revolutionary, enunciation": "it is literature that produces an active solidarity in spite of skepticism and if the writer is in the margins or completely outside his or her fragile community, this situation allows the writer all the more the possibility to express another possible community and to forge the means for another consciousness and another sensibility."[15] In novels such as *The Bluest Eye, Sula, Beloved,* and *Jazz*, a localized individual concern—Pecola's problem, Sula's heresy, Sethe's haunting, Joe and Violet's violence—sets into motion a dialogic of memory in which the individual concern is decentered and becomes the enunciation of the collective.

A fourth significant characteristic of minor literature is that it makes language "vibrate with a new intensity" partly deriving from "*terms that connote pain.*" Deleuze and Guattari refer to "an intensive utilization [of language] that makes it take flight along creative lines of escape," "us[ing] syntax in order to cry, to give a syntax to the cry."[16] One of the most remarkable elements of Morrison's prose is the sensational or visceral evocation of pain; its power stems from the author's ability to translate the experience of political inequities and wrongs with lyrical effect.

Toni Morrison's fiction makes us reevaluate individuals via the complex sociopolitical history that bespeaks them. Her novels aim to redistribute the pressure of accountability from the axis of the individual to that of the collective. Her art draws its imperatives from personal and collective histories: the maternal and paternal inheritance of a working-class consciousness with southern roots; the black aesthetic movement of the 1960s with its reclamation of oral traditions of storytelling and folk music as authentic modes of cultural expression; the liberation narrative of black history itself. As an African American novelist within the American literary tradition, Morrison interrogates national identity and reconstructs social memory. It is a truism of contemporary understanding that public identity is the product of nationalism, whose work it is to link a people dispersed by difference to a common past. As historians such as Benedict Anderson have pointed out, this common past is not simply there to access but is made available by imagined or constructed narratives of the nation. However—and this is a central question Morrison's work addresses—what happens to the identity of a group within a nation built upon its marginalization?

Further, in what ways can a marginalized identity construct its own knowledge? What new modes of narration are required to voice its presence? It is not surprising that Toni Morrison's literary project has affinities with the tasks of historiography. Writing the past, in historian Michael Roth's words, "is one of the crucial vehicles for reconstructing or reimagining a community's connections to its traditions. This is especially true for groups who have been excluded from the mainstream national histories that have dominated Western historiography, and who have suffered a weakening of group memory as part of their experience of modernity."[17]

Morrison's project of remembering must be appreciated in the context of the privatization of individual memory. As Michael Roth notes, "memory in modernity is seen less as a public, collective function than as a private, psychological faculty: it is imagined by philosophers and doctors from the eighteenth century on as being internal to each of us, at the core of the psychological self. We are what we remember. . . . But the psychologization of memory makes it extremely difficult for people to share the past, for them to have confidence that they have a collective connection to what has gone before." In Morrison's novels memory "becomes a locus of struggle over the boundary between the individual and the collective." The novels exploit the idiosyncratic compositions of individual memory, the unique particularities of personal reminiscence, only to re-collect them in the frame of a larger, unfolding history. Michael Lambek and Paul Antze observed that "the rise of popular therapeutic discourse in North America has gone hand in hand with widespread political disengagement." As they succinctly put it, "historical trauma is displaced by individual drama," resulting in "a shift in moral focus from collective obligations to narratives of individual suffering."[18] Morrison means to reverse this pattern. As her various characters attest, their lives do not make sense outside history: the meaning of personal suffering is available only within a collective temporality.

The post-Faulknerian American novel is of a genre that allows for the detailed exploration of interiority—a hallmark of Morrison's fiction, with its array of characters the reader comes to know with astonishing intimacy. In fact, Morrison's appeal and achievement lies in her ability to create individuals, with all their idiosyncracies, while anchoring subjectivity *in a collective history* without which it would have little meaning. This achievement stems from an ideological position not readily available from the position of bourgeois individualism. As Kumkum Sangari notes, "Individuality is a truly connective definition—that which connects the subject to a collectivity—so that it is the richness of contextualization that *sets off* the notion of personal particularity and differentiates the individual, rather than the social collectivity itself as being subject to the unique perception of the bourgeois individual." Morrison pays a great deal of attention to individual consciousness; we are made to see what constitutes a particular character's subjectivity and what diminishes or augments the humanity of that character. But in that appraisal Morrison compels us to evaluate not just the individual but the entire complex sociopolitical history that constitutes the individual. What Toni Morrison said in 1976 of Gayl Jones's first novel, *Corregidora,* is most applicable to her own work: what "accounts for the success" is "the weight of history working itself out in the life of one, two, three people: I mean a large idea, brought down small, and at home, which gives it a universality and a particularity which makes it extraordinary."[19]

Morrison's novels allow us to examine the quality of human relationships under the constraints of historical processes and social relations, in the context of a collective. The emphasis on the interiority of her characters, the acknowledgment and enactment of desire in all its unruly forms, becomes a way of countering the diminishing of the subordinated, alienated self. Morrison remarked in a television interview that people often say her characters appear larger than life; she countered that they are "*as* large as life, not larger. Life *is* large."[20] That individuals' large desires remain unfulfilled or thwarted creates the ambience of loss—a loss that adds powerful affect to the critique of history.

Through the evocation of specific, historicized landscapes of loss and erosion, the reader is made to see in individual loss—usually incurred by exceeding social limits—the limitations of the socius. It is thus that emotions of loss become charged with the intelligence of a critique. By endowing pain—itself mute and inchoate and all too personal—with a narrative that is as intelligible as it is social, Morrison makes room for recovery that is at once cognitive and emotional, therapeutic and political. Loss is both historicized and mourned so that it acquires a collective force and a political understanding. Morrison's fictive circles of sorrow invite readers to become *conscious* of the terrain of their lives, to re-cognize the terrain as not simply individual or personal but as thoroughly social, traversed by the claims of the past, occupied by conflicting ideologies of identity (class, gender, race, nationhood) that give rise to the boundaries of the self. In the novels, the place of the individual is de-isolated, the boundaries of the self shown to be permeated by the collective struggle of historical agents who live the long sentence of history by succumbing to (repeating), contesting, and remaking it.

Each novel charts a destruction recalled through the mnemonic prisms of multiple characters; the story of destruction and loss becomes a historical and political testimony that we as readers participate in as belated witnesses. As the story of loss is transferred to us, we become its interpreters, collaborating in the work of understanding. Each novel draws us into its circles of sorrow with the imperative to make sense; we do so by yielding our own knowledge of destruction and loss, by struggling alongside the characters. Unlike the healing transference between client and analyst in the consulting room—where the healing is private and concealed—the literary therapeutic narrative is social and collective, opening out into the politics of the world. The strategy of Morrison's novels is always to make sense of the individual psyche and memory in wider social and political terms. As a chronicler of African American experience, Morrison's contribution has been to create, in the face of public dissociation of a painful past, a space where the traumatic material may find a coherent articulation and a collective dimension. Her novels create a "public space of trauma," a space Laurence Kirmayer defined as "provid[ing] a consensual reality and collective memory through which the fragments of personal memory can be assembled, reconstructed, and displayed with a tacit assumption of validity." The construction of such a space is all the more urgent given "the failure of the world to bear witness." "The social world fails to bear witness for many reasons. Even reparative accounts of the terrible things that happen to people (violations, traumas, losses) are warded off because of their capacity to to create vicarious fear and pain and because they constitute a threat to social and political arrangements."[21]

The work of recovery in Morrison's fiction entails not only the representation of a knowledge excised from dominant understanding, but also the healing from a history that has visited trauma upon its subjects. The function of collective memory in Toni Morrison's work is political as well as therapeutic. As Roth notes, "In addition to establishing a we-group, claiming a legacy of op-

pression can enable individuals to work through the traumas of their collective and personal histories. The avoidance of a painful past or the failure to recognize its lasting effects often creates disabling patterns of behavior that only cause further pain." As recent studies of trauma relating to the experience of Holocaust survivors have shown, healing depends on the validation of traumatic events. The traumatized do not heal under suppression (amnesia), although forgetting is a characteristic response to trauma. Trauma's unconscious (pathological) mode of expression is to repeat itself, to reenact in a different guise what has never been redressed or represented. The survivor, in the words of Dori Laub, "is not truly in touch either with the core of his traumatic reality or with the fatedness of its reenactments, and thereby remains entrapped in both." What frees the survivor from this entrapment entails the "therapeutic process . . . of constructing a narrative, of reconstructing a history and essentially, of re-externalizing the event." This is precisely what Toni Morrison does. Shoshana Felman's remarks on literature as testimony clarify the relationships between narrative, history/trauma, and healing that are central to Morrison's writing: "the task of the literary testimony is . . . to open up in that belated witness [the reader] . . . the imaginative capability of perceiving history—what is happening to others—in one's own body, with the power of sight (of insight) usually afforded only by one's own immediate physical involvement."[22] Toni Morrison's highly visceral and sensuous prose effects this immediacy of experience.

* * *

Addressing the social changes taking place in Europe in the early part of the twentieth century, Walter Benjamin observed that the useful "art of storytelling is reaching its end because the epic side of truth, wisdom, is dying out." Contrasting the oral tradition of storytelling with the written one of the novel, Benjamin remarked that what is eminently present in the former and missing in the latter is the tale's offering of counsel. For him, this move from oral to written is an organic process in which something is both lost and gained: "nothing would be more fatuous than to want to see in it merely a 'symptom of decay,' let alone a 'modern' symptom. It is, rather, only a concomitant symptom of the secular productive forces of history, a concomitant that has quite gradually removed narrative from the realm of living speech and at the same time is making it possible to see a new beauty in what is vanishing." Similarly, Morrison notes the demise of a grounding world view within urban African American communities dislocated from ancestral wisdom and communal forms of expression. A sense of responsibility and urgency characterizes Morrison's comments: "for larger and larger numbers of black people, this sense of loss has grown, and the deeper the conviction that something valuable is slipping away from us, the more necessary it has become to find some way to hold on to the useful past without blocking off the possibilities of the future." Present in Morrison's expressed need to hold on to certain cultural forms of the past is a framework of cultural domination within which these cultural forms have played an oppositional role. Thus Morrison hopes to have her fiction accomplish/replace "what the music did for blacks": "the music kept us alive, but it's not enough anymore. My people are being devoured."[23]

Morrison's invocation of black music is significant, for it is related to a nonbourgeois consciousness not co-opted by the dominant culture. LeRoi Jones wrote that in the face of "the persistent calls to oblivion made by the mainstream of the society," music "was the one vector out of African culture impossible to eradicate. It signified the existence of an Afro-American, and the existence of an Afro-American culture." The musical consciousness was displaced as integration into white America compelled the marginalization of such cultural forms. Hence, for the middle class to have "gotten 'free' of all the blues tradition" was to have been deprived of a vital sense of connection to the resistant traditions of the past. Paule Marshall's *Praisesong for the Widow* is an eloquent and moving account of a black couple, the Johnsons, who had done just that—"gotten 'free'"—and found they had lost an integral part of themselves. The widowed Avey Johnson recalls the significance of the music that had been abandoned in their haste to leave behind a life of poverty and limitations: "Something vivid and affirming and charged with feeling had been present in the small rituals that had once shaped their lives. . . . Something in those small rites, an ethos they held in common, had reached back beyond her life and beyond Jay's to join them to the vast unknown lineage that had made their being possible." And this link, these connections, heard in the music and in the praisesongs, "had both protected them and put them in possession of a kind of power." They spent their lives in pursuit of a different kind of power, one promised by assimilation, a house in the white suburbs; "running with the blinders on they had allowed that richness, protection and power to slip out." Avey bitterly mourns the loss: "What kind of bargain had they struck?"[24]

Marshall's Jay Johnson has much in common with Morrison's Macon Dead, the patriarch in *Song of Solomon* who is driven to amass worldly goods with a compulsion born of the insecurity of dispossession. In a scene of nostalgic hearkening, Macon Dead stands hidden outside his sister Pilate's home, his head pressed to the window, watching and listening as Pilate sings the blues with her daughter and granddaughter, Reba and Hagar. His distance from that setting becomes the measure of his own cultural and spiritual alienation. Hagar demonstrates what Morrison means when she claims, "the music kept us alive, but it's not enough anymore." Hagar is easy prey to an urban consumer culture, a world in which Pilate's song is muted and her wisdom marginalized. Hence Morrison's emphatic statement: "There has to be a mode to do what the music did for blacks." Historically, these expressive cultural forms have been means of forging a collective black consciousness, of keeping alive an awareness of oppression and resistance, of soul force. In wanting her novels to perform the function of black music, Morrison intends her art to forge a historical consciousness, to embody and create a communal intersubjectivity.

In the following passage from *The Bluest Eye*, Morrison reveals something about her own craft: "The pieces of Cholly's life could become coherent only in the head of a musician. Only those who talk their talk through the gold of curved metal, or in the touch of black and white rectangles and taut skins . . . would know how to connect the heart of a red water melon to the asafetida bag . . . to the fists of money to the lemonade in a mason jar . . . and come up with what all of that meant in joy, in pain, in anger, in love, and give it its final and pervading ache of freedom." Words seek to accomplish the emotive-cognitive resonance belonging to music; what we audition in Morrison's novels is the "pervading ache of freedom." This ache accounts for what in Morrison's prose might appear as linguistic extravagance. This pervading ache is "the insistent pressure of *freedom* as the *absent horizon*"—the point Kumkum Sangari made regarding Gabriel García Márquez's narratives, in which absent freedom is "precisely that which is made present and possible by its absence—the lives that people have never lived *because* of the lives they are forced to live or have chosen to live. That which is desired and that which exists, the sense of abundance and the sense of waste, are dialectically related."[25]

In Toni Morrison's art we witness the lyric gesture and force of a minor literature doing the difficult work of decolonization, demystification, and social redress within the dominant language. In attempting to account for the compelling power of this particular literature, I want to add the word *soul,* the dimension least theorized in literary criticism and more acknowledged in music. Toni Morrison is one of the most soulful literary soloists of our time. Explaining the "emotional substance" of jazz, Paul Berliner makes the following comment: "Part and parcel of originality and taste is a performance's 'soul,' its 'spirituality,' its 'integrity of expression.' . . . Soulful performances embody such affective qualities as pathos, intensity, urgency, fire, and energy. . . . Musicians use the term *energy* both literally and figuratively. Just as it requires energy to produce and project sounds on musical instruments, it requires energy for performers to draw upon feelings as they infuse sounds with emotion. Moreover, the sound waves themselves comprise a form of energy that touches listeners physically, potentially also touching them emotionally." Morrison inscribes her own awareness of the energetic properties of sound; consider these lines from **Beloved**: the singing "voices of women searched for the right combination, the key, the code, the sound that broke the back of words. Building voice upon voice until they found it, and when they did it was a wave of sound wide enough to sound deep water and knock the pods off chestnut trees. It broke over Sethe and she trembled like the baptized in its wash." The dimension of sound in language is potentially a musical or harmonic dimension, an ethereal register in which even the written voice can sing. Here, I can do no more than acknowledge that harmonic dimension in Toni Morrison's prose; its source is the spiritual principle of liberation that animates her writing, a principle I have attempted to elucidate here in its historic, social, and political terms.[26]

Notes

1. Howard Winant, "Postmodern Racial Politics in the United States: Difference and Inequality," *Socialist Review* (January-March, 1990), 121; Margaret Croyden, "Toni Morrison Tries Her Hand at Playwriting," in *Conversations with Toni Morrison,* ed. Danille Taylor-Guthrie (Jackson, Miss., 1994), 218, 220; Morrison, *Playing in the Dark,* 65, 117, 13.

2. Raymond Williams, *Marxism and Literature* (Oxford, 1977), 193; Hortense J. Spillers, "Afterword: Cross-Currents, Discontinuities: Black Women's Fiction," *Conjuring: Black Women's Fiction, and Literary Tradition,* ed. Hortense Spillers and Marjorie Pryse (Bloomington, Ind., 1985), 250; Barbara Smith, "Toward a Black Feminist Criticism," in *Feminist Criticism and Social Change,* ed. Judith Newton and Deborah Rosenfelt (New York, 1985), 4.

3. Morrison, "What the Black Woman Thinks About Women's Lib," *New York Times Magazine,* August 22, 1971, p. 15; Alice Walker, *In Search of Our Mothers' Gardens* (New York, 1983), xi.

4. Toni Morrison, "The Language Must Not Sweat," Interview with Thomas LeClair in *Conversations,* 120, 121; Toni Morrison, "Rootedness: The Ancestor as Foundation," in *Black Women Writers at Work, 1950-1980,* ed. Mari Evans (Garden City, N.Y., 1984), 340; Susan Willis, *Specifying: Black Women Writing the American Experience* (Madison, Wis., 1987), 83-109; Wilfred Sheed, "Improbable Assignment: Tar Baby," *Atlantic* (April, 1981), 119.

5. Morrison, interview with Charles Ruas, in *Conversations,* 105.

6. Toni Morrison, qtd. in Bonnie Angelo, "The Pain of Being Black," *Time,* May 22, 1989, p. 120; Wahneema Lubiano, in a paper on black cultural nationalism delivered at the Modern Language Association Convention (New York, 1992).

7. Helen Tiffin, "Post-Colonialism, Post-Modernism and the Rehabilitation of Post-Colonial History," *Journal of Commonwealth Literature,* XXIII (1988), 171; Thiongo, *Decolonizing the Mind,* 87; Chinua Achebe, *Hopes and Impediments: Selected Essays* (New York, 1988), 44.

8. Eva Cherniavsky, "Subaltern Studies in a U. S. Frame," *Boundary 2,* XXIII (1996), 85-110.

9. Robert Allen, *Black Awakening in Capitalist America* (Garden City, N.Y., 1970), 2; Harold Cruse, *Rebellion or Revolution?* (New York, 1968), 76-77; Gayatri Chakravarty Spivak, "Rani of Sirmur," in *Europe and Its Others: Proceedings of the Essex Conference on the Sociology of Literature, July, 1984,* ed. Francis Barker, *et al.* (2 vols.; Colchester, Eng., 1985), I, 130; Morrison, *Playing in the Dark, passim.*

10. Saty a Mohanty, "The Epistemic Status of Cultural Identity: On *Beloved* and the Postcolonial Condition," *Cultural Critique,* XXIV (Spring, 1993), 67; Kumkum Sangari and Sudesh Vaid, qtd. in R. Radhakrishnan, "Nationalism, Gender, and the Narrative of Identity," in *Nationalisms and Sexualities,* ed. Andrew Parker, Mary Russo, *et al.* (New York, 1992), 79.

11. Morrison, *The Nobel Lecture.*

12. Williams, *Marxism and Literature,* 210.

13. Deleuze and Guattari, *Toward a Minor Literature,* 16, 19, 18.

14. *Ibid.,* 17.

15. *Ibid.,* 17.

16. *Ibid.,* 22, 26 (authors' emphasis).

17. Benedict Anderson, *Imagined Communities: Reflections on the Origin and Spread of Nationalism* (New York, 1983); Michael Roth, *The Ironist's Cage: Memory, Trauma, and the Construction of History* (New York, 1995), 10.

18. Roth, *The Ironist's Cage*, 9; Paul Antze and Michael Lambek, eds. *Tense Past: Cultural Essays in Trauma and Memory* (New York, 1996), xx, xxiv.

19. Kumkum Sangari, "Politics of the Possible," *Cultural Critique*, VII (Fall, 1987); Morrison, "Intimate Things in Place," interview with Robert Stepto, in *Conversations*, 29.

20. Toni Morrison, *Toni Morrison,* an RM Arts Production, 1987.

21. Laurence Kirmayer, "Landscapes of Memory: Trauma, Narrative, and Dissociation," in *Tense Past*, 190, 192.

22. Roth, *The Ironist's Cage*, 10-11; Dori Laub, "Bearing Witness, or the Vicissitudes of Listening," in *Testimony: Crises of Witnessing in Literature, Psychoanalysis, and History*, ed. Shoshana Felman and Laub (New York, 1991), 69; Felman, "Camus' The Plague, or a Monument to Witnessing," in *Testimony*, 108.

23. Walter Benjamin, *Illuminations*, trans. Harry Zohn, ed. Hannah Arendt (New York, 1968), 87; Toni Morrison, "Rediscovering Black History," *New York Times Magazine*, August 11, 1974, p. 14; Morrison, "The Language Must Not Sweat," 121.

24. LeRoi Jones, *Blues People* (New York, 1963), 131, 176; Paule Marshall, *Praisesong for the Widow* (New York, 1983) 137, 139.

25. Sangari, "Politics of the Possible," 176.

26. Paul Berliner, *Thinking in Jazz: The Infinite Art of Improvisation* (Chicago, 1994) 255-56; Toni Morrison, *Beloved* (New York, 1987), 261.

TITLE COMMENTARY

The Bluest Eye

PIN-CHIA FENG (ESSAY DATE 1998)

SOURCE: Feng, Pin-chia. "The Gaze of *The Bluest Eye*." In *The Female Bildungsroman by Toni Morrison and Maxine Hong Kingston: A Postmodern Reading*, pp. 51-75. New York: Peter Lang, 1998.

In the following excerpt, Feng discusses Morrison's treatment of race, power, and black conformity to white beauty standards in The Bluest Eye, *noting the novel's anti-Bildungsroman properties.*

The visual image of a splintered mirror, or the corridor of split mirrors in blue eyes, is the form as well as the content of *The Bluest Eye.*

—Toni Morrison, "**Memory, Creation, and Writing**"

The Bluest Eye tells a story of a black girl, Pecola Breedlove, who wants blue eyes and is raped by her own father. Haunted by the memory of Pecola's tragedy, the first-person narrator, Claudia MacTeer, attempts to make sense of the incident in retrospect. The novel is not only Pecola's story but Claudia's as well. It is also a story for girls growing up without positive images of themselves reflected in the mirror held up by mainstream society, and constantly under the gaze of the blue eye of dominant ideology. And the reader is the one to piece together the fragments of the girls' personal, cultural, and racial experiences to understand the political message Morrison has inscribed in her haunting novel.

The Bluest Eye can be read as a double *Bildungsroman*, in which Claudia's narrative of *Bildung* is deployed as a contrast to Pecola's.[1] The idea of a "double *Bildungsroman*" is first suggested in Jerome Buckley's reading of *The Mill on the Floss* entitled "George Eliot—Double Life."[2] Charlotte Goodman coins the term "male-female double *Bildungsroman*" for the developmental plot of a male-female pair.[3] This double form, Goodman contends, is able to emphasize the way in which rigid gender roles restrict the full development of women and men alike (31). Susan Fraiman's model of "counternarratives" in the novel of development by British women writers further diverts from Goodman's androgynous vision and underscores the rifts and incongruities between the coveted male model of development and the female counter one. Central to both Goodman's and Fraiman's theoretical models is a critique of the gender dichotomy imposed by society.

In the fictional world of *The Bluest Eye*, however, Toni Morrison focuses instead on racial dichotomy. She weaves the contrasts and comparisons around a pair of black girls to highlight the compounding work of racism as well as sexism and classism on the *Bildung* of black girls. Claudia grows up to tell the story, while Pecola "grows down" and sinks into madness.[4] The novel proper records the intersection of Pecola's and Claudia's narratives of *Bildung*: a single year of their lives which marks both girls' "coming of age"—from the autumn of 1940 to the "fall" of 1941—the year in which Pecola's incestuous rape takes place. What happens in that year are not isolated events but events closely connected to the racial and cultural memories of black Americans. Whether the two girls' development is "successful" is measured against the degree of assimilation to white ideology of the *Bildung* they achieve. But contrary to the prototypical plot of the male *Bildungsroman*, Claudia survives to tell the story by resisting social and racial conformity. Pecola fails the test precisely because of her unconditional internalization of the dominant ideology. Thus even in her first attempt at the novel form Morrison not only highlights the racial factor in Afro-

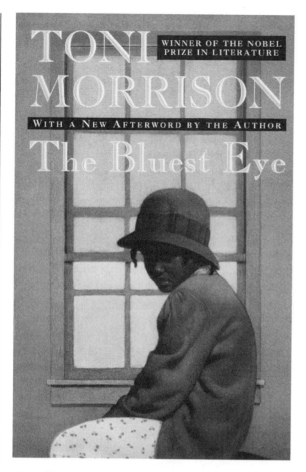

Cover illustration of *The Bluest Eye*.

American developmental plot but also deconstructs the plot of social integration inherent in the male *Bildungsroman*.

Furthermore, this novel challenges the developmental patterns of the typical *Bildungsroman* that Buckley has specified. From the outset Morrison creates a pseudo-chronological framework based on the natural transition of four seasons. This simulacrum of lineality is nevertheless constantly interrupted by the emergence of broken pieces of past experiences. This kind of narrative fragmentation reflects a characteristic discursive discontinuity of modernist and postmodernist writing. This mode of fragmentary writing, what Susan Willis identifies as "the four-page formula" for black women writers, also embodies the story-telling tradition in Afro-American culture (*Specifying* 14). The intrusion of past experiences into the present signifies a return of the repressed that the two protagonists are forced to reckon with.

Morrison achieves the effect of narrative fragmentation in **The Bluest Eye** through the use of multiple narrative voices. Even within Claudia's first-person narrative the voice is divided between different perspectives of Claudia-as-a-child and of a somewhat "mature" Claudia. The outer framework of the novel inscribes a "mature" Claudia who looks backward at one of the most significant years of her childhood and attempts to exorcize the experience of pain by reconstructing the nature of this pain that lives in her memory. This outer frame is further deconstructed by Morrison's use of a third-person omniscient narrator. As Valerie Smith points out, the apparently objective omniscient narrator fills in for the reader information that the characters have no access to (125). The omniscient narrator also vicariously acts out Claudia's, even Morrison's, desire for revenge on the dominant society. In her television interview with Bill Moyers, Morrison assigns one of the reasons for Pecola's tragedy to her unconditional acceptance of the "master narrative"—the dominant discourse represented by the Dick-and-Jane primer at the beginning of the novel. The primer, which can be regarded as one of Barthes's cultural codes, functions as the standard discourse of *Bildung* provided by the mainstream culture. Susan Fraiman observes the attraction of the standard *Bildungsroman* to women in her theory of counternarratives. In **The Bluest Eye** Morrison both portrays the attractiveness of the Dick-and-Jane narrative to the black community and deconstructs element by element the false ideology of this white, middle-class discourse. By allowing the narrator to dissect the primer into fragments, Morrison enacts Claudia's desire to dismember the white dolls and partially releases the pressure of discursive violence and racial confrontation.

Neither Claudia nor the narrator, nevertheless, can get to the *how* of Pecola's story. The narrative stance of the "mature" Claudia is still repressive since she could not bear to look into the *why* of Pecola's tragedy. And the narrator also chooses to "show" *how* the tragedy occurs rather than to "tell" *why*. Only the reader attentive to the heteroglossic narrative voices can start the analytical process of breaking the resistance and come to the *why* through piecing together the narrative of *how*.

The role of the reader is of great importance in Morrison's literary creation. The text is "the map" for the reader's participation, as Morrison proclaims in **"Memory, Creation, and Writing"** (389). And the writer's duty is to provide the places and spaces for the reader to participate in (**"Rootedness"** 341). The emphasis on the "reader's response" is further underlined in Morrison's analysis of her own works. In "**Unspeakable Things Unspoken**," Morrison indicates that the purposeful simplicity of the opening line of *The Bluest Eye*, coming directly from black women's language of gossip, is meant to establish a conspiratorial relationship between the narrator and the reader, and a sudden and instant intimacy between the reader and the page. This aura of conspiracy and familiarity, however, is immediately undermined by the question of reliability provoked by Claudia's child-like logic in linking Pecola's rape to the nonappearance of marigolds in 1941. Claudia and Frieda have attempted to find a logical explanation for the unnaturalness they have witnessed. If they have any success, as Morrison points out, it will be "in transferring the problem of fathoming to the presumable adult reader, to the inner circle of listeners" (19-22). This careful design on Morrison's part to engage the reader indicates that the reader must be the final "private eye" to ferret out the *why* of Pecola's tragedy.

In Claudia's haunting story there is also an immanent sense of guilt for failing to save Pecola's baby and the hapless mother. This kind of guilt originates in female bonding and empathy. In Alice Walker's *Possessing the Secret of Joy* the protagonist Tashi's analyst Raye, an Afro-American woman herself, mutilates her gum in order to understand Tashi's pain of genital castration. Tashi sees Raye's action as "intuitively practicing an ageless magic, the foundation of which was the ritualization, or the acting out, of empathy" (131). In this guise, the healer Raye becomes for the resisting Tashi someone she can bond with and one who can release her repressed memory. That kind of female bonding happens in *The Bluest Eye*, too. Claudia and Frieda, while trying to save Pecola's unborn baby by burying the seeds and their hard-earned money, practice the same kind of magical ritual of empathy. The MacTeer sisters' sacrifice creates a bond between them and the unhappy Pecola. By implication, Morrison suggests that in order to work for the possibility of social healing, the reader, too, needs to practice this emphathetic magic. The only saving grace for Pecola, perhaps, is the reader's attentiveness to the voice within the silence, as Kogawa has suggested in *Obasan*. What follows is this reader's attempt to work the magic of empathy and piece together the splintered mirror in the novel to trace the *why* of one black girl's tragic end and another's narrow escape.

I. Pecola Breedlove

Pecola Breedlove's story builds upon Morrison's specific recollection of how she felt upon hearing that a black girl in her neighborhood prayed for blue eyes ("**Memory**" 388). Pecola is the narrative embodiment of this prayer; and as Claudia states, "the horror at the heart of her yearning is exceeded only by the evil of fulfillment" (158). In her schizophrenic state Pecola imagines herself with the bluest eyes of all. It is not difficult to see her as a victim of the external society. Patrice Cormier-Hamilton, for instance, claims that *The Bluest Eye* serves as an example of "black naturalism" and in the character of Pecola Morrison most emphatically "incorpoartes the naturalist theme of the 'waste of individual potential' due to environmental circumstances" (115). Some critics, however, regard Pecola's end as a triumph. For example, Chiwenye Ogunyemi, arguing from a "womanist" position, maintains that Pecola's madness allows her to acquire "an interior spiritual beauty symbolized by the bluest eye." "Madness," contends Ogunyemi, "becomes a temporary aberration preceding spiritual growth, healing, and integration." (74).

It is hard to chime in with Ogunyemi's optimistic tone since she fails to analyze the ideological connotation behind the bluest eye. Pecola *is* the ultimate victim of "the bluest eye." In spite of the fact that her insanity reverses her previous invisibility and forces her presence on her community, Pecola's final appearance in the novel is metaphorically "a winged but grounded bird, intent on *the blue void* it could not reach—could not even see—but which filled the valleys of the mind" (158, italics mine). This "blue void" represents a "lack" inside Pecola that has grounded her fledgling development—a desire that is impossible to fulfill because it originates in an external standard imposed by the dominant society and impossible to forget since Pecola has fully internalized her own deficiency. Not unlike her slave foremothers who have been judged as morally deficient because of their supposed "lack" of (white) True Womanhood,[5] Pecola suffers this psychological lack because her biological difference is designated as inferior in the hegemonic discourse of white supremacy.

This "blue void" also represents the monolithic bluest eye of the external world that has consumed Pecola. The bluest eye of the title signifies the monovision of American society that perceives minority people as the "Other" and privileges only a white physical standard. From

Pecola's prayer for "blue eyes" to the one final irreducible eyeball of "the bluest eye" like a gigantic social monitor, Morrison suggests an accentuating movement of the closing-in of dominant society on the self-definition of the non-white. This monolithic bluest eye represents what bell hooks calls "the imperial gaze—the look that seeks to dominate, subjugate, and colonize" generated from a white supremacist culture (*Black Looks* 7). The "void" in Pecola's life reflects what hooks calls the "gaps" in the psyche of black people—the gaps "where mindless complicity, self-destructive rage, hatred, and paralyzing despair enter"—conditioned by this relentless monovision (*Black Looks* 4).

This "void" is also created by an experience of "mirror stage," in Lacanian terms. While looking into the mirror that a white society holds up to her, Pecola cannot see "the ideal image," that is, one with blue eyes, in her own reflection. Pecola has internalized the dominant ideology of ideal beauty, the Law of the White Fathers, so deeply that the unbridgeable difference between her and the objectified image of standard beauty obliterates what little self image she has, thus creating a paradoxically invisible yet imprisoning "blue void" around her. Hence Pecola's entrance into the Symbolic order ironically marks her mental and physical destruction.

The central trope of Pecola's narrative is indeed the eye, as Wilfred Samuels and Clenora Hudson-Weems contend (17). Pecola is completely reified by what Jean-Paul Sartre calls *le regard* (the Look), the gaze of the dominant definition of her as an "Other." In their critical assessment of *The Bluest Eye*, Samuels and Hudson-Weems use Sartre's notion of *le regard* to explicate the self-objectification of Pecola and her family. The Breedloves are characters who "use others to escape their own responsibility to define themselves" (8) and try to live up to an external image imposed on them by mainstream society. Pecola's self-abnegation is an especially castrating act of "Bad Faith" because she objectifies herself into a "being-for-the-other" instead of being a subjective "being-for-self" (18). From wanting *blue eyes* to being overwhelmed by *the bluest eye*, Pecola becomes the protagonist of an anti-*Bildungsroman* that illustrates *how* a mentally colonized black girl fails to negotiate her personal, cultural and racial experiences and finally resorts to the protection of madness.[6]

Pecola's narrative of (anti-)*Bildung* is modeled after Greek tragedy, yet rooted in Afro-American community. Like Hurston who writes about the inner world of black life, Morrison situates her first novel in the black community with a very limited appearance of white characters. Morrison stages the descent into madness of this Afro-American anti-heroine in a way similar to a predestined Greek "hero." For instance, Pecola's story is outlined at the very beginning by the "mature" Claudia. This unconventional narrative technique locks Pecola in an unbreakable discursive prison and creates a sense of the overdetermination of Pecola's fate. After providing the reader with this plot summary, Morrison then upstages Pecola through the side door in the narrative proper as a "case"—a girl who has been put outdoors by her reckless father—which establishes Pecola's status as a marginal figure even in her own community. All these theatrical devices contribute to make Pecola an object of the gaze for the reader and reflect upon Pecola's self-objectification, yet curiously make her remain invisible to characters around her at the same time.

Two factors contribute to Pecola's theatrical "invisible presence" in the novel. One is that Morrison renders Pecola consistently silent, even in her own narrative of (anti-) *Bildung*. Another is Pecola's parental heritage of racial neurosis introduced in the two embedded stories of Pauline and Cholly Breedlove. Coming right before Pecola's rape, these two pieces of stories appear to be direct causes of Pecola's tragedy. Appearing at almost the end of the novel, Pauline's and Cholly's narratives serve as a discursive return of the repressed past to show how the parents' traumatic experiences with a racist society are visited upon the children. To understand fully *how* Pecola "grows down," therefore, we must reverse the process of narrative repression and look at her parents' stories first.

From her mother, Pecola learns to love and internalize white ideology. What characterizes Pauline Breedlove as a mother is her lack of maternal affection. The section about Pauline comes right after an episode in which she humiliates and neglects the burned Pecola to comfort "the little pink-and-yellow" Fisher girl. Yet by allowing Pauline to have her own voice in the novel, Morrison shows that Pauline was once full of dreams and feelings. Her lack of love, as represented by the loss of her "rainbow," is not natural but emerges out of her "education" in a society saturated with class and racial inequality.

Pauline's story is an embedded narrative of anti-*Bildung* within Pecola's story. After separating from her own folks and migrating to the North with Cholly, Pauline has her first "education" in the movies, from which she refreshes her dreams of romantic love and becomes initiated to the standard of physical beauty represented by the white visual icons on the silver screen. As the narrator comments, the notions of romantic love and physical beauty are "[p]robably the most destructive ideas in the history of human thought. Both originated in envy, thrived in insecurity, and ended in disillusion" (97). The ray of light coming from the projector, as Madonne M. Miner points out, resembles a gigantic eyeball that reflects white male vision (186). Being black *and* female render Pauline totally insignificant within this visual scope. Lacking other alternatives, Pauline is forced to identify with this blinding gaze.

Pauline is seduced by glamorous illusions produced by the Hollywood film industry into a figural identification with the white ideology of beauty. In *Alice Doesn't,* Teresa de Lauretis focuses on the centrality of "the look" in cinema and dissects the process of the double figural identification to seduce the female spectator into acceptance of femininity. The woman in a narrative cinema, de Lauretis contends, "is framed by the look of the camera as icon, or object of gaze: an image made to be looked at by the spectator, whose look is relayed by the look of the male character(s)" (139). By seeing through the eye of the hero,

> the female spectator identifies with both the subject and the space of the narrative movement, with the figure of movement and the figure of its closure, the narrative image. Both are figural identifications, and both are possible at once; more, they are concurrently borne and mutually implicated by the process of narrativity. This manner of identification would uphold both positionalities of desire, both active and passive aims: desire for the other, and the desire to be desired by the other. This is in fact the operation by which narrative and cinema solicit the spectators' consent and seduce women into femininity: by a double identification, a surplus of pleasure produced by the spectators themselves for cinema and for society's benefit.
>
> (143)

From de Lauretis's theory of identification we may infer that for an ethnic woman, the seduction into "white femininity" is a process of "triple identification" which allows her to identify with not only the gaze, the subject of the movement (white male hero) and the narrative image (white heroine) but also with the power and privilege represented by the white skin. Pauline's figural identification with the white visual icons is exemplified in her attempt to dress her hair like

Jean Harlow (97). Her disappointment brought on by her lost tooth alone breaks her illusion of this figural identification. But the spell of Hollywood is still on her, which only makes her sink lower and into acceptance of her own ugliness. Pauline is a black female spectator who fails to cultivate what bell hooks calls a decolonizing "oppositional gaze" (*Black Looks* 116).

Another part of Pauline's education is the "denigrification" of her mind. Pauline Breedlove is the very example of mental colonization that Franz Fanon has analyzed in his *Black Skin, White Masks.* In his interpretation of the psychological and existential alienation of black people, Fanon argues that black people's "inferiority complex" is the outcome of "a double process." The black feel inferior in a white hegemonic society primarily because of their economic disadvantage. This sense of materialist incompetence leads to a severe damage of the psyche when black people internalize, even epidermalize, this inferiority (11). In an oversimplified fashion, Fanon claims that all black women want to be white "because the Negress feels inferior that she aspires to win admittance into the white world" (60). "In this endeavor," Fanon writes, "she will seek help of a phenomenon that we shall call *affective erethism*" (60). Pauline's identification with the power of her white employers while dealing with the creditors and service people who looked down upon her when she went to them on her own behalf shows her racial inferiority complex. And her contentment over the nickname they have assigned her does reveal a symptom that is close to *affective erethism.*[7] These symptoms of Pauline's mental colonization and her willing submission to the seductive power of the white look illustrate the overwhelming power of dominant ideology and testify to the difficult *Bildung* of an ethnic woman. Pauline's process of denigrification prefigures Pecola's subjugation to the white gaze.

At the end of her "process of becoming" Pauline enters faithfully into the role of "an ideal servant," a female Uncle Tom so to speak, and alienates her own family. She is finally suffering from what Fanon calls "a collapse of the ego" (154).[8] Before her education in the movies, Pauline has refused to give up her husband for her white mistress. As she says in her first-person voice, "*it didn't seem none too bright for a black woman to leave a black man for a white woman*" (95). But when racial ideology sinks in, Pauline is sadly transformed. By giving up her family and retreating into the private world of snow-white beauty and order in the Fisher household, Pauline cuts the final link to her racial identity. Worst of all, she passes on these symptoms of racial neurosis to Pecola, into whom she beats "a fear of growing up, fear of other people, fear of life" (102).

The paternal influence on Pecola also contributes to her invisibility. Cholly Breedlove's story is another version of the return of the repressed past to haunt people in the present. Cholly has been educated by racism to assert his manhood on the defenseless. His mentality comes very close to what Paulo Freire has illustrated in *The Pedagogy of the Oppressed*. Freire studies the "adhesion" of the oppressed to the oppressor:

> But almost always, during the initial stage of the struggle, the oppressed, instead of striving for liberation, tend themselves to become oppressors, or "sub-oppressors." The very structure of their thought has been conditioned by the contradictions of the concrete, existential situation by which they were shaped. Their ideal is to be men; but for them, to be men is to be oppressors. This is their model of humanity.
>
> (29-30)

Nowhere is this model more revealing than in Cholly's traumatic sexual initiation. The narrator actually tells the story twice—of Cholly being surprised by two white hunters with flashlights during his first sexual act, and how he transfers his shame and hatred onto his helpless partner. The narrator first mentions this episode in the bushes passingly (37). Later, however, the narrator examines Cholly's consciousness thoroughly:

> Never did he once consider directing his hatred toward the hunters. Such an emotion would have destroyed him. They were big, white, armed men. He was small, black, helpless. . . . For now, he hated the one who had created the situation, the one who bore witness to his failure, his impotence. The one who he had not been able to protect, to spare, to cover from the round moon glow of the flashlight. The hee-hee-hee's.
>
> (119)

By telling Cholly's story twice the narrator simulates the nature of his mental repression. She also implicitly comments on what underlies Cholly's pathetic mental measurement of his size, color and power against his real enemy, which again reminds us of Fanon's "inferiority complex." Cholly's transference of anger onto the helpless Darlene also illustrates his desperate clinging to the shred of manhood under the threat of racial emasculation. Even when he has learned to hate those "big" white men, Cholly continues to inflict his own frustration on his fellow oppressed. This is typical in his relation with Pauline in the declining stage of their marriage. He treats her with

violence since "[s]he was one of the few things abhorrent to him that he could touch and therefore hurt. He poured out on her the sum of all his inarticulate fury and aborted desires" (37). Using the same mentality he also hurts and pours out his desire onto his own daughter.

Cholly commits the rape of Pecola based on his reaction to his own sense of guilt and impotence faced with Pecola's "young, helpless, hopeless presence" (127). Parentless from his birth, Cholly has difficulty committing himself to family responsibility. Rejected at fourteen by his supposed father, Cholly turns dangerously "free," free in a negative sense that he is uprooted from his own community, as represented by his Aunt Jimmy and old man Blue. Without positive parental role models and sufficient contact with the healthy influence of his agrarian community, Cholly is ill prepared for his paternal role. His financial frustration with work and emotional tumult with Pauline after his northern migration further contribute to Cholly's inability to keep his family "indoors."

The rape of Pecola is directly caused by this rootlessness. In his drunken state Cholly identifies Pecola with Pauline in the gesture of scratching her leg, which triggers his violent tenderness. The young Pecola evokes Cholly's tenderness because he sees her both as an image of young Pauline, his first love, and his unprotected daughter. This conflation of familial roles (mother and daughter) and paradoxical emotions (protectiveness and destruction) characterizes the entire episode of the rape and underlines the confusion of kinship within the Breedlove family.[9] Some critics contend that Pecola may not simply be a victim but a participant in the rape (Gibson 171). But Pecola's ambiguous reaction speaks to her extreme hunger for love and again underscores the disruption of familial structure. Morrison's surrealist style in this rape episode creates a dream-like sensation that is grotesquely "romantic." Maybe Pecola needs to "breed love" so much that she momentarily suspends her moral sensibility and turns to respond to Cholly's sexual violation, which makes her incestuous story even more gruesome. Whether Morrison is actually writing an intertextual revision of the "Trueblood episode" in Ralph Ellison's *Invisible Man*, as Michael Awkward contends or not (62), her undertaking of this taboo subject in conjunction with symptoms of racial neurosis shows her determination to uncover the repressed historical and social memory of the Afro-American community through her writing.

What intrigues me, and is overlooked almost by all critics, is the missing narrative about Pecola's brother. In the primer, brother Dick appears only once, which may explain Sammy's absence. Still, this runaway boy's "escape" from narrative confinement remains a mystery. The only line he has in the novel is to urge his mother to kill Cholly, which provides another twist to the Freudian Oedipus complex but most of all highlights the prevailing element of violence in the Breedlove household (39). His appearance/disappearance therefore deconstructs the happy "normative" family structure in the Dick-and-Jane mode. Moreover, Sammy's disappearance represents a loose thread in Pecola's narrative of (anti-) *Bildung*. It even subtly suggests a possible repetition of the fate of Cholly Breedlove—another homeless, parentless "free" black boy on the run, and another future family tragedy looming on the horizon.

Besides her parental heritage, what also makes Pecola invisible in her own story is her passivity and most of all, her silence. Except for her conversation with the three prostitutes and final schizophrenic soliloquy, the reader only catches a few glimpses of her inner consciousness mediated by a third-person narrator. Each of these momentary revelations of Pecola's thoughts marks a traumatic experience. The first of these moments is Pecola's reaction to the brutal fight between her parents. The second one records her racial encounter with a white store owner. The last one appears in Pecola's admiration of Geraldine's gold-and-green house right before she was expelled from this "paradise." Morrison provides us with these three moments of entrance into Pecola's mind as specimens of her personal, racial, and cultural experiences.

Pecola's personal experience is marked by violence and lovelessness, as represented by the brutal but darkly formal "battle" between her parents in their storefront home. Here Morrison is recording the derogatory impact of family violence on young children through Sammy's and Pecola's reactions to the fight. While her brother Sammy escapes their violent home by running away, Pecola's reaction is "restricted by youth and sex" (38). Here Morrison reiterates a common theme in women's fiction about the lack of physical mobility for a heroine. Confined by her immobility, Pecola resorts to passively praying for disappearance. But her eyes would not go away. For the first time in the novel Pecola's intense desire for blue eyes, which is implicit in her insatiable consumption of milk from the Shirley Temple cup,

and her rationalization for this desire are revealed: she wants blue eyes so she can be beautiful and her family will be transformed miraculously into a loving one. But her hope for the miracle built upon a childish logic only leads to self-objectification. The omniscient narrator observes, "She would see only what there was to see, the eyes of other people" (40). Pecola merely manages to objectify herself by the gaze of the Look.

The obstacles to Pecola's development are not only youth and sex but also racism. The reader's second entrance into Pecola's consciousness follows right after the fight between the Breedloves and Pecola's prayer for disappearance. Pecola's encounter with Mr. Yacobowski echoes the discourse of invisibility in Ellison's *Invisible Man*. Like Ellison's anonymous hero, Pecola is unseen because people refuse to see her. Pecola's invisibility is an evidence of her lack of self image when facing the dominant white society. But whereas Ellison's hero blames his invisibility to the construction of white people's "*inner eyes,* those eyes with which they look through their physical eyes upon reality" (7), Pecola's locates the source of "the vacuum" and "absence of human recognition" of Yacobowski's eyes in her own blackness:

> It has an edge; somewhere in the bottom lid is the distaste. She has seen it lurking in the eyes of all white people. So, The distaste must be for her, her blackness. All things in her are flux and anticipation. But her blackness is static and dread. And it is the blackness that accounts for, that creates, the vacuum edged with distaste in white eyes.
>
> (42)

The vacancy in Yacobowski's blear-dropped blue eyes foretells the "blue void" that is going to consume Pecola at the end. Morrison points out in a *Time* interview with Bonnie Angelo that white European immigrants gain their entrance into American society by sharing a common contempt for black people and "becoming American is based on an attitude: an exclusion of me" (120). Bearing this brunt of racial contempt, Pecola becomes nonexistent to the middle-aged white immigrant storekeeper. Sensing this personal threat, Pecola reacts to the white distaste by trashing the dandelions as "ugly" and "weeds," with which she just has had one of her rare moments of intimacy. She also consumes the Mary Jane candy purchased from the white man's store, more for the smiling white face, blond hair and blue eyes on the wrapping than for the taste of caramel and peanut butter. "To eat the candy is somehow to eat the eyes, eat Mary Jane. Love Mary Jane. Be Mary Jane," (43) the narrator reveals Pecola's inner consciousness. This double reaction again reflects Pecola's parental heritage—transferring anger to the defenseless and the internalization of white ideology.

Pecola's humiliation in Geraldine's house provides the reader a glimpse of the derogatory side of Afro-American culture in the name of "uplifting the race." Zora Neale Hurston delineates the psychology of the black middle class who have internalized white ideology and snubbed their own people in "My People! My People!":

> the well-bred Negro has looked around and seen America with his eyes. He or she has set himself to measure up to what he thinks of as the white standard of living. He is conscious of the fact that the Negro in America needs more respect if he expects to get any acceptance at all. Therefore, after straining every nerve to get an education, maintain an attractive home, dress decently, and otherwise conform, he is dismayed at the sight of other Negroes tearing down what he is trying to build up. It is said everyday, "And that good-for-nothing, trashy Negro is the one the white people judge us all by. They think we're all just alike. My people! My people!"
>
> (23)

This looking up to white standard and looking down upon "trashy" blacks manifest another kind of mental colonization and develop a tension of mutual distrust between the black middle class and the poor black. Geraldine represents this false sense of racial uplifting. Here Morrison openly criticizes black women like Geraldine who attained middle-class status through learning "how to do white man's work with refinement" and "how to get rid of funkiness. The dreadful funkiness of passion, the funkiness of nature, the funkiness of the wide range of human emotions" (68). The "funkiness," as Susan Willis contends, originates in the discontinuity between past and present (*Specifying* 84)—the past of an agrarian South that needs to be kept out in this Northern industrial town. Pecola's appearance in Geraldine's house is like a return of the repressed funkiness. And Geraldine's hysteria is triggered by an instinctive sense of how easily her simulacrum of a bourgeois urbanity can be shattered and turned to waste. In view of her loveless relationship with her husband and child, the light-skinned Geraldine is the crystallization of this proper but passionless, unnatural and emotionless "colored" bourgeoisie. Through Geraldine's education of Junior about the difference between "colored people and niggers," Morrison also criticizes the falsity of a caste system based on skin color and the danger of over-assimilation. "The line between colored and nigger was not always clear;" the narrator speaks in the tone of all the Geraldines, "subtle and telltale signs threatened to erode it, and the watch had to be constant" (71). These subtle and telltale signs, Morrison implies, are the threat of return of the repressed Afro-American experiences that will disrupt the false facade of bourgeois respectability at any minute.

Pecola's encounter with this "colored" respectability is as devastating as her experience of racism. Even after her humiliating "false spring" experience with the high-yellow dream-child Maureen Peal, Pecola remains dominated by the ideology of the Look. Inside Geraldine's house we see Pecola's unrestrained admiration of the appearance of middle-class respectability represented by the Bible, lace dollies, the decorated picture of Jesus, and potted plants. In spite of her misery after being bullied by Junior she finds consolation in the cat's "blue eyes." Her exile from the gold-and-green "paradise" is under the full gaze of Jesus's "sad and unsurprised eyes" (76). In both cases Morrison underscores Pecola's self-objectification through stressing the influence of alien "eyes" on her. As Ho Wen-ching aptly argues, since she is trapped in "the bifurcate situation of 'I' versus 'them,' Pecola in her endeavour to transcend the I/them bifurcation has come to equate 'I' with 'eye'" (4). She pays for this mistaken identification with her own sanity.

Right before her final breakdown, Pecola, desperately trying to save her world by getting the bluest eyes, visits the self-claimed spiritual adviser Soaphead Church. The atrocity of Soaphead's tricking Pecola into poisoning an old dog is comparable only to Cholly's rape of Pecola. Both Soaphead and Cholly act out of oxymoronic feelings of sympathetic tenderness and destructive violence. Moreover, Soaphead's West Indian past as a mulatto descendant of an English nobleman at once suggests the heterogenous experiences of black diaspora and an implied colonial discourse that has not been fully developed in *The Bluest Eye*. In Soaphead we observe how an offspring and victim of colonization turns into a victimizer. Soaphead transfers his legacy of misery of being a colonized into Pecola. An act which, like Cholly's transference of anger unto Darlene and Pauline, intensifies the sense of multiple jeopardy of being, black, being female, and being a social underclass in the text.

Ugly to herself, invisible to the white, and funky to the "colored," Pecola remains undeveloped and a victim to the labyrinth of her multiple experiences. In her madness Pecola becomes a fixture around the garbage heap, which bleakly reflects on another of her paternal heritages since as a newborn Cholly was abandoned in a dumpster. The difference between the father and daughter is that there is no Aunt Jimmy, as in the case of Cholly Breedlove, to rescue Pecola.

II. Claudia Macteer

In "Lady No Longer Sings the Blues," Madonne M. Miner compares the rape of Pecola to the archetypal rape story of Philomela. Unlike the rape victim in the classical myth, however, silent Pecola does not find her "voice" in her insanity. Claudia, and her creator Morrison, are the ones who weave the telling tapestry. Claudia's first-person narrative serves as counter-discourse to Pecola's story of silent victimization. Her narrative voices function as "choral note" in Greek tragedy, as Morrison herself contends (**"Rootedness"** 341.) Claudia is also a would-be Afro-American "griot" figure who passes on wisdom through storytelling. As Janie reveals the story of her growth with "that oldest human longing—self revelation" in *Their Eyes Were Watching God* (18), Claudia consciously retells the story that changes herself and her community permanently. In her storytelling Claudia is also reminiscent of the compulsive storyteller in Coleridge's supernatural narrative poem *The Rime of the Ancient Mariner*. Claudia's sense of guilt for not saving Pecola and her child is the albatross around her neck that propels her to repeat the story. She actually undergoes a process of self-healing when retelling this painful experience of her past. The self-division in her narrative reveals the construction of her personal *Bildungsroman* even as she is apparently telling Pecola's story. Claudia herself, like the reader, becomes sadder but wiser once the unspeakable tale is spoken.

Claudia starts her story, as Morrison herself identifies, with mimicking adult black women on the porch or in the back yard and trying to be grown-up about the shocking information of Pecola's incestuous rape (**"Unspeakable"** 21). Although she appears to be still childish in believing the rape as the cause of the disappearance of marigolds, there is a marked difference between Claudia's behavior before and after the rape. The heaviness of her language is one evidence. In the prologue Claudia states, "What is clear now is that all of that hope, fear, lust, love, and grief, nothing remains but Pecola and the unyielding earth" (9). With this note marking an aura of postlapsarian sterility, the "mature" Claudia proposes to tell *why* but immediately takes refuge in *how*. Clearly Claudia's own sense of guilt still prevents her from looking into the real reasons for Pecola's tragedy. But Claudia cannot reach a certain maturity without first coming to terms with the disintegration of Pecola, and moreover, her own helplessness to revoke Pecola's tragic fate.

The narrative of prelapsarian Claudia is in direct contrast to Pecola's in the aspects of personal, racial, and cultural experiences. Although Claudia is of the same class as Pecola, her family works hard to keep themselves "indoors." Unlike Pecola, Claudia learns love, self-respect, and a sense of security from her parents. The MacTeer house resembles what bell hooks terms "homeplace," the site of resistance to white supremacy and the space for renewal and self-recovery (*Yearning* 41). Claudia describes her parents in the "Autumn" and "Winter" sections of the novel. But the temper of the weather only reflects the stress that the MacTeers have to endure in the face of poverty and depression. Inside, Claudia's parents are fighters who lovingly guard their family.

Mrs. MacTeer's unselfish maternal love is the very opposite of the barrenness and self-righteousness of Pauline. Claudia's memory of her sickness during the autumn is oxymoronically "a productive and fructifying pain." Mrs. MacTeer's sustaining "thick and dark" love is the medicine that helps her daughter to fight for her health. Hence in spite of the bitter weather Claudia confesses that "when I think of autumn I think of somebody with hands who does not want me to die" (14). Mrs. MacTeer's maternity also extends to Pecola, whom she dutifully takes in as a case. Significantly, it is Mrs. MacTeer who assumes the maternal role and helps Pecola to adjust to the "horror" of her first menstruation. Mrs. MacTeer is also closely connected to her Afro-American roots, as exemplified in her constant singing of the blues, which are songs that channel personal suffering and forge "a communal consciousness" for the Afro-American, as Angela Davis observes (12).

Unlike Cholly who only inflicts pain on the helpless, Claudia's father functions as his family's guardian. Claudia describes her father in the epithets of winter:

> My daddy's face is a study. Winter moves into it and presides there. His eyes become a cliff of snow threatening to avalanche; his eyebrows bend like black limbs of leafless trees. His skin takes on the pale, cheerless yellow of winter sun; for a jaw he has the edges of a snowbound field dotted with

stubble; his high forehead is the frozen sweep of the Erie, hiding currents of gelid thoughts that eddy in darkness. Wolf killer turned hawk fighter, he worked night and day to keep one from the door and the other from under the windowsills.

(52)

But next in Claudia's portrayal he suddenly turns into the very opposite of wintriness and becomes a "Vulcan guarding the flames" to keep his family warm. From Claudia's poetic illustration we detect a strong sense of security in the MacTeer household. Just like the healing power of the mother's hands, Mr. MacTeer battles to keep his family from harm. So when the tenant Mr. Henry sexually molested Frieda, Mr. MacTeer threw the girls' tricycle at his head, knocked him off the porch, and tried to gun him down. This incident with Mr. Henry has a realistic equivalence in Morrison's own life. In an interview with Rosemarie K. Lester, Morrison describes her first racial encounter as the time when her father pushed a white stalker downstairs and threw a bike at him (50). By transferring this sense of racial triumph onto MacTeer, Morrison creates a strong, responsible father figure who serves as a sharp contrast to the "free" Cholly Breedlove.

But most importantly, Claudia has a sister. Unlike Pecola's nonexistent brother, Claudia is closely bonded with Frieda. Together the MacTeer sisters combat adversity. For example, they always did their Candy Dance to make their white neighbor jealous (63). Claudia even starts her storytelling with a plural "we" to signify the experiences she and her sister have shared together. Therefore, when Frieda is molested, Claudia is empathic to her fear of being "ruined" (81). We might smile at the sisters' naivete about sexuality, but Frieda's molestation puts the MacTeer girls in the similar position with Pecola as potential victims. What differentiates Claudia's from Pecola's narrative of victimization, however, is the father's protection and Claudia's resistance.

Claudia escapes victimization partially because she resists the racial ideology of white physical supremacy, although as a child she could not articulate exactly the work of mental colonization around her. Her hatred of the mass media icon Shirley Temple and her desire to dismember white baby dolls, even white girls, manifest this resistance which takes a destructive channel:

I had only one desire: to dismember it. To see what it was made [of], to discover the dearness, to find the beauty, the desirability that has escaped me, but apparently only me. Adults, older girls, shops,

magazines, newspapers, window signs all the world had agreed that a blue-eyed, yellow-haired, pink-skinned doll was what every girl child treasured.

(20)

Claudia's ignorance of this "desirability" is what keeps her from racial neurosis. In her state of innocence, she is immune from the inferiority complex that Fanon has diagnosed. So when she encounters Maureen Peal, a "colored" embodiment of the white doll, Claudia is just curious about what "the *Thing*" is that makes Maureen beautiful. At this stage Claudia is still in love with her self image and feels comfortable in her skin, as the narrator informs us (62). Claudia's desire to understand "the *Thing*" appears to be a positive act of exposing a racist unconsciousness that dominant society has hammered into the minds of minority people. However, the intensity of Claudia's reaction to the dolls and the Maureen Peals make the reader pause. In her violent response we see the backfire of racism which in real life becomes hurtful racial uprisings. Then again, what other channels do black people have to express their frustration and anger? In Claudia's childish reaction we detect a tragic reality that violence generates violence.

In time, Claudia, too, will experience the same kind of racial vertigo as Pecola does. She will sense the same kind of "blue void" that has consumed Pecola. Only the gaze of the bluest eye is reflected in the brown eyes around her:

Dolls we could destroy, but we could not destroy the honey voices of parents and aunts, the obedience in the eyes of our peers, the slippery light in the eyes of our teachers when they encountered the Maureen Peals of the world.

(61-2)

And she, too, will be educated by this sense of racial "lack" through a mirror stage of racial inferiority into unconditional admiration of white beauty once she reaches "the turning point" in the development of her psyche. Here Morrison injects a pessimistic note into Claudia's and all minority girls' narratives of *Bildung*. None can escape mental contamination and colonization as long as minority people see through the "eye" of mainstream ideology.

But before Claudia's racial innocence is "ruined" by commodified racial ideology, she feels closely connected to her blackness. For instance, her simple wish for Christmas is to indulge her senses in Big Mama's kitchen with Big Papa playing the violin (21). That is, Claudia would rather have close bonding to her own cultural community on the most special day of the year. Unlike Pecola, who is practically an outsider, Claudia is rooted within the context of her Afro-American community. Claudia's rootedness is represented by the MacTeer girls' sifting through the gossip they overheard to learn practical, though often discredited, wisdom. Claudia describes the dances of gossiping voices around her:

> sound meets sound, curtsies shimmers, and retires. Another sound enters but is upstaged by still another: the two circle each other and stop. Sometimes their words move in lofty spirals; other times they take strident leaps, and all of it is punctuated with warm-pulsed laughter—like the throb of a heart made of jelly.
>
> (16)

The combination of music, visual effects, and taste in the description of gossip provides an immediacy of the abundant sensuality, as in Paule Marshall's kitchen table conversations. In the orality, musicality and imaginativeness of gossip Morrison finds the real metaphor for a "black quality" that she is striving for in her writing, as she has indicated in an interview with Nellie McKay (427). In **The Bluest Eye** Morrison creates her own "speakerly text," in the term of Henry Louis Gates, Jr.

But gossip, like the community itself, is double-edged. They can both be sustaining and devastating. The feelings of disgust, shock, outrage, even excitement, but total lack of compassion in the gossip about Pecola and the rape represent the negative side of gossip and the community. Claudia voices a disappointment in her community in this regard: when she and Frida try to look for "eyes creased with concern" about the unfortunate Pecola, they see "only veils" (148). The contrast between an omnipresent gaze of the blue eyes and the veiled apathy of the brown eyes further highlights the hostile environment to the growth of a black girl. In "Trajectories of Self-Definition," Barbara Christian classifies Morrison's **The Bluest Eye** as belonging to the second phase of contemporary Afro-American women's writing in which "the black community itself becomes a major threat to the survival and empowerment of women" (24). The unsympathetic community, therefore, also contributes to the general sterility in the fall of 1941.

So by the end of her narrative Claudia learns her lesson about racial ideology and her own community as an accomplice in upholding this ideological construct:

> This soil is bad for certain kind of flowers. Certain seeds it will not nurture, certain fruit it will not bear, and when the land kills its own volition, we acquiesce and say the victim had no right to live.
>
> (160)

Claudia's marigolds may not live; but she survives to tell the stories of two black girls. Claudia's fall, in a sense, is a fortunate fall (*felix culpa*) since innocence is a sign of "degenerate acquiesce," as Terry Otten contends (4). By dividing Claudia into an innocent child and an older and wiser person, Morrison inscribes Claudia's *Bildung* into the novel which counterpoints Pecola's decline.

Morrison sees a weakness of form in her first novel. The combination of seasonal cycles and fragments of the primer, Morrison observes in retrospect, does not sufficiently handle the silence at its center: "The *void* that is Pecola's 'unbeing'." ("**Unspeakable Things Unspoken**" 22, italic mine). But Morrison does represent the void in the shape of a consuming vortex, with the intersection of Claudia and Pecola's lives at the center. Pecola is drawn into the abyss because of her passivity; Claudia surfaces because she resists the pull. Furthermore, by transferring Pecola from "unbeing" to a "being" in her schizophrenic hallucination, Morrison makes a political inquiry into the nature of *Bildung* for black girls—*How* come a black girl can only *see* herself with imagined blue eyes? In **The Bluest Eye** Morrison reveals the detriment of oppression through the tragedy of one black girl. She also explores the role that the ideology of "whiteness" plays in the imagination and real life of black people.[10] While political activists campaign for civil rights and power for black people, Morrison locates the source of black powerlessness in white racism and black acquiescence. But she also implies that neither racial whitewash nor chanting the slogan of "Black is Beautiful" is enough to counteract the Look. The former only intensifies the neurotic symptoms of racial inferiority complex; the latter is just a reversal of the mainstream ideology of "White *is* Beautiful." Morrison writes to challenge the reader's literary imagination and social consciousness. She also writes to open the eyes of both dominant and minority communities. Thus Morrison, even in her first attempt, fulfills her self-assigned mission for the novelist, to write a fiction that is both *political* and *beautiful* ("**Rootedness**" 345).

Notes

1. Elliott Butler-Evans has a similar reading of the novel. He sees Morrison develop dominant themes through the interplay of two narratives: Claudia's rite of passage and Pecola's disintegration (66). Joanne Frye and

Linda Krumholz also argue that Claudia narrates not only the destruction of Pecola but also her own self-formation.

2. Buckley not only compares the development between Maggie and her brother but also draws a parallel of this competing double plot with the real-life sibling disagreement between Eliot and her brother.

3. Out of her analysis of *Wuthering Heights, The Mill on the Floss, My Antonia, The Mountain Lion,* and *them,* Goodman deduces that the structure of the "male-female double *Bildungsroman*" is circular, tripartite. Its typical plot starts from the shared prelapsarian childhood experience of a male and a female protagonist, to the separation in adolescence and young adulthood, and ends with a final reunion with a reaffirmation of androgynous wholeness (30).

4. I borrow the term of "growing down" from Annis Pratt and Barbara White's "The Novel of Development" to illustrate Pecola's anti-*Bildung*. Pratt and White identify a generic double bind in female *Bildungsroman* that the female protagonists oftentimes regress from full participation in adult life rather than progressing towards maturity (36).

5. See Hazel Carby's *Reconstructing Womanhood* (20).

6. bell hooks gives a vivid portrayal of the damaged psyche of black people faced with the Look: "for black people, the pain of learning that we cannot control our images, how we see ourselves (if our vision is not colonized), or how we are seen is so intense that it rends us. It rips and tears at the seams of our efforts to construct self and identity. Often it leaves us ravaged by repressed rage, feeling weary, dispirited, and sometimes just plain old brokenhearted. These are the gaps in our psyche that are the spaces where mindless complicity, self-destructive rage, hatred, and paralyzing despair enter" (*Black Looks* 3-4).

7. Nicknaming functions as personal recognition in black communities. Pauline's attachment to the Fisher family, as Trudier Harris points out, is guided by a perversion of this function (20). Ironically, the Fishers give her this generic nickname not out of intimacy but out of convenience, as the plantation masters used to treat their slaves, which explains Claudia's antagonism when the Fisher girl calls Pauline by her nickname while even Pauline's family call her Mrs. Breedlove (86).

8. Fanon points out, "When the Negro makes contact with the white world, a certain sensitizing action takes place. If his psychic structure is weak, one observes a collapse of the ego. The black man stops behaving as an *actional* person. The goal of his behaviour will be The Other (in the guise of the white man), for the Other alone can give him worth" (154).

9. Madonne M. Miner sees this breaking down of familial boundaries as archetypal. She argues that "the female must fear a loss of identity as the family loses it boundaries—or, more accurately, as the male transgresses these boundaries" (178).

10. In her analytical essay *Playing in the Dark* Morrison explores the other end of the question—how racial ideology and "blackness" influence the literary imagination of the white masters.

Works Cited

Angelo, Bonnie. "The Pain of Being Black: An Interview with Toni Morrison." *Time* 22 May 1989: 120-22.

Awkward, Michael. "Roadblocks and Relatives: Critical Vision in Toni Morrison's *The Bluest Eye.*" *Critical Essays on Toni Morrison.* Ed. Nellie McKay. Boston: G. K. Hall, 1988. 57-68.

Barthes, Roland. "The Death of the Author." *Image-Music-Text.* Trans. Stephen Heath. New York: Hill & Wang, 1977. 142-8.

——. *S/Z.* Trans. Richard Miller. New York: Hill and Wang, 1974.

Buckley, Jerome Hamilton, *Season of Youth: The Bildungsroman from Dickens to Golding.* Cambridge: Harvard UP, 1974.

Butler-Evans, Elliott. *Race, Gender and Desire: Narrative Strategies in the Fiction of Toni Cade Bambara, Toni Morrison and Alice Walker.* Philadelphia: Temple UP, 1989.

Carby, Hazel V. *Reconstructing Womanhood: The Emergence of the Afro-American Woman Novelist.* New York: Oxford UP, 1987.

Christian, Barbara. "Trajectories of Self-Definition: Placing Contemporary Afro-American Women's Fiction." *Conjuring: Black Women, Fiction, and Literary Tradition.* Eds. Majorie Pryse and Hortense Spillers. Bloomington: Indiana UP, 1985. 233-48.

Cormier-Hamilton, Patrice. "Black Naturalism and Toni Morrison: The Journey Away from Self-Love in *The Bluest Eye.*" *MELUS* 19.4 (Winter 1994): 109-27.

Davis, Angela Y. "Black Women and Music: A Historical Legacy of Struggle." *Wild Women in the Whirlwind.* Ed. Joanne M. Braxton and Andren Nicoln Mclaughlin. New Brunswick, N.J.: Rutgers UP, 1990. 3-21.

De Lauretis, Teresa. *Alice Doesn't: Feminism, Semiotics, Cinema.* Bloomington: Indiana UP, 1984.

Ellison, Ralph. *Invisible Man.* 1947. New York: Signet, 1952.

Fanon, Franz. *Black Skin, White Masks.* Trans. Charles Lam Markmann. New York: Grove Press, 1967.

Fraiman, Susan. *Unbecoming Women: British Women Writers and The Novel of Development.* New York: Columbia UP, 1993.

Freire, Paulo. *Pedagogy of the Oppressed.* Trans. Myra Bergman Ramos. New York: Herder and Herder, 1972.

Frye, Joanne S. *Living Stories, Telling Lives: Women and the Novel in Contemporary Experience.* Ann Arbor: U of Michigan P, 1986.

Gibson, Donald. "Text and Countertext in Toni Morrison's *The Bluest Eye.*" *Toni Morrison: Critical Perspectives Past and Present.* Eds. Henry Louis Gates, Jr. and K. A. Appiah. New York: Amistad, 1993. 159-74.

Goodman, Charlotte. "The Lost Brother, the Twin: Women Novelists and the Male-Female Double *Bildungsroman.*" *Novel* 17.1 (1983): 28-43.

Harris, Trudier. *Fiction and Folklore: The Novels of Toni Morrison.* Knoxville: The U of Tennessee P, 1991.

Ho, Wen-ching. "In Search of A Female Self: Toni Morrison's *The Bluest Eye* and Maxine Hong Kingston's *The Woman Warrior, American Studies* 17.3 (1987): 1-44.

hooks, bell. *Black Looks: Race and Representation.* Boston: South End Press, 1991.

———. *Yearning: Race, Gender, Cultural Politics.* Boston: South End Press, 1990.

Hurston, Zora Neale. "My People! My People!" *Mother Wit and the Laughing Barrel.* Ed. Alan Dundes. Englewood Cliffs: Prentice Hall, 1973. 23-33.

———. *Their Eyes Were Watching God.* 1937. Urbana and Chicago: U of Illinois P, 1987.

Kogawa, Joy. *Obasan.* 1981. Boston: Godine, 1984.

Krumholz, Linda Joan. "Ritual, Reader, and Narrative in the Works of Leslie Marmon and Toni Morrison." Diss. U of Wisconsin-Madison, 1991.

Marshall, Paule. "From the Poets in the Kitchen." *New York Times Book Review* 9 January 1983: 3.

McKay, Nellie. "An Interview with Toni Morrison." *Contemporary Literature.* 24 (Winter 1983): 413-29.

Miner, Madonne. "Lady No longer Sings the Blues: Rape, Madness and Silence in *The Bluest Eye.*" *Conjuring: Black Women Fiction and Literary Tradition.* Ed. Majorie Pryse and Hortense J. Spillers. Bloomington, Indiana: Indiana UP, 1985. 176-91.

Morrison, Toni. *The Bluest Eye.* 1970. New York: Washington Square Press, 1972.

———. *Playing in The Dark: Whiteness and the Literary Imagination.* Cambridge: Harvard UP, 1992.

———. "Rootedness: The Ancestor as Foundation." *Black Women Writers, 1950-1980: A Critical Evaluation.* Ed. Mari Evans. Garden City, N.Y.: Anchor Press, 1984.

———. "Unspeakable Things Unspoken: The Afro-American Presence in American Literature." *Michigan Quarterly Review* 38 (Winter 1989): 1-34.

Ogunyemi, Chiwenye. "Womanism: The Dynamics of the Contemporary Black Female Novel in English." *Signs* 11 (1985): 63-80.

Otten, Terry. *The Crime of Innocence in the Fiction of Toni Morrison.* Columbia: U of Missouri P, 1989.

Samuels, Wilfred D. and Clenora Hudson-Weems. *Toni Morrison.* Boston: Twayne Publishers, 1990.

Smith, Valerie. "Toni Morrison's Narratives of Community." *Self Discovery and Authority in Afro-American Narrative.* Cambridge, Mass.: Harvard UP, 1987. 122-53.

———. "Black Feminist Theory and the Representation of the 'Other'." *Changing Our Own Words.* Ed. Cheryl Wall. New Brunswick: Rutgers UP, 1989. 38-57.

Walker, Alice. *Possessing the Secret of Joy.* New York: HBJ, 1992.

Willis, Susan. *Specifying: Black Women Writing the American Experience.* Madison: The U of Madison P, 1987.

FURTHER READING

Bibliographies

Middleton, David L. *Toni Morrison: An Annotated Bibliography.* New York: Garland Publishing, Inc., 1987, 186 p.

Includes considerable criticism on Morrison's first four novels, as well as other writings, interviews, and anthologies.

Mix, Debbie. "Toni Morrison: A Selected Bibliography." *Modern Fiction Studies* 39, nos. 3-4 (fall-winter 1993): 795-818.

Bibliography covering selected criticism on Morrison's novels.

Criticism

Beaulieu, Elizabeth Ann. "Gendering the Genderless: The Case of Toni Morrison's *Beloved.*" *Obsidian II* 8, no. 1 (spring-summer 1993): 1-17.

Examines the blurring of conventional notions of gender in Beloved.

Bell, Bernard W. "*Beloved*: A Womanist Neo-Slave Narrative; or Multivocal Remembrances of Things Past." In *Critical Essays on Toni Morrison's "Beloved,"* edited by Barbara H. Solomon, pp. 166-76. New York: G. K. Hall & Co., 1998.

Examination of Beloved *as a black feminist text that gives voice to those silenced by slavery.*

Bidney, Martin. "Creating a Feminist-Communitarian Romanticism in *Beloved*: Toni Morrison's New Uses for Blake, Keats, and Wordsworth." *Papers on Language & Literature* 36, no. 3 (summer 2000): 271-301.

Contends that critics generally ignore Morrison's regeneration of the work of the major British romantic poets in Beloved.

Dickerson, Vanessa D. "Summoning SomeBody: The Flesh Made Word in Toni Morrison's Fiction." In *Recovering the Black Female Body: Self-Representations by African American Women,* edited by Michael Bennett and Vanessa D. Dickerson, pp. 195-216. New Brunswick, N.J.: Rutgers University Press, 2001.

Analysis of how Morrison's characters recover and repossess the black female body.

Duvall, John N. "Descent in the 'House of Chloe': Race, Rape, and Identity in *Tar Baby.*" In *The Identifying Fictions of Toni Morrison,* pp. 99-117. New York: Palgrave, 2000.

Discusses the importance of Morrison's fourth novel, the critically neglected Tar Baby, *and its intertextual references to the Book of Genesis.*

Eckard, Paula Gallant. "Toni Morrison." In *Maternal Body and Voice in Toni Morrison, Bobbie Ann Mason, and Lee Smith,* pp. 33-37. Columbia: University of Missouri Press, 2002.

Explores how Morrison combines myth and reality in her treatment of maternal experience in The Bluest Eye, Sula, *and* Beloved.

Furman, Jan. "Black Girlhood and Black Womanhood: *The Bluest Eye* and *Sula.*" In *Toni Morrison's Fiction,* pp. 12-33. Columbia, S.C.: University of South Carolina Press, 1996.

Explores the roles that black girls and women in The Bluest Eye *and* Sula *play within their respective communities.*

Galehouse, Maggie. "'New World Woman': Toni Morrison's *Sula.*" *Papers on Language & Literature* 35, no. 4 (fall 1999): 339-62.

Explores the independent nature of Sula's *title character and raises questions about her accessibility to the reader.*

Gillespie, Diane and Missy Dehn Kubitschek. "Who Cares? Women-Centered Psychology in *Sula.*" In *Toni Morri-*

son's Fiction: Contemporary Criticism, edited by David L. Middleton, pp. 61-91. New York: Garland, 1997.

Praises Morrison's representation of female psychological development in Sula.

Iyasere, Solomon O. and Marla W. Iyasere, eds. *Understanding Toni Morrison's Beloved and Sula: Selected Essays and Criticisms of the Works by the Nobel Prize-winning Author.* Troy, N.Y.: Whitston Pub. Co., 2000, 381 p.

Thorough examination of Morrison's works, including a lengthy bibliographic resource.

McDowell, Deborah E. "'The Self and the Other': Reading Toni Morrison's *Sula* and the Black Female Text." In *Critical Essays on Toni Morrison,* edited by Nellie Y. McKay, pp. 77-90. Boston: G. K. Hall & Co., 1988.

Maintains that in Sula, *Morrison creates a different kind of identity for the black female in America.*

McKay, Nellie. "An Interview with Toni Morrison." *Contemporary Literature* 24, no. 4 (winter 1983): 413-29.

McKay talks with Morrison about black women's writing and her first four novels.

Mitchell, Angelyn. "'Sth, I Know That Woman': History, Gender, and the South in Toni Morrison's *Jazz.*" *Studies in the Literary Imagination* 31, no. 2 (fall 1998): 49-60.

Asserts that in Jazz, *Morrison fuses her primary concerns: the lives of black women and the historical circumstances of life in the South.*

Peterson, Nancy J. "Toni Morrison Double Issue." *Modern Fiction Studies* 39, nos. 3-4 (fall-winter 1993): 461-794.

A special double issue containing essays by a variety of critics on Morrison's novels and her place in the literary canon.

Rigney, Barbara Hill. *The Voices of Toni Morrison.* Columbus: Ohio State University Press, 1991, 127 p.

Examination of Morrison's position within the discourses of both race and gender.

Storhoff, Gary. "'Anaconda Love': Parental Enmeshment in Toni Morrison's *Song of Solomon.*" *Style* 31, no. 2 (summer 1997): 290-309.

An examination of the dysfunctional families—both matriarchal and patriarchal—that populate Song of Solomon.

Taylor-Guthrie, Danille, ed. *Conversations with Toni Morrison,* Jackson: University Press of Mississippi, 1994, 293 p.

Collection of interviews and conversations between Morrison and various authors and critics including Alice Childress, Robert Stepto, Gloria Naylor, and Bill Moyers.

Trace, Jacqueline. "Dark Goddesses: Black Feminist Theology in Morrison's *Beloved.*" *Obsidian II* 6, no. 3 (winter 1991): 14-30.

Discussion of specific qualities of black feminism and theology in Beloved *treating Morrison's use of goddess mythology and its contribution to a new theology for African American women.*

Wagner, Linda W. "Toni Morrison: Mastery of Narrative." In *Contemporary American Women Writers: Narrative Strategies,* edited by Catherine Rainwater and William J. Scheick, pp. 191-204. Lexington: University Press of Kentucky, 1985.

Critical assessment of the narrative techniques employed by Morrison in her first four novels.

OTHER SOURCES FROM GALE:

Additional coverage of Morrison's life and career is contained in the following sources published by the Gale Group: *African-American Writers,* Eds. 1, 2; *American Writers: The Classics,* Vol. 1; *American Writers Supplement,* Vol. 3; *Authors and Artists for Young Adults,* Vols. 1, 22; *Beacham's Encyclopedia of Popular Fiction: Biography and Resources,* Vol. 2; *Black Literature Criticism; Black Writers,* Eds. 2, 3; *Concise Dictionary of American Literary Biography, 1968-1988; Contemporary Authors,* Vols. 29-32R; *Contemporary Authors New Revision Series,* Vols. 27, 42, 67, 113; *Contemporary Literary Criticism,* Vols. 4, 10, 22, 55, 81, 87, 173; *Contemporary Novelists,* Ed. 7; *Contemporary Popular Writers; Dictionary of Literary Biography,* Vols. 6, 33, 143; *Dictionary of Literary Biography Yearbook,* 1981; *DISCovering Authors; DISCovering Authors: British Edition; DISCovering Authors: Canadian Edition; DISCovering Authors Modules: Most-studied, Multicultural, Novelists* and *Popular Writers; DISCovering Authors 3.0; Encyclopedia of World Literature in the 20th Century,* Ed. 3; *Exploring Novels; Feminist Writers; Literary Movements for Students,* Vol. 2; *Literature and Its Times,* Vols. 2, 4; *Literature and Its Times Supplement,* Ed. 1; *Literature Resource Center; Major 20th-Century Writers,* Eds. 1, 2; *Modern American Women Writers; Novels for Students,* Vols. 1, 6, 8, 14; *Reference Guide to American Literature,* Ed. 4; *St. James Guide to Young Adult Writers; Short Stories for Students,* Vol. 5; *Something about the Author,* Vols. 57, 144; *Twayne's United States Authors;* and *Twentieth-Century Romance and Historical Writers.*

JOYCE CAROL OATES

(1938 -)

(Also has written under the pseudonym Rosamond Smith) American novelist, short story writer, poet, playwright, essayist, critic, and editor.

One of America's most prolific and versatile contemporary writers, Oates began her literary career in 1963. Since then she has published more than twenty-five novels; hundreds of short stories in both collections and anthologies; nearly a dozen volumes of poetry; several books of nonfiction, literary criticism, and essays; and many dramas and screenplays. Writing in a dense, elliptical style that ranges from realistic to naturalistic to surrealistic, Oates concentrates on the spiritual, sexual, and intellectual malaise of modern American culture in her fiction, exposing the darker aspects of the human condition. Her tragic and violent plots abound with incidents of rape, incest, murder, mutilation, child abuse, and suicide, and her protagonists often suffer as a result of the conditions of their social milieu or their emotional weaknesses. This is especially true of her female characters, who are portrayed as dysfunctional, passive, and vulnerable to exploitation and abuse in a male-dominated society. For this reason feminist critics consider Oates a controversial figure, because she has created few strong, independent female role models in her numerous works.

BIOGRAPHICAL INFORMATION

Born in Lockport, New York, Oates was raised on her grandparents' farm in Erie County, a region that is represented in much of her fiction as Eden County. A bookish, serious child, she first submitted a novel to a publisher at the age of fifteen. Oates attended Syracuse University on a scholarship and graduated Phi Beta Kappa in 1960; the following year she earned a master's degree at the University of Wisconsin and married Raymond Smith, a former English professor. From 1962 to 1968 the couple lived in Detroit, where Oates taught at the University of Detroit and published her first novels, short story collections, and poetry. She also witnessed the 1967 race riots in Detroit, which inspired her National Book Award-winning novel *them* (1969). Shortly thereafter, Oates accepted a teaching position at the University of Windsor, Ontario, staying until 1978, when she was named a writer-in-residence at Princeton University; she joined the faculty there as a professor in 1987. Despite the responsibilities of an academic career, Oates has actively pursued writing, publishing an average of two books a year in various genres since the publication of her first book, the short story collection *By the North Gate* (1963). Her early novels consistently earned nominations for the National Book Award, while her short fiction won several individual O. Henry Awards and the O. Henry Special Award for Continuing Achievement in both 1971 and 1986.

Oates has written poetry and is a regular contributor of essays and stories to scholarly journals, periodicals, and anthologies. She is also a respected literary critic whose work presents logical, sensitive analyses of her subjects. In 1987 she published the widely admired nonfiction study *On Boxing*, which led to at least one television appearance as a commentator for the sport. During the 1990s Oates gained additional recognition as a playwright for producing many plays off-Broadway and at regional theaters, including *The Perfectionist* (1993), which was nominated by the American Theatre Critics Association for best new play in 1994.

MAJOR WORKS

With Shuddering Fall (1964), Oates's first novel, foreshadows her preoccupation with violence and darkness, describing a destructive romance between a teenage girl and a thirty-year-old stock car driver that ends with his death by accident. Oates's best known and critically acclaimed early novels form an informal trilogy exploring three distinct segments of American society: *A Garden of Earthly Delights* (1967) chronicles the life of a migrant worker's daughter in rural Eden County; *Expensive People* (1967) exposes the superficial world of suburbia; and *them* presents the violent, degrading milieu of an inner-city Detroit family. Oates's novels of the 1970s explore American life and cultural institutions, combining social analysis with vivid psychological portraits of frustrated characters ranging from a brilliant surgeon (1971; *Wonderland*), a young attorney (1973; *Do with Me What You Will*), and the widow of a murdered conservative politician (1975; *The Assassins*) to religious zealots (1978; *Son of the Morning*) and distinguished visiting poets and feminist scholars (1979; *Unholy Loves*). Her short stories of this period, most notably in *Marriages and Infidelities* (1972), and *Where Are You Going, Where Have You Been?* (1974), considered by many to be her best work, concern themes of violence and abuse between the sexes. "Where Are You Going, Where Have You Been," for instance, tells of the sexual awakening of a romantic girl by a mysterious man, Alfred Friend; this story is considered a masterpiece of the modern short form and was adapted for film.

Oates's novels of the early 1980s—*Bellefleur* (1980), *A Bloodsmoor Romance* (1982), and *Mysteries of Winterthurn* (1984)—exploit the conventions of nineteenth-century Gothic literature as they examine such sensitive issues as crimes against women, children, and the poor, and the influence of family history on shaping destiny; likewise, many of her short stories rely on gothic elements, including those collected in *Haunted* (1994) and *First Love* (1996). Most of Oates's fiction of the 1980s features more explicit violence than does her earlier fiction, which tends more toward psychological afflictions, but psychological obsessions nevertheless persist. In *Marya* (1986), for example, a successful academic searches for her alcoholic mother who had abused her as a child, and in *You Must Remember This* (1987), a former boxer commits incest with his niece during the McCarthyist 1950s. Oates's works of the 1990s continue to address relations between violence and the cultural realities of American society. Other topics addressed in Oates's works include racism, affluence, alienation, poverty, classism, sexual-political power dynamics, feminism, success, serial killers, and familial conflicts. The series of mysteries published under the pseudonym of Rosamond Smith—*Lives of the Twins* (1988), *Soul/Mate* (1989), *Nemesis* (1990), *Snake Eyes* (1992), and *You Can't Catch Me* (1995)—concern the psychopathic exploits of aberrational academics.

CRITICAL RECEPTION

Commentators note that Oates occupies a controversial position in the feminist literary tradition. Her female characters are not considered feminist in nature: they are often dependent and passive and withdraw from sexual and emotional connections instead of articulating their needs and frustrations. Moreover, the abuse of women—sexually, physically, and emotionally—has been a recurring theme in Oates's work. Feminist critics view these female characters as masochistic and note the lack of strong, independent female role models in her fiction. Despite the general disregard of Oates as a feminist writer, a number of commentators have defended the feminist sensibility underlying much of her fiction. They trace her changing portrayals of gender power in her later work, contending that her more recent novels focus on the power of female bonds and self-discovery. A few critics have maintained that Oates's embittered portrayal of gender relations accurately mirrors a male-determined society. Although some critics have dismissed her gothic fiction as whimsical, others have suggested that it invigorates the gothic literary tradition, particularly feminist critics who often have likened Oates's ghosts to the cultural status of "invisible woman."

PRINCIPAL WORKS

By the North Gate (short stories) 1963

With Shuddering Fall (novel) 1964

The Sweet Enemy (drama) 1965

Upon the Sweeping Flood and Other Stories (short stories) 1966

Expensive People (novel) 1967

A Garden of Earthly Delights (novel) 1967

Women in Love and Other Poems (poetry) 1968

Love and Its Derangements and Other Poems (poetry) 1970

The Wheel of Love and Other Stories (short stories) 1970

Wonderland (novel) 1971

Marriages and Infidelities (short stories) 1972

Angel Fire (poetry) 1973

Do with Me What You Will (novel) 1973

The Goddess and Other Women (short stories) 1974

Miracle Play (drama) 1974

Where Are You Going, Where Have You Been?: Stories of Young America (short stories) 1974

The Assassins: A Book of Hours (novel) 1975

Childwold (novel) 1976

Triumph of the Spider Monkey: The First Person Confession of the Maniac Bobby Gotteson as Told to Joyce Carol Oates (novella) 1976

Son of the Morning (novel) 1978

Cybele (novel) 1979

Unholy Loves (novel) 1979

Bellefleur (novel) 1980

Angel of Light (novel) 1981

Contraries: Essays (nonfiction) 1981

A Sentimental Education (short stories) 1981

A Bloodsmoor Romance (novel) 1982

Invisible Woman: New and Selected Poems, 1970-1972 (poetry) 1982

Mysteries of Winterthurn (novel) 1984

Solstice (novel) 1985

Marya: A Life (novel) 1986

You Must Remember This (novel) 1987

Lives of the Twins [as Rosamond Smith] (novel) 1988

(Woman) Writer: Occasions and Opportunities (nonfiction) 1988

American Appetites (novel) 1989

Soul/Mate [as Rosamond Smith] (novel) 1989

The Time Traveler (poetry) 1989

Because It Is Bitter, and Because It Is My Heart (novel) 1990

I Lock the Door upon Myself (novel) 1990

Nemesis [as Rosamond Smith] (novel) 1990

The Rise of Life on Earth (novel) 1991

I Stand Before You Naked (drama) 1991

Black Water (novel) 1992

Heat: And Other Stories (short stories) 1992

Snake Eyes [as Rosamond Smith] (novel) 1992

Foxfire: Confessions of a Girl Gang (novel) 1993

The Perfectionist (drama) 1993

What I Lived For (novel) 1994

Will You Always Love Me? and Other Stories (short stories) 1995

You Can't Catch Me [as Rosamond Smith] (novel) 1995

Zombie (novel) 1995

First Love: A Gothic Tale (novel) 1996

Tenderness (novel) 1996

We Were the Mulvaneys (novel) 1996

Double Delight [as Rosamond Smith] (novel) 1997

Man Crazy (novel) 1997

My Heart Laid Bare (novel) 1998

Broke Heart Blues: A Novel (novel) 1999

The Collector of Hearts: New Tales of the Grotesque (short stories) 1999

Starr Bright Will Be with You Soon [as Rosamond Smith] (novel) 1999

Where I've Been, and Where I'm Going: Essays, Reviews, and Prose (essays and nonfiction) 1999

Blonde (novel) 2000

Faithless: Tales of Transgression (short stories) 2001

Middle Age: A Romance (novel) 2001

Beasts (novel) 2002

Big Mouth & Ugly Girl (novel) 2002

I'll Take You There (novel) 2002

Bad Girls (drama) 2003

The Faith of a Writer: Life, Craft, Art (nonfiction) 2003

Freaky Green Eyes (novel) 2003

Small Avalanches and Other Stories (short stories) 2003

Tattooed Girl (novel) 2003

Where is Little Reynard? (juvenilia) 2003

I Am No One You Know (short stories) 2004

PRIMARY SOURCES

JOYCE CAROL OATES (ESSAY DATE 1999)

SOURCE: Oates, Joyce Carol. "Where Is an Author?" In *Where I've Been, and Where I'm Going*, pp. 3-8. New York: Plume, 1999.

In the following essay, Oates debates the question of how much information a reader should know about the author of a work and finds the label of "woman writer" to be restrictive and frustrating.

The artist's life is his work, and this is the place to observe him.

—Henry James

It all came together between the hand and the page.
—Samuel Beckett (on the composition of *Waiting for Godot*)

Why do we write? Why do we read? Why is "art" crucial to human beings?

The engine that gives its mysterious inner life to a work of art must be the subterranean expression of a wish, working its way to the surface of narrative. In fairy tales and legends, the "wish" is often explicit: for a rendering of justice rare in life, for romance in the face of improbability, for a happy ending. In a more sophisticated art, the "wish" may be so buried as to be unacknowledged by the artist, or even repudiated. "Never trust the artist," D. H. Lawrence warned in his iconoclastic *Studies in Classic American Literature* (1923). "Trust the tale. The proper function of a critic is to save the tale from the artist who created it." Often, writers don't know what they're writing until they've completed it. For some of us, the composition of any sustained, structured work would not be possible if there wasn't a secret code or connection between the story (or what we call for lack of a more precise term "story") and an interior, hidden pattern. A sense, in a way visual, of the story's trajectory: where it begins, where it ends, its dominant images and tone. Though the act of writing can be emotionally volcanic, a white-hot frenzy in the initial process of creation, in its later stages, those of revision, recasting and restructuring, it is the most icy-cold of activities. "So cold, so icy, that one burns one's fingers on him! Every hand that touches him receives a shock. That is why some think he is burning hot." This aphorism of Friedrich Nietzsche's suggests the formalist's self-conception: the self as viewed from within. To present emotionally dynamic material is to confess that one *has felt,* and perhaps extremely, but is *not now feeling,* emotion.

Is the artist, by temperament, a perpetual antagonist to the crowd? the state? the prevailing ethos? This collision of the ethical/tribal/familial world and the world of the individual; the world of the individual soul and the universe of sheer numbers—"laws" of nature: This is the drama that arrests me, and haunts me, in life as in writing; in reverie, most keenly during insomniac fugues when "I" seems to dissolve, and an impersonal kernel of being, primarily one of inquiry, emerges. (For me, these fugues began in early adolescence.) In asking, like Lewis Carroll's child-heroine Alice, *Who am I?* am I really asking *Who, or what, is this "I" that asks this question, asked repeatedly, with such hope, yet perhaps futilely, through human history?* Is this "I" unique—or is it in essence identical with the multitude of other "I"s?—as we are presumably composed of identical matter, turn and turn about, mineral deposits from the stars of how many trillions of years ago, in varying compositions, except never varying in our temporality: "Oh Life, begun in fluent Blood, / And consummated dull!" (Emily Dickinson, 1130, c. 1868)

Or is this, too, a fiction?—an artfully constructed and sculpted wish? In the collision of the personal and the impersonal, in the arena where language and silence touch, the possibility of art arises like flame.

In 1969, the influential if much-misunderstood Michel Foucault published a speculative essay, "What Is an Author?" A kind of thought-experiment, generated perhaps more by political bias than disinterested aesthetic inquiry, this famous essay considered the ontological status of the writer; one might say, undermined it. (Yet only in theory, for since Foucault's time no writers, including theorists of the Foucault school, have surrendered their names on the spines of their books, nor their advances and royalties. As in hothouse plantings, bibliographies of even obscure writers flourish; but the plantings are discreetly fenced off from one another, and named.) Still the debate over what is called "authorial presence" continues, and has not been resolved, for, in such debates, it is language, or a critical vocabulary, that is at stake, and not a quantifiable reality. Roland Barthes and Jacques Derrida have argued, though not this succinctly, for the "death of the author"—the theoretical claim that "there is nothing outside the text"—"there is no center or integrated core from which we can say a piece of literature issues." (There is no Mozart from whom the music issues; there is the Mozartian text, which shares with other Mozartian texts certain characteristics, like voiceprints, or fingerprints, but no essential identity.)[1]

One might stand the theory on its head, as in a phantasmagoric scenario in which any and all things written by a "historic individual" (with name, fingerprints, DNA, etc.) are part of the oeuvre of the writer; not merely the revised, polished hardcover books he/she has nurtured into being with such determination. Certainly, collectors of manuscripts act upon this assumption, appalling to the writer: They are willing to pay high sums of money for minor work, juvenilia, letters tossed off in unguarded moments, mere jottings—for, one might argue, these are the truer testaments of the elusive self, because unmediated. If you are a writer of reputation you may argue eloquently, like T. S. Eliot, that art is in fact the "extinction of personality"; nonetheless, any original manuscript of yours, in your own inimitable hand, any embarrassing love letters, diary entries, in Eliot's case anti-Semitic and misogynist pornographic fantasies, will be worth far more than any chastely printed book with your name stamped on the spine. For human beings seem to honor instinctively the individual sui generis, despite philosophical theories arguing the nonexistence of individuals. To escape the prison house of identity, writers have often fled to pseudonyms in the hope that the text will be, simply, a text, with an anonymous-sounding name attached to which no prior assumptions accrue. To begin again!—to be born again!—not as an author, but purely as a text!

Yet it's symptomatic of our profoundly secularized era that, French theory and the "New" Historicism to the contrary, any and all biographical data can be applied to the writer as a "historic" individual; nothing too obscure, too mundane, too trivial, too demeaning is ruled out as an instrument of illumination into the writer's motive. (A well-regarded academic-literary journal recently printed an essay on Sylvia Plath's last poems interpreted in the light of premenstrual tension, for instance.) Massive contemporary biographies, bloated with unedited taped interviews, bury their ostensible subjects beneath a vertiginous mass of data, and the writer's forlorn plea *The artist's life is his work, and this is the place to observe him* is ignored. Yet, most writers will acknowledge that

they do not inhabit their books—the more clinical term is "texts"—once they have completed them; they—we—are expelled from them like any other reader, for the act of composition is time-bound, and time is an hourglass that runs in one direction only. To consider the text as an art work is to acknowledge that there can be nothing outside the text. Authorial intentions have long been dismissed from serious critical consideration, though outside the lecture hall there may be intense, gossipy interest in such old riddles as the nature of Henry James's wound, did an individual named "Shakespeare" write the body of work attributed to "Shakespeare" or is someone else "Shakespeare," is the "I" of the next poem you read the poet or an invented persona? As Michel Foucault reasonably asks, "What difference does it matter who is speaking?"

What difference does it make to know that Marcel Proust was a homosexual? Does this biographical information alter the text of Proust's great novel?—does it expand the text?—detract from the text?—qualify, or enhance, its greatness? Can it be argued that Oscar Wilde's *The Picture of Dorian Gray,* written by a homosexual, is a more subtle, codified work of fiction than the identical novel would have been had Wilde been heterosexual? No matter the plea embodied in the question "What difference does it make?" it seems, in fact, to make a difference to most readers.

For the feminist critic, it makes a considerable difference to know that the text has been authored by a woman: For a woman's discourse will presumably differ from a man's, even if the texts are identical. If the author is a woman, her text has very likely been generated by "female rage"; her art work may be intimately related to her body. To protest against such narrow corseting of motive is to deny one's gender-identity. Far from erasing identity, this popular strategy of criticism has reenforced identity by means of gender. Does a woman, in fact, possess a special language, distinct from male language? Or is it purely Woman, and no individual, who possesses such a language? And what of the "androgynous" artist? As a writer, and a woman, or a woman, and a writer, I have never found that I was in possession of a special female language springing somehow from the female body, though I can sympathize with the poetic-mystic yearning that might underlie such a theory. To be marginalized through history, to be told repeatedly that we lack souls, that we aren't fully human, that we're "unclean," therefore can't write, can't paint, can't compose music, can't do philosophy, math, science, politics, power in its myriad guises—the least of our compensations should be that we're in possession of some special gift brewed in the womb and in mother's milk. For the practicing woman writer, feminist/gender criticism can be wonderfully nurturing, for obvious reasons: Texts by women are read attentively and sympathetically; "lost" writers are continually rediscovered, and wrongly dismissed writers (Kate Chopin, for instance) are given the respectful scrutiny they deserve. On the most practical level, as the feminist critic Elaine Showalter has said, "The best thing the feminist can do for women's writing is to buy women's books."

Yet this criticism, for all its good intentions, can be restrictive as well, at least for the writer who is primarily a formalist, and for whom gender is not a pressing issue in every work. (As a writer who happens to be a woman, I choose to write about women, and I choose to write from the perspective of women; but I also choose to write about men, and I choose to write from the perspective of men; with the confidence that, dissolving myself into the self of a fictitious other, I have entered a dimension of consciousness that is not my own in either case, and yet legitimate.) Surely it is an error to reduce to a genitally defined essence any individual, whether a woman or a man; for the (woman) writer, it is frustrating to be designated as a "woman writer"—a category in relationship to which there is no corresponding "man writer."

To return to the question "Where is an author?"—we might say, with Henry James, that the artist's life is his work, yet this is not quite the same thing as saying that the artist's work is his life, for of course it can be only part of that life, and possibly, for some artists, even the gifted, not the most valued part of that life. We might argue that there must be an ontological distinction between the writer-as-creator-of-texts and the living person, the medium of the art. The work is thus the artist. The artist is a component of an aesthetic object, a product, printed or processed or in some way made into an artifice—"artificial." The individual is born of nature, but the artist is born of that individual, yearning to transcend the merely "natural" and to make complete that which, existentially, is forever incomplete, unrealized. We might argue that all books, fiction, poetry, nonfiction, have been created by pseudonymous selves in the process of that creation, and if the name on the dust jacket is identical

with the historic name, that is not the same thing as saying that the name on the dust jacket *is* the historic individual.

Where is the author?—in the work, of course.

Which is not to say that the author of the author (i.e., the historic self) doesn't exist too; at least provisionally.

Notes

1. Wolfgang Amadeus Mozart is our paragon of genius. This letter suggests the genius as oddly passive, a vessel to be filled from the unconscious.

> When I am, as it were, completely myself, entirely alone, and of good cheer . . . it is on such occasions that my ideas flow best and most abundantly. *Whence* and *how* they come, I know not; nor can I force them. . . .

> When I proceed to write, the committing to paper is done quickly enough, for everything is . . . already finished. . . . But why my productions take from my hand that particular form and style that makes them *Mozartish,* and different from the works of other composers, is probably owing to the same cause which renders my nose so large or so aquiline, or, in short, makes it Mozart's, and different from those of other people. For I really do not study or aim at originality.
>
> (trans. Edward Holmes)

Yet Mozart's most dazzling compositions are readily identified as of his musical era; for even a genius is a child of his time.

GENERAL COMMENTARY

LINDA WAGNER-MARTIN (ESSAY DATE 1995)

SOURCE: Wagner-Martin, Linda. "Panoramic, Unpredictable, and Human: Joyce Carol Oates's Recent Novels." In *Traditions, Voices, and Dreams: The American Novel since the 1960s,* edited by Melvin J. Friedman and Ben Siegel, pp. 196-209. Newark: University of Delaware Press, 1995.

In the following essay, Wagner-Martin traces Oates's changing portrayal of women and gender power in her novels.

Although Joyce Carol Oates must be named among America's most successful contemporary novelists, she remains strangely marginalized. The value of her fiction keeps getting displaced, subsumed under arguments about who she is, what her concerns as a writer really are, what role her fiction plays in the paradigm of current literature. Throughout a sprawling labyrinth of reviews and personal interviews, Oates has long evinced her belief that the novelist's function is moral and at least partly didactic. The writer observes culture, lamenting its travesties and tragedies. He or she uses technical virtuosity to write effectively about any theme, any character, any concern. Oates has frequently been compared with Faulkner because of her command of craft, her technical daring, her general artistic sophistication—and her admittedly dark vision of human possibility.

That she is a woman writer is probably less significant than that she draws from all kinds of belief and "knowledge." Yet her gender has skewed reviews of her books throughout her career, beginning in 1964 with **With Shuddering Fall.** She recently wrote that "the impulse to create, like the impulse to destroy is utterly mysterious." It is "one of the primary mysteries of human existence."[1] Once those mysteries are accepted, and the power of the sub (or supra) conscious acknowledged, the writer's work becomes chameleon. It is then realistic, fantastic; labored, effusive; predictable, oblique; naturalistic, mythic; utopian, dystopian; generic, avant-garde; exaggerated, understated. Each of these terms has been used at some point in Oates's career to describe her fiction. Panoramic in theme, unpredictable in method, her writing reflects the human condition as she acknowledges it to be in the latter third of this century. For the most part, her assessment of that human condition is critical. Hence her recent novels have charted themes that society as a whole would rather ignore. Among these are sexual abuse, incest, and the enslavement of physical passion and its consequent betrayal.

One of Oates's most controversial stands within her fiction is that culture is male-determined. In her fiction, women do what they do because of the men of power in their lives. Women are wives, fearful of what their husbands will think or do. They are unquestioning in their submission, or they are young women or adolescents waiting to trap the man who fathers their child, learning early the tricks of sexual manipulation. Or, they are children, sensing where family power lies and responding to the (usually male) sources of it. There are few families anywhere in Oates's fictions that are not male-dominated. There are few women or female adolescents who have lives of their own; their ambition rather is to keep their man, whether father or lover, happy. Because of this schema of domination, most of Oates's main characters are male. They are the determinants of the culture; their actions and decisions count in the lives of all Oates's characters. Oates is often criticized for writing about powerless women and for focusing her attention on men, yet the American culture she describes is still male-dominated. It is in this context of describing gender power that Oates's fiction of the 1980s begins to differ from her earlier work.

Oates's **Marya, A Life** (1986) ostensibly creates a different milieu for the title character. In Marya's "night of patchy dreams, strangers' voices, rain hammering on the tarpaper roof close overhead,"[2] the reader realizes that Marya's union organizer father has been killed. Marya comes to understand the meaning of his death—and the depletion of her family's economic and human resources—later. This occurs when her mother takes her into the morgue and she sees a body, but the body "hadn't any face that you could recognize" (p. 11). Abandoned by their mother, Marya and her two young brothers live with her father's people. Sexually abused during the years she is eight, nine, and ten by her cousin Lee, "who liked her" (he is twelve, thirteen, and fourteen), Marya learns to exist by going "into stone." From her early life on, Marya typifies Oates's fragile, damaged characters, who are often so numbed by the pain of their existence that they perform at what appear to be subhuman levels.

Oates's fiction of the 1980s increasingly focuses on the subhuman, not as a criticism of these characters but as a criticism of the society that forms them. Many are as dehumanized as Richard Wright's Bigger Thomas in *Native Son* (1940). But Oates's most brutalized characters are women. Victimized by older male relatives—fathers, uncles, cousins—and unprotected by the obtuse or blandly uncaring women of their families, Marya and Enid, the protagonists of her shattering novel **You Must Remember This** (1987), barely survive their frequent psychic mutilations. **You Must Remember This** begins with Enid's suicide attempt: "She swallowed forty-seven aspirin tablets between 1:10 A.M. and 1:35 A.M. locked in the bathroom of her parents' rented house. . . . She stood five feet three inches tall in her bare feet, she weighed eighty-nine pounds."[3] Victimized by her adored young uncle, Enid acts out the horrifying fear that she—though innocent—will be found out, that her uncle will be discovered, that (most realistic of Oates's plot machinations) she will come to enjoy this evil. Wearing her thin silver chain with the Virgin Mary stamped on the medal, she dresses herself all in white like a bride and goes to find death. She seeks the death she has convinced herself she deserves, the death only she can control. Through her chosen death, she will finally come to some kind of power. Oates's poignant cry for women to have control of their bodies and their lives shapes both *Marya, A Life* and *You Must Remember This.*

In both books, Oates resolves her tormented narratives through reconciliations of daughters with mothers, through resolutions of the matriarchal bond. The books are unlike *A Garden of Earthly Delights* or *them,* two of Oates's earlier novels in which mothers are perpetrators of male coercion. These two more recent books explore the ways women come to know both their "selves" and their potential as women in contemporary culture. Even in these efforts, however, Oates's women are very male-dependent. Marya goes through countless debilitating relationships with men, including a dying priest, as well as teachers and other lovers. Like Enid, she leads her life with a relentless subtext of romance, watching for the man who will make her dreams come true—despite the fact that she never dreams. Marya is too numb to have a normal subconscious life. Oates portrays one of her heroine's early high school romances so that the reader is reminded of the cultural imperative for Marya's behavior: "In the beginning she had pursued him [Emmett Schroeder]. . . . Falling in love—'romance' of one kind or another—behaving like all the other girls. . . . Her 'feeling' for boys, for men, was largely a matter of daydreaming" (p. 101).

Both Marya and Enid have accepted what Oates, in her preface to *You Must Remember This,* describes as the "green of romance, of nostalgia, of innocence." Oates's working title for *You Must Remember This* was "The Green Island," retained here as a subsection title. It provides an image that pulls together the notion of the fresh innocence of adolescence with the highly romanticized fantasy of being shipwrecked on an island with someone. The metaphor of life as some uncontrollable sea and of a woman's safety dependent on her being rescued by a man (any man, regardless of the source of his power) prompts most of Oates's women characters' behavior.

Growing up through a 1950s girlhood that was itself dominated by this myth, Oates knew too well that conventional wisdom Marya and Enid accepted. She has referred to both these novels as her "most personal" books. She also has compared herself as an adolescent to Enid, "The contours of whose soul so resemble my own," not in the experience of sexual abuse but in the painful development of an independent psyche.[4] Women in the world Oates depicts in *You Must Remember This* (carefully dated 1946-56) followed the injunctions of their culture: "You *Must* Remember This" is not only the title of a maudlin, mindlessly romantic ballad, but it is also a prescription for living the female life. A woman's role was to serve, to listen, to follow orders, and not to originate anything.

> He instructed her to hold still. Not to move. *Not to move.*
>
> And not to look at him either. Or say a word.
>
> (*Marya,* p. 15)

> She remembered his voice, Don't tell anybody will you.
>
> (*Remember,* p. 4)

> "Get in! Close the door!" Felix said. . . . He was nerved up, angry. "Does your father know you hitch rides?" he asked. . . . It's cheap and it's asking for trouble—I don't want any niece of mine doing it. . . . You led me on, acting the way you did fooling around the way you did you knew damn well what you were doing didn't you!—and now I see you out on the street hitching rides! . . .
>
> He lit another cigarette, he let her cry for a while, then said, "It's stopped raining," though in fact it hadn't quite stopped yet. "You can get out now, Enid. Get out."
>
> (*Remember,* pp. 130-32)

Even as adults, Oates's women characters continue these patterns; they are frozen in the psychological states abuse has created for them. In Marya's later relationship with Professor Fein, she again takes orders and lets herself be manipulated. She is used and reused, both sexually and professionally. Yet it is the much older and cynical Fein who tells her that she must find her mother. The novel builds to that predictable ending, but the effect of Marya's finding her mother is left ambiguous. She has written to the woman she has not seen since childhood, and her mother has replied. In the novel's last scene Marya prepares to open her mother's letter:

> As if a dream secret and prized in her soul had blossomed outward, taking its place, asserting its integrity. . . . She placed the envelope carefully on a table and sat in front of it staring, smiling, a pulse beating in her forehead. How odd to see her name—Marya Knauer—*her* name in a handwriting that belonged to her mother, a handwriting she did not recognize.
>
> Marya, this is going to change your life, she thought, half in dread.
>
> Marya, this is going to cut your life in two.
>
> (p. 275)

The ending of *You Must Remember This* is much more ambiguous. Oates's layered structure has Enid leaving for college, the appropriate demise of Felix, the reunion of her parents (which culminates in an almost powerless sexual act), and the poignant letter from Enid's brother, Warren. In following his example (leaving "home"), Enid has saved herself—the reader supposes. But Warren's closing letter to Enid expresses the unpredictable—and ungovernable—power of physical passion:

> Strange isn't it—how "love" seems to carry with it no knowledge. The people I have loved most in my lifetime (including you) I haven't known at all. Nor have they known me.
>
> The blood ties are so powerful and deep and mute. Something terrifying there. How we feel about one another—even about the house on East Clinton Street—so strange, helpless, paralyzing and exciting both. It's only away where people don't know me or haven't known me for very long that I am *myself*.
>
> (p. 416)

In *You Must Remember This*, Warren takes a positive maternal role. Although Enid's mother does find a professional life for herself—in her sewing and designing, her physically leaving the house—the ending of the novel shows her once again locked in the sex act, repeating her husband's hesitant profession of love. But she has provided for Enid the beautiful quilt the latter takes with her to school; it is an emblematic gift of women's understanding and power (albeit worked in the wedding ring pattern). The ending of Oates's 1987 novel seems to countermand the comparatively simple ambivalence of *Marya, A Life*.

Elaine Showalter, in her essay on Oates and this novel, finds Marya's reaching back "to find the mother who has abandoned her, and to reclaim a matrilineage that is both painful and empowering,"[5] to be mostly positive. Showalter states that for Marya to deny "the mother's country . . . is to be a permanent exile" (p. 152). Yet she also acknowledges—in response to the grim tone of the book—that Marya's gesture of reconciliation is not itself a panacea.

> The community of women is not idyllic, but torn by rage, competition, primal jealousies, ambiguous desire, and emotional violence, just like the world in which women seem subordinate to and victimized by men.

In this comment, and in other reviews of *You Must Remember This*, critics have again taken up their pastime of making Joyce Carol Oates into a feminist writer. One of the reasons *Marya, A Life* and *You Must Remember This* were well received is that in these books comparatively strong women characters endured, even succeeded, though undeniably damaged by the gender struggles of their culture. It seemed to Oates's many readers as if she had become more interested in the problems of women and might be moving toward writing about fully achieving women protagonists. (The thirty-five years of Oates's career as novelist have engendered a tapestry of criticism about the absence of feminist themes in her writing.[6])

Oates has repeatedly spoken to the conflicts of being both writer and woman—not about any inherent conflict in being a woman who writes, but about critics' reaction to women writers. In her essay "(Woman) Writer: Theory and Practice," she stated: "She is likely to experience herself, from within, as a writer primarily: perhaps even a writer exclusively. . . . When the writer is alone with language and with the challenging discipline of creating an art by way of language alone, she is not defined to herself as 'she.'"[7] Oates then declares—though less militantly than she might have in either the 1960s or the 1970s (as she has no desire to discount her female being and psyche): "Is memory gender-bound? Are impressions filtered through the prism of gender? Is there a distinctly female voice?—or even a conspicuously feminine voice?" (p. 23).

Most of Oates's essays and prefaces that deal with the gender issue have been negations of the Gilbert and Gubar position that now dominates the critical world. This view suggests that women writers suffer under an "anxiety of authorship" different from, and more intense than, the anxieties of male writers. Oates is confident enough of both her vision and her voice to downplay the effects gender has on the writer's natural state of hesitancy. Hence when Oates herself writes about *Marya, A Life*, she sees the importance of the closing episode: She perceives Marya's attempt to find her mother as less a matriarchal connection (the search for parent become thoroughly gender based) than a humane one. Oates states that Marya's action is positive because she makes the choice "finally"; she chooses "not to accept the terms of their [her] own betrayal."[8] She acts against the betrayer, the parent who happens to be mother rather than father.

Some critics believed they were seeing some pattern of more self-assertive women protagonists in Oates's 1980s fiction. For them, her 1989 novel, *American Appetites*, reversed whatever tendency they might have anticipated. Ian McCullough, highly esteemed research Ph.D., and his wife, Glynnis, author of successful cookbooks, lead a chic upper middle-class social and intellectual life. Disturbed only by the emotional vicissitudes of Bianca, their nineteen-year-old, their life runs to predictable busyness: Ian leads a remote, conventional intellectual life; Glynnis punctuates her suburban days with short-lived affairs—several with Ian's best friends. When Ian becomes fascinated by Sigrid Hunt, one of Glynnis's young protégées who had formerly been a dancer, the outer fabric of their life is shredded by Glynnis's jealousy. After Glynnis's quasi-accidental death, the reader is left to determine motives for Ian, Sigrid, and Bianca—motives for their subsequent behavior, not for their actual or fantasized complicity in Glynnis's death.

Despite the semblance of power each woman in this novel pretends, none is self-actualizing. Glynnis arranges not only her husband's existence but also a great many other people's. (One key anecdote is her memory of having sex with Ian's best friend, Denis, just minutes before the two of them go to lunch with their respective spouses as a foursome.) Bianca's defiance of her mother is a move against that awesome control. Her "present" for her father's fiftieth birthday is the parodic sexual dance, and it provides a useful glimpse into her understanding of the forces that motivate adult culture. Glynnis sits at the center of the web that shapes life in Hazelton-on-Hudson. Hence the shattered glass in the picture window represents Glynnis's webs or lines of power, as well as the actual cracks in the glass as she falls through it to her death.

Rather than equating Glynnis's control with strength, however, Oates shows how frightened Glynnis is once she suspects that Ian might have a lover. His asexuality, which had shown itself in occasions of impotence throughout their twenty-six-year marriage, now becomes more threatening than any overt hostility. In her drunken, violent response to him, Glynnis shows the hidden passions, the hungers, that had prompted so many of her actions in the past. By making Glynnis the proprietor of foods, cooking, and homes, Oates aligns the natural hungers for food and sex with the matriarchy.

Lest the reader miss the horror of Glynnis's complicated life because of the coolly understated prose, Oates underscores the vapidity of suburban women's lives. She does so by creating a macabre affair between Ian and Meika (whose older husband, Vaughn, had been one of Glynnis's lovers) soon after Ian is accused of Glynnis's murder. Meika, like Glynnis, is every bit the predator. By the close of **American Appetites,** Ian is living with Sigrid and planning a marriage, and Meika and Ian's attorney, Ottinger, are living together. Sexual liaisons are reasonless, impermanent, destructive,

Oates's novel warns, but they are an expected part of all hearty and elite "American appetites." Her listeners understand full well the pathetic confession Sigrid makes on the witness stand: "I was caught up in this love affair which seemed to be sucking all the life from me. It was just a state I had drifted into . . . a pathological state of the soul."[9]

The closing coda has two of Ian's best friends (one is Denis, the lover Glynnis has taunted him about) come for a lunch that Sigrid has prepared. She has unwittingly contributed to a closed male camaraderie that shuts her out and makes her only a sexual object. The incident shows the mystery and the impenetrability of every human relationship. Supposedly Ian's best friend, Denis, has lied to him about his affair with Glynnis. Both lunch guests, Denis and Malcolm Oliver, have been Meika's lovers. Ian has no idea why he plans to marry Sigrid. He says in a later part of the scene, "I will blow my brains out when the season turns" (p. 337). The rapacity—conscious or unconscious—of these upstanding male professionals lies just under their veneer of accomplishment and wit.

Oates foreshadows our bleak knowledge that Sigrid will be left to bear the loss—and probably the guilt—of Ian's death by having her speak only once during the male-dominated luncheon. In that scene she tells the story of her dancing the role of the doomed Princess Creon in *Medea,* an oblique parallel to her triangle with Ian and Glynnis. Just as Medea in her bitter jealousy sends the princess the beautiful poisoned gifts that melt her flesh from her bones, so Glynnis has given Sigrid the anguishing work of caring for Ian. She is covered by his body in the sex act just as Princess Creon was by the poisoned robes. Sigrid states that "the Princess is so innocently vain, or . . . vainly innocent, she accepts the gifts immediately, and puts them on, and preens in front of a mirror, and dies an agonizing death" (p. 327).

Becoming lovers the night of Ian's acquittal, Sigrid and he as couple are the immediate result of Ian's fear *of* death (his own) and his fear *from* the death (of Glynnis). His fear gives him a sexual power that he had earlier lost. The *Medea* narrative also suggests incest—in that it includes the Princess's father, the Creon who—in trying to remove her flaming garments—also dies. Oates uses many references to Ian's and Sigrid's ages, to Sigrid's estrangement from her father, to Bianca's estrangement from Ian, and to Sigrid's appearance at the luncheon "like a tall somber child in a nightgown"; the allusions suggest that the sexual bond between Ian and Sigrid, as their names suggest, is incestuous. Sigrid has already had one abortion; the next fruit of her passionate involvements will be Ian's death. The reader is reminded of Ian's irrational binary statement to Nick Ottinger as they wait for the jury to bring in its verdict: "I will blow my brains out . . . or I will get married again and begin my life over." "I will blow my brains out or I will marry" (pp. 328, 330).

As if to illustrate her statements about gender-determined imaginations, Oates creates in *American Appetites* a novel in which gender is less important than morality. Men and women alike break codes of marriage and friendship and professional loyalty. Only the "innocently vain, or vainly innocent"—Ian, Bianca, and to a lesser degree Sigrid—can be hurt by disillusion: What does marriage "mean"? What does family "mean"? *American Appetites,* one of the most graphically bitter of Oates's novels, implies that language—like the social and moral codes it represents—"means" nothing. The most chilling scene in the novel is Denis's lying to Ian about his former relationship to the now-dead Glynnis.

As Sigrid's single narrative suggests, the misleading and oversimplified romance script is to blame for much of the novel's and the culture's sorrow. Dissatisfied with professions and roles, women look for fulfillment in sexual relationships. Sigrid's life was such a paradigm, and one can assume Glynnis's was, too. As Sigrid says, "at the time I became involved in this love affair, I was feeling ill-used and embittered about losing my job at Vassar" (p. 313). The appetites of Oates's characters are explicable, however, not only in terms of the late twentieth-century culture but also as ramifications of primordial gender patterns. In Oates's 1979 novel *Cybele,* she established the same patterns, creating in the unaware Edwin Locke a precursor of the equally unaware Ian McCullough.

Her *Cybele* is the story of a middle-aged man whose quick and destructive love affairs with a half-dozen women lead to the actual death with which the novel opens. At forty-four, Edwin Locke was a prosperous businessman, stable in his love for his wife, Cynthia, and his two sons. The family is part of an established suburban social group. At forty-six, he is depleted from sexual and drug experimentation, living on the fringe of society, ready to become a child molester. The explanation for Locke's perversion is given by the mysterious narrator of the novel, the *I* of Chapter One ("*In Memoriam.* Edwin Locke") and of subsequent brief references, Cybele. With characteristic whimsy, Oates gives the reader no way of identifying the narrator except through the title.

Cybele is the great earth mother, nature goddess, mother of the gods, and wife of Cronus. She is known also as Demeter, Rhea, Op, protectress of the wild things of the earth. But she is probably best known in mythology for her relationship with Attis. Jealous of his turn to other women, Cybele drives him mad so that he castrates himself. He dies under a pine tree, where violets eventually grow. In other versions of the myth, Attis, like Adonis, is killed by a boar. Spring was the season for Attis to be celebrated because he was the god of vegetation. Other objects or images connected with the Cybele-Attis myth are the lions that either accompanied Cybele or drew her chariot, the drum or cymbals she carried, and the dancing and wild music used to celebrate her being. (Without extensive elaboration, it is clear that *American Appetites* makes use of a great many of these characteristics.)

Oates's narrator/author points out in chapter 1 that the story will accelerate greatly as it continues. It assumes the form of dance itself, so that by the end of the narrative "no one will see him [Locke] at all and he certainly will have lost even his incomplete vision of himself."[10] The novel fulfills that promise, so that the last chapters become more and more fragmented and less connected to previous segments. As Locke changes lovers rapidly, we know less and less about them and about his state of mind. Oates's narrative method changes to show the precipitous changes in the man and in his social behavior.

The character of Edwin Locke can be read as an ironic recreation of seventeenth-century philosopher John Locke, creator of the idea of the pleasure principle. The travesty which the search for pleasure becomes in *Cybele* is far removed from the ideal balance that Locke wrote about in 1690 in *An Essay Concerning Human Understanding.* Oates's Locke exemplifies the horrors of ignorance, of the equation of sexual pleasure with "love," and of a male's complete ego absorption in the sexual act, without thought for his partner. "He knows only that the October night is beautiful, that the future lies all before him, rich with the surprise, the continual shock, of sensual pleasure; it lies in wait for him. The past does not exist. The past is falling away, moment by moment, helpless to impede him. . . . *this is why we are born,* Edwin Locke thinks" (p. 98). No other human being is important to this man; his ego has become the center; what matters is his experience, his sensual pleasure. The rest of *Cybele* chronicles a succession of meaningless relationships—with a hint of homosexual, group, and child partners. These illustrate the indiscriminate search that obsesses Locke.

That search finally becomes faceless. A body is any body, and all sex partners become

> An immense hill into which he wants to burrow. Head-first. Trembling with desire. Sobbing with desire. And the hill becomes flesh, and the flesh seems to flinch from his violence, his need, whimpering as if it were alive; but still he forces himself into it. Like this! Like this! Like this! And as he forces himself into it it does give way, it succumbs, he pounds at it with his head, plunging, burrowing, half-choking with the rage of his desire, until he has penetrated my very core.

Cybele's speech gives her identity away to the reader: "my" very core is the feminine principle, the earth mother, who first entices and then traps irretrievably. The passage above continues,

> And then the flesh, which has parted for him, in fear of him, begins to contract.

> And horribly, he is caught in me. Trapped.

> Swallowed alive!

> He screams for help, for release. But of course no one hears. His screams are not audible, nor is there anyone to hear. For I have him now, I have him fast, and tight, in the hot tight blood-thrumming depths of me, and he will never withdraw, no matter how frantically he struggles to get free, no matter how valiantly his poor strained heart beats: I have him, I have him forever.

> (pp. 200-201)

Oates continues, "it's the oldest story in the world, isn't it?" She reinforces the image of Cybele, waiting till Locke plays himself out, winding to the inevitable end of the saga—his own death.

Death comes to Locke not by castration, which has been gradual throughout the novel in various episodes of impotence, but by scissor stabs to the heart. The real seat of passion, this change from the Attis legend implies, is the heart and not the genitals. Locke dies from the scissor injuries, but he is immolated as well, burned after his murderer "dribbles" gas over his body "with a certain ceremonial grace." Locke's death occurs, Cybele makes clear, because he hadn't "the insight. He never understood." His burned body, found by the very children he would have liked to use as sex partners, is finally mistaken for that of a dog. It is not only bereft of gender distinctions, but also of humanity.

In *Mysteries of Winterthurn* (1984),[11] Oates creates another of these men for whom sexual passion is all-important. Xavier Kilgarvan, the detective-hero of *Mysteries,* is as passionately foolhardy as Edwin Locke or Ian McCullough. Xavier, at sixteen, falls irresistibly in love with his distant cousin Perdita. Because of horrible crimes occurring in his cousin's home, Xavier (with the idealism suggested by his named saint, Francis Xavier) becomes a detective. Oates gives the reader scene after scene in which conventional religious accouterments carry sinister meaning. For example, the cherubs surrounding the Virgin Mary in a ceiling painting attempt to seduce Xavier as he keeps watch in the murder bower, just as Perdita has earlier enticed him to the attic of her home where Xavier eventually finds wire-choked infant bodies swaddled and laid in bureau drawers. The sensual and depraved grow from, or into, the religious, as Oates follows the familiar Gothic interpretation of humanity's quest for emotional gratification.

Although the novel falls into three seemingly separate tales—horrific accounts of strange and never-solved crimes—*Mysteries* is the story of Xavier and his obsessive passion for Perdita. Ironically—or with the mockery of narrative conventions so obvious throughout Oates's work—the novel has a "happy ending" as Perdita and Xavier finally marry. When Xavier gives up his occupation as detective, however, the reader assumes that he becomes a lost man. But this irony is never apparent, and the reader—lulled by the conventions of the genre—gives a sigh of relief when the marriage occurs. The reader is convinced that Xavier's efforts have finally paid off in this long-anticipated but unexpected reward.

If anything, *Mysteries* is a comic novel—although the relationship of Erasmus Kilgarvan to his oldest daughter, Georgina (the self-styled poet Iphigenia), is difficult to read as comedy. Incest is one way of murdering the child, just as Agamemnon tried to sacrifice his daughter to the gods. In her description of Georgina as Emily Dickinson, Oates carefully underplays the macabre. Instead, she makes an important comment about family power structures, the coercion by the religious community, and the impossibility of women using their talents and finding freedom—unless that freedom is sanctioned by patriarchal power.

Her *Mysteries of Winterthurn,* like its triad genre novels *Bellefleur* and *A Bloodsmoor Romance,* shows Oates's easy versatility. Such a deviation from her usual intense naturalism or fantasy as to be found in this trio proves again that Oates's writing, collectively, merits the same kind of explicative and diverse critical methodology that is generally applied to Thomas Pynchon's fiction. The chief difference between the two writers is that Oates's sense of humor is even more madcap. She directs her humor at the most sacred cultural and literary conventions while offering so few clues that her fiction becomes a great, wry mystery. In *Mysteries of Winterthurn* she gives the reader the most rational of frameworks: "Editor's Notes," "Postscripts," "Epilogues," and the detective-novel tradition itself. It proves an organization that suggests ends and reliable conclusions (the three-part, separate mystery structure) and a sane narrative voice that describes a seemingly sane detective figure. What we are left with, however, is a completely inexplicable novel; it is not one of the mysteries explained in any way. We also are left with an ever-widening rift between the rational and the irrational: in the case of Xavier, it is between the psychic health we associate with sanity and his own brand of passionate madness. Oates's *Mysteries* then is a conundrum of literary conventions, even to the concrete poems created by the entries in her table of contents.

To see these two earlier novels—*Cybele* and *Mysteries of Winterthurn*—in the light of Oates's three later fictions—*Marya, A Life, You Must Remember This*, and *American Appetites*—is to see how differently she has come to approach the same themes. These include sexual passion and enthrallment, the cultural adoption of the panacea of sex, and the underlying destruction of women's freedom as a result of these attitudes about sexuality during the later 1980s. What might have once become a text that could evoke some humor has become fiction of the highest possible seriousness. Oates is convinced that her writing mirrors life and that life exists in some part to teach and to admonish. This conviction has given her many readers these embittered and embittering novels about women's lives, lived in the strangleholds of the men their culture has empowered. It is not a satisfying vision, but it is a true one. And Oates is once again fulfilling her own role as Cassandra in the panorama of contemporary American fiction.

Notes

1. Joyce Carol Oates, *(Woman) Writer, Occasions and Opportunities* (New York: E. P. Dutton, 1988), p. 3.

2. Joyce Carol Oates, *Marya, A Life* (New York: Berkeley, 1988), p. 1.

3. Joyce Carol Oates, *You Must Remember This* (New York: Harper & Row, Perennial Library, 1988), p. 3.

4. Oates, *(Woman) Writer*, pp. 379-80.

5. Elaine Showalter, "Joyce Carol Oates: A Portrait," *Ms* (March 1986), reprinted in *Modern Critical Views, Joyce Carol Oates*, ed. Harold Bloom (New York: Chelsea House, 1987), pp. 137-45. See esp. p. 137.

6. See my collection, *Critical Essays on Joyce Carol Oates* (Boston: G. K. Hall, 1979), especially the Introduction and essays by Charles Lam Markmann, Sanford Pinsker, Eileen Bender, and Joanne V. Creighton. See also Victor Strandberg, "Sex, Violence, and Philosophy in *You Must Remember This*," *Studies in American Fiction* 17 (Spring 1989): 3-17.

7. Oates, *(Woman) Writer*, pp. 22-23.

8. Ibid., p. 378.

9. Joyce Carol Oates, *American Appetites* (New York: E. P. Dutton, 1989), p. 314.

10. Joyce Carol Oates, *Cybele* (Santa Barbara, CA: Black Sparrow Press, 1979), pp. 11-12.

11. Joyce Carol Oates, *Mysteries of Winterthurn* (New York: E. P. Dutton, 1984).

TITLE COMMENTARY

Do With Me What You Will

JOSEPH PETITE (ESSAY DATE AUGUST 1986)

SOURCE: Petite, Joseph. "A Predator in Liberationist Clothing." *Journal of Evolutionary Psychology* 7, nos. 3-4 (August 1986): 245-48.

In the following essay, Petite investigates the repressed nature of the female characters in Do with Me What You Will.

In *Do With Me What You Will* Joyce Carol Oates, it has been argued, creates the truly independent woman. Noting that the novel is dedicated to a member of the national board of the National Organization of Women, Patricia Hill Burnett, Constance Denne says of the book: "Its subject is the raising of a young woman's consciousness and her liberation. Elena . . . breaks through to a higher level of awareness, and, integrated, affirms not only what she wants but also how she will get it."[1] Christopher Lehmann-Haupt also sees Elena as liberated, suggesting that since she and her mother, Ardis, are anything but passive, the title is ironic. He finds Elena's decision to leave her husband for Morrissey "an uncompromising assertion of her newly discovered self."[2] A reviewer for *Publisher's Weekly* concurs; this is the story of Elena's liberation. Choosing Morrissey, he says, is the "love through which she begins at last to be her own person."[3]

Critics, however, have failed to notice the direct contradiction between the liberationist rhetoric supplied to Elena and Ardis and the facts of the novel. Elena merely improves on her mother's techniques for exploiting men. The fact is that her "victory," her domination of Jack, has won her nothing. Not only isn't she the new woman Denne describes, she isn't even new in Oates' fiction. Like Clara in *A Garden of Earthly Delights*, she thinks of male/female relations as an adversary process. Like Maureen in *them* Elena is alienated from men and frigid. Like many of Oates' women, Elena has traded for security, only to find herself lonely.[4] Even in her affair with Jack her object is security not liberation. Ardis tutors Elena in alienation from men; men are "machines."

> 'If it's one thing I can't understand,' she said, 'it's men mauling me. It's very annoying, it's boring. You won't like it either. You try to think of something else but you can't. Men are like machines, they're like automatic washers that must go through certain cycles, one after the other, it's all predictable and boring . . . for women who have no imagination, who can't think of anything better to do with their lives, maybe it's all right for them, but not for someone like me.'[5]

Machines is precisely how the frigid Maureen in *them* sees men. In response to a man's sexual advances, Maureen reflects that, "a man was like a machine: one of those machines at the laundromat where she dragged the laundry. There were certain cycles to go through."[6] In talking of male/female relationships in her fiction, Oates repeats her own words a great deal.

Rather than being liberated, Elena is trained to see men as providers, though Ardis camouflages this manipulation by convincing herself of her own philosophical depth: "'We're our own ideas, we make ourselves up; some women let men make them up, invent them, fall in love with them they're helpless to invent themselves . . . but not me, I'm nobody's idea but my own'" (p. 72). Obviously Ardis considers herself a woman of "imagination." The facts, however, indicate she is not at all liberated. When we first meet mother and daughter they are scheming to get financial security from Mr. Karman by convincing him that it is his idea that they should be "protected" by him (p. 72). Knowing his need to be their benefactor, Ardis cynically uses the word "belong," (employed by so many of Oates' women) only here it is obvious that she has no intention of being a helpless dependent: "'I want Elena and myself to have your name, yes. And then some day I want to be your wife, I want to belong to you'" (p. 62). The critics have too easily taken

these words at face value, and have failed to explore the larger picture of male/female interaction in Oates' work.

Rather than being liberated, Ardis is guilty, just as men are, of exploiting the opposite sex. However, in spite of the success of the plan with Marvin, Elena is lonely. Her emotions are so twisted by Ardis' teaching that she is frigid, and ironically views her own absence of response as a sign that she is in control of both her husband and her lover. Certainly exploitation is not a sign of personality growth, nor is the inability to respond.

Elena is aware that her marriage is arranged by Ardis, that "her life is being prepared" (p. 97). Ardis, frank about the exploitation, tells her plainly, "'You're set for life'" (p. 10). Marvin, the typical Oates husband, is at work "all the time, maybe sixteen hours a day" (p. 115). Elena's contribution to the marriage is to let Marvin go through his cycles: "When he made love to her in the months afterward, she felt no pain, no alarm; she felt nothing, but drifted like this, absolutely still, gentle, opened to him and empty" (p. 119). When he asks if she loves him, she knows the game has to be played if the male is to continue to protect her: "She realized that she was expected to answer him. And so she whispered, 'Yes,' and wondered if it was the right word, the magical word he wanted" (p. 119). This could just as easily be the scene between Clara and Revere in *A Garden of Earthly Delights* where Clara "lets" Revere love her in order to remain under his protection. In return for Revere's "strength" to count on, "She . . . (gives) herself over to him"[7] "telling him what he wanted to hear and letting him love her" (p. 260).

Elena's description of the emotional arrangement in her marriage leaves no room for doubt about its emptiness: "'It isn't any of my business, his life. It belongs to him. It's private. I've lived with him for only a small part of his life, I'm just a fraction of it . . . I belong to him but he doesn't belong to me'" (p. 375).

Elena's alienation from men carries over into her affair with Morrissey. She holds herself back. "So he made love to her: she felt the love being made, forced, generated out of his misery as a physical creature, grinding itself into her" (p. 344). Not responding to a man, she believes, gives her power over him. In her marriage she also reaches a point where she uses sex to defeat her husband: "She has eluded him, she had established a kind of triumph over him" (p. 414). It is after this "victory" that she leaves Marvin.

Elena feels "a feverish certainty" about her liberation; "she did not need anyone, she did not love anyone, she was free" (p. 536). Interestingly, of all of Oates' women Elena most resembles Clara and Maureen, two women whose emotional lives are stunted precisely because they are alientated from men. They are unable to love, if love means sharing, and Elena describes herself as free beause she does not love. Elena's move is not into "adulthood," but into herself, and is therefore destructive.

At the end of the novel Elena believes she has broken her bonds. If she loves, she believes it will not be because she is slavishly dependent on a man, but because she chooses to love. Initiating a relationship, she feels is the equivalent of being adult and male, and it is in this sense that she admires maleness. Yet we see that her real interest is not simply in initiating a relationship; it is in dominating, and the object is still security. Though she believes she "loathes" this role, she finds it an expression of "freedom." Making Morrissey fall in love with her is a victory, proof of her power and control:

> She did not need love. But if she wanted love she must have Morrissey. . . . Never in her life had she conquered any territory, achieved any victories. Never. Never had she been selfish, never evil or adult. And now if she wanted Morrissey she would cross over into adulthood to get him, into the excitement of evil. Extending her freedom as men do, making a claim . . . claiming a man . . . almost against his will, forcing him. It saddened her, it was degrading. Spiritually she loathed it. As a woman she loathed it. Yet there was an excitement in the risk she would run.
>
> (p. 544)

Her freedom, it seems, is definable only in terms of her ability to take freedom away from a man. Elena wants not freedom to be herself, to love and be loved as a whole person; she wants control. While at the end she is free of male influence, she is still obsessed with her original need to protect herself. She has not reached a new level of awareness. She has simply adopted male habits of domination. Her liberation is only rhetorical. A predator is no less a predator because she is female and spouts liberationist dogma.

Notes

1. Constance Denne: "Joyce Carol Oates' Women," *Nation*, 219 (December 7, 1974), pp. 597-599. All future references will be in parentheses.

2. Christopher Lehmann-Haupt: "Stalking the Eternal Feminine," *New York Times* (15 October 1973), p. 35.

3. Anon. Review of *Do With Me What You Will*, *Publisher's Weekly*, 204 (20 August 1973), p. 84.

4. See my article, "The Marriage Cycle of Joyce Carol Oates," *The Journal of Evolutionary Psychology*. Vols. V and VI.

5. Joyce Carol Oates: *Do With Me What You Will* (New York: 1973), p. 70. All future references will be in parentheses.

6. Joyce Carol Oates: *them* (New York: 1969), p. 209.

7. Joyce Carol Oates: *A Garden of Earthly Delights* (New York: 1966), p. 223. All future references will be in parentheses.

Foxfire: Confessions of a Girl Gang

BRENDA DALY (ESSAY DATE 1996)

SOURCE: Daly, Brenda. "How Does 'I' Speak for 'We'?: Violence and Representation in *Foxfire: Confessions of a Girl Gang*." In *Lavish Self-Divisions: The Novels of Joyce Carol Oates*, pp. 205-22. Jackson: University Press of Mississippi, 1996.

In the following essay, Daly views Foxfire *to be a novel about girls who utilize language to defend themselves against male-perpetrated violence.*

Through its narrator, Madeleine "Maddy" Wirtz, *Foxfire, Confessions of a Girl Gang*[1] explores the complex relationship between language and violence. Fifty-year-old Maddy, a member of FOXFIRE (always spelled in caps) from age thirteen to age seventeen, uses her notes and memories—as well as some flights of imagination—to chronicle the gang's adventures from 1952 to 1956. "It was a time of violence against girls and women," Maddy explains, "but we didn't have the language to talk about it then" (100). In retrospect, Maddy—who has completed college and now works as an astronomer's assistant—understands that the girls in FOXFIRE had no language for the violence perpetrated against them; however, as narrator, Maddy has a different problem: how can she tell the gang's story—that is, how can an "I" speak for a "we"—without doing violence to, without denying the voices of, the women she once loved? This question is of critical importance because the gang was formed so that collectively its members would have the power to resist the violence perpetrated against them. Under the leadership of Margaret "Legs" Sadovsksy, the FOXFIRE gang devised a range of creative strategies, many of them verbal, to defend themselves against sexual harassment and violence. As Legs tells Maddy, "It's a state of undeclared war, them hating us, men hating us no matter our age or who the hell we are but nobody wants to admit it, not even *us*." (101).

Angelina Jolie in a scene from the film adaptation of
Foxfire.

To defend themselves against male violence,
the girls in FOXFIRE must first admit what adults,
especially males in positions of authority, refuse
to acknowledge: institutionally sanctioned violence toward women, violence perpetuated by the
silences in public discourses. As Teresa de Lauretis
argues, the silence of male-dominated discourses—
the way language "names certain behaviors and
events as violent, but not others" (240)—is one
way that "violence is en-gendered in representation" (240). To illustrate her point, de Lauretis
cites the work of feminist social scientists Wini
Breines and Linda Gordon, who explain that as
long as no word existed for "family violence,"
medical professionals usually ignored the causes
of a patient's injuries, returning wives and children
to their abusers, thereby perpetuating domestic
violence. Again citing Breines and Gordon, De
Lauretis argues that the use of gender-neutral
language in most studies of incest perpetuates
sexual violence by obscuring the fact that "in cases
of incest as well as cases of child sexual abuse, 92
per cent of the victims are female and 97 per cent
of the assailants are male" (242). What is at stake,

de Lauretis emphasizes, is whether the social
order—in this case the family—is to be "maintained or to be dismantled" (242). The violence
engendered by such presumably "neutral" institutional discourse has a direct bearing upon the lives
of poor teenage girls, such as those depicted in
Foxfire, many of whom, while running away from
violent or neglectful families, become vulnerable
to sexual violence on the street.

The traditional canon of literature also constitutes a form of violence, as Judith Fetterley asserts,
because "through what is taught and how it is
taught, our educational system ratifies boys' sense
of agency and primacy, their sense of themselves
as subjects, particularly as defined *against* their
sense of girls as objects" ("'Not in the Least
American'" 880). By contrast, Maddy is striving to
define her subjectivity, not by making the girls in
FOXFIRE into mute objects, but by establishing
their claims to language and agency, along with
her own. Strictly speaking, Maddy's voice occupies
an "intermediate" zone between personal and
communal narration. Maddy is, in fact, not the
protagonist—that role belongs to Legs—but she is
telling her own story and, at the same time, the
gang's. As Susan Lanser points out, narrative
individualism has prevented analysis of this
"intermediate" type of narrator: one who is
"reconstructing the life of another woman but is
in some sense the protagonist herself, not simply
an eye witness or an autobiographer" (21). At the
same time, Maddy's narrative authority comes
from her membership in a community that,
contradictorily, has authorized her to write the
gang's history, but not to tell it. In my view, Maddy's style of communal narration, her attempt to
create an "I" that can speak nonviolently for a
"we," is born out of her recognition that violence,
whether linguistic or physical, arises from a desire
for stability, certainty, and control.

"For the violator," as Laura Tanner says in
Intimate Violence, "violence may come to serve as
a temporary affirmation of an unstable self, a
material manifestation of a disembodied ideology,
an expansion of one's own insubstantial form out
into an alien world" (4). Even though Maddy's
authority is already unstable because of her gender
and class, she reveals her uncertainties as a narrator: she is striving to avoid representational
violence by acknowledging that, even as she attempts to tell the "Truth," she doubts that it is
possible to do so. She admits that, at times, she is
not simply reporting an event, but inventing it,
while at other times she admits to losing control
over the narrative. As narrator, Maddy's voice is

structurally superior to others in the gang, but she refuses to claim linguistic agency by denying other points of view. Sometimes, for example, Maddy makes it obvious that Legs has a different point of view. Furthermore, Maddy's authority is clearly contingent upon her position in the community; Legs is always first in command of the FOXFIRE gang.

As Maddy relates, the girls of FOXFIRE refuse to become the blank screens of male desire or violence. Working together, under the capable guidance of Legs, they devise a game called "hook and bait" to trap the men who would buy them for sex. Invented primarily to meet a desperate need—to raise capital to pay the gang's living expenses—the game also provides the pleasures of revenge. Their strategy is simple but effective: while one girl acts as the attractive "bait" with which to "hook" the male gaze—as if she were merely a blank screen for male desire—the rest of the gang watches, waiting for the right moment to attack. The object of the game is not to kill or injure, but to demand money from men willing to treat them as commodities. The tricky part of the game is, of course, timing the attack to catch the man with his pants down, just before the girl who is playing "bait" can be forced to turn a trick. It is Margaret "Legs" Sadovsky, the gang's remarkable leader, who invents the game following a job interview that turns into an attempted seduction. Because Legs was "fed up with the kinds of jobs available in Hammond for young women with her qualifications" (225), she had dressed as a man[2] to interview for a position as an encyclopedia salesman. When the interviewer, mistaking Legs for a young ("feminine") man, tries to seduce "him," she draws her knife. To save himself, the injured Mr. Rucke bribes Legs by giving her all he has.

"Just something that got snagged on my *hook*" (232), Legs explains upon returning to FOXFIRE with Rucke's money, watch, ring, camera, even some marijuana. Though she didn't get the job, the interview inspires the invention of the money-making game, "hook and bait." In a chapter called, "FOXFIRE HOOKING: A Miscellany, Winter 1955-56," Maddy describes the disguises worn by gang members who play "bait"—it may be "an alone-looking girl of about seventeen years of age, pretty freckled face and curly red hair" (233) or "the one with dead-white skin and luscious lips, big sloe eyes, sleek black hair" (234) or "a shapely girl with eye-catching platinum blond hair waved and curled like Marilyn Monroe's" (236). The gang stages the game in different settings—at a train depot, a hotel, and an inn—and they hook a variety of "fatherly" men: a man with "a fatherly, an avuncular look to him" (233), a man who takes "the hook in his smug little purse of a mouth" (234) with the comment, "I have a daughter myself" (235), and another man who is "a good Catholic husband and father" (236). When Maddy plays the bait, "sitting in the Trailways station glancing through a newspaper" (239), a man "with a fatherly-bullying smile" almost wins the game by leading Maddy, in a manner "snug and fatherly" (244) into an isolated alley. By the time FOXFIRE arrives to defend her, she is already swallowing blood.

Despite its dangers, the gang plays this tricky game quite successfully, hooking "fatherly" men who read them as blank screens, as bodies without voices, as "bad daughters" who function as currency to be circulated by the fathers. According to the homosocial rules of "hooking," the prostitute circulates as daughter/currency among men; however, FOXFIRE turns the tables, rewriting the rules of the game. As Elaine Scarry observes, voice and body historically have been understood as "paired opposites," a structural relationship "between the disembodied torturer (at times no more than a voice) and the (speechless) victim who is all body," a relationship that is "played out again in biblical history with a God who is all voice and in Marxist economic theory with its remote commands issued by a disembodied capitalist class" (quoted in Morris 251). Since these paired opposites—voice and body—are gendered, a (woman) writer finds herself in a different relationship to language; as de Lauretis points out, Nietzsche can speak from the position of woman, because that place is "vacant" (239). The novel makes this point most powerfully when Legs decides to kidnap a wealthy businessman and hold him for ransom. At this moment, when FOXFIRE attempts to turn a male body into a commodity—a body that the gang hopes to circulate like currency—the novel raises questions about the ethics of violence.

I will return to this ethical issue after first illustrating how the gang plays the language game—that is, how they fight sexual violence with words. I begin my analysis of the novel's word games with the gang's rewriting of the body in its ritual of membership. As Maddy reports, FOXFIRE is a linguistic creation, born during a formal swearing-in ceremony. The ceremony takes place on New Year's Day, 1953, when four girls arrive at the home of Legs (also "Sheena") Sadovsky: Goldie (also "Boom-Boom") Betty Siefried; Lana Loretta

Maguire; Rita (also "Red or Fireball") Elizabeth O'Hagan; and Madeleine (also "Maddy," "Monkey" or "Killer") Faith Wirtz. All wear black, and all wear crosses around their necks, as instructed by Legs. Once all have entered her bedroom, which is darkened except for five burning candles, Legs distributes five shot glasses filled with whiskey, "with priestly decorum" (39). Next, in an "incantatory" voice, and in language she probably borrowed from conversations with a "retired" priest, she leads them in this secret oath: "Do you solemnly swear to consecrate yourself to your sisters in FOXFIRE *yes I swear* to consecrate yourself to the vision of FOXFIRE *I do, I swear* to think always of your sisters as you would they would think of you *I do* in the Revolution of the Proletariat that is imminent in the Apocalypse that is imminent in the Valley of the Shadow of Death and under torture physical or spiritual *I do*" (39-40). The girls must also swear, "never to betray your FOXFIRE sisters in thought word or deed never to reveal FOXFIRE secrets" (39-40), a promise Maddy clearly breaks by writing the FOXFIRE confessions.

Following this swearing-in ceremony—a playfully serious parody of religious, civic, and legal ceremonies that traditionally confer power on men—Legs produces an "elegant silver ice pick" (40) with which she writes the gang's emblem upon her own body. Maddy, who is last in the ceremony, asks Legs to tattoo her left shoulder: "At first it was a tattoo of blood, oozing blood-droplets, points of pain on the pale tender flesh of Maddy's left shoulder," but after the bleeding stopped, they rubbed alcohol into their wounds and used red dye to form the flame-tattoo; then, "while the bleeding was fresh, they pressed together eagerly to mingle their blood their separate bloods" (41). In this ceremony they become "blood sisters," as Legs says, in a serious parody of homosocial rituals in which men celebrate their collective power. And in the Dionysian frenzy that follows—when Goldie is pulling down Legs's bra and giving Lana "a jungle-cat bite of a kiss," when Rita is "pressing her grapefruit-sized bare breasts against Goldie's smaller taut breasts and someone dribbled whiskey on Rita's breasts and licked it off" (42). This parody of ceremonies—those rituals in which language is an action conferring power—is not a pale imitation, but an aggressive recontextualization, a carnivalization of language by which the FOXFIRE gang appropriates linguistic power for itself.

I deliberately choose Mikhail Bakhtin's term *carnivalization* because, as Patricia Yaeger points

out in *Honey-Mad Women*, we must turn to Bakhtin, rather than Foucault, if we are to find a theory of transgressive practices that liberates not only words but speakers, speakers such as the young women in *Foxfire*. In Yaeger's view, as in mine, "There is little room in Foucault's system for the linguistic play affirmed, say, in Bakhtin's descriptions of insult and parody. According to Bakhtin, such transgressive practices allow not only words, but speakers themselves to be released 'from the shackles of sense,' to define moments within discourse when we are able 'to enjoy a period of play and complete freedom and to establish unusual relationships'" (Bakhtin, *Rabelais and His World* 423; qtd. in Yaeger 89). Although the gang enjoys only a short period of such playful freedom, they celebrate by writing on a variety of surfaces—on paper or placards, on cars, buildings, or cakes, as well as on their own flesh—and with a variety of materials—with crayons and ink, blood and frosting, paint and nail polish, ice picks and an old Underwood typewriter. They also use different genres—tattoos, graffiti, letters, and a ransom note. During these carnival moments, the gang radically reverses the position of women: FOXFIRE claims collective agency through acts of violent inscription, thereby rejecting the role of mute body, often violently inscribed by men. The novel depicts a number of these reversals.

One such reversal—also depicted as a scene of recognition between women—takes place in a chapter called "Black Eye" when Maddy's mother opens the bathroom door, which has a broken lock, to see her daughter standing before the mirror. Because it is early in the morning and both mother and daughter are half-naked, they can read what is written on the other's body: Maddy is inscribed with the "beautiful FOXFIRE tattoo . . . my tattoo so lurid and flamey red exposed for Momma to see," while her mother is inscribed with a "big purplish-orangish black eye as if a giant's fist has walloped her good on the right side of her face" (58). Although both mother and daughter have been written upon, the flame on Maddy's shoulder is a reversal, a mirror image, of the black eye inscribed by the male "giant." Men possess the power of a giant, not only because of greater physical strength, but because of economic dominance. For example, Maddy's mother has been widowed by war, but she cannot earn enough to support herself and her daughter. Yet her husband's family offers her no financial help. In fact, when Maddy asks her uncle for a favor—she wants an old Underwood he has put out with the trash—he tries to force her into providing sexual favors in exchange for the typewriter.

A second scene occurs when Legs, newly released from a girls' detention center and employed by the Park Service, accidentally comes upon a "dwarf" woman named Yetta. Legs is helping to clear underbrush at the edge of Cassadaga Park when she grows thirsty. At that moment she spots a house attached to a tavern, that happens to be closed. When no one answers her knock on the door of the house, she goes to the back yard looking for an outside faucet. There she sees a strange woman "child-size but not child-proportioned with a long torso and a misshapen back, and her face, not ugly exactly, but strange, sort of twisted like her spine" (198). What is most shocking to Legs is that "this woman is wearing a dog collar around her neck and the collar is attached to a lightweight chain which is attached to a clothesline" (198). Although Legs is a "giant" in the eyes of her gang—a mythical figure with powers usually attributed only to heroic males—Yetta is actually a mirror image of the many "dwarfing" experiences of abuse that Legs has experienced at home, at school, at work, and in a girls' detention center. Drawn to those who cannot defend themselves, imagining herself as a protector of women, Legs returns with Goldie to observe what happens to Yetta at night. Hiding in the bushes, the girls are horrified by what they see: Yetta lying "naked, spread-eagle, a terrible sight to see her with her wrists and ankles tied to the bed's four posters so her deformed body is completely exposed and completely open . . . and one by one men come into the room" (200 Oates's ellipsis).

The attachment of the tavern to a house underscores the close relationship between commercial and family violence—the latter a form of violence that, as stated above, didn't even exist until feminists named it.[3] Legs and Goldie try to prevent family violence when they return to the house where they confront a "bear-size" man who identifies himself as Yetta's brother. Boldly, since the two girls are alone, Legs argues that "there are laws prohibiting such things, abuse, forced prostitution" (200), but Yetta's brother retorts angrily that "it's none of her fucking business what people do in the privacy of their own home" (200). Unfortunately, because Legs has been abused by many figures of authority—father, principal, judge, prison guards—she does not trust them enough to ask for their help. Nonetheless, she returns, alone, to the scene of the crime. Again she watches men enter Yetta's room where "one by one bare-assed their genitals swollen, penises

stiffened into rods, mounting the dwarf-woman, the woman-that's-a-body, one by one pumping their life into her, evoking those cries" (202), and her rage flares. Recalling the words of Father Theriault, a defrocked and alcoholic priest who speaks "of capitalism of the curse of human beings apprehending one another as commodities the tragedy is that men and women not only use one another as things but use themselves, present themselves, sell themselves . . . as things" (202-3 Oates's ellipsis), Legs sets fire to the house and tavern. The fox's fire burns. In this instance, words of protest have proven to be useless. In the next chapter, called "FOXFIRE DREAM/FOXFIRE HOMESTEAD," Legs manages to finance a mortgage on an old farmhouse that, in sharp contrast to Yetta's, protects the FOXFIRE "family"—as they define themselves—from abusive men.

Almost all of the early FOXFIRE triumphs recorded by Maddy are to some degree verbal victories. For example, in their first adventure the girls cover with graffiti the car of a middle-aged math teacher who has been sexually harassing Rita "Red" O'Hagan. By age eleven, Rita had "the contours and proportions of a woman" (23), as well as a certain "conspicuous female helplessness" (25) and as a result had already begun attracting unwanted male attention. At age twelve, for example, her own brothers, along with older boys from the Viscounts gang, had made her "the object of certain acts performed upon her, or to her, or with her, for most of a long August afternoon" (25). However, when Mr. Buttinger, her ninth-grade teacher, not only made fun of Rita's mistakes but was observed "sometimes drawing his thick beefy hands against her breasts quickly and seemingly accidentally" (29), the gang decided to act. The next time Buttinger forced Rita to stay after school, they were ready: they painted "tall lurid red letters" on the back and passenger side of his 1949 Ford. During his drive home, Buttinger feels himself "running the gauntlet of witnesses, some of them students" (31), but, out of dread, waits until he arrives home to read the words that have made a "spectacle" of him: "I AM NIGGER LIPS BUTTINGER IM A DIRTY OLD MAN MMMMMM GIRLS!!! I TEACH MATH & TICKLE TITS IM BUTTINGER I EAT PUSSY" and mysteriously, on the bumper, "FOXFIRE REVENGE!" (31). Shortly afterward, Buttinger retires from teaching.

FOXFIRE's next triumph is also, in part, a matter of possessing the word—in this case, owning a typewriter. When Maddy Wirtz tries to buy her uncle's used Underwood, with which she plans to chronicle the gang's adventures, the gang saves her from his attempt at sexual blackmail. Uncle "Wimpy," as they call him, demands five dollars for the machine even though it had been put out on the curb with the garbage; "I'm a businessman, sweetie," he says, "I'm not the goddamed Salvation Army" (61). Maddy returns with borrowed money, but once again he raises the price—this time to eight dollars. Then, after teasing his niece for an hour, "He brought her hand against the front of his trousers: against his bulging crotch" (67). She manages to get away, and, after consulting with her gang, returns. Uncle Wirtz mistakenly interprets her return as signaling a willingness to submit to his sexual demands. This time, however, she has brought along the gang who wait, hidden, ready to attack when signaled. Just as Wimpy unzips his pants exposing "a red boiled sausage," Maddy "scrambles to her feet, tugs at the blind to release it so it flies up to the ceiling," calling for the attack: "they have a board they're using as a battering ram, within seconds the window is broken, shards of glass go flying, it's an explosion, it's festive, the girls of FOXFIRE piling through the window like young dogs eager for the kill, there's Legs, there's Goldie, there's Lana, there's fierce little hot-eyed Fireball, and Maddy's one of them, five girls springing on Wimpy Wirtz caught frozen in astonishment and disbelief, gaping, pants open and penis exposed, big as a club but already it's beginning to wilt, and retreat. And they're on him" (76).

Inflamed by their success, the gang finds great pleasure in writing FOXFIRE's "secret flame-tattoo in red crayon or ink or nail polish just a few inches high on a locker or a desk or a window at school" (80), or drawing "a giant flame five feet in height in bright red-blood paint on these surfaces: the eastern side of the railroad viaduct above Mohawk Street; the southern side of the Sixth Street bridge; the wall facing Fairfax Avenue of the boarded-up Tuller Bros. warehouse; the brick wall facing Ninth Street of the high school; the tattered billboard high on stilts overlooking the Northern Pacific railroad yard!" (80). Their next adventure, a protest against a pet shop's mistreatment of animals, is also a triumph of words. They drive customers away by carrying picket signs bearing the words, "TYNE PETS IS CRUEL TO ANIMALS," "IF YOU LOVE ANIMALS DON'T SHOP HERE," "SHAME SHAME SHAME," "HAVE MERCY ON ME," and "HELP ME PLEASE" (92). It is a tactic they have learned from local unions, but they add an unusual twist, disguising their identities by wearing Halloween masks: "Legs has a crafty fox mask, Goldie has a snarling wolf mask, Lana has a

snooty cat mask, Rita has a panda mask, and Maddy, naturally, has a puckish monkey mask" (92). This carnivalesque moment, in which the costumed young women assert the transformational power of the word, illustrates what Yaeger calls "the animality of the letter" even as the gang calls attention to the violence of representation: the fact that, historically, man's flight from the body has been predicated upon his identification of woman as body, animal, nature.

Of course, FOXFIRE does not define its protest in such academic rhetoric, yet Legs's sympathetic identification with Yetta, as well as the gang's with the animals at the Tyne Pet Shop, indicates a desire to transform that violent binary hierarchy: voice/body, writing/text, culture/nature, man/woman. Of course, the gang's desire for transformation includes economic hierarchies as well. As Legs understands, the power of words is not enough. FOXFIRE must have a home of its own and an adequate income. Indeed, the demise of FOXFIRE is brought about primarily (though not exclusively) by the gang's lack of a strong economic base. However, in its heady early days the gang usually managed to find ways, as well as words, to triumph over their oppressors. Halloween is such a triumphant occasion. "ITEM. Hallowe'en: the sisters of FOXFIRE in disguise as gypsies in long black skirts, exotic scarves and jewelry, wearing black domino masks travel miles away to uptown Hammond to go trick-or-treating in the affluent residential neighborhoods" (93). While trick-or-treating they acquire quite a bit of loot, "but their real mission as Legs envisions it is to familiarize themselves with alien territory—the world of the 'propertied bourgeoisie'" (95). They write their Halloween graffiti on the plate glass windows of business establishments: Lana writes, "SATAN LIVES," Maddy prints, "BEWARE THE CAT," and Legs scrawls, "NO ESCAPE NO MERCY $$$$ IS SHIT ABOMINATION DEATH" (94). In this and other episodes, the novel emphasizes the point that the gang performs its subversive acts not simply as women, but as poor women.[4]

Indeed, it is largely because she is poor and untrained in good-girl submissiveness that Legs is "detained" in Red Bank State Correctional Facility for Girls. Yes, she had pulled a knife to defend a new gang member from harassment by members of the Viscount gang, and, yes, she had stolen a car to make her getaway, but most of FOXFIRE had gone along for the ride. However, Legs is clearly their leader, and the judge must punish someone: "Legs drew what is called an indeterminate sentence, five months *minimum*, no stated *maximum*" (130) which she had the audacity to declare "*unconstitutional*" (131). In the eyes of her gang, the fact that Legs is incarcerated only raises her stature. As Oates comments, "She begins as a young girl and ascends to a kind of mythic state, at least in the minds of her Foxfire sisters" (Karpen 6). Despite her mythic attributes, Legs finally collides with the patriarchal power that cages young women—institutional power personified by principal Morton Wall, Judge Oldacker, and her father Ab Sadovsky. Though known for his public drinking and fighting, Ab Sadovsky appears in court not to support his daughter but to testify against her. Like Yetta, Legs is caged and—because she imagines herself always in flight, running like a horse,[5] climbing like a cat, even flying like a hawk—such confinement drives her almost mad.

As John Crowley says, "Legs Sadovsky is a brilliant creation—wholly heroic, wholly convincing, racing for her tragic consummation impelled by a finer sensibility and a more thoughtful daring than is usually granted to the tragic male outlaws we love and need" (6). In one legendary exploit, Legs climbs a sixty-foot water tower, defeating all male contenders for the prize money: seventy-five dollars. In another climbing exploit, Legs tries to escape from Red Bank: "skinny and snakey-agile she pushes herself through a crack between buildings" until she reaches "the wall—she doesn't hesitate, leaps up grasping at raw blunt featureless cinderblock, leaps up like a doe shot in the heart, leaps up, up, grabbing and grasping and falling back" (151). Once apprehended, her resistance only increases her prison time. However, Legs finally becomes "tractable; reasonable; obedient; good" (174) following a visit from her father, during which the sadistic man told Legs that her mother had tried to abort her. Meanwhile, the other Legs—though isolated, injured, and caged—watches "the sparrow hawks riding the air in the blue of morning," and "suddenly she was among them her arms that ached from being twisted up behind her back were wings dark-feathered powerfully muscled wings and she ascended the air, the cinderblock wall fell away" (170-71).

Legs vows, "*No one and nothing will touch me, ever again. If anybody is to kill it will be me*" (174). Although she loves Legs, Maddy cannot make such a vow. The division between Legs and Maddy over the attempt to kidnap a wealthy businessman is the result, to a large degree, of their different experiences: because Maddy's father is dead, she has not experienced paternal violence as Legs has, nor has Maddy been subjected to the violence of prison as Legs has. But their conflict can also be attributed to differences in their personalities. Both yearn for escape, but Maddy's flights tend to be primarily verbal while Legs's are primarily physical. Oates says, "The book is supposed to be a kind of dialectic between romance and realism. . . . I had originally imagined Legs Sadovsky with a great deal of motion, flying across rooftops, able to jump long distances. Probably, in a larger sense, I was writing a romance, and Legs is one of those figures out of myth" (Karpen 6). Legs is the romantic figure, but the dialectic between romance and realism, between heavenly transcendence and earthly bonds, between the freedom of flight and the pull of gravity, is intensified by Maddy's narrative strategies. As an adolescent, Maddy, the voice of "realism," was no match for Legs. Maddy tells us, "Legs talked, I listened, always I was mesmerized listening to her, always and forever" (15); "I wasn't hoping to analyze Legs' account of what had befallen her, I never tried, those early years," she says. "I wouldn't have granted Maddy Wirtz such authority!" (16).

Maddy gradually acquires a sense of her own authority, not the authority of mastery but of the imagination. As a girl, she had "loved to study maps, maps of the solar system, and the Earth, but maps too of local regions" (8); she loved writing lunar names; and she had been excited by "numbers invisible and inviolate never to be contaminated nor even touched by their human practitioners" (28). Like Legs, Maddy loves freedom, but while Legs chooses the power of moving physically through space, Maddy prefers the power of moving mentally through time and space. Maddy does, in fact, become a scientist whose work is "the contemplation and quantification of rock-debris" (322), but she returns to earth—and to the body—through the act of writing her memoir. "Writing a memoir is like pulling your own guts out inch by slow inch" (99), she says. Sadly, since the gang had pledged itself to secrecy: "Never never tell" (3, 7, 319) the act of writing is itself a betrayal of Legs and of FOXFIRE. In fact, from the start, Legs had regarded Maddy's flights of imagination as a betrayal of their friendship. Once, observing a family buying a Christmas tree, Maddy had said innocently to Legs, "There's something about other people isn't there—you'd like to know who they are?—you'd like to know who they are—you'd like to *be* them, maybe?" (21). Legs had answered, "You'd betray your friends, huh, not giving a shit about anybody who knows you and your true friend not some fucking stranger, huh?" (21).

Conflict emerges once again when Legs is released from Red Banks. Maddy senses, not without jealousy, that Legs "knows things I don't know, now" (187). For example, Legs has been brutally beaten by a female guard, and she knows now, as she tells Maddy, "that we do have enemies, yeah men are the enemy but not just men, the shock of it is that girls and women are our enemies too sometimes" (180). However, the final break between Legs and Maddy occurs when Maddy refuses to participate in the plot to kidnap a wealthy capitalist. Since Maddy's rescue during the game of "hook and bait," she recognizes that the gang's use of violence has escalated—"*Since that terrible night. I was afraid of you I guess. You saved my life but I was afraid of you having seen you hit him the way you did*" (253)—and she rejects, finally, the very American—and very male—role of romantic outlaw. Here, I believe, Maddy speaks for her author. Although Maddy is not an autobiographical character, Oates acknowledges, "I'm very much like Maddy" (Karpen 6). It is through the narrator's voice, as well as Maddy's refusal to commit a violent (or potentially violent) criminal act, that the novel makes its ethical point: when women take power, they must not simply identify with it but redefine it. Maddy's refusal to write the ransom note constitutes a betrayal of FOXFIRE, but it also marks her rejection of violence as a tactic. Her decision is primarily ethical; however, it also turns out to be practical for, in this way, Maddy avoids becoming an accessory to kidnapping.

From the start, the crime seems doomed to fail. A major problem is that the gang's carefully chosen male victim—Whitney Kellogg, Jr.—refuses to cooperate: he refuses, for example, to speak to his wife on the phone, using words dictated by his captors. A strong-willed man, he simply refuses to speak to anyone and, in this instance, silence is, ironically, more powerful than words. Another problem is that, though Legs has promised not to use violence, a new member of the gang, V. V. the Enforcer, disobeys orders and shoots their stubborn captive, seriously injuring him. At this point Legs draws the line: she calls an ambulance, ending the game. Idealistic and protective to the end, she orders all those not directly involved to run away before she drives off with V. V., Lana, and Goldie in the gang's car, LIGHTNING BOLT. It is a conclusion reminiscent of and even more ambiguous than the movie *Thelma and Louise*. For, since LIGHTNING BOLT might actually have made it across the Cassadaga bridge—in fact, "is never sighted again, so far as law enforcement authorities can determine" (316)—Legs may still live. This mystery is heightened in the novel's "Epilogue," in which Maddy returns to Hammond some years later. At this time, a now-married Rita shows Maddy a newspaper photograph taken on April 22, 1961, in which a woman—"a figure distinctly American, tall, slender, blond, male? female?"—appears to be listening intently to "a stiff bearded military figure, Fidel Castro" (324). But they can't be certain. And since much of the action in *Foxfire* occurs in Maddy's narration, the ambiguities persist.

As Maddy records the adventures of FOXFIRE, it becomes evident that the gang has nurtured her gift for words. "Rightly or wrongly," as Maddy says, she was perceived as "having the power of words" because she got good grades in writing and because she could "talk fast" (5). The close relationship between a woman's ability to fight back and her ability to talk back is established not only in many of the gang's adventures but also through Maddy's narrative technique. For example, words play an important part in the gang's final adventure (or misadventure): Maddy's refusal to write the ransom note illustrates a refusal to turn a male body into a commodity. Because Maddy begins many chapters by commenting directly upon the act of writing, her narration not only heightens the dialectic between realism and romance, it also problematizes notions of authority and truth. For example, Maddy acknowledges that she may not achieve unity or consistency in her authorial role. She says, for example, "Whoever's reading this, if anyone is reading it: does it matter that our old selves are lost to us as surely as the past is lost, or is it enough to know yes we lived then, and we're living now, and the connection must be there?" (179). She also acknowledges that she does not have complete control of the writing process. For example, in the novel's final part, five chapters are given the same title: "The Plot (I)," "The Plot (II)," "The Plot (III)," "The Plot (IV)," and "The Plot (V)"—as if a single plot cannot tell the truth, the whole truth. And she begins one chapter: "I was certain this morning I'd be writing about our FOXFIRE DREAM/FOXFIRE HOMESTEAD" (195). In this chapter, called "The Paradox of Chronology/Dwarf-Woman," Maddy supposedly "records" the encounter between Yetta and Legs; however, Maddy admits that she did not witness the actual event. How reliable, then, is her "chronicle," as she sometimes calls it?

And what, exactly, is a "fact"? She speculates openly, "If it were not for language, could we lie?" (196). As a scientist—though she admits that she

288

is not an astronomer, but only an astronomer's assistant—Maddy raises complex questions about the relationship between language, memory, imagination, and truth. For example, she says: "There's the paradox of chronology which arises when you try to record events of historical veracity; the problem of transcribing a document like this notebook is that it's a memoir or a confession where you have not the power to invent episodes, people, places, 'plot,' etc. but must set everything down as it occurred. Not imagination but memory is the agent but language is the instrument in all cases and can language be trusted?" (195-96). Admitting that the episode of the dwarf-woman was "never actually glimpsed by Maddy Wirtz," she hints at the desire prompting her to invent the dwarf-woman episode and to position it just before the chapter, "FOXFIRE DREAM/FOXFIRE HOMESTEAD." She says, "The paradox of chronology is hateful because you are always obliged to seek out earlier causes than what's at hand" (196). As Maddy knows, establishing causality is primarily a matter of careful sequencing: what happens first, it is assumed, causes what happens next. In this instance, Maddy's sequencing of events establishes the victimization of Yetta as a cause of the gang's desire for revenge against violent men. Here, by implying that revenge is the motive, Maddy contradicts an earlier statement that she is writing the gang's history to refute certain *"distortions and misunderstandings,"* such as, "Like we did evil for evil's sake, and for revenge" (3).

Of course, it is Maddy the fifty-year-old scientist-writer, not the thirteen-year-old gang member, who understands that language structures our notions of authority, truth, and social relationships. Looking at her record of the gang's adventures—defined by adolescent Maddy as a "historical document in which Truth would reside forever" (3)—the adult woman observes: "Never does Maddy record in her notebook her own doubts of herself, or of FOXFIRE" (239). Her youthful idealism—her still developing ethical sense and intense loyalty to FOXFIRE—would have made any confession of doubt difficult. While the adolescent Maddy grows intensely anxious during Legs's absence—and admits that without "certain interests of mine like reading about the stars, and Time, yes I guess and typing on the old Underwood typewriter I loved, I would not have known who I was at all. Even maybe, whether I *was*" (167)—the adult writer acknowledges, "For every fact transcribed in these CONFESSIONS there are a dozen facts, a hundred facts, my God maybe a thousand left out. . . . Can you

tell the truth if it isn't the *entire* truth" (99). Even chronology, Maddy realizes, is a fiction, a language effect. She says, "Because one thing rises out of something that came before it, or many things that came before it, so it's like a big spiderweb in Time going back forever and ever, no true beginning or any promise of an end in the way in those years it was believed the Universe was" (99). While the adolescent Maddy desired certainty from math and science—"the world of Numbers that doesn't change, immutable facts, celestial bodies" (100)—the adult acknowledges: "For all material things, we have learned in the twentieth century, are but the processes of invisible force-fields" (221).

As an author, as a writer who is presumably confessing the Truth, Maddy's reflections upon the composing process point to the instability of self, truth, and authority. Even the heavens, which once promised Maddy a stable place to drift—the very names, "OCEAN OF STORMS SEA OF TRANQUILITY LAKE OF DREAMS LAKE OF DEATH" (163) providing a sanctuary from her "scary loose slipping-down life" (166)—turn out to be constantly in flux. For the adult Maddy, the lunar names function instead as a code for the loneliness that Maddy felt in the absence of Legs but that she could not openly express. Another chapter, "A Short History of the Heavens," serves a similar metaphorical purpose. As an adolescent, Maddy had memorized certain facts—so desperate to *learn* to *memorize* things she believed to be permanent" (137)—which she now lists: reports of "fiery stones" falling from the sky in Rouen, France, in 1594; of "raining-burning rocks" falling in Salem Falls, Connecticut, in 1923; or of an object shaped like a "pineapple with wings" observed in Puce, Ontario, in 1951 (135-36). Now, such "facts" have become a code for Maddy to confess the powerful passions of her youth: her feeling, for example, that when Legs fell to the earth, it was as if the sky itself had fallen. "What is a meteorite?—it's the metallic substance of a meteoroid that has survived its swift, violent passage to earth through the earth's atmosphere. A meteoroid?—small planets or chunks of planets that, passing into the earth's atmosphere, become incandescent; sometimes trail flame" (136). To Maddy, Legs is a burning star, a meteorite or a meteoroid, an asteroid who fell to the earth.

Although science no longer provides certainty for Maddy, her use of scientific discourse allows Oates to create an evolutionary context in which to situate her analysis of human violence. As Oates says, the novel is a dialectic between romance and realism, a dialectic between the language of romance, in which giant-sized humans possess godlike powers, and the evolutionary language of science. While an individual life may appear gigantic in romantic contexts, the novel re-imagines an individual human life in an evolutionary context, as part of "a big spiderweb in Time." In a chapter called "Homo Sapiens," Oates situates the problem of human violence in just such an evolutionary context. Viewing "THE TREE OF LIFE: EVOLUTION" (102), Legs expresses indignation at such a vision of humanity—"Christ you'd think our hot-shit species would count for more than *that*" (102-3)! Maddy responds somewhat differently. At first "fascinated by how complex the tree is, how multiple its branches" (102), Maddy's faith in God is shaken by evidence that not just a single human being but an entire species can die out. The thought occurs to Maddy: "*Homo sapiens* is no big deal! and it doesn't look as if there's any logic to it, the TREE OF LIFE, man's position on the tree, *Homo sapiens: thinking man:* created by what humanoid God in His own image?" (102). What, exactly, does it mean for women to take on power within such an evolutionary context?

Through the novel's representation of violence—particularly as played out in the figures of Legs and Maddy—*Foxfire* considers a range of narrative possibilities. During their visit to the museum, for example, Legs and Maddy talk about the terrible things happening to females, things most girls didn't dare to think or talk about: the rape and strangling of a nineteen-year-old nursing student; a pregnant woman stabbed to death in her house; a serial killer charged with the death of eight girls; a little girl "slashed by some madman with a razor" (100). And Legs dares to say, "They hate us, y'know?—the sons of bitches! This is proof they hate us, they don't even know it probably, most of them, but they hate us" (101). Within an evolutionary context, the only sane option is for homo sapiens to give up romantic illusions—illusions of omnipotence, autonomy, and control. Maddy's communal narrative strategies, in concert with a plot that ends with the probable demise of FOXFIRE, emphasize the limits of human power, mental or physical. The plot also dramatizes how Legs's desire for revenge—the kidnapping plot is motivated by revenge, not just economic need—leads to destruction, to violence and death, while Maddy's communal narration encourages readers to reflect upon the possibility that fear, not strength, motivates Legs's desire for conquest of a "man." According to Jessica Benjamin, the desire for omnipotence—a desire

evident in the self presented in psychology and philosophy—is rooted in the fear of dependency upon others.

The fear of dependency can also be discerned in the linguistic habit of splitting the self into a privileged disembodied (male) voice and a repressed (m)other. It is through this type of psychic splitting, as de Lauretis points, that "violence is en-gendered in representation" (240). One consequence of such representational violence, as Carolyn Heilbrun says, is that "women have been deprived of the narratives, or the texts, plots, or examples by which they might assume power over—take control of—their own lives" (17). As Heilbrun says, "Women's exercise of power and control, and admission and expression of anger necessary to that exercise, has until recently been declared unacceptable" (17). *Foxfire, Confessions of a Girl Gang* portrays women as capable of exercising power and control, capable of expressing the unacceptable. Just as Virginia Woolf recognized that, if she wished to write, she must "kill" the Victorian Angel in the House, Oates understands that to open a creative space for women's voices, she must transform those representations of "woman" as a speechless, tortured victim into representations of women who, together, claim their voices and their agency. Ironically, given *Foxfire*'s critique of the romantic outlaw, the novel's dialectical motion also advances the argument that in order to take power over her own life, a woman must become an outlaw; she must, in community with other women, transgress sociolinguistic codes that position her outside language. The dialectic between romance and realism in *Foxfire*, as represented in the figures of Legs and Maddy, illustrates the paradox, quoted in Heilbrun's *Writing a Woman's Life,* that "all women must destroy in order to create."[6]

Notes

1. According to Oates, a movie based on *Foxfire* will be out in 1996. The name "Foxfire" may be an allusion to the original *Foxfire Books,* edited by Eliot Wigginton. Written by Eliot's students, the stories and articles in the *Foxfire Books* are about their own working-class mountain community. Tragically, although Wigginton mentored his young writers and found a publisher for them, he was later imprisoned for sexually molesting some of them. On the topic of Wigginton's sexual abuse of children, see Guy Osborne's "Eliot Wigginton: A Meditation."

2. This cross-dressing is reminiscent of Constance Philippa Zinn's transformation into a man called Philippe Fox in Oates's *A Bloodsmoor Romance.*

3. See Breines and Gordon's "The New Scholarship on Family Violence." They open by saying, "Only a few

decades ago, the term 'family violence' would have had no meaning: child abuse, wife beating, and incest would have been understood but not recognized as serious social problems" (490).

4. The fact that they are white women does not become a divisive issue until later, following Legs's release from a girls detention center, when the members of FOX-FIRE do not welcome her new African-American friends, Marigold and Tama. In the detention center itself, as Legs observes, some women are white, some black, but all are poor.

5. Legs is described as "running now, leaping and flying across the rooftops of the brownstone row houses descending the street toward the invisible river, she's a horse, a powerful stallion all hooves, flying mane, tail, snorting and steamy-breathed" (12). For an earlier version of Legs, see the story "The Witness," which opens Oates's collection *Last Days*. Significantly, an even earlier occurrence of this image of the horse can be found in *A Garden of Earthly Delights*, but in association with a male, Carleton Walpole.

6. Heilbrun is quoting Myra Jehlen's "Archimedes and the Paradox of Feminist Criticism" (583).

FURTHER READING

Bibliography

Lercangée, Francine. *Joyce Carol Oates: An Annotated Bibliography.* New York: Garland Publishing, 1986, 272 p.

Complete, well-annotated bibliography of works by and about Oates, through 1986.

Biography

Johnson, Greg. *Invisible Writer: A Biography of Joyce Carol Oates.* New York: Dutton, 1998, 492 p.

Biography of Oates which describes how Oates's upbringing, her career stopovers in Detroit and Princeton are mythologized in her fiction. An admirer of Oates, Johnson also portrays the occasionally unflattering dimension of his subject.

Criticism

Bender, Eileen Teper. *Joyce Carol Oates, Artist in Residence.* Bloomington, Ind.: Indiana University Press, 1987, 207 p.

Examines the works of Oates.

Bloom, Harold. *Joyce Carol Oates.* New York: Chelsea House Publishers, 1987, 164 p.

Offers a critical interpretation of Oates

Chell, Cara. "Un-Tricking the Eye: Joyce Carol Oates and the Feminist Ghost Story." *Arizona Quarterly* 41, no. 1 (spring 1985): 5-23.

Provides a feminist interpretation of Bellefleur, A Bloodsmoor Romance, *and* Mysteries of Winterthurn.

Creighton, Joanne V. "Unliberated Women in Joyce Carol Oates's Fiction." *World Literature Written in English* 17, no. 1 (April 1978): 165-75.

Surveys the range of female characters who fail in their quest for personal liberation in Oates's novels and short fiction.

Daly, Brenda. "'How Do We [Not] Become These People Who Victimize Us?': Anxious Authorship in the Early Fiction of Joyce Carol Oates." In *Anxious Power: Reading, Writing, and Ambivalence in Narrative by Women,* edited by Carol J. Singley and Susan Elizabeth Sweeney, pp. 235-52. Albany: State University of New York Press, 1993.

Contends that Oates's early fiction exhibits a "pattern of authorial self-division that conforms to gender conventions."

————. "Sexual Politics in Two Collections of Joyce Carol Oates's Short Fiction." *Studies in Short Fiction* 32, no. 1 (winter 1995): 83-93.

Maintains that the short story collections The Wheel of Love *and* Last Days *illustrate that Oates's feminist writings have the potential to transform gender roles.*

————. *Lavish Self-Divisions: The Novels of Joyce Carol Oates.* Jackson: University Press of Mississippi, 1996, 278 p.

Thematic analysis of Oates's novels through the 1980s.

Goodman, Charlotte. "Women and Madness in the Fiction of Joyce Carol Oates." *Women & Literature* 5, no. 2 (fall 1977): 17-28.

Surveys the psychologically disturbed female characters in Oates's fiction.

Petite, Joseph. "A Predator in Liberationist Clothing." *Journal of Evolutionary Psychology* 7, nos. 3-4 (August 1986): 245-48.

Petite investigates the repressed nature of the female characters in Do with Me What You Will.

Wesley, Marilyn C. "Father-Daughter Incest as Social Transgression: A Feminist Reading of Joyce Carol Oates." *Women's Studies* 21, no. 3 (1992): 251-64.

Considers the recurring theme of father-daughter incest in Oates's fiction.

————. "Reverence, Rape, Resistance: Joyce Carol Oates and Feminist Film Theory." *Mosaic* 32, no. 3 (September 1999): 75-85.

Applies feminist film theory to Oates's short story "The Girl."

OTHER SOURCES FROM GALE:

Additional coverage of Oates's life and career is contained in the following sources published by the Gale Group: *American Writers Supplement,* Vol. 2; *Authors and Artists for Young Adults,* Vols. 15, 52; *Authors in the News,* Vol. 1; *Beacham's Encyclopedia of Popular Fiction: Biography & Resources,* Vol. 2; *Beacham's Guide to Literature for Young Adults,* Vol. 11; *Bestsellers,* Vol. 89:2; *Concise Dictionary of American Literary Biography, 1968-1988; Contemporary Authors,* Vols. 5-8R; *Contemporary Authors New Revision Series,* Vols. 25, 45, 74, 113; *Contemporary Literary Criticism,* Vols. 1, 2, 3, 6, 9, 11, 15, 19, 33, 52, 108, 134; *Contemporary Novelists,* Ed. 7; *Contemporary Poets,* Ed. 7; *Contemporary Popular Writers; Contemporary Women Poets; Dictionary of Literary Biography,* Vols. 2, 5, 130; *Dictionary of Literary Biography Yearbook,* 1981; *DISCovering Authors; DISCovering Authors: British Edition; DISCovering Authors: Canadian Edition; DISCovering Authors Modules: Most-studied Authors, Novelists,* and *Popular Writers; DISCovering Authors 3.0; Encyclopedia of World Literature in the 20th Century,* Ed. 3; *Exploring Short Stories; Feminist Writers; Literature and Its Times,* Vol. 4; *Literature Resource Center; Major 20th-Century Writers,* Eds. 1, 2; *Modern American Women Writers; Novels for Students,* Vol. 8; *Reference Guide to American Literature,* Ed. 4; *Reference Guide to Short Fiction,* Ed. 2; *St. James Guide to Horror, Ghost & Gothic Writers; Short Stories for Students,* Vol. 17; *Short Story Criticism,* Vol. 6; *Supernatural Fiction Writers,* Vol. 2; *Twayne's United States Authors;* and *World Literature Criticism.*

SYLVIA PLATH

(1932 - 1963)

(Also wrote under the pseudonym Victoria Lucas)
American poet, novelist, short story writer, essayist,
memoirist, and scriptwriter.

Plath is widely considered one of the most
emotionally evocative and compelling American poets of the postwar period. Although Plath
gained only modest critical success during her
lifetime, after her suicide at the age of thirty and
the subsequent publication of her poetry collection *Ariel* (1965) she achieved widespread acclaim
as a poet. This status was affirmed when Plath's
posthumously published *Collected Poems* (1981)
was awarded the Pulitzer Prize for poetry in 1982.
Plath also wrote a semi-autobiographical novel
titled *The Bell Jar* (1963), which, like her poetry,
reveals an intensely personal struggle with self-consciousness, bold metaphors for death and
sexuality, and a pioneering examination of societal
limitations experienced by women. A complicated
literary personality whose biography is nearly
impossible to disentangle from her writing, Plath
has often been regarded as a confessional poet,
though her deeply personal lamentations often
achieve universality through mythic allusion and
archetypal symbolism. Viewed as a cathartic
response to her divided personae as an artist,
mother, and wife, Plath's works have been heralded by feminist critics for illuminating the

personal and professional obstacles faced by
women in the mid-twentieth century. These factors, combined with her tragic death, have made
Plath an iconic figure whose popular fame has
nearly equaled her literary acclaim.

BIOGRAPHICAL INFORMATION

Plath was born in Boston, Massachusetts, on
October 27, 1932, the eldest child of Otto Emil
and Aurelia Plath. Her father was a German immigrant who served as a professor of entomology
at Boston College. An undiagnosed diabetic, Otto
died in 1940 after complications resulting from
surgery to amputate his leg. His death devastated
Plath, who was then eight years old, and the sense
of betrayal she felt following his passing would
later become a major theme in her writing. While
in her teens, Plath began to publish poetry and
short fiction in various magazines, including *Seventeen* and the *Christian Science Monitor*. A precocious and highly motivated student, she received
a scholarship and attended Smith College beginning in 1950. There, she continued to earn academic distinction and in 1953 she was selected to
serve as a student editor for *Mademoiselle* magazine
in New York City. Due to the stressful conditions
of the guest editorship and the subsequent rejection of her application to a Harvard short story
class taught by Frank O'Connor, Plath lapsed into
a severe depression which culminated in her first

suicide attempt. After overdosing on sleeping pills, she was hospitalized and received psychiatric care, including electroshock therapy to treat her depression. Plath convalesced and received outpatient psychiatric treatment for several months before returning to Smith College and graduating *summa cum laude* with a degree in English in 1955. That same year, Plath received a Fulbright scholarship and enrolled in Newnham College in Cambridge, England. There, she met English poet Ted Hughes, whom she married after a brief courtship in 1956. After completing her master's degree at Cambridge in 1957, Plath settled with Hughes in the United States, where she taught English at Smith College and attended poetry workshops given by Robert Lowell at Boston University. In 1959 Plath and Hughes returned to England, where she gave birth to their first child, Freida. Her first book of poetry, *The Colossus*, appeared in 1960. In 1961 she began work on *The Bell Jar*, which was published in London two years later under the pseudonym Victoria Lucas. In 1962 Plath gave birth to a second child, Nicholas. That same year, she learned that Hughes was having an affair with another woman, and the two separated. During the divorce proceedings, Plath moved to a London apartment with her two children, where she became increasingly despondent. On February 11, 1963, she committed suicide by inhaling gas from her kitchen stove.

MAJOR WORKS

Commentators have generally agreed that Plath's literary oeuvre is remarkable for its unrestrained emotional intensity and its ubiquitous incorporation of personal detail inspired by the author's own life experiences. *The Bell Jar*, Plath's only novel, is perhaps her most explicitly autobiographical work. It recounts events strikingly similar to Plath's demanding student internship at *Mademoiselle*, her suicide attempt, and her subsequent psychiatric rehabilitation. The novel's protagonist, Esther Greenwood, becomes dissatisfied with her work at a New York magazine and struggles to develop her self-identity in opposition to conventional female roles. After strained encounters with several men who attempt either to manipulate or to subjugate Esther, she leaves New York and returns home, where she becomes depressed and attempts suicide. Esther is then hospitalized and undergoes electroshock treatment, eventually improving enough to return to school, although another breakdown threatens. Throughout the book, Esther seeks her own identity by comparing herself to other feminine

archetypes whom she encounters, including a benevolent female doctor who is instrumental in her rehabilitation and a lesbian acquaintance who ultimately commits suicide. In the course of the novel, Esther also ponders the traditional expectations placed upon women and displays a strong aversion to the prospect of a stifling domestic existence as a mother and housewife.

Critics have observed that Plath's first poetry collection, *The Colossus*, displays an overriding preoccupation with estrangement, motherhood, and fragmentation within contemporary society. Many have further asserted that the collection demonstrates Plath's mastery of traditional literary forms while bearing the influence of confessional poets such as Robert Lowell and Anne Sexton. Several of the poems in this collection introduce Plath's obsession with the symbol of the father figure, who is treated with scorn and rage but who is also invoked as a muse. The starkly direct poems in *Ariel*—many of which were written in the months and weeks prior to Plath's death—address similar subjects to those in *The Colossus* but display a more distinctive voice and a less formal style. Critics have pointed out that psychic distress is signaled through brutal self-revelation, violent imagery, and macabre associations, including disconcerting references to Nazis and the Holocaust. "Lady Lazarus" features a speaker who addresses "Herr Doktor" and references lampshades that Nazi torturers fashioned from the skin of their victims. The poem's central metaphor, the resurrected Lazarus from the Bible, has often been read as a reference to a woman who has survived several suicide attempts. The closing declaration of the woman's ability to "eat men like air" sounds a note of revenge against the male figure the speaker identifies as her "Enemy." Similar references are found in "Daddy," where the poetic voice associates both her father and husband with Nazism and herself with Jewish victims of the Holocaust. The title poem, "Ariel," displays Plath's intricate use of color imagery. It encompasses a forceful move from darkness to light that has been interpreted as a woman speaker transforming herself into the male image of the arrow. The poet's ongoing fascination with death is sounded in many of the *Ariel* poems, including "Edge," which presents a vision of a dead woman holding two dead children and noting the woman's "smile of accomplishment."

CRITICAL RECEPTION

Most critics have acknowledged that Plath's poems display an accomplished technical acumen and a brilliant, yet stark insight into severe psychological disintegration and harrowing existential anxiety. Many have also asserted that despite its overall gravity, her poetry exhibits an appealing undercurrent of irony and dark humor in its treatment of morbid themes. However, some commentators have objected to what they perceive as Plath's histrionic display of emotion, inaccessible personal allusions, and nihilistic obsession with death. These critics have further averred that her use of horrific events as metaphors for personal anguish might be considered gratuitous and inappropriate. Regardless of the critical debate about the merit of Plath's themes and motifs, feminist scholars have championed the poet for her pioneering efforts to expose the absurdity of conventional feminine models and her attempts to establish equal footing for women writers in a male-dominated publishing industry. Indeed, critics have identified *The Bell Jar* as a groundbreaking female version of the typically masculine coming-of-age novel and hailed the book's incisive portrayal of the frustrations felt by a talented and ambitious young woman in a profession dominated by men. At least one critic, Diane S. Bonds, has challenged this notion, arguing that Esther's experience represents the concept of a separative model of selfhood. Bonds concluded that because Esther fails to cultivate a network of positive, non-hierarchical relations, especially with other women, within the challenging parameters of her masculine environment she is likely to re-experience the alienation that led to her suicide attempt. Joyce Carol Oates (see Further Reading) has also written of this alienation in Plath's poetry, contending that it represents outmoded Romantic ideas that identify the human condition as one of isolated competition. In this context, Oates has characterized Plath's poems as "regressive fantasies" that speak of a separate self rather than a universal one. Most feminist critics have affirmed, however, that insurmountable masculine oppression is what led to Plath's obsessive preoccupation with alienation. Kathleen Margaret Lant has asserted that "Ariel" serves as an analogy for Plath's role as a woman poet and argues that the female speaker's attempt to transform herself into a more masculine figure ultimately proves futile. Similarly, other scholars have discussed "Lady Lazarus" in the context of this struggle, with Maureen Curley (see Further Reading) contending that the poem serves as a commentary on the difficulties faced by female artists and Laura Johnson Dahlke (see Further Reading) concluding that the speaker's conflict with "Herr Doktor" represents a struggle against male dominance that ultimately ends in defeat. Christina Britzolakis has extended this gender conflict to society as a whole, arguing that Plath addresses a much larger issue than mere feelings of alienation and futility in the face of male domination. According to Britzolakis, Plath's poetry can be seen as an exhibition of ironic self-reflection in response to the widespread cultural objectification of women as mere commodities for mass consumption.

PRINCIPAL WORKS

The Colossus (poetry) 1960

Three Women: A Monologue for Three Voices (radio play) 1962

The Bell Jar [originally published under pseudonym Victoria Lucas] (novel) 1963

Ariel (poetry) 1965

Crossing the Water: Transitional Poems (poetry) 1971

Crystal Gazer and Other Poems (poetry) 1971

Winter Trees (poetry) 1971

Letters Home: Correspondence, 1950-1963 (letters) 1975

The Bed Book (juvenilia) 1976

Johnny Panic and the Bible of Dreams, and Other Prose Writings [edited by Ted Hughes] (short stories, prose, and diary entries) 1977; also published as *Johnny Panic and the Bible of Dreams: Short Stories, Prose, and Diary Excerpts* [enlarged edition] 1979

Collected Poems (poetry) 1981

The Journals of Sylvia Plath, 1950-1962 (diaries) 1982

Sylvia Plath's Selected Poems (poetry) 1985

Plath: Poems (poetry) 1998

The Unabridged Journals of Sylvia Plath, 1950-1962 (journals) 2000

PRIMARY SOURCES

SYLVIA PLATH (NOVEL DATE 1963)

SOURCE: Plath, Sylvia. *The Bell Jar*, pp. 215-23. 1963. Reprint. New York: Perennial Classics, 1999.

In the following excerpt from The Bell Jar, *the protagonist, Esther Greenwood, reflects on motherhood as she visits a doctor's office to be fitted for a birth-control device.*

I waited for the doctor, wondering if I should bolt. I knew what I was doing was illegal—in Massachusetts, anyway, because the state was cram-jam full of Catholics—but Doctor Nolan said this doctor was an old friend of hers, and a wise man.

"What's your appointment for?" the brisk, white-uniformed receptionist wanted to know, ticking my name off on a notebook list.

"What do you mean, *for*?" I hadn't thought anybody but the doctor himself would ask me that, and the communal waiting room was full of other patients waiting for other doctors, most of them pregnant or with babies, and I felt their eyes on my flat, virgin stomach.

The receptionist glanced up at me, and I blushed.

"A fitting, isn't it?" she said kindly. "I only wanted to make sure so I'd know what to charge you. Are you a student?"

"Ye-es."

"That will only be half-price then. Five dollars, instead of ten. Shall I bill you?"

I was about to give my home address, where I would probably be by the time the bill arrived, but then I thought of my mother opening the bill and seeing what it was for. The only other address I had was the innocuous box number which people used who didn't want to advertise the fact they lived in an asylum. But I thought the receptionist might recognize the box number, so I said, "I better pay now," and peeled five dollar notes off the roll in my pocketbook.

The five dollars was part of what Philomena Guinea had sent me as a sort of get-well present. I wondered what she would think if she knew to what use her money was being put.

Whether she knew it or not, Philomena Guinea was buying my freedom.

"What I hate is the thought of being under a man's thumb," I had told Doctor Nolan. "A man doesn't have a worry in the world, while I've got a baby hanging over my head like a big stick, to keep me in line."

"Would you act differently if you didn't have to worry about a baby?"

"Yes," I said, "but . . ." and I told Doctor Nolan about the married woman lawyer and her Defense of Chastity.

Doctor Nolan waited until I was finished. Then she burst out laughing. "Propaganda!" she said, and scribbled the name and address of this doctor on a prescription pad.

I leafed nervously through an issue of *Baby Talk*. The fat, bright faces of babies beamed up at me, page after page—bald babies, chocolate-colored babies, Eisenhower-faced babies, babies rolling over for the first time, babies reaching for rattles, babies eating their first spoonful of solid food, babies doing all the little tricky things it takes to grow up, step by step, into an anxious and unsettling world.

I smelt a mingling of Pablum and sour milk and salt-cod-stinky diapers and felt sorrowful and tender. How easy having babies seemed to the women around me! Why was I so unmaternal and apart? Why couldn't I dream of devoting myself to baby after fat puling baby like Dodo Conway?

If I had to wait on a baby all day, I would go mad.

I looked at the baby in the lap of the woman opposite. I had no idea how old it was, I never did, with babies—for all I knew it could talk a blue streak and had twenty teeth behind its pursed, pink lips. It held its little wobbly head up on its shoulders—it didn't seem to have a neck—and observed me with a wise, Platonic expression.

The baby's mother smiled and smiled, holding that baby as if it were the first wonder of the world. I watched the mother and the baby for some clue to their mutual satisfaction, but before I had discovered anything, the doctor called me in.

"You'd like a fitting," he said cheerfully, and I thought with relief that he wasn't the sort of doctor to ask awkward questions. I had toyed with the idea of telling him I planned to be married to a sailor as soon as his ship docked at the Charlestown Navy Yard, and the reason I didn't have an engagement ring was because we were too poor, but at the last moment I rejected that appealing story and simply said "Yes."

I climbed up on the examination table, thinking: "I am climbing to freedom, freedom from fear, freedom from marrying the wrong person, like Buddy Willard, just because of sex, freedom from the Florence Crittenden Homes where all the poor girls go who should have been fitted out like me, because what they did, they would do anyway, regardless. . . ."

As I rode back to the asylum with my box in the plain brown paper wrapper on my lap I might have been Mrs. Anybody coming back from a day in town with a Schrafft's cake for her maiden aunt or a Filene's Basement hat. Gradually the suspicion that Catholics had X-ray eyes diminished, and I grew easy. I had done well by my shopping privileges, I thought.

I was my own woman.

The next step was to find the proper sort of man.

GENERAL COMMENTARY

CHRISTINA BRITZOLAKIS (ESSAY DATE 1999)

SOURCE: Britzolakis, Christina. "The Spectacle of Femininity." In *Sylvia Plath and the Theatre of Mourning*, pp. 135-56. Oxford: Clarendon Press, 1999.

In the following essay, Britzolakis surveys Plath's poems as examples of ironic self-analysis in response to the cultural objectification femininity as a commodity fit for mass consumption.

Although Plath is often celebrated as the poet of anguished authenticity, she can equally be seen as harnessing the expressive conventions of the lyric cry for a language of elaborate inauthenticity. Her rhetoric encodes a spectacular relation between poet and audience, foregrounding questions of sexuality and power in ways which have only recently begun to be acknowledged. The later Plath in particular makes her distinctive black comedy by crossing Orphic myths of the inspired poet with an ironic deployment of stereotypes of alienated or objectified femininity. In this chapter, I shall argue that the ironic specularity or self-reflexivity at work in Plath's language is an effect not merely of literary history, or of the literary market, but also of a culture of consumption in which images of women circulate as commodities. The visual objectification of femininity has now become a familiar theme of feminist cultural criticism and practice, especially in the area of film and photography.[1] Long before notions of the 'gaze' became current in cultural debate, however, Plath's poetry explored the ambivalent alignments of woman with both consumer and commodity.

The Spectacle of Femininity: The Question of Style

One of the stock themes of Plath criticism is the stylistic transformation which the *Ariel* poems represent in relation to *The Colossus*: from an academic formalism heavily influenced by the New Critics towards a more colloquial, immediate voice, depending less on discursive logic than on a logic of elliptically juxtaposed, startling images.

FROM THE AUTHOR

JOURNAL ENTRY
November 7, 1959, Saturday. . . .

Dangerous to be so close to Ted day in day out. I have no life separate from his, am likely to become a mere accessory. Important to take German lessons, go out on my own, think, work on my own. Lead separate lives. I must have a life that supports me inside. This place a kind of terrible nunnery for me. I hate our room: the sterile white of it, the beds filling the whole place. Loved the little crowded Boston apartment, even though J. Panic visited me there.

What horrifies me most is the idea of being useless: well-educated, brilliantly promising, and fading out into an indifferent middle-age. Instead of working at writing, I freeze in dreams, unable to take disillusion of rejections. Absurd. I am inclined to go passive, and let Ted be my social self. Simply because we are never apart. Now, for example: the several things I can do apart from him: study German, write, read, walk alone in the woods or go to town. How many couples could stand to be so together? The minute we get to London I must strike out on my own. I'd be better off teaching than writing a couple of mediocre poems a year, a few mad, self-centered stories. Reading, studying, "making your own mind" all by oneself is just not my best way. I need the reality of other people, work, to fulfill myself. Must never become a mere mother and housewife. Challenge of baby when I am so unformed and unproductive as a writer. A fear for the meaning and purpose of my life. I will hate a child that substitutes itself for my own purpose: so I must make my own.

Plath, Sylvia. "Boston 1958-1959." In *The Journals of Sylvia Plath*. New York: Dial Press, 1982, pp. 328-29.

Alicia Ostriker sees this change of style as a form of 'Americanization'. A risk-taking technique which insists on the 'cutting edge' of immediate factual reality, 'a kind of journalism of obsessions', is, she argues, a peculiarly American one, also practised by Thoreau, Whitman, Williams, and Frost.[2] The language of Plath's later poems undoubtedly draws upon the 'flashy' naturalistic idiom of contemporary American speech. But this change of stylistic register cannot be seen merely in terms of liberation from a tradition-bound academicism, which thereby inserts Plath into another tradition: that of American literary anti-traditionalism. The project of 'making it new', of renewing and paring down the language of poetry, is a feature shared by a range of different modernisms. It has even been seen as part of the definition of literary history itself.[3] The narrative of Plath's stylistic development as a process of leaving behind or shedding the trappings of literary history is therefore a deceptive one, even when Plath's own figurative strategies seem to underwrite it.

For some of Plath's critics, as we have seen, the stylistic 'break-through' of *Ariel* is part of a narrative of authentic self-realization or self-destruction. For others, however, it unleashes charges of theatricality and sensationalism. For example, David Shapiro deplores her reliance on cliché, hyperbole, and melodrama; Hugh Kenner claims that 'all her life, a reader had been someone to manipulate', and Philip Hobsbaum identifies her 'faults of style' as 'verbal conceit' and 'emotive sensationalism'.[4] The later Plath has even been seen as an aestheticist, a poet of decadent sensation rather than of immediacy. One of the most striking features of her later style is, after all, the foregrounding of the individual detail, often at the expense of the larger syntactic unit. In 1968, Arthur K. Oberg, noting the recurrent *fin-de-siècle* iconography in Plath's work, hailed her as the prophet of 'a new Decadence'. He saw certain features of the *Ariel* poems as axiomatically Decadent: the association of aesthetic perfection with death; the attraction towards stasis and 'sculpted form'; the 'self-generating and self-sustaining' quality of the images; the internalization of objective reality and consequent 'loss of an available world'; and the 'histrionic exhibition of herself and her wounds'.[5]

The critical debate about Plath tends to be organized around an opposition between expressive depths and tawdry surfaces, between 'high' and 'low' culture. Yet it is this very opposition which her 'Decadent' style puts into question, since it situates itself as part of a culture in which self-revelation or self-expression has itself become a cliché. Plath cannot, as Jacqueline Rose has pointed out, be 'made into an emblem for the flight of poetry—poetry as the expression of a transcendent selfhood, poetry as rising above the dregs of the culture which it leaves behind'.[6] Although at one level her Decadent tactics, such as the decomposition of 'organic' narrative into individual detail, purport to remove the artist from 'vulgar' or prosaic reality, at another they are revealed as entirely compatible with popular culture. They form part of a verbal landscape saturated with visual spectacle and the melodramatic plots of mass culture. The Decadent cult of artifice, performance, and libidinal excess becomes a metaphor for the aestheticization of everyday life in consumer culture, which, indeed, it anticipates.

Plath's formation as a poet coincides with the point at which modernism began, in the 1950s, to be canonized and institutionalized within the Anglo-American academy. At the same time, a debate about the origins and effects of mass culture was in progress, tending to position it as the antagonist of true culture.[7] Clement Greenberg's opposition between true art and kitsch, Dwight MacDonald's description of mass culture as a 'spreading ooze', and Theodor Adorno's critique of the 'culture industry' all contributed to the prestige of modernist anxiety and alienation during the Cold War, as a trope of aesthetic resistance to totalitarian ideologies.[8] The category of the 'classic' was being constituted in reaction against, but also as a product of, consumer society. High culture was thought to be in need of protection and custody, if the mass media with their 'unchecked circulation of high and low' were not to have 'the effect of transforming all culture into mass culture'.[9]

Plath's various styles imply a self-consciously appropriative and factitious, 'postmodern' relation to literary tradition; her poetry seems to *consume* culture as a random assortment of styles which circulate promiscuously. In a famous essay, 'Postmodernism, or the Cultural Logic of Late Capitalism', Frederic Jameson sets up an opposition between 'pastiche', which he sees as characteristically postmodernist, and 'parody', which is properly modernist; while the latter assumes a norm, from which it deviates, the former is neutral and unmotivated, void of the critical distance which is capable of positing a norm, that is, 'blank parody'.[10] Pastiche embraces the depthlessness of the simulacrum; it presupposes 'the effacement . . . of the older (essentially high-modernist) frontier between high culture and so-called mass or commercial culture'.[11] By contrast, parody clings to modernism's adversary role as a critique of social reality.[12]

The element of pastiche in Plath's work turns 'style' into a dialogue with commodity culture that undermines the hierarchies of value implicit in the concept itself. However, Jameson's opposition between parody and pastiche, like the larger opposition of modernism and postmodernism to which it is linked, is notoriously difficult to sustain, and nowhere more so than in relation to Plath. If at one level her poems embrace the depthlessness of popular culture, at another they are, in the words of Terry Eagleton's 1985 rejoinder to Jameson's essay, 'still agonizedly caught up in metaphysical depth and wretchedness, still able to experience psychic fragmentation and social alienation as spiritually wounding'.[13] I am not arguing, then, that Plath's work abolishes critical distance in some postmodernist carnival of schizophrenic 'intensities'. On the contrary, through the dominant trope of 'confession' Plath charts the operations of power upon the subject and upon language in intensely negative terms.

Style and the Woman

As a writer, Plath framed herself, and was framed, within a highly gendered literary market in which 'pulp' writing was associated with femininity and truly literary writing with masculinity. Andreas Huyssen has pointed out the historical tendency of modernism to position mass culture as its feminine 'other'. The 'imaginary femininity' assumed by many male modernist artists repudiates the strenuously active, self-defining bourgeois subject of modernity, while maintaining 'the exclusion of real women from the literary enterprise and . . . the misogyny of bourgeois patriarchy itself'.[14] Flaubert's famous statement, 'Madame Bovary, c'est moi' positions 'woman (Madame Bovary) . . . as reader of inferior literature—subjective, emotional and passive— while man (Flaubert) emerges as writer of genuine authentic literature—objective, ironic, and in control of his aesthetic means'.[15] With the institutionalization of modernism, and the consequent watering down of its oppositional status, this distinction—always a defensive and imperilled gesture, as Huyssen shows—becomes well-nigh impossible to maintain. Moreover, many of the ethical imperatives, such as the internalization of patriarchal authority, which structure the separate constitution and validation of male and female subjectivity in bourgeois society, are themselves eroded by the culture of consumption.[16] Images of women circulate in both modernism and 'mass' culture as objects of identification and desire. As we have seen, Plath ironizes this collusion by exploiting the association of femininity with masquerade, with seduction and false representation. In her poems, the speaking subject invents and reinvents herself as an ensemble of staged and theatrical identities which range across both high and low culture.

Amongst the images of women which appear most frequently in Plath's poetry are those of the prostitute, the female performer and the mechanical woman. In male-authored *fin-de-siècle* literature, these figures serve, as Rita Felski has pointed out, as emblems of a crisis of modernity, signalling an ambivalent response to the rationalizing, technological vision of capitalist progress.[17] Plath appropriates these images for her exploration of the fractured and crisis-ridden identities of woman as poet, wife, mother, consumer, and commodity-spectacle. In '**Fever 103°**', for example, the quasi-cinematic 'cutting' from one apparently self-generating image to another corresponds to a series of rhetorical masks assumed by the peaking subject, who remodels herself endlessly, sometimes in the image of masculine desire, sometimes in that of her own. Performance and intoxication seem to feed upon each other in a kind of erethism of images, plotting a transcendence parodically redefined as an erotic, indeed orgasmic event. The parody of spiritual purgation and transcendence evokes Baudelaire's poem 'Élévation', in which the poet counsels his spirit to 'Ascend beyond the sickly atmosphere ¦ To a higher plane, and purify yourself'.[18] The speaker of '**Fever 103°**' arrogates to herself both the disease and the cure, the foggy, splenetic resentment of the time-bound self and the virile aspiring spirit. As in '**Ariel**', the shedding of layers of 'impure' selfhood is seen as an autoerotic process. Notwithstanding its powerful sexual charge, this self-delighting language is fuelled by a Nietzschean will to appearance. The speaker becomes, successively, a lover 'flickering' with the fever of desire, a starved ascetic or saint who is 'too pure' for lovers, and an exotic *object d'art* with a high market value ('My head a moon ¦ Of Japanese paper, my gold beaten skin ¦ Infinitely delicate and infinitely expensive'). She oscillates between the positions of artist and artefact, consumer and commodity. Amongst the explicitly theatrical incarnations assumed are the *fin-de-siècle* figure of the dancer Isadora Duncan, and the Virgin Mary. These roles are explicitly assumed *for an audience*, for the lover/reader to whom the poem is addressed:

The beads of hot metal fly, and I, love, I

Am a pure acetylene
Virgin
Attended by roses,

By kisses, by cherubim,
By whatever these pink things mean.
Not you, nor him,

Not him, nor him
(My selves dissolving, old whore petticoats)—
To paradise.

The culminating moment in which the 'I' asserts its transcendence is a revelation of pure kitsch—'I ¦ Am a pure acetylene ¦ Virgin'. The conceit yokes together the 'white heat' of industrial technology with the Madonna's halo, parodying the Marian iconography of submissiveness and meekness; this is a Virgin burning with the fiercely corrosive, precisely directed flame of a blowtorch. Hyperbole in Plath's work tends to align itself with kitsch, which Theodor Adorno calls 'a parody of catharsis'.[19] In this case it is a *cult* image that has been mechanically reproduced, making it the very apotheosis of insincerity: the virgin Mary as prostitute.

The self as pure invention, as the libidinally charged 'flickering' play of images: what could be more postmodern than this? Yet to represent these disposable 'selves' as 'old whore petticoats', i.e. as prostitution, is to invoke an older, ethical language of modernity. In exploiting the creative possibilities of illusion and spectacle—in producing herself as an ensemble of images for an audience—the speaker risks colluding in her own cultural objectification. Her ironic pleasure in this process is revealed as intimately in league with commodity fetishism. In 'A Birthday Present', the power of endless self-transformation is attributed to the mysterious object of the title, which is feminized through recurrent images of veiling and unveiling. The mystical, even transcendent character of the birthday present recalls Marx's description of commodity fetishism.[20] It marks a shift towards a non-representational aesthetic; the status of 'nature' is no longer given, no longer rooted in a recognizable life-world, but uncanny. As Elizabeth Wright argues, the uncanny 'makes us see the world not as ready-made for description, depiction or portrayal (common terms used to say what an artist or writer does), but as in a constant process of construction, deconstruction and reconstruction'.[21] This uncanny world, where nature threatens to do a disappearing act, is also the world of commodity culture, which thrives on images which endlessly veil and defer the truth.

Yet the seductive variety of the birthday present conceals a relentless logic of abstract equivalence, the logic of the 'adding machine', which erases all distinctive attributes of self and world.

Walter Benjamin's essay, 'The Work of Art in the Age of Mechanical Reproduction', famously argues that photographic technology transforms the mode of reception of art, abolishing what he calls the aura of the artefact, the cultic distance between the artefact and its viewer.[22] In Plath's later poetry the pathos of lyric subjectivity is constantly undercut by the reproduced image. The element of compulsive visualization, the piling up of images with what Calvin Bedient calls an 'optic desperation', cannot be understood in terms of print culture alone.[23] These images have a hallucinatory vividness inseparable from a culture saturated and erotically charged with simulacra. In 'Fever 103°' the lines 'Greasing the bodies of adulterers ¦ Like Hiroshima ash and eating in. ¦ The sin. The sin' allude to a scene in Alain Resnais's film *Hiroshima Mon Amour* (1961). Exotic and brilliantly coloured plants and flowers, including spotted orchids, camellias ('Fever 103°'), tiger lilies ('The Night Dances'), and sea anemones ('Lesbos') form a décor, a Decadent iconography drawn from the collective imaginary of the mass media. The phantasmagoria of *Ariel* implies an ambiguous interdependence between aesthetic appearance and commodity fetishism.

Movie Nightmares

What I have called the 'phantasmagoria' of Plath's poems is, in part, an effect of her ironic exploitation of the 'sensationalist' or 'subliterary' resources of the Gothic mode. M. L. Rosenthal complains that poems such as 'Stopped Dead', 'The Tour', 'Eavesdropper', and 'A Secret', 'are hard to penetrate in their morbid secretiveness', 'make a weirdly incantatory black magic against unspecified persons and situations', and 'often seem to call for biographical rather than poetical explanations'.[24] These 'weird' scenarios recycle key motifs of Gothic popular culture, drawing on cinematic as well as literary texts, to probe the nightmarish underside of the Cold War suburban dream of normality. Their satirical target, like that of many contemporary thrillers and horror films, is the stifling family-centred and ethnocentric conformity of the 1950s small-town idyll. Frederic Jameson points out that 'Gothics are . . . ultimately a class fantasy (or nightmare) in which the dialectic of privilege and shelter is exercised: your privileges seal you off from other people, but by the same token they constitute a protective wall through which you cannot see, and behind which therefore all kinds of envious forces may be imagined in the process of assembling, plotting, preparing to give assault; it is, if you like, the shower-curtain syndrome (alluding to *Psycho*)'.[25]

The cross-cutting of images in Plath's later poems generates a series of quasi-cinematic narrative moments. In 'Berck-Plage', 'A green pool opens its eye, ¦ Sick with what it has swallowed—¦ Limbs, images, shrieks.' Another horror-film moment occurs in 'A Birthday Present' when a dismembered body turns up in the innocuous guise of a birthday present: 'Let it not come by the mail, finger by finger.' Old love letters are described as 'unroll(ing) ¦ Sands where a dream of clear water ¦ Grinned like a getaway car' ('Burning the Letters'). In 'Stopped Dead', the speaker addresses a murderous male companion, 'out cold' beside her in a car 'hung out over the dead drop' of a cliffside. The 'Eavesdropper' peers through windows, harbouring murderous designs on her neighbours, in a malicious parody of the suburban ethos of good-neighbourliness which recalls Hitchcock's *Rear Window* (1953).

The paradigmatic Gothic film scenario converts the threatened murder or victimization of a woman into fetishistic spectacle. Many of Plath's poems work ironic variations and reversals on this theme. 'Stopped Dead', for example, echoes the plot of Hitchcock's *Shadow of a Doubt* (1943), where the young suburban heroine, Charlie, finds out that her beloved and long-lost uncle, newly arrived in 'our town', is the murderer of wealthy widows. 'Who do you think I am, ¦ Uncle, uncle? Sad Hamlet, with a knife? ¦ Where do you stash your life?' asks the poem's speaker. In *Shadow of a Doubt*, Uncle Charlie is indeed a 'sad Hamlet, with a knife', who at one point makes a speech railing against the corruption of women which has turned the world into a 'foul sty', 'a filthy, rotting place'. By threatening to expose his criminal identity ('I know a secret about you, Uncle Charlie'), the heroine uncovers his psychic weak spot, the paranoid instability that underlies his violence towards women.[26]

'The Detective' draws upon the conventions of the detective story or film, in which a purely instrumental, masculine rationality typically applies itself to that most Poe-like and Hitchcock-like of themes, the murder of a woman. In its drive to construct an intelligible narrative, a 'case', the detective story must annihilate the materiality of the body. The woman's mouth, breasts, children, and finally 'the brown motherly furrows, the whole estate' undergo a 'vaporization'; Holmes

and Watson 'walk on air'. In 'The Courage of Shutting-Up', the figure of the artistic-scientific male expert is replaced by that of the tattooist, representative of the 'primitive' aesthetic rituals of popular culture: 'A great surgeon, now a tattooist, ¦ Tattooing over and over the same blue grievances, ¦ The snakes, the babies, the tits ¦ On mermaids and two-legged dreamgirls'.

For Plath, the world of 'two-legged dreamgirls' is the suburban ideal home, occupied by the perfect couple, where the sanitizing language of ladies' magazines reigns. In the surreal marital drama of 'A Secret' a 'dwarf baby' is discovered imprisoned in the bureau drawer where the 'lingerie' should be. The emergence of this monster unleashes a disgusting female sexuality: 'It smells of salt cod, you had better ¦ Stab a few cloves in an apple, ¦ Make a sachet or ¦ Do away with the bastard'. In 'The Tour', the *Ladies' Home Journal* world of domesticity, women's work, and women's talk is satirized by the baleful mimicry of a witch-like persona who conjures madness in the familiar. The 'maiden aunt', who is shown round the speaker's house, becomes the victim of a gleeful circus sideshow of horror. This cartoon Gothic uses the nursery-rhyme rhythms and italicized verbal gestures of children's books:[27]

O I shouldn't put my finger in *that*
Auntie, it might bite!
That's my frost box, no cat,
Though it *looks* like a cat, with its fluffy stuff,
    pure white.
You should see the objects it makes!
Millions of needly glass cakes!

Fine for the migraine and bellyache. And *this*
Is where I kept the furnace,
Each coal a hot-cross stitch—a *lovely* light!
It simply exploded one night,
It went up in smoke.
And that's why I have no hair, auntie, that's why
    I choke
Off and on, as if I just had to retch.

The exploding oven and the refrigerator which hovers between wild animal and domestic 'appliance' mock a suburban cult of normality underpinned by a paranoid fantasy of absolute instrumental control over nature. As in 'Kindness', there is a bitter confrontation between an older woman cast as the guardian of convention, and a younger, resentful, initiate into domesticity. The satirical malice directed against the female culture of domesticity and housework gains its edge from Plath's own powerful and disillusioned investments in this very culture.

In 'Eavesdropper' the parodic target is the suburban ethos of good-neighbourliness, a world of spying and prying *doppelgängers*. In this Browningesque monologue, a *tour de force* of extreme solipsism and paranoia, the speaker arrogates to herself witch-like powers, such as the ability to kill her neighbours through sympathetic magic. The dystopian setting of '**Eavesdropper**' is 'a desert of cow people ¦ Trundling their udders home ¦ To the electric milker, the wifey, the big blue eye ¦ That watches, like God, or the sky ¦ The ciphers that watch it'. In this bizarrely involuted and flattened vision, people become automata, 'cyphers' that can be permutated with the animals they farm and the machines they operate, under the surveillance of an all-seeing 'big blue eye'. The 'schizophrenic' perspective of these poems produces a quasi-Brechtian alienation effect, confronting the reader with a world locked into the frozen grimace of cliché.

Writing from the Heart: True Confessions

One of the most distinctive features of Plath's later poetry is the predominance of the first person singular, the strongly inflected 'I', which has often led critics to see her as a 'Confessional' poet. The 'Confessional' view of Plath groups her with Robert Lowell, Anne Sexton, and John Berryman as part of a movement towards a poetics of disclosure. It takes its cue from Plath's remark in a 1962 interview with Peter Orr that she had been 'excited' by Lowell's *Life Studies* (1959), with its 'intense breakthrough into very serious, very personal emotional experience'.[28] The 'Confessional' thesis configures the diverse careers of these poets around a shared moment of revolt against the New Critical orthodoxies (especially the doctrine of poetic impersonality) in which they had been schooled. The term 'Confessional' itself was first used in 1959 by M. L. Rosenthal, in a review of Lowell's *Life Studies*.[29] In *The New Poets* (1967), he expanded the review into a general thesis about contemporary poetry: 'the private life of the poet himself, especially under stress of psychological crisis, becomes a major theme. Often it is felt at the same time as a symbolic embodiment of national and cultural crisis.'[30] In *Life Studies,* Lowell had broken New Critical taboos by reconstructing details of his family history within a loosely psycho-historical interpretive framework. Rosenthal assumed, as did Al Alvarez, that the consequences of modernization—consumer society, mass culture, technology, and global warfare—were implacable enemies of poetic subjectivity, squeezing it into a corner where only subjective neurosis could prove the poet's au-

tonomy: 'The intensity and purity of a realization are the measure of poetic sense and success. Thus the alienated sensibility reclaims the world on its own terms.'[31] To hear himself speak, the poet must purify his insights, filtering out the noise of the mass media and the clash of social idioms. Yet the notion of a 'Confessional' style is, of course, inconceivable without the culture of True Confessions, of journalistic scandal and popularized Freudianism. While reacting against the New Critical distinction between the 'speaker' or 'persona' and the poet as biographical individual, between public and private, the earliest theorists of confessional poetry reinstated at another level the New Criticism's founding hierarchical oppositions between subjective value and society, inner authenticity and external facticity.[32]

Recent restatements of the 'Confessional' thesis have continued to align it, as Rosenthal and Alvarez had done, with the earlier Romantic-Symbolist conception of the *poète maudit,* and to organize it around the exemplary case of Robert Lowell. Paul Breslin sees Plath's poetry as bent on the self-destructive pursuit of absolute authenticity, yet at the same time finds her guilty of rhetorical manipulation and sensationalism, of 'teasing the reader with half-veiled revelations' instead of transmuting autobiography into myth; her poetry constitutes 'a damning indictment of the whole confessional project'.[33] Jeffrey Meyers sees Lowell and his contemporaries in heroic-masculine terms as a Nietzschean cursed generation, cultivating extremities of experience and aggressively competing with each other in the art of madness.[34] The complex negotiations of gender, literary tradition, contemporaneity, and popular culture at work in the trope of 'confession' have therefore remained largely unexamined.

Amongst Plath's papers at Smith College is a typescript about her participation in a contest to write a 'true confession', which I quote below:

> friday I got an idear. I am now in the midst of writing the biggest true Confession I have ever written, all for the remote possibility of gaignigh (that word the lady said is gaining, as in weight) filthy lucer. a contest in True Story is in the offing, with all sorts of Big Money prizes. being a most mercenary individual, because money can buy trips to europe, theaters, chop-houses, and other Ill Famed what-nots, I am trying out for it. all you have to do, the blurb ways is write the story of your life or somebody else's life from the heart. and a sexy old heart it is. grammar and spelling mistakes won't count in the judging, says the rules, only it must be written in english, and not on onion skin paper or in pencil . . . anyhow, sylvia just finished the roughdraft of a whopping

True Confession of over 40 (you can count them) pages, trying to capture the style, and let me tell you, my supercilious attitude about the people who write Confessions has diminished. it takes a good tight plot and a slick ease that are not picked up overnight like a cheap whore, so tomorrow, I rewrite the monstrosity I have just illegitimately (everything gets done amid great conflict) delivered.[35]

This confession about writing a 'true Confession' generates two versions of the authorial subject: a 'good girl' and a 'bad girl'. Whereas the former sees writing as an end in itself, the latter is a 'mercenary individual' who writes for motives of 'filthy lucer'. Popular culture is explicitly feminized; to write true confessions 'from the heart' is to become a gross body addicted to the fleshly pleasures of consumption ('that word the lady said is gaining, as in weight'). Even the mass of typographical and/or spelling errors seems to ventriloquize the sloppy, dissolute identity of 'sylvia' the trash writer, who is denied the dignity of a capital letter, and whose narrative is reduced to the abstract exchange value of 'over 40 pages'. Most importantly, writing for mass consumption is seen as *prostitution,* which at the end of the passage gives rise to a monstrous and illegitimate birth. Yet it is also an important avenue to professional success and financial security; although it invalidates the writer's aesthetic pretensions, it gives her a certain amount of economic muscle in the literary market-place. The metaphor of prostitution marks Plath's ambivalence towards popular culture and her investment in High Modernist rituals of impersonality, which stressed the importance of transmuting the raw materials of personality into the perfection of art. As a 1956 letter to Aurelia Plath (*LH* 211) puts it: 'When I say I *must* write, I don't mean I *must* publish. There is a great difference. The important thing is the aesthetic form given to my chaotic experience, which is, as it was for James Joyce, my kind of religion, and as necessary for me . . . as the confession and absolution for a Catholic in church.' Whereas mass culture is stigmatized by association with the debased tastes of the female consumer, literary culture becomes the site of a sacred authority.[36]

The trope of self-revelation assumes a listener. In Plath's later poems, the positing of an authentic 'I' tends to slide into theatre, into what George Steiner calls a *'rhetoric of sincerity'*.[37] The poet's unstable and ambiguous relationship to her audience is anticipated by Baudelaire, who famously accosts his reader in the introductory poem to *Les Fleurs du mal* as 'Hyprocrite lecteur,—mon semblable,—mon frère'.[38] Plath echoes Baudelaire's line in '**Eavesdropper**', where the voyeurism of the prying neighbour caricatures the 'confessional' complicity between poet and reader: 'Toad-stone! Sister-bitch! Sweet neighbour!'. Her later poems are often addressed to a named or unnamed interlocutor, a 'You' whose implied presence shapes the poem's narrative ('**The Other**', '**A Birthday Present**', '**A Secret**', '**The Applicant**', '**Daddy**', '**Medusa**', '**Lesbos**', '**Stopped Dead**', '**Eavesdropper**'), and whose relation to the 'I' is defined by various modalities of antagonism, rejection, or disavowal. This register of demand inscribes the speaking subject as structurally incomplete, or 'jealous', dependent upon a loved/ hated other: a lover, a father, a mother, a reader.

Michel Foucault's analysis of cultural history gives confession a central place as the discursive structure that has historically constituted the notion of a subject possessing interiority, deep feelings, and a personal history. The Christian apparatus of confession is seen as the catalyst for a proliferating discourse about sexuality which has the effect not of liberating but of policing identity, and especially sexual identity, within the dominant structures of the 'episteme'.[39] True Confessions popular culture can be seen in these terms as a Freudianized discourse of licensed transgression or scandal, centred on the spectacle of the pure/impure, redeemed/prostituted female body. In the era of Senator McCarthy's witch-hunts, the word 'confession' had, in addition, a powerful political resonance, linking insurgent, inadequate, or deviant sexuality with Communism. Another social apparatus of confession in the 1950s, of which Plath had intimate and traumatic knowledge, was, of course, institutional psychiatry, a technology for the 'cure' of psychic disorder.

Many of Plath's later poems are organized around tropes of institutional or bureaucratic violence which summon up a nightmare vision of a wholly organized and administered world. In these dystopian scenarios of confession, the 'I' alternates between the positions of confessor and penitent. Confession is linked with machines that literally inscribe the flesh with a text: 'The secret is stamped on you, ¦ Faint, undulant watermark. ¦ Will it show in the black detector?' ('**A Secret**'); 'O adding machine—¦ Is it impossible for you to let something go and have it go whole? ¦ Must you stamp each piece in purple, ¦ Must you kill what you can?' ('**A Birthday Present**'). '**The Other**' is made up of a sequence of surreal images of crime, detection, and interrogation, circulating between speaker and addressee, and undermining the distinction between them. In '**The Jailer**', the

PLATH

FEMINISM IN LITERATURE: A GALE CRITICAL COMPANION, VOL. 6   303 speaker declares herself an 'Indeterminate criminal' who 'die[s] with variety—¦ Hung, starved, burned, hooked'. In **'The Applicant'** she satirically assumes the voice of a corporate 'Big Brother' interviewing a candidate for admission to the organization. A grotesque assortment of anatomical substitutes and surgical prostheses become the qualifications required for 'marriage' to the corporation, recalling D. H. Lawrence's 'Editorial Office', in which an applicant for the post of literary critic is asked if he has been surgically sterilized.[40] The 'corporate' voice is crossed with the rhythms of the pop song and advertising jingle; a mannequin-like 'ideal woman' is presented to the applicant in a bitter echo of Cliff Richard's 1959 hit song 'Livin' Doll': 'A living doll, everywhere you look. ¦ It can sew, it can cook, ¦ It can talk, talk, talk.'[41] The woman is a mechanical appliance which accrues exchange value like a market investment. At the same time she is a commodity-spectacle to be consumed, a fetishistic 'poultice' or anodyne for masculine lack: 'You have a hole, it's a poultice. ¦ You have an eye, it's an image.' In this Kafkaesque world, the 'image' of a reified and sanitized femininity—of the mechanical woman—plays a crucial role in cementing the paranoid-bureaucratic relationship between applicant and organization. It serves as metaphor for a wider violence of which the applicant is victim as well as perpetrator.

'Lady Lazarus' and Literary History

Although Plath's 'confessional' tropes are often seen in terms of a Romantic parable of victimization, whether of the sensitive poetic individual crushed by a brutally rationalized society, or of feminist protest against a monolithic patriarchal oppressor, her self-reflexivity tends to turn confession into a parody gesture or a premiss for theatrical performance. The central instance of the 'confessional' in her writing is usually taken to be **'Lady Lazarus'**. M. L. Rosenthal uses the poem to validate the generic category: 'Robert Lowell's 'Skunk Hour' and Sylvia Plath's **'Lady Lazarus'** are true examples of 'confessional' poetry because they put the speaker himself at the centre of the poem in such a way as to make his psychological shame and vulnerability an embodiment of his civilization.'[42] The confessional reading of the poem is usually underpinned by the recourse to biography, which correlates the speaker's cultivation of the 'art of dying' with Plath's suicidal career. Although Plath is indeed, at one level, mythologizing her personal history, the motif of suicide in **'Lady Lazarus'** operates less as self-revelation than as a theatrical *tour de force*, a music-hall routine.

With **'Daddy'**, **'Lady Lazarus'** is probably the single text in the Plath canon which has attracted most disapproval on the grounds of a manipulative, sensationalist, or irresponsible style. Helen Vendler, for example, writes that 'Style (as something consistent) is meaningless, but styles (as dizzying provisional scepticism) are all . . . Poems like **'Daddy'** and **'Lady Lazarus'** are in one sense demonically intelligent, in their wanton play with concepts, myths and language, and in another, and more important, sense, not intelligent at all, in that they wilfully refuse, for the sake of a cacophony of styles (a tantrum of style), the steady, centripetal effect of thought. Instead, they display a wild dispersal, a centrifugal spin to further and further reaches of outrage.'[43] Here, the element of 'wilful' pastiche in **'Lady Lazarus'** is measured against a normative ideal of aesthetic detachment. Yet the poem's ironic use of prostitution as the figure of a particular kind of theatricalized self-consciousness—of the poet as, in Plath's phrase, 'Roget's trollop, parading words and tossing off bravado for an audience' (*JP* 214)—calls for a reading which takes seriously what the poem does with, and to, literary history.

Like **'Lesbos'**, **'Lady Lazarus'** is a dramatic monologue which echoes and parodies 'The Love Song of J. Alfred Prufrock'. The title alludes, of course, not only to the biblical story of Lazarus but also to Prufrock's lines: 'I am Lazarus, come from the dead, ¦ Come back to tell you all, I shall tell you all'. Like Eliot, Plath uses clothing as a metaphor for rhetoric: the 'veil' or 'garment' of style. By contrast with Eliot's tentative hesitations, obliquities, and evasions of direct statement, however, Plath's poem professes to 'tell all'. Lady Lazarus deploys a patently alienated and manufactured language, in which the shock tactic, the easy effect, reign supreme. Her rhetoric is one of direct statement ('I have done it again'), of brutal Americanisms ('trash', 'shoves', 'the big strip tease', 'I do it so it feels like hell', 'knocks me out'), of glib categorical assertions and dismissals ('Dying is an art, like everything else'), and blatant internal rhymes ('grave cave', 'turn and burn'). As Richard Blessing remarks, both **'Lady Lazarus'** and **'The Applicant'** are poems that parody advertising techniques while simultaneously advertising themselves.[44] The poet who reveals her suffering plays to an audience, or 'peanut-crunching crowd'; her miraculous rebirths are governed by the logic of the commodity. Prufrock is verbally overdressed but feels emotionally naked and exposed, representing himself as crucified before the gaze of the vulgar mass. Lady Lazarus, on the other hand, incarnates the 'holy prostitution of the soul' which Baudelaire found in the experience of being part of a crowd; emotional nakedness is itself revealed as a masquerade.[45] The 'strip-tease' artist is a parodic, feminized version of the symbolist poet sacrificed to an uncomprehending mass audience.[46] For Baudelaire, as Walter Benjamin argues, the prostitute serves as an allegory of the fate of aesthetic experience in modernity, of its 'prostitution' to mass culture. The prostitute deprives femininity of its aura, its religious and cultic presence; the woman's body becomes a commodity, made up of dead and petrified fragments, while her beauty becomes a matter of cosmetic disguise (make-up and fashion). Baudelaire's prostitute sells the *appearance* of femininity. But she also offers a degraded and hallucinated memory of fulfilment, an intoxicating or narcotic substitute for the idealized maternal body. For the melancholic, spleen-ridden psyche, which obsessively dwells on the broken pieces of the past, she is therefore a privileged object of meditation. She represents the loss of that blissful unity with nature and God which was traditionally anchored in a female figure.[47] Instead, Benjamin argues, the prostitute, like commodity fetishism, harnesses the 'sex-appeal of the inorganic', which binds the living body to the realm of death.[48]

Lady Lazarus is an allegorical figure, constructed from past and present images of femininity, congealed fantasies projected upon the poem's surface. She is a pastiche of the numerous deathly or demonic women of poetic tradition, such as Poe's Ligeia, who dies and is gruesomely revivified through the corpse of another woman. Ligeia's function, which is to be a symbol, mediating between the poet and 'supernal beauty', can only be preserved by her death.[49] Similarly, in Mallarmé's prose poem 'Le Phénomène Futur', the 'Woman of the Past' is scientifically preserved and displayed at a circus sideshow by the poet.[50] For Plath, however, the woman on show, the 'female phenomenon' is a revelation of unnaturalness instead of sensuous nature, her body gruesomely refashioned into Nazi artefacts. Lady Lazarus yokes together the canonical post-Romantic, symbolist tradition which culminates in 'Prufrock', and the trash culture of True Confessions, through their common concern with the fantasizing and staging of the female body:

I rocked shut

As a seashell.
They had to call and call
And pick the worms off me like sticky pearls.

The densely layered intertextual ironies at work in these lines plot the labyrinthine course of what Benjamin calls 'the sex appeal of the inorganic' through literary history. They echo Ariel's song in *The Tempest,* whose talismanic status in Plath's writing I have already noted. Plath regenders the image, substituting Lady Lazarus for the drowned corpse of the father/king. The metaphor of the seashell converts the female body into a hardened, dead, and inorganic object, but at the same time nostalgically recalls the maternal fecundity of the sea. The dead woman who suffers a sea change is adorned with phallic worms turned into pearls, the 'sticky', fetishistic sublimates of male desire. In Marvell's poem of seduction, 'To His Coy Mistress', the beloved is imagined as a decaying corpse: 'Nor, in thy marble vault shall sound ¦ My echoing song: then worms shall try ¦ That long-preserved virginity: ¦ And your quaint honour turn to dust; ¦ And into ashes all my lust.'[51] In T. S. Eliot's *The Waste Land,* the refrain 'Those are pearls that were his eyes' is associated with the drowned Phoenician sailor, implicit victim of witch-like, neurotic, or soul-destroying female figures, such as Madame Sosostris and Cleopatra.[52]

Lady Lazarus stages the spectacle of herself, assuming the familiar threefold guise of actress, prostitute, and mechanical woman. The myth of the eternally recurring feminine finds its fulfilment in the worship and 'martyrdom' of the film or pop star, a cult vehicle of male fantasy who induces mass hysteria and vampiric hunger for 'confessional' revelations.[53] Lady Lazarus reminds her audience that 'there is a charge, a very large charge ¦ For a word or a touch ¦ Or a bit of blood ¦ Or a piece of my hair or my clothes.' It is as if Plath is using the Marilyn Monroe figure to travesty Poe's dictum in 'The Philosophy of Composition' (1846) that 'the death of a beautiful woman is, unquestionably, the most poetical topic in the world'.[54] The proliferation of intertextual ironies also affects the concluding transformation of **'Lady Lazarus'** into the phoenix-like, man-eating demon, who rises 'out of the ash' with her 'red hair'. This echoes Coleridge's description of the possessed poet in 'Kubla Kahn': 'And all should cry Beware! Beware! His flashing eyes, his floating hair!'[55] The woman's hair, a privileged fetish-object of male fantasy, becomes at once a badge of daemonic genius and a flag of vengeance.

It is tempting to read these lines as a personal myth of rebirth, a triumphant Romantic emergence of what Lynda Bundtzen calls the female 'body of imagination'.[56] The myth of the transcendent-demonic phoenix seems to transcend the dualism of male-created images of women, wreaking revenge on 'Herr Doktor', 'Herr God', and 'Herr Lucifer', those allegorical emblems of an oppressive masculinity. Yet Lady Lazarus's culminating assertion of power—'I eat men like air'—undoes itself, through its suggestion of a mere conjuring trick. The attack on patriarchy is undercut by the illusionistic character of this apotheosis which purports to transform, at a stroke, a degraded and catastrophic reality. What the poem sarcastically 'confesses', through its collage of fragments of 'high' and 'low' culture, is a commodity status no longer veiled by the aura of the sacred. Lyric inwardness is 'prostituted' to the sensationalism of 'true confession'. The poet can no longer cherish the illusion of withdrawing into a pure, uncontaminated private space, whose immunity from larger historical conflicts is guaranteed by the 'auratic' woman. As I shall argue in the next chapter, for Plath the female body, far from serving as expiatory metaphor for the ravages of modernity, itself becomes a sign whose cultural meanings are in crisis.

Notes

1. See Laura Mulvey's pioneering essay, 'Visual Pleasure and Narrative Cinema', *Screen*, 16, 3 (Autumn 1975), 6-18. Mulvey later qualified her binary opposition between active male spectators and passive female objects of the gaze in 'Afterthoughts on "Visual Pleasure and Narrative Cinema"', in *Visual and Other Pleasures* (Basingstoke: Macmillan, 1989), 29-37. See also Rachel Bowlby, *Just Looking: Consumer Culture in Dreiser, Gissing and Zola* (London: Methuen, 1985), 27-34; Griselda Pollock, *Vision and Difference: Femininity, Feminism and the Histories of Art* (London: Routledge, 1988); Kaja Silverman, *The Acoustic Mirror: The Female Voice in Psychoanalysis and Culture* (Bloomington, Ind.: Indiana University Press, 1988); and Laura Mulvey, 'Some Thoughts on Fetishism in the Context of Contemporary Culture', *October*, 65 (Summer 1993), 3-20.

2. Alicia Ostriker, '"Fact" as Style: The Americanization of Sylvia', *Language and Style*, 1, 3 (Summer 1968), 201-11. See also Stanley Plumly, 'What Ceremony of Words', in Alexander (ed.), *Ariel Ascending*, 13-25.

3. Paul de Man, 'Literary History and Literary Modernity', in *Blindness and Insight*, 142-65.

4. David Shapiro, 'Sylvia Plath: Drama and Melodrama', in Lane (ed.), *Sylvia Plath*, 45-53; Hugh Kenner, 'Sincerity Kills', in Lane (ed.), *Sylvia Plath*, 33-44; Philip Hobsbaum, 'The Temptation of Giant Despair', *Hudson Review*, 25 (Winter 1972-3), 612.

5. Arthur K. Oberg, 'Sylvia Plath and the New Decadence', in Edward Butscher (ed.), *Sylvia Plath* (London: Peter Owen, 1979), 177-85.

6. Jacqueline Rose, *The Haunting of Sylvia Plath* (London: Virago, 1991), 8.

7. The contributors to Bernard Rosenberg and David Manning White (eds.), *Mass Culture: The Popular Arts in America* (New York: The Free Press, 1957), included Ortega y Gasset, Dwight Macdonald, Leslie Fiedler, Irving Howe, Theodor Adorno, and Marshall McLuhan.

8. Clement Greenberg, 'Avant-Garde and Kitsch', in Rosenberg and White (eds.), *Mass Culture*, 98-107; Dwight MacDonald, 'A Theory of Mass Culture', ibid. 59-73; Theodor Adorno, 'The Culture Industry: Enlightenment as Mass Deception' (1944), in Theodor Adorno and Max Horkheimer, *Dialectic of Enlightenment*, trans. John Cumming (London: Verso, 1979), 120-67.

9. Jed Rasula, 'Nietzsche in the Nursery: Naïve Classics and Surrogate Parents in Postwar American Cultural Debates', *Representations*, 29 (Winter 1990), 51. See also Andrew Ross, *No Respect: Intellectuals and Popular Culture* (New York: Routledge, 1989), 42-64.

10. Frederic Jameson, 'Postmodernism, or, the Cultural Logic of Late Capitalism', *New Left Review*, 146 (1984), 65.

11. Jameson, 'Postmodernism', 54.

12. Jameson's view of the 'critical' vocation of modernism is indebted to Theodor Adorno's notion of a modernist 'dissonance' which 'negates' or criticizes reified social relations. See Adorno, *Aesthetic Theory*, trans. C. Lenhardt (London: Routledge and Kegan Paul, 1984).

13. Terry Eagleton, 'Capitalism, Modernism and Postmodernism', in *Against the Grain: Essays 1975-1985* (London: Verso, 1986), 143.

14. Andreas Huyssen, 'Mass Culture as Woman: Modernism's Other', in *After the Great Divide: Modernism, Mass Culture, Postmodernism* (London: Macmillan, 1988), 45.

15. Huyssen, *After the Great Divide*, 46.

16. See Craig Owens, 'The Discourse of Others: Feminists and Postmodernism', in Hal Foster (ed.), *Postmodern Culture* (London: Pluto Press, 1985), 57-82; Linda Nicholson (ed.), *Feminism/Postmodernism* (New York: Routledge, 1990); Margaret Ferguson and Jennifer Wicke (eds.), *Feminism and Postmodernism* (Durham, NC: Duke University Press, 1992).

17. Rita Felski, 'The Counterdiscourse of the Feminine in Three Texts by Wilde, Huysmans, and Sacher-Masoch', *PMLA* 106, 5 (1991), 1094-105.

18. Charles Baudelaire, *Les Fleurs du mal*, trans. Richard Howard (London: Picador Classics, 1987), 14.

19. Adorno, *Aesthetic Theory*, 340.

20. Karl Marx, 'The Fetishism of Commodities and the Secret Thereof', in *Karl Marx: A Reader*, ed. Jon Elster (Cambridge: Cambridge University Press, 1986), 63-75.

21. Elizabeth Wright, 'The Uncanny and Surrealism', in Peter Collier and Judy Davies (eds.), *Modernism and the European Unconscious* (Cambridge: Polity Press, 1990), 265.

22. Walter Benjamin, 'The Work of Art in the Age of Mechanical Reproduction', in *Illuminations,* trans. Harry Zohn (London: Fontana, 1973), 211-44.

23. Calvin Bedient, 'Sylvia Plath, Romantic', in Lane (ed.), *Sylvia Plath,* 10.

24. M. L. Rosenthal, *The New Poets: American and British Poetry Since World War II* (New York: Oxford University Press, 1967), 88.

25. Frederic Jameson, *Postmodernism, or, the Cultural Logic of Late Capitalism* (London: Verso, 1991), 289.

26. *Shadow of a Doubt* (Alfred Hitchcock, 1943), cited by Tanya Modleski, *The Women Who Knew Too Much: Hitchcock and Feminist Theory* (New York: Methuen, 1988), 108.

27. See, in particular, Ted Hughes's *Meet My Folks!* (London: Faber and Faber, 1961).

28. Sylvia Plath, 'Interview' (30 Oct. 1962), in Peter Orr (ed.), *The Poet Speaks* (London: Routledge and Kegan Paul, 1966), 167-8. The interview notes the influence not only of Lowell's *Life Studies,* but also of Anne Sexton, with whom Plath had attended Lowell's poetry seminar in Boston in 1958. On the impact of Sexton's poems on *Ariel,* see Heather Cam, '"Daddy": Sylvia Plath's Debt to Anne Sexton', *American Literature,* 59, 3 (1987), 29-31, and Ian Hamilton, *Robert Lowell* (New York: Random House, 1982), 183.

29. M. L. Rosenthal, 'Poetry as Confession', *Nation,* 190 (1959), 154-5.

30. Rosenthal, *The New Poets,* 15. Al Alvarez's preferred term was 'Extremist Poetry'. See Alvarez, 'Beyond all This Fiddle' (1967), in *Beyond All This Fiddle: Essays 1955-1967* (London: Allen Lane, 1968), 3-21.

31. Rosenthal, *The New Poets,* 17. See also Al Alvarez, 'The Fate of the Platypus' (1958), in *Beyond All This Fiddle,* 59-66, and A. R. Jones, 'Necessity and Freedom: The Poetry of Robert Lowell, Sylvia Plath and Anne Sexton', *Critical Quarterly,* 7 (Spring 1965), 11-30.

32. See Walter Kalaidjan, *Languages of Liberation: The Social Text in Contemporary American Poetry* (New York: Columbia University Press, 1989).

33. Paul Breslin, *The Psycho-Political Muse: American Poetry since the Fifties* (Chicago: University of Chicago Press, 1987), 97, 99. For another attack on Plath as exemplar of the worst excesses of 'Confessional' poetics, see Hobsbaum, 'The Temptation'.

34. Jeffrey Meyers, *Manic Power: Robert Lowell and his Circle* (London: Macmillan, 1987).

35. Sylvia Plath, 'Typescript on writing a true confession', Unpublished Journals, 5 Apr. 1953, Smith. Typographical and spelling errors are transcribed.

36. Compare Cleanth Brooks's reference to 'the young lady who confesses to raptures over her confessions magazine' in *The Well-Wrought Urn* (New York: The Cornwell Press, 1947), 233.

37. George Steiner, 'Dying is an Art', in Newman (ed.), *The Art of Sylvia Plath,* 212. Emphasis added.

38. Charles Baudelaire, *The Complete Verse* (London: Anvil Press, 1968), i. 54.

39. See Michel Foucault, *The History of Sexuality,* i, trans. Robert Hurley (Harmondsworth: Penguin, 1990). See also Jeremy Tambling, *Confession: Sexuality, Sin and the Subject* (Manchester: Manchester University Press, 1990).

40. D. H. Lawrence, *The Complete Poems* (Harmondsworth: Penguin, 1977), 582.

41. The song, whose chorus-line is, 'Got myself a walking, talking living doll', was at number 1 in the British hit parade for four weeks, 1-29 Aug. 1959. See Paul Flattery, *The Illustrated History of Pop* (London: New English Library, 1973), 129.

42. Rosenthal, *The New Poets,* 82.

43. Helen Vendler, 'An Intractable Metal', in Alexander (ed.), *Ariel Ascending,* ii. See also Breslin, *The Psycho-Political Muse,* 108-9.

44. Richard Allen Blessing, 'The Shape of the Psyche: Vision and Technique in the Late Poems of Sylvia Plath', in Lane (ed.), *Sylvia Plath,* 68.

45. Charles Baudelaire, 'Les Foules' (1861), in *The Poems in Prose,* trans. Francis Scarfe (London: Anvil Press, 1989), 59.

46. References to prostitution are more explicit in the drafts of the poem. Draft 1, p. 2, includes the lines: 'Yessir, yessir ¦ Though the doctors say its rare ¦ Each time I rise, I rise a bloody virgin'. Alternatives given for the deleted phrase 'bloody virgin' are 'blooming virgin' and 'sweet whore'. Draft 1, p. 4, includes the lines: 'And there is a charge, a very large charge ¦ For a night in my bed'. Ariel Poems MSS, 23-9 Oct. 1962, Smith.

47. See Walter Benjamin, *Charles Baudelaire: A Lyric Poet in the Era of High Capitalism* (London: New Left Books, 1973), 56, 166, 171-2, and 'Central Park', trans. Lloyd Spencer, *New German Critique,* 34 (Winter 1985), 1-27.

48. Benjamin, *Charles Baudelaire,* 166. On Benjamin's use of the prostitute figure, see Angelika Rauch 'The *Trauerspiel* of the Prostituted Body, or Woman as Allegory of Modernity', *Cultural Critique,* 10 (Fall 1988), 77-88; Christine Buci-Glucksmann, 'Catastrophic Utopia: The Feminine as Allegory of the Modern', in Catherine Gallagher and Thomas Laqueur (eds.), *The Making of the Modern Body* (Berkeley and Los Angeles: University of California Press, 1987), 220-9; and Susan Buck-Morss, 'The Flaneur, the Sandwichman and the Whore: The Politics of Loitering', *New German Critique,* 39 (Fall 1986), 99-140.

49. Edgar Allan Poe, 'Ligeia' (1838), in *Tales of Mystery and Imagination* (London: Dent, 1908), 155-69.

50. Stéphane Mallarmé, *Mallarmé's Prose Poems: A Critical Study,* trans. and ed. Robert Greer Cohn (Cambridge: Cambridge University Press, 1987), 23-9.

51. Andrew Marvell, *The Complete Poems,* ed. Elizabeth Story Donno (Harmondsworth: Penguin Classics, 1985), 51.

52. Eliot, *Collected Poems,* 63-79.

53. Marilyn Monroe's death on 5 Aug. 1962 antedates the composition of 'Lady Lazarus' (23-9 Oct. 1962). 'Lesbos' (18 Oct.) also contains allusions to the star system: 'In New York, in Hollywood, the men said, / Through? ¦ Gee baby, you are rare.' ¦ You acted, acted, acted for the thrill.'

54. Edgar Allan Poe, *Poems and Essays* (London: Dent, 1927), 170.

55. S. T. Coleridge, *Samuel Taylor Coleridge*, ed. H. J. Jackson (Oxford: Oxford University Press, 1985), 103-4.

56. Lynda K. Bundtzen, *Plath's Incarnations: Woman and the Creative Process* (Ann Arbor: University of Michigan Press, 1983), 43.

Bibliography

1. Primary Sources

(A) MANUSCRIPTS

Sylvia Plath, 'Typescript on writing a True Confession', Unpublished Journals, 5 Apr. 1953.

2. Secondary Sources

Adorno, Theodor, *Aesthetic Theory* (1970), trans. C. Lenhardt (London: Routledge and Kegan Paul, 1984).

———and Horkheimer, Max, *Dialectic of Enlightenment* (1944), trans. John Cumming (1972) (London: Verso, 1979).

Alexander, Paul (ed.), *Ariel Ascending: Writings about Sylvia Plath* (New York: Harper and Row, 1985).

———*Rough Magic: A Biography of Sylvia Plath* (New York: Viking Penguin, 1991).

Alvarez, A., *Beyond All this Fiddle: Essays* 1955-1967 (London: Allen Lane, 1968).

Baudelaire, Charles, *The Complete Verse*, 2 vols., trans. Francis Scarfe (London: Anvil Press, 1986).

———*Les Fleurs du mal* (1857), trans. Richard Howard (London: Picador Classics, 1987).

———'Les Foules' (1861), *The Poems in Prose*, trans. Francis Scarfe (London: Anvil Press, 1989).

Bedient, Calvin, 'Sylvia Plath, Romantic', in Lane (ed.), *Sylvia Plath*, 3-18.

Benjamin, Walter, 'The Work of Art in the Age of Mechanical Reproduction', in *Illuminations* (1955), trans. Harry Zohn (London: Fontana, 1973), 211-44.

———*Charles Baudelaire: A Lyric Poet in the Era of High Capitalism*, trans. Harry Zohn (London: New Left Books, 1973).

———'Central Park', trans. Lloyd Spencer, *New German Critique*, 34 (Winter 1985), 1-27.

Blessing, Richard Allen, 'The Shape of the Psyche: Vision and Technique in the Late Poems of Sylvia Plath', in Lane (ed.), *Sylvia Plath*, 57-73.

Bowlby, Rachel, *Just Looking: Consumer Culture in Dreiser, Gissing and Zola* (London: Methuen, 1985).

Breslin, Paul, *The Psycho-Political Muse: American Poetry since the Fifties* (Chicago: University of Chicago Press, 1987).

Brooks, Cleanth, *The Well Wrought Urn* (New York: The Cornwall Press, 1947).

Buci-Glucksmann, Christine, 'Catastrophic Utopia: The Feminine as Allegory of the Modern', in Catherine Gallagher and Thomas Laqueur (eds.), *The Making of the Modern Body* (Berkeley: University of California Press, 1987), 220-9.

Buck-Morss, Susan, 'The Flaneur, the Sandwichman and the Whore: The Politics of Loitering', *New German Critique*, 39 (Fall 1986), 99-140.

Bundtzen, Lynda K., *Plath's Incarnations: Woman and the Creative Process* (Ann Arbor: University of Michigan Press, 1983).

Butscher, Edward (ed.), *Sylvia Plath: The Woman and the Work* (London: Peter Owen, 1979).

Cam, Heather, '"Daddy": Sylvia Plath's Debt to Anne Sexton', *American Literature*, 59, 3 (October 1987), 29-31.

Coleridge, Samuel Taylor, *Samuel Taylor Coleridge*, ed. H. J. Jackson, The Oxford Authors (Oxford: Oxford University Press, 1985).

Collier, Peter, and Davies, Judy, (eds.), *Modernism and the European Unconscious* (Cambridge: Polity Press, 1990).

Eagleton, Terry, 'Capitalism, Modernism and Postmodernism', in *Against the Grain: Essays* 1975-1985 (London: Verso, 1986), 131-47.

Eliot, T. S., *Collected Poems* 1909-1962 (London: Faber and Faber, 1936).

Felski, Rita, 'The Counterdiscourse of the Feminine in Three Texts by Wilde, Huysmans, and Sacher-Masoch', *PMLA* 106, 5 (1991), 1094-1105.

Ferguson, Margaret, and Wicke, Jennifer (eds.), *Feminism and Postmodernism* (Durham, NC: Duke University Press, 1992).

Flattery, Paul, *The Illustrated History of Pop* (London: New English Library, 1973).

Foster, Hal (ed.), *Postmodern Culture* (London: Pluto Press, 1985).

Foucault, Michel, *The History of Sexuality*, trans. Robert Hurley, 3 vols. (Harmondsworth: Penguin, 1990), i.

Greenberg, Clement, 'Avant-Garde and Kitsch' (1946), in Bernard Rosenberg and David Manning White (eds.), *Mass Culture: The Popular Arts in America* (New York: The Free Press, 1957), 107-20.

Hamilton, Ian, *Robert Lowell: A Biography* (New York: Random House, 1982).

Hobsbaum, Philip, 'The Temptation of Giant Despair', *Hudson Review*, 25 (Winter 1972-3), 597-612.

Hughes, Ted, *Meet My Folks!* (London: Faber and Faber, 1961).

Huyssen, Andreas, 'Woman as Mass Culture: Modernism's Other', in Andreas Huyssen, *After the Great Divide: Modernism, Mass Culture, and Postmodernism* (Basingstoke: Macmillan, 1988), 44-62.

Jameson, Frederic, 'Postmodernism, or, the Cultural Logic of Late Capitalism', *New Left Review*, 146 (July-Aug. 1984), 53-92.

———*Postmodernism, or, the Cultural Logic of Late Capitalism* (London: Verso, 1991).

Jones, A. R., 'Necessity and Freedom: The Poetry of Robert Lowell, Sylvia Plath and Anne Sexton', *Critical Quarterly*, 7 (Spring 1965), 11-30.

Kalaidjan, Walter, *Languages of Liberation: The Social Text in Contemporary American Poetry* (New York: Columbia University Press, 1989).

Kenner, Hugh, 'Sincerity Kills', in Lane (ed.), *Sylvia Plath*, 33-44.

Lane, Gary (ed.), *Sylvia Plath: New Views on the Poetry.* Baltimore: Johns Hopkins University Press, 1979.

Lawrence, D. H., *The Complete Poems of D. H. Lawrence*, ed. Vivian de Sola Pinto and Warren Roberts, 2 vols. (London: Heinemann, 1964).

MacDonald, Dwight, 'A Theory of Mass Culture', in Rosenberg (ed.), *Mass Culture*, 59-73.

Mallarmé, Stéphane, *Mallarmé's Prose Poems: A Critical Study*, trans. and ed. Robert Greer Cohn (Cambridge: Cambridge University Press, 1987).

De Man, Paul, *Blindness and Insight: Essays in the Rhetoric of Contemporary Criticism* (London: Methuen, 1983).

——'Literary History and Literary Modernity', in *Blindness and Insight*, 142-65.

Marvell, Andrew, *The Complete Poems*, ed. Elizabeth Story Donno (Harmondsworth: Penguin, 1972; rpt. 1985).

Marx, Karl, 'The Fetishism of Commodities and the Secret Thereof', in *Karl Marx: A Reader*, ed. Jon Elster (Cambridge: Cambridge University Press, 1986), 63-75.

Meyers, Jeffrey, *Manic Power: Robert Lowell and his Circle* (London: Macmillan, 1987).

Modleski, Tanya, *The Women Who Knew Too Much: Hitchcock and Feminist Theory* (New York: Methuen, 1988).

Mulvey, Laura, 'Visual Pleasure and Narrative Cinema', *Screen*, 16, 3 (Autumn 1975), 6-18.

——'Afterthoughts on "Visual Pleasure and Narrative Cinema"' (1981), in Laura Mulvey, *Visual and Other Pleasures* (Basingstoke: Macmillan, 1989), 29-37.

Newman, Charles (ed.), *The Art of Sylvia Plath: A Symposium* (Bloomington, Ind.: Indiana University Press, 1970).

Nicholson, Linda (ed.), *Feminism/Postmodernism* (New York: Routledge, 1990).

Oberg, Arthur, 'Sylvia Plath and the New Decadence', *Chicago Review*, 20, 1 (1968), 66-73. Rpt. in Butscher (ed.), *Sylvia Plath*, 177-85.

Orr, Peter (ed.), *The Poet Speaks* (London: Routledge and Kegan Paul, 1966).

Ostriker, Alicia, '"Fact" as Style: The Americanization of Sylvia', *Language and Style*, 1 (Summer 1968), 201-12. Rpt. as 'The Americanization of Sylvia', in Wagner (ed.), *Critical Essays*, 97-109.

Owens, Craig, 'The Discourse of Others: Feminists and Postmodernism', in Hal Foster (ed.), *Postmodern Culture* (London: Pluto Press, 1985), 57-82.

Plumly, Stanley, 'What Ceremony of Words', in Alexander (ed.), *Ariel Ascending*, 13-25.

Poe, Edgar Allan, *Tales of Mystery and Imagination* (London: Dent, 1908; rpt. 1981).

——'The Philosophy of Composition', in *Poems and Essays* (London: Dent, 1927; rpt. 1987), 163-77.

Pollock, Griselda, *Vision and Difference: Femininity, Feminism and the Histories of Art* (London: Routledge, 1988).

Rasula, Jed, 'Nietzsche in the Nursery: Naïve Classics and Surrogate Parents in Postwar American Cultural Debates', *Representations*, 29 (Winter 1990), 50-77.

Rose, Jacqueline, *The Haunting of Sylvia Plath* (London: Virago, 1991).

Rosenberg, Bernard, and White, David Manning (eds.), *Mass Culture: The Popular Arts in America* (New York: The Free Press, 1957).

Rosenthal, M. L., 'Poetry as Confession', *Nation*, 190 (1959), 154-5.

——*The New Poets: American and British Poetry Since World War II* (New York: Oxford University Press, 1967).

Ross, Andrew, *No Respect: Intellectuals and Popular Culture* (New York: Routledge, 1989).

Shapiro, David, 'Sylvia Plath: Drama and Melodrama', in Lane (ed.), *Sylvia Plath*, 45-53.

Silverman, Kaja, *The Acoustic Mirror: The Female Voice in Psychoanalysis and Culture* (Bloomington, Ind.: Indiana University Press, 1988).

Steiner, George, 'Dying is an Art' (1965), in Newman (ed.), *The Art of Sylvia Plath*, 211-18.

Tambling, Jeremy, *Confession: Sexuality, Sin and the Subject* (Manchester: Manchester University Press, 1990).

Vendler, Helen, 'An Intractable Metal', *New Yorker*, 57 (15 Feb. 1982), 124-38. Rpt. in Alexander (ed.), *Ariel Ascending*, 1-12.

Wagner, Linda (Wagner-Martin) (ed.), *Critical Essays on Sylvia Plath* (Boston: G. K. Hall, 1984).

Wright, Elizabeth, 'The Uncanny and Surrealism', in Collier and Davies (eds.), *Modernism and the European Unconscious*, 265-82.

LINDA WAGNER-MARTIN (ESSAY DATE 1999)

SOURCE: Wagner-Martin, Linda. "Plath's Poems about Women." In *Sylvia Plath: A Literary Life*, pp. 95-105. New York: St. Martin's, 1999.

In the following chapter from her critical biography of Plath, Wagner-Martin offers an overview of Plath's poems involving female figures, noting the poet's emphasis on the themes of physical perfection, fertility, barrenness, and motherhood.

Even while the reader can find in Hughes's lists some themes that would feed into Plath's poetry, the discrepancy between those collective lists and the poems she began writing, and continued to write, starting in 1959 is noticeable. Whereas most of Hughes's ideas for subject matter were historically or geographically based, with a strong component of trees, animals, and natural scenes, many of the poems Plath wrote during these years were about women—women either achieving or non-achieving, and particularly women either fertile or barren. Working directly from Frazer's premise in *The Golden Bough* that pregnant women bespeak fertility, she crafted poems that glowed with positive imagery about both pregnancy and about babies. And working just as directly from the polar opposite concept in the same source, that a barren wife "infects" her husband's garden with her own sterility, she wrote repeatedly about barren women who were unfruitful by their own doing: a woman who had had abortions became, for Plath, the Other. (Nothing is simple here: we have Plath's comment in her college journal that "I do not want primarily to be a mother,"[1] and biographer Paul Alexander contends that Plath had aborted their first child, a few months after her marriage to Hughes.)[2] As a corollary to the barren women theme, Plath also wrote several poems that criticized the artifical ways women maintained their beauty (e.g., **"Face Lift," "The Rival"**).

A systematic emphasis on physical beauty was inherent in this set of poems, for the 1950's privileged the thin, the emaciated, the ill-nourished. Because of her height, Plath could carry somewhat more weight than the Twiggy model-thin women who starved themselves to be fashionable; but at the time she delivered Frieda, her weight—usually 135 to 137 pounds—had climbed to 155; when Nicholas was born in January, 1962, Plath weighed 170 pounds. Although she remained attractive in her pregnancy (one of Ted's friends wrote that as the time neared for Frieda's birth Sylvia was "a woman blazing with life and good spirits"),[3] her use of the adjective "cow-like" in several of her poems about babies and mothering reflected the way she knew society would view her large, nursing, body. It was a new problem for her, one that stemmed entirely from maternity and its processes.[4]

From early childhood, Plath had been a "good eater." As her journal entries and letters to her family show, she finds food—and eating it—interesting. She grew up very conscious of the cost of things; knowing that the Sunday roast cost $0.41 a pound made her feel as if she were eating pennies. Similarly, her childhood letters from camp are hardly more than descriptions of what food has been served at each meal, and the comment that she ate it all.[5] As a college woman, her life was still ruled by necessary economies (one has only to look at the accounting of what she spent in each year at Smith to see the way she tracked minute amounts of, for instance, $2 for postage stamps, or $1.50 for cleaning).[6]

Chary about any spending, Plath would not invest money in food and then leave it on her plate. Because she and Hughes had so little spendable income, especially during the early years of their marriage, her habits of accounting for every dollar were reinforced. She loved the luxuries—London's "sour cream and cream cheese"[7] not to mention the Fortnum and Mason chicken pies—but she knew they were just that, luxuries. It also seems plausible that the fierce argument she had with her sister-in-law occurred over the fact that Plath was usurping a daughter's place, perhaps by eating too much.[8]

To a surprising extent in Plath's later poems, this dichotomy of the thin, mannequin styled woman set against the comfortably well-fed motherly female is played out. In a 1961 poem, **"Heavy Women,"** she describes the "Irrefutable, beautifully smug / As Venus . . ." women settling in "their belling dresses." Their pregnancies bring such satisfaction that they smile to themselves, listening "for the millennium, / The knock of the small, new heart." Nature blesses them too, in other ways, as Plath writes that "Over each weighty stomach a face / Floats calm as a moon or a cloud." Hooded in "Mary-blue," these women live happy and contented lives among their "Pink-buttocked infants." At a distance, "far off, the axle of winter / Grinds down."[9]

Written just a week earlier, **"Morning Song"** re-creates the joyous mothering occasioned by the infant who wakes during the night. Although the mother-persona describes herself as "cow-heavy and floral / In my Victorian nightgown," her significant quality is her ability to hear, to sense her newborn's need. "I wake to listen: A far sea moves in my ear. / / One cry, and I stumble from bed . . ."[10] Disdainful of what fashion-conscious observers might think of the motherly body, the persona knows that her love for the child is the essential characteristic.

During that same week, Plath writes the poem titled **"Barren Woman,"** and it interestingly reverts to the intricate images of some of her earlier poems. The opening word is "Empty" and the structure the poet then envisions is museum-like, echoing, "blind to the world." Even the flowers here, which are forbidding lilies, "Exhale their pallor like scent." A place of deadness, the space that the barren woman represents is the site not of celebration but a place where "nothing can happen."[11] For a short poem, **"Barren Woman"** consists of a great many images, all underscoring the notion of being barren, fruitless.

"Face Lift," which Plath admitted was about Dido Merwin's plastic surgery (and about which Dido later recalled Plath's curiosity),[12] extends the themes of the measures the barren woman will take to enhance her beauty. Written in the voice of the woman who has had the surgery, the poem recounts her much-married history, the easy anesthesia, and the secrecy of the hospitalization: "For five days I lie in secret, / Tapped like a cask, the years draining into my pillow. / Even my best friend thinks I'm in the country . . ." The net result is, as the persona says with elation, "I grow backward. I'm twenty." In the last stanza of the poem, addressing her former self as "Old sock-face, sagged on a darning egg,"[13] she wishes that self dead. Although the persona has been reborn, the irony of the poet's tone undermines her self-congratulation.

Plath wrote to friends late in 1962, after Hughes had left Court Green to live in London with Asia Wevill, "the woman he is with is on her third husband and has had so many abortions she can't have children. She is part of this set of barren women . . . that I am glad to get rid of. I guess I am just not like that . . ."[14]

Wrestling with the fact that her sister-in-law had accused her of being selfish and piggish, Plath wrote a poem about the beautiful Olwyn titled simply "The Rival." In draft, the poem consists of three sections, but only the first appears in *Ariel* and *Collected Poems.* Although Plath never saw her sister-in-law again after the argument of the 1960 Christmas in Yorkshire,[15] she knew that the closeness that existed between Ted and his older sister was not going to be diminished by physical absence—that her beautiful sister-in-law was, in fact, a rival.

The poem is filled with vivid yet metallic images of the invasive woman, "Ticking your fingers on the marble table, looking for cigarettes . . . dying to say something unanswerable."[16] Given to debasing people, "making stone out of everything," preying on everyone ("No day is safe from news of you"), the rival remains her exquisite self. It is in this 1961 poem that Plath reinforces the pattern of identifying the moon with coldness, with inhuman responses; yet when the rival is compared with the moon, the rival is even less human. This is the poem's decisive opening: "If the moon smiled, she would resemble you. / You leave the same impression / Of something beautiful, but annihilating."

Part 2 of the poem contrasts the aloof beauty with the speaker, a woman "corruptible as a loaf of bread," whose virtue is that she has "a baby you like." The rival sits beguilingly in a distant room, while the young mother "crawled on all fours, A sow or a cow" to play with the smiling child. Living away from England, the rival now writes to them "with loving regularity," her let-

ters—typically filled with "dissatisfactions"—are "expansive as carbon monoxide."[17]

Part 3 describes the persona's longing to escape from the force of the rival's personality. Her home is filled with the killing gas of memory; the horizon is preoccupied with the rival, and the sea "keeps washing you up like an old bone." The truth is that the rival is as indestructible as a diamond. Yet because the diamond is such a valued object, the persona will wear her at the center of her forehead, marked forever as a victim.

In the corner of the first page of the draft, Plath has listed other poem titles; "**The Rival**" comes first, followed immediately by "**Face Lift.**" In a pattern strangely prescient, Plath has set up the contrast that she will write about and around almost to the time of her death. Late in 1962, with "**Mary's Song**" she returns to the mother theme, but this time the mother persona is obsessed with the possible harm the world may do to her child. For all its crystalline beauty, the poem "**Child**" also echoes with tones of worry and fear; its closing image leaves the reader with "this troublous / Wringing of hands, this dark / Ceiling without a star."[18] As Plath had written in "**Winter Trees,**" her life is now absorbed by "Memories growing, ring on ring / Knowing neither abortions nor bitchery,"[19] and therefore, "Truer than women."

Closely related to "**Winter Trees**" is Plath's poem "**Brasilia,**" the manuscripts of which show the kind of intertextual borrowing that occurs in many of the very late poems. (Lines deleted from the center of "**Brasilia**" become the opening stanza of "**Childless Woman,**" a different kind of contrast—sharper, bloodier, dominated by the blood-letting spider which utters "nothing but blood— / Taste it, dark red!")[20] The watchful mother in "**Brasilia**" who swims under the defenseless child is herself a prehistoric fish, an "old coelacanth . . . Out-of-date and bad luck to the fisherman / Nearly extinct." Once she too dies off, the child will be "one of the new people / motherless, fatherless."[21] What he awaits will be the destruction she sees on the horizon.

One of Plath's most moving poems, "**For a Fatherless Son,**" also draws from imagery of destruction, trees that carry death rather than life, and the core image of the child's life, the absence of his father. The shifts of focus and mood in the poem's opening lines lead the reader through the simple statement of loss, intensifying in the "death tree" metaphor. The contrast of the baby's grabbing the mother's nose—emphasized with unexpected words such as "dumb" and "stupidity" to suggest his voicelessness—brings the reader back to normalcy, but only for a time. Quickly into stanza three, the poet describes the way the child will "touch what's wrong."[22] As if she cannot pull back herself from the edge of her realization, she lists in a crabbed series three surrealistic images: "The small skulls, the smashed blue hills, the godawful hush." Replete with the -s linkage—small, skulls, smashed, hills, hush—the poet takes the reader away from the 1's in the first image, drawing the poem to the hush of its ending. The turn of the last line cannot counteract the assonantal mood of quiet sorrow, of absence both literal and metaphoric.

While in these manuscripts, the mother has also left the child, the finished poems give the woman a living identity. In the poem **"Childless Woman,"** forbiddingly, the woman "achieves" a body that is "ivory,"[23] bloodless, as she becomes herself a rose—and, significantly, not a live woman. In **"Amnesiac,"** Plath points to the pretended forgetfulness of the husband/father, the man who has left his family, so that he can "travel, travel, travel" with "the red-headed sister he never dared to touch." Here she fuses the barren woman of the affair with his forbidden sister (emphasizing for the reader, "Barren, the lot are barren!"), and turns the poem into a comedy as the two travel with "scenery / Sparking off their brother-sister rears."[24]

In **"The Fearful,"** Plath is even more direct: she accuses the woman in question of hating "The thought of a baby— / Stealer of cells, stealer of beauty— / / She would rather be dead than fat , / Dead and perfect, like Nefertit . . ."[25] And the protagonist of **"Lesbos"** also suffers from having "blown your tubes like a bad radio / Clear of voices and history."[26] The reader is not surprised when this woman suggests to her friend, the poet-persona, that she get rid of both her kittens and her small daughter.

A long poem, **"Lesbos"** includes a number of unexplained references, but the last section describes the persona-mother's reaction to the woman who continually advises her: "Now I am silent, hate / Up to my neck, / Thick, thick. / I do not speak. / I am packing the hard potatoes like good clothes, / I am packing the babies, / I am packing the sick cats . . ." Persisting in her only real ambition—to be a good mother to the children she has borne—the persona has to leave the sterile woman, relinquishing her offer of friendship, wiping her out of her consciousness.

In March of 1962, all the knowledge Plath had acquired about pregnancy and childbirth, and social attitudes toward both, came to fruition in her magnificent—and radical—radio play about three women in a hospital maternity ward. Because Hughes had made both good money and important literary contacts through the BBC productions of his radio plays, Sylvia was eager to become one of their playwrights. Douglas Cleverdon was a talented, earnest producer, responsible for airing Dylan Thomas's *Under Milkwood,* a work Plath had long admired. To know Cleverdon would be exciting, she thought, and the subject matter of the unique **"Three Women"** was certainly near to hand—and her own. She had only birthed Nicholas Farrar a short six weeks earlier.

What Plath achieves in choosing three different kinds of pregnancies—one miscarriage, one full-term delivery in which the unmarried mother would give the baby up for adoption, and one delivery in which the mother would take the child and raise it—is the canvas for a spectrum of physical experiences and attitudes. The bereavement of the woman who miscarries is poignant, separated as she is from her husband and the men of the office in which she works. Male behaviors here are truly obtuse, and metaphorically, men's bodies are described as flat. Or in the monologue of the woman, "That flat, flat, flatness from which ideas, destructions, / Bulldozers, guillotines, white chambers of shrieks proceed, / Endlessly proceed . . ."[27]

It is the Third Voice that has no place for the child. Surprised by her pregnancy, she repeats, "I wasn't ready." Angry at the smug male doctors who deliver these children, wanted or unwanted, she contends, "what if they found themselves surprised, as I did? / They would go mad with it." Her anger subsiding, she watches her "red, terrible girl," "crying," "furious," Scratching at my sleep like arrows, / Scratching at my sleep, and entering my side." Her leave-taking is an amazing poem. Packing the clothes "of a fat woman I do not know," she is surprised—now—at how vulnerable she has become: "I am a wound walking out of hospital. / I am a wound that they are letting go." Pained and hollow, she realizes that "I leave my health behind. I leave someone / Who would adhere to me: I undo her fingers like bandages: I go."

The heart of the long poem rests in the solemn happiness of the First Voice, the woman who gives birth to a long-wanted child. As she speaks before delivery of her time ("I am slow as the world. I am very patient"), she brings the gentle humor of fulfillment into the juxtaposed tones of the work: "When I walk out, I am a great event. / I do not have to think, or even rehearse. / What happens in me will happen without attention . . . / Leaves and petals attend me. I am ready."

When her pains begin, fear overtakes her equanimity; the "calm before something awful" is shattered. "A seed about to break," she feels the first tug of the "cargo of agony . . . inescapable, tidal." After the long labor,

> There is no miracle more cruel than this.
> I am dragged by the horses, the iron hooves.
> I last. I last it out. I accomplish a work . . .

Hard-earned satisfaction suffuses the mother's reaction as she sees the boy. She hardly notices the "red lotus [that] opens in its bowl of blood;" rather, she croons to the angry infant:

> What did my fingers do before they held him?
> What did my heart do, with its love?
> I have never seen a thing so clear.
> His lids are like the lilac-flower
> And soft as a moth, his breath.
> I shall not let go.
> There is no guile or warp in him. May he keep
>   so.

Amid the two other women's complaints, this lullaby of the First Voice continues, almost to the end of the poem. One of the most beautiful lyrics in twentieth-century poetry occurs toward the end of "Three Women," in the passage of the loving mother which begins, "How long can I be a wall, keeping the wind off? / How long can I be / Gentling the sun with the shade of my hand . . ."

Never predictable because of the juxtaposition of the three voices, speaking at very different emotional places and tempos, "Three Women" conveys women's reactions to childbirth or miscarriage with more variety than the uninitiated might expect. Sheer hatred darkens the speech of the Second Voice, the woman who has miscarried again and again. Her vengefulness takes in the patriarchal world, including her husband. She is hopelessly self-centered: "I am bled white as wax, I have no attachments. / I am flat and virginal, which means nothing has happened . . . It is I. It is I— / Tasting the bitterness between my teeth. The incalculable malice of the everyday."

The vacuity after the pain of leave-taking saddens the reader. Will the Third Voice ever come to be human again? The birth of her child is only a fast-fading memory: "I had an old wound once, but it is healing. / I had a dream of an island, red with cries. / It was a dream, and did not mean a thing."

The secure joy of the First Voice, as she watches her son sleep, both begins and ends the poem. "I am reassured. I am reassured . . . I am simple again. I believe in miracles." Her blessing for her child is that he be normal, not exceptional. Wanting to protect him, feeling powerless to keep him innocent, the voice explains, "It is the exception that interests the devil. It is the exception that climbs the sorrowful hill." Rather, her wish is that he be common, "To love me as I love him, / And to marry what he wants and where he will."

A strange ending for the First Voice, so soon recovered from the ordeal of childbirth: would she be worried about her son's marriage, unless she were haunted by thoughts that her husband's family does not love her, and perhaps that her family does not think she has made a suitable match either. Or perhaps the persona herself worries about the suitability of that match, fraught as it is with angry fights and physical brutality? As focused as the text manages to be on the three child-bearing women and their poetry, their responses to the life events that are handed to them, fated for them, elements of Plath's own life at the time manage to creep in. While she keeps the woman who miscarries from being objectionable in herself, recasting her as a sympathetic woman rather than an intentionally barren one, she clearly favors the pregnant woman who takes her child home to care for. Women who give birth assume a lifetime of responsibility, with love to leaven the weight of that care. There could be no equivocation about that responsibility—or about that love.

To be considered along with these autobiographical emphases is the pattern Sandra Gilbert finds that connects "Three Women," or "Three Voices" as it was originally titled, with the three women characters in Virginia Woolf's novel, *The Waves*. With some remarkable similarities between the language of Susan, Rhoda and Jinny and Plath's three speakers, and with knowledge of the fact that she much admired and loved Woolf's work, Gilbert's point is plausible.[28] It also is comforting to see that a woman writer would turn to another women writer for imaginative help in creating effective and poetically real female characters. As a composite of Plath's hospital experience, her reading life, and her own emotional understanding of becoming a mother, "Three Women" is the most impressive long poem Plath had written, or would write. It was also a powerful precursor to the later works that also evolved from her conceptualization of a single idiomatic voice. Here, the voices are largely calm and sympathetic. But the stridency and despair of the Second Voice will soon become all too familiar.

By the late fall of 1962, the time of "**The Munich Mannequins**" (a poem which was earlier titled "**The Bald Madonnas**"), Plath becomes more autobiographical as she assigns a German cast to the beautiful, heartless barren woman. (Because of the distinctively ethnic name of Hughes's new lover, Assia Guttman Wevill, Plath chose to describe objectionable things as German in many of her late poems; she also takes onomatopoetic jabs at the sibilance of "Assia.") After its revealing title, this stark poem opens, "Perfection is terrible, it cannot have children."[29] The poem is loaded with metaphors of coldness, poisonous gas, sterility, snow, and nakedness (and the sibilance of the s's in *sulfur loveliness, smiles, sacrifice* and *snow,* used three times in key positions to signal death). Spreading like a poison gas, the mannequin's inhumanity infects her male companion; together, in "Munich, morgue between Paris and Rome," the two lovers are pictured as "Naked and bald in their furs, / Orange lollies on silver sticks," but—because they have frustrated the life force— 'Intolerable, without mind.'

This poem connects subliminally with another written in January of 1963, called enigmatically "**Totem**," a recitation of various kinds of killings that seem to take place in Smithfield. The killings go beyond hog butchery, however, and include the killings of children as well as the rabbits that have become Plath's own totem for innocence. As the persona notes tersely, "There is no mercy in the glitter of cleavers."[30] As might be expected in the context of her other writing, "**Totem**" contains abortion imagery, as well as a litany of sacrifice ritual from Radin's African folktales. The Anansi spider returns, mirrors chart events, cobras hypnotize the viewer, and death seems inescapable.

In several of Plath's February poems, among the last half dozen she composed before her suicide, the dichotomous imaging of good-mother, not-mother disappears. Absorbed into a less angry and less tenuous way of looking at the world, Plath's categories meld into larger notions of calm. In "**Kindness**," the poet cryptically describes the acts of the good godmother caring for the children, "Sweetly picking up pieces!," and bringing the persona "a cup of tea / Wreathed in steam."[31] Caring for equates with the *tenderness* that Plath has long used as a positive description in her writing. Even without the intertextual response to Hughes's BBC play about dead rabbits and the rab-

bit killer carrying two roses to his new lover, "**Kindness**" rings a different chord in her gallery of women's portraits. As the concluding line of the poem emphasizes, it is Dame Kindness who proffers her beloved children to the persona: "You hand me two children, two roses." That this line is given the closing position, one of sure emphasis, undercuts the importance of the previous two lines, which are often quoted, "The blood jet is poetry, / There is no stopping it." In effect, the presence of the two children does stop that blood loss, or at least blunts it. If the persona were in a position to choose, the structure of the poem— with its ending line restatement of "two children"—makes clear what her choice would be.

"**Edge**," the last poem attributed to Plath before her suicide is also about a mother and her children. Drawing from the opening line of "**The Munich Mannequins**," that "Perfection is terrible," here the persona shifts her lens. Terrible it may be, or perhaps it is "terrible" in the sense of creating terror as a parallel to "awful" as a means of inspiring awe, but the poem opens with a sentence that has a clearly positive effect, "The woman is perfected."[32] A significant change occurs in the composition of this poem from draft stage to final version: in the draft, the perspective is of viewers high above the scene, looking down on the body of a dead woman. At that time the poem was titled "Nuns in Snow" and the observers are nuns, traveling as if on a pilgrimage to view the dead woman. From that perspective, the later countless images of a woman's being nunlike, being pure, coalesce in the impact of this tautly crafted work.

Critic Mary Kurtzman notes that Plath relied on her knowledge of the Tarot cards (a Western Tarot based on the Hebrew Cabala, replicating the 22 paths on the Cabalistic Tree of Life, each standing for a "state of consciousness and spiritual unfolding") throughout her last years of writing, using the pack as an organizing principle as early as the chapter arrangement of *The Bell Jar.* She attributes the positive effect of "**Edge**" to the fact that its details and form suggest that Plath was drawing on the High Priestess card as model, and the role of the High Priestess was to experience the "highest possible union with the Goddess or God (Tarot divinities are both female and male)." Such union is labeled "Isis perfected" and Kurtzman notes that someone wrote ISIS on the final typescript of the poem "**Edge**."[33]

She also speaks to the choice of the word "illusion" and concludes that Plath was explaining that, although the Scorpio sign which was her astrological marker might suggest a fated suicide, such a link was illusory: Kurtzman then reads the poem's last four lines as the reason for the suicide, which may well have been chosen to avoid another hospitalization, complete with its terrorizing electroconvulsive shock. As the blacks "crackle and drag" in the treatment, the woman would lose the heart of her life—both the full creative powers of her mind, and, as a socially mandated result, the custody of her beloved children. In the poem, the woman has protectively folded her children back into her body—from which they came.

The poem's imagery suggests that her symbolically taking the children back is as natural as a rose closing its petals at night; her act is part of that necessity that mother's lives are governed by. Had the poem been longer, had the woman persona been given speech before her death, she might have echoed the moving lines from the ["**Three Women**"]'s First Voice:

> How long can my hands
> Be a bandage to his hurt, and my words
> Bright birds in the sky, consoling, consoling?
> It is a terrible thing
> To be so open: it is as if my heart
> Put on a face and walked into the world.[34]

If only the child could be spared that world, if only the poem's persona could have been spared it. But, if Kurtzman is correct about the symbology of **"Edge"** (and other of Plath's late poems), the persona here has "accomplished" what she set out to do, find a mystical unity with the spiritual world, and she has thereby finally escaped—by journeying to the edge of the known world—that world that so increasingly frustrated her, and her writerly ambition.

Notes

1. Sylvia Plath, *Journals*, p. 74.

2. Paul Alexander, *Rough Magic*, p. 252.

3. Daniel Huws, Comments on 1987 Wagner-Martin manuscript.

4. Marilyn Yalom in her *Maternity, Mortality and the Literature of Madness* touches on this only obliquely; somewhat strangely, though perhaps reflective of the 1950s attitudes about maternity, Plath's letters do not mention her physical appearance during or after pregnancy.

5. Sylvia Plath, various letters from childhood and adolescence to her mother, The Lilly Library, Indiana University.

6. Sylvia Plath, notebooks, Smith College Rare Books Room archive.

7. Sylvia Plath, letter to Helga Huws, October 30, 1961.

8. Paul Alexander, *Rough Magic*, p. 252.

9. Sylvia Plath, "Heavy Women," *Collected Poems*, p. 158.

10. Sylvia Plath, "Morning Song," *Collected Poems*, pp. 156-7.

11. Sylvia Plath, "Barren Woman," *Collected Poems*, p. 157.

12. Dido Merwin, "Vessel of Wrath: A Memoir of Sylvia Plath," Appendix II, Anne Stevenson, *Bitter Fame*, pp. 329-30. I have numerous letters from Ms. Merwin written during the mid-1980s attesting to her consistent view of Plath's character.

13. Sylvia Plath, "Face Lift," *Collected Poems*, pp. 155-6. See Susan Van Dyne's discussion of this poem in *Revising Life*.

14. Sylvia Plath, letter to Helga and Daniel Huws, late December, 1962.

15. Paul Alexander makes this claim in *Rough Magic*, p. 252.

16. Sylvia Plath, "The Rival," *Collected Poems*, pp. 166-7, and manuscript drafts (of the three-section poem) from The Lilly Library, Indiana University. Quotations not from the published poem are from the manuscript.

17. The metallic imagery is reinforced with the description of the rival's "steel complexion," which connects with the inhuman "people with torsos of steel" in "Brasilia.'

18. Sylvia Plath, "Child," *Complete Poems*, p. 265.

19. Sylvia Plath, "Winter Trees," *Complete Poems*, pp. 257-8. In manuscript, the line is "No face-lifts, abortions, affairs." (New York Public Library, Berg Collection, poetry exhibition, 1996).

20. Sylvia Plath, "Childless Woman," *Collected Poems*, p. 259.

21. Sylvia Plath, "Brasilia," manuscript drafts in the Berg Collection, New York Public Library; final version in *Collected Poems*, pp. 258-9.

22. Sylvia Plath, "For a Fatherless Son," *Collected Poems*, pp. 205-6. In manuscript, the poem was titled "For a Deserted One" (Smith College Rare Books Archive).

23. Sylvia Plath, "Childless Woman," *Collected Poems*, p. 259.

24. Sylvia Plath, "Amnesiac," *Collected Poems*, pp. 232-3; manuscript versions, Smith College Rare Book Room.

25. Sylvia Plath, "The Fearful," *Collected Poems*, p. 256.

26. Sylvia Plath, "Lesbos," *Collected Poems*, pp. 227-30; a poem written about the same time, "The Tour," has less vitriolic imagery, but it still writhes with irritation at superior women and their attitudes.

27. Sylvia Plath, "Three Women," *Collected Poems*, pp. 176-87; individual quotations are not cited in notes. That spring Plath wrote to Olwyn that she was excited to be doing "longer stuff," and happy to be back in her study, which she calls "my poultice, my balm, my absinthe" (undated, 1962, p. 1, Lilly Library, Indiana University).

28. Sandra M. Gilbert, "In Yeats' House: The Death and Resurrection of Sylvia Plath," *Critical Essays on Sylvia Plath*, ed. Linda W. Wagner, pp. 217-18.

29. Sylvia Plath, "The Munich Mannequins," *Collected Poems*, pp. 262-3.

30. Sylvia Plath, "Totem," *Collected Poems*, pp. 215-16.

31. Sylvia Plath, "Kindness," *Collected Poems*, pp. 269-70.

32. Sylvia Plath, "Edge," *Collected Poems*, pp. 272-3, and draft versions housed at Smith College Rare Books Archive. See Van Dyne, *Revising Life*, and Mazzaro, *Postmodern American Poetry*, p. 162.

33. Mary Kurtzman, "Plath's 'Ariel' and Tarot," *Centennial Review*, Summer 1988, pp. 286-95.

34. Sylvia Plath, "Three Women," *Collected Poems*, p. 185.

Bibliography

Primary

Plath, Sylvia, *The Collected Poems of Sylvia Plath*, ed. Ted Hughes. New York: Harper & Row, 1981.

———, *The Journals of Sylvia Plath*, ed. Frances McCullough. New York: Dial Press, 1982.

Extensive manuscript material and correspondence at both the Lilly Library, Indiana University, and the Rare Books Room, Smith College (the largest Plath archives), as well as University of Texas, The Harry Ransom Humanities Research Collection; Emory University Rare Books Room; the Houghton Library at Harvard University; and the Berg Collection, New York Public Library. The author's own file of interview transcriptions, correspondence, and other materials date from 1982 to 1996.

Secondary

Alexander, Paul, *Rough Magic*. New York: Viking, 1991.

Gilbert, Sandra M., "In Yeats' House: The Death and Resurrection of Sylvia Plath," *Critical Essays on Sylvia Plath*, ed. Linda W. Wagner, pp. 204-22.

Kurtzman, Mary, "Plath's 'Ariel' and Tarot," *Centennial Review*, 32 (Summer 1988), pp. 286-95.

Mazzaro, Jerome, "The Cycles of History: Sylvia Plath (1932-1963)," *Post-modern American Poetry*. Urbana: University of Illinois Press, 1980, pp. 139-66.

Stevenson, Anne, *Bitter Fame: A Life of Sylvia Plath*. Boston: Houghton Mifflin, 1989.

Van Dyne, Susan R., *Revising Life: Sylvia Plath's Ariel Poems*. Chapel Hill: University of North Carolina Press, 1993.

Wagner, Linda W., ed. *Critical Essays on Sylvia Plath*. Boston: G. K. Hall, 1984.

TITLE COMMENTARY

"Ariel"

KATHLEEN MARGARET LANT (ESSAY DATE WINTER 1993)

SOURCE: Lant, Kathleen Margaret. "The Big Strip Tease: Female Bodies and Male Power in the Poetry of Sylvia Plath." *Contemporary Literature* 34, no. 4 (winter 1993): 620-70.

In the following excerpt, Lant asserts that "Ariel" is an analogy for Plath's role as a woman poet and argues that the female speaker's attempt to transform herself into a more masculine figure ultimately proves futile.

The work which most perfectly embodies Plath's conflicting sets of figures concerning power and nakedness is **"Ariel"** (October 1962), for this poem shows how Plath's metaphorical universes collide but also how her mutually exclusive systems of representation give rise to some of the most effective and beautiful poetry she wrote. Plath noted in her journal that she was privileged to listen to Auden discuss his view of Shakespeare's Ariel as representative of "the creative imaginative" (*Journals* 77), so one might assume that in this poem she is revealing something about her own view of creativity. (17) What is curious is that the creativity which emerges so energetically here is ultimately undone within the context of the poet's own presentation of that creativity.

M. L. Rosenthal points to the basic conflict of the poem in observing that "In a single leap of feeling, it identifies sexual elation (in the full sense of the richest kind of encompassment of life) with its opposite, death's nothingness" (74). In fact, however, Plath is not conflating two opposing states of being; instead she is capering dangerously between metaphorical designs which seem to consume the poem from within. Obviously the movement of the poem is very powerful and very positive since the speaker proceeds from stillness and ignorance ("Stasis in darkness" [239]) toward light at a very rapid pace. The speaker moves with some potent force—a horse, a sexual partner, some aspect of herself—which compels her, and given the title and Plath's remarks concerning Auden, we can assume that this force must relate to some aspect of Plath's creative self. The speed of the journey is such that the earth "Splits and passes" before the speaker, and even those delicious and tempting enticements that come between the creator and her work are not enough to impede her; they may be "Black sweet blood mouthfuls," but the speaker of the poem consigns them to the category "Shadows," things which threaten the vision (light) and power of her creative surge.

The female force of the poem flies through air, and suddenly she begins to engage in that most essential of poetic acts—at least for the writers of Plath's generation; she removes those restrictions which threaten her gift. She tosses her clothing off like a rebellious Godiva and rides free, fast, unclothed, and fully herself toward her goal:

> White
> Godiva, I unpeel—
> Dead hands, dead stringencies.

(239)

And she reaches a moment of apparent transcendence: "And now I Foam to wheat, a glitter of seas." Her epiphany is associated with traditionally female symbols. (We might make a connection between the wheat and Demeter, goddess of agriculture, or between wheat and the mother earth. The sea, moreover, certainly seems closely connected with female cycles and with the female symbol of the moon.) Her moment of triumph, moreover, is conveyed in verbs which may suggest—if sexuality is at all to be considered appropriate here—female rather than male sexuality. To foam and to glitter have arguably much more resonance when considered in terms of female orgasm than in terms of male orgasm. The energy of these verbs is great, but it is a more sonorous and sustained energy than a directed, explosive, and aimed burst. To make use of Luce Irigaray's paradigm, woman's sexuality and woman's pleasure are not "one" but "plural" because "woman has sex organs more or less everywhere" (28).

But now the speaker enters a different metaphorical paradigm. Her final "stringency" is removed, "The child's cry / / Melts in the wall," and she can become more powerful only by moving her fully exposed (naked) female self toward the power which she so covets, the power of light and heat and vision—the sun. To make this journey she must transform herself from wheat and water to something much more dangerous and traditionally powerful—an arrow. And here Plath is forced—by the desire of her speaker to assert herself, to move and fly—to appropriate an inappropriate figure for her speaker's flight: the speaker of "Ariel" becomes an arrow. She transforms herself into the most potent figure of the patriarchal symbolic order—the phallus. The arrow is clearly a figure Plath associates, somewhat resentfully, with masculine power. In *The Bell Jar,* Buddy Willard's mother tells him that a man is "an arrow into the future" and that a woman needs to be "the place the arrow shoots off from" (79). Esther's response to Buddy's reiteration of Mrs. Willard's platitudes is that she, Esther, wants to be that arrow: "I wanted change and excitement and to shoot off in all directions myself" (92). In "**Ariel**," Plath demonstrates the consequences for the female artist of such proud and self-affirming desires when these desires are couched in the only symbolic structures available to her.

While the speaker of the poem may call herself the arrow, while she might arrogantly lay claim to that title, she is still female, still the wheat and the water, still naked and exposed and vulnerable. It is important to note that once the speaker begins her flight, she is no longer the arrow; her femaleness has ineluctably reasserted itself. Inescapably female, she is

> The dew that flies
> Suicidal, at one with the drive
> Into the red
>
> Eye, the cauldron of morning.
> (240)

And dew must be consumed by the power of the sun. The speaker of the poem is fully aware that her urgent desire for the power she has arrogated for herself is destructive to her as a woman, for she refers quite deliberately to her journey as suicidal. What is perhaps most tragic about both the speaker of this poem and about Sylvia Plath as the creator of that speaker is that the impulse toward self-disclosure, the desire to move toward the eye/I of awareness, is destined to destroy both of them. In Western culture the unclothed female, whether it be the self-disclosing creator or the emblematic and naked female subject, can be a symbol only of vulnerability and victimization, even when the audience to the glorious and hopeful unveiling is the self.

Placing "**Ariel**" in a feminist context, Sandra Gilbert argues that the "Eye" toward which this poem moves is "the eye of the father, the patriarchal superego which destroys and devours with a single glance" ("Fine, White Flying Myth" 259). But such a reading, by ignoring the play on words of "eye" and "I," leaves unremarked a central ambiguity in the poem and underestimates Plath's commitment to her female subject and her wild and creative commitment to her own art. The speaking subject here is not just moving toward a powerful male entity, the sun; Plath's speaker is moving implosively toward herself as well, toward the eye/I that has become the center of her universe, the focus of her attention. The tragedy of Plath's work, however, is that she has conceived of this overwhelmingly omnipotent figure in the only metaphors available to her—those of the masculine poetic tradition. In this tradition, power is the sun/god, as Gilbert has observed, and to be fully revealed before him, to be naked before this God, is the most transcendently powerful act a human can perform. But when you are female, when you burn with your own sun and expose yourself confidently to that sun, you are consumed. Your body, your self, is still vulnerable. It will be destroyed. The most telling irony of the poem is that the masculine God of patriarchal discourse has been displaced here by the "I" which is the speaker herself. And the female speaker has become the phallic arrow which impels itself toward that sun. But such a journey into knowledge will prove deadly—because the language, the signifiers of that journey dictate that it must be so for the speaking subject who is still "dew," still female. Even when the father is replaced, his words speak for him, his language secures his position: the dew will be dispersed by the sun.

Clearly, the energies and anomalies of Plath's poetry can be related to her experiences as a poet who is also a woman. Sympathetic feminist critics, attempting to explain the tensions of a poem such as "**Ariel**," have seen Sylvia Plath as a victim of what Suzanne Juhasz calls "the double bind of the woman poet" (1): "Plath suffered in an extreme form from the woman artist's need to reconcile her two roles, woman and poet; from the necessity of living with what may seem her two selves" (88). Juhasz feels that Plath struggled in her poetry with this wrenching conflict but that she never resolved it, adding, "Her death . . . proves the impossibility of what she set out to do" (114). Paula Bennett refers as well to opposing forces in Plath's work when she asserts that Plath was troubled by "the conflict between the needs of her gender and the requirements of her genre" (My Life 99). While Bennett concludes that these internal conflicts finally destroyed Plath, Lynda Bundtzen, who also finds Plath's work indelibly marked by the tensions Plath felt as woman and writer, asserts that her best works represent a resolution of the conflicts she experienced between "her art and her life." Bundtzen goes on to observe that in her last poems Plath reimagines a world where she could live as a woman and an artist: "She translates social and psychological constraints on women into physical and sexual terms, so that we come to understand not only what it may feel like to live in a woman's body, but also how this affects her inventive freedom and control of the world around her" (42). Bundtzen's more positive readings notwithstanding, the overwhelming force of most such studies seems to fall with those who find Plath endlessly conflicted in her creativity.

Works Cited

Bennett, Paula. *My Life a Loaded Gun: Dickinson, Plath, Rich, and Female Creativity.* Urbana: U of Illinois P, 1990.

Bundtzen, Lynda K. *Plath's Incarnations: Woman and the Creative Process.* Women and Culture Ser. Ann Arbor: U of Michigan P, 1983.

Gilbert, Sandra M. "A Fine, White Flying Myth: The Life/ Work of Sylvia Plath." *Shakespeare's Sisters: Feminist Essays on Women Poets.* Ed. Sandra M. Gilbert and Susan Gubar. Bloomington: Indiana UP, 1979. 245-60.

Juhasz, Suzanne. *Naked and Fiery Forms: Modern American Poetry by Women, A New Tradition.* New York: Harper, 1976.

Newman, Charles, ed. *The Art of Sylvia Plath: A Symposium.* Bloomington: Indiana UP, 1970.

Plath, Sylvia. *The Bell Jar.* New York: Harper, 1971.

——. *The Collected Poems.* Ed. Ted Hughes. New York: Harper, 1981.

——. *The Journals of Sylvia Plath.* Ed. Frances McCullough and Ted Hughes. New York: Dial, 1982.

Rosenthal, M. L. "Sylvia Plath and Confessional Poetry." Newman 69-76.

The Bell Jar

DIANE S. BONDS (ESSAY DATE 1990)

SOURCE: Bonds, Diane S. "The Separative Self in Sylvia Plath's *The Bell Jar.*" *Women's Studies* 18, no. 1 (1990): 49-64.

In the following essay, Bonds examines how Esther Greenwood, the protagonist of The Bell Jar, *represents the concept of a separative model of selfhood and contends that because Esther fails to cultivate a network of positive, non-hierarchical relations, especially with the other women, she is likely to re-experience the alienation that led to her suicide attempt.*

As Paula Bennett has written, Sylvia Plath's **The Bell Jar** offers a brilliant evocation of "the oppressive atmosphere of the 1950s and the soul-destroying effect this atmosphere could have on ambitious, high-minded young women like Plath."[1] It has not been widely recognized, however, that the "soul-destroying effect" of Plath's social context is dramatized as vividly by the putative recovery of the heroine as by her breakdown and attempted suicide. The novel presents the transformation of Esther Greenwood from a young woman who hates the idea of serving men in any way to one who appears to earn her exit from the asylum by committing herself, albeit unwittingly, precisely to that project. In the first half of the novel, the pervasive imagery of dismemberment conveys the alienation and self-alienation leading to Esther's breakdown and suicide attempt. In the second half of the novel a pattern of symbolic rebirth is superimposed on a narrative which in its details suggests that Esther purchases her "new" self by the discontinuance of any relations that might threaten by means of intimacy or tenderness the boundaries of a self conceived as an autonomous entity, as a separate and "separative" self.

Contemporary feminist theory has questioned the validity of this model of the self. Catherine

Keller, for example, has recently drawn on theology, philosophy, psychology (including the work of Nancy Chodorow and Carol Gilligan), and literature, to demonstrate in impressive detail the historic collusion between the notion of a separate subject or bounded, autonomous self and the cultural forces that have oppressed women.[2] *The Bell Jar* vividly illustrates that collusion by proposing, through its representation of Esther's recovery, an ideal of a self uncontaminated by others. But such a conception of the self denies the undeniable: the relationality of selfhood. The recovery which Plath constructs for her heroine reenacts the dismemberments obsessively imaged in the first half of the novel; I would argue that it merely leaves Esther prey to defining herself unwittingly and unwillingly in relation to all that remains to her: culturally-ingrained stereotypes of women. Critics for the most part seem to have brought to the novel the same assumptions about the self which inform Plath's book, assumptions deriving from a separative model of the self.[3] Thus they have failed to recognize what the novel has to teach about the effects of our cultural commitment to that model.

In the first part of Plath's novel, both the commitment to the separative self and the effects of that commitment are woven into the text through the pervasive imagery of dismemberment. This imagery suggests Esther's alienation and fragmentation as well as a thwarted longing for relatedness with others and for a reconnection of dismembered part to whole. A signal example of this imagery is the image of a cadaver head which occurs on the first page of the novel:

> I kept hearing about the Rosenbergs over the radio and at the office until I couldn't get them out of my mind. It was like the first time I saw a cadaver. For weeks afterward, the cadaver's head—or what there was left of it—floated up behind my eggs and bacon at breakfast. . . . I felt as though I was carrying that cadaver's head around with me on a string, like some black, noseless balloon stinking of vinegar.[4]

This image anticipates and comprehends the disembodied faces that Esther repeatedly encounters, faces always associated with the threat of the loss of self. She repeatedly confronts her own unrecognized or distorted image in the mirror, mistaken on one occasion for "a big, smudgy-eyed Chinese woman" (16), looking "like a sick Indian" (92) on another; a third time, in the hospital after her suicide attempt, she thinks she is looking at a picture of another person, unrecognizably male or female, "with their hair . . . shaved off and sprouted in bristly chicken-feather tufts all over

FROM THE AUTHOR

JOURNAL ENTRY, 1959
SUNDAY: OCTOBER 4:

Marilyn Monroe appeared to me last night in a dream as a kind of fairy godmother. An occasion of "chatting" with audience much as the occasion with Eliot will turn out, I suppose. I spoke, almost in tears, of how much she and Arthur Miller meant to us, although they could, of course, not know us at all. She gave me an expert manicure. I had not washed my hair, and asked her about hairdressers, saying no matter where I went, they always imposed a horrid cut on me. She invited me to visit her during the Christmas holidays, promising a new, flowering life.

Plath, Sylvia. Excerpt from "12 December 1958 - 15 November 1959." *The Unabridged Journals of Sylvia Plath 1950-1962*, pp. 513-14. New York: Anchor Books, 2000.

their head" (142). The faces of others hover over her or float in front of her eyes with startling frequency: the face of Buddy Willard hanging over her after her skiing accident, announcing with some satisfaction "'You'll be stuck in a cast for months'" (80); the face of Joan Gilling floating before her, bodiless and smiling, like the face of the Cheshire cat" (192), an image that comes to Esther immediately before she learns of Joan's suicide by hanging; on the next page her mother's face floating "to mind, a pale reproachful moon" (193).

It is possible that the precursor of these and other apparently disembodied heads is the head of the baby born in the traumatic episode in which Buddy Willard, a medical student, takes Esther into the delivery room to witness a birth. The episode, a flashback, is permeated with images of dismemberment: the stomach of the woman in labor sticks up so high that her face cannot be seen; the baby's head is the first thing to appear in the delivery, "a dark fuzzy thing" that emerges "through the split, shaven place between [the woman's legs], lurid with disinfectant" (53). The images of dismemberment seem to be linked as well to the image of "a baby pickled in laboratory jar" (10-11) which occurs at the end of the first chapter. If, as Jung has taught us, the baby is an archetypal symbol of the self in crisis, then the image of the pickled baby, along with the images of dismembered body parts, accurately conveys the nature of Esther's crisis: each of the various paths open to her will require that she dispense with, leave undeveloped, some important part of herself. Imagistically the novel makes this point through scenes like that in the delivery room where the emergence of the infant's head is accompanied by the "decapitation" of the mother.

Thus at the beginning of the novel, as Esther walks along the New York streets "wondering what it would be like, being burned alive all along your nerves" (1), her musing is not merely a response to the electrocution of the Rosenbergs but to her own growing sense of alienation from the cultural demands and images of women with which she is daily bombarded during her guest editorship at *Ladies' Day*. These seem implicitly to reinforce the lessons of the preceding year, especially those of her relationship with Buddy Willard, suggesting that she must mutilate or deform herself through mating, marriage, and motherhood. It is not entirely surprising then that she begins to see the city as a collocation of dismembered body parts: "goggle-eyed headlines" stare up at her "on every street corner and at the fusty, peanut-smelling mouth of every subway" (1). Her friend Doreen, too, is presented as such a collocation: "bright white hair standing out in a cotton candy fluff and blue eyes like transparent agate marbles, hard and polished and just about indestructible, and a mouth set in a sort of perpetual sneer" (4), "long, nicotine-yellow nails" (4) and the breasts which pop out of her dress later at Lenny's apartment (14). The dismembered animal parts that decorate that apartment—the white bearskins, the "antlers and buffalo horns and [the] stuffed rabbit head" with its "meek little grey muzzle and the stiff, jackrabbit ears" (12)—are tokens of the sexual hunt in which it is assumed all the young guest editors at *Ladies' Day* will gladly play their parts, oozing enthusiasm, like Betsy, about learning the latest way "to make an all purpose neckerchief out of mink tails" (23).

Feeling as "cut off" as these excised animal parts from the culture which expects her participation in this hunt, Esther is haunted by images suggesting the self-mutilations of marriage and motherhood. She recalls the way in which Buddy Willard's mother weaves a beautiful rug only to detroy its beauty in a matter of days by using it as a kitchen mat. The message is clear to Esther: ". . .

I knew that in spite of all the roses and the kisses . . . what [a man] secretly wanted when the wedding service ended was for [the wife] to flatten out underneath his feet like Mrs. Willard's kitchen mat" (69). Her reaction against this form of mutilation is clear in her violent sensitivity upon her return home to the presence of Dodo Conway, a neighbor who had gone to Barnard and who is now pregnant with her seventh child. The vision of Dodo, "not five feet tall, with a grotesque, protruding stomach. . . . Her head tilted happily back, like a sparrow egg perched on a duck egg" (95), elicits from Esther the following reaction: "Children made me sick. . . . I couldn't see the point of getting up. I had nothing to look forward to" (96).

Esther sees Dodo as a grotesque collection of unrelated and incompatible parts, a vision which we may read as a projection of her own sense of self. It is crucial to emphasize at this point in the argument, however, that the imagery of dismemberment in **The Bell Jar** does not simply communicate Esther's psychic disturbance or a set of feelings characterizing a certain point in her history; the imagery also implies a certain model of the self. Imagery focusing our attention on part-whole relations (or dis-relations) presupposes that the self is a bounded entity, something with separate and distinct existence and of which certain kinds of things may be said: it is a whole; it may have parts or members; if some of these parts or members are removed, then the entity is not whole; neither are the severed parts, from this perspective, wholes. The model of the self implied by the imagery of dismemberment, in short, coincides with the model of a bounded self, an autonomous subject, that has dominance in our culture.

The notion of a separate, bounded self of course corresponds to our sense of being locked into our own bodies, of being separate and distinct entities. But it is important to stress that the model of an autonomous bounded self does not represent the only way in which the self may be conceived, and according to some theorists it does not represent the most accurate way of conceiving selfhood. Catherine Keller compellingly argues for the possibility of a relational model of selfhood that does not preclude a sense of differentiated identity or imply, as some feminists have argued, submersion of the self in others. Based on the assumption that the self is constituted in and through relationships with others, the relational model rejects subject-object dualism (and the system of hierarchical oppositions in which it is embedded), and it recognizes the fluid, permeable boundaries of self.[5] Conceived then not as an entity, but as a nexus of relations, the self might be imaged through metaphors of webs and linkages. Conceived not as a substance, but as a process, it might be imaged through metaphors of fluidity.

Or, conversely, a predominance of images of webs, linkages, process and fluidity, might imply an entirely different conception of the self from that informing *The Bell Jar.* That such metaphors are absent from Plath's novel suggests how thoroughly dominated by the separative model was the novelist's imagination. One image of linkage, of apparent significance because of its location in the last paragraph of the novel, is qualified by the paragraph which precedes it:

> Pausing, for a brief breath, on the threshold I saw the silver-haired doctor . . . and the pocked, cadaverous face of Miss Huey, and eyes I thought I had recognized over white masks.

> The eyes and the faces all turned themselves toward me, and guiding myself by them, as by a magical thread, I stepped into the room.
> (199-200)

The reminder in the image of Miss Huey of the cadaver head which obsesses Esther, the recalled image of eyes floating over masks—there is little qualitative difference between the vision represented here and that at the beginning of the novel, though the narrator's tone may have changed. The magical thread does not so much provide a link to others constitutive of the self as it does a line to those who hold the power of release from daily confrontation with the self and its agonies.

Despite the ambiguities of the closing of *The Bell Jar,* critics have been surprisingly willing to accept that Esther is in some positive sense "reborn" even if her future is uncertain. In the final episode, when Esther readies herself to meet the board of doctors who will certify her release from the hospital, she behaves as if she is preparing for a bridegroom or a date; she checks her stocking seams, muttering to herself "Something old, something new. . . . But," she goes on, "I wasn't getting married. There ought, I thought, to be a ritual for being born twice—patched, retreaded, and approved for the road, I was trying to think of an appropriate one . . .' (199). Critics who have been willing to see a reborn Esther have generally done so without ever questioning the propriety of the reference to a "retread" job.[6] Linda Wagner, for example, ignores this passage and concentrates on subsequent paragraphs,

where the image of an "open door and Esther's ability to breathe are," Wagner writes, "surely positive images."[7] Susan Coyle writes that the tire image "seems to be accurate, since the reader does not have a sense of [Esther] as a brand-new, unblemished tire but of one that has been painstakingly reworked, remade"; Coyle claims that Esther has taken steps that "however tentative, do lead her toward an authentic self that was previously impossible for her."[8] Not only do the comments of Coyle and Wagner ignore the implication of choosing the tire image in the first place; they also miss an affinity of the passage with one I quoted earlier in which Esther views wifehood in terms of service as a kitchen mat. The tire, like a kitchen mat, presents us with a utilitarian object, easily repaired or replaced, as a metaphor for a woman. It is worth observing that a patched, retreaded tire may be ready for the road, but somewhere down the highway the owner can expect a flat. Now "flatten out" is exactly what Esther suspects—or had suspected—women do in marriage. Yet it is precisely for marriage that Esther seems confusedly to be preparing herself in the final episode as she straightens her seams. It is true that she withdraws her reference to marriage, but despite her disclaimer, it seems to me, a retread job can only be a travesty of rebirth.

The metaphor of rebirth or a second birth is thus especially suspicious because of the way in which the tire image obliquely forces us to associate Esther's new lease on life with role expectations that contributed to her breakdown in the first place: the domestic servitude that Esther painfully recognizes "as a dreary and wasted life for a girl with fifteen years of straight A's" (68). Although Esther's breakdown may have sources lying buried in the past along with her father, the novel makes it sufficiently clear that she is torn apart by the intolerable conflict between her wish to avoid domesticity, marriage and motherhood, on the one hand, and her inability to conceive of a viable future in which she avoids that fate, on the other.

Plath's inability to resolve that conflict in her own life is well known. In an essay entitled "Sylvia Plath's 'Sivvy' Poems: A Portrait of the Poet as a Daughter," Marjorie Perloff concludes:

> The first shock of recognition produced by Sylvia Plath's 'independence' from her husband and her mother was the stimulus that gave rise to the *Ariel* poems. But given the 'psychic osmosis' between herself and Aurelia Plath . . . given the years of iron discipline during which Sylvia had been her

mother's Sivvy, the touching assertion [in "**Medusa**"] that 'There is nothing between us' could only mean that now there would be nothing at all.[9]

Whatever the biographical validity of Perloff's argument, it may help us to define a pattern that has not been discerned in *The Bell Jar.* Esther's movement toward her breakdown entails a series of rejections of or separations from women who, though they may be associated with some stereotype of womanhood unacceptable to Esther, have nurtured some important aspect of her evolving identity; as I want to show, the supposed cure which she undergoes is actually a continuation of a pattern in which Esther severs relations precisely with those whose presence "in" her self has been constitutive. Such a series of rejections may dramatize a deluded notion that an autonomous and "authentic" self may be derived through purging the self of the influence of others, but there is good reason to suppose that the process actually means that little or nothing would remain to Esther, as means of modeling identity, except forms of womanhood offered to her by the very stereotypes she has sought to elude. The irony here is that in the attempt to avoid dismemberment, disfiguration or mutilation of the self, the heroine undergoes a process of self-dismemberment.

The novel provides another metaphor for the process I am describing in the repeated binge-and-purge episodes of the first portion of the novel. In chapter 2, Esther vicariously participates in Doreen's debauche with Lenny, then returns to the hotel and a bath of purification; the pattern is repeated when Doreen returns, to pass out in a pool of her own vomit. Chapter 4 presents another purgative cleansing; after gorging on caviar at a luncheon, Esther is leveled by food poisoning, an experience which makes her feel "purged and holy and ready for a new life" (39). Shortly after this purgation, she announces: "I'm starving" (40).

In somewhat a similar manner, I am arguing, Esther embraces relations with most of the women in the novel only to cast them off, as if they constituted a foreign presence within the purity of her own identity, some threat to her integrity. Doreen, for example, speaks to her with a voice "like a secret voice speaking straight out of [her] own bones" (6), but after the evening in Lenny's apartment, Esther decides to have nothing to do with her. A similar pattern is repeated with every female character in the novel, including Dr. Nolan, the psychiatrist who brings about Esther's recovery, and Esther's mother.

Esther's aversion from her mother is obvious, ascending in stridency from the mild understatement, "My own mother wasn't much help" (32) to the murderous fantasy inspired by sharing a room with her mother: one sleepless night, after staring at "the pin curls on her [mother's] head glittering like a row of little bayonets" (100), Esther comes to feel that the only way she can escape the annoying sound of her mother's faint snore "would be to take the column of skin and sinew from which it rose and twist it to silence between [her] hands" (101). Even though Esther at one point wishes that she had a mother like Jay Cee, the editor for whom she works at *Ladies' Day,* her ambivalence toward Jay Cee and other women who have nurtured her talents is profound—and it appears to derive, quite simply, from their supposed unattractiveness to men. Of Jay Cee, Esther says ". . . I liked her a lot. . . . [She] had brains, so her plug-ugly looks didn't seem to matter" (5); but sentences later, after admitting that she cannot imagine Jay Cee in bed with her husband, Esther changes her attitude abruptly: "Jay Cee wanted to teach me something, all the old ladies I ever knew wanted to teach me something, but I suddenly didn't think they had anything to teach me" (5). A similar reflection recurs near the end of the novel in a scene where the lesbian Joan Gilling lounges on Esther's bed in the asylum and Esther's revery seems to lump the unattractive, the manless, and the woman-loving together. She remembers:

> . . . the famous woman poet at my college [who] lived with another woman—a stumpy old Classical scholar with a cropped Dutch cut. When I told the poet that I might well get married and have a pack of children someday, she stared at me in horror. "But what about your *career*?" she had cried.
>
> My head ached. Why did I attract these weird old women? There was the famous poet, and Philomena Guinea, and Jay Cee, and the Christian Scientist lady, and lord knows who, and they all wanted to adopt me in some way, and, for the price of their care and influence, have me resemble them.
>
> (180)

This passage focuses our attention on the immersion of Plath/Esther in what Adrienne Rich has called the "compulsory heterosexuality," the pervasive heterosexism, of our culture.[10] It also reinforces our awareness that despite her intelligence, imagination and professional ambition, Esther's sense of identity as a woman is predicated on finding "the right man."

That Esther categorizes Jay Cee, Philomena Guinea, and the woman poet at college (who is never named)—along with the Christian Scientist lady whom she does not know—as weird old women who want to save her is a way of rejecting these women's very real contributions and potential contributions to her own evolving identity. The claim would seem to be at least partly a projection of her own desire to be saved from becoming like these women with whom she shares certain talents, capacities, and interests. I want to suggest that there may be a kind of psychic dismemberment signified by the separation of self thus from one's nurturers; denying their influence is like peeling off layers of her own self—or cutting off important members. It is especially important to notice in this regard that the point where Esther turns her back on Jay Cee coincides with the diminishment of her sense of competence, which becomes increasingly worse as the weeks pass in New York. In rejecting the "weird old women" who want to save her, she appears to become increasingly disempowered; that is, she appears to lose touch with the talents and skills that these women nurtured.

Esther's recovery involves a reinstitution of the problems that led to her breakdown. If, as I have already suggested, the reconstructed Esther is a retreaded tire doomed to go flat (and probably on the same highway that brought her to the asylum in the first place), that is partly because her cure perpetuates the disease. The recovery process of this heroine merely extends the series of separations from or rejections of others which seems to have played an important part in bringing about her breakdown.

By the closing pages of the novel, two meaningful relations with women are open to Esther, relations with her friend, Joan Gilling, and her psychiatrist, Dr. Nolan. The first of these relations is terminated decisively by the character's suicide, which renders irreversible Esther's prior rejection of that character. In the penultimate scene of the novel, Esther attends Joan's funeral, wondering, she tells us, "what I thought I was burying" and listening to the insistent "brag of [her own] heart"—"I am, I am, I am" (198-99). Since Esther springs to new life as Joan is buried, it would be difficult not to conclude that Plath is putting aside, burying, some unacceptable part of her heroine: Esther has even explicitly identified Joan as "the beaming double of my old best self" (167). Like the metaphor of a retread, however, this comment exemplifies "the uncertainty of tone" that, according to Rosellen Brown, "manages to trivialize . . . [the novel's] heavy freight of pain."[11] If the passage hints Esther's awareness that her "old

best self" is peculiarly vulnerable to disintegration precisely because of the intolerable psychic conflict produced by trying to meet cultural expectations of women, it also—to the extent that it is sarcastic—distances Esther from Joan and from the painful feelings that she shares with Joan.

Until the revelation that Joan is involved in a lesbian relationship, that young woman is associated with a potential for intimacy that seems more positive than negative. Joan replaces, as Esther's neighbor, Miss Norris, with whom Esther shares an hour of "close, sisterly silence" (156). Joan's intimacy with Dee Dee is associated with improving health (*pace* Vance Bourjaily, who writes that a "relapse" is indicated by Joan's "lesbian involvement"[12]—the novel simply contradicts this). Esther even feels free to curl up on Joan's bed on first encountering her at the asylum, though she admits to having known Joan at college only "at a cool distance" (160).

After discovering Joan with Dee Dee, however, Esther's treatment of Joan begins to be marked by a blatant cruelty, as when Esther tells Joan, "'I don't like you. You make me want to puke, if you want to know'" (180). A less explicit cruelty, implicating not merely the character Esther but the author Plath, pervades the scene where Joan seeks medical attention for Esther's hemorrhaging after Esther's encounter with Irwin. Esther/Plath clearly has one eye on humiliating Joan. Because Joan is allowed to surmise that the bleeding is some mysterious menstrual problem rather than connected to Esther's loss of virginity, she is made to look like a bumbler. She has difficulty explaining the problem clearly enough to get emergency aid, a problem which of course increases the danger to Esther, but a pun seems more important here than prompt medical assistance. When Joan asks about the man who has dropped Esther off, Esther says: "I realized that she honestly took my explanation at face value . . . and his appearance [was] a mere prick to her pleasure at my arrival." The oddity of her mentioning, in circumstances where every beat of her heart "pushed forth another gush of blood" (189), Joan's pleasure at her arrival is matched by what looks like a kind of desperation to hide from Joan the cause of the hemorrhaging.

The peculiarities of this scene create ambiguities about Esther's motives and suggest confusion on Plath's part. Still Plath's imagery hints at a causal link between Esther's hemorrhaging and Joan's death. Often described before this episode in terms of horse imagery, Joan is here described as a "myopic owl" (190) in an image that appears paradoxically to reveal what it intends to obscure: Joan's knowledge of the cause of Esther's suffering and the trauma of the rejection that Esther's suffering represents. Similarly, the structuring of the narrative implies a link between Joan's death and Esther's rebirth. Before she gets to the Emergency Room, Esther remembers "a worrisome course in the Victorian novel where woman after woman died, palely and nobly, in torrents of blood, after a difficult childbirth" (189). The birth that is brought about here, however, is not that of a strong new self but of an Esther who gives in to her fear of the love and nurturance of women—exemplified by Joan's role as nurse in this scene—an Esther who buries her capacity for identification with women and accepts the very stereotypes which have been the source of her pain.

As "the only purely imagined event in the book,"[13] the inclusion of Joan's unexpected and unprepared for suicide immediately following this episode, is, as Paula Bennett has written, "necessitated not by the novel's plot, themes, or characters but by Plath's own emotional understanding of her text. Joan, the woman who loves other women and who, therefore, can pursue a career and independent life without benefit of man or marriage, must be disposed of if the demons that haunt Plath's/Esther's mind are to be exorcised as well. . . ."[14] The nature of those demons may partly be implied by the descriptions of the lesbians in the novel: not only the "stumpy" old Classical scholar, already mentioned, but the "matronly-breasted senior, homely as a grandmother and a pious Religion major, and a tall, gawky freshman with a history of being deserted at an early hour in all sorts of ingenious ways by her blind dates" (179). Such images indicate the "weirdness," the unattractiveness, to Plath of any female behavior deviating from heterosexual, patriarchal norms: Esther says of Joan, "It was like observing a Martian, or a particularly warty toad" (179).

It seems a kind of narrative reaction to these images that in the episode following those in which they occur, Esther has herself fitted with a diaphragm. So compelling is the logic of her desire to avoid pregnancy that we do not feel spurred to ask why she would at this point want to have anything to do with a man in the first place. But it should be noted that her encounters with men have been nearly devastating: her father deserts her by dying when she is very young; much more recently in the novel, she is knocked down in the mud, mauled, practically raped by a man who marks her face with blood; in another, a flashback to an occasion where she ends up inspecting Buddy Willard's genitals, all she can think of is "turkey neck and turkey gizzards" (55). The man she sets out to seduce (Constantin) falls asleep unaroused by her, and the male psychiatrist to whom she turns for help practically electrocutes her. This pattern of pain and disappointment is merely confirmed by her experience with Irwin, who creates for her, in deflowering her, a possibly life-threatening medical emergency.

It is a sad irony that precisely at the point in *The Bell Jar* where the action seems to call for at least a temporary turning away from men or from seeing herself in relation to male sexuality, if only to provide for some period of reflection and healing on Esther's part, the novel turns more decisively than ever away from women and toward men. Critics have not, however, generally recognized this irony; the typical reaction has been to accept at face value that the purchase of a diaphragm is an important step in the direction of independence. While contraception surely frees Esther from fears which no women should have to suffer, my argument is that we need to question the validity of the notion of independence offered through this episode.

In killing off Joan, Plath cancels for Esther the possibility of tenderness—outside the relatively impersonal therapeutic relationship—clearly symbolized by Joan's lesbianism. That possibility is named by Dr. Nolan, the only character in the novel treated with unambiguous respect. When Esther asks this psychiatrist "What does a women see in a woman that she can't see in a man," Dr. Nolan replies with one definitive, authoritative word: "Tenderness" (179). Plath dramatizes both the yearning for tenderness in Esther and the way in which Esther is cut off from that yearning, but there seems to be little authorial awareness of the disjunction. The novel presents the possibility of tenderness between women in a story Esther recounts about two "suspected" lesbians at her college: "'Milly was sitting on the chair and Theodora was lying on the bed, and Milly was stroking Theodora's hair'" (180). An image of this sort of caress occurs at another point in the novel, significantly in connection with a male who is probably a homosexual.[15] When Constantin, the simultaneous interpreter whom Esther fails to seduce in New York, reaches out at the end of the evening to touch her hair she feels "a little electric shock" and tells us: "Ever since I was small I loved feeling somebody comb my hair. It made me go all sleepy and peaceful" (70). This touch is arguably the only tenderness Esther experiences in the novel, yet her response to the similar contact between Milly and Theodora is this: "I was disappointed. . . . I wondered if all women did with women was lie and hug" (180).

In her aversion to Joan, Esther denies what the text nonetheless reveals: the possibility of a healing "tenderness" and "weirdness" that the relation of Joan and Dee Dee represents. As we have seen, this denial is authorially endorsed by Plath's invention of Joan's suicide. Suggesting that Joan represents Esther's "suicidal self" or—more exotically but no more helpfully—"the inverted Victorian side of Esther," critics with a Freudian orientation have linked Esther's recovery to a splitting off of an unacceptable portion of the self dramatized by Joan's suicide.[16] While a splitting off undoubtedly occurs, the nature of what is split off is ultimately ambiguous. Furthermore, *splitting off* appears to be a major symptom of the disorder from which Esther suffers. The novel dramatizes a tragic self-dismemberment in which the heroine, because of her very strengths and aspirations, appears to split off those components of herself that represent patriarchally-defined expectations of women, projecting these aspects of herself on her mother, her grandmother, Dodo Conway, Mrs. Willard, and the young women who are guest editors with her at *Ladies' Day,* especially Doreen and Betsy. Although she consciously rejects the influence of these others, she must still unconsciously be dominated by the patriarchal images of womanhood that she rejects; otherwise she would not need *also* to split off those qualities and impulses in herself that do *not* meet patriarchal expectations—all that goes counter to conventional femininity and is therefore "weird." These she projects upon Jay Cee, Philomena Guinea, the unnamed famous poet at her college, and finally Joan. Her systematic rejection of these leaves her quite possibly "with nothing" in the same sense that, as Perloff argues, Plath was left with nothing after rejecting the beliefs she inherited from her mother.

Dr. Nolan appears to play a special role in Esther's "cure," but several reservations about that role ought to be made. Combining the attributes of patriarchally-defined femininity and professional accomplishment, Dr. Nolan is set forth by some readers as an ideal role model for Esther, but the last thirty years have taught us to question this sort of image which can merely compound the oppression of women by leading them to assume expectations traditionally held of men as well as those held of women: Plath herself provides a highly visible example of the tragic consequences of uncritically embracing this model which encourages the belief that women can "have it all." Furthermore, the novel leaves ambiguous the extent of Nolan's contribution to the recovery. Although the trust she engenders in Esther undoubtedly counts for a great deal, the electroshock therapy and the psychic dismemberment involved in the process appear to get equal if not more credit for Esther's improvement. Finally, whatever the depth of Esther's indebtedness to Dr. Nolan, the relationship appears to be largely terminated by Esther's release from the hospital.

Thus, at the end of the novel, far from having moved in the direction of an "authentic self," Esther has been systematically separated from the very means by which such a self might be constituted: relationships with others. Her high heels and "red wool suit flamboyant as [her] plans" (199) clearly signal a renewed and energized willingness to enter the sexual hunt that so dispirited her during her summer in New York. Esther's seeming preparation to reenter the hunt for "the right man" is accompanied by the strong suggestion that the right man is one with whom she may avoid emotional attachment. (Esther says gleefully, after realizing that Irwin's voice on the phone means nothing to her and that he has no way of getting in touch with her again, "I was perfectly free" [198].) In other words, Esther's identity, the boundary of her self, has been secured by her isolation.

The Bell Jar makes apparent the oppressive force (at least for women) of the model of separative selfhood which dominates patriarchal culture. The novel dramatizes a double bind for women in which, on the one hand, an authentic self is one that is presumed to be autonomous and whole, entire to itself and clearly bounded, and yet in which, on the other hand, women have their identity primarily through relationship to a man. It is the increasing tension of this double bind for Esther which results in her breakdown; her release from the asylum, I have argued, is marked by a restoration of the double bind at a different and tolerable level of tension. The experiences of both Esther and Joan suggest that escape is not possible through conscious rejection of the expectation that a woman find herself in a man; in my reading, Plath's novel hints that the expectation is, in that instance, likely to be heeded at a more deeply unconscious level. (This would be a possible explanation of Joan's unexpected suicide, and the idea is supported by the imagery of the closing episode as I have analyzed it.) Yet the other alternative, to reject the model of separative self-hood and embrace a relational model, in-volves—in the cultural context portrayed by Plath—the restoration of the traditional plight of women: subservience to or submersion in others.

The way out of the dilemma is a relational conception of selfhood in a world of non-oppressive, non-hierarchical relations. But we do not live in such a world (yet), and our culture offers few means of imaging non-oppressive, non-hierarchical relationality. It is in signaling the paucity of such means, the unavailability of such images at least to someone like Plath but by extension to many women in our culture, that *The Bell Jar* has special importance. Images of lateral relationships among women, i.e. images of female friendship, provide one means, but as I have argued, Plath seems compelled in this novel eventually to reject all such images. In this context, the introduction of Joan specifically as a lesbian becomes very important. Joan's lesbianism and suicide appear to belong to a small number of "invented" features of the novel. That Plath rejects Joan by killing her off is a sign of the novelist's domination by the cultural norms that, I believe, destroyed her; that she created Joan as a lesbian in the first place, however, especially in a novel so dominated by autobiographical fact, might plausibly be viewed as a last desperate imaginative reaching toward some viable image of non-hierarchical relationality. Having rejected all the other woman-woman relationships available to her from her experience, Plath turns finally to invention, which—controlled by stereotype as it is—proves no more successful than autobiographical fact.

It is important for feminist critics to discern such emancipatory impulses or gestures wherever they occur in women's writing. We need to bring them into focus and to assess where they succeed and the conditions of their success or failure. But I would suggest that critics are less than well-equipped to undertake such work if they remain uncritical of their own discourse, for example, the way in which it is permeated with terminology implying that the self is an autonomous, bounded entity. Paula Bennett, who rightly calls the ending of *The Bell Jar* "unbearably factitious," provides an example of such terminology when she writes that ". . . Plath herself seems to have gained little from her experience at the psychiatric hospital. She returned to Smith . . . hollow and uninte-grated at her core."[17] Bennett's language here ("hollow," "core"), founded as it is upon the dichotomy of inner and outer, implies subject-object dualism and all the patriarchally-freighted oppositions that it brings in its wake. It is difficult to write about the self in our culture without making use of terms implying the very dualisms on which patriarchy is founded. Yet if we cannot entirely dispense with such terminology—and I do not believe that we very well can—we can be aware of its metaphoric nature and of the assumptions that it covers.

When we become aware of the limits of our metaphors for selfhood, we become more attuned to those employed by the writers we study. Only when such awareness is brought to bear upon *The Bell Jar,* for instance, do we become fully appreciative of the way in which the novel dramatizes the destructive effects of a commitment to the separative model of the self. When such awareness is brought to bear upon the writing of women less tragically constricted than Plath by stereotypes of women, it may enable us to discern alternative metaphors and images for the self, the very means by which the dominant model of the self in our culture may be transformed into one conducive to the validation of women.

Notes

1. Paula Bennett, *My Life a Loaded Gun: Female Creativity and Feminist Poetics* (Boston: Beacon, 1986), p. 124.

2. Catherine Keller, *From a Broken Web: Separation, Sexism, and Self* (Boston: Beacon, 1987). The term "separative self" is taken from Keller, p. 9; also see p. 26. The groundwork for feminist questioning of models of the self is provided in Nancy Chodorow, *The Reproduction of Mothering: Psychoanalysis and the Sociology of Gender* (Berkeley: University of California Press, 1978) and Carol Gilligan, *In a Different Voice: Psychological Theory and Women's Development* (Cambridge: Harvard University Press, 1982). Also relevant is Mary Beth Field Belenky, Blythe McVicker Clinchy, Nancy Rule Goldberger and Jill Mattuck Tarrule, *Women's Ways of Knowing: The Development of Self, Voice, and Mind* (New York: Basic Books, 1986).

3. The only critic I am aware of who has raised a question about the consequences of Plath's commitment to the bounded, individualistic ego is Joyce Carol Oates in "The Death Throes of Romanticism," in *Ariel Ascending: Writings About Sylvia Plath,* ed. Paul Alexander (New York: Harper, 1985), pp. 26-45. The poet Louise Glück has alluded to an obsession with boundaries in Plath; see "Invitation and Exclusion," *Antaeus,* 47 (Autumn 1982), 154.

It is interesting that Paula Bennett, whose reading of the novel corresponds to mine in many details, claims that for Plath "the only way to life was through fusion and the *consequent erasure of the separate self*" (115, emphasis added). The separative impulse that I trace in this essay and the longing for fusion, Bennett's concern in the passage quoted, appear to be two aspects—two alternating consequences—of the model of the self I am calling the separative model. The relational model sketched in Keller's book relieves the self of oscillation between such poles.

4. Sylvia Plath, *The Bell Jar* (New York: Harper, 1971), p. 1. Subsequent references to Plath's novel with be cited parenthetically in the text.

5. This is Keller's thesis; see, for example, 2-4, 153-54.

6. Two treatments of the novel by critics skeptical about Esther's recovery are Bennett's chapter on the novel in *My Life a Loaded Gun* and Lynda K. Bundzen, *Plath's Incarnations: Woman and the Creative Process* (Ann Arbor: The University of Michigan Press, 1983), pp. 109-56.

7. Linda W. Wagner, "Plath's *Bell Jar* as *Female Bildungsroman*," *Women's Studies*, 12 (1986), 64.

8. Susan Coyle, "Images of Madness and Retrieval: An Exploration of Metaphor in *The Bell Jar,*" *Studies in American Fiction*, 12 (1984), 171.

9. Marjorie Perloff, "Sylvia Plath's 'Sivvy' Poems: A Portrait of the Poet as Daughter," in *Sylvia Plath: New Views on the Poetry*, ed. Gary Lane (Baltimore: Johns Hopkins, 1979), p. 175.

10. See Adrienne Rich, "Compulsory Heterosexuality and Lesbian Existence" in *Blood, Bread and Poetry: Selected Prose, 1979-1985* (New York: Norton, 1986), pp. 23-75.

11. Rosellen Brown, "Keeping the Self at Bay," in *Ariel Ascending: Writings About Sylvia Plath*, ed. Paul Alexander (New York: Harper, 1985), p. 122.

12. Vance Bourjaily, "Victoria Lucas and Elly Higginbottom," in *Ariel Ascending*, ed. Paul Alexander (New York: Harper, 1985), p. 138.

13. Edward Butscher, *Sylvia Plath: Method and Madness* (New York: Seabury, 1976), p. 342. Quoted by Bennett, p. 130.

14. Bennett, p. 130.

15. Bourjaily, p. 149.

16. Christopher Bollas and Murray M. Schwartz, "The Absence at the Center: Sylvia Plath and Suicide," *Sylvia Plath: New Views on the Poetry*, ed. Gary Lane (Baltimore: Johns Hopkins University Press, 1979), p. 200; Gordon Lameyer, "The Double in Sylvia Plath's *The Bell Jar,*" *Sylvia Plath: The Woman and the Work*, ed. Edward Butscher (New York: Dodd, 1977), p. 159.

17. Bennett, p. 132, p. 131. My point is not to fault Bennett's terminology but to suggest that we be aware of the implications of the metaphors we use in our criticism. Both Wagner and Coyle use language implying the separative model of selfhood in contexts that demand closer scrutiny of such metaphors than does Bennett's argument.

FURTHER READING

Bibliography

Tabor, Stephen. *Sylvia Plath: An Analytical Bibliography.* Westport, Conn.: Meckler Publishing, 1987, 268 p.

A helpful bibliography of essential works by and about Plath.

Biographies

Alexander, Paul. *Rough Magic: A Biography of Sylvia Plath,* New York: Viking, 1991, 402 p.

Hayman, Ronald. *The Death and Life of Sylvia Plath,* Secaucus, N.J.: Carol Publishing Group, 1991, 235 p.

A biography of Plath considered by critics to be empathetic and thorough.

Malcolm, Janet. *The Silent Woman: Sylvia Plath and Ted Hughes,* New York: A. A. Knopf, 1994, 207 p.

Highly regarded psychoanalytic study of Plath's life and work that examines the shortfalls and conflicts involved in any biographical endeavor.

Middlebrook, Diane. *Her Husband: Hughes and Plath—A Marriage.* New York: Viking, 2003, 361 p.

Provides an assessment of the partnership between Ted Hughes and Plath, asserting that the strong creative impulses within both poets resulted in a dynamic and powerful combination.

Stevenson, Anne. *Bitter Fame: A Life of Sylvia Plath,* London: Viking, 1989, 413 p.

A comprehensive account of Plath's life and literary career.

Wagner-Martin, Linda. *Sylvia Plath: A Biography,* New York: St. Martin's Press, 1987, 282 p.

Biography of Plath providing access to previously unseen journals and letters.

Criticism

Alexander, Paul, ed. *Ariel Ascending: Writings about Sylvia Plath,* New York: Harper and Row, 1985, 217 p.

A collection of criticism on Plath's life and writing, including essays by Helen Vendler, Alicia Ostriker, Joyce Carol Oates, Rosellen Brown, and others.

Axelrod, Stephen Gould. *Sylvia Plath : The Wound and the Cure of Words,* Baltimore, Md: Johns Hopkins University Press, 1990, 257 p.

Provides criticism through the means of "a biography of the imagination."

Bentley, Paul. "'Hitler's Familiar Spirits': Negative Dialectics in Sylvia Plath's 'Daddy' and Ted Hughes's 'Hawk Roosting'." *Critical Survey* 12, no. 3 (2000): 27-38.

Addresses Plath's use of Holocaust imagery in "Daddy" and compares the poem to Hughes's "Hawk Roosting," another poem that is often interpreted as a commentary on events in World War II.

Butscher, Edward. *Sylvia Plath, Method and Madness,* New York: Seabury Press, 1976, 388 p.

A critical and biographical study of Plath's writings and her life.

Curley, Maureen. "Plath's 'Lady Lazarus'." *Explicator* 59, no. 4 (summer 2001): 213-14.

Maintains that "Lady Lazarus" serves as a poetic commentary on the difficulties faced by female artists and also contends that the poem plays upon a second biblical character named Lazarus in addition to the well-known figure that Jesus returned to life.

Dahlke, Laura Johnson. "Plath's 'Lady Lazarus'." *Explicator* 60, no. 4 (summer 2002): 50-2.

Asserts that the speaker's conflict in "Lady Lazarus" with the Herr Doktor character represents a struggle against male dominance that ultimately ends in defeat, despite the defiant closing lines of the poem.

Hedley, Jane. "Sylvia Plath's Ekphrastic Poetry." *Raritan* 20, no. 4 (spring 2001): 37-73.

Focuses on Plath's poems that concern visual works of art.

Kendall, Tim. *Sylvia Plath: A Critical Study,* London: Faber and Faber, 2001, 235 p.

Book-length study of Plath that emphasizes her writing rather than the biographical details of her life.

Oates, Joyce Carol. "The Death Throes of Romanticism." *Southern Review,* 9, no. 3 (summer 1973): 501-22.

Identifies Plath as part of the Romantic tradition in literature, seeing her poetry as a representation of outmoded ideas that identify the human condition as one of isolated competition.

Rose, Jacqueline. *The Haunting of Sylvia Plath.* Cambridge, Mass.: Harvard University Press, 1992, 288 p.

Psychoanalytic study examining Plath's life and work, focusing on feminism in relation to her writing, among other topics.

Van Dyne, Susan R. *Revising Life: Sylvia Plath's Ariel Poems.* Chapel Hill: University of North Carolina Press, 1993, 206 p.

A feminist examination of many of the poems in Ariel, *focusing on the processes of their writing and revision.*

Vendler, Helen. "Sylvia Plath: Reconstructing the Colossus." In *Coming of Age as a Poet: Milton, Keats, Eliot, Plath,* pp. 115-54. Cambridge, Mass.: Harvard University Press, 2003.

Examines the poem "Edge" in an effort to defend Plath's work against charges that it lacked vision and suffered from contradictions.

Wagner, Erica. *Ariel's Gift: Ted Hughes, Sylvia Plath, and the Story of Birthday Letters,* New York: W. W. Norton and Company, 2001, 256 p.

Critical study presenting analysis of Plath's poetry and life through a study of Ted Hughes' poetry.

Wagner-Martin, Linda. *Sylvia Plath: A Literary Life,* New York: St. Martin's Press, 1999, 171 p.

Examines the process by which Plath developed herself as a writer, including analysis of her early reading and writing habits.

Wagner, Linda W. "Plath's *The Bell Jar* as Female *Bildungsroman." Women's Studies* 12, no. 1 (1986): 55-68.

Maintains that The Bell Jar *fits into the tradition of youthful coming-of-age novels, though it also stands apart because the protagonist is female.*

Zivley, Sherry Lutz. "Sylvia Plath's Transformations of Modern Paintings." *College Literature* 29, no. 3 (summer 2002): 35-56.

Analyzes Plath's poems that were inspired by paintings by Henri Rosseau, Paul Klee, and others.

OTHER SOURCES FROM GALE:

Additional coverage Plath's life and career is contained in the following sources published by the Gale Group: *American Writers Retrospective Supplement,* Vol. 2; *American Writers Supplement,* Vol. 1; *Authors and Artists for Young Adults,* Vol. 13; *Beacham's Encyclopedia of Popular Fiction: Biography and Resources,* Vol. 3; *Concise Dictionary of American Literary Biography, 1941-1968; Contemporary Authors,* Vols. 19-20; *Contemporary Authors New Revision Series,* Vols. 34, 101; *Contemporary Authors Permanent Series,* Vol. 2; *Contemporary Literary Criticism,* Vols. 1, 2, 3, 5, 9, 11, 14, 17, 50, 51, 62, 111; *Dictionary of Literary Biography,* Vols. 5, 6, 152; *DISCovering Authors; DISCovering Authors: British Edition; DISCovering Authors: Canadian Edition; DISCovering Authors Modules: Most-studied Authors* and *Poets; DISCovering Authors 3.0; Encyclopedia of World Literature in the 20th Century,* Ed. 3; *Exploring Novels; Exploring Poetry; Feminist Writers; Literature and Its Times,* Vol. 4; *Literature Resource Center; Major 20th-Century Writers,* Eds. 1, 2; *Modern American Women Writers; Novels for Students,* Vol. 1; *Poetry Criticism,* Vols. 1, 37; *Poetry for Students,* Vols. 1, 15; *Poets: American and British; Reference Guide to Young Adult Writers; Something about the Author,* Vol. 96; *Twayne's United States Authors; World Literature Criticism;* and *World Poets.*

ADRIENNE RICH

(1929 -)

American poet, essayist, and critic.

An important poet of the post-World War II era, Rich is praised for her lyrical and highly crafted poems in which she explores a variety of socially relevant subjects, including feminism and lesbianism. Rich is also an influential essayist whose numerous prose works have advanced theories of feminist criticism. An early proponent of societal change that reflects the values and goals of women, Rich is credited with articulating one of the most profound poetic statements of the feminist movement.

BIOGRAPHICAL INFORMATION

Rich was born in Baltimore, Maryland, to Dr. Arnold Rich, a respected pathologist and professor at Johns Hopkins University Medical School, and Helen Rich, a classical pianist and composer. According to the educational beliefs of her father, Rich was schooled at home under the tutelage of her mother until the fourth grade. She showed an early interest in writing and was encouraged by her father to peruse his extensive collection of Victorian literature. Rich graduated from Radcliffe College in 1951, and her first volume of poetry, *A Change of World,* was chosen by W. H. Auden for the Yale Series of Younger Poets award. The fol-

lowing year Rich won a Guggenheim Fellowship and traveled to Europe and England. In 1953 she married Harvard University economist Alfred H. Conrad, and the couple settled in Cambridge, Massachusetts. Rich gave birth to a son in 1955 and that same year saw the publication of her second poetry collection, *The Diamond Cutters, and Other Poems.* By 1959 Rich was the mother of three sons and had little time for writing. Though she wrote sporadically when her children were young, Rich was unhappy with the quality of work she produced. In 1963, however, she published *Snapshots of a Daughter-in-Law,* a collection of poems drawn from the fragments of writing she had compiled over eight years. This volume is widely considered her breakthrough work because of its overt delineation of female themes. In 1966 Rich and her family moved to New York City, where she became involved in the civil rights and antiwar movements. By 1969 she had become estranged from her husband, who committed suicide the following year. During the early 1970s Rich devoted much of her time to the women's movement and began identifying herself as a radical feminist. In 1973 her eighth poetry collection, *Diving into the Wreck,* won the National Book Award. Defying what she perceived to be the patriarchal organization on which the competition was founded, Rich refused the award as an individual; however, she accepted it collectively with fellow nominees Audre Lorde and Alice

Walker. In 1979 she moved to Montague, Massachusetts, with Michelle Cliff, a distinguished Caribbean-American fiction and essay writer, where the two coedited the lesbian feminist journal *Sinister Wisdom.* In 1997 she was awarded the Academy of American Poets Wallace Stevens Award. Also that year, Rich was awarded a National Medal for the Arts, to be presented at a ceremony by President Bill Clinton; Rich refused to accept the award, criticizing public policies and governmental priorities as a whole. She wrote a short essay explaining her actions, which was published in the *Los Angeles Times* books section on August 3, 1997. Rich currently lives in northern California.

MAJOR WORKS

Rich's poetry is generally divided into discrete phases that reflect the evolutionary nature of her canon. The highly crafted verse structures and portrayal of such themes as alienation and loss in her first two collections, *A Change of World* and *The Diamond Cutters,* evince Rich's early affinities with modernist poets. In *Snapshots of a Daughter-in-Law,* considered her first transitional work, Rich departed from the formalism of her earlier volumes by employing free verse and overtly portraying women's themes. Rich began the next phase of her poetic career with the collections *Necessities of Life* (1966), *Leaflets* (1969), and *The Will to Change* (1971). These works focus on the relationship between private and public life and openly reject patriarchal culture and language. *Diving into the Wreck,* Rich's second major transitional work, stands as a radical feminist critique of contemporary society. Many of the poems in this volume assert the importance of reinventing cultural standards in feminist terms and focus on the need for women to achieve self-definition. Her next collections, *The Dream of a Common Language* (1978) and *A Wild Patience Has Taken Me This Far* (1981), are considered lyrical celebrations of the accomplishments of women. In these works Rich examines the lives of historical female figures as well as the everyday experiences of ordinary women. In *Your Native Land, Your Life* (1986), *Time's Power* (1989), and *An Atlas of the Difficult World* (1991), Rich addresses new issues—such as her Jewish heritage and the effects of the Holocaust on her life and work—while continuing to develop feminist ideals. In her most recent collections of poetry, *Dark Fields of the Republic* (1995),

Midnight Salvage (1999), and *Fox* (2001), Rich focuses on "the interfold of personal and public experience."

In *Of Woman Born: Motherhood as Experience and Institution* (1976)—a volume of essays frequently considered her most forceful statement of radical feminism—Rich discusses the alienation and anger that she contends women experience in their roles as mothers in a patriarchal society. A second collection of essays, *On Lies, Secrets, and Silence* (1979), contains prose that furthers her feminist aesthetic, including her most noted essay, "When We Dead Awaken: Writing as Re-Vision," in which Rich clarifies the need for female self-actualization. In *Blood, Bread, and Poetry* (1986) Rich continues to explore issues of lesbianism while focusing on such topics as racial identity and racism. In *What Is Found There: Notebooks on Poetry and Politics* (1993) Rich argues for the importance of poetry as a "social art" throughout human experience. *Arts of the Possible: Essays and Conversations* (2001) collects some of Rich's best-known essays and adds several new works to her canon.

CRITICAL RECEPTION

Since the publication of *Diving into the Wreck,* most critics have analyzed Rich's work as an artistic expression of feminist politics. While many reviewers have praised her ability to write effectively in numerous verse forms, others have faulted the content of her poems as didactic. Critical commentary on Rich's work has reflected the polemics of her verse; critics who adhere to Rich's politics frequently commend her poems unconditionally, while those who disagree with her radical feminism disavow her work. Additionally, there has been no conclusive appraisal of her canon as Rich continually revises her views and asserts her new approaches to contemporary issues. Most critics concur, however, that Rich's intelligent and innovative portrayals of women have contributed significantly to the feminist movement.

PRINCIPAL WORKS

A Change of World (poetry) 1951

The Diamond Cutters, and Other Poems (poetry) 1955

Snapshots of a Daughter-in-Law: Poems, 1954-1962 (poetry) 1963; revised edition, 1967

Necessities of Life: Poems, 1962-1965 (poetry) 1966

Selected Poems (poetry) 1967

Leaflets: Poems, 1965-1968 (poetry) 1969

The Will to Change: Poems, 1968-1970 (poetry) 1971

Diving into the Wreck (poetry) 1973

Poems: Selected and New, 1950-1974 (poetry) 1975

Of Woman Born: Motherhood as Experience and Institution (criticism) 1976

The Dream of a Common Language: Poems, 1974-1977 (poetry) 1978

On Lies, Secrets, and Silence: Selected Prose, 1966-1978 (criticism) 1979

A Wild Patience Has Taken Me This Far: Poems, 1978-1981 (poetry) 1981

The Fact of a Doorframe: Poems Selected and New, 1950-1984 (poetry) 1984

Blood, Bread, and Poetry: Selected Prose, 1979-1985 (criticism) 1986

Your Native Land, Your Life (poetry) 1986

Time's Power: Poems, 1985-1988 (poetry) 1989

An Atlas of the Difficult World: Poems, 1988-1991 (poetry) 1991

What Is Found There: Notebooks on Poetry and Politics (criticism) 1993

Dark Fields of the Republic: Poems, 1991-1995 (poetry) 1995

Midnight Salvage: Poems, 1995-1998 (poetry) 1999

Arts of the Possible: Essays and Conversations (essays and interviews) 2002

Fox: Poems, 1998-2000 (poetry) 2003

What Is Found There: Notebooks on Poetry and Politics (nonfiction) 2003

PRIMARY SOURCES

ADRIENNE RICH (ESSAY DATE OCTOBER 1972)

SOURCE: Rich, Adrienne. "When We Dead Awaken: Writing as Re-Vision." In *Adrienne Rich's Poetry: Texts of the Poems, the Poet on Her Work, Reviews and Criticism,* edited by Barbara Charlesworth Gelpi and Albert Gelpi, pp. 90-8. New York: W. W. Norton & Company, 1975.

In the following essay, originally published in the journal College English *in October, 1972, Rich encourages readers to reexamine texts by and about women in order to come to a new understanding of women as artists and individuals.*

Ibsen's *When We Dead Awaken* is a play about the use that the male artist and thinker—in the process of creating culture as we know it—has made of women, in his life and in his work; and about a woman's slow struggling awakening to the use to which her life has been put. Bernard Shaw wrote in 1900 of this play:

> [Ibsen] shows us that no degradation ever devized or permitted is as disastrous as this degradation; that through it women can die into luxuries for men and yet can kill them; that men and women are becoming conscious of this; and that what remains to be seen as perhaps the most interesting of all imminent social developments is what will happen "when we dead awaken".[1]

It's exhilarating to be alive in a time of awakening consciousness; it can also be confusing, disorienting, and painful. This awakening of dead or sleeping consciousness has already affected the lives of millions of women, even those who don't know it yet. It is also affecting the lives of men, even those who deny its claims upon them. The argument will go on whether an oppressive economic class system is responsible for the oppressive nature of male/female relations, or whether, in fact, the sexual class system is the original model on which all the others are based. But in the last few years connections have been drawn between our sexual lives and our political institutions, which are inescapable and illuminating. The sleepwalkers are coming awake, and for the first time this awakening has a collective reality; it is no longer such a lonely thing to open one's eyes.

Re-vision—the act of looking back, of seeing with fresh eyes, of entering an old text from a new critical direction—is for us more than a chapter in cultural history: it is an act of survival. Until we can understand the assumptions in which we are drenched we cannot know ourselves. And this drive to self-knowledge, for woman, is more than a search for identity: it is part of her refusal of the self-destructiveness of male-dominated society. A radical critique of litterature, feminist in its impulse, would take the work first of all as a clue to how we live, how we have been living, how we have been led to imagine ourselves, how our language has trapped as well as liberated us; and how we can begin to see—and therefore live—afresh. A change in the concept of sexual identity is essential if we are not going to see the old political order re-assert itself in every new revolution. We need to know the writing of the past, and know it differently than we have ever known it; not to pass on a tradition but to break its hold over us.

For writers, and at this moment for women writers in particular, there is the challenge and promise of a whole new psychic geography to be explored. But there is also a difficult and dangerous walking on the ice, as we try to find language and images for a consciousness we are just coming into, and with little in the past to support us. I want to talk about some apects of this difficulty and this danger.

Jane Harrison, the great classical anthropologist, wrote in 1914 in a letter to her friend Gilbert Murray:

> By the by, about "Women," it has bothered me often—why do women never want to write poetry about Man as a sex—why is Woman a dream and a terror to man and not the other way around? . . . Is it mere convention and propriety, or something deeper?[2]

I think Jane Harrison's question cuts deep into the myth-making tradition, the romantic tradition; deep into what women and men have been to each other; and deep into the psyche of the woman writer. Thinking about that question, I began thinking of the work of two 20th-century women poets, Sylvia Plath and Diane Wakoski. It strikes me that in the work of both Man appears as, if not a dream, a fascination and a terror; and that the source of the fascination and the terror is, simply, Man's power—to dominate, tyrannize, choose, or reject the woman. The charisma of Man seems to come purely from his power over her and his control of the world by force, not from anything fertile or life-giving in him. And, in the work of both these poets, it is finally the woman's sense of *herself*—embattled, possessed—that gives the poetry its dynamic charge, its rhythms of struggle, need, will, and female energy. Convention and propriety are perhaps not the right words, but until recently this female anger and this furious awareness of the Man's power over her were not available materials to the female poet, who tended to write of Love as the source of her suffering, and to view that victimization by Love as an almost inevitable fate. Or, like Marianne Moore and Elizabeth Bishop, she kept human sexual relationships at a measured and chiselled distance in her poems.

One answer to Jane Harrison's question has to be that historically men and women have played very different parts in each others' lives. Where woman has been a luxury for man, and has served as the painter's model and the poet's muse, but also as comforter, nurse, cook, bearer of his seed, secretarial assistant and copyist of manuscripts, man has played a quite different role for the female artist. Henry James repeats an incident which the writer Prosper Mérimée described, of how, while he was living with George Sand,

> he once opened his eyes, in the raw winter dawn, to see his companion, in a dressing-gown, on her knees before the domestic hearth, a candlestick beside her and a red *madras* round her head, making bravely, with her own hands, the fire that was to enable her to sit down betimes to urgent pen and paper. The story represents him as having felt that the spectacle chilled his ardor and tried his taste; her appearance was unfortunate, her occupation an inconsequence, and her industry a reproof—the result of all of which was a lively irritation and an early rupture.[3]

I am suggesting that the specter of this kind of male judgment, along with the active discouragement and thwarting of her needs by a culture controlled by males, has created problems for the woman writer: problems of contact with herself, problems of language and style, problems of energy and survival.

In rereading Virginia Woolf's *A Room Of One's Own* for the first time in some years, I was astonished at the sense of effort, of pains taken, of dogged tentativeness in the tone of that essay. And I recognized that tone. I had heard it often enough, in myself and in other women. It is the tone of a woman almost in touch with her anger, who is determined not to appear angry, who is *willing* herself to be calm, detached, and even charming in a roomful of men where things have been said which are attacks on her very integrity. Virginia Woolf is addressing an audience of women, but she is acutely conscious—as she always was—of being overheard by men: by Morgan and Lytton and Maynard Keynes and for that matter by her father, Leslie Stephen. She drew the language out into an exacerbated thread in her determination to have her own sensibility yet protect it from those masculine presences. Only at rare moments in that essay do you hear the passion in her voice; she was trying to sound as cool as Jane Austen, as Olympian as Shakespeare, because that is the way the men of the culture thought a writer should sound.

No male writer has written primarily or even largely for women, or with the sense of women's criticism as a consideration when he chooses his materials, his theme, his language. But to a lesser or greater extent, every woman writer has written for men even when, like Virginia Woolf, she was supposed to be addressing women. If we have come to the point when this balance might begin to change, when women can stop being haunted, not only by "convention and propriety" but by internalized fears of being and saying themselves, then it is an extraordinary moment for the women writer—and reader.

I have hesitated to do what I am going to do now, which is to use myself as an illustration. For one thing, it's a lot easier and less dangerous to talk about other women writers. But there is something else. Like Virginia Woolf, I am aware of the women who are not with us here because they are washing the dishes and looking after the children. Nearly fifty years after she spoke, that fact remains largely unchanged. And I am thinking also of women whom she left out of the picture altogether—women who are washing other people's dishes and caring for other people's children, not to mention women who went on the streets last night in order to feed their children. We seem to be special women here, we have liked to think of ourselves as special, and we have known that men would tolerate, even romanticize us as special, as long as our words and actions didn't threaten their privilege of tolerating or rejecting us according to *their* ideas of what a special woman ought to be. An important insight of the radical women's movement, for me, has been how divisive and how ultimately destructive is this myth of the special woman, who is also the token woman. Every one of us here in this room has had great luck—we are teachers, writers, academicians; our own gifts could not have been enough, for we all know women whose gifts are buried or aborted. Our struggles can have meaning only if they can help to change the lives of women whose gifts—and whose very being— continue to be thwarted.

My own luck was being born white and middle-class into a house full of books, with a father who encouraged me to read and write. So for about twenty years I wrote for a particular man, who criticized and praised me and made me feel I was indeed "special." The obverse side of this, of course, was that I tried for a long time to please him, or rather, not to displease him. And then of course there were other men—writers, teachers—the Man, who was not a terror or a dream but a literary master and a master in other ways less easy to acknowledge. And there were all those poems about women, written by men: it seemed to be a given that men wrote poems and women frequently inhabited them. These women were almost always beautiful, but threatened with the loss of beauty, the loss of youth—the fate worse than death. Or, they were beautiful and died young, like Lucy and Lenore. Or, the woman was like Maud Gonne, cruel and disastrously mistaken,

and the poem reproached her because she had refused to become a luxury for the poet.

A lot is being said today about the influence that the myths and images of women have on all of us who are products of culture. I think it has been a peculiar confusion to the girl or woman who tries to write because she is peculiarly susceptible to language. She goes to poetry or fiction looking for *her* way of being in the world, since she too has been putting words and images together; she is looking eagerly for guides, maps, possibilities; and over and over in the "words' masculine persuasive force" of literature she comes up against something that negates everything she is about: she meets the image of Woman in books written by men. She finds a terror and a dream, she finds a beautiful pale face, she finds La Belle Dame Sans Merci, she finds Juliet or Tess or Salomé, but precisely what she does not find is that absorbed, drudging, puzzled, sometimes inspired creature, herself, who sits at a desk trying to put words together.

So what does she do? What did I do? I read the older women poets with their peculiar keenness and ambivalence: Sappho, Christina Rossetti, Emily Dickinson, Elinor Wylie, Edna Millay, H. D. I discovered that the woman poet most admired at the time (by men) was Marianne Moore, who was maidenly, elegant, intellectual, discreet. But even in reading these women I was looking in them for the same things I had found in the poetry of men, because I wanted women poets to be the equals of men, and to be equal was still confused with sounding the same.

I know that my style was formed first by male poets: by the men I was reading as an undergraduate—Frost, Dylan Thomas, Donne, Auden, MacNiece, Stevens, Yeats. What I chiefly learned from them was craft. But poems are like dreams: in them you put what you don't know you know. Looking back at poems I wrote before I was 21, I'm startled because beneath the conscious craft are glimpses of the split I even then experienced between the girl who wrote poems, who defined herself in writing poems, and the girl who was to define herself by her relationships with men. **"Aunt Jennifer's Tigers,"** written while I was a student, looks with deliberate detachment at this split. In writing this poem, composed and apparently cool as it is, I thought I was creating a portrait of an imaginary woman. But this woman suffers from the opposition of her imagination, worked out in tapestry, and her life-style, "ringed with ordeals she was mastered by." It was important to me that Aunt Jennifer was a person as distinct from myself as possible—distanced by the formalism of the poem, by its objective, observant tone—even by putting the woman in a different generation.

In those years formalism was part of the strategy—like asbestos gloves, it allowed me to handle materials I couldn't pick up barehanded. (A later strategy was to use the persona of a man, as I did in **"The Loser."**) I finished college, published my first book by a fluke, as it seemed to me, and broke off a love affair. I took a job, lived alone, went on writing, fell in love. I was young, full of energy, and the book seemed to mean that others agreed I was a poet. Because I was also determined to have a "full" woman's life, I plunged in my early twenties into marriage and had three children before I was thirty. There was nothing overt in the environment to warn me: these were the fifties, and in reaction to the earlier wave of feminism, middle-class women were making careers of domestic perfection, working to send their husbands through professional schools, then retiring to raise large families. People were moving out to the suburbs, technology was going to be the answer to everything, even sex; the family was in its glory. Life was extremely private; women were isolated from each other by the loyalties of marriage. I have a sense that women didn't talk to each other much in the fifties—not about their secret emptinesses, their frustrations. I went on trying to write; my second book and first child appeared in the same month. But by the time that book came out I was already dissatisfied with those poems, which seemed to me mere exercises for poems I hadn't written. The book was praised, however, for its "gracefulness"; I had a marriage and a child. If there were doubts, if there were periods of null depression or active despairing, these could only mean that I was ungrateful, insatiable, perhaps a monster.

About the time my third child was born, I felt that I had either to consider myself a failed woman and a failed poet, or to try to find some synthesis by which to understand what was happening to me. What frightened me most was the sense of drift, of being pulled along on a current which called itself my destiny, but in which I seemed to be losing touch with whoever I had been, with the girl who had experienced her own will and energy almost ecstatically at times, walking around a city or riding a train at night or typing in a student room. In a poem about my grandmother I wrote (of myself): "A young girl, thought sleeping, is certified dead."[4] I was writing very little, partly from fatigue, that female fatigue of suppressed anger and the loss of contact with her own being; partly from the discontinuity of female life with its attention to small chores, errands, work that others constantly undo, small children's constant needs. What I did write was unconvincing to me; my anger and frustration were hard to acknowledge in or out of poems because in fact I cared a great deal about my husband and my children. Trying to look back and understand that time I have tried to analyze the real nature of the conflict. Most, if not all, human lives are full of fantasy—passive daydreaming which need not be acted on. But to write poetry or fiction, or even to think well, is not to fantasize, or to put fantasies on paper. For a poem to coalesce, for a character or an action to take shape, there has to be an imaginative transformation of reality which is in no way passive. And a certain freedom of the mind is needed—freedom to press on, to enter the currents of your thought like a glider pilot, knowing that your motion can be sustained, that the buoyancy of your attention will not be suddenly snatched away. Moreover, if the imagination is to transcend and transform experience it has to question, to challenge, to conceive of alternatives, perhaps to the very life you are living at that moment. You have to be free to play around with the notion that day might be night, love might be hate; nothing can be too sacred for the imagination to turn into its opposite or to call experimentally by another name. For writing is re-naming. Now, to be maternally with small children all day in the old way, to be with a man in the old way of marriage, requires a holding-back, a putting-aside of that imaginative activity, and seems to demand instead a kind of conservatism. I want to make it clear that I am *not* saying that in order to write well, or think well, it is necessary to become unavailable to others, or to become a devouring ego. This has been the myth of the masculine artist and thinker; and I repeat, I do not accept it. But to be a female human being trying to fulfill traditional female functions in a traditional way *is* in direct conflict with the subversive function of the imagination. The word traditional is important here. There must be ways, and we will be finding out more and more about them, in which the energy of creation and the energy of relation can be united. But in those earlier years I always felt the conflict as a failure of love in myself. I had thought I was choosing a full life: the life available to most men, in which sexuality, work, and parenthood could coexist. But I felt, at 29, guilt toward the people closest to me, and guilty toward my own being.

I wanted, then, more than anything, the one thing of which there was never enough: time to think, time to write. The fifties and early sixties were years of rapid revelations: the sit-ins and marches in the South, the Bay of Pigs, the early anti-war movement, raised large questions—questions for which the masculine world of the academy around me seemed to have expert and fluent answers. But I needed desperately to think for myself—about pacifism and dissent and violence, about poetry and society and about my own relationship to all these things. For about ten years I was reading in fierce snatches, scribbling in notebooks, writing poetry in fragments; I was looking desperately for clues, because if there were no clues then I thought I might be insane. I wrote in a notebook about this time:

> Paralyzed by the sense that there exists a mesh of relationships—e.g. between my anger at the children, my sensual life, pacifism, sex, (I mean sex in its broadest significance, not merely sexual desire)—an interconnectedness which, if I could see it, make it valid, would give me back myself, make it possible to function lucidly and passionately. Yet I grope in and out among these dark webs.

I think I began at this point to feel that politics was not something "out there" but something "in here" and of the essence of my condition.

In the late fifties I was able to write, for the first time, directly about experiencing myself as a woman. The poem was jotted in fragments during children's naps, brief hours in a library, or at 3 a.m. after rising with a wakeful child. I despaired of doing any continuous work at this time. Yet I began to feel that my fragments and scraps had a common consciousness and a common theme, one which I would have been very unwilling to put on paper at an earlier time because I had been taught that poetry should be "universal," which meant, of course, non-female. Until then I had tried very much *not* to identify myself as a female poet. Over two years I wrote a 10-part poem called **"Snapshots of a Daughter-in-Law,"** in a longer, looser mode than I'd ever trusted myself with before. It was an extraordinary relief to write that poem. It strikes me now as too literary, too dependent on allusion; I hadn't found the courage yet to do without authorities, or even to use the pronoun "I"—the woman in the poem is always "she." One section of it, No. 2, concerns a woman who thinks she is going mad; she is haunted by voices telling her to resist and rebel, voices which she can hear but not obey.

The poem **"Orion,"** written five years later, is a poem of reconnection with a part of myself I had felt I was losing—the active principle, the energetic imagination, the "half-brother" whom I projected, as I had for many years, into the constellation Orion. It's no accident that the words "cold and egotistical" appear in this poem, and are applied to myself. The choice still seemed to be between "love"—womanly, maternal love, altruistic love—a love defined and ruled by the weight of an entire culture; and egotism—a force directed by men into creation, achievement, ambition, often at the expense of others, but justifiably so. For weren't they men, and wasn't that their destiny as womanly love was ours? I know now that the alternatives are false ones—that the word "love" is itself in need of re-vision.

There is a companion poem to **"Orion,"** written three years later, in which at last the woman in the poem and the woman writing the poem become the same person. It is called **"Planetarium,"** and it was written after a visit to a real planetarium, where I read an account of the work of Caroline Herschel, the astronomer, who worked with her brother William, but whose name remained obscure, as his did not.

In closing I want to tell you about a dream I had last summer. I dreamed I was asked to read my poetry at a mass women's meeting, but when I began to read, what came out were the lyrics of a blues song. I share this dream with you because it seemed to me to say a lot about the problems and the future of the woman writer, and probably of women in general. The awakening of consciousness is not like the crossing of a frontier—one step, and you are in another country. Much of woman's poetry has been of the nature of the blues song: a cry of pain, of victimization, or a lyric of seduction. And today, much poetry by women—and prose for that matter—is charged with anger. I think we need to go through that anger, and we will betray our own reality if we try, as Virginia Woolf was trying, for an objectivity, a detachment, that would make us sound more like Jane Austen or Shakespeare. We know more than Jane Austen or Shakespeare knew: more than Jane Austen because our lives are more complex, more than Shakespeare because we know more about the lives of women, Jane Austen and Virginia Woolf included.

Both the victimization and the anger experienced by women are real, and have real sources, everywhere in the environment, built into society. They must go on being tapped and explored by poets, among others. We can neither deny them, nor can we rest there. They are our birth-pains, and we are bearing ourselves. We would be failing each other as writers and as women, if we neglected or denied what is negative, regressive, or Sisyphean in our inwardness.

We all know that there is another story to be told. I am curious and expectant about the future of the masculine consciousness. I feel in the work of the men whose poetry I read today a deep pessimism and fatalistic grief; and I wonder if it isn't the masculine side of what women have experienced, the price of masculine dominance. One thing I am sure of: just as woman is becoming her own midwife, creating herself anew, so man will have to learn to gestate and give birth to his own subjectivity—something he has frequently wanted woman to do for him. We can go on trying to talk to each other, we can sometimes help each other, poetry and fiction can show us what the other is going through; but women can no longer be primarily mothers and muses for men: we have our own work cut out for us.

Notes

1. G. B. Shaw, *The Quintessence of Ibsenism* (Hill and Wang, 1922), p. 139.

2. J. G. Stewart, *Jane Ellen Harrison: A Portrait from Letters* (London, 1959), p. 140.

3. Henry James, "Notes on Novelists" in *Selected Literary Criticism of Henry James*, ed. Morris Shapira (London: Heineman, 1963), pp. 157-58.

4. "Halfway," in *Necessities of Life.*

GENERAL COMMENTARY

CATHARINE STIMPSON (ESSAY DATE SPRING-SUMMER AND FALL-WINTER 1985)

SOURCE: Stimpson, Catharine. "Adrienne Rich and Lesbian/Feminist Poetry." *Parnassus* 12-13, nos. 2-1 (spring-summer and fall-winter 1985): 249-68.

In the following essay, Stimpson traces the development of lesbian and feminist themes throughout Rich's poetic career.

. . . it is the subjects, the conversations, the facts we shy away from, which claim us in the form of writer's block, as mere rhetoric, as hysteria, insomnia, and constriction of the throat.[1]

Four years after . . . (Adrienne Rich) published her first book, I read it in almost disbelieving wonder; someone my age was writing down my life . . . I had not known till then how much I had wanted a contemporary and a woman as a speaking voice of life. . . .[2]

"Lesbian." For many, heterosexual or homosexual, the word still constricts the throat. Those "slimy" sibilants; those "nasty" nasalities. "Lesbian" makes even "feminist" sound lissome, decent, sane. In 1975, Adrienne Rich's reputation was secure.[3] She might have eased up and toyed with honors. Yet, she was doing nothing less than seizing and caressing that word: "lesbian." She was working hard for "a whole new poetry" that was to begin in two women's "limitless desire."[4]

Few poetic things could be more difficult—even for a writer of such fire, stone, and fern. For the "intense charge of the word *lesbian*, and . . . all its deliquescences of meaning . . . ," (*On Lies, Secrets, and Silence* 202) necessarily provoke readings that are potent, but confused, confusing, and contradictory. Some of us read Rich with disbelieving wonder. Imagine being a mother, in court, on the stand, in the dock, during a child custody case. Your husband's lawyer asks, with brutal repetition, "When did you first kiss this woman?" Imagine, then, the gratitude and relief of hearing . . . [*The Dream of a Common Language: Poems 1974-1977*, p. 59].

Yet, others read with wondrous disbelief. Alicia Ostriker, my colleague, pugnaciously declared Rich's "myth" of female sexuality "too narrow":

"I find the Lesbian Imperative offensively totalitarian, and would prefer to defend human diversity as well as human liberty."[5]

To add to the mess, even some of the supporters and defenders of Rich's sexual ideology find the call for a "whole new poetry" an emblazoned naiveté. *Surely,* they whisper nervously, she must know about our post-structural awareness of the nature of the sign. *Surely,* she must realize that language is a fiction, not a transparent vehicle of truth; that signifiers are bits and bytes of an arbitrary system, not elements in a holistic union of word and idea, word and thing. *Surely,* she must now admit that this system creates the human subject, not the other way around.[6] Others grumble that Rich's theory contradicts her poetic practice. The first is new, the second old. Rhetorically, she is more like—well, Robert Lowell—than Gertrude Stein. Rich undermines her calls for action, Marjorie Perloff claims, because of her ". . . conservative rhetoric, a rhetoric indistinguishable from the Male Oppressor."[7]

This messiness is ironic—if only because Rich herself is radiantly clear. She is, of course, one of a number of outspoken lesbian poets of the last part of the American Century. She resists being laid down as the star track in what ought to be a multiple-trek tape of the language of such women as Judy Grahn, Susan Griffin, Marilyn Hacker, Audre Lorde, Susan Sherman. "To isolate what I write," she has warned, "from a context of other women writing and speaking feels like an old, painfully familiar critical strategy."[8] Yet, I want, in gratitude and relief, to spell out how she has moved from the constriction of the throat to the construction of the page.

Before the 1970s, Rich had published poems about the feelings, social relations, and mythic promise of women. **"Women"** (1968) sees three sisters ". . . sitting / on rocks of black obsidian," versions of the fates. (*Poems Selected and New, 1950-1974*, 109) Deromanticizing heterosexual love, Rich had written of the strains and loneliness within marriage. Symbolically, she had put aside a 1962 poem, **"For Judith, Taking Leave."**[9] Here a speaker longingly memorializes another woman, Judith: ". . . a singular event . . . a beautiful thing I saw." (*PSN* [*Poems Selected and New, 1950-1974*,] 132) The speaker praises feminist predecessors who "suffered ridicule" for them. Then, in the middle of the poem, she calls out. . . .*PSN*, 132].

Only to add, as the line runs on to the next, "with two men—."

In the early 1970s, Rich riskily uncoiled the repressed sexual and psychological materials that she had once coiled and from which she had subsequently recoiled. She announces that release in **"Re-forming the Crystal."** Addressed to a man, it gives him his due, and discharge. The speaker first imagines what male sexuality, "desire / centered in a cock," might feel like. However, she passes on, old identity gone. Voice at once tough and exultant, she states, "my photo on the license is not me. . . ." (*PSN*, 228) She will move, a key word in Rich's vocabulary of action, to ". . . the field of a poem wired with danger . . . into the cratered night of female memory. . . ." Women now live to the nerves' limit with women. Inevitably, some poems counterpoint past identity with present; tradition with radical change. **"For L. G.: Unseen for Twenty Years"** ruefully wonders who, and where, a male homosexual might be. He and the speaker had been boon travelling companions twenty years before, when both were turning to men.

Significantly, **"Re-forming the Crystal"** alternates vertical columns of "poetry" with paragraphs of "prose." For Rich was producing controversial, influential prose as well as poetry. From 1981 to 1983, she and Michelle Cliff were to edit *Sinister Wisdom,* a lesbian/feminist journal. Rich, a sophisticated student of the genetics of the text, coher-

ently crossed autobiography with biography; polemic with scholarship; political theory with literary criticism.[10] In part, her transgressions of generic conventions are the deconstructive gestures of post-modernism—without much manic play or ludic romps. In greater part, her mingling of "subjective" and "objective" genres, advocacy and argument, demonstrates her belief in their inseparability. Her style also emblemizes the position of contemporary, educated women. No longer forced to choose between public or private lives, women can lead both—at once. No longer forced to choose between writing about public or private concerns, women can take on both—at once.[11]

Rich had consistently been "a poet of ideas,"[12] of hewn arguments as well as images. Now her ideas, doubly sited, could reinforce and annotate each other. In its totality, her work is that of a kind of conceptual artist. What is disturbing and dazzling is not the familiar notion of a conceptual artist, but the content of her ideas. Rich's lesbian/feminism reveals both the steely, stubborn logic of the geometrician (or the convert) and the sinuousness of imaginative reason. Those who insist that she is the Great Generalissima of Lesbian Poetry resist granting her her habitual gift for pragmatic self-revision and subtlety. ". . . the subject of truth," she noted in 1975. "There is nothing simple or easy about this idea. There is no 'the truth,' 'a truth'—truth is not one thing, or even a system. It is an increasing complexity." (*LSS* [*On Lies, Secrets, and Silence,*] 187) Yet, she consistently walks out from the cultural space in which the libraries of her father and of Harvard University had enclosed her. She announces the primacy of a woman's perspective and of women as subjects. The eye of the female writing "I" fastens on the presence of a woman. The voice of the inquiring woman asks of herself and other women: ". . . how she came to be for-herself and how she identified with and was able to use women's culture, a women's tradition; and what the presence of other women meant in her life." (*LSS*, 158)

Rich, as other feminists were doing, insists upon an idea of time as a tragic process, a fall into patriarchy. However, she promises, we can reverse that process. We can outwrestle, outwit, and feminize time. Skillfully, Rich splices two mutually enhancing narratives together that dramatize her idea of time's procession. The first is that of the self. In her prose, Rich persistently tests her generalizations against her own experiences. In her poetry, she articulates experience and discovers its meaning. Though the poetic self has a vast capacity for experiences, it reveals itself, rather than develops, in time. Indeed, a measure of development is the degree of revelation. So convinced, Rich assumes the primacy of the primal self. Appropriately, then, "**Natural Resources**" brilliantly extends the trope of the woman miner, as both rhetorical and historical figure. The miner excavates experience to find buried strata. In other passages, Rich is a Dickinsonian surgeon, ". . . cutting away / dead flesh, cauterizing old scars. . . ." (*DCL* [*The Dream of a Common Language: Poems 1974-1977*,] 70) She rips away the tissue that covers old wounds, old traumas, to recover the origins of self and pain.

In her narrative, Rich is a child whom two women (one white, one black) first love before they turn her over to the father. The reality of the maternal body gives way to the "charisma" of the father's ". . . assertive mind and temperament. . . ."[13] Her reward for their rejection, and her loss, is his approval and the power of language, the conviction that ". . . language, writing, those pages of print could teach me how to live, could tell me *what was possible.*" (*LSS*, 200) She becomes a child-of-the-word, unable to see that those pages veil and erase the feminine. Rich is no fan of psychoanalysis, but its tales and that of her passage from the tender passions of the realm of the mother to the symbolic order of the domain of the father half-echo each other.

Educated, a published poet, her father's pride, Rich then rejects the father—to marry a man he despises. She bears three sons. As Rich knows, but never exploits, the sheer masculinity of her heterosexual experience (the husband, the long marriage, the sons) burnishes her credibility as a witness of, and for, lesbianism. That credibility challenges a popular perception that lesbians are maculately sterile—either because they are butches, imitation men, or femmes, who will never receive the sperm of real men.

Rich's second narrative is that of any child, female or male. For them, "The mother-child relationship is the essential human relationship." (*Of Woman Born: Motherhood as Experience and Institution,* 127) Binding the two are the sucking mouth, the milky nipple, the mutual gaze. Then, the father—his demands, commands, needs, and seductions—will pick at those bonds; pick up his children and possess them all in a "savagely fathered and unmothered world." (*PSN*, 237) Heterosexual institutions damage both sons and daughters, but, Rich insists, in the crucial axiom of feminist theory, they damage women far more

than men. Those institutions embody sufficient psychological, economic, social, and legal power to *compel* heterosexuality.[14] That compulsion redirects women away from the first and most profound object of love, the mother. Rich writes: "Probably there is nothing in human nature more resonant with charges than the flow of energy between two biologically alike bodies, one of which has laid in amniotic bliss inside the other, one of which has labored to give birth to the other. The materials are here for the deepest mutuality and the most painful estrangement." (*OWB* [*Of Woman Born: Motherhood as Experience and Institution,*] 225-26)

To redeem her past, and to begin her future, Rich must return to the mother's body, in memory or with other women. So must all women. Their sources are their natural resources. In a 1963 poem about marriage, Rich, in one of the crazy intuitive flashes we label the cognitive gift of poetry, describes wanting husband to be mother . . . ["Like This Together," (*FD*) *The Fact of a Doorframe: Poems Selected and New 1950-1984*].[15]

Not until she becomes a lesbian is she content; not until then can desire fulfill its needs. In *Twenty-One Love Poems,* she writes of her female lover's . . . [tongue and fingers. . . . *DCL,* 32].

The fecundity of woman is such that she can also give birth to and mother herself. Her body can be her "crib"; she can be her own "midwife." She can then become a matrix that mothers others, through personality or the page. Some evidence: in 1975, Nancy Milford, the writer, read through Rich's poetry. She had a dream of the person within "**Diving into the Wreck.**" A maternal figure was walking towards, and empowering, her: ". . . naked, swaying, bending down . . . her full breasts brushing my cheek, moving toward my mouth . . . The hands of that diving woman become our own hands, reaching out, touching, holding; not in sex but in deliverance. That is the potency of her poetry. . . ."[16]

As Rich grounds women's thoughts and feelings in their bodies, she *naturalizes* them. Her poetry harvests the earth and the elements for its metaphors: the cave; trees; plants; flowers; fields; the volcano, at once peak to ascend and crater into which to descend, breast and genitals, cervix, womb. Rich, too, has absolute competence in composing a poem, in arranging implosive patterns of rhythm and sound. Because the quality of her verbal music and choreography is so assured, a reader learns to trust the palpability of a poem;

its replication of the intellectual and emotional movements of experience.

Because of the pressure and magnetism of her metaphors; because of the surprising physicality of her lines; and because of her contempt for patriarchal culture, especially in its modern and urban forms, Rich may seem to be endorsing a feminized primitivism. However, she is far too intelligent a grammarian of reality to parse it into two opposing spheres of "nature" and "culture," and clamor only for the pristine ecological purities of the first. She constructs houses on her land. Rich's dream, her imaginative vision, is of an organic, but freeing, unity among body, nature, consciousness, vision, and community. Unequivocally, lyrically, she asks women to think through their maternal flesh and their own bodies, ". . . to connect what has been so cruelly disorganized—our great mental capacities, hardly used; our highly developed tactile sense; our genius for close observation; our complicated, pain-enduring, multi-pleasured physicality." (**OWB**, 284) In a leap of faith, she wants women to become the presiding geniuses of their bodies in order to create new life—biologically and culturally. Their thoughts and visions will transform politics, ". . . alter human existence," sustain a "new relationship to the universe." (**OWB**, 285-86)

The primal bonds among mothers, sisters, and daughters are the soil from which lesbianism grows. Lesbianism does mean women's erotic passion. Indeed, the most explicitly erotic lyric in **Twenty-One Love Poems** is "**(The Floating Poem, Unnumbered),**" as if physical passion drifts and runs like a deep current through the seas of the connection between "I" and "you" in the sequence. However, Rich declares, in a move that lesbian/feminism, but not the culture-at-large, accepts, the lesbian cannot live only in and with love. "I want to call this, life." Rich writes, "But I can't call it life until we start to move / beyond this secret circle of fire. . . ." (**DCL**, 9) Moreover, a lesbianism that is more than a treasured carnality is a synecdoche for any female sexuality. Rich, like Monique Wittig, projects ". . . lesbian love (a)s a paradigm of female sexuality that is neither defined by men nor exploited by a phallocentric political system."[17]

Even more than a fancily labelled metaphor, even more than a schematized paradigm, lesbianism forms a "continuum," a range of "woman-identified" activities that embraces eros, friendship and intensity between women, resistance to gynephobia, and female strength. A woman can love men, live with men, and inhabit a point on this continuum—if she has managed some distance from patriarchal heterosexuality. For its imprisoning institutions have ripped daughters from mothers; lobotomized and slashed women's psychological, cultural, and political energies. As the brief accumulates in "**Compulsory Heterosexuality,**" Rich mourns: "The denial of reality and visibility to women's passion for women, women's choice of women as allies, life companions, and community; the forcing of such relationships into dissimulation and their disintegration under intense pressure have meant an incalculable loss to the power of all women *to change the social relations of the sexes, to liberate ourselves and each other.*" (657) "**Transcendental Etude,**" a chiselled monument of a poem, dedicated to Michelle Cliff, elegizes "rootless, dismembered" women, whose "Birth stripped our birthright from us, / tore us from a woman, from women, from ourselves." (**DCL**, 75)

If women are to change themselves and their social relations, if they are to liberate themselves and each other, they must revivify that lesbianism hidden or denied, feared or despised. Lesbianism is an imperative, not because Rich imposes it, but because it is a wellspring of identity that must be sprung if women are to claim any authentic identity at all. "It is the lesbian in us who is creative, for the dutiful daughter of the fathers in us is only a hack." (**LSS**, 201) I remember Rich giving us these words, quietly, tautly, in a New York hotel ballroom, in 1976, at a panel at the Modern Language Association. She leaned forward from a dais, where three other poets were also sitting: June Jordan, Audre Lorde, Honor Moore. I was on a chipped and gilded chair, between two scholar/critics: one a divorced mother, heterosexual, who called herself a lesbian out of political sympathy, a radical feminist act of the late 1960s and early 1970s; the second a married mother, about to begin a secret love affair with a woman, who rarely (if ever) spoke about lesbianism. "Right on," said the first. Enigmatically, the second looked at the husband next to her. Grinning, with the casualness of marriage, he affectionately slapped her thigh. There we were—an imperfect, blurry shadow of Rich's continuum.

Deftly, Rich's theories of female sexuality invert the accusatory slander that lesbianism is "unnatural." To Rich, what is "unnatural" is not the presence, but the absence, of women's bodies, to be "homesick . . . for a woman. . . ." (**DCL**, 75) In the 1970s, her theories were influenced by, and influences on, the cultural feminism that was a powerful strain in feminist thinking, particularly about sexuality, culture, and identity.[18] Reconstituting and eroticizing nineteenth-century ideologies of gender, with their endorsement of "female" and "male" spheres, cultural feminism tends to divide the world into female and male; to idealize female sexuality and being, and to demonize male sexuality and doing. Ironically, some of the principles of cultural feminism gravitate toward a conservative ideology that prefers divinely authorized gender roles and "female" and "male" behaviors that fit squarely into them. However, cultural feminism's preference for women's communities, its commitment to women's self-determination, and its loathing of patriarchal heterosexuality dismay, and repel, right-wing flappers in the Eagle Forum and their ilk.

To discover that female sexuality and being, women are to nurture natural, but defaced and obliterated, capacities for nurture and for nature itself. With the help of scholars and artists, they are to unearth primal images of these capacities, and of rituals with which to celebrate them. Some of Rich's most poignant, lambent poems present the poet as a priestess in a service with a lost script; in a liturgy with missing words. In "Toward the Solstice," she laments that she does not know "in what language to address / the spirits that claim a place / beneath these low and simple ceilings." (DCL, 69) She fears that she has forgotten or failed to say the "right rune"; to "perform the needed acts. . . ." (70)

Such theories were to serve neither abstract debate (a "male" activity) nor mere poetic need (a self-indulgent sport). On the contrary. They were to be designs for action and for communal life. As a result, cultural feminists have taken sides in some of the most volatile political quarrels within United States feminism: How separate from the rest of society are women's groups to be? What is the relationship of feminism to other political movements and to the New Left? What is the meaning of pornography? What, if anything, should be done to banish it? Many of Rich's poems refer immediately to those fights. The controversial "For Ethel Rosenberg," for example, speaks vocatively to "Ethel Greenglass Rosenberg" . . . [(WP) A Wild Patience Has Taken Me This Far].[19]

"Take back the night" is a slogan and rallying cry for the anti-pornography movement that cultural feminism has conceived and organized. The words have inspired women. They flatten Rich's poem. Their presence gives some critics permission to tsk-tsk and scold Rich for letting a political agenda master a poet's imagination. She might legitimately scorn their motives and the blatancy of the division they invent between politics and poetry. However, she, too, is warily aware of any domination of her imagination. She fears the hunters, trappers, and wardens of the mind. One of her toughest poems, "North American Time," written in the gritty style of much of A Wild Patience, starts . . . [FD, 324].

Something hardens the difficulty of interweaving a passionate fidelity to a politics that wants to change the laws of history; to the imagination; and to the unconscious, which nourishes the imagination as mother does the child: the very terms of Rich's politics. For lesbian/feminism, the casting of the world as a duality of dominating male and damaged female carries the virus of a double threat: it reduces the world to a duality; it reduces women to a monolith. Rich distrusts the false universal, especially among women, who are to think more specifically than men. A resonant section of "Natural Resources," the 1977 revision of "Diving Into the Wreck," rejects the words "humanism" and "androgyny." They are falsely universal; therefore, universally false.

Rich has wonderfully escaped the nets she fears, the "impasse" at which some critics pin her.[20] In part, she does so because of the Jamesian (William) belief in change that has marked all her work. We must live in an Einsteinian world of flux and chance that has neither "center nor circumference."[21] We must work and wish for a world, not as it is, but as it might be. Yet, we must respond to time present as it presents and represents itself. Because errors and lapses can stain our responses, we must abandon dreams of purity, of final cures, of a process with an end.

Logically, then, responsibly, the lesbian/feminist Rich has continued to rewrite her sense of self and politics; to question what it means to "cast my lot" in the world and to be "accountable." More and more deeply, she has engaged the structures and pain of racism. She has said that the Civil Rights Movement of the 1960s lifted her ". . . out of a sense of personal frustration and hopelessness."[22] However, the 1970s had to teach her the harsh stiffness of her own "racist blinders." Black women's response to Of Woman Born had to school her in her ignorance about them.[23] Rich believes that political poetry emerges from the self's encounter with the world. Her explorations of race start with her black nurse, her other mother. Necessarily, she cannot rest there. She must go on to still other structures, other pains, of domination. Racism is inseparable from still another vise and vice of modern politics: colonialism. "To understand colonization," she writes, with self-consciousness and some self-contempt, "is taking me / years." (*A Wild Patience Has Taken Me This Far,* 55)

Some of Rich's most ambitious lesbian/feminist poems speak for all women and mourn their suffering, affliction, and powerlessness: **"From an Old House in America," "Culture and Anarchy," "For Julia in Nebraska."** Like Rich's poems about her grandmothers, they offer women their history; the arts of their endurance. Because Rich fuses women with nature, especially with the land, a history of people is a pangyneric record of place as well.

However, the recognition of racism and colonialism demands that Rich issue a series of ironic, searing, yet empathetic poems about cultivated white women with the disadvantages of sex but the advantages of class and race. A tart observation, "No room for nostalgia here," opens **"Turning the Wheel,"** an extraordinary 1981 sequence in which Rich returns to a desert landscape. (*WP* 52-59) The wheel belongs to both a modern woman driving her car and a Native American woman creating her pottery. The speaker sees a "lesbian archaeologist," studying shards, who asks ". . . the clay all questions but her own." She imagines, too, a letter that Mary Jane Colter might have written home. Colter, an architect and designer, planned buildings at the Grand Canyon for the Santa Fe Railroad. She both preserved and appropriated Native American culture. Two years later, in **"Education of a Novelist,"** Rich calls across time to another Southern writer, Ellen Glasgow. She condemns Glasgow for not teaching her black nurse, Lizzie Jones, to read, but confesses: . . . [*FD*, 317].

Lesbian/feminist politics remain, but Rich's perceptions expand upon them. She thinks, not only of male domination, but of a system of iron patterns of power that wheel and deal and work together. Pornography violently debases and exploits women, but its nauseating "objectification" of women also warns us against slavery—of anyone by anyone.[24]

Rich now wants, in women, both "difference and identity." Women share the architecture of their bodies, the humiliation and mutilation of those bodies. What "fuses my anger now . . . ," she wrote in 1978, ". . . is that we were told we were utterly different." (*LSS*, 310) Yet, as race proves, so obviously, so profoundly, women differ, too. With delicate audacity, Rich pushes at the boundaries of those differences, pushes for the specific, and particular. As she does so, she uncovers, and must enter, still another buried part of herself: her Jewishness, the faith of father, husband, and first woman lover. She circles back to Jerusalem, the original City on the Hill. *Sources,* perhaps her most fragmented but suggestive book, exhumes that past. Rich affirms her "powerful" and "womanly" choices; a "powerful, womanly lens"—in brief, the domain of the mother.[25] However, *Sources* returns to the domain of the fathers, and to their vulnerability and pain. Arnold Rich, her father, was the outwardly successful, assimilated son of a Jewish shoe merchant from Birmingham, Alabama. Powerful and arrogant patriarch though he was, he also bore "the suffering of the Jew, the alien stamp." (15) Her mother carried the cultural genes of the Christianity that would stamp Jews out.

Then, with immense dignity, Rich writes to Alfred Conrad, the husband who committed suicide. She has had ". . . a sense of protecting your existence, not using it merely as a theme for poetry or tragic musings." (32) Now, for the first time, she believes he might hear her. "No person," her elegy ends, "should have to be so alone. . . ." (33) She has passed through the moral and psychological process that some of her most magnificent poems—**"The Phenomenology of Anger," "Integrity"**—envision: that between wildness and patience, rage and pitying compassion, fire and water and tears. She has completed the hardest of swings between "Anger and tenderness: my selves." (*WP,* 9)[26]

That fusion of the moral and the psychological, the ethical and the emotional, marks Rich. Her writing inflects a stable vocabulary of the good that flows, as feminism itself does, from principles of the Enlightenment, radical democracy, and a redemptive domesticity: freedom; choice; truth; a lucidity as clear as water pouring over rocks; gentleness, an active charity, swabbing "the crusted stump." (*DCL,* 63) The last of *Twenty-One Love Poems* asserts . . . [*DCL,* 36].

As insistently, Rich's writing asks how to reconcile the claims of autonomy (being free, having will) and the claims of connection (being together, having unity). Connections fuse within the self, between lover and beloved, with others. "Sometimes I feel," she wrote in 1982, "I have seen too long from too many disconnected angles: white, Jewish, anti-Semite, racist, anti-racist, once-married, lesbian, middle-class, feminist, exmatriate Southerner, *split at the root.*"[27] She longs, then, for wholeness, for touch, a desire the hand signi-

ON THE SUBJECT OF...

ANGER AND THE STATUS OF VICTIM IN RICH'S POETRY

While, in "The Burning of Paper Instead of Children," the poet and poetry are virtually consumed from within, in this poem the poet's analysis of her anger as phenomenon allows the fire to be expressed in condemnation of the most horrible atrocities, and to forge a new language and consciousness. Rich's "dream of a common language" depends first of all on the capacity to create a new subjectivity which avoids the threats of "madness" and "suicide," to refine anger to an "acetylene" intensity and focus, and then to share that new consciousness with others who "burn" similarly under the weight of oppression. In poems like "Nightbreak," where her body becomes the Vietnamese village, or "Planetarium," where she similarly becomes the receptacle for radio signals, Rich takes the status of victim into her own consciousness and even her own body. She forges a new, feminist subjectivity based on the rejection rather than imposition of oppression, the identification with rather than opposition to "the enemy."

Greenwald, Elissa. "The Dream of a Common Language: Vietnam Poetry as Reformation of Language and Feeling in the Poems of Adrienne Rich," *Journal of American Culture* 16, no. 3, (fall 1993): 97-102.

fies. The hand. It holds the pen, clasps the child, finds the lover, sews the quilt, cleans the pot, dusts the house. For Rich, hands hammer nails, empty kettles, catch babies leaping from the womb, work vacuum aspirators, stroke "sweated temples" (both body and sanctuary), steer boats. (*WP,* 9) The hand also knots in anger, smashes in pain. As palms are the canvas of our life-lines, so the figure of the hand backs Rich's vision.

Before the 1960s, her lesbian/feminism was, if not inconceivable, unspeakable. Yet, if her ideas are contemporary, her sense of the poet is not. For Rich refuses to sever poetry from prophecy, those morally driven, passionately uttered visions of things unseen and foreseen, and poetry from

witnessing, those morally driven, passionately uttered insights into actions seen. What she said of Dickinson she might have said of herself:

"Poetic language . . . is a concretization of the poetry of the world at large, the self, and the forces within the self . . . there is a more ancient concept of the poet (as well) . . . she is endowed to speak for those who do not have the gift of language, or to see for those who—for whatever reasons—are less conscious of what they are living through." (*LSS,* 181)[28] She is painfully aware that she cannot control what might happen to her words after she chooses them, but she is accountable for that choice, and for her accuracy.

Rich's lesbian/feminism helps to sculpt her role as prophet and witness. Because patriarchal culture has been silent about lesbians and "all women who are not defined by the men in their lives,"[29] the prophet/witness must give speech to experience for the first time. This is one meaning of writing a whole new poetry. However, patriarchal culture has not been consistently silent. Sometimes, it has lied about lesbians. The prophet/witness must then speak truth to, and about, power. At other times, patriarchal culture has distorted or trivialized lesbians. The prophet/witness must then use and affirm ". . . a vocabulary that has been used negatively and pejoratively."[30] She must transvalue language.

Necessarily, the prophet/witness is a performer. She demands an audience, primarily of women. However, the ideology of lesbian/feminism is suspicious of star turns. Rich herself writes in **"Transcendental Etude"** . . . [*DCL,* 74].

The performing Rich—unlike Walt Whitman or Jeremiah—has more stamina than flash; more intensity than ebullience. She is a laser rather than an explosion of fireworks. She will speak, but in **"North American Time,"** a grim, colloquial meditation on the poet's responsibility, she says, self-deprecatingly . . . [*FD,* 327].

She will also speak, if possible, to an audience of many women. She is allusive and intricate, but rarely elusive and snobby. In part, she has the clarity of classical poetry. In part, she has the clarity of one who wishes to be heard.[31]

But what language will she speak? Clearly, Rich believes in the power of language to represent ideas, feelings, and events. Although she writes about film and photography, she is no postmodern celebrant of the visual media. She fears that mass TV induces passivity, atrophies the literacy and language we need to "take on the most complex, subtle, and drastic re-evaluation ever attempted of the condition of the species." (*LSS*, 12) Her dream of a common language is of *words*, a shared cultural frame and thread, communal and quotidian, "hewn of the commonest living subtance" as well as "violent, arcane." (*PSN*, 232)

Yet, the lesbian/feminist poet cannot accept language that smoothly. What is she to do with the fact that the powerful have used language to choke and to erase her? To mystify and to disguise? Some French theoreticians of *écriture féminine* advocate stealing, and then, flying away with the oppressor's speech. That theft and that escape are acts of re-appropriation and control. Certainly, in her references to male poets—yes, even to Robert Lowell, Rich shows her authority.[32] More fervently, Rich selects female experience—the body; mothers, daughters, and granddaughters; lesbianism; women's history—as her subject. Men, too, have written such experiences up and down, but men, because they are men, have been false prophets, narcissistic and perjuring witnesses.

Sadly, that selection offers little ease. For what is Rich, who believes in poetry, to do with the fact that lesbian/feminism has naturalized female experience? That lesbian/feminism has rooted female experience less in language than in things, objects, inarticulate but pregnant silences? Rich's poetry itself shows how craftily she handles the issue. First, she reduces the physical presence of language on the page. She wipes away diacritical marks, the busyness of syntax. Then, she alternates words with blank spaces—for breathing, for gazing. As she pushes language towards silence, she does to the verbal image what Nathalie Sarraute (or, in her way, Jane Austen) does to narrative. Yet, she refuses silence. She has words, and doubts-in-words.

Read "**The Images.**" (*WP*, 3-5) The poem is a series of six sections, each an irregular series of staggered three- or four-line sections. The eye cautions the reader against regularities, sonorities. Two women are in bed. In the "pain of the city," the speaker turns. Her hand touches her lover "before language names in the brain." The speaker chooses touch, but not this city, where both images of women, and the looks of men, string women out and crucify them.

The speaker then recognizes that she has romanticized language, music, art, "frescoes translating / violence into patterns so powerful and pure / we continually fail to ask are they true for us." In contrast, when she now walks among "time-battered stones," she can think of her lover. She has gone to the sea, among flowering weeds, and drawn a flower. She has been "mute / innocent of grammar as the waves." There, feeling "free," she has had a vision of a woman's face and body. Her breasts gaze at the poet; the poet at her world. Rich writes . . . ["**The Images,**" *WP*, 3-5].

"Free of speech" is, of course, a syntactical pun. For the speaker is both free from speech, and, now, free to speak. She comes home, "starving / for images," a body in need of culture. She and her lover, as they remember each other in sleep, will "reassemble re-collect re-member" the lost images of women in the past. They will do the work of Isis, but for Isis, not Osiris. As the culture's images seek to "dismember" them, they will fight the war of the images.

The poem's last lines then recall the picture that the speaker has drawn: a thorn-leaf guarding a purple-tongued flower. Perhaps the picture represents only a flower on a beach. Perhaps not, too. For the thorn leaf can signify the lovers' vigilance in protecting the purple-tongued flower of the vulva, of their sexuality, and of their speech. The thorn is the anger that guards their tenderness, and their poetry.

Language lies. Language invents. Poetry lies. Poetry invents. Rich accepts that "truth." Writing tells stories that matter. Writing gives us images from the mind and of the body, for the relief of the body and the reconstruction of the mind. Rich accepts that "truth" as well. If some words ("lesbian") constrict the throat, say them. Open them up. Only then can we speak enough to wonder seriously if language lies, because it is language; if language invents, because it is language, or if language lies because people are liars who invent to control, rather than to dream. and justly please.

Notes

1. Adrienne Rich, "It Is the Lesbian in Us . . . ," *On Lies, Secrets, and Silence,* hereafter *LSS,* (New York: W. W. Norton and Co., 1979), p. 201.

2. Helen Vendler, "Ghostlier Demarcations, Keener Sounds," *Adrienne Rich's Poetry,* ed. Barbara Charlesworth Gelpi and Albert Gelpi, hereafter *ARP,* (New York: W. W. Norton and Co., Norton Critical Edition, 1975), p. 160. Vendler's essay was originally published in *Parnassus,* II, 1 (Fall/Winter 1973). As Marjorie Perloff has pointed out to me in conversation, Rich is the only living poet who is the subject of a Norton critical anthology.

3. In 1975, when *ARP* appeared, Rich also published *Poems Selected and New, 1950-1974,* hereafter *PSN,* (New York: W. W. Norton and Co.). Mark that the first poem is "Storm Warnings", the last "From an Old House in America," which ends, "Any woman's death diminishes me."

4. Adrienne Rich, *The Dream of a Common Language: Poems 1974-1977,* hereafter *DCL* (New York: W. W. Norton and Co., 1978), p. 76.

5. *Writing Like a Woman* (Ann Arbor: University of Michigan Press, 1983), p. 121.

6. Rachel Blau DuPlessis, *Writing beyond the Ending: Narrative Strategies of Twentieth-Century Women Writers* (Bloomington: Indiana University Press, 1985), pp. 138-9, expresses this position most sympathetically, in an elegant exegesis of Rich, which discusses the poetics of her lesbian/feminism.

7. Marjorie Perloff, "Private Lives/Public Images," *Michigan Quarterly Review,* 22 (January 1983), 132. My essay, "Curing: Some Comments on the Women's Movement and the Avant-Garde," compares Stein and Rich. Manuscript read at the University of Houston, March, 1985, and at the University of California/Irvine, May, 1985, forthcoming in a collection of essays about the avant-garde, edited by Sandy Friedan and Richard Spuler, Munich: Fink (sic).

8. Adrienne Rich, "'Comment' on Susan Stanford Friedman," *Signs: Journal of Women in Culture and Society,* 9, 4 (Summer 1984), 737. Friedman's article, "'I go where I love': An Intertextual Study of H. D. and Adrienne Rich," appeared in *Signs,* 9, 2 (Winter 1983), 228-245. Elly Bulkin, "'Kissing/Against the Light': A Look at Lesbian Poetry," *Lesbian Studies: Present and Future,* ed. Margaret Cruikshank (Old Westbury, New York: Feminist Press, 1982), 32-54, is a solid survey. For analyses of other genres, see Bonnie Zimmerman, "The Politics of Transliteration: Lesbian Personal Narratives," *Signs,* 9, 4 (Summer 1984), 663-682, and my "Zero Degree Deviancy: The Lesbian Novel in English," *Critical Inquiry,* Special Issue, "Writing and Sexual Difference," ed. Elizabeth Abel, 8, 2 (Winter 1981), 363-379.

9. See, too, Bulkin, 45-46.

10. Marilyn R. Farwell, "Adrienne Rich and Organic Feminist Criticism," *College English,* 39, 2 (October 1977), 191-203, analyzes Rich's literary criticism.

11. I have adapted this idea from one of the most competent studies of Rich, her development, and relationship to Anne Bradstreet and Emily Dickinson as Puritan American women writers: Wendy Martin, *An American Triptych* (Chapel Hill: University of North Carolina Press, 1984), p. 5.

12. Ostriker, *Writing Like A Woman,* p. 102.

13. Adrienne Rich, *Of Woman Born: Motherhood as Experience and Institution,* hereafter *OWB* (New York: W. W. Norton and Co., 1976), p. 219.

14. Rich writes of this most fully in "Compulsory Heterosexuality and Lesbian Existence," hereafter *CH, Signs: Journal of Women in Culture and Society,* 5, 4 (Summer 1980), 631-660. The founding editor of *Signs,* I had asked Rich, over a white tablecloth at lunch in a Chinese restaurant on the Upper West Side of New York City, if she would be generous enough to contribute. I respected, and feared, her intellectual purity. I hoped she would not find me an academic muddle. Yes, she said, she had an article, about heterosexuality and lesbianism. The essay was one of the most famous *Signs* published. For extended comment, read "Viewpoint," by Ann Ferguson, Jacquelyn N. Zita, and Kathryn Pyne Addelson, *Signs,* 7, 1 (Autumn 1981), 158-199.

15. "Like This Together," *The Fact of a Doorframe: Poems Selected and New 1950-1984,* hereafter *FD* (New York: W. W. Norton and Co., 1984), pp. 62-63.

16. "This Woman's Movement," *ARP,* p. 202.

17. Martin, p. 211.

18. Alice Echols, "The New Feminism of Yin and Yang," *Powers of Desire: The Politics of Sexuality,* ed. Ann Snitow, Christine Stansell, and Sharon Thompson (New York: Monthly Review Press, 1983), pp. 439-459, gives an informed, if not throbbingly sympathetic, account of 1970s cultural feminism. She has published a version in "The Taming of the Id: Feminist Sexual Politics, 1968-1983," *Pleasure and Danger: Exploring Female Sexuality,* ed. Carole S. Vance (Boston: Routledge and Kegan Paul, 1984), pp. 50-72. Together, the books represent new directions in the feminist debate about female sexuality in the 1980s, largely toward a theory of female sexuality as a source of pleasure, fantasy, delight. Elizabeth Wilson, "Forbidden Love," *Feminist Studies,* 10, 2 (Summer 1984), 213-226, is an intriguing English parallel.

19. "For Ethel Rosenberg," *A Wild Patience Has Taken Me This Far,* hereafter *WP* (New York: W. W. Norton and Co., 1981), p. 29.

20. Perloff, 136, for one.

21. Martin, p. 9.

22. "Split at the Root," *Nice Jewish Girls: A Lesbian Anthology,* ed. Evelyn Torton Beck (Watertown: Persephone Press, 1982), p. 81. Rich notes the extent of her debt to her friendship with Audre Lorde and her life with Michelle Cliff for her understanding of racism, and of "passing."

23. "Response," *Sinister Wisdom* 14 (Summer 1980), 104-05. Rich thanks Elly Bulkin, who helped open a public debate in lesbian/feminism about racism and Mary Daly's work.

24. Adrienne Rich, "Afterword," *Take Back the Night,* ed. Laura Lederer (New York: William Morrow and Co., 1980), p. 314.

25. *Sources,* hereafter *S* (Woodside, California: The Heyeck Press, 1983).

26. I suggest that Rich has refined a poetics of anger and tenderness in a line that begins with the two stresses of the spondee, or, occasionally, a trochee, and then relaxes into her controlled, but flexible, iambic feet. Look at the phrase "Anger and tenderness" itself.

27. "Split at the Root," p. 83. Rich's work is evidence for Alicia Ostriker's typology of women's poetry: ". . . the quest for autonomous self-definition; the intimate treatment of the body; the release of anger; and . . . for want of a better name, the contact imperative." The latter craves unity, mutuality, continuity, connection, touch. "The Nerves of a Midwife: Contemporary American Women's Poetry," *Parnassus,* 6, 1 (Fall/Winter 1977), 73, 82-83.

28. Albert Gelpi, "Adrienne Rich: The Poetics of Change," *ARP,* p. 148, persuasively casts Rich as prophet and scapegoat.

29. "Three Conversations," *ARP,* p. 112.

30. "An Interview: Audre Lorde and Adrienne Rich," in Audre Lorde, *Sister Outsider* (Trumansburg, New York: The Crossing Press, 1984), p. 112.

31. Several critics comment on Rich's clarity, e.g. Martin, p. 169; Suzanne Juhasz, *Naked and Fiery Forms, Modern American Poetry by Women: A New Tradition* (New York: Harper Colophon Books, 1976), pp. 178-180, 202. In her memoir of Rich as teacher, a sort of performance, Joyce Greenberg says: ". . . there was nothing of the actress, nothing of the performer about her." "By Woman Taught," *Parnassus*, 7, 2 (Spring/Summer 1979), 91.

32. Joanne Feit Diehl, "'Cartographies of Silence': Rich's *Common Language* and the Woman Writer," *Feminist Studies*, 6, 3 (Fall 1980), 545, confronts the issue of Lowell and Rich. My comments about Rich and language owe much to this essay.

TITLE COMMENTARY

Diving into the Wreck

ERICA JONG (REVIEW DATE JULY 1973)

SOURCE: Jong, Erica. "Visionary Anger." *Ms.* 2, no. 1 (July 1973): 30-4.

In the following review, Jong outlines the feminist concerns of Diving into the Wreck, *highlighting such themes as the patriarchy, femininity, and androgyny.*

"If I read a book and it makes my whole body so cold no fire can ever warm me, I know *that* is poetry. If I feel physically as if the top of my head were taken off, I know *that* is poetry. . . . Is there any other way?"

—Emily Dickinson

The test of a good book of poetry for me is that it makes me want to write. It reawakens that part of myself which poems come from; it makes my pen itch to be on the paper; it warms me, chills me, and fills my head with first lines.

This is not surprising, because that-place-which-poems-come-from is shared by all poets, all people. It is not the exclusive property of one individual. Call it the muse, or call it the collective unconscious, it is our shared source—though each poet taps it somewhat differently. And it is a place beyond ego, beyond the narrow distinctions of *yours* and *mine*. A good book of poetry makes me want to write again because it reestablishes my connection with that source. It strips away the petty obstacles which the cowardly superego imposes (the fear of self-exposure, the worry about what the family will think, the terror of criticism) and it puts me in touch with that deeper part of myself which speaks boldly because it is not speaking only for *my* self.

Adrienne Rich's *Diving into the Wreck* is a good book in that most fundamental sense. By "good" I mean "alive." Emily Dickinson once asked whether her poems "lived"; she did not ask whether they were "good." And "alive" or "dead" still seems a far more pertinent criterion than "good" or "bad." This book lives. I have put my ear to its chest; I have felt its moist breath on my neck; I have heard the beating wings of the muse nearby.

Diving into the Wreck is Adrienne Rich's seventh collection and probably her best. I say "probably" because each of her books (starting with the first Yale Younger Poets Award volume) has been so accomplished and probing in its own way that ranking them seems silly. Her first book, *A Change of World* (1951), was very much of its world. It was full of perfectly crafted poems which speculated on the relationship between life and art (as accomplished, craft-conscious poets did in those days). And yet even then, she was original and piercing in a way most of her contemporaries were not. There was a striking honesty about her poems and a willingness to deal with disillusion and disappointment that was rare for so young a poet.

In her second book, there appeared a poem which I loved when I was in college and still love now. It was called "Living in Sin," and it was a perfect blend of irony and grimness. It also pointed the way toward the deeper exploration of women which has characterized Adrienne Rich's recent work. [. . . "Living in Sin," from *The Diamond Cutters*].

A remarkable poem to have written at any time, but especially remarkable for the mid-fifties. I quote it not only to show how powerful Adrienne Rich's writing was from the beginning, but also to demonstrate that this poet was "contending with a woman's demons" long before it became fashionable to do so. Like all good poets, she was prophetic because she was in touch with her own feelings.

The line of development from "Living in Sin" to *Diving into the Wreck* is a serpentine line, yet there has never been any question where Adrienne Rich is going. Along the way, there have been great numbers of extraordinary poems that never flinched from dealing with sexuality, hunger, motherhood, loneliness, blood and revolution in both the personal and the public senses. If you read *Diving into the Wreck* and then go back and consider the books before it (*A Change of World, The Diamond Cutters, Snapshots of a Daughter-in-Law, Necessities of Life, Leaflets,* and *The Will To Change*), I think you will see that

ON THE SUBJECT OF...

one of Adrienne Rich's most recurrent themes has always been the relationship between poetry and patriarchy.

Poetry and patriarchy. The problems of woman in a patriarchal society. That is, in part, what **Diving into the Wreck** is about. Yet it is not about patriarchy in a narrowly political sense. Rich is one of very few poets who can deal with political issues in her poems without letting them degenerate into social realism, because her notion of politics is not superficial; it is essentially psychological and organic. We all give lip-service to this concept of politics, yet few of us truly understand it. We all claim to believe that political oppression and personal feelings are related, and yet a great deal of the self-consciously polemical poetry that has come out of the Women's Movement reads like a generalized rant and it lacks any sort of psychological grounding. The poet has not really looked into herself and told it true. She has been content to echo simplistic slogans.

Adrienne Rich's concept of patriarchy has nothing simplistic about it. Her feminism is a natural extension of her poetry because, for her, feminism *means* empathy. And empathy is the essential tool of the poet. It is akin to the quality Keats called "negative capability"—that unique gift for projecting oneself into other states of consciousness. If Rich sees the role of the poet and the role of the revolutionary as totally compatible, it is because she understands that the most profound revolutions will come from the development of our capacity for empathy.

In a brilliant essay entitled **"The Anti-Feminist Woman,"** (The *New York Review of Books,* November 30, 1972), she summed this up in these words:

I believe that feminism must imply an imaginative identification with all women (and with the ghostly woman in all men) and that the feminist must, because she can, extend this act of the imagination as far as possible.

The phrase "the ghostly woman in all men" is crucial. Rich is alarmed not only by the outward signs of discrimination against women in our patriarchal culture, but also by the way this culture suppresses the nurturant qualities in men, in children, and in societal institutions. She is a feminist because she feels "endangered, psychically and physically, by this society, and because [she believes] we have come to an edge of history when men—insofar as they are embodiments of the patriarchal idea—have become dangerous to children and other living things, themselves included." Her feminism is far more radical and far-reaching than equal-pay-for-equal-work or the establishment of fifty-fifty marriages. It envisions a world in which empathy, mothering, "a concern for the quality of life," "a connection with the natural and the extrasensory order" will not be relegated to women (who then have no power to implement these concerns on a practical level), but will be encouraged in the society at large.

So she is not talking only about discrimination against women, but about discrimination against the *feminine*.

(By the *feminine* I mean the nurturant qualities in all people—whatever their sex. I realize that the term is unsatisfactory and reflects the sexism of our language. The real nature of the feminine and the masculine can never be ascertained until we have a truly equitable social order. Adrienne Rich, however, does seem to be convinced that the feminine principle is more nurturant and the masculine more competitive. I think she might also agree that this need not *always* be so. But her main point seems to be that after too many centuries of uncontested phallic power, we need to right the balance. Women may have to take over for a while to save men from their own self-destructiveness. Eventually, though, Rich would probably hope for a world in which gentle, strong men and gentle, strong women could work together in harmony.)

Her poems reflect this concern with the feminine. But since they are poems, not tracts, they reflect it in a subtle way. The first poem in the book, "Trying To Talk With A Man," establishes the theme of destructive masculine power versus the "underground river" which women have represented in our desert of a culture. . . . ["Trying to Talk With A Man," *Diving into the Wreck*].

The imagery of bombs, testings, laceration, and thirst evokes the landscape of emergency in which we all live. The "dull green succulents" and the "underground river" are opposed to the "condemned scenery," the "ghost town," and the "dry heat" of masculine power. The woman speaker feels more helpless with the man than without him; her nurturant and intellectual power "forcing its way between deformed cliffs," is less pervasive than the man's—though for both of them, it is the only chance for redemption. The time is now. The "condemned scenery" is our culture. The question at the end of the poem is whether we will survive the test, whether we will realize soon enough that the danger lies in ourselves, in our own mistaken priorities.

Again and again the dead end of male civilization is dramatized in these poems . . . [see poems in *Diving into the Wreck*].

But the poems are not only about dead ends. They are about loneliness and the various forms it takes: the loneliness of being a woman in a male-dominated culture, the loneliness of being a life-giver in a world that is in love with death, the loneliness of being on artist, an outsider, a survivor. Human loneliness is one of the great themes in all the arts, and Adrienne Rich depicts it more intensely here than in any other recent book I know. But she also shows that loneliness can be the beginning of rebirth. The woman, because she stands outside the death-dealing culture and its power games, can be a visionary who points the way to redemption. And these poems are also very much about redemption: about sister giving birth to sister, and woman giving birth to herself. For instance, in "The Mirror in Which Two Are Seen As One" . . . [see "The Mirror in Which Two Are Seen As One"].

The speaker of this book is a survivor. She has all the pain of the survivor, but she also has the survivor's unique vision. The subterranean life of the book, which flows through its images, is full of scars, faults, stains, deserts, leaking blood rotting logs, ruined cities, and wrecked ships. The survivor-poet dives into this wreckage and tries to salvage meaning and a new life. She must give birth to herself and to her sisters, and she must also try to save man from himself—though she spends her own life energy endlessly in trying: "The waste of my love goes on this way / trying to save you from yourself."

If I've made this sound as though the speaker of these poems is a sort of Wonder Woman determined to rescue the world by heroic feats, then I've misled you. Rich *does* imply that women are strong and must learn to be even stronger (which is one of the glorious things about her book—especially after reading all those so-called feminist novels in which women are depicted as helpless victims); but the speaker of these poems need not be seen exclusively as a woman, even as a Wonder Woman. She could be *any* outsider, any person who is alienated from our destructive culture, any life-giver (female or male) who wishes to raise a voice against death-worship and the waste of love.

In fact, some of the most interesting poems in the book are those in which Rich imagines an androgynous creature who transcends conventional maleness and conventional femaleness and walks through the city like a stranger—*my visionary anger cleansing my sight / and the detailed perceptions of mercy / flowering from that anger* . . . ["The Stranger"].

In "Diving into the Wreck," the title poem, it is the androgyne who dives into the wreck *to see the damage that was done / and the treasures that prevail* . . . ["Diving into the Wreck,"].

This stranger-poet-survivor carries "a book of myths" in which her/his "names do not appear." These are the old myths of patriarchy, the myths that split male and female irreconcilably into two warring factions, the myths that perpetuate the battle between the sexes. Implicit in Rich's image of the androgyne is the idea that we must write new myths, create new definitions of humanity which will not glorify this angry chasm but heal it. Rich's visionary androgyne reminds me of Virginia Woolf's assertion that the great artist must be mentally bisexual. But Rich takes this idea even further: it is not only the artist who must make the emphatic leap beyond gender, but *any* of us who would try to save the world from destruction.

Though it is extremely important, the androgynous vision is not unique to Rich. However, if you read closely and follow the patterns of metaphors in these poems, you will find another fascinating cluster: those of fire and burning. The speaker of the poems describes herself at one point as "wood with a gift for burning"; and women are often described in terms of fire imagery. Matchsticks, glowing coals, and blazing wood leap through the pages of this book. The survivor-poet burns, yet her burning leaves her unconsumed. The poet as sacred flame—one might almost say. The poet as hearthkeeper. The visionary who lights the dark world by her own burning. Her burning, however, is never a destructive burning, never a vengeful self-immolation. There is nothing of the widow jumping on the funeral pyre here, and nothing like Sylvia Plath's obsession with suicide almost for its own sake. This burning is an affirmation. The fire is a temple- or a hearth-fire. It might even be the sacred flame at Delphi which women guarded.

If you follow the fire imagery still more speculatively and try to see the old myths with an unjaundiced eye, you may even conclude that Adrienne Rich's survivor-poet is a kind of Prometheus. I was, in particular, reminded of a passage in Freud's *Civilization and Its Discontents* which has always intrigued me. In it, Freud is ruminating on the origin of fire and its eventual domestication. Of course he never stops to consider that Prometheus may have been a woman, but had he fewer patriarchal prejudices, his own evidence might have led him to that conclusion:

> It is as though primal man had the habit, when he came in contact with fire, of satisfying an infantile desire connected with it, by putting it out with a stream of his urine. The legends that we possess leave no doubt about the originally phallic view taken of tongues of flame as they shoot upward. Putting out fire by micturating—a theme to which modern giants, Gulliver in Lilliput and Rabelais' Gargantua, still hark back—was therefore a kind of sexual act with a male, an enjoyment of sexual potency in a homosexual competition. The first person [nota bene] to renounce this desire and spare the fire was able to carry it off with him [sic] and subdue it to his [sic] own use. By damping down the fire of his own sexual excitation, he had tamed the natural force of fire. This great cultural conquest was thus the reward for his [sic] renunciation of instinct. Further, it is as though woman had been appointed guardian of the fire which was held captive on the domestic hearth, because her anatomy made it impossible for her to yield to the temptation of this desire.

The first *person* to renounce this self-indulgence would have been the domesticator of fire, and Freud automatically assumes it to have been a man—who then *gave* it to a woman to guard. But the logical conclusion of his own evidence is a bit different. Women, who are not interested in things like competing with each other to piss out fires, would more likely have been the tamers of fire. Far from being the passive receptors of a force tamed by men, women were probably the fire-givers and later, its guardians. Ergo: Prometheus was a woman.

So twisted are our myths that it will take generations of new scholars to begin to untangle them. But the exploration has begun. Adrienne Rich's poems are not just a dirge for a dead order but a celebration of a new age of discovery. No review can hope to do justice to the richness and variety of *Diving into the Wreck*. Every poem in the book matters. Read them.

FURTHER READING

Criticism

Bere, Carol. "The Road Taken: Adrienne Rich in the 1990s." *Literary Review* 43, no. 4 (summer 2000): 550-61.

   Provides a thematic overview of Rich's poetry published during the 1990s.

Dickie, Margaret. *Stein, Bishop, and Rich: Lyrics of Love, War, and Place.* Chapel Hill, N.C.: University of North Carolina Press, 1997, 234 p.

   Critical analysis of Rich's poetry.

Eagleton, Mary. "Adrienne Rich, Location, and the Body."[1] *Journal of Gender Studies* 9, no. 3 (November 2000): 299-312.

   Examination of the theoretical significance of "Notes toward a Politics of Location" in relation to Rich's poetry, illustrating how the essay situates Rich's physical body as both a personal and a public location of white female Jewish subjectivity.

Flynn, Gale. "The Radicalization of Adrienne Rich." *Hollins Critic* 11, no. 4 (October 1974): 1-15.

   Traces the evolution of Rich's feminist ideology throughout her life and career.

Henneberg, Sylvia. "'The Slow Turn of Consciousness': Adrienne Rich's Family Plot." *Women's Studies: An Interdisciplinary Journal* 27, no. 4 (1998): 347-58.

   Explores Rich's treatment of family in her work.

Morris, Adelaide. "'Saving the Skein': The Structure of *Diving into the Wreck*." *Contemporary Poetry* 3, no. 2 (summer 1978): 43-61.

   Analyzes the formal and thematic structure of Diving into the Wreck.

Ostriker, Alicia. "Her Cargo: Adrienne Rich and the Common Language." *The American Poetry Review* 8, no. 4 (July-August 1979): 6-10.

   Examines the feminist poetics of The Dream of a Common Language.

Rupp, Leila J. "Women's History in the New Millennium: Adrienne Rich's 'Compulsory Heterosexuality and Lesbian Experience': A Retrospective." *Journal of Women's History* 15, no. 3 (autumn 2003): 7-89.

   Reviews Rich's work in relation to feminist literary theory.

Templeton, Alice. *The Dream and the Dialogue: Adrienne Rich's Feminist Poetics,* Knoxville: University of Tennessee Press, 1995, 193 p.

Discusses the mutual influence of contemporary feminism and Rich's poetics upon each other.

Van Dyne, Susan R. "The Mirrored Vision of Adrienne Rich." *Modern Poetry Studies* 8, no. 1 (spring 1977): 140-73.

Examines the evolving relationship between the personae and the politics of Rich's poetry.

Yorke, Liz. *Adrienne Rich: Passion, Politics, and the Body.* Thousand Oaks, Calif.: Sage Publications, 1998, 176 p.

Surveys Rich's feminist prose writings.

OTHER SOURCES FROM GALE:

Additional coverage of Rich's life and career is contained in the following sources published by the Gale Group: *American Writers Retrospective Supplement,* Vol. 2; *American Writers Supplement,* Vol. 1; *Concise Dictionary of American Literary Biography Supplement; Contemporary Authors,* Vols. 9-12R; *Contemporary Authors New Revision Series,* Vols. 20, 53, 74; *Contemporary Literary Criticism,* Vols. 3, 6, 7, 11, 18, 36, 73, 76, 125; *Contemporary Poets,* Ed. 7; *Contemporary Southern Writers; Contemporary Women Poets; Dictionary of Literary Biography,* Vols. 5, 67; *DISCovering Authors Modules: Poets; DISCovering Authors 3.0; Encyclopedia of World Literature in the 20th Century,* Ed. 3; *Exploring Poetry; Feminist Writers; Literature Resource Center; Major 20th-Century Writers,* Ed. 1, 2; *Modern American Women Writers; Poetry Criticism,* Vol. 5; *Poetry for Students,* Vol. 15; *Poets: American and British; Reference Guide to American Literature,* Ed. 4; and *World Poets.*

ANNE SEXTON

(1928 - 1974)

American poet, playwright, author of children's books, short story writer, and essayist.

Sexton is among the most celebrated poets of the confessional school. Her highly emotional, self-reflexive verse, characterized by preoccupations with childhood guilt, mental illness, motherhood, and female sexuality, is distinguished for its stunning imagery, artistry, and remarkable cadences. An unlikely latecomer to the literary scene, Sexton underwent a rapid metamorphosis from suburban housewife to major literary figure in the early 1960s. Sexton's art and life—culminating in her suicide—converged with the convictions of the contemporary feminist movement, drawing attention to the oppressive, circumscribed existence of women in middle-class American society.

BIOGRAPHICAL INFORMATION

Born Anne Gray Harvey in Newton, Massachusetts, Sexton was the youngest of three daughters raised in an upper-middle-class home near Boston. Her mother, a housewife and daughter of a published author, had aspired to be a poet in her own right, and Sexton struggled throughout her life with a sense of competition with her mother, a tension that routinely appears in Sex-

ton's poetry. In 1947 Sexton graduated from Rogers Hall preparatory school for girls, where her first poetry appeared in the school yearbook. After a year at Garland Junior College, a finishing school in Boston, she eloped with Alfred Muller "Kayo" Sexton II. Following an impulsive marriage that endured separations and infidelities, the couple divorced in 1973. From 1949 to 1952 Sexton worked as a model—notably for the esteemed Hart modeling agency in Boston—as well as a lingerie salesperson and bookstore clerk while Kayo served in the Navy Reserve during the Korean War. Sexton gave birth to her first daughter, Linda Gray, in 1953, followed by a second daughter, Joyce Ladd, in 1955. After the arrival of Joyce, Sexton suffered from postpartum depression and attempted suicide for the first time in 1956. She was hospitalized and underwent psychiatric treatment, losing custody of her children after her release, when she was forced to return to her parents' home to live for a time. According to Sexton, these events precipitated her return to poetry writing after years of ignoring her interest and talent. Both her psychiatrist and a priest she went to for spiritual guidance supported her decision to write about her experiences. "God is in your typewriter," the priest reportedly told her. In 1957 Sexton joined a poetry workshop headed by John Holmes at the Boston Center for Adult Education, where she befriended Maxine Kumin, who would also become a distinguished poet. The following year Sexton received a scholarship to attend the Antioch Writers' Conference to study under W. D. Snodgrass. Later that year, she enrolled in Robert Lowell's writing seminar at Boston University, where she was introduced to Sylvia Plath, and in 1959 she participated in the Bread Loaf Writers Conference with the assistance of a Robert Frost fellowship. Her first volume of poetry, *To Bedlam and Part Way Back* (1960), received a National Book Award nomination, as did her second volume, *All My Pretty Ones* (1962), which also won the Levinson Prize from *Poetry* magazine. After an appointment at the Radcliffe Institute from 1961 to 1963, Sexton received an American Academy of Arts and Letters fellowship and traveled to Europe. She received a Ford Foundation grant for residence with the Charles Playhouse in Boston in 1964. Sexton also collaborated with Kumin on a series of children's books. Her next major volume of poetry, *Live or Die* (1966), received a Pulitzer Prize and Shelley Award from the Poetry Society of America in 1967. Shortly after the publication of *Love Poems* (1969), she was awarded a Guggenheim fellowship to complete her only dramatic work, *Mercy Street,* produced off-Broadway by the American Place Theatre in 1969. The recipient of honorary degrees from Harvard and Radcliffe, Sexton gave frequent poetry readings and taught creative writing at Boston University from 1970 until her death. During the 1970s Sexton's mental and physical health deteriorated, exacerbated by addictions to alcohol and sleeping pills. She committed suicide by carbon monoxide poisoning in 1974.

MAJOR WORKS

As a confessional poet, Sexton's writing is in many ways a candid autobiographic record of her struggle to overcome the feelings of guilt, loss, inadequacy, and suicidal despair that tormented her. Informed by years of psychotherapy, Sexton's carefully crafted poetry often addresses her uncertain self-identity as a daughter, wife, lover, mother, and psychiatric patient. Her first volume, *To Bedlam and Part Way Back,* consists of poems written shortly after her confinement in a mental hospital. "The Double Image," among the most accomplished works of the volume, is a sequence of seven poems describing Sexton's schism with her mother in the imagery of two portraits facing each other from opposite walls. "Unknown Girl in the Maternity Ward," which concerns an unwed mother who prepares to abandon her illegitimate child, alludes to Sexton's guilt over los-

ing custody of her children. Another significant poem in the book, "For John, Who Begs Me Not to Enquire Further," is Sexton's response to John Holmes's criticism of her transgressive subject matter, representing Sexton's defense of the confessional mode and her own poetic voice. The poems of *All My Pretty Ones* further illustrate Sexton's aptitude for invoking musical rhythms and arresting imagery. The volume contains the often-anthologized poems "The Truth the Dead Know," "All My Pretty Ones," "The Abortion," and "Letter Written on a Ferry while Crossing Long Island Sound," all of which concern feelings of loss. "With Mercy for the Greedy," also from this volume, anticipates Sexton's proclivity for Christian motifs in much of her subsequent work. The poems of *Live or Die* explore Sexton's ongoing vacillation between life and maternal responsibility and her attraction to suicide. Her obsession with death, a prominent recurring theme in all her work, is explicit in the poems "Sylvia's Death," about Sylvia Plath's suicide, and "Wanting to Die," countered by the life-affirming poem "Live" at the end of the volume. Also included are such well-known poems as "Flee on Your Donkey," "Menstruation at Forty," "The Addict," "Little Girl, My Stringbean, My Lovely Woman," a tender paean to her daughter, and "Somewhere in Africa," a eulogy on the death of Holmes. Less concerned with psychic trauma, *Love Poems* contains verse ranging from elegant depiction of erotic desire in "The Breast," "Song for a Lady," and "Eighteen Days Without You," praise for womanhood in "In Celebration of My Uterus," the pain of love's end in "For My Lover, Returning to His Wife," "You All Know the Story of the Other Woman," and "The Ballad of the Lonely Masturbator," and her relationship with her husband in "Loving the Killer." In *Transformations* (1971), a collection of loosely reinterpreted Grimms fairy tales, Sexton relied upon biting satire and dark humor to shatter the notion of happy or conventional endings. Sexton's late volumes reveal the poet's mounting anguish, coloring her work with an increasing morbidity and overriding religiosity. The themes of alienation, death, and deliverance are evident in "The Death of the Fathers" and "The Jesus Papers" in *The Book of Folly* (1972), "The Death Baby" and "O Ye Tongues," a sequence of psalms, in *The Death Notebooks* (1974), and "The Rowing Endeth," the final poem of the overtly religious volume *The Awful Rowing Toward God* (1975), in which the speaker arrives at "the island called God" to play a hand of cards with the deity himself. The balance of Sexton's poetry is collected in the posthumous volumes *45 Mercy Street* (1976) and *Words for Dr. Y* (1978).

CRITICAL RECEPTION

Sexton is recognized as a significant American poet of the postwar era. Widely praised for the forceful imagery, compelling associations, affective elegiac tone, and meticulously arranged tonal patterns of her best verse, she is considered among the most talented representatives of the first generation of confessional poets, along with Lowell and Plath. Critics frequently comment on the dual nature of Sexton's poetry as a cathartic process and destructive urge. While many find courage in Sexton's willingness to transmute painful experience and taboo topics into art, others have condemned such themes as exhibitionist and inappropriate. James Dickey wrote of Sexton's poems in his now-famous review of *To Bedlam and Part Way Back*, "One feels tempted to drop them furtively into the nearest ashcan, rather than be caught with them in the presence of such naked suffering." Despite the limitations of Sexton's unabashed self-scrutiny, many critics discern profound archetypal motifs in her work, particularly allusions to the Oedipus myth in themes of incest and the relentless search for forbidden truth and her complex handling of her own search for spiritual meaning in *The Awful Rowing Toward God*. A celebrity and trenchant poet whose frank discussion of sexuality and mental illness offered liberating honesty for many, Sexton remains among the most important female poets of her generation.

PRINCIPAL WORKS

To Bedlam and Part Way Back (poetry) 1960

All My Pretty Ones (poetry) 1962

Eggs of Things [with Maxine Kumin] (juvenilia) 1963

More Eggs of Things [with Kumin] (juvenilia) 1964

Selected Poems (poetry) 1964

Live or Die (poetry) 1966

Love Poems (poetry) 1969

Mercy Street (play) 1969

Joey and the Birthday Present [with Kumin] (juvenilia) 1971

Transformations (poetry) 1971

The Book of Folly (poetry) 1972

O Ye Tongues (poetry) 1973

The Death Notebooks (poetry) 1974

The Awful Rowing Toward God (poetry) 1975

The Wizard's Tears [with Kumin] (juvenilia) 1975

45 Mercy Street (poetry) 1976

Anne Sexton: A Self-Portrait in Letters (letters) 1977

Words for Dr. Y: Uncollected Poems with Three Stories (poetry and short stories) 1978

The Complete Poems (poetry) 1981

No Evil Star: Selected Essays, Interviews, and Prose (essays, interviews, and prose) 1985

Selected Poems of Anne Sexton (poetry) 1988

PRIMARY SOURCES

ANNE SEXTON (ESSAY DATE NOVEMBER 1973)

SOURCE: Sexton, Anne. "All God's Children Need Radios." In *No Evil Star: Selected Essays, Interviews, and Prose*, edited by Steven E. Colburn, pp. 23-32. Ann Arbor: The University of Michigan Press, 1985.

In the following essay, originally published as "A Small Journal" in Ms. *magazine in November, 1973, Sexton chronicles her experiences during the months preceding and following her mother's death.*

Roses

NOV. 6, 1971

Thank you for the red roses. They were lovely. Listen, Skeezix, I know you didn't give them to me, but I like to pretend you did because, as you know, when you give me something my heart faints on the pillow. Well, someone gave them to me, some official, some bureaucrat, it seems, gave me these one dozen. They lived a day and a half, little cups of blood, twelve baby fists. Dead today in their vase. They are a cold people. I don't throw them out, I keep them as a memento of my first abortion. They smell like a Woolworth's, half between the candy counter and the 99-cent perfume. Sorry they're dead, but thanks anyhow. I wanted daisies. I never said, but I wanted daisies. I would have taken care of daisies, giving them an aspirin every hour and cutting their stems properly, but with roses I'm reckless. When they arrive in their long white box, they're already in the death house.

Trout

SAME DAY

The trout (brook) are sitting in the green plastic garbage pail full of pond water. They are Dr. M's trout, from his stocked pond. They are doomed. If I don't hurry and get this down, we will have broken their necks (backs?) and fried them in the black skillet and eaten them with our silver forks and forgotten all about them. Doomed. There they are nose to nose, wiggling in their cell, awaiting their execution. I like trout, as you know, but that pail is too close and I keep peering into it. We want them fresh, don't we? So be it. From the pond to the pail to the pan to the belly to the toilet. We'll have broccoli with hollandaise. Does broccoli have a soul? The trout soil themselves. Fishing is not humane or good for business.

Some Things Around My Desk

SAME DAY

If you put your ear close to a book, you can hear it talking. A tin voice, very small, somewhat like a puppet, asexual. Yet all at once? Over my head JOHN BROWN'S BODY is dictating to EROTIC POETRY. And so forth. The postage scale sits like a pregnant secretary. I bought it thirteen years ago. It thinks a letter goes for 4 cents. So much for inflation, so much for secretaries. The calendar, upper left, is covered with psychiatrists. They are having a meeting on my November. Then there are some anonymous quotations Scotch-taped up. *Poets and pigs are not appreciated until they are dead.* And: *The more I write, the more the silence seems to be eating away at me.* And here is Pushkin, not quite anonymous: *And reading my own life with loathing, I tremble and curse.* And: *Unhappiness is more beautiful when seen through a window than from within.* And so forth. Sweeney's telegram is also up there. *You are lucky,* he cables. Are you jealous? No, you are reading the Town Report, frequently you read something aloud and it almost mixes up my meditations. Now you're looking at the trout. Doomed. My mother's picture is on the right up above the desk. When that picture was taken, she too was doomed. You read aloud: *Forty-five dog bites in town.* Not us. Our dog bites frogs only. *Five runaways and five stubborn children.* Not us. Children stubborn but not reported. The phone, at my back and a little to the right, sits like a general (German) (SS). It holds the voices that I love as well as strangers, a platoon of beggars asking me to dress their wounds. The trout are getting peppier. My mother seems to be looking at them. Speaking of the phone, yesterday Sweeney called

from Australia to wish me a happy birthday. (Wrong day. I'm November ninth.) I put my books on the line and they said, "Move along, Buster." And why not? All things made lovely are doomed. *Two cases of chancres,* you read.

Eat and Sleep

NOV. 7, 1971

Today I threw the roses out, and before they died the trout spawned. We ate them anyhow with a wine bottled in the year I was born (1928). The meal was good, but I preferred them alive. So much for gourmet cooking. Today the funeral meats, out to Webster (you call it Ethan Frome country) for a wake. *Eat* and *Sleep* signs. World War II steel helmets for sale. There was a church with a statue of a mother in front of it. You know, one of those mothers. The corpse clutched his rosary and his cheek bumped the Stars and Stripes. A big man, he was somebody's father. But what in hell was that red book? Was it a prayer book or a passport at his side? Passports are blue, but mine has a red case. I like to think it's his passport, a union card for the final crossing. On the drive back, fields of burst milkweed and the sun setting against hog-black winter clouds. It was a nice drive. We saw many *Eat* and *Sleep* signs. Last night the eater, today the sleeper.

Mother's Radio

NOV. 8, 1971

FM please and as few ads as possible. One beside my place in the kitchen where I sit in a doze in the winter sun, letting the warmth and music ooze through me. One at my bed too. I call them both: *Mother's Radio.* As she lay dying her radio played, it played her to sleep, it played for my vigil, and then one day the nurse said, "Here, take it." Mother was in her coma, never, never to say again, "This is the baby," referring to me at any age. Coma that kept her under water, her gills pumping, her brain numb. I took the radio, my vigil keeper, and played it for my waking, sleeping ever since. In memoriam. It goes everywhere with me like a dog on a leash. Took it to a love affair, peopling the bare rented room. We drank wine and ate cheese and let it play. No ads please. FM only. When I go to a mental hospital I have it in my hand. I sign myself in (voluntary commitment papers) accompanied by cigarettes and mother's radio. The hospital is suspicious of these things because they do not understand that I bring my mother with me, her cigarettes, her radio. Thus I am not alone. Generally speaking mental hospitals are lonely places, they are full of TV's and medications. I have found a station that plays the hit tunes of the nineteen-forties, and I dance in the kitchen, snapping my fingers. My daughters laugh and talk about bobby socks. I will die with this radio playing—last sounds. My children will hold up my books and I will say good-bye to them. I wish I hadn't taken it when she was in a coma. Maybe she regained consciousness for a moment and looked for that familiar black box. Maybe the nurse left the room for a moment and there was my mama looking for her familiars. Maybe she could hear the nurse tell me to take it. I didn't know what I was doing. I'd never seen anyone die before. I wish I hadn't. Oh Mama, forgive. I keep it going; it never stops. They will say of me, "Describe her, please." And you will answer, "She played the radio a lot." When I go out it plays—to keep the puppy company. It is fetal. It is her heartbeat—oh my black sound box, I love you! Mama, mama, play on!

Little Girl, Big Doll

NOV. 10, 1971

Out my window, a little girl walking down the street in a fat and fuzzy coat, carrying a big doll. Hugging it. The doll is almost as large as a basset hound. The doll with a pink dress and bare feet. Yesterday was my birthday and I excised it with bourbon. No one gave me a big doll. Yesterday I received one yellow wastebasket, two umbrellas, one navy pocketbook, two Pyrex dishes, one pill pot, one ornate and grotesque brown hamper. No doll. The man in the casket is gone. The birthday is gone, but the little girl skipped by under the wrinkled oak leaves and held fast to a replica of herself. I had a Dye-dee doll myself, a Cinderella doll with a crown made of diamonds and a Raggedy Ann with orange hair and once on my sixth birthday a big doll, almost my size. Her eyes were brown and her name was Amanda and she did not welcome death. Death forgot her. (For the time being.)

Daddy Sugar

NOV. 15, 1971

O. called the night before my birthday, sticking his senile red tongue into the phone. Yet sentimental too, saying how it was forty-three years ago, that night when he paced the floor of my birth. I never heard of my father pacing the floor—a third child, he was bored. Isn't pacing

limited to fathers? That's the point, isn't it! Maybe O. is my biological father, my daddy sugar and sperm. It ruined my birthday, to be claimed at forty-three by O. Just last Christmas, around the twentieth of December, he arrived out here with a secret package—my photo at sixteen (I never gave it to him. Mother must have given it to him!) and a lock of my baby hair. Why would Mother give a lock of baby hair to bachelor-family-friend-O.? He said, "I don't want to die with the evidence!" And then he drove off. Later, on the phone we promise to meet for lunch and have a confession hour. But I shy away. I am like Jocasta who begs Oedipus not to look further. I am a dog refusing poisoned meat. It would be poison he pumped into my mother. She who made me. But who with? I'm afraid of that lunch—I would throw up the vichyssoise if he said: "Happy birthday, Anne, I am your father."

Brown Leaves

NOV. 16, 1971

Out my window: some wonderful blue sky. Also I see brown leaves, wrinkled things, the color of my father's suitcases. All winter long these leaves will hang there—the light glinting off them as off a cow. At this moment I am drinking. At this moment I am very broke. I called my agent but she wasn't there, only the brown leaves are there. They whisper, "We are wiser than money; don't spend us." . . . And the two trees, my two telphone poles, simply wait. Wait for what? More words, dummy! Joy, who is as straight as a tree, is bent today like a spatula. I will take her to the orthopedic man. Speaking of suitcases, I think of my childhood and Mutnick Forever. Christmases, every single year, my father tearing off the red wrapping and finding a Mark Cross two-suiter, calf, calf the color of the oak leaves—and thinking of the wool supplier, Mr. Mutnick, who gave him this yearly goodie—he'd cry, "Mutnick Forever." That sound, those two words meant suitcases, light tan, the color of dog shit but as soft as a baby's cheek and smelling of leather and horse.

Breathing Toys

NOV. 18, 1971

The gentle wind, the kind gentle wind, goes in and out of me. But not too well. Walking a block—just say from Beacon to Commonwealth—or over at B. U., I lean against the building for wind, gasping like a snorkel, the crazy seizure of the heart, the error of the lungs. Dr. M.

wants me to go into his hospital for tests, come January. He's a strange one, aside from his stocked trout pool he keeps saying, "I want to save a life!" The life being mine. Last time we met he said, "You'll be an old hag in three years!" What does he mean? A yellow woman with wax teeth and charcoal ringlets at her neck? Or does he only mean the breathing—the air is hiding, the air will not do! An old hag, her breasts shrunken to the size of pearls? My lungs, those little animals, contracting, drowning in their shell. . . . Joy is still down. Meals float up to her. (I am the cork.) She lies on her mattress with a board under it and asks, "Why me?" Her little toes wriggling on the roof, her head lolling over the TV, her back washing like sand at low tide. As I've said elsewhere: the body is meat. Joy, will you and I outlive our doctors or will we oblige, sinking downward as they turn off the flame? As for me, it's the cigarettes, of course. I can't give them up any more than I can give up Mother's radio. I didn't always smoke. Once I was a baby. Back then only Mother smoked. It hurts, Mama, it hurts to suck on the moon through the bars. Mama, smoke curls out of your lips and you sing me a lullaby. Mama, mama, you hurt too much, you make no sense, you give me a breathing toy from World War II and now you take it away. Which war is this, Mama, with the guns smoking and you making no sense with cigarettes?

Dog

NOV. 19, 1971

"O Lord," they said last night on TV, "the sea is so mighty and my dog is so small." I *heard* dog. You say, they said *boat* not *dog* and that further *dog* would have no meaning. But it does mean. The sea is mother-death and she is a mighty female, the one who wins, the one who sucks us all up. *Dog* stands for me and the new puppy, Daisy. I wouldn't have kept her if we hadn't named her Daisy. (You brought me daisies yesterday, not roses, daisies. A proper flower. It outlives any other in its little vessel of water. You must have given them to me! If you didn't give them to me, who did?) Me and my dog, my Dalmatian dog, against the world. "My dog is so small" means that even the two of us will be stamped under. Further, dog is what's in the sky on winter mornings. Sun-dogs springing back and forth across the sky. But we dogs are small and the sun will burn us down and the sea has our number. Oh Lord, the sea is so mighty and my dog is so small, my dog whom I sail with into the west. The sea is mother, larger than Asia, both lowering their large breasts onto the coastline. Thus we ride on her praying for good moods and a smile in the heavens. She is mighty, oh Lord, but I with my little puppy, Daisy, remain a child.

Too complicated, eh?

Just a thought in passing, just something about a lady and her dog, setting forth as they do, on a new life.

Thanksgiving in Fat City

NOV. 25, 1971

The turkey glows. It has been electrified. The legs huddle, they are bears. The breasts sit, dying out, and the gizzard waits like a wart. Everyone eats, hook and sinker, they eat. They eat like a lady and a bear. They eat like a drowning dog. The house sits like the turkey. The chimney gasps for breath and the large, large rock on the front lawn is waiting for us to move into it. It is a large mouth. Autograph seekers attend it. They mail it letters, postage due. They raise their skirts and tease it. . . . It is a camera, it records the mailman, it records the gasman, it records the needy students, it records the lovers, serious as grandmothers, it records the sun and the poisonous gases, it records the eaters, the turkey, the drowned dog, the autograph seekers, the whole Hollywood trip. Meanwhile I sit inside like a crab at my desk, typing pebbles into a boat.

A Life of Things

DEC. 2, 1971

They live a life of things, Williams said. This house is stuffed like a pepper with things: the painted eyes of my mother crack in the attic, the blue dress I went mad in is carved on the cameo. Time is passing, say the shoes. Afrika boots saying their numbers, wedding slippers raining on the attic floor. The radiator swallows, digesting its gallstones. The sink opens its mouth like a watermelon. Hadn't I better move out, dragging behind me the bare essentials: a few pills, a few books, and a blanket for sleeping? When I die, who will put it all away? Who will index the letters, the books, the names, the expendable jewels of a life? Things sweat in my palm as I put them each carefully into my mouth and swallow. Each one a baby. Let me give the jar of honey, the pickles, the salt box to my birthday. Let me give the desk and its elephant to the postman. Let me give the giant bed to the willow so that she may haunt it. Let me give the hat, the Italian-made Safari hat, to my dog so that she may chew off her puppyhood.

Finally let me give the house itself to Mary-who-comes. Mary-who-comes has scoured the floors of my childhood and the floors of my motherhood. She of the dogs, the army of dogs, old English Sheep dogs (best of show), fifteen altogether, their eyes shy and hidden by hair, their bodies curled up wool. Mary-who-comes may have my house: the Lenox for her dogs to lap, the kitchen for breeding, the writing room for combing and currying. Mary will have a temple, a dog temple, and I will have divorced my things and gone on to other strangers.

Found Topaz

DEC. 10, 1971

The sherry in its glass on the kitchen table, reflecting the winter sun, is a liquid topaz. It makes a tinkerbelle light on the wall. Sea light, terror light, laugh light. . . . There is less and less sherry, a cocktail sherry, very light, very good. It keeps me company. I am swallowing jewels, light by light. To celebrate this moment (it is like being in love) I am having a cigarette. Fire in the mouth. Topaz in the stomach.

Oatmeal Spoons

SAME DAY

I am still in the kitchen, feeling the heat of the sun through the storm window, letting Mother's radio play its little tunes. Dr. Brundig is away, a week now, and I'm okay, I'm sanforized, above ground, full of anonymous language, a sherry destiny, grinning, proud as a kid with a new drawing. I'm flying invisible balloons from my mailbox and I'd like to give a party and ask my past in. And you—I tell you how great I feel and you look doubtful, a sour look as if you were sucking the ocean out of an olive. You figure, she's spent fifteen years attending classes with Dr. Brundig and her cohorts, majoring in dependence. Dr. M. (trout man, lung man) asked me, "What is your major problem? Surely you know after fifteen years?"

"Dunno."

"Well," he said, "Did you fall in love with your oatmeal spoon?"

"There was no oatmeal spoon."

He caught on.

Angels Wooly Angels

JAN. 1, 1972, 12:30 A.M.

I feel mild. Mild and kind. I am quite alone this New Year's Eve for you are sick: having fallen in love with the toilet, you went on an opium voyage and fell asleep before the New Year. I heard it all down here in the kitchen on Mother's radio—Times Square and all that folly. I am drinking champagne and burping up my childhood: champagne on Christmas Day with my father planting corks in the ceiling and the aunts and uncles clapping, Mother's diamonds making mirrors of the candlelight, the grandmothers laughing like stuffed pillows and the love that was endless for one day. We held hands and danced around the tree singing our own tribal song. (Written in the eighteen hundreds by a great, great uncle.) We were happy, happy, happy. Daddy crying his MUTNICK FOREVER and the big doll, Amanda, that I got. . . . All dead now. The doll lies in her grave, a horse fetus, her china blue eyes as white as eggs. Now I am the wife. I am the mother. You are the uncles, the grandmothers. We are the Christmas. Something gets passed on—a certain zest for the tribe, along with the champagne, the cold lobster hors d'oeuvres, the song. Mother, I love you and it doesn't matter about O. It doesn't matter who my father was; it matters who I *remember* he was. There was a queen. There was a king. There were three princesses. That's the whole story. I swear it on my wallet. I swear it on my radio. See, Mother, there are angels flying over my house tonight. They wear American Legion hats but the rest of them is wool, wool, that white fluffy stuff Daddy used to manufacture into goods, wool, fat fleecy wool. They zing over the telephone wires, their furry wings going *Hush, hush*. Like a mother comforting a child.

GENERAL COMMENTARY

ANNE SEXTON AND MAXINE KUMIN, ELAINE SHOWALTER, AND CAROL SMITH (INTERVIEW DATE 15 APRIL 1974)

SOURCE: Sexton, Anne, and Maxine Kumin, Elaine Showalter, and Carol Smith. "With Maxine Kumin, Elaine Showalter, and Carol Smith." In *No Evil Star: Selected Essays, Interviews, and Prose*, edited by Steven E. Colburn, pp. 158-79. Ann Arbor: The University of Michigan Press, 1985.

In the following interview, originally conducted on April 15, 1974, and first published in the journal Women's Studies *in 1976, Sexton discusses her personal and professional friendship with Kumin with respect to the rise of the women's movement and the literary successes of both poets.*

Max and I
two immoderate sisters,

two immoderate writers,
two burdeners,
made a pact.
To beat death down with a stick.
To take over.

—Anne Sexton, "**The Death Baby**"

This conversation [April 15, 1974] between four women is about the friendship of Maxine Kumin and Anne Sexton, a friendship which began in the late 1950s, when they studied together in a poetry workshop in Boston led by John Holmes. Because they had young children, and were often unable to get out of the house, they developed a process of "workshopping" poems on the telephone, supplying for each other both detailed criticism and warm support. Both women won Pulitzer Prizes for books of poems. Anne Sexton in 1967 for **Live or Die**, and Maxine Kumin in 1973 for *Up Country: Poems of New England.* Their poetic styles are completely different; Kumin's poetry is exact, formal, intensely crafted, while Sexton wrote dramatically about breakdown and death. On October 4, 1974, Anne Sexton killed herself at her home in Weston, Massachusetts.

We met Anne and Maxine before their poetry reading at Douglass College, and asked to talk with them together, not in the form of a traditional interview, but more as something relaxed and spontaneous. So the reader should not expect to find any theories of art, or formal or technical problems, examined here. Instead we hear the voices of Annie and Max, taped in a motel room in New Brunswick, New Jersey, on an April afternoon, interrupting each other, joking, remembering.

[*Kumin*]: *Meeting Anne was really fantastic. When I met Annie she was a little flower child, she was the ex-fashion model. She wore very spiky high heels—*

[Sexton]: Well, that was the age.

[*Kumin*]: *Yes, it was. Well, she was totally chic, and I was sort of more frumpy.*

[Sexton]: You were the most frump of the frumps. You had your hair in a little bun.

[*Kumin*]: *I was the chief frump. She was really chic and she wore flowers in her hair.*

[*Showalter*]: *Where did you model? I remember reading that, and then it dropped out of your blurbs.*

[Sexton]: It's called the Hart Agency, in Boston.

[*Kumin*]: *She was a Hart girl. At any rate, we met at the Boston Center for Adult Education where we had each come to study with John Holmes.*

[Sexton]: I came trembling, thinking, oh dear god, with the most ghastly poems. Oh god, were they bad!

[*Kumin*]: *Well . . . I don't know if that's true.*

[Sexton]: Oh, oh, Maxine, horrible, horrible. Anyway, your impression of me was—?

[*Kumin*]: *And my impression of Anne was—I don't know what my impression was. I was very taken with her. I think we were each very taken with each other.*

[Sexton]: Now, wait a minute. You were scared of me.

[*Kumin*]: *I was terrified of her. I had just had my closest friend commit suicide, in a postpartum depression. Gassed herself.*

[Sexton]: I wasn't writing about that right off.

[*Kumin*]: *Now, wait a minute. I'm just saying why I was scared.*

[Sexton]: Why should you know I had anything to do with it?

[*Kumin*]: *Well, I knew your history.*

[Sexton]: How?

[*Kumin*]: *You were very open about the fact, of why you had begun to write poetry, and how you had started to write poetry. You had just gotten out of the mental hospital. And something in me very much wanted to turn aside from this. I didn't want to let myself in for that again, for that separation. And Anne is still very much more flamboyant and open a person than I am. I'm much more closed up, restrained. I think this is certain, although much less so now than then.*

[Sexton]: Can I say? Since your analysis—you're quite a changed person.

[*Kumin*]: *Yes, since my analysis.*

[Sexton]: I mean, she's gotten attractive and yummy. Before her hair was pulled back and in a bun—

[*Showalter*]: *I wouldn't have recognized you, Maxine, from your pictures.*

[Sexton]: No pictures are good. She was attractive then, she was attractive then; just a bad picture.

[*Kumin*]: *The picture on the novel coming out next year is a really good picture of me and my dog. I recommend that picture.*

[Sexton]: She keeps saying, look at my dog. As if the dog were more important.

[Kumin]: *He is kind of spectacular. Anyway, Anne and I met, and we drove into this class together. For a long time, she used to pick me up and—*

[Sexton]: Not at the beginning I didn't. I can remember, it was funny. I remember you going to a reading at Wellesley College and you picking me up. I had on sandals. You said, look, she has prehensile toes. I've never forgotten it. And I said, look, anytime you want me to go to a reading or anything (because I was desperate then) I'll do anything. And I started to drive Maxine to the Adult Center.

[Kumin]: *And from that we began to go to all sorts of readings together. Actually the reading at Wellesley College was Marianne Moore.*

[Sexton]: Remember her? Because she kept contradicting and saying, now don't handle a line this way, don't do that, that's very bad, you know, and don't end-stop here.

[Kumin]: *She mumbled so. She read so badly. She was a character, in her tricorner hat and her great black robe.*

[Sexton]: Do you remember going to hear Robert Graves? Dear god, he was ghastly!

[Kumin]: *Now look, we are not here to talk about people who were ghastly readers or we'll be here all night.*

[Showalter]: *Was John Holmes in charge of that workshop?*

[Kumin]: *Yes, John Holmes was teaching a little workshop, for anybody. It was available to the world, whoever wanted to come. And we would all try our poems. And this, I think, is how Anne and I learned to work by hearing a poem, because we didn't bring copies. John would sit at the head of the table and shuffle through the poems.*

[Sexton]: He didn't do anything alphabetically.

[Kumin]: *And we would all sit there dying, hoping to be chosen.*

[Sexton]: Oh, you'd pray to be chosen.

[Showalter]: *Not afraid to have a poem read?*

[Sexton]: No, not afraid, wanting to be chosen.

[Kumin]: *And he would read your poem, and the class would then discuss it.*

[Sexton]: And he would.

[Kumin]: *And he would.*

[Sexton]: Now we have to go into the fact that as it grew later—well, we used to go out afterwards. John didn't drink.

[Kumin]: *John was a former alcoholic.*

[Sexton]: I don't think I drank myself. I don't think I drank much then, really. I had a beer.

[Kumin]: *But he was really on the wagon. He had been a severe alcoholic. And then after that we broke off from the Boston Center, and we formed our own group.*

[Sexton]: But I didn't.

[Kumin]: *You certainly did. When we broke off?*

[Sexton]: I was seeing Robert Lowell.

[Kumin]: *No, that was much later. That was after John was dead.*

[Sexton]: No, wait a minute. I'm very sorry. I was going, to Robert Lowell's class, and still John's, without you. Begging for the approval that Daddy would never give. Why was I so masochistic?

[Showalter]: *Was John Holmes a difficult person for a woman to work with?*

[Sexton]: John Holmes didn't approve of a thing about me. He hated my poetry. I remember, even after Maxine had left, and I was still with Holmes, there was a new girl who came in. And he kept saying, oh, let us see *new* poems, *new* poems. We need them. And here I was giving him things that were later anthologized forever. I mean, really good poems.

[Smith]: *Didn't Holmes write comic verse as well, himself? And think you should move in the direction of comic verse, Maxine?*

[Sexton]: No, no, she started with comic verse.

[Kumin]: *I had already graduated from comic verse, Carol. I had started by writing light verse; that's how I became a poet. I started writing light verse for the slicks when I got pregnant with Danny, for a year.*

[Sexton]: Maxine, it was two or three years, it was no one year.

[Kumin]: *Wait a minute—he's now twenty-one. So it was twenty-one years ago. And I made a pact with myself that if I didn't sell anything by the time this child was born, I would chuck all my creative discontents. And in about my eighth month I started really landing with little four-liners, there, here and everywhere. Saturday Evening Post and Cosmo-*

politan, *and so on. Then someone told me about John Holmes's class at the Center and in great fear and trembling I went and met Anne. We did that thing at the Center for a year and then we broke off and started a workshop of our own.*

[Sexton]: It was at least two years.

[*Showalter*]: *And who was in the second workshop?*

[*Kumin*]: *It consisted of Sexton, Kumin, George Starbuck, Sam Albert, and John Holmes. And for a little while, Ted Weiss.*

[Sexton]: He was there for a while. And do you remember? the night we laughed so hard we were screaming, over women's girdles? I mean, we were hysterical. Ted Weiss was in Boston, and John wanted to bring him into the class, and he was nice. I'll never forget how we laughed. He just got us all onto women's girdles. I mean, in its own way it is a bit vulgar, and yet to me it isn't really vulgar at all. It's beauty, it's the girdle that's corrupting her. It was funny. But—I have to point this out, and you must too—John found me evil.

[*Kumin*]: *But I think it should also be said, that the reason for John's reaction, we guess, is that his first wife had been mentally ill, and had killed herself.*

[Sexton]: But I was writing about this subject. He kept saying, no no, too personal, or you musn't, or anything. Everything he said about my poems was bad, almost altogether. And yet, from the beginning, from the class, from him, I learned. And from Maxine. I must say Maxine, my best teacher—although for a while I was copying Maxine's flaws. I don't know how, I didn't know they were hers, although now I can see they were someone else's, an inversion here, or a noun. I got over that. I remember, I didn't know her very well. I wrote **"Music Swims Back to Me."** I was playing a record, a 45, and I was leaning over my husband who was building a hi-fi set. I was climbing over him, in the kitchen, because I wrote in the dining room—I didn't really have a place to write, I wrote on a card table—to put on the 45 again. It's necessary to hear that song, because the song was taking me back to the mental institution where it constantly played. It was a very early poem, and I had broken all my ideas of what a poem should be, and I go to Maxine—very formal—we don't know each other very well. We hadn't started writing together yet. And I said, could you—? We sat together in the living room, stiffly on the couch. Sunday. It was a Sunday. And I said, is this a poem? And she said, yes.

[*Kumin*]: *Well, I get points for knowing it. I don't know how I knew it.*

[Sexton]: She knew. She knew. She responded. I had done this crazy thing, written this poem. Always Maxine responded to my poetry. Not John, but Maxine, although in spite of herself. Because it was hard for her.

[*Kumin*]: *Yes, it was hard. Here was my Christian academic daddy saying, stay away from her. She's bad for you.*

[*Showalter*]: *Did he actually say that?*

[Sexton]: He would write letters saying, she's evil. He did, he said, be careful of her.

[*Kumin*]: *Oh, yes, he would write me letters. He was my patron; he got me a job at Tufts.*

[Sexton]: And for me, he was my daddy, but he was the daddy who was saying, you are no good.

[*Kumin*]: *And the fantastic thing is that it did not come between us. Of course, John then died terribly, terribly. He was told that his aches and pains were mental, that he needed a psychiatrist; meanwhile he had throat cancer and it had metastasized. Had totally invaded his chest and shoulders. I remember him talking about a shawl, a cape of pain. And he started drinking again. It was awful, awful.*

[Sexton]: It was awful. I remember calling his wife, Doris, and saying, what is it, what is it? He's not going to *die*, is he? And she said, well, it's funny, it's like psychiatry. What could she say?

[*Smith*]: *Who's that?*

[*Kumin*]: *She was a very good foil for John, because she's very warm, very outgoing, and she supplied a lot of things that John didn't. He was really quite reserved. I thought of him as very New England.*

[Sexton]: I remember one night Sam and me going to John's. It was sleeting out, but we make it. And he's on his way out—and he's so happy we were going out. I think maybe that moment he forgave me a little.

[*Kumin*]: *I was then teaching at Tufts, but we all read at Tufts, in the David Steinman series.*

[Sexton]: I never did. No, he wasn't going to ask *me*.

[*Kumin*]: *We used to go to parties at John's after all those readings—after John Crowe Ransom, and after Robert Frost. Frost said, don't sit there mumbling in the shadows, come up here closer. By then he was very deaf. And I was so awed.*

[*Smith*]: *Was it out of that early relationship that you both began to work together?*

[Sexton]: Yes, because we had to listen.

[Kumin]: *Because we had to listen to John Holmes read the poems—copies were not provided—and then we worked together on the telephone.*

[Sexton]: In our own workshop later we made copies. But then we worked on the phone. And sometimes my kids would be climbing all over me, and I'd say, shh! poem! Maxine! and I'd block my ear, and I could hear it. I could grasp the whole thing, and say change this, change that.

[Showalter]: *Did you see it?*

[Kumin]: *Later. Maybe the following week, if we could get together, if one of us had a sitter.*

[Sexton]: She means did we see it in our minds. No, no, I just knew. I could tell the poem, and I could tell what she wanted to do. We still do it.

[Showalter]: *You don't have to anymore. This was just because you couldn't get out of the house?*

[Sexton]: Yes, because our kids were too small.

[Kumin]: *Yes. We did eventually do this wicked thing. We put in a second line, because our husbands complained that we were always on the phone.*

[Sexton]: We used to talk for two hours sometimes.

[Showalter]: *When was it that you put in the phone? Was it before or after the Radcliffe Institute?*

[Kumin]: *Probably just then, because we both probably felt flush and important.*

[Smith]: *And you would talk about each other's poems, workshop each other's poems?*

[Sexton]: Yes, and also talk about our emotions and our feelings and what the day was like, what was going on.

[Smith]: *When you heard each other's poems, you said before you could enter the consciousness of the other person.*

[Sexton]: Well, you see, we never tried to make the other sound like ourselves. We always saw in the other's voice, I'm sure of it.

[Kumin]: *We started with a recognition for and a respect for that separate identity. I would never meddle with what Anne is doing. I might be able to help her find a more effective way to do what she's doing.*

[Showalter]: *Did you ever find your own writing began to shade into the other person?*

[Kumin]: *No, no, we're different.*

[Sexton]: You can tell we're completely different.

[Showalter]: *Yes, but was there ever a period when there was a struggle?*

[Sexton]: No, there was never a struggle. It was natural, it wasn't hard.

[Kumin]: *It seems to be so normal. It wasn't ever an issue.*

[Sexton]: There was never any struggle. Don't you see—you enter into the voice of the poet, and you think, how to shape, how to make better, but not, how to make like me.

[Kumin]: *I think there is one conviction about the writing of a poem Anne and I share, although we may have come to it by separate routes. We both have very strong feelings about a poem ending definitively. We don't like poems that trail off. Real closure.*

[Sexton]: We both do. Oscar Williams said, anyone can write a poem, but who can end it? It's like slamming the door. And I said, you mean like having sex without orgasm? He didn't like that remark.

[Showalter]: *Do you do this exchanging with your novels as well, Maxine?*

[Kumin]: *Anne reads sections. I ask a lot from her when I write prose, but not as much these days.*

[Showalter]: *Is the poetry workshopping diminishing too? Do you do this less, need this less, than you used to?*

[Sexton]: No, not as long as we're writing.

[Kumin]: *I think the difference is that perhaps this year I haven't been writing as much.*

[Sexton]: I haven't been writing as much either; I've been having an upsetting time.

[Kumin]: *I think the intensity is the same, but the frequency has changed.*

[Sexton]: But just the other day Maxine said, well, that's a therapeutic poem, and I said, for god's sake, forget that. I want to make it a real poem. Then I forced her into helping me make it a real poem, instead of just a kind of therapy for myself. But I remember once a long time ago a poem called **"Cripples and Other Stories."** I showed it to my psychoanalyst—it was half done—and I threw it in the wastebasket. Very unusual because I usually put them away forever.

But this was in the wastebasket. I said, would you by any chance be interested in what's in the wastebasket? And she said, wait a minute, Anne. You could make a real poem out of that. And you know how different that is from Maxine's voice.

[Kumin]: *I happen to really love that poem.*

[Sexton]: Really? I hate it. Although it's good. It reads well. But we're different temperatures, Maxine and I. I have to be warmer. We can't even be in the same room.

[Kumin]: *I'm always taking my clothes off and Anne is putting on coats and sweaters.*

[Sexton]: But you must remember it's not just a poetic relationship. It's been a great bond of friendship, growing, I suppose developing, deeper and deeper. I mean, if one of us is sick, the other is right there. We tell each other everything that's going on. I tell her a dream to remember it, almost. Used to—I haven't been lately. We've both been so busy this year, we've kind of drifted apart, but it's because—

[Smith]: *When you talk about a poem, do you talk about ideas or techniques?*

[Kumin]: *Usually we don't start without a draft.*

[Sexton]: Well—I remember you talking to me about **"Eighteen Days Without You,"** helping me with the plot, the cabin. Although in the end I used none of it.

[Kumin]: *You had started though. You knew the shape.*

[Sexton]: No I didn't. I have the worksheets. First of all you had an apartment in Watertown and then I make it a cabin in Groton. Yet, she's fictionalized, helping me fictionalize the setting for the lovers. She did one thing, I did another. She started me.

[Kumin]: *It's always been this way.*

[Sexton]: Now can I tell this very personal thing, which we can cross out?

[Kumin]: *Probably not, but go ahead.*

[Sexton]: We might just be talking, and I'd say, we're just talking. Why the hell aren't we writing? And we'd get a line, a concept. I'd say, I'll call you back in twenty minutes. It is the most stimulating thing. It's a challenge. We've got this much time, and goddam it, I'm going to have something there. We hang up. In twenty-five minutes I call back. Have you got anything? She sure does. And so have I. It forces us. It's the challenge of it. And with the workshop we had, we always had two poems, sometimes three.

[Kumin]: *There were certain people who need not be mentioned who always went over their allotted time span. My kids, when they would see some activity around the house would say, oh, the poets! now we'll never get any sleep! And they would fight for the privilege of sleeping over the garage, which was at the farthest remove, because the poets were so noisy. The poets came together and fought.*

[Sexton]: We'd scream and yell. Sam Albert said to Anne Hussey: There was no one who fought harder for her words in workshop than Anne Sexton and then went home and changed them. But I would fight—it was like they were taking my babies away from me. Actually I would write down who said what—like Max, no, George, this—and there were certain people I respected more. But Sam could be good at a sort of instinctive thing.

[Kumin]: *Well, we were a good group. George was icily cerebral. George would be sitting there counting the syllabics. But I could point to lines that I changed because of George. We've grown in different directions. We were very open and raw and new then. We were all beginners.*

[Sexton]: I think I had my first book published then. But the one time we didn't speak about writing poems was about John. We didn't workshop, we didn't talk, we were suddenly separate.

[Smith]: *Because your relationships with him were different?*

[Sexton]: Yes, and I suppose our love for him was different.

[Kumin]: *Grief is private.*

[Sexton]: But our grief was never private in any other way. It was just with him, because he loved you, he didn't love me, and it probably made you feel guilty. Anyway, we discussed nothing. She wrote one poem, I wrote another. Mine was called **"Somewhere in Africa."**

[Showalter]: *Has anything that's come out from the women's movement made you see the relationship you have in a different way?*

[Sexton]: You see, when we began, there was no women's movement. We were it.

[Kumin]: *And we didn't know it.*

[Showalter]: *Because the relationship you have, and the relationship of Hallie and Sukey in* The Passions of Uxport *is totally new.*

[Sexton]: I want to say—that is not me in *The Passions of Uxport.*

[Kumin]: *But certainly it takes something from our friendship.*

[Showalter]: *There are very few relationships in books that are like it. Women are generally supposed to destroy each other.*

[Sexton]: I do support Maxine, although I've been a little weaker—

[Kumin]: *Of course you do. When I was writing my first novel, Anne was in Europe on a Prix de Rome. I sent Annie air mail, what? Forty pages? Three chapters. I said, please wherever you are, drop everything, read this, get back in touch with me. I don't know what I'm doing. Am I writing a novel? And Anne read it.*

[Sexton]: I started to cry. I was with Sandy. We had just driven out of Venice and I read the three chapters from *The Dooms of Love*, and I cried. She could do it.

[Kumin]: *I had to do all that without her. I think though that we're always proud of ourselves that we're not dependent on the relationship. We're very autonomous people, but it is a nurturing relationship.*

[Showalter]: *What difference would it have made if there had been a women's movement?*

[Kumin]: *We would have felt a lot less secretive.*

[Sexton]: Yes, we would have felt legitimate.

[Kumin]: *We both have repressed, kept out of the public eye that we did this.*

[Sexton]: I mean, our husbands, we could have thrown it at them.

[Showalter]: *Why did you feel so ashamed of this mutual support?*

[Sexton]: We did. We were ashamed. We had to keep ourselves separate.

[Kumin]: *We were both struggling for identity.*

[Sexton]: Also, it's a secret, we didn't want anyone to know. But I think it's time to acknowledge it.

[Smith]: *The separateness is evident and obvious.*

[Sexton]: You should put that in, because the people who read this might never have read us, and think we're alike. I said to Maxine, write a book called *Up Country*.

[Kumin]: *Yes, you did. You tell yours and I'll tell mine.*

[Sexton]: I said write those country poems. It will be a book. Have it illustrated.

[Showalter]: *By Barbara Swan. That's one of the external things that connects you, one of the few visible signs. Barbara Swan's illustrations for* Up Country, **Transformations, The Death Notebooks, Live or Die.**

[Sexton]: She was at the Radcliffe Institute.

[Kumin]: *We were all there in the same year. Annie wrote the first transformation, and I said, god, that's fantastic. You could do a whole book of these. And Annie said I couldn't possibly. That's the only one, I know it. Of course, by the next day she had written another one. When she was done she said, what can I call it? And I said, call it* **Transformations.**

[Sexton]: Right in the middle I started a novel and you said, put that novel down and finish that book of poems! And thank you.

[Kumin]: *We titled each other's books. I titled* **Transformations**—

[Sexton]: It's a crappy title (*laughing*).

[Kumin]: *I love it.*

[Sexton]: And I named *Up Country.*

[Showalter]: *You said you knew that could be a book. When you write do the poems come separately, or in a rush as a book?*

[Sexton]: She had it in her to write masses of these country poems. I knew it.

[Showalter]: *How do you organize the poems in the books?*

[Sexton]: Well, we look at each other's things and say, do I have a book or do I not have a book? And we say, help me, help me, or this is crap.

[Smith]: *I assume* Up Country *came thematically. In the author's note you have to* **Live or Die,** *you say you're going to publish the poems chronologically. Were you interested in them as biography?*

[Sexton]: No, I just thought it might be vaguely interesting to someone to see what dates they were written. They were all dated in the manuscripts, you see.

[Smith]: *How did they come together as a book?*

[Sexton]: I remember George reading it, and there was no last poem. He said, all you need is a poem saying hello. And I wrote "**Live.**"

[Kumin]: *Funny how we both went back to George. I sent George the manuscript of my third book, and he read through it with a great deal of care.*

[Sexton]: Some of his comments were damn wrong. He said, no one can write about operations but Anne Sexton. How ridiculous. A totally different kind of operation. I encouraged her to write it.

[*Showalter*]: *There were a lot of nineteenth-century women writers who had partnerships like that, and critics tried to make them rivals. Charlotte Brontë once delayed the publication of a novel so it wouldn't come out at the same time as Elizabeth Gaskell's.*

[Sexton]: Of course. We have books coming out at the same time next year.

[*Kumin*]: *We just found out.*

[Sexton]: It's all right. Maxine used to be horrified if we came out in the same year. But we're not compared.

[*Showalter*]: *In a larger sense, now there's a female renaissance in poetry.*

[*Kumin*]: *Thank God. I think the fact that women are coming out of the closet is one of the most positive things that's happened in the century. Maybe the only good thing in a fucked-up world. I see such immense changes in women's perceptions. I grew up in an era when you went to a cocktail party and measured your success by how many men spoke to you. I really identified much more with the male side, but now I have such a feeling of sisterhood. I find that wherever I go, I meet splendid women, and I'd a hell of a lot rather be with them.*

[Sexton]: You know, this is also your analysis.

[*Kumin*]: *Yes, and the fact that I have two grown daughters with full-blown careers, and they have raised my consciousness. It was the work that I did with the analyst that helped me get past my awful difficulties with my own mother.*

[Sexton]: She had no close women friends, but I broke the barrier, because I'm a terrible breaker of barriers.

[*Showalter*]: *Did you have a lot of close women friends?*

[Sexton]: Yes.

[*Showalter*]: *But in your books you have generations of women—the mother, the grandmother, the daughter. There aren't any women friends in it.*

[Sexton]: You do see Max, and lists of names. There are the dedications.

[*Showalter*]: *But then there are the blood relationships that are difficult, love you have to win back.*

[Sexton]: My mother was very destructive. The only person who was very constructive in my life was my great-aunt, and of course she went mad when I was thirteen. It was probably the trauma of my life that I never got over.

[*Showalter*]: *How did she go mad?*

[*Kumin*]: *Read **"Some Foreign Letters."***

[Sexton]: That doesn't help. Do you know **"The Hex"**? **"Anna Who Was Mad"** in **Folly**? Notice the guilt in them. But the hex is a misnomer. I had tachycardia and I thought it was just psychological.

[*Showalter*]: *Were you named for her?*

[Sexton]: Yes, we were namesakes. We had love songs we would sing together. She cuddled me. I was tall, but I tried to cuddle up. My mother never touched me in my life, except to examine me. So I had bad experiences. But I wondered with this that every summer there was Nana, and she would rub my back for hours. My mother said, women don't touch women like that. And I wondered why I didn't become a lesbian. I kissed a boy and Nana went mad. She called me a whore and everything else.

I think I'm dominating this interview.

[*Kumin*]: *You are, Anne.*

[*Showalter*]: *Maxine, in* The Passions of Uxport *you describe the death of a child from leukemia—a death which has haunted me ever since. Do you think it's more difficult for a woman to write about the death of a child?*

[*Kumin*]: *In all my novels there's a death. In* The Abduction *there's a sixteen-year-old who dies in a terrible car crash. Perhaps as a mother I have a fear of a loss of a child.*

[Sexton]: We all know that a child going is the worst suffering.

[*Kumin*]: *Many years ago, my brother lost a child, and I remember this terrible Spartan funeral. That's the funeral in* The Passions of Uxport, *when he says the Hebrew prayer for the dead.*

[Sexton]: Do you remember we were young and going to a place called the New England Poetry Club, the first year we won the prizes, first or second. We were terrified. It was our first reading. Maxine's voice was trembling so, we couldn't hear her.

[*Kumin*]: *I couldn't breathe.*

[Sexton]: I couldn't stand up, I was shaking so. I sat on the table.

[*Kumin*]: *I wonder if there was a trembling in us— the wicked mother, or the wicked witch, or whatever those ladies were to us.*

[Showalter]: *They were all women?*

[Kumin]: *There were a few squashy old men.*

[Sexton]: There were young men too. John was there. Sam was there.

[Showalter]: *Did you have trouble with women writers of another generation? In Louise Bogan's* Letters—*she says about Anne? She doesn't seem to have been able to accept the subjects.*

[Kumin]: *This was the problem with a great many people. Women are not supposed to have uteruses, especially in poems.*

[Sexton]: To me, there's nothing that can't be talked about in art. But I hate the way I'm anthologized in women's lib anthologies. They cull out the "hate men" poems, and leave nothing else. They show only one little aspect of me. Naturally there are times I hate men, who wouldn't? But there are times I love them. The feminists are doing themselves a disservice to show just this.

[Kumin]: *They'll get over that.*

[Sexton]: Yes, but by then, they won't be published. Therefore they've lost their chance.

[Showalter]: *When I anthologized you in my book,* Women's Liberation and Literature, *I chose* "Abortion," "Housewife," *and* "For My Lover on Returning to His Wife." *And I like all those poems very much; I'd choose them again.*

[Sexton]: "For My Lover" is a help. It doesn't cost very much money to get "Housewife"—you can get it cheap. A strange thing—"a woman *is* her mother." That's how it ends. A housecleaner—washing herself down, washing the house. It was about my mother-in-law.

[Showalter]: *A woman is her mother-in-law.*

MAXINE KUMIN (ESSAY DATE 1981)

SOURCE: Kumin, Maxine. "How It Was: Maxine Kumin on Anne Sexton." In *The Complete Poems,* by Anne Sexton, pp. xix-xxxiv. Boston: Houghton Mifflin Company, 1981.

In the following essay, Kumin reminisces about her relationship with Sexton, providing an overview of Sexton's life and career.

Anne Sexton as I remember her on our first meeting in the late winter of 1957, tall, blue-eyed, stunningly slim, her carefully coifed dark hair decorated with flowers, her face skillfully made up, looked every inch the fashion model. And indeed she had briefly modeled for the Hart Agency in Boston. Earrings and bracelets, French perfume, high heels, matching lip and fingernail gloss bedecked her, all intimidating sophistications in the chalk-and-wet-overshoes atmosphere of the Boston Center for Adult Education, where we were enrolled in John Holmes's poetry workshop. Poetry—we were both ambitious beginners—and proximity—we lived in the same suburb—brought us together. As intimate friends and professional allies, we remained intensely committed to one another's writing and well-being to the day of her death in the fall of 1974.

The facts of Anne Sexton's troubled and chaotic life are well known; no other American poet in our time has cried aloud publicly so many private details. While the frankness of these revelations attracted many readers, especially women, who identified strongly with the female aspect of the poems, a number of poets and critics—for the most part, although not exclusively, male—took offense. For Louis Simpson, writing in *Harper's Magazine,* "Menstruation at Forty" was "the straw that broke this camel's back." And years before he wrote his best-selling novel, *Deliverance,* which centers on a graphic scene of homosexual rape, James Dickey, writing in the *New York Times Book Review,* excoriated the poems in All My Pretty Ones, saying "It would be hard to find a writer who dwells more insistently on the pathetic and disgusting aspects of bodily experience . . ." In a terse eulogy Robert Lowell declared, with considerable ambivalence it would seem, "For a book or two, she grew more powerful. Then writing was too easy or too hard for her. She became meager and exaggerated. Many of her most embarrassing poems would have been fascinating if someone had put them in quotes, as the presentation of some character, not the author." Sexton's work rapidly became a point of contention over which opposing factions dueled in print, at literary gatherings, and in the fastnesses of the college classroom.

And yet the ground for Sexton's confessional poems had been well prepared. In 1956, Allen Ginsberg's *Howl* had declaimed:

> I saw the best minds of my generation destroyed
> by madness,
> starving hysterical naked
>
> . . . . .
>
> . . . on
> the granite steps of
> the madhouse with shaven heads and
> harlequin speech of
> suicide, demanding instantaneous
> lobotomy,
> and who were given instead the concrete void
> of insulin metrasol

electricity hydrotherapy psychotherapy oc-
cupational therapy
    pingpong & amnesia . . .

At the time Sexton began to work in the confessional mode, W. D. Snodgrass had already published his prize-winning collection, *Heart's Needle,* which included details of his divorce and custody struggle. Sylvia Plath and Robert Lowell were hammering out their own autobiographical accounts of alienation, despair, anomie, and madness. John Berryman, deceiving no one, charmingly protested in a prefatory note that the Henry of *The Dream Songs* "is essentially about an imaginary character (not the poet, not me) . . . who has suffered an irreversible loss and talks about himself sometimes in the first person, sometimes in the third, sometimes even in the second . . ." The use of *le moi* was being cultivated in fashionable literary journals everywhere. It seems curious that the major and by far most vitriolic expressions of outrage were reserved for Sexton.

Someone once said that we have art in order not to die of the truth, a dictum we might neatly apply to Sexton's perspectives. To Hayden Carruth, the poems "raise the never-solved problem of what literature really is, where you draw the line between art and documentary."

While Louise Bogan and Joyce Carol Oates for the most part appraise Sexton favorably, Mona Van Duyn finds Sexton's "delineation of femaleness so fanatical that it makes one wonder, even after many years of being one, what a woman is . . ." Muriel Rukeyser, who sees the issue as "survival, piece by piece of the body, step by step of poetic experience, and even more the life entire . . . ," finds much to praise, for instance singling out **"In Celebration of My Uterus"** as "one of the few poems in which a woman has come to the fact as symbol, the center after many years of silence and taboo."

Over and over in the critical literature dealing with the body of Sexton's work, we find these diametrical oppositions. The intimate details divulged in Sexton's poetry enchanted or repelled with equal passion. In addition to the strong feelings Anne's work aroused, there was the undeniable fact of her physical beauty. Her presence on the platform dazzled with its staginess, its props of water glass, cigarettes, and ashtray. She used pregnant pauses, husky whispers, pseudoshouts to calculated effect. A Sexton audience might hiss its displeasure or deliver a standing ovation. It did not doze off during a reading.

Anne basked in the attention she attracted, partly because it was antithetical to an earlier generation's view of the woman writer as "poetess," and partly because she was flattered by and enjoyed the adoration of her public. But behind the glamorously garbed woman lurked a terrified and homely child, cowed from the cradle onward, it seemed, by the indifference and cruelties of her world. Her parents, she was convinced, had not wanted her to be born. Her sisters, she alleged, competed against and won out over her. Her teachers, unable to rouse the slumbering intelligence from its hiding place, treated her with impatience and anger. Anne's counterphobic response to rejection and admonishment was always to defy, dare, press, contravene. Thus the frightened little girl became a flamboyant and provocative woman; the timid child who skulked in closets burst forth as an exhibitionist declaiming with her own rock group; the intensely private individual bared her liver to the eagle in public readings where almost invariably there was standing room only.

Born Anne Gray Harvey in 1928, she attended public school in Wellesley, Massachusetts, spent two years at Rogers Hall preparatory school, and then one year at Garland Junior College in Boston. A few months shy of her twentieth birthday, she eloped with Alfred Muller Sexton II (nicknamed Kayo), enrolled in a Hart Agency modeling course, and lived briefly in Baltimore and San Francisco while her husband served in the Navy. In 1953, she returned to Massachusetts, where Linda Gray Sexton was born.

The first breakdown, diagnosed as postpartum depression, occurred in 1954, the same year her beloved great-aunt Anna Ladd Dingley, the Nana of the poems, died. She took refuge in Westwood Lodge, a private neuropsychiatric hospital that was frequently to serve as her sanctuary when the voices that urged her to die reached an insistent pitch. Its director, Dr. Martha Brunner-Orne, figured in Anne's life as a benevolent but disciplinary mother, who would not permit this troubled daughter to kill herself.

Nevertheless, seven months after her second child, Joyce Ladd Sexton, was born in 1955, Anne suffered a second crisis and was hospitalized. The children were sent to live with her husband's parents; and while they were separated from her, she attempted suicide on her birthday, November 9, 1956. This was the first of several episodes, or at least the first that was openly acknowledged. Frequently, these attempts occurred around Anne's birthday, a time of year she came increasingly to dread. Dr. Martin Orne, Brunner-Orne's son, was the young psychiatrist at Glenside Hospital who attended Anne during this siege and treated her for the next seven years. After administering a series of diagnostic tests, he presented his patient with her scores, objective evidence that, despite the disapproving naysayers from her past, she was highly intelligent. Her associative gifts suggested that she ought to return to the writing of poetry, something she had shown a deft talent for during secondary school. It was at Orne's insistence that Anne enrolled in the Holmes workshop.

"You, Dr. Martin" came directly out of that experience, as did so many of the poems in her first collection, *To Bedlam and Part Way Back.* On a snowy Sunday afternoon early in 1957, she drove to my house to ask me to look at "something." Did she dare present it in class? Could it be called a poem? It was "Music Swims Back to Me," her first breakaway from adolescent lyrics in rhyming iambic pentameter.

Years later, when it seemed to her that all else in her life had failed—marriage, the succor of children, the grace of friendship, the promised land to which psychotherapy held the key—she turned to God, with a kind of stubborn absolutism that was missing from the Protestantism of her inheritance. The God she wanted was a sure thing, an Old Testament avenger admonishing his Chosen People, an authoritarian yet forgiving Father decked out in sacrament and ceremony. An elderly, sympathetic priest she called on—"accosted" might be a better word—patiently explained that he could not make her a Catholic by fiat, nor could he administer the sacrament (the last rites) she longed for. But in his native wisdom he said a saving thing to her, said the magic and simple words that kept her alive at least a year beyond her time and made *The Awful Rowing Toward God* a possibility. "God is in your typewriter," he told her.

I cite these two examples to indicate the influence that figures of authority had over Anne's life in the most elemental sense; first the psychiatrist and then the priest put an imprimatur on poetry as salvation, as a worthy goal in itself. I am convinced that poetry kept Anne alive for the eighteen years of her creative endeavors. When everything else soured; when a succession of therapists deserted her for whatever good, poor, or personal reasons; when intimates lost interest or could not fulfill all the roles they were asked to play; when a series of catastrophes and physical illnesses assaulted her, the making of poems remained her one constant. To use her own metaphor, "out of used furniture [she made] a tree." Without this rich, rescuing obsession I feel certain she would have succeeded in committing suicide in response to one of the dozen impulses that beset her during the period between 1957 and 1974.

Sexton's progress in Holmes's workshop in 1957 was meteoric. In short order her poems were accepted for publication in *The New Yorker, Harper's Magazine,* and the *Saturday Review.* Sam Albert was in that class, and Ruth Soter, the friend to whom "With Mercy for the Greedy" is dedicated. Through Holmes, we met George Starbuck at the New England Poetry Club. A year later, five of us joined together to form a workshop of our own—an arrangement that lasted until Holmes's untimely death from cancer in 1962. During this period, all of us wrote and revised prolifically, competitively, as if all the wolves of the world were at our backs. Our sessions were jagged, intense, often angry, but also loving. As Holmes's letters from this period make abundantly clear, he decried the confessional direction Anne's poems were taking, while at the same time acknowledging her talent. Her compulsion to deal with such then-taboo material as suicide, madness, and abortion assaulted his sensibilities and triggered his own defenses. Convinced that the relationship would harm my own work, he warned me to resist becoming involved with Anne. It was the only advice he gave me that I rejected, and at some psychic cost. Anne and I both regarded Holmes as an academic father. In desperate rebuttal, Anne wrote "For John, Who Begs Me Not to Enquire Further." A hesitant, sensitive exploration of their differences, the poem seeks to make peace between them.

Virtually every poem in the *Bedlam* book came under scrutiny during this period, as did many of the poems in *All My Pretty Ones.* There was no more determined reviser than Sexton, who would willingly push a poem through twenty or more drafts. She had an unparalleled tenacity in those early days and only abandoned a "failed" poem with regret, if not downright anger, after dozens of attempts to make it come right. It was awesome the way she could arrive at our bimonthly sessions with three, four, even five new and complicated poems. She was never meek about it, but she did listen, and she did respect the counsel of others. She gave generous help to her colleagues, and she required, demanded, insisted on generous response.

As a result of this experience, Anne came to believe in the value of the workshop. She loved growing in this way, and she urged the method on her students at Boston University, Colgate, Oberlin, and in other workshops she conducted from time to time.

During the workshop years, we began to communicate more and more frequently by telephone. Since there were no message units involved in the basic monthly phone-company fee—the figure I remember is seven dollars—we had a second phone line installed in our suburban homes so that we could talk at will. For years we conducted our own mini-workshops by phone, a working method that does much to train the ear to hear line breaks, internal rhymes, intentional or unwanted musical devices, and so forth. We did this so comfortably and over such an extended period of time that indeed when we met we were somewhat shy of each other's poems as they appeared on the page. I can remember often saying "Oh, so *that's* what it looks like," of a poem I had heard and visualized through half-a-dozen revisions.

Over the years, Anne's lines shortened, her line breaks became, I think, more unpredictable, and her imagery grew increasingly surreal. Initially, however, she worked quite strictly in traditional forms, believing in the value of their rigor as a forcing agent, believing that the hardest truths would come to light if they were made to fit a stanzaic pattern, a rhyme scheme, a prevailing meter. She strove to use rhyme unexpectedly but always aptly. Even the most unusual rhyme, she felt, must never obtrude on the sense of the line, nor must the normal word order, the easy tone of vernacular speech, be wrenched solely to save a rhyme.

The impetus for creation usually came when Anne directly invoked the muse at her desk. Here, she read favorite poems of other poets—most frequently Neruda—and played certain evocative records over and over. One I remember for its throaty string section was Respighi's "Pines of Rome." Music acted in some way to free her to create, and she often turned the volume up loud enough to drown out all other sounds.

But for all the sought-after and hard-won poems Anne wrote—in this connection, I recall the arduous struggle to complete "**The Operation**," "**All My Pretty Ones**," "**Flee on Your Donkey**"—a number were almost totally "given" ones. "**Riding the Elevator into the Sky**," in *The Awful Rowing*, is an example. The newspaper article referred to in the opening stanza suggested the poem; the poem itself came quite cleanly and easily, as if written out in the air beforehand and then transcribed onto the page with very few alter-

ations. Similarly arrived at, "**Letter Written on a Ferry While Crossing Long Island Sound**" began at the instant Anne sighted the nuns on an actual crossing. The poem was written much as it now appears on the page, except for minor skirmishes required to effect the closure in each stanza. "**Young**" and "**I Remember**" were also achieved almost without effort. But because Anne wanted to open *All My Pretty Ones* with a terse elegy for her parents, one shorn of all autobiographical detail, "**The Truth the Dead Know**" went through innumerable revisions before arriving at its final form, an *a b a b* rhyme scheme that allows little room for pyrotechnics.

For a time, it seemed that psychiatrists all over the country were referring their patients to Anne's work, as if it could provide the balm in Gilead for every troubled person. Even though it comforted and nurtured her to know that her poems reached beyond the usual sphere of belles lettres, she felt considerable ambivalence about her subject matter. Accused of exhibitionism, she was determined only to be more flamboyant; nevertheless, the strict Puritan hiding inside her suffered and grieved over the label of "confessional poet." For instance, when she wrote "**Cripples and Other Stories**" (in *Live or Die*), a poem that almost totally "occurred" on the page in an hour's time, she crumpled it up and tossed it into the wastebasket as if in embarrassment. Together we fished it out and saved it, working to make the tone more consistent and to smooth out some of the rhythmically crude spots. Into this sort of mechanical task Anne always flung herself gladly.

The results were often doubly effective. I remember, for instance, how in "**The Operation**" she worked to achieve through rhyme and the shaping of the poem's three parts a direct rendition of the actual experience. The retardation of rhyming sounds in those short, rather sharply end-stopped lines, in the first section, for example (*leaf, straw, lawn: car, thief, house, upon*), add to the force of metaphor in the poem—the "historic thief," the "Humpty-Dumpty," and so on. Or, to take another poem, "**Faustus and I**," in *The Death Notebooks,* was headed for the discard pile. It was a free-verse poem at the outset and had what seemed to me a malevolently flippant tone. Often when stymied for a more articulate response to one of her poems I disliked, I suggested, "Why don't you pound it into form?" And often the experiment worked. In the case of the Faustus poem, the suggestion was useful because the rhyme scheme gave the subject a dignity it demanded and because the repetitive "pounding" elicited a level of language, of metaphor, that Anne had not quite reached in the earlier version.

Sexton had an almost mystical faith in the "found" word image, as well as in metaphor by mistake, by typo, or by misapprehension. She would fight hard to keep an image, a line, a word usage, but if I was just as dogged in my conviction that the line didn't work, was sentimental or mawkish, that the word was ill-suited or the image trite, she would capitulate—unless she was totally convinced of her own rightness. Then there was no shaking her. Trusting each other's critical sense, we learned not to go past the unshakable core, not to trespass on style or voice.

Untrammeled by a traditional education in Donne, Milton, Yeats, Eliot, and Pound, Anne was able to strike out alone, like Conrad's secret sharer, for a new destiny. She was grim about her lost years, her lack of a college degree; she read omnivorously and quite innocently whatever came to hand and enticed her, forming her own independent, quirky, and incisive judgments.

Searching for solutions to the depressive episodes that beset her with dismaying periodicity, Anne read widely in the popular psychiatric texts of the time: interpretations of Freud, Theodore Reik, Philip Rieff, Helena Deutsch, Erik Erikson, Bruno Bettelheim. During a summer-school course with Philip Rahv, she encountered the works of Dostoevski, Kafka, and Thomas Mann. These were succeeded by the novels of Saul Bellow, Philip Roth, and Kurt Vonnegut. But above all else, she was attracted to the fairy tales of Andersen and Grimm, which her beloved Nana had read to her when she was a child. They were for her, perhaps, what Bible stories and Greek myths had been for other writers. At the same time that she was being entertained and drawn into closer contact with a kind of collective unconscious, she was searching the fairy tales for psychological parallels. Quite unaware at first of the direction she was taking, she composed the first few "transformations" that comprise the book of that name. The book evolved very much at my urging, and gathered momentum as it grew. It struck me that Anne's poems based on fairy tales went one step further than contemporary poets' translations from languages they did not themselves read but apprehended through a third party. Their poems were *adaptations;* hers were *transformations.*

Thematically, Anne's concern in *Transformations* was a logical extension of the material she dealt with in the confessional genre, but this time with a society-mocking overlay. Her attention focuses on women cast in a variety of fictive roles: the dutiful princess daughter, the wicked witch, the stepmother. We see the same family constellations in a fairy-tale setting, ranging from the Oedipal explorations of **"The Frog Prince"** to the stage-set adultery of **"The Little Peasant."** The poems are replete with anachronisms from pop culture: the Queen in **"Rumpelstiltskin"** is "as persistent / as a Jehovah's witness"; Snow White "opened her eyes as wide as Orphan Annie"; and Cinderella in her sooty rags looks like Al Jolson. Moreover, the conventional happily-ever-after endings receive their share of sardonic jibes. Cinderella and her prince end up as "Regular Bobbsey Twins. / That story." And the princess and her husband in **"The White Snake"** are condemned by way of a happy ending to "a kind of coffin, / a kind of blue funk."

Despite Houghton Mifflin's initial misgivings about publishing it, *Transformations* was widely acclaimed for its balance between the confessional and the fable. It was a new lode to mine. I hoped that by encouraging Anne to continue to look outside her own psyche for material, she might develop new enthusiasms to match the one she felt for the brothers Grimm.

And indeed her impulse to work in fable continued in *The Book of Folly,* where, in addition to three prose inventions, Sexton created the sequence of poems she called **"The Jesus Papers."** These are more searching, more daring than the early Jesus poems (**"In the Deep Museum,"** **"For God While Sleeping,"** **"With Mercy for the Greedy"**) from *All My Pretty Ones,* in which it seemed to be the cruelty of the crucifixion itself that fascinated her. Now we have a different voice and a different Jesus, however humanized, however modernized—a Jesus who still suffers knowingly in order to endure.

Jesus, Mary, angels as good as the good fairy, and a personal, fatherly God to love and forgive her, figure ever more prominently in the late poems. Always Sexton explores relentlessly the eternal themes that obsess her: love, loss, madness, the nature of the father-daughter compact, and death—the Death Baby we carry with us from the moment of birth. In my view, the sequence entitled **"The Death of the Fathers,"** a stunning investigation of these latter two themes, is the most successful part of *The Book of Folly.* It would be simplistic to suggest that the Oedipal theme overrides all other considerations in Sexton's work, but a good case might be made for viewing her poems in terms of their quest for a male authority figure to love and trust. Yeats once said that "one poem lights up another," and in Sexton's poetry the reader can find the poet again and again identifying herself through her relationship with the male Other, whether in the person of a lover or—in the last, hasty, and often brilliant poems in *The Awful Rowing,* which make a final effort to land on "the island called God"—in the person of the patriarchal final arbiter.

The poems in *Transformations* mark the beginning of a shift in Sexton's work, from the intensely confessional to what Estella Lauter, in a fascinating essay, "Anne Sexton's 'Radical Discontent with the Order of Things,'" has termed the "transpersonal." In retrospect, it seems to me that the broad acceptance *Transformations* eventually earned in the marketplace (after hesitant beginnings) reinforced Sexton's deeply rooted conviction that poems not only could, but had to be, made out of the detritus of her life. Her work took on a new imaginative boldness. She experimented with a variety of persona/poems, particularly involving God figures, revisited the crucifixion stories, reworked the creation myth and ancient psalms, and even planned a book-length bestiary, which was only partially realized. Her perception of her place in the canon of American letters was enhanced, too, by the success of *Transformations.* Inscribing a copy of *The Book of Folly* for me in 1972, she wrote: "Dear Max—From now on it's OUR world."

She began to speak of herself as Ms. Dog, an appellation that is ironic in two contexts. We were both increasingly aware of the Women's Movement. To shuck the earlier designations of Miss and Mrs. was only a token signal of where we stood, but a signal nonetheless. Dog, of course, is God in reverse. The fact that the word worked both ways delighted Sexton much as her favorite palindrome, "rats live on no evil star," did. There was a wonderful impudence in naming herself a kind of liberated female deity, one who is "out fighting the dollars."

In the collections that followed *Transformations,* images of God proliferate, crossing all boundaries between man and woman, human and animal; between inner and outer histories of behavior. It was slippery material, difficult to control. Not all the poems Anne arrived at in this pursuit of self-definition and salvation succeed; of this she was well aware. Whenever it came down to a question of what to include, or what to drop from a forthcoming collection, Anne agonized at length. It was our practice over the years to sit quietly with each other on the occasion of the ar-ranging of a book, sorting through groups of poems, trying out a variety of formats, voting on which poems to save and which to discard. In a kind of despondency of the moment, suffering the bitter foretaste of reviews to come, Anne frequently wanted to jettison half the book. But I suspect this was a way she had of taking the sting out of the selection process, secure in the knowledge that she and I would always rescue each other's better poems; even, for the right reasons, rescue those flawed ones that were important psychically or developmentally. We took comfort from Yeats's "lighting-up," allowing the poems to gain meaning and perspective from one another.

When Anne was writing *The Awful Rowing* at white heat in January and February of 1973, and the poems were coming at the rate of two, three, even four a day, the awesome pace terrified me. I was poet-in-residence at Centre College in Danville, Kentucky; we had agreed in advance to split the phone bill. Fearing a manic break, I did everything I could to retard the process, long-distance, during our daily hour-long calls. The Sexton who had so defiantly boasted, in her Ms. Dog phase, "I am God la de dah," had now given way to a ravaged, obsessed poet fighting to put the jigsaw pieces of the puzzle together into a coherence that would save her—into "a whole nation of God." Estella Lauter states that "her vision of Him as the winner in a crooked poker game at the end of that book is a sporting admission of her defeat rather than a decisive renewal of the Christian myth." On one level, I agree. But on another, even more primitive level, God the poker-player was the one living and constant Daddy left to Sexton out of the "Death of the Fathers." Of course he held the crooked, winning hand.

Though the reviewers were not always kind to Anne's work, honors and awards mounted piggyback on one another almost from the moment of the publication in 1960 of her first book, *To Bedlam and Part Way Back.* The American Academy of Letters Traveling Fellowship in 1963, which she was awarded shortly after *All My Pretty Ones* was published and nominated for the National Book Award, was followed by a Ford Foundation grant as resident playwright at the Charles Playhouse in Boston. In 1965, Anne Sexton was elected a Fellow of the Royal Society of Literature in Great Britain. *Live or Die* won the Pulitzer Prize in poetry in 1967. She was named Phi Beta Kappa poet at Harvard in 1968 and accorded a number of honorary doctoral degrees.

Twice in the 1960s, and twice more in the 1970s, Anne and I collaborated to write books for children. *Eggs of Things* and *More Eggs of Things* were constructed within the constraints of a limited vocabulary. *Joey and the Birthday Present* and *The Wizard's Tears* were more fanciful excursions into the realm of talking animals and magical spells. Our work sessions were lighthearted, even casual. We took turns sitting at the typewriter; whoever typed had the privilege of recording or censoring the dialogue or description as it occurred to us. Three or four afternoon workouts sufficed for a book. We were full of generous praise for each other's contributions to the story line and to the exchanges of conversation. It was usually summer. We drank a lot of iced tea and squabbled amiably about how to turn the *Wizard*'s townspeople into frogs, or about which of us actually first spoke the key line in *Joey*: "And they both agreed a birthday present cannot run away." Sometimes we explored plans for future collaborations. We would do a new collection of animal fables, modeled on Aesop. We would fish out the rejected sequel to *More Eggs*, entitled *Cowboy and Pest and the Runaway Goat*, and refurbish it for another publisher. Sexton enthusiastically entertained these notions, as did I. Working together on children's books when our own children were the age of our projected readership kept us in good rapport with each other's offspring. It provided a welcome breathing space in which nothing mattered but the sheer verbal play involved in developing the story. Indeed, we regressed cheerfully to whatever age level the text required, and lost ourselves in the confabulation.

But between the publication of new books and the bestowal of honors fell all too frequently the shadow of mental illness. One psychiatrist left. His successor at first succumbed to Sexton's charm, then terminated his treatment of her. She promptly fell downstairs and broke her hip—on her birthday. With the next doctor, her hostility grew. Intermediary psychiatrists and psychologists came and went. There seemed to be no standard for dealing with this gifted, ghosted woman. On Thorazine, she gained weight, became intensely sun-sensitive, and complained that she was so overwhelmed with lassitude that she could not write. Without medication, the voices returned. As she grew increasingly dependent on alcohol, sedatives, and sleeping pills, her depressive bouts grew more frequent. Convinced that her marriage was beyond salvage, she demanded and won a divorce, only to learn that living alone created an unbearable level of anxiety. She returned to West-

ABOUT THE AUTHOR

DIANE MIDDLEBROOK COMMENTS ON SEXTON'S LIFE
At the time Anne Sexton wrote *The Awful Rowing toward God*, she was preparing to leave her marriage of twenty-five years. Her husband, Kayo, a wool salesman whose hobbies were hunting and fishing, had never taken much interest in poetry or poets. Both daughters—Joy now age 18, Linda 20—had left the family home for boarding school and college. Like many couples of their era, Anne and Kayo found that the departure of their children opened a void across which they measured how little else they had in common. Moreover, career success had given Anne Sexton the confidence and financial security to make divorce a viable option.

Middlebrook, Diane. "Anne Sexton: The Making of *The Awful Rowing Toward God*," in *Rossetti to Sexton: Six Women Poets at Texas,* edited by Dave Oliphant, pp. 223-35. Austin: University of Texas at Austin, 1992.

wood Lodge, later spent time at McLean's Hospital in Belmont, Massachusetts, and finally went to the Human Resources Institute in Brookline, Massachusetts. But none of these interludes stemmed her downward course. In the spring of 1974, she took an overdose of sleeping pills and later remonstrated bitterly with me for aborting this suicide attempt. On that occasion she vowed that when she next undertook to die, she would telegraph her intent to no one. A little more than six months later, this indeed proved to be the case.

It seems presumptuous, only seven years after her death, to talk about Anne Sexton's place in the history of poetry. We must first acknowledge the appearance in the twentieth century of women writing poetry that confronts the issues of gender, social role, and female life and lives viewed subjectively from the female perspective. The earlier world view of the poet as "the masculine chief of state in charge of dispensing universal spiritual truths" (Diane Middlebrook, *The World Into Words*) has eroded since World War II, as have earlier notions about the existence of universal truths themselves. Freed by that cataclysm from their clichéd roles as goddesses of hearth and bedroom, women began to write openly out of their own experiences. Before there was a Women's Movement, the underground river was already flowing, carrying such diverse cargoes as the poems of Bogan, Levertov, Rukeyser, Swenson, Plath, Rich, and Sexton. [I have omitted from this list Elizabeth Bishop, who chose not to have her work included in anthologies of women poets.]

The stuff of Anne's life, mercilessly dissected, is here in the poems. Of all the confessional poets, none has had quite Sexton's "courage to make a clean breast of it." Nor has any displayed quite her brilliance, her verve, her headlong metaphoric leaps. As with any body of work, some of the later poems display only ragged, intermittent control, as compared to **"The Double Image," "The Operation,"** and **"Some Foreign Letters,"** to choose three arbitrary examples. The later work takes more chances, crosses more boundaries between the rational and the surreal; and time after time it evokes in the reader that sought-after shiver of recognition.

Women poets in particular owe a debt to Anne Sexton, who broke new ground, shattered taboos, and endured a barrage of attacks along the way because of the flamboyance of her subject matter, which, twenty years later, seems far less daring. She wrote openly about menstruation, abortion, masturbation, incest, adultery, and drug addiction at a time when the proprieties embraced none of these as proper topics for poetry. Today, the remonstrances seem almost quaint. Anne delineated the problematic position of women—the neurotic reality of the time—though she was not able to cope in her own life with the personal trouble it created. If it is true that she attracted the worshipful attention of a cult group pruriently interested in her suicidal impulses, her psychotic breakdowns, her frequent hospitalizations, it must equally be acknowledged that her very frankness succored many who clung to her poems as to the Holy Grail. Time will sort out the dross among these poems and burnish the gold. Anne Sexton has earned her place in the canon.

DIANE MIDDLEBROOK (ESSAY DATE WINTER 1984)

SOURCE: Middlebrook, Diane. "Becoming Anne Sexton." *Denver Quarterly* 18, no. 4 (winter 1984): 23-34.

In the following essay, Middlebrook explores the significance of Sexton's first attempted suicide with respect to the direction of her literary career and her roles as mother, daughter, and writer.

Anne Gray Harvey became Mrs. Alfred Muller Sexton II on August 16, 1948, after eloping from the family home in Weston, Massachusetts, to be married before a justice of the peace in North Carolina. She was nineteen years old. According to her, an action equally precipitous and defiant changed her identity nine years later into Anne Sexton, poet. On her twenty-eighth birthday in 1956 she attempted suicide. A month later she began writing poetry; two and a half years later her first book was published with the title, *To Bedlam and Part Way Back* (1960). "It was," she said, "a kind of rebirth at twenty-nine."[1]

A large collection of manuscripts and correspondence makes it possible to reconstruct the years 1956-1960 in enough detail to conclude that while Anne Sexton's professional development was both rapid and improbable, her success, like that of most writers, resulted from a combination of talent, hard work and well-timed good luck. But Sexton always claimed that her career as a poet had the shape of a story; and that it opened not with the event of writing her first poem, but with the suicide attempt that separated her from a former life. In the following pages I want to explore the ways in which her emphasis on suicide expresses an ambivalence Sexton learned from her mother, a writer's daughter, regarding the roles of mother, daughter, and writer.

Sexton began telling, in print, the story of how she became a writer after she was well on the way to being famous, in "craft interviews" published mainly in literary journals between 1965 and 1976[2]. In each, Sexton found an occasion to remind the questioner that poetic truth is not "just factual." A preference for poetic truth seems to have determined the selection of details she provides about her beginnings as a poet. Particularly artful is the lengthy interview that appeared in *Paris Review* shortly after Sexton received the Pulitzer Prize for Poetry in 1967. In four paragraphs she discloses much of what she ever had to say about the origins of her vocation.

> Until I was twenty-eight I had a kind of buried self who didn't know she could do anything but make white sauce and diaper babies. I didn't know I had any creative depths. I was a victim of the American Dream, the bourgeois, middle-class dream. All I wanted was a little piece of life, to be married, to have children. I thought the nightmares, the visions, the demons would go away if there was enough love to put them down. I was trying my damnedest to lead a conventional life, for that was how I was brought up, and it was what my husband wanted of me. But one can't

build little white picket fences to keep nightmares out. The surface cracked when I was about twenty-eight. I had a psychotic break and tried to kill myself.

She began writing as a form of therapy, Sexton told the interviewers:

> I said to my doctor at the beginning, "I'm no good; I can't do anything; I'm dumb." He suggested I try educating myself by listening to Boston's educational TV station. He said I had a perfectly good mind. [. . .] One night I saw I. A. Richards on educational television reading a sonnet and explaining its form. I thought to myself, I could do that, maybe; I could try. So I sat down and wrote a sonnet. The next day I wrote another one, and so forth. My doctor encouraged me to write more. "Don't kill yourself," he said. "Your poems might mean something to someone else someday." That gave me a feeling of purpose, a little cause, something to *do* with my life, no matter how rotten I was. [. . .]
>
> After I'd been writing about three months, I dared to go into the poetry class at the Boston Center for Adult Education taught by John Holmes. I started in the middle of the term, very shy, writing very bad poems, solemnly handing them in for eighteen others in the class to hear. The most important aspect of the class was that I felt I belonged somewhere. When I first got sick and became a displaced person, I thought I was quite alone, but when I went into the mental hospital, I found I wasn't, that there were other people like me. It made me feel better—more real, sane. I felt, "These are my people." Well, at the John Holmes workshop that I attended for two years, I found I belonged to the poets, that I was *real* there, and I had another, "These are my people."

Asked whether she had never tried her hand at poetry before age twenty-eight, Sexton acknowledged writing little beside light verse for family occasions.

> I wrote some serious stuff in high school; however, I hadn't been exposed to any of the major poets, not even the minor ones. [. . .] I read nothing but Sara Teasdale. I might have read other poets but my mother said as I graduated from high school that I had plagiarized Sara Teasdale. I had been writing a poem a day for three months, but when she said that, I stopped.[3]

From a factual point of view, this account of her development is incomplete and inexact: Sexton condenses the time periods and exaggerates the severity of the mental breakdown. But the narrative or storytelling truth is substantial. Suddenly, in 1956, through a cracked surface a buried self emerged and began looking for something to do. Like many of the housewives Betty Friedan was interviewing for her book *The Feminine Mystique*,[4] Sexton experienced the home as a sphere of confinement and stultification. Her usage three times in two paragraphs indicates that for her the verb *do* meant action in a social realm other than the family. Among both mental patients and poets she found she felt "more real, sane"; and it was within the realm of psychotherapy that she discovered and began to develop her talents. In the hospital she learned with infinite relief that as a mad housewife she was not merely the selfish monster she knew herself to be at home. She discovered that she belonged to a social category with its own language, its own system of symbol-making. Melville said of Ishmael in *Moby Dick* that a whaling ship was his Harvard College and his Yale. So too for Anne Sexton were Westwood Lodge and the Boston Center for Adult Education. In these institutions she began to grasp both madness and metaphor as symbol systems, and to cultivate an understanding of them as ways of exploring and expressing her existence.

Sexton amplifies this arresting association between mental hospital and poetry class in both a letter and an early poem, **"For John, Who Begs Me Not to Enquire Further."** Addressed to her teacher at the Boston Center, the poem tells him that an asylum was the site of her first real education.

> in that narrow diary of my mind,
> in the commonplaces of the asylum
> [. . .] the cracked mirror
> or my own selfish death
> outstared me.
>   [. . .]
>
> And if you turn away
> because there is no lesson here
> I will hold my awkward bowl
> with all its cracked stars shining
> like a complicated lie.
>   [. . .]
>
> This is something I would never find
> in a lovelier place, my dear,
> although your fear is anyone's fear,
> like an invisible veil between us all . . .
> and sometimes in private,
> my kitchen, your kitchen,
> my face, your face.[5]

In the poem **"For John,"** the reference to a cracking surface she uses in the interview appears as a metaphor for a kind of writing and a kind of speech. Her mind itself is a diary; the commonplaces of the asylum, a field of meanings she has learned to interpret in therapy and in the study of poetry. The poem is about the discovery of signs. Two years before her suicide attempt in 1956, Sexton had begun consulting a doctor in order to deal with recurring depression. Among other forms of treatment she undertook psychotherapy—sometimes called the "talking cure": the process of verbalizing or free association in which the psyche is coaxed to disclose its private symbolisms. The "buried self" thus uncovered is a linguistic self whose associations and metaphors are, in theory, keys to the origins of the illness.

Listening to the primitive speech of the buried self in herself and other mental patients, Sexton discovered what she later called "language," the convention-exploding imposition of new meanings on clusters of words produced by urgent personal associations. "It is hard to define," she wrote a friend.

> When I was first sick I was thrilled [. . .] to get into the Nut House. At first, of course, I was just scared and crying and very quiet (who me!) but then I found this girl (very crazy of course) (like me I guess) who talked language. What a relief! I mean, well . . . someone! And then later, a while later, and quite a while I found out that [her psychiatrist] talked language [. . .] I don't know who else does. I don't use it with everyone. No one of my whole street, suburb neighbors.[6]

In the interview, Sexton positions the proto-poet beneath what can be observed on the surface: "I didn't know I had any creative depths." The surface was a mirror reflecting back to parents and husband "the American dream" girl. Not appropriate for exposure were other dreams: nightmares, visions, demons; when the mirror "cracked," these were released for speculation in therapy and poetry. Sexton referred to the releasing event as a "psychotic break." She was of course aware that "psychotic" had a specific meaning in psychiatry that did not apply to her case. By 1968 a variety of diagnostic labels had been attached to Sexton's ongoing mental illness—"hysteric," "psychoneurotic," "borderline," and "alcoholic"—but "psychotic" was not among them.[7] For the purposes of the interview, however, the term implied a significant poetic lineage. It connected her not only to such luminous contemporaries as Robert Lowell, Theodore Roethke, John Berryman, Delmore Schwartz, and Sylvia Plath, but Eliot and Pound, and, before the age of mental hospitals, Rimbaud, Baudelaire, Coleridge and others whose careers in poetry had included, in Rimbaud's widely-translated words, "a lengthy, immense and systematic derangement of the senses." As she said to the interviewer, "These are my people."

Sexton's term "break," then, has a range of references in the story of her transformation from housewife into poet. Most obviously, it denotes her break into language and into the fellowship of poets, much assisted by the lucky breaks of having at her disposal the resources of literary Boston, and an affluent, cooperative family to take over the responsibilities of childcare and housekeeping. I want to pause, though, over what is concealed in Sexton's emphasis on discontinuity and transformation. For to become a poet did not mean for Anne Sexton breaking away from family ties, or breaking up a marriage. Rather than breaking out of the conventions of what she called "the bourgeois, middle class dream," Sexton found ways to break into the meanings repressed there, and bring them over into brilliant metaphors. By 1968 when she granted the *Paris Review* interview, Anne Sexton was established as the poet of female bedlam. But in person Sexton presented to the world the carefully maintained image of an ordinary middle-class woman on whom unexpected fame has fallen. She kept a wardrobe of long dresses for important readings, and made entrances in them like an actress. Except during her severest illnesses, Sexton visited her hairdresser weekly and tinted her hair to cover the gray. Photographs invariably show large diamonds on both manicured hands. Despite her protestations that she was a "victim of the bourgeois, middle-class dream," Sexton maintained its insignia to furnish context for her art. Garbed in her finery, cigarette in hand, Anne Sexton mounted the stage and took the podium to speak lines uniting the buried self with her social stereotype, the suburban housewife.

Earlier I suggested that Sexton's account of her origins was incomplete as well as inexact. Now I want to turn to the question of what she left out or glossed over: the relevance of literary forebears, and most pertinently, the role her mother played in shaping Sexton's literary vocation.

In the fairy-tale version of her life reported to the interviewer, Sexton's suicide attempt precipitates the turn of the plot. Like the Briar Rose and the Snow White of her poems based on Grimm, Sexton wakened from the numb, death-like state of a drug overdose into a new life. The doctor's confidence in her intelligence conflicted with the family drama in which Sexton had been assigned the role of the dumb daughter. The sense of being rotten, purposeless, dumb was of course an issue in Sexton's therapy, where it was treated as a symptom. But in the story she told of her transformation from housewife into poet, it was linked directly to a struggle with her mother over being a writer.

Anne's mother, always called Mary Gray, was the "adored" only child born late in life to Jane Dingley and Arthur Gray Staples in the small town of Lewiston, Maine. Mary Gray's father was editor of the *Lewiston Evening Journal*. A genteel man of letters, he collected his weekly editorials in several books of essays; on his retirement a eulogistic book of memoirs was published in his honor. One of his books survives in Anne Sexton's library with an inscription by Mary Gray: "to the author's youngest grandchild [. . .] from the author's daughter."[8]

Mary Gray was not a published author herself, but in a family which assigned older members younger namesakes and appointed family members different roles, Mary Gray and Arthur Gray formed the literary cohort. Several years after her mother's death from cancer in 1959, Sexton discussed the alliance of mother and grandfather with her psychiatrist. Your father always spoke of your mother as a writer, the doctor reminded her. And your grandfather published some books. Were they any good? "The opposite way my poetry is good—folksy—human—He wasn't original—he was homespun—[. . .] My mother must have had a tremendous Oedipus complex—she imitated him—grandfather drank a lot." The doctor pursued the question of mother's writing. Grandfather ran a newspaper; did mother work on it? "She never worked at anything—she wrote letters, charming letters. I can't spell." Sexton goes on to comment that Mother had beautiful handwriting and wrote the girls "elegant" excuses for school absences—but "she never really wrote real letters—she just composed letters."[9]

He wasn't original; she just composed. The question, Who are the writers in the family? evokes from Sexton distinctions similar to those that appear in the interview: those people (the family), my people (the poets); the conventional, the real. A feeling of rivalry with her mother had grown especially intense in the period following Sexton's recovery from the suicide attempt of 1956. Diary entries suggest that Sexton, who had only a high school education, thought of enrolling in college courses and broached the subject with Mary Gray. "Mother says she won't help pay for any college," Sexton noted. "Also said she got highest marks ever recorded on I. Q. test at Wellesley College. In other words there is nothing I could do to equal her genius."[10] But the conflict between mother and daughter that counted most in Sexton's discovery of her own genius had occurred much earlier, at the time of Anne's graduation from Rogers Hall. Anne had been writing poems; two were published in the school yearbook. Anne's sister Blanche validated Anne's memory that Mary Gray at that time accused

Anne of plagiarism. Another girl had been expelled from Rogers Hall for submitting her father's work as her own; the scandal may have elicited Mary Gray's suspicions about Anne. She sent a sheaf of Anne's writing to "someone she knew in New York," for an expert opinion.[11] He assured Mary Gray that the work was original, but from Anne's point of view, the damage was irreversible. Her account of this episode to the *Paris Review* indicates she believed Mary Gray's intervention ended a phase of development and effected a moratorium that lasted ten years. No one else's encouragement would have mattered to her, Sexton insisted. "My mother was top billing in that house."[12]

Mary Gray expressed her sense of being an author's daughter by composing inscriptions, notes and verses to accompany gifts and celebrate special occasions. Given that Sexton was from a young age a scrapbook keeper and hoarder of letters, it is interesting that very few of Mary Gray's manuscripts in these genres survived among Anne Sexton's papers. But three of them which Sexton did save—a letter and two short poems—suggest ways in which Mary Gray served as both censor and precursor during the evolution of Sexton's identity as a poet. All are undated, but from internal evidence all seem to be responses to Sexton's second suicide attempt, which took place in May, 1957, after she had begun writing poetry.

Mary Gray's letter, shattered by long dashes, sounds far from "composed." It poses the predictable question of a parent to a suicidal offspring: where have I failed you?

> We have always been a two-way radio, with perhaps one exception—Do *you* suppose subconsciously you feel—that *if* you don't please ME you are losing an anchor? I would not know—but I have a feeling that your love for me and my "sympatica" for you—could be licking you—[. . .]
>
> *You*—Anne—my sweet daughter find life unattractive—Sometimes I do, *too*—and cry and cry—all full of self-pity and utter misery—So I can understand how you feel—Yet—you have something to give—*a* word—The word—a beautiful appreciation of what life—nature—and human relationship does [. . .] Every time you look at Joy—or Kayo—or me—or Linda with love in your heart *You* are happy—when you think of yourself and all of your failings you are *un*happy—It happens to me—today—tomorrow—End of sermon—*Bless you darling*—Your very *im*perfect mother.[13]

In the forward drive of feeling, she addresses Anne as both a daughter and a mother and, identifying with both positions, expresses the point of view that the mother's responsibility requires the sacrifice of the daughter's point of view. Daughter finds life unattractive; but mother's duty is "to give—a word—The word—a beautiful appreciation." Closing from the "motherly" position, Mary Gray's letter seems to justify Sexton's claim that the way she was brought up required the suppression of demons, "if there was enough love to put them down." Mary Gray's poems, however, speak from the other, the demonic position. One ends in unambiguous identification with the daughter's despair: "with you I am a frail / Expression of the will to fail." The other, titled "Misery," contains a vivid portrait of Anne returning to consciousness from a drug overdose:

> She lay there very still and much too cool
> And though she hoped disaster yet could fool
> A mortal. But often her red tongue
> Kept flicking at her lips. How very young
> She seemed to me and when those long white
> toes
> Exposed among the bedclothes rose
> They told me she was on this plane
> So I could love her desperately again.[14]

The daughter's deathwish places the mother in a double bind, damned whether the daughter dies, or lives to be loved "desperately again." Yet it is disaster that inspires poetry, and the "author's daughter" in the mother who writes it.

Sexton viewed Mary Gray's poems not as messages of compassion, but as outrageous appropriations of the position of writer in the family, according to a letter she wrote poet James Wright about a year after Mary Gray's death. "When my mother wrote me these poems it was to show me that she too could write. But she was a little too late, thank God—I already knew I could do better than this. I remember, now, the scorn with which I read these." Proving she could, indeed, do better, Sexton "improved" the poem "Misery" a bit in process of retyping it for her mentor to read, undermining her rival and improving her own standing as an author's daughter at the same time.[15]

Sexton's unending rivalry with Mary Gray illuminates yet another meaning in the metaphor of "breaking" by which Sexton characterized the liberation of her talent. Accusing Anne of plagiarism at an early age, then "proving" Anne's originality by consulting a specialist, Mary Gray effectively halted her development as "the author's granddaughter," writer of "elegant excuses" and verse in the manner of Sara Teasdale. What survived to be uncovered as the "real" poet required breaking with the conventions that identify poetry with "beautiful appreciation"; yet she had her convention-imposing mother to

thank. Breaking with convention meant, among other things examined here, breaking mother's code. For Mary Gray's communications suggest an identification of Daughter with unacceptable subjectivity, with self-centered authority—with poetry of the sort written by both Sexton and Mary Gray; and Mother with its repression.

The struggle to comprehend the contradiction between the roles of mother and daughter as she had learned them from Mary Gray provided Sexton the subject of what is arguably her most important early poem, **"The Double Image"** [*CP* [*The Complete Poems*] pp. 35-42], written in 1958. Addressed to her younger daughter, Joy, the poem is an explanation of why Sexton "chose two times / to kill myself" rather than live within the family as Joy's mother. "Why did I let you grow in another place" than the family home? The answer is a long autobiographical poem incorporating many factual details about the period between July 1956, when Joy was sent to live with her paternal grandmother, and November 1958, when "you stay for good [. . .] You learn my name [. . .] You call me *mother*." The poem has a roughly chronological structure, and recounts that Sexton had been hospitalized, attempted suicide, convalesced in her parents' home; that her mother had been diagnosed and treated for breast cancer, blaming Sexton for the illness; that Sexton had attempted suicide a second time. Sexton condenses and interprets these events in the course of developing the rich metaphor of the poem's title. The double image is in fact a pair of portraits, of Mary Gray and Anne, painted during convalescence. In implication it is the situation of the mother in relation to the daughter she was and has; and the situation of the daughter, who must both separate from and approximate the mother.

Sexton speaks in the poem *as a daughter to a daughter, against* the dominance of mothers. Motherhood in this poem is depicted in images of invasion of personal boundaries, and in the imposition of conventions—as in these lines characterizing Anne's return to the family home, infantilized by illness.

> Part way back from Bedlam
> I came to my mother's house in Gloucester,
> Massachusetts. And this is how I came
> to catch at her; and this is how I lost her.
> I cannot forgive your suicide, my mother said.
> And she never could. She had my portrait
> done instead.
>
> I lived like an angry guest,
> like a partly mended thing, an outgrown child.
> I remember my mother did her best.

> She took me to Boston and had my hair restyled.
> Your smile is like your mother's, the artist said.
>
> (*CP* p. 37)

The mother's effort to remake the daughter in her own image and dissolve the boundaries between their identities has a tragic outcome when the daughter's unforgiven deathwish shows up in the mother's aging body. "As if death were catching," Mary Gray developed cancer; following hospitalization for a mastectomy, she had her own portrait painted in a pose like that of Anne's portrait: "matching smile, matching contour." When, toward the end of the poem, Sexton returns to the question of "why I would rather / die than love," she offers Joy as an answer these symbolic portraits.

> In north light, my smile is held in place,
> the shadow marks my bone.
> What could I have been dreaming as I sat there,
> all of me waiting in the eyes, the zone
> of the smile, the young face,
> the foxes' snare.
>
> In south light, her smile is held in place,
> her cheeks wilting like a dry
> orchid; my mocking mirror, my overthrown
> love, my first image. She eyes me from that face
> that stony head of death
> I had outgrown.
> [. . .]
>
> And this was the cave of the mirror,
> that double woman who stares
> at herself, as if she were petrified.
>
> (*CP* pp. 40-41)

Across a passageway in the parental home the generations eye each other, reproductions, surfaces concealing the nightmares of the recent past in both their lives. In this complex of images—of the cave of the mirror, the zone of the smile, the implication of receiving and passing on womanhood as a fatal legacy—is condensed material that fills book after book of poetry by Anne Sexton. And the last lines of "The Double Image" beautifully extend the implications of the metaphor, as Sexton ruefully acknowledges that she has stepped into the mother's position.

> we named you Joyce
> so we could call you Joy.
> [. . .]
>
> I needed you. I didn't want a boy,
> [. . .]
>
> I, who was never quite sure
> about being a girl, needed another
> life, another image to remind me.
> And this was my worst guilt; you could not cure
> nor soothe it. I made you to find me.
>
> (*CP* pp. 41-42)

Doubleness now denotes not only proliferation, but duplicity. Naming a daughter for a desirable state of mind, like having her portrait painted, appropriates the daughter's identity, turns her into a mirror; implies that the struggle to separate will have to be violent: cracked mirror, psychotic break. In this poem, Sexton apparently concurs with the assumption that her suicide attempt has been a pathological rather than a creative form of separation. But the "guilt" she accepts at the end of the poem does not refer to her suicide attempt. It refers to the guilt of mothers who wish to reproduce themselves in daughters. For all its tenderness, the poem's point of view is catastrophic: the birth of a child turns the daughter into a mother; if the daughter, a buried self, emerges it must be to kill herself or the mother. Or the mother's image.

In the psychiatric interrogation of her deathwish that began in 1956, Sexton was to grasp that inability to separate from her mother was a central issue in her pathology. In the symbolic structures of her art, however, the hunger for mothering and the boundariless connection to the restless daughter in the repressed mother was fertile ground for exploring the interconnectedness of suffering and love, particularly across the generations of women in a family. Sexton acknowledged this complex debt, in which her pathology and her gift were interdependent, in the enclosure that accompanied her Christmas gift to Mary Gray in 1957:

> Dear Mother, Here are some forty-odd pages of the first year of Anne Sexton, Poet. You may remember my first sonnet written just after Christmas a year ago. I do not think all of these are good. However, I am not ashamed of them. [. . .] I love you. I don't write for you, but know that one of the reasons I do write is that you are my mother.
>
> (*L* [*Anne Sexton: A Self-Portrait in Letters*] pp. 31, 33)

"The Double Image," which Sexton claimed as the first poem in which she had truly found her voice as a writer,[16] was not to be written for another two years, after zealous work in the mastery of poetics. But by the end of 1956 Sexton had begun the process of separation and rebirth as the unique talent who for eighteen more years survived her own impulse to self-destruction: Anne Sexton, Poet.

Notes

1. "Interview with Anne Sexton (1965)," by Patricia Marx, in *Anne Sexton: The Artist and Her Critics*, ed. J. D. McClatchy (Bloomington: Indiana University Press, 1978), p. 30.

2. *Anne Sexton: The Artist and Her Critics* contains a complete list of such interviews, pp. 292-293.

3. "The Art of Poetry: Anne Sexton (1968)," interview with Barbara Kevles, in *Anne Sexton: The Artist and Her Critics*, pp. 3-7.

4. In the introduction to the tenth anniversary edition of *The Feminine Mystique*, Friedan describes the origins of this groundbreaking study: "In 1957, getting strangely bored with writing articles about breast feeding and the like for *Ladies' Home Journal*, I put an unconscionable amount of time into a questionnaire for my fellow Smith graduates of the class of 1942, thinking I was going to disprove the current notion that education had fitted us ill for our roles as women. But the questionnaire raised more questions than it answered [. . .] The suspicion arose as to whether it was the education or the role that was wrong" (New York: W. W. Norton & Company, Inc., 1974), p. 2.

5. "For John, Who Begs Me Not to Enquire Further," *The Complete Poems*, ed. Linda Gray Sexton, with a foreword by Maxine Kumin (Boston: Houghton Mifflin Company, 1981), pp. 34-35. Further quotations from this edition will be annotated *CP*.

6. *Anne Sexton: A Self-Portrait in Letters*, ed. Linda Gray Sexton and Lois Ames (Boston: Houghton Mifflin Company, 1977), pp. 244-245. Further quotations from this edition will be annotated *L*.

7. These diagnostic labels appear in Sexton's hospital records, and in transcripts of tape-recorded therapy sessions she kept from January, 1961 to May, 1964. The latter are deposited as restricted materials in the Anne Sexton Archive, Humanities Research Center, The University of Texas, Austin, and quoted with the permission of Linda Sexton.

8. Inside cover of Arthur G. Staples, *Just Talks on Common Themes* (Lewiston, Maine: J. Scudney Publishing Co., 1920). Copy in the collection of Linda Sexton.

9. Entry in Anne Sexton's therapy transcript June 12, 1962. Quoted from restricted material in the Anne Sexton Archive, Humanities Research Center, The University of Texas, Austin, with the permission of Linda Sexton.

10. Holograph notes on loose calendar pages dated February 14-19, 1957; filed among letters to her psychiatrist deposited as restricted materials in the Anne Sexton Archive, Humanities Research Center, The University of Texas, Austin, and quoted with the permission of Linda Sexton.

11. Interview with Blanche Harvey Taylor, Scituate, Massachusetts, April 27, 1983.

12. "Art of Poetry: Anne Sexton," p. 5.

13. Sexton, Anne, Miscellaneous file, Humanities Research Center, The University of Texas, Austin.

14. Sexton, Anne, Recipient: from Harvey, Mary Gray Staples, Humanities Research Center, The University of Texas, Austin. I have reproduced Mary Gray's first two lines as written; the uses of "to" and "And" seem to be errors.

15. Wright, an established poet slightly older than Sexton, had become her lover and mentor; both relationships were conducted chiefly in an enormous correspondence, much of which has been lost. However, Sexton kept a carbon of this undated letter in a file reserved for notes written in the course of therapy with the psychiatrist who had proposed writing poetry. Quoted from restricted materials, Humanities Research Center, The University of Texas, Austin, with permission from Linda Sexton.

16. Letter to W. D. Snodgrass, November 26, 1958, *L.* p. 43.

TITLE COMMENTARY

The Complete Poems

DERYN REES-JONES (ESSAY DATE WINTER 1999)

SOURCE: Rees-Jones, Deryn. "Consorting with Angels: Anne Sexton and the Art of Confession." *Women* 10, no. 3 (winter 1999): 283-96.

In the following essay, Rees-Jones analyzes the authenticity and aesthetic "truth" of Sexton's confessional poetry and role as feminist poet, discussing the boundaries and intersections between the private and public realms, the writer and reader, and male and female.

Structuralist and poststructuralist rethinking of the relationship between author, text and reader presents an interesting problem when it comes to the idea of confessional poetry. The lyric poem's particularly resonant history in setting up a fixed dyadic relationship between self and other acts as an especially receptive and intimate stage for the dramatization of such an enterprise as the search for 'truth'. And yet how *can* we read the confessional 'properly' in an age when the 'author is dead'? For unlike autobiography, which purports to document factual and emotional truth, and which embeds its 'I' within a narrative, confessional poetry hovers in a kind of no man's land between documentary experience on the one hand, and fiction on the other, establishing itself as a mode which ostensibly unites the borders of the relationship between the 'I' who speaks and the 'I' who is spoken about. Yet as James Merrill has pointed out: 'Confessional poetry . . . is a literary convention like any other, the problem is to make it *sound* as if it were true.'[1] If autobiography can be read as a narrative which fashions a truth about the history of the self, then surely we must read the confessional poem as an aesthetic of truth, the terms of its own nature determined exactly by its very authenticity—an authenticity which paradoxically is as subject to 'tinkerings', as Lowell called them, as of any other piece of creative writing.

My preoccupation here is with three aspects of the confession and its importance to lyric poetry written by women, particularly in relation to the work of the North American poet Anne Sexton. First, authenticity and related issues of truth are particularly charged in a reading of women's texts when an authenticity of suffering becomes entangled with the quest for an establishment of a female writing 'identity'. Second, the borders between private and public, between male and female, between that which can and cannot be said, and the place where the two intersect are interesting because, although the experience of the confessional poem is of an intensely personal, extreme and often transgressive nature, part of its aesthetic must also consist of some kind of sympathetic union that disturbs the usual boundaries between poet and reader. The poem allows what the reader is forbidden: it puts into words the unspeakable, the unsayable. Third, I am interested in the relationship Sexton has with the confessional genre, and the way she relates to the confessional model as constructed largely by male poets, particularly the poet Robert Lowell, who tutored Sexton at a formative point in her career.

Intimately related to these issues is Sexton's role as a feminist, or protofeminist, poet. Sexton's mental illness and its expression via her poetry offers a difficult model of femininity, both for the reader and for the woman poet who writes after her. Diane Middlebrooke's important and controversial biography of Sexton has shown, through its use of the tapes made of her psychoanalytic sessions—from which some of the poems (those she referred to as her transference poems) draw—how close some of the links are between poem and therapeutic material. To what degree, then, is it reasonable to ask whether Sexton's private experience of suffering is one which is understandable or recognizable in the wider realm?

In her introduction to **The Complete Poems,** Maxine Kumin suggests that women readers did in fact identify with the extremity of Sexton's experience[2], and that it was this graphic exposé of female experience that left male reviewers uncomfortable or outraged:

> The facts of Anne Sexton's troubled and chaotic life are well known; no other American poet in our time has cried aloud publicly so many private details. While the frankness of these revelations attracted many readers, especially women, who identified strongly with the female aspect of the poems, a number of poets and critics—for the most part, although not exclusively male—took offence. For Louis Simpson, writing in *Harper's Magazine*, '**Menstruation at Forty**' was 'the straw that broke the camel's back.' And years before he wrote his best-selling novel, *Deliverance*, which centres on a graphic scene of homosexual rape,

James Dickey, writing in *The New York Times Book Review*, excoriated the poems in **All My Pretty Ones**, saying 'It would be hard to find a writer who dwells more insistently on the pathetic and disgusting aspects of bodily experience . . .' In a terse eulogy Robert Lowell declared, with considerable ambivalence it would seem, 'For a book or two, she grew more powerful. Then writing was too easy or too hard for her. She became meager and exaggerated. Many of her most embarrassing poems would have been fascinating if someone had put them into quotes, as the presentation of some character, not the author.'[3]

This issue of embarrassment is an interesting one—Lowell, for example, makes extensive use of the quotation, Berryman adopts a persona—and highlights one of the crucial differences between Sexton's work and the work of her male confessing contemporaries. For the male poet the act of confession may be figured as a transgression against a preconceived notion of the masculine as controlled, ordered and rational. For the woman poet, however, the transgression works on a double model. On the one hand it offers a liberation from stereotypical representations of women (the Angel in the House, the paragon of sexual and domestic virtue) while on the other hand it may actually reinforce patriarchal anxieties about women's fury and madness, desire and dirtiness, and reinscribe them in the ostensible service of liberation. Without in any way negating or trivializing the anguish or difficulties of the male confessional, or the powerfulness of the poetry, it seems fair to say that the male confessional is radical precisely because it can be seen to be exploring new territories of the male psyche; it breaks down patriarchal notions of masculinity while at the same time offering an extremity of experience as a testimony of suffering that equates with prophecy and 'strength', and yet may also be disclaimed. The male confessional speaks as representative of the suffering of his time and his nation. His pain is seen to be of both personal and global relevance. If this confessing poet is Robert Lowell, a poet whose family is part of the political ruling class, the implications are perhaps even more extreme; the fact that Lowell served as a figurehead for the so-called Confessional group also supports this conjecture.

The woman who confesses is, however, frequently read as testifying only to her own anguish and her own 'weakness'; she is simply revealing the awfulness of femininity which was 'known' to be there all along, and which, in the most simplistic terms, has led to her oppression in the first place. In speaking what she believes to be a personal truth she is making a spectacle of herself,

Anne Sexton with her daughters Joy and Linda in her home in Newton, Massachusetts, 1962.

throwing an already precarious subjectivity into a heightened state of prominence and vulnerability. And it is here we see the exact nature of the problem: for if the woman poet *does* remain silent, if the awfulness of her confessional truth is such that it will serve only to oppress her further, she is left where she started, and cannot speak at all. Alternatively, she can speak a version of the self which also confirms a certain kind of femininity—that of beauty, passivity, orderliness and self-control—but which nevertheless fails to 'tell it like it is'.

Furthermore Sexton's departure from the more straightforwardly autobiographical poems of her early work—poems such as '**You, Doctor Martin**' (*CP* [*The Complete Poems*], 3-4) or '**Said the Poet to Her Analyst**' (*CP*, 12-13)—are an attempt to circumlocute the difficulties of writing the purely personal *as a woman*. Her use of the angel acts as a cypher for the confessional, which still allows her a voice of anguish and suffering, but adds to it a dimension of androgyny which removes it from being a direct expression of her female self. The angel is both her and not her, the

good self and the bad self, the human and the transcendent. From writing to a 'you' who listens—the male figure of authority, the teacher, the psychiatrist, the doctor or even the lover—Sexton shifts her muse from the external, her necessary other, to an internal muse who dramatizes her dilemma, and who offers an imago which allows her to speak both to and about herself. Thus she presents a self which is both real and unreal, honest yet mystical, both male and female, me and not me.

The representation of femininity is a concern raised by the poet Elizabeth Bishop in a letter to Lowell in 1960 in which she describes Sexton as having

> a bit too much romanticism and what I think of as the 'our beautiful old silver' school of female writing, which is really boasting about how 'nice' we were. V. Woolf, E. Bowen, R. West, etc.—they are all full of it. They have to make quite sure that their reader is not going to misplace them socially, first, and that nervousness interferes constantly with what they think they'd like to say. I wrote a story at Vassar that was too much admired by Miss Rose Peebles, my teacher, who was very proud of

being an old-school Southern lady—and suddenly this fact about women's writing dawned on me, and has haunted me ever since.[4]

Bishop's comment, perhaps testimony at least as much to her aesthetics of reserve as to her gender, and which, given when it was written, can only refer to Sexton's first collection *To Bedlam and Part Way Back* (1960), seems a curious one to make about a poet who would later be notorious for breaking a variety of social taboos. The construction of an approved female self is one which clearly causes Bishop herself some anxiety. Rereading *To Bedlam and Part Way Back,* which came out of Sexton's experiences of two mental breakdowns, and her hospitalization and attempted suicide in 1956, it is easy to detect the nervousness that Bishop identifies. In this first collection Sexton interestingly also offers a defence of her use of the confessional mode in **'For John, Who Begs Me Not to Enquire Further'**. She writes:

> I tapped my own head;
> it was a glass, an inverted bowl.
> It is a small thing
> to rage in your own bowl.
> At first it was private.
> Then it was more than myself;
> it was you, or your house
> or your kitchen.
> And if you turn away
> because there is no lesson here
> I will hold my awkward bowl,
> with all its cracked stars shining
> like a complicated lie,
> and fasten a new skin around it
> as if I were dressing an orange
> or a strange sun.
> Not that it was beautiful,
> but that I found some order there.

(*CP,* 34-5)

The poem, addressed to John Holmes who ran the creative-writing class which she, Kumin and others attended in 1957, is an eloquent plea for the 'complicated lie' of the confession. Echoing Blake and obliquely engaging with some of the images of shadowy femininity which dominate *The Book of Thel* (1789),[5] the poem also links up with the epigraph Sexton uses for the volume, a letter from Schopenhauer to Goethe dated November 1815, which reads:

> It is the courage to make a clean breast of it in the face of every question that makes the philosopher. He must be like Sophocles's Oedipus, who, seeking enlightenment concerning his terrible fate, pursues his indefatigable enquiry, even when he divines that appalling horror waits him in the

ABOUT THE AUTHOR

SEXTON'S POETRY ACCORDING TO CRITIC LIZ PORTER HANKINS

Mrs. Sexton reliably and openly confesses in her work; she seldom, if ever, yields to distortion or illusion. Her poems reflect the intimacy and complexity of her life and her struggle; she dares to set it in verse with the same force with which she lived it. Although many critics have been drawn to Mrs. Sexton's attraction to madness, they have repeatedly failed to deal with her femininity—her intimate search into herself for redemption. She found her answer in her work, not in suicide, through search and affirmation. Her solution lies in the long journey into herself when she transcends in verse the limitations of the physical and when the temple of her body becomes her ideological universe. She summons usage and experience, the world, through her body poetry.

Hankins, Liz Porter. "Summoning the Body: Anne Sexton's Body Poems," in *Midwest Quarterly* 28, no. 4 (summer 1987): 511-24.

answer. But most of us carry in our heart the Jocasta who begs Oedipus for God's sake not to inquire further . . .

In this strange reversal of genders, Sexton positions herself as Oedipus, her mentor as Jocasta. Writing, Sexton seems to be pointing out, is about taking oneself to the horror of one's own fate. But what exactly is that fate? Finding one's identity, in what had seemed a certain world, to be not what one had thought? Discovering that sexual relations between men and women are not what had been previously imagined? In her essay on abjection, *Powers of Horror,* Julia Kristeva sees Oedipus as a scapegoat figure: 'Entering an impure city—a miasma—he turns himself into *agos,* defilement, in order to purify it and to become *katharmos.* He is thus a purifier by the very fact of being *agos.*'[6] Might then the confessing poet, who transgresses the borders of the spoken, also speak for and cleanse the generation for which he or she speaks? Sexton's poem, however, also testifies to the recreation of something other than the self that testifies. The 'complicated lie' involves the construction of another self. It also allows for broadening the sense of suffering beyond the purely personal to an exchange of experience between men and women, Oedipus and Jocasta. As **'For John, Who Begs Me Not to Enquire Further'** ends:

> . . . Your fear is anyone's fear,
> like an invisible veil between us all . . .
> and sometimes in private,
> my kitchen, your kitchen,
> my face, your face.

How then does Sexton attempt to negotiate the pitfalls of representing femininity within the confessional mode? One way is by using the figure of the angel. Sexton first uses the angel in *To Bedlam and Part Way Back* in 'The Waiting Head' (*CP*, 31-2). Here it is the glanced image of a figure that becomes an alter ego:

> Surely I remember the hooks
>
> of her fingers curled on mine, though even now
> will not admit the times I did avoid this street,
> where she lived on and on like a beached fig
> and forgot us anyhow;
> visiting the pulp of her kiss, bending to repeat
> each favor trying to comb out her mossy wig
> and forcing love to last. Now she is always dead
> and the leather books are mine. Today I see the
>   head
>
> move like some pitted angel, in that high
>   window.

This representation of a self who is both the poet and not the poet sets the ground for later poems in which the angel acts as a figure of otherness. But perhaps Sexton's most difficult and pivotal use of the angel is to be found in her poem **'Consorting with Angels'** (*CP*, 111-12) which appeared in 1963:

> I was tired of being a woman,
> tired of the spoons and the pots,
> tired of my mouth and my breasts,
> tired of the cosmetics and silks.
> There were still men who sat at my table,
> circled around the bowl I offered up.
> The bowl was filled with purple grapes
> and the flies hovered in for the scent
> and even my father came with his white bone.
> But I was tired of the gender of things.
>
> Last night I had a dream
> and I said to it . . .
> 'You are the answer.
> You will outlive my husband and my father.'
> In that dream there was a city made of chains
> where Joan was put to death in man's clothes
> and the nature of the angels went unexplained,
> no two in the same species,
> one with a nose, one with an ear in its hand,

> one chewing a star and recording its own orbit,
> each one like a poem obeying itself,
> performing God's functions,
> a people apart.
>
> 'You are the answer,'
> I said, and entered,
> lying down on the gates of the city.
> Then the chains were fastened around me
> and I lost my common gender and my final
>   aspect.
> Adam was on the left of me
> and Eve was on the right of me,
> both thoroughly inconsistent with the world of
>   reason.
> We wove our arms together
> and rode under the sun.
> I was not a woman anymore,
> not one thing or the other.
>
> O daughters of Jerusalem,
> the king has brought me into his chamber
> I am black and I am beautiful.
> I've been opened and undressed.
> I have no arms or legs.
> I'm all one skin like a fish.

This enigmatic poem sees the speaker interrogating gender constructions in relation to her own sexuality, and ultimately rejecting stereotypical masculine or feminine gender constructions in favour of a mutilated and limbless but nevertheless desiring subject. This creature with whom we are left presents difficulties: limbless, the torso is left with nothing and the bodily parts which define her difference (the breasts, the vagina) and the points of similarity (the legs, arms, hands, feet) are sacrificed in favour of a fish-like skin. The speaker is tired of the feminine masquerade, 'the cosmetics and the silks' as well as the mouth and breasts. (This mutilation of the body might be compared to a later poem by Lowell, 'Seals', in which the speaker of the poem offers a kind of prayer that 'If we must live again, not us; we might / go into seals'. Like the torso, the seals are virtually limbless and fishy, yet the image of the seal, though androgynous, is one which seems less ambiguously positive: 'we'd handle ourselves better: / able to dawdle, able to torpedo, / all at home in our three elements, / ledge, water and heaven'.[7])

Accordingly the speaker of the poem also rejects stereotypical woman's adoption of 'masculine' behaviour (as figured by Joan of Arc who is put to death in a man's clothes in the city of chains), as well as the masculine itself: the husband and the potentially abusive father with his threatening 'white bone'. Instead she identifies her gender with the angels, which in the poem seem to mark difference itself (there are 'no two in the same species'). Here the 'I' of the poem has 'lost' her 'common gender and my final aspect'; she is not a 'woman anymore / not one thing or the other'. The poem also directly alludes to Blake's *Marriage of Heaven and Hell*:

> [S]oon we saw seven houses of brick: one we enter'd; In it were a number of monkeys, baboons, & all of that species, chain'd by the middle, grinning and snatching at one another, but witheld by the shortness of their chains: However I saw that they sometimes grew numerous, and then the weak were caught by the strong, and with a grinning aspect, first coupled with & then devour'd, by plucking off first one limb and then another, till the body was left a helpless trunk: this after grinning & kissing it with seeming fondness, they devour'd too . . .[8]

Sexton is clearly allying herself with a visionary, mystical tradition, yet one which, like Blake's interrogational and satirical approach to the writings of Swedenborg, takes a stance against texts which inscribe masculinity to the exclusion of the feminine. Blake's scenario, however, offers a much more horrific and grotesque vision than Sexton's. The trunk or torso that Sexton leaves us with is not finally devoured: what is left is an image of woman as orifice—the mouth, the vagina and the anus—orifices which ingest, engulf, expel. Yet, unlike Lowell's image in the poem 'Seals', this figure does not represent the freedom of androgyny in the sense of a merger of masculine and feminine sexual characteristics; rather it represents a vision of an all encompassing or even engorging sexuality.

The speaker of the poem defines herself in terms which link her directly to the woman speaker of the *Song of Songs*, depending heavily as Sexton's poem does on its intertextual reference to the *Songs*. Sexton's figure is clearly sexual, and clearly powerful, and is interestingly echoed by Lowell's 'Mermaid Emerging' (*The Dolphin*, 1973):

> Mermaid, why are you another species?
> 'Because, you, I, everyone is unique.'
> Does anyone ever make you do nothing; you're
>   not chained.
> I am a woman or I am a dolphin,
> the only animal man really loves,
> I spout the smarting waters of joy in your face—
> rough weather fish, who cuts your nets and
>   chains.

The interplay between Sexton and Lowell here is an interesting one, and it is important to point out here that, while Lowell is an important figure to Sexton, she is equally as important to him as a poet. What seems to connect these images, one mutilated, one transformed, the other a mythical creature which is both one thing and another, is

that they seem to represent for both poets an escape from the fixity of sex roles. But although the speaker of Sexton's poem places herself between Adam and Eve, we are ultimately left with a figure who is simultaneously and paradoxically identifying with a woman's sexuality (at the expense of a mutilation of her human characteristics, her arms and her legs) through her identification with the speaker of the *Song of Songs*: a figure who is both 'black and beautiful', but who also denies that she is female ('I am no more a woman / than Christ was a man'). Sexton's use of the line break is neatly juxtaposed by a final image of the woman who, Christ-like, achieves an in-between state, between the male and the female, the human and the divine, through the act of suffering. Clearly, then, '**Consorting with Angels**' cannot be simply read as a confessional poem: its surreal, apocalyptic vision, its biblical borrowing, all serve to destabilize any sense of a straightforwardly 'authentic' self who is examined in the retelling of a 'true' event.

By the ***Book of Folly*** (1972) the preoccupation with angels is growing, as Sexton's six-poem sonnet sequence, '**Angels of the Love Affair**', reveals. Written in May and June of 1971, the title of the collection is taken from Ecclesiastes 1:17: 'I gave my heart to know wisdom, and to know madness and folly: I perceived that this also is a vexation of the spirit. For in much wisdom is much grief and he that increaseth knowledge increaseth sorrow.' Again Sexton is using a biblical source as a way of criticizing patriarchal restrictions on femininity. But even as she offers a criticism of religion, she is also representing it, through the figure of the angel, as a source of solace. The epigraph to the '**Angels of the Love Affair**' (*CP*, 332-6) asks: 'angels of the love affair, do you know that other, the dark one, that other me?' With their setting up of 'Contraries', rather than binary oppositions, these poems are influenced not only by Blake but by the work of the Chilean poet Pablo Neruda, whom Sexton met in London in 1967 and whose work she had been reading for a considerable time.[9] With often shockingly graphic details charting mental illness, bodily disease and desperation, these are poems about the horrors of the genesis of the self. The angels of the sequence look both to Blake's 'I heard an Angel singing',[10] and, certainly in the first poem, to Neruda's 'Ode to Fire'.[11] Using prayers or invocations, Sexton maintains the binary opposition established in previous angel poems, between black and white, in a progressive exploration of the establishment of a female identity. This time, however, it is an opposition between heat and cold, and red and white: images of fire and ice, and red and white appear throughout the sequence, as blood, as rubies, as raspberries, a mouth, blizzards, sugar, a face. Both colours are represented ambiguously: if white is representative of the clean sheets of the second sonnet, it is also the blizzard of the fifth; if red is the 'little bits of dried blood' or the blood that 'buzzes like a hornet's nest' it is also the fruit of childhood and the red mouth of the kiss. Like Blake's use of 'Contraries', Sexton is clearly using opposites in order to deconstruct them in a way which is reminiscent of her deconstruction of fixed gender roles.

In the first poem of the sequence, '**Angel of Fire and Genitals**' (*CP*, 332-3), the speaker of the poem asks

> do you know slime,
> that green mama who first forced me to sing,
> who put me first in the latrine, that pantomime
> of brown where I was beggar and she was king?

The sonnet introduces elemental imagery, in this case fire, which is followed in the next three sonnets by earth, wind and water imagery. The 'Angel of Fire' might refer in particular to two angels: the seraph who placed burning coals on Isaiah's lips to relieve him of his silence, and Uriel, whose name means 'Fire of God' and who is thought to be the angel who stands outside the Garden of Eden with his sword of flames. These two powerful images are suggestive of the connection between speech, and saying the right thing (Isaiah was punished for not naming his child the name that God had wanted), and sexuality (the angel was placed outside Eden once Adam and Eve, having eaten of the Tree of Knowledge, had been exiled). Uniting these two images at the beginning of the sequence sets up these two relationships between speech and sexuality, and traces Sexton's ongoing anxiety over the representation of herself as a woman who 'speaks the poem'.

Throughout the sequence there is a repetition of the word 'hole', clearly here associated with feminine sexuality. Homophonically 'hole', which is also 'whole', denotes a sense both of emptiness and completeness. The angel leaves her sense of self in a position of liminality which both refutes and embraces the female sex. This sense of liminality, of dilemma and anxiety about the positioning of the self, also potentially offers a position of power. Being neither one thing nor the other, it might be said that one also creates for oneself the possibility of continual freedom; the stasis implicit in the position also offers the continual possibility

of movement. Yet the first four angel sonnets end on an image of stasis or petrifaction: 'Mother of fire, let me stand at your devouring gate'; 'I have known the tuck-in of a child / but inside my hair waits the might I was defiled'; 'I stand in stone shoes as the world's bicycle goes by'; 'Your arms are cut and bound by bands / of wire. Your voice is out there. Your voice is strange. / There are no prayers here. There is no change.'

The angels seem to offer an escape from this stasis, each poem offered up to the angel like a prayer. And yet it is as if this is a prayer that will never be answered. Sexton writes in the third sonnet:

> Angel of flight, you soarer, you flapper, you
>   floater,
> you gull that grows out of my back in the
>   dreams I prefer,
>
> stay near. But give me the totem. Give me the
>   shut eye
> where I stand in stone shoes as the world's
>   bicycle goes by.
>
> > (*CP*, 334)

And in the sixth:

> . . . I hear my lungs fill and
>   expel
> as in an operation. But I have no one left to tell.
> > (*CP*, 335)

These painful and difficult poems nevertheless seem to indicate some kind of progression from the images of abjection in the earlier poems, so that the body of the complete woman in the sixth sonnet, '**Angel of Beach Houses and Picnics**' (*CP*, 335-6), sunbathing nude at the end of the sequence, offers some semblance of hope for a return to the lean, young, healthy and politicized self:

> Once I sunbathed in the buff, all brown and
>   lean,
> watching the toy sloops go by, holding court
> for busloads of tourists. Once I called breakfast
>   the sexiest
> meal of the day. Once I invited arrest
>
> at the peace march in Washington. Once I was
>   young and bold
> and left hundreds of unmatched people out in
>   the cold.

Increasingly, as we have seen, Sexton's experimentation with the figure of the angel allows her direct access to 'the word' of other male poets, as well as to the power of divinity itself. Sexton's use of the angel, like Blake's, gives her access to powerful images from Christian iconography. The angel acts as a powerful muse which allows her to 'consort', with all the ambiguities of pleasure and collusion that that word contains. In 'The Fallen Angels' (*CP*, 430-1), included in 'The Awful Rowing towards God' (1975), the angel has become a metaphor for writing itself:

> They come on to my clean
> sheet of paper and leave a Rorschach blot.
> They do not do this to be mean,
> they do it to give me a sign
> they want me, as Aubrey Beardsley once said,
> to shove it around until something comes.
>
> Clumsy as I am,
> I do it.
> For I am like them—
> both saved and lost,
> tumbling downward like Humpty Dumpty
> off the alphabet.

In 'Talking to Sheep' (*CP*, 484-6), a poem that appeared in the posthumous collection *45 Mercy Street* (1976), and which has strong echoes of 'Consorting with Angels', Sexton seems to sum up her career as a confessional. It begins:

> My life
> has appeared unclothed in court,
> detail by detail,
> death-bone witness by death-bone witness,
> and I was shamed at the verdict
> and given a cut penny
> and the entrails of a cat.
> But nevertheless I went on
> to the invisible priests,
> confessing, confessing
> through the wire of hell
> and they wet upon me in that phone booth

The father's white bone from 'Consorting with Angels' has become a death-bone. The invisible priests seem to represent a disembodied male who metamorphoses into the faceless person at the end of the telephone to whom she confesses her poems. As Kumin notes, the telephone played an important part in Sexton's writing process:

> During the workshop years we began to communicate more and more frequently by telephone . . . a working method which does much to train the ear to hear line breaks, internal rhymes, intentional or unwanted musical devices, and so forth. We did this comfortably and over such an extended period of time that indeed when we met we were somewhat shy of each other's poems as they appeared on the page.
>
> (*CP*, xxv)

Perhaps the telephone here works as symbolic umbilicus—the curly loop which acts as life-line of communication between the two women—the poems arising out of long, intimate and faceless conversations almost as if taking place between priest and confessor: 'Whoever God is', explains Sexton, 'I keep making telephone calls to him.

I'm not sure that's religion. More desperation than faith in such things.'[12] Such a comment seems to set in motion the idea of the speaker and listener of the lyric. And yet we see Sexton again looking to a male poet in order to establish a poetic self— for her poem also appears to echo James Dickey's 'The Sheep Child' (1966)—which, while still addressing her problematic relationship with confessional writing, sets up a dynamic between the author's own (albeit heavily intertextually plundering) work and that of a male writer. Dickey (as we have heard) had been a fierce critic of Sexton's work, and had written several searing reviews of her previous collections. The two poets met for the first time in December 1965, and formed an intense friendship which, on Dickey's part at least, bordered on infatuation; Sexton is clearly addressing Dickey via his poem. 'The Sheep Child', with humour and tenderness, gives voice to the child of a union between a man and a sheep 'this thing that's only half / Sheep like a woolly baby / Pickled in alcohol because / those things can't live his eyes / Are open but you can't stand to look'.[13] In Sexton's poem she is representing the poetic self as being as much a hybrid as Lowell's mermaid or Dickey's sheep, as she is a Jesus, the good shepherd, who suffers so that others may be redeemed. Yet writing as a woman involves a necessary mutilation of herself in public, and she becomes a circus freak, neither woman nor man:

> . . . My *breasts are off me*.
> The transvestite whispering to me,
> over and over, *My legs are disappearing*.
> My mother, her voice like water,
> saying *Fish are cut out of me*.
> My father,
> his voice thrown into a cigar,
> *A marble of blood rolls into my heart*.
> My great aunt,
> her voice,
> thrown into a lost child at the freaks' circus,
> *I am the flame swallower*
> *but turn me over in bed*
> *and I am the fat lady*.

The poem's positioning of the woman poet is oddly reminiscent of the positioning of the hysteric at one of Charcot's Tuesday gatherings at the Salpetriere in Paris, when his 'patients' were hypnotized and asked to perform a variety of tricks. Is this, Sexton seems to be asking, her status as performer of her work.[14] For Sexton the role of the woman poet and the confessional is a difficult one. And yet the speaker of the poem—the woman who writes—appears to have few alternatives:

> It was wise, the medical men said,
> wise to cry *Baa* and be smiling into your mongoloid hood,

while you simply tended the sheep.
Or else to sew your lips shut
and not let a word or a deadstone sneak out.

Reading Sexton clearly presents difficulties. In crying 'baa', rather than identifying with the mother or the father, the 'ma' or the 'pa', but also refusing its simple-mindedness, by becoming the black sheep, Sexton embraces the most difficult alternative. She attempts to speak the horror in which she finds herself, but also attempts 'to push around' that horror on the page in a way which may make it relevant to others, and particularly relevant to a generation of women suffering, to various degrees, the effects of patriarchy. Increasingly for Sexton the poem is not simply an expression of suffering, but an attempt to purge, to disinherit her experience. Whereas Lowell remembers, and places the self he describes within the bounds of specific time and specific history, merging the boundaries between public and private experience, and John Berryman fabulizes and dramatizes, Sexton's confessional, as her work progresses, acts as a compulsive repetition and re-enactment of suffering, which hauls trauma into the moment of writing itself. As she herself acknowledges in **'Talking to Sheep'**, 'I keep making statues / of my acts, carving them with my sleep'. Because of this it might be tempting to read Sexton's writing as a solely therapeutic act, a reading which indeed ties in with the direct relationship that can be drawn between her writing and her psychiatric treatment and ensuing therapy. Yet Sexton's poetic is so much more than this. Her interrogation of femininity and gender in relation to her writing, her desire to transform the horror of personal experience into wider realms—the relations between men and women, male and female, the human and the divine—is an ambitious one that prefigures and, in a sense, allows much of the poetry arising from the women's movement in the 1970s. Her poetry does not always, perhaps, offer a clearly positive feminist model, yet her bravery, her erratic power, suggests a model of confession which is about the desire and impossibility of cleansing and atonement in a secular context; it is one which works on the borders of existence, and sometimes even poetry itself. Sexton's work attempts to refigure the self as a model of power that moves her from the horror of silence to the horror of suffering at a mythic level as well as a personal one; a suffering which, in *Powers of Horror*, Kristeva describes as

> . . . the place of the subject. Where it emerges, where it is differentiated from chaos. An incandescent, unbearable limit between inside and outside, ego and other. The initial, fleeting grasp:

'suffering', 'fear,' ultimate words sighting the crest where sense topples over into the senses, the 'intimate' into nerves.[15]

Notes

1. Marjorie Perloff, *Robert Lowell,* Ithaca, NY: Cornell University Press, 1973, p. 80.

2. Some of Sexton's readers were in mental institutions themselves. See *Anne Sexton: A Self-Portrait in Letters,* ed. Linda Gray Sexton and Lois Ames, with a new foreword by Linda Gray Sexton, Boston: Houghton Mifflin, 1991, p. 276.

3. Anne Sexton, *The Complete Poems,* ed. and with a foreword by Maxine Kumin, Boston: Houghton Mifflin, 1981, p. xx (henceforth *CP*).

4. Elizabeth Bishop, *One Art: The Selected Letters,* ed. and introd. Robert Giroux, London: Pimlico, 1994, pp. 386-7.

5. See *Blake's Poetry and Designs,* ed. Mary Lynn Johnson and John E. Grant, New York: Norton, 1979, plate 1, p. 61: 'Does the Eagle know what is in the pit? / Or wilt thou go ask the Mole: / Can wisdom be put in a silver rod? / Or Love in a golden bowl.'

6. Julia Kristeva, *Powers of Horror: An Essay on Abjection,* trans. Leon S. Roudiez, New York: Columbia University Press, 1982, p. 84.

7. *Robert Lowell's Poems: A Selection,* ed. with an introduction and notes by Jonathan Raban, London: Faber, 1984, p. 142.

8. *Blake's Poetry and Designs,* plates 19 and 20, p. 97.

9. Kumin describes Sexton's working method in the introduction to *The Complete Poems*: 'the impetus for creation usually came when Anne directly invoked the muse at her desk. Here, she read favorite poems of other poets—most frequently Neruda—and played certain evocative records over and over' (*CP*, xxvi).

10. *Motto to the Songs of Innocence and Experience* in *Blake's Poetry and Designs,* p. 187: 'I heard an Angel singing / When the day was springing / Mercy Pity Peace / Is the world's release'.

11. See Pablo Neruda, *Odes to Opposites,* ed. Ferris Cook, trans. Ken Krabbenhoft, New York: Little, Brown and Co., 1995, pp. 76-7. 'Of all / my friends / and / enemies, / you're / the hardest to handle. / Everybody else / carries you tied up, / a demon in their pockets, / a hurricane locked away / in boxes and decrees. / But not me. I carry you right alongside me, / and I'm telling you this: / It's high time / you showed me / what you can do. / Open up, let down / your tangled / hair, / leap up and singe / the heights of heaven.'

12. Diane Middlebrooke, *Anne Sexton: A Biography,* London: Virago, p. 355.

13. James Dickey, *Poems 1957-1967,* London: Rapp and Carroll, 1967, pp. 252-3.

14. Sexton's insecurity about her own credibility within a male domain had resulted in her sly reprimand of Ted Hughes in a much earlier letter (1967) in which she displays an anxiety about her positioning as woman, as poet and as confessional: 'It looks as if I will be the only female poet at the festival (not counting Ginsberg!) . . . is that so? How strange. I look drawn

and haggard now, I will be no addition. I will work on a tan. Not, of course, that you asked me because I was another sex. No. That is another lump I dislike[:] "female poets lump," the "confessional lump," or the "Lowell, Sexton, Plath lump" (see *Anne Sexton: A Self Portrait in Letters*, p. 308).

15. Kristeva, p. 141.

FURTHER READING

Bibliography

Northouse, Cameron, and Thomas P. Walsh. *Sylvia Plath and Anne Sexton: A Reference Guide*. Boston, Mass.: G. K. Hall, 1974, 143 p.

Annotated checklist of publications about Sexton and her work, dated but valuable.

Biographies

Middlebrook, Diane. *Anne Sexton: A Biography*. London: Vintage, 1992, 528 p.

Reconstructs Sexton's life and interprets her works based on audiotapes of the poet's psychotherapy sessions, which has prompted controversy in some quarters.

Sexton, Linda Gray. *Searching for Mercy Street: My Journey Back to My Mother, Anne Sexton*. Boston, Mass.: Little, Brown, 1994, 307 p.

Biography of Sexton by her daughter.

Criticism

Furst, Arthur, and Linda Gray Sexton. *Anne Sexton: The Last Summer*, New York: St. Martin's Press, 2000, 128 p.

Contains photographs taken during the summer before Sexton's suicide and includes previously unpublished letters and early drafts of poems.

George, Diana Hume. "How We Danced: Anne Sexton on Fathers and Daughters." *Women's Studies* 12, no. 2 (1986): 179-202.

Traces the development of the father-daughter motif throughout Sexton's poetry in terms of the social structures and psychoanalytic traditions of Western culture.

———. "The Poetic Heroism of Anne Sexton." *Literature and Psychology* 33, nos. 3-4 (1987): 76-88.

Identifies Sexton's poetic persona with the mythical figure of Oedipus, interpreting the thematic recurrence of infancy and parent-child relationships in Sexton's works within the context of feminist psychoanalytic revisions of the ancient myth.

Johnson, Greg. "The Achievement of Anne Sexton." *Hollins Critic* 21, no. 2 (June 1984): 1-13.

Provides an overview of Sexton's poetry in terms of a search for identity, both personal and social.

Long, Mikhail Ann. "As If Day Had Rearranged into Night: Suicidal Tendencies in the Poetry of Anne Sexton." *Literature and Psychology* 39, nos. 1-2 (1993): 26-41.

Demonstrates that the entire canon of Sexton's poetry is founded upon her desire to die and informed by suicidal thoughts.

McClatchy, J. D., ed. *Anne Sexton: The Artist and Her Critics*. Bloomington: Indiana University Press, 1978, 297 p.

Documents and interprets Sexton's work through previously published interviews with Sexton, a revision of "Elizabeth Gone," personal reflections by those who knew her, including Robert Lowell and Maxine Kumin, early reviews by noted writers, and several overview essays on her works.

Morton, Richard E. *Anne Sexton's Poetry of Redemption: The Chronology of a Pilgrimage*. Lewiston, Maine: Edwin Mellen Press, 1989, 137 p.

Examines Sexton's poetry.

Ostriker, Alicia. "That Story: Anne Sexton and Her Transformations." *American Poetry Review* 11, no. 4 (July-August 1982): 11-17.

Discusses the significance of Transformations, *comparing the volume with respect to the themes and structure of Sexton's other works.*

Wagner-Martin, Linda. *Critical Essays on Anne Sexton*. Boston: G. K. Hall, 1989, 254 p.

Contains reviews, essays, and reminiscences tracing the critical reputation of Sexton and her poetry.

OTHER SOURCES FROM GALE:

Additional coverage of Sexton's life and career is contained in the following sources published by the Gale Group: *American Writers Supplement*, Vol. 2; *Concise Dictionary of American Literary Biography, 1941-1968*; *Contemporary Authors*, Vols. 1-4R, 53-56; *Contemporary Authors Bibliographical Series*, Vol. 2; *Contemporary Authors New Revision Series*, Vols. 3, 36; *Contemporary Literary Criticism*, Vols. 2, 4, 6, 8, 10, 15, 53, 123; *Dictionary of Literary Biography*, Vols. 5, 169; *DISCovering Authors*; *DISCovering Authors: British Edition*; *DISCovering Authors: Canadian Edition*; *DISCovering Authors Modules: Most-studied Authors* and *Poets*; *DISCovering Authors 3.0*; *Encyclopedia of World Literature in the 20th Century*, Ed. 3; *Exploring Poetry*; *Feminist Writers*; *Literature Resource Center*; *Major 20th-Century Writers*, Eds. 1, 2; *Modern American Women Writers*; *Poetry Criticism*, Vol. 2; *Poetry for Students*, Vols. 4, 14; *Poets: American and British*; *Reference Guide to American Literature*, Ed. 4; *Something about the Author*, Vol. 10; *Twayne's United States Authors*; and *World Literature Criticism*.

GERTRUDE STEIN

(1874 - 1946)

American playwright, autobiographer, poet, novelist, and essayist.

A major American writer associated with literary Modernism and Cubist painting, Stein is noted for her avant-garde approach to language and literature. Rejecting patriarchal literary traditions, Stein produced novels, plays, and poetry known for their obscurity and characterized by multiplicity of meanings and absence of punctuation. Her most famous, and most successful, work is her 1933 autobiography *The Autobiography of Alice B. Toklas,* named for her lifelong companion.

BIOGRAPHICAL INFORMATION

The youngest of five children, Stein was born in Allegheny, Pennsylvania, on February 3, 1874, into a wealthy Jewish family. Her parents, Daniel Stein and Amelia Keyser Stein, moved the family to Europe a year after Stein's birth; they spent three years in Vienna and two in Paris before returning to America where they took up residence in Oakland, California. The education of the Stein children—particularly the two youngest, Gertrude and her brother Leo—during this period was chaotic, consisting of a combination of public schooling and private tutors. Stein was an avid reader and she supplemented her meager formal education by reading extensively on her own. After her mother's death in 1888 and her father's in 1891, Stein was raised by her oldest brother Michael, who took a relaxed approach to his duties as guardian of his younger siblings. Stein developed an especially close relationship with her brother Leo, two years her senior, and when Leo went to Harvard University in 1892, Stein decided to follow him. She entered Harvard's women's division in 1893, a year before it became Radcliffe College, and studied under the psychologist William James. Upon graduation, Stein again followed her brother's academic career path, enrolling in Johns Hopkins Medical School. She left in 1902 without earning a degree, and the following year she and Leo moved to Paris. Their home at 27, rue de Fleurus, became a salon frequented by the leading writers and artists of the time, among them Pablo Picasso, Henri Matisse, Guillaume Apollinaire, and Jean Cocteau. In 1913, Leo moved out of the apartment, partly because of disagreements with his sister about art and literature, including Stein's own writing, but chiefly because of Stein's relationship with Alice B. Toklas, who had moved in with the brother and sister in 1909. Stein described Toklas as her "wife" and the two became lifelong companions; Stein and Leo, who became a prominent art critic, never spoke again.

Stein wrote in her studio at night after her guests had departed, producing her first novella in

1903 (unpublished until 1950) and her first published book, *Three Lives,* in 1909. During World War I, Stein and Toklas, subjected to shortages of both food and fuel in wartime Paris, fled to Majorca for a year. They returned to Paris in 1916 and became involved in the war effort. Stein bought a truck, learned to drive, and transported hospital supplies to wounded French and American soldiers for the remainder of the war. Stein characterized the international community of writers in Paris after the war as "the lost generation," but she and Alice rejected their way of life in favor of a conventional bourgeois existence. Rather than frequenting the bars and cafes fashionable with the expatriates, the couple entertained their friends—among them Sherwood Anderson, Ernest Hemingway, and F. Scott Fitzgerald—at home. The 1920s and 1930s were Stein's most productive years and also marked the high point of her literary reputation. Her work was published in a variety of small literary magazines, usually without compensation. Her first, and only, popular and commercial success came with the publication of the best-selling *The Autobiography of Alice B. Toklas* (1933). Following its very favorable reception in America, Stein embarked on a six-month lecture tour of various colleges and universities, among them Harvard and the University of Virginia. Her tour was also a success, and she was finally courted by an American publisher, Bennett Cerf of Random House.

In 1939, Stein and Toklas lived at their summer residence in the farming village of Bilignin, near the Swiss border. Even after France fell, the pair resolved to stay there for the remainder of the war even though their status as Jews and as American nationals made that a dangerous choice. Despite some close calls, they survived the occupation and returned to Paris at the end of 1944, where they began entertaining American G.I.s in their home. Stein's hectic lifestyle began to exhaust her, and she became seriously ill while vacationing in Luceau. She was diagnosed with cancer and underwent an unsuccessful operation for her condition. Stein died July 27, 1946, and was buried in Pere Lachaise Cemetery; Toklas, who died twenty-one years later, was laid to rest by her side.

MAJOR WORKS

Although Stein was an extraordinarily prolific writer who produced works in a wide variety of genres, her best known text remains *The Autobiography of Alice B. Toklas,* a memoir of her early years in Paris up to and including her involvement with the literary community of expatriates in the 1920s. The work was a Literary Guild selection and appeared in a series of four installments in *Atlantic Monthly.* Unlike most of her other works, *The Autobiography* was considered highly readable. In contrast was Stein's personal favorite, the novel *The Making of Americans* which was widely deemed long, rambling, and repetitious, and although the author compared it to *Remembrance of Things Past,* it was judged far too eccentric to find an audience. Assessed as equally difficult was the only volume of poems published during her lifetime, *Tender Buttons* (1914). The work is divided into three sections: "Objects," "Food," and "Rooms," and is considered by many scholars to be Stein's erotic tribute to Toklas.

Her dramatic works, most of them written in her unique experimental style, include *What Happened* (1913), *Ladies' Voices* (1916), and *A Circular Play* (1920). *Four Saints in Three Acts* (1934), which was scored by Virgil Thomson, was one of the few plays by Stein to be produced during her lifetime. She also collaborated with Thomson on 1947's *The Mother of Us All,* a drama based on the life and work of Susan B. Anthony.

Stein's essays on literature, such as *Lectures in America* (1935) and *Narration* (1935), and her memoirs of historical periods and events, such as *Wars I Have Seen* (1945) and *Brewsie and Willie* (1946), were produced in a more conventional, and therefore more accessible, style. Like her autobiography, these works were far more popular with both readers and critics than her more innovative texts.

CRITICAL RECEPTION

Although Stein was forced to underwrite the expenses of her first published work herself, *Three Lives* was well received by American critics who especially praised the story "Melanctha." However, the reception of what Stein considered her masterpiece, *The Making of Americans,* was negative, and she was unable to find an English or American publisher until fourteen years after she completed the book. The majority of her work was considered far too eccentric for most readers and most of it was published at her own expense. Critics and literary scholars objected to Stein's experiments with language and syntax and by her deliberate violations of the standard conventions—both thematic and stylistic—of virtually every literary genre. Her intricate patterns of repetition and her failure to use punctuation made her writing not just challenging, but according to some critics, unreadable.

These same violations of literary norms, though, are what feminist scholars have found most praiseworthy in Stein's body of work. They consider her experimental use of language and forms to be a conscious rejection of the patriarchal literary tradition, and find her treatment of sexuality and gender roles to be bold and innovative. Wendy Steiner (see Further Reading) claims that although Stein was read only as a cult figure at the time of her death, forty years later she had been elevated to a position within the American literary canon largely due to increased attention from feminist critics. Bettina L. Knapp reports on Stein's complicated relationship to feminism, claiming that while Stein was "not an overt subscriber to feminism," in some of her poetry she "clearly displays her ire against the patriarchal Judeo-Christian society."

Ironically, although Stein rejected conventional notions of femininity in her own life, she often advocated a traditional role for other women. Her essay "Degeneration in American Women," written in 1901 or 1902 and recently analyzed by Brenda Wineapple, makes this clear. According to Stein, "the only serious business of life in which [the female] cannot be entirely outclassed by the male is that of child bearing," although she did allow for a limited number of exceptions—herself included. Janice L. Doane (see Further Reading) points out discrepancies between Stein's 1898 essay, "The Value of a College Education for Women," and her polemical 1904 novel *Fernhurst*. According to Doane, in the novel "Stein rejects . . . through her narrator's speech, the defenses of women's colleges which she had previously endorsed so wholeheartedly" in the essay. For Doane, by insisting on essential differences between men and women, Stein put herself in the difficult position of "reserving a special place for herself as an anomaly in terms of traditional categories. She is a woman speaking as a man . . ." Claudia Roth Pierpont concurs, reporting that Stein had been persuaded by a friend to write the paper on women's education; for Stein herself, though, "the last thing she was interested in was the cause of women's rights."

PRINCIPAL WORKS

Three Lives (novellas) 1909

What Happened: A Five Act Play (drama) 1913

Tender Buttons: Objects, Food, Rooms (poetry) 1914

Ladies' Voices (drama) 1916

A Circular Play. A Play in Circles (drama) 1920

Geography and Plays (prose and dramas) 1922

The Making of Americans (novel) 1925

Composition as Explanation (essay) 1926

Useful Knowledge (nonfiction) 1928

A Lyrical Opera Made by Two (drama) 1928

Useful Knowledge (nonfiction) 1928

Lucy Church, Amiably (drama) 1930

Before the Flowers of Friendship Faded Friendship Faded: Written on a Poem by Georges Hugnet (drama) 1931

How to Write (essay) 1931

Say It with Flowers (drama) 1931

Operas and Plays (drama) 1932

The Autobiography of Alice B. Toklas (autobiography) 1933

Four Saints in Three Acts (libretto) 1934

Lectures in America (lectures) 1935

Narration (lecture) 1935

Everybody's Autobiography (autobiography) 1937

The World Is Round (novel) 1939

Ida (novel) 1941

Wars I Have Seen (nonfiction) 1945

Brewsie and Willie (nonfiction) 1946

Selected Writings of Gertrude Stein (prose) 1946

Four in America (prose) 1947

The Mother of Us All (drama) 1947

Things as They Are (novel) 1950

The Yale Edition of the Unpublished Works of Gertrude Stein. 8 vols. (novels, poetry, essays, lectures, and novellas) 1951-1958

Fernhurst, Q.E.D., and Other Early Writings (novel, short story, and essays) 1971

PRIMARY SOURCES

GERTRUDE STEIN (ESSAY DATE C. OCTOBER 1901)

SOURCE: Stein, Gertrude. "Degeneration in American Women." In *Sister Brother: Gertrude and Leo Stein,* by Brenda Wineapple, pp. 411-14. New York: G. P. Putnam's Sons, 1996.

In the following essay, written sometime between October 1901 and early 1902, Stein discusses the problems of sterility and low birth rates among American women, outlining the physiological and voluntary causes which she attributes to the abandonment of maternal ideals.

In an article published in the *Journal of the American Medical Association* October 5, 1901, Dr. Engellman [*sic;* the spelling of Engelmann's name varies throughout] discusses the alarming increase in sterility among American women. He finds that in the United States there is a higher sterility and a lower fecundity than in any other country outside of France and for the native American population the condition is worse than in France. The data that he uses are his own experience in private practice and in the dispensaries of St. Louis consisting of 1700 cases, series of carefully compiled statistics from Boston, Massachusetts and Michigan and the census records.

The facts are as follows:

The normal rate of sterility in foreign countries is eleven percent. In America over twenty percent of the women are childless. The highest fecundity among American born is to be found in St. Louis and that consists of 2.1 children to a marriage a lower rate of fecundity than than [*sic*] is to be found anywhere outside of Paris. In Boston the fecundity is 1.7 & in Michigan it is in the last few years 1.8. It has been slowly decreasing in every state in the union. This can be profitably contrasted with Franklin's estimate for his contemporaries of eight children to a normal marriage and Malthus's estimate of 5.2 children to a marriage in America.

In private practice in St. Louis Engelmann finds among the Americans of American parentage 1.7 children to a marriage and Americans of foreign parentage 1.9 children to a marriage. Among college women the results are still worse the average number of children to a marriage being 1.3 children to 1.6 while the non college woman of the same class and in the same city gives a record of 2.1. In England we find the same result among college women the average college woman's marriage producing 1.5 children while the non-college women in the same class of society average 4.2 children to a marriage.

Engelmann divides his cases among the laboring classes into those of foreign birth and those born in America. Among the foreign population the percent of sterility is 17 while in one generation of residence in America it rises to 26 percent and in the second generation becomes the apparent normal percentage for the modern American that is about 23 percent. In private practice in St. Louis he finds it to be about 23 percent and for college graduates 25. In Massachusetts we find the same discrepancy between the foreign and the native born population. The foreign born portion of the community shows 13.3 percent of the women sterile while the native population shows a percentage of 20.3 which in Boston runs up to 23.7. Now let us contrast these figures with those of foreign countries. In Paris the percentage of sterility is 27.3, in Berlin the sterility among the higher classes is 25.7 while among the laboring classes it is only 15 percent. These figures are rather appalling for these two cities have always been considered the most complete type of degeneration from the standpoint of fecundity and yet Berlin shows a better percent and Paris only a slightly worse one than obtains throughout America among the native population. From England we get the following figures, among the higher classes 16.4 percent among villagers 9.6 percent and among college alumnae 27.6 percent.

About 25 percent of all this sterility can be attributed to disease caused by the male for the rest as Dr. Engellmann concludes the barrenness in the large majority of cases is independent of physical causes as evidenced by the astonishing increase in sterility in this country with the marked increase in progress of gynecology which should control sterility were it due to disease and physical causes. Instead of that we have passed to a fecundity less and a sterility greater than any country except France. In considering the question of the causes for the marked increase in sterility among American women one fact cannot be too often dwelt upon. The fact that the normal period of fertility for a woman is from her eighteenth to her forty fifth year and that unless labor has so to speak cleared a passage, from her twenty fifth year on there is a gradual hardening of all her genitalia making conception rarer, miscarriages more frequent and labor much more dangerous. The first labor of a woman at thirty is always a much more serious matter than in the case of a young woman. This fact is one that must be kept constantly in mind when one is considering the causes of sterility among American women.

In considering the causes of sterility it is best to divide them into two classes,

1. Physiological sterility.

2. Voluntary sterility. These two classes must again be divided into

A. Absolute sterility by which we mean women who have never conceived.

B. Relative sterility that is women who have never come to term. The causes of phisiological [*sic*] sterility of the absolute variety are the impotence on the part of the male, anatomical malformation on the part of the female, gonnorheal [*sic*] infection of the female and gynecological operations. The relative physiological sterility is due either to a syphilitic infection of the female or to congenital weakness. All these causes together with miscarriages due to obscure puerperal infections combine to make up the eleven percent sterility that one may call the normal sterility among civilised races and which is known as Simpson's law of sterility. In addition to these causes for physiological sterility which we may perhaps call the normal causes of sterility among civilized peoples there are a set of causes bringing about physiological sterility both of the absolute and relative type which are due to the education and habits of life that obtain among the American women of to day.

The first point is that of the prevailing tendency to delay marriages until a woman's period of fertility is almost half over and the dangers and difficulties of conception and labor have become markedly increased. The second point is that in our modern system of education the heaviest mental strain is put upon the girl when her genitalia is making its heaviest physical demand and when her sexual desires are being constantly stimulated without adequate physiological relief, a condition that obtains to a very considerable extent in our average American college life. All these causes induce of necessity a weakening of the genitalia and a consequent increase of absolute and relative physiological sterility. The third point is the incessant strain and stress that the modern woman endeavoring to know all things, do all things and enjoy all things undergoes. This condition of life must of necessity lead to weakness and inadequacy of the genitalia as the whole physical scheme of the woman is directed toward fitness for propagation.

If these conditions only obtained among the upper classes in this country one might deplore but one could afford to disregard them for after all a nation never depends upon its upper classes but as will be noted in the statistics given by Engellmann there is not that immense difference in the percentage of sterility and fecundity in this country between the upper and lower classes that we find in all European countries. In America what the upper classes do the middle classes do and what is true of the middle class holds for the laboring classes and so we find in this country a uniform sterility and lack of fecundity varying very little from the top to the bottom.

The second and more important class of sterility is the voluntary type. It is this kind of sterility and lack of fecundity that that [*sic*] is so markedly increasing in America among all classes of the population. This type of sterility is of course all due to moral causes and these are so numerious [*sic*] that one can hardly do more than give the headings.

Voluntary sterility consists first of the absolute type that due to methods of prevention of conception and the relative type that of the criminal abortion. As both these types of sterility are due to the same moral causes they may be considered together.

Two classes of the community I imagine are chiefly responsible for the increased knowledge of methods of prevention among the laboring classes. On the one hand the charity workers with misdirected zeal and false ideals have spread as far as in them lay the knowledge of methods of prevention. The constantly increasing use of the dispensaries and the knowledge there obtained has helped to spread this feeling that prevention should be indulged in. As one old negress put it, "I had twenty children I would not do that now any more I know too much." Let us now consider a few of the causes that have led to the disrepute into which the ideal of maternity has fallen and see what can be said for them.

In the first place among the educated classes in this country, that is among the educated women and among the pseudo educated women there is a strong tendency to what we may call the negation of sex and the exaltation of the female ideal of moral and methods and a condemnation and abhorrence of virility.

By this statement is meant the tendency of the modern American woman to mistake her education her cleverness and intelligence for effective capacity for the work of the world. In consequence she underestimates the virile quality because of its apparent lack of intelligence. In the moral world she also finds herself the superior because on account of the characteristic chivalry of the American man the code of morality which her sheltered life has developed seems adequate for the real business of life and it is only rarely that she learns that she never actually comes in contact with the real business and that when she does the male code is the only possible one. All this of course leads to a lack of respect both for the matrimonial and maternal ideal for it will only be when women succeed in relearning the fact that the only serious business of life in which they cannot be entirely outclassed by the male is that of child bearing that they will once more look with respect upon their normal and legitimate function. Of course it is not meant that there are not a few women in every generation who are exceptions to this rule but these exceptions are too rare to make it necessary to subvert the order of things in their behalf and besides if their need for some other method of expression is a real need there is very little doubt but that the opportunity of expression will be open to them.

Another very important cause for the low rate of fecundity lies in the modern morbid responsibility for offspring. This is true in America for both parents. There is a foolish conviction abroad that the parents can raise one or two children better than half a dozen can raise themselves. This fallacy is due to the same cleverness of the American woman which has just ben [sic] mentioned and makes her mistake a knowledge of facts for training in method and makes her believe it possible for her to learn by a few lectures the things one only gets after years spent day after day in the daily round of working, listening and waiting. This conviction produces the type that is the terror to the trained professional mind, the intelligent mother. When this generation learns over again the truth that the training of children should on the one hand consist of a back ground in the home of a tradition that stands for honesty and right living and that for the rest it should in the hands of the trained professional the morbid responsibility, for the offspring will disappear [sic]. On the paternal side the responsibicity [sic] takes the form of the onviction [sic] that one should bear children only when you can remove them as far as humanly possible from the normal conditions of a struggle for existence.

The prevailing pessimism that characterizes the modern community and carries with it a ceaseless desire for amusement and a consequent incrnase [sic] in the expense of living is another of the important causes for the marked increase in sterility. The American population seems to have completely lost sight of the fact that the exercise of ones [sic] normal functions of living, walking, talking, thinking, being, eating and drinking is an endless joy of a healthy human being. As Jasper Petulengro puts it in answer to Lavengro's melancholy "There's night and day brother both sweet things, sun moon and stars brother all sweet things, there is likewise the wind on the heath. Life is very sweet brother who would wish to die." No in the development [sic] of the play instinct and the feeling of joy in the world one must look for a counteracting force against the prevailing

pessimism and the consequent voluntary sterility. Another important element to be considered is the characteristic inefficiency in household matters of the lower class American woman. She is incapable for the most part of cooking sewing or any of the household duties for which her European sisters are famous. Her housekeeping is expensive and the food she supplies her family is not for the most part nutritious. Besides she does not want to increase her labors by her normal maternal functions. Just to cite one case that is extremely characteristic. A woman the wife of a railroad conductor and a very worthy person has been married for five years. Her husband is very fond of children and wants them the woman however refuses on account of the bother. She has within the last two years voluntarily brought about two miscarriages. This is not an isolated case but can be matched in any street and house in any city in the union. It is this point that cannot be too much insisted upon that this condition does not prevail among the better classes alone but that it is true of every class of the American population and that there is in no portion of the community that lives its fair quota of population except the foreign and this virtue is lost by the first generation born in America.

To conclude: unless the American woman can be made once more to realize that the ideal of maternity is the only worthy one for her to hold, until she can be made to realize that no work of hers can begin to compensate for the neglect of that function we are going the same way as France except that with true American push we are going France considerably better and a few years are showing a worse record than she has after ages of degenerative civilization. In discussing this subject one inevitably thinks of the picture of Brush in the Boston museum that of the mother with the lusty child in her arms. She is worn and weary but the vigorous struggling baby in her arms transfigures her weariness and changes it from a sacrifice to the purest pride.

GENERAL COMMENTARY

MARY E. GALVIN (ESSAY DATE 1999)

SOURCE: Galvin, Mary E. "'This Shows It All': Gertrude Stein and the Reader's Role in the Creation of Significance." In *Queer Poetics: Five Modernist Women Writers*, pp. 37-50. Westport, Conn.: Praeger, 1999.

In the following essay, Galvin analyzes the purpose and significance of Stein's subversion of traditional assumptions about literary language, form, and precedents in terms of her position as lesbian writer.

Next to Sappho, Gertrude Stein (1874-1946) is probably the most famous lesbian writer in recorded literary history. However, although the nature and duration of her relationship with Alice B. Toklas has long been common knowledge, until recently most Stein critics when considering her work have chosen either to disregard politely Stein's sexual "difference" or to act as if this "difference" in Stein really made her no different from other "men of genius": that she simply assumed the male role and acted out her relationship with Alice heterosexually, in the timeworn tradition of the great poet and his companion/servant/muse.

In either case, we can see heterosexist assumptions operating to erase the significance of lesbian existence in the creation of modern literature. The first approach simply ignores sexuality and gendered positions as relevant in reading Stein. This is a surprisingly "generous" move when we consider that the gender of the writer has been taken into account critically since the days of Plato and Aristotle. Yet with Stein, many critics seem to have been content to accept her as an honorary "man," in the generic, universal sense. Stein's inclusion within the canon of modernist poetry depends on a willingness to disregard her gender and her sexuality, except perhaps to note in passing that she is one of the few "female" participants in the category, "Significant Writers of the 20th century."[1]

The second approach, to acknowledge Stein's lesbian existence but recast it in bourgeois, heterosexual terms, helps bring her life, if not her work, into the realm of the "thinkable." Critics favorable to Stein attempt to render her life respectable in these terms, while those who insist on her lunacy find that her inability to be authentically heterosexual constitutes the source of great "anxiety" in both her writings and her life. Both of these positions assume a fundamental heterosexuality, which, even if it is somehow strayed from, is still the standard.

The idea that a lesbian is really a man trapped in a woman's body, is only one of several ways that the straight mind can acknowledge lesbian existence and yet still manage to dismiss it as culturally or epistemologically insignificant. By acknowledging a "difference" that is in fact the same, the straight mind, with its limited range of what is thinkable psychosexually, does not need to make any structural shifts in order to accommodate anything "other" than that which is already contained within the perameters of its dichotomies.

In more recent years, with the rise of feminist literary criticism and the increasingly visible lesbian and gay liberation movement, it has become more acceptable to discuss Stein's lesbianism as a relevant factor in any critical assessment of her life and work. One of the more popular strategies for reading Stein as lesbian is to insist that there is a Steinian code by which she can speak to Alice erotically, without drawing censure from her larger public.

Advocates of this hermeneutic approach often claim that although Stein's code is arbitrary, it can be cracked, and once we have our cribsheet filled in, we can readily interpret everything from her frequency of orgasm to her guilt complex at having failed heterosexually oriented familial expectations. While the motives for devising such an ingenious critical approach to Stein may be genuine in terms of accepting, even honoring, the lesbian behind the "man of genius," the major shortcoming of this method is that it rests on principles that are antithetical not only to Stein's approach to composition, but also to her articulation of a nonhierarchically based lesbian existence.[2]

Gertrude Stein was a relentless advocate of what she termed "democracy." While this particular term, along with its counterpart, "equality," have been perhaps irretrievably corrupted for us late-twentieth-century readers, conceptually, the ideas these terms represent are still quite fresh. In more contemporary terms, Stein's "democracy" translates into our grappling with the nonhierarchical, the nonpatriarchal, with new ways of thinking that embrace multiplicity.

Indeed, such a discourse is very strange to our patriarchally entrenched linguistic consciousness, and many readers have felt intimidated, or even threatened, by Stein's strange discourse. For example, her aversion to punctuation has been received with varying degrees of hostility and confusion, yet she avoided it because she found it to be too directive. As Judy Grahn says about Stein's use of (or lack of) commas, "She thought this was condescending to and undermining of the independence of mind of the reader."[3] By eschewing grammatical structuring, with its privileging of the noun-verb phrase and its insistence on temporal closure, Stein was extending this democratic attitude toward language itself.

To some extent, the hostility some readers have felt toward Stein's irreverent deconstruction of "meaning" and her abdication of the privileged position of knowing (authority) is understandable, in light of how much of our social order depends on such principles. Usually, the occurrence of certain expected structures constitutes its own sort of "code," which allows the reader certain short-cuts to comprehension. Without these structures in place, people tend to feel ungrounded, sensing that all their assumptions about reality and their place in it have been dislocated. In many ways, this is analogous to how lesbian existence is received under heterosexism. To acknowledge the presence and difference of lesbian existence, even unconsciously, is unsettling of the "comfort" provided by heterosexist structures.

On an unconscious level, then, the fact that Stein actually was a lesbian and not particularly secretive about it probably fed into the critical resistance toward accepting the challenge of her experiments. This resentment can sometimes take the form of feeling excluded, as if one were being left out of the joke.

We can see why some believe she was writing in a secret lovers' language to Alice. But if this were true, why would she bother to seek publication and to elicit responses from many readers, even of the unpublished manuscripts? While it is true that Alice was probably the first reader to take her seriously and the one to give her the most support most consistently (her brother Leo mocked her), there is no reason to presume she was writing only for Alice.

From the outset of her writing career, Gertrude Stein was outside the literary establishment. Trained in psychology and medicine, and subsequently living in Paris, she was an interloper in the field of American letters. The writing she produced, always composed of relatively simple words and phrases, drew directly from colloquial diction; Stein's use of a finite vocabulary eschewed the use of "literary" diction. Through a combination of repetition and variation, Stein found she could create emphasis and degrees of emotional intensity without relying heavily on adjectives and nouns to further her descriptions. In this way she could begin to move away from the categorizing tendencies of these particular parts of speech.

By abandoning nominalism, a staple of traditional literary poetics, Stein also severed her dependence on metaphor. If she felt any clarification was necessary, she would repeat her "meaning" (her original word choice) in a slightly different verbal context. In this way, she avoided drawing resemblances between two dissimilar beings, since doing so would have falsified the unique being of the person, place, or thing described. Stein was always acutely aware of the variety, the multiplicity of identity, of "being."

Thus, her writing, always in an American idiom, defies hermeneutic approaches in its repetitive, sparsely punctuated, and illogical form, yet manages to engage us through its effective use of sound and tone. This kind of writing is best read aloud, for it is then that we can fully appreciate the "insistence" for which she was aiming:

> They did then learn many ways to be gay and
>   they
> were then being gay being quite regular in being
> gay, being gay and they were learning little
> things, little things in ways of being gay, they
> were very regular then, they were learning very
> many little things in ways of being gay, they
>   were
> being gay and using these little things they were
> learning to have to be gay with regularly gay
>   with
> then and they were gay the same amount they
>   had
> been gay.[4]

While it is exceedingly popular to consider Stein a singular "genius" existing in isolation without connection to poetic predecessors, particularly other lesbian or even female predecessors, I see Stein as a direct descendant of Dickinson. In her linguistic experimentation, Stein, like Dickinson, often plays with the multiplicity of language: its ability for ambiguity, equivocation, and unstable meanings.

In both poets, we can witness a propensity for disrupting categorical distinctions, and therefore the "truths" they establish. Whereas Dickinson does leave just enough traditional structure in place to make interpretation feasible, Stein pushes her poetics of disruption into the realm of the rationally unrecognizable.

If Dickinson's poetics are like a ghost that haunts convention, displacing objects and expectations, then Stein's poetics are like a volcanic eruption, permeating and undermining structure and form on every level, from the "balanced completion" of the sentence to that of the paragraph, through genres, and ultimately addressing the larger assumptions of culture and tradition itself.

One such set of assumptions that Stein's writing undermines is the concept of literary language and form, and the need for critical interpretation. The passage quoted above, taken from **"Miss Furr and Miss Skeene,"** is fairly self-evident in its content. Only if one is operating from a critical base that assumes the symbolic, that sense is concealed rather than revealed through language, can one be puzzled by the "meaning" of the passage. It's "about" two women who learn how to be gay and then do so "regularly." The "difficulty" in reading this passage comes only when a reader refuses the obvious and retreats to the familiarity of heterosexist assumption. Of course, Stein is playing with this propensity to think "straight" in her choice of the word "gay," which puns directly on the different, but not mutually exclusive, denotations accorded the word.

In "The There That Was and Was Not There," contemporary lesbian poet and theorist Judy Grahn writes: "For years I thought: 'She is difficult,' until one day it occurred to me to say it the other way: 'She is easy. I am difficult.' . . . Suppose it is not that she is veiled and obscure but that we, her readers, are. We are veiled by our judgments" (Grahn, 5).

Of course, the veil of heterosexism works to obscure the lesbian content of **"Miss Furr and Miss Skeene,"** but the obscurity is not inherent in Stein's use of language. In a further example of this cultural obscurantism, many readers have taken the presence of "some dark and heavy men" as well as "some who were not so heavy and some who were not so dark" to imply that Helen Furr and Georgine Skeene had heterosexual liaisons. But just the fact that the two women knew and "sat with" some men does not mean they are not lesbian. Contrary to popular mythology, lesbians do not hate men and often have friendships as well as other relationships with a variety of men. And these men could, of course, be gay men. The fact that some of these men were "dark and heavy" (and some were not!) could contradict another heterosexist stereotype—that gay men tend to be pale and thin as well as lispy and limp-wristed. When Stein mentions these male associates of Helen and Georgine, she states, "They were regular then, they were gay then, they were where they wanted to be then, where it was gay to be then, they were regularly gay then."

In her personal life, Stein was not "in the closet." Anyone who came to visit her understood the nature of the relationship between Alice and herself. In fact, her overt lesbianism eventually became a source of great distress for Ernest Hemingway, who would have preferred her to be more closeted. There is little reason to assume she was closeted in her writing. In her subject matter, Stein tended to draw on the "actualities" around her—people, objects, and events she had known.

Yet, even as she drew on these "actualities," it is really the use of language itself and its interactions with consciousness that constitutes her main theme. Unlike her contemporaries the imagists,

Stein's concern with consciousness led her to abandon any pretense of "objectivity." Hers is a writing of intersubjectivity—and the psychosexual aspect of her own subjectivity was decidedly lesbian.

One of the accusations hurled at Stein by her detractors is that her writing is solipsistic, self-occupied, and self-centered. Yet in her search for the "bottom nature" of her characters, for the "essence" of objects and foods, she was really seeking to discover and record the inner being, the consciousness of the world around her. Paradoxically, she realized, particularly in writing her first "poetry" cycle **Tender Buttons,** that the only access she could have to these other "inner beings" was through her own consciousness. Thus, she discarded the illusion of objective knowing and its concomitant poetics of "objective" description, and located her writing firmly within her own consciousness as it played in contemplation across the surface of its subject. This "self-centering," as Judy Grahn calls it, ironically, was not self-occupied, but was geared toward what she termed "listening."

Stein herself always considered her writing to be accessible to anyone who would listen. She believed strongly in the intelligence of her readers, and in publishing her writing, she was inviting her readers to listen alongside her to the inner being of the subject at hand, as well as to the play of her own consciousness in its encounter with her subject. Thus, the subjectivity in her writing is not solipsistic, but an extension of subjectivity from and to others, a layering of multiple subjectivities. In order to create this writing of intersubjectivity, she knew she had to forego any attempt at representationality. Not only would a poetics of resemblance compromise the unique inner being of her subject matter, but it would also burden her language with associations and meanings that would interfere with the immediate experience of "listening."

In this one aspect, at least, Gertrude Stein was not unlike many of her contemporaries, who were concerned with divesting the English language of its cultural baggage and reclaiming its poetic possibilities from an overwrought sentimentality. But while others were occupied with wresting new meanings from the language to express the radical sentiments of a new age, Stein went a step further, attempting to divest language from the burden of representationality itself.

In **"Patriarchal Poetry,"** Stein explores the traditional role of linear sequence in the creation of "meaning." Rather than de*lineating* her comprehension of the way this discourse functions, however, Stein simply demonstrates her knowledge through parody:

> What is the difference between a fig and an
> apple. One comes before the other. What is the
> difference between a fig and an apple one comes
> before the other what is the difference between a
> fig and an apple one comes before the other.
> When they are here they are here too here too
>   they are here too. When they are here they
>   are
> here too when they are here they are here too.
>   As out in it there.
>   As not out not out in it there as out in it out
> in it there as out in it there as not out in it
> there as out in as out in it as out in it there.
>   Next to next next to Saturday next to next
>   next
> to Saturday next to next next to Saturday.
>   This shows it all.[5]

Patriarchal language, and by extension heterocentric thinking, depend on a categorical approach toward identity. In this passage, Stein demonstrates her understanding of how the concept of "difference" depends on a dichotomous distinction that hangs on the simple negative "not."

Typically, in this system of discourse, "not out" is equivalent to "in it." Yet, this is only part of the story. The initial passage, "What is the difference between a fig and an apple. One comes before the other" illustrates the role temporality plays in categorical concepts of identity. This temporal structure is usually maintained through the linear sequence of grammar. Thus, when she plays with the distinction between "out" and "in" without the guiding structure of grammatical subordination, Stein shows us that the distinction cannot hold through a simple dichotomous negation alone. Such a distinction must also exist in a larger structural context, one that privileges a certain notion of time as linear sequence.

Taken together, these combined elements of patriarchal poetry, definition through exclusion, and adherence to "proper" sequence, allow the arrogant and grandiose claim to complete knowledge: "This shows it all." At the same time, by parodying the certitude of such a technique, Stein herself is claiming to have uncovered something important about the way such a poetics defines a consciousness. Her playful traversal of linguistic boundaries has enabled Stein to reveal these boundaries at work in our consciousness. Thus, her writing also "shows it all."

In her explorations of linguistic structure in its relation to consciousness, Stein returned again and again to the problem of grammar. For it is here that we find the keystone to both linear and hierarchical thinking:

> In Stein's work the linear plot inherent in English language sentences falls away. The noun is no longer the all-important main character surrounded by subservient modifiers and dependent articles and clauses, the verb is no longer a mounted hero riding into the sentence doing all the action, while the happy or tragic ending of objective clause waits in the wings with appropriate punctuation to lead us through the well-known plot to the inevitable end period.
>
> She let the characters (which in some of her writing are parts of speech or numbers, not people or other creatures) spin out from their own internal natures as she let them happen from within themselves rather than placing them in an externally directed context. She discovered them as she uncovered them layer by layer through the rhythms of their speech or parts of speech, and the patterns of their daily lives, she listened to them as her eyes listened to Cezanne's intensity of color, carrying this idea of equality further to where everything in a given field is seen as equally vital, life is perceived as a dance in which every element contributes to every other.
>
> (Grahn, 11)

Throughout her career, Stein experimented with various ways to achieve this effect. As she herself has written, she took her initial cue from Cezanne, Matisse, Picasso, and other early modernist painters. Stein began converting words from bearers of meaning and identity into plastic entities, treating them in their purely sensory character. She did this by arranging them next to each other, setting up and exploring spatial and tactile relations among them rather than the more conventional syntactic, semantic, logical ones.

For the reader, these relations can only occur in the present moment, since they are unique to the text, yet do not depend on what precedes or follows in it. The absence of a linear syntax (on the level of the sentence) or a narrative progression (on the level of overall structure) strips the text of any temporal reference to anything else in the text.

Thus, in reading her text, we must inhabit the "continuous present" of the text at all times. Since this focus on language without the linear structure of past-present-future is so foreign to our typical ways of thinking through language, Stein brings to the forefront of our awareness the linguistic structures on which our thinking usually depends. Through what is absent, we become conscious of the role linguistic structures usually play in our creation of "meaning."

When the text frustrates our attempts to formulate a coherency of significance, we are made aware of the extent to which our "consciousness," as it is socially constructed through language, depends on the concepts of meaning and identity to hold it together. Any "meaning" that may arise from reading Stein's text stems from the confluence of linguistic habit with the reader's subjectivity, which includes personal experience, outside knowledge, and leaps of the imagination, all interacting within the context provided by the text itself.

Just as she sought to work nonhierarchically within the linguistic field of her writings, Stein also sought to establish a nonhierarchical relation to her readers. Stein's poetics of intersubjectivity depends on the participation of the reader, with her culturally inculcated desire for meaning and the openness of her own consciousness as it plays across the text in search of this meaning.

By taking words from their expected context and placing them outside the confines of typical grammatical structure, Stein is creating a linguistic space where words can be more flexible. Taken out of the clearly defined roles of a patriarchal discourse, they begin to resonate with their own potential, as the reader is thwarted in her attempt to determine the author's intent.

Since Stein is not interested in conveying any definitive "meaning" through her text, her writing is void of the patriarchal concept of the author's "intent." Rather, Stein seeks only to convey the play of her consciousness through language. She is abdicating her "authority" over "meaning," thereby subverting a hierarchical power and creating a more "democratic" relationship to her reader.

In playing fiercely with the multiplicity of language, Stein breaks down the distinction between author and reader in the search for "meaning." The absence of exact meaning is for Stein a space she opens up into a broad vista of significance, which she invites the reader to step inside to experience together with her, in the only time the text allows, the continuous present. The fluidity of language use she achieves by foregoing the hierarchizing structures of grammar allows each word in the text to reverberate with possible significances, and the reader's participation is crucial in this process.

Even when Stein's work focuses on her relationship with Alice, she invites us to participate in her play of consciousness as its language dances across the page. In what is perhaps her "most lesbian" poem, "Lifting Belly," Stein calls her disruptive poetics of intersubjectivity into action, so that the reader is invited into a lesbian world, the world viewed through a lesbian consciousness.

It is clearly evident that Alice played an important part in Stein's life, art, and sense of personal identity. Early on, in her portrait of Melanctha, Stein observed that everyone has loving in them and that this loving is a central aspect of identity. Nearly ten years later, in "Lifting Belly," Stein chose to write about the significance of the particular kind of loving she and Alice shared, and to explore the effects this loving was having on her own sense of being.[6]

Written while Gertrude and Alice were staying in Majorca during the First World War, the poem centers on the daily life and conversation shared by the two lovers. Although Alice had already been living with Stein for about seven years, Leo had moved out of 27 Rue de Fleuris only the previous year. The time period in which "Lifting Belly" was written (1915-1917) constitutes what must have been a "honeymoon" period in their relationship. Thus, it is fitting that the poem Stein wrote during this period comprises her fullest linguistic exploration of her relationship with Alice.

The poem places the two women in relationship with each other, and with the world and people around them. As they converse on various subjects with varying degrees of seriousness and silliness, they return again and again to the title phrase, "Lifting Belly."

Grammatically, the phrase constantly shifts roles. It is an action, a person, an event, and more. While the phrase has an obvious sexual connotation, Stein places it in an wide array of contexts so that the words begin to multiply with significances never before imagined. Thereby she destabilizes and expands its "meaning." Everything the lovers discuss in the poem is discussed in relation to "Lifting Belly." "Lifting Belly" becomes the lens through which the lovers view and speak of the world. It is their lesbian consciousness:

> Lifting belly is an occasion. An occasion to
> please me. Oh yes. Mention it.
> Lifting belly is courteous.
> Lifting belly is hilarious, gay and favorable.
> Oh Yes it is.
> Indeed it is not a disappointment.
> Not to me.
> Lifting belly is such an incident. In one's life
> Lifting belly is such an incident in one's life.
> I don't mean to be reasonable.
> Shall I say thin.
> This makes me smile.
> Lifting belly is so kind.
>
> (*Yale*, 10)

ABOUT THE AUTHOR

WINEAPPLE DISCUSSES STEIN'S
RELATIONSHIP TO FEMINISM

Gertrude Stein was iconoclastic, intelligent, and querulous. Her prose cleansed both the language and our habits of reading it. But willing to comment on and contradict herself with an insouciance positively Whitmanesque, in our day she has herself become something of a cipher, seized by those who found in her prose, and then in her person, the shibboleth of a cause. But she was neither the Mother Goose of Montparnasse nor the Mother of Us All.

Was she a feminist? "Degeneration" renders the question obsolete. Its author was brash, untried, and rife with the conflicts a more poised Stein would later conceal or convert into literary muscle: she who would never be a mother advised motherhood; she who would be virtually canonized as one of the most creative and liberated women of the century counseled the mundane and conservative—but not for herself. And this lesbian Jew who loved democracy, inspiring women and men to discover themselves, also spoke a nativist language, urging white middle-class American women to submit to a round of putative or biological givens.

The paradoxes of "Degeneration" are the paradoxes of Gertrude Stein, neither radical nor philistine, feminist nor foul; in "Degeneration" she is a twenty-eight-year-old woman grappling with her life and on its threshold. She is alive, complex, jam-packed with contradiction—and the biographer's true find.

Wineapple, Brenda. Excerpt from "Gertrude Stein: Woman Is a Woman Is." *The American Scholar* 67 (winter 1997): 107-12.

It is fairly common knowledge among lesbians and gay men that the process of "coming out" involves more than simply acknowledging and deciding whether or not to act on one's sexual inclinations. Because the decision to "come out" is made in the context of a culture that is hostile, or at best indifferent, to nonheterosexual choosing, this "personal" decision affects our relationship with the culture at large.

Coming out necessarily entails a "difference of view," since to accept the dominant view would render our lesbianism "impossible." This difference of view has been described by Audre Lorde as an "erotic knowledge," a knowledge that "empowers us, becomes a lens through which we scrutinize all aspects of our existence."[7] In **"Lifting Belly,"** Stein is both celebrating and exploring the power of this erotic knowing in her life. She wants to share with us, her readers, the effects of "such an incident in one's life."

> Lifting belly is such an experiment.
> We were thoroughly brilliant.
> If I were a postman I would deliver letters. We
> call them letter carriers.
> Lifting belly is so strong. And so judicious.
> Lifting belly is an exercise.
> Exercise is very good for me.
> Lifting belly necessarily pleases the latter.
> Lifting belly is necessary.
> Do believe me.
> Lifting belly quietly.
> It is very exciting.
> Stand.
> Why do you stand.
> Did you say you thought it would make any
> difference.
> Lifting belly is not so kind.
> Little places to sting.
> We used to play star spangled banner.
> Lifting belly is so near.
> Lifting belly is so dear.
> Lifting belly all around.
> Lifting belly makes a sound.
>
> (*Yale*, 13-14)

In devising techniques that are decidedly unlike traditional "patriarchal poetry," Stein does not set out to describe her relationship with Alice for us; a descriptive voice would automatically cast the reader as an outsider to the relationship. Rather, she wants to draw us into the play of her lesbian consciousness. She does this by bringing us into the poem as active participants in the wordplay of the language. For, above all, **"Lifting Belly"** is playful.

As she explores the eroticism of vision she shares with Alice, Stein also explores and celebrates the language in its erotic possibilities. The poem abounds with rhymes, homonyms, and associational relations among words and phrases. Bristling with what today might be called *jouissance*, Stein's text is an energy field, and we are invited to dance within the charged atmosphere of instability and overdetermination of meaning.

> This is the way I see it.
> Lifting belly can you say it.

Lifting belly persuade me.
Lifting belly persuade me.
You'll find it very easy to sing to me.
What can you say.
Lifting belly set.
I can not pass a door.
You mean odor.
I smell sweetly.
So do you.
Lifting belly plainly.
Can you sing.
Can you sing for me.
Lifting belly settled.
Can you excuse money.
Lifting belly has a dress.
Lifting belly in a mess.
Lifting belly in order.
Complain I don't complain.
She is my sweetheart.
Why doesn't she resemble an other.
This I cannot say here.
Full of love and echoes. Lifting belly is full of
    love.

                  (**Yale**, 30-31)

While it may be tempting to read **"Lifting Belly"** as a "dialogue" between lovers, the text itself resists such a reading. One of the greatest hindrances to a dialogic approach is that the poem is devoid of quotation marks or any other clear differentiation of speakers. The effect of the absence of clear reference marks is similar to that of Dickinson's ambiguously referenced pronouns: in both poets, ambiguity allows for a richly evocative multiplicity of significance. To try to sort out which lines can be attributed to which lover is not only impossible, but undoes what Stein has accomplished. Throughout **"Lifting Belly,"** she is not trying to exclude the reader, but to create a shared linguistic space.

Rather than struggling to reassert an order intentionally eschewed by Stein, the poem might be more fruitfully engaged by giving ourselves over to the text as it is written. While it is true that the poem conveys a sense of intimacy between the lovers, the lack of attributive punctuation works toward inviting the reader into this intimacy. We must bring our own consciousness, full of imagination and inventiveness, into the text.

We cannot stand outside the poem in judgment of its "meaning" or its structure; we must participate in the construction of its "meaning" or else it remains meaningless. **"Lifting Belly"** is about relationship, the relationship shared by Gertrude and Alice, and the difference their lesbianism made in their relationship to the world, their consciousness of the world, and the events around them. Through a complex strategy of presenting

us with a "dialogue" lacking quotation marks, in which a continually repeated and redefined "subject" ("lifting belly") is discussed with a determinedly ambiguous reference to other subjects, Stein makes the reader a participant in the conversation rather than an eavesdropper. In this way, Stein draws her readers into a relationship with her lesbian loving and perceiving. She is inviting us into the continuum of lesbian existence.

Lifting belly is so kind.
Darling wifie is so good.
Little husband would.
Be as good.
If he could.
This was said.
Now we know how to differ.
From that.
Certainly.
Now we say.
Little hubbie is good.
Every Day.
She did want a photograph.
Lifting belly changed her mind.
              Lifting belly changed her
    mind.
Do I look fat.
Do I look fat and thin.
Blue eyes and windows.
You mean Vera.
Lifting belly can guess.
Quickly.
Lifting belly is so pleased.
Lifting Belly seeks pleasure.
And she finds it altogether.

                  (**Yale**, 49)

In **"Lifting Belly,"** Stein brings to the forefront the play of the signifier as it joyfully traverses the boundaries of logic and identificatory meaning. Just as Stein's nontraditional use of language allowed her to experiment with nonhierarchically based forms of expression, her lesbian connection with Alice allowed her to experiment with nonhierarchical forms of human relationships.

Throughout the poem, several "roles" are mentioned: baby, pussy, caesar, bunny, husband, wife, mother, man, bird. But the lack of quotation marks makes it impossible to know which of the lovers to attribute lines to, so that the ambiguity of the speaker's identity feeds into the ambiguity of the roles named. The taking on of sexual/gender roles in the poem is arbitrary and temporary. Stein is playing with our expectations for such roles to be stable and consistent, just as she disrupts our expectations in regard to the grammatical functions of words. By inviting the reader into her linguistic dance, she is inviting us to experience the playful construction of identity, as consciousness, sexuality, and language collide within the energy field that is her text.

In the meantime listen to Miss Cheatham.
In the midst of writing.
In the midst of writing there is merriment.

                                        (*Yale*, 54)

Notes

1. For an excellent historical overview of Stein criticism, see Michael J. Hoffman, *Critical Essays on Gertrude Stein* (Boston: G. K. Hall, 1986). Richard Bridgman, *Gertrude Stein in Pieces* (New York: Oxford University Press, 1970) and Shari Benstock, *Women of the Left Bank* (Austin: University of Texas Press, 1986) were indispensable to me in writing this chapter.

2. I am indebted to Benstock for her argument advocating a reassessment of this approach and for the suggestiveness of her own reading strategy, particularly as delineated in *Women of the Left Bank,* 158-193. For approaches that favor this "lesbian hermeneutics," see Bridgman, *Gertrude Stein in Pieces*; Elizabeth Fifer, *Rescued Readings: A Reconstruction of Gertrude Stein's Difficult Texts* (Detroit: Wayne State University Press, 1992); Sandra M. Gilbert and Susan Gubar, *No Man's Land, Volume 1* (New Haven, Conn.: Yale University Press, 1988); Lisa Ruddick, "A Rosy Charm: Gertrude Stein and the Repressed Feminine," in Hoffman, *Critical Essays*, 225-240; Cynthia Secor, "Gertrude Stein: The Complex Force of Her Femininity," in *Women, the Arts, and the 1920's in Paris and New York*, eds. Kenneth W. Wheeler and Virginia Lee Lussier (New Brunswick, N. J.: Rutgers University Press, 1982), 27-35; and Catherine R. Stimpson, "Gertrice/Altrude: Stein, Toklas, and the Paradox of the Happy Marriage," in *Mothering the Mind*, eds. Ruth Perry and Martine Watson Brownley (New York: Holmes and Meyer, 1984), "Gertrude Stein and the Transposition of Gender" in *The Poetics of Gender*, ed. Nancy K. Miller (New York: Columbia University Press, 1986), "The Mind, the Body, and Gertrude Stein," in *Critical Inquiry* 3, no. 3 (Spring 1977): 489-506, and "The Somagrams of Gertrude Stein" in *Poetics Today* 6, nos. 1-2 (1985): 67-80.

3. Judy Grahn, *Really Reading Gertrude Stein* (Freedom, Calif.: Crossing Press, 1989), 10.

4. *Selected Writings of Gertrude Stein*, ed. Carl Van Vechten (New York: Vintage Books, 1972), 566.

5. *The Yale Gertrude Stein*, ed. Richard Kostelanetz (New Haven, Conn.: Yale University Press, 1980), 128.

6. For an insightful and specifically lesbian reading of this poem, see Rebecca Mark's introduction to *Lifting Belly*, published in book form by Naiad Press, 1989.

7. Audre Lorde, *Sister Outsider* (Trumansburg, N. Y.: Crossing Press, 1984) 57.

CLAUDIA ROTH PIERPONT (ESSAY DATE 2000)

SOURCE: Pierpont, Claudia Roth. "The Mother of Confusion: Gertrude Stein." In *Passionate Minds: Women Rewriting the World*, pp. 33-49. New York: Alfred A. Knopf, 2000.

In the following essay, Pierpont narrates key events of Stein's life, highlighting their influence upon her writings.

"Pablo & Matisse have a maleness that belongs to genius," Gertrude Stein scrawled in a notebook, sometime in her early Paris years, about the two painters she planned to join in re-creating Western art. She was an aspiring writer just past thirty when she met the paired geniuses, in 1905, and their spectacular audacity helped her to determine her own ambitions: to overturn the nineteenth century's constraining rules and prejudices, and to find new words for people's secret inner lives. Stein—a Jewish woman who'd studied psychology at Harvard—had fled America to join her brother on the Left Bank in 1903, to write an anguished novel while he painted mediocre nudes. It was at that moment, when modern art was being born, that the Steins began to buy the best and most shocking paintings; before long, the best and most unshockable people were stopping by to view their riotous, thick-hung walls—and were staying for dinner. Although Leo had begun the collection, Gertrude was the one Picasso wanted to paint and the one he called Pard, using some cowboy slang he'd picked up in American comic strips. Casting off her stays and starting a new novel, she began to think it possible that she, too, might be a genius—that she might do in words what Picasso and Matisse had done in paint—and if maleness was a necessary part of it, well: "*moi aussi* perhaps," as she added in her notebook. That was not a problem but an opportunity to demonstrate a truth of her own secret inner life.

The first decade of the new century was barely over before she had achieved a version of her goal: the first indubitably modern literary style. Before James Joyce—as she volubly insisted all her life—before Dada or Surrealism, before Bloomsbury or the *roman fleuve*, Gertrude Stein was writing books and stories that were formally fractured, emotionally inscrutable, and, above all, dauntingly unreadable. This achievement has given the Library of America a particularly difficult task in assembling two hefty volumes of Stein's selected works. How best to represent her legacy? It is often forgotten that Stein commanded a broad literary range, from the psychological realism of her earliest fiction to the journalistic accounts of life in occupied France during the Second World War. The work that made her famous and still earns her canonical status is, of course, the barrage of janglingly repetitive lyric obfuscation that has come to be known as Steinese. "A rose is a rose is a rose is a rose," she wrote, with the philosophic kick of a nursery Wittgenstein. "The sister was not a mister," she warned, out on a sexual edge, and then provided her own commentary: "Was this a surprise. It was." Although she did not write "Yes!

We Have No Bananas," it isn't surprising that the song has been accused of betraying her influence.

It was by perpetrating such suspiciously significant nonsense, somewhere between the studies of Freud and the logic of the Red Queen—**"Before the Flowers of Friendship Faded Friendship Faded"** one cautionary title runs—that Stein entered our language as the bard of a culture of confusion, the vastly imperturbable mother of an age that had given up on answers. Yet no one took more vivid pleasure in the questions than she did, or set them out in a more brilliant company, beginning with the famous salon where she gathered Picasso and Matisse and Braque (who was so strong and so amiable that he would help the janitor hang the bigger pictures) and Derain and Juan Gris and Apollinaire. And after the Great War had blown this brilliant world apart, her rooms filled with charter members of the next cultural resurgence, and then the next, as there entered Hemingway, Fitzgerald, Cocteau, Tchelitchev, Christian Bérard, Cecil Beaton, Thornton Wilder, Virgil Thomson, and Richard Wright. For decades, there seemed no end to her gifts of renewal. She was host, sponsor, critic, instigator, frequently foe, and sometimes friend again of some of the century's finest provocateurs, and it was often hard to tell whether her life was a party or a revolution. But her intent was serious ("desperately" serious, as Alice B. Toklas put it), and she knew all along that the stakes were as high as the opposition was fierce, albeit nervous. "They needn't be so afraid of their damn culture," she erupted early on, and, for once, hung back in estimating her powers: "It would take more than a man like me to hurt it."

How did a girl born in Allegheny, Pennsylvania, in 1874 turn into such a disruptive fellow? Her grandparents had sailed from Germany to Baltimore in time to take opposing sides in the Civil War—a difference of opinion that she thought well established the Stein familial spirit. She was the youngest of five, although she seems to have felt herself to be the youngest of seven, so often did she dwell on two siblings who had died before she was born—an infant boy and a stillborn girl—and without whose deaths neither she nor her brother Leo would have been brought into the world. Both Leo and Gertrude had perceived some regret on their parent's parts at the quality of the substitution. This was one of the things that drew the youngest pair so close together, along with the knowledge that they were smarter than everyone else they knew.

The family moved from Allegheny to Vienna when Gertrude was a baby, and then to Paris (where she added French to her English and German) and, finally, to the wilds of Oakland, California, in 1880, when Daniel Stein forbade his children to speak any language but "pure" American English. A cold and domineering man of minimal formal education, he went on to make a small fortune by investing in San Francisco cable cars, and provided well for the children whose lives he overloaded with tutors and lessons and ambitions. Leo recalled his childhood as a torturous regime lived out under his father's disapproval, while his softhearted mother was too weak to make any difference; Gertrude would only allow that she considered it a foolish idea to have had an unhappy anything, let alone something as important as a childhood.

But there can have been little room for bluster back in 1886, when their mother began to show symptoms of abdominal cancer. Years of wasting pain and withdrawal turned Milly Stein into something of a household wraith before she died in 1888, when her younger daughter was fourteen. In *The Making of Americans*, the massive novel Gertrude Stein wrote about her family—the first stunningly original disaster of modernism, finished in 1911, written as though from deep within a halting, troubled mind—she suggests that Milly's illness had rendered her so nearly invisible that neither her husband nor her children noticed when she finally disappeared.

> Sometimes then they would be good to her, mostly they forgot about her, slowly she died away among them and then there was no more of living for her, she died away from all of them. She had never been really important to any of them. . . . Mostly for them she had no existence in her and then she died away and the gentle scared little woman was all that they ever after remembered of her.

Stein's notebooks, however, tell a different story: "All stopped after death of mother."

In fact, the household fell into chaos, while eighteen-year-old Bertha struggled to make up for a maternal presence that no one else would even acknowledge was missing. But if Gertrude had thought her mother negligible, she found her older sister sorely disgusting: "pure female," she wrote in her notebook for *The Making of Americans*, "sloppy oozy female . . . good, superior, maternal." Alone and untended, Gertrude left high school—her most thorough early biographer, Brenda Wineapple, states that she simply vanished from all records—and plunged into what she later called her "dark and dreadful" days. She took to reading with a kind of violence, buying piles of books (often with advice from Leo) and gulping them in great haphazard quantities. And she developed an almost equally violent need for food—"books and food, food and books, both excellent things," she wrote. Her discovery of food as a way back to early childhood, to "the full satisfied sense of being stuffed up with eating," marked her first divergence from the ways of her beloved Leo, who was just discovering how much he preferred to starve.

The case against Daniel Stein was set out many times by his two youngest children. They hated him, and yet they respected his power; they feared him, yet they wanted to be like him, if only for self-protection. More ambiguously, *The Making of Americans* contains some bizarrely dreamlike scenes that, among Stein scholars, have long raised the question of incest. (In the clearest example, a grown daughter accuses her father of having introduced her to an unnamed vice, and her words cause him to fall down paralyzed.)

In 1995 the biographer Linda Wagner-Martin, having studied Gertrude's notes for the novel, concluded that it was Bertha who had been sexually approached by their father: Gertrude wrote of his "coming in to her one night, to come and keep him warm." Complicating matters further, Gertrude elaborated by referring to a similar incident she had undergone with an uncle, her father's brother Solomon. "Scene like the kind I had with Sol," she wrote, and added, in a strangulated shorthand, "like me what he tried to do." Whatever actually took place, it is striking that just at those moments when she approaches what she cannot say, even in her own notes, this cautious writer begins to sound like quintessential Gertrude Stein. "Fathers loving children young girls," she goes on, and it appears that at least one branch of modern literary style may derive from a fearful evasion of meaning, and from the necessary invention—and wasn't that necessity "pure female"?—of a secret code.

"Then our life without a father began, a very pleasant one" was Stein's typically cloudless way of addressing the death of Daniel Stein—by apoplexy, three years after the death of his wife. Certainly his death precipitated a release of productive energy in his younger daughter. In 1893 she followed Leo to Harvard—this was a year before the Harvard Annex for Women became Radcliffe College—where, studying English and psychology, she turned out a quantity of notebooks in which her private turmoils were forced into traditional narrative forms. Her idols were

George Eliot and Henry James, but her first work to be published was **"Normal Motor Automatism,"** a psychological report she produced under the aegis of William James, who was doubtless responsible for rerouting her toward psychology as a science rather than, as in his brother's work, psychology as an aspect of literature.

In 1898 she went on to medical school at Johns Hopkins, planning to study the mysterious female affliction known as hysteria. Freud's book on the subject had been published three years before, but the frailties of women had preoccupied Stein since her childhood. Now she found refuge in the theory, not uncommon at the time, that a few rare women are born exceptions to their sex. To be extremely accomplished or intelligent or determined—to aspire to genius—was to be, by definition, less female. Although a friend persuaded her to present a public paper on the benefits of women's education, the last thing she was interested in was the cause of women's rights. As far as she could see, the only thing most women excelled at was having babies.

She did well in her first years of medical school, when the work centered on the classroom and the lab, but she had a great deal of difficulty when it came to visiting wards filled with sick human beings. And then, in her third year, she fell passionately in love with a young Bryn Mawr graduate who was permanently attached to another female medical student. The woman was responsive yet elusive. Instead of studying, Gertrude pined; she planned her life around seeing her beloved, or not seeing her. Sabotaged by the very parts of herself that she had been trying to cut off—the emotional, the uncontrolled—she failed her final exams and did not graduate. But by then, of course, she claimed she didn't care. She no longer wished to be a doctor. She had discovered that the only way to relieve her suffering was by writing. She was a novelist after all.

Virginia Woolf believed that no woman had succeeded in writing the truth of the experience of her own body—that women and language both would have to change considerably before anything like that could happen. She also believed that those who struggled toward the liberation of language—like herself and Stein and Eliot and Joyce—were bound to fail at least as often as they succeeded, and in this respect she judged Stein's "contortions" a generational misfortune. Woolf was eight years Stein's junior, and in many ways her experience and ambitions ran a parallel course: the death of her mother when she was thirteen; the influence of her dangerously overbearing father; the sexual "interference" inflicted by her stepbrothers; her love of women; her literary interest in male and female aspects of character and in an androgynous ideal. Also, like Stein, Woolf had enough money to write exactly as she pleased, and that was surely a major factor in allowing these two individuals, so different in their gifts and temperaments, to become the opposing poles of risk-all modern writing in a woman's voice.

The anguished novel Stein wrote when she joined her brother in Paris was an account of the love affair that had been tearing her apart. Stein's first full literary achievement, **Q.E.D.**—standing for *quod erat demonstrandum,* the conclusion of a geometric proof—was one of the few works she never tried to publish; although not explicitly erotic, it was plainly open about the fact that all three members of its sexual triangle were women. No explanations, no apologies, no wells of loneliness. Stein seems to have written the book as a kind of exorcism, incorporating in it actual letters and conversations, with the goal of restoring her serenity and never losing it again.

The book is fascinating not only for the information it provides about Stein but for the Jamesian acuity of its psychological portraits. It is hard to predict how far Stein might have gone in adapting this tradition—she was then twenty-nine—but the autobiographical narrator hints at why the attempt would be abandoned. She has always had a "puritanic horror" of passion, she confesses, and the pain of this love affair has rendered it absolute. "You meant to me a turgid and complex world," she rebukes her beloved—protesting also against the Jamesian tasks of emotional probing and dissection—before she heads off for a better or at least more soothing world of "obvious, superficial, clean simplicity." What she didn't know yet was how to find it.

After a year of frantic travelling, Gertrude moved in permanently with Leo in his apartment on the Rue de Fleurus. Because her erudite brother didn't approve of **Q.E.D.**, she wrote only late at night, hurrying to bed just before dawn so the birds would not keep her awake. During ordinary hours she was more than ever Leo's pupil, with everything to learn about the flourishing art of painting. When Leo took her to see the work of a young Spanish painter in a gallery owned by a former circus clown, she initially refused to chip in her share of the funds required to make a purchase. She thought the long figure of a nude woman had ugly, monkeylike legs and feet. The dealer offered to cut off the offending parts and

sell just the head, but the strange Americans eventually returned and bought the whole thing. Picasso's *Woman with a Bouquet of Flowers* was soon followed into the Steins' salon by many other Picassos, as well as Matisses and Cézannes. But, most important, it was followed by Picasso himself, who thought Leo a dreadful bore but recognized in Gertrude a companion spirit. He had barely met her when he asked to paint her portrait. Uncharacteristically, he struggled with the subject mightily: after more than eighty sittings, he wiped out the naturalistic head and quit. He returned to the canvas only months later, and what he finally produced was not Gertrude Stein as she then appeared—no one thought the portrait looked like her—but the grandly masked *monstre sacré* she would become once she had forged her genius and had paid the price.

It was while she was sitting for her portrait, in the spring of 1906, that Stein thought out much of the book that first won her literary renown. Inspired by Flaubert's meticulously understated *A Simple Heart* (which Leo had set her to translate as an exercise in French), Stein's **Three Lives** is a trio of stories about the grim existences of three women—two German-born servants and one poor black—who drift toward their fates in the airless atmosphere of a small American city. Stein's achievement was to make the writing seem as if shaped by the inner states of her characters: the childishly simple diction of those who had never willingly opened a book, the repetitiveness of those who had not much to think about or who were unused to being heard. The book was not published until 1909, and then in a tiny edition that Stein paid for herself. The reaction was astounding on almost any scale. "A very masterpiece of realism" was the general tenor of reviews. Many writers and critics began to see Stein's little book as the start of a truly American, unliterary literature, homely and vernacular and existentially unpresuming—a response suggesting that many writers and critics knew no more of the people she was supposedly writing about than Gertrude Stein did.

Like everything that she had written (but had not published) up until then, **Three Lives** is about Stein's autobiographical obsessions. Here are the vile but attractive father and the mother whose death is hardly noticed, the better-loved dead babies, and a continuous replaying of the tormented love affair, complete with psychological observations transposed from **Q.E.D.** But there is a change: the narrative voice is now so apathetic and the emotional temperature so low that it's no wonder the characters seem half-unconscious. The cause is not their social downtroddenness but the fact that *Three Lives* catches Stein in the very act of administering the emotional anesthesia that marked her style forever after.

The success of *Three Lives* coincided with two other important developments in Stein's life: Picasso's return from a summer in Spain with his first Cubist canvases, and the deepening of her relationship with Alice B. Toklas. The result was an explosion that shattered all her effortful old forms. The sudden outpouring of small, fragmented "portraits" and other glittering esoterica is usually said to have been inspired by—depending on one's source or one's inclination—either her desire to write like a Cubist or her need to conceal the erotic joy of her new attachment. Certainly, Cubism was vital to Stein, because it provided her with an intellectual rationale for doing exactly what she already urgently wanted and needed to do: keep her eyes on the surface. Facet it, mirror it, spin it around, and repeat it ad infinitum, but never go back underneath.

* * *

When Gertrude first met Alice in the fall of 1907, she thought her the same type of "pure female" as her sister Bertha, and she was wary. "She listens, she is docile, stupid and she owns you," runs one notebook entry. A tiny, brittle woman, dressed in exotic fringed shawls that seemed to emphasize her ever-remarked-on Semitic features—"an awful Jewess, dressed in a window-curtain" was Mary Berenson's typical assessment—Alice also gave signs of possessing, according to Gertrude, "an exquisite and keen moral sensibility." And there was no doubt that she knew a genius when she met one. (Actually, she claimed that she heard a bell ring whenever she met one.) Furthermore, she was absolutely certain (now that she'd seen it) of the world in which she wanted to live. This was a very different world from the one she'd come from, back in San Francisco, where for the past ten years—since her mother's death, when she was nineteen—she'd borne the domestic burdens of a household made up of her father, her grandfather, and her younger brother. None of whom she, gladly, ever saw again.

Stein and Toklas were formally "married" in the summer of 1910, outside Florence, and that fall Alice moved into the Stein ménage on the Rue de Fleurus. And so it was that Alice B. Toklas "came to be happier than anybody else who was living then," as Stein wrote in *Ada,* a biographical portrait of her bride. Because Alice, for the first time since the death of her mother, had someone to tell her charming stories to: "some one who was loving was almost always listening." Listening and loving, loving and listening—the paired satisfactions now nearly replaced books and food. Notably, at this time Leo began to display symptoms of chronic deafness, and to starve himself in fasts that lasted as long as thirty days; he claimed to be writing a book on painting, but he couldn't produce a word. Just as Gertrude was becoming the man that being a genius required her to be ("I am very fond of yes sir," she wrote), Leo was turning into the very model of the mysteriously afflicted, hysterical woman she had once been so interested in trying to cure. But no longer.

With someone now listening to her so well, Gertrude began to pour out words without hesitation, revision, or second thoughts. Privately, there are the sweet-breathed burps and coos of utter infantile contentment: "Lifting belly fattily / Doesn't that astonish you / You did want me / Say it again / strawberry." The work she offered to the world made even fewer concessions to standards of sense and communication:

> One whom some were certainly following was one who was completely charming. One whom some were following was one who was charming. One whom some were following was one who was completely charming. One whom some were following was one who was certainly completely charming.

So runs the first paragraph of Stein's "portrait" of Picasso, which was published by Alfred Steiglitz (along with her "portrait" of Matisse) in *Camera Work* in 1912, a year before the Armory Show introduced modern art to *le tout* New York—with loans from the Stein collection—and made Gertrude Stein about as notorious as the painters whose outrageous principles she was said to share. ("The name of Gertrude Stein is better known in NY today than the name of God!" Mabel Dodge Luhan wrote to her ecstatically, and Stein replied, "Hurrah for *gloire.*") She didn't mind that most of her fame came in the form of parody and ridicule. "They always quote it," she pointed out in what may be her most truly modern observation, "and those they say they admire they do not quote."

All this was too much for Leo. He had hated Cubism from the start, and he didn't hang back from declaring Gertrude's work "Godalmighty rubbish." By late 1913 brother and sister were no longer speaking, and he soon moved out. The collection of paintings was divided more or less equitably, with Gertrude taking the Picassos and

Leo the Renoirs; they split the Cézannes between them. (Picasso painted her an apple to make up for one of the Cézannes she lost.) Although Leo later tried to resume contact, she did not respond. "I have very bad headaches and I don't like to commit to paper that which makes me very unhappy," she wrote in one of her notebooks. More than thirty years remained of their lives, but Gertrude and Leo never spoke again. Alice claimed that Gertrude had simply forgotten all about him.

Stein had won enormous freedoms, but she chose to confine herself to a comfortably narrow space. In the midst of sexually explosive Paris, where the members of Natalie Barney's lesbian circle flaunted their glamour and their liaisons and their belly-dancing parties, Gertrude and Alice ran a salon that was a model of middle-class decorum. Despite occasional unorthodoxies of dress—Alice's window curtains, Gertrude's tents—and the Roman-emperor haircut Gertrude eventually got, they played the roles of two charmingly eccentric ladies who just happened to be man and wife (a fact as perfectly obvious to all as it was presumed unmentionable).

The effects of self-confinement on Stein's writing, however, were cruel. Beyond the occasional flash of wit or happy juxtaposition, her chains of words and repetitions come to suggest an animal's relentless pacing—cramped and dulled and slightly desperate. One feels that just outside the strict boundaries imposed by her pen lurked fathers and brothers and arguments and wars. In life, she could be head-on and courageous. During the First World War, she imported a Ford van and learned to drive it (except in reverse) to deliver supplies to hospitals all over France, and after the war she and Alice wrote to the many lonely American soldier "godsons" they had adopted. But nowhere in Stein's "literary" writing did she take in the experience: the wounded, the fear, the tenderness. She was writing less then anyway, giving over much of her time to advising and instructing (and sometimes to feeding and supporting) a group of young writers who found their way to her fabled door; in the twenties, as if by decree, the painters dispersed and the writers appeared. Among these, first in place and most fiercely devoted, was the twenty-three-year-old Ernest Hemingway, who sat at her feet and learned to write like a man.

"Gertrude Stein and me are just like brothers," Hemingway crowed to Sherwood Anderson in 1922. He brought her his stories to read and criticize, and they talked for hours while his wife, Hadley, was none too gracefully monopolized by Alice. (Holding off "wives of geniuses" was a stressful part of Alice's occupation; some had to be cornered behind large pieces of furniture.) He credited "Miss Stein" with getting him to give up newspaper reporting and to concentrate on his serious writing. He commended her method of analyzing places and people. And it was on the Rue de Fleurus that he was advised to go to Spain to see the bullfighting.

In 1925 reviewers of Hemingway's first volume of stories, *In Our Time*, recognized stylistic debts to Stein that were unmistakable: drastically short and unadorned sentences, repetition, a "naiveté of language" that suggested a complex, inarticulate emotional state. But for Hemingway the style clearly served as a kind of dam against an opposing sentimental pressure that was rarely if ever felt in Stein's prose. The new American hero was syntactically disengaged, because he'd been through hell and had already felt too much; his semiautism was part of his sexual equipment in a world in which physical courage was destiny and the only truly frightful things were women and emotion. Virginia Woolf—who used "virile" as an insult—particularly deplored Hemingway's exaggeration of male characteristics, for which she blamed the "sexual perturbations" of the times. (This was in 1927, and she was reviewing his aptly titled collection *Men Without Women*.) Woolf might have felt differently if she had traced the most famously virile of modern styles to its origins in the work of a woman—albeit a woman who liked to call herself "a roman and Julius Caesar and a bridge and a column and a pillar" (when all Virginia ever called Vita was "a lighthouse").

Are there male and female characteristics in writing? Male and female sentences? Is the comma a languishing feminine ruse, draining the strength of the tough male verb into a miasma of girlish uncertainties? Writing is self-exposure, and in the postsuffrage, neo-Freudian twenties the fear of what might get exposed was everywhere. Stein believed that the use of a comma was degrading and a sign of weakness because after all you ought to know yourself when you needed to take a breath. Woolf suggested that any woman who wrote in a terse, short-winded style was probably trying to write like a man. But at the heart of their difference is the fact that Woolf didn't see why a woman should want to do anything like a man; feminine generosity was life itself, and the necessary source of male achievement. One could hardly get further from Stein's perception of the sexes' division of properties. The two women met once—at a party in London, in 1926—and the revulsion was mutual. On Woolf's part, this was a matter of class and snobbery. "Jews swarmed," she wrote of the event in a letter to her sister. On Stein's part, there was defensiveness and bravado, surely based on a perception of the chilly atmosphere and perhaps, too, on the glaringly anomalous presence of a purely female genius.

By the late twenties, Stein and Hemingway had battled often, and they finally parted ways. She never spoke of what had come between them; he could hardly stop speaking of it. Sometimes he claimed that it was Alice, jealous of his relationship with Gertrude ("I always wanted to fuck her and she knew it"), who had caused the break. He also claimed that after Gertrude went through menopause she wanted no men around her except homosexuals—her "feathered friends," as he called all those whom he resented for usurping his place in the nest. Undeniably, there had been a change in the salon. Although Gertrude and Alice were as reserved as ever, they did live increasingly within a kind of tacit homosexual freemasonry. Indeed, it seems to have been this very reserve which was part of the attraction for such cautious old-world gentlemen as Frederick Ashton and Virgil Thomson and others from the highly sexually encoded worlds of music and theater and dance. In Stein's new role as a professional collaborator writing opera and ballet librettos, and also as a friend, she seems to have developed the appeal of a more or less inverted Mae West: a good-humored woman in male drag, a warm and wise mama who not only took in all her gay sons but was gay herself.

None of which was known to the public, of course, when *The Autobiography of Alice B. Toklas,* written in 1932, suddenly turned the world's most famously obscure writer into the best-selling author of a Literary Guild selection. From the start, Stein had thought of the *Autobiography*—actually it is her own biography, written from the dazzled point of view of her companion—as an embarrassingly traditional, moneymaking venture, on a different level from the meaningfully experimental work she still composed at night. In fact, this magical book doesn't resemble anything else in Stein's work—or, for that matter, anything else in American literature. Its only models seem to be those other famed "Alice" books, by Lewis Carroll, and the social surrealism of Oscar Wilde, which further muddles the question of the sexual significance of a writer's style.

The book is a modern fairy tale: the story of a golden age of art in Paris, when geniuses regularly came to dinner and were cleverly seated opposite their own paintings so that everyone was made especially happy, although everyone was happy anyway—this was back before death and divorce and success—and Henri Rousseau played the violin and Marie Laurencin sang, and Frédéric of the Lapin Agile wandered in and out with his donkey. And into the middle of this wonderland walks the sensible American Alice B. At her very first dinner, she finds herself next to Picasso, who gravely asks her to tell him whether she thinks he really does look like her President Lincoln. "I had thought a good many things that evening," she reports quite as gravely, "but I had not thought that." Ever temperate, Alice is the quiet but quizzical eye at the heart of the storm. Her equanimity, like her pleasure, is absolute. The book indulges in some small revenge—Leo is not mentioned by name, Hemingway is imputed to be a coward—and it leaves us with a sense of loss that is as profound as it is muted. Once, there was so much life all around that one had to hurry to bed before dawn to have any hope of sleep: "There were birds in many trees behind high walls in those days, now there are fewer."

With the book's success, Stein fell into a profound depression. Even her new *gloire* didn't help, at first; she was fifty-nine, she was having her first major success, and it was for the wrong thing. In *Four in America,* a particularly reader-resistant work she completed about this time, she rose—briefly, rather thrillingly—to a clear explanation of her intended goals and values:

> Now listen! Can't you see that when the language was new—as it was with Chaucer and Homer—the poet could use the name of a thing and the thing was really there? He could say "O moon," "O sea," "O love," and the moon and the sea and love were really there. And can't you see that after hundreds of years had gone by and thousands of poems had been written, he could call on those words and find that they were just wornout literary words? . . .

> Now listen! I'm no fool. I know that in daily life we don't go around saying 'is a . . . is a . . . is a . . .' Yes, I'm no fool; but I think that in that line the rose is red for the first time in English poetry for a hundred years.

Alas for good intentions. When Stein returned to America for the first time in thirty years, in 1934, to attend a performance of Virgil Thomson's opera (to her libretto) *Four Saints in Three Acts,* she also gave a series of lectures around the country. Directly exhorting her audience, Stein made headlines (MISS STEIN SPEAKS TO BEWILDERED 500) but clearly failed to win the understanding she was after. The work of the woman who claimed to believe so fervently in the immediacy of language and the recovery of meaning remained synonymous with obscurity and confusion. (In the 1935 movie *Top Hat,* Ginger Rogers giggled that an indecipherable telegram "sounds like Gertrude Stein.") Any attempt to assess Stein's literary achievement raises many old questions—not only about her judgment and credibility but about the relationship of theory to art in the troubled history of modernism.

When Stein and Toklas returned to Paris in the spring of 1935, Toklas took it upon herself to ship copies of Stein's manuscripts back to America for safekeeping. This was the full extent of their preparations for the possibility of hard times ahead in Europe. Stein couldn't believe that anything would really happen, and certainly not to them—two elderly Jewish ladies with a bit of fame and no political interests. Their political indifference was now dangerously compounded by Stein's long-standing way of handling all serious unpleasantness: pretend it isn't there, and then tumble into nonsense or baby talk, so that perhaps it will be persuaded that you are not there, either—or, at least, that you are not a reasonable target. In her early Paris days, she had written to a friend who had apparently mentioned the Russian pogroms against the Jews, "The Russians is very bad people and the Czar a very bad man." In the mid-thirties, her thoughts about Hitler were hardly more sophisticated. She and Alice were staying in the countryside, at Bilignin, in 1939, when war broke out. They hurried to Paris in order to close up their apartment. Then, taking one Cézanne and Gertrude's Picasso portrait, they returned—against all advice—to Bilignin, which soon fell under the jurisidiction of Vichy. And there they spent the war.

How did they survive? Largely, it seems, through a French admirer and friend who was appointed head of the Bibliothèque Nationale under the Occupation and issued several requests that they not be disturbed. They lived quietly and scrounged for food; they sold the Cézanne and liked to tell visitors surprised at the quality of their dinner that they were eating it. They watched the German army march into the land and, a long and burning time later, straggle out; German soldiers were billeted for a time in their house, as were American GIs when at last they arrived. This experience is recounted clearly and movingly in a book Stein completed in 1944, entitled ***Wars I Have Seen.*** Sadly, the book is out of print, and its failure to meet a modernist criterion has kept it from inclusion in the Library of America compila-

Gertrude Stein (left) arriving in New York aboard the *S. S. Champlain* with her secretary and companion Alice B. Toklas.

tion. Yet it is one of the few of Stein's works that might be called essential, because it tells the ending of the fairy tale.

There is much here that is richly, lovingly observed, about the women's daily life and that of their neighbors and about French pragmatism and courage. Typically, whatever could not be lovingly observed is passed over—or nearly so. For now history almost catches up with Gertrude Stein, and forces her into confrontation. One feels her struggling with the effort not to look away: the very term "collabo"—which is all she manages to spit out of it—causes her to stumble on the page, falling into a repetitive stutter that seems not a mannerism but a kind of seizure. Her attempt to address anti-Semitism begins with an early memory of the Dreyfus Affair, but she hasn't advanced beyond a sentence when she segues into senseless babble: "He can read acasias, hands and faces. Acasias are for the goat. . . ." "Acasia" is not even a word (and Stein never made up words; she thought such arrogant idiocy to be the province of Joyce). "Acacia" is the name of a tree, but "aphasia" means the loss of the ability to speak. It is as though Stein were making her own diagnosis, or as though a part of her reason were watching the rest of her mind run away.

After the war, back in Paris, the famous salon was filled with GIs eating Alice's chocolate ice cream. Gertrude wrote down what they said and how they said it as though they were the new poets of the age. She adored them, she celebrated them: they were, after all, young men and heroes. But something in her attitude was changing. Along with the ice cream, she dispensed correction; she worried that the great liberators were taken in by the flattery and politeness of the postwar Germans, or that they saw the world in terms of movies. By and large, it seems to have dawned on her that there was a lot these callow demigods ought to learn before the world was put in the hands of men, even the best and noblest men, ever again.

Although she was over seventy and weak with cancer, Stein was very eager to work. In late 1945 she began a second opera project with her old friend Virgil Thomson. It was his idea that the setting be the American nineteenth century; it was her idea that the hero be a heroine, the suffragist Susan B. Anthony. Stein completed the libretto for **The Mother of Us All** just before her death, in July 1946. Although the work is predictably baffling, Stein maintains an exceptionally strong dramatic focus on the character of Susan B. She had done a considerable amount of historical research—shocking in itself, given her usual methods—and it is Anthony's public concerns that dominate the text: the disparities between the sexes, and her passionate conviction that women are stronger and must lead.

For men are afraid, Stein's heroine observes: "They fear women, they fear each other, they fear their neighbor, they fear other countries and then they hearten themselves in their fear by crowding together and following each other, and when they crowd together and follow each other they are brutes, like animals who stampede." As for women, they are afraid not for themselves but only for their children: "that is the real difference between men and women." Stein shows Susan B. at the end of her life, when she knows that all her work has failed. She has helped to win the vote for black men, but she will die before it is granted to women, white or black. When someone attempts to comfort her by saying that women will vote someday, her despair only deepens: she dreads that when women have the vote they, too, will become afraid—that they will become like men.

How astonishing that Stein can now voice her lifelong wish—"women will become like men"—as a dreaded possibility. A new sense of the value of what women had traditionally done and been may even have given her succor in these last months, as she looked back on her own life as the mother of so much and so many. Perhaps by then she had realized that in her years of giving and feeding and advising and encouraging and (is there another word for it?) mothering—in the continual dispersal of herself to men whom she loved and admired, to geniuses and soldiers and cowards alike—she had inadvertently lived the life of the most profoundly womanly of women, and that it had been good.

TITLE COMMENTARY

Tender Buttons

BETTINA L. KNAPP (ESSAY DATE 1990)

SOURCE: Knapp, Bettina L. "*Tender Buttons*: Cubism and an Alchemical Linguistic Trajectory." In *Gertrude Stein*, pp. 111-35. New York: Continuum, 1990.

In the following essay, Knapp discusses the themes, style, and technique of Tender Buttons *with those of cubism, interpreting the volume's three parts in terms of the writing process, sexuality, and psychology.*

Tender Buttons (1914) may be regarded as one of Stein's most innovative and most esoteric works. Like the alchemist who transmutes his metals and records his findings in iconographic representations, ciphers, and diagrams, Stein projects her continuously altering mental meanderings, meditations, visions, and free associations onto real objects, foods, and rooms. First viewed as distinct substances, the images she observes, like the chemical combinations studied by those ancient scientists, are depicted with great "exactitude."

Working with the word, rather than with the alchemists' metals, Stein's lexicon, when externalized and placed on the white sheet of paper, is explicit and redolent with clarity. Such clarity, however, is a strategy, a subterfuge, a springboard for the spawning of infinite associations and analogies.

Like the alchemists who purified the baser elements (lead) with which they worked by putting them through triturating tests, so Stein also experimented with words, requiring them to go through her version of trial by fire and water. Words that had become atrophied through centuries of use and misuse were dismembered, mutilated, stripped of their traditional and logical meanings, relationships, analogies, memories, and associations. Dross was shorn while the core, the primitive essence and melody, was retained by Stein to decant into fresh and heteroclite conjunctions of words. Such a process allowed her to receive the old word(s) in the *now,* as it had once existed long ago; in its pristine purity, dazzling, sparkling, glowing, ready for incantation in melody—in the poem.

Alchemists, who had to maintain strict secrecy concerning their experiments in order to protect themselves against persecution by the Roman Catholic Church, which believed their discoveries might in some way lessen its authority, coded their records, writing them in symbols, glyphs, and iconic signs. Stein, unwilling to reveal her most private thoughts and feelings to an unfeeling and destructive public, was likewise secretive. Accordingly, *Tender Buttons,* is a confluence of word/signs—a *mystery.*

For some, this slim volume may be looked upon as a *religious* work, but only insofar as the word *religion* is understood in its original Latin sense—Latin *religare:* to root, to bind, to link back, to reconnect with a collective past. Never, when referring to Stein, is it to be associated with organized religion. In this regard, *Tender Buttons,* divided into three parts—Objects, Food, and Rooms—may be viewed as an inner trajectory, Stein's descent into being, into the collective unconscious, the source of creation.

Painterly factors are also evident in *Tender Buttons.* Cézanne's influence, as previously noted, is primordial. As he had believed it was more important for the artist to reveal geometric structures hidden behind objects than to delineate the objects concretely, so Stein adopted a similar method with regard to the function of words. Once terms had been pared down to their essentials, the skeleton structure and bone marrow of the word and work could come forth full-blown.

Cézanne's attempt to "re-create nature" by simplifying forms, reducing them to their basic geometric equivalents, led to certain distortions, as in *Mont Sainte-Victoire* (1885-87). Likewise did Stein's signs, symbols, and glyphs appear disfigured, deformed, and because of such altered appearances, were disorienting to the viewer. Cézanne, after divesting his canvases of traditional perspective, allowed new spatial patterns to emerge, leading him to delineate objects from shifting rather than from a single point of view. The resulting interaction between flat planes, which encouraged minute transitional color tones to oscillate one against another, gave the observer the impression of vibrating surfaces. In like manner did Stein divest her words of perspective and hierarchies, endowing them, once juxtaposed, with continuous motility, and not allowing one to assume greater importance than another. Indeed, so active and vital did they become both as single and sequenced units, that she played one "lively word" against or with another in a *continuous present.*

Cézanne's views were also significant in the spawning of cubism. There were, understandably, affinities between Stein's writings, most specifically *Tender Buttons,* and the canvases of such friends as Picasso, Braque, and Gris. Like them, she emphasizes still lifes, with their commonplace objects like potatoes or asparagus, which also have their cerebral and spiritual equivalents. When embedded in the sentence, a potato or an asparagus is conveyed two-dimensionally, flatly, without adjectives; nor is memory called upon since it serves to highlight one or another element within a grammatically self-contained speech unit. Thus did Stein dispense, as had Cézanne and the cubists even more radically, with perspective and the illusion of depth. Fragmentation and dissociation of traditional literary forms and conventions allowed her the psychological and aesthetic freedom to re-create fresh verbal compositions, and in so doing, expand and implement their impact on the reader. Like the cubists also, she did not attempt to find meaning in the group of objects depicted in *Tender Buttons.* What was of import to her was the need to convey ideas and feelings relating to these forms in terms of their mass, color, texture, and line.

Stein had come a long way since *Three Lives* and *The Making of Americans* and the universal types ("bottom nature"), which she attempted to portray non-mimetically, by means of the repetitive use of verbs of being, genderless pronouns, prepositions, and conjunctions. What she now sought to capture was the *perception* of that *single moment* when the mind comes into contact with the object of its consciousness, and the sensory experience it then conveys in a continuous present. Each such occurrence is viewed by Stein as unique: no memory of a past or of a special type. Stein's mental leaps, requiring intense concentration and discipline on her part, revealed an ability to verbalize and sensorialize the effect of the shock or head-on collision between consciousness and the object of its focus in a present reality.[1]

Tender Buttons, like cubist painting, is representational. Yet, paradoxically, its gleanings are increasingly abstract and hermetic. Words used to replicate an object emerge arbitrarily. There is, then, no defining or ordering of them into readily understandable groupings. As Picasso, Braque, and Gris created their *collages,* so Stein brought forth her own pictorial reality in the word, which she viewed as a *thing* in and of itself. Unlike the cubists in their collages, she did not include fragments of newspapers, cigarette wrappers, tickets, and other sundry objects drawn from the everyday world in her writings. Her architectonic structures were built instead on polysemous words.

In *Tender Buttons,* therefore, words are for the most part non-referential, non-relational, non-ideational, non-illusionist. Devoid of descriptions and for the most part unintelligible to those whose world is limited to rational reasoning, the forward movement of Stein's lexicon is triggered by an inner necessity—by some mysterious energy. Although she did away with most of the connective signs of discourse (conjunctions, prepositions, pronouns, articles, etc.), she reintegrated the noun, the very grammatical device she had abolished in an earlier work, *The Making of Americans* (see chapter 6). Why use the superfluous? She wrote: "A noun is a name of anything, why after a thing is named write about it."[2] In time, her views changed.

> And then, something happened and I began to discover the name of things, that is not discover the names but discover the things the things to see the things to look at and in so doing I had of course to name them not to give them new names but to see that I could find out how to know that they were there by their names or by replacing their names. And how was I to do so. They had their names and naturally I called them by the names they had and in doing so having begun looking at them I called them by their names with passion and that made poetry, I did not mean it to make poetry but it did, it made the Tender Buttons, and the Tender Buttons was very good poetry it made a lot more poetry.[3]

Since Stein names the thing and its qualities, but does not deal with the thing itself, her language is forcibly abstract.[4] In that concrete nouns and adjectives are linked to one another in new and what appears to be arbitrary diagrammatical order and in a variety of arrangements, with seem-

ingly no relationship to the world of contingencies, to decipher such poetry is difficult and depends for the most part upon the depth of the reader's projection.

Although *Tender Buttons,* like the works of the ancient alchemists, is a *vas hermeticum,* let us explore associationally some poems in the collection. First, its oxymoronic title. Both qualitative and quantitative, abstract and concrete, the appeal is to the eye, the pictorial element, rather than to the ear and sound, as in her *Portraits.* The eye, identified with the archetype of consciousness, is associated with the intellect and the cognitive use of words. It has also been identified, since ancient Egyptian times, with the spirit and soul; thus does it become instrumental in creating the sacred space (*temenos*) within which the glyphs will be imprinted. In that the eye is the organ that orders, selects, and differentiates levels of reading and understanding, the aura and vibrations it experiences pave the way for its relationships with the object (or objects) depicted in the poem.

The noun *button* (from the Old French, *boton*), is a bud, sprout, shoot, tendril; *bouter* means to push, eject. It may also be associated with a knob that one pushes as on a bell, or turns to open a door; with a button on clothing; or a pimple. That Stein appends the adjective *tender* (Latin *tener*) to buttons, adds a metatextual quality to the title. Buttons, as metaphor, represent something that is growing, burgeoning; its shoots and tendrils emerging from the earth, however, are still tender and must be cared for. *Tender,* therefore, suggests something malleable, easily cut, divided, masticated, vulnerable to feeling and affection. It was Mlle. de Scudéry who, in seventeenth-century France, dreamed up the *Carte du Tendre,* representing the various paths by which one could gain access to the land of love. Isn't this exactly what interests Stein? "Poetry is doing nothing but using losing refusing and pleasing and betraying and caressing nouns."[5]

By its very ambiguity, this metatextual title has almost infinite connotations, stemming from both matriarchal and patriarchal worlds. Divested of normal order, context, function, and semantics, the associations evoked by the title, along with the poems included in the volume, have been liberated from the limitations imposed upon them by the world of contingencies. As the eye focuses on the roundness of the button, the object may be used as a meditative device, taking the reader into a space/time continuum. From this vantage point, Stein took yet another revolutionary step in her stylistic ways.

Having freed herself, as she explained in *The Geographical History of America,* from her obsession with "human nature" that she now associates with linearity and the workaday world, she has penetrated another dimension, that of the "human mind," or the transpersonal realm that one may call the collective unconscious. From this new and more detached vantage point, she succeeded in endowing common, everyday objects—dress, petticoat, etc.—with a revitalized existence, thus transforming what had been dormant or latent into something with *livingness.* Not necessarily was the object's strictly utilitarian use focused upon in *Tender Buttons*; rather, and most importantly for her, it was its essence that was revealed in the work of art. Marcel Duchamp had also expanded the simply functional nature of an object in his masterpiece *Urinal*; as had Picabia, picking out objects from the five-and-dime store, then signing his name to them, after which he labeled them works of art.

Stein's new verbal iconography, as revealed in *Tender Buttons,* transgressed the limitations imposed upon language. Disorientation resulting from her realignments of words and verbal patternings, triggered new sensations born from her humanization of the inhuman material world. Her inner trajectory, unlike Charles Baudelaire's in *The Flowers of Evil,* which was accomplished in six steps, or Dante's, in nine spheres, is undertaken in three. Segments from each level—from the world of Objects, to the domain of Food, and finally to the inner sanctum of Rooms—will be explained in terms of the writing process, sexuality, and psychology.

Step 1. Objects

Objects (Latin *objectum: jactere,* something thrown in the way of the observer), suggests anything that one sees, that affects the senses, occupies the mind, calls for attention, and sets a goal. Grammatically, objects indicate nouns or substantives that directly or indirectly receive the action of a verb; philosophically, anything that can be known or perceived by the mind. The verb, *to object,* means to oppose, expose, protest, remonstrate, expostulate, and demur. Such associations, and the many more that come to mind, suggest an intensely active, aggressive, excited, powerful, and even hostile mood on Stein's part. She seems ready to explode, to give vent, to expel her new and loving vision of language.

The fifty-eight poems included under the rubric "Objects" deal with visible, tangible, and commonplace items. Stein's asyntactical placements and alignments of words into melodic patterns and rhythms, trigger an emotional response in the reader as does a puzzle, acrostic, logogriph, or anagram. In so doing, the poems titillate, frustrate, as well as bedazzle the mind.

"A CARAFE, THAT IS A BLIND GLASS"

> A kind in glass and a cousin, a spectacle and nothing strange a single hurt color and an arrangement in a system to pointing. All this and not ordinary, not unordered in not resembling. The difference is spreading.

The carafe—like the alchemist's crucible—is and contains mysterious elements. A bottle with a flaring lip used to hold beverages, wine, blood, or any liquid, it may be viewed in Stein's linguistic scheme as an *ideogram*: a picture, symbol, or sign used to represent a thing or an idea. No longer merely utilitarian, it has become an object of contemplation and meditation.

Pictorially, the carafe suggests the female body with its rounded, uterine-looking container at the bottom and the spreading outer lip or vagina at the top, which permits the entrance and exit of substances. Such an association is valid since Toklas moved into rue de Fleurus when Stein was composing *Tender Buttons.* It was the first time that either women had experienced a reciprocal love relationship. Unable to contain the joy of their union and fearful of revealing her sexual pleasures openly, she resorted to the ideogram to celebrate the excitement, joys, and fruitful nature of the female body. .

Blind, indicating an inability to see in the outer realm, and therefore easy deception by appearances, permits on the other hand greater perception into those darkened, murky, and sometimes forbidding inner spheres. Homer, Tiresias, and Oedipus are all associated with blindness, the latter figure having gouged out his eyes in order to fathom the depth of his crimes. Were such emotions implicit in Stein's lesbian relationship? It is doubtful that she still felt guilt. Certainly, her pleasure encouraged her to intone her delight in poetry but always in a mitigated, restrained, and hermetic manner, thereby protecting herself from the aspersions of others. Was her love blind?

The description of *glass* a blind is a personification. It is opaque in its understanding of outer elements, but transparent for those who can peer inwardly, for the poet who knows how to secrete the contents of the glass. When hand blown, glass may be looked upon as an art object, worthy of admiration for its beauty, luster, color, tone—as is a beloved. If broken or chipped, as happens in relationships, the cutting, hard, and bruising edge may draw blood. The references to *glass* also suggests "spectacle"—*eyeglasses* make for better sight—but also a *spectacle,* an eye-catching public or theatrical display, an object of curiosity or contempt about which one may speculate. Because of Stein's sexual proclivities and her literary objections and rebellions against staid grammatical and syntactical conventions, she was vulnerable and open, like the carafe, to public shame were she to make a "spectacle" of herself.

"A kind in glass and a cousin," suggests a qualitative relationship, rooted in kindness and understanding. It may also intimate a type of bond to which a relative may be kindly disposed, though such a "spectacle" might lead some "to pointing" their finger at the object of their ire, thus casting opprobrium on the couple in question, despite the fact that there is "nothing strange" about such "an arrangement" or "system." Singly or individually, people "hurt" others for any reason at all—a different literary "system" or unusual sexual proclivities. In so doing, they draw blood ("color"), the "color," referring to wine contained in the carafe, which brings merriment, or as in communion, commemorates a bond or sacrament, thus uniting what had been divided and transforming the temporal into the atemporal. "A single hurt color" implies the pain of blood issuing from a cut or from menstruation, mirroring the bruising lot of women who are looked down upon in a patriarchal "system." Yet, this very liquid contained in the carafe/uterus is the sine qua non of life, that which permits its continuation. Redness, which intimates embarrassment and "not ordinary" passion is catalytic, but "not unordered," dissimilar "in not resembling" the behavior of the majority. While "The difference" between Stein's way as a lesbian poet and society may be increasing or "spreading," this sentence also refers to the lips of the vagina/carafe that, when opened up, allow the mysteries hidden within its liquid body to be decanted.

"GLAZED GLITTER"

Although a mood of jubilation and excitement also prevails in **"Glazed Glitter,"** a warning is offered to those who take the world of appearances at face value:

Nickel, what is nickel, it is originally rid of a cover.

The change in that is that red weakens an hour. The change has come. There is no search. But there is, there is that hope and that interpretation and sometime, surely any is unwelcome, sometime there is breath and there will be a sinecure and charming very charming is that clean and cleansing. Certainly glittering is handsome and convincing.

There is no gratitude in mercy and in medicine. There can be breakages in Japanese. That is no programme. That is no color chosen. It was chosen yesterday, that showed spitting and perhaps washing and polishing. It certainly showed no obligation and perhaps if borrowing is not natural there is some use in giving.

The alliteration in the poem's title, **"Glazed Glitter,"** and the previous poem's **"Glass,"** suggests an object with a mirrorlike, sparkling, glossy, and highly polished surface. Although hard and immobile, like fired clay or enamel, its bedazzling, scintillating, flickering, and rippling exterior infuse it with life and dynamism. Let us recall that alchemists used *nickel,* a silvery hard ductile metallic element capable of a high polish and resistance to corrosion, in their scientific transmutations. Because of its gray/silvery tones, it was likened to lead, a base or unrefined metal, identified by alchemists with Saturn, the God of Time, and thus of death. The German *kupfer* (nickel), deceptively labeled copper, accounts for the "red" in the second sentence, perhaps referring to the moon, thus symbolizing change when identified with the woman's monthly menses. With the flow of time, the once-brilliant coloration "weakens an hour," growing paler and more feeble with each passing moment.

"The change in that is that red weakens an hour," indicates flux and aging as well as the desire to be forthright and open, to be "rid of a cover." In that nickel is also change (five-cent piece) that passes from hand to hand, it is a common denominator, facilitating commercial transactions in the everyday world. So should the word and its object be plain and commonplace. "The change has come" implies a change in time but also of monetary values, referring perhaps to Stein's financial transactions with her brother. Their once-glittering and bedazzling works of art, food for spirit and soul, had, when sold, taken on functional value. A question of tender, they now resemble the impure and leaden metals rather than the solely golden and aesthetic ones. "There is no search" now for higher worth—that of eternal values in art. Yet, there is "hope" in the "interpretation" and aftermath of such a transaction, though "sometimes, surely any is welcome." The mention of "breath" (*pneuma*), a sublimating force, refers to spiritual and creative powers within a being; others see it as a "sinecure" to be viewed as a disease, *sine cure*, that is, without a cure. Idleness is "charming," as Leo and Stein knew only too well. Relationships change, however; emotions and passions have a "cleansing" factor; they "clean" away the rubble, the dross, allowing for the essence of kinship to emerge: "Certainly glittering is handsome and convincing."

That "There is no gratitude in mercy and in medicine," intimates Stein's loss of expectation in science, relying more deeply at present on feelings as her guide. The "breakages in Japanese" may refer to Leo's collection of Japanese prints, also broken up during the division, thus mirroring the shattering of the brother/sister friendship. It was not so intended; there was "no programme" for such a happening. Nor was choice involved. Things had to be cleared up: anger, which "showed spitting," also viewed as a cleansing process for Orientals, reinforces Stein's frequent use of "washing and polishing," cleansing and cleaning. Nor was there any "obligation" that she share her life/art with her brother; no "borrowing," henceforth, between them. Her anger has dissipated. The need to be generous is uppermost now, "yet may there be some use in giving."

Stein seems to have traversed her Rubicon. The "glazed glitter" that prevails since Toklas moved to 27, rue de Fleurus, brightening, cleaning, and cleansing her life, bringing to it unheard of beauty, polish, and glitter, thus extracts the silvery and reddened tones from the object/life. The matriarchate had taken full sway over the patriarchate with its "handsome and convincing" autocracy of monetary values.

"A BOX"

In "**A Box**," viewed as a feminine symbol because of its containing/uteruslike quality, may also be identified with the cranium, the home of secret, fragile, precious, but also fearful elements. Protective as well as imprisoning, the brain case is the seat of potentiality, the origin of infinite riches, but also of distress, disease, and all of life's iniquities. Yet, as in Pandora's box, there is hope. When identified with a coffin, as in Osiris' case, the box symbolizes decay that, in alchemical view, is the locus for transformation from unregenerate to productive matter.

What emerges from within Stein's box? Ideas, feelings, sensations revolving around a human body? a brain? Qualitative factors, implicit in the poems already analyzed, reappear: "kindness," for example, may be so unexpected for some as to elicit "redness" or blushing; "rudeness," may provoke the "redness" of rage. The "rapid" barrage involving the "same question" also provokes anger, redness, and rudeness. The "eye," the organ of enlightenment and perception, probes the emotions that surge forth. Its careful "research" and "selection," painful at times, eliminates the "cattle" or multiple riches that exist within the box/cranium and the box/body. "Cattle" may also suggest domestication: these animals, considered property, are raised for the masses, that is, society's lowest common denominator. "Cattle" are like the commonest of objects Stein uses in her ideograms and cubists in their paintings. She succeeds in creating a work of art by her discerning placement of these objects in her poem, thus altering both their meaning and focus. A writer, like a cook who cleans food by stripping it of its dross, must peer critically into everything that emanates from his box/cranium and box/body: idea, emotion, sensation. The conscious mind must control, edit, classify each single moment of experience. Never should emotions be allowed entry into the written work without having first been probed and purified by the eagle "eye." The first syllable of "Question," indicates a *quest*, a search, thus underscoring the mental operation of "selection," the notion of looking, finding, seeking, spying, thereby separating the wheat from the chaff. The multiple alliterations, (*r, s, c, s, q, p*), underscoring sibilants, labials, gutturals, palatals, sound out the intense struggle existing within the *box:* "rudimentary" contents within the unconscious, which seek so desperately to surface.

What does "order" outside of the box, that is, in the world, imply? What is the "white" (Steinese baby talk for right) "way" for the "cattle" to take themselves or be taken out of the pasture? The virgins, referring to traditional values concerning the body and mind, like "cattle" do not like to be led out of their secure and contented ways. Enclosed within the pasture, however, virginal views "disappoint" both the thinking and sexually active person. So, too, is it easier for the writer to adhere to conventional ways (imitate the nineteenth-century techniques) and for the virgin to experience the normal (heterosexual) act of intercourse, "suggesting a pin" rather than to try the different (lesbian) way. The world outside of the boxed-in world may disorient, one may lose one's way and go "round" in circles, thus paving the way for a visionless, nondifferentiated, intellectually and sexually blinding life. Cut off from dangers, one is also severed from the excitement engendered by "a fine substance strangely." Withdrawal encourages vulnerability to hurt, but also to pleasure of the most "rudimentary" kind. Reactions, therefore, must "be analysed," cognized, contemplated, sifted, pruned. The discovery of "strangely" delicate, subtle, sensitive elements within being are to be pinpointed. All factors in the life process are invited to be scrutinized: the "green point," suggesting fertility; the "red," implying pain and menstruation. Each factor must serve to transform what remains latent and dormant within the "box" into active forces, be it in the domain of art or in human relationships.

"PETTICOAT"

Although not an overt subscriber to feminism, Stein, in her one-line poem, "A Petticoat," clearly displays her ire against the patriarchal Judeo-Christian society with its hierarchy of unsavory and deficient values. While emphasizing the fine dividing line between acceptable ways—the pure, virginal "light" and "white"—as opposed to the usually black "ink spot," she is referring to the writer who strays from conventional ways and is considered a "disgrace" to society. The spot left from "menstruation," viewed as unclean, symbolizes a rejection of women. Yet, both have their "rosy charm." Who better than Stein understood the meaning of "disgrace"? Her writings had been refused by so many publishers, her ideas and behavior discredited. She was an outcast. Yet, even in pain, straying out of the "pasture" held its "rosy charm" for the writer and the woman.

"Peeled Pencil. Coke" and "This Is This Dress, Aider" are two essentially pornographic poems. The first consists of three words, "Rub her coke." An example of Stein's stripping of phonemes down to their bare essentials, the alliterated title, "Peeled Pencil," suggests another kind of fruitful defloration: the readying of the vagina for the insertion of the dildo. The creative process is implicit in the phallic symbol of the pencil: as used by the poet, this instrument serves to make its mark on the paper. In the old days, pencils had to be peeled to be sharpened. As layer upon layer was being pulled off, its slender black cylinder essence was made ready to "pin" point the author's glyphs on the virginal page. Like the sexual, so the writing process arouses passion. Excitement

reaches such a pitch that some feel as if their windpipe had been blocked, causing near strangulation.

To Rub, an active verb, defined as subjecting to back and forth or circular action with pressure and friction, as in cleaning, polishing, and smoothing, also suggests the hand massaging the surface of the body, thus generating friction and heat. The writer likewise encounters difficulties as she moves her hand across the page in an effort to smooth and polish the words in the manuscript. So, in alchemy, after the flammable, volcanic, ebullient powers have surged forth, distillation must take place. "Coke," the residue of coal and used as fuel, is what remains following the burning, triturating, or cleansing operation. In Stein's poem, "coke" symbolizes the transformatory round that must take place for the quintessential experience (the poem or sexual act) to make its mark on body, psyche, and intellect. Only after the raw or primitive experience has been lived can "coke" be extracted: that active substance that fuels both the sexual and creative process. "Coke," short for cocaine, acts as a local anesthetic and induces intoxication as well—something Stein never abided. Lucidity was her guide. Rather than "Coke," implying cock and coitus, she uses cunnilingus for sexual fulfillment.

"THIS IS THIS DRESS, AIDER"

In "This Is This Dress, Aider," Stein not only decorticates her words of conventional meaning, but uses, as always, onomatopeias and multiple puns to strengthen the point she is trying to make. The noun *Dress,* an outer garment that serves to hide the body, used as a verb, depicts the act of covering, hiding, secreting—a sexually exciting thought. Like a fetish, the dress as object is endowed with its own energy and magical qualities, thus transmuting the image into a tantalizing power. A feeling of "distress" (*this dress*) counters the joyous mood of anticipation, opening up the writer to the fear and frustration arising from her partner's built-in inhibitions, which prevent sexual fulfillment.

> Aider why aider why whow, whow stop touch, aider whow, aider stop the muncher, muncher, munchers.

> A jack in kill her, a jack in, makes a meadowed king, makes a to let.

"Aider," is Alice, the active participant in this poem. Like eiderdown, her presence is soft, pliable, and comforting. It is she who comes to the poet's *aid* and *aids her.* As the poet's scientific and medical side ponders the question as to "why" rapture takes place during coitus, she realizes that for highs to reach their peak, intellectuality must be stripped. To yield fully to instinct and to feeling, to basic or primitive elements, allows her to go beyond the state of reason and self-control. Rapturously and repeatedly, she expresses her glee: "whow whow stop touch, aider whow, aider stop." No longer is voice subverted; on the contrary, it is allowed to sing out the overwhelming, almost trancelike state she now experiences. The word *muncher,* someone who chews with relish, is an onomatopeia, its nasals and fricatives suggesting the action involved in oral sex and the sonorities accompanying such labial activities.

Fairy tales about Jack the Giant Killer, Jack and the Beanstalk, Jack Sprat, Jack-in-the-box, and many more, although frightening and humorous to children and adults, also trigger the imagination. So the writer's fantasy world is likewise aroused by the thought of sexual play, and the sensations evoked *aid* her in finding the word that will replicate the experience. A *jack,* is also a mechanical and portable device for exerting pressure or lifting a heavy body a short distance. The emphasis on this twice-mentioned "a jack in" recalls a similar heaving or hoisting motion in Stein's later **"Lifting Belly,"** referring in both cases to the use of the dildo to bring on a climax. The word *meadowed,* associated with a tract of moist low-lying grassland, may be a metaphor for pubic hair. "King," ruler, master, and center of all he surveys, suggests the male partner—in this case, Stein, who always considered herself man, potentate, supreme consciousness, and creative principle, while Toklas was the woman, the homebody, and subservient in every way.

Step 2. Food

Stein's second step in her initiatic journey into the wonder-working elements of nature and of language, deals with food. Fuel for the body/mind, such nourishment as is mentioned in the fifty-one poems included in this section represents Mother Nature as both vital and destructive. The giver of life and energy, she sees to the propagation of the vegetal and animal worlds with which Stein now deals. Such a focalization suggests a need to regress to a primitive mode: the nonhuman psyche, the instinctual domain, in order to root out the very substance of word and sexual experience. Stein's desire to deal with common everyday entities such as foods replicates a similar movement on the part of the writer to "flatten out" poetic themes, as Arthur Rimbaud and Jules Laforgue had accomplished before her. In order to succeed, the writer

must immerse herself in primal waters and bathe in the very source of existence. Only then can such vital questions as life and death be posed. These notions had always haunted Stein. Now, for the first time, they would no longer be posed from an intellectual, scientific, or philosophical point of view, but viscerally, via Mother Nature's fertility rites.

For the alchemist, food was energy—that is, the fire or catalyst needed to perform the operation that transmuted base metal into sublime gold. To effect such a change was arduous and painful, requiring the burning and water operations that stripped and cleansed the problem, thus isolating it from other elements. Stein's poetic needs may be examined similarly. Her intense search in the domain of language took her from the outer world, "the glazed glitter," into the very heart of physical being. Her trajectory, she believed, had helped her better assess her needs and her worth, thus aiding in the transmuting of feeling into its authentic container, the *word.*

Food also has a qualitative factor appended to it. Identified with agressivity, it is the mouth's task first to take it from the outside world, then masticate ("muncher"), ingest, digest, and finally eliminate it. So, too, must the word be internalized, experienced, sensed, palpated, prior to its implantation into the poem. Life and the creative process, then, require a combative, invasive, and militant stance.

"MILK"

A symbol for abundance and fertility, milk is nature's sustaining force par excellence. For mystics, such as the Orphics, it spells immortality; for the Druids, it was used for curative purposes. The inconographic representations of Isis, Hera, and Mary nursing their young, represent Mother Nature in her most fructifying form. The *Philosophical Stone* (Spiritual God), the summation of the alchemical operation, was referred to as "Virgin's Milk," for it brought immortality.

> Climb up in sight climb in the whole utter needles and a guess a whole guess is hanging. Hanging hanging.

The vertical act of climbing to the breast or "utter" (udder) to suck out the fluid of life—a natural act for infants—requires effort, exertion, striving. Stein's verbal portrait, **"Picasso"** comes to mind: her admiration for his valiant and continuous struggle in contrast to "Matisse" who, once fame was his, abandoned the battle and renounced the challenge. Be it in the artistic or love process, contention is crucial; passivity, lethargy, an inability to concentrate and focus on one's goal, is death.

The word *utter*, closely allied in Stein's punning ways to a cow's udder, conflates the intellectual and the physical worlds. Without such sucking activity, the physical energy needed in the practical as well as the poetic worlds would be wanting. That the cow image is implicit in utter/udder is not, in Stein's view, a derogatory epithet attached to womankind. On the contrary, having recourse to it in many of her writings, she uses it to symbolize the nourishing aspect of Mother Earth.

"Needles," used repeatedly in the first section of Stein's work, are phallic images, suggesting pain during the act of penetration. In that they are also employed in sewing, designed to bind together bits of disparate cloth, they fuse the heteroclite. Likewise, the word is interwoven or intertwined into the text. To needle someone is to annoy, upset; but the energy aroused in such activity is catalytic. It is worth recalling that the cubists stuck pins and nails into their collages, introducing a non-painterly element onto the canvases, thus rejecting while also expanding the prevailing logocentric definition of art. Nor are Stein's texts devoid of such puncturing and piercing objects. Hurt necessarily plays a role in the creative process as well as in human relationships.

"A guess a whole guess is hanging" implies the world of the unknown that comes into being as the milk of life is suckled. Nor are the sexual pleasures derived from such an act to be overlooked by the sensualist that Stein was. *Guess* (from Middle English *gessen*) suggests *get*, which like *Climb*, allows for the fulfillment of the wishing, wanting, and needing. The food (omitting the g leaves *essen*, to eat in German) within the "hanging" breast endows the one who "climbs" with energy, to be expended in sexual, philosophical, or literary activity. Within milk/breast exists the potential for life; within it *hangs* the fate of the human (intellect) and animal (body) species.

"Hanging hanging" is a reference to breasts in general and, in particular, Stein's pendulous ones. Within them resides the unknown, the unforeseen—that creative power that makes her world go round. Metaphors for security, tenderness, intimacy, breasts are an offering as well as a refuge.

"POTATOES"

Stein's three poems dealing with potatoes, a spherical, bulbous root nourished within the heart of Mother Earth, visualize the notion of growth and creativity. That the French equivalent for potato, *pomme de terre*, or apple of the earth, is the terrestrial counterpart of paradise's forbidden fruit that hangs from the tree of knowledge, conflates what had been severed according to Genesis. Unlike the spiritual fruit that leads to transgression, the *potato* yields knowledge of another sort: it permits an ingestion of earthly and everyday matter, thus serving to fructify both mind and body. Existential, the potato symbolizes this present life—the *now*—rather than the Christian's view of future heavenly domain.

> POTATOES "Real potatoes cut in between."
>
> POTATOES "In the preparation of cheese, in the preparation of crackers, in the preparation of butter, in it."
>
> ROAST POTATOES "Roast potatoes for."

The three poems focus on the preparation of potatoes: from the raw and cutting phase, the cooking operation, to its final state in the serving.

The image in the first poem, reminiscent of Georgia O'Keefe's many opening or severed flowers, replicates the dividing and severing process in making the potato ready for eating. The cutting open of the vegetable opens up its secret parts to the light of the eye. So, too, may the "cut in between" be applied to other areas, needing no profound decoding since its message is more than obvious. In terms of the poet, however, to articulate requires a cutting up, a trimming and slimming of syllables in the preparation of the word's implantation into the text.

That "cheese" and "butter" in the second poem are added in the cooking process not only increases the vegetable's succulence, but in that they are milk products, they increase its nutritive powers. So, too, must the poet include foreign materials, as had the cubists, to enrich a text. "Crackers" are not only a dry crispy bread product made of leavened or unleavened bread used to mop up the delectable sauce from a dish or platter, but they also make snapping or crackling noises. To the combination of potatoes, cheese, and butter, a feast for the taste buds, is added the agreeable crackling sonorities from the "crackers" being eaten, but also those emanating from the oven as the "roast" (referred to in the third poem) is cooking, thus also becoming food for the ear. *Crackers* broken down into *crack-er* (her), has a sexual allusion, referring back to "the cut in between" in the first poem; and to the effort made by the poet, cracking her brain to come out with the proper combination of words to be added during the cooking process.

"ASPARAGUS"

That a fat and ungainly woman is alluded to as a sack of potatoes, an image that can readily be applied to Stein, may help to explain the poem entitled "**Asparagus**," referring, perhaps to Toklas's thinness.

> Asparagus in a lean in a lean to hot. This makes it art and it is wet wet weather wet weather wet.

Asparagus, (Greek *spargan*) meaning to swell, is iconographically tall and pencil-like, and thus a phallic symbol. A perennial plant of the lily family having many-branched stems and minute scalelike leaves, the asparagus is cultivated for its edible shoots. No longer dealing with an invisible and secret world with regard to the potato, Stein broaches an ocular and delectable one. That the object depicted is "lean" suggests skinniness, but also the act of inclining, bending, or casting one's weight to one side for support. In these cases, it alludes to Toklas: her skeletal appearance, her subservience, her bending and fawning when in the presence of her deity; also the awkwardness of the sexual position when making love to Stein. The "hot" refers to the heat brought on by the rubbing operation during the sexual encounter; the "wet wet weather," to the perspiration resulting from such friction; and "wet weather wet," to the vaginal fluids discharged preceding and following the climax. There may also be a literary allusion: the efforts expended by Stein as she leans first on one word or artistic form and then another. The intensity poured into the choices she must make in the writing process generates bodily heat, liquidity, and when completed, moments of Dionysian ecstasy.

"CHICKEN"

Stein's many poems dealing with meats (roast beef, mutton, sausages, chicken) take us into the animal world, antithetical to Platonists and Christians who prize spirituality rather than instinctuality. Not so for Stein who loved animals, and especially dogs. In keeping with Western values, to allude to the animal in an individual is to refer to what is base or, in alchemical terms, is leaden and unrefined in that person. Yet, it is the animal as *libido,* raw energy, that empowers creation.

The "**Chicken**," the title Stein gave to four poems, is a barnyard animal, not too clean, not too bright, and easily scared. It may also refer to the coward, the young woman as a term of endearment, or to a prostitute, as well as to the young male homosexual.

The "**Pheasant**," unlike the common chicken, is a sought-after game bird known for its long sweeping tail and brilliant feathers. On the other hand, the chicken is "a peculiar bird," different, curious, odd, known for its eccentricities. Used in some religious, initiatory, and divinatory rites by shamans, the chicken symbolizes death and resurrection. In Orphic rituals, it is associated with the dog, friendly to humans. According to the ancient Egyptians and Greeks, the chicken leads the dead to the lower worlds—psychologically, to inner (unconscious) realms.

That Stein emphasizes the words *dirty* and *third* intimates an association between Christianity's (Trinity) view of dirt and women (the chicken is identified with the female). The emphasis placed by revealed religions on purity and virginity was anathema to Stein, as was their view of dirt as being synonymous with evil. Dirt and evil are implicit in the world of differentiation, thus of earthly existence. To reject these aspects of life is to seek to escape into the pristine purity of an afterlife, without ever knowing terrestrial joy. The same may be said of the writer's approach to his art. For Stein, all themes, all words, from the most commonplace to the most ethereal, fueled her pen providing they were picked, prepared, and served on the proper platter.

Like a collage, cooking and writing require the introduction of other ("more") foods into the dinner or completed text. Various plants in the mustard family, like "**Cress**," add a pungent flavor to the meat; as do "**Potato**" and "**Loaves**" of bread. The combination of foods and seasoning, like that of letters in a word or morphemes in a text, enhance the visual beauty of the arrangement on the platter as well as its aroma and taste during its ingestion.

As previously noted, eating is an aggressive act that in the case of the pheasant and chicken begins with the catching, continues with the killing of the bird (sticking), and then the depluming (sticking), cleansing of the inside ("sticking"); and then the "sticking" of it into the mouth, masticating, pulverising, digesting it. The repetition of *stick,* its strident sibilants, hostile dentals, grating gutturals, and ferocious fricatives, stick the ear with a medley of unpleasant cacophonies, thus replicating the murderous intent of the eater. This same analogy may be applied to sexuality, for example, during a sadistic act, with all of the "extra" "sticking" devices needed to bring on the climax. Nor should the writer be discouraged from entering into verbal sadomasochistic play, in the annexing, rejecting, and redefining of terms. For everything, positive and negative, must participate in the feast that is writing.

Stein has taken the *mystery* of matter from the world of objects to that of plants and animals. Her third step will deal with the inner sanctum, viewed in terms of body and mind (both conscious and unconscious). Like the alchemist working in silence in his laboratory, so the verbal draftsman fashions, shapes, colors, and texturizes his words, clauses, sentences, and paragraphs. The labors in both cases are conducted in the secret realms of remote climes.

Step 3. Rooms

The heart of the transformatory process takes place in the room/chamber/cavern. In ancient Egypt, initiates entered the most secret vaults within the pyramid to undergo their initiatory rituals: the transformation of the potential or unformed into the fulfilled and formed. Such a conversion was looked upon as a death of the old self and the birth of the new, purified, and elevated one.

The room in **Tender Buttons** represents that solitary area within the psyche into which libido (energy) withdraws in order to revitalize what has become worn and arid within being. Comparable to the womb, where the seed is nourished, or the vaginal area where the climax may be experienced, or the mind, replete with ideas, the room provides the seclusion and separation from the outside world that is crucial to the evolution of an individual.

Withdrawing into an inner space permits Stein to cut herself off from the excitement of the workaday world that drains and deletes her energies. Within the peace and security of her own mind/room, or vaulted cranium, Stein is able to sense and think authentically. Thus does she feel able to transmute the fruit of her meditations into the word. Within the mind (conscious and unconscious spheres) she learns to see, hear, listen, and palpate in a space/time continuum; thus does she feel competent to reorganize volume, space, and form, and all other inconstants. No limitations are imposed upon the senses, now reactivated by the inflow of energy into the psyche.

The tangled terminology and rescrambling of ideas and notions occurring in **"Rooms,"** no longer made up of separate poems, but divided into paragraphs, is as esoteric, perhaps even more so, than the previous sections. No better paradigm of Stein's ambiguous views can be offered than her repeated use of *centre.* She warns ("Act so that

there is no use in a centre") against imprisonment within a rationally conceived *centre:* that is, within concepts. According to Cézanne's vision of composition, the painter's and the writer's goal is to portray each object and all of its parts in positions that are equally responsive to his sensibility and to the livingness of his observation. All hierarchies within the frame, as well as the frame itself, are abolished. The center, therefore, is no longer the center of focus of anything; nor is it to be regarded as an organizing principle.[6] No frame; no point of reference; no boundaries. A poem has no more a center than does a canvas. The cubists' dictum is: an "object is an object"; its place in the composition is "decentralized"; its ideations and iconography are transformed into the object of the composition.

The same is true of the *centre* in **"Rooms"** if viewed three-dimensionally, that is, as the focalizing point on a classical compositional canvas or the suspenseful line in a poem or novel. When viewed four-dimensionally, however, as in such age-old religious symbolic images as the Star of David, Cross, Circle, and so on, the *centre* is everywhere and nowhere. Some mystics refer to this transpersonal *centre* existing within a space/time continuum as the Principle, Absolute, or God. Pascal, quoting Hermes Trismegistus, wrote, "God is a sphere the center of which is everywhere and the circumference nowhere." Stein, the nonbeliever, as God/the artist, must reach the creative center living inchoate and transpersonally within her. In this most sacred and unknowable region exists the beginning and end of all things in an eternal *now.* Forever spawning and disintegrating, life exists as a continuously reshuffling, redirecting, rebalancing, and rekindling process.

> If the centre has the place then there is distribution. That is natural. There is a contradiction and naturally returning there comes to be both sides and the centre. That can be seen from the description.

Active and dynamic, the writer who plunges into a continuously shifting, expanding, and unlimited inner space, know *chaos* (the *void*). As conveyed in Genesis and in many creation myths, including Hesiod's *Theogony,* such fomenting mass yields, paradoxically, new insights while concomitantly dismantling nonfunctioning ones. Words, when inhabiting this dark, moist, and unlimited realm, expand in meaning, sensation, texture, and coloration. As their consistencies alter, so does their impacting upon other phonemes and morphemes in the sentence. Although word is one, it is made up of individual letters, each possessing its own identity, confluence, sensation, rhythms, and blendings, thus acting and reacting on the rest "of the herd" as the poet Stéphane Mallarmé used to say.

Body, psyche, and mind are energized by Stein's intuitive forays into and out of her *centre*. A redistribution in the placement of words in the sentence detaches them from conventional use, thus redefining them and pushing them to the extreme limit of language. Because of Stein's paratactical intervals, aided and abetted by her omission of punctuation, subjects, and objects, and the addition of a plethora of puns, extreme syntactical distortion and incomprehensibility are the result.

Metaphors, analogies, and associations to the pleasure and pain involved in the sexual and literary acts, for example, pepper the entire text: *stress, distress, pain, joy, accomplishing, lifting, voice, centre, spreading, black line, distribution, kneeling, opening, rubbing, erection, swelling, open, four, startling, starving, husband, betrothed, sleeping, size, torn, sack, hangings, movement, bed, disorder, funnel, cape, conundrum, torn, target, breath, window, milk, water, empty, flower, cutting, clean, pecking, petting, asparagus, fountain,* and so forth.

Coitus is alluded to in and of itself, but also its effect on mind and body is also suggested. The tremulous sensations triggered by climaxes and the sensual excitement generated, activates the poetic process. Described as an alchemical operation, Stein writes: "Burnt and behind and lifting a temporary stone and lifting more than a drawer."

The fire of passion produced during the sexual act heightens the flame or electric spark, which in turn, and in keeping with the alchemical process, not only burns off impurities, but dries out all moisture. Only "burnt" or charred remains are left "behind" (posterior), that is, the word's quintessence. Like a precious diamond, the word is no longer embedded in black carbon, but is polished, glittering, and gleaming with incandescent emotions, now that the old and unproductive perceptions and sensations have been killed.

The reborn and recrystallized insights are "lifting" (sexually and creatively) the poet into new areas of feeling and of expression. The "stone" that was raised suggests the removal of a veil: inhibitions have been dropped, adding to the impetus of the electric charge. An androgynous element, stone constitutes the wholeness and fullness of the primordial state, which has now been made accessible. But the experience of the sexual and verbal act, like unrefined and unshaped "stone," must be smoothed and polished, thus fulfilling its goal—the transformation of brute matter into the work of art. "Drawer," a boxlike entity used for storage, may be opened or closed. In like manner, ideas and feelings may be covertly or overtly conveyed in a poem. Stein's use of the comparison *more* suggests her increasing self-confidence in her talent as a writer.

Sight, always crucial for Stein, be it in her observation of paintings or words, is explicit in the following sentence:

> No eye-glasses are rotten, no window is useless and yet if air will not come in there is a speech ready, there always is and there is no dimness, not a bit of it.

Within the secret space that is the room, the use of such devices as "eye-glasses" not only enhance vision, but protect the eye from the dirt outside. Since the "window" for Plato represents an opening onto the soul, such apertures increase the reception of Light from the spirit, senses, and mind on a variety of levels. Thus, every "window" serves the poet. Like eyeglasses, the "window," inviting air (spirit) to permeate formerly enclosed quarters, expands horizons. The eye/window may now indulge in a dual activity: to look *out* onto the world and *within,* into the deepest recesses of the *room:* body, psyche, soul. The world, like all other concrete or abstract notions, alters in meaning, consistency, texture, and coloration depending upon the light shed on it during the observing process. Such a seeing and looking activity is crucial. Such voyeurism helps her convey the carnality of language in social discourse.

"Air," a sublimated element, suggests height, spirituality, flight, an amorphous condition rather than the previously solid material principle. Such alteration of focus implies spiritual growth, an ability to abstract and conceptualize problems by divesting them of earthly entanglements. Air may be identified with "breath" (Hebrew *ruh*), the spirit of God as it moved over primordial waters in the beginning of time and created the world (Gen. 1:2). With breath, according to Judeo-Christian and Hindu belief, came the word and speech (John 1:1; Rig-Veda 1:164). Those who can see into matter and spirit sense the word; for them "there always is and there is no dimness, not a bit of it."

In another entry, Stein writes: "The time when there is not the question is only seen when there is a shower. Any little thing is water." Experienced as transpersonal and immanent, *time,* like the creative instinct, is both temporal and atemporal.

As for the word imprinted on the page and embedded in matter, it too becomes abstracted, as thought. *Question* (from the Latin, *quaestio*), identified with *quest* (Latin *quaestus*), indicates a continuous search or process leading to fulfillment. The spirit of interrogation, so crucial to the writer, vanishes when the sensate world submerges the rational sphere. Yet, it has its positive attributes. Like the Flood, a "shower," identified with emotion, inundates. On the other hand, for the alchemist and poet, the water operation both solves and dissolves. In so doing, the unsolvable problem vanishes. What had been a stumbling block has been liquefied, as sugar or salt when placed in a bowl of water. A smoother or more objective and comprehensive attitude may therefore come into being. Problems, now viewed in particles, may be divided, thereby altering perspectives and approaches to them. The particular, rather than the whole, comes under scrutiny. If, however, currents are too swift, the "shower" leads to drowning, regression, and loss of identity. "Any little thing is water" suggests that rigid, fixated, and solidified attitudes and their accompanying words may be turned into a solution—that is, be allowed to flow freely. The poet, then, is given the freedom to evaluate and reevaluate, to position and reposition them, thus bringing a new reality into being.

There is no end to the meanings and interpretations one may glean on reading *Tender Buttons*. Each word imprinted on the page may trigger in the reader ideas, melodies, rhythms, colorations, codes, and the infinite reverberations to which these give rise. Stein's inner journey or descent into the mystic's *centre*, as conveyed in *Tender Buttons*, was a breakthrough—a turning point in her life as woman and writer. Successful in subverting the Westerner's logic and habitual modes of rumination, always anathema to her, she discovered her own working order. First visualizing her object, she then interiorized it by way of the cooking operation, through which she assimilated its energy. Finally, like the good alchemist she was, she sublimated and abstracted its contents, after which it was ready to be embedded in the text. Her bristling treatment of discourse and syntax, her polysemous meanings and meanderings, her subvocal nonsense, and her verbal and ideational fragmentations were spectacular examples of what could be called the cubist language.

As cubist and alchemist, Stein, the word stripper, offers her bewitching, puzzling, and frustrating brew to contemporary readers. May each and every one plunge into its infinite waters.

Notes

1. Randa K. Dubnick, *The Structure of Obscurity: Gertrude Stein, Language, and Cubism* (Urbana: University of Illinois Press, 1984), 35.

2. Stein, "Poetry and Grammar," *Lectures in America*, 209.

3. Ibid., 235.

4. Walker, *Making of a Modernist*, 132.

5. Stein, "Poetry and Grammar," 231.

6. Katz, "Matisse, Picasso, and Gertrude Stein," *Four Americans in Paris*, 52.

"Patriarchal Poetry"

LINDA S. WATTS (ESSAY DATE 1996)

SOURCE: Watts, Linda S. "'Reject Rejoice Rejuvenate': Gertrude Stein's Feminist Critique of Spiritual and Literary Tradition." In *Rapture Untold: Gender, Mysticism, and the 'Moment of Recognition' in Works by Gertrude Stein*, pp. 131-44. New York: Peter Lang, 1996.

In the following essay, Watts explicates the literary and spiritual politics of the essay "Patriarchal Poetry," investigating the feminist implications of Stein's syntax and typology for patriarchal language.

They do not ask what is religion but I do. I ask what is religion. I cannot ask too often, what is religion.

Gertrude Stein, *The Geographical History of America*

With its polemical title, **"Patriarchal Poetry,"** this 1927 Stein text, invites a political reading. By no means does Stein avail herself of didacticism, here any more than she does elsewhere. Still, there can be little question that one of Stein's accomplishments in this now often-quoted composition is commentary on and subversion of patriarchal poetry. As she notes in this and other writings, Stein considers language to be a belief system in itself, comparable in that sense to a religion. Invoking the images of Catholicism, she writes of "Patriarchal poetry and fish on Friday, Patriarchal poetry and birds on Sunday," linking the rituals of language and religion. (PP, [**"Patriarchal Poetry"**] 259) When treated with such reverence, language cannot change. Without change, language loses its vitality, becoming merely "worn-out literary words."[1] With an unexamined vocabulary, it also becomes a conservative social and political force. In her own writing, and particularly in a piece such as **"Patriarchal Poetry,"** Stein rebels from literary traditions. To write as it has been written is to serve Mammon, and so Stein makes it her task to build a second, or alternative, form of literature, in which she "serves God" by resisting outside influence.[2]

Stein's declaration to serve "God" rather than "Mammon" is somewhat misleading, however, insofar as Stein's ideal writer serves no master but herself. Recall her insistence that creativity is "not being blown into you, it is very much your own."[3] Creativity (and responsibility for that creativity) resides within the individual. A writer's creative authority must be her own; she cannot inherit it or receive it from some altogether external mystical force. Since Stein views writing as a solitary enterprise, even the influence of literary predecessors is best avoided. In much the same way Stein advises the individual against deference to canonical law in religious matters, she characterizes the writer "serving God" as one who, while writing, "does not remember" her literary forebears. The great books are a chronicle of, rather than a substitute for, creative talent. Laboring under the weight of a literary inheritance, the writer faces the task of revivifying language. That challenge becomes greatest when the poet uses words grown weak from repeated use.

Stein calls for the poet to speak not with old images, but rather with a new diction. Using the familiar Romantic symbol of a "nightingale," ("Ode to a Nightingale") Stein chastises the derivative poet, saying "Not to such a pretty bird." (**PP**, 257) Just as she maintains that a new poetic image may appear ugly at first, Stein implies that an overused image may be all too pretty.

> Compare something else to something else. To be rose. Such a pretty bird. Not to such a pretty bird. Not to not to not to such a pretty bird. Not to such a pretty bird. Not to such a pretty bird. As to as to not to as to and such a pretty bird.
>
> (**PP**, 257)

Stein expresses boredom with the stock images of poetic tradition, as she urges poets to "Compare something else to something else." Metaphors lose their power if used so often that they are simply another name for the object described. To clarify her point, Stein supplies underused alternatives for animal imagery (which also functions for Stein as sexual imagery), including the "fish" and the "cow," two images which appear frequently throughout Stein's work.

The writer must renew poetic language. Stein's objection to literary inheritance is not offered simply as a means for avoiding poetic clichés, though, but also stems from her awareness of the conservative function a literary canon serves. By elevating literary greats, the canon forms a hierarchy which reflects the class and gender hierarchies of a society. When honoring that canon, writers defer to and perpetuate not only literary styles, but also the ideologies, both social and political, those styles encode. In this respect, Stein's indictment of patriarchal poetry anticipated feminist challenges to the literary canon by contemporary feminist writers, critics, theorists, and activists.

As a case in point, Stein identifies this literary inheritance ["Their origin and their history" (**PP**, 263)] as masculinist, and is quick to note that her own language, literary standards, and literary influences are largely if not exclusively male in origin. While such women as George Eliot, Charlotte Perkins Gilman, and Louisa May Alcott impress Stein, the bulk of her references are to men: Carlyle, Dante, DeFoe, Fielding, Flaubert, Scott, Smollett, Shakespeare, Sterne, Swift, Wordsworth, Meredith, Hardy, and Trollope. While Gertrude Stein's immersion in male writing is indisputable, some would say inescapable, she does not accept blindly these writers' techniques, perceptions, models, or hierarchies. Stein writes as one keenly aware not only of the possibilities opened by past writers, but also the options their language and actions deny to her. To these limitations, **"Patriarchal Poetry"** stands as her manifesto. To alternative possibilities, it stands as her blueprint.

It is significant that Stein assigns a name to the works representing this traditional literature, for traditional literature does not acknowledge what it cannot classify. With her capitalization of that name, Stein makes the tradition seem even more staid and static. This 1927 composition takes the shape of a series of assertions, many of which begin by invoking the name, "Patriarchal poetry," as in "Patriarchal poetry makes no mistake." (**PP**, 263) For patriarchs, names imply status over people and possession of things. ["Come to a distance and it still bears their name." (**PP**, 264)] Patriarchs preside over traditional literature, and so "Patriarchal Poetry is named patriarchal poetry." (**PP**, 293) Each time speakers use the name, they reassert possession. In this way, patriarchs also may assure their own honor by insisting that "Patriarchal poetry be often praised often praised." (**PP**, 279) In order for Stein to set out an alternative literature, then, she must see to it that Patriarchal poetry is "renamed." (**PP**, 289)

Stein has numerous reasons for resisting traditional literature. The chief issue Stein takes with Patriarchal Poetry concerns its rigid order: "Patriarchal poetry should be this. . . ." (**PP**, 281) Stein mocks that order with its endless language rules: "Which is why is why is why. . . ." (**PP**, 262) In much the same way that St. Ignatius of Loyola in **Four Saints in Three Acts** imposes upon religion a hierarchical and paramilitary order,

ABOUT THE AUTHOR

ELYSE BLANKLEY ON STEIN'S INFLUENCE IN THE LITERARY WORLD

Although she was not to enjoy widespread acclaim until *The Autobiography of Alice B. Toklas* was published in 1934, by the mid-20s Stein's early works had helped shape the literary development of Anderson, Fitzgerald, Wilder, and Hemingway, all of whom would later change or had already begun to alter the course of twentieth-century letters. Even Joyce was not immune to Stein's "little sentences." Indeed, the sweeping and fundamental linguistic changes suggested by *Tender Buttons* are echoed in Joyce's final work; but where Joyce's encyclopedic *Finnegans Wake*, the universal dictionary of language, is actually an index of fathers (Sterne, Aristotle, Shakespeare, Vico, etc.) sustained and upheld by a monumental cross-referencing of western civilization, Stein's work refers back to no one but herself.

Blankley, Elyse. Excerpt from "Beyond the 'Talent of Knowing': Gertrude Stein and the New Woman." In *Critical Essays on Gertrude Stein*, edited by Michael J. Hoffman, pp. 196-209. Boston: G. K. Hall & Co., 1986.

patriarchs expect poets to fall in step: "Patriarchal poetry left left left right left," **(PP, 294)** because "This is what order does." **(PP, 262)** Patriarchal poetry, with its rules and arbitrary distinctions, reduces creativity to habit. There are so many rules to follow that all "Patriarchal poetry is the same." **(PP, 264)** Art becomes too routinized. Writing, after all, it not a set order like a menu or a calendar:

> . . . and not meat on Monday patriarchal poetry and meat on Tuesday. Patriarchal poetry and venison on Wednesday. Patriarchal poetry and fish on Friday. Patriarchal poetry and birds on Sunday Patriarchal poetry and beef on Tuesday patriarchal poetry and fish on Wednesday Patriarchal poetry and eggs on Thursday patriarchal poetry and carrots on Friday patriarchal poetry and extras on Saturday patriarchal poetry and venison on Sunday Patriarchal poetry and lamb on Tuesday patriarchal poetry and jellies on Friday patriarchal poetry and turkeys on Tuesday.
>
> **(PP, 259)**

Language rules produce standardization, and so "Patriarchal poetry makes it as usual," "Patriarchal poetry one two three." **(PP, 274)** If a writer is to become part of patriarchal poetry, s/he must accept its rankings, too, for Patriarchal poetry "makes no mistake in estimating the value to be placed upon the best and most arranged of considerations." **(PP, 272)** The writer must respect the literary canon and "Remember all of it too." **(PP, 271)** The canon must perpetuate itself in memory and deed.

It is, then, at the very least, convenient that Stein's spiritualized view of "creative" writing requires no knowledge of literary tradition or precedent. In so defining her ideal writer, Stein undermines the patriarchal shape of literary practice, recognition, and memory. By her standards, an original writer exists outside literary tradition, and need not fit into social categories to which that tradition's tribute has been exclusive. Stein's genius perceives in an "unhabitual way," free from the tethers of a literary past. Her expression is limited only by her creativity, and the value of her work resides not in its adherence to literary precedent, but rather in its own creative moment.

In comparing traditional (or patriarchal) literature to a religion, Stein does not overlook the connection between a literary canon and a religious canon. In her challenge to patriarchal poetry, Stein takes on the Bible, itself a sacred text. In particular, she deconstructs the gender roles of Genesis, asking

> What is the difference between a fig and an apple.
> One comes before the other.
>
> **(PP, 276)**

Stein questions the distinction between Adam and Eve, making the difference between the two figures no greater than "the difference between a fig and an apple." At the same time, Stein uses the Biblical story to illustrate the tyrannies of a tradition ruled by "One [who] comes before the other." Patriarchal poetry is not superior to new poetry simply because it preceded the less traditional form. Indeed, by exposing arbitrary distinctions (such as that between Adam and Eve, or old and new poetry), Stein renders such attempts at classification meaningless. She asks of such distinctions:

> What is the result.
>
> The result is that they know the difference between instead and instead and made and made and said and said.
>
> **(PP, 264)**

Stein constructs oppositions with equal terms so that an "initial boundary" melts away. (**PP**, 258) For Stein, there exist no absolute distinctions, and so she challenges the binary oppositions underpinning attempted distinctions.

Stein dispenses with the literary inheritance to which she refers as "**Patriarchal Poetry.**" When finished, she resolves "Never to mention [or name] patriarchal poetry altogether." (**PP**, 263) The act of building an alternative literature liberates her from literary precedent, for that alternative "makes patriarchal poetry apart" rather than central. (**PP**, 265) As the name "**Patriarchal Poetry**" implies, Stein regards literary tradition as masculinist and laden with the perspectives of male domination. Such literature stands as a male province. Stein hopes to see "Patriarchal Poetry interdicted," (**PP**, 287) so that authors, especially women, might have options instead of simply being "Assigned to Patriarchal Poetry." (**PP**, 265) As Stein writes of this gender split, she encourages another mode of writing, particularly for women.

> Let her try,
> Never to be what he said.
>
> (**PP**, 269)

Stein provides women writers with an alternative form of expression, in which they are no longer mere character/subjects of male writers, but rather valued contributors to literature. As she sets aside Patriarchal Poetry, Stein reprises her communion hymn, "When this you see remember me." Here she asserts that, "When this you see remember me should never be added to that." (**PP**, 282) To incorporate Stein in an existing (androcentric) literary canon would be to miss the point of her literary counter strategy and her efforts to see "Patriarchal Poetry replaced." (**PP**, 291) Stein writes of literary tradition "undone," (**PP**, 259) and needful of "rearrangement," (**PP**, 267) and "rectification." (**PP**, 264) Consequently, she considers it no tribute to be assimilated into patriarchal poetry.

Stein does not dismiss patriarchal poetry entirely ["These words containing as they do neither reproaches nor satisfaction. . . ." (**PP**, 265)]. She concedes to men that, "Patriarchal poetry might be what they wanted." (**PP**, 273) Stein does insist, however, that "Patriarchal Poetry makes mistakes" she finds unacceptable, and to which she does not wish herself or others to be subject. (**PP**, 280) Therefore, Stein calls for a new form of expression. Undaunted by anticipated objections from a male proponent of Patriarchal Poetry, Stein declares with the power of Biblical genesis, "If he is not used to it he is not used to it, this is the beginning." (**PP**, 362) With this declaration, Stein inaugurates a celebration of women's emancipation from patriarchal poetry, an emancipation whose impulses are plain in Stein's call to "reject rejoice rejuvenate." (**PP**, 262) Stein reclaims language from the patriarchal and oppressive uses to which it has been put. For this reason, she fills the piece with words in which the pre-fix "re-" depicts regeneration.

> Patriarchal Poetry reclaimed renamed replaced and gathered together as they went in and left it more where it is in when it pleased when it was pleased when it can be pleased to be gone over carefully and letting it be a chance for them to lead to lead not only by left but by leaves.
>
> (**PP**, 289)

By speaking in terms of claims, Stein points out the proprietary relation of patriarchal poetry to literary production. Indeed, within the composition, Stein appears to struggle with the patriarchs for power: "When this you see give it to me." (**PP**, 298) In renaming and replacing patriarchal poetry, Stein empowers new authors, providing "a chance for them to lead."

Naming as the Exercise of Power

Stein is best known, then, for her challenge to conventional syntax and word use. Stein's criticisms of androcentric religion must be understood as related to her challenge to androcentric language. In one of her works, "**Woodrow Wilson**," (1920), Stein makes explicit her critique of language as an instrument whose power is comparable to religion: "How can a language alter. It does no it is an altar."[4] Her affront to reader expectation was so dramatic that many readers accused her of writing in code, or in a personal language they termed "Steinese." Even the headline of Stein's *New York Times* obituary suggests her notoriety in this regard:

> Gertrude Stein Dies in France, 72
> American Author Was Known for Her
> 'A Rose is a Rose is a Rose' Literary Style
> FIRST BOOK INTELLIGIBLE
> Two Biographies Also Written in Lucid Form
> Composed Plays and Opera Libretto.[5]

Where Stein disturbs the orderly literary language of tradition, though, she does so purposefully, making points not only about language, but also about the culture of which that language is both a part and an expression. For example, Stein had an aversion to nouns, or, as she refers to the noun, "the name of anything."[6] In a sharp tone she reserved for impertinent questioners at universities, Stein states the basis for her objection.

Now listen! Can't you see that when the language was new—as it was with Chaucer and Homer—the poet could use the name of a thing and the thing was really there? . . . And can't you see that after hundreds of years had gone by and thousands of poems had been written he could call on those words and find that they were just wornout literary words?[7]

Like other modernists, Stein argued that writers inherit from their literary forebears old words, tired from overuse. It is the task of the writer to restore language. For Stein, nouns represent the greatest challenge. It becomes her passion, for Stein maintains that great writing requires passion, to replace the noun. As Stein seeks models for this work, she rediscovers Walt Whitman. Here was someone who had done away with nouns. Stein writes of Whitman,

He wanted really to express the thing and not call it by its name. He wanted really wanted to express the thing and not call it by its name. He worked very hard at that, and he called it Leaves of Grass because he wanted it to be as little a well known name to be called upon passionately as possible.[8]

Stein takes note of Whitman, separating him from traditions of patriarchal poetry by determining that "creating it without naming it, was what broke the rigid form of the noun."[9] The noun must be reconsidered.

Stein considers the overused noun as a symptom of excess in traditional literature. Each time an author applies a noun, s/he claims the right to create something by assigning to it a name. In this way, authors may employ nouns as instruments of authority.

Think of all that early poetry, think of Homer, think of Chaucer, think of the Bible and you will see what I mean you will really realize that they were drunk with nouns, to name to know how to name earth sea and sky and all that was in them was enough to make them live and love in names, and that is what poetry is it is a state of knowing and feeling a name.[10]

Stein links these nouns as acts of literary and religious creation. To name an object ("earth sea and sky and all that"), or assign to it an identity, is to create it. Fellow writer Anäis Nin also objected to the gender-coding of creativity (and so, generative power), whether earthly or divine, as male:

As to this "I am God," which makes creation an act of solitude and pride, this image of God alone making sky, earth, sea, it is this image which has confused woman.[11]

It is telling that Stein describes writers "drunk with nouns" in much the same way that she

might describe one who is 'drunk with power'. The poet has the power to (re)create the world through language. Stein argues that with time's passage, however, writers have exhausted the possibilities of nouns, or names of things. Stein does not reject nouns so much as she laments the manner in which nouns become conventional through continued use, losing the freshness of meaning.

Stein's alternative to using conventional nouns requires the writer to engage passionately with objects s/he might otherwise choose to render with clichés. Only through contemplation can the writer break the habits of naming, for "*slowly* if you feel what is inside that thing you do not call it by the name by which it is known."[12] Stein takes the overused noun, then, as a sign that a writer lacks the necessary level of engagement with subject matter. Nouns permit a writer to fall back on conventional meanings and symbolisms. They require no immediate experience of those meanings by the author. For Stein, writing instead should proceed from an intimate relationship to a subject. Explaining this difference, Stein draws on the emotion she believes to be universally experienced through love relationships. She writes, "Everybody knows that [engaged writing] by the way they do when they are in love and a writer should always have that intensity about whatever is the object about which he writes."[13] According to Stein. love names, spontaneous and emotional, should replace traditional poetic nouns.

In this regard, Stein takes special interest in the application of nouns to people. Such nouns reduce human beings to references. She is aware of the degree to which these references tend to target specific populations on the basis of race, class, gender, ethnicity, and creed. In literature, for example, Stein notes that convention dictates that certain cultural groups be relegated to the background of one's fiction. In one instance, Stein claims (somewhat playfully), "I am afraid that I can never write the great American novel . . . so I have to content myself with niggers and servant girls and the foreign population generally."[14] Stein's statement is no doubt a specific reference to her characters in *Three Lives*: the Good Anna, the Gentle Lena, and Melanctha. Despite America's claims of pluralism, when it comes to designating great literature, Stein observes that only works featuring members of the dominant group may receive consideration. It is most irregular for a work such as *Three Lives* to focus on three such characters and tell their life stories instead of reducing them to hidden references (in keeping with their confinement to servile and secondary positions in the world outside fiction). On the basis of race, class, gender, ethnicity, and creed, such individuals occupy the margins of an elite literary tradition. Within her own works, however, Stein frequently features those not part of the dominant population. In her letters, Stein refers to this process of shifting literary emphasis as making "foreground background."[15] It is a subversive act.

Stein's objection to nouns, then, is not purely literary. As Stein reveals the sense in which these individuals (and authors who choose to write about them in this way) fall outside literature's "ideological scripts," she also uncovers the role language itself plays in their marginalization. Stein recognized that language serves the interests of those with the authority to apply language to (classify) others. The result is a political process of nomenclature, in which the powerful name the powerless. Regardless, for example, of how many racial groups exist, the privileged status of whites in the literary canon reduces all other races to non-whites, forming a binary opposition. The same is true of gender, in which case there are males and not-males; class, in which there are haves and have-nots; ethnicity, in which there are Europeans and Orientals; and religion, in which there is Christianity and everything else. Once relegated to this secondary status (not-*x*), an individual's characteristics blur, rendering them interchangeable with any other member of that secondary group. They are equal in their perceived inferiority. This political process of naming interested Stein early in her career. It takes a striking form, for instance, in the revisions to the manuscript of **The Making of Americans.** Referring to a study by Leon Katz of the manuscript sources for Stein's epic novel, Richard Bridgman argued that

> By the time she was working on **The Making of Americans,** Gertrude Stein had already become ambivalent about her Jewishness. In successive revisions, the qualification "Jewish" became, first, "German," and then "middle-class."[16]

Although it may be true that Gertrude Stein was "ambivalent about her Jewishness," her series of substitutions suggests how, for Stein, the categories of analysis (religion, ethnicity, and class) are interchangeable examples of the ways in which typological systems may tag groups for "oppression."[17] Human complexity may be reduced to a label based on a single perceived characteristic: black, woman, Jew, lesbian, German, and the life. This particular example further demonstrates that a single individual may fit into numerous such classifications at once. (Stein herself was both a German-American and a Jewish-American.) In this way, the individual may represent a target on multiple bases. Throughout her career, then, whether writing about an "apostle of the middle class" or a "chinese christian," Stein calls attention to the embattled status of individuals on the basis of race, gender, class, ethnicity, or religion.

One might doubt that someone of Stein's wealth, status, and eventual fame could understand or identify with society's outsiders, yet Stein did have reason to see the culture through an outsider's eyes. She was a woman, a Jew, a lesbian, an expatriate, and, due to her unconventional writing style, a self-proclaimed literary "outlaw."[18] At the very least, one can say that Stein experienced anti-Semitism and homophobia firsthand. Although Stein herself does not make many references to anti-Semitism, testimony by those around her strongly suggests its influence on her life. Leo Stein, her brother, writes frequently about his own "Jew complex," or "pariah complex" which dates back to childhood in California. In an autobiographical writing, he remembers that "There were almost no Jewish families in East Oakland and most of the time I was the only Jewish boy in school."[19] Gertrude Stein's memories of Oakland were probably not altogether different from her brother's. Once she went away to Cambridge, there are indications that Stein's college years, too, may have been marred with anti-Jewish sentiment. In his correspondence with Gertrude Stein, Arthur Lachman makes quips and remarks which hint at their shared experiences of anti-Semitism at Cambridge. In one such letter, Lachman writes from his new home in Eugene, Oregon, telling Stein, "My Hebraic descent is pretty generally known, as I have freely told it. There is quite a colony of your co-religionists here—I am sure you would feel quite at your ease."[20] Stein also encountered objections to her lesbianism. She shared this information with Samuel Steward, who recalls the conversation:

> "It bothers a lot of people," Gertrude said. "But like you said, it's nobody's business, it [the objection] came from the Judeo-Christian ethos, especially Saint Paul the bastard, but he was complaining about youngsters who were not really that way, they did it for money, everybody suspects us or knows but nobody says anything about it.[21]

As the above case reveals, Stein also was aware of the hostility of Catholicism to her own way of life. Stein knew very well what it was to be rejected and judged harshly by others' standards.

It was in this spirit that Stein described singer Paul Robeson as one who "knew american values and american life as only one in it but not of it could know them."[22] No one knows the structure of a society better than one forced to occupy its lowest ranks ("in it but not of it"). As a black man, Robeson knew all too well. Stein, too, was aware of the inequalities in American society, such as those based on race and class, by which individuals are born into oppression. She links this caste system to one's name, noting that, "After all occupation and your name and where you were born and what your father's business was is a thing to know about any one, at least it is for me."[23] Stein shares her society's curiosity about others' lineage, and acknowledges that such information often may be deduced from a name. As a result, she rebels against the tendency to emphasize the surname (or patrifocal family name), deciding that it is of "no importance."[24] Instead, in keeping with her interest in religion, Stein turns to the given (or Christian) name, which she maintains still "does . . . denote [individual] character and career."[25] Stein sees nomenclature and religion as related, for when one places faith in nomenclature, it becomes a religion. Stein writes, "Names and religion are always connected just like that. Nobody interferes between names and religion."[26] She also engages in some wordplay between naming and religion, observing that religion is "Just as necessary to know . . . as to know your name so that you can come when you are called."[27] With her pun on the word "calling," Stein suggests that both names and religion identify the individual to others.

Not only is Stein intrigued by names, but she also feels compelled to imagine what life would be like if one had a different name. In this way, Stein resists the static identity a name represents.

> I do ask some, I would ask every one, I do not ask somebecause I am quite certain that they would not like me to ask it, I do ask some if they would mind it if they found out that they did not have the name they had then and had been having been born not in the family living they are then living in, if they had been born illegitimate. I ask some and I would ask every one only I am quite certain very many would not like to have me ask it if they would like it, if they would very much dislike it, if they would make a tragedy of it, if they would make a joke of it, if they found they had in them blood of some kind of a being that was a low kind to them.[28]

To change one's name is to change one' station. In this case, Stein asks how an individual would respond to being renamed as someone with less status ("illegitimate," "a low kind to them"). This same principle of renaming guides Stein's efforts in *Four in America,* a work she regarded as

"the history of some one if his name had not been the name he had."[29] With playful impertinence, Stein approaches the great figures of American history, subverting the authority of those great (male) names by renaming them as each other.

> If Ulysses S. Grant had been a religious leader who was to become a saint what would he have done. If the Wright brothers had been artists that is painters what would they have done. If Henry James had been a general what would he have had to do. If General Washington had been a writer that is a novelist what would he do.[30]

This juggling of identity forms the hypothetical premise of *Four in America.* In an individual's name, Stein sees her/his destiny.

Typologies as Naming Processes

Stein was particularly interested in the relationship between names and character. Within her writing about human typologies, Stein discusses individual characters in terms of social categories: race, ethnicity, class, gender, and religion. Like her ideas about naming, Stein's use and subversion of human typologies must be viewed in social context. Influencing her thinking were numerous figures, among them William James, George Santayana, Hugo Münsterberg, Josiah Royce, and Otto Weininger. All five studied and sought to classify the shapes of human consciousness. Although it would not be until 1924 that America would pass the National Origins Quota Law, and not until 1926 that natural law, social Darwinism, and nativism would combine to produce such institutional results as the American Eugenics Society, efforts to explain personality and individual character already divided the nation's theorists of human nature. Even those who opposed Eugenics, its principles and practices, and its campaign for genetic character improvement, argued over the source of human temperament and character. Some sought in their findings justification for cultural stereotypes.

Into this climate of controversy, Stein introduces her typological works, her own inquiry into human identity. Stein is far from an activist, yet the implication of her texts' representations of cultural stereotypes and social inequalities forms the basis for a debate concerning the author's intentionality. While John Malcolm Brinnen finds Stein's characterization an emblem of "the struggle within character that gives character its peculiar force," and Edmund Wilson comments on Stein's "grasp of the organisms, contradictory and indissoluble, which human personalities are," other readers, including Milton Cohen and Richard

Bridgman, consider this union of psychological typology and literary characterization wrong-minded, even reprehensible.[31] They read Stein's typology as an endorsement of stereotypes and prejudice. However, these criticisms fail to weigh adequately Stein's critical distance from the human typologies about which she writes. In **"The Gradual Making of *The Making of Americans,"*** Stein notes this distinction between typology and fact. She writes that, "Types of people I could put down but a whole human being felt at one and the same time, in other words while in the act of feeling that person was very difficult to put into words."[32] At best, Stein could record a human type, a single image of the multiplicity residing within an individual. Given that Stein knew herself to be incapable of complete description, it is doubtful that she ever intended her character types to display the fullness of human complexity. To the contrary, her characters are tracings, and rather transparent ones at that, laid down to help readers imagine the difficult process by which one would assemble the layers of human identity. By critiquing her own descriptive impulses, Stein demonstrated to herself and to her readers the inadequacies of character typology. While Stein never prefaced her use of character types, she trusted that her critical perspective would be clear in the language itself. Stein writes, "I was sure that in a kind of a way the enigma of the universe could in this way be solved. That after all description is explanation. . . ."[33] The critical debate over Stein's typological characterization raises issues regarding what Stein's descriptive typologies explain.

Typologies in Stein's writing hold political implications, but not those usually claimed by Stein's critics. By equating human beings through their "bottom nature," Stein urges a chronicle to include all of society's members, "a history of every one."[34] Of *The Making of Americans,* a book which shares the experiments of *Three Lives,* Gertrude Stein reflects, "I could finally describe really describe every kind of human being that ever was or is or would be living."[35] With her literary typologies, Stein suggests that any system purporting to "describe every kind of human being" must be reductive, for it deals with groups rather than individuals. Her "types" thus mock the attribution of characteristics on the basis of race, gender, religion, class, and ethnicity. Gertrude Stein's characterizations, such as those in *Q.E.D.,* reveal the power struggles and alienating effects of human nature so defined, for in a world where oth-

ers constitute the "abjectly familiar type," one feels "no need of recognizing their existence" as individuals.[36]

Religion as Case Study

In many of her works, Stein directs the reader's attention to typologies of religious feeling, particularly as defined by William James. Such practices are most conspicuously present during two phases of Stein's career, (1) the early period (1895-1911), represented by such familiar works as the Radcliffe Themes, *The Making of Americans,* and ***Quod Erat Demonstrandum,*** and (2) the less familiar period of the 1920s, represented by **"Lend a Hand or Four Religions,"** *Lucy Church Amiably,* ***Four Saints in Three Acts,*** and **"Patriarchal Poetry."** In both phases, Stein employs religious language and ideas in ways which may be as important to the study of culture as they are to the study of literature. Stein's response to religious authority (whether that of theology, clergy, doctrine, or deity) offers a case-study in the writer's challenge to patriarchy. In the early writings, such as the Radcliffe themes, *The Making of Americans,* and ***Quod Erat Demonstrandum,*** Stein challenges androcentric religion, with its patriarchal and hierarchical authority structure. Stein's objections to androcentric religion temper her enthusiasm for existing faiths. While Stein's religious ideas owe much to Catholicism, even her earliest writings are openly critical of some Catholic beliefs and practices. By the 1920s, Stein meliorates this conflict, making selective use of those elements of Catholicism compatible with her own views. In her writings of the twenties, Stein goes further to reject existing religions, advocating instead an individualized, woman-identified religion in which first-hand spiritual experience becomes the individual's quest. This alternative form of religion resists the hierarchical constructions of religious faith, in which clergy mediate religious experience. In Stein's alternative spirituality, religious doctrines and rules of morality no longer suppress the individual's spirit. One goal of such quest is spiritual union, whether it be unity of self or union with another. For Stein, this symbolic surrender of the individual's will to spiritual union remains distinct from blind obedience to church dogma, because it preserves the individual's insight.

In her writings of the 1920s, such as **"Patriarchal Poetry,"** Stein takes issue with the gendered, hierarchical, and deferential structure of literary narrative. In this piece in particular, Stein presents a treatise on women's emancipation from a literary inheritance under girded by the same gender oppression found in other acts of androcentric language. In much the way that *Four Saints in Three Acts* establishes parallels between the mystic and the artist, Stein conjoins these figures in **"Patriarchal Poetry"** to call for an alternative spiritual life and an alternative literature. Finally, Stein's alternatives to restrictive spiritual and literary traditions distinguish themselves by incorporating unabashed forms of sensuality and sexuality, forms which previously required the cloak of more traditional images of passion as religious ecstasy and Platonic love. Erotic writing, another medium for the Stein's experimentations with a non-patriarchal, woman-identified spirituality, allowed Stein to elaborate on her ideas concerning the analogies between sexual and spiritual love. Regardless of Stein's encoding of sexual meanings, many of these writings were not published until after her death. While the period from 1915-1919 proved a prolific time for Stein's erotic writing, she continued to write in this mode later in her literary career. During the twenties, she added to their number related compositions, including **"A Sonatina Followed By Another"** (1921), **"As A Wife Has a Cow: A Love-Story"** (1923), and **"A Lyrical Opera Made By Two"** (1928). In these works, Stein presents anything but a patriarchal view of women's sexuality, particularly as expressed among women. That is to say, Stein celebrates sex, pronounces her pleasure in sex, declares her entitlement to write about sexual love among women, expands her discussion of homosexual marriage, and pays tribute to that marriage by likening it to spiritual union. Love, as Stein represents it, is redemptive. Her erotic poetry, like her spiritual writings, open a world of women's possibilities and pleasures. With these texts, Stein begins to demonstrate what it might mean to "live and love in names" liberated from an androcentric language.

Notes

1. Gertrude Stein, *Four in America, v-vi.*
2. Gertrude Stein, *Lectures in America,* 54.
3. Gertrude Stein, quoted in Thornton Wilder's "Introduction" to *Four in America,* xi.
4. Gertrude Stein, *Useful Knowledge,* 108.
5. *New York Times,* July 28, 1946, 40.
6. Gertrude Stein, *Lectures in America,* 233.
7. Gertrude Stein, *Four in America, v-vi.*
8. Gertrude Stein, *Lectures in America,* 241.
9. Ibid. 237.
10. Ibid. 233. Note that within this passage, Stein regards the Bible primarily as a work of literature. She does the same in Lecture 2 of *Narration.*
11. Anäis Nin quoted in Sandra Gilbert, "Patriarchal Poetry and Women Readers: Reflections on Milton's Bogey." *PMLA* 93 (1978): 368.
12. Gertrude Stein, *Lectures in America,* 210.
13. Ibid. 210.
14. George Knox, "The Great American Novel: Final Chapter." *American Quarterly* 21:4 (Winter 1969): 679.
15. Gertrude Stein to Carl Van Vechten, August 1923, reprinted in Edward Burns, ed., *The Letters of Gertrude Stein and Carl Van Vechten, 1913-1946* (New York: Columbia University Press, 1986) 87.
16. Richard Bridgman, *Gertrude Stein in Pieces,* 161.
17. Gertrude Stein, *Lucy Church Amiably,* 101.
18. Gertrude Stein, *Composition as Explanation,* 8-9.
19. Leo Stein, *Journey Into the Self* [*Being the Letters, Papers and Journals of Leo Stein* (New York: Crown Publishers, 1950)]:, 175, 199.
20. Arthur Lachman to Gertrude Stein, Dec. 21, 1897, YCAL.
21. Samuel Steward, ed. *Dear Sammy,* 55.
22. Gertrude Stein, *Autobiography of Alice B. Toklas,* 292.
23. Gertrude Stein, *Everybody's Autobiography,* 204.
24. Gertrude Stein, *Four in America,* 3.
25. Ibid. 7.
26. Gertrude Stein, *Four in America,* 7.
27. Gertrude Stein, *Geographical History of America,* 29.
28. Gertrude Stein, *The Making of Americans,* 351.
29. Gertrude Stein, *Narration,* 28-29.
30. Gertrude Stein, *Four in America,* 2.
31. John Malcolm Brinnen, *The Third Rose: Gertrude Stein and Her World* (Boston: Little, Brown and Co., 1959) 60; Edmund Wilson, *Axel's Castle: A Study in the Imaginative Literature of 1870-1930* (New York: Charles Scribner's Sons, 1931) 238; Milton A. Cohen, "Black Brutes and Mulatto Saints: The Racial Hierarchy of Stein's 'Melanctha,' "*Black American Literature Forum* 18:3 (Fall 1954): 119-121, and Richard Bridgman, *Gertrude Stein in Pieces.* Cohen contends that the characterizations of "Melanctha," for example, were "tainted by cultural bias" consistent with the vast cultural chasm dividing middle-class, white medical students [such as Stein] from the poor blacks they treated [here, the fictional Melanctha]." (119); Cohen also cited Richard Bridgman's contention of Stein's bigotry, that *Three Lives* "swarms with clichés about the happy, promiscuous, razor-fighting, church-going darky." This issue has resurfaced with the publication of Sonia Salvidar-Hull's "Wrestling Your Ally: Stein, Racism, and Feminist Critical Practice," in Mary Lynn Broe and Angela Ingram, eds., *Women Writing in Exile* (Chapel Hill: University of North Carolina Press, 1989) 181-198.
32. Gertrude Stein, "The Gradual Making of *The Making of Americans,*" reprinted in Meyerowitz, ed., *Writings and Lectures,* 88.

33. Ibid. 86.

34. Stein writes, "always this comes to be clear about them, the history of them of the bottom nature in them, the nature of natures mixed up in them to make the whole of them in anyway it mixes up in them. Sometime then there will be a history of every one." Gertrude Stein, *The Making of Americans*, reprinted in Meyerowitz, ed., *Writings and Lectures*, 84.

35. Ibid. 127.

36. Gertrude Stein, *Early Writings*, 53.

Bibliography

Manuscript Sources

Gertrude Stein Papers. Yale Collection of American Literature (YCAL). Beinecke Rare Book and Manuscript Library. Yale University, New Haven, Connecticut.

Selected Publications By Gertrude Stein

The Autobiography of Alice B. Toklas. New York: Vintage Books, 1933, 1961.

Composition As Explanation. Garden City, New York: Doubleday and Co., Inc., 1928.

Everybody's Autobiography. New York: Cooper Square Publishers, Inc., 1971.

Fernhurst, Q.E.D., and Other Early Writings. Introduction by Leon Katz. New York: Liveright Publishing Corporation, 1971.

Four in America. Introduction by Thornton Wilder. New Haven, Connecticut: Yale University Press, 1947.

Four Saints in Three Acts. New York: The Modern Library, 1934.

The Geographical History of America or The Relation of Human Nature to the Human Mind. Intro. by Thornton Wilder. New York: Random House, 1936.

Lectures in America. New York: Random House, 1935.

Lucy Church Amiably. Paris: Imprimerie "Union," 1930.

The Making of Americans: The Hersland Family. New York: Harcourt, Brace and Company, 1934.

Narration: Four Lectures by Gertrude Stein. intro. by Thornton Wilder. Chicago: University of Chicago Press, 1935.

Useful Knowledge. New York: Payson and Clarke Ltd., 1928.

Publications Treating Gertrude Stein

Bridgman, Richard. *Gertrude Stein in Pieces*. New York: Oxford University Press, 1970.

Brinnen, John Malcolm. *The Third Rose: Gertrude Stein and Her World*. Boston: Little, Brown and Company, 1959.

Meyerowitz, Patricia, ed. *Gertrude Stein: Writings and Lectures, 1911-1945*. Intro. by Elizabeth Sprigge. London: Peter Owen Ltd., 1967.

Steward, Samuel. ed. *Dear Sammy: Letters From Gertrude Stein*. Boston: Houghton Mifflin Co., 1977.

FURTHER READING

Bibliography

Liston, Maureen R. *Gertrude Stein: An Annotated Critical Bibliography*, Kent, Ohio: Kent State University Press, 1979, 230 p.

Thorough listing of criticism on Stein's work.

Biographies

Knapp, Bettina L. *Gertrude Stein*, New York: Continuum, 1990, 201 p.

Covers Stein's life as an exile, incorporating criticism of some of her most famous works.

Kostelanetz, Richard. Introduction to *The Gertrude Stein Reader: The Great American Pioneer of Avant-Garde Letters*, edited by Richard Kostelanetz, pp. i-xxxvii. New York: Cooper Square Press, 2002.

Provides an overview of Stein's life and career.

Sprigge, Elizabeth. *Gertrude Stein: Her Life and Work*, London: Hamish Hamilton, 1957, 277 p.

Details Stein's life in America and Europe and offers commentary on some of her works.

Criticism

Burke, Carolyn. "Gertrude Stein, the Cone Sisters, and the Puzzle of Female Friendship." In *Writing and Sexual Difference*, edited by Elizabeth Abel, pp. 221-42. Chicago: University of Chicago Press, 1982.

Examines Stein's fictional treatment of female friendship based on her own relationship with Claribel and Etta Cone.

Chessman, Harriet Scott. "*Ida* and the Twins." In *The Public Is Invited to Dance: Representation, the Body, and Dialogue in Gertrude Stein*, pp. 167-98. Stanford, Calif.: Stanford University Press, 1989.

Discusses Stein's use of the concept of twins in her 1941 novel Ida.

Doane, Janice L. "*Fernhurst*: Place and Propriety." In *Silence and Narrative: The Early Novels of Gertrude Stein*, pp. 32-51. Westport, Conn.: Greenwood Press, 1986.

Relates the narrator's search for a cohesive self-identity in Fernhurst *to Stein's own shifting positions regarding the place and purpose of higher education for women.*

Fifer, Elizabeth. "Father, Brother, Lover, Other: Gertrude Stein and the Search for Identity." In *Rescued Readings: A Reconstruction of Gertrude Stein's Difficult Texts*, pp. 22-45. Detroit: Wayne State University Press, 1992.

Discusses identity issues in The Mother of Us All, The Making of Americans, *and* Geography and Plays.

Gibbs, Anna. "Helene Cixous and Gertrude Stein: New Directions in Feminist Criticism." *Meanjin* 38, no. 3 (spring 1979): 281-93.

Identifies similarities in the works of Cixous and Stein, despite the initial appearance of little common ground between them in their relationships to feminism and feminist criticism.

Johnson, Manly. "Stein Arose." *Lost Generation Journal* 2, no. 1 (winter 1974): 3-7.

Offers a brief overview of Stein's literary philosophy.

Modern Fiction Studies, Special Issue: Gertrude Stein 42, no. 3 (fall 1996): 469-680.

Features critical discussions of different aspects of Stein's life and works by a wide variety of critics.

Murphy, Margueritte S. "Gertrude Stein's *Tender Buttons*: Beyond Description: A New Domestic Language." In *A Tradition of Subversion: The Prose Poem in English from Wilde to Ashbery*, pp. 137-67. Amherst: University of Massachusetts Press, 1992.

Discusses interpretive difficulties surrounding Tender Buttons.

Pladott, Dinnah. "Gertrude Stein: Exile, Feminism, Avant-Garde in the American Theatre." In *Modern American Drama: The Female Canon*, edited by June Schlueter, pp. 111-29. Rutherford, N.J.: Fairleigh Dickinson University Press, 1990.

Examines Stein's contributions to American drama as a woman, a Jew, a lesbian, and an expatriate.

Ruddick, Lisa. "*Tender Buttons*: Woman and Gnosis." In *Reading Gertrude Stein: Body, Text, Gnosis*, pp. 190-252. Ithaca, N.Y.: Cornell University Press, 1990.

Contends that Tender Buttons *lends itself to interpretation and understanding far more than has been generally acknowledged.*

Steiner, Wendy. Introduction to *Lectures in America*, by Gertrude Stein, pp. ix-xxvii. Boston: Beacon Press, 1985.

Demonstrates how Stein's work, particularly Lectures in America, *both anticipated and influenced pop art and postmodernism.*

Stimpson, Catharine R. "Gertrude Stein and the Lesbian Lie." In *American Women's Autobiography: Fea(s)ts of Memory*, edited by Margo Culley, pp. 152-66. Madison: University of Wisconsin Press, 1992.

Explores Stein's dual reputation as a popular writer and as a transgressive figure in the sexual and literary realms.

Weiss, M. Lynn. *Gertrude Stein and Richard Wright: The Poetics and Politics of Modernism.* Jackson, Miss.: University Press of Mississippi, 1998, 150 p.

Bio-critical review of Stein and Richard Wright.

OTHER SOURCES FROM GALE:

Additional coverage of Stein's life and career is contained in the following sources published by the Gale Group: *American Writers*; *American Writers: The Classics*, Vol. 2; *Concise Dictionary of American Literary Biography, 1917-1929*; *Contemporary Authors*, Vols. 104, 132; *Contemporary Authors New Revision Series*, Vol. 108; *Dictionary of Literary Biography*, Vols. 4, 54, 86, 228; *Dictionary of Literary Biography Documentary Series*, Vol. 15; *DISCovering Authors*; *DISCovering Authors: British Edition*; *DISCovering Authors: Canadian Edition*; *DISCovering Authors Modules: Most-studied Authors, Novelists, and Poets*; *DISCovering Authors 3.0*; *Drama Criticism*, Vol. 19; *Encyclopedia of World Literature in the 20th Century*, Ed. 3; *Exploring Short Stories*; *Gay & Lesbian Literature*, Ed. 1; *Literature Resource Center*; *Major 20th-Century Writers*, Eds. 1, 2; *Modern American Women Writers*; *Nonfiction Classics for Students*, Vol. 4; *Poetry Criticism*, Vol. 18; *Reference Guide to American Literature*, Ed. 4; *Reference Guide to Short Fiction*, Ed. 2; *Short Stories for Students*, Vol. 5; *Short Story Criticism*, Vol. 42; *Twayne's United States Authors*; *Twentieth-Century Literary Criticism*, Vols. 1, 6, 28, 48; *World Literature Criticism*; and *World Poets*.

AMY TAN

(1952 -)

American novelist, essayist, and author of children's books.

Tan's two best-known novels, *The Joy Luck Club* (1989) and *The Kitchen God's Wife* (1991), both showcase the complex and often difficult relationships between mothers and daughters—specifically immigrant mothers and their American-born daughters. Focusing on the nuances of culture and language—issues she discusses explicitly in her essay "Mother Tongue" (1990)—Tan uses humor and traditional oral conventions to explore generational disconnections among women.

BIOGRAPHICAL INFORMATION

Tan was born in 1952 in Oakland, California, to parents who had immigrated to the United States from China separately in 1947 and 1949. Tan was strongly influenced by her mother's storytelling about the family's Chinese heritage, and she later used oral storytelling as a narrative device in her fiction. Tan's older brother and her father both died of brain cancer in the late 1960s. After their deaths, her mother moved the family to Europe to escape what she believed to be the evil of their "diseased house" in California. The family settled first in the Netherlands and then in Montreux, Switzerland. Tan finished high school at the College Monte Rosa Internationale, where she was considered an outsider among the children of ambassadors, tycoons, and princes. Filled with anger and resentment at the loss of her father and brother, Tan rebelled and fell in with a group of drug-dealing social outcasts; she was arrested when she was sixteen years old. She later planned to elope to Australia with a mental patient who claimed to be a German army deserter. Shortly thereafter, her mother moved the family back to the United States.

Tan entered Linfield College in Oregon, where she intended to study medicine but decided to pursue a degree in English instead, much to her mother's dismay. She transferred to San Jose State University, where she earned a bachelor of arts degree in 1973. The following year she received a master's degree in English and linguistics. Tan enrolled in the doctoral program at the University of California at Berkeley, but withdrew from the program in 1976 after the murder of her best friend and a subsequent relapse into a period of anger and depression. From 1976 to 1981 she worked as a language-development specialist for disabled children. She edited a medical journal and worked as a technical writer in the 1980s.

Tan's first novel, *The Joy Luck Club*, brought her acclaim, and rose quickly on *The New York Times* bestseller list. She followed her initial success with another critically and popularly admired novel, *The Kitchen God's Wife*. Her other novels include *The Hundred Secret Senses* (1995) and *The Bonesetter's Daughter* (2001). Tan has also written a collection of essays and several children's works.

MAJOR WORKS

Through sixteen interconnected stories told by four immigrants from China and their four American-born daughters, *The Joy Luck Club* illuminates the nature of mother-daughter relationships in both cultures. An important theme in the novel is the impact of past generations on the present. The structure, in which the daughters' eight stories are interwoven with those of the mothers, implies that the older generation may hold a key to resolving the problems of the young. *The Kitchen God's Wife* also concerns mother-daughter relationships, but focuses on only one family and the tension between a woman named Winnie Louie and her daughter Pearl, who have persistently kept secrets from each other. Once they begin to reveal their secrets, they establish a connection. In *The Hundred Secret Senses* Tan delineates the relationship between two sisters: Olivia, an American-born daughter of a Chinese father, and Kwan, her older Chinese-born sister from her father's first marriage. Kwan's mystical belief in the existence of ghosts and previous lives clashes with Olivia's pragmatic attachment to the concrete and real. In *The Bonesetter's Daughter* an American-born Chinese woman named Ruth finds two packets of writings in Chinese calligraphy, and learns that they are the memoirs of her mother, who suffers from Alzheimer's disease and has written down events of her life before her disease renders her incapable of doing so. Ruth works with a translator to decipher her mother's writing, and discovers details concerning her mother's past in the remote mountains of China.

CRITICAL RECEPTION

Tan's work has achieved both popular and critical acclaim, and appeals to her largely female readership because of her ability to illustrate the common breakdown in communication that occurs between women of different generations. Critics have praised her complex narratives and storytelling as well as her poetic use of language in the evocation of a woman's search for identity within languages and stories that are often not of her own making.

PRINCIPAL WORKS

The Joy Luck Club (novel) 1989

The Kitchen God's Wife (novel) 1991

The Moon Lady (juvenilia) 1992

The Joy Luck Club [with Ronald Bass] (screenplay) 1993

Sagwa, the Chinese Siamese Cat (juvenilia) 1994

The Hundred Secret Senses (novel) 1995

The Bonesetter's Daughter (novel) 2001

The Opposite of Fate: A Book of Musings (essays) 2003

PRIMARY SOURCES

AMY TAN (ESSAY DATE 1990)

SOURCE: Tan, Amy. "Mother Tongue." In *The Best American Short Stories 1991*, edited by Joyce Carol Oates, pp. 196-202. New York: Ticknor and Fields, 1991.

In the following essay, originally published in The Threepenny Review *in 1990, Tan explains her youthful embarrassment of and adult pride in her Chinese mother's use of English.*

I am not a scholar of English or literature. I cannot give you much more than personal opinions on the English language and its variations in this country or others.

I am a writer. And by that definition, I am someone who has always loved language. I am fascinated by language in daily life. I spend a great deal of my time thinking about the power of language—the way it can evoke an emotion, a visual image, a complex idea, or a simple truth. Language is the tool of my trade. And I use them all—all the Englishes I grew up with.

Recently, I was made keenly aware of the different Englishes I do use. I was giving a talk to a large group of people, the same talk I had already given to half a dozen other groups. The nature of the talk was about my writing, my life, and my book, ***The Joy Luck Club.*** The talk was going along well enough, until I remembered one major difference that made the whole talk sound wrong. My mother was in the room. And it was perhaps the first time she had heard me give a lengthy speech, using the kind of English I have never used with her. I was saying things like, "The intersection of memory upon imagination" and "There is an aspect of my fiction that relates to thus-and-thus"—a speech filled with carefully wrought grammatical phrases, burdened, it suddenly seemed to me, with nominalized forms, past perfect tenses, conditional phrases, all the forms of standard English that I had learned in school and through books, the forms of English I did not use at home with my mother.

Just last week, I was walking down the street with my mother, and I again found myself conscious of the English I was using, the English I do use with her. We were talking about the price of new and used furniture and I heard myself saying this: "Not waste money that way." My husband was with us as well, and he didn't notice any switch in my English. And then I realized why. It's because over the twenty years we've been together I've often used that same kind of English with him, and sometimes he even uses it with me. It has become our language of intimacy, a different sort of English that relates to family talk, the language I grew up with.

So you'll have some idea of what this family talk I heard sounds like, I'll quote what my mother said during a recent conversation which I videotaped and then transcribed. During this conversation, my mother was talking about a political gangster in Shanghai who had the same last name as her family's, Du, and how the gangster in his early years wanted to be adopted by her family, which was rich by comparison. Later, the gangster became more powerful, far richer than my mother's family, and one day showed up at my mother's wedding to pay his respects. Here's what she said in part:

"Du Yusong having business like fruit stand. Like off the street kind. He is Du like Du Zong—but not Tsung-ming Island people. The local people call putong, the river east side, he belong to that side local people. That man want to ask Du Zong father take him in like become own family. Du Zong father wasn't look down on him, but didn't take seriously, until that man big like become a mafia. Now important person, very hard to inviting him. Chinese way, came only to show respect, don't stay for dinner. Respect for making big celebration, he shows up. Mean gives lots of respect. Chinese custom. Chinese social life that way. If too important won't have to stay too long. He come to my wedding. I didn't see, I heard it. I gone to boy's side, they have YMCA dinner. Chinese age I was nineteen."

You should know that my mother's expressive command of English belies how much she actually understands. She reads the *Forbes* report, listens to *Wall Street Week,* converses daily with her stockbroker, reads all of Shirley MacLaine's

books with ease—all kinds of things I can't begin to understand. Yet some of my friends tell me they understand 50 percent of what my mother says. Some say they understand 80 to 90 percent. Some say they understand none of it, as if she were speaking pure Chinese. But to me, my mother's English is perfectly clear, perfectly natural. It's my mother tongue. Her language, as I hear it, is vivid, direct, full of observation and imagery. That was the language that helped shape the way I saw things, expressed things, made sense of the world.

Lately, I've been giving more thought to the kind of English my mother speaks. Like others, I have described it to people as "broken" or "fractured" English. But I wince when I say that. It has always bothered me that I can think of no way to describe it other than "broken," as if it were damaged and needed to be fixed, as if it lacked a certain wholeness and soundness. I've heard other terms used, "limited English," for example. But they seem just as bad, as if everything is limited, including people's perceptions of the limited English speaker.

I know this for a fact, because when I was growing up, my mother's "limited" English limited *my* perception of her. I was ashamed of her English. I believed that her English reflected the quality of what she had to say. That is, because she expressed them imperfectly her thoughts were imperfect. And I had plenty of empirical evidence to support me: the fact that people in department stores, at banks, and at restaurants did not take her seriously, did not give her good service, pretended not to understand her, or even acted as if they did not hear her.

My mother has long realized the limitations of her English as well. When I was fifteen, she used to have me call people on the phone to pretend I was she. In this guise, I was forced to ask for information or even to complain and yell at people who had been rude to her. One time it was a call to her stockbroker in New York. She had cashed out her small portfolio and it just so happened we were going to go to New York the next week, our very first trip outside California. I had to get on the phone and say in an adolescent voice that was not very convincing, "This is Mrs. Tan."

And my mother was standing in the back whispering loudly, "Why he don't send me check, already two weeks late. So mad he lie to me, losing me money."

And then I said in perfect English, "Yes, I'm getting rather concerned. You had agreed to send the check two weeks ago, but it hasn't arrived."

Then she began to talk more loudly. "What he want, I come to New York tell him front of his boss, you cheating me?" And I was trying to calm her down, make her be quiet, while telling the stockbroker, "I can't tolerate any more excuses. If I don't receive the check immediately, I am going to have to speak to your manager when I'm in New York next week." And sure enough, the following week there we were in front of this astonished stockbroker, and I was sitting there red-faced and quiet, and my mother, the real Mrs. Tan, was shouting at his boss in her impeccable broken English.

We used a similar routine just five days ago, for a situation that was far less humorous. My mother had gone to the hospital for an appointment, to find out about a benign brain tumor a CAT scan had revealed a month ago. She said she had spoken very good English, her best English, no mistakes. Still, she said, the hospital did not apologize when they said they had lost the CAT scan and she had come for nothing. She said they did not seem to have any sympathy when she told them she was anxious to know the exact diagnosis, since her husband and son had both died of brain tumors. She said they would not give her any more information until the next time and she would have to make another appointment for that. So she said she would not leave until the doctor called her daughter. She wouldn't budge. And when the doctor finally called her daughter, me, who spoke in perfect English—lo and behold—we had assurances the CAT scan would be found, promises that a conference call on Monday would be held, and apologies for any suffering my mother had gone through for a most regrettable mistake.

I think my mother's English almost had an effect on limiting my possibilities in life as well. Sociologists and linguists probably will tell you that a person's developing language skills are more influenced by peers. But I do think that the language spoken in the family, especially in immigrant families which are more insular, plays a large role in shaping the language of the child. And I believe that it affected my results on achievement tests, IQ tests, and the SAT. While my English skills were never judged as poor, compared to math, English could not be considered my strong suit. In grade school I did moderately well, getting perhaps B's, sometimes B-pluses, in English and scoring perhaps in the sixtieth or seventieth percentile on achievement tests. But those scores were not good enough to override the opinion that my true abilities lay in math and science, because in those areas I achieved A's and scored in the ninetieth percentile or higher.

This was understandable. Math is precise; there is only one correct answer. Whereas, for me at least, the answers on English tests were always a judgment call, a matter of opinion and personal experience. Those tests were constructed around items like fill-in-the-blank sentence completion, such as, "Even though Tom was _____, Mary thought he was _____." And the correct answer always seemed to be the most bland combinations of thoughts, for example, "Even though Tom was shy, Mary thought he was charming," with the grammatical structure "even though" limiting the correct answer to some sort of semantic opposites, so you wouldn't get answers like, "Even though Tom was foolish, Mary thought he was ridiculous." Well, according to my mother, there were very few limitations as to what Tom could have been and what Mary might have thought of him. So I never did well on tests like that.

The same was true with word analogies, pairs of words in which you were supposed to find some sort of logical, semantic relationship—for example, "*Sunset* is to *nightfall* as _____ is to _____." And here you would be presented with a list of four possible pairs, one of which showed the same kind of relationship: *red* is to *stoplight, bus* is to *arrival, chills* is to *fever, yawn* is to *boring.* Well, I could never think that way. I knew what the tests were asking, but I could not block out of my mind the images already created by the first pair, *"sunset* is to *nightfall"*—and I would see a burst of colors against a darkening sky, the moon rising, the lowering of a curtain of stars. And all the other pairs of words—red, bus, stoplight, boring—just threw up a mass of confusing images, making it impossible for me to sort out something as logical as saying: "A sunset precedes nightfall" is the same as "a chill precedes a fever." The only way I would have gotten that answer right would have been to imagine an associative situation, for example, my being disobedient and staying out past sunset, catching a chill at night, which turns into feverish pneumonia as punishment, which indeed did happen to me.

I have been thinking about all this lately, about my mother's English, about achievement tests. Because lately I've been asked, as a writer, why there are not more Asian Americans represented in American literature. Why are there few Asian Americans enrolled in creative writing programs? Why do so many Chinese students go into engineering? Well, these are broad sociological questions I can't begin to answer. But I have noticed in surveys—in fact, just last week—that Asian students, as a whole, always do significantly better on math achievement tests than in English. And this makes me think that there are other Asian-American students whose English spoken in the home might also be described as "broken" or "limited." And perhaps they also have teachers who are steering them away from writing and into math and science, which is what happened to me.

Fortunately, I happen to be rebellious in nature and enjoy the challenge of disproving assumptions made about me. I became an English major my first year in college, after being enrolled as pre-med. I started writing nonfiction as a freelancer the week after I was told by my former boss that writing was my worst skill and I should hone my talents toward account management.

But it wasn't until 1985 that I finally began to write fiction. And at first I wrote using what I thought to be wittily crafted sentences, sentences that would finally prove I had mastery over the English language. Here's an example from the first draft of a story that later made its way into *The Joy Luck Club*, but without this line: "That was my mental quandary in its nascent state." A terrible line, which I can barely pronounce.

Fortunately, for reasons I won't get into today, I later decided I should envision a reader for the stories I would write. And the reader I decided upon was my mother, because these were stories about mothers. So with this reader in mind—and in fact she did read my early drafts—I began to write stories using all the Englishes I grew up with: the English I spoke to my mother, which for lack of a better term might be described as "simple"; the English she used with me, which for lack of a better term might be described as "broken"; my translation of her Chinese, which could certainly be described as "watered down"; and what I imagined to be her translation of her Chinese if she could speak in perfect English, her internal language, and for that I sought to preserve the essence, but neither an English nor a Chinese structure. I wanted to capture what language ability tests can never reveal: her intent, her passion, her imagery, the rhythms of her speech and the nature of her thoughts.

Apart from what any critic had to say about my writing, I knew I had succeeded where it counted when my mother finished reading my book and gave me her verdict: "So easy to read."

GENERAL COMMENTARY

VICTORIA CHEN (ESSAY DATE 31 MARCH 1995)

SOURCE: Chen, Victoria. "Chinese American Women, Language, and Moving Subjectivity." *Women and Language* 13, no. 1 (31 March 1995): 3-9.

In the following essay, Chen discusses the effects on Chinese American women of "dual cultural enmeshment," particularly where language is concerned, as it is explored in works by Tan and Maxine Hong Kingston.

It was not until the 1970s that Asian American literature became recognized as a separate canon and a "new tradition" of writing. While this "new" form of expression created a new political consciousness and identity, the images and stories that abound in pioneer literature such as Maxine Hong Kingston's *The Woman Warrior* and *China Men* are paradoxically located in "recovered" ethnic history (Lim, 1993, p. 573). More recently, Amy Tan's *The Joy Luck Club* also takes the reader through a journey back to a specific set of ethnic memories as the mothers in the stories interweave their experiences struggling for survival and dignity in China and for coherence and hope in America. Part of the reason for the celebration of Asian American women's literature is that it provides an alternative way to think about issues such as language, subjectivity, cultural voice, and ethnic/gender identity.

For Chinese American women such as Kingston, Tan, and the female characters in *The Joy Luck Club*, speaking in a double voice and living in a bicultural world characterize their dual cultural enmeshment. While striving to maintain a relationship with their Chinese immigrant parents, the Chinese American daughters also live in a society where one is expected to speak in a "standard" form of English and to "succeed" in the middle class Euro-American way. For Kingston and Tan, writing about their immigrant mothers' neglected pasts and their own tumultuous presents becomes a powerful way to create their own identities as Chinese Americans and to confront the dilemma of living biculturally in a society that insists on a homogeneous identity. If a language indeed is instrinsically connected with a form of life, and speaking and writing in a given language necessitates one to participate in that cultural world, how then do these Chinese American women authors position themselves in linguistic/cultural borderlands through the use of language? What are some forms of language and life that make their storytelling possible and intelligible? How do different languages function in their own lives and in their storytelling? How do they use languages to interweave and mediate their, multiple identities? This essay attempts to address some of these issues. I will draw upon essays written about Kingston and Tan as well as narratives from *The Joy Luck Club* and *The Woman Warrior* in my discussion.

Amy Tan (1991) in her essay **"Mother Tongue"** discusses that as someone who has always loved language, she celebrates using "all the Englishes I grew up with" (p. 196) in her living and her writing. The English that she hears from her mother, despite it's "imperfection," has become their "language of intimacy, a different sort of English that relates to family talk, the language I grew up with" (p. 197). There is a discrepancy, both linguistically and culturally, between the "standard" English that she learns from school and uses in her professional world and the "simple" and "broken" English (p. 201) that is used in her interaction with her mother. However, as Tan points out, speaking her mother's version of English gives her bicultural insight and strength, and she sees the beauty and wisdom in her mother's language: "Her language, as I hear it, is vivid, direct, full of observation and imagery" (p. 198); "I wanted to capture what language ability tests can never reveal: her intent, her passion, her imagery, the rhythms of her speech and the nature of her thoughts" (p. 202). Kingston also grew up in two languages, her family's Chinese dialect and the public American English in which she was educated. *The Woman Warrior* reveals the disjunction that Kingston experienced in moving between these two languages. While her mother marked her growing up with stories of nameless Chinese women, multiple cultural ghosts, Kingston wrote, "To make my waking life American-normal . . . I push the deformed into my dreams, which are in Chinese, the language of impossible stories" (Kingston, 1977, p. 102). The entire book is devoted to Kingston's ongoing struggle to enter the Chinese cultural world composed of impossible stories and to figure out what it meant to be a Chinese American woman in this society.

Tan's *The Joy Luck Club* is a segmented novel, set in San Francisco in the 1980s, powerfully blending the voices of four Chinese immigrant mothers and their American-born daughters. The book opens with story of a swan and a woman sailing across an ocean toward America saying, "In America I will have a daughter just like me. But over there . . . nobody will look down on her, because I will make her speak only perfect American English. And over there she will always be too

full to swallow any sorrow! She will know my meaning . . ." (Tan, 1989, p. 17). The tale symbolizes not only the geographic separation from the woman's motherland but also the alienation later felt by both the mother and daughter in America. The woman's desire for her daughter to speak perfect American English foregrounds the problems and difficulties of communicating and translating between the different languages that they speak. The American dream eventually eludes the immigrant woman beyond her best intentions. Mastering this imaginary perfect English for the American-born daughter turns out not to be a simple ticket to American success. This linguistic competency, ironically, signifies her departure from her mother (and her motherland), deepening the chasm between generations and cultures. Moreover, learning to speak perfect American English may also entail the complex journey of "successful" acculturation which often masks the racism and sexism that belie the American dream.

Although Tan's essay celebrates the two Englishes with which she grew up, and that dual languages and cultures can indeed enrich and enlighten one's life, coherence and double voice do not always come without personal struggle and emotional trauma. As we enter the hyphenated world of the "Chinese-American" women in *The Joy Luck Club*, much of the mothers' and daughters' conversations seem to be focused on debating, negotiating, and wandering between the two disparate cultural logics. Lindo shared her daughter's concern that she cannot say whether her Chinese or American face is better: "I think about our two faces. I think about my intentions. Which one is American? Which one is Chinese? Which one is better? if you show one, you must always sacrifice the other" (Tan, 1989, p. 266). Tan (1990), in her essay **"The Language of Discretion,"** pointed out a special kind of double bind attached to knowing two languages and vehemently rebelled against seeing cultural descriptions as dichotomous categories: "It's dangerous business, this sorting out of language and behavior. Which one is English? Which is Chinese? . . . Reject them all!" (p. 28). "Having listened to both Chinese and English, I also tend to be suspicious of any comparisons between Chinese and English languages." Tan argued: "Typically, one language—that of the person doing the comparing—is often used as the standard, the benchmark for a logical form of explanation" (p. 29).

Speaking a language is inherently political. In the case of Chinese American women, while straddling and juggling along the fault lines of gender and culture, the truth is that the two Englishes that Tan cherished are not valued equally in this society. Despite the creative use of imaginative metaphors in her English, as Tan humorously presented, her mother would never score high in a standard English test that insists on one correct way of linguistic construction. It is no secret that in much of our social discourse and communication practice, the myth persists that what counts as the "normal" standards and criteria for comparing and discussing cultural difference is still the mainstream Eurocentric mode of thinking and doing. In her writing about Asian American women's experience of racism, Shah (1994) said, "For me, the experience of 'otherness,' and formative discrimination in my life, has resulted from culturally different people thinking they were culturally central; thinking that my house smelled funny, that my mother talked weird, that my habits were strange. They were normal; I wasn't" (pp. 151-152). Similarly, in a discussion of the difficult dialogues between black and white women, Houston (1994) points out that when a white woman says "We're all alike," she usually means "I can see how you, a black woman, are like me, a white woman." She does not mean "I can see how I am like you." In other words, whether explicitly or implicitly, "just people" often means "just white people" (p. 137).

Language and identity are always positioned within a hierarchical power structure in which the Chinese American immigrants' form of life has never been granted a status equal to that of their European counterparts in the history of this country. It is one thing to embrace the philosophical wisdom of "having the best of both worlds" but another to confront the real ongoing struggle between languages and identities that most Chinese Americans experience. Bicultural identity cannot be reduced to two neutral, pristine, and equal linguistic domains that one simply picks and chooses to participate in without personal, relational, social, and political consequences. We need to understand the tension and conflict between generations of Chinese American women within the ideological cultural context of racial and sexual inequality and their ongoing contestation of their positions in it.

Through Tan's storytelling in **The Joy Luck Club,** the meaning of "perfect English" is transformed from the mother's naive American dream to the daughter's awakening bicultural disillusionment, as the daughter June laments: "These kinds of explanations made me feel my mother and I spoke two different languages, which we did. I talked to her in English, she answered back in Chinese" (Tan, 1989, pp. 33-34), and later, "My mother and I never really understood one another. We translated each other's meanings and I seemed to hear less than what was said, while my mother heard more" (p. 37). The lack of shared languages and cultural logics remains a central theme throughout all the narratives in Tan's book. This absence transcends the simple linguistic dichotomies or cultural misunderstandings; both mothers and daughters are negotiating their relational and social positions and contesting their identities as Chinese American women in the languages that can enhance or undermine their power, legitimacy, and voice.

In a similar vein, in *The Woman Warrior* Kingston describes "abnormal" discourse as constructed and experienced by both parents and children in her family. The children in Kingston's family often spoke in English language which their parents "didn't seem to hear"; "the Chinese can't hear American at all; the language is too soft and Western music unhearable" (Kingston, 1977, p. 199). Exasperated and bemused by their Chinese aunt's behavior, the children told each other that "Chinese people are very weird" (p. 183). Angry at the fact that the Chinese were unable, unwilling, or did not see the need to explain things to the children, Kingston writes, "I thought talking and not talking made the differences between sanity and insanity. Insane people were the ones who couldn't explain themselves" (p. 216). While the Chinese American children were frustrated by the impenetrable wisdom spoken or unspoken in the Chinese language, the parents teased the children about the way they spoke in the "ghosts" language and of the craziness and absurdity of doing things in American ways. Insane and absurd in what language(s) and from what cultural perspective(s)? Who has the authority to tell Kingston that Chinese girls are worthless growing up in a society that is supposed to be more egalitarian and liberating for women? What constitutes "normal" and "abnormal" discourse for Chinese American women? What price do they have to pay for being a full participant in either or both cultural worlds?

One intriguing feature in learning to speak and hear incommensurate languages is the process of adjudicating conflicting voices. In Chinese American families, communication can often be characterized by a lack of a shared universe of discourse or a set of mutually intelligible vocabularies. For Kingston, even attempting to engage in a meaningful dialogue with her parents about her confusions and their conflicts became a problem, as she told us, "I don't know any Chinese I can ask without getting myself scolded or teased" (Kingston, 1977, p. 238). Silent and silenced, Kingston was angry at the sexist trivialization of her intellectual interests and academic accomplishment. She writes, "I've stopped checking 'bilingual' on job applications. I could not understand any of the dialects the interviewer at China Airlines tried on me, and he didn't understand me either" (p. 239). Family language almost became a "burden" as Kingston strived to make sense of what it meant to occupy two linguistic and cultural spaces as a Chinese American woman in a patriarchal system. Could her surrender allude to the disappointment and frustration that Chinese Americans as a group feel within the larger society?

In Tan's novel, when one of the daughters, June, did not comply with her mother's wishes, her mother shouted at her in Chinese: "Only two kinds of daughters. Those who are obedient and those who follow their own mind! Only one kind of daughter can live in this house. Obedient daughter!" (Tan, 1989, p. 142). The mother's injunction is an enactment of her personal power within the family structure, and in this language and cultural logic, June is powerless even if she could speak "perfect" American English, which would give her positional power in a different situation.

Toward the end of the book when Kingston finally confronted her mother with her long list of feelings of guilt being a Chinese American daughter, the linguistic gap and cultural intranslatability resonated throughout their shouting match. Angry, frustrated, hurt, sad, and disappointed, Kingston realized that the confrontation was futile: "And suddenly I got very confused and lonely because I was at the moment telling her my list, and in the telling, it grew. No higher listener. No listener but myself" (Kingston), p. 237). Once again, their voices did not intermesh, and neither could enter the cultural logic that was specifically structured within the primary language that they spoke. There was no possibility for Kingston to articulate her silence, nor was there space for displaying her mother's good intentions. The celebration of the multiple languages and polyphonic voices seemed elusive. Two generations of women were ultimately torn apart and yet inextricably bonded by the unspeakable cultural tongue. Each in their own way sounded strange, incoherent, crazy, abnormal, and stubborn to the other.

The end of the story of the swan in **The Joy Luck Club** says, "Now the woman was old. And she had a daughter who grew up speaking only English and swallowing more Coca-Cola than sorrow. For a long time now the woman had wanted to give her daughter the single swan feather and tell her, 'This feather may look worthless, but it comes from afar and carries with it all my good intentions.' And she waited, year after year, for the day she could tell her daughter this in perfect American English" (Tan, 1989, p. 17). As one of the mothers, Lindo, lamented, "I wanted my children to have the best combination, American circumstances and Chinese character. How could I know these two things do not mix?" (Tan, p. 265).

If indeed Chinese Americans are steeped in two languages and two forms of life, one public and dominant, another private and submerged, what is the symbolic significance of using these languages, as constructed from various social positions? For the immigrant parents, educating their American-born children to speak the family language is a way to continue the cultural tradition and to instill ethnic pride. Speaking a private language is also an attempt to mark one's difference from the mainstream culture and to resist racism, hegemony, and the overwhelming power of homogenization in this society. In Tan and Kingston's storytelling, speaking Chinese also becomes simply functional for the older immigrants who do not want to participate or/and are not perceived as full participants in the public language. As a result, they remain outsiders within the system: their use of private language marks the central feature of their identity.

Although for many American-born Chinese, using family language can affirm their cultural ties to their ancestors, Kingston also grew up hearing all the derogatory comments about girls in Chinese, the language of foreign and impossible stories to her ear. While speaking her family dialect gives her a sense of connection and intimacy, the private language also symbolizes the oppression, confusion, frustration, madness, and silence that were associated with her coming of age. Using English to speak and write signifies Kingston's rebellion against the patriarchal tradition; it forced her to take a non-Chinese and non-female position in her family and community. For Chinese identity and gives them a legitimate cultural voice to claim for a space in this society. English gives them a means to assert their independence and a tool to fight against sexism and racism that they encounter. Trinh Minh-ha, in an interview, insisted that identity remains as a political/personal strategy of resistance and survival; "the reflexive question asked . . . is no longer: who am I? but when, where, how am I (so and so)?" (Parmar, 1990, p. 72).

It is important to remember that a discussion of uses of language needs to be understood in a political context. Chinese Americans strive for polyphonic coherence within a society that celebrates conformity and homogeneity despite its rhetoric of diversity and pluralism. To mainstream ears, Chinese languages may sound a cacophony of unfamiliar tones and words; this unintelligibility can be associated with foreignness, exotic cultural others, lack of education, or powerlessness. This perceived absence of a shared language and culture (and therefore of disparate social and national interests) can lead to hostility or discrimination toward Chinese Americans.

Through the use of language we create and maintain our social relationships. We accomplish this goal only if an intersubjective discourse exists so that our words and actions are intelligible to others within the community. In Chinese American bicultural experience, this shared language often cannot be taken for granted. In *The Woman Warrior,* Kingston confronted her mother about telling her that she was ugly all the time, to which her mother replied, "That's what we're supposed to say. That's what Chinese say. We like to say the opposite" (Kingston, 1977, p. 237). Here in the mother's language, "truth" is characterized by the logic of the opposite; this "indirect" approach works only if one knows how to hear the statement within the context of a certain kind of relationship. Saying the opposite is what the mother felt obligated to perform; in fact, it was the only language that she could use in order to demonstrate her affection and care for her daughter. Unfortunately, lacking the cultural insight to reverse the logic of her mother's statement, Kingston felt shamed, outraged, and was in turn accused by her mother of not being able to "tell a joke from real life"; her mother shouts at her, "You're not so smart. Can't even tell real from false" (p. 235). Real from false in what language? Where does the humor of this apparent joke for the mother—and humiliation for the daughter—lie in perfect American English?

In *The Joy Luck Club,* the young women's innocence, ignorance, and apathy toward their mothers' language seemed to frighten the mothers. June tried to understand her three aunties at the mah jong table:

> And then it occurs to me. They are frightened. In me, they see their own daughters, just as ignorant, just as unmindful of all the truths and hopes they have brought to America. They see daughters who grow impatient when their mothers talk in Chinese, who think they are stupid when they explain things in fractured English. They see that joy and luck do not mean the same to their daughters, that to these closed American-born minds "joy luck" is not a word, it does not exist. They see daughters who will bear grandchildren born without any connecting hope passed from generation to generation.
>
> (Tan, 1989, pp. 40-41)

Failure to translate between languages can cost emotional turmoil; it can also silence someone who depends on the English translation to negotiate or accomplish his/her goals. In one of the stories in *The Joy Luck Club,* the daughter Lena was unable to translate her mother's words to her Caucasian stepfather who did not speak Chinese. Since Lena understood the Chinese words spoken by her mother but not the implications, she made up something in her translation and as a result rewrote her mother's story in that episode. Tan intentionally constructed this scene to illustrate the nature of the mother-daughter relationship. Lena was ignorant of both the story that her mother was hinting at and of the Chinese language that her mother was speaking. Kingston's and Tan's writings are characterized by untold stories written in untranslatable language between the two generations of women. McAlister (1992) argued that by failing to translate between languages and stories, Chinese American daughters can participate in the silencing of their mothers. This position seems incongruous in view of Tan's overall agenda in her storytelling. By having all the women narrate their own stories, Tan treats language not just as a tool to reflect upon the past or to celebrate the present, but as a political means to allow Chinese American women to articulate their silenced lives, their otherwise voiceless positions in this society.

Tan writes *The Joy Luck Club* in a language that demands the reader recognize the distinctness of each character, each story and voice, and each mother-daughter relationship. The women in her creation are not just nameless, faceless, or interchangeable Chinese Americans. The interrelated narratives make sense only if readers can discern the specificities of each woman's story as located within the novel. Therefore, "Tan confronts an Orientalist discourse that depends on the sameness of Chinese difference" (McAlister, 1992, p. 110). By granting subjectivity to each woman, Tan compels each to tell her own story in her own words, thus (re)creating the meanings of her life. The mother-daughter tensions as constructed in their own discourse are fraught with complexities of racial, gender, and class issues, not just the simple binary opposition of Americanness and Chinesesness, mothers and daughters.

The ability to tell one's own story, to speak one's mind, is the best antidote to powerlessness. Tan's writing instills agency and visibility in Chinese American women. The silence is broken, and their new voices are constructed in collective storytelling, a language of community, without denying or erasing the different positions such collaboration encounters. In a similar vein, Kingston gave the no name woman in her mother's storytelling a voice and a life, a permanent place in American culture; she immortalized this silent woman through her writing: "My aunt haunts me—her ghost drawn to me because now, after fifty years of neglect, I alone devote pages of paper to her" (Kingston, 1977, p. 19). Both Tan and Kingston allow their female characters to reclaim and recreate their identity. "Storytelling heals past experiences of loss and separation; it is also a medium for rewriting stories of oppression and victimization into parables of self-affirmation and individual empowerment" (Heung, 1993, p. 607). It is possible to celebrate the present without forgetting the past. In an interview when Kingston was contrasting her own American voice in *Tripmaster Monkey* and her translation of Chinese voices in her previous two books, she said, "When I wrote *The Woman Warrior* and *China Men,* as I look back on it, I was trying to find an American language that would translate the speech of the people who are living their lives with the Chinese language. They carry on their adventures and their emotional life and everything in Chinese. I had to find a way to translate all that into a graceful American language, which is my language" (Chin, 1989-1990, p. 71). Perhaps the boundary between Kingston's two languages/voices is not so clear; of *Tripmaster Monkey,* [a Chinese poet] she said that "I was writing in the tradition of the past" (Chin, p. 64). "And I spent this lifetime working on roots. So what they were saying was that I was their continuity" (Chin, p. 65).

Both Kingston's and Tan's writings point to the multiplicity and instability of cultural identity for Chinese American women, oscillating and crisscrossing between different Englishes and Chinese dialects that they speak. Although cultural borderlands can be a useful metaphor for "home" for these individuals, we must realize that this home does not rest in a fixed location, nor is it constructed in any one unified language or perfect American English. Neither of the authors

is searching for definitive Chinese American voice. Through interweaving their own bicultural tongues and multiple imaginative voices, Kingston and Tan focus on women's experiences in their writings and position their uses of languages as central to our understanding of Chinese American women's bicultural world.

Ultimately we see the transformation of double voice in both *The Woman Warrior* and *The Joy Luck Club.* As Trinh put it nicely, ". . . the fact one is always marginalized in one's own language and areas of strength is something that one has to learn to live with" (Parmar, 1990, p. 71). Therefore, fragmentation in one's identity becomes "a way of living with differences without turning them into opposites, nor trying to assimilate them out of insecurity" (pp. 71-72). Chinese American women need to cultivate not simply multiple subjectivities but also the ability to move between different languages and positions. As Trinh suggested, this fluidity is a form of challenge and reconstruction of power relations, and women need to learn to use language as a poetic arena of struggle of possibility for transformation. "Ethnic identity is twin skin to linguistic identity—I am my language" (Anzaldua, 1987, p. 59). Unless Chinese American women acknowledge and celebrate all the Englishes that they grew up with, they cannot accept the legitimacy of their bicultural identity. When asked if she still felt the same contradictions that the protagonist did in *The Woman Warrior,* Kingston said "No, no. I feel much more integrated . . . It takes decades of struggle. When you are a person who comes from a multicultural background it just means that you have more information coming in from the universe. And it's your task to figure out how it all integrates, figure out its order and its beauty. It's a harder, longer struggle" (Chin, 1989-1990, p. 63).

M. MARIE BOOTH FOSTER (ESSAY DATE 1996)

SOURCE: Foster, M. Marie Booth. "Voice, Mind, Self: Mother-Daughter Relationships in Amy Tan's *The Joy Luck Club* and *The Kitchen God's Wife.*" In *Women of Color: Mother-Daughter Relationships in 20th-Century Literature,* edited by Elizabeth Brown-Guillory, pp. 208-27. Austin: University of Texas Press, 1996.

In the following essay, Foster examines the importance of individual voice in the development of Chinese American women's identities, especially within the mother-daughter relationship as Tan portrays it in her novels.

In *The Joy Luck Club* and *The Kitchen God's Wife,* Amy Tan uses stories from her own history and myth to explore the voices of mothers and daughters of Chinese ancestry. Each woman tells a story indicative of the uniqueness of her voice. Mary Field Belensky, in *Women's Ways of Knowing,* argues that voice is "more than an academic shorthand for a person's point of view . . . it is a metaphor that can apply to many aspects of women's experience and development. . . . Women repeatedly used the metaphor of voice to depict their intellectual and ethical development; . . . the development of a sense of voice, mind, and self were intricately intertwined" (18). In Tan's fiction, the daughters' sense of self is intricately linked to an ability to speak and be heard by their mothers. Similarly, the mothers experience growth as they broaden communication lines with their daughters. Tan's women are very much like the women Belensky portrays in *Women's Ways of Knowing*: "In describing their lives, women commonly talked about voice and silence: 'speaking up,' 'speaking out,' 'being silenced,' 'not being heard,' 'really listening,' 'really talking,' 'words as weapons,' 'feeling deaf and dumb,' 'having no words,' 'saying what you mean,' 'listening to be heard'" (18). Until Tan's women connect as mothers and daughters, they experience strong feelings of isolation, a sense of disenfranchisement and fragmentation. These feelings often are a result of male domination, as Margery Wolf and Roxanne Witke describe in *Women in Chinese Society* (1-11).

A photo that is in part a pictorial history of Tan's foremothers is the inspiration for many of her portrayals of women. Tan writes in **"Lost Lives of Women"** of a picture of her mother, grandmother, aunts, cousins:

> When I first saw this photo as a child, I thought it was exotic and remote, of a faraway time and place, with people who had no connection to my American life. Look at their bound feet! Look at that funny lady with the plucked forehead. The solemn little girl was in fact, my mother. And leaning against the rock is my grandmother, Jing mei. . . . This is also a picture of secrets and tragedies. . . . This is the picture I see when I write. These are the secrets I was supposed to keep. These are the women who never let me forget why stories need to be told.
>
> (90)

In her remembrances, Tan presents Chinese American women who are forging identities beyond the pictures of concubinage and bound feet, women encountering new dragons, many of which are derived from being "hyphenated" American females. She views mother-daughter relationships in the same vein as Kathie Carlson, who argues, "This relationship is the birthplace of a woman's ego identity, her sense of security in the world, her feelings about herself, her body and other women. From her mother, a woman receives her first impression of how to be a woman" (xi).

The Joy Luck Club and *The Kitchen God's Wife* are studies in balance—balancing hyphenation and the roles of daughter, wife, mother, sister, career woman. In achieving balance, voice is important: in order to achieve voice, hyphenated women must engage in self-exploration, recognition and appreciation of their culture(s), and they must know their histories. The quest for voice becomes an archetypal journey for all of the women. The mothers come to the United States and have to adapt to a new culture, to redefine voice and self. The daughters' journeys become rites of passage; before they can find voice or define self they must acknowledge the history and myth of their mothers—"her-stories" of life in China, passage to the United States, and assimilation. And each must come to grips with being her mother's daughter.

The Joy Luck Club is a series of stories by and about narrators whose lives are interconnected as a result of friendship and membership in the Joy Luck Club: Suyuan and Jing-mei Woo, An-mei Hsu and Rose Hsu Jordan, Lindo and Waverly Jong, and Ying-ying and Lena St. Clair. The stories illuminate the multiplicity of experiences of Chinese women who are struggling to fashion a voice for themselves in a culture where women are conditioned to be silent. The stories are narrated by seven of the eight women in the group—four daughters and three mothers; one mother has recently died of a cerebral aneurysm. Jing-mei, nicknamed June, must be her mother's voice. The book is divided into four sections: Feathers from a Thousand Li Away, The Twenty-six Malignant Gates, American Translation, and Queen Mother of the Western Skies. Each chapter is prefaced with an introductory thematic tale or myth, all of which tend to stress the advice given by mothers.

Tan tells her mother's stories, the secret ones she began to tell after the death of Tan's father and brother in *The Kitchen God's Wife*. Patti Doten notes that Tan's mother told stories of her marriage to another man in China and of three daughters left behind when she came to the United States in 1949 (14), a story that is in part remembered in *The Joy Luck Club* with An-mei's saga. In *The Kitchen God's Wife*, a mother and daughter, Winnie Louie and Pearl Louie Brandt, share their stories, revealing the secrets that hide mind and self—and history—and veil and mask their voices. Winnie Louie's tale is of the loss of her mother as a young girl, marriage to a sadistic man who sexually abused her, children stillborn or dying young, a patriarchal society that allowed little room for escape from domestic violence (especially against the backdrop of war), and her flight to America and the love of a "good man." Daughter Pearl Louie Brandt's secrets include her pain upon the loss of her father and the unpredictable disease, multiple sclerosis, that inhibits her body and her life.

Tan's characters are of necessity storytellers and even historians, empowered by relating what they know about their beginnings and the insufficiencies of their present lives. Storytelling—relating memories—allows for review, analysis, and sometimes understanding of ancestry and thus themselves. The storytelling, however, is inundated with ambivalences and contradictions which, as Suzanna Danuta Walters argues, often take the form of blame in mother-daughter relationships (1).

Voice balances—or imbalances—voice as Chinese American mothers and daughters narrate their sagas. Because both mothers and daughters share the telling, the biases of a singular point of view are alleviated. Marianne Hirsch writes, "The story of female development, both in fiction and theory, needs to be written in the voice of mothers as well as in that of daughters. . . . Only in combining both voices, in finding a double voice that would yield a multiple female consciousness, can we begin to envision ways to live 'life afresh'" (161). Tan's fiction presents ambivalences and contradictions in the complicated interactions of mothers' and daughters' voices.

Regardless of how much the daughters try to deny it, it is through their mothers that they find their voice, their mind, their selfhood. Voice finds its form in the process of interaction, even if that interaction is conflict. "Recognition by the daughter that her voice is not entirely her own" comes in time and with experiences (one of the five interconnecting themes referred to by Nan Bauer Maglin in *The Literature of Matrilineage* as a recurring theme in such literature [258]). The experiences in review perhaps allow the daughters to know just how much they are dependent upon their mothers in their journey to voice. The mothers do not let them forget their own importance as the daughters attempt to achieve self-importance.

As Jing-mei "June" Woo tells her story and that of her deceased mother, the importance of the mother and daughter voices resonating, growing out of and being strengthened by each other,

is apparent in her state of confusion and lack of direction and success. Perhaps her name is symbolic of her confusion: she is the only daughter with both a Chinese and an American name. As she recalls life with her mother, Jing-mei/June relates that she is constantly told by her mother, Suyuan Woo, that she does not try and therefore cannot achieve success. June's journey to voice and balance requires self-discovery—which must begin with knowing her mother. June has to use memories as a guide instead of her mother, whose tale she tells and whose saga she must complete. She must meet the ending to the tale of life in China and daughters left behind that her mother has told her over and over again, a story that she thought was a dark fairy tale.

The dark tale is of a previous life that includes a husband and daughters. Suyuan's first husband, an officer with the Kuomintang, takes her to Kweilin, a place she has dreamed of visiting. It has become a war refuge, no longer idyllic. Suyuan Woo and three other officers' wives start the Joy Luck Club to take their minds off the terrible smells of too many people in the city and the screams of humans and animals in pain. They attempt to raise their spirits with mah jong, jokes, and food.

Warned of impending danger, June's mother leaves the city with her two babies and her most valuable possessions. On the road to Chungking, she abandons first the wheelbarrow in which she has been carrying her babies and her goods, then more goods. Finally, her body weakened by fatigue and dysentery, she leaves the babies with jewelry to provide for them until they can be brought to her family. America does not make Suyuan forget the daughters she left as she fled. June Woo secretly views her mother's story as a fairy tale because the ending always changed. Perhaps herein lies the cause of their conflict: neither mother nor daughter listens to be heard, so each complains of not being heard. June Woo's disinterest and lack of knowledge of her mother's history exacerbate her own voicelessness, her lack of wholeness.

At a mah jong table where, appropriately, June takes her mother's place, she is requested by her mother's friends to go to China and meet the daughters of her mother. Thus her journey to voice continues and begins: it is a journey started at birth, but it is only now that she starts to recognize that she needs to know about her mother in order to achieve self-knowledge. She is to tell her sisters about their mother. The mothers' worst fears are realized when June asks what she can possibly tell her mother's daughters. The mothers see their daughters in June's response, daughters who get irritated when their mothers speak in Chinese or explain things in broken English.

Although it startles her mother's friends, June's question is a valid one for a daughter whose relationship with her mother was defined by distance that developed slowly and grew. According to June, she and her mother never understood each other. She says they translated each other's meanings: she seemed to hear less than what was said, and her mother heard more. It is a complaint leveled by mothers and daughters throughout *The Joy Luck Club* and later in *The Kitchen God's Wife.* Both women want to be heard, but do not listen to be heard. They must come to understand that a voice is not a voice unless there is someone there to hear it.

Jing-mei is no longer sitting at the mah jong table but is en route to China when she summons up memories of her mother that will empower her to tell the daughters her mother's story. In the title story and in the short story "A Pair of Tickets," she occupies her mother's place in the story-telling, much as she occupies it at the mah jong table, and she is concerned with the responsibilities left by her mother. In her own stories, "Two Kinds" and "Best Quality," she is concerned with her selves: Jing-mei and June—the Chinese and the American, her mother's expectations and her belief in herself. Her stories are quest stories, described by Susan Koppelman in *Between Mothers and Daughters* as "a daughter's search for understanding" of her mother and herself (xxii). As June makes soup for her father, she sees the stray cat that she thought her mother had killed, since she had not seen it for some time. She makes motions to scare the cat and then recognizes the motions as her mother's; the cat reacts to her just as he had to her mother. She is reminded that she is her mother's daughter.

According to Judith Arcana in *Our Mothers' Daughters,* "we hold the belief that mothers love their daughters by definition and we fear any signal from our own mother that this love, which includes acceptance, affection, admiration and approval does not exist or is incomplete" (5). It does not matter to Jing-mei that she is not her mother's only disappointment (she says her mother always seemed displeased with everyone). Jing-mei recalls that something was not in balance and that something always needed improving for her mother. The friends do not seem to care; with all of her faults, she is their friend. Perhaps it is a

FROM THE AUTHOR

TAN ON HER EXPERIENCE WITH DEPRESSION

In many ways, I consider depression my legacy. There's a photograph of my grandmother in China in 1921. She's with three other women in her family. Every woman in the picture committed suicide. The belief was that if you killed yourself, your ghost could come back and wreak havoc on those who had wronged you.

I first tried to kill myself when I was 6. I remember feeling deeply unhappy, although I can't remember why. So I took a butter knife from the kitchen and dragged it across my wrists. I tried to slice through my skin, but it hurt too much, so I stopped. Looking back, I realize I must have had some form of depression by then.

I never told anyone how bad I felt as a child. My mother had her own problems. She was very dramatic in her depression—she would throw the furniture upside down, things would be smashed. She always threatened to commit suicide. Once, she opened the door of a moving car and threatened to jump out. I don't know what my father thought about it all. I remember one day when she had overturned the furniture, he quietly left the house and took me with him. We never talked about what my mother had done. I would cry, and he would comfort me but not say anything.

Later, Mom had reason to be depressed. When I was 14, my brother Peter and my father, who was a Baptist minister and an electrical engineer, were both diagnosed with brain tumors. Peter died in July 1967, at 16; my father died six months later. My mother believed there was a curse on our family. My younger brother John and I lived with the notion that we too might die at any time.

People Weekly 55, no. 18 (7 May 2001): 85-87.

"daughter's" expectations that June uses to judge her mother. Suyuan tells the rebellious June that she can be the best at anything as she attempts to mold her child into a piano-playing prodigy. She tells June she's not the best because she's not trying. After the request by the Joy Luck Club mothers June, in really listening to the voice of her mother as reserved in her memory, discovers that she might have been able to demonstrate ability had she tried: "for unlike my mother I did not believe I could be anything I wanted to be. I could only be me" (154). But she does not recognize that the "me" is the one who has made every attempt to escape development. The pendant her late mother gave her is symbolic. It was given to her as her life's importance. The latter part of the message is in Chinese, the voice of wisdom versus the provider of American circumstances.

In archetypal journeys, there is always a god or goddess who supports the "traveler" along his or her way. In **The Kitchen God's Wife,** Lady Sorrowfree is created by Winnie Louie, mother of Pearl, when the Kitchen God is determined by her to be an unfit god for her daughter's altar, inherited from an adopted aunt. The Kitchen God is unfit primarily because he became a god despite his mistreatment of his good wife. A porcelain figurine is taken from a storeroom where she has been placed as a "mistake" and is made into a goddess for Pearl, Lady Sorrowfree. Note Winnie's celebration of Lady Sorrowfree:

> I heard she once had many hardships in her life. . . . But her smile is genuine, wise, and innocent at the same time. And her hand, see how she just raised it. That means she is about to speak, or maybe she is telling you to speak. She is ready to listen. She understands English. You should tell her everything. . . . But sometimes, when you are afraid, you can talk to her. She will listen. She will wash away everything sad with her tears. She will use her stick to chase away everything bad. See her name: Lady Sorrowfree, happiness winning over bitterness, no regrets in this world.
>
> (414-415)

Perhaps Tan's mothers want to be like Lady Sorrowfree; they are in a sense goddesses whose altars their daughters are invited to come to for nurturance, compassion, empathy, inspiration, and direction. They are driven by the feeling of need to support those daughters, to give to them "the swan" brought from China—symbolic of their her-stories and wisdom, and the advantages of America, like the mother in the preface to the first round of stories. In the tale, all that is left of the mother's swan that she has brought from China after it is taken by customs officials is one feather; the mother wants to tell her daughter that the feather may look worthless, but it comes from her homeland and carries with it all good intentions. But she waits to tell her in perfect English,

in essence keeping secrets. The mothers think that everything is possible for the daughters if the mothers will it. The daughters may come willingly to the altar or may rebelliously deny the sagacity of their mothers.

The mothers struggle to tell their daughters the consequences of not listening to them. The mother in the tale prefacing the section "Twenty-six Malignant Gates" tells her daughter not to ride her bike around the corner where she cannot see her because she will fall down and cry. The daughter questions how her mother knows, and she tells her that it is written in the book *Twenty-six Malignant Gates* that evil things can happen when a child goes outside the protection of the house. The daughter wants evidence, but her mother tells her that it is written in Chinese. When her mother does not tell her all twenty-six of the Malignant Gates, the girl runs out of the house and around the corner and falls, the consequence of not listening to her mother. Rebellion causes conflict—a conflict Lady Sorrowfree would not have to endure. June Woo and Waverly Jong seem to be daughters who thrive on the conflict that results from rebellion and sometimes even the need to win their mother's approval. June trudges off every day to piano lessons taught by an old man who is hard of hearing. Defying her mother, she learns very little, as she reveals at a piano recital to which her mother has invited all of her friends. June notes the blank look on her mother's face that says she has lost everything. Waverly wins at chess, which pleases her mother, but out of defiance she stops playing until she discovers that she really enjoyed her mother's approval. As an adult she wants her mother to approve of the man who will be her second husband; mother and daughter assume the positions of chess players.

Tan's mothers frequently preach that children are to make their mothers proud so that they can brag about them to other mothers. The mothers engage in fierce competition with each other. Suyuan Woo brags about her daughter even after June's poorly performed piano recital. All of the mothers find fault with their daughters, but this is something revealed to the daughters, not to the community.

Much as Lindo Jong credits herself with daughter Waverly's ability to play chess, she blames herself for Waverly's faults as a person and assumes failures in raising her daughter: "It is my fault she is this way—selfish. I wanted my children to have the best combination: American circumstances and Chinese character. How could I know these things do not mix?" (289). Waverly knows how American circumstances work, but Lindo can't teach her about Chinese character: "How to obey parents and listen to your mother's mind. How not to show your own thoughts, to put your feelings behind your face so you can take advantage of hidden opportunities. . . . Why Chinese thinking is best" (289). What she gets is a daughter who wants to be Chinese because it is fashionable, a daughter who likes to speak back and question what she says, and a daughter to whom promises mean nothing. Nonetheless, she is a daughter of whom Lindo is proud.

Lindo Jong is cunning, shrewd, resourceful; Waverly Jong is her mother's daughter. Waverly manages to irritate her mother when she resists parental guidance. Judith Arcana posits that "some daughters spend all or most of their energy trying futilely to be as different from their mothers as possible in behavior, appearance, relations with friends, lovers, children, husbands" (9). Waverly is a strategist in getting her brother to teach her to play chess, in winning at chess, in gaining her mother's forgiveness when she is rude and getting her mother's acceptance of the man she plans to marry. Lindo proudly reminds Waverly that she has inherited her ability to win from her.

In literature that focuses on mother/daughter relationships, feminists see "context—historical time and social and cultural group" as important (Rosinsky, 285). Lindo relates in "The Red Candle" that she once sacrificed her life to keep her parents' promise; she married as arranged. Chinese tradition permits Lindo's parents to give her to Huang Tai for her son—to determine her fate—but Lindo takes control of her destiny. On the day of her wedding, as she prepares for the ceremony, she schemes her way out of the planned marriage and into America, where "nobody says you have to keep the circumstances somebody else gives to you" (289).

It takes determination to achieve voice and selfhood, to take control of one's mind and one's life from another, making one's self heard, overcoming silence. Lindo does not resign herself to her circumstances in China. Waverly reveals that she learns some of her strategies from her mother: "I was six when my mother taught me the art of invisible strength. It was a strategy for winning arguments, respect from others, and eventually, though neither of us knew it at the time, chess games" (89). Therein lies Lindo's contribution to her daughter's voice.

Lindo uses the same brand of ingenuity to play a life chess game with and to teach her daughter. Adrienne Rich writes in *Of Woman Born*: "Probably there is nothing in human nature more resonant with charges than the flow of energy between two biologically alike bodies, one which has lain in amniotic bliss inside the other, one which has labored to give birth to the other. The materials are there for the deepest mutuality and the most painful estrangement" (226). Lindo has to contend with a headstrong daughter: "'Finish your coffee,' I told her yesterday. 'Don't throw your blessings away.' 'Don't be old-fashioned, Ma,' she told me, finishing her coffee down the sink. 'I'm my own person.' And I think, how can she be her own person? When did I give her up?" (290).

Waverly is champion of the chess game, but she is no match for her mother in a life chess game. She knows her chances of winning in a contest against her mother, who taught her to be strong like the wind. Waverly learns during the "chess years" that her mother was a champion strategist. Though she is a tax attorney able to bully even the Internal Revenue Service, she fears the wrath of her mother if she is told to mind her business: "Well, I don't know if it's explicitly stated in the law, but you can't ever tell a Chinese mother to shut up. You could be charged as an accessory to your own murder" (191). What Waverly perceives as an impending battle for her mother's approval of her fiancé is nothing more than the opportunity for her mother and her to communicate with each other. She strategically plans to win her mother's approval of her fiancé, Rick, just as if she is playing a game of chess. She is afraid to tell her mother that they are going to be married because she is afraid that her mother will not approve. The conversation ends with her recognition that her mother also needs to be heard and with her mother's unstated approval of her fiancé. Waverly Jong recognizes her mother's strategies in their verbal jousts, but she also recognizes that, just like her, her mother is in search of something. What she sees is an old woman waiting to be invited into her daughter's life. Like the other mothers, Lindo views herself as standing outside her daughter's life—a most undesirable place.

Sometimes Tan's mothers find it necessary to intrude in order to teach the daughters to save themselves; they criticize, manage, and manipulate with an iron fist. An-mei Hsu and Ying-ying St. Clair play this role. "My mother once told me why I was so confused all the time," says Rose

Hsu during her first story, "Without Wood" (212). "She said that I was without wood. Born without wood so that I listened to too many people. She knew this because she had almost become this way" (212). Suyuan Woo tells June Woo that such weaknesses are present in the mother, An-mei Hsu: "Each person is made of five elements. . . . Too little wood and you bend too quickly to listen to other people's ideas, unable to stand on your own. This was like my Auntie An-mei" (19). Rose's mother tells her that she must stand tall and listen to her mother standing next to her. If she bends to listen to strangers, she'll grow weak and be destroyed. Rose Hsu is in the process of divorce from a husband who has labeled her indecisive and useless as a marriage partner. She is guilty of allowing her husband to mold her. He does not want her to be a partner in family decisions until he makes a mistake in his practice as a plastic surgeon. Then he complains that she is unable to make decisions: he is dissatisfied with his creation. Finding it difficult to accept divorce, she confusedly runs to her friends and a psychiatrist seeking guidance.

Over and over again her mother tells her to count on a mother because a mother is best and knows what is inside of her daughter. "A psycheatricks will only make you hulihudu, make you heimongmong" (210). The psychiatrist leaves her confused, as her mother predicts. She becomes even more confused as she tells each of her friends and her psychiatrist a different story. Her mother advises her to stand up to her husband, to speak up. She assumes the role of Lady Sorrowfree. When Rose does as her mother advises, she notices that her husband seems scared and confused. She stands up to him and forces him to retreat. She is her mother's daughter. She listens to her mother and finds her voice—her self.

Like the other mothers, An-mei demonstrates some of the qualities of "Lady Sorrowfree." An-mei is concerned that her daughter sees herself as having no options. A psychologist's explanation is "to the extent that women perceive themselves as having no choice, they correspondingly excuse themselves from the responsibility that decision entails" (Gilligan, 67). An-mei was "raised the Chinese way": "I was taught to desire nothing, to swallow other people's misery, to eat my own bitterness" (241). She uses the tale of the magpies to indicate that one can either make the choice to be in charge of one's life or continue to let others be in control. For thousands of years magpies came to the fields of a group of peasants just after they had sown their seeds and watered them with their

tears. The magpies ate the seeds and drank the tears. Then one day the peasants decided to end their suffering and silence. They clapped their hands and banged sticks together, making noise that startled and confused the magpies. This continued for days until the magpies died of hunger and exhaustion from waiting for the noise to stop so that they could land and eat. The sounds from the hands and sticks were their voices. Her daughter should face her tormentor.

An-mei tells stories of her pain, a pain she does not wish her daughter to endure. Memory is, in part, voices calling out to her, reminding her of what she has endured and of a relationship wished for: "it was her voice that confused me," "a familiar sound from a forgotten dream," "she cried with a wailing voice," "voices praising," "voices murmuring," "my mother's voice went away" (41-45). The voices of her mothers confused her. She was a young girl in need of a mother's clear voice that would strengthen her circumstances and her context. The voices remind her, in "Scar," of wounds that heal but leave their imprint and of the importance of taking control out of the hands of those who have the ability to devour their victims, as in the story "Magpies." A scar resulting from a severe burn from a pot of boiling soup reminds her of when her mother was considered a ghost: her mother was dead to her family because she became a rich merchant's concubine. With time the scar "became pale and shiny and I had no memory of my mother. That is the way it is with a wound. The wound begins to close in on itself, to protect what is hurting so much. And once it is closed, you no longer see what is underneath, what started the pain" (40). It is also the way of persons attempting to assimilate—the wounds of getting to America, the wounds of hyphenation, close in on themselves and then it is difficult to see where it all began.

An-mei remembers the scar and the pain when her mother returns to her grandmother Poppo's deathbed. Upon the death of Poppo, she leaves with her mother, who shortly afterward commits suicide. Poppo tells An-mei that when a person loses face, it's like dropping a necklace down a well: the only way you can get it back is to jump in after it. From her mother An-mei learns that tears cannot wash away sorrows; they only feed someone else's joy. Her mother tells her to swallow her own tears.

An-mei knows strength and she knows forgetting. Perhaps that is why her daughter tells the story of her loss. It is Rose Hsu who tells the story of her brother's drowning and her mother's faith that he would be found. She refuses to believe that he is dead; without any driving lessons, she steers the car to the ocean side to search once more for him. After her son Bing's death, An-mei places the Bible that she has always carried to the First Chinese Baptist Church under a short table leg as a way of correcting the imbalances of life. She gives her daughter advice on how to correct imbalances in her life. The tale prefacing the section "Queen of the Western Skies" is also a fitting message for Rose Hsu. A woman playing with her granddaughter wonders at the baby's happiness and laughter, remembering that she was once carefree before she shed her innocence and began to look critically and suspiciously at everything. She asks the babbling child if it is Syi Wang, Queen Mother of the Western Skies, come back to provide her with some answers: "Then you must teach my daughter this same lesson. How to lose your innocence but not your hope. How to laugh forever" (159).

Like all the other daughters, Lena must recognize and respect the characteristics of Lady Sorrowfree that are inherent in her mother, Ying-ying. Ying-ying describes her daughter as being devoid of wisdom. Lena laughs at her mother when she says "arty-tecky" (architecture) to her sister-in-law. Ying-ying admits that she should have slapped Lena more as a child for disrespect. Though Ying-ying serves as Lena's goddess, Lena initially does not view her mother as capable of advice on balance. Ying-ying's telling of her story is very important to seeing her in a true mothering role; her daughter's first story makes one think that the mother is mentally unbalanced.

Evelyn Reed in *Woman's Evolution* writes: "A mother's victimization does not merely humiliate her, it mutilates her daughter who watches her for clues as to what it means to be a woman. Like the traditional foot-bound Chinese woman, she passes on her affliction. The mother's self-hatred and low expectations are binding rags for the psyche of the daughter" (293). Ying-ying, whose name means "Clear Reflection," becomes a ghost. As a young girl she liked to unbraid her hair and wear it loose. She recalls a scolding from her mother, who once told her that she was like the lady ghosts at the bottom of the lake. Her daughter is unaware of her mother's previous marriage to a man in China twenty years before Lena's birth. Ying-ying falls in love with him because he strokes her cheek and tells her that she has tiger eyes, that they gather fire in the day and shine golden at night. Her husband opts to run off with another woman during her pregnancy, and she aborts the

baby because she has come to hate her husband with a passion. Ying-ying tells Lena that she was born a tiger in a year when babies were dying and because she was strong she survived. After ten years of reclusive living with cousins in the country, she goes to the city to live and work. There she meets Lena's father, an American she marries after being courted for four years, and continues to be a ghost. Ying-ying says that she willingly gave up her spirit.

In Ying-ying's first story, "The Moon Lady," when she sees her daughter lounging by the pool she realizes that they are lost, invisible creatures. Neither, at this point, recognizes the importance of "listening harder to the silence beneath their voices" (Maglin, 260). Their being lost reminds her of the family outing to Tai Lake as a child, when she falls into the lake, is rescued, and is put on shore only to discover that the moon lady she has been anxiously awaiting to tell her secret wish is male. The experience is so traumatic that she forgets her wish. Now that she is old and is watching her daughter, she remembers that she had wished to be found. And now she wishes for her daughter to be found—to find herself.

Lena, as a young girl, sees her mother being devoured by her fears until she becomes a ghost. Ying-ying believes that she is already a ghost. She does not want her daughter to become a ghost like her, "an unseen spirit" (285). Ying-ying begins life carefree. She is loved almost to a fault by her mother and her nursemaid, Amah. She is spoiled by her family's riches and wasteful. When she unties her hair and floats through the house, her mother tells her that she resembles the "lady ghosts . . . ladies who drowned in shame and floated in living people's houses with their hair undone to show everlasting despair" (276). She knows despair when the north wind that she thinks has blown her luck chills her heart by blowing her first husband past her to other women.

Lena, Ying-ying's daughter, is a partner in a marriage where she has a voice in the rules; but when the game is played, she loses her turn many times. Carolyn See argues that "in the name of feminism and right thinking, this husband is taking Lena for every cent she's got, but she's so demoralized, so 'out of balance' in the Chinese sense, that she can't do a thing about it" (11). In the introductory anecdote to the section "American Translation," a mother warns her daughter that she cannot put mirrors at the foot of the bed because all of her marriage happiness will bounce back and tumble the opposite way. Her mother takes from her bag a mirror that she plans to give the daughter as a wedding gift so that it faces the other mirror. The mirrors then reflect the happiness of the daughter. Lena's mother, as does Rose's mother, provides her with the mirror to balance her happiness; the mirror is a mother's advice or wisdom. It is Lena's mother's credo that a woman is out of balance if something goes against her nature. She does not want to be like her mother, but her mother foresees that she too will become a ghost; her husband will transform her according to his desires. Ying-ying recalls that she became "Betty" and was given a new date of birth by a husband who never learned to speak her language. Her review of her own story makes her know that she must influence her daughter's "story" that is in the making. Lena sees herself with her husband in the midst of problems so deep that she can't see where the bottom is. In the guise of a functional relationship is a dysfunctional one. Her mother predicts that the house will break into pieces. When a too-large vase on a too-weak table crashes to the floor, Lena admits that she knew it would happen. Her mother asks her why she did not take steps to keep the house from falling, meaning her marriage as well as the vase.

The goddess role becomes all important to Ying-ying as she becomes more determined to prevent her daughter from becoming a ghost. She fights the daughter that she has raised, "watching from another shore" and "accept[ing] her American ways" (286). After she uses the sharp pain of what she knows to "penetrate [her] daughter's tough skin and cut the tiger spirit loose," she waits for her to come into the room, like a tiger waiting between the trees, and pounces. Ying-ying wins the fight and gives her daughter her spirit, "because this is the way a mother loves her daughter" (286). Lady Sorrowfree helps her "charge" achieve voice.

From the daughter with too much water, to the mother and daughter with too much wood, to the tiger ghosts and just plain ghosts, to the chess queens, Tan's women in *The Joy Luck Club* find themselves capable of forging their own identities, moving beyond passivity to assertiveness—speaking up. They are a piece of the portrait that represents Amy Tan's family history—her own story included; they are, in composite, her family's secrets and tragedies. Tan is unlike some Asian American writers who have had to try to piece together and sort out the meaning of the past from shreds of stories overheard or faded photographs. As in her stories, her mother tells her the stories and explains the photographs. Bell Gale Chevigny writes that "women writing about

other women will symbolically reflect their internalized relations with their mothers and in some measure re-create them" (80). From Tan's own accounts, her interaction with her mother is reflected in her fiction.

Tan's women with their American husbands attempt often without knowing it to balance East and West, the past and the future of their lives. A level of transcendence is apparent in the storytelling, as it is in *The Kitchen God's Wife*. Mothers and daughters must gain from the storytelling in order to have healthy relationships with each other.

In *The Kitchen God's Wife*, Winnie Louie and her daughter Pearl Louie Brandt are both keepers of secrets that accent the distance that characterizes their relationship. Pearl thinks after a trip to her mother's home: "Mile after mile, all of it familiar, yet not this distance that separates us, me from my mother" (57). She is unsure of how this distance was created. Winnie says of their relationship: "That is how she is. That is how I am. Always careful to be polite, always trying not to bump into each other, just like strangers" (82). When their secrets begin to weigh down their friends who have known them for years, who threaten to tell each of the other's secrets, Winnie Louie decides that it is time for revelation. The process of the revelation is ritual: "recitation of the relationship between mother and daughter," "assessment of the relationship," and "the projection of the future into the relationship" (Koppelman, xxvii). At the same time revelation is a journey to voice, the voice that they must have with each other. Again, voice is a metaphor for speaking up, being heard, listening to be heard. No longer will stories begin as Pearl's does: "Whenever my mother talks to me, she begins the conversation as if we were already in the middle of an argument" (11). That they argue or are in conflict is not problematic; it is the "talks to" that should be replaced with "talks with." As much as Pearl needs to know her mother's secrets, Winnie Louie needs to tell them in order to build a relationship that is nurturing for both mother and daughter.

Pearl's secret is multiple sclerosis. At first she does not tell her mother because she fears her mother's theories on her illness. What becomes her secret is the anger she feels toward her father, the inner turmoil that began with his dying and death. Sometimes the mother's voice drowns the voice of the daughter as she attempts to control or explain every aspect of the daughter's existence. "If I had not lost my mother so young, I would not have listened to Old Aunt," says Winnie Louie (65) as she begins her story. These might also be the words of her daughter, though Pearl's loss of mother was not a physical loss. The opportunity for the resonating of mother and daughter voices seems to be the difference between balance and imbalance. American circumstances are to be blamed for the distance; the need to keep secrets grows out of the perceived necessity of assimilation and clean slates. Because her mother was not there, Winnie "listened to Old Aunt" (65). Winnie Louie's dark secret begins with her mother, who disappeared without telling her why; she still awaits some appearance by her mother to explain. Her mother's story is also hers: an arranged marriage—in her mother's case, to curb her rebelliousness; realization that she has a lesser place in marriage than purported; and a daughter as the single lasting joy derived from the marriage. The difference is that Winnie's mother escaped, to be heard from no more.

Winnie's family abides by all of the customs in giving her hand in marriage to Wen Fu: "Getting married in those days was like buying real estate. Here you see a house you want to live in, you find a real estate agent. Back in China, you saw a rich family with a daughter, you found a go-between who knew how to make a good business deal" (134). Winnie tells her daughter, "If asked how I felt when they told me I would marry Wen Fu, I can only say this: It was like being told I had won a big prize. And it was also like being told my head was going to be chopped off. Something between those two feelings" (136). Winnie experiences very little mercy in her marriage to the monstrous Wen Fu.

Wen Fu serves as an officer in the Chinese army, so during World War II they move about China with other air force officers and their wives. Throughout the marriage, Winnie knows abuse and witnesses the death of her babies. She tries to free herself from the tyranny of the marriage, but her husband enjoys abusing her too much to let her go. Her story is a long one, a lifetime of sorrow, death, marriage, imprisonment, lost children, lost friends and family. Jimmie Louie saves her life by helping her to escape Wen Fu and to come to the United States. She loves Jimmie Louie and marries him. The darkest part of her secret she reveals to Pearl almost nonchalantly: Pearl is the daughter of the tyrant Wen Fu.

The daughter asks her mother: "Tell me again . . . why you had to keep it a secret." The mother answers: "Because then you would know. . . . You would know how weak I was. You would think I was a bad mother" (398). Winnie's actions and response are not unexpected. She is every mother who wants her daughter to think of her as having lived a blemish-free existence. She is every mother who forgets that her daughter is living life and knows blemishes. Secrets revealed, the women begin to talk. No longer does Winnie have to think that the year her second husband, Jimmie Louie, died was "when everyone stopped listening to me" (81). Pearl knows her mother's story and can respect her more, not less, for her endurance. She is then able to see a woman molded by her experiences and her secrets—a woman who has lived with two lives. With the tiptoeing around ended, the distance dissipates. By sharing their secrets, they help each other to achieve voice. The gift of Lady Sorrowfree is symbolic of their bonding; this goddess has all of the characteristics of the nurturing, caring, listening mother. Her imperfections lie in her creation; experiences make her. She has none of the characteristics of the Kitchen God.

The story of the Kitchen God and his wife angers Winnie Louie; she looks at the god as a bad man who was rewarded for admitting that he was a bad man. As the story goes, a wealthy farmer, Zhang, who had a good wife who saw to it that his farm flourished, brought home a pretty woman and made his wife cook for her. The pretty woman ran his wife off without any objection from the farmer. She helped him use up all of his riches foolishly and left him a beggar. He was discovered hungry and suffering by a servant who took him home to care for him. When he saw his wife, whose home it was, he attempted to hide in the kitchen fireplace; his wife could not save him. The Jade Emperor, because Zhang admitted he was wrong, made him Kitchen God with the duty to watch over people's behavior. Winnie tells Pearl that people give generously to the Kitchen God to keep him happy in the hopes that he will give a good report to the Jade Emperor. Winnie thinks that he is not the god for her daughter. How can one trust a god who would cheat on his wife? How can he be a good judge of behavior? The wife is the good one. She finds another god for her daughter's altar, Lady Sorrowfree. After all, she has already given her a father.

Even as Winnie tells her story, one senses that the women are unaware of the strength of the bond between them that partly originates in the biological connection and partly in their womanness. Storytelling/revealing secrets gives both of them the opportunity for review; Winnie Louie tells Pearl that she has taught her lessons with love, that she has combined all of the love that she had for the three she lost during the war and all of those that she did not allow to be born and has given it to Pearl. She speaks of her desire "to believe in something good" (152), her lost hope and innocence: "So I let those other babies die. In my heart I was being kind. . . . I was a young woman then. I had no more hope left, no trust, no innocence" (312). In telling her story, she does not ask for sympathy or forgiveness; she simply wants to be free of the pain that "comes from keeping everything inside, waiting until it is too late" (88).

Perhaps this goddess, Lady Sorrowfree, to whom they burn incense will cause them never to forget the importance of voice and listening. On the heels of listening there is balance as both Winnie and Pearl tell their secrets and are brought closer by them. East and West, mother and daughter, are bonded for the better. Arcana notes that "mother/daughter sisterhood is the consciousness we must seek to make this basic woman bond loving and fruitful, powerful and deep . . ." (34). It ensures that women do not smother each other and squelch the voice of the other or cause each other to retreat into silence.

In exploring the problems of mother-daughter voices in relationships, Tan unveils some of the problems of biculturalism—of Chinese ancestry and American circumstances. She presents daughters who do not know their mothers' "importance" and thus cannot know their own; most seem never to have been told or even cared to hear their mothers' history. Until they do, they can never achieve voice. They assimilate; they marry American men and put on American faces. They adapt. In the meantime, their mothers sit like Lady Sorrowfree on her altar, waiting to listen. The daughters' journeys to voice are completed only after they come to the altars of their Chinese mothers.

Works Cited

Arcana, Judith. *Our Mothers' Daughters.* Berkeley: Shameless Hussy Press, 1979.

Belensky, Mary Field, et al. *Women's Ways of Knowing.* New York: Basic Books, 1986.

Blicksilver, Edith. *The Ethnic American Woman: Problems, Protests, Lifestyle.* Dubuque, Ia.: Kendall/Hunt Publishing, 1978.

Carlson, Kathie. *In Her Image: The Unhealed Daughter's Search for Her Mother.* Boston: Shambhala, 1990.

Chevigny, Bell Gale. "Daughters Writing: Toward a Theory of Women's Biography." *Feminist Studies* 9 (1983): 79-102.

Chodorow, Nancy. *Feminism and Psychoanalytic Theory.* New Haven: Yale University Press, 1989.

Doten, Patti. "Sharing Her Mother's Secrets." *Boston Globe,* June 21, 1991, E9-14.

Friday, Nancy. *My Mother/My Self.* New York: Delacorte Press, 1977.

Gardiner, Judith Kegan. "Mind Mother: Psychoanalysis and Feminism." In *Making a Difference: Feminist Literary Criticism,* ed. Gayle Greene and Coppélia Kahn, 113-145. New York: Methuen, 1985.

Gilligan, Carol. *In a Different Voice.* Cambridge, Mass.: Harvard University Press, 1982.

Hirsch, Marianne. *The Mother-Daughter Plot: Narrative, Psychoanalysis, Feminism.* Bloomington: Indiana University Press, 1989.

Hirsch, Marianne, and Evelyn Fox Feller. *Conflicts in Feminism.* New York: Routledge, 1990.

Kim, Elaine H. *Asian American Literature: An Introduction to the Writings and Their Social Context.* Philadelphia: Temple University Press, 1982.

Koppelman, Susan. *Between Mothers and Daughters, Stories across a Generation.* New York: Feminist Press at the City University of New York, 1985.

Maglin, Nan Bauer. "The Literature of Matrilineage." In *The Lost Tradition: Mothers and Daughters in Literature,* ed. Cathy N. Davidson and E. M. Broner, 257-267. New York: Frederick Ungar, 1980.

Marbella, Jean. "Amy Tan: Luck But Not Joy." *Baltimore Sun,* June 30, 1991, E-11.

"Mother with a Past." *Maclean's* (July 15, 1991): 47.

Reed, Evelyn. *Woman's Evolution.* New York: Pathfinder Press, 1975.

Rich, Adrienne. *Of Woman Born: Motherhood as Experience and Institution.* New York: Norton, 1976, 1986.

Rosinsky, Natalie M. "Mothers and Daughters: Another Minority Group." In *The Lost Tradition: Mothers and Daughters in Literature,* ed. Cathy N. Davidson and E. M. Broner, 281-303. New York: Frederick Ungar, 1980.

See, Carolyn. "Drowning in America, Starving in China." *Los Angeles Times Book Review,* March 12, 1989, 1, 11.

Spence, Jonathan D. *The Search for Modern China.* New York: W. W. Norton, 1990.

Tan, Amy. *The Joy Luck Club.* New York: Ivy Books, 1989.

———. *The Kitchen God's Wife.* New York: G. P. Putnam's Sons, 1991.

———. "Lost Lives of Women." *Life* (April 1991), 90-91.

Walters, Suzanna Danuta. *Lives Together/Worlds Apart: Mothers and Daughters in Popular Culture.* Berkeley: University of California Press, 1992.

Wolf, Margery, and Roxanne Witke. *Women in Chinese Society.* Stanford: Stanford University Press, 1975.

Yamada, Mitsuye. "Invisibility Is an Unnatural Disaster: Reflections of an Asian American Woman." In *This Bridge Called My Back: Writings of Radical Women of Color,* ed. Cherríe Moraga and Gloria Anzaldúa, 35-40. Latham, N.Y.: Kitchen Table/Women of Color Press, 1982.

TITLE COMMENTARY

The Joy Luck Club

CATHERINE ROMAGNOLO (ESSAY DATE SPRING 2003)

SOURCE: Romagnolo, Catherine. "Narrative Beginnings in Amy Tan's *The Joy Luck Club*: A Feminist Study."[1] *Studies in the Novel* 35, no. 1 (spring 2003): 89-107.

In the following essay, Romagnolo argues that the "master narratives" imposed on The Joy Luck Club *have resulted in incomplete readings of the novel. She suggests that a return to the fundamental narrative beginning can result in a fuller reading of the novel's ideological implications.*

Like virginity, literary introductions are often seen as an awkward embarrassment, an obstacle to be overcome as quickly as possible in order to facilitate vital experiences. On the other hand, "the first time" is a supremely privileged moment, to be lingered over, contemplated, and cherished. Which is the more telling conception we can only begin to imagine.

—Steven Kellman, "Grand Openings and Plain"

Even feminist narratology . . . has tended to focus on women writers or female narrators without asking how the variables "sex," "gender," and "sexuality" might operate in narrative more generally.

—Susan S. Lanser, "Queering Narratology"

Few extensive studies of narrative beginnings exist, and not one takes a feminist perspective. Offering almost exclusively formalist readings, existing analyses neglect the ideological implications of beginnings, especially as they relate to gender, race, and cultural identity.[2] Even as scholars overlook ideological valence in narrative beginnings, their own readings often indicate, perhaps unexpectedly, that social and cultural concerns adhere to any conception of beginnings. For example, Steven Kellman, one of the first to study narrative beginnings in an extended analysis, evokes ways that cultural bias is embedded in these studies. The sexualized metaphor he uses to illustrate the trouble inherent in starting a literary text testifies to this bias. The problem with his description arises when one considers the historical importance placed on female purity and virginity in numerous cultures. Not only is the conception of virginity as an "awkward embarrassment" a specifically heteronormatively masculinist perspective, but it also posits the proverbial pen-as-penis, page/text-as-female-body metaphor with whose ideological valences we are all familiar. Furthermore, the analogy obscures cultural differences that shape the relationship of a given individual to gendered sexuality. Similarly, A. D.

Tsai Chin and Tamlyn Tomita in the 1993 film production of *The Joy Luck Club.*

Nuttall, while recognizing that his text on narrative beginnings is a "spectacle of alternating (male) authority and (male) sequence [that] will certainly be unpleasing to some people,"[3] never interrogates this exclusively white male focus (vii). These studies serve as examples of the way gender concerns, however invisible, are often already linked to beginnings. They invite us to examine seriously the identificatory variables that have been elided and to take up the challenge identified by Susan S. Lanser to explore how social categories operate in narrative (250).

The Joy Luck Club by Amy Tan is an ideal vehicle with which to begin such a project.[4] It is suggestive of a new way to look at narrative beginnings, one that emphasizes a destabilization of conceptions of history that exclude women, particularly those of non-European descent. This way of reading narrative beginnings encourages an interrogation of the relevance of both European American and Asian American cultural and national origins for Asian American female subjects, as well as promoting a resistance to the notion of an alternatively authentic origin. If we attend to the ideological significance of beginnings in Tan's novel, a critique of the very concept of origins—especially in its relation to "American," "Chinese," and "Chinese American" identity—becomes apparent. Moreover, doing so illuminates the discursive constructedness of authenticity, origins, and identity, thereby problematizing reductive cultural representations of female, American, and Asian American subjectivity. Building on recent scholarship about Asian American literature and subjectivity, which has suggested that *The Joy Luck Club* has been misread,[5] this essay attempts to extend, if not disrupt, the readings of many scholars from different disciplines who impose certain kinds of master narratives onto this novel.[6] While these readings are not so much "wrong" as they are incomplete, an examination of this text's narrative beginnings can at once help us to theorize narrative with an attentiveness to difference and to recognize this help as integral to the cultural work Tan's novel performs.

Narrative beginnings, as suggested by the example of *The Joy Luck Club,* assume a symbolic primacy in relation to social identity. Because, as Tan's text demonstrates, they represent one way to conceptualize origins and contest the representational inadequacies of patriarchal, nationalist rhetoric, narrative beginnings often take on figurative status as metaphorical origins and embody the significance of origins in nationalist discourse. Origins and their relation to national identity and questions of authenticity are discussed by a wide variety of cultural and literary critics working in such diverse fields as post-colonial studies, U.S. minority discourse, and feminist theory. Such scholarship has interrogated the recovery of authentic cultural, literary, and historical origins, a nationalist recovery initially embarked upon in an effort to reveal the falsity of stereotypical conceptions of identity and to propose an "authentic" representation in their place. Although a thorough overview is beyond the scope of this essay, this scholarship broadly asserts that the importance placed upon authenticity can lead to discrimination and exclusion. Norma Alarcón et al., for example, explicate the problems associated with nationalism and the "denial of sexual or racial difference" within the nation-state (1). Etienne Balibar theorizes the ironic connection between racism and nationalism, even within what he calls "nationalism of the dominated" (45). And Dana Takagi, in the context of Asian American studies, contends that a fixation upon reclaiming authentic origins can occlude the

experiences of marginalized members of a community: "At times, our need to 'reclaim history' has been bluntly translated into a possessiveness about the Asian American experience or perspectives as if such experiences or perspectives were not diffuse, shifting, and often contradictory" (33). In conjunction with such critiques of origins as grounds for social identity, many similarly oriented critics maintain the importance of narrative and narrative form to explicating gender, nation formation, national identity, and individual subjectivity. For example, Lisa Lowe argues that formal attributes of Asian American narratives express "an aesthetic of 'disidentification' and 'infidelity'" (32). Through formal and thematic "contradictions," she explains, this aesthetic critiques exclusionary conceptions of American and Asian American cultural identity. Contributing to such critical debates, my study of Amy Tan's novel demonstrates the importance of focusing on *narrative beginnings,* specifically, as sites at which these questions about origins, authenticity, and narrative converge.

Using Tan's text as a point of entry, I propose a more fully elaborated way of defining narrative beginnings in order to facilitate understanding of their ideological function and textual significance. Theorists such as Gerald Prince, Nuttall, and James Phelan have defined narrative beginnings in various ways. Prince, for example, defines them as "the incident[s] initiating the process of change in a plot or action . . . not necessarily follow[ing] but . . . necessarily followed by other incidents" (10). Nuttall, on the other hand, chooses to narrow his discussion to the actual opening lines and/or pages of a narrative text, claiming that these openings are "naturally rooted, are echoes, more or less remote, of an original creative act" (viii). Phelan, taking another approach, breaks his understanding of opening lines and/or pages into four separate categories: "exposition . . . initiation . . . introduction . . . entrance" (97). These definitions, while useful, fall short of distinguishing the different ways that beginnings may be conceptualized in narrative fiction. In effect, they have been unable to yield a discussion of the many ideological functions a beginning may serve within a narrative. The example of *The Joy Luck Club,* however, can serve as a source of critical insight from which we might generate a broader framework for the consideration of narrative beginnings. Working with Tan's novel, then, I schematize a critical paradigm for the study of four categories of narrative beginnings:

Structural Narrative Openings—The beginning pages or lines of a narrative, as well as the opening pages/lines of chapters or section breaks. This beginning is the most easily identified and most frequently studied.

Chronological Narrative Beginnings—The chronologically earliest diegetic moments in a narrative. Often there exist several simultaneously occurring textual moments that compete, in a sense, for the status of chronological beginning.

Causal Beginnings—The diegetic moment or moments that represent the catalyst for the main action within a narrative. They initiate or set into motion the conflict of the narrative.

Thematic Origins—The topic of origins or beginnings when it is interrogated or explored by the characters, narrator, or by the author her/himself. This beginning occurs on the story or content level of a narrative.

By working through this particularized framework that Tan's novel helps us to formulate, I propose that we can advance our understanding of both this text in particular and the broader narratological as well as cultural matters it thematizes.

Structural Narrative Openings: Repetition and Revision

The Joy Luck Club begins with what has been described by Asian American writer and cultural critic Frank Chin as a "fake" myth of origin:

> Then the woman and the swan sailed across an ocean many thousands of *li* wide, stretching their necks toward America. On her journey she cooed to the swan: "In America I will have a daughter just like me. But over there nobody will say her worth is measured by the loudness of her husband's belch. Over there nobody will look down on her, because I will make her speak only perfect American English. And over there she will always be too full to swallow any sorrow! She will know my meaning, because I will give her this swan—a creature that became more than what was hoped for."
>
> (3)

This "fake Chinese fairy tale" is so described both because, according to Chin, it overstates the misogyny of Chinese society, and because it represents a misappropriation, a "faking," of Chinese culture (2). The implication of this misappropriation, Chin argues, is that Chinese Americans—particularly women—like Tan and her characters are so assimilated that they have lost touch with their "Chinese" cultural origins. Consequently, they have produced new feminized "versions of these traditional stories," which in trying to pass themselves off as authentic only

represent a further "contribution to the stereotype," a stereotype which facilitates the emasculation of Asian American men (3).

We may take this myth to exemplify the structural opening, that is, the beginning lines/pages of Tan's novel. While other theories of narrative beginnings might identify this section of the text as the beginning, its purpose is not as self-evident as might be suggested. It is neither a "fake fairy tale" nor an "echo of an original creative act" (Nuttall viii). In fact, while the structural opening of *The Joy Luck Club* may initially appear to be trying (and failing, according to Chin) to establish and mythologize an authentic and originary moment of immigration from China to U.S.A. for the "Joy Luck aunties," it, in fact, disrupts the very notion of authenticity, especially in regards to origins. Although the first half of the myth seems to imply an unproblematic transition between Chinese and American cultures, by its ending, the contradiction between an idealized version of assimilation to "American" subjectivity and the fragmentation of identity that historically marks immigrant experiences becomes clear: "But when she arrived in the new country, the immigration officials pulled her swan away from her, leaving the woman fluttering her arms and with only one swan feather for a memory. And then she had to fill out so many forms she forgot why she had come and what she had left behind." Instead of either idealizing an essential Asian origin or mythologizing a melting-pot ideology of U.S. immigration, Tan's structural narrative opening marks the way "America" strips the woman of her past, her idealized hopes for the future in the United States, and excludes her from an "American" national identity: the woman is still waiting "for the day she could tell her daughter this [narrative] in perfect American English" (3). By opening with a fabricated myth of origin, Tan's novel foregrounds the ideological implications of a search for beginnings and exemplifies the importance of narrative beginnings to an understanding of this text.

As Chin's response attests, Tan invokes a mythic sensibility in these opening lines, yet undermines the authority of nationalist myths of origin that attempt to uncover an uncorrupted past ethnic identity in which the members of the nation can "rediscover their authentic purpose" (Hutchinson 123). Through an ironic use of mythic form, language, and tone, Tan utilizes repetition for subversion. Repetition in this sense is a performance, which has "innovation," to use Trinh Minh-Ha's term, as its goal. Trinh explains:

Recirculating a limited number of propositions and rehashing stereotypes to criticize stereotyping can . . . constitute a powerful practice . . . Repetition as a practice and a strategy differs from incognizant repetition in that it bears with it the seeds of transformation . . . When repetition reflects on itself as repetition, it constitutes this doubling back movement through which language . . . looks at itself exerting power and, therefore, creates for itself possibilities to repeatedly thwart its own power, inflating it only to deflate it better.

(190)

Tan's opening myth utilizes mythic characters such as "The old woman" juxtaposed with historically rooted figures like immigration officials. It invokes mythic situations seemingly ungrounded in time such as a journey across an ocean "many thousands of li wide" contrasted by modern cultural icons like Coca Cola. Her myth, then, reflects upon itself as national mythology, revised. In its self-reflexivity and difference, this formal and generic repetition serves to deflate the power of the so-called original. That is, by mimicking supposedly authentic nationalist mythologies, the self-consciously illegitimate status of Tan's myth exposes the inability of any nationalist project to recover a genuinely original, pure cultural history. Like Homi Bhabha's concept of mimicry, Tan's myth "problematizes the signs of racial and cultural priority, so that the 'national' is no longer naturalizable" (87). Because culture is always hybrid, any project that asserts purity must necessarily be "fake." This "fakeness" should not, however, be read as inauthenticity, but as a deconstruction of the very concept of authenticity.

The self-conscious repetition and revision of Tan's myth simultaneously destabilizes the notion of an authentic cultural origin (which gives rise to essentialist conceptions of gendered and racialized identities) and dislodges stereotypical representations of Chinese culture. For although the language of this structural opening might evoke a mythological aura, in its content, Tan's opening myth reflects the hybridity of immigrant subjectivity. That is, it signifies the historical "relationships of unequal power and domination" (Lowe 67) that accompany Chinese immigration to the United States. Moreover, it combines and interrogates stereotypically "Chinese" cultural symbols like the swan and "American" cultural emblems like Coca Cola: "Now the woman was old. And she had a daughter who grew up speaking only English and swallowing more Coca Cola than sorrow." In such cases, Tan utilizes overdetermined cultural symbols, which most readers would recognize as the trite, even clichéd, images that have come to signify the respective cultures. And yet, because of the way in which they are deployed, the repetition of these stereotypes cannot take hold as authentic representations; their authority is subverted. The symbol of the swan, stereotypically representative of Chinese women as graceful, silent, and docile, is hybridized and re-appropriated within Tan's narrative. It comes to symbolize both the woman's past ("the old woman remembered a swan she had bought many years ago in Shanghai for a foolish sum") and her idealized hopes for the future as an American ("I will give her this swan—a creature that became more than what was hoped for"). In combining these contradictory impulses or desires (nativism and assimilation), the symbol becomes unstable, unfixed, never to be resolved within Tan's revisionist myth. Furthermore, as this symbol (the swan) is torn away from the old woman when she reaches the United States, we apprehend both the historical violence of immigration as well as the illusory nature of nativist and assimilationist mythology: "She forgot why she had come and what she had left behind" (3).

Tan also invokes a stereotypical emblem of Americanness in the materialistic and modern cultural icon, Coca Cola. Yet, like the symbol of the swan, this sign is already unstable and dislocated from its supposed referent. For, while Coca Cola has come to represent "Americanness," in fact, in this period of late-capitalism the corporation of Coca Cola is found throughout the world. The transnational character of this icon registers the economic and cultural imperialism entailed in the success of Americanization on a global scale, while contradicting its status as American; for, it both is and is not American. This instability continuously interrogates what it means to be "American." That is, the Coca Cola icon does not have as its referent some real originary "America," but alludes to a popular representation of Americanness as tied especially to diversity ("I'd like to buy the world a Coke"). This image is not only a cultural myth unto itself; it also points back to other media representations of America, which refer back yet again to the popular representation of America in "melting pot" ideology, a construction which has historically contributed to the elision of a United States that is, in reality, fraught with racial contradictions. Thus, through the chain of signifiers set in motion by the Coca Cola icon, Tan's myth not only subverts the authority of cultural symbols, but confirms cultural identity to be discursively constructed. Finally, through the placement of these icons in an opening narrative which undermines its own status as a myth of origin, *The Joy Luck Club* structurally reaffirms the inadequacy of such "authentic" cultural symbols to represent the "original essence" of their cultures. The final effect of this myth, then, is not a reconciliation of contradictions—assimilation and nativism—but a dialogic representation of an immigrant experience that struggles with both of these impulses.

By positioning an obviously spurious myth at the structural opening of *The Joy Luck Club,* Tan gives her own text a false originary moment and thus further critiques the notion of origins. The duplicity of this opening structurally and symbolically undermines the text's status as an "immigration novel" that could somehow refer to and represent the "authentic" female immigrant experience. That is, by placing a false myth of origin—which refers only to other illusory origins—in the inaugural pages of her text, Tan implies metaphorically that the novel can never be said to recover any sort of authentic, definitive experience. In searching for the originary moment of Tan's writing, contrary to the "original creative act" that Nuttall finds in his dynasty of white-male authors, one finds an obvious "fake," a performative, symbolic repetition of an originary moment, which itself is discursively constructed (viii). Through this self-conscious performance, the novel argues that any claims of ethnic and/or national authenticity are suspect; they can only be said to allude intertextually to other discursive constructions.

Tan's structural opening is additionally significant in that it acts as a synecdoche for the thematic concerns of the novel. Through its preoccupation with a search for authenticity, origin, and/or the defining moment of one's identity, the story helps us to recognize links between structure and thematic origins. This thematic interest in beginnings is placed in dialogue with the text's structural openings, reinforcing its cultural critique. For example, Suyuan Woo, who has already died as the novel opens, has spent her entire life in an unsuccessful quest to recover the fateful moment when she left her babies on the roadside in Kweilin while fleeing from the invasion of Japanese soldiers. Symbolically, she tells her daughter Jing Mei (June): "The East is where things begin, . . . the direction from which the sun rises, where the wind comes from" (22). An-Mei Hsu is also preoccupied with a quest. Her narrative tells the story of an attempt to recover the source of her psychic pain as well as a search for a mother who was absent for much of her childhood. She

speaks of this past as a wound: "That is the way it is with a wound. The wound begins to close in on itself, to protect what is hurting so much. And once it is closed, you no longer see what is underneath, what started the pain" (40). And Ying Ying St. Clair, who is similarly in search of a lost self, remembers the sense of loss that accompanied her youth: "The farther we glided, the bigger the world became. And I now felt I was lost forever" (79).[7]

Despite the almost compulsive search for origin and identity displayed by the stories within this novel, each quest in its own way repudiates the existence of its goal. For example, although Suyuan claims that the East is where all begins, we learn that this "East" is not static; in fact, it moves and changes just as her Kweilin story changes each time she tells it. Although June takes her mother's place on the East side of the mah jong table, the East shifts places: "Auntie Ying throws the dice and I'm told that Auntie Lin has become the East wind. I've become the North wind, the last hand to play. Auntie Ying is the South and Auntie An-Mei is the West" (23). Similarly, An-Mei learns that underneath the multiple layers of memory that compose one's sense of self, there is no authentic core: "you must peel off your skin, and that of your mother, and her mother before her. Until there is nothing. No scar, no skin, no flesh" (41). And Ying Ying finds that although as she ages she feels closer and "closer to the beginning" of her life, that beginning, that origin is fluid—not fixed, but variable. She suggests this fluidity in speaking of the traumatic day in her childhood when she falls from a boat and is separated from her family. This moment in her life comes to represent, for her, the origin of her loss of self and the beginning, in a sense, of her adult life: "And I remember everything that happened that day because it has happened many times in my life. The same innocence, trust, and restlessness; the wonder, fear, and loneliness. How I lost myself" (83). Further undermining any sense of fixed origins, Ying Ying's beginning also represents an end, a loss; for her, coming to a recognition of one's self entails a loss of a sense of wholeness.[8] The quests embarked upon by these women, therefore, repudiate the ability to recover any type of static identity which might solidify exclusionary conceptions of gendered and racialized subjectivity; at the same time, however, they stress the importance of the histories of these characters to their ongoing sense of agency, highlighting an idea of history as not completely knowable, but nevertheless significant to the discursive construction of identity.

Alternative Structural Openings: Authenticity and Truth

Although Tan's introductory tale possesses great significance, it merely represents the first of the structural narrative openings in her novel. In fact, *The Joy Luck Club* is constructed in such a manner that it has at least four section openings and sixteen chapter openings (four sections each with four chapters). Moreover, each of the characters has at least two narratives (which with the exception of Suyuan, each narrates herself) and each of these narratives has at least one opening of its own, not necessarily coinciding with the opening pages of a section or a chapter; thus, the number of conceivable structural narrative openings is quite large. Although these separate stories are tied to one another through content and theme, each on its own arguably qualifies as a narrative with individual structure including an opening and a closing, however open that closing may be. (It seems to me that a reader could start this text at any one of these openings and still comprehend the narrative.) This proliferation of structural openings, in combination with the text's use of thematic origins, undermines the concept of an originary moment in obvious ways. That is, because each opening represents a new structural beginning, it signifies a challenge, contradicting any claim the first opening might make as the originary moment of the text. Thus, this repetition of openings symbolically represents the way in which a search for origins/authentic beginnings uncovers multiple possibilities, none clearly the most privileged, each possible origin continually displacing/deferring the privilege onto other possibilities.

Furthermore, it becomes clear in a close reading of these alternative openings that many are, in and of themselves, revisionist originary myths working to destabilize essentialist notions of authenticity and truth. The opening to the second section of the novel, "The Twenty-Six Malignant Gates," for example, expresses a seemingly ambiguous message about cultural mythology and truth. For, while it exposes the book *The Twenty-Six Malignant Gates* as simply a fairy tale intended to keep young children obedient, this tale proves itself to be quite powerful. The mother in the opening narrative uses the myth in *The Twenty-Six Malignant Gates* to bolster her authority and support what she views to be best for her child—staying close to home: "'Do not ride your bicycle

around the corner.' . . . 'I cannot see you and you will fall down and cry and I will not hear you.' 'How do you know I'll fall?' whined the girl. 'It's in a book, *The Twenty-Six Malignant Gates,* all the bad things that can happen to you outside the protection of this house.'" If we read this opening as a comment on the use of mythology in nationalist projects, Tan's revisionist myth can be seen as illustrative of the way in which the invocation of an "authentic" mythology/past may be used to manipulate subjects of a nation into loyalty to the "mother" country:

> "Let me see the book."
>
> "It is written in Chinese. You cannot understand it. That is why you must listen to me."
>
> "What are they, then?" The girl demanded. "Tell me the twenty-six bad things."
>
> But the mother sat knitting in silence.
>
> "What twenty-six!" shouted the girl.
>
> The mother still did not answer her.
>
> "You can't tell me because you don't know! You don't know anything!"
>
> (87)

Similar to the recovery or enforcement of a national language and the naturalization of ethnic and national identity, the mother's use of the "mother-tongue" (Chinese) in her invocation of this myth implies that the daughter's ethnic purity is questionable while simultaneously reinforcing the legitimacy of the myth. Both uses, then, are attempts to prevent the daughter from questioning the authority of the myth and to assert the daughter's inferiority to the mother's authenticity. The daughter, in recognizing and rejecting this authority and authenticity, exposes the actual status and purpose of the myth and in the process suggests a goal of nationalist mythology.

Yet, while the first half of this narrative seems to subvert claims of originality and truth, the ending of the narrative appears, at first, to reinforce the power of the very myth the opening exposes. Although the daughter uncovers the constructed nature of *The Twenty-Six Malignant Gates,* the prophecy her mother claims to extract from this myth comes to fruition: "And the girl ran outside, jumped on her bicycle, and in her hurry to get away, she fell before she even reached the corner" (87). Clearly, we are not to suppose that the myth actually predicted this child's injury; instead, we understand this ending to represent the ability of the myth to enter the child's imagination and prompt her to attribute her fall to the story's premonitory power. Thus, the narrative argues that the power of national mythology lies in the subject's imagination, not in some intrinsic truth.

Chronological and Causal Beginnings: History and Time

While the numerous structural openings of this novel are, like the structural openings of all novels, clearly located in fixed textual positions, the chronological beginning of Tan's narrative is not. The earliest diegetic moment is, perhaps, easy to identify in a single linear narrative; but, a text like *The Joy Luck Club* is difficult to view as a single entity at all. It seems more appropriate to refer to the text's *narratives*. And yet, even when we recognize their plurality, the actual earliest moments, or chronological beginnings, of all of these narratives are elusive. This fact is represented structurally in the complex chronological arrangement of Tan's text, as well as thematically in each of the stories. The numerous flashbacks and concurrent narratives that characterize the chronological organization of *The Joy Luck Club* challenge the idea of history as linear and objectively knowable. Each section of the text is narrated from a different perspective, many of the incidents occurring simultaneously. For example, through flashbacks, we learn about Lindo Jong's first arranged marriage, which coincides with Suyuan Woo's experience in Kweilin. Both stories take place during the Japanese invasion of China, and yet the two experiences are markedly different. For Lindo, the war remains a backdrop to her personal experiences, while, for Suyuan, the war represents a catalyst for a personal tragedy from which she will never fully recover. We cannot choose one woman's experience as more representative than the other's, nor can we choose one view of the war's impact over another. In understanding these simultaneously occurring events and experiences as equally important, we as readers will find it impossible to choose one as the definitive chronological beginning of the novel. This non-linear structure, accordingly, undermines the teleology often associated with traditional narrative sequence, which, as feminist theorists like Margaret Homans, Nancy K. Miller, and Rachel Blau DuPlessis have asserted, is linked to restrictive conceptions of femininity.[9] The novel combines what is traditionally seen as the "personal" history of women with the typically male-centered "public" history of war, destabilizing the hierarchical relationship between these seemingly opposing narratives. It undermines a nationalist conception of history as progress, as a "shared real or imagined past . . . [that] defines the present in the trajectory toward a common future" (Moallem and Boal 251).[10] This conception of history is reinforced by nationalist narrative, which as Mary N. Layoun argues, strives "to give the impression of coherence" (251). And, as Alarcón, Kaplan, and Moallem explain, this coherence is enmeshed in patriarchy, engendering exclusion of women from participation in the nation-state, which according to these critiques, is the "central site of 'hegemonic masculinity'" (Alarcón et al. 1). Tan's structure counters this narrative by depicting the many disjointed trajectories that history takes through the stories of these individual women. Unlike national historical myths, which tend to imply progress toward either successful immigration/assimilation or a return to authentic cultural origins, the directions that history takes in the stories of Tan's women cannot be perceived in terms of progress. Instead, the movements from China to the United States and back to China are lateral, significant because of the material effects they have upon the women of Tan's story. Thus, the text implies a more complex understanding of the relationship among cultural origins, history, and the development of individual female and cultural identities.

Just as a chronological beginning to the novel itself is impossible to locate, so too are the causal beginnings of the individual characters' narratives. Causal beginnings, like chronological beginnings, are especially elusive in modern and postmodern narratives. These narrative moments are not connected to any fixed textual location or to any particular place in time. Borrowing from Prince's definition of a "narrative beginning" (Prince 10), they are instead defined as the moment or moments in a story that represent the catalyst for the main action. This beginning is clearly the most subjective in that each reader may have his/her own interpretation of what qualifies as the catalyst. And yet, despite its subjective nature, it can be key in identifying important cultural work being performed by a text. As *The Joy Luck Club* progresses, we read a narrative about each mother-daughter relationship first from the daughter's perspective and then from the mother's. Inhibiting the reader's ability to locate a causal beginning to the struggles within each mother/daughter narrative, the text structurally and causally links each daughter's present problems directly to her own childhood in the United States as well as to her mother's past in China. For example, in "American Translation" we hear from Lena's point of view about her unhappy marriage to Harold.

And later in "Queen Mother of the Western Skies" we read about the same situation from her mother Ying Ying's viewpoint. Ying Ying attributes her daughter's instability in the present directly to her own past weakness: "Now I must tell my daughter everything. That she is the daughter of a ghost. She has no *chi*. This is my greatest shame. How can I leave this world without leaving her my spirit?" (286). Lena, however, finds a different origin to her present marital strife, seeing it as something she deserves for mistakes made as a child: "I still feel that somehow, for the most part, we deserve what we get . . . I got Harold" (168). The mothers return to their Chinese roots to understand their daughters' present strife, while the daughters locate the origin of their pain in their American childhoods. Neither causal beginning is placed in a more structurally prominent position; nor is one legitimized by content over the other. The novel leaves the reader vacillating between two causes, two origins of the daughters' identities; it thereby disrupts a sense of sequentiality, portraying identity as "simultaneously" constructed, a state of being described by Ketu H. Katrak as a "simultaneous present of being both here and there . . . challeng[ing] the linearity of time and specificity of space by juxtaposing . . . here and now . . . with histories and past geographies" (202). The text, therefore, acknowledges an integral continuity between the past in China and the present in the United States.

Thematic Origins: Subjectivity and Deferral

The representation of thematic origins is, perhaps, best illustrated through the repetition of Suyuan Woo's "Kweilin" story, a self-created myth of origin, which she and other characters begin to tell over and over again. Like Tan's novel itself, the deferred telling of Suyuan's full story can be read as manifesting a compulsion to recover the defining moment of one's identity at the same time her tale refutes the possibility of such a recovery. June searches for knowledge of her own beginnings through her mother's story, in much the same way that Suyuan attempts to recover her whole self by repetitively beginning her originary story. June describes her mother's obsession with the telling of this story:

> Joy Luck was an idea my mother remembered from the days of her first marriage in Kweilin, before the Japanese came. That's why I think of the Joy Luck as her Kweilin story. It was the story she would always tell me when she was bored, when there was nothing to do . . . This is when my mother would take out a box of old ski sweat-

ers sent to us by unseen relatives from Vancouver. She would snip the bottom of a sweater and pull out a kinky thread of yarn, anchoring it to a piece of cardboard. And as she began to roll with one sweeping rhythm, she would start her story. Over the years she told me the same story, except for the ending, which grew darker, casting long shadows into her life, and eventually into mine.

(7)

Significantly, like the yarn of the sweaters Suyuan unravels, she dismantles the complex weave of her story each time she begins to tell it, re-forming it, like the balls of yarn she tightly winds, into a new and re-usable shape constructed from the substance of the previous form. Suyuan's story and the way that she relates it thematically represent the text's conception of the past and its connection to individual identity; for the organized pattern of the sweater may also be read to symbolize both History and authentic subjectivity. Like Suyuan, Tan's novel attempts to snip the threads that hold these tightly knitted structures together, unraveling them as it constructs new ideas of history and identity which are at once subjective, personal, and polymorphous.

Just as the story evolves when Suyuan tells it to June, it is also significantly altered by the several characters who advance the narrative after Suyuan's death, each storyteller attempting to decipher the "truth" of this originary story. And yet, the novel asserts no version of this narrative as definitive, just as it posits no authoritative representation of history; each remains in dialogue with the other, none on its own signifying an essential truth. The concepts of storytelling and history, then, are directly connected to one another, as we see when closely examining the final telling of the Kweilin story. When June travels to China to meet her sisters, her father again begins to tell her mother's story, this time attempting to close it. In its final version, however, the historical event of the invasion of Kweilin by Japanese soldiers seems to permeate the "personal" story of Suyuan's lost babies. This conflation of the personal and historical dismantles the dichotomy of personal/private vs. historical/public and interrogates notions of truth and the power of representation:

> "Japanese in Kweilin? says Aiyi [June's Aunt]. "That was never the case. Couldn't be. The Japanese never came to Kweilin."

> "Yes, that is what the newspapers reported. I know this because I was working for the news bureau at the time. The Kuomintang often told us what we could say and could not say. But we knew the Japanese had come into Kwangsi Province. We had sources who told us how they had captured

the Wuchang-Canton railway. How they were coming overland, making very fast progress, marching toward the provincial capital."

(321)

The contradictions between personal experiences and documented history exemplified by this passage clearly exhibit the text's play with notions of history and objectivity, for they make apparent the fact that the representation of historical events is as manipulable and subject to questions of power as storytelling. Thus, by complicating notions of historical objectivity and truth, Tan examines the way in which political power affects the representation of historical events as well as an understanding of individual subjectivity.

The completion of Suyuan's story is continually deferred in an attempt to recover an irretrievable past which represents her unknowable beginning. The deferral of this narrative, however, may also be seen to signify an anxiety over representation, which, as we have seen, is a theme continually worked through in Tan's novel. The inability of the other *Joy Luck Club* characters to tell Suyuan's story in its entirety, therefore, symbolizes the impossibility of depicting an authentic subject through language. This same anxiety is expressed when June's aunties tell her that she must visit her sisters and tell them of her mother: "What will I say? What can I tell them about my mother? I don't know anything. She was my mother" (31). June's apprehension, expressive of the novel's concern with the representation of subjectivity, is never quelled and the question of how to represent an authentic subject is not definitively answered. Instead, the metaphoric search for an authentic and stable identity represented by the search for origins in the Kweilin story is, like the story itself, destined to remain infinitely fragmented and ultimately irretrievable, for it refers only to other discursive representations whose "truth" can never be discerned.

Although we as readers learn more about Suyuan each time the Kweilin story is begun, we never receive the complete story, only fragments that we must try to piece together to compose the whole narrative. The text, nonetheless, renders this act of construction impossible, for it mixes fact, myth, and incomplete memories seemingly indiscriminately among the narrative pieces. Accordingly, neither the reader nor June can distinguish between them: "I never thought my mother's Kweilin story was anything but a Chinese fairy tale" (12). Although we might suspect much about the origins of the Joy Luck Club to be fable, neither the text nor Suyuan distinguishes this ele-

ment of the narrative as more or less truthful than the other fragments. Moreover, June's interpretation of the new versions of the story (told by her aunties and her father) are inextricably colored by her previous knowledge. Instead of referring to a "real" event for her, the story as told by her mother's friends only refers back to stories her mother had told her. She remembers the refrain from one of those stories ("You are not those babies") and can only think of her sisters the way they were represented in her mother's narratives, as babies:

> The babies in Kweilin. I think. I was not those babies. The babies in a sling on her shoulder. Her other daughters. And now I feel as if I were in Kweilin amidst the bombing and I can see these babies lying on the side of the road, their red thumbs popped out of their mouths, screaming to be reclaimed. Somebody took them away. They're safe. And now my mother's left me forever, gone back to China to get these babies.
>
> (29)

Even Suyuan's knowledge of her own story is intertextual, for it refers back to prior versions of the story as well as to other narratives, all of which are inseparably combined with the language of fairy tale and myth:

> Oh, what good stories! Stories spilling out all over the place! We almost laughed to death. . . . We feasted, we laughed, we played games, lost and won, we told the best stories. And each week, we could hope to be lucky. That hope was our only joy. And that's how we came to call our little parties Joy Luck.
>
> (11-12)

The language used here, like that of the first opening myth, ironically mimics the language of fairy tale causing the line between fact and fiction to be irreparably blurred for both June and the reader. We cannot always separate what is performance from what is factual, thus we are forced to interrogate our own notions of truth, as well as the nature of history and identity.

It only appears to be ironic that I wish to conclude my discussion of narrative beginnings in *The Joy Luck Club* with a look at the ending of the novel; for it seems clear that these beginnings have resonance throughout the entirety of the novel, its close being no exception. It has been argued that Tan's text ends on a note of reconciliation, forcing to quiescence all of the contradictions and interrogations raised throughout; however, if we choose to examine the ending(s) in light of the novel's many beginnings, such a reading is, perhaps, dislodged. That is, by focusing on the way the beginnings of this text foreground a search for origins, we see that the endings to the many narratives actually leave the conclusion of this quest quite open.

Because the endings of Suyuan's and June's stories are the most easily perceived as conciliatory, it is on their conclusions that I will focus most closely. Suyuan's search as well as the telling of her story, as I have intimated, is displaced onto June throughout the text. And although it might be argued that this quest achieves resolution through June's trip to China, the fact that Suyuan dies before returning herself to China means that she can never be said to have actually achieved her goal; symbolically, she never recovers her origins. Instead, the displacement of this achievement onto June leaves it indefinitely deferred, the goal eternally displaced. Similarly, June's search for her mother/origin is displaced onto her sisters. When she finally reaches China she sees her mother in the faces of her two sisters ("Together we look like our mother. Her same eyes, her same mouth, open in surprise to see, at last, her long-cherished wish"); however, the text acknowledges that the daughters "look like," or signify their mother, but they are not actually her (332). June, therefore, can only recover the sign of her mother/origin, never her actual mother. Additionally, although the daughters, as representatives of their mother, see her "long-cherished wish" come to fruition, Suyuan herself does not.

Finally, in much the same way the denouement of June and Suyuan's story is displaced and deferred, so are the resolutions of the other mother-daughter stories. For, none of these narratives actually end in resolution. Like the other stories, Waverly and Lindo's narrative ends with unresolved questions: "What did I lose? What did I get back in return? I will ask my daughter what she thinks" (305). Certainly, adhered to these questions is a hope for future answers, but no real sense of closure. Instead, the perception of closure comes exclusively through June and Suyuan's story, which, as we have seen, simultaneously offers and rescinds this sense of resolution for the reader. Thus, by giving a sense of closure without "real" resolution, Tan's novel subverts the notion that the contradictions set up by both the content and form of her novel can be reconciled. For as Trinh has argued: "Closures need not close off; they can be doors opening onto other closures and functioning as ongoing passages to an elsewhere (-within-here) . . . The closure here . . . is a way of letting the work go rather than of sealing it off" (15).

Narrative beginnings in *The Joy Luck Club* invoke questions about origins, cultural identity, individual subjectivity, gendered identity, and history; they, therefore, enable a critical interrogation and reconfiguration of these ideas. Destabilizing a nationalist conception of cultural, national, and historical subjectivity, which relies heavily upon the recovery of origins, Tan's text suggests an alternative narrative based upon a feminist, contingent, contradictory, and heterogeneous conception of history. The understanding that narrative beginnings are integrally connected to questions of narrativity and social identity undermines notions of authentic subjectivity accomplished through the recovery of an originary historical moment. This study, through an illustrative reading of *The Joy Luck Club,* stresses the necessity of focusing instead on a broader, more fluid sense of the historical and material conditions giving rise to gendered and racialized subjectivities. This way of considering narrative beginnings is vital to ensuring that we attend to difference on all levels and in all formal elements of narrative, a focus which helps to make visible the roles these cultural factors play in our critical reading and writing practices.

Notes

1. I would like to acknowledge the help and support of the following mentors, friends, and colleagues: Kandice Chuh, Brian Richardson, Emily Orlando, and Scott A. Melby.

2. Although Edward Said's *Beginnings* is an example of an extensive philosophical examination of the concept of beginnings, Said does not include in this study a consideration of the formal functions of beginnings within narratives; nor does he consider the implications of social identity in relation to formal beginnings.

3. Nutall's use of parentheses in this statement is particularly telling in that it seems to reveal a certain reluctance to admit that his all-male study may not be universally representative.

4. This study of narrative beginnings in *The Joy Luck Club* is part of a larger project on beginnings in women's literature. The framework for the larger project has been derived through my examination of Tan's text.

5. See Lisa Lowe, Melani McAlister, and Malini Johar Schueller for discussions of the misreading of Tan's novel. Lowe, for example, points to the tendency of *The Joy Luck Club* to be appropriated as a text that "privatizes social conflicts and contradictions" by figuring "broader social shifts of Chinese immigrant formation" as a "generational conflict" and "'feminized' relations between mothers and daughters" (78). She has asserted that *The Joy Luck Club* actually critiques the way this trope of mother-daughter relationships has become a symbol for Asian American culture and has rendered cultural and class differences in conceptions of gender invisible (80). Malini Johar

Schueller uses Lisa Lowe's theories of ethnic and racial subjectivity to discuss how Tan's text works to "affirm a politics of resistance and difference," and to emphasize the "discursive nature of gender and ethnic identity" (74). Also see Patricia Hamilton and Yuan Yuan, who both offer alternative, perhaps less universalizing, readings of the "generational conflict."

While, as my examples show, many scholars have recently sought to look beyond the generational conflict that so clearly underestimates this text's complexity, most have not recognized the important role narrative form plays in *The Joy Luck Club*. I will be stressing this role.

6. For example, some feminist scholars, such as Bonnie Braindlin and Gloria Shen, read Tan's text as a universal exploration of mother-daughter relationships. Similarly, such scholars of American literature as Walter Shear tend to identify *The Joy Luck Club* as an example of the "successful-immigrant" narrative. And still further, many scholars of Asian American literature such as Sau-Ling Cynthia Wong read Tan's text as a narrative which encourages orientalist views of the Chinese American community.

7. Although there is not space to discuss each example, all of Tan's characters are involved in a search for an origin of some type. Each daughter, for example, searches in some way for her own origins as she seeks to know her mother. Furthermore, as Schueller has noted, this search for mothers may be interpreted as a metaphoric search for the motherland.

8. Each character's search for a definitive moment of identity formation is similarly undermined. For instance, although each daughter comes closer to a complete knowledge of her mother, she can never fully achieve her goal, for much of the mother's past is unknowable. Moreover, the mothers only represent a small portion of the daughters' discursively constructed identities, which are variously formed by the stories their mothers tell, their education in U.S. schools, and their exposure to the media's representations of their cultural heritage.

9. Although many feminist scholars of narrative assert that sequential narrative form is inherently conservative and restrictive, this essay takes the position that narrative form in and of itself is without inherent ideological value; the ideological valences are instead attributable to the "social uses that can be made of [narrative form]," to use Margaret Homan's words (7). See Brian Richardson in his recent essay "Linearity and Its Discontents: Rethinking Narrative Form and Ideological Valence," where he discusses this issue extensively, arguing against those who would assert inherent political value in literary form.

10. For scholarship on narratives of nationalism, see *Between Woman and Nation*, eds. Kaplan et al.

Works Cited

Alarcón, Norma et al. "Introduction: Between Woman and Nation." *Between Woman and Nation: Nationalisms, Transnational Feminisms, and the State*. Eds. Caren Kaplan, Norma Alarcón, and Minoo Moallem. Durham: Duke UP, 1999.

Balibar, Etienne and Immanuel Wallerstein. *Race, Nation, Class: Ambiguous Identities*. New York: Verson, 1991.

Bhabha, Homi K. *The Location of Culture*. New York: Routledge, 1994.

Braendlin, Bonnie. "Mother/Daughter Dialog(ic)s In Around and About Amy Tan's *The Joy Luck Club*." *Synthesis: An Interdisciplinary Journal* 1.2 (Fall 1995): 41-53.

Chin, Frank. "Come All Ye Asian American Writers of the Real and the Fake." *An Anthology of Chinese American and Japanese American Literature*. Eds. Jeffrey Chan et al. New York: Penguin, 1991.

DuPlessis, Rachel Blau. *Writing Beyond the Ending: Narrative Strategies of Twentieth-Century Women Writers*. Bloomington: Indiana UP, 1985.

Hamilton, Patricia L. "Feng Shui, Astrology, and the Five Elements: Traditional Chinese Belief in Amy Tan's *The Joy Luck Club*." *MELUS* 24.2 (Summer 1999): 125-45.

Homans, Margaret. "Feminist Fictions and Feminist Theories of Narrative." *Narrative* 2 (1994): 3-16.

Hutchinson, John. "Cultural Nationalism and Moral Regeneration." *Nationalism*. Eds. John Hutchinson and Anthony B. Smith. New York: Oxford UP, 1994. 122-31.

Katrak, Ketu H. "South Asian American Literature." *An Interethnic Companion to Asian American Literature*. Ed. Kingkok Cheung. Cambridge: Cambridge UP, 1997. 192-218.

Kellman, Steven G. "Grand Openings and Plain: The Poetics of First Lines." *Sub-Stance* 17 (1977): 139-47.

Lanser, Susan S. "Queering Narratology." *Ambiguous Discourse: Feminist Narratology and British Women Writers*. Chapel Hill: U of North Carolina P, 1996. 250-61.

Layoun, Mary N. "A Guest at the Wedding." *Between Woman and Nation*. Eds. Caren Kaplan et al. Durham: Duke UP, 1999. 92-107.

Lowe, Lisa. *Immigrant Acts*. Durham: Duke UP, 1996.

McAlister, Melani. "(Mis)Reading *The Joy Luck Club*." *Asian America: Journal of Culture and the Arts* 1 (1992): 102-18.

Miller, Nancy K. "Emphasis Added: Plots and Plausibilities in Women's Fiction." *PMLA* 96 (1981): 36-48.

Moallem, Minoo and Iain A. Boal. "Multicultural Nationalism and the Poetics of Inauguration." *Between Woman and Nation*. Eds. Caren Kaplan et al. Durham: Duke UP, 1999. 243-63.

Nuttall, A. D. *Openings: Narrative Beginnings from the Epic to the Novel*. Oxford: Clarendon Press, 1992.

Phelan, James. "Beginnings and Endings: Theories and Typologies of How Novels Open and Close." *Encyclopedia of the Novel*. Ed. Paul Schellinger. Chicago: Fitzroy Dearborn, 1998. 96-99.

Prince, Gerald. *A Dictionary of Narratology*. Lincoln: U of Nebraska P, 1987.

Richardson, Brian. "Linearity and its Discontents: Rethinking Narrative Form and Ideological Valence." *College English*. 2000.

Said, Edward W. *Beginnings*. New York: Basic Books Inc., Publishers, 1975.

Schueller, Malini Johar. "Theorizing Ethnicity and Subjectivity: Maxine Hong Kingston's *Tripmaster Monkey* and Amy Tan's *The Joy Luck Club*." *Genders* 15 (Winter 1992): 72-85.

Shear, Walter. "Generational Differences and the Diaspora in *The Joy Luck Club*." *Critique* 34.3 (Spring 1993): 193-99.

Shen, Gloria. "Born of a Stranger: Mother-Daughter Relationships and Storytelling in Amy Tan's *The Joy Luck Club*." *International Women's Writing: New Landscapes of Identity*. Westport: Greenwood P, 1995. 233-44.

Takagi, Dana Y. "Maiden Voyage: Excursion into Sexuality and Identity Politics in Asian America." *Asian American Sexualities: Dimensions of the Gay and Lesbian Experience*. Ed. Russell Leong. New York: Routledge, 1996. 21-37.

Tan, Amy. *The Joy Luck Club*. New York: Ivy Books, 1989.

Trinh, T. Minh-Ha. *When The Moon Waxes Red: Representation, Gender, and Cultural Politics*. New York: Routledge, 1991.

Wong, Sau-Ling Cynthia. "'Sugar Sisterhood': Situating the Amy Tan Phenomenon." *The Ethnic Canon: Histories Institutions, and Interventions*. Ed. David Palumbo-Liu, Minneapolis: U of Minnesota P, 1995. 175-210.

Yuan, Yuan. "The Semiotics of China Narratives in the Con/ Texts of Kingston and Tan." *Critique* 40.3 (Spring 1999): 292-303.

FURTHER READING

Criticism

Bow, Leslie. "*The Joy Luck Club* by Amy Tan." In *A Resource Guide to Asian American Literature*, edited by Sau-ling Cynthia Wong and Stephen H. Sumida. New York: Modern Language Association of America, 2001, 345 p.

A bio-critical essay, with bibliography, concerned with The Joy Luck Club.

Braendlin, Bonnie. "Mother/Daughter Dialog(ic)s In Around and About Amy Tan's *The Joy Luck Club*." *Synthesis: An Interdisciplinary Journal* 1, no. 2 (fall 1995): 41-53.

Offers a feminist approach to assessing Tan's depiction of mother-daughter relationships.

Cooperman, Jeanette Batz. *The Broom Closet: Secret Meanings of Domesticity in Postfeminist Novels by Louise Erdrich, Mary Gordon, Toni Morrison, Marge Piercy, Jane Smiley, and Amy Tan*. New York: Peter Lang Publishing, 1999, 239 p.

Examines domestic rituals as they appear in novels by major contemporary women writers, including Tan.

Heung, Mariña. "Daughter-Text-Mother/Mother-Text: Matrilineage in Amy Tan's *Joy Luck Club*." *Feminist Studies* 19, no. 3 (fall 1993): 597-616.

Asserts that "despite Tan's explicit embrace of a daughter's perspective, The Joy Luck Club *is remarkable for foregrounding the voices of mothers as well as of daughters."*

Houston, Marsha. "Women and the Language of Race and Ethnicity." *Women and Language* 17, no. 1 (spring 1995): 1-7.

Traces the importance of multiple languages in The Joy Luck Club *and Maxine Hong Kingston's* The Woman Warrior.

Huntley, E. D. *Amy Tan: A Critical Companion*. Westport, Conn.: Greenwood Publishing Group, 1998, 184 p.

Collection of essays covering numerous aspects of Tan's work.

Nagel, James. *The Contemporary American Short-Story Cycle: The Ethnic Resonance of Genre*. Baton Rouge, La.: Louisiana State University Press, 2001, 297 p.

Examines ethnicity in The Joy Luck Club.

Souris, Stephen. "'Only Two Kinds of Daughters': Inter-monologue Dialogicity in *The Joy Luck Club*." *MELUS* 19, no. 2 (summer 1994): 99-124.

Uses dynamic reader models to illustrate how readers are challenged to find the interconnections in The Joy Luck Club.

Wachtel, Eleanor. "Amy Tan." In *Writers and Company*, pp. 273-89. New York: Harcourt Brace and Company, 1993.

Interview in which Tan discusses the impact of her mother on her work; the role of women in Chinese society; and how differences between Chinese and American behavior have influenced her writing.

OTHER SOURCES FROM GALE:

Additional coverage of Tan's life and career is contained in the following sources published by the Gale Group: *American Writers Supplement*, Vol. 10; *Asian American Literature*; *Authors and Artists for Young Adults*, Vols. 9, 48; *Beacham's Encyclopedia of Popular Fiction: Biography and Resources*, Vol. 3; *Bestsellers*, Vol. 89:3; *Concise Dictionary of American Literary Biography Supplement*; *Contemporary Authors*, Vol. 136; *Contemporary Authors New Revision Series*, Vols. 54, 105; *Contemporary Literary Criticism*, Vols. 59, 120, 151; *Contemporary Novelists*, Ed. 7; *Contemporary Popular Writers*, Ed. 1; *Dictionary of Literary Biography*, Vol. 173; *DISCovering Authors Modules: Multicultural, Novelists*, and *Popular*; *DISCovering Authors 3.0*; *Exploring Novels*; *Feminist Writers*; *Literature and Its Times*, Vols. 3, 5; *Major 20th-Century Writers*, Ed. 2; *Novels for Students*, Vols. 1, 13, 16; *Reference Guide to American Literature*, Ed. 4; *St. James Guide to Young Adult Writers*; *Short Stories for Students*, Vol. 9; and *Something about the Author*, Vol. 75.

ALICE WALKER

(1944 -)

American novelist, short story writer, essayist, poet, critic, editor, and author of children's books.

The acclaimed writer of the Pulitzer Prize-winning novel *The Color Purple* (1982), Walker has asserted that for her writing is a way to correct wrongs that she observes in the world, and that she has dedicated herself to delineating the unique dual oppression from which black women suffer: racism and sexism. Her work is an exploration of the individual identity of the black woman; in it she examines how embracing her identity and bonding with other women affects the health of her community at large. Walker describes this kinship among women as "womanism," as opposed to feminism.

BIOGRAPHICAL INFORMATION

Walker was born February 9, 1944, and grew up, along with seven older brothers and sisters in Eatonton, Georgia, where her father was a share-cropper. When she was eight years old, one of her brothers accidentally shot her with his BB gun, leaving her scarred and blind in one eye until age fourteen when she underwent surgery to remove the scar tissue. The disfigurement made Walker shy and self-conscious, and she turned to writing as a means of expressing herself. Though Walker

had a tenuous relationship with her father, she notes that she respected her mother's strength and perseverance in the face of poverty, and she recalls how hard her mother worked in her garden to create beauty in even the shabbiest of conditions. Despite a disadvantaged childhood, Walker earned a scholarship to Spelman College. She attended Spelman for two years, became disenchanted with what she considered a puritanical atmosphere there, and transferred to Sarah Lawrence College in Bronxville, New York, to complete her education. While at Sarah Lawrence, Walker wrote her first collection of poetry, *Once* (1968), in reaction to a traumatic abortion she experienced during her senior year of college. Walker shared the poems with one of her teachers, poet Muriel Rukeyser, whose agent found a publisher for them.

After college, Walker moved to Mississippi to work as a teacher and a civil rights advocate. In 1967 she married Melvyn Leventhal, a Jewish civil rights attorney; they became the first legally married interracial couple to reside in Jackson, Mississippi. Walker and Leventhal had a daughter, Rebecca; they divorced in 1976. While working in Mississippi, Walker discovered the writings of Zora Neale Hurston, an author whose works greatly influenced Walker's later work. Walker eventually edited a collection of Hurston's fiction called *I Love Myself When I Am Laughing . . . and Then Again When I Am Looking Mean and Impressive: A Zora Neale Hurston Reader* (1979). In addition to poetry, Walker has written short stories, collected in *In Love and Trouble* (1973) and *You Can't Keep a Good Woman Down* (1981), and several novels, most notably *The Color Purple,* which received both the Pulitzer Prize and the American Book Award.

MAJOR WORKS

Walker's first novel, *The Third Life of Grange Copeland* (1970), introduces many of the themes that became prevalent in her later work, particularly the domination of powerless women by equally powerless men. The novel follows three generations of a black southern family of sharecroppers and its patriarch, Grange Copeland, as they struggle with racism and poverty. In Grange's "first life" he tortures his wife until she commits suicide. His son Brownfield inherits Grange's sense of helplessness and hatred, and eventually murders his own wife. In Grange's "second life" he attempts to escape to the industrial North. Walker does not present industrial labor as a viable solution to the poverty of the South, however, and in his "third life" Grange returns to his southern home. At the end of the novel, Grange has become a compassionate man who longs to atone for the legacy of hate he has left his family, attempting to help his granddaughter Ruth escape from her father (Brownfield) and the South as a gesture of his remorse. Another prominent theme in Walker's fiction deals with the ways in which black women seek "wholeness" and this quest's impact on the health of the community. The attempt at wholeness comes from remaining true to one's self and fighting against the constraints of society, as portrayed in the stories from Walker's collection *In Love and Trouble.*

Walker's novel *Meridian* (1976) is considered an autobiographical work. The title character is born in the rural South, like Walker, and uses education as a means of escape. Pregnant and married to a high school dropout, Meridian struggles with thoughts of suicide or killing her child, but eventually decides to give the child up and attend college. After graduating, she enters an organization of black militants in Mississippi, but realizes she is not willing to kill for the cause. With this knowledge she resolves to return to rural Mississippi to help its residents struggle against oppression.

In *The Color Purple,* Walker uses an epistolary form to create a woman-centered focus for her novel. The letters span thirty years in the life of Celie, a poor southern black woman. Celie is victimized physically and emotionally by her stepfather, who repeatedly rapes her and then takes their children away from her, and by her husband, an older widower who sees her more as a mule than as a wife. Celie's letters are written to God and to Celie's sister Nettie, who escaped a similar life by becoming a missionary in Africa. Celie overcomes her oppression with the intervention of an unlikely ally, her husband's mistress, Shug Avery. Shug helps Celie find self-esteem and the courage to leave her marriage. By the end of the novel, Celie is reunited with her children and her sister.

The Temple of My Familiar (1989) is an ambitious novel recording 500,000 years of human history. The novel's central character, Miss Lissie, is a goddess from primeval Africa who has been incarnated hundreds of times throughout history. She befriends Suwelo, a narcissistic university professor whose marriage is threatened by his need to dominate and sexually exploit his wife. Through a series of conversations with Miss Lissie and her friend Hal, Suwelo learns of Miss Lissie's innumerable lives and experiences—from the prehistoric world in which humans and animals lived in harmony under a matriarchal society to slavery in the United States—and regains his capability to love, nurture, and respect himself and others.

In *Possessing the Secret of Joy* (1992), Walker examines the practice of female genital mutilation. The novel focuses on Tashi, a woman who willingly requests the ritual, in part because she is unaware of what the ceremony involves. Since discussion of the ritual is taboo in her culture, Tashi is ignorant of the profound impact the procedure will have on her life. This ritual is further examined in *Warrior Marks* (1994), a nonfiction account of this ceremony that is still practiced in many parts of the world. Walker also collaborated with Indian filmmaker Pratibha Parmar to produce a film with the same title. The book covers the making of the film as well as bringing to light the consequences of this practice.

CRITICAL RECEPTION

There are several widely debated aspects of Walker's writing. One such aspect is her portrayal of black male characters as archetypes of black men in modern society. Many reviewers condemn her portrayals of black men as unnecessarily negative, pointing to the vile characters in some of her work and to her own comments about black men as evidence of enmity on her part. Other critics assert that the author, in presenting flawed characters, reveals typical shortcomings in the hope that real people burdened with these flaws will recognize themselves in her stories and strive to improve. Some reviewers also assert that Walker's work contains positive images of black men that are often ignored by critics. Beyond her portrayal of black men, some reviewers have found fault with Walker's characterization in general, opposing her tendency to refer to characters only with pronouns, thereby encouraging readers to consider the characters exemplary of anyone to whom that pronoun could apply. Finally, Walker's work is often viewed as political in intent, at times to the detriment of its literary value.

In contrast, reviewers praise works such as *In Love and Trouble* for balancing the art of storytelling with political concerns. Critics commend Walker's use of oral storytelling tradition, finding her work most convincing when she employs anecdotal narrative. Overall, critics commend her ability to incorporate a message within her narratives. Critics have also lauded *Warrior Marks* for its exposure of the practice of female genital mutilation. Walker's work consistently reflects her concern with racial, sexual, and political issues—particularly with the black woman's struggle for spiritual survival. Addressing detractors who fault her "unabashedly feminist viewpoint," Walker explained: "The black woman is one of America's greatest heroes. . . . Not enough credit has been given to the black woman who has been oppressed beyond recognition."

PRINCIPAL WORKS

Once: Poems (poetry) 1968

The Third Life of Grange Copeland (novel) 1970

Five Poems (poetry) 1972

In Love and Trouble: Stories of Black Women (short stories) 1973

Revolutionary Petunias and Other Poems (poetry) 1973

Langston Hughes: American Poet (juvenile nonfiction) 1974

Meridian (novel) 1976

Good Night Willie Lee, I'll See You in the Morning (poetry) 1979

I Love Myself When I Am Laughing . . . and Then Again When I Am Looking Mean and Impressive: A Zora Neale Hurston Reader [editor] (fiction) 1979

You Can't Keep a Good Woman Down: Stories (short stories) 1981

The Color Purple (novel) 1982

In Search of Our Mothers' Gardens: Womanist Prose (essays) 1983

Horses Make a Landscape Look More Beautiful: Poems (poetry) 1984

Living by the Word: Selected Writings, 1973-1987 (essays) 1988

To Hell with Dying (juvenile fiction) 1988

The Temple of My Familiar (novel) 1989

Finding the Green Stone (juvenile fiction) 1991

Her Blue Body Everything We Know: Earthling Poems, 1965-1990 (poetry) 1991

Possessing the Secret of Joy (novel) 1992

Warrior Marks: Female Genital Mutilation and the Sexual Blinding of Women [with Pratibha Parmar] (nonfiction) 1994

The Same River Twice: Honoring the Difficult: A Meditation on Life, Spirit, Art, and the Making of the Film "The Color Purple," Ten Years Later (essays) 1996

Anything We Love Can Be Saved: A Writer's Activism (essays) 1997

By the Light of My Father's Smile (novel) 1998

The Way Forward Is with a Broken Heart (short stories) 2000

Absolute Trust in the Goodness of the Earth (poetry) 2003

A Poem Traveled Down My Arm: Poems & Drawings (poetry) 2003

Now Is the Time to Open Your Heart (novel) 2004

PRIMARY SOURCES

ALICE WALKER (POETRY DATE 1971)

SOURCE: Walker, Alice. "'Women' and 'For My Sister Molly Who in the Fifties.'" In *Revolutionary Petunias & Other Poems*, pp. 5, 16-9. New York: Harcourt Brace Jovanovich, Inc., 1971.

In the following poems, Walker admires the feminist struggles of the previous generation of women and of her courageous, adventurous sister.

"Women"

They were women then
My mama's generation
Husky of voice—Stout of
Step
With fists as well as
Hands
How they battered down
Doors
And ironed
Starched white
Shirts
How they led
Armies
Headragged Generals
Across mined
Fields
Booby-trapped
Ditches
To discover books
Desks
A place for us
How they knew what we
Must know
Without knowing a page
Of it
Themselves.

. . . . .

"For My Sister Molly Who in the Fifties"

Once made a fairy rooster from
Mashed potatoes
Whose eyes I forget
But green onions were his tail
And his two legs were carrot sticks
A tomato slice his crown.
Who came home on vacation
When the sun was hot
and cooked
and cleaned
And minded least of all
The children's questions
A million or more
Pouring in on her
Who had been to school
And knew (and told us too) that certain
Words were no longer good
And taught me not to say us for we
No matter what "Sonny said" up the
road.
FOR MY SISTER MOLLY WHO IN THE FIFTIES
Knew Hamlet well and read into the night
And coached me in my songs of Africa
A continent I never knew
But learned to love
Because "they" she said could carry
A tune
And spoke in accents never heard
In Eatonton.
Who read from *Prose and Poetry*
And loved to read "Sam McGee from Tennessee"
On nights the fire was burning low
And Christmas wrapped in angel hair

And I for one prayed for snow.
WHO IN THE FIFTIES
Knew all the written things that made
Us laugh and stories by
The hour   Waking up the story buds
Like fruit. Who walked among the flowers
And brought them inside the house
And smelled as good as they
And looked as bright.
Who made dresses, braided
Hair. Moved chairs about
Hung things from walls
Ordered baths
Frowned on wasp bites
And seemed to know the endings
Of all the tales
I had forgot.

. . . . .

WHO OFF INTO THE UNIVERSITY
Went exploring   To London and
To Rotterdam
Prague and to Liberia
Bringing back the news to us
Who knew none of it
But followed
crops and weather
funerals and
Methodist Homecoming;
easter speeches,
groaning church.
WHO FOUND ANOTHER WORLD
Another life   With gentlefolk
Far less trusting
And moved and moved and changed
Her name
And sounded precise
When she spoke.   And frowned away
Our sloppishness.
WHO SAW US SILENT
Cursed with fear   A love burning
Inexpressible
And sent me money not for me
But for "College."
Who saw me grow through letters
The words misspelled   But not
The longing   Stretching
Growth
The tied and twisting
Tongue
Feet no longer bare
Skin no longer burnt against
The cotton.
WHO BECAME SOMEONE OVERHEAD
A light   A thousand watts
Bright and also blinding
And saw my brothers cloddish
And me destined to be
Wayward
My mother remote   My father
A wearisome farmer
With heartbreaking
Nails.
FOR MY SISTER MOLLY WHO IN THE FIFTIES
Found much
Unbearable
Who walked where few had
Understood   And sensed our

Groping after light
And saw some extinguished
And no doubt mourned.
FOR MY SISTER MOLLY WHO IN THE FIFTIES
Left us.

GENERAL COMMENTARY

RUTH D. WESTON (ESSAY DATE SPRING-SUMMER 1992)

SOURCE: Weston, Ruth D. "Who Touches This Touches a Woman: The Naked Self in Alice Walker." *Weber Studies* 9, no. 2 (spring-summer 1992): 49-62.

In the following essay, Weston contrasts Walker's verse with that of Walt Whitman, finding that Walker presents a uniquely feminist perspective on love, sexuality, and self-worth.

In *The New York Times Book Review* for March 9, 1986, Alicia Ostriker celebrates American women poets who refuse to be limited by the masculine ideal of "universal," meaning nonfemale, poetry. Ostriker believes that the writing of these women poets during the last twenty-five years constitutes a shaping force in American poetry. Their passionate, intimate poems "defy divisions between emotion and intellect, private and public, life and art, writer and reader," reminding us, she says, of the frank sexuality of Walt Whitman's poems, so aptly characterized by his own words: "Camerado, this is no book, / Who touches this touches a man." Such an impulse is alive today in both the poems and the stories of Alice Walker. Her work has been previously linked to Whitman's because of both poets' celebration of the common problems that unite and divide people (Gernes 93-94), yet hers is a uniquely feminist—Walker would say "womanist" (*In Search* xii) perspective.

Whitman assumed his personal experience to be the universal experience, but it was more precisely the masculine universal. Walker writes about black women with the authority of the universal female experience, an experience made complex and contradictory by the phenomenon of love. Although some black critics, like Ishmael Reed, charge that white feminists' interest in black women's writing constitutes "intellectual fraud" (qtd. in Watkins 36), which exploits black women and undermines the black community (Watkins 36; qtd. in Sharpe et al 149), Patricia Sharpe and her colleagues explain white feminists' ability for cross-racial identity. Initially recognizing the basis of such identity in anthropological theories of female "liminality" as a locus of power (See

FROM THE AUTHOR

WALKER ON THE IMPORTANCE OF BLACK FEMALE VOICES

When we look back over our history it is clear that we have neglected to save just those people who could help us most. Because no matter what anyone says, it is the black woman's words that have the most meaning for us, her daughters, because she, like us, has experienced life not only as a black person, but as a woman; and it was *different* being Frederick Douglass than being Harriet Tubman—or Sojourner Truth, who only "looked like a man," but bore children and saw them sold into slavery.

I thought of the black women writers and poets whose books—even today—go out of print while other works about all of us, less valuable if more "profitable," survive to insult us with their half-perceived, half-rendered "truths." How simple a thing it seems to me that to know ourselves as we are, we must know our mothers' names. Yet, we do not know them. Or if we do, it is only the names we know and not the lives.

And I thought of the mountain of work black women must do. We must work as if we are the last generation capable of work—for it is true that the view we have of the significance of the past will undoubtedly die with us, and future generations will have to stumble in the dark, over ground we should have covered.

Walker, Alice. Excerpt from "A Letter to the Editor of *Ms.*" (1974). In her *In Search of Our Mothers' Gardens: Womanist Prose*, pp. 273-77. New York: Harcourt Brace Jovanovich, 1983.

Mascia-Lees et al), they have recently refined their analysis by pointing out women's common experience of victimization. These critics argue that:

> [W]e, as white feminists, are drawn to black women's visions because they concretize and make vivid a system of oppression . . . [and] abuse. . . . [And further, that] it has not been unusual for white women writers to seek to understand their oppression through reference to the atrocities experienced by other oppressed

groups. Sylvia Plath, for example, likened her feelings of rejection . . . by her father to the treatment of Jews under Nazism. . . .

(Sharpe et al 146)

Alice Walker's song of the self, although ultimately a celebration (Davis 38-53), differs from Whitman's not only in expected ways due to their respective genders, races, and eras. It differs more basically in the fact that, in Walker's fiction and poetry of the Black experience, many women are almost entirely ignorant of love, never having been allowed to share it. What is more, they do not know, much less celebrate, themselves. When they are abused—and they often are—they do not know the value of the self that has been violated. Celebrations, in such circumstances, are necessarily infused with an irony completely alien to Whitman's *Leaves of Grass* period, when he envisioned an ideal equality between men and women.

Even in relationships between women, Walker often shows the undervalued selves of women. In the story **"Everyday Use,"** Maggie suffers psychological scars long after physical healing from burns in a fire set by Dee, her older sister. When the citified and condescending Dee comes to visit, Maggie feels ugly and hides behind the door, providing a graphic symbol of the physical and psychological disfigurement of women that is an important theme in Walker's writing. Similarly, low self-esteem also leads Roselily, in the story that bears her name, to marry the Muslim who will take her away from her home, promising her rest and freedom from the hard work she has always known. But Walker's narrative is laced with images of the new bondage that awaits Roselily in a culture which undervalues women, images which reveal the irony of her hope to be "Free! In robe and veil" (*In Love* 7).

Walker does not ignore the black man's search for self-worth, a theme she explores in **The Third Life of Grange Copeland**; but the casualties of that search are the wives of Grange and Brownfield Copeland. Not only because they are influenced by a macho male white culture (Wallace; qtd. in Sharpe et al 147), but because they are also frustrated in their own claim to manhood, Grange and Brownfield in turn deny their women's every assertion of self-worth. Thus, when Mem raises the family's standard of living, Brownfield systematically destroys first her health and then her spirit. Finally, he blows her face away with a shotgun (172), literally effacing her identity. That Walker intends the scene as an affirmation of the universality of female cultural effacement is clear from her statement in the "Afterword" to the novel that

Mem, "after the French la même, meaning 'the same,'" was so named because the actual murder victim Walker based the story on "in relation to men was . . . symbolic of all women" (344).

The theme of regressive violence within black families is seen even earlier in the poems that reveal how the exigencies of the Civil Rights movement of the 1960s helped Alice Walker to come to terms with personal wounds. An example that she herself has pointed to is that of her poem **"The Democratic Order: Such Things in Twenty Years I Understood"**:

> My father
> (back blistered)
> beat me
> because I
> could not
> stop crying.
> He'd had
> enough 'fuss'
> he said
> for one damn
> voting day.
>
> (*Once* 43)

Although Walker's relationship with her father was not good, the matter of the poem is not strictly autobiographical (Walker *Living* 11), yet it creates an idealized father character that allows her to displace her anxiety about her own father while the poem speaks to the general cultural frustrations that are vented upon women.

In the novel **Meridian,** however, the field of anxiety is broadened to include anxiety about men as sexual "partners." The adolescent Meridian, like many of Walker's female protagonists, becomes afraid of males as soon as she is seen as fair game by boys at school. She submits to Eddie's sexual needs not because they respond to her own but because they

> saved her from the strain of responding to other boys or even noting the whole category of Men. . . . This . . . was probably what sex meant to her; not pleasure but a sanctuary. . . . It was resting from pursuit.
>
> (54-55)

These women are ignorant of the joy of offering themselves as inherently valuable gifts, perhaps, because, as Barbara Christian points out, for such abused women "the body can become the tomb of the mind, [and similarly] the mind's anguish can diminish the body;" thus, Christian continues, Meridian's own guilt for "not living up to her mother's expectations about motherhood," combined with frustration at her sense of powerlessness, results in progressively more serious physical problems: "blue spells," then loss of sight, then temporary paralysis (**Black Women** 216). The world has touched women who have suffered similar experiences, perhaps indelibly marked them, but they are out of touch with themselves.

Celie, in **The Color Purple,** learns both psychological and literal touching of the self. Through her relationships with other women in the novel, she gets in touch with her moral and physical self. Jealous of Sophia's physical strength and sense of authority, and frustrated at her own lack of either quality, Celie strikes out at her by repeating to Harpo the advice his father had given him about how to make his wife obey him: "Beat her" (43). Celie rationalizes:

> I like Sophia, but she don't act like me at all. If she talking when Harpo and Mr.____ come in the room, she keep right on. If they ast her where something at, she say she don't know. Keep talking.
>
> I think bout this when Harpo ast me what he ought to do to her to make her mind. I don't mention how happy he is now. How three years pass and he still whistle and sing. I think bout how every time I jump when Mr.____ call me, she look surprise. And like she pity me.
>
> Beat her. I say.
>
> (43)

When Harpo tries to beat Sophia and gets beaten himself, Celie realizes her culpability but can only turn her guilt inward. When she is abused by her husband, Celie again internalizes her anger. She can't sleep, she feels like throwing up, and finally she feels nothing. Ironically, it is Sophia who calls her to moral responsibility, not only for allowing herself to encourage male brutality to women, but ultimately to responsibility for her own life. Celie's usual response to a beating from the man she calls only Mr.____ has been, "But he my husband. I shrug my shoulders. This life soon be over, I say. Heaven last all ways." Sophia advises, "You ought to bash Mr.____ head open. . . . Think bout heaven later" (47). It is only when Celie can externalize her anger, can dare to express herself in spite of the fact that her father has forbidden her to speak, that she begins her journey toward selfhood by writing a revised self, by literally touching pen to paper to release her creative energy.

But the rite of passage comes through a different sort of literal touching of the self, in Celie's sexual awakening by Shug Avery. Although Celie has been raped repeatedly by her father and has given birth to two children by him, and although she is now married to Mr.____, she is, according to Shug, still a virgin (79). In other words, she has never known, or even realized there could be, sexual pleasure for a woman. Thus her most significant initiation into human sexuality is by her husband's mistress, and the lesbian lovemaking that follows is Celie's first experience of erotic love. To Celie, "it feel like heaven is what it feel like, not like sleeping with Mr.____ at all" (110). At last she is put in touch with her own body and her own needs. She learns to associate pleasure, not pain, with human touch. Thus, although women's relationships with men have impeded female self-development, their bonds with women, even literary bonds (Sadoff 4-26), can provide positive correctives. And certainly Celie's rite of passage provides the kind of cultural deconstruction that is a symbol of "emotive power" like those used by African women "mythmakers creating viable and meaningful new images of and for women" (Sharpe et al 145-46).

Even in the face of the painful disjunctions of life, Walker's emphasis is always on the inherent yearning for unity in all life of body and mind, of flesh and spirit, and especially of male and female. Thus in the title poem of **Horses Make a Landscape Look More Beautiful,** the most important element of the poem is the "s" in **"Horses,"** a fact which is evident from the incident that provided the impetus for the poem. Walker tells the story of a horse's wild suffering when deprived of his mate, and of his look that was "piercing, . . . full of grief . . ., [and] human" (**Living** 7). And the cruelty Walker sees in the humans who took away the mare after stud service seems an ironic reflection on the frequency of cruelty she notes among humans, who continually rupture their own intimate relationships. In the "Introduction" to her volume of poems entitled **Good Night Willie Lee, I'll See You in The Morning,** she states the basic need for human touch, a need which will, she says, "call out [one's] own heart for review" (vi). The complex theme common to the poems in this book is that of the perennial conflict of woman's two basic needs, which have historically been mutually exclusive: the need for intimacy with a man but also the need for mental and physical integrity. By "call[ing] out [one's] heart for review" in these poems, Walker shows us the state of the heart of woman. We see the continuing vulnerability of heart and body, but we also see hints of an emerging awareness of woman's equal need, and increasing ability, to resist abuse. It is as though Walker's book, published in 1979, is her answer to Adrienne Rich's call to action in her 1972 essay "When We Dead Awaken": a call not only for women writers to express anger at their victimization by men, but also a call for women to stop permitting the abuse, to take responsibility for their lives, to exchange the imposition of pain for what Rich calls the self-actuated "birth-pains [of] bearing ourselves" (25). And indeed, as Barbara Christian has shown, Walker's work contributes to, and perhaps represents the epitome of, a rapidly-developing theme in Afro-American women's writing: that of female self-development and self-definition ("Trajectories" 233-248).

The destructive results of a woman's need for a love relationship with a man are seen in Walker's poems through images of pain and death, suggesting the physical and mental stress on a woman in this double bind. Her conflicting needs cause "a painful knot in her back;" or they come up like weeds.

> Through cracks in the conversation.
> Through silences in the dark.
> Through everything you thought was concrete.
> Such needful love has to be chopped out
> or forced to wilt back
> poisoned by disapproval
> from its own soil.
>
> (*Good Night* 2-3)

A reviewer of Walker's first volume of poems, entitled *Once* (1968), noticed the juxtaposition of images of the world's brutality with images of great tenderness (Walsh 20). In that book, however, the contrasting expressions were not often identified with sex; and sometimes they did not even appear in the same poem. Compare, for example, the soft eroticism of "**The Smell of Lebanon**," from the sequence of "impossible love" poems, with the following bitter passage from the long title poem "**Once**":

> I remember
> seeing
> a little girl,
> dreamingperhaps,
> hit by
> a
> van truck
> "That nigger was
> in the way!" the
> man
> said
> to
> understanding cops. . . .
>
> (*Once* 35)

Perhaps the volume's most emphatic ironic contrast comes in "**Karamojans**," where the poet suggests the inherent native African beauty and dignity, which has been spoiled by poverty and disease. Throughout the poem, images of the fineness of human beings are undercut by those of

the world's brutal realities, as stanzas two and eight will suffice to show:

> The Noble Savage
> Erect
> no shoes on his
> feet
> His pierced ears
> Infected.
>
> . . . . .
>
> How bright the little
> girl's
> Eyes were!
> a first sign of
> Glaucoma.
>
> (*Once* 20, 22)

The simple, perhaps even clichéd, vocabulary is elevated by the poem's sustained technique of ironic negation, a technique that also occurs in the title poem "**Once**," where the reality of the Southern jailer "in grey" negates, for the Civil Rights demonstrators, the "Green lawn / . . . picket fence / flowers / . . . [and] the blue sky" (*Once* 23). The continual juxtaposition of positive and negative images produces an overriding antiphonal style in both the poems and the prose, a style apparent, for example, in the title poem of *Revolutionary Petunias*; in the structure of the stories "**Roselily**" and "**The Child Who Favored Daughter**" (*In Love*); and in the alternating voices of Celie and Nettie, which "encompass and interconnect all the characters" in *The Color Purple* (Fifer 156).

This ironic antiphony underlies what are perhaps Walker's most striking images of negation: those which occur in poems which express love's mental anguish in terms of physical pain or danger: Loving a man is analogous to bearing a "knife that presses / without ceasing / against [a woman's] heart" (*Good Night* 10); to being "in limbo" (11), to being "afflicted" to the point of "murder[ing] the man" (13); to having one's life "shredded / by an expert" (15). Often, however, a woman endures sexual pain that has nothing to do with love. A recurring reference in Walker's poems is to the rape her great-great-grandmother suffered at age eleven. A poem entitled "**The Thing Itself**," from the volume *Horses Make a Landscape Look More Beautiful*, is the poet's vision of that experience. It includes these lines:

> There was no
> pornography
> in her world
> from which to learn
> to relish the pain.
> (She was the thing
> itself.)
>
> (62)

Nowhere is the body of the poem more at one with the female body than in Walker's **"Early Losses: A Requiem,"** in which the poet, in the persona of a nine-year-old African girl sold into slavery, mourns the loss of her childhood friend but also the loss of her own childhood:

> . . . Omunu vanished
> down a hole that
> smelled of blood and
> excrement and death
> and I was "saved"
> for sport among
> the sailors of the crew.
> Only nine, upon a ship. My mouth
> my body a mystery
> that opened with each tearing
> lunge.
>
> (*Good Night* 28)

In this volume of poems we touch a woman in pain.

But mitigating the pain expressed are also flashes of the spirited woman that is Alice Walker. For example, in **"Janie Crawford"**:

> I love the way Janie Crawford
> left her husbands the one who wanted
> to change her into a mule
> and the other who tried to interest her
> in being a queen
> a woman unless she submits is neither a mule
> nor a queen
> though like a mule she may suffer
> and like a queen pace
> the floor.
>
> (*Good Night* 18)

We also see a "moody woman / [with] temper as black as [her] brows / as sharp as [her] nails" (19). We see her trying to survive with a dream different from that of her grandmother, who longed only for some comfort in her poor life, and yet trying to maintain some connection with her heritage, as she says in "Talking to my grandmother . . .,"

> I must train myself to want
> not one bit more
> than what i need to keep me alive
> working
> and recognizing beauty
> in your
> so nearly
> undefeated face.
>
> (*Good Night* 46-47)

And there is the resurgent good humor in poems such as **"Every Morning,"** the poet's rebuke to a sleepy, complaining body:

> "Don't you see that person
> staring at you?" I ask my breasts,
> which are still capable
> of staring back.

> "If I didn't exercise
> you couldn't look up
> that far. . . .
>
> (*Horses Make* 16)

Although the volume *Horses Make a Landscape Look More Beautiful* received mixed reviews, some readers alleging its "pathos" ("Private Voices" 19), banality (*Publishers'* 71), "forced" quality (*Virginia Quarterly* 57), or even racism (Disch 6), such poems as **"Every Morning"** speak both for Walker and her readers to the subject that Adrienne Rich said she herself addressed in writing "Planetarium": "the relief of the body / and the reconstruction of the mind" (30).

Contrary to charges of her insensitivity to black men, typified by the comments of Tony Brown (2), of her sexist polemic, according to Charles Johnson (107), or of both and more (Cheatwood; qtd. in Walker *Living* 88), Walker, as she herself has reminded us (*Living* 80), extends that same opportunity for relief and reconstruction to her male characters—to Grange Copeland, to Harpo, to Albert, and even to Mister. Yet there is no more false (that is, sexless) "universality" in Alice Walker's writing than there was false modesty in Walt Whitman's frankly sexual poems, notwithstanding even Walker's own cogent claim that all races suffered (and by implication still suffer) from the experience of slavery: "We are the African and the trader. We are the Indian and the settler . . ., the slaver and the enslaved . . ." (*Living* 89). To admit these common human afflictions is not to deny Chikweyne Okonjo Ogunyemi's claim that "black womanist writers . . . are committed to the survival and wholeness of their entire people, female and male" (qtd. in Sharpe et al 143). Yet in her fiction and poems, it is nevertheless the nerves and bodies and minds of Walker's female characters that are laid bare—to each other, to themselves, and to the reader. On the page in black and white (pun intended, in the spirit of Walker's own use in **"African Images"** *Once* 7), the complex self of woman is naked and exposed, in the misery of its pain or the celebration of its worth. Alice Walker's writing will never be mistaken for that of Whitman; for who touches this touches a woman.

Works Cited

Brown, Tony. "Tony Brown's Comments: The Color of Purple is White." *The Herald* 1 Jan. 1986: 2.

Christian, Barbara. *Black Women Novelists: The Development of a Tradition, 1892-1976.* Westport, CT.: Greenwood Press, 1980.

———. "Trajectories of Self-Definition: Placing Contemporary Afro-American Women's Fiction." *Conjuring: Black*

Women, Fiction, and Literary Tradition. Ed. Majorie Pryse and Hortense Spillars. Bloomington: Indiana U P, 1985. 233-248.

Davis, Thadious M. "Alice Walker's Celebration of Self in Southern Generations." *Women Writers of the Contemporary South.* Ed. Peggy Whitman Prenshaw. Jackson: U P of Mississippi, 1984. 38-53.

Disch, Tom. "The Perils of Poesy." *Book World* 30 Dec. 1984: 6.

Fifer, Elizabeth. "Alice Walker: The Dialect & Letters of The Color Purple." *Contemporary American Women Writers: Narrative Strategies.* Ed. Catherine Rainwater and William J. Scheick. Lexington: U P of Kentucky, 1985. 155-71.

Gernes, Sonia. *America* 152.4 (2 Feb. 1985): 93-94; qtd. in Pratt, Louis H. and Darnell D. Pratt, *Alice Malsenior Walker: An Annotated Bibliography: 1968-1986.* Westport, CT: Meckler, 1988.

Johnson, Charles. *Being & Race: Black Writing Since 1970.* Bloomington: Indiana U P, 1988.

Mascia-Lees, Frances E., Pat Sharpe, and Colleen B. Cohen. "Double Liminality and the Black Woman Writer." *American Behavioral Scientist* 31 (Sept.-Oct. 1987): 101-14.

Ostriker, Alicia. "American Poetry, Now Shaped by Women." *New York Times Book Review.* 9 Mar. 1986: 1, 28-30.

"Private Voices." *Books and Bookmen* Sept. 1985: 19.

Publishers Weekly 24 Aug. 1984: 71.

Reed, Ishmael. *Reckless Eyeballing.* New York: St. Martin's, 1986.

Rich, Adrienne. "When We Dead Awaken: Writing as Re-Vision." *College English* 34:1 (Oct. 1972): 18-25.

Sadoff, Dianne F. "Black Matrilineage: The Case of Alice Walker and Zora Neale Hurston." *Signs* 11.1 (Autumn 1985): 4-26.

Sharpe, Patricia, F. E. Mascia-Lees, and C. B. Cohen. "White Women and Black Men: Differential Responses to Reading Black Women's Texts." *College English* 52:2 (Feb. 1990): 142-53.

Virginia Quarterly Review 61:2 (Spring 1985): 57.

Walker, Alice. *The Color Purple.* 1982. New York: Washington Square, 1983.

——. *Good Night Willie Lee, I'll See You in The Morning.* 1979. Harvest/Harcourt Brace Jovanovich, 1984.

——. *Horses Make a Landscape Look More Beautiful.* New York: Harcourt Brace Jovanovich, 1984.

——. *In Love and Trouble: Stories of Black Women.* New York: Harcourt Brace Jovanovich, 1974.

——. *In Search of Our Mother's Gardens.* New York: Harcourt Brace Jovanovich, 1984.

——. *Living By the Word: Selected Writings, 1973-1987.* New York: Harcourt Brace Jovanovich, 1988.

——. *Meridian.* New York: Harcourt, 1976.

——. *Once.* New York: Harcourt Brace World, 1968.

——. *Revolutionary Petunias & Other Poems.* New York: Harcourt Brace Jovanovich, 1973.

——. *The Third Life of Grange Copeland.* 1970. Rpt. New York: Pocket Books, 1988.

Wallace, Michele. *Black Macho and the Myth of the Superwoman.* New York: Warner, 1979.

Walsh, Chad. "A Present Rooted in the Past." *Book World* 3 Nov. 1968: 20.

Watkins, Mel. "Sexism, Racism and Black Women Writers." *New York Times Book Review* 15 June 1986: 1, 35-37.

Whitman, Walt. "So Long." *Leaves of Grass.* 1860. Rpt. *Eight American Writers: An Anthology of American Literature.* Ed. Norman Foerster and Robert P. Falk. New York: Norton: 1963. 1137-38.

KEITH BYERMAN (ESSAY DATE 2000)

SOURCE: Byerman, Keith. "Gender and Justice: Alice Walker and the Sexual Politics of Civil Rights." In *The World Is Our Home: Society and Culture in Contemporary Southern Writing,* edited by Jeffrey J. Folks and Nancy Summers Folks, pp. 93-106. Lexington: The University Press of Kentucky, 2000.

In the following essay, Byerman considers the interrelationship between racial discrimination and gender relations in Walker's fiction, contending that she uses the mid-twentieth-century civil rights movement in the South to explore current issues of gender and power.

In her novel **Meridian** (1976), Alice Walker depicts a northern white civil rights worker very concerned with her impulse to see southern blacks as aesthetic objects: "To Lynne, the black people of the South were Art. . . . 'I will pay for this,' she often warned herself. 'It is probably a sin to think of a people as Art.' And yet, she would stand perfectly still and the sight of a fat black woman singing to herself in a tattered yellow dress, her voice rich and full of yearning, was always—God forgive her, black folks forgive her—the same weepy miracle that Art always was for her" (128).

This essay argues that for Walker herself, just as for her character, southern black folk are Art, in the sense that they serve as a fixed standard by which to measure the moral significance and achievements of the central actors in her narratives about civil rights. It is necessary to understand that region and class are as important as race in establishing this standard. Those who retain their status of being close to the land, with a southern mind-set that rejects abstraction, are the model.[1] This does not mean that Walker has a nostalgic view, though she may have a romantic one. The folk she presents are capable of change and of political action; it is simply that change must be connected to concrete experience.

Corollary to this narrative concern is the related issue of sexuality; desire in Walker's stories tends to produce distortions of itself in that characters generate abstractions of the sexual Other that they then manipulate out of motives of class or race ideology. In this case, the folk become the standard by consistently demonstrating innocent desire in the concreteness and authenticity of their relationships. Consistently in the texts under consideration here—the last part of *The Third Life of Grange Copeland* (1970), *Meridian,* and "**Advancing Luna—and Ida B. Wells**" (1981)—a complicated modern (even modernist) way of being and doing is set over against a folk model of (relatively) simple virtue in matters of gender and racial justice, and the modern approach is found wanting. Part of the problem is, in fact, that the modern characters confuse and conflate matters of desire and of justice.

The earliest version of this pattern occurs late in Walker's first novel, *The Third Life of Grange Copeland.* The book as a whole is almost naturalistic in its depiction of the repetition of racial hatred and attacks on women. It sets up a social pattern in which the powerlessness of black men in the face of white hostility leads them to victimize black women, especially their wives. Grange, having undergone an earlier transformation, has established his farm as a fortress to protect himself and his granddaughter Ruth from the effects of white racism and black self-destructiveness. While most of the novel is devoted to narratives of domestic violence, interracial antagonism, and self-hatred, it turns, in the penultimate chapter, to a story of civil rights.

Each of the episodes in the chapter links a sensual experience to the effort to attain justice, with the implication, at this stage in Walker's writing, that civil rights is an object of desire in the personal as well as political sense. Into Grange's sanctuary, through the device of television, come images of the civil rights movement. The initial viewing is contextualized by being presented as an item on the news, specifically the *Huntley-Brinkley Report.* Before the message, Ruth notes the messengers: "She became almost fond of Chet Huntley and David Brinkley, especially David Brinkley, who was younger than Chet and whose mouth curved up in a pleasingly sardonic way" (231). This representation of white male authority as "pleasing" marks a break from the images of whiteness that dominate the book. Brinkley's presence in Grange's fortress, through the media, is also a breakdown of the black man's separatist principles, principles developed over a lifetime of abuse, self-hatred, and racial intimidation. The

visual image is at once intrusive and distant, allowing Ruth and Grange to come to terms with it without directly engaging it.

They receive their knowledge of the movement through these white images. When the narrator comments that "integration appealed to Ruth in a shivery, fearful kind of way" (231), the term "integration" can be understood as applying to the cross-racial experience of media producer and consumer as well as to the movement that is depicted. Moreover, the language of the appeal— "shivery, fearful"—can be linked as easily to sensual experience as to political activity. Thus it can be argued that Ruth is in part seduced into belief. At the same time, the medium keeps the events at a distance from her reality, allowing her to encounter them safely. Change can come to her in an attractive package, not in the dangerous action that shaped her grandfather's attitudes and behaviors.

The extent of this generational difference is apparent in the story of Fred Hill, an old friend of Grange's. He is killed, and Grange concludes that it is because his grandson "is making news" by trying to integrate the schools. The shooting is officially labeled a suicide, though no gun is found. For Grange, this is evidence that the world will not and cannot change. For his granddaughter, the interest is elsewhere:

> "Tried to get into one of the cracker schools?"
>
> "And did he make it?"
>
> Grange leaned back his head and looked at the ceiling, his chair tilted back on two legs. "Naw," he said, "he didn't make it. How you going to study in a cracker school with half your granddaddy's head missing?"
>
> "Well," said Ruth, attempting to see a bright side, "you don't need your granddaddy's head to study. You just need your own."
>
> (234)

The assumption that there is a "bright side" to the story reflects a sanitized, dehistoricized relation to reality that is reinforced by the media. Ironically, it can be contended that it is also one means by which hope can be sustained, especially in the primarily secularized world in which Walker's characters operate. Without the church as a source of faith, the only alternatives seem to be ahistorical optimism and experiential despair.

Desire, politics, and history come together in the culminating scene of the chapter. The movement from television physically enters their realm when two couples, one black and one white, appear at the farm to encourage Grange to register to vote. The young black man is someone Ruth has seen in town with the demonstrators. The sensual nature of her response is evident even to her grandfather: "Grange looked over at Ruth. She was standing at the edge of the porch with one arm around a roof support. Her eyes were shining! He could almost feel the hot current that flowed through her, making her soft young body taut and electric with waiting" (237). Her desire continues throughout the scene, even when she learns that the young man is married to the pregnant woman with him. She reacts with a twinge of jealousy and then regret. It remains for her a "charged" moment, in which desire reinforces admiration for political activism.

What is important here is the innocence of Ruth's response to the young man, a response not followed in either **Meridian** or "**Advancing Luna.**" This difference reflects Walker's representation of the folk as pure. The black activists in this novel are themselves part of the folk. They are locals whose families Grange knows well. They are engaged in the movement, not out of some abstract notion of virtue or justice but because it serves the needs of their community. Helen's father was killed trying to vote, and her mother was evicted from her lifelong home for aiding the activists. What is evident is their simple belief in the cause and their attendant refusal to be discouraged or dissuaded by hostility or resistance. Grange's life experience does not permit a sharing of their faith, but it does inspire a protective impulse: "He felt a deep tenderness for the young couple. He felt about them as he felt about Dr. King: that if they'd just stay with him on his farm he'd shoot the first cracker that tried to bother them. He wanted to protect them, from themselves and from their dreams as much as from the crackers. He would not let anybody hurt them, but at the same time he didn't believe in what they were doing. Not because it wasn't worthy and noble and inspiring and good, but because it was impossible" (241).

Through the black couple the young whites are granted standing. Because they are with the blacks and because they have also been threatened for their efforts, their commitment cannot be doubted. Ruth immediately accepts them, but Grange cannot overcome his suspicion, especially of the white woman. She represents for him the opposite side of desire, a racialized, gendered object used to justify oppression and violence against blacks. In his view, the white woman cannot be separated from this objectification. Ironically, his position is the correlative of that of white

racists, who call one of the women participating in the march "you nigger-fucking whore" (235). In both instances, she is an eroticized image distorted for purposes of power. She cannot be an individual self. In this text, the figure of the white woman is the measure of the moral enlightenment of the characters. Grange recognizes the limitations of his own feelings but cannot quite get over them. They are too deeply embedded in his personal experiences and cultural conditioning.

The relatively straightforward interaction of gender, race, and civil rights in **Grange Copeland** is deeply complicated in **Meridian** and "**Advancing Luna,**" in part because of Walker's decision to distinguish between the folk and the activists. By making this distinction, she can introduce questions of motive that challenge some of the conventional wisdom about the movement. She can retain a fixed moral standard while examining modern, secular characters and perspectives. The key figures in both of the later narratives have no direct links to the folk but must establish such links primarily through the movement itself. The quality of the connection is one measure of the moral development of the central characters.

But aspects of life in the modern world—education, cosmopolitanism, individualism, urbanization, middle-class culture—work against such connections by focusing on private rather than communal concerns. Whatever their political commitment and ideals, modern characters bring into the movement their personal conflicts and desires and find ways to play them out.

The three central figures in **Meridian**—Meridian Hill, Truman Held, and Lynne Rabinowitz—are educated young people who participate in civil rights activities out of a complex of motives that include idealism, guilt, self-assertion, and rebellion. Each is in some way self-absorbed. Meridian cannot come to terms with her own mother; Truman believes in his own importance; Lynne seeks to escape her northern bourgeois life by identifying the black folk as "Art." In contrast, the folk, whether local young men, poor families, or the religious elderly, are characterized by simple dignity, honor, and love; they can be confused or troubled by circumstances, but their underlying moral strength is never in doubt.

On matters of both desire and politics, the position of the folk community is very clear. In terms of sexuality, they are not tempted to dehumanize others. For example, after raping Lynne, Tommy Odds urges a group of young men active in the movement to sexually assault "it." "'It? *It?*' [Altuna] said. 'What *it* you talking about? That ain't no *it*, that's Lynne'" (162). Similarly, the refusal of some to register to vote is never the result of cowardice or indifference; they simply make it clear that they have higher priorities: God, family, or personal honor. Lynne attempts to argue with a mother of the church; she succeeds only in offending her by insisting that God has not gotten her anything of value. When Truman and Meridian try to register a husband whose wife is dying, he questions the purpose of registering, given his need to care for her and their son on his meager earnings. This time, instead of arguing, the activists bring back groceries for the family. Some time later, apparently after the wife has died, the husband comes bearing gifts and signs the registration list. In these cases and many others throughout the novel, the spiritual and moral strength of the folk is asserted and demonstrated.

In one sense, it could be argued that for them civil rights as an ideology and a movement is largely irrelevant. As Truman and Meridian admit in their recruiting visits, voting will have little immediate or direct impact on individual lives. The people who sign up do so largely out of gratitude for the kindness and attention of the civil rights workers rather than because they have any belief in the efficacy of the political system. At the same time, the folk do not question the moral power of the movement or the courage of the activists. But that power and courage already exist within the people, so the movement cannot transform their basic character; it can only confirm it.

In contrast, because the central characters and others are not part of the folk, they are subject to a variety of inconsistencies, self-induced problems, moral quandaries, and complications of race, gender, sexuality, and class. They cannot simply *be*, as the folk can; they must do and think and become and desire. If desire is the response to a lack or absence, as contemporary theory suggests, then it may be said to be the primary motivation for the key characters of the novel.

For Truman Held, desire is connected to status. He prefers, in his conversations with Meridian, to speak French because "he believed profoundly that anything said in French sounded better, and he also believed that people who spoke French were better than people (*les pauvres, les misérables!*) who did not" (95). She responds positively to him in part because he is clearly more sophisticated than other black men she has known: "He was a man who fought against obstacles, a man who could become anything, a man whose very words

were unintelligible without considerable thought" (96). This last phrase suggests the irony with which he is viewed by the narrator, since it refers to the fact that Meridian knows very little French, not to the profundity of Truman's ideas. This commitment to white culture extends to his preference for northern white women. He tells Meridian, in an especially cruel moment, that he is attracted to them "because they read *The New York Times*" (141). The cruelty is based on his awareness that she has led a provincial life, with little access to the privilege inherent in the lives of the exchange students. Sex becomes the means by which he vicariously joins the world of white privilege; it is vicarious because his relationships do not literally enable him to enter the realm of white status and wealth. When Lynne's parents, for example, learn of their marriage, they disown her and her offspring. Moreover, Truman loses interest in her once she becomes his wife rather than a precious, almost unattainable object of desire.

He consistently links his sexual impulses to ideology. He justifies his interest in white students with his interpretation of W. E. B. Du Bois's writings, though how he does so is not made clear in the text. Later, he connects his abandonment of Lynne to a return to his racial roots. His artistic efforts are large images of black women with oversized breasts. While creating these Black Madonnas, he is living in New York with a young white woman from Alabama. Yet he cannot sustain the actual black woman in his life, Meridian, as an object of desire or as an actual person. When he returns to her three years after marrying Lynne, he claims that he should have married her instead. But she is no longer impressed by his words or superior tone. When he makes his claim, she insists that it is because it has now become fashionable to be associated with black women, not white ones. Then she turns his denial against him:

"Because I'm black?"

"Because you're *you*, damn it! The woman I should have married and didn't!"

"Should have *loved,* and didn't," she murmured.

And Truman sank back staring, as if at a lifeboat receding in the distance.

(138)

While Truman makes the narcissistic error of equating personal desire with political agenda and is repeatedly shocked by his self-delusion, both Meridian and Lynne link the personal and political in different ways.[2] Both of them are damaged by Truman's arrogance, but they also suffer because of their complex motivations for and responses to social activism. For Lynne, who grows up in a privileged northern Jewish environment that was both protected and standardized, the South and especially the black folk there represent vitality and creativity.

Lynne's need to escape that northern life is not a desire to become southern herself; she never in the course of the novel loses the individualistic, secular assertiveness that she brought with her from the North. Rather, she wishes to exploit the geographic, racial Other to satisfy her personal and cultural lack in a variation of what George Frederickson has called "romantic racialism" (97-129). Her Jewishness is part of her sensibility as well. She grows up in a post-Holocaust world that suppresses the knowledge of suffering so that children like her can develop in a state of carefully maintained innocence. She responds by seeking out suffering, but suffering that has been reified: "Mississippi—after the disappearance of the three civil rights workers in 1964—began to beckon her. For two years she thought of nothing else. If Mississippi is the worst place in America for black people, it stood to reason, she thought, that the Art that was their lives would flourish best there" (130). The South for her, then, is a living museum. Denied the narrative of her own people's great horror, in part because it is too real to be subjected to aesthetic control, she turns to a parallel experience that has both immediacy and distance.

The problem with Lynne's approach is her refusal to accept the humanity of those she has constructed as art objects. She cannot grasp the ambivalence created by her own whiteness, which produces a volatile mix of desire and hostility. She fails to understand the effect her presence has on both blacks and whites in the South. Tommy Odds blames her for the loss of his arm in an act of racial violence; by being with a group of black men, she endangered them. Through a conversation with Odds, Truman is able to understand the attitudes of blacks toward Lynne: "To them she was a route to Death, pure and simple. They felt her power over them in their bones; their mothers had feared her even before they were born. Watching their fear of her, though, he saw a strange thing: They did not even see her as a human being, but as some kind of large, mysterious doll. A thing of movies and television, of billboards and car and soap commercials. They liked

her hair, not because it was especially pretty, but because it was long. To them, *length* was beauty" (137).

In an important reversal, Lynne, as the white woman, is herself made into an object, but a dangerous, taboo one. The fact that she is northern and Jewish does not change this attitude. In the South, White Woman is a category nearly overwhelming in ideological, social, and erotic significance. The white woman who aligns herself with blacks is seen as a race traitor and whore by whites, who read her association with an "inferior," "promiscuous" race as the lowest form of profanation. Blacks, regardless of their individual views of her, retain a clear perception of her symbolic power in southern society. Her motives *must* be questioned because affiliation with her is deeply problematic. At the same time, her significance (and danger) can make her a powerful object of desire, less in the sexual than in the political sense. A sexual attack on her is an attack on the basis of white supremacy. It is simultaneously an act of revenge and rebellion, though in one sense it reinforces racism by accepting the premise of contamination. To have a white woman is to "ruin" her for white men.

Thus Tommy Odds's rape of Lynne expresses his personal rage and allows him to engage in a political act. He can vent his hostility toward whites without committing a suicidal attack on the white men who shot him. But the assault on her is a strangely safe act. She is already viewed as racially promiscuous by the white community simply by being where she is; attacking her will not affect their views in the least. Moreover, he is reasonably certain that she will not seek justice: "She wished she could go to the police, but she was more afraid of them than she was of Tommy Odds, because they would attack young black men in the community indiscriminately and the people she wanted most to see protected would suffer" (162). The very motives and circumstances that necessitated the movement generally and Lynne's participation specifically make it impossible for her to seek justice. The very power of her whiteness precludes her resistance to sexual violence. Moreover, her aestheticist view of black life holds even during the assault:

> She lay . . . thinking of his feelings, his hardships, of the way he was black and belonged to people who lived without hope; she thought about the loss of his arm. She felt her own guilt. . . . She did not any longer resist but tried instead to think of Tommy Odds as he was when he was her friend and near the end her arms stole around his neck, and before he left she told him she forgave him

and she kissed his slick rounded stump that was the color of baked liver, and he smiled at her from far away, she did not know him.

(159)

As Elliott Butler-Evans has noted: "If the novel's racial politics demands that it explore Tommy Odds's behavior within the context of racial oppression, it is also committed to investigating Lynne's status as victim. That issue is somewhat ambiguously presented through the graphic detail of the rape coupled with Lynne's commitment to the 'correct' political attitude, even at the expense of her own welfare" (122).

Rape is transmuted into a permissible effect of black suffering and white penance for that suffering. Lynne denies him the humanity of being responsible for an act of violence. Her embrace of him turns assault into fulfilled desire, apparently for both of them. He can both satisfy his sexual need for the white woman and express his hostility toward the white world; she can be the sacrifice that links her to black suffering. By kissing his stump, which approximates the phallus, she submits to black (male) authority and thus escapes the guilt associated with her whiteness. At the same time, she can sustain her image of black experience in something like its purity.

Significantly, neither Truman nor Meridian wants to hear her story, in part because they, too, wish to construct a version of the folk that serves their private purposes while permitting them to interpret themselves as benefactors. Meridian is the most extreme example of this. Her responses to the world are shaped in part by guilt, first the guilt of having "stolen" something from her mother and, second, the guilt of having abandoned her son to pursue her education. Hers is the dilemma of the modern woman: how is it possible to live an individually meaningful life in a world that still demands loyalty to traditional roles? What she has "stolen" from her mother, simply by being her child, is independence and individuality. She exacerbates the problem by giving up her own child; she in effect discredits the sacrifice made by her mother (cf. Callahan 159; Daly 254-55).

This conflict about maternity inspires Meridian's commitment to the civil rights movement. She seeks, in effect, the social equivalent of her mother's sacrifice. She takes in and identifies with the outcasts in the college community. She has an abortion when Truman loses his interest in her, but she never tells him. She offers to die for the movement but is uncertain of her willingness to kill. When she is rejected by her revolutionary

friends for her ambivalence, she chooses to return to the rural South, even though that form of activism has become passé. During all this time, her health is fragile, and she consistently enters catatonic states after her public challenges to authority. In this sense, her repudiation of her mother's life in truth reenacts its sacrificial quality.

Her work with the folk has a healing effect on her over time. In her encounters with them, there is little evidence of ethical or political principles being transmitted in either direction. The people are particularly empowered by her actions. She sees herself as doing *for* them: "They *appreciate* it when somebody volunteers to suffer" (25). They are consistently shown to be simply good people who must be led. Even the transformative religious service near the conclusion of the novel reveals a largely passive people. After the grieving father has spoken his ritual three words—"My son died"—on the anniversary of the young activist's death, Meridian has an insight into the congregation's response to his call: "The people in the church . . . were saying, 'we are slow to awaken to the notion that we are only as other women and men, and even slower to move in anger, but we are gathering ourselves to fight for and protect what your son fought for on behalf of us. If you will let us weave your story and your son's life into what we already know—into the songs, the sermons, the 'brother and sister'—we will soon be so angry we cannot help but move'" (199).

Meridian's voicing of their feelings itself suggests the text's limited faith in the power of the folk. She, though an outsider, must speak for them. Moreover, it is the expression of a desire to be fulfilled at some future point, not the planning of an action in the present (cf. Hall). In fact, implicit in the statement is justification for inaction: "if your son should come again," they could act; but, of course, resurrection is not to be expected. The weaving of narrative must precede any movement into the social realm. It is Meridian's insight into her own situation, not that of the congregation, that is the focus of narrative attention. *She* now understands the circumstances under which she could take a life. She claims spiritual maternity by asserting that she could kill to save the boy and others like him. Her role is that of nurturer, protector, and culture-bearer. The revolutionaries do the fighting, and Meridian provides the music that makes sense of the struggle and that saves the soul of the people. "When they stop to wash off the blood and find their throats too choked with the smell of murdered flesh to sing, I will come forward and sing from memory songs they will need once more to hear" (201). The people themselves have no role in this tremendous effort on their behalf. They are kept outside of history, an object of contemplation and a source of inspiration for the fighters and artists of the revolution. For Meridian, in slight contrast to Lynne, it is not the folk but the souls of black folk that are Art (cf. Hall 104).

Given her understanding and commitment in this passage, it is significant that Meridian is absent herself from the end of the novel. Her efforts for the people and her overcoming of maternal guilt by interpreting those efforts as maternal have healed her. And having been healed, she walks away. She leaves Truman to take over guiding the people and in the process healing himself. This transition suggests that what happens to the individual is more important than the community or society. Meridian has been the guide, not so much for the folk as for those modern individuals—Truman, Lynne, Anne-Marion—who are no longer part of the community and who suffer as a result. Once the self-healing occurs, there is no longer a responsibility to the people. Social action is a form of therapy; community improvement is merely a means to a private end.

The furthest remove from community comes in "Advancing Luna—and Ida B. Wells." The story develops the logic of the rape of Lynne depicted in **Meridian**. The narrator is a young black woman who spent a brief time one summer doing voter registration work. It was here that she met Luna, who had come to Georgia for the same purpose. They work together until the narrator takes advantage of a fellowship opportunity to visit Africa. Later, they meet again in New York, and it is on this occasion that Luna describes the rape.

Almost no attention is paid in the story to civil rights activities. In fact, the narrator comments that the effort "seems not only minor, but irrelevant" (88). The focus of this part of the story is on the narrator's smugness and world-weariness. She describes the extent to which she takes for granted the efforts on behalf of the students by the local people, including the danger to which their assistance subjects them. The movement becomes simply the occasion to explore the politics of rape and race. Implicit in this analysis, however, is the view, similar to that established in **Meridian,** that the movement is more interesting in terms of what it reveals about young activists and about ideology than what it says about its effects on black southerners. As in the previous work, the folk are not delineated in any depth;

they are simply there in their saintly being—patient, courageous, understanding.

Unlike them, the modern young volunteers must deal with larger moral and political issues. When the rape is first described to the narrator, she immediately turns to critical commentary on the sexual politics of Eldridge Cleaver and LeRoi Jones, both of whom she attacks for advocating the rape of white women. When Luna tells of her attack and the narrator asks why she had not screamed, the white woman responds, "You know why" (92). This comment leads into the narrator's imaginary conversation with Ida B. Wells, the turn-of-the-century antilynching activist. Wells consistently urged blacks to protect their sons, fathers, and husbands against accusations of sexual assault because such accusations endangered not only individuals but entire communities. Just as Lynne had done, Luna chooses protection of blacks over punishment of her assailant. In this instance, though, the narrator is more interested in her own conflicts and in the ideological implications of the assault than in the emotional and psychological states of either victim or victimizer (cf. McKay). In fact, the narrative effectively diminishes both of these figures. Luna is consistently described as childlike, while Freddie Pye seems almost bestial in his unattractiveness and inarticulateness. Such reduction allows the argument with Wells over the writer's need to depict reality as she finds it, regardless of the social or racial consequences. "'No matter what you think you know, no matter what you feel about it, say nothing. And to your dying breath!' Which, to my mind, is virtually useless advice to give a writer" (94). The literary rights of the individual must supersede whatever consequences might develop for the community. Just as the narrator walked away from activism to pursue her private agenda, so here she ignores history to enable self-expression.

Having rejected the sexist aspects of black nationalism and the suppressions of Wells, the narrator now turns on Luna: "And yet the rape, the knowledge of the rape, out in the open, admitted, pondered over, was now between us. (And I began to think that perhaps—whether Luna had been raped or not—it had always been so; that her power over my life was exactly the power *her word on rape* had over the lives of black men, over *all* black men, whether they were guilty or not, and therefore over my whole people)" (95).

The question of power takes priority over the question of rape; Luna in this passage is not a distinct character but White Woman, though it is precisely her racial power that she resists using. The narrator refuses to engage the complexity of a situation that positions Luna closer to Ida B. Wells (and implicitly to "my whole people") than the narrator herself. Not surprisingly, the two women grow apart, though not before Freddie Pye appears in their apartment coming out of Luna's bedroom one morning. We also learn that the narrator goes back to the South because of "the need to return, to try to understand, and write about, the people I'd merely lived with before" (97). She does not describe the impact of the return, choosing instead to end the story proper at this point.

In a metafictional move, Walker offers several appendices to the narrative that attempt to specify its ideological significance. One addition locates the existing ending in the context of current reality, "a society in which lynching is still reserved, at least subconsciously, as a means of social control" (98). But this "unresolved" conclusion cannot support the narrator's vision of what the society ought to be and so, after a brief comment that again deprecates Luna's efforts at racial understanding ("A very straight, clear-eyed, coolly observant young woman with no talent for existing outside her own skin" [99]), she offers "Imaginary Knowledge," an alternative ending. In this version, she depicts Freddie and Luna engaging in a night-long conversation about their lives and the rape. Importantly, she focuses on Freddie's coming to the North as an "exhibit" of what southern oppression had done to black men. When he has done his part at a fund-raiser, he is abandoned by both his black and white sponsors, who clearly want nothing to do with his real life. After Freddie has described this situation, this ending stops with the comment that it would now be Luna's turn to talk and that she needed to understand the rape and her response to it. But this conversation is never presented, though in some sense it would seem to be the key to the story.

Instead of granting voice to Freddie and Luna about their central experience, the narrator turns to a "Postscript" that undermines what has just been offered. In Cuba, the narrator tells the story, but her listener objects that she has been unable to imagine true evil. He speculates that Freddie was a government agent paid to disrupt the civil rights movement by acts of sexual violence. Though the narrator seeks to qualify this scenario, she clearly is attracted by it. By positioning it as the actual conclusion to the narrative, she grants it considerable authority. In this sense, what began as an attempt to understand a crucial aspect of the sexual-racial dynamic of the South and the movement becomes a political commentary far removed from its beginnings. The narrator is ultimately concerned with the ideological underpinnings of her story rather than with the people and experiences of the South. Freddie Pye, as an emblem of the southern folk, is cast either as the Pathetic Victim of southern oppression and northern exploitation or as the Dark Villain, much like the black beast of racist imagination. He is, in other words, Art.

In "The Black Writer and the Southern Experience," Walker says, "In large measure, black Southern writers owe their clarity of vision to parents who refused to diminish themselves as human beings by succumbing to racism" (19). Ironically, what we see in her fiction of the civil rights movement is a focus on the individual, especially the modern individual, alienated from the folk in some way, whether through media, representation, education, guilt, or artistic impulse. The attraction to the people is consistently motivated by some private need, and when that need is met, the folk become irrelevant. Black southern life is primarily an aesthetic idea and ideal by which to measure those who are doing the truly important work in life, struggling for virtue and justice within modern consciousness. Unlike Ernest Gaines, who also writes of the South and the movement of the mid-twentieth century, as an artist Alice Walker is not particularly interested in the complexities of southern people or the social movements of the region. Rather, she sees them as a means to explore current issues of gender and power. She generates sympathy or antipathy about them depending on the requirements of ideology and modern character development. Like her character Lynne, Walker as author sees black folk as Art; unlike that character, however, she does not acknowledge her aesthetic hegemony.

Notes

1. For other interpretations of Walker's views on the South and civil rights, see Butler (two articles), Daly, Donaldson, Ensslen, Hall, and Manvi.

2. On interracial friendships in *Meridian*, see Jones and Porter.

Works Cited

Butler, Robert James. "Alice Walker's Vision of the South in *The Third Life of Grange Copeland*." *African-American Review* 27.2 (1993): 195-204.

——. "Visions of Southern Life and Religion in O'Connor's *Wise Blood* and Walker's *The Third Life of Grange Copeland*." *College Language Association Journal* 36.4 (1993): 349-70.

Butler-Evans, Elliott. "History and Genealogy in Walker's *The Third Life of Grange Copeland* and *Meridian*." *Alice Walker: Critical Perspectives Past and Present*. Ed. Henry Louis Gates Jr. and K. A. Appiah. New York: Amistad, 1993. 105-25.

Callahan, John F. "The Hoop of Language: Politics and the Restoration of Voice in *Meridian*." *Alice Walker: Modern Critical Views*. Ed. Harold Bloom. New York: Chelsea House, 1989. 153-84.

Daly, Brenda O. "Teaching Alice Walker's *Meridian*: Civil Rights According to Mothers." *Narrating Mothers: Theorizing Maternal Subjectivities*. Ed. Brenda O. Daly and Maureen T. Reddy. Knoxville: U of Tennessee P, 1991. 239-57.

Donaldson, Susan. "Alice Walker's *Meridian*, Feminism, and the 'Movement.'" *Women's Studies* 16.3-4 (1989): 317-30.

Ensslen, Klaus. "Collective Experience and Individual Responsibility: Alice Walker's *The Third Life of Grange Copeland*." *The Afro-American Novel Since 1960*. Ed. Peter Bruck and Wolfgang Karrer. Amsterdam: Gruner, 1982. 189-218.

Frederickson, George M. *The Black Image in the White Mind: The Debate on Afro-American Character and Destiny, 1817-1914*. New York: Harper, 1971.

Hall, Christine. "Art, Action and the Ancestors: Alice Walker's *Meridian* in Its Context." *Black Women's Writing*. Ed. Gina Wisker. New York: St. Martin's, 1993. 96-110.

Jones, Suzanne W. "Dismantling Stereotypes: Interracial Friendships in *Meridian* and *A Mother and Two Daughters*." *The Female Tradition in Southern Literature*. Ed. Carol S. Manning. Urbana: U of Illinois P, 1993. 140-57.

Manvi, Meera. "The Second Reconstruction and the Southern Writer: Alice Walker and William Kelley." *Literature and Politics in Twentieth Century America*. Ed. J. L. Plakkoottam and Prashant K. Sinha. Hyderabad: American Studies Research Centre, 1993. 92-98.

McKay, Nellie Y. "Alice Walker's 'Advancing Luna—and Ida B. Wells': A Struggle Toward Sisterhood." *Rape and Representation*. Ed. Lynn A. Higgins and Brenda R. Silver. New York: Columbia UP, 1991. 248-60.

Porter, Nancy. "Women's Interracial Friendships and Visions of Community in *Meridian*, *The Salt Eaters*, *Civil Wars*, and *Dessa Rose*." *Tradition and the Talents of Women*. Ed. Florence Howe. Urbana: U of Illinois P, 1991. 251-67.

Walker, Alice. "Advancing Luna—and Ida B. Wells." *You Can't Keep a Good Woman Down*. New York: Harcourt Brace Jovanovich, 1981. 85-104.

———. "The Black Writer and the Southern Experience." *In Search of Our Mothers Gardens*. New York: Harcourt Brace Jovanovich, 1983. 16-21.

———. *Meridian*. New York: Harcourt Brace Jovanovich, 1976.

———. *The Third Life of Grange Copeland*. New York: Harcourt Brace Jovanovich, 1970.

TITLE COMMENTARY

"Everyday Use"

BARBARA T. CHRISTIAN (ESSAY DATE 1994)

SOURCE: Christian, Barbara T. Introduction to *"Everyday Use": Alice Walker*, edited by Barbara T. Christian, pp. 3-17. New Brunswick, N.J.: Rutgers University Press, 1994.

In the following essay, Christian investigates Walker's use of the quilt metaphor in her fiction—especially in Walker's story "Everyday Use"—and underscores the role of quilting in African American literature and African women's culture.

Although Alice Walker's **"Everyday Use"** was published in 1973, in the early phase of her writing career, it is a cornerstone in her large and distinguished opus—one that consists, to date, of five novels, five volumes of poetry, two essay collections, two children's books, and two short-story collections. For it is in this story and in her classic essay **"In Search of Our Mothers' Gardens"** (1974) that Walker first articulates the metaphor of quilting to represent the creative legacy that African Americans have inherited from their maternal ancestors. Walker's exploration of that metaphor is not only an abiding contribution to African American literature, as well as to American women's culture, it is also the basis of the forms she has used in her works, especially in her novels, including **The Third Life of Grange Copeland** (1970), the Pulitzer Prize-winning **The Color Purple** (1982), and her most recent, **Possessing the Secret of Joy** (1992).

During the twenty years since this story was published, critics have explored the quilt as the major metaphor in Walker's works. In *Black Women Novelists, The Development of a Tradition, 1892-1976* (1980), I called Walker's first two novels "quilts" and named the chapter on these works "Novels for Everyday Use."[1] In "Alice Walker: The Black Woman Artist as Wayward" (1981), reprinted in this volume [*"Everyday Use": Alice Walker*], **"Everyday Use"** is pivotal to my reading of Walker. Houston Baker and Charlotte Pierce Baker critique my analysis of the quilt motif in African American culture and in **"Everyday Use"** in their essay, "Patches: Quilts and Community in Alice Walker's 'Everyday Use'" (1985), also reprinted here.

In the 1980s, partially inspired by Walker's works, many studies, including those by cultural and feminist critics such as Elaine Showalter, explored the relationship between the quilt as metaphor and American literature and culture. In her book *Sister's Choice,* named after Walker's name for Celie's quilt in **The Color Purple,** Showalter investigates the history of the quilt in relation to American culture, ranging from nineteenth-century women's literature to the AIDS Quilt so important in contemporary culture.

African American women writing today have also responded to Walker's metaphor of the quilt as an articulation of women's culture, notably Toni Morrison in *Beloved* in her subtle use of the orange piece in the quilt that Baby Suggs looks to for color,[2] and Gloria Naylor in *Mama Day* in her dramatization of the construction by the "matriarch," Mama Day, of her quilt as the history of her family and community.[3] In her essay, "Sister's Choice: Quilting Aesthetics in Contemporary African American Women's Fiction," included in this volume, Margot Anne Kelley traces that motif in the novels of Walker, Morrison, and Naylor.[4] Even a popular magazine, *Newsweek,* has acknowledged the importance of the quilt in its articles on African American writers, as, for example, in Margo Jefferson's review of Toni Morrison's *Song of Solomon.*[5]

In her essay **"In Search of Our Mothers' Gardens,"** published in 1974 before the rise of Cultural Studies, Walker celebrates the creative legacy, symbolized by the quilt that women like her mother had bestowed on her and other contemporary black women writers. In this essay, Walker searches for literary models of her own, as Virginia Woolf does in *A Room of One's Own.* Instead of analyzing the reasons why women had not created great art, as Woolf—an upper-class British white woman—does, Walker wonders whether, instead of looking for a clearly defined African American female tradition of 'art,' perhaps we should look for the female folk creativity that sustained our maternal ancestors. When she looks "low," Walker finds quilts like the one she saw in the Smithsonian Institution, composed by an "anonymous black woman" who lived in an almost invisible past, yet who created a work of art valued for its passion and imagination. What Walker, a contemporary black woman writer, stresses in her appreciation of such examples of the creativity of nearly anonymous black Southern women like her mother is their ability to devise something beautiful and functional out of throwaways, from what the society considers to be waste. **"In Search of Our Mother's Gardens"** beautifully complements Walker's short story **"Everyday Use."** In both pieces she uses the metaphor of the quilt to represent the pivotal role Southern

Oprah Winfrey and Willard E. Pugh in a scene from the film adaptation of *The Color Purple.*

black women played in the development of African American culture. The ability to transform nothing into something, central to these women's creativity, is the critical theme of **"Everyday Use."**

In **"Everyday Use,"** as in **"In Search of Our Mothers' Gardens,"** Walker alludes to the process of quilting as a basis for "high art." Walker's own literary process is, in fact, developed on that model of quilting, for she consistently stitches together short units in patterns of recurring imagery to create her novels, the first three in particular: **The Third Life of Grange Copeland** her patchwork quilt,[6] **Meridian** her crazy quilt,[7] and **The Color Purple** her sister quilt.

In **The Third Life of Grange Copeland,** Walker uses the novel form to explore the complexities of the relationships between poverty, racism, and gender oppression in the life of a black Southern sharecropping family, the Copelands. More generally, Walker confronts the question of how to change the destructive pattern comprising the lives of many black sharecroppers to a pattern of creativity and wholeness.[8] In **Grange Copeland** she demonstrates the ways in which the oppression the men face sometimes results in cruelty to wives and the destruction of children. In the first part of the novel, Walker graphically lays out the bleak pattern of life for Grange, the father, who comes to hate the white man so much he has no space to love his own family. In the second part, Grange's son Brownfield repeats that same pattern of despair, resulting in his murder of Mem, his wife. But in the third part of the novel, Grange, now a grandfather, is able to change the motifs in the pattern that had made up the quilt of his life. He learns, in his third life, that the possibility of "surviving whole" resides not in his hatred of whites but in his love for his granddaughter, Ruth, his reverence for the land, and his African American Southern heritage.

In *Meridian*, published in 1976, two years after "Everyday Use," Walker improvises more freely to create a crazy quilt, juxtaposing the histories of Southern blacks and Native Americans, and the motifs of violence throughout American history as well as in the decade of the 1960s, with the life of Meridian, an "ordinary lower middle class Southern woman." At first the quilt of change she constructs seems incoherent, but by arranging a pattern of patches for Meridian's growing up (one being the way in which girls are made to feel that their only goal is to be biological mothers) in apparently random relationship to patches evoking the collective, often violent history of the sixties (with the assassinations of President John F. Kennedy and the Reverend Martin Luther King, Jr.), Walker in fact creates a quilt of the Civil Rights Movement. As she focuses on the Movement's refusal to violate life and extends its philosophy of non-violence to include the nurturing of life, she creates a pattern that suggests a quality usually ascribed to mothers as central to all those who would be revolutionaries.

Walker employs another pattern of quilting in *The Color Purple* to embody the history and culture of women, for the entire novel is written as a series of letters, a form which feminist historians have found to be a major source of women's history. Walker's composition of a quilt of sisterhood is signalled in the novel by her choice of the name "Sister's Choice" for the quilt her central character, Celie, is stitching.

Walker's choice of these various quilting techniques for her three novels is related to the project she proposed for herself in the early 1970s. In her interview in 1973 with critic Mary Helen Washington, Walker described the three "cycles" of black women that she was about to explore in the early seventies. The first type of black woman character Walker felt was missing from pre-1970s American literature were those "who were cruelly exploited, spirits and bodies mutilated, relegated to the most narrow and confining lives, sometimes driven to madness"—a succinct description of the Copeland women in Walker's first novel as well as of many of the young protagonists of *In Love and Trouble.* The women of Walker's second cycle are those who are not so much physically abused as they are psychically conflicted as a result of wanting to be part of mainstream American life—for example, Walker's sister in the poem "**For My Sister Molly Who in the Fifties**" (reprinted in this volume), or early twentieth-century writers Nella Larsen and Zora Neale Hurston, who suffered from "contrary instincts" in their need to be recognized as "real" writers in order to express themselves and their people. In Walker's third cycle are those black women who come to a new consciousness about their right to be themselves and to shape the world. The title character in Walker's second novel *Meridian* is a woman who moves in that direction, but who suffers from the restrictions imposed by the world in which she lives. Thus Meridian's need to be a part of a Movement, a struggle for change. It is Celie, Shug, and Sophia in Walker's third novel, *The Color Purple,* as well as some of the women in her second collection of stories, *You Can't Keep a Good Woman Down* (1981), who achieve the wholeness of Walker's third cycle of women. Yet, while most of the third-cycle women appear in works published after *In Love and Trouble,* there are some older women in Walker's early fiction, Washington notes, who are clearly and completely themselves.

As early as 1973, in "Everyday Use," Walker presents women of all three cycles. Maggie is the scarred sister who does not know her own worth. Her mother tells us that she walks like "a lame animal, perhaps a dog run over by some careless person rich enough to own a car." In contrast to Maggie, Dee is very much like the women of Walker's second cycle. It is true that she does not want to assimilate into white society, and that at first glance she appears to have a sense of her own selfhood. Yet it is clear from her mother's description of her growing up that she detests her family and her people's past—until it is fashionable to appreciate them. While her mother is, from time to time, fascinated by Dee's desire to win in the world, Mrs. Johnson understands Maggie's value and her love for her family, and she is critical of Dee's denigration of her past. As someone who understands herself, her right to be herself, Mrs. Johnson is one of those older women in Walker's fiction who prefigures the women of the third cycle she would so beautifully portray in *The Color Purple.* And it is significant that in "Everyday Use" it is the older mother figure, a woman who must have learned much about her own worth from her grandma Dee, who passes on that tradition of self-hood to the scarred black women of Walker's first cycle.

"Everyday Use" is also critical to Walker's work in that it is the pivotal story in her first short-story collection, *In Love and Trouble: Stories of Black Women* (1973). As its title indicates, this book placed African American women's voices at the center of the narrative, an unusual position at that time. *The Third Life of Grange Copeland,* Walker's first book of fiction, is told primarily from the point of view of Southern black men, but the stories in Walker's next publication, *In Love and Trouble,* are narrated from the point of view of women. *In Love and Trouble* is linked to *The Third Life of Grange Copeland* because the Copeland women, Margaret and Mem, like the younger protagonists of the short stories, are very much "in trouble." Thus, *In Love and Trouble* represents an important shift in Walker's work: from then on, women will occupy the center of her narratives. In one of her first interviews (with John O'Brien, included in this volume), Walker tells us that she is "preoccupied with the spiritual survival, the survival *whole* of [her] people," and that she is "committed to exploring the oppressions, the insanities, the loyalties, and the triumphs of black women."

Most reviewers of *In Love and Trouble* were aware of the distinctly new emphasis Walker placed on African American women. Barbara Smith, in her review in *Ms.,* was exuberant about Walker's ability to "explore with honesty the texture and terrors of black women's lives."[9] Mel Watkins, in *The New York Times Book Review,* characterized these stories as "perspective minatures, snapshorts that capture their subjects at crucial and revealing moments"[10]—qualities seldom found at that time in writings about African American women. Still, few reviewers were then aware of the importance "Everyday Use" would have in Walker's opus, either as a harbinger of the importance of the quilt in her work or as a new beginning in the creation of African American Southern women as subjects in their own right.

Walker's attention to black women's voices in *In Love and Trouble* is especially significant in that perhaps for the first time in contemporary United States literary history, a writer featured a variety of *Southern* black women's perspectives. In so doing, Walker had to confront the variety of stereotypes which had shaped earlier accounts of black Southern women. Walker was certainly aware of the traditional stereotypes of "the mammy" and "the wench" that had developed during slavery, for these stereotypes continued to have currency in twentieth-century American culture.[11] No doubt, she was also aware of the ways in which these stereotypes had become standard in American literature, a conspicuous example being William Faulkner's portrait of Dilsey in *The Sound and the Fury* (1929). A descendant of the historical representation of slave mammies, Dilsey has little life outside of the terrain of her employers, the Compsons. She has no black context, little family or life of her own, and exists only to enhance her white folks' lives. So incensed was Walker by this character that she called the portrayal of Dilsey, in one of her interviews, an "embarrassment" to black people.[12]

But Walker not only had to contend with American white authors' constructions of Southern black women, she had to revise African American men's representations of these women. She clearly appreciated Jean Toomer's haunting portraits of African American Southern women's sexuality in his masterpiece, *Cane* (1923), for she named her second novel, *Meridian* (1976), after Toomer's "The Blue Meridian" (1933), his prophetic poem about women and men, the earth and survival. Yet Toomer's women are silent, their sense of themselves and their condition interpreted by a male narrator.

Walker did discover a writer who allowed her Southern black women to speak. While writing **"The Revenge of Hannah Kemhuff,"** another story in *In Love and Trouble,* Walker accidently came upon the works of Zora Neale Hurston, another black Southern woman writer, who, in 1937, published *Their Eyes Were Watching God,* a novel which emphasized a Southern black woman's search for her own voice. In one of her later essays, Walker tells us that *"There is no book more important to me than this one* (including Toomer's *Cane,* which comes close, but from what I recognize is a more perilous direction)."[13] Hurston's works were to inspire Walker, not only because of their use of black folk English, which clearly influenced Walker's use of black folk English in *The Color Purple,* but also because of Hurston's abiding respect for Southern black folk. Understanding the importance of Hurston's legacy to American literature, Alice Walker would be a major force in the rediscovery of her maternal ancestor's works, to the extent that today, in significant measure because of her efforts, Hurston is considered a great American writer.[14] Walker's discovery of Hurston and the inspiration she drew from her literary maternal ancestor exemplifies the critical role models play in the development of young writers, as well as the importance of passing on the literary tradition of black people in educational institutions.

Walker's first collection of short stories was not only influenced by past stereotypes of black women in American literature, it was also very much affected by the present within which she was living. "Everyday Use" is, in part, Walker's response to the concept of heritage as articulated by the black movements of the 1960s. In that period, many African Americans, disappointed by the failure of integration, gravitated to the philosophy of cultural nationalism as the means to achieve liberation. In contrast to the veneration of Western ideas and ideals by many integrationists of the 1950s, Black Power ideologues emphasized the African cultural past as the true heritage of African Americans. The acknowledgment and appreciation of that heritage, which had too often been denigrated by African Americans themselves as well as by Euro-Americans, was a major tenet of the revolutionary movements of the period. Many blacks affirmed their African roots by changing their "slave names" to African names, and by wearing Afro hair styles and African clothing. Yet, ideologues of the period also lambasted older African Americans, opposing them to the lofty mythical models of the ancient past. These older men and women, they claimed, had become Uncle Toms and Aunt Jemimas who displayed little awareness of their culture and who, as a result of the slave past, had internalized the white man's view of blacks. So while these 1960s ideologues extolled an unknown ancient history, they denigrated the known and recent past. The tendency to idealize an ancient African past while ignoring the recent African American past still persists in the Afrocentric movements of the 1990s.

In contrast to that tendency, Walker's "Everyday Use" is dedicated to "your grandmama." And the story is told by a woman many African Americans would recognize as their grandmama, that supposedly backward Southern ancestor the cultural nationalists of the North probably visited during the summers of their youth and probably considered behind the times. Walker stresses those physical qualities which suggest such a person, qualities often demeaned by cultural nationalists. For this grandmama, like the stereotypical mammy of slavery, is "a large big-boned woman with rough, manworking hands," who wears "flannel nightgowns to bed and overalls during the day," and whose "fat keeps [her] hot in zero weather." Nor is this grandmama politically conscious according to the fashion of the day: she never had an education after the second grade, she knows nothing about African names, and she

eats pork. In having the grandmama tell this story, Walker gives voice to an entire maternal ancestry often silenced by the political rhetoric of the period. Indeed, Walker tells us in "In Search of Our Mothers' Gardens" that her writing is part of her mother's legacy to her, that many of her stories are based on stories *her* mother told her. Thus, Walker's writing is her way of breaking silences and stereotypes about her grandmothers', mothers', sisters' lives. In effect, her work is a literary continuation of a distinctly oral tradition in which African American women have been and still are pivotal participants.

Other African American women writers have also been aware of the ways in which the cultural nationalist rhetoric attempted to erase the importance of these ancestors. Toni Cade Bambara in her short story "My Man Bovanne," published in the early seventies, also critiques the demeaning of older black women.[15] Bambara's story, however, takes place in the urban North, rather than the rural South, and her character, Hazel, is a decidedly urban woman. In contrast, Walker's story emphasizes the rural Southern roots of African American heritage.

Mrs. Johnson, Walker's grandmama, typifies the elder protagonists in *In Love and Trouble*. Southern contentions about family, community, the general society, even their conscious understanding of who they *should* be, hem them in. But, denying the passive images of Southern black women accepted by our society, these women actively seek to be themselves; they are often, therefore, in conflict with social restrictions rooted in racist and sexist ideologies and may appear crazed or at least contrary. Walker underlines these internal conflicts by introducing *In Love and Trouble* with quotations from two seemingly unrelated figures: the west African writer Elechi Amadi and the early twentieth-century German poet Rainer Maria Rilke. Both excerpts stress that "everything in nature grows and defends itself in its own way," and "is characteristically and spontaneously itself," against all opposition. In using an excerpt from a West African writer about the restrictions imposed on a young girl, as well as an excerpt from a European writer, Walker challenges the stereotypes of women, especially of older women within black societies, as well as the racism these women must confront within white societies. When Mrs. Johnson yanks the old quilts away from Dee/Wangero, the seemingly educated and politically correct daughter, and gives them to Maggie, the scarred and supposedly backward daughter who would put them to everyday use, she might appear unreasonable or contrary.[16] Yet her act is in keeping with her own knowledge of the meaning of the quilts, the spirit that they embody, and her need to make decisions based upon her own values.

Alice Walker is well aware of the restrictions of the African American Southern past, for she is the eighth child of Georgia sharecroppers. Born in 1944, she grew up during that period when, as she put it, apartheid existed in America.[17] For in the 1940s and 1950s, when segregation was the law of the South, opportunities for economic and social advancement were legally denied to Southern blacks. Walker was fortunate to come to adulthood during the social and political movements of the late fifties and sixties. Of her siblings, only she, and a slightly older sister, Molly, were able even to imagine the possibility of moving beyond the poverty of their parents. It is unlikely that Alice Walker would have been able to go to college—first at Spelman, the African American woman's college in Atlanta, and then at Sarah Lawrence, the white woman's college near New York City—if it had not been for the changes that came about as a result of the Civil Rights Movement. Nor is it likely that she, a Southern black woman from a poor family, would have been able to become the writer that she did without the changes resulting from the ferment of the Black and Women's movements of the 1960s and early 1970s.

While Walker was a participant in these movements, she was also one of their most astute critics. As a Southerner, she was aware of the ways in which black Southern culture was often thought of as backward by predominantly Northern Black Power ideologues, even as they proclaimed their love for black people. She was also acutely aware of the ways in which women were oppressed within the Black Power Movement itself, even as the very culture its participants revered was so often passed on by women. Walker had also visited Africa during her junior year of college and had personally experienced the gap between the Black Power advocates' idealization of Africa and the reality of the African societies she visited.

One of Walker's distinctive qualities as a writer is the way she plays on one idea in different modes, in much the same way that a musical idea in jazz is explored through different instruments. Walker's instruments are literary genres: the poem, the short story, the essay, the novel. Her first publication, a book of poetry called *Once* (1968), criticizes the uses the Black Power Movement made of Africa, particularly the movement's tendency to turn Africans into artifacts, an objec-

tion she develops in her third novel, *The Color Purple,* and in her fifth novel, *Possessing the Secret of Joy.* Ironically, the name given to Walker by Africans during her trip there was Wangero, a name she uses for herself in *Once* and for the educated sister in "Everyday Use."

Names are extremely important in African and African American culture as a means of indicating a person's spirit. During the 1960s Walker criticized the tendency among some African Americans to give up the names their parents gave them—names which embodied the history of their recent past—for African names that did not relate to a single person they knew. Hence the grandmama in "Everyday Use" is amazed that Dee would give up her name for the name Wangero. For Dee was the name of her great-grandmother, a woman who had kept her family together against great odds. Wangero might have sounded authentically African but it had no relationship to a person she knew, nor to the personal history that had sustained her.

Walker has always been concerned with the ways in which artifacts of the African American past are celebrated by black political ideologues while the people who created them are not—a theme she develops in many of the short stories in *In Love and Trouble.* Perhaps that volume's most succinct expression of the theme is "Everyday Use." She would continue to explore the same theme in her later work. For example, the grandmama in "Everyday Use" has many qualities in common with Gracie Mae Stills, the blues singer in Walker's short story "1955," published eight years later in the volume *You Can't Keep a Good Woman Down.* Both women appear to be traditional mammy figures, but they are in fact the creators and guardians of the culture. By contrast, the young Celie in *The Color Purple* is in many ways like the scarred sister, Maggie, in "Everyday Use," but, as Thadious Davis notes in an essay included in this volume, Celie, created some ten years later, is able to acquire her own voice.

In "Everyday Use," by contrasting a sister who has the opportunity to go to college with a sister who stays at home, Walker reminds us of the challenges that contemporary African American women face as they discover what it means to be truly educated. The same concern appears in many of her works. For example, in "For My Sister Molly Who in the Fifties," she explores the conflicts that can result from an education that takes a woman away from her cultural source. Like Molly, Dee/Wangero in "Everyday Use" is embarrassed by her folk. She has been to the

North, wears an Afro, and knows the correct political rhetoric of the 1960s, but she has little regard for her relatives who have helped to create that heritage. Thus, she does not know how to quilt and can only conceive of her family's quilts as priceless artifacts, as *things,* which she intends to hang on her wall as a means of demonstrating to others that she has "heritage." On the other hand, Maggie, the supposedly uneducated sister, who has been nowhere beyond the supposedly uneducated black South, loves and understands her family and can appreciate its history. She knows how to quilt and would put the precious quilts to "everyday use," which is precisely what, Walker suggests, one needs to do with one's heritage. For Maggie, the quilts are an embodiment of the *spirit* her folk have passed on to her.

It is worth noting that Walker, in interviews as well as in her dedication to *In Search of Our Mothers' Gardens,* refers to herself as scarred, perhaps because of the tragedy she endured at the age of eight when her brother accidently shot her with a BB gun and left her blind in one eye.[18] The two sisters in "Everyday Use," then, are related to different aspects of Walker's own personal experience as an African American woman scarred by the poverty of her origins, and as a African American woman whose awareness of the richness of the culture of her origins causes her to question the meaning of her education in prestigious American colleges.

Because Walker came from a background of poverty and social restriction, she also experienced first hand those values through which the grandmama and Maggie transformed the little they had into much more, so that they might survive. As important, Walker understood that poor people needed beauty in their lives and went to great lengths to create it. Although Walker's mother worked long hours in the fields and as a domestic, she cultivated beautiful gardens, artfully told stories, and created beautiful, functional quilts out of scraps. In creating beauty in the media available to them, Walker's mother and other "ordinary" African American women not usually considered artists were, in face, models of creativity for young African American women who now have the opportunity to become artists.

In Alice Walker's works, from *Once* (1968) to *Possessing the Secret of Joy* (1992), the pieces of the ancestors' quilts continue to be restitched. As the essays in this volume suggest, the figure of this older African American woman who knows the patterns of the past and therefore knows how to stitch together patterns for the future—a

perspective first enunciated in "Everyday Use"—is central to our understanding of African American culture as well as that culture we call American. While there are differences between the patterns of African American quilts and those of other American women, as Margot Kelly's essay delineates, there are also the powerful similarities between these apparently disparate cultures, as Elaine Showalter points out. Without question, a significant number of American writings published in the last decade have illuminated ways in which "ordinary" Americans used female folk creations to articulate distinct American cultures. In that same decade, more and more American writings are focussed on women's voices, women as subjects. By emphasizing the power and variety of African American women's voices, Walker forecast the primary focus of an entire generation of African American women writers, who, in the 1970s and 1980s, published more fiction than they ever had, fiction in which they consistently constructed themselves as major actors in the world. Walker's literary works and the wisdom she exhibited in articulating the legacy of African American female creativity symbolized by the quilt helped bring about this significant development in American literature.

Notes

1. Barbara T. Christian, "Novels for Everyday Use," in *Black Women Novelists, the Development of a Tradition, 1892-1976* (Westport: Greenwood Press, 1980), pp. 180-238.

2. Toni Morrison, *Beloved* (New York: Alfred A. Knopf, 1987).

3. Gloria Naylor, *Mama Day* (New York: Ticknor and Fields, 1988).

4. Margot Anne Kelley, "Quilting Aesthetics in Contemporary African-American Women's Fiction," in *Quilt and Metaphor,* ed. Judy Elsley and Cheryl Torsney (Columbia: University of Missouri Press, forthcoming). It appears for the first time in this volume.

5. Margo Jefferson, "Across the Barricades" *Newsweek* 87, (31 May 1976): 71-72.

6. Claudia Tate, "Interview with Alice Walker," in *Black Women Writers at Work,* ed. Claudia Tate (New York: Continuum, 1983), pp. 175-187.

7. Tate, "Interview with Alice Walker."

8. See Barbara T. Christian, "Novels for Everyday Use," in *Black Women Novelists.*

9. Barbara Smith, "The Souls of Black Women," *Ms.* 2 (February 1974): 42.

10. Mel Watkins, *The New York Times Book Review* 123, #42, Section 1 (17 March 1974): 40-41.

11. See, for example, Barbara T. Christian, "Shadows Uplifted," in *Black Women Novelists,* pp. 1-34.

12. Alice Walker, "Alice Walker and *The Color Purple*," BBC production, 1986.

13. Alice Walker, "Zora Neale Hurston: A Cautionary Tale," introduction to *I Love Myself When I'm Laughing . . . And Then Again When I Am Looking Mean and Impressive: A Zora Neale Hurston Reader* (Old Westbury, New York: Feminist Press, 1979).

14. See Alice Walker, "In Search of Zora Neale Hurston," *Ms.* 2, no. 11 (March 1975).

15. See Toni Cade, "My Man Bovanne," *Gorilla My Love: Short Stories* (New York: Random House, 1972).

16. See Barbara Christian, "The Contrary Women of Alice Walker," *The Black Scholar* (March-April 1981): 21-30.

17. For a succinct biography of Alice Walker, see Barbara T. Christian, "Alice Walker," *Dictionary of Literary Biography, Vol. 33: Afro-American Fiction Writers After 1955*, ed. Thadious Davis and Trudier Harris (Detroit: Gale Research Company, 1984), pp. 257-270.

18. Alice Walker, dedication to *In Search of Our Mothers' Gardens: Womanist Prose* (New York: Harcourt Brace Jovanovich, 1983). The dedication reads: "To My Daughter Rebecca / Who saw in me / what I considered / a scar / And redefined it / as / a world."

The Color Purple

WINIFRED MORGAN (ESSAY DATE 1997)

SOURCE: Morgan, Winifred. "Alice Walker: *The Color Purple* as Allegory." In *Southern Writers at Century's End*, edited by Jeffrey J. Folks and James A. Perkins, pp. 177-84. Lexington: The University Press of Kentucky, 1997.

In the following essay, Morgan discusses The Color Purple *as an allegory that represents the traditional gender role of women as constituting slavery.*

Since the 1982 publication of **The Color Purple,** Alice Walker has continued to publish essays, poetry, and fiction. She has also maintained a high profile in news media for her role in spearheading a campaign against the primarily African practice of female genital mutilation, clitorectomy. Regardless of these accomplishments, Walker remains best known for **The Color Purple.** Since its publication, buoyed up by the enthusiastic support of feminists and black studies departments, the novel has enjoyed considerable success. This was true both before and after Stephen Spielberg's cinematic revisioning of the novel.[1] Walker's novel certainly has appealing qualities which generally sell—strongly drawn characters, a sense that these characters embody the experience of many people, memorable contrasts between the oppressors and oppressed, a downtrodden central character who overcomes both horrendous abuse and deprivation to bloom into a strong person, and, above all, an optimistic, some say a fairy-tale, ending.

ABOUT THE AUTHOR

BARBARA SMITH ON *THE COLOR PURPLE*
The fact that a book with a Black Lesbian theme by a Black woman writer achieved massive critical acclaim, became a bestseller, and was made into a major Hollywood film is unprecedented in the history of the world. It is *The Color Purple* which homophobes and antifeminists undoubtedly refer to when they talk about how "many" books currently have both Black Lesbian subject matter and an unsparing critique of misogyny in the Black community. For Black Lesbians, however, especially writers, the book has been inspirational. Reading it we think it just may be possible to be a Black Lesbian and live to tell about it. It may be possible for us to write it down and actually have somebody read it as well.

Smith, Barbara. An excerpt from "The Truth That Never Hurts: Black Lesbians in Fiction in the 1980s." In *Feminisms: An Anthology of Literary Theory and Criticism*, edited by Robyn R. Warhol and Diane Price Herndl, pp. 691-712. New Brunswick, N.J.: Rutgers University Press, 1991.

Whether they praise or condemn the novel, few readers react with less than passion to Alice Walker's **The Color Purple.** The considerable critical disagreement which has developed about the novel reflects these emotional responses. Beginning with the novel's publication and continuing through the 1985 premiere of the film version, one group of reviewers and critics has lavished praise even as others have questioned both the novel's and the film's artistic validity, particularly their verisimilitude, and their depiction of black men.[2]

From the first reviews to the most current criticism, writers have analyzed, adulated, and excoriated the novel's structure. A number of scholars, with a glance toward Terry Eagleton's comments on the epistolary novel in *The Rape of Clarissa*, have concentrated on Walker's use of letters. Most (for example, Gates) find the choice fortuitous, allowing Walker to move beyond the limitations of first-person narration while still encouraging readers to identify with the central character. Most critics also find Nettie's letters the least satisfying part of the novel.[3] A few critics (for example, Katz and Heraldson, in Bloom) enjoy the use Walker makes of this inherently didactic form usually associated with eighteenth-century tomes. They believe that Walker uses this traditional, even old-fashioned form, to overturn expectations of traditional social structures.

Still other writers have placed the novel in the existential tradition (Christophe) and that of the parable (Scholl). Yet the most obvious tradition that the novel belongs to beyond that of the epistolary novel is that of the slave narrative. The common narrative pattern encountered in slave narratives—an innately good, morally superior person is unjustly confined and maltreated by a corrupt individual; through heroic efforts, the victim escapes and lives to tell the tale and to work against the evil institution—continues to influence African-American literature almost a century and a half after the legal abolition of chattel slavery in the United States.[4] In fact, Walker's echoing of that form[5] accounts for a good deal of the angry reaction to the novel since black men, accustomed to seeing themselves vindicated in African-American literature, encounter little vindication in this novel.

Although critics have made much of the tie between *The Color Purple* and the slave-narrative tradition, concentrating on the similarities between the form of this novel and that of slave narratives may distract critics from the novel's allegorical possibilities, what Hernton refers to an "ironic analogy" between racism and sexism. A traditional definition reminds students that allegory is

> a form of extended METAPHOR in which objects, persons and actions in a NARRATIVE are equated with meanings that lie outside the NARRATIVE itself. . . . *Allegory* attempts to evoke a dual interest, one in the events, characters, and settings presented, and the other in the ideas they are intended to convey or the significance they bear. The characters, events, and settings may be historical, fictitious, or fabulous; *the test is that these materials be so employed that they represent meanings independent of the action described in the surface story.*
>
> [Harmon and Holman 12; my italics in the last clause]

With this novel, Alice Walker joins other late-twentieth-century feminists in building up, and on, an allegorical construct which personifies the traditional gender roles of woman as constituting slavery.[6] In fact, Kathleen Barry even equates domestic abuse and incest with slavery: "*Female sexual slavery is present in ALL situations where*

women or girls cannot change the immediate conditions of their existence; where regardless of how they got into those conditions they cannot get out; and where they are subject to sexual violence and exploitation" (40; Barry's italics and caps).

Not only does the novel play upon the form of traditional slave narratives, as an allegory *The Color Purple* provides a devastating critique not only of racism but also of the sexism that has doubled the burden of those women whom Zora Neale Hurston has one of her characters call the "mules of men."[7] Furthermore, the novel speaks against all forms of oppression. Readers do not have to be poor, black, ugly, unable to cook, or female to feel its central character's plight.

A striking allegorical representation of a kind of continuing slavery occurs in *The Color Purple*. Unnerving similarities exist between Celie's twentieth-century existence in the early part of the novel and that of her slave ancestors and other black women's lives under slavery. Before the novel opens, Celie's birthright has been stolen as her stepfather, Alphonso, has usurped her inheritance. If, as a sage in one of the medieval Spanish *ejemplos* argues, stealing is "the greatest villainy," then that is what has been practiced against Celie. Not only has her stepfather taken over her inheritance, his physical and sexual abuse have almost obliterated her sense of self. Hence, when fourteen-year-old Celie attempts to write her first "letter to God," her second sentence begins with a false start as she crosses out "I am." The adolescent Celie's rape by the man she believes is her father parallels the rape of slave women whom plantation theory considered "children" of the patriarchal owner. In common with generations of slave women, Celie then has her infant daughter and son taken from her. Her stepfather tells her that they are dead when, in fact, he has given—perhaps sold—them to a childless couple.

Five or six years later, when he hopes to unleash his sexual abuse on her younger sister, Nettie, Alfonso connives to get rid of Celie by having a neighbor, Mr. _____, a widower with four children, marry her. During their negotiations, Alfonso's description, "she ain't fresh," identifies Celie with milk-producing animals, and the way he makes her turn around for Mr. _____ to examine her body recalls the way slave women were bought and sold. Like them, Celie is handed on to Mr. _____ for reasons slave women were bought—their ability to endure hard physical labor and their potential as sexual objects.

In common with her ancestors, Celie is lied to and lied about. In fact, her stepfather tells Mr. _____ that "She tell lies" (10). Until Celie finally breaks loose from Mr. _____—whom she refuses to, perhaps dare not, call by his first name, Albert—she is almost constantly abused and intimidated by him. Celie spends her first day of married life fleeing Mr. _____'s twelve-year-old son, who nonetheless manages to wound her in her head with the rock he throws at her. She then cooks dinner under primitive conditions and untangles the long-neglected hair of Mr. _____'s little daughters. When night comes, she spends her time thinking about her sister, Nettie, and Shug Avery while Mr. _____ is "on top" (13) of her. Mr. _____, it quickly turns out, is a brute who alternates between beating her and beating his children (22). Living with Mr. _____'s brutality, Celie inures herself to maltreatment and tells herself she is a "tree" (22). "I don't say nothing. . . . What good it do? I don't fight, I stay where I'm told. But I'm alive" (21). Celie lacks power and skill. All she can do is survive and persevere. All she retains of ego is her "voice," and in the presence of her masters, that she keeps silent.

The stories of the other black women in the novel provide variations on Celie's story. They also serve as catalysts. As a matter of fact, from the first mention of Sophie twenty pages into the novel, Celie's existence *starts* to improve—if only because she has someone to talk to. The intersection of the other women's lives with that of Celie allows her for the first time to envision other possibilities. First Sophie, then Shug, but even Mary Agnes (Squeak) and Nettie move from being dominated to liberated. Each of them starts out "freer" than Celie, but none travels quite as far as she. As Shug comments to Mr. _____'s brother, Tobias, "All women's not alike" (52).

The Color Purple looks at what the dynamics of power between men and women, and particularly between some black men and women, currently achieve. The novel finds them so appalling that they evoke the image of conditions under slavery. No other image has quite the same potential for inciting horror, repulsion, and anger among African-Americans. Having raised this dreadful specter and dramatized the similarities between slavery and patriarchy, the novel, in effect, asks, "Can men and women find 'another way' of dealing with one another? What might this new dynamic look like? How might it come about?" The novel then pictures a world in which such new relationships might unfold. The novel's

allegory implies that if such changes and new relationships could occur in the life of the downtrodden, humanly almost obliterated Celie, surely a new life with different alternatives could be possible for anyone.

In a sense each person's life, even that of a single cell, recapitulates that of the entire race. Yet Celie's experience in the first two-thirds of Alice Walker's *The Color Purple*—until she leaves Mr._____ and moves to Memphis with Shug and Grady—has such specific parallels with the experiences of slave women that the novel emerges as an allegory of the black woman's experience of slavery in America. Calvin Hernton labels the novel "an emulation of the slave narrative" (3). But as an allegory, and not merely a novel utilizing "a classical (primal) literary genre" (Hernton 3), the novel becomes an even stronger statement of the parallels between the domestic slavery found in some homes and marriages and the situation of black women under the system of chattel slavery existing in the United States before the Civil War. Although he never actually uses the word *allegory*, Hernton does interpret the novel as an allegory of patriarchy (13-14). Celie's declaration of independence from Mr. _____ contrasts with her earlier comment that "I don't fight. . . . But I'm alive" and echoes what is probably the best known epiphany found in the slave narrative genre, Douglass's insight into Covey's tyrannous reign (Douglass 81).[8] When Celie turns on Mr. _____ and challenges him with the warning that "Anything you do to me, already done to you. . . . I'm pore, I'm black, I may be ugly and can't cook. . . . But I'm here" (176), she changes her life dramatically. "What women want" is respect. But then that is what all human beings want and need. The ending of the novel projects "what might be" if men and women respected one another.

One wonders whether the novel's allegorical message helps to explain its popularity, which took even Walker by surprise. Readers respond to this novel at an emotional level, suggesting that something is influencing them at a subliminal as well as a conscious level. One explanation might be that in *The Color Purple*, Walker has written an apparently realistic novel that also functions as an allegory of the slave woman's experience. But since the story does not, after all, take place during slavery times, readers are left with the impression that for some black women, at least, their condition after slavery hardly changed. Orlando Patterson's definition of slavery resonates with a chilling familiarity when one thinks about Celie's situation at the opening of the novel. As Patterson explains, "on the level of personal relations . . . *slavery is the permanent, violent domination of natally alienated and generally dishonored persons*" (13).[9] Although not born a slave, as the novel opens, for all practical intents and purposes, Celie is a slave.

One has to ask "Why has the condition of women like Celie changed so little?" Many people respond that racism alone does not explain this fact. Both the excitement and the outrage that the novel has generated are understandable, even to be expected, when one realizes that inadvertently or not, the novel lends itself to an allegorical interpretation explicating the lives of many poor black women both during and after slave times. The fragmented, epistolary, almost inchoate early part of the novel also deflects readers from suspecting that Walker might be using a seemingly outdated technique like allegory. By setting the novel in the not-too-distant past, Walker makes clear that slavery did not end with the Emancipation Proclamation nor even with the end of the American Civil War. Nor—despite the novel's apparently happy ending—does slavery end until people grow into an appreciation of themselves within a human community. Celie's story starts in slavery but goes on to suggest not so much how slave women of the antebellum period could choose to be free (they could not) as how those who continue to suffer a kind of slavery might participate in their own emancipation.

The central narrative in *The Color Purple* certainly works as an allegory, and the allegorical nature of the novel may help to explain why critics delight in finding multiple interpretations. It mimics aspects of the slave-narrative pattern because it harks back to a defining experience in African-American culture: the unavoidable historical fact of chattel slavery. But Walker seems to use that experience as a foil or mirror, forcing her readers to acknowledge the equally formative experience of sexism under patriarchy.[10]

Unlike the "temptation" which C. S. Lewis warns readers to avoid lest they attend to an allegory's larger meaning to the detriment of its poetry, to find allegory in *The Color Purple* in no way encourages readers to attend to an intellectual abstraction or any other kind of construct in preference to the novel's verisimilitude. On the contrary, most readers are far more likely to get so caught up in the fiction's highly charged details that they ignore any larger significance. Yet, in fiction as in poetry, "the more concrete and vital the [work] is, the more hopelessly complicated it will become in analysis: but the imagination receives it as a simple—in both senses of the word" (Lewis 345).

Yet the critical reaction to *The Color Purple* illustrates that, however easy it is to summarize its plot, the novel is not simple. That Walker should have produced a work with allegorical overtones flows organically from her rural Southern upbringing in which the tradition of African-American religious music has always spoken symbolically. Allegory works through symbols, and as Don Cameron Allen reminds readers, symbols allow communication that is larger than simple reality. "It is also the nature of the symbol to communicate to others those intuitions which seize us" (Swann and Krupat 566). The emotional reaction to the novel seems to suggest that many readers have felt that it speaks to their intuitions. Allegory, according to Angus Fletcher, has been "omnipresent in Western literature" as long as there has been such an entity, and often the surface of an allegorical tale works perfectly well by itself but achieves greater depth with interpretation. In any case, allegory serves to get past defenses, to speak to those intuitions of which Allen speaks, intuitions that might otherwise be repressed.

By its nature allegory is open to interpretation. Since readers respond to a piece of literature and interpret it according to individual experiences, not surprisingly, contemporary readers do indeed find *The Color Purple* a "moral tale" as Walker originally subtitled the novel. While, *of course,* the novel reflects the experience of only a portion of black women, enough of them relate to the central character's vicissitudes that, for example, during the movie's showing in some theaters, black women's voices sang out their encouragement of Celie. On the one hand, many African-American women could reasonably interpret *The Color Purple* as an allegory of both the racial and sexual oppression that black women have endured during and since slavery. Many white women, on the other hand, respond to the novel as a "womanist" (with its emphasis on choosing a course of action rather than accepting one's fate as biologically predetermined) allegory. Anyone can read the novel as an allegory of every human being's need for respect.

The novel's most adamant critics have objected to its supposed lack of realism and what they insist are vicious stereotypes of black men. But if *The Color Purple* is allegorical, the criticism of the novel as a fairy tale or unrealistic or improbable loses some of its validity. *The Color Purple* is about reclaiming one's history, gifts, inheritance, language, skills, song, and voice—and thereby throwing off the yoke of slavery. Though the action in the early part of the novel closely parallels that of black women under slavery, the novel's conclusion has moved far beyond that. Questions both about whether it is unfair that some black men are depicted as violent and whether the story achieves adequate historical accuracy are beside the point. As an allegory, the novel does not have these as primary concerns. In any case, why cannot the story of a poor black woman's liberation also help to set free others of both sexes, all classes, and all races?

Notes

1. The movie subtly alters and even subverts some of the novel's feminism, but that's another essay. As Jacqueline Bobo reminds readers, "the film is a commercial venture produced in Hollywood by a white male according to all of the tenets and conventions of commercial cultural production in the United States" ("Cultural Readers" 93).

2. See, for example, Bartelme, Baumgaertner, Bovoso, Graham, Heyward, Hiers, Kelley, Pinckney, Prescott, Dinita Smith, Tickle, Towers, and Watkins.

3. See, for example, Barbara Christian's comments in an early essay on Walker (in Evans 470).

4. During the early 1990s, William L. Andrews led NEH Summer Seminars at the University of Kansas exploring how this tradition functions in African-American literature. I was fortunate to be part of the 1991 seminar.

5. The assumption that *The Color Purple* echoes the slave narrative is so common as to be almost a truism. See, for example, Awkward and Hernton.

6. This is, of course, hardly a new connection, since radical eighteenth-century feminists insisted on the same similarities. More recently, Kari Winter's *Subjects of Slavery, Agents of Change* delineates some of the parallel strategies utilized by women slave narrators and women writers of gothic fiction. Winter's book also carefully delineates the limits of the rhetoric linking women under slavery and other, for the most part, less harsh patriarchal forms of domination.

7. In *Their Eyes Were Watching God*, Janie's grandmother gives this warning to the still youthful, romantic central character.

8. This is, of course, the section of Douglass's autobiography where he determines to fight back. In an extended brawl he beats the bully Covey; and years later, recalling his insight from that experience, Douglass muses that "I now resolved that, however long I might remain a slave in form, the day had passed forever when I could be a slave in fact. I did not hesitate to let it be known of me, that the white man who expected to succeed in whipping, must also succeed in killing me" (81).

9. In David Brion Davis's explanation, "the slave has three defining characteristics: his [sic] person is the property of another man, his will is subject to his owner's authority, and his labor or services are obtained through coercion." Without irony, Davis goes on to note that "various writers have added that slavery must be 'beyond the limits of the family relations'"(31).

10. Michael Awkward explores what he believes is Walker's conscious construction in *The Color Purple* of a tale about black women's creativity in order to counter false images developed over the years in the fiction of black men. Her portrayal, even if a "dream" or "utopian," nonetheless offers a picture of what a black community that had advanced beyond patriarchy might look like (163-64).

FURTHER READING

Bibliographies

Banks, Erma Davis, ed. *Alice Walker, an annotated bibliography, 1968-1986*. New York: Garland Pub., 1989, 210 p.

Offers an annotated bibliography.

Bow, Leslie. *Alice Malsenior Walker: An Annotated Bibliography, 1968-1986*, Westport, Conn.: Meckler, 1988, 162 p.

Provides an annotated bibliography.

Criticism

Barnett, Pamela E. "'Miscegenation,' Rape, and 'Race' in Alice Walker's *Meridian*." *Southern Quarterly* 39, no. 3 (spring 2001): 65-81.

Addresses the issue of interracial rape in Meridian *and explores the repercussions of the issue on African American women in the novel and in American society.*

Bradley, David. "Novelist Alice Walker Telling the Black Women's Story." *New York Times Book Review* (8 January 1984): 25-37.

An extensive biographical profile of Walker, interspersed with critical analyses of her work.

Callaloo 12, no. 12 (spring 1989).

Special issue devoted to Walker, with essays and reviews by Theodore O. Mason Jr., Joseph A. Brown, and Keith Byerman.

Dieke, Ikenna, ed. *Critical Essays on Alice Walker*. Westport, Conn.: Greenwood Press, 1999, 226 p.

Collection of critical essays.

Gourdine, Angeletta K. M. "Postmodern Ethnography and the Womanist Mission: Postcolonial Sensibilities in *Possessing the Secret of Joy*." *African American Review* 30, no. 2 (1996): 237-44.

Explores Possessing the Secret of Joy *"as ethnographic, predicated upon and beholden to the legacy of Western anthropology's relationship to and conscription of Africa and blackwomen's bodies."*

Pollitt, Katha. "Stretching the Short Story." *New York Times Book Review* (24 May 1981): 9, 15.

Praises Walker's willingness to explore controversial topics in You Can't Keep a Good Woman Down, *but faults her perceived tendency to depict all black women as victims of racism and sexism.*

Steinem, Gloria. "Alice Walker: Do You Know This Woman? She Knows You." In *Outrageous Acts and Everyday Rebellions*, pp. 259-75. New York: Holt, Rinehart and Winston, 1983.

Offers a feminist appreciation of Walker's literary career.

Washington, Mary Ellen. "An Essay on Alice Walker." In *Sturdy Black Bridges: Visions of Black Women in Literature,* edited by Roseann P. Bell, Bettye J. Parker, and Beverly Guy-Sheftall, pp. 133-49. Garden City, N.Y.: Anchor Books, 1979.

Views Walker as an apologist and spokesperson for black women, and examines the author's preoccupation with her subject matter.

Viswanathan, Meera, and Evangelina Manickam. "Is Black Woman to White as Female Is to Male?: Restoring Alice Walker's Womanist Prose to the Heart of Feminist Literary Criticism." *Indian Journal of American Studies* 28, nos. 1-2 (winter-summer 1998): 15-20.

Discusses Walker as a black feminist and situates her feminist writings within the tradition of feminist literary criticism.

OTHER SOURCES FROM GALE:

Additional coverage of Walker's life and career is contained in the following sources published by the Gale Group: *African-American Writers,* Eds. 1, 2; *American Writers Supplement,* Vol. 3; *Authors and Artists for Young Adults,* Vols. 3, 33; *Beacham's Encyclopedia of Popular Fiction: Biography and Resources,* Vol. 3; *Bestsellers,* Vol. 89:4; *Black Literature Criticism; Black Writers,* Eds. 2, 3; *Concise Dictionary of American Literary Biography, 1968-1988; Contemporary Authors,* Vols. 37-40R; *Contemporary Authors New Revision Series,* Vols. 9, 27, 49, 66, 82; *Contemporary Literary Criticism,* Vols. 5, 6, 9, 19, 27, 46, 58, 103, 167; *Contemporary Novelists,* Ed. 7; *Contemporary Popular Writers; Contemporary Southern Writers; Dictionary of Literary Biography,* Vols. 6, 33, 143; *DISCovering Authors; DISCovering Authors: British Edition; DISCovering Authors: Canadian Edition; DISCovering Authors Modules: Most-studied, Multicultural, Novelists, Poets,* and *Popular Writers; DISCovering Authors 3.0; Encyclopedia of World Literature in the 20th Century,* Ed. 3; *Exploring Novels; Exploring Short Stories; Feminist Writers; Literature and Its Times,* Vol. 3; *Literature Resource Center; Major 20th-Century Writers,* Eds. 1, 2; *Modern American Women Writers; Novels for Students,* Vol. 5; *Poetry Criticism,* Vol. 30; *Reference Guide to American Literature,* Ed. 4; *Reference Guide to Short Fiction,* Ed. 2; *St. James Guide to Young Adult Writers; Short Stories for Students,* Vols. 2, 11; *Short Story Criticism,* Vol. 5; *Something about the Author,* Vol. 31; *Twayne's United States Authors;* and *World Literature Criticism Supplement.*

EDITH WHARTON

(1862 - 1937)

(Full name Edith Newbold Jones Wharton) American short story writer, novelist, critic, autobiographer, travel writer, and poet.

Best known as a novelist of manners, Wharton chronicled the cruel excesses of American genteel society both at home and abroad at the beginning of the twentieth century in works ranging from *The House of Mirth* (1905) and *Ethan Frome* (1911) to *The Age of Innocence* (1920) and *The Buccaneers* (1938). Her carefully crafted, psychologically complex fiction also reflects a concern for the status of women in society and for the moral decay she observed beneath the outward propriety of the social elite. Critics have often compared her subject matter, tone, and style with those of Henry James, her friend and mentor, but Wharton has also received recognition for her original observations on the conflict between social convention and the inner self.

BIOGRAPHICAL INFORMATION

Born into a wealthy New York City family, Wharton was privately educated by a series of governesses and tutors both at home and abroad, who schooled her in foreign languages and European culture. As a child, she displayed a marked interest in writing and literature, from which her

socially ambitious mother attempted to dissuade her. Nevertheless, Wharton finished her first novella at the age of fourteen and anonymously published some verse in the *Atlantic Monthly* four years later. As an upper-class initiate, she witnessed the shift of power and wealth from the hands of New York's established gentry to the Industrial Revolution's nouveau riche, whom she considered to be cultural philistines obsessed with status rather than character and upon whom she modeled many of her most memorable fictional characters and situations. In 1885, she married the Boston banker Edward Wharton, who shared few of her interests or opinions and never understood her affinity for literature. Assuming the public responsibilities of society matron during her marriage, Wharton traveled widely with her husband and maintained fashionable homes in Manhattan, Newport, and Paris. However, she gradually grew dissatisfied with society life and disillusioned with marriage, so she sought personal fulfillment by writing in private. Many of these early poems and stories first appeared in *Scribner's Magazine*, and her best fiction of the period was collected in *The Greater Inclination* (1899), whose critical reception not only surprised her but also steeled her resolve to hone her literary skills. Subsequently, Wharton published the novel *The Valley of Decision* (1902), the story collection *The Descent of Man* (1904), and *The House of Mirth*, which established her critical and popular reputation as a leading writer of the era. Wharton's professional success, along with her husband's eroding sanity and marital infidelity, prompted her in 1907 to take up permanent residence in France and in 1913 to divorce her husband, which greatly pained her. Once she settled in France, however, Wharton produced some of the most notable works of her career, including the short story collections *The Hermit and the Wild Woman* (1908), *Tales of Men and Ghosts* (1910), and *Xingu and Other Stories* (1916) as well as the novels *Ethan Frome, The Reef* (1912), *The Custom of the Country* (1913), and *Summer* (1917). During World War I, Wharton organized war relief efforts for refugees, for which she earned the French Legion of Honor, and wrote propaganda for the Allies as well as the undistinguished war novels *The Marne* (1918) and *A Son at the Front* (1923). Following the armistice, Wharton resumed her literary career, and in 1921 she became the first woman to win the Pulitzer Prize for her novel *The Age of Innocence,* which she followed with *The Mother's Recompense* (1925) and the best-selling *Twilight Sleep* (1927). During the last decade of her life, Wharton continued to write short stories and novels, many of which reflect her growing disillusionment with postwar America and the Jazz Age, most notably the novels *Hudson River Bracketed* (1929) and *The Gods Arrive* (1932). In 1934, she published her autobiography, *A Backward Glance.* Wharton died at St. Brice-sous-Foret in 1937, leaving behind the unfinished manuscript of her final novel, *The Buccaneers,* which was published in 1938.

MAJOR WORKS

A number of thematic concerns characterize Wharton's works. A central theme is the repressive nature of genteel society in the United States, especially for women who usually endured diminished roles in courtship rituals and marriage arrangements. For example, in the short story "The Last Asset," a mother sanctions her daughter's engagement to a wealthy Frenchman as a means of restoring her own social position, while in "The Letters," a wife painfully reevaluates her marriage after she discovers her unopened love letters in her husband's desk. The novel *House of Mirth* also examines the limited and narrow roles for women in high society. In this novel, twenty-nine-year-old Lily Bart has beauty and social connections but lacks both money and a husband to secure her place in society. In order to remedy these circumstances she pursues two men: one is rich but outside her class, the other socially acceptable

but relatively poor. As her fortunes decline and the privileges of her milieu recede, she is either unable or unwilling to commit to either gentleman and instead overdoses on sleeping pills. Another common theme in Wharton's fiction illumines the limitations of society upon personal freedom for women and men alike, usually in ironic terms. Attempts to circumvent social convention through adultery and divorce often prove futile in her stories, demonstrating how social codes thwart the possibility of meaningful human relationships. For instance, the short story "Autres Temps . . ." focuses on an expatriate American woman ostracized by her community for her divorce twenty years earlier. She returns to her former neighborhood after learning of her own daughter's divorce and quick remarriage in the same place. Assuming her daughter suffers a similar fate, she soon discovers that community standards have changed, but society still cannot tolerate her actions because they occurred in different times and under different mores. In "Souls Belated," a woman leaves her husband for another man only to have her hopes for a life unfettered by conventional mores destroyed when her lover proposes marriage and a return to their former social circle. Similarly, *The Age of Innocence* centers on the conflict between the personal desires and social obligations of representative members of high society, exploring issues of hypocrisy and fidelity. Set in New York City in the 1870s, the novel delineates the relationship that develops between Newland Archer, a socially prominent young lawyer engaged to wed the respectable May Welland, and the Countess Ellen Olenska, who has left her unfaithful Polish husband and returned as an outsider to the old New York society into which she was born. A cousin of Welland, Olenska possesses European sophistication and a self-confidence that both attracts and threatens Archer. Torn between the predictable world of propriety and tradition to which he and his fiancée belong and the personal freedom and fulfillment that he imagines a life with Olenska represents, Archer ultimately marries Welland, unable or unwilling to break either his moral code or flout social convention. However, a number of social meetings present Archer and Olenska with the possibility of establishing a more intimate relationship, which Welland dashes with the announcement of her pregnancy. Consequently, Olenska returns to Europe, and Archer stays behind, resigned to a life as faithful husband, loving father, and upstanding citizen. The novel concludes years later as the widowed Archer travels to Europe with his grown son. Despite realizing that he finally has the social freedom and opportunity to engage in a relationship with Olenska, Archer decides not to pursue a reality that might disappoint a lifetime of dreams. Many critics have suggested that the moral, social, and intellectual dilemmas that confront Archer and Olenska mirror similar experiences in Wharton's personal and professional lives, as do other characters and situations in her oeuvre. One of Wharton's best-known and most popular works, *Ethan Frome,* is set in the aptly-named village of Starkfield in the hill country of rural New England and portrays a world that offers no satisfactory escape from a loveless marriage. This novella examines the frustration and limitations imposed on individuals by poverty and strict adherence to social codes concerning decency, propriety, and loyalty, particularly as they impinge upon male-female relationships, and suggests that infidelity invariably leads to further unhappiness. The narrative is mainly told through a series of flashbacks from the perspective of the title character's employee, who is fascinated by the fifty-two-year-old crippled Frome and seeks information about his history from the villagers. The narrative gradually reveals that twenty-four years before the narrator encounters him, Frome and his hypochondriac wife Zeena opened their home to Zeena's destitute young cousin, Mattie Silver. As time passes, Mattie and Frome fall in love in sight of Zeena's jealous eyes. Zeena eventually decides that Mattie must leave, and Frome reluctantly complies, bound to his jealous wife by his sense of duty. On the way to the train station, Frome and Mattie profess their love for each other and impulsively decide to go sledding. Unable to accept the idea of a lifetime of separation from Frome, Mattie suggests that they commit suicide by crashing their sled into an elm, but as they hurtle downhill, Frome is distracted by a vision of his wife and fails to steer the sled squarely into the tree, leaving the pair severely crippled and dependent upon Zeena to care for them. Because of their poverty and immobility, Ethan, Zeena, and Mattie are unable to improve their situation, spending interminable hours together in the decaying farmhouse.

CRITICAL RECEPTION

Despite the popular appeal and critical acclaim of both *Ethan Frome* and *The Age of Innocence* throughout most of the twentieth century, readers and critics have often failed to acknowledge essential concerns in Wharton's fiction and have dismissed her as an outdated novelist of manners whose settings, style, and slow-moving pace belong to the nineteenth century. With the rise of the women's movement in the 1970s, criticism began to focus on Wharton's expression of feminist issues, occasionally to the exclusion of Wharton's other concerns, yet feminist scholarship has also diversified approaches to her work, focusing on its implications for contemporary feminism in particular and American culture in general. For example, some critics have investigated Wharton's portrayals of women's political status at the turn of the century, particularly in connection with the woman's suffrage movement during the decades surrounding World War I, while others have contrasted her fictional representation of women's culture with the literary aesthetics that inform the writings of such early twentieth-century New England female regional writers as Sarah Orne Jewett and Kate Chopin. In addition, commentators have explained the influence of literary naturalism on Wharton's fiction in light of the deterministic themes that characterize the works of such American masters as Mark Twain and William Dean Howells. Although Wharton's works underwent a period of relative neglect during the mid-twentieth century, most contemporary critics have rehabilitated Wharton's canon as a significantly vital link between the morally and psychologically oriented works of the late nineteenth century and the iconoclastic realism of the early twentieth-century's Lost Generation.

PRINCIPAL WORKS

The Decoration of Houses [with Ogden Codman, Jr.] (nonfiction) 1897

The Greater Inclination (short stories) 1899

The Touchstone: A Story (novella) 1900; published in England as *A Gift from the Grave: A Tale*

Crucial Instances (short stories) 1901

The Valley of Decision: A Novel (novel) 1902

Sanctuary (novella) 1903

The Descent of Man (short stories) 1904

Italian Villas and Their Gardens (essays) 1904

The House of Mirth (novel) 1905

Italian Backgrounds (memoirs) 1905

The Fruit of the Tree (novel) 1907

Madame de Treymes (novella) 1907

PRIMARY SOURCES

EDITH WHARTON (NOVEL DATE 1905)

SOURCE: Wharton, Edith. Chap. 1 in *The House of Mirth.* New York: Charles Scribner's Sons, 1905.

In the following first chapter from Wharton's novel The House of Mirth, *Wharton introduces readers to Miss Lily Bart and Mr. Selden, the two protagonists of the novel, and addresses several of the customs of the period, including Miss Bart's desire for a flat of her own in New York.*

Selden paused in surprise. In the afternoon rush of the Grand Central Station his eyes had been refreshed by the sight of Miss Lily Bart.

It was a Monday in early September, and he was returning to his work from a hurried dip into the country; but what was Miss Bart doing in town at that season? If she had appeared to be catching a train, he might have inferred that he had come on her in the act of transition between one and another of the country-houses which disputed her presence after the close of the Newport season; but her desultory air perplexed him. She stood apart from the crowd, letting it drift by her to the platform or the street, and wearing an air of irresolution which might, as he surmised, be the mask of a very definite purpose. It struck him at once that she was waiting for some one, but he hardly knew why the idea arrested him. There was nothing new about Lily Bart, yet he could never see her without a faint movement of interest: it was characteristic of her that she always roused speculation, that her simplest acts seemed the result of far-reaching intentions.

An impulse of curiosity made him turn out of his direct line to the door, and stroll past her. He knew that if she did not wish to be seen she would contrive to elude him; and it amused him to think of putting her skill to the test.

"Mr. Selden—what good luck!"

She came forward smiling, eager almost, in her resolve to intercept him. One or two persons, in brushing past them, lingered to look; for Miss Bart was a figure to arrest even the suburban traveller rushing to his last train.

Selden had never seen her more radiant. Her vivid head, relieved against the dull tints of the crowd, made her more conspicuous than in a ballroom, and under her dark hat and veil she regained the girlish smoothness, the purity of tint, that she was beginning to lose after eleven years of late hours and indefatigable dancing. Was it really eleven years, Selden found himself wondering, and had she indeed reached the nine-and-twentieth birthday with which her rivals credited her?

"What luck!" she repeated. "How nice of you to come to my rescue!"

He responded joyfully that to do so was his mission in life, and asked what form the rescue was to take.

"Oh, almost any—even to sitting on a bench and talking to me. One sits out a cotillion—why not sit out a train? It isn't a bit hotter here than in

Mrs. Van Osburgh's conservatory—and some of the women are not a bit uglier." She broke off, laughing, to explain that she had come up to town from Tuxedo, on her way to the Gus Trenors' at Bellomont, and had missed the three-fifteen train to Rhinebeck. "And there isn't another till half-past five." She consulted the little jewelled watch among her laces. "Just two hours to wait. And I don't know what to do with myself. My maid came up this morning to do some shopping for me, and was to go on to Bellomont at one o'clock, and my aunt's house is closed, and I don't know a soul in town." She glanced plaintively about the station. "It IS hotter than Mrs. Van Osburgh's, after all. If you can spare the time, do take me somewhere for a breath of air."

He declared himself entirely at her disposal: the adventure struck him as diverting. As a spectator, he had always enjoyed Lily Bart; and his course lay so far out of her orbit that it amused him to be drawn for a moment into the sudden intimacy which her proposal implied.

"Shall we go over to Sherry's for a cup of tea?"

She smiled assentingly, and then made a slight grimace.

"So many people come up to town on a Monday—one is sure to meet a lot of bores. I'm as old as the hills, of course, and it ought not to make any difference; but if I'M old enough, you're not," she objected gaily. "I'm dying for tea—but isn't there a quieter place?"

He answered her smile, which rested on him vividly. Her discretions interested him almost as much as her imprudences: he was so sure that both were part of the same carefully-elaborated plan. In judging Miss Bart, he had always made use of the "argument from design."

"The resources of New York are rather meagre," he said; "but I'll find a hansom first, and then we'll invent something." He led her through the throng of returning holiday-makers, past sallow-faced girls in preposterous hats, and flat-chested women struggling with paper bundles and palm-leaf fans. Was it possible that she belonged to the same race? The dinginess, the crudity of this average section of womanhood made him feel how highly specialized she was.

A rapid shower had cooled the air, and clouds still hung refreshingly over the moist street.

"How delicious! Let us walk a little," she said as they emerged from the station.

They turned into Madison Avenue and began to stroll northward. As she moved beside him, with her long light step, Selden was conscious of taking a luxurious pleasure in her nearness: in the modelling of her little ear, the crisp upward wave of her hair—was it ever so slightly brightened by art?—and the thick planting of her straight black lashes. Everything about her was at once vigorous and exquisite, at once strong and fine. He had a confused sense that she must have cost a great deal to make, that a great many dull and ugly people must, in some mysterious way, have been sacrificed to produce her. He was aware that the qualities distinguishing her from the herd of her sex were chiefly external: as though a fine glaze of beauty and fastidiousness had been applied to vulgar clay. Yet the analogy left him unsatisfied, for a coarse texture will not take a high finish; and was it not possible that the material was fine, but that circumstance had fashioned it into a futile shape?

As he reached this point in his speculations the sun came out, and her lifted parasol cut off his enjoyment. A moment or two later she paused with a sigh.

"Oh, dear, I'm so hot and thirsty—and what a hideous place New York is!" She looked despairingly up and down the dreary thoroughfare. "Other cities put on their best clothes in summer, but New York seems to sit in its shirtsleeves." Her eyes wandered down one of the sidestreets. "Someone has had the humanity to plant a few trees over there. Let us go into the shade."

"I am glad my street meets with your approval," said Selden as they turned the corner.

"Your street? Do you live here?"

She glanced with interest along the new brick and limestone house-fronts, fantastically varied in obedience to the American craving for novelty, but fresh and inviting with their awnings and flower-boxes.

"Ah, yes—to be sure: THE BENEDICK. What a nice-looking building! I don't think I've ever seen it before." She looked across at the flat-house with its marble porch and pseudo-Georgian facade. "Which are your windows? Those with the awnings down?"

"On the top floor—yes."

"And that nice little balcony is yours? How cool it looks up there!"

He paused a moment. "Come up and see," he suggested. "I can give you a cup of tea in no time—and you won't meet any bores."

Her colour deepened—she still had the art of blushing at the right time—but she took the suggestion as lightly as it was made.

"Why not? It's too tempting—I'll take the risk," she declared.

"Oh, I'm not dangerous," he said in the same key. In truth, he had never liked her as well as at that moment. He knew she had accepted without afterthought: he could never be a factor in her calculations, and there was a surprise, a refreshment almost, in the spontaneity of her consent.

On the threshold he paused a moment, feeling for his latchkey.

"There's no one here; but I have a servant who is supposed to come in the mornings, and it's just possible he may have put out the tea-things and provided some cake."

He ushered her into a slip of a hall hung with old prints. She noticed the letters and notes heaped on the table among his gloves and sticks; then she found herself in a small library, dark but cheerful, with its walls of books, a pleasantly faded Turkey rug, a littered desk and, as he had foretold, a tea-tray on a low table near the window. A breeze had sprung up, swaying inward the muslin curtains, and bringing a fresh scent of mignonette and petunias from the flower-box on the balcony.

Lily sank with a sigh into one of the shabby leather chairs.

"How delicious to have a place like this all to one's self! What a miserable thing it is to be a woman." She leaned back in a luxury of discontent.

Selden was rummaging in a cupboard for the cake.

"Even women," he said, "have been known to enjoy the privileges of a flat."

"Oh, governesses—or widows. But not girls—not poor, miserable, marriageable girls!"

"I even know a girl who lives in a flat."

She sat up in surprise. "You do?"

"I do," he assured her, emerging from the cupboard with the sought-for cake.

"Oh, I know—you mean Gerty Farish." She smiled a little unkindly. "But I said MARRIAGE-ABLE—and besides, she has a horrid little place, and no maid, and such queer things to eat. Her cook does the washing and the food tastes of soap. I should hate that, you know."

"You shouldn't dine with her on wash-days," said Selden, cutting the cake.

They both laughed, and he knelt by the table to light the lamp under the kettle, while she measured out the tea into a little tea-pot of green glaze. As he watched her hand, polished as a bit of old ivory, with its slender pink nails, and the sapphire bracelet slipping over her wrist, he was struck with the irony of suggesting to her such a life as his cousin Gertrude Farish had chosen. She was so evidently the victim of the civilization which had produced her, that the links of her bracelet seemed like manacles chaining her to her fate.

She seemed to read his thought. "It was horrid of me to say that of Gerty," she said with charming compunction. "I forgot she was your cousin. But we're so different, you know: she likes being good, and I like being happy. And besides, she is free and I am not. If I were, I daresay I could manage to be happy even in her flat. It must be pure bliss to arrange the furniture just as one likes, and give all the horrors to the ash-man. If I could only do over my aunt's drawing-room I know I should be a better woman."

"Is it so very bad?" he asked sympathetically.

She smiled at him across the tea-pot which she was holding up to be filled.

"That shows how seldom you come there. Why don't you come oftener?"

"When I do come, it's not to look at Mrs. Peniston's furniture."

"Nonsense," she said. "You don't come at all—and yet we get on so well when we meet."

"Perhaps that's the reason," he answered promptly. "I'm afraid I haven't any cream, you know—shall you mind a slice of lemon instead?"

"I shall like it better." She waited while he cut the lemon and dropped a thin disk into her cup. "But that is not the reason," she insisted.

"The reason for what?"

"For your never coming." She leaned forward with a shade of perplexity in her charming eyes. "I wish I knew—I wish I could make you out. Of course I know there are men who don't like me—one can tell that at a glance. And there are others who are afraid of me: they think I want to marry them." She smiled up at him frankly.

"But I don't think you dislike me—and you can't possibly think I want to marry you."

"No—I absolve you of that," he agreed.

"Well, then—?"

He had carried his cup to the fireplace, and stood leaning against the chimney-piece and looking down on her with an air of indolent amusement. The provocation in her eyes increased his amusement—he had not supposed she would waste her powder on such small game; but perhaps she was only keeping her hand in; or perhaps a girl of her type had no conversation but of the personal kind. At any rate, she was amazingly pretty, and he had asked her to tea and must live up to his obligations.

"Well, then," he said with a plunge, "perhaps THAT'S the reason."

"What?"

"The fact that you don't want to marry me. Perhaps I don't regard it as such a strong inducement to go and see you." He felt a slight shiver down his spine as he ventured this, but her laugh reassured him.

"Dear Mr. Selden, that wasn't worthy of you. It's stupid of you to make love to me, and it isn't like you to be stupid." She leaned back, sipping her tea with an air so enchantingly judicial that, if they had been in her aunt's drawing-room, he might almost have tried to disprove her deduction.

"Don't you see," she continued, "that there are men enough to say pleasant things to me, and that what I want is a friend who won't be afraid to say disagreeable ones when I need them? Sometimes I have fancied you might be that friend—I don't know why, except that you are neither a prig nor a bounder, and that I shouldn't have to pretend with you or be on my guard against you." Her voice had dropped to a note of seriousness, and she sat gazing up at him with the troubled gravity of a child.

"You don't know how much I need such a friend," she said. "My aunt is full of copy-book axioms, but they were all meant to apply to conduct in the early fifties. I always feel that to live up to them would include wearing book-muslin with gigot sleeves. And the other women—my best friends—well, they use me or abuse me; but they don't care a straw what happens to me. I've been about too long—people are getting tired of me; they are beginning to say I ought to marry."

There was a moment's pause, during which Selden meditated one or two replies calculated to add a momentary zest to the situation; but he rejected them in favour of the simple question: "Well, why don't you?"

She coloured and laughed. "Ah, I see you ARE a friend after all, and that is one of the disagreeable things I was asking for."

"It wasn't meant to be disagreeable," he returned amicably. "Isn't marriage your vocation? Isn't it what you're all brought up for?"

She sighed. "I suppose so. What else is there?"

"Exactly. And so why not take the plunge and have it over?"

She shrugged her shoulders. "You speak as if I ought to marry the first man who came along."

"I didn't mean to imply that you are as hard put to it as that. But there must be some one with the requisite qualifications."

She shook her head wearily. "I threw away one or two good chances when I first came out—I suppose every girl does; and you know I am horribly poor—and very expensive. I must have a great deal of money."

Selden had turned to reach for a cigarette-box on the mantelpiece.

"What's become of Dillworth?" he asked.

"Oh, his mother was frightened—she was afraid I should have all the family jewels reset. And she wanted me to promise that I wouldn't do over the drawing-room."

"The very thing you are marrying for!"

"Exactly. So she packed him off to India."

"Hard luck—but you can do better than Dillworth."

He offered the box, and she took out three or four cigarettes, putting one between her lips and slipping the others into a little gold case attached to her long pearl chain.

"Have I time? Just a whiff, then." She leaned forward, holding the tip of her cigarette to his. As she did so, he noted, with a purely impersonal enjoyment, how evenly the black lashes were set in her smooth white lids, and how the purplish shade beneath them melted into the pure pallour of the cheek.

She began to saunter about the room, examining the bookshelves between the puffs of her cigarette-smoke. Some of the volumes had the ripe tints of good tooling and old morocco, and her eyes lingered on them caressingly, not with the appreciation of the expert, but with the pleasure in agreeable tones and textures that was one of her inmost susceptibilities. Suddenly her expression changed from desultory enjoyment to active conjecture, and she turned to Selden with a question.

"You collect, don't you—you know about first editions and things?"

"As much as a man may who has no money to spend. Now and then I pick up something in the rubbish heap; and I go and look on at the big sales."

She had again addressed herself to the shelves, but her eyes now swept them inattentively, and he saw that she was preoccupied with a new idea.

"And Americana—do you collect Americana?"

Selden stared and laughed.

"No, that's rather out of my line. I'm not really a collector, you see; I simply like to have good editions of the books I am fond of."

She made a slight grimace. "And Americana are horribly dull, I suppose?"

"I should fancy so—except to the historian. But your real collector values a thing for its rarity. I don't suppose the buyers of Americana sit up reading them all night—old Jefferson Gryce certainly didn't."

She was listening with keen attention. "And yet they fetch fabulous prices, don't they? It seems so odd to want to pay a lot for an ugly badly-printed book that one is never going to read! And I suppose most of the owners of Americana are not historians either?"

"No; very few of the historians can afford to buy them. They have to use those in the public libraries or in private collections. It seems to be the mere rarity that attracts the average collector."

He had seated himself on an arm of the chair near which she was standing, and she continued to question him, asking which were the rarest volumes, whether the Jefferson Gryce collection was really considered the finest in the world, and what was the largest price ever fetched by a single volume.

It was so pleasant to sit there looking up at her, as she lifted now one book and then another from the shelves, fluttering the pages between her fingers, while her drooping profile was outlined against the warm background of old bindings, that he talked on without pausing to wonder at her sudden interest in so unsuggestive a subject. But he could never be long with her without trying to find a reason for what she was doing, and as she replaced his first edition of La Bruyère and turned away from the bookcases, he began to ask himself what she had been driving at. Her next question was not of a nature to enlighten him. She paused before him with a smile which seemed at once designed to admit him to her familiarity, and to remind him of the restrictions it imposed.

"Don't you ever mind," she asked suddenly, "not being rich enough to buy all the books you want?"

He followed her glance about the room, with its worn furniture and shabby walls.

"Don't I just? Do you take me for a saint on a pillar?"

"And having to work—do you mind that?"

"Oh, the work itself is not so bad—I'm rather fond of the law."

"No; but the being tied down: the routine—don't you ever want to get away, to see new places and people?"

"Horribly—especially when I see all my friends rushing to the steamer."

She drew a sympathetic breath. "But do you mind enough—to marry to get out of it?"

Selden broke into a laugh. "God forbid!" he declared.

She rose with a sigh, tossing her cigarette into the grate.

"Ah, there's the difference—a girl must, a man may if he chooses." She surveyed him critically. "Your coat's a little shabby—but who cares? It doesn't keep people from asking you to dine. If I were shabby no one would have me: a woman is asked out as much for her clothes as for herself. The clothes are the background, the frame, if you like: they don't make success, but they are a part of it. Who wants a dingy woman? We are expected to be pretty and well-dressed till we drop—and if we can't keep it up alone, we have to go into partnership."

Selden glanced at her with amusement: it was impossible, even with her lovely eyes imploring him, to take a sentimental view of her case.

"Ah, well, there must be plenty of capital on the look-out for such an investment. Perhaps you'll meet your fate tonight at the Trenors'."

She returned his look interrogatively.

"I thought you might be going there—oh, not in that capacity! But there are to be a lot of your set—Gwen Van Osburgh, the Wetheralls, Lady Cressida Raith—and the George Dorsets."

She paused a moment before the last name, and shot a query through her lashes; but he remained imperturbable.

"Mrs. Trenor asked me; but I can't get away till the end of the week; and those big parties bore me."

"Ah, so they do me," she exclaimed.

"Then why go?"

"It's part of the business—you forget! And besides, if I didn't, I should be playing bezique with my aunt at Richfield Springs."

"That's almost as bad as marrying Dillworth," he agreed, and they both laughed for pure pleasure in their sudden intimacy.

She glanced at the clock.

"Dear me! I must be off. It's after five."

She paused before the mantelpiece, studying herself in the mirror while she adjusted her veil. The attitude revealed the long slope of her slender sides, which gave a kind of wild-wood grace to her outline—as though she were a captured dryad subdued to the conventions of the drawing-room; and Selden reflected that it was the same streak of sylvan freedom in her nature that lent such savour to her artificiality.

He followed her across the room to the entrance-hall; but on the threshold she held out her hand with a gesture of leave-taking.

"It's been delightful; and now you will have to return my visit."

"But don't you want me to see you to the station?"

"No; good bye here, please."

She let her hand lie in his a moment, smiling up at him adorably.

"Good bye, then—and good luck at Bellomont!" he said, opening the door for her.

GENERAL COMMENTARY

LINDA WAGNER-MARTIN (ESSAY DATE 1996)

SOURCE: Wagner-Martin, Linda. "Prospects for the Study of Edith Wharton." *Resources for American Literary Study* 22, no. 1 (1996): 1-15.

In the following essay, Wagner-Martin surveys the critical reception of Wharton's writings since the mid-1970s, highlighting the diversity of approaches to her work and its implications for contemporary feminism.

To assert that serious criticism of the writing of Edith Wharton began with R. W. B. Lewis's 1975 *Edith Wharton: A Biography* would be an

exaggeration. Yet for many readers and scholars of the 1980s and the 1990s, this single book—and its attendant publicity and awards—led to waves of reevaluation. In the long run, the attention meant that Wharton's work would be assessed in the context of the later twentieth century, rather than the earlier, a shift that has been healthy in a number of ways.

Following the Lewis biography by just two years was Cynthia Griffin Wolff's *A Feast of Words: The Triumph of Edith Wharton,* a more psychologically based study of not only Wharton's life and writing, but also the integral relationship between the two. The acclaim for Wolff's book signaled both a wide popular market for scholarship on Wharton and a hunger for information about the supposedly remote and austere "Mrs. Wharton" among women scholars who thought of themselves as feminist. In the project of the 1970s and 1980s, to reclaim and—in Adrienne Rich's term—to revision writing by women, reading Wharton's novels and short stories was truly a "feast."

In the early 1980s, the now-flourishing Edith Wharton Society was formed. Its leadership arranged panels on Wharton's work at existing professional conferences and at several important meetings devoted entirely to discussions of Wharton (in Lenox, Massachusetts; New York; Paris; and, most recently, New Haven, Connecticut). Part of the society's mission was to institute a journal—first known as *The Edith Wharton Newsletter* but now titled *The Edith Wharton Review.* Included regularly in the journal, which was often edited by Annette Zilversmit, was a comprehensive bibliography prepared by Alfred Bendixen. The excellent leadership in Wharton studies continues, providing both information and support to scholars interested in her work.

I emphasize the society and its publication because Wharton studies had previously been marked by an air of dutifulness. Good and generous work had been done by many critics, among them E. K. Brown, Percy Lubbock, Vernon L. Parrington, Edmund Wilson, Blake Nevius, and Irving Howe. However, their writings so obviously championed Wharton, aimed so apparently at creating a solid, scholarly reputation for her, that some readers were skeptical. Was Wharton being placed in the canon because professors of American literature taught no other women fiction writers? One might have suggested this when Arthur Mizener wrote a chapter on Wharton's *The Age of Innocence* in his 1967 *Twelve Great American Novels*: Wharton was the only woman writer included.

Graduate students were not rushing to write dissertations on Edith Wharton; undergraduates were not eager to read her fiction. The atmosphere surrounding the study of Wharton—like that surrounding the study of Ellen Glasgow—was one of nostalgia. Yes, Wharton was a novelist of manners and, yes, she had been one of the best of the local color writers. Yes, those of us interested in the New York scene in the 1870s and 1880s—particularly those of us interested in the narratives of the socially elite—would continue to read her novels. Nonetheless, there was little passion attached to the study of her writing. The person who "did Wharton" in most English departments was probably the aging woman teacher whose publications were counted but seldom read. The assumption, even as late as the 1970s, was that women writers were of little interest to those faculty members who taught Wordsworth, Chaucer, and Hemingway—writers the study of whose work was the real business of English departments.

This is not to say that James Tuttleton's 1972 *The Novel of Manners in America* was obsolete, but rather that new ways of viewing the written text had begun to eclipse those based on existing literary classifications. A knowledge of history became less important a consideration for even Wharton's most-acclaimed novel, **The Age of Innocence,** winner of the Pulitzer Prize for Fiction in 1921. In addition, the usual way of establishing that Wharton belonged among the great American writers—because, in E. K. Brown's words, she was "at ease in a man's world" and was, therefore, a gentlemanly novelist rather than a woman writer—had fallen into disrepute. No matter how often she had been labeled "Mrs. Wharton," Edith Newbold Jones was coming into her rightful place in American letters as a great woman writer. During the late 1970s, readers focused more intently on Wharton as woman writer—traveling widely, living abroad in France, and succeeding as a bestselling author until her death in 1937.

The figuration of Edith Wharton as a striking and powerful woman, a woman who accrued power both because of her ability to create memorable, sympathetic protagonists and because of the clear financial success of her fiction, appeared on the horizon of Wharton studies in ways that embarrassed some literary critics. Better that Wharton remain the dignified upper-class woman whose personal energy terrified the more leisurely Henry James. (Even though Millicent Bell had clarified the relationship between James and Wharton in her 1965 study, the tendency to reduce Wharton to James's apprentice lingered.)

Better that readers continue to negate the fiery intelligence and feeling that made Wharton's writing more forceful than many other turn-of-the-century and modernist fictions.

The past twenty years of criticism, drawing partially on the biographies, have created a new sense of Edith Wharton as woman writer. They have brought innovative critical perspectives to some of her fiction, although a great deal of her extensive oeuvre remains neglected. Even though Alfred Bendixen claims in his 1993 bibliographic essay that Wharton's place as major novelist is firmly established ("New Directions" 20), a great quantity of work remains to be done. In this essay, I will suggest only a few of the kinds of explorations that would be fruitful.

All Americanists recognize that criticism of Edith Wharton is at a far different place from that of Walt Whitman or Ernest Hemingway—that is, truly canonized writers. For them, the scaffolding of good bibliographies, good biographies, and good collections of essays and letters has long been in place. The tools so necessary to excellent scholarship, then, are already accessible. So far as research on Wharton is concerned, the past decade has brought improvement in such resources. To Marlene Springer's 1976 reference guide to both Wharton and Kate Chopin (the combination of the two writers reflective of the amount of work then being done—as well as of publishers' views of the importance of these writers) came other listings of secondary criticism (Tuttleton, "Edith Wharton"; Springer and Gilson; Bendixen, "A Guide," "New Directions," "Recent Wharton Studies," "Wharton Studies," "The World"; Joslin, "Edith Wharton at 125"; and Lauer and Murray). To Vito J. Brenni's 1966 bibliography came Stephen Garrison's 1990 descriptive work, published in the Pittsburgh series. And to help make research for Wharton students somewhat manageable, in 1992 Tuttleton, Lauer, and Murray brought out the useful *Edith Wharton: The Contemporary Reviews* in the Cambridge series. Of all twentieth-century writers, Wharton had amassed a huge, almost underscribed, body of reviews. Because she lived abroad during many of the years she published, she herself had been unable to collect the newspaper and magazine commentaries extant. Tracing these materials and collecting representative reviews has been a valuable project.

What now exists suggests further lacunae that need to be filled. Scholars would benefit from having a volume—or several volumes—of retrospective critical essays, drawing from the quantity of excellent recent work as well as those essays already published in Irving Howe's 1962 collection. Millicent Bell's recent *The Cambridge Companion to Edith Wharton,* with essays by Gloria Erlich, Elaine Showalter, William Vance, Elizabeth Ammons and others, begins to fill that need. Such a collection begins the process of making standard Wharton criticism easily available to students. Today, doing research on Wharton remains an arduous library task, and an *Edith Wharton: Six Decades of Criticism* (or perhaps *Seven Decades*) would at least begin to describe some patterns in the commentary.

Even more valuable would be a collection of Wharton's own reviews and occasional essays. Perhaps her 1925 **The Writing of Fiction** could be republished in conjunction with her comments on her art from both reviews and letters; an *Edith Wharton on Writing* would help readers understand the author's pose of modest irony, which she tended to assume whenever she discussed her craft (see Wegener). It goes without saying that publication of Wharton's previously unpublished writings will also be both desirable and, eventually, necessary. The interest provoked by R. W. B. Lewis's inclusion (as an appendix to his biography) of Wharton's "Beatrice Palmato" fragment, a previously unknown fiction about father-daughter incest, suggests the need to publish materials that remain inaccessible. When Cynthia Griffin Wolff found the Palmato fragment in the Yale Wharton collection, she asked Lewis—whose book was to be in print before her own—to make the work available. Many scholars are less generous; to ensure that interested parties have access to materials, we should both publish these materials and catalog them.

An obvious gap in resources for Wharton scholarship is the lack of either print or on-line catalogues for the largest manuscript and correspondence collections: the Beinecke collection at Yale; the Harry Ransom Humanities Research Center collection at the University of Texas, Austin; and the Lilly Library collection at Indiana University. Also of interest are materials in the Firestone Library at Princeton, the Houghton Library and the Pusey Library at Harvard, the Villa I Tatti (Bernard Berenson's former home in Florence, which is now the Harvard Center for Renaissance Studies), and other collections. Access to these materials is now dependent upon actually visiting the site, an expensive and time-consuming process for researchers.

One of the most dramatic illustrations of scholars' lack of awareness of what a collection held was the discovery in the early 1980s that the Harry Ransom Humanities Research Center at Texas had, in 1980, purchased the three hundred letters written by Wharton to her lover Morton Fullerton (Gribben, Colquitt). Presumed to have been destroyed, the cache of poignant, passionate letters had an immense impact, both on the biography of the author and on readings of her fiction. Eighty of the letters were published, at least partially, in the Lewises' 1988 **The Letters of Edith Wharton,** and Shari Benstock and other recent critics and biographers have made great use of the collection (see Benstock's appendix in *No Gifts From Chance: A Biography of Edith Wharton* on the history of the discovery).

The difficulty of trying to publish a meaningful sample of Edith Wharton's letters is apparent: she wrote hundreds, perhaps thousands, of letters. Lewis recounts that, on one instance in 1924, Wharton returned from a short trip to find sixty-five letters (three days' mail) waiting for her (*Letters* 3). Most of her correspondents were not famous, of course, so many of her letters are simply lost. Of the four thousand pieces of correspondence that the Lewises located, they could print only a tenth, four hundred, in their volume. That volume has since been supplemented by Lyall Powers's collection of the James-Wharton letters, but much more of Wharton's correspondence needs to be made available. Literally hundreds of letters from Wharton to Sara Norton, Gaillard Lapsley, Bernard and Mary Berenson, and others exist; it appears that, regrettably, either Wharton or the recipients destroyed her letters to Percy Lubbock and Walter Berry.

The impact made by the discoveries of both the "Beatrice Palmato" fragment and Wharton's letters to Fullerton suggests a pervasive problem within Wharton studies. Perhaps because the earlier critical history of response to Wharton's work followed such predictable patterns, new pieces of information have a great potential to change the existing body of work. The shock value of discoveries, then, depends as much on their effect on the critical givens as on their intrinsic meaning. Accordingly, criticism of Wharton and her work tends to plateau, to halt in pools of agreement, while evidence that supports new information is put forth. This tendency is especially noticeable because publication outlets for criticism about Wharton are relatively few: when one reads essays in the Society publication, or in *American Literary Realism, American Literature,* or *Studies in American Fiction,* the same material is often repeated—or at least alluded to.

Such a pattern suggests another problem within Wharton studies: even current criticism tends to reify its past history. Discussions of Wharton's various uses of irony, for example, always a significant tactic for this writer, still return to Blake Nevius's excellent early work. Those considerations could be grounded as easily in the more recent work on irony of such critics as Wayne Booth and Linda Hutcheon. In other words, today's scholars might study Wharton's work by using theories of critics who do not treat Wharton's work. One instance of reliance on non-Whartonians is Kathy Miller Hadley's 1993 book, *In the Interstices of the Tale: Edith Wharton's Narrative Strategies,* which discusses Wharton's narrative achievements from **The Reef** to **The Mother's Recompense** and **The Children,** using such feminist narratological approaches as those given in Rachel Blau DuPlessis's *Writing Beyond the Ending* and work by Sandra M. Gilbert and Susan Gubar. Others are essays by Ellie Ragland Sullivan (a psychoanalytic reading) and D. Quentin Miller (a language-based narratological reading).

More diverse critical approaches would seem to be particularly useful in dealing with Wharton's women characters, and with themes that must be characterized as women-centered (as in **The Mother's Recompense** or **Twilight Sleep,** for example). Dale M. Bauer's 1994 study, *Edith Wharton's Brave New Politics,* shows the kinds of wide-ranging information provided by a serious look at social, philosophical, and medical issues contemporary with Wharton's fictions from **Summer** through the late 1920s. As useful as Bauer's 1988 Bakhtinian reading of Wharton was (*Female Dialogics*), *Brave New Politics* breaks more—and newer—ground. It places Wharton's late writing in the mainstream of philosophical and biological theories of reproduction and eugenics, as well as such less often scrutinized currents of popular culture as the self-help movement, the marriage market, and the public obsession with film stars. Bauer here draws Wharton as a novelist keenly aware of the foibles of modernism, an author far different from the aging woman said to be past her peak as writer.

A different kind of contextualization occurs in Shari Benstock's 1986 *Women of the Left Bank: Paris, 1910-1940.* In this rich study of more than a dozen women's lives, Benstock both describes the existences of expatriate women and shows the way insistent parallels from their lives create a culture that shaped much of twentieth-century modernism. In this context, Wharton was one of the most essential figures of European and American modernity. Similarly, Elizabeth Ammons's 1992 study, *Conflicting Stories: American Women Writers at the Turn into the Twentieth Century,* juxtaposes what might appear to be singular, even unique, lives into parallel patterns. Her sometimes harsh criticism of privileged white culture, represented in part by Wharton, is a long-overdue corrective to critical views of what is normative about modernist writing.

While *Women of the Left Bank* and *Conflicting Stories* have been immensely important in helping readers place Wharton and her work, two books by Susan Goodman have had as their aim the further surrounding of Wharton with her own immediate cultural context. In her 1990 *Edith Wharton's Women: Friends and Rivals,* Goodman explores key relationships between Wharton and other women, pointing out that many of her most intimate letters were to women correspondents. In her 1994 study of the men who comprised what she terms *Edith Wharton's Inner Circle,* Goodman again provides a quantity of previously uncollected information to show Wharton's deep interest in aspiring artists, and her genuine gift for friendship with achieving people (many of them, given the cultural climate of her time, male).

For all this attention to the context of Wharton's life as a writer, however, much criticism of the work itself remains myopic. It is as if readers find Wharton's characters so fascinating, her plots so involving, that many are unwilling to discuss more than one text, or more than one character, at a time. Yet some of the best earlier studies of Wharton's works (McDowell; Lawson; Ammons, *Edith Wharton's Argument*; Wershoven, Gimbel) surveyed most of her novels. Much recent criticism of Wharton tends, in contrast, to be New Critical. At its best, as in essays by D. Quentin Miller, Sherrie A. Inness, and Jean Frantz Blackall, or the book by Catherine M. Rae, close readings of texts are never outdated. Some publishers' formats call for readings of single texts (Springer on **Ethan Frome,** Wagner-Martin on **The House of Mirth** and **The Age of Innocence**). For students trained in various kinds of criticism, however, the close-reading approach makes Wharton's work seem less interesting than works by her peers—Virginia Woolf, Willa Cather, Djuna Barnes, Katherine Mansfield—who have received attention from scholars whose critical practices are more diverse.

Partly because of the reification of past criticism, coupled with an emphasis on close-reading techniques, it has been difficult to change—or even modify—the ways in which Wharton's best-known texts are read. Male characters still occupy the center of critical attention, for example. (An index of the power of the male-focused interpretations of the novels was the kind of attention Judith Sensibar's 1988 essay in *American Literature*—questioning Wharton's view of "the bachelor type"—received [and see Holbrook].) Readings are still dominated by the view that Wharton was as good a writer as she was largely because she *was* one of the boys, voiced in studies by Percy Lubbock and others through Lewis's biography, although countered by Goodman in her book on Wharton's male circle. This view discounts the issue of whether or not she was influenced by Henry James by contending that in some ways she *was* Henry James—or at least Walter Berry.

A corollary to the problem that Wharton is identified with male writers is that earlier criticism often identified her with her male protagonists. Such identification causes immense problems for today's readers, who are accustomed to having women writers, like writers of color, identify themselves proudly rather than disguise their gender and race. The logical autobiographical correspondence in *The Reef*, for example, is between Wharton and some composite of Sophy Viner and Anna Leath—just as in *The Age of Innocence* the logical correspondence is between Wharton and Ellen Olenska. The traditional reading of the latter novel, however, is to identify the author with Newland Archer (Mizener, Parrington, Lewis; but see Benstock, *No Gifts,* and Wagner-Martin, Introduction). Any attempt to rescue Wharton's work from long-entrenched perspectives will require serious investigation of her treatment of gender roles and new kinds of analyses of both female and male characters.

The impulse to give Edith Wharton as writer the characteristics and attributes of a male author is understandable: "raising" women writers into the largely male canon was most often accomplished in this way. Nonetheless, a 1995 book by Carol J. Singley proves just how weak a strategy this division of writers' traits into male and female is. *Edith Wharton: Matters of Mind and Spirit* establishes Wharton's crucial involvement in the compelling intellectual, philosophical, and religious debates of her times (i.e., Wharton assumes an intellectual—and perhaps "male"—role in her culture). Singley combines biography, cultural history, and focused readings of a number of texts—short stories as well as such novels as *The Reef, Summer, The Age of Innocence, Hudson River Bracketed,* and others.

Singley treats this body of work in conjunction with wide-ranging discussions of Wharton's knowledge of, and responses to, Darwinian science, aestheticism, rationalism, and such religious movements as Calvinism, Catholicism, and transcendentalism. She often presents the more abstract contextualizations through her readings of Wharton's texts. Through her discussion of "**The Angel at the Grave,**" for example, the reader comes to understand why Wharton preferred rationalism to William James's pragmatism. Similarly, in Singley's reading, *Ethan Frome* illustrates not realism so much as Calvinism, showing "both a personal and cultural defeat" (122) while *The Reef* posits a kind of feminine wisdom and power, *Summer* evokes Emersonian beliefs, and *Hudson River Bracketed* and *The Gods Arrive* explore Catholicism.

Singley deals with a myriad of ideas in *Edith Wharton: Matters of Mind and Spirit*—information about Wharton's affinity with George Eliot, discussion of the scientists and philosophers Wharton called her "Awakeners" (Henry Coppée, William Hamilton, Blaise Pascal, and Charles Darwin), the pervasive New York Episcopalian social (if not religious) forms. She has written a comprehensive study of Wharton and her intellectual times, and I would group this book with Dale Bauer's 1994 study of Wharton and politics and Kathy Fedorko's 1995 *Gender and the Gothic in the Fiction of Edith Wharton* to create an impressive paradigm for future directions in Wharton criticism. Each book gives an immense amount of new factual information, providing contexts that few Wharton critics have ever associated with her work. Because each scholar has written widely not just on Wharton, but also on other American writers, the systematic application of the factual material to Wharton's writing is managed with balance and acumen. This is not to say these three studies avoid the controversial; sometimes large claims are made, but they are palatable because the reader has confidence in the scholarship. These three books are filled with the evidence of diligent work. No one has taken short cuts. Even more to the point, Singley, Bauer, and Fedorko are keenly imaginative, so that the quantities of facts are put to expert use.

Such a triumverate implicitly answers a somewhat petulant 1989 essay by a dedicated Wharton scholar. James Tuttleton's *New Criterion* defense of R. W. B. Lewis's work on Wharton—the ostensible purpose for his publishing "The Feminist Takeover of Edith Wharton"—met with much less opposition than did his assumption that only women scholars could be feminist, and that all women scholars, by virtue of biology, were feminist. That a great amount of the best criticism on Wharton's work is currently being done by women scholars is apparent, but the critical persuasion of at least some of these scholars is far from feminist, or it is feminist in so broad a sense as to be comparatively meaningless. If one defines feminist to mean using a methodology dependent on the work of the French feminist critics Kristeva and Cixous, or British or American scholars influenced by them, then very little current criticism on Wharton's work is feminist.

In surveying significant publications during the 1980s and the 1990s, however, I have noted (with some initial surprise) that women scholars have written a number of these works (what follows is a very limited list; for more inclusion, see Bendixen's bibliographic essays). One explanation for this phenomenon is that women scholars are likely to be pushed to try newer methodologies—perhaps because they are looking for strategies that allow their text-based readings more sophistication. It also appears that some of the most interesting criticism on Wharton's works in the 1980s was economically grounded: Wai-chee Dimock's "Debasing Exchange: Edith Wharton's *The House of Mirth*" in *PMLA* for 1985 became an instant reference point (and see DuBow, Kaplan, and Robinson). Much more study of Wharton and the literary marketplace could be undertaken.

A quantity of criticism in the 1980s and 1990s insists that Wharton's writing be read as a woman's text (Gilbert and Gubar, Herndl), while one approach to that kind of reading is the mythic (Donovan's *After the Fall*; Waid's *Edith Wharton's Letters from the Underworld*). Other interesting attempts to fuse the diverse elements of Wharton's *oeuvre* are made from the perspective of the author's use of space (Fryer's *Felicitous Space*) and of the domestic trope of the house (Chandler's *Dwelling in the Text*).

Excellent work on Wharton as a local color writer (Donovan, *Local Color*), or the opposite of that classification (Campbell), has set the pace for what may prove to be one of the most helpful ways of reading Wharton—that of as a practitioner of the Gothic. Martha Banta's 1994 essay, "The Ghostly Gothic of Wharton's Everyday World," extends work done by Lynette Carpenter and Kathy Fedorko into the field of anthropology. Fedorko's 1995 book, a consummate and convincing study of the way the trope of horror/suspense informs a great deal of Wharton's writing, not merely her identifiable ghost stories, provides yet another point of departure for critics who question the finality of existing readings. In *Gender and the Gothic in the Fiction of Edith Wharton*, Fedorko uses feminist archetypal theory to explore the ways in which Wharton adopts Gothic elements as a means of describing the nature of feminine and masculine ways of knowing and being, thereby dramatizing the tension between them. Fedorko's reading of six novels and sixteen stories, written in four different periods of Wharton's career, provides the reader with plausible and, in many cases, new interpretations.

The apparent genre study, in the case of Wharton's writing, provides a workable format to delineate freshly observed patterns in the work. Much more extensive investigation needs to be done on Wharton's memoirs and travel writing (excellent models are the 1987 essay by Mary Suzanne Schriber and the 1990 book by Janet Goodwyn). Barbara A. White's careful work on Wharton's short stories (*Edith Wharton*) revisits her important two-part essay on incest in Wharton's writing and perhaps her life ("Neglected Areas"). More attention needs to be given to Wharton's novellas and short stories. Like James, Wharton wrote a great deal and well in shorter forms, yet most critical attention has gone to her novels. Evelyn E. Fracasso's 1994 study reads many of the short stories from Wharton's dominant trope of imprisonment; it also deals with the figurative imprisonment of fear, often that of the supernatural. Useful in this connection would be studies of Wharton's reading, particularly her reading of the Gothic tale.

Recent book-length studies of Wharton's work have helped to change the direction of future critical investigation. Incorporating psychoanalytic methodologies, both Gloria Erlich and Lev Raphael assume somewhat atypical stances toward Wharton and her work: Raphael's *Edith Wharton's Prisoners of Shame: A New Perspective on Her Neglected Fiction* scrutinizes such texts as **The Touchstone, Sanctuary, The Glimpses of the Moon,** her war writing, and the later fiction, discerning the pattern of shame (in affect theory) that marks so many of her characters' behaviors. While Raphael does not make what might seem logical biographical extensions, Erlich, in her 1992 *The Sexual Education of Edith Wharton*, continues various interrogations about, not only incest, but also the full extent of Wharton's relationship—or lack of relationship—with Fullerton.

Much of the impetus for excellent criticism seems, in Wharton's case, to remain biographical. The R. W. B. Lewis biography of Edith Wharton remains in print, and, in 1995, the Radcliffe Biography Series brought out a new edition of

Cynthia Griffin Wolff's *A Feast of Words: The Triumph of Edith Wharton,* a book that includes a new introduction and several of Wolff's previously uncollected essays. Also useful as treatments of Wharton's life and work are Katherine Joslin's clearly written and always accurate *Edith Wharton,* Margaret B. McDowell's much-revised edition of her earlier *Edith Wharton,* and Eleanor Dwight's *Edith Wharton: An Extraordinary Life,* the best illustrated of the recent biographies. Superior even to these is Shari Benstock's *No Gifts from Chance: A Biography of Edith Wharton.*

An assiduously drawn portrait of Wharton as woman writer, Benstock's creation pulls together strands of aesthetics, biography, cultural history, and feminist insight into the problems of Wharton's dilemma. Plagued by issues of class, race, and sexuality, the writer led a life more often disguised than transparent. In a period when being unlettered was fashionable, Wharton was truly well educated; when being poor was not onerous, Wharton was wealthy; when being sexually adventurous was fashionable, Wharton had little opportunity for any kind of sensual exploration. Benstock's achievement is not in adding to the chorus of lament for Edith Wharton, but in showing how her writing became her joy, and how she conceived of herself and her life, her strength. The immense amount of new material, the calmly evocative style, and the obvious clarity of judgment make *No Gifts from Chance* the starting point for the next twenty years of Wharton criticism.

In conclusion, I would remind readers that much work remains to be done. We would all benefit from more attention to manuscripts. There is also the fact that Wharton's novels were often serialized before they were published entire; criticism that deals with the history of the publication of her work, as well as criticism that deals with manuscript revision, such as Alan Price's essay on **The Age of Innocence,** would be useful. Recent collections of essays (see Bendixen and Zilversmit, Joslin and Price), as well as past special issues of *College Literature* and *Women's Studies,* provide a number of insights into the critical health of the Wharton project; more such collections would continue to build a body of solid Wharton criticism (see Werlock). Attention to the various film versions of Wharton's texts also interests many readers, and much could be learned about cultural history and the perceptions of women characters in women's fiction through further study in that area. The 1993 publication of Wharton's early novella, **Fast and Loose,** in conjunction with her unfinished last work, **The Buccaneers,** edited by

Viola Hopkins Winner (or in its somewhat bastardized 1993 form, completed by Marion Mainwaring), also suggests the keen interest in whatever material remains unpublished (plays, translations, essays, fiction). It seems clear that—nearly sixty years after her death—Edith Wharton has once again become an American author to be reckoned with.

Works Cited

Ammons, Elizabeth. *Conflicting Stories: American Women Writers at the Turn into the Twentieth Century.* New York: Oxford UP, 1992.

——. *Edith Wharton's Argument with America.* Athens: U of Georgia P, 1980.

Banta, Martha. "The Ghostly Gothic of Wharton's Everyday World." *American Literary Realism* 27.1 (1994): 1-10.

Bauer, Dale M. *Edith Wharton's Brave New Politics.* Madison: U of Wisconsin P, 1994.

——. *Female Dialogics: A Theory of Failed Community.* Albany: State U of New York P, 1988.

Bell, Millicent, ed. *The Cambridge Companion to Edith Wharton.* New York: Cambridge UP, 1995.

——. *Edith Wharton and Henry James: The Story of Their Friendship.* New York: George Braziller, 1965.

Bendixen, Alfred. "A Guide to Wharton Criticism, 1976-1983." *Edith Wharton Newsletter* 2 (1985): 1-8. [Comments also by others]

——. "New Directions in Wharton Criticism: A Bibliographic Essay." *Edith Wharton Review* 10.2 (1993): 20-24.

——. "Recent Wharton Studies: A Bibliographic Essay." *Edith Wharton Newsletter* 3 (1986): 5, 8-9.

——. "Wharton Studies, 1986-1987: A Bibliographic Essay." *Edith Wharton Newsletter* 5 (1988): 5-8, 10.

——. "The World of Wharton Criticism: A Bibliographic Essay." *Edith Wharton Review* 7.1 (1990): 18-21.

Bendixen, Alfred, and Annette Zilversmit, eds. *Edith Wharton: New Critical Essays.* New York: Garland, 1992.

Benstock, Shari. *No Gifts from Chance: A Biography of Edith Wharton.* New York: Scribners, 1994.

——. *Women of the Left Bank: Paris, 1900-1940.* Austin: U of Texas P, 1986.

Blackall, Jean Frantz. "Edith Wharton's Art of Ellipsis." *Journal of Narrative Technique* 17 (1987): 145-61.

Booth, Wayne C. *A Rhetoric of Irony.* Chicago: U of Chicago P, 1974.

Brenni, Vito J. *Edith Wharton: A Bibliography.* Morgantown, VA: McClain Printing, 1966.

Brown, E. K. "Edith Wharton: The Art of the Novel." *The Art of the Novel: From 1700 to the Present Time.* Ed. Pelham Edgar. New York: Macmillan, 1933. 196-205.

Campbell, Donna M. "Edith Wharton and the 'Authoresses': The Critique of Local Color in Wharton's Early Fiction." *Studies in American Fiction* 22 (1994): 169-83.

Carpenter, Lynette. "Deadly Letters, Sexual Politics, and the Dilemma of the Woman Writer: Edith Wharton's 'The House of the Dead Hand.'" *American Literary Realism* 24.2 (1992): 55-69.

Chandler, Marilyn. *Dwelling in the Text: Houses in American Fiction.* Berkeley: U of California P, 1992.

Colquitt, Clare. "Unpacking Her Treasures: Edith Wharton's 'Mysterious Correspondence' with Morton Fullerton." *Library Chronicle of the University of Texas at Austin* ns 31 (1985): 73-107.

Dimock, Wai-chee. "Debasing Exchange: Edith Wharton's *The House of Mirth.*" *PMLA* 100 (1985): 783-92.

Donovan, Josephine. *After the Fall: The Demeter-Persephone Myth in Wharton, Cather, and Glasgow.* University Park: The Pennsylvania State UP, 1989.

——. *Local Color: A Woman's Tradition.* New York: Ungar, 1983.

Dubow, Wendy M. "The Businesswoman in Edith Wharton." *Edith Wharton Review* 8.2 (1991): 11-18.

DuPlessis, Rachel Blau. *Writing Beyond the Ending: Narrative Strategies of Twentieth-Century Women Writers.* Bloomington: Indiana UP, 1985.

Dwight, Eleanor. *Edith Wharton: An Extraordinary Life.* New York: Henry A. Abrams, 1994.

Erlich, Gloria C. *The Sexual Education of Edith Wharton.* Berkeley: U of California P, 1992.

Fedorko, Kathy A. *Gender and the Gothic in the Fiction of Edith Wharton.* Tuscaloosa: U of Alabama P, 1995.

Fracasso, Evelyn E. *Edith Wharton's Prisoners of Consciousness.* New York: Greenwood, 1994.

Fryer, Judith. *Felicitous Space: The Imaginative Structures of Edith Wharton and Willa Cather.* Chapel Hill: U of North Carolina P, 1986.

Garrison, Stephen. *Edith Wharton: A Descriptive Bibliography.* Pittsburgh: U of Pittsburgh P, 1990.

Gilbert, Sandra M., and Susan Gubar. *No Man's Land.* Vol. 2 of *Sexchanges.* New Haven, CT: Yale UP, 1989.

Gimbel, Wendy. *Edith Wharton: Orphancy and Survival.* New York: Praeger, 1984.

Goodman, Susan. *Edith Wharton's Inner Circle.* Austin: U of Texas P, 1994.

——. *Edith Wharton's Women: Friends and Rivals.* Hanover, NH: UP of New England, 1990.

Goodwyn, Janet. *Edith Wharton: Traveller in the Land of Letters.* London: Macmillan, 1990.

Gribben, Alan. "'The Heart Is Insatiable': A Selection from Edith Wharton's Letters to Morton Fullerton, 1907-1915." *Library Chronicle of the University of Texas at Austin* ns 31 (1985): 7-18.

Hadley, Kathy Miller. *In the Interstices of the Tale: Edith Wharton's Narrative Strategies.* New York: Peter Lang, 1993.

Herndl, Diane Price. *Invalid Women: Figuring Feminine Illness in American Fiction and Culture 1840-1940.* Chapel Hill: U of North Carolina P, 1993.

Holbrook, David. *Edith Wharton and the Unsatisfactory Man.* New York: St. Martin's, 1991.

Howe, Irving, ed. *Edith Wharton: A Collection of Critical Essays.* Englewood Cliffs, NJ: Prentice-Hall, 1962.

Hutcheon, Linda. *Irony's Edge: The Theory and Politics of Irony.* New York: Routledge, 1995.

Inness, Sherrie A. "Nature, Culture, and Sexual Economics in Edith Wharton's *The Reef.*" *American Literary Realism* 26.1 (1993): 76-90.

Joslin, Katherine. *Edith Wharton.* New York: St. Martin's, 1991.

——. "Edith Wharton at 125." *College Literature* 14.3 (1987): 193-206.

Joslin, Katherine, and Alan Price, eds. *"Wretched Exotic": Essays on Edith Wharton in Europe.* New York: Peter Lang, 1993.

Kaplan, Amy. *The Social Construction of American Realism.* Chicago: U of Chicago P, 1988.

Lauer, Kristin O., and Margaret P. Murray. *Edith Wharton: An Annotated Secondary Bibliography.* New York: Garland, 1990.

Lawson, Richard H. *Edith Wharton.* New York: Ungar, 1976.

Lewis, R. W. B. *Edith Wharton: A Biography.* New York: Harper & Row, 1975.

Lubbock, Percy. *Portrait of Edith Wharton.* New York: Appleton-Century-Crofts, 1947.

McDowell, Margaret B. *Edith Wharton.* Boston: Twayne, 1976; revised, 1990.

Miller, D. Quentin. "'A Barrier of Words': The Tension between Narrative Voice and Vision in the Writings of Edith Wharton." *American Literary Realism* 27.2 (1994): 11-22.

Mizener, Arthur. *Twelve Great American Novels.* New York: New American Library, 1967.

Nevius, Blake. *Edith Wharton: A Study of Her Fiction.* Berkeley: U of California P, 1961.

Parrington, Vernon L. "Our Literary Aristocrat." *The Pacific Review* 2 (1921): 157-60.

Powers, Lyall H., ed. *Henry James and Edith Wharton, Letters: 1900-1915.* New York: Scribners, 1990.

Price, Alan. "The Composition of Edith Wharton's *The Age of Innocence.*" *Yale University Library Gazette* 55 (1980): 22-30.

Rae, Catherine M. *Edith Wharton's New York Quartet.* Lanham, MD: UP of America, 1984.

Raphael, Lev. *Edith Wharton's Prisoners of Shame: A New Perspective on Her Neglected Fiction.* New York: St. Martin's, 1991.

Robinson, Lillian S. "The Traffic in Women: A Cultural Critique of *The House of Mirth.*" *Edith Wharton, "The House of Mirth."* Ed. Shari Benstock. New York: St. Martin's, Bedford Books, 1994. 340-58.

Schriber, Mary Suzanne. "Edith Wharton and Travel Writing as Self-Discovery." *American Literature* 59 (1987): 257-67.

Sensibar, Judith. "Edith Wharton Reads the Bachelor Type: Her Critique of Modernism's Representative Man." *American Literature* 60 (1988): 575-90.

Singley, Carol J. *Edith Wharton: Matters of Mind and Spirit.* New York: Cambridge UP, 1995.

Springer, Marlene. *Edith Wharton and Kate Chopin: A Reference Guide.* Boston: G. K. Hall, 1976.

——. *"Ethan Frome": A Nightmare of Need.* New York: Twayne, 1993.

Springer, Marlene, and Joan Gilson. "Edith Wharton: A Reference Guide Updated." *Resources for American Literary Study* 14 (1984): 85-111.

Sullivan, Ellie Ragland. "The Daughter's Dilemma: Psychoanalytic Interpretation and Edith Wharton's *The House of Mirth.*" *Edith Wharton, "The House of Mirth."* Ed. Shari Benstock. 464-81.

Tuttleton, James W. "Edith Wharton." *American Women Writers: Bibliographical Essays.* Ed. Maurice Duke, Jackson R. Bryer, and M. Thomas Inge. Westport, CT: Greenwood, 1983. 71-107.

——. "The Feminist Takeover of Edith Wharton." *The New Criterion* 7.7 (1989): 6-14.

——. *The Novel of Manners in America.* Chapel Hill: U of North Carolina P, 1972.

Tuttleton, James W., Kristin O. Lauer, and Margaret P. Murray, eds. *Edith Wharton: The Contemporary Reviews.* New York: Cambridge UP, 1992.

Wagner-Martin, Linda. *"The Age of Innocence": A Novel of Ironic Nostalgia.* New York: Twayne, 1996.

——. *"The House of Mirth": A Novel of Admonition.* Boston: Twayne, 1990.

——. Introduction. *The Age of Innocence.* New York: Washington Square P, 1995. vii-xxiv.

Waid, Candace. *Edith Wharton's Letters from the Underworld.* Chapel Hill: U of North Carolina P, 1991.

Wegener, Frederick. "Edith Wharton and the Difficult Writing of The Writing of Fiction." *Modern Language Studies* 25.2 (1995): 60-79.

Werlock, Abby H. P. "Whitman, Wharton, and the Sexuality in *Summer.*" *Speaking the Other Self: New Essays on American Women Writers.* Ed. Jeanne Campbell Reesman. Forthcoming.

Wershoven, Carol. *The Female Intruder in the Novels of Edith Wharton.* Rutherford, NJ: Fairleigh Dickinson UP, 1982.

Wharton, Edith. *The Age of Innocence.* New York: Appleton, 1920.

——. "The Angel at the Grave." *The Best Short Stories of Edith Wharton.* Ed. Wayne Andrews. New York: Scribners, 1958. 117-32.

——. *The Buccaneers: A Novel by Edith Wharton.* Completed by Marion Mainwaring. New York: Penguin, 1993.

——. *The Children.* New York: Appleton, 1928.

——. *The Collected Short Stories.* 2 vol. Ed. R. W. B. Lewis. New York: Scribners, 1968.

——. *Ethan Frome.* New York: Scribners, 1911.

——. *Fast and Loose & The Buccaneers.* Ed. Viola Hopkins Winner. Charlottesville: UP of Virginia, 1993.

——. *The Glimpses of the Moon.* New York: Appleton, 1922.

——. *The Gods Arrive.* New York: Appleton, 1932.

——. *The House of Mirth.* New York: Scribners, 1905.

——. *Hudson River Bracketed.* New York: Appleton, 1929.

——. *The Letters of Edith Wharton.* Ed. R. W. B. Lewis and Nancy Lewis. New York: Scribners, 1988.

——. *The Mother's Recompense.* New York: Appleton, 1925.

——. *The Reef.* New York: Appleton, 1912.

——. *Sanctuary.* New York: Scribners, 1903.

——. *Summer.* New York: Appleton, 1917.

——. *The Touchstone.* New York: Scribners, 1900.

——. *Twilight Sleep.* New York: Appleton, 1927.

——. *The Writing of Fiction.* New York: Scribners, 1925.

White, Barbara A. *Edith Wharton: A Study of the Short Fiction.* Boston: Twayne, 1991.

——. "Neglected Areas: Wharton's Short Stories and Incest." *Edith Wharton Review* 8.1 (1991): 3-12; and 8.2 (1991): 3-10, 32.

Wilson, Edmund. "Justice to Edith Wharton." *The Wound and the Bow.* New York: Oxford UP, 1947. 195-213.

Wolff, Cynthia Griffin. *A Feast of Words: The Triumph of Edith Wharton.* New York: Oxford UP, 1977. Reissued (expanded) New York: Addison Wesley, 1995.

SCOTT EMMERT (ESSAY DATE AUTUMN 2002)

SOURCE: Emmert, Scott. "Drawing-Room Naturalism in Edith Wharton's Early Short Stories." *Journal of the Short Story in English,* no. 39 (autumn 2002): 57-71.

In the following essay, Emmert explains the influence of literary naturalism on Wharton's early short stories, showing the connections between the formal elements of short fiction and the deterministic themes of naturalism.

In her biography of Edith Wharton, Cynthia Griffin Wolff discusses the ways in which the nineteenth-century upper-class girl was encouraged to deny her feelings, particularly sexual ones. As a young girl of that class, Wharton was pressured into early self-denial. One of the primary lessons Wharton learned was that "[s]ociety had decreed that 'nice' young women didn't really *have* feelings to be explained: if you did have feelings— well, then, obviously you weren't 'nice.' Lady-like behavior demanded the total suppression of instinct." As a reaction against her repressed upbringing, young Edith Jones turned to books and to "making up" stories. Her "lifelong love of words," Wolff insists, "sprang from her early emotional impoverishment," and nothing terrified young Edith more than the prospect of remaining forever mute, which was connected in her mind with the existence of "helpless" animals (Wolff 37, 27 and 25)[1].

The notion of being seen and not heard was applied especially to female children of Wharton's class. Wolff summarizes Wharton's training in proper gender roles with the simple infinitive "to be." Young women were meant to be looked at and admired, and they were not expected "to do" much more than fulfill that ornamental role. Independent action and opinion were not fostered in female children, and early on Wharton learned to suppress her "impulse 'to do'" (Wolff 42). Indeed, a portrait of Wharton done when she was five years old displays her in a luxurious blue dress and standing next to a vase of flowers; her long red hair drapes one shoulder, over which the girl gives the viewer a coy look. The painting freezes the child in a purely decorative posture[2].

The need to present a proper appearance oppressed Wharton. Her first short story, written when she was eleven, contains in its first paragraph the line: "'Oh, how do you do, Mrs. Brown?' said Mrs. Tomkins. 'If only I had known you were going to call I should have tidied up the drawing room.'" When Edith's mother, Lucretia, glanced at the story, she returned it to her daughter with the acidic remark, "Drawing rooms are always tidy" (Wharton **Backward Glance,** 73). Her words are borne out by an 1884 photograph of the interior of Lucretia Jones's house on West Twenty-Fifth Street, shown in the R. W. B. Lewis biography of Wharton. The visible rooms are nothing if not rigidly ordered.

Wharton's literary rebellion against the stifling nature of these rooms results in what could be termed "drawing-room naturalism". Repeatedly in her short fiction, female characters are depicted in a variety of narrow spaces in which they suffer the restrictions of social decorum. Wharton made an explicit connection between the rooms of a large house and the psychology of upper-class women in **"The Fulness of Life"** (1893) when the protagonist muses:

> "I have sometimes thought that a woman's nature is like a great house full of rooms: there is the hall, through which everyone passes in going in and out; the drawing room, where one receives formal visits; the sitting room, where the members of the family come and go as they list; but beyond that, far beyond, are other rooms, the handles of whose doors perhaps are never turned; no one knows the way to them, no one knows whither they lead; and in the innermost room, the holy of holies, the soul sits alone."
>
> (14)[3]

The deterministic element in Wharton's fiction is social, and it is made concrete by her presentation of spaces such as drawing rooms in which formal requirements impinge upon a woman's individual needs and desires.

A careful student of the literary marketplace, Wharton first began publishing fiction during the development of literary naturalism in America. Although she eschewed the usual subject matter of naturalist fiction, several of her early short stories, those published around the turn of the nineteenth century, may be considered naturalistic because they present characters who are aware of the social forces arrayed against them, forces that prevent them from expressing original thoughts or becoming autonomous selves. These characters may wish to be realist characters in possession of an essential self, but they are pressured into living as naturalist characters subject to a tyranny of appearance that grants them limited agency. While realist characters are allowed a self-defining ability to act—permitted "to do" first in order "to be" themselves—Wharton's characters, especially her female characters, are often allowed merely "to be" passive constructions of external forces[4].

Although the scholarship on Wharton's involvement in literary naturalism appears mainly in connection with her novels, a common property in all of her fiction is the dramatization of the inability to act or the insufficiency of action. That such a dramatization is especially clear in her short stories results largely from the greater sense of restriction the form allows. Wolff has identified Wharton's frequent use of "enclosed space" to suggest the limited options of her characters (60). But in addition to depicting a variety of enclosures—rooms in houses and compartments on trains, for example—Wharton's short stories become restrictive spaces themselves. Andrew Levy argues that Wharton took thematic advantage of the short story form, because "[a]mong prose genres, it is most like an enclosed space, most concentrated in form. Among *all* genres, it is most 'locked,' requiring the synthetic closure of an impact-filled beginning and a dramatic conclusion" (65).

The connection between form and deterministic theme is often stronger in short stories than it is in novels, and Wharton made effective use of this connection in her short fiction. As Philip Fisher and June Howard have noted, naturalist novels are frequently structured by plots of decline in which a character degenerates physically, socially, and even morally over an extended period of time. Such a plot served most obviously to give form to Theodore Dreiser's *Sister Carrie* (1900) and Frank Norris's *Vandover and the Brute* (1914) (Fisher 169-78; Howard 63-69). In addition to the plot of decline, Fisher finds the structure of naturalist novels to be dependent upon different "temporary worlds" through which characters carry their desires and seek their identities (138-53). Short stories, in contrast, cannot easily form narrative with the plot of decline or with a series of temporary worlds. Their length makes it nearly impossible to present the span of time needed to make plausible a character's gradual degeneration, and at best a short story may focus successfully on a limited number of settings. The short story form nonetheless provides advantages to naturalist writers. A story's limited length and formal compression allow for a keener dramatization of the oppositional forces arrayed against naturalist characters. Often the sense of restriction and entrapment felt by these characters is more dramatic and less ambiguous in short stories than in novels. While critics (e.g., Richard A. Kaye and Lori Merish) often identify certain of Edith Wharton's early novels as only partially committed to literary naturalism, in a number of her early short stories Wharton's commitment to extending naturalism to the social sphere is reflected by the unambiguous deterministic plight of her characters, a plight that is apparent both formally and thematically.

Wharton embraced the short story form, eventually producing nine story collections; furthermore, she admitted to struggling with the structural demands of the novel. She wrote, in a letter to Robert Grant in 1907, that the need to view a novel "more architectonically" required her to "sacrifice . . . the small incidental effects that women have always excelled in, the episodical characterisation, I mean." Appreciating the "smaller realism" made possible by the story form, Wharton confesses to possessing "the sense of authority with which I take hold of a short story" (**Letters,** 124). And, significantly, in chapter two of **The Writing of Fiction,** entitled "Telling a Short Story," Wharton elucidates a clear distinction between short fiction and the novel, demonstrating a cogent understanding of the short story's aesthetic requirements.

Among those requirements is the story's dependence on "situation" rather than "on the gradual unfolding of the inner life of its characters" to which the novel is devoted (**Writing of Fiction,** 48 and 42). Characters in short stories, then, will possess less of an individual "inner life" which must be sacrificed to the story's "situation." In Wharton's stories, that dramatic situation often centers on the ways in which characters are deprived of an inner life; thus the form of the

ON THE SUBJECT OF...

WHARTON'S FEMINISM

Wharton was not by any standard measure a feminist. The muse's tragedy is not the fact that she is not a poet herself but that the poet never loved her as a woman. The public speaker is ridiculously bad at the work she can't bear to give up. But no one between Nietzsche and Simone de Beauvoir was so ruthlessly clear in depicting the deforming effects of social history on the human female, in examining the dreadful methods she has been constrained to use in order to obtain the trivial things she has been taught to want. And no one has given us so many ways to love and to hate, often simultaneously, the weak, manipulative, pitiful, dangerous, and beautiful creatures this history produced.

Pierpont, Claudia Roth. An excerpt from "Cries and Whispers." *New Yorker* (2 April 2001): 68.

story aids Wharton in enacting a principal theme: that is, the psychological confinement of her characters. Wharton writes that "the characters engaged" in short stories "must be a little more than puppets; but apparently, also, they may be a little less than individual human beings" (**Writing of Fiction,** 47). The ways in which her characters are puppets and not fully autonomous selves is central in many of Wharton's early short stories, which arguably makes them her most naturalistic fictions.

While recognition of the early influence of literary naturalism on Wharton's fiction is relatively recent, the critical case for such an influence now enjoys acceptance. Indeed, Donna M. Campbell has identified a naturalist impulse in Wharton's first published short story, "**Mrs. Manstey's View**" (1891), which depicts an aging widow living a cramped and lonely existence in a small room. Mrs. Manstey fails to prevent the construction of a building extension that threatens the view from her single window. Often in her short stories, Wharton explores the illusion of independent action, and the dramatic use of this exploration is present in her fiction from the beginning. "**Mrs. Manstey's View**" ironically dramatizes the false belief in autonomy by presenting a protagonist who dies while under the delusion that her actions have been successful. Arguing for an analysis of Wharton as a writer "caught in the historical shift between local color and naturalism," Campbell discovers in this often overlooked story the threatening nature of the "landscape of naturalism", of an urban Hydra that recalls the fiction of Frank Norris and Stephen Crane (152-3).

Even though it indicates Wharton's interest in an ironic donnée, **"Mrs. Manstey's View"** does not reflect the aesthetic control of the more mature author. That literary maturity is reflected in other stories by a deft merging of irony with narrative voice to implicate the reader more closely in the realization of a character's limitations. As critics have noted, Wharton's best short stories require the reader's active, inferential engagement to "meet her halfway and fill in the gaps" of meaning (White 24). Wharton's frequent use of ellipses has been interpreted as an attempt to "entice the reader to enter into imaginative collaboration" with the narrator (Blackall 145), and her reliance in her stories on "situation" over complex plot emphasizes thematic significance more than action. In addition, her preference for the third-person limited point of view, strictly focalized through a central consciousness, tends to place readers immediately within an interpretive situation, instantly involving them with a single character's vision and, usually flawed, judgment. For Wharton the limited vision of the "reflector," the character from whose point of view the story is told, should be strictly enforced; as she wrote in *The Writing of Fiction,* a short-story writer should "never . . . let the character who serves as reflector record anything not naturally within his register" (46). Naturalist novelists, preferring omniscient narrators and making frequent use of authorial commentary, often create distance between a novel's characters and its readers, who are positioned as spectators[5]. Wharton's limited reflectors, in contrast, create kinship between protagonists and readers, for both find themselves in similar interpretive situations.

The limits of the reflector have thematic significance in the story **"The Other Two"** (1904), which is told from the point of view of Waythorn, a New York City stockbroker who has recently married a twice-divorced woman. The story's irony derives from the reader's growing awareness of Waythorn's limited understanding of his wife's past. He believes that he knows Alice even as his view of her changes, but as Barbara A. White

notes, the story's frequent use of economic imagery makes apparent the "limitations of his vision" (17). Even though they tend to be as restricted as Wharton's female characters, her male characters are often deluded by their own sense of importance, a sense that is reinforced by their social and economic position[6].

Secure in his position as husband and successful businessman, Waythorn is confident that he understands his new wife, an understanding the reader initially has no reason to doubt. He appreciates her stable personality and "perfectly balanced nerves". Early in the story, as Waythorn waits for Alice to come down to dinner, he stands before "the drawing-room hearth" thinking of her "composure," one that "was restful to him; it acted as ballast to his somewhat unstable sensibilities" (380). Although she has been divorced from two men, Alice appears unperturbed by society's negative view of divorce. Waythorn admires her "way of surmounting obstacles without seeming to be aware of them," (381) but his admiration of her apparent mastery of external circumstances blinds him to the fact that Alice is adept at masking her own feelings. When she appears for dinner, Alice wears "her most engaging tea gown" but "she had neglected to assume the smile that went with it" (382). Concerned about her daughter's health and about a visit from the girl's father, Alice naturally cannot appear cheerful. Waythorn tells her "to forget" her concern, and he is later confident "that she had obeyed his injunction and forgotten" (382-83). In fact, as White points out, Waythorn may simply be accepting Alice's outward composure as a sign that she has indeed forgotten her maternal worries. But Alice, the story makes clear, is an accomplished pretender.

To make Waythorn happy, Alice pretends to be "serene and unruffled"; she works hard to appear like "a creature all compact of harmonies" (385, 386). At first, Waythorn is untroubled by Alice's previous marriages because he believes these relationships have left her unaffected. Alice's past intrudes upon Waythorn's harmony, however, when he must allow Haskett, the first husband, to enter "his" house to visit Lily, the daughter Haskett had with Alice—and when he has to begin a business relationship with Varick, Alice's second husband. In a significant scene, Alice mistakenly pours cognac into Waythorn's coffee, forgetting that it was Varick who preferred such a drink. Aware of Varick's preference, Waythorn begins to be disturbed by Alice's history: "He had fancied that a woman can shed her past like a man. But now he saw that Alice was bound to hers both by the circumstances which forced her into continued relation with it, and by the traces it had left on her nature" (393).

Waythorn's opinion of his wife is changed but not deepened by this revelation, for she simply becomes a different kind of possession to him. At first, he thought of her as a rare object "whom Gus Varick had unearthed somewhere" (381). He believes that her outward poise reflects her inner life, and he basks in the comfort of her attentions. After close association with her previous husbands, however, Waythorn scorns Alice, likening her to a common thing. "She was 'as easy as an old shoe,'" he thinks, "a shoe that too many feet had worn" (393). At this point for Waythorn, Alice no longer possesses an essential self: "Alice Haskett—Alice Varick—Alice Waythorn—she had been each in turn, and had left hanging to each name a little of her privacy, a little of her personality, a little of the inmost self where the unknown god abides" (393). Waythorn thus considers himself only a partial investor in Alice; he "compared himself to a member of a syndicate. He held so many shares in his wife's personality and his predecessors were his partners in the business" (393). From being an object that belonged to him exclusively, Alice has changed for Waythorn into a "third of a wife" in which he owns stock.

By perceiving of her as an object or an investment, Waythorn denies to Alice the possibility of an essential identity. Only his valuation of her matters to him, a valuation that she must constantly seek to maintain. **"The Other Two"** is not merely, as R. W. B. Lewis terms it, a "comedy of manners" (134); it is, rather, an indication of the ways by which a woman is divested of a coherent sense of self when she must always act in accordance with a man's expectations. White argues that "when she is viewed independently of Waythorn," Alice presents "an identity in shreds" (16).

Ironically, of course, a judgmental Waythorn is blind to his own limitations. He does not perceive the full meaning of Alice's reactions upon her meeting with both Haskett and Varick in the library. Surprised to see her ex-husbands in the same room with her current spouse, Alice betrays her emotions. Although she greets Varick "with a distinct note of pleasure," the sight of Haskett causes her "smile" to fade "for a moment" (395-96). She quickly regains her mask, however, and Waythorn remains oblivious to his wife's true feelings. Both Waythorn and Alice, the reader eventually discerns, are locked into fixed roles. They are not husband and wife but collector and possession. Waythorn has enough discernment to ap-

preciate Alice's "value" to him, but his utilitarian viewpoint prevents him from appreciating any of her possibly unique qualities.

The terror of discovering oneself at the mercy of societal dictates afflicts both male and female characters in Wharton's stories. The male protagonist of **"The Line of Least Resistance"** (1900), for instance, discovers the social costs of divorcing an unfaithful wife and recognizes his lack of freedom. More often, however, Wharton's social victims are intelligent women who recognize society's deleterious effect on their personal development. Such is the case with Mrs. Clement Westall in **"The Reckoning"** (1902) who is stripped of legal identity and emotional security when her husband asks for a divorce in order to marry another woman. In an equally evocative story, Mrs. Vervain of **"The Dilettante"** (1903) is forced to confront her vacant sense of self.

For seven years, Vervain has been the subject of Thursdale's oppressive training in emotional reticence and equivocation. Thursdale prides himself on his apt pupil: "He had taught a good many women not to betray their feelings, but he had never before had such fine material to work with" (412). The story begins with Thursdale about to meet with Mrs. Vervain to discuss his fiancée, Miss Gaynor. Thursdale loves Miss Gaynor, in part because she cannot control her emotions. He has introduced his fiancée to his pupil and been delighted by the "naturalness with which Mrs. Vervain had met Miss Gaynor" (412). Of course, Mrs. Vervain's "natural" reaction was to suppress her own feelings, and Thursdale once again goes to her to continue their game. Upon entering the familiar house, Thursdale notes "the drawing room [which] at once enveloped him in that atmosphere of tacit intelligence which Mrs. Vervain imparted to her very furniture" (413). Introduced early as a metaphor for Mrs. Vervain herself, this room will be instrumental in her ultimate self-revelation.

"The Dilettante" has been interpreted as a "feminist revenge story" in that Mrs. Vervain succeeds by tricking Thursdale into revealing an undisguised emotion, and—perhaps—gains a triumph by ending his engagement with Miss Gaynor (White 59). Mrs. Vervain tells Thursdale that Miss Gaynor has come to visit a second time, and in his anxious desire to learn the outcome of that visit, Thursdale declares, "You know I'm absurdly in love" (414). Further twisting the knife, Mrs. Vervain confronts Thursdale with his sin of withholding a genuine affection from her. But although she informs him plainly that he "always *hated . . .* to have things happen: you never would let them," Thursdale, from whose point of view the story unfolds, misses her implication, considering her words to be "incoherent" (415). Mrs. Vervain tells Thursdale that Miss Gaynor has come to her to discover whether she and Thursdale had been lovers. When Mrs. Vervain tells the truth—that she and Thursdale have never had a sexual relationship—Miss Gaynor appears disappointed. She has apparently looked into Thursdale's "past" for evidence of a genuine passion, but having found none, Mrs. Vervain intimates, Miss Gaynor will likely break her engagement. Naturally, Thursdale despairs until Mrs. Vervain offers a potential solution. She urges him to lie about their relationship, to suggest that they have indeed been lovers. She offers him, in short, her social reputation, and the offer momentarily strips away all pretenses: "It was extraordinary how a few words had swept them from an atmosphere of the most complex dissimulations to this contact of naked souls" (418). For once, they have shown their true feelings.

The ambiguous ending complicates the story, making it difficult to accept revenge as its subject[7]. It is not certain whether Miss Gaynor has in fact visited Mrs. Vervain a second time or whether she has sent a letter to Thursdale to break off their engagement. Mrs. Vervain could have fabricated the entire incident, and it is she who suggests that Miss Gaynor may have written to Thursdale. Nor is it certain that Thursdale intends to break the engagement himself, lest he turn Miss Gaynor into another Mrs. Vervain. Thus both the success of Mrs. Vervain's revenge and the possibility of Thursdale's moral growth are left in doubt.

A more obvious theme inheres in the story's last sentence, which occurs after Thursdale leaves: "The door closed on him, and she hid her eyes from the dreadful emptiness of the room" (419). Representing her inner self, the "empty" drawing room forces Mrs. Vervain to acknowledge her lack of individuality. The social propriety she and Thursdale have practiced has led Mrs. Vervain to suppress emotion and passion, to deny the expression of any personal desire that could make her unique. In her drawing room, a barren site devoid of warmth, Mrs. Vervain recognizes a confinement of spirit. By internalizing Thursdale's training never to betray an emotion, she comes to betray herself. Set within a single room that takes on metaphorical significance, **"The Dilettante"** deftly merges form and theme.

Wharton's highly praised **"Souls Belated"** (1899) is perhaps her best illustration of the social restrictions women and men encounter when they try to establish a relationship outside of marriage. The story's naturalism is evident, as both main characters, Lydia and Gannett, have their personal freedom curtailed by social decorum. The first story by Wharton to make extensive use of the "prison cell" metaphor (Lewis 87), **"Souls Belated"** presents a female character who desires an identity outside of the socially determined one, but who is ultimately imprisoned by social approval.

Lydia, whose lack of a last name figures her absence of identity (White 58), has been living with Gannett, a successful writer not her husband. Her divorce from Tillotson has just been granted, so she is presumably free to marry Gannett. But for Lydia, independence lies in not having to marry, in not having to follow the staid morality of society. She becomes angry when Gannett assumes that she will indeed marry him. Instead, she intends to pursue her version of personal liberty. Marriage to Tillotson revealed to her the dreary obligation of "doing exactly the same thing every day at the same hour" (106). Meeting Gannett relieves her of this "dull" life, and she revels in a new-found freedom, even though she pretends "to look upon him as the instrument of her liberation" (107) when in fact she recognizes that to be truly free she must leave Gannett. Lydia is fully aware that social propriety restricts her individuality, but she remains committed to living according to her own code. "Of course one acts as one can," she tells Gannett, "as one must, perhaps—pulled by all sorts of invisible threads; but at least one needn't pretend, for social advantages, to subscribe to a creed that ignores the complexity of human Motives—that classifies people by arbitrary signs, and puts it in everybody's reach to be on Mrs. Tillotson's visiting list" (110-11). As this passage suggests, Lydia resists social determinism, its iron grip of propriety, its insistence on uniformity, and its desire to render people in the simplest of terms.

Although to express her autonomy Lydia refuses to marry Gannett, nevertheless she soon finds herself trapped in a naturalist environment. At the Hotel Bellosguardo, the other guests assume she is married to Gannett, and she does not disabuse them of that assumption. The hotel's social order is policed by Lady Susan Condit who presupposes that Lydia is Mrs. Gannett. Lydia's security is threatened, however, when Mrs. Cope tries to blackmail her into revealing what Cope's young companion, Lord Trevenna, has revealed to Gannett. Knowledge is the source of Mrs. Cope's power over her young lord; she needs to control him to ensure he will marry her once her divorce is final. Perceiving that she and Lydia are "both in the same box," (118) Mrs. Cope threatens to expose the truth that Lydia and Gannett are not married. Even after Mrs. Cope's threat is averted, however, Lydia realizes that she enjoys the security of respectability, even though having to pretend she is married belies her sense of freedom. Gannett again asks her to marry him, but she refuses, knowing that society will still reject her because she has been married before. To society she will appear to be a social pariah whom Gannett has rehabilitated.

The story's last section alters the point of view by narrating events from Gannett's perspective instead of Lydia's, one of the few instances in Wharton's short fiction of a change in focalization. The effect creates more distance between Lydia and the reader. But as we see her from the outside only, Lydia's restriction comes sharply into focus (White 59). As she tries to leave Gannett, he watches from a window while she retreats from the steam launch and returns to the hotel. Implying that they will be married, the story's ending intimates that Lydia will have to give up not caring about society's opinion, which has been the principal expression of her desire for a free will.

This last section of the story also allows the sympathy Gannett feels for Lydia to register keenly with the reader. Earlier in the story Gannett appears incapable of understanding Lydia's arguments for personal freedom; as the narration dryly notes, "Nothing is more perplexing to a man than the mental process of a woman who reasons her emotions" (111). But watching her from the window, Gannett perceives "the cruelty he had committed in detaching her from the normal conditions of life" (125). Gannett may certainly be taking too much credit for ending Lydia's marriage and severing her from "normal" social relations, but he does sympathize with her limited choices: "Even had his love lessened, he was bound to her now by a hundred ties of pity and self-reproach; and she, poor child, must turn back to him as Latude returned to his cell" (125). While aware that he and Lydia are "two separate beings," Gannett nevertheless recognizes the hard fact of their being "bound together in a *noyade* of passion that left them resisting yet clinging as they went down" (125).

The story's title implies the pathos of Gannett's and Lydia's "belated" attempt to live independently of social opinion, thereby possessing their souls. In the end, they will presumably travel to Paris to be married, for neither of them can resist society's pressure to conform. At one point early in the story, Lydia expressed their mutual contempt for conformity:

> "We neither of us believe in the abstract 'sacredness' of marriage; we both know that no ceremony is needed to consecrate our love for each other; what object can we have in marrying, except the secret fear of each that the other may escape, or the secret longing to work our way back gradually—oh, very gradually—into the esteem of the people whose conventional morality we have always ridiculed and hated?"
>
> (110)

Even in a hotel as remote as the Bellosguardo that "conventional morality" prevails, denying independent action and the prerogatives of self-definition.

In these stories, Wharton's social or drawing-room naturalism poignantly dramatizes the struggle of individuals to resist a socially constructed sense of self. That struggle for individuality occurs amid impersonal social forces that prevent self-definition. Confined in drawing-rooms and in the compressed space of the short story form itself, Wharton's characters are often abruptly stripped of their affected autonomy. As a result, her characters have more in common with the powerless naturalist character that Lee Clark Mitchell identifies than with realist characters who exhibit mastery over, or at least successfully negotiate, social forces.

Wharton understood, furthermore, that characters in short stories are by necessity more limited than characters in novels. Yet, for Wharton this requirement offers a thematic opportunity in that she is able to use her short story characters as symbols of socially determined lives. Recently, narrative theorists have argued that characters in short stories may be interpreted more readily as symbols than characters in novels. Charles E. May, for example, argues that characters in short fiction are often "symbolic projections" that serve aesthetic and thematic functions (66-7). These characters frequently act according to the needs of a story's plot and theme, becoming "stylized figures rather than 'real people'" (64). As a naturalist writer, Wharton is interested in portraying static, socially determined characters without an essential identity, figures of determinism. This portrayal is assisted by the short story's formal requirements vis-à-vis characterization[8].

Social determinism remains a consistent theme in Wharton's stories throughout her career, as she continued to take advantage of the short story's compressed form to dramatize the limited inner lives of her characters and their inability to control personal destiny[9]. Wharton shared this struggle for autonomy with her protagonists, but she eventually discovered freedom in the creation of art. She found a way "to do" and not simply "to be". On the small canvas of much of her short fiction, however, Wharton's characters are arrested in passive poses while nonetheless offering an appeal to the reader's sympathy. Readers of these stories may share with characters such as Lydia and Gannett the disturbing recognition of an illusory free will, of the absence of hope for a unified selfhood.

Notes

1. Shari Benstock provides a different view of Wharton's childhood and her mother's reaction to her desire to "make up" stories and to play as a "tomboy," 20-21.

2. This painting, done by Edward Harrison May, hangs in the National Portrait Gallery in Washington, D.C. It is dated 1870, but Benstock identifies Edith's age as five years, (13).

3. Page references refer to volume one of R. W. B. Lewis's edition of Wharton's collected stories.

4. Lee Clark Mitchell argues persuasively for the essential difference between autonomous and self-defining realist characters and passive naturalist characters whose sense of self is determined by external circumstance, 1-33.

5. See Howard and Rachel Bowlby on naturalist novels as spectacle.

6. On the self-importance of Wharton's male characters, see Elsa Nettels, 252.

7. Indeed, White ultimately rejects the revenge theme entirely, 59.

8. See also Suzanne Hunter Brown's theory that the "[t]echnical factors" of short stories "lead many short-story writers to project an individual's nature as an essential given," 199.

9. See, for example, the often anthologized "Roman Fever" (1934) in which a woman's actions, inspired by jealously and hatred, result in a sudden realization that strips her of an assumed superiority.

Works Cited

Benstock, Shari. *No Gifts from Chance: A Biography of Edith Wharton.* New York: Charles Scribner's Sons, 1994.

Blackall, Jean Frantz. "Edith Wharton's Art of Ellipsis." *Journal of Narrative Technique* 17 (1987): 145-62.

Bowlby, Rachel. *Just Looking: Consumer Culture in Dreiser, Gissing and Zola.* New York: Methuen, 1985.

Brown, Suzanne Hunter. "The Chronotope of the Short Story: Time, Character, and Brevity." *Creative and Critical Approaches to the Short Story.* Ed. Noel Harold Kaylor, Jr. Lewiston, NY: Edwin Mellen Press, 1997. 181-213.

Campbell, Donna M. *Resisting Regionalism: Gender and Naturalism in American Fiction, 1885-1915.* Athens: Ohio UP, 1997.

Fisher, Philip. *Hard Facts: Setting and Form in the American Novel.* New York: Oxford UP, 1985.

Howard, June. *Form and History in American Literary Naturalism.* Chapel Hill: U of North Carolina P, 1985.

Kaye, Richard A. "Textual Hermeneutics and Belated Male Heroism: Edith Wharton's Revisions of *The House of Mirth* and the Resistance to American Literary Naturalism." *Arizona Quarterly* 52 (1995): 87-116.

Levy, Andrew. *The Culture and Commerce of the American Short Story.* Cambridge: Cambridge UP, 1993.

Lewis, R. W. B. *Edith Wharton: A Biography.* New York: Harper & Row, 1975.

May, Charles E. "Metaphoric Motivation in Short Fiction: 'In the Beginning Was the Story.'" *Short Story Theory at a Crossroads.* Ed. Susan Lohafer and Jo Ellyn Clarey. Baton Rouge: Louisiana State UP, 1989. 62-73.

Merish, Lori. "Engendering Naturalism: Narrative Form and Commodity Spectacle in U. S. Naturalist Fiction." *Novel* 29 (1996): 319-45.

Mitchell, Lee Clark. *Determined Fictions: American Literary Naturalism.* New York: Columbia UP, 1989.

Nettels, Elsa. "Gender and First-Person Narration in Edith Wharton's Short Fiction." *Edith Wharton: New Critical Essays.* Ed. Alfred Bendixen and Annette Zilversmit. New York: Garland, 1992. 245-60.

Wharton, Edith. *A Backward Glance.* New York: D. Appleton-Century, 1934.

———. *The Collected Stories of Edith Wharton.* Vol. 1. Ed. R. W. B. Lewis. New York: Charles Scribner's Sons, 1968.

———. *The Letters of Edith Wharton.* Ed. R. W. B. Lewis and Nancy Lewis. New York: Collier Books, 1988.

———. *The Writing of Fiction.* New York: Charles Scribner's Sons, 1925.

White, Barbara A. *Edith Wharton: A Study of the Short Fiction.* New York: Twayne, 1991.

Wolff, Cynthia Griffin. *A Feast of Words: The Triumph of Edith Wharton.* 2nd ed. Reading, Mass.: Merloyd Lawrence, 1995.

TITLE COMMENTARY

Ethan Frome

MARY V. MARCHAND (ESSAY DATE 2001)

SOURCE: Marchand, Mary V. "Cross Talk: Edith Wharton and the New England Women Regionalists." *Women's Studies: An Interdisciplinary Journal* 30 (2001): 369-95.

In the following essay, Marchand explores the gendered nature of the style and theme of Ethan Frome, *contrasting the novel's representation of women's culture with the literary aesthetics and feminist politics of early twentieth-century New England female regional writers.*

To read through the contemporary reviews of Edith Wharton's work is to be struck by the contradictory assessments of her attitude toward her female characters. It is not unusual to find among reviews of the same novel praise for Wharton's "sympathetic delineation of her heroine's character, her acute analysis of women's minds," and the complaint that these "pictures of American women for harshness of uncharity are difficult to parallel."[1] Equally open to dispute, apparently, was the gender of her writing. In their chapter on Wharton in *Some Modern Novelists* (1918), Helen and Wilson Follett allude to a long-standing debate over whether Wharton, "of all women, [writes] most like a man" (291). For the Folletts, the putative masculine qualities of Wharton's fiction—its balance, asperity, detachment—are "but a species of protective coloring adopted in order to escape being obviously a woman" (292). Her fiction, they conclude, "escapes the limitations of both sexes, of sex itself. It is fundamentally sexless" (200). More recently, feminist scholars have clarified how Wharton's representations of women issue from her "argument with America," to use Elizabeth Ammons's fine phrase, her sympathetic, complex and often deeply pessimistic assessment of the plight of American women. And yet Wharton scholarship continues to exhibit a startling array of conclusions regarding Wharton's women. Janet Malcolm's characterization of Wharton as "the woman who hated women," and of her work as pervaded with "profound misogyny," has been largely dismissed as bizarre and capricious, and yet not all objections to Wharton are of this cruder variety. Among the more sophisticated is James W. Tuttleton's argument that the sweeping nature of Wharton's satire and her social conservatism resist any lopsided account of her social and political views.[2] In light of the ambiguities surrounding both Wharton's attitudes toward women and the "sex" of her own writing, it is perhaps not surprising that several recent critics have discovered in the Demeter-Persephone myth an apt text for understanding Wharton's mind and work.[3] This image of the daughter who divides her year between the world of the mother and the province of the father, which appears throughout Wharton's own writings, implicitly allows us to both view her as one of then "key figures" in the feminist debates of her day (Ammons, *Argument* ix) and acknowledge certain stubborn facts, including the revelation by her most recent biographer that when she endowed a scholarship for students of design she stipulated that the recipient be male: women had "much better stay at home and mind the baby" (qtd. in Benstock 387). All of this taken together begins to suggest why Wharton's work continues to represent a challenge to feminist criticism.

I want to argue that the vexed question of Wharton's representations of women and her ties to the feminist debates of her day cannot be adequately posed apart from investigation of her rival affiliations as an elite cultural critic and as a woman writer with high art ambitions. The burden of my argument is that certain developments in both the argument for women's rights and against the spread of what Henry Canby would decry as "vast," "engulfing" middlebrow culture irrevocably complicated the commitments of writers like Wharton who had ties to both the feminist and cultural debates of her day. In contrast to an earlier generation, who generally linked political emancipation to the ideal of the assimilated woman, many in this generation of activists articulated their vision of women's rights in terms of the superior contributions of womanliness to the public sphere. It was precisely the intolerable prospect of the widening influence of the "feminine" in public life that stimulated antifeminist rhetoric among the cultural elite, who tended in their writings to conflate the political demands of activists with the undisciplined feminine tastes linked to the spread of middle- and lowbrow culture. This overlap between sexual and cultural politics gave rise to "cross talk" between the two; because the debate over the political uses of women's culture also concerned the boundaries between high- and lowbrow tastes, these sexual and cultural politics continually interfered with one another. This volatile cross talk characterizes much of Wharton's fiction, its presence shaping and disrupting her representations of women and her attitude toward the presence of the feminine in American politics and letters.

Many of these tensions are played out in Wharton's relationship with New England women writers, whose regionalist fiction came to Wharton as an active term in these tense overlapping debates concerning the political and aesthetic standing of women's culture. Cross talk finds its virtual embodiment in her 1911 novel **Ethan Frome**, which much more closely reads and rewrites the tradition of New England women writers than previously recognized. Wharton's acerbic reflections on these women writers are well known, as is her claim, renewed over the years, that her own small body of New England fiction was written in response to their writings. And

Michelle Pfeiffer and Daniel Day-Lewis in the film adaptation of *The Age of Innocence*.

while a few critics have pursued the broader significance of Wharton's claim to revise the local color tradition, this essay explores how meaning in **Ethan Frome** accrues through an elaborate system of differences from these regionalist texts. The novel's polemical intertextuality, which I argue ultimately entangles Wharton in telling contradictions and challenges current understandings of both the gendering of **Ethan Frome** and Wharton's place in the gendering of literary history.

I. The Politics and Aesthetics of Women's Culture

The nature of Wharton's feminism clearly depends on the historical character of the arguments available to her. Restoring some of the complexity to these arguments entails distinguishing between the more conservative rhetoric of so-called social feminists[4] and the radicalism of Charlotte Perkins Gilman, Harriot Stanton Blatch, and others. The various positions activists maintained frequently turned on the controversial question of the role of women's culture in further-

ing one or another of "woman's causes." Largely acquiescing in the premise of essential sex differences and sexually determined roles, social feminists sought to enlarge these roles by appealing to the potentially superior contributions of women's culture to the public sphere. We see this gender consciousness reflected in Rheta Childe Dorr's assertion in *What Eight Million Women Want* (1910) that "women now form a new social group, separate, and to a degree homogenous"; "they have evolved a group opinion and a group ideal" (5). In translating domestic virtues to serve a larger context, social feminists, including many suffragists (social feminists included "antis" as well), had the force of progressive ideology behind them. Having taken up the social policy issues and public services that were once the province of women, a newly domesticated state bolstered in turn the activists' claims that women were uniquely fitted to serve the state as Municipal Housekeepers.[5] As suffrage historian Aileen Kraditor observes of this crucial alignment of progressive and sexual politics, the cultural piety that "home was woman's sphere was now an argument not against women suffrage but in favor of it, for government was now 'enlarged housekeeping'" (68).

While scholars continue to dispute the compatibility of women's culture and feminist politics,[6] the decision among "sex-conscious feminists," as one dissenting suffragist called them, to take the "sex line" was a storm center in Wharton's day as well. Where social feminists accepted in large part received notions of sex differences, often, in fact, emphasizing them, Gilman, for example, considered most of these differences manifestations of "excessive sex-distinction."[7] Where social feminists demanded equality on the basis of their essential womanliness, Gilman argued for women's rights on the conviction that "the whole area of human life is outside of, and irrelevant to, the distinctions of sex" (*Home* 217). Gilman's conviction that centuries-long economic dependence had crippled women also put her deeply at odds with social feminists over the sensitive issue of the present state of women's culture. Where social feminists propounded the alternative virtues of women's culture and female values to an acquisitive nation, Gilman argued that because her "economic position is reactionary and unjust," woman "reacts injuriously upon industry, upon art, upon science, discovery, and progress" (120).

Wharton's work suggests that she shared many of Gilman's assumptions. Like Gilman, her partial repudiation of essentialism sharpened her skepticism about whether the politics of women's culture could contribute to any real adjustment in women's status. Social feminist separatist strategies and their limitations emerge as the major theme in Wharton's chapter on **"Frenchwomen and Their Ways"** in *French Ways and Their Meaning* (1919), which insists that despite "her 'boards' and clubs and sororities, her public investigation of everything under the heavens from the 'social evil' to baking-powder, and from 'physical culture' to the newest esoteric religion," the American woman is "a Montessori infant" who lives in a "kindergarten" (101). For Wharton the salient feature of these "seemingly influential lives" and "independent activities" is that they are all conducted in a separate female realm, where women are confined in "improved" public but no less restrictive surroundings. She subsequently points out, through the example of French women of various classes, the benefits that accrue for women when the sexes are instead fully integrated. Among members of the leisure class, it is

the salon that promotes an extraordinary degree of interaction between the sexes, based as it is "on the belief that the most stimulating conversation in the world is that between intelligent men and women who see each other often enough to be on terms of frank and easy friendship" (117). Together with Susan Goodman's arresting portrait of Wharton as the "extraordinary" woman in an otherwise male circle of intimates, these glowing tributes to acts of individualist assimilation and integration into male institutions suggest just how deeply at odds Wharton was with the values of women's culture.

But the debate over women's culture arose simultaneously in another context. Lawrence W. Levine's and Paul DiMaggio's historical studies of the "sacralization" of the arts reveal the growing chasm between highbrow and lowbrow culture. Partly in response to social developments associated with modernity, including the new reign of money (embodied for Wharton in the colossal fortunes and philistine tastes of the "invaders from Pittsburgh," the "barbarians from the West"), the old bourgeoisie sought to define "legitimate" culture that they could control. Wharton is in many ways exemplary of the elite cultural critic. Nowhere is this more evident than in the ways her views on the artist and intellectual as guardian of high culture come to involve her in a tendency to stigmatize low- and middlebrow tastes as feminine.

While it is true, as Tania Modleski has observed, that images of women and the feminine seem invariably to turn up at the center of explanations for the debasement of tastes, there is also an historically specific basis for the gender inscriptions of this era's cultural criticism: the first mass women's movement. What especially interests me is that the spread of low- and middlebrow culture, persistently described in terms of a feminine threat, is somehow associated with the prospect of women's emancipation. What seems clear is that the presence of a politicized women's culture—the power of this new social group, in Dorr's words, to advance feminine values, opinions, and ideals—fed high art anxiety over the boundaries between high and low culture, and suggests why elite critics tended in their writings to collapse women's political demands with the feminine presence that ostensibly threatened the conditions surrounding the production and consumption of high art in America. There is a kind of confusion in the writings of many conservative intellectuals at turn of the century, but one that becomes intelligible in light of the cross talk between the gender inscriptions of the era's political and aesthetic struggles. It is precisely because the culture circulated both a feminist critique of women's culture and antifeminist rhetoric directed against women's share in the decline of taste, that challenging the politics of women's culture left Wharton vulnerable to antifeminist appropriation.

Recognizing the vexed relationship between Wharton's feminism and her cultural criticism returns us to **Ethan Frome** with a new awareness of how this cross talk shaped her response to the New England women writers, a tradition that, by its subject, was inscribed at the intersection of these debates.

II. Wharton and the New England Authoresses

In an introduction to a 1922 edition of **Ethan Frome**, Wharton indicates that she conceived of the novel as a corrective to the fiction of the local colorists, whose work she felt had only "a vague botanical and dialectical [. . .] resemblance to the harsh and beautiful landscape," a landscape she knew from her years living and touring in the Berkshires. And again in **A Backward Glance** (1934), Wharton recalls that both **Ethan Frome** and **Summer** were formed in reaction to the "rose-and-lavender productions" of New England's "favourite authoresses" (1003). She writes, "For years I had wanted to draw life as it really was . . . utterly unlike that seen through the rose-coloured spectacles of my predecessors, Mary Wilkins and Sarah Orne Jewett" (1002). While these remarks are well known, critics have tended to either interpret them loosely or discount them altogether as disingenuous.[8] And indeed, the problem with Wharton's alleged contrast between her own grim story and that of the local colorists is that Wharton singles out Jewett and Wilkins, whose fiction adheres to the tenets of realism.

However, recent scholarship on American women regionalists, which has clarified the extent to which their work forms a distinct and coherent tradition,[9] a tradition that relies on what Josephine Donovan has called a "feminine literary mode" in its depictions of a rich, women-based culture, brings to light a central impulse behind **Ethan Frome**, one until now not sufficiently clear: Wharton's novel is both a structural and thematic response to the matrifocality of these regionalist texts. It is, inextricably, an aesthetic and political response; this popular tradition of women's writing at once embodies the feminist strategies Wharton opposed and constituted one source of the feminine presence in arts and letters that she and other elite critics repudiated.

I argue that **Ethan Frome** rewrites many of the shared conventions of regionalist fiction, but there are good reasons to suspect that she was more narrowly responding to Jewett's work. Few authors were as closely identified with this tradition as Jewett, whose 1896 novel *The Country of the Pointed Firs* was hailed early on as a masterpiece of the genre. Moreover, as Richard Brodhead reveals, Jewett shared Wharton's high art aspirations. In *Culture of Letters,* his illuminating account of this tradition's location in late nineteenth-century social and cultural space, he demonstrates that regional writing was a project exquisitely attuned to the needs of the upper class. For elite readers of the *Atlantic* and *Harper's,* fictional excursions in coastal Maine and rural Vermont performed the important cultural work of allowing these readers to "rehears[e] the leisured outlook that differentiated [them] as a social group" (144). In Brodhead's account, Jewett and a small circle of intellectuals and artists formed a women's community that was not separate from the high art literary establishment but "nested" in it (156). But if Jewett challenged the (masculinist) norms that limited the woman artist's access to high culture, she did so under distinctly feminine auspices, an aspect of her work and career that Brodhead tends to underplay. Again and again in the reviews of her fiction, one encounters views like those expressed by Edward Garnett in a 1903 essay, in which Jewett's art is embraced as "exceedingly feminine." "She has that characteristically feminine patience with human nature which is intimately enrooted in a mother's feeling" (qtd. in Sherman 266).

In this light, Jewett came to Wharton as a figure with the admixture of sameness and difference that would compel Wharton not, as Brodhead suggests, to sidestep Jewett, the sketch, and the regional subject (175), but to engage them head on. In almost every dimension, **Ethan Frome** reveals its intertextual dependence. As many critics have observed of the matrifocality of the New England women regionalists' texts, despite the significant differences among them, they all point towards a conception of women's community more fully realized than that of any previous generation of women writers. Their work repeatedly inscribes a compelling vision of a female realm, what Donovan in *New England Local Color Literature* has broadly characterized as a "counter world of their own, a rural realm that existed on the margins of patriarchal society, a world that nourished strong, free women" (3). This vision culminates in *Pointed Firs*, where the absent, dead, or taciturn men only serve to highlight the richness of the community of single and widowed women, a community traditionally marginalized in the romantic novel. In her deepening relationship with Dunnet Landing's two great matriarchs, Mrs. Todd and Mrs. Blackett, the urban female narrator learns, and we through her, that in Marjorie Pryse's words, "there still exists a country—a world—where the vision of women is not only vital, but can be shared" ("Introduction" xix).

In ***Ethan Frome,*** Wharton subverts this vision of a benevolent rural matriarchy. If New England women's fiction took as its premise that the country is a place where "strong, authentic women flourished" (Donovan 104), in Starkfield not only do both men and women falter, but the effects of rural life are strangely magnified and turn threatening in the women. We learn that Ethan's mother "got queer and dragged along for years weak as a baby" when the stage stopped traveling past the Frome farmstead (68). The details of Zeena's own obscure illnesses are too well known to need recounting, and yet Ethan observes of her case that it is merely the most notable in a "community rich in pathological instances" (98). When Zeena grows increasingly taciturn, he wonders if, like his mother, she too is "turning queer": "Women did, he knew. Zeena, who had at her fingers' end the pathological chart of the whole region, had cited many cases of the kind while she was nursing his mother; and he himself knew of certain lonely farm-houses in the neighborhood where stricken creatures pined, and of others where sudden tragedy came of their presences" (99). Here Wharton characterizes women's sickliness as decidedly threatening, and the sympathetic image of "stricken creatures" turns ominous with Ethan's recollections that these women brought "sudden tragedy" to their households.

Ethan immediately associates Zeena with these darkly mysterious tragedies; he observes her "shut face" and feels the "chill of forebodings" (99). And certainly her psychosomatic illnesses bring a measure of tragedy to their marriage, forestalling his plans to move to a larger city (98), depleting their meager funds in her "therapeutic excursions," and ultimately furnishing Zeena with unassailable grounds for dismissing Mattie from the household. Nearly every female character, however, is subject to Wharton's insistence on projecting the rural matriarchite as a menacing community of women. This insistence is most

evident in Mattie's transformation. The prevailing narrative tension, which derives from the explicit and forcible contrast between Zeena's gray, pinched aspect and Mattie's rosy beauty, is grotesquely resolved in the novel's vivid final tableaux, where the two women are rendered indistinguishable. Here the lines are no longer drawn with Mattie and Ethan on one side and sadistic Zeena on the other; it is clearly Ethan "shut up there'n that one kitchen" with two embittered women (155). As Ammons observes, this scene projects Zeena and Mattie as one woman, as the witch or shrew (*Argument* 66). Mattie in effect becomes Zeena, much as Zeena replaces Ethan's mother. Together these women fall under the category of "queer" women whose presence brings tragedy.

In this context, even Ethan's encounters with genial old Mrs. Hale, whose sympathetic words check him in mid-flight from Starkfield, and the widow Homan, whose prescient query when Ethan buys glue from her—"I hope Zeena ain't broken anything she sets store by" (115)—only sharpens his dread of Zeena discovering that her prize pickle dish was broken during his dinner alone with Mattie, assume a threatening aspect. The community of women in Jewett's novel, for whom "tact is after all a kind of mindreading" (46), and whose "constant interest and intercourse" have forged "golden chains of love and dependence" (90), becomes in Wharton's hands a community of women that seemingly act in concert to expose the romantic subplot and head off the male protagonist's escape from village life. To focus too narrowly on Zeena or discount the harsh depiction of women as expressive of male fears ignores the disturbing implication that women in general finally entrap Ethan; it ignores as well the novel's concluding sentiment, uttered, after all, not by the male narrator but by Mrs. Hale.[10] She compares the Fromes "up at the farm" with the Fromes "down in the graveyard" and grimly concludes that at least "down there [. . .] the women have got to hold their tongues" (156).

For many women regionalists, the imagined world of women's community is strengthened by and sustains in turn rural traditions of folk knowledge. The opposition between rural and urban life frequently finds literary expression in what Donovan describes as the deep tensions between women's preindustrial forms of knowledge—herbology, witchcraft, mysticism—and the male scientific-technological knowledge that "threatened to recolonize the matriarchal world of the New England local colorists forever" (*New England*

236). These ancient matriarchal powers are famously embodied in Mrs. Todd, the "Sybil" and herbalist at the center of *Pointed Firs*. Her "rustic pharmacopoeia," with its mysterious plants and pungent odors, resonates for the narrator with "a dim sense and remembrance of something in the forgotten past [. . . of] sacred and mystic rites, and [. . .] some occult knowledge handed with them down the centuries" (3-4). Jewett and other women regionalists understood women's collective life to take shape through these shared forms of knowledge, and the narrative is crisscrossed by and organized around visits to and by Mrs. Todd to dispense advice and herbs to the women of Dunnet Landing.

In *Ethan Frome*, Wharton retains this association between women and rural traditions of healing only to turn it on its head. We need to recognize in Zeena's nursing skills (98), Mrs. Hale's "doctoring," her "authority on symptoms and treatment" (99), and the community "rich in pathological cases," Wharton's ferocious satire of the occult knowledge promoted by Jewett and others as an important facet of the vitality of community life. Through Zeena in particular, Wharton satirizes the tradition of women's healing as the other side of a hypochondriacal concern for one's own health. While Ethan is initially "shamed and dazzled" by Zeena's mastery of the sick-bed duties (97), Wharton subsequently exposes her interest in medicine as neurotic, her knowledge acquired from "absorbed observation of her own symptoms" (98). Wharton seems to have grasped what the women local colorists perhaps perceived only implicitly, that these rural traditions of knowledge formed the basis for matriarchal power, and Zeena's power over Ethan derives almost entirely from her familiarity with the rituals of illness and death. Her efficient handling of the duties surrounding his mother's sickness and death instills in Ethan a sense of gratitude mingled with obligation, "magnif[ying] his sense of what he owed her" (97). Zeena further uses the authority of her mysterious illness both to bring Mattie to the farm and then to send her away when she recognizes her as a rival. Throughout the novel, woman's involvement with illness and death is systematically portrayed as destructive, and women's lore, which operates in Jewett's novel to create a community, as collective neurosis.

For many women regionalists, the tensions between rural and urban, between women's traditions and male scientific-industrial knowledge, were irreconcilable. In this, Wharton concurs.

Matriarchal authority flourishes only in the absence of technology, either in Starkfield the rural pocket of twenty years ago or Starkfield of the present day, when, as the narrator observes, winter effectively rolls back progress. Wharton registers rural women's resistance to the encroaching modern world in Zeena's refusal to leave Starkfield for a larger city, where she would "suffer a complete loss of identity," an identity that we are told derives entirely from her "sickliness" (98). Rural women's traditions are indeed threatened by the modern world, Wharton implies, but it is a loss of identity she refuses to romanticize.

The vision in *Pointed Firs* of rural Maine as a counterreality to urban life can be traced back to the woman visitor-narrator. A frequent device in this body of women's fiction, the figure of the "insider-outsider" suggests what Pryse has described as the modern woman's "metaphysical isolation," her alienation from the female-identified realm ("Introduction xi"). This distance is subsequently diminished through the narrative's invocation of community life. An ambivalent member of the modern world, the narrator of *Pointed Firs* discovers a women's community that has retained much of its preindustrial character, and thus its potency, and she discovers in the oracular Mrs. Todd no less than "a force of Nature [that] gave her cousinship to the ancient deities" (199). As part of the process of reconnecting with this world of the ancestral mothers—a process she compares to falling in love (1)—she serves as erstwhile apprentice to her landlady, temporarily setting aside her own work in order to imbibe Mrs. Todd's folk wisdom, attend to the community's stories, and participate in its rites.

In polemical contrast to New England women's fiction, where the vision of a transcendent female realm frequently issues from the woman visitor's own yearning for female ties, *Ethan Frome*'s male visitor-narrator is primed for sympathetic identification with the male protagonist, who shares many of his "tastes and acquirements," including an interest in science and technology (70). Most importantly, he identifies with Ethan's thwarted ambition to escape village life, his touchingly modest aspiration to "live in town, where there were lectures and big libraries and 'fellows doing things'" (98). The novel is set in motion not, as in Jewett's work, by the narrator's desire to partake of "rustic simplicities," but by his determination to learn what hindered Ethan's flight from Starkfield (66).

This unapologetic representative of modern technology, an engineer whose stay in Starkfield is connected with his job at a nearby power station, Wharton's narrator is the very figure women local colorists decried as the "burglar in paradise" (Donovan, *New England* 120) and he exhibits none of the woman visitor's nostalgia for rural life. In his attitude towards the pastoral myth, Wharton seizes on the chance to neatly invert the poles of New England local color fiction. Progress, growth, the technology available to rural locations: these developments, he argues, bring life to small towns, and when winter temporarily turns back progress, the inhabitants must confront once again the void, the "negation" of life (65). Wharton transvalues the regionalists' opposition between rural and urban, but she leaves the gendering of this dialectic intact, consistently identifying the male characters with scientific-industrial knowledge and suggesting that the bonds between men are formed on the basis of this knowledge. A shared interest in engineering supplies the initial and vital tie between Ethan and the narrator, and borrowing the visitor's volume of popular science affords Ethan a rare and liberating glimpse of the modern world outside Starkfield's narrow confines. So, too, a year of physics at Worcester technological college has left a deep impression that is indissolubly connected with images of male mentors, of the "friendly professor of physics" who helped Ethan in the lab, and the minister who befriended him and lent him books. The patriarchal forms of knowledge that the regionalists decried as the greatest threat to the female sanctuary, Wharton projects as her protagonist's only means of escape from this realm.

A final trace of the novel's thematic connections with local color fiction appears in the images of women as failed housekeepers and in the scenes of failed domesticity. The novel repeatedly encourages the reader to assess the female characters in light of domestic virtues. While Ethan initially perceives Zeena as possessing "all the household wisdom that his long apprenticeship had not instilled in him" (97), every trace of this wisdom disappears with the onset of her illness. Nor does Mattie exhibit any of the traditional domestic talents. Ethan sees her at certain key points as a paragon of household efficiency, but this is largely belied by his own observation that while love may awaken "a dormant instinct" in her, Mattie had "no natural turn for housekeeping. [. . .] Domesticity in the abstract did not interest her" (80). Wharton suggests the failure of domesticity in the image of the farmstead's squalid kitchen. Even with Zeena's absence, when the kitchen appears "warm and bright," Ethan

characterizes it as a "poor place, not 'spruce' and shining as his mother had kept it in his boyhood" (96). The narrator's sentiments echo Ethan's when he renders his first impression of the Frome kitchen. "Even for that part of the country," he observes, it "was a poor-looking place" (152). This is all by way of preparing us for Mrs. Hale's final pronouncement on the tragedy: "It's bad enough to see the two women sitting there—but *his* face, when he looks around that bare place, just kills me. [. . .] You see, I can look back and call it up in his mother's day, before their troubles" (154). In its implication that Ethan's suffering is best gauged by the bleakness of his kitchen, the remark reflects how the text repeatedly measures the tragedy against domestic norms.

Here, too, understanding the significance Wharton attaches to the image of the home as a "poor-looking place" entails giving full weight to her declared intention of writing against New England women's fiction. In "Distilling Essences: Regionalism and Women's Culture," Pryse has shown how women's culture as rendered by the regionalists effectively dismantles the concept of home as women's proper place and of "mother" as defined by separate spheres ideology. In these texts, she argues, women have turned to "domesticating public space" (7), and "mother" has become a "model of generativity that links generations," a model that moves motherhood beyond biology (10-11). We see this put to startling effect in *Pointed Firs*, where women's domesticity has little to do with men, marriage, or even children. This strategy is reflected as well in the representation of Mrs. Todd, "mateless and appealing" (131), but also in the portrayal of her mother, Mrs. Blackett. On one level, their lives of sewing, visiting, cooking, nurturing, and healing are fully consonant with traditional expectations of women, and yet these domestic duties, translated to serve the larger context of the community, operate as reasons for leaving the privatized home and family.

The specific nature of Ethan's dream, the dream of perfect domesticity, reveals Wharton's grasp of the challenge Jewett's work and the notion of women's culture presented to a narrow conception of women's sphere. The text is full of wistful allusions to warm kitchens and domestic intimacy. As Ethan and Mattie walk home from a dance, he fantasizes about a kitchen where he and Mattie could sit side-by-side at the stove, a "little enclosure" that would provide him with a much longed for sense of "continuance and stability" (88). This fantasy of perfect domesticity materializes at the very center of the narrative in their one evening alone in the house: "She set the lamp on the table, and he saw that it was carefully laid for supper, with fresh dough-nuts, stewed blueberries and his favourite pickles in a dish of gay red glass. A bright fire glowed in the stove and the cat lay stretched before it, watching the table with a drowsy eye. Ethan was suffocated with the sense of well-being" (103). In this scene, Wharton draws on all of the kitchen's powerful associations with domestic comfort. She subsequently underscores her intentions here, calling attention to "the ancient implications of conformity and order" embodied in this "warm lamp-lit room" (104). In keeping with these "ancient implications," the characters rediscover the pleasure of playing out conventional gender roles. Ethan basks in his new-found aura of "protection and authority"; Mattie sits blushing in maidenly modesty with her eyes downcast (104). Thus, while Jewett quietly maneuvers her female protagonists out of the home, Wharton puts them back in the kitchen. In the interest of systematically overturning the regionalist project, Wharton's text occupies the conservative position of reasserting women's ties to the home, a rhetorical move that as I discuss below ultimately renders the text deeply at odds with itself.

In addition to thematic connections of this sort, I want to postulate that **Ethan Frome** reveals an intertextual dependence that is structural as well. In her study of Jewett's critical theory, Donovan suggests that early on she worried about her relation to the novel form: "I can furnish the theatre, and show you the actors, and the scenery, and the audience, but there never is any play!" (qtd. in Donovan, "Notes" 218). As Donovan describes it, Jewett eventually resolves this in favor of cultivating a "feminine literary mode," one that rejects the conventional plot as inadequate for reflecting women's experience, and adopts instead a "plotless" structure that scholars have described as "centric" and "weblike."[11] Jewett and other women who wrote within the genre of narratives of community, as Sandra Zagarell has called it, organized their depictions of community and the bonds between women around the transactions of village life, the exchange of visits, its hospitalities, rites and rituals. This orientation toward the viewpoint of the community is exemplified by the narrators and female protagonists. Through their attentiveness to the stories of the community, their willingness to include other voices in their texts, they exhibit what Marcia Folsom has characterized as the "empathic style" and

Zagarell as the exceptional "porousness" of these narratives (515). In *Pointed Firs,* Jewett's narrator makes room for, among others, Captain Littlepage's haunting tale of the "waiting place," Joanna's story as jointly reconstructed by Mrs. Todd and Mrs. Fosdick, and Mrs. Todd's own account of her marriage.

When we turn back to Wharton's novel, we find that she employs a male narrator as her "sympathizing intermediary" ("Introduction" 260), and perhaps no aspect of the novel has given rise to more discussion than his status in the text. Criticism of this narrative device, which goes back at least as far as John Crowe Ransom's "Character and Characters," suggests this is the weak point of the novel. Despite Wharton's claim that the narrative is composed in part of the details supplied the narrator by various villagers, each of whom "contributes just so much as he or she is capable of understanding" (260), they actually furnish very little of the story. Instead, his "vision" of the story, as it is called (74), seems improbably pieced together from one night's stay at the Frome farmstead. One way to make sense of this awkward construction and the value Wharton attached to it (she defends it in a preface to the novella, a foreword to the play, and again in her autobiography) is to consider how it renegotiates the important elements of Jewett's narrative: this narrator's "vision" is both irreducibly his own—not, as in Jewett's novel, porous or truly collaborative—*and* objective. Indeed, in her discussions of the novel Wharton insists that this story yields up the hard truth overlooked by the regionalists, and she attributes this to the narrator's capacity for "seeing all around" the characters. "Only the narrator," she maintains, "has scope enough to see it all, to resolve it back into simplicity, and to put it in its rightful place among his larger categories" ("Introduction" 260). This brings us to a potentially alienating aspect of Wharton's thought: while she almost certainly conceived of the novel as a male version of a conventionally female narrative, she did not then view this version as partial or limited. The combination of the male point of view and the sympathetic male center and subject makes this an extraordinarily pro-male story, but instead of emphasizing the distortions that inhere in the narrator's perspective, Wharton's reflections on the novel invariably assign wider truth and greater objectivity to his "vision" of the events.

The chief question raised by what I have argued thus far is why Wharton so insistently overturns the conventions associated with this tradition of women's writing. A partial explanation lies with Amy Kaplan's insight that Wharton's interest in the profession of authorship involved distancing herself from the "volubility and commercial success of the domestic tradition of American women novelists" (43). In this light, it is perhaps not surprising that Wharton repeatedly links the writing of this novel with her emergence as a professional writer. "It was not until I wrote **Ethan Frome**," she claims in her autobiography, "that I suddenly felt the artisan's full control of his implements" (**Backward** 209). And the deep note of tragedy sounded in **Ethan Frome**, which critics have not failed to connect to Wharton's tumultuous personal life, is somehow belied by "the greatest joy" and "fullest ease" she says she brought to the writing of the novella, and the "fatuous satisfaction" she reports feeling as she read over its proofs (**Backward** 209; qtd. in Lewis 297).

But **Ethan Frome** also occupies a similar place in the growing body of cultural criticism to that of Henry James's "Speech and Manners of American Women" and F. Marion Crawford's "False Taste in Art," sharing their tendency to disparage popular forms by invoking the specter of a politicized women's culture. In linking the women's regionalist tradition, with its emphasis on the exalted value of femaleness, with popular tastes and inferior art, **Ethan Frome** recalls the web of signification that turns up at the center of antifeminist rhetoric directed at public women. To the extent that Wharton's narrative acquires meaning in asserting its opposition to this tradition, Wharton was engaged in the novella in an act of cultural criticism, one intent on using the putative aesthetic threat of a politicized women's culture to shore up the fledgling distinctions between high-, low- and middlebrow tastes.

If **Ethan Frome** discloses the interests and affiliations of both the elite critic and the woman writer with high art aspirations, these interests are ultimately complicated by the feminist context of Wharton's concerns. The significant thematic subversion of the text occurs in its idealized descriptions of domesticity. Wharton is intent in these scenes on reasserting the domestic ideology that Jewett and her female protagonists struggled to dismantle, but she cannot sustain the sentimental mode these scenes demand. In passages like the one cited above describing the details of the supper table, the clichéd prose and the discordant note struck by the allusion to suffocation inevitably introduce an antithetical interpretation of Ethan's domestic fantasy as a sentimental and, finally, disabling ideal.

ON THE SUBJECT OF...

COMPARISON OF *THE REEF* **AND** *ETHAN FROME*

The Reef is perhaps the most Jamesian of Wharton's novels. Artistically it falls short of the superb economy and control manifested in *Ethan Frome*; however, if it is a less successful work than its predecessor, it is at the same time much more ambitious in scope. *Ethan Frome* deals with the tragic and sterile renunciation of sexuality; *The Reef* attempts to deal with the complex personal and social implications of acting on one's sexual impulses, and it examines this question as it pertains to both men and women. For its time, *The Reef* was an audacious experiment.

Wolff, Cynthia Griffin. An excerpt from *Dictionary of Literary Biography, Volume 9: American Novelists, 1910-1945*. A Bruccoli Clark Layman Book. Edited by James J. Martine, Saint Bonaventure University. The Gale Group, 1981. pp. 126-42.

Wharton's dilemma emerges most clearly in connection with the gender roles defined by domestic ideology. In the interest of overturning the nondomestic images of women in Jewett's work, Wharton uses the crucial kitchen scene as the occasion for projecting exemplary male and female behavior. When the pickle-dish breaks, Ethan sheds his characteristic passivity for the conventional male role and Mattie becomes the very image of appealing feminine weakness: she immediately breaks into tears, looks to Ethan's greater authority with "stricken eyes," and when he commands her in a "voice of sudden authority" to give him the pieces of glass, she contentedly defers to him. The scene's resolution stops just short of parody: "Completely reassured, she shone on him through tear-hung lashes, and his soul swelled with pride as he saw how his tone subdued her. [. . .] Except when he was steering a log down the mountain to his mill he had never known such a thrilling sense of mastery" (106). As in the stock description of the domestic scene, the sentimental mode of "tear-hung lashes" and the ludicrous comparison of subduing women to steering logs introduce a note of irony that makes reading these scenes straight almost impossible. The false note struck by these exaggeratedly male and female postures reveals Wharton at cross purposes with her own text. In writing against women's fiction, Wharton reasserts the prevailing sexual codes that prize submissiveness in women and mastery in men, but the clichéd prose betrays her skepticism about these roles.

Wharton's ambivalence is even more visible in her treatment of Mattie's plight after Zeena replaces her with a hired girl. Her distraught cry as Ethan drives her to the station—"where'll I go if I leave you? I don't know how to get along alone"—invokes the grim specter of her plight prior to working for the Fromes. Wharton touches illuminatingly on the orphaned girl's inadequate training for self-support: she could "trim a hat, make molasses candy, recite 'Curfew shall not ring tonight,' and play 'The Lost Chord' and pot-pourri from 'Carmen,'" but her health broke down when she tried stenography, book-keeping, and clerking at a department store (92). Wharton explicitly links Mattie's economic plight to her lack of professional training and the social conventions that trained her instead for her dependent status as a decorative object. And like the clichéd prose Wharton falls back on in projecting the domestic scene, this signals the text's major contradictions. If Jewett advocates through her protagonists the necessity of self-reliance, Wharton, at least on one level, reassures us that if men and women conform to the "ancient implications" of the ideology of separate spheres, the "true woman" will be taken care of by the masterful man. Yet Mattie's harrowing predicament, pointing as it does to the necessity for self-support and nondomestic work for women, undermines this conservative thematic insistence on the value of specifically feminine virtues and ideals.

In *Ethan Frome,* cross talk thus manifests itself as Wharton's ambivalence towards domesticity. Starting from the premise that she declares in the novel her high art allegiance by systematically overturning the conventions of a popular tradition of women's writing—a strategy that entailed in this instance endorsing separate spheres ideology—I argue that Wharton could not entirely erase from the text her commitment to nondomestic work for women and her concern that social feminism, in accepting women's link to the home and domestic virtues, had failed in this regard. Thus the novel shows Wharton as a more complicated figure, even a deeply conflicted one, devoted, on the one hand, to asserting her class culture against the rising factions of the middle

THE HOUSE OF MIRTH

BY

EDITH WHARTON

WITH ILLUSTRATIONS BY A. B. WENZELL

NEW YORK
CHARLES SCRIBNER'S SONS
MDCCCCV

Title page of *The House of Mirth,* published in 1905.

class (whose tastes she stigmatizes as feminine) while, on the other hand, offering an alternative feminism that seeks to subvert, not simply revaluate, conventional female identity.

At one level *Ethan Frome* makes vivid the sororophobic tensions in her work. When one tries to put Wharton back into a tradition of women's literary community, somehow she ends up testing the limits of the familial idiom that Helena Michie argues feminist discourse has come to rely on. She becomes, as in Donovan's analysis, the "rebellious but male-identified daughter" (*After* 44). It is tempting to measure only the losses incurred in her rejection of a female-identified realm—the "emotional alienation from the maternal bower" (83) that Donovan alludes to, the loneliness that emerges as part of Goodman's complex portrait of Wharton as the only woman in the inner circle (16-17). But Wharton's response to women's culture was also the other side of her ambition to be a self-made man,[12] an ambition that situates her within a different feminism. Perhaps one of Wharton's most telling comments was that it was "doubtful if a novelist of one race can ever really penetrate into the soul of another" ("Great American" 157). Strikingly, she seems not to have held similar doubts about adopting the sex of another. In **Ethan Frome** and almost all of her first-person narratives, Wharton wrote as a man. Unlike Jewett, who would advise Willa Cather that "when a woman writes in a man's character,—it must always, I believe be something a masquerade" (*Letters* 246), Wharton apparently felt one could successfully mask one's presence in a text as male.[13] What does it say about Wharton's conception of the nature and extent of sex differences that unlike racial characteristics, which she argued would inevitably "peep disconcertingly through the ill-fitting disguise," sex attributes could be convincingly shed and adopted? As a successful literary cross dresser—the woman author the Folletts tell us was widely regarded as writing "most like a man"—Wharton defied what Nina Baym has characterized as the contract between women writers, reviewers and readers: "women may write as much as they please providing they define themselves as women writing when they do so," whether by "tricks of style," "choice of subject matter" or tone (257). This, then, is the singularity of Wharton, if we may believe the Folletts: she produced writings that, by their style, threatened to abolish the frontiers between male and female writing. If Jewett's art reconciled alternatives separated by the dominant theories of art—a feminine realism—it is not, it seems to me, to force the meaning of Wharton's ambition to be a self-made man to see there the program of an aesthetic that would situate her above the plane of ordinary alternatives. Whether, in the terms of her contemporaries, Wharton's writings were perceived as convincingly male or fundamentally sexless, they formed a rebuke to the scientific and cultural orthodoxies that asserted the leading role of sex in explaining human differences. Thus the polemical intertextuality of **Ethan Frome** reveals Wharton's necessarily complicated and vexed relationship with women's culture, but it also frees us to begin to appreciate the creative transgression embodied in the specter of Wharton as a literary cross dresser.

Notes

1. The contemporary reviews have been collected by Tuttleton *et al.*

2. As its title suggests, Tuttleton's "The Feminist Takeover of Edith Wharton" is occasionally marred by strenuousness.

3. Lewis first notes Wharton's "lifelong obsession" with this legend (*Edith* 495). See also Donovan and Waid. Psychobiographies of Wharton reveal how this gender split might have its roots in her childhood relationship with a cold and critical mother and loving and permissive father (see Wolff 9-54; Erlich 16-49).

4. I use "conservative" advisedly here, taking my lead from historical accounts that suggest just how successfully the forces militating against women's rights had defined the terms of the debate. See, for example, Russett's stunning account of how the science of sex difference limited the kinds of challenges mounted against the secondary status of women; O'Neill 3-48; Kraditor 123-62.

5. This is Baker's thesis in "The Domestication of Politics."

6. Here as elsewhere I am relying on DuBois's definition of women's culture as "the broad-based commonality of values, institutions, relationships, and methods of communication, focused on domesticity and morality and particular to late eighteenth- and nineteenth-century women" (Walkowitz 29).

7. Darwin's legacy in Gilman's work is well documented, as is her fascination with the gynecocentric theories of Lester Ward, but Russett convincingly argues that "Gilman's suspicion that there existed a bedrock residuum of sex distinction played second fiddle, nonetheless, to her exasperation with the social overemphasis on sexual distinction" (13).

8. For important exceptions to this failure to ascribe much subtlety to Wharton's assessment of this fiction, see Donovan, *After the Fall* (43-82), Waid's convincing analysis of the possible relation between *Summer* and Wilkins's "Old Woman Magoun" (85-172), and Campbell.

9. My discussion of Jewett and the conventions of the regionalist genre is informed by Donovan, *New England* and "Notes"; Fetterley and Pryse; Pryse, "Distilling" and "Introduction"; Zagarell, and Boone. An early and implicitly dissenting view of the significance of this tradition is represented in Wood's pungent essay. A recent collection of essays on Jewett's *Pointed Firs* renders more complexly her depictions of women's culture. See in particular Zagarell's and Ammons's essays on the political and racial implications of the novel's reliance on the idiom of community.

10. See Hovey, for example, whose argument was conceived in part as a rebuttal to recent readings that discover in the female characters the novella's real victims and that trace the distorted images of women back to the narrative's masculine perspective (see Ammons's discussion of both rural women's harder lot and the male narrator's role in unlocking the "deepest, the psychosexual level, of *Ethan Frome*," "the fear that woman will turn into witch", *Argument* 74; and Goodman's argument that the narrator's perspective precludes sympathetic awareness of Zeena's plight, *Friends* 72).

11. See Boone's illuminating discussion of the "centric structures" in what he calls the "novel of female community." Ammons argues that *Pointed* combines a linear plot with a "weblike structure," a fusion of forms that neatly embodies the fruitful tensions in Jewett's work between the city as the world of "modern 'masculinized' opportunities" and the "affectional

world of women" (58, 54). See also Donovan, "Notes"; Zagarell; Folsom; Fetterley and Pryse. Bell argues that the importance of Jewett's work might lie with how it resists any easy link between gender and genre.

12. Lubbock notes that someone once referred to Wharton as a "self-made man" and that she enjoyed repeating the remark (11).

13. Nettels notes that Jewett employed a male narrator in the short story "Hallowell's Pretty Sister" only to be strongly advised against this by Howells: "it appears to me impossible that you should do successfully what you've undertaken in it. [. . .] When it comes to casting the whole autobiographical being in a character of the alien sex, the line is distinctly drawn" (qtd. in Nettels 245).

Works Cited

Ammons, Elizabeth. *Conflicting Stories: American Women Writers at the Turn into the Twentieth Century.* New York: Oxford UP, 1991.

——. *Edith Wharton's Argument with America.* Athens: U of Georgia P, 1980.

——. "Jewett's Witches." *Critical Essays on Sarah Orne Jewett.* Ed. Gwen L. Nagel. Boston: G. K. Hall, 1984. 165-84.

——. "Material Culture, Empire, and Jewett's *Country of the Pointed Firs.*" *New Essays on The Country of the Pointed Firs.* Ed. June Howard. Cambridge: Cambridge UP, 1994. 81-99.

Baker, Paula. "Domestication of Politics: Women and American Political Society, 1780-1920." DuBois and Ruiz 66-91.

Baym, Nina. *Novel, Readers, and Reviewers: Responses to Fiction in Antebellum America.* Ithaca: Cornell UP, 1984.

Bell, Michael Davitt. "Gender and American Realism in *The Country of the Pointed Firs.*" *New Essays on the Country of the Pointed Firs.* Ed. June Howard, Cambridge: Cambridge UP, 1994. 61-80.

Benstock. Shari. *No Gifts From Chance.* New York: Scribner's, 1994.

Boone, Joseph Allen. *Tradition Counter Tradition: Love and the Form of Fiction.* Chicago: U of Chicago P, 1987.

Brodhead, Richard. *Culture of Letters: Scenes of Reading and Writing in Nineteenth-Century America.* Chicago: U of Chicago P, 1993.

Campbell, Donna M. "Edith Wharton and the 'Authoresses': The Critique of Local Color in Wharton's Early Fiction." *Studies in American Fiction* 22 (1994): 169-83.

Donovan, Josephine. *After the Fall: The Demeter-Persephone Myth in Wharton, Cather, and Glasgow.* University Park: Penn State UP, 1989.

——. *New England Local Color Literature: A Women's Tradition.* New York: Ungar, 1983.

——. "Sarah Orne Jewett's Critical Theory: Notes Toward a Feminine Literary Mode." Nagel 212-25.

DuBois, Ellen Carol, and Vicki L. Ruiz, eds. *Unequal Sisters.* New York: Routledge, 1990.

Erlich, Gloria. *The Sexual Education of Edith Wharton.* Berkeley: U of California P, 1992.

Fetterley, Judith, and Marjorie Pryse. "Introduction." *American Women Regionalists, 1850-1910.* New York: Norton, 1982. 11-20.

Fields, Annie, ed. *The Letters of Sarah Orne Jewett.* Boston: Houghton, 1911.

Follett, Helen Thomas, Wilson Follett. *Some Modern Novelists: Appreciations and Estimates.* New York: Holt, 1919.

Folsom, Marcia McClintock. "Tact is a Kind of Mind-Reading: Empathic Style in Sarah Orne Jewett's *The Country of the Pointed Firs.*" *Critical Essays on Sarah Orne Jewett.* Ed. Gwen L. Nagel. Boston: G. K. Hall, 1984. 76-89.

Gilman, Charlotte Perkins. *The Home: Its Work and Influence.* 1903. Urbana: U of Illinois P, 1972.

Goodman, Susan. *Edith Wharton's Inner Circle.* Austin: U of Texas P, 1994.

Hovey, R. B. "*Ethan Frome*: A Controversy about Modernizing It." *American Literary Realism, 1870-1910* 19.1 (1986): 4-19.

Howard, June, ed. *New Essays on The Country of the Pointed Firs.* Cambridge: Cambridge UP, 1994.

Jewett, Sarah Orne. *The Country of the Pointed Firs.* 1896. New York: Norton, 1981.

Kraditor, Aileen. *The Ideas of Women Suffrage Movement, 1890-1920.* New York: Columbia UP, 1965.

Levine, Lawrence W. *Highbrow/Lowbrow: The Emergence of Cultural Hierarchy in America.* Cambridge: Harvard UP, 1988.

Lewis, R. W. B. *Edith Wharton: A Biography.* New York: Harpers, 1975.

Lubbock, Percy. *Portrait of Edith Wharton.* New York: Appleton, 1947.

Malcolm, Janet. "The Woman Who Hated Women." *New York Times Book Review* 16 Nov. 1986: 11-12.

Michie, Helena. *Sororophobia: Differences Among Women in Literature and Culture.* New York: Oxford UP, 1992.

Modleski, Tania. "Femininity as Mas(s)querade: A Feminist Approach to Mass Culture. *High Theory/Low Culture.* Ed. Colin McCabe. New York: St. Martin's, 1986. 37-52.

Nagel, Gwen L., ed. *Critical Essays on Sarah Orne Jewett.* Boston: G. K. Hall, 1984.

Nettels, Elsa. "Gender and First-Person Narration in Edith Wharton's Short Fiction." *Edith Wharton: New Critical Essays.* Eds. Alfred Bendixen and Annette Zilversmit. New York: Garland, 1992. 245-60.

Pryse, Marjorie. "'Distilling Essences': Regionalism and 'Women's Culture.'" *American Literary Realism, 1870-1910* 25.2 (1993): 1-15.

——. "Introduction." *Country of the Pointed Firs.* New York: Norton, 1981. 5-14.

Ransom, John Crowe. "Characters and Character." *American Review* 6 Jan. 1936: 271-88.

Russett, Cynthia Eagle. *Sexual Science: The Victorian Construction of Womanhood.* Cambridge: Harvard UP, 1989.

Sherman, Sarah Way. *Sarah Orne Jewett, an American Persephone.* Hanover: UP of New England, 1989.

Tuttleton, James. "The Feminist Takeover of Edith Wharton." *New Criterion* March 1989: 1-9.

Tuttelton, James W., Kristin O. Lauer, and Margaret P. Murray, eds. *Edith Wharton: The Contemporary Reviews.* Cambridge: Cambridge UP, 1992.

Waid, Candace. *Edith Wharton's Letters from the Underworld.* Chapel Hill: U of North Carolina P, 1991.

Walkowitz, Judith R., ed. "Politics and Culture in Women's History: A Symposium." *Feminist Studies* 6.1 (1980): 26-63.

Wegener, Frederick, ed. *The Uncollected Critical Writings.* Princeton: Princeton UP, 1996.

Wharton, Edith. *A Backward Glance. Novellas and Other Writings.* New York: Library of America, 1933. 767-1069.

——. *Ethan Frome. Novellas and Other Writings.* New York: Library of America. 61-156.

——. *French Ways and Their Meaning.* New York: Appleton, 1919.

——. "The Great American Novel." *The Uncollected Critical Writings.* Ed. Frederick Wegener. Princeton: Princeton UP, 1996. 151-59.

——. "Introduction to *Ethan Frome.*" *The Uncollected Critical Writings,* Ed. Frederick Wegener. Princeton: Princeton UP, 1996. 259-61.

——. *The Letters of Edith Wharton.* Eds. R. W. B. Lewis and Nancy Lewis. New York: Scribner's, 1988.

——. "The Writing of *Ethan Frome.*" *The Uncollected Writings.* Ed. Frederick Wegener. Princeton: Princeton UP, 1996. 261-63.

——. "Foreword to *Ethan Frome: A Dramatization of Edith Wharton's Novel.*" *The Uncollected Writings.* Ed. Frederick Wegener. Princeton: Princeton UP, 1996. 263-64.

Wolff, Cynthia Griffin. *A Feast of Words: The Triumph of Edith Wharton.* New York: Oxford UP, 1977.

Wood, Ann Douglas. "The Literature of Impoverishment: The Women Local Colorists in America, 1865-1914." *Women's Studies* 1 (1972): 3-45.

Zagarell, Sandra A. "*Country's* Portrayal of Community and the Exclusion of Difference." *New Essays on the Country of the Pointed Firs.* Ed. June Howard. Cambridge: Cambridge UP, 1994. 39-60.

——. "Narrative of Community: The Identification of a Genre." *Signs* 13.3 (1988): 498-527.

FURTHER READING

Bibliographies

Garrison, Stephen. *Edith Wharton: A Descriptive Bibliography.* Pittsburgh, Pa.: University of Pittsburgh Press, 1990, 514 p.

Provides a descriptive bibliography.

Lauer, Kristin O. and Margaret P. Murray. *Edith Wharton: An Annotated Bibliography.* New York: Garland Pub., 1990, 528 p.

Offers an annotated bibliography.

Biographies

Benstock, Shari. *No Gifts From Chance: A Biography of Edith Wharton.* New York: Charles Scribner's Sons, 1994, 546 p.

Biography of Wharton.

Coolidge, Olivia. *Edith Wharton, 1862-1937.* New York: Charles Scribner's Sons, 1964, 221 p.

Biography of Wharton.

Dwight, Eleanor. *Edith Wharton: An Extraordinary Life.* New York: Abrams, 1994, 296 p.

Biography of Wharton.

Lewis, R. W. B. *Edith Wharton: A Biography.* New York: Harper & Row, 1975, 592 p.

Definitive biography of Wharton.

McDowell, Margaret B. *Edith Wharton.* Boston: Twayne, 1976, 158 p.

Provides a biographical and critical overview of Wharton's life and career.

Singley, Carol J., editor. *A Historical Guide to Edith Wharton.* New York: Oxford University Press, 2003, 302 p.

Offers a biographical and critical examination of Wharton.

Wolff, Cynthia Griffin. *A Feast of Words: The Triumph of Edith Wharton.* New York: Oxford University Press, 1977, 453 p.

Offers a biographical and critical analysis of Wharton's career.

Criticism

Anderson, Hilton. "Edith Wharton as Fictional Heroine." *South Atlantic Quarterly* 69, no. 1 (winter 1970): 118-23.

Highlights the parallels between Wharton's heroines and her own life.

Bell, Millicent, ed. *The Cambridge Companion to Edith Wharton,* New York: Cambridge University Press, 1995, 210 p.

Gathers critical essays on various aspects of Wharton's oeuvre.

Brooks, Kristina. "New Woman, Fallen Woman: The Crisis of Reputation in Turn-of-the-Century Novels by Pauline Hopkins and Edith Wharton." *Legacy* 13, no. 1 (1996): 91-111.

Compares and contrasts the figures of the Victorian "fallen woman" and the modern "new woman" as models of female identity represented in The House of Mirth *and Pauline Hopkins's* Contending Forces: A Romance Illustrative of Negro Life North and South.

Erlich, Gloria C. "The Female Conscience in Wharton's Shorter Fiction: Domestic Angel or Inner Demon?" In *The Cambridge Companion to Edith Wharton,* edited by Millicent Bell, pp. 98-116. New York: Cambridge University Press, 1995.

Traces the representation of the female conscience in Wharton's short stories to the literary conventions of sentimental fiction and to the internalized voice of the author's own mother.

Fedorko, Kathy A. *Gender and the Gothic in the Fiction of Edith Wharton.* Tuscaloosa: University of Alabama Press, 1995, 198 p.

Investigates the use and revision of literary Gothic conventions in Wharton's realistic novels "to explore the tension between feminine and masculine ways of knowing and being."

French, Marilyn. Introduction to *The House of Mirth,* by Edith Wharton. New York: Berkley Books, 1981.

A general foreword on Wharton, this introduction was also printed in the Berkley Books edition of Summer *and treats feminist concerns in Wharton's canon.*

————. Introduction to *The Reef,* by Edith Wharton, pp. v-ix. London: Virago Press, 1983.

Explicates the central theme of The Reef, *commenting on the novel's setting and main characters in relation to it.*

Heller, Tamar. "Victorian Sensationalism and the Silence of Maternal Sexuality in Edith Wharton's *The Mother's Recompense.*" *Narrative* 5, no. 2 (May 1997): 135-42.

A study of the plot and theme of The Mother's Recompose *in light of the conventions of Victorian melodrama and sensationalism, tracing the aesthetic and ideological implications of the novel to its literary predecessors.*

Herman, David. "Style-Shifting in Edith Wharton's *The House of Mirth.*" *Language and Literature* 10, no. 1 (February 2001): 61-77.

Shows that the gendered social styles of speech in The House of Mirth *accounts for the antagonistic relationships between men and women in daily life.*

Jessup, Josephine Lurie. "Edith Wharton: Drawing-Room Devotee." In *The Faith of Our Feminists,* pp. 14-33. New York: Richard R. Smith, 1950.

Examines male-female conflicts in Wharton's fiction.

Jurecic, Ann. "The Fall of the Knowledgeable Woman: The Diminished Female Healer in Edith Wharton's *The Fruit of the Tree.*" *American Literary Realism, 1870-1910* 29, no. 1 (fall 1996): 29-53.

Analyzes the characterization of Justine Brent in The Fruit of the Tree *in terms of a contrast between the conventions of literary realism and sentimental fiction.*

Lidoff, Joan. "Another Sleeping Beauty: Narcissism in *The House of Mirth.*" *American Quarterly* 32, no. 5 (winter 1980): 519-39.

Contends that The House of Mirth *is "a romance of identity" that portrays Lily Bart as a self-obsessed child-woman whose maturation destroys her.*

Marchand, Mary V. "Death to Lady Bountiful: Women and Reform in Edith Wharton's *The Fruit of the Tree.*" *Legacy* 18, no. 1 (2001): 65-78.

Elucidates the feminist subtext that informs the structure of The Fruit of the Tree, *focusing on the connection between the conventions of early twentieth-century women's writings and industrial reform objectives.*

McDowell, Margaret B. "Viewing the Custom of Her Country: Edith Wharton's Feminism." *Contemporary Literature* 15, no. 4 (autumn 1974): 521-38.

Traces the evolution of feminist concerns implicit in Wharton's writings, noting her changing attitudes toward women throughout her life.

McGowan, Marcia Phillips. "Female Development as Subtext in Edith Wharton's Final Novels." *Connecticut Review* 15, no. 2 (fall 1993): 73-80.

Examines Hudson River Bracketed *and* The Gods Arrive *as encoded fictions of female development, or examples of the bildungsroman form.*

McManis, Jo Agnew. "Edith Wharton's Hymns to Respectability." *Southern Review* 7, no. 4 (October 1971): 986-93.

Analyzes the theme of female self-sacrifice in Wharton's novels, assessing the motives of the characters.

Orr, Elaine Neil. "Negotiation Our Text: The Search for Accommodations in Edith Wharton's *The House of Mirth.*" In *Subject to Negotiation: Reading Feminist Criticism and American Women's Fictions,* pp. 27-45. Charlottesville: University Press of Virginia, 1997.

Reviews previous feminist readings of The House of Mirth *and Lily Bart's characterization, showing that the novel's themes of marriage and sorority are represented as interrelated rather than as a choice between options available to women.*

Pierpont, Claudia Roth. "Cries and Whispers." *New Yorker* (4 April 2001): 66-75.

Reviews the two-volume Collected Stories, *detailing Wharton's life and career in terms of the stories' plots, themes, and characters.*

Wagner-Martin, Wendy. *The Portable Edith Wharton.* New York: Penguin Books, 2003, 656 p.

Work dedicated to Wharton, includes bibliography.

Williams, Deborah. "Threats of Correspondence: The Letters of Edith Wharton, Zona Gale, and Willa Cather." *Studies in American Fiction* 25, no. 2 (autumn 1997): 211-39.

Examines selected correspondence between Wharton, Willa Cather, and Zona Gale to illustrate each writer's strategy of identification with and separation from their public personae as women writers.

————. "Introduction: 'Strangled with a Petticoat.'" In *Not in Sisterhood: Edith Wharton, Willa Cather, Zona Gale, and the Politics of Female Authorship,* pp. 1-10. New York: Palgrave, 2001.

Examines the reasons behind Wharton's and Cather's hostility toward fellow women writers, contrasting their attitudes with that of Gale, whose feminist literary accomplishments remain largely unknown.

Woods, Susan L. "The Solace of Separation: Feminist Theory, Autobiography, Edith Wharton, and Me." In *Creating Safe Space: Violence and Women's Writing,* edited by Tomoko Kuribayashi and Julie Tharp, pp. 27-46. Albany: State University of New York Press, 1998.

Analyzes the gendered spatial signifiers in The Mother's Recompense *in terms of the heroine's struggles to articulate her voice and place in patriarchal society.*

OTHER SOURCES FROM GALE:

Additional coverage of Wharton's life and career is contained in the following sources published by the Gale Group: *American Writers; American Writers: The Classics,* Vol. 2; *American Writers Retrospective Supplement,* Vol. 1; *Authors and Artists for Young Adults,* Vol. 25; *Beacham's Encyclopedia of Popular Fiction: Biography & Resources,* Vol. 3; *Concise Dictionary of American Literary Biography, 1865-1917; Contemporary Authors,* Vol. 132; *Dictionary of Literary Biography,* Vols. 4, 9, 12, 78, 189; *Dictionary of Literary Biography Documentary Series,* Vol. 13; *DISCovering Authors; DISCovering Authors:*

British Edition; *DISCovering Authors: Canadian Edition; DIS-Covering Authors Modules: Most-studied Authors* and *Novelists; DISCovering Authors 3.0; Encyclopedia of World Literature in the 20th Century,* Ed. 3; *Exploring Short Stories; Literature and Its Times,* Vols. 2, 3; *Literature and Its Times Supplement,* Ed. 1; *Literature Resource Center; Major 20th-Century Writers,* Eds. 1, 2; *Modern American Women Writers; Novels for Students,* Vols. 5, 11, 15; *Reference Guide to American Literature,* Ed. 4; *Reference Guide to Short Fiction,* Ed. 2; *St. James Guide to Horror, Ghost & Gothic Writers; Short Stories for Students,* Vols. 6, 7; *Short Story Criticism,* Vol. 6; *Supernatural Fiction Writers; Twayne's United States Authors; Twentieth-Century Literary Criticism,* Vols. 3, 9, 27, 53, 129; *20th Century Romance and Historical Writers;* and *World Literature Criticism.*

VIRGINIA WOOLF

(1882 - 1941)

English novelist, critic, essayist, short story writer, diarist, autobiographer, and biographer.

A critically acclaimed novelist and essayist, Woolf was a founding member of the intellectual circle known as the Bloomsbury Group. Her most famous works include the novels *Mrs. Dalloway* (1925) and *To the Lighthouse* (1927), and the essay *A Room of One's Own* (1929).

BIOGRAPHICAL INFORMATION

Woolf was born Adeline Virginia Stephen on January 25, 1882, in London. Her parents were Leslie Stephen, editor of the *Dictionary of National Biography* and Julia Prinsep Jackson Duckworth Stephen. Both parents had been married before and had children from those unions. Together, the Stephens had three other children in addition to Virginia: Vanessa, born in 1879; Thoby, born in 1880; and Adrian, born in 1883. Woolf was educated at home where she had free access to her father's extensive library. In 1895 her mother died, and Woolf experienced the first of many psychological breakdowns that would plague her throughout her life. Her half sister Stella, thirteen years Woolf's senior, assumed management of the household, a position she relinquished to Vanessa two years later. In 1904 Leslie Stephen died, and

Woolf attempted suicide after suffering a second psychological crisis. During her recuperation, her sister Vanessa moved the family to the bohemian Bloomsbury section of London, where Woolf began her writing career and where the Thursday evening gatherings with Thoby's Cambridge friends constituted the beginning of the Bloomsbury Group. During this time the four Stephen siblings traveled, in 1904 to Paris and Italy, and two years later to Greece, where Woolf and Thoby both contracted typhoid fever; the illness proved fatal for Thoby.

In 1912 Woolf married Leonard Woolf—one of the original Bloomsbury members recently returned from a seven-year period of civil service in Ceylon. Soon afterwards suffered a serious mental breakdown involving another suicide attempt; she remained in severe mental distress for the next three years. During this period, Woolf completed her first novel, *The Voyage Out*, published in 1915. Two years later, the Woolfs established their own publishing company in the basement of their home; the Hogarth Press published not only Woolf's work, but those of T. S. Eliot, Katherine Mansfield, and Sigmund Freud, among others. In 1920, through a series of letters to the editor of the *New Statesman*, Woolf engaged in a dispute over women's intellectual abilities with Desmond MacCarthy, a member of the Bloomsbury Group who wrote under the name "Affable Hawk." She pursued the subject in greater depth at the end of the decade with her feminist essay *A Room of One's Own.* Throughout the 1920s and 1930s, Woolf continued writing and publishing, producing several more novels and a number of essays. In 1941, fearing the onset of another psychological breakdown, Woolf committed suicide by filling her pockets with rocks and drowning herself in the River Ouse.

MAJOR WORKS

Although Woolf wrote a number of short stories, her best-known fiction has always been her novels, particularly *Mrs. Dalloway, To the Lighthouse,* and to a lesser extent, *Orlando* (1928) and *The Waves* (1931). *Mrs. Dalloway,* frequently compared to James Joyce's 1922 work *Ulysses,* is an expansion of "Mrs. Dalloway in Bond Street," a short story Woolf produced for *Dial* magazine in 1923. The events of the plot occur over a period of twenty-four hours in the life of society hostess Clarissa Dalloway and culminate in a large, elaborate party. The work is not only a critique of the social system, but deals as well with issues of madness and suicide through Woolf's characterization of Septimus Smith, a psychological casualty of the war. *To the Lighthouse,* a family novel with obvious connections to Woolf's own early life, involves Mr. and Mrs. Ramsay, thinly disguised versions of her parents. Notwithstanding the subtitle's claim that *Orlando* is a biography, it is, in fact, a novel featuring an androgynous main character said to be modeled after Woolf's friend and reputed lover, Vita Sackville-West. *The Waves,* a complicated exploration of the inevitable mutability of human life, is perhaps Woolf's most complex work, considered by some, including her husband, to be her masterpiece.

Woolf explored issues of sex, gender, and feminism to some degree in her novels, particularly *Orlando,* and in her short stories, particularly "A Society." However, she most thoroughly articulated her ideas on the equality of women in her essays, especially *A Room of One's Own* and *Three Guineas* (1938). Both books explore male power and the injustices associated with it; Woolf especially criticizes the lack of legal rights, educational opportunities, and financial independence for women. Unlike some of her contemporaries, however, Woolf did not believe that women should strive to be like men. She believed, rather, that men should take on some of the characteristics associated with women.

CRITICAL RECEPTION

Woolf's works were well received during her lifetime, and recent interest in specific Woolf texts has been revived by feminist scholars who claim Woolf as one of their own. Most current feminist scholarship centers on her *A Room of One's Own* and *Three Guineas.* Harold Bloom has claimed "puzzled" when these essays are considered "political theory, the genre invoked by literary feminists for whom Woolf's polemics have indeed assumed scriptural status." For Bloom, Woolf's "religion (no lesser word would be apt) was Paterian estheticism: the worship of art," rather than feminism. Herbert Marder cautions that the two texts should not be considered merely tracts and that they have a great deal in common with Woolf's novels. For Marder, "the tracts fade into fiction, the fiction echoes the tracts; and the continuity is so pronounced that it seems necessary to read every book by Virginia Woolf in the context of her work as a whole" in order to fully appreciate her as a feminist. Thus Marder traces the development of her feminist theories from her earliest novels, *The Voyage Out* and *Night and Day* (1919). Similarly, Toril Moi situates the early articulation of Woolf's concept of androgyny in the novel *To the Lighthouse,* in which the author "illustrates the destructive nature of a metaphysical belief in strong, immutably fixed gender identities—as represented by Mr. and Mrs. Ramsay." It was clear to Woolf, Moi asserts, "that the goal of the feminist struggle must precisely be to deconstruct the death-dealing binary oppositions of masculinity and femininity." Rachel Bowlby (see Further Reading) contends that Woolf's work is both embraced and derided by critics in general and by feminist critics in particular. According to Bowlby, feminist scholars who celebrate her work consider her "exemplary both in the sense of exceptional . . . and as an example," while Woolf's detractors claim that her work fits in "all too well with patriarchal norms, literary or social, to which authentic women's writing should by definition be opposed." Bowlby herself characterizes Woolf as a feminist writer who questioned masculinity and patriarchy in all aspects of her work.

PRINCIPAL WORKS

The Voyage Out (novel) 1915

Two Stories [with Leonard Woolf] (short stories) 1917

Kew Gardens (short stories) 1919

Night and Day (novel) 1919

Monday or Tuesday (short stories) 1921

Jacob's Room (novel) 1922

Mr. Bennett and Mrs. Brown (essay) 1924

The Common Reader (criticism) 1925

Mrs. Dalloway (novel) 1925

To the Lighthouse (novel) 1927

Orlando: A Biography (novel) 1928

A Room of One's Own (essay) 1929

The Waves (novel) 1931

The Common Reader: Second Series (criticism) 1932

Flush: A Biography (fictional biography) 1933

The Years (novel) 1937

Three Guineas (essays) 1938

Roger Fry: A Biography (biography) 1940

Between the Acts (novel) 1941

The Death of the Moth, and Other Essays (essays) 1942

A Haunted House, and Other Short Stories (short stories) 1943

The Moment, and Other Essays (essays) 1947

The Captain's Death Bed, and Other Essays (essays) 1950

A Writer's Diary (journal) 1953

Hours in a Library (essay) 1957

Granite and Rainbow (essays) 1958

Collected Essays. 4 vols. (essays) 1966-67

Mrs. Dalloway's Party: A Short Story Sequence (short story) 1973

The Diary of Virginia Woolf. 5 vols. (diaries) 1974-84

The Letters of Virginia Woolf. 6 vols. (letters) 1975-80

Moments of Being (autobiographical essays) 1976

The Complete Shorter Fiction of Virginia Woolf (short stories) 1985

PRIMARY SOURCES

VIRGINIA WOOLF (REVIEW DATE 25 JANUARY 1905)

SOURCE: Woolf, Virginia. Review of *The Feminine Note in Fiction*, by W. L. Courtney. In *The Essays of Virginia Woolf, 1904-1912*, Volume I, edited by Andrew McNeillie, pp. 15-17. London: Hogarth Press, 1986.

In the following review, which originally appeared in the newspaper Guardian *on January 25, 1905, Woolf rebuts the principal points of Courtney's argument concerning women's writing, concluding that the book raises more questions than it answers.*

Mr Courtney is certain that there is such a thing as the feminine note in fiction; he desires, moreover, to define its nature in the book before us, though at the start he admits that the feminine and masculine points of view are so different that it is difficult for one to understand the other. At any rate, he has made a laborious attempt; it is, perhaps, partly for the reason just stated that he ends where he begins[1]. He gives us eight very patient and careful studies in the works of living women writers, in which he outlines the plots of their most successful books in detail. But we would have spared him the trouble willingly in exchange for some definite verdict; we can all read Mrs Humphry Ward, for instance, and remember her story, but we want a critic to separate her virtues and her failings, to assign her right place in literature and to decide which of her characteristics are essentially feminine and why, and what is their significance. Mr Courtney implies by his title that he will, at any rate, accomplish this last, and it is with disappointment, though not with surprise, that we discover that he has done nothing of the kind. Is it not too soon after all to criticise the 'feminine note' in anything? And will not the adequate critic of women be a woman?

Mr Courtney, we think, feels something of this difficulty; his introduction, in which we expected to find some kind of summing-up, contains only some very tentative criticisms and conclusions. Women, we gather, are seldom artists, because they have a passion for detail which conflicts with the proper artistic proportion of their work. We would cite Sappho and Jane Austen as examples of two great women who combine exquisite detail with a supreme sense of artistic proportion. Women, again, excel in 'close analytic miniature work;'[2] they are more happy when they reproduce than when they create; their genius is for psychological analysis—all of which we note with interest, though we reserve our judgment for the next hundred years or bequeath the duty to our successor. Yet it is worth noting, as proof of the difficulty of the task which Mr Courtney has set himself, that he finds two at least of his eight women writers 'artists'[3]—that two others possess a strength which in this age one has to call masculine, and, in fact, that no pair of them come under any one heading, though, of course, in the same way as men, they can be divided roughly into schools. At any rate, it seems to be clear according to Mr Courtney that more and more novels are written by women for women, which is the cause, he declares, that the novel as a work of art is disappearing. The first part of his statement may well be true; it means that women having found their voices have something to say which is naturally of supreme interest and meaning to women, but the value of which we cannot yet determine. The assertion that the woman novelist is extinguishing the novel as a work of art seems to us, however, more doubtful. It is, at any rate, possible that the widening of her intelligence by means of education and study of the Greek and Latin classics may give her that sterner view of literature which will make an artist of her, so that, having blurted out her message somewhat formlessly, she will in due time fashion it into permanent artistic shape. Mr Courtney has given us material for many questions such as these, but his book has done nothing to prevent them from still remaining questions.

Notes

1. A review in the *Guardian*, 25 January 1905, of *The Feminine Note in Fiction* (Chapman & Hall, 1904) by W. L. (William Leonard) Courtney (1850-1928), philosopher, journalist, and sometime fellow of New College, Oxford. See Editorial Note, p. xxii.

2. Courtney, Intro., p. xxxv.

3. The two writers Courtney describes as artists are Mrs Humphry Ward (Mary Augusta Ward, 1851-1920): p. 32, where he talks of her work in terms of the visual arts, and p. 40, where he refers to the 'artistic excellence' of *Lady Rose's Daughter* (1903); and John Oliver Hobbes (Mrs Pearl Craigie, 1867-1906): p. 51, and p. 53, where she is described as 'an artist assured of her powers'. The other writers he discusses are: Lucas Malet, Gertrude Atherton, Margaret Louisa Woods, Mrs E. L. Voynich, Elizabeth Robins (see '*A Dark Lantern*' below), and Mary E. Wilkins (see '*The Debtor*' below).

VIRGINIA WOOLF (LETTER DATE 16 OCTOBER 1920)

SOURCE: Woolf, Virginia. "Letter to the Editor, *The New Statesman*." In *Congenial Spirits: The Selected Letters of Virginia Woolf*, edited by Joanne Trautmann Banks, pp. 124-27. London: Hogarth Press, 1989.

In the following letter, which originally appeared in the magazine New Statesman *on October 16, 1920, Woolf responds to comments made by Desmond MacCarthy—"Affable Hawk"—regarding the intellectual inferiority of women by offering a number of historical precedents that contributed to such a conclusion.*

To The Editor, The New Statesman
[*Hogarth House, Richmond*]

[16 October 1920][1]

Sir,

To begin with Sappho. We do not, as in the hypothetical case of Burns suggested by 'Affable Hawk', judge her merely by her fragments.[2] We supplement our judgement by the opinions of those to whom her works were known in their entirety. It is true that she was born 2,500 years ago. According to 'Affable Hawk' the fact that no poetess of her genius has appeared from 600 B.C. to the eighteenth century proves that during that time there were no poetesses of potential genius. It follows that the absence of poetesses of moderate merit during that period proves that there were no women writers of potential mediocrity. There was no Sappho; but also, until the seventeenth or eighteenth century, there was no Marie Corelli and no Mrs Barclay.[3]

To account for the complete lack not only of good women writers but also of bad women writers I can conceive no reason unless it be that there was some external restraint upon their powers. For 'Affable Hawk' admits that there have always been women of second or third rate ability. Why, unless they were forcibly prohibited, did they not express these gifts in writing, music, or painting? The case of Sappho, though so remote, throws, I think, a little light upon the problem. I quote J. A. Symonds:

Several circumstances contributed to aid the development of lyric poetry in Lesbos. The customs of the Aeolians permitted more social and domestic freedom than was common in Greece. Aeolian women were not confined to the harem like Ionians, or subjected to the rigorous discipline of the Spartans. While mixing freely with male society, they were highly educated and accustomed to express their sentiments to an extent unknown elsewhere in history—until, indeed, the present time.[4]

And now to skip from Sappho to Ethel Smyth.

'There was nothing else [but intellectual inferiority] to prevent down the ages, so far as I can see, women who always played, sang and studied music, producing as many musicians from among their number as men have done,' says 'Affable Hawk'. Was there nothing to prevent Ethel Smyth from going to Munich [Leipzig, actually]? Was there no opposition from her father? Did she find that the playing, singing and study of music which well-to-do families provided for their daughters were such as to fit them to become musicians? Yet Ethel Smyth was born in the nineteenth century. There are no great women painters, says 'Affable Hawk', though painting is now within their reach. It is within their reach—if that is to say there is sufficient money after the sons have been educated to permit of paints and studios for the daughters and no family reason requiring their presence at home. Otherwise they must make a dash for it and disregard a species of torture more exquisitely painful, I believe, than any that man can imagine. And this is in the twentieth century. But, 'Affable Hawk' argues, a great creative mind would triumph over obstacles such as these. Can he point to a single one of the great geniuses of history who has sprung from a people stinted of education and held in subjection, as for example the Irish or the Jews? It seems to me indisputable that the conditions which make it possible for a Shakespeare to exist are that he shall have had predecessors in his art, shall make one of a group where art is freely discussed and practised, and shall himself have the utmost of freedom of action and experience. Perhaps in Lesbos, but never since, have these conditions been the lot of women. 'Affable Hawk' then names several men who have triumphed over poverty and ignorance. His first example is Isaac Newton. Newton was the son of a farmer; he was sent to a grammar school; he objected to working on the farm; an uncle, a clergyman, advised that he should be exempted and prepared for college; and at the age of nineteen he was sent to Trinity College, Cambridge. (See D.N.B.)[5] Newton, that is to say, had to encounter about the same amount of opposition that the daughter of a country solicitor encounters who wishes to go to Newnham in the year 1920. But his discouragement is not increased by the works of Mr Bennett, Mr Orlo Williams and 'Affable Hawk'.

Putting that aside, my point is that you will not get a big Newton until you have produced a considerable number of lesser Newtons. 'Affable Hawk' will, I hope, not accuse me of cowardice if I do not take up your space with an enquiry into the careers of Laplace, Faraday, and Herschell, no compare the lives and achievements of Aquinas and St Theresa, nor decide whether it was Mill or his friends who was mistaken about Mrs Taylor.[6] The fact, as I think we shall agree, is that women from the earliest times to the present day have brought forth the entire population of the universe. This occupation has taken much time and strength. It has also brought them into subjection to men, and incidentally—if that were to the point—bred in them some of the most lovable and admirable qualities of the race. My difference with 'Affable Hawk' is not that he denies the present intellectual equality of men and women. It is that he, with Mr Bennett, asserts that the mind of woman is not sensibly affected by education and liberty; that it is incapable of the highest achievements; and that it must remain for ever in the condition in which it now is. I must repeat that the fact that women have improved (which

'Affable Hawk' now seems to admit), shows that they may still improve; for I cannot see why a limit should be set to their improvement in the nineteenth century rather than in the one hundred and nineteenth. But it is not education only that is needed. It is that women should have liberty of experience; that they should differ from men without fear and express their difference openly (for I do not agree with 'Affable Hawk' that men and women are alike); that all activity of the mind should be so encouraged that there will always be in existence a nucleus of women who think, invent, imagine, and create as freely as men do, and with as little fear of ridicule and condescension. These conditions, in my view of great importance, are impeded by such statements as those of 'Affable Hawk' and Mr Bennett, for a man has still much greater facilities that a woman for making his views known and respected. Certainly I cannot doubt that if such opinions prevail in the future we shall remain in a condition of half-civilised barbarism. At least that is how I define an eternity of dominion on the one hand and of servility on the other. For the degradation of being a slave is only equalled by the degradation of being a master.

Yours, etc., Virginia Woolf

Notes

1. 'Affable Hawk' (Desmond MacCarthy) had not been convinced by Virginia's arguments and had written a rebuttal, to which Virginia replied the following week.

2. MacCarthy had suggested that Robert Burns too might be considered a great poet if, like Sappho, his work had survived only in fragments.

3. The popular novelists Marie Corelli (Mary Mackay, 1855-1924) and Florence Barclay (1862-1921).

4. From John Addington Symonds' *Studies of the Greek Poets* (1873).

5. The *Dictionary of National Biography,* whose first editor, 1882-91, was Leslie Stephen.

6. Mrs Taylor, whom MacCarthy used to support his argument along with the others named in this sentence, married John Stuart Mill in 1851. The philosopher thought her his superior in every way, but his friends disagreed with him.

GENERAL COMMENTARY

HERBERT MARDER (ESSAY DATE 1968)

SOURCE: Marder, Herbert. "Causes." In *Feminism & Art: A Study of Virginia Woolf,* pp. 5-30. Chicago: University of Chicago Press, 1968.

In the following essay, Marder discusses Woolf's personal philosophy and ideas about women and feminism in rela-

tion to developments in English social history and the beginnings of the feminist movement.

1

In the years immediately preceding Virginia Woolf's birth, the legal status of English women was essentially the same as it had been in the middle ages. Their rights as individuals were severely limited. Married women could not dispose of the money they earned, or enter into valid contracts. They could be deprived of a say in the upbringing of their children. In one celebrated case, a husband, upon being estranged from his wife, sent the children to live with his mistress and refused to permit the mother to see them. He was entirely within his rights, and the act which was passed in 1839 as a result of this case only permitted the Lord Chancellor to grant custody to the mother until the children were seven years old. The law continued to assume that there could be no divergence of interest between man and wife. A woman could not sue her husband or hold him to an agreement that would have been legally binding under any other circumstances. "By marriage," says Blackstone, "the very being or legal existence of the woman is suspended, or at least it is incorporated or consolidated into that of the husband, under whose wing, protection and cover she performs everything. . . . My wife and I are one and I am he."[1]

If these facts do not prove Virginia Woolf's claim that English women have always been an oppressed class, they at least suggest that the state was willing to aid and abet domestic tyranny. A distinction must be made, of course, between kinds of behavior that are legally permissible and kinds of behavior that are common or habitual. But where the law discriminates, people will usually be found to take advantage of the fact. Mid-nineteenth-century criminal records in England show an average of nearly fifteen hundred cases a year of aggravated assault committed by husbands against their wives. There must have been a great many more incidents that were never reported. No matter how brutally a husband treated his wife, she was legally bound to keep his house and share his bed.

Nevertheless, it is difficult to generalize about the position of women during this period. It was a time of social change. Whatever the restrictions placed upon Victorian women, there were also new opportunities open to them. Setting aside Victoria herself, the careers of the Brontë sisters, Florence Nightingale, Elizabeth Barrett Browning, and George Eliot show that a woman of genius was no longer doomed to die in obscurity and be buried at the crossroads, as Virginia Woolf said would have happened to Shakespeare's sister if she had had a gift for dramatic literature. There is another indication that Victorian women had some power and influence in the many reforms that were enacted during the last two decades of the nineteenth century, while Virginia Woolf was growing up. The year of her birth, 1882, was also the year of The Married Women's Property Act, an important step in the economic emancipation of women. One of its provisions was that "a married woman shall be capable of acquiring, holding and disposing by will . . . of any real or personal property as her separate property . . . without the intervention of any trustee."[2] Three years later, a crusading newspaper editor revealed the existence of a thriving white slave trade which sent young British girls to houses of prostitution abroad. By setting the age of consent at thirteen, the law in effect encouraged seduction, making things easier for the pimps and madames. When this became widely known, the age of consent was raised to sixteen. The following year women for the first time won the right to act as guardians of their own children in case of the father's death. In 1891 the courts decided that "a husband had no right to carry off his wife by force or to imprison her until she submitted to his wishes."[3] If the British patriarch could no longer legally treat his wife as chattel, custom still gave him a powerful influence over all her actions. But by the beginning of this century, when Virginia Woolf was eighteen, "British women were, in the main, free, both in their persons and their properties . . . and the Women's Movement was nearing its height."[4]

The effects of this growing women's movement are apparent in the literature of the time. Many important writers were influenced by feminist ideas, and a significant part of the social criticism in Victorian novels has to do with the grievances of women. Novelists and poets created a succession of remarkable female characters such as Charlotte Brontë's Jane Eyre, Elizabeth Barrett Browning's Aurora Leigh, George Eliot's Dorothea Brooke, Thomas Hardy's Tess of the d'Urbervilles. Probably the most effective literary statement of the feminine dilemma was *A Doll's House*, which was first performed in 1879. The example of Ibsen's Nora could not be so easily ignored as the protests of feminists, and that is why *A Doll's House* aroused so much indignation among conservatives. More and more people were seeing the point, that although women might be quiet, they were not necessarily satisfied with their lot in life.

Ibsen's conclusions were similar to those which Virginia Woolf stated, fifty years later, in *A Room of One's Own.* Jotting down some "Notes for the Modern Tragedy," before beginning to write *A Doll's House,* Ibsen observed that

> there are two kinds of spiritual law, two kinds of conscience, one in man, and another, altogether different, in woman. They do not understand each other; but in practical life the woman is judged by man's law as though she were not a woman but a man.
>
> The wife in the play ends by having no idea of what is right or wrong; natural feeling on the one hand, belief in authority on the other, have altogether bewildered her.
>
> A woman cannot be herself in the society of the present day, which is exclusively masculine society, with laws framed by men and with a judicial system that judges feminine conduct from a masculine point of view.[5]

By the 1890's Ibsen's plays were being produced in London, where Hardy was shocking middle-class readers with his attacks on the prevailing sexual morality, and a self-styled Ibsenite, George Bernard Shaw, was writing *Mrs. Warren's Profession* and *Candida.*

The "new woman" was making her appearance in popular novels such as Grant Allen's *The Woman Who Did* and H. G. Wells's *Ann Veronica.* The provocative title of Allen's 1895 bestseller is a fair clue to its content. This book capitalized on advanced ideas about marriage and female emancipation by combining them with a melodramatic plot. H. G. Wells's heroine, like Grant Allen's, is determined to retain her independence and freedom of action, but both young women soon find themselves involved in love affairs, and events unfold in predictable fashion. There is an element in *Ann Veronica* which was absent from the earlier novel. While Herminia Barton of *The Woman Who Did* found it necessary to suffer alone for the sake of her principles, Ann Veronica, a few years later, can join a feminist society. When her love life becomes too complicated, she takes part in a militant protest which results in her being sent to prison. This is no tragedy, however, merely a prelude to connubial bliss.

Virginia Woolf (then Virginia Stephen) read Wells's books, and agreed with the liberal and high-minded sentiments which they expressed. Nevertheless, she had reservations about Wells as a novelist because of what seemed to her his misguided attempts to combine art and propaganda.[6] Although she was determined to have her say in the controversy about women's rights, she was equally determined to keep didacticism out of her novels.

The generation to which Virginia Stephen belonged was the first to enjoy on a large scale the freedoms for which the feminists had been fighting. Her youth coincided with a turning point in the history of the feminist movement. She had been born early enough to know Victorian England from personal experience, as well as from contact with her elders. Her memories of that patriarchal society, ruled by a queen who was implacably hostile to the feminist movement, were vivid and disturbing. In their home life the Stephens, like most middle-class Victorian families, composed a patriarchal society in miniature. The father, a somewhat distant and majestic figure, was the center around whom everything revolved, the arbiter whose austere judgments shaped his ambitious daughter's opinion of herself. By the time that young girl had become a young woman her world had changed almost beyond recognition. Women had won the vote and penetrated the masculine professions. The girl herself was becoming known as a writer—a writer, moreover, whose aestheticism was at the furthest possible remove from her father's philosophy.

But such breaks with the past are rarely as complete as they seem. Leslie Stephen's daughter, like many of her contemporaries, rejected Victorian ideas of propriety, but in doing so she displayed a form of moral earnestness derived from the Victorians themselves. Her pursuit of the good and the beautiful was in keeping with her father's example; her intense intellectuality revealed the influence of that irascible and kindly old man. Her career itself seems vaguely to echo his. Leslie Stephen was an eminent man of letters who had overcome a nervous weakness in his youth by means of strict self-discipline. When Virginia was born, he was the editor of one of the most respected British periodicals, the *Cornhill Magazine,* and she grew up in the midst of fashionable literary society. The family's friends were dignitaries and famous men, such as James Russell Lowell (her godfather), Thomas Hardy, Henry James, George Meredith. In making her way in the world as a young woman, Virginia had to contend with her own mental instability. She managed, nevertheless, to establish herself at the center of literary society. Bloomsbury friends such as E. M. Forster, Lytton Strachey, Maynard Keynes, and Roger Fry formed a brilliant group, comparable to that which had frequented her father's house. The more closely one looks, the more clearly one perceives in her career, the effects of the training which she received as a girl. All of her attitudes, including her feminism, as it developed in later life, are related to this class and family background—particularly the influence of her father and his ideas.

One writer, in emphasizing the importance of this paternal inheritance, has pointed out that although "in her physical beauty, temperament and imagination she certainly resembled her mother . . . such an endowment may be greatly modified by environment. Leslie Stephen, like other strong, opinionated Victorian men, was a formidable piece of environment."[7] It must be kept in mind that her mother died when Virginia was thirteen. From that time until Leslie Stephen's death in 1904, he was the dominant influence in her life. After the loss of her mother, Virginia, who had always been delicate, suffered a nervous breakdown, and it was decided that she should be educated at home. Her father was her intellectual guide, she read the books on his shelves, and those which he brought home for her from the London Library. Leslie Stephen was a distinguished literary critic and biographer, as well as the historian of English thought in the eighteenth century and the utilitarians. Young Virginia read all of English literature, and her first impressions were colored by memories of her father's terse judgments, and his disconcerting way of chanting poetry to himself. The fictional portrait which she drew of him many years after his death in **To the Lighthouse** reveals the complexity of the emotions which he aroused in her. She commented on his influence—and her own ambivalence—in her dairy: "Father's birthday. He would have been 96, 96, yes, today and could have been 96, like other people one has known: but mercifully was not. His life would have entirely ended mine. What would have happened? No writing, no books;—inconceivable. . . . I must read him some day. I wonder if I can feel again, I hear his voice, I know this by heart."[8] Especially in his later years, Stephen was at times a household tyrant like Mr. Ramsay. Within the limits determined by his principles, he was a broadminded man, but his attitude toward women and the family, like his relationship with his children, displays some interesting contradictions.

As a political liberal Stephen believed that women should be assured equality under the law. In writing the life of his friend, Henry Fawcett, he described a point of view with which he sympathized. Fawcett, he said, was "a chivalrous supporter of women's rights." Whether or not women were actually the equals of men in any particular field of endeavor seemed to him beside the point. The competition should give "the prize to the most vigorous, but [Fawcett] was righteously indignant when it was so contrived as to impose additional burdens on the feeblest." Stephen further explained his friend's views in another passage: "He did not, I think, anticipate any great change in the ordinary career of women—he admitted that, for the most part, it would continue to lie chiefly in the domestic circle; but his sense of justice revolted against the virtual condemnation of a large number of women in every class to inability to use their faculties freely."[9]

The cautiously progressive sentiments of this passage were echoed by Stephen in his essay on "Forgotten Benefactors." He was very willing to grant women all sorts of rights, but he was not enthusiastic about the prospect of their using them. He believed that women's place was in the home. This attitude is implicit in an anecdote he told about a friend who had confided to him that she felt ashamed when she compared the scope of her own work in the domestic sphere with that of her husband, a politician. Stephen was not inclined to see the matter in this light. He wrote:

> No one, I hope, could assert more willingly than I, that the faculties of women should be cultivated as fully as possible, and that every sphere in which their faculties can be effectively applied should be thrown open to them. But the doctrine sometimes tacitly confounded with this, that the sphere generally assigned to women is necessarily lower or less important than others is not to be admitted. . . . The domestic influence is, no doubt, confined within narrower limits; but then, within those limits it is incomparably stronger and more certain of effect. The man or woman can really mould the character of a little circle, and determine the whole life of one little section of the next generation.[10]

Stephen was more interested in defining the value of domestic service than in considering the implications of his friend's complaint. In proving the dignity and importance of woman's work, he tended to ignore or minimize the dissatisfaction of the women who had to do it.

A belief in the importance of domestic life and the integrity of the family formed an important part of Stephen's philosophy. In "Forgotten Benefactors" he wrote: "The degree in which any ethical theory recognizes and reveals the essential importance of the family relation is, I think, the best test of its approximation to the truth. . . . To those activities which knit families together, which help to enlarge the highest ideal of domestic life, we owe a greater debt than to any other kind of conduct. . . . The highest services of this kind are rendered by persons condemned, or perhaps I should say privileged, to live in obscurity."[11] Whatever his sympathy for women who felt that they had been prevented from using or developing their faculties, Stephen could not wholeheartedly support reforms that would give them a chance to do so. The family relation was of paramount importance to him, and domestic life, as he understood it, could not exist unless women stayed at home.

In another passage of "Forgotten Benefactors," Stephen expressed his veneration for his second wife, the mother of Virginia and the prototype of Mrs. Ramsay. "A lofty nature which has profited by passing through the furnace acquires claims not only upon our love but upon our reverence. . . . We cannot attempt to calculate the value of this spiritual force which has moulded our lives, which has helped by a simple consciousness of its existence to make us gentler, nobler, and purer in our thoughts of the world . . . which has constantly set before us a loftier ideal than we could frame for ourselves."[12] He went on to liken this ennobling influence to the light of the sun, of whose essential importance to us "we are apt to be unconscious . . . until some accident makes us realize the effect of its eclipse." In a letter written to his children after the death of his second wife he ranked her achievement in life high above his own: "Had I fully succeeded and surpassed all my contemporaries in my own line, what should I have done? I should have written a book or two which might be read by my contemporaries and perhaps by the next generation. . . . Now I say, advisedly, that I do not think such an achievement as valuable as hers."[13] "That man is unfortunate," he believed, "who has not a saint of his own."[14]

Leslie Stephen's veneration of his second wife, and the importance which he attributed to the domestic sphere were obviously related. The home was the precinct in which his saint was enshrined; its existence made possible the operation of her special kind of sanctity. The family was needed to call forth her qualities, as she was needed to fill it with her ennobling influence. But a desire to worship woman as a higher moral influence tends, in real life, to restrict her freedom almost as much as a conviction of her inferiority. It is not uncommon to wish one's saint to remain on her pedestal so that one can go on worshipping her. The Victorian father often claimed to be protecting his wife or daughter when he was really protecting his image of her. Leslie Stephen, though on the whole a reasonable man, was capable of becoming a grim and threatening incarnation of the Victorian father.

As far as sex was concerned Stephen's position was that of the strict moralist. Once again, his strictures were connected with his belief in the importance of the domestic sphere, for sexual purity was the basis of stable family life. Noël Annan says as much in his study of Stephen: "Like other Victorian moralists [Stephen] sees loose-living and lust as the hooks which clutch at man and make him lower than the angels. Man can be saved from himself by woman: feminine innocence will rouse man from sensuality. . . . Because the institutions of marriage and the family will perish, and society with them, unless we eradicate 'brutalizing and anti-social instincts' all social forces must be directed to the inculcation of chastity."[15] The pattern is clear: the need to believe in the moral superiority of women; the faith in the sanctity of the family; the prohibition against loose-living lest the purity of women and the stability of the home be endangered—these attitudes made Leslie Stephen cling to the Victorian proprieties. He remained faithful, emotionally at least, to the old order which was rapidly becoming a thing of the past.

Stephen's attitude toward sex also entered into his position as a critic. He prized masculinity very highly and despised effeminacy. Thus, one of the most serious defects which he found in the works of such women novelists as the Brontës and George Eliot was their failure to create believable male characters. Their "men were often simply women in disguise."[16] The corresponding failures of male writers to create plausible female characters seem to have troubled him far less. For Leslie Stephen, writes Annan, "the opposite of masculine is not feminine but morbid."[17]

Stephen's response to effeminacy was that of the red-blooded Victorian Englishman. The slightest hint of inversion provoked the bully in him. In her mature years Virginia Woolf rebelled against this attitude. Her circle of artists and intellectuals included a number of homosexuals, and she and her friends took it for granted that a person's sex life is a private matter concerning only himself. Leslie Stephen's whole concept of sexual attributes, and especially his belief in the importance of masculinity, was repugnant to her. But while she rejected her father's ideas, Virginia Woolf found it harder to discard the emotional legacy he had left her. Here and there in her books she displays traces of severity, not to say priggishness, befitting the daughter of a knighted Victorian moralist. Her novels, too, are marked by a more than average reticence about sex. Leslie Stephen measured the value of works of art by their moral significance. His daughter's aestheticism, like her belief in sexual freedom, contained a considerable degree of ambivalence. Perhaps it is precisely because her aestheticism was an overreaction against her father's moralizing that she could not, within its limits, do full justice either to her social interests or her artistic values. The need to moralize remained strong in her, but it was submerged and displaced. In the 1920's, and even later, when she had become a novelist with an international reputation, she still carried on the struggle with her father's ghost. The composition of *To the Lighthouse,* with its fictionalized portraits of both her parents, was a rite she needed to perform in order to free herself. "I used to think of him and mother daily," she noted, ". . . I was obsessed by them both, unhealthily; and writing of them was a necessary act."[18] Shortly after finishing *To the Lighthouse* she produced her most extravagant book, *Orlando,* and wrote in *A Room of One's Own* that the creative faculty is based on the union of masculine and feminine elements. The artist's mind is androgynous, and not, as Leslie Stephen had contended, solidly masculine or feminine.

In 1932 Virginia Woolf wrote a brief reminiscence of her father. She described him affectionately but with a considerable degree of detachment. He was a man, she said, who could be alarmingly opinionated and admirably magnanimous, who inspired both love and resentment. "His daughters, though he cared little enough for the higher education of women," had the same freedom as his sons to follow whatever professions they chose. "If at one moment he rebuked a daughter sharply for smoking a cigarette—smoking was not in his opinion a nice habit in the other sex—she had only to ask him if she might become a painter, and he assured her that so long as she took her work seriously he would give her all the help he could. He had no special love for painting; but he kept his word. Freedom of that sort was worth thousands of cigarettes."[19] After the death of her father, Virginia Woolf became a habitual smoker of cigars.

The generation to which Virginia Woolf belonged was in revolt against Victorianism. Mrs. Woolf was extremely sensitive to the present, that is to say, to the spirit of modernism. She was also linked to the past by unusually strong bonds. Her father had believed in a certain kind of moral strenuousness, and although Virginia and her

friends were serious young people, it was almost a point of honor with them to adopt an attitude as far removed as possible from that of their elders. Here is the way John Maynard Keynes expressed it in an essay entitled, "My Early Beliefs": "We repudiated entirely customary morals, conventions, and traditional wisdom. We were, that is to say, in the strict sense of the term, immoralists. We recognized no moral obligation on us, no inner sanction, to conform or to obey."[20] Virginia Woolf's iconoclasm differed somewhat from that of her friends in being based on a feminist rationale. Moreover, her commitment to the present was modified by her need to preserve her ties with the past. This conjunction of modernism and traditionalism was responsible for the characteristic tone of her prose, and for its special fascination.

Almost every writer on Virginia Woolf has commented on the fundamental dualism in her work. Unlike some of her contemporaries, she wished not only to criticize the tradition which she had inherited, but in a sense to renew it. Her goal was to write in such a way as to satisfy the utilitarian philosophy of her father, while remaining true to the artistic mood of her own generation. The former demanded that her books contribute something to the welfare of mankind, the latter taught her that every work of art is autonomous, a purely aesthetic skirmish in the struggle to achieve "significant form." The moralist in Virginia Woolf is most in evidence in her feminist writings, and the aesthete in her novels; neither is entirely lacking in anything she wrote.[21]

2

Leslie Stephen's death in 1904 led to a dramatic change in his daughter's way of life. She moved from Kensington to Bloomsbury, that is, from middle-class domestication to high-brow bohemianism. Other things being equal, there is no doubt about which of these worlds she preferred. The loss of her father was a harrowing experience, but in later life she looked back upon it almost with a sense of relief. As she observed in her diary,[22] she was now free to have the career that would otherwise have been denied her. The four orphaned Stephen children, all in their twenties, set up house together. Soon Virginia was getting to know a group of Thoby's brilliant Cambridge friends, among them Leonard Woolf, her future husband. The sensitive, sheltered girl suddenly found herself an independent woman who could earn one pound ten shillings and sixpence by scribbling a few pages and sending them to an editor, a fact that amazed and delighted her. She sold her first reviews and was encouraged to think seriously of becoming a writer.

This crucial moment in Virginia Stephen's life coincided, almost exactly, with the beginning of the heroic phase of the women's movement. Suffrage societies had been in existence for about forty years, but they had attracted relatively little attention. In 1903 a new society, the Women's Social and Political Union (WSPU) was founded by Emmeline Pankhurst in Manchester. Mrs. Pankhurst and her followers were radicals. They believed that women must fight for their emancipation, using whatever means were available to them. To be sure, they could not overthrow the government, but they could infiltrate meetings and heckle speakers who were opposed to their cause. They could demand that every candidate for public office commit himself on the subject of women's rights. They could march on Parliament in tens of thousands, provoking the police to arrest them and filling the prisons. In short, they could keep up a steady, vigorous harassment of the authorities who had prevented women's suffrage bills from being enacted in Parliament. Mrs. Pankhurst's militant policy came to be self-sustaining. The more violent the militants grew, the more police action they provoked, the more publicity they attracted. Notoriety did no harm at all to the WSPU; its membership grew rapidly. Money flowed into the national office, making possible still more spectacular protests which in their turn generated still more publicity. With its emphasis on civil disobedience, Mrs. Pankhurst's movement inevitably produced its martyrs: one woman threw herself under the horses' hoofs at a fashionable race course and was killed. Many others, imprisoned for resisting police or throwing rocks through windows, went on hunger strikes and were forcibly fed. For nine years, from 1905 to 1914, the militants kept the cause of women's rights in the public eye. Again and again their demands were rejected, but it was impossible to ignore them, or to deny the fanatical heroism of their leaders.

The period 1911-13, when the militant agitation reached its peak, was another time of transition for Virginia Stephen. In 1912, the year of her marriage to Leonard Woolf, social critic and socialist, she was thirty years old and finishing her first novel.[23] As her husband soon discovered, Virginia Woolf's mental equilibrium, which had broken down several times during her youth, was still extremely precarious. Not only did the condition of her health preclude any strenuous activity, such as taking part in protests and rallies, but it made even a normal active life potentially dangerous. She would always have to avoid undue excitement.

Leonard Woolf has movingly described his wife's mental illness and the precautions which they had to take throughout their married life. As long as Virginia Woolf lived "a quiet, vegetative life, eating well, going to bed early . . . she remained perfectly well."[24] But if she were subjected to any mental or physical strain "serious danger signals" would appear—"a peculiar 'headache' low down at the back of the head, insomnia, and a tendency for the thoughts to race." If these symptoms were not checked at once by rest and seclusion in a darkened room they would grow much worse. Four times in her life they led to nervous breakdowns which continued for months or years. An attack came on not long after her marriage. At one point she fell into a coma for two days and at another tried to commit suicide by taking an overdose of veronal. While in the depressive state, she was subject to delusions and fits of violence, and required the care of two trained nurses. There was constant danger, during these periods of insanity, that she would try to kill herself.

Aside from her health, there was another important factor which kept Virginia Woolf from joining public demonstrations. As much as she sympathized with the aims of the suffragists, she could not share their enthusiasm for political action; she found something antipathetic in the idea of marching in a protest or even sitting on a committee. She was a lady and a highbrow—aristocratic, aloof. On the other hand, she was unusually sensitive to any slight on account of her sex. The mere thought of being discriminated against could make her physically ill. This extreme sensitivity brought her close, at times, to the militant suffragists, though she differed from them in many of her assumptions.

Her attitude toward the question of women's rights was never simple and straightforward. Her energies were directed differently from the majority of feminists who were concerned mainly with eliminating specific abuses and not much interested in trying to discover the causes of tyranny. If her attitude was less practical than theirs, her vision was more comprehensive. Long after women had won the vote she was at work with her pen, shaping a role for herself, making her own contribution to "The Cause." Her labors resulted in the two long and impassioned essays, *A Room of One's Own* and *Three Guineas*. These books are not merely tracts, but, in one way or another, touch on all the matters that vitally concerned her. And because she would never restrict herself to one genre at a time, they often have something in common with her novels. The tracts fade into fiction, the fiction echoes the tracts; and the continuity is so pronounced that it seems necessary to read every book by Virginia Woolf in the context of her work as a whole. Her attitude as a feminist was intimately bound up with her attitude as an artist. When we unravel the intricacies and describe the contradictions of the one, we are led toward an understanding of the other.

Virginia Woolf's first two novels contain most of the important themes of her fiction, themes which reveal her preoccupation with the problems of women. They also seem to reveal uncertainties connected with her early married life. The heroines of *The Voyage Out* and *Night and Day* are both afraid to marry. In each case the crucial question is whether a young woman can succeed in satisfying her emotional and intellectual needs within the framework of married life. The question is never satisfactorily answered. The conclusion of *The Voyage Out* seems, from one point of view, to reflect an inability to come to grips with the heroine's dilemma. Rachel Vinrace, a talented girl devoted to her books and music—and given to dreaming—goes on a voyage to South America, where she meets, and eventually becomes engaged to, an aesthetic young man. The lovers are dismayed by the social pressures on them to transform their relationship into a conventional courtship. They are deeply apprehensive about marriage, but before they can discover whether their fears are justified, Rachel grows ill and dies. This ending, which emphasizes the arbitrariness of fate, is not altogether satisfactory. The reader suspects that Rachel was too jealous of her independence to marry anyone, and that the novelist has evaded the implications of this fact. One critic has summed up the theme as "the hesitation a girl of spirit and breeding felt at yielding in marriage to one of the traditionally dominant sex."[25]

Night and Day deals even more explicitly with the problems of marriage. In general outline it is a social comedy about lovers who are separated by a series of misunderstandings, and finally united when their true feelings become known. But *Night and Day* is more reminiscent of one of Shaw's problem plays than it is of *Evelina* or *Pride and Prejudice*. It is an intellectual romance. The main obstacle separating the lovers is Katharine Hilbery's inability to make up her mind, because what she wants out of life is apparently so different from what society expects her to want. Like Rachel Vinrace, she is terrified of marriage. She is so confused, moreover, that she has permitted herself to become engaged to a conventional male who expects his wife to devote herself to raising children and managing servants. Katharine finally escapes this life by breaking off her engagement and marrying Ralph Denham, an angry young man who believes that men and women need not interfere with each other even though married. *Night and Day* is a kind of fictional laboratory in which the author is testing ways of adapting old social forms to new needs. Unfortunately, Virginia Woolf once again stops short of answering the crucial question. Katharine and Ralph's experiment, the marriage in which they are to live both together and apart, is to take place in a nebulous future after the close of the novel. Like *The Voyage Out, Night and Day* ends with an evasion.

The feminist movement is a definite presence in both these books. In *Night and Day* one of the main characters works as the unpaid secretary of a suffrage society. Having been disappointed in love, Mary Datchet decides to devote her life to the cause, to become a professional feminist. Virginia Woolf contrasts the drab existence of the social reformer with Katharine's more glamorous private experiment in self-reform. Mary's suffrage society is mainly an object of satire. The total effect is interesting; women's problems are taken seriously, but the feminist societies are not. Both too much and too little is made of feminism as a theme—too much for it to remain mere background; too little for it to become a significant part of the fictional pattern. It seems that the writer has failed to resolve her own uncertainties and achieve a coherent point of view.

In method and outlook *The Voyage Out* and *Night and Day* belong to the pre-1914 era. But most of Virginia Woolf's working life fell in the interim between the two world wars, in the years after women had won the vote. And after her first novels she rarely commented directly on social problems in her fiction. She confined such comments to the essays she regularly wrote. Works of art, she believed, should say what cannot be said by other means. They should reveal the hidden realities from which social problems spring, without engaging in social analysis. Virginia Woolf tried in her mature novels to penetrate unexplored regions of the ordinary and habitual. Fear and tyranny begin, she observed, in the casual moments that compose people's lives from hour to hour, from day to day. The most esoteric truths are concealed in the most commonplace experiences. As she pursued these truths, Virginia Woolf's novels became increasingly plotless, fragmented, and evocative.

Night and Day had dealt with the problem of marriage somewhat analytically—by isolating it for study. **Mrs. Dalloway** and **To the Lighthouse** dealt with it impressionistically. These novels of the decade following World War I contain vivid pictures of family life and domestic tyranny, but they do not converge on a central "problem." Virginia Woolf was attempting here to capture moments of sensibility in order to reveal the inner lives of her characters. She wished to convey, as precisely as possible, what it feels like to be a particular individual—Clarissa Dalloway or Mrs. Ramsay—at half past two on an ordinary day. Her awareness of social problems is still present, but it has been absorbed into a broader range of ideas, connected with many levels of experience. The advantage lies with the maturer novels. There is more reality in the delicate impressions and convolutions of **To the Lighthouse** than in the elaborate representation of **Night and Day**. Nevertheless, in spite of this new emphasis on the texture of experience, Virginia Woolf never allows us to forget that her characters have suffered certain disadvantages, if women, and enjoyed certain privileges, if men. The essential differences between these two "classes," as she called them, were always on her mind.

In **Mrs. Dalloway** and **To the Lighthouse** it is mainly her descriptions of masculine tyranny which remind us that Virginia Woolf was a feminist. These books of her middle period reveal an increasing interest in the minds of the oppressors. The desire for power over others, she seems to be saying, always does incalculable harm. One suspects that Mr. Ramsay, for instance, is at least partially responsible for his wife's untimely death. An even more representative patriarch is Sir William Bradshaw, the fashionable doctor whose insensitivity plays a decisive part in causing the suicide of Septimus Smith. Behind these portraits there is a sense of general evil: Septimus has been shellshocked in a war that confirmed the feminist charge of masculine brutality. Virginia Woolf's preoccupation with the causes of this evil finally led her beyond the bounds of fiction.

Having completed **To the Lighthouse** she began working on a fantasy in a much lighter vein, which became **Orlando**. At the same time she was preparing two lectures, delivered at Newnham and Girton in 1928, which became the basis of **A Room of One's Own. Orlando** and **A Room of One's Own** represent a summing up of Virginia Woolf's feminist ideas as of the late twenties. The two books have in common not only their emphasis on the bi-sexuality of the artist but their good humor and whimsicality; in writing **A Room of One's Own** Virginia Woolf was fully aware of the dangers that beset the controversialist and made every effort to avoid them. But, though she carefully excluded strident tones, her commitment to the cause of women's rights was perfectly serious.

In **Orlando,** fantasy became a means of emphasizing the inner life of her hero-heroine; liberated from the demands of strict rationality, Virginia Woolf could glance satirically at the position of women in different ages and poke fun at masculine pedantry. Orlando's famous change of sex about halfway through the novel allowed her to comment shrewdly on relations between the sexes. It is only in **A Room of One's Own,** however, that the broader outlines of her feminist doctrine begin to appear. The original subject of the lectures here revised and expanded was "Women and Fiction," but Virginia Woolf had used this subject as a point of departure for a general discussion of the woman question. The resulting tract, constantly enlivened, or diluted, with fiction, can be described as a feminist fantasy. It begins with the story of a visit to two colleges, one for men, the other for women. In the men's college, the narrator says, she dined on sole, partridge, and "a confection which rose all sugar from the waves." The same evening, in the dining hall of the women's college, she had been served a supper of beef, custard and prunes. Two scenes had been evoked in her mind, the first of "kings and nobles" bringing "treasure in huge sacks" and the second of "lean cows and a muddy market and withered greens."

Virginia Woolf's main contention in this book is that in order to write "a woman must have money and a room of her own." That is, she must have the same opportunities as men to pursue her interests, to be free of material cares. Trying to answer the question, "Why are women so poor?" Virginia Woolf discusses the trouble they have had in earning a living. She comments indignantly on the position of English women at various times in history and glances at the books written about them, mainly by men. On the whole, women have failed to create great works of art, she says, because they have been denied an opportunity to develop their faculties. The one field in which they have made substantial contributions is literature—and for very good reasons. It was possible to keep them out of academies and institutes, but no one could bar them from the writing-desk or forbid the use of pen and paper. Nevertheless, in spite of the genius of women like Jane Austen, George Eliot, the Brontës, the exploration of truly feminine modes of expression has never seriously been attempted. Such an undertaking, Virginia Woolf predicted, would have important implications for the art of fiction as a whole. Here her feminism and her attitude as a critic came into conjunction. For she believed that novelists, especially women novelists, had often been misled by the prevailing masculine bias, and that in order for creation to take place there must be a meeting, a fusion of masculine and feminine elements. One-sidedness causes the spirit to atrophy. Ideally, the artist should be androgynous, like Orlando. Virginia Woolf concluded, therefore, by emphasizing the importance of cooperation between the sexes. She looked forward to a time when life would become ordered and harmonious, when men and women would finally succeed in sharing their wisdom.

On the whole *A Room of One's Own* creates an impression of wit and urbanity. In spite of misgivings about the patriarchs, Virginia Woolf could still permit herself to be optimistic. In her later works this was no longer true. As the 1930's wore on she became increasingly appalled by social injustice. She could not look at the world with equanimity. Her old horror of masculine authority was magnified by constant reports of tyranny and aggression. She no longer felt the inclination to indulge in literary "escapades," such as the one that had produced *Orlando.* She could not be good-humored about concentration camps, and she was more concerned than ever about injustices to women. For the condition of her sex seemed to her a sign of a universal danger that was growing steadily greater.

The Years and *Three Guineas,* works which are the culmination of her writings on women, reveal this darker mood. Published in 1937 and 1938, they may be considered companion volumes, like *Orlando* and *A Room of One's Own*: Virginia Woolf actually referred to them as "one book" in her diary.[26] These two pairs of companion volumes complement each other, presenting her ideas about women from different points of view. They range from sociology to fictional biography, from saga to fantasy, and occasionally approach poetry. Between them they contain essentially all of Virginia Woolf's ideas about the position of women. *A Room of One's Own* and *Three Guineas* are deliberate formulations of these ideas; *Orlando* and *The Years* are fictional and do not teach anything (Virginia Woolf was a firm believer in the separation of art and propaganda) but nevertheless reflect the thought of the essays. While *Orlando* and *A Room of One's Own* pay a great deal of attention to the inner life, the emphasis in the two later books is explicitly on women in relation to society. Their total effect, however, is not to exclude psychological comment; on the contrary, in *The Years* Virginia Woolf succeeded brilliantly in revealing the minds of her characters by indirect methods.

The Years is a fictional saga tracing the disappearance of the Victorian system of family life which had been described in *To The Lighthouse*; it is documentation, in a sense, for *Three Guineas,* in which Virginia Woolf formulated a feminist program based on her observations of society. To put it another way, we can infer the state of mind that inspired the program set forth in *Three Guineas* from this grim view of society. The novel follows members of three related family groups from 1880 to "the present day," that is, 1937. The Victorian family (the Pargiters have seven children), which seems to be so stable at the beginning of the novel, is shown to be in a state of decadence. The father visits his mistress while his wife lies dying; the daughters are frustrated and desperate. Although the rituals of respectability continue to be practiced, no one is quite sure any longer what they mean. People hide their dissatisfaction, even from themselves; Victorian society is sinister—a world in which lies fester. By the end of the novel the various family groups have been all but disbanded, many of the children have remained unmarried, most are living in isolation; the evils inherent in the old tradition have done their work. In the last chapter all the surviving characters and their children and grandchildren gather at a party, a kind of family reunion, which serves to sharpen our sense of time passing and of that revolution in society which has shaken and dispersed the Pargiters.

Given the simple chronological scheme of *The Years* and its emphasis on physical realities, it was possible for Virginia Woolf to bring in the movement for social and political reforms in a way that would have been jarring in her earlier novels. Eleanor is active in philanthropic organizations and the feminist movement; one sister has romantic dreams of becoming a revolutionary; another goes to jail as a suffragette. Changes in the status of women are suggested during the finale by the introduction of Eleanor's niece—a young lady doctor who is dedicated to her work and interested in little else. An awareness of political and social issues pervades *The Years,* as it does so many works of the thirties. The reforming societies, moreover, in spite of their activity, have not succeeded in getting at the root of the problem, and we are aware, as the book closes, that England is threatened by dictatorship from abroad.

The rise of fascism appalled Virginia Woolf. She consistently interpreted this political development in terms of her ideas about the position of women. Thus, when she set out to discuss the causes of the European crisis in *Three Guineas,* the book, as it were of itself, became an exposition of feminist doctrine. Improving the lot of women and opposing tyranny were identified in her mind. The early feminists had been fighting in essentially the same cause, she maintained, as contemporary democrats and anti-fascists.

Three Guineas opens with an anecdote. Virginia Woolf has received a letter asking her to contribute to a society for the prevention of war. The book is in the form of a reply, explaining why she has decided to send money elsewhere first—to a fund for rebuilding a women's college, to a society for helping women enter the professions—before considering the appeal of the antiwar society. Her position is that the causes of war are to be found in the conventional education given to young people. They are brought up, for instance, to accept the exploitation of the female sex. Furthermore, women are excluded from national office, which results in an imbalance in the state, an inherent bias in favor of masculine traits such as acquisitiveness and pugnacity. The evil must be attacked, she concludes, at the points where it originates. The "room of one's own" demanded in the earlier tract here has become an education that accords realistically with the feminine nature; the emphasis on an independent income has been transformed into an appeal for equal opportunity in the professions. In the course of her argument Virginia Woolf presents a documented survey of women's grievances. She casts a critical eye on essentially masculine institutions, such as the universities, the church, the army, and asserts that the fascist state is the apotheosis of virility. Finally she presents a series of practical proposals to the "daughters of educated men" based on her contention that woman has always been essentially an "outsider," a second-class citizen deprived of wealth and power. The exclusion of women from leadership in the state has helped them to preserve their moral superiority and fitted them to undertake a civilizing mission. Women in the professions, she says, should form a new, semimonastic, noncompetitive order; they should help to educate young people in the arts

of peace. Since they are by nature pacifists, they should engage in passive resistance to all preparations for war and refuse in any way to abet the belligerent males. If necessary, women should decline, like Lysistrata, to breed sons for cannon fodder.

Both *A Room of One's Own* and *Three Guineas* were written at a time when the ardor of the feminists had died down and public interest had waned. In 1936 one feminist leader wrote: "Modern young women know amazingly little of what life was like before the war, and show a strong hostility to the word 'feminism' and all which they imagine it to connote."[27] For many young women feminism was a dead issue, or perhaps a kind of reproach—something they had to live down. For Virginia Woolf, who belonged to an earlier generation, it was still very much alive. The world crisis, which made the claims of the feminists seem trivial to most people, only confirmed for her the importance of the women's movement. She was deeply interested in social and political issues, but she brought her own interpretation of history to bear on them. The position of her sex was a principle axis along which she attempted to plot contemporary events. Attitudes deriving from the pre-World War I era of militant feminism seem to have remained latent in her, coming to the surface during the twenties and thirties. She had never had a chance to work off her resentments in political action. E. M. Forster may have been implying something of the kind when he said, a bit apologetically: "In my judgment there is something old-fashioned about this extreme feminism; it dates back to her suffragette youth of the 1910's, when men kissed girls to distract them from wanting the vote, and very properly provoked her wrath."[28] We must come back to the fact that Virginia Woolf's youth coincided with the pioneering era of feminism in order to see her attacks on the patriarchy in perspective. When she touched on the subject of women's rights, she frequently displayed the intensity, the touchiness, the "angularity," as she herself expressed it, of the pioneer.

Virginia Woolf considered the subjugation of women both cause and symptom of a fundamental imbalance in society. Her concern began with a sense of personal grievance; it ended with a consciousness of public responsibility. Inequality in the home had its counterpart in the political sphere; the problems of the family reflected those of the state. Lack of wholeness in the modern world was an implicit theme in almost everything she wrote. In her books she attempted to reconcile fact and imagination, masculine reason and feminine intuition. The following chapters are about her efforts to do so.

Notes

1. Quoted by Ray Strachey, *The Cause* (London, 1928), p. 15.

2. Great Britain, *Parliamentary Papers* (1882), *Bills: Public,* vol. 4, p. 13.

3. W. Lyon Blease, *The Emancipation of English Women* (London, 1913), p. 140.

4. Strachey, *The Cause,* pp. 223-24.

5. Quoted by Donald Clive Stuart in *The Development of Dramatic Art* (New York, 1937), p. 575.

6. See her well-known attacks on Wells, Galsworthy, Bennett, in "Modern Fiction," *The Common Reader,* and "Mr. Bennett and Mrs. Brown," *The Captain's Death Bed.*

7. Hilda Ridley, "Leslie Stephen's Daughter," *Dalhousie Review,* 33 (Spring, 1953): 65.

8. *A Writer's Diary,* November 28, 1928, p. 135.

9. *The Life of Henry Fawcett* (London, 1886), pp. 173, 177.

10. *Social Rights and Duties* (London, 1896), 2: 249-51.

11. *Ibid.,* 2: 244, 245-46.

12. *Ibid.,* 2: 256, 258.

13. Quoted by Desmond MacCarthy in *Memories* (New York, 1953), pp. 93-94.

14. "Forgotten Benefactors," *Social Rights and Duties,* 2: 264.

15. *Leslie Stephen: His Thought and Character in Relation to His Time* (Cambridge, Mass., 1952), p. 228.

16. "George Eliot," *Hours in a Library* (New York, 1904), 4: 163.

17. *Leslie Stephen,* p. 226.

18. *A Writer's Diary,* November 28, 1928, p. 135.

19. "Leslie Stephen" in *The Captain's Death Bed,* p. 71. In spite of Leslie Stephen's tolerance of his daughter's artistic ambitions, he appears at times to have been less than reasonable. "When Stephen discusses sex," Noël Annan observes, "he begins to shriek: then he rushes in, fists milling, like a small boy in a temper, and most of his blows go wide" (*Leslie Stephen,* p. 229). Aileen Pippett recounts a typical incident in the family life of the Stephens, after Virginia's mother had died: "When her father made a scene and almost reduced Vanessa to tears, it was terrible for Virginia to have to excuse him for being so majestic and so unreasonable. It was also belittling to his real dignity that they knew he would be sorry later on and would reproach himself bitterly and need to be comforted because he was such an unkind father." *The Moth and the Star: A Biography of Virginia Woolf* (Boston, 1955), p. 26.

20. *Essays and Sketches in Biography* (New York, 1956), p. 252.

21. Clive Bell comments on Virginia Woolf's occasional tendency to discourage her friends from pursuing the arts: "Sometimes it seemed to me that Virginia had inherited from her immediate ancestors more than their beauty and intelligence. Every good Victorian knew that a young man should have a sensible profession, something solid and secure, which would lead naturally to a comfortable old age and a fair provision for the children. In her head Virginia knew perfectly well that to give such advice to Lytton [Strachey] or Duncan [Grant] was absurd; but Virginia, like the merest man, was not always guided by reason." *Old Friends* (New York, 1957), p. 100.

22. See p. 11 above.

23. *The Voyage Out* was completed in February, 1913, and published in 1915. See Leonard Woolf, *Beginning Again* (New York, 1964), p. 87.

24. *Ibid.,* p. 76.

25. Edwin Berry Burgum, "Virginia Woolf and the Empty Room," *The Novel and the World's Dilemma* (New York, 1947), p. 125.

26. "That's the end of six years floundering, striving, much agony, some ecstasy: lumping *The Years* and *Three Guineas* together as one book—as indeed they are." *A Writer's Diary,* June 3, 1938, p. 284. Cf. the entry for May 21, 1935 (pp. 240-41): "Oddities of the human brain: woke early and again considered dashing off my book on Professions [*Three Guineas*], to which I had not given a single thought these 7 or 8 days. Why? This vacillates with my novel [*The Years*]—how are they both to come out simultaneously."

27. Ray Strachey, "Introduction," *Our Freedom and Its Results* (London, 1936), p. 10.

28. "Virginia Woolf," *Two Cheers for Democracy* (New York, 1951), p. 255.

Bibliography

1 By Virginia Woolf

(Where an edition other than the first has been used, the original date of publication is given in parentheses.)

Between the Acts. New York: Harcourt, Brace, 1941.

The Captain's Death Bed and Other Essays. London: Hogarth Press, 1950.

The Common Reader. New York: Harcourt, Brace, 1925.

The Common Reader. 2nd ser. London: Hogarth Press, 1948 (1932).

Contemporary Writers. New York: Harcourt, Brace and World, 1966.

"A Cookery Book," Review of *The Cookery Book of Lady Clark of Tillypronie,* edited by Catherine Frances Frere. *TLS,* November 25, 1909, p. 457.

The Death of the Moth and Other Essays. New York: Harcourt, Brace, 1942.

Flush: A Biography. New York: Harcourt, Brace, 1933.

Granite and Rainbow: Essays. London: Hogarth Press, 1958.

A Haunted House and Other Short Stories. London: Hogarth Press, 1953 (1943).

"The Intellectual Status of Women." Letter to the editor, *New Statesman,* October 16, 1920, pp. 45-46.

"Introduction," *Mrs. Dalloway.* New York: Modern Library, 1928.

Jacob's Room. London: Hogarth Press, 1960 (1922).

"Julia Margaret Cameron." Introduction to *Victorian Photographs of Famous Men and Fair Women,* by Julia Margaret Cameron. London: Hogarth Press, 1926.

"Lady Hester Stanhope." Review of *Lady Hester Stanhope,* by Mrs. Charles Roundell. *TLS,* January 20, 1910, p. 20.

"Men and Women." Review of *La Femme anglaise au XIXe Siècle et son Evolution d'après le Roman anglais contemporain,* by Leonie Villard. *TLS,* March 18, 1920, p. 182.

The Moment and Other Essays. London: Hogarth Press, 1952 (1947).

Monday or Tuesday. New York: Harcourt, Brace, 1921.

"More Carlyle Letters." Review of *The Love Letters of Thomas Carlyle and Jane Welsh,* edited by Alexander Carlyle. *TLS,* April 1, 1909, p. 126.

Mrs. Dalloway. London: Hogarth Press, 1960 (1925).

Night and Day. New York: Harcourt, Brace, 1931 (1919).

Orlando: A Biography. New York: Harcourt, Brace, 1928.

Roger Fry: A Biography. New York: Harcourt, Brace, 1940.

A Room of One's Own. New York: Harcourt, Brace, 1929.

"A Scribbling Dame." Review of *The Life and Romances of Mrs. Eliza Haywood,* by George Frisbie Whicher. *TLS,* February 17, 1916, p. 78.

Three Guineas. London: Hogarth Press, 1952 (1938).

To the Lighthouse. New York: Harbrace Modern Classics, 1959 (1927).

Virginia Woolf and Lytton Strachey: Letters. Edited by Leonard Woolf and James Strachey. New York: Harcourt, Brace, 1956.

The Voyage Out. New York: Blue Ribbon Books, 1920 (1915).

The Waves. London: Hogarth Press, 1955 (1931).

A Writer's Diary (Extracts from the Diary of Virginia Woolf). Edited by Leonard Woolf. New York: Harcourt, Brace, 1953.

The Years. New York: Harcourt, Brace, 1937.

BARBARA CURRIER BELL AND CAROL OHMANN (ESSAY DATE 1974)

SOURCE: Bell, Barbara Currier, and Carol Ohmann. "Virginia Woolf's Criticism: A Polemical Preface." In *Feminist Literary Criticism: Explorations in Theory,* second edition, edited by Josephine Donovan, pp. 48-60. Lexington: University Press of Kentucky, 1989.

In the following essay, which originally appeared in the journal Critical Inquiry *in 1974, Bell and Ohmann examine Woolf's body of literary criticism, describing the methods and principles that inform it.*

In her novels, and those are what most of her readers know best, Virginia Woolf habitually aims at creating moments of freedom, moments when the self, breaking bonds and vaulting bounds, arrives at an unqualified intensity of thought and emotion. Clarissa Dalloway, on a London morning in spring, feels herself lifted on "waves of divine vitality." "It [is] very, very dangerous," she thinks, but without any regret, "to live even one day." Lily Briscoe, toward the close of **To the Lighthouse,** is oppressed by Mr. Ramsay's demands: he is a widower, and hence aggrieved; she is a woman and owes him, he would insist, solace. She cannot, she will not oblige: she'd gotten up that morning to paint. But suddenly, forgetting him and forgetting herself, she sees, and remarks, that his boots are beautiful. For the moment Lily and Mr. Ramsay are unlocked from the past and convention. They reach, together, "the blessed island of good boots." Percival, in **The Waves,** has a power over the other characters that may surely be tied to the image he appears to present of perfectly habitual, perfectly unconscious self-expression. He need not study Shakespeare's plays; he simply understands them; he appears to be at home, and at large, in a brave new world. And even Eleanor Pargiter, in **The Years,** wakes from the constriction of nearly a lifetime to ask, "And now? . . . And now?" She is at once ripe and ready.

As a novelist, Virginia Woolf has taken, and takes, some wrist-slapping. By some of her contemporaries she was viewed, as E. M. Forster said, in an image that condensed many a small-minded complaint: she was viewed as the Invalid Lady of Bloomsbury. And we have heard that just a few seasons ago, when the idea was first put to them, the committee of assorted academic eminences that plans the programs for the English Institute said no to a suggestion for a series of papers on Woolf; she was, some of them asserted, not good enough for the Institute, which has traditionally assembled at Columbia and, most recently, at Harvard. But time may do much and indeed has already done very much to praise Virginia Woolf as the creator of **Mrs. Dalloway, To the Lighthouse, The Waves,** and **Between the Acts.**

Our purpose is to discuss her criticism, and at the same time to praise, even to celebrate, that. Her criticism is less well known than her fiction. It's been neglected, and deserves much more attention than it's gotten.[1] In passing, we might make the guess—we consider it quite a reasonable one—that it has been easier for professional academics to praise, or even only to notice, a woman novelist, than it has been to accept a woman critic.

As a critic, Virginia Woolf has been called a number of disparaging names: "impressionist," "bellelettrist," "raconteur," "amateur." Here is one academic talking on the subject: "She will survive, not as a critic, but as a literary essayist recording the adventures of a soul among congenial masterpieces. . . . The writers who are most downright, and masculine, and central in their approach to life—a Fielding or a Balzac—she for the most part left untouched. . . . Her own approach was at once more subterranean and aerial, and invincibly, almost defiantly, feminine."[2] In other words: Virginia Woolf is not a critic; how could she be? She is a woman. From its beginning, criticism has been a man's world. This is to say not only that males have earned their living as critics, but, more importantly, that the conventionally accepted ideals of critical method are linked with qualities stereotypically allotted to males: analysis, judgment, objectivity. Virginia Woolf has had a poor reputation as a critic not merely because her sex was female, but because her method is "feminine." She writes in a way that is said to be creative, appreciative, and subjective. We will accept this description for the moment, but will later enlarge on it, and even our provisional acceptance we mean to turn to a compliment.

Virginia Woolf's difference from conventional critics is precisely one reason, we would argue, why she should be praised. She is not almost defiantly feminine; she is beyond a doubt defiantly feminine. She is in revolt against the established terms and tones of literary study. Researching for a book on literary history, she had this experience, which she records in her diary:

> Yesterday in the Public Library I took down a book of X.'s criticism. This turned me against writing my book. London Library atmosphere effused. Turned me against all literary criticism: these so clever, so airless, so fleshless ingenuities and attempts to prove—that T. S. Eliot for example is a worse critic than X. Is all literary criticism that kind of exhausted air?—book dust, London Library, air. Or is it only that X, is a second hand, frozen fingered, university specialist, don trying to be creative, don all stuffed with books, writer? . . . I dipped for five minutes and put the book back depressed. The man asked, "What do you want, Mrs. Woolf?" I said a history of English literature. But was so sickened I couldn't look. There were so many.[3]

Or again, she writes:

> [Do not] let us shy away from the kings because we are commoners. That is a fatal crime in the eyes of Aeschylus, Shakespeare, Virgil, and Dante, who, if they could speak—and after all they can—would say, "Don't leave me to the wigged and

gowned. Read me, read me for yourselves." They do not mind if we get our accents wrong, or have to read with a crib in front of us. Of course—are we not commoners, outsiders?—we shall trample many flowers and bruise much ancient grass. . . . [But] let us trespass at once. Literature is no one's private ground; literature is common ground.[4]

No other twentieth century critic has approached literature with less explicit "system" and more sympathy than Virginia Woolf. Trespassers, she knew, had to stay aloof from all critical schools, to differ from them all. In her diary, she frequently expressed a wish to break new ground.

> I feel . . . at the back of my brain that I can devise a new critical method; something far less still and formal than [what has been done before]. . . . There must be some simpler, subtler, closer means of writing about books, as about people, could I hit upon it.[5]

Although she was never finally satisfied with herself, she did write criticism that is truly revolutionary. In what follows, we will try to describe the most significant terms of her revolt.

She solves, first of all, the problem of how to address her readers amiably and unpretentiously, and her solution is crucial to her overall success as a critic. For she is not traditionally authoritarian, not an eminence, not a lecturer in her mode of relationship to her audience. Instead of the stance of omniscience, which is a stance that is often uncongenial to women writers (it never did Charlotte Brontë any good, Emily avoided it, and George Eliot assumed it with success only, perhaps, because her dominant emotional tone was one of suffering compassion and hence not altogether at odds with conventional requirements for women)—instead of the stance of omniscience, Woolf invents "the common reader," and employs that *persona* convincingly. When she says "we," she means *we,* rhetorically asserting the existence of a community, but, in fact, by that rhetoric and the other devices we will note, working to create a community.

"We" are readers, not critics or scholars. "We" are English men and women who read for pleasure and for inspiration when "we" can get it. "We" are tolerant but not permissive; "we" laugh and cry but "we" are not fickle, "our" sentiments have limits; "we" believe in common virtues; "we" like fantasy in measurable doses; "we" are worldly-wise but not world-weary; "we" are of "our" age but ours could be any age;[6] "we" constantly question and argue with writers the minute they assume too much, or pretend wisdom, or get too far from the facts of daily life. "['We' are] guided by an instinct to create for ['ourselves'], out of whatever odds and ends ['we'] can come by, some kind of whole—a portrait of a man, a sketch of an age, a theory of the art of writing.'"[7] But "we" do not like labels. "We" do not care about the difference between the pre-Romantics and the post-Romantics, or between a novelist of manners and a novelist of sentiment. "We" may, in the end, accept assumptions, or morals, or fantasies, but not without good reason. "We" are suspicious of books "for we have our own vision of the world; we have made it from our own experience and prejudices, and it is therefore bound up with our own vanities and loves. It is impossible not to feel injured and insulted if tricks are played and our private harmony is upset."[8] When we do make a judgment, we make it forthrightly and simply.

> The Edwardians have developed a technique of novel-writing which suits their purpose; they have made tools and established conventions which do their business. But those tools are not our tools, and that business is not our business. For us those conventions are ruin, those tools are death.[9]

Her "common reader" helps Woolf to produce critical essays that are exceptionally readable, clear, and vivid. Thanks to "us," her essays move smoothly and quickly, for the common reader's reactions seem to dictate most of her commentary, even though the truth, of course, is exactly the opposite: she has shaped or elicited the reactions she posits.[10] Her continual consciousness of "the common reader" is especially useful to Woolf in essays on abstract aesthetic topics. "We" prevent her from becoming too general, or pedantic, or confusing. "We" ask hard questions like "What is art?" or "How should one read a book?" and demand outright answers. Also, "we" are a source that generates imagery. Woolf, of course, uses a great deal of imagery in her criticism; the fact has been often observed, but by no means (or seldom) connected with the common reader. First of all, we like imagery. In an effort to please us, Woolf uses it as liberally as cooks use seasoning. Second, we need imagery. Many of the ideas Woolf puts forth, particularly in the aesthetic essays, are essentially abstruse, and images are the fastest, most concrete and effective means of explanation—that is, if they are of a certain kind: either simple, or striking, or both.[11]

An essay titled "**The Elizabethan Lumber Room**" will do as an extended example here.[12] It offers an introduction to Woolf's favorite period, discussing the *zeitgeist,* the quires of poetry, prose, and drama, and their characteristic evolution. It might be a syllabus for a seminar at Columbia or Harvard. But it is more winning than most seminars. It offers a highly imaginative alternative to conventional literary criticism.

The essay is a review of Hakluyt's famous book, *Early Voyages, Travels, and Discoveries of the English Nation.* In her very first sentence, Woolf puts herself on our level of acknowledging, "These magnificent volumes are not often, perhaps, read through." We nod. We have not often, or even ever read through Hakluyt; we do belong in the community that Woolf invokes. Then, Woolf involves us further with her metaphor of the lumber room; it is exactly the simple and striking kind of image we like and need:

> [Hakluyt] is not so much a book as a great bundle of commodities loosely tied together, an emporium, a lumber room strewn with ancient sacks, obsolete nautical instruments, huge bales of wool, and little bags of rubies and emeralds. One is for ever untying this packet here, sampling that heap over there, wiping the dust off some vast map of the world, and sitting down in semi-darkness to snuff the strange smells of silks and leathers and ambergris, while outside tumble the huge waves of the uncharted Elizabethan sea.

Hakluyt's expeditions, Woolf goes on to tell us, were manned by "apt young men" who loved to explore and trade for treasure. They told the mysterious and wondrous tales that Hakluyt recorded as truth. Here, knowing our liking not only for imagery but also for narrative, Woolf tells us some of these tales.

> The Earl of Cumberland's men, hung up by adverse winds off the coast of Cornwall for a fortnight, licked the muddy water off the deck in agony. And sometimes a ragged and wornout man came knocking at the door of an English country house and claimed to be the boy who had left it years ago to sail the seas. . . . He had with him a black stone, veined with gold, or an ivory tusk, or a silver ingot, and urged on the village youth with talk of gold strewn over the land as stones are strewn in the fields of England.

At one level, Woolf is entertaining us, but at another, she is instructing us, for these tales were, after all, a major source for Elizabethan literature. "All this," she writes, "the new words, the new ideas, the waves, the savages, the adventures, found their way naturally into the plays which were being acted on the banks of the Thames." The extravagant spirit that fabricated them is the same extravagant spirit that buoys us up through so many Elizabethan writings. In the words of the essay:

> Thus, with singing and with music, springs into existence the characteristic Elizabethan extravagance; the dolphins and lavoltas of Greene; the

hyperbole, more surprising in a writer so terse and muscular, of Ben Jonson. Thus we find the whole of Elizabethan literature strewn with gold and silver; with talk of Guiana's rarities, and references to that America . . . which was not merely a land on the map but symbolized the unknown territories of the soul.

The next section of the essay, in which Woolf weighs two important Elizabethan genres against each other, effortlessly continues from her opening metaphor. The magic spirit of the lumber room inspired poetry, but was bad for prose. She writes, "Rhyme and metre helped the poets to keep the tumult of their perceptions in order. But the prose writer, without these restrictions, accumulated clauses, petered out interminable catalogues, tripped and stumbled over the convolutions of his own rich draperies." From this point, Woolf moves to the next with another image, "The stage was the nursery where prose learnt to find its feet."

Now, having covered prose, poetry, and drama, and having explained the reason for drama's importance, she begins slowly to trace the evolution *out* of Elizabethan literature: "The publicity of the stage and the perpetual presence of a second person, were hostile to that growing consciousness of one's self . . . which, as the years went by, sought expression." As necessarily as a pendulum swing, the pressure of the outside world caused writers to reflect upon themselves, but with the old imagery intact. Woolf quotes Sir Thomas Browne: "'The world that I regard is myself; it is the microcosm of my own frame that I cast mine eye on; for the other I use it but like my globe, and turn it round sometimes for my recreation.'" "'We carry with us the wonders we seek without us; there is all Africa and her prodigies in us.'" She leads us to sympathize with Browne: she involves us with her picture of him in the same way she involved us with her picture of Hakluyt, his covers shut before his conclusion. "In short, as we say when we cannot help laughing at the oddities of people we admire most, he was a character, and the first to make us feel that the most sublime speculations of the human imagination are issued from a particular man, whom we can love." Again, we nod; we identify; we fully consent to her use of "we."

At the very end of her essay, Woolf repeats the lumber room metaphor. Only now, instead of being an image for Hakluyt's book—the outside world that so excited Elizabethans—it is an image for the mind of Sir Thomas Browne—the inside world that so intrigued writers of the seventeenth century. "Now," she writes, "we are in the pres-

ence of sublime imagination; now rambling through one of the finest lumber rooms in the world—a chamber stuffed from floor to ceiling with ivory, old iron, broken pots, urns, unicorns' horns, and magic glasses full of emerald lights and blue mystery." The lumber room has served to beguile us in the beginning of the essay, to guide us throughout, and to give us a rich sense of unity at the end. Yet, like the symbols of great poetry, it has never preached to us directly.

Though "the common reader" was Virginia Woolf's most dramatic critical innovation—and probably the most important to *her*—she made other experiments in criticism to escape tradition. She pushed, for example, a certain kind of biographical criticism to its frontier. "Try to become the author," she advises herself, and thinks further, "Were I another person I would say to myself, Please write criticism; biography; invent a new form for both."[13] Woolf's search for a new combination of criticism and biography might be thought of as representing her attachment to that old critical dictum, "The style is the man." In a number of her essays, she personifies the works of a writer; so she presents us not with a series of texts but with some*one,* a man or a woman.

She makes a person, for instance, out of Goldsmith's essays, and calls the person Goldsmith. "The Citizen [in Goldsmith's volume *The Citizen of the World*] is still a most vivacious companion as he takes his walk from Charing Cross to Ludgate Hill . . . Goldsmith keeps just on the edge of the crowd so we can hear what the common people are saying and note their humours. Shrewdly and sarcastically he casts his eye, as he saunters on, upon the odd habits and sights that the English are so used to that they no longer see them."[14] The point is that "Goldsmith," in this passage, is actually Goldsmith's book.

Woolf had sense enough to think about the appropriateness of her technique carefully, so that the debate about biographical criticism has been enriched by her thoughts. Considering Henley, a man who, according to her, wrote the most mechanical sort of biographical criticism, she said, "There are times when we would sweep aside all biography and all psychology for the sake of a single song or a single poem expounded and analysed phrase-by-phrase."[15] Finally in favor of her biographical tendencies as a critic, however, she said that a writer never stops being a writer, even when he does not write; "the pith and essence of [a person's] character . . . shows itself to the observant eye in the tone of a voice, the turn of a head, some little phrase or anecdote picked up in passing."[16] If the tiniest, vaguest clues can show a person's essence, then Woolf was surely justified in reading from book to author and back again. In her essay **"Personalities,"** she analyzes again her brand of criticism, offering the following justification and quite sensible reservation about it:

> The people whom we admire most as writers . . . have something elusive, enigmatic, impersonal about them. . . . In ransacking their drawers we shall find out little about them. All has been distilled into their books. The life is thin, modest, colourless, like blue skimmed milk at the bottom of the jar. It is the imperfect artists who never manage to say the whole thing in their books who wield the power of personality over us.[17]

In other words, bringing the life of the writer *to* the work or deducing personality *from* a work may be more or less appropriate, more or less revelatory, according to the nature of the biography or the *oeuvre* under scrutiny. Woolf may not have succeeded in inventing a new form in her mixture of biography and criticism: at the least, we remember Johnson's *Lives of the Poets,* Lamb's *Essays of Elia,* or Hazlitt's *Table Talk,* and we may even recall *Hours in a Library,* written by Sir Leslie Stephen, Woolf's father. She did, however, overtake her predecessors in the devotion and the grace with which she practised it.

Of course, Woolf habitually moved out of criticism coupled with biography into pure biography. Many of her essays review letters, memoirs, autobiographies, biographies. Her interest in these latter stretches further, and is a further instance of her revolt against tradition: she writes repeatedly on works outside the standard canon of English literature. She suggests that the word "literature" might well be redefined, as we find it undergoing redefinition today, to include popular or miscellaneous writing of all periods.[18] And she takes women writers quite seriously, going out of the conventional way to notice them and give notice of them. Roughly 20 percent of her published essays are about women writers directly. Roughly the same proportion again are indirectly concerned with the frustrating limits that conventional society places on women's personal and literary lives. An essay on Dorothy Osborne's *Letters,* for example, stresses that the literary talents of women could only begin, historically, to find expression in what we might call "underground" writing. In "Madame de Sévigné," she looks anew at a famous "token woman"; in "Sara Coleridge," sketches the difficulties of a literary daughter; and in "Poe's Helen," emphasizes Helen far more than Poe.

The features of Woolf's criticism we have been concerned with are all, we would argue, strategies in a single campaign: an effort to take books down from library shelves and put them into the hands of her ideal community, the common readers. And to talk about them outside the walls of lecture rooms. And to talk about them, finally, in such a way that they matter, not in literary history, but in our lives.

Woolf has, as we noted at the beginning, been called "subjective," and we accepted the term with its apparently pejorative overtones. But the acceptance was only temporary, and we want now to return to it so as to redefine it.

In 1923, beginning to revise a number of essays for publication in the collection she titled **The Common Reader,** Woolf wrote in her diary, "I shall really investigate literature with a view to answering certain questions about ourselves."[19] Not "myself," but "ourselves." She is not a subjective critic in the sense that she refers to her own life in her critical essays.[20] She does not, for instance, mention that she knew some of the contemporary authors she wrote about; and, as an early biographer remarked, "No one would guess from reading '**The Enchanted Organ'** that the woman whose selected letters she was reviewing had been not only Miss Thackeray, Mrs. Richmond Ritchie but also Aunt Annie [the sister of Sir Leslie Stephen's first wife]."[21] It would be impossible to learn from Woolf's criticism about her daily routine or her friends or her marriage or her mental illness or her work for the Women's Cooperative Guild. Yet her work may be called subjective in this broader sense, that she sees literature as a series of personal transactions, a series of encounters between people writing and people reading, and she urges us to see both literature and popular culture that way ourselves.

Learning, she knows, is by no means necessarily a humanizing experience. In the biography of Dr. Bentley, head of Trinity College, Cambridge, she tells us, Bentley is described as extraordinarily learned, knowing Homer by heart, reading Sophocles and Pindar the way we read newspapers and magazines, spending his life largely in the company of the greatest of the Greeks. And yet, in his life, she says, "we shall [also] find much that is odd and little that is reassuring. . . . The man who should have been steeped in beauty (if what they say of the Classics is true) as a honey-pot is ingrained with sweetness was, on the contrary, the most quarrelsome of mankind."[22] He was aggressive; he was coercive; he bullied and threatened his academic staff at Trinity and beyond a doubt did the same to students. Did the Society of Trinity College dare to think he spent too much of the college funds on the staircase of his own lodging? Did they perceive that he stole food, drink and fuel from the college stores? Then let them look at their jobs and their other preferments. And so on and on and on.

Nonetheless, Woolf's essays imply, over and over again, that learning can be a humanizing experience. And here we turn back to our beginning. Far from merely recording the adventures of a soul among masterpieces, Woolf's criticism always exerts a standard of judgment, seldom explicit but nonetheless there, informing her essays, evident in the selection of her details as well as the choices of her *persona* and her rhetoric. In *A Room of One's Own,* she speaks of Shakespeare's mind as a mind without "obstacle," a mind "unimpeded" and "incandescent," free to produce works of art. Such works "seem to stand there complete by themselves," which is to say not only that form and content beautifully accord, but that the works do not break or unseam to show, say, an anger that is only personal or a grievance merely local. And John Paston, reading in Norfolk with the sea to his left and the fen to his right, saw in Chaucer fields and skies and people he recognized, but seldom rendered more brightly, more clearly, "rounded and complete." Chaucer's mind, too, was "free to apply its force fully to its object."[23] On the other hand, reading Charlotte Brontë's novels,[24] Woolf finds material not germane to fictional design, not consistent with the predominant point of view and style. There are interpolations of self-defense and interjections of indignation—indignation about, for example, the lot of the English governess. The explanation for these anomalies, Woolf suggests, can be found by moving back beyond the work of art to the mind that made it, and there is the life "cramped and thwarted," pressed into uncongenial services and attitudes that frustrated the impulse of genius to express itself, "whole and entire." While Woolf's criticism of Brontë is in some ways adverse, it is, nonetheless, basically sympathetic. What was, evokes hauntingly the image of what might have been. And more, what should have been. The critical ideal applied to Shakespeare, Chaucer and Brontë is the same ideal of the free self that Woolf expresses in her novels, a self breaking bonds and vaulting bounds, a self arriving at the furthest intensity of thought and emotion.

In this last sense, then, Woolf's criticism may without injury be called subjective or personal. Its function is to humanize our lives, to urge a libera-

tion and wholeness of self. It is a brilliant and graceful protest against any narrower, more abstract, or merely professional critical purpose. To put the case concretely, as she habitually did, it is a brilliant and graceful protest against one of the pictures she drew in *A Room of One's Own*: Professor von X., engaged in writing a "monumental work." Professor von X. is heavy in build, his eyes are very small, his complexion is red with anger, and he "jabs" with his pen at his paper "as if he were killing some noxious insect."[25]

Notes

1. Not many readers of Woolf know how *much* criticism she published: somewhere near 400 articles. Her first publications were reviews, and at certain times in her life she financed her novels with her criticism. Of her critical work, produced for leading journals and sometimes anonymous, only about one-third has been published in collections.

2. Louis Kronenberger, *The Republic of Letters* (New York: Alfred A. Knopf, 1955), p. 249.

3. *A Writer's Diary,* ed. Leonard Woolf (New York: Harcourt Brace, 1953), p. 337.

4. "The Leaning Tower," *The Moment and Other Essays,* ed. Leonard Woolf (1st ed., 1947), reprint (London: Hogarth Press, 1964), p. 125.

5. *A Writer's Diary,* p. 172.

6. Woolf knew that the way people read depends on the age they belong to, but she could evoke the spirit of each age so strongly as to make her readers peripatetic through time. See "The Countess of Pembroke's Arcadia" and "The 'Sentimental Journey'" on Sidney's *Arcadia* and Sterne's *Sentimental Journey* in *The Common Reader,* 2d ser. (London: Hogarth Press, 1932).

7. "The Common Reader," *The Common Reader,* 1st ser. (Harvest ed.; New York: Harcourt, Brace, 1956), p. 1.

8. "Robinson Crusoe," *Common Reader,* 2d ser., p. 53.

9. "Mr. Bennett and Mrs. Brown," *The Captain's Death Bed,* ed. Leonard Woolf (London: Hogarth Press, 1950), pp. 103-4.

10. In considering whether or not Woolf is successful at making us identify with "we," the common reader, one should constantly remember how cautious Woolf herself was about claiming success. To her, the common reader was always an experiment, never a foregone conclusion. In entries for 1929, 1930, 1931, 1933, 1937, 1940, her diary contains constant self-doubts as she challenges herself to do better. See *Writer's Diary,* pp. 140, 156, 172, 203-4, 275, 324.

11. The process by which Woolf shaped her essays around key images can be pieced together through a reading of her ms. drafts, many of which can be found in the Berg Collection of the New York Public Library. It is fascinating. She would start out with a subject, begin writing down information and thoughts on it more or less at random, trying several different ways into it. As she rambled along, invariably an image would turn up. When it did, and if it was a good one, she would seize on it. From that moment, she would know she

had the key to the essay it seems, for the essay's final form would usually be determined by the image's being placed at its opening, climax, end, or any combination of those.

12. *Common Reader,* 1st ser., pp. 40-48.

13. *A Writer's Diary,* p. 272.

14. "Oliver Goldsmith," *Captain's Death Bed,* p. 12.

15. "Henley's Criticism," *Times Literary Supplement,* February 24, 1921, p. 123.

16. "Sterne," *Granite and Rainbow,* ed. Leonard Woolf (London: Hogarth Press, 1960), p. 167; "The New Biography," ibid., p. 153.

17. *The Moment and Other Essays,* p. 138.

18. In an article called "Towards a Feminist History," *Female Studies V: Proceedings of the Conference Women and Education: A Feminist Perspective,* ed. Rae Lee Siporin (Pittsburgh: KNOW, 1972), pp. 49-52, Linda Gordon describes a radical new perspective on history which she illustrates at one point by writing, "Imagine, if you can, the story of the court of Louis XIV as told by one of his scullery maids, based on kitchen rumors and occasional glimpses of the lower edges of the court hierarchy." Virginia Woolf fostered just this kind of radical perspective on literature by emphasizing the role of affect in writing. She operated on the assumption that literature is not just the "great works," but is anything people write to fulfill themselves, whatever that means, in whatever way.

19. *A Writer's Diary,* p. 59.

20. Woolf's private point of view is as carefully hidden in her criticism as it is in her novels. In that sense, her achievement in one form is much the same as that in the other.

21. Aileen Pippett, *The Moth and the Star* (Boston: Little, Brown, 1953), p. 188.

22. "Outlines (II: Dr. Bentley)," *Common Reader,* 1st ser., p. 195.

23. "The Pastons and Chaucer," *Common Reader,* 1st ser., p. 14.

24. *A Room of One's Own* (New York: Harcourt, Brace, 1929), pp. 71-72.

25. Ibid., p. 52.

TORIL MOI (ESSAY DATE 1985)

SOURCE: Moi, Toril. "Who's Afraid of Virginia Woolf? Feminist Readings of Woolf." In *"Mrs. Dalloway" and "To the Lighthouse": Virginia Woolf,* edited by Su Reid, pp. 87-97. New York: St. Martin's Press, 1993.

In the following excerpt, which comprises the second part of the introduction to her 1985 treatise Sexual/Textual Politics, *Moi outlines a way of reading Woolf's texts according to French feminist theories, which significantly diverge from the aesthetic categories of most Anglo-American feminist critics.*

Woolf seems to practise what we might now call a 'deconstructive' form of writing, one that engages with and thereby exposes the duplicitous nature of discourse. In her own textual practice, Woolf exposes the way in which language refuses to be pinned down to an underlying essential meaning. According to the French philosopher Jacques Derrida, language is structured as an endless deferral of meaning, and any search for an essential, absolutely stable meaning must therefore be considered metaphysical. There is no final element, no fundamental unit, no *transcendental signified* that is meaningful *in itself* and thus escapes the ceaseless interplay of linguistic deferral and difference. The free play of signifiers will never yield a final, unified meaning that in turn might ground and explain all the others.[1] It is in the light of such textual and linguistic theory that we can read Woolf's playful shifts and changes of perspective, in both her fiction and in **Room**, as something rather more than a wilful desire to irritate the serious-minded feminist critic. Through her conscious exploitation of the sportive, sensual nature of language, Woolf rejects the metaphysical essentialism underlying patriarchal ideology, which hails God, the Father or the phallus as its transcendental signified.

But Woolf does more than practise a non-essentialist form of writing. She also reveals a deeply sceptical attitude to the male-humanist concept of an essential human identity. For what can this self-identical identity be if all meaning is a ceaseless play of difference, if *absence* as much as presence is the foundation of meaning? The humanist concept of identity is also challenged by psychoanalytic theory, which Woolf undoubtedly knew. The Hogarth Press, founded by Virginia and Leonard Woolf, published the first English translations of Freud's central works, and when Freud arrived in London in 1939 Virginia Woolf went to visit him. Freud, we are tantalisingly informed, gave her a narcissus.

For Woolf, as for Freud, unconscious drives and desires constantly exert a pressure on our conscious thoughts and actions. For psychoanalysis the human subject is a complex entity, of which the conscious mind is only a small part. Once one has accepted this view of the subject, however, it becomes impossible to argue that even our conscious wishes and feelings originate within a unified self, since we can have no knowledge of the possibly unlimited unconscious processes that shape our conscious thought. Conscious thought, then, must be seen as the 'overdetermined' manifestation of a multiplicity of structures that intersect to produce that unstable constellation the liberal humanists call the 'self'. These structures encompass not only unconscious sexual desires, fears and phobias, but also a host of conflicting material, social, political and ideological factors of which we are equally unaware. It is this highly complex network of conflicting structures, the anti-humanist would argue, that produces the subject and its experiences, rather than the other way round. This belief does not of course render the individual's experiences in any sense less real or valuable; but it does mean that such experiences cannot be understood other than through the study of their multiple determinants—determinants of which conscious thought is only one, and a potentially treacherous one at that. If a similar approach is taken to the literary text, it follows that the search for a unified individual self, or gender identity or indeed 'textual identity' in the literary work must be seen as drastically reductive.

It is in this sense that Elaine Showalter's recommendation to remain detached from the narrative strategies of the text is equivalent to not reading it at all. For it is only through an examination of the detailed strategies of the text on all its levels that we will be able to uncover some of the conflicting, contradictory elements that contribute to make it precisely *this* text, with precisely these words and this configuration. The humanist desire for a unity of vision or thought (or as Holly puts it, for a 'noncontradictory perception of the world'[2]) is, in effect, a demand for a sharply reductive reading of literature—a reading that, not least in the case of an experimental writer like Woolf, can have little hope of grasping the central problems posed by pioneering modes of textual production. A 'non-contradictory perception of the world', for Lukács's Marxist opponent Bertolt Brecht, is precisely a reactionary one.

The French feminist philosopher Julia Kristeva has argued that the modernist poetry of Lautréamont, Mallarmé and others constitutes a 'revolutionary' form of writing. The modernist poem, with its abrupt shifts, ellipses, breaks and apparent lack of logical construction is a kind of writing in which the rhythms of the body and the unconscious have managed to break through the strict rational defences of conventional social meaning. Since Kristeva sees such conventional meaning as the structure that sustains the whole of the symbolic order—that is, all human social and cultural institutions—the fragmentation of symbolic language in modernist poetry comes for her to parallel and prefigure a total *social* revolution. For Kristeva, that is to say, there is a *specific practice of writing* that is itself 'revolutionary', analogous to sexual and political transformation,

and that by its very existence testifies to the possibility of transforming the symbolic order of orthodox society from the inside.[3] One might argue in this light that Woolf's refusal to commit herself in her essays to a so-called rational or logical form of writing, free from fictional techniques, indicates a similar break with symbolic language, as of course do many of the techniques she deploys in her novels.

Kristeva also argues that many women will be able to let what she calls the 'spasmodic force' of the unconscious disrupt their language because of their strong links with the pre-Oedipal mother-figure. But if those unconscious pulsations were to take over the subject entirely, the subject would fall back into pre-Oedipal or imaginary chaos and develop some form of mental illness. The subject whose language lets such forces disrupt the symbolic order, in other words, is also the subject who runs the greater risk of lapsing into madness. Seen in this context, Woolf's own periodic attacks of mental illness can be linked both to her textual strategies and to her feminism. For the symbolic order is a patriarchal order, ruled by the Law of the Father, and any subject who tries to disrupt it, who lets unconscious forces slip through the symbolic repression, puts her or himself in a position of revolt against this regime. Woolf herself suffered acute patriarchal oppression at the hands of the psychiatric establishment, and **Mrs. Dalloway** contains not only a splendidly satirical attack on that profession (as represented by Sir William Bradshaw), but also a superbly perspicacious representation of a mind that succumbs to 'imaginary' chaos in the character of Septimus Smith. Indeed Septimus can be seen as the negative parallel to Clarissa Dalloway, who herself steers clear of the threatening gulf of madness only at the price of repressing her passions and desires, becoming a cold but brilliant woman highly admired in patriarchal society. In this way Woolf discloses the dangers of the invasion of unconscious pulsions as well as the price paid by the subject who successfully preserves her sanity, thus maintaining a precarious balance between an overestimation of so-called 'feminine' madness and a too precipitate rejection of the values of the symbolic order.

It is evident that for Julia Kristeva it is not the biological sex of a person, but the subject position she or he takes up, that determines their revolutionary potential. Her views of feminist politics reflect this refusal of biologism and essentialism. The feminist struggle, she argues, must be seen historically and politically as a three-tiered one, which can be schematically summarised as follows:

1 Women demand equal access to the symbolic order. Liberal feminism. Equality.

2 Women reject the male symbolic order in the name of difference. Radical feminism. Femininity extolled.

3 (This is Kristeva's own position.) Women reject the dichotomy between masculine and feminine as metaphysical.

The third position is one that has deconstructed the opposition between masculinity and femininity, and therefore necessarily challenges the very notion of identity. Kristeva writes:

> In the third attitude, which I strongly advocate—which I imagine?—the very dichotomy man/woman as an opposition between two rival entities may be understood as belonging to *metaphysics*. What can 'identity', even 'sexual identity', mean in a new theoretical and scientific space where the very notion of identity is challenged?[4]

The relationship between the second and the third positions here requires some comment. If the defence of the third position implies a total rejection of stage two (which I do not think it does), this would be a grievous political error. For it still remains *politically* essential for feminists to defend women *as* women in order to counteract the patriarchal oppression that precisely despises women *as* women. But an 'undeconstructed' form of 'stage two' feminism, unaware of the metaphysical nature of gender identities, runs the risk of becoming an inverted form of sexism. It does so by uncritically taking over the very metaphysical categories set up by patriarchy in order to keep women in their places, despite attempts to attach new feminist values to these old categories. An adoption of Kristeva's 'deconstructed' form of feminism therefore in one sense leaves everything as it was—our positions in the political struggle have not changed—but in another sense radically transforms our awareness of the nature of that struggle.

Here, I feel, Kristeva's feminism echoes the position taken up by Virginia Woolf some sixty years earlier. Read from this perspective, **To the Lighthouse** illustrates the destructive nature of a metaphysical belief in strong, immutably fixed gender identities—as represented by Mr and Mrs Ramsay—whereas Lily Briscoe (an artist) represents the subject who deconstructs this opposition,

MRS. DALLOWAY

VIRGINIA WOOLF

PUBLISHED BY LEONARD & VIRGINIA WOOLF AT THE HOGARTH PRESS, 52 TAVISTOCK SQUARE, LONDON, W.C.
1925

Title page of *Mrs. Dalloway*, published in 1925.

perceives its pernicious influence and tries as far as is possible in a still rigidly patriarchal order to live as her own woman, without regard for the crippling definitions of sexual identity to which society would have her conform. It is in this context that we must situate Woolf's crucial concept of androgyny. This is not, as Showalter argues, a flight from fixed gender identities, but a recognition of their falsifying metaphysical nature. Far from fleeing such gender identities because she fears them, Woolf rejects them because she has seen them for what they are. She has understood that the goal of the feminist struggle must precisely be to deconstruct the death-dealing binary oppositions of masculinity and femininity.

In her fascinating book *Toward Androgyny*, published in 1973, Carolyn Heilbrun sets out her own definition of androgyny in similar terms when she describes it as the concept of an 'unbounded and hence fundamentally indefinable nature'.[5] When she later finds it necessary to distinguish androgyny from feminism, and therefore implicitly defines Woolf as a non-feminist, her distinction seems to be based on the belief that only the first two stages of Kristeva's three-tiered struggle could count as feminist strategies. She acknowledges that in modern-day society it might be difficult to separate the defenders of androgyny from feminists, 'because of the power men now hold, and because of the political weakness of women'[6] but refuses to draw the conclusion that feminists can in fact desire androgyny. As opposed to Heilbrun, I would stress with Kristeva that a theory that demands the deconstruction of sexual identity is indeed authentically feminist. In Woolf's case the question is rather whether or not her remarkably advanced understanding of feminist objectives prevented her from taking up a progressive political position in the feminist struggles of her day. In the light of *Three Guineas* (and of *A Room of One's Own*), the answer to this question is surely no. The Woolf of *Three Guineas* shows an acute awareness of the dangers of both liberal and radical feminism (Kristeva's positions one and two), and argues instead for a 'stage three' position; but despite her objections she ends up firmly in favour of women's right to financial independence, education and entry into the professions—all central issues for feminists of the 1920s and 1930s.

Nancy Topping Bazin reads Woolf's concept of androgyny as the *union* of masculinity and femininity—precisely the opposite, in fact, of viewing it as the deconstruction of the duality. For Bazin, masculinity and femininity in Woolf are concepts that retain their full essential charge of meaning. She thus argues that Lily Briscoe in *To the Lighthouse* must be read as being just as feminine as Mrs Ramsay, and that the androgynous solution of the novel consists in a *balance* of the masculine and the feminine 'approach to truth'.[7] Herbert Marder, conversely, advances in his *Feminism and Art* the trite and traditional case that Mrs Ramsay must be seen as an androgynous ideal in herself: 'Mrs Ramsay as wife, mother, hostess, is the androgynous artist in life, creating with the whole of her being'.[8] Heilbrun rightly rejects such a reading, claiming that:

> It is only in groping our way through the clouds of sentiment and misplaced biographical information that we are able to discover Mrs Ramsay, far from androgynous and complete, to be as one-sided and life-denying as her husband.[9]

The host of critics who with Marder read Mrs Ramsay and Mrs Dalloway as Woolf's ideal of femininity are thus either betraying their vestigial sexism—the sexes are fundamentally different and should stay that way—or their adherence to what Kristeva would call a 'stage two' feminism: women

are different from men and it is time they began praising the superiority of their sex. These are both, I believe, misreadings of Woolf's texts, as when Kate Millett writes that:

> Virginia Woolf glorified two housewives, Mrs Dalloway and Mrs Ramsay, recorded the suicidal misery of Rhoda in *The Waves* without ever explaining its causes, and was argumentative yet somehow unsuccessful, perhaps because unconvinced, in conveying the frustrations of the woman artist in Lily Briscoe.[10]

A combination of Derridean and Kristevan theory, then, would seem to hold considerable promise for future feminist readings of Woolf. But it is important to be aware of the political limitations of Kristeva's arguments. Though her views on the 'politics of the subject' constitute a significant contribution to revolutionary theory, her belief that the revolution within the subject somehow prefigures a later social revolution poses severe problems for any materialist analysis of society. The strength of Kristevan theory lies in its emphasis on the politics of language as a material and social structure, but it takes little or no account of other conflicting ideological and material structures that must be part of any radical social transformation. It should nevertheless be emphasised that the 'solution' to Kristeva's problems lies not in a speedy return to Lukács, but in an integration and transvaluation of her ideas within a larger feminist theory of ideology.[11]

A Marxist-feminist critic like Michèle Barrett has stressed the materialist aspect of Woolf's politics. In her introduction to *Virginia Woolf: Women and Writing,* she argues that:

> Virginia Woolf's critical essays offer us an unparalleled account of the development of women's writing, perceptive discussion of her predecessors and contemporaries, and a pertinent insistence on the material conditions which have structured women's consciousness.[12]

Barrett, however, considers Woolf only as essayist and critic, and seems to take the view that when it comes to her fiction, Woolf's aesthetic theory, particularly the concept of an androgynous art, 'continually resists the implications of the materialist position she advances in *A Room of One's Own*' (p. 22). A Kristevan approach to Woolf, as I have argued, would refuse to accept this binary opposition of aesthetics on the one hand and politics on the other, locating the politics of Woolf's writing *precisely in her textual practice*. That practice is of course much more marked in the novels than in most of the essays.

Another group of feminist critics, centred around Jane Marcus, consistently argue for a radical reading of Woolf's work without recourse to either Marxist or poststructuralist theory. Jane Marcus claims Woolf as a 'guerrilla fighter in a Victorian skirt',[13] and sees in her a champion of both socialism and feminism. Marcus's article 'Thinking back through our mothers', however, makes it abundantly clear that it is exceptionally difficult to argue this case convincingly. Her article opens with this assertion:

> Writing, for Virginia Woolf, was a revolutionary act. Her alienation from British patriarchal culture and its capitalist and imperialist forms and values, was so intense that she was filled with terror and determination as she wrote. A guerrilla fighter in a Victorian skirt, she trembled with fear as she prepared her attacks, her raids on the enemy.[14]

Are we to believe that there is a causal link between the first and the following sentences—that writing was a revolutionary act for Woolf *because* she could be seen to tremble as she wrote? Or should the passage be read as an extended metaphor, as an image of the fears of *any* woman writing under patriarchy? In which case it no longer tells us anything specific about Woolf's particular writing practices. Or again, perhaps the first sentence is the claim that the following sentences are meant to corroborate? If this is the case, the argument also fails. For Marcus here unproblematically evokes biographical evidence to sustain her thesis about the nature of Woolf's writing: the reader is to be convinced by appeals to biographical circumstances rather than to the texts. But does it really matter whether or not Woolf was in the habit of trembling at her desk? Surely what matters is what she wrote? This kind of emotionalist argument surfaces again in Marcus's extensive discussion of the alleged parallels between Woolf and the German Marxist critic Walter Benjamin ('Both Woolf and Benjamin chose suicide rather than exile before the tyranny of fascism'[15]). But surely Benjamin's suicide at the Spanish frontier, where as an exiled German Jew fleeing the Nazi occupation of France he feared being handed over to the Gestapo, must be considered in a rather different light from Woolf's suicide in her own back garden in unoccupied England, however political we might wish her private life to be? Marcus's biographical analogies strive to establish Woolf as a remarkable individual, and so fall back into the old-style historical-biographical criticism much in vogue before the American New Critics entered the scene in the 1930s. How far a radical feminist approach can simply take over such traditional methods untransformed is surely debatable.

We have seen that current Anglo-American feminist criticism tends to read Woolf through traditional aesthetic categories, relying largely on a liberal-humanist version of the Lukácsian aesthetics, against which Brecht so effectively polemicised. The anti-humanist reading I have advocated as yielding a better understanding of the political nature of Woolf's aesthetics has yet to be written. The only study of Woolf to have integrated some of the theoretical advances of poststructuralist thought is written by a man, Perry Meisel, and though it is by no means an anti-feminist or even an unfeminist work, it is nevertheless primarily concerned with the influence on Woolf of Walter Pater. Meisel is the only critic of my acquaintance to have gasped the radically deconstructed character of Woolf's texts:

> With 'difference' the reigning principle in Woolf as well as Pater, there can be no natural or inherent characteristics of any kind, even between the sexes, because all character, all language, even the language of sexuality, emerges by means of a difference from itself.[16]

Meisel also shrewdly points out that this principle of difference makes it impossible to select any one of Woolf's works as more representative, more essentially 'Woolfian' than any other, since the notable divergence among her texts 'forbids us to believe any moment in Woolf's career to be more conclusive than another'. It is a mistake, Meisel concludes, to 'insist on the coherence of self and author in the face of a discourse that dislocates or decentres them both, that skews the very categories to which our remarks properly refer'.[17]

The paradoxical conclusion of our investigations into the feminist reception of Woolf is therefore that she has yet to be adequately welcomed and acclaimed by her feminist daughters in England and America. To date she has either been rejected by them as insufficiently feminist, or praised on grounds that seem to exclude her fiction. By their more or less unwitting subscription to the humanist aesthetic categories of the traditional male academic hierarchy, feminist critics have seriously undermined the impact of their challenge to that very institution. The only difference between a feminist and a non-feminist critic in this tradition then becomes the formal political perspective of the critic. The feminist critic thus unwittingly puts herself in a position from which it becomes impossible to read Virginia Woolf as the progressive, feminist writer of genius she undoubtedly was. A feminist criticism that would do both justice and homage to its great mother and sister: this, surely, should be our goal.

Notes

[Toril Moi's *Sexual/Textual Politics: Feminist Literary Theory* made a wide range of readers and students aware that the work of Hélène Cixous, Luce Irigaray, and, especially, Julia Kristeva might be directly related to the reading of other texts. The essay printed here is most of the second half of Moi's Introduction. In the first half Moi laments the lack of admiration accorded, at her time of writing, by feminist critics to Woolf, whom she calls 'this great feminist writer' (*Sexual/Textual Politics,* p. 2) and 'the greatest British woman writer of this century' (p. 8). She argues that critics such as Elaine Showalter, whose influential *A Literature of Their Own* (1977) had accused Woolf of failing to present readers with a strong representation of her suffering as a woman, are making naïve demands of Woolf's texts. With Showalter's work she specifically groups Patricia Stubbs's *Women and Fiction. Feminism and the Novel 1880-1920* (Brighton, 1981) and Marcia Holly's essay 'Consciousness and Authenticity: Toward a Feminist Aesthetic' (1975) (see note 2 below). Comparing these three with the Marxist critic Georg Lukács (see note 9 below), Moi argues that they work from the 'humanist' belief that individuals are fixed entities who have defined experiences which can be objectively observed; and that they simplistically demand that women's writing should give an 'authentic' and realistic account of women's observed experience.

In the second part of her Introduction, reprinted here, Moi opposes this idea of the individual to that of the French theorists. Here she argues that consciousness is fluid, and constructed by forces of which the individual is unaware. She proposes a way of reading that sees the text as a place in which consciousness is enacted, not as a representation of objective experience; and argues that Woolf's writing must be read in this way. Ed.]

1. [In her original note Moi refers readers, for an introduction to Derrida's thought and to other forms of deconstruction, to Christopher Norris, *Deconstruction: Theory and Practice* (London and New York, 1982). Ed.]

2. [Moi is referring to Marcia Holly, 'Consciousness and Authenticity: Toward a Feminist Aesthetic', in Josephine Donovan (ed.), *Feminist Literary Criticism. Explorations in Theory* (Lexington, 1975), pp. 38-47. Ed.]

3. [Moi writes, in a note to the original essay, that this presentation of Kristeva's position is based on her *La*

Révolution du langage poétique (Paris, 1974). Selections from this, in translation, appear in Toril Moi (ed.), *The Kristeva Reader* (Oxford, 1986), pp. 89-136. Ed.]

4. [This quotation is from Kristeva's essay 'Le Temps des Femmes' (Paris, 1979), translated as 'Women's Time' in Toril Moi (ed.), *The Kristeva Reader,* p. 209. Ed.]

5. Carolyn G. Heilbrun, *Toward Androgyny. Aspects of Male and Female in Literature* (London, 1973), p. xi.

6. Ibid., pp. xvi-xvii.

7. Nancy Topping Bazin, *Virginia Woolf and the Androgynous Vision* (New Brunswick NJ, 1973), p. 138.

8. Herbert Marder, *Feminism and Art. A Study of Virginia Woolf* (Chicago and London, 1968), p. 128.

9. *Toward Androgyny,* p. 155.

10. Kate Millett, *Sexual Politics* (1969; London, 1977), pp. 139-40.

11. [In the earlier part of the Introduction (*Sexual/Textual Politics,* pp. 4-6) Moi compared Showalter's demand for 'a powerful expression of personal experience in a social framework' in feminist writing with the 'proletarian humanism' of Lukács. Of Lukács's work she particularly cites, in a note, his 'Preface' in *Studies in European Realism. A Sociological Survey of the Writings of Balzac, Stendhal, Zola, Tolstoy, Gorki and Others* (London, 1972), pp. 1-19. Ed.]

12. Michèle Barrett (ed.), *Virginia Woolf: Women and Writing* (London, 1979), p. 36.

13. Jane Marcus (ed.), *New Feminist Essays on Virginia Woolf* (Nebraska and London, 1981), p. 1.

14. Ibid., p. 1.

15. Ibid., p. 7.

16. Perry Meisel, *The Absent Father. Virginia Woolf and Walter Pater* (New Haven, 1980), p. 234.

17. Ibid., p. 242.

HAROLD BLOOM (ESSAY DATE FALL 1994)

SOURCE: Bloom, Harold. "Feminism as the Love of Reading." *Raritan* 14, no. 2 (fall 1994): 29-42.

In the following essay, Bloom centers on Woolf's passion for reading as the defining feature of her literary criticism, demonstrating the influence of Walter Pater's aestheticism upon her feminist politics.

Sainte-Beuve, to me the most interesting of French critics, taught us to ask as a crucial question of any writer in whom we read deeply: What would the author think of us? Virginia Woolf wrote five remarkable novels—***Mrs. Dalloway*** (1925), ***To the Lighthouse*** (1927), ***Orlando*** (1928), ***The Waves*** (1931), and ***Between the Acts*** (1941)— which are very likely to become canonical. These days she is most widely known and read as the supposed founder of "feminist literary criticism," particularly in her polemical ***A Room of One's***

Own (1929) and *Three Guineas* (1938). Since I am not yet competent to judge feminist criticism, I will center here upon only one element in Woolf's feminist writing, her extraordinary love for and defense of reading.

Woolf's own literary criticism seems to me very mixed, especially in her judgment of contemporaries. To regard Joyce's *Ulysses* as a "disaster," or Lawrence's novels as lacking "the final power which makes things entire in themselves," is not what we expect from a critic as erudite and perceptive as Woolf. And yet one could argue that she was the most complete person of letters in England in our century. Her essays and novels expand the central traditions of English literature in ways that freshen beyond any possible reach of her polemics. The preface to *Orlando* begins by expressing a debt to Defoe, Sir Thomas Browne, Sterne, Sir Walter Scott, Lord Macaulay, Emily Brontë, DeQuincey, and Walter Pater, "to name the first that come to mind." Pater, the authentic precursor, or "absent father," as Perry Meisel calls him, might have headed the list, since *Orlando* is certainly the most Paterian narrative of our era. Like Oscar Wilde's and the young James Joyce's, Woolf's way of confronting and representing experience is altogether Paterian. But other influences are there as well, with Sterne perhaps the most crucial after Pater. Only Pater seems to have provoked Woolf to some anxiety; she very rarely mentions him and ascribes the model for her "moments of being" not to Pater's "privileged moments" or secularized epiphanies but rather oddly to Thomas Hardy, or to Joseph Conrad at his most Paterian. Perry Meisel has traced the intricate ways in which Pater's crucial metaphors inform both Woolf's fiction and her essays. It is an amiable irony that many of her professed followers tend to repudiate esthetic criteria for judgment, whereas Woolf herself founded her feminist politics upon her Paterian estheticism.

There may be other major writers of our century who loved reading as much as Woolf did, but no one since Hazlitt and Emerson has expressed that passion so memorably and usefully as she did. A room of one's own was required precisely for reading and writing in. I still treasure the old Penguin edition of *A Room of One's Own* that I purchased for ninepence in 1947, and I go on musing about the passage I marked there, which brings together Jane Austen and Shakespeare as a kind of wished-for, composite precursor:

> I wondered, would *Pride and Prejudice* have been a better novel if Jane Austen had not thought it

necessary to hide her manuscript from visitors? I read a page or two to see; but I could not find any signs that her circumstances had harmed her work in the slightest. That, perhaps, was the chief miracle about it. Here was a woman about the year 1800 writing without hate, without bitterness, without fear, without protest, without preaching. That was how Shakespeare wrote, I thought, looking at *Antony and Cleopatra*; and when people compare Shakespeare and Jane Austen, they may mean that the minds of both had consumed all impediments; and for that reason we do not know Jane Austen and we do not know Shakespeare, and for that reason Jane Austen pervades every word that she wrote, and so does Shakespeare. If Jane Austen suffered in any way from her circumstances it was in the narrowness of life that was imposed upon her. It was impossible for a woman to go about alone. She never travelled; she never drove through London in an omnibus or had luncheon in a shop by herself. But perhaps it was the nature of Jane Austen not to want what she had not. Her gift and her circumstances matched each other completely. But I doubt whether that was true of Charlotte Brontë, I said . . .

Was Woolf, in this respect, more like Austen or more like Charlotte Brontë? If we read *Three Guineas* with its prophetic fury against the patriarchy, we are not likely to decide that Woolf's mind had consumed all impediments; yet when we read *The Waves* or *Between the Acts* we may conclude that her gift and her circumstances matched each other completely. Are there two Woolfs, one the precursor of our current critical maenads, the other a more distinguished novelist than any woman at work since? I think not, although there are deep fissures in *A Room of One's Own*. Like Pater and like Nietzsche, Woolf is best described as an apocalyptic esthete, for whom human existence and the world are finally justified only as esthetic phenomena. As much as any writer ever, be it Emerson or Nietzsche or Pater, Virginia Woolf declines to attribute her sense of self to historical conditioning, even if that history is the endless exploitation of women by men. Her selves, to her, are as much her own creation as are *Orlando* and *Mrs. Dalloway,* and any close student of her criticism learns that she does not regard novels or poems or Shakespearean dramas as bourgeois mystifications or as "cultural capital." No more a religious believer than Pater or Freud, Woolf follows her estheticism to its outer limits, to the negativity of a pragmatic nihilism and of suicide. But she cared more for the romance of the journey than for its end, and she located what was best in life as her reading, her writing, and her conversations with friends, preoccupations not those of a zealot.

Will we ever again have novelists as original and superb as Austen, George Eliot, and Woolf, or a poet as extraordinary and intelligent as Dickinson? Half a century after Woolf's death, she has no rivals among women novelists or critics, though they enjoy the liberation she prophesied. As Woolf noted, if ever there has been Shakespeare's sister, it was Austen, who wrote two centuries ago. There are no social conditions or contexts that necessarily encourage the production of great literature, though we will be a long time learning this uncomfortable truth. We are not being flooded with instant masterpieces these days, as the passage of even a few years will show. No living American woman novelist, of whatever race or ideology, compares in esthetic eminence to Edith Wharton or to Willa Cather; nor have we a current poet within range of Marianne Moore or Elizabeth Bishop. The arts are simply not progressive, as Hazlitt noted in a wonderful fragment of 1814, where he remarks that "the principle of universal suffrage . . . is by no means applicable to matters of taste"; Woolf is Hazlitt's sister in sensibility, and her immense literary culture shares little with the current crusade mounted in her name.

* * *

It is difficult, at this time, to maintain any kind of balance or sense of proportion in writing about Woolf. Joyce's *Ulysses* and Lawrence's *Women in Love* would seem to be achievements well beyond even *To the Lighthouse* and *Between the Acts,* and yet many current partisans of Woolf would contest such a judgment. Woolf is a lyrical novelist: *The Waves* is more prose poem than novel, and *Orlando* is best where it largely forsakes narrative. Herself neither a Marxist nor a feminist, according to the informed testimony of her nephew and biographer, Quentin Bell, Woolf is nevertheless an Epicurean materialist, like her precursor Walter Pater. Reality for her flickers and wavers with every fresh perception and sensation, and ideas are shades that border her privileged moments.

Her feminism (to call it that) is potent and permanent precisely because it is less an idea or composite of ideas and more a formidable array of perceptions and sensations. Arguing with them is to sustain defeat: what she perceives and what she experiences by her sensibility is more finely organized than any response I can summon. Overwhelmed by her eloquence and her mastery of metaphor, I am unable—while I read it—to dispute *Three Guineas,* even where it makes me wince. Perhaps only Freud, in our century, rivals

Woolf as a stylist of tendentious prose. *A Room of One's Own* has a design on its reader, and so does *Civilization and Its Discontents,* but no awareness of the design will save the reader from being convinced while he or she undergoes the polemical magnificence of Freud and of Woolf. They are two very different models of persuasive splendor: Freud anticipates your objections and at least appears to answer them, while Woolf strongly insinuates that your disagreement with her urgency is founded upon imperceptiveness.

I am puzzled each time I reread *A Room of One's Own,* or even *Three Guineas,* as to how anyone could take these tracts as instances of "political theory," the genre invoked by literary feminists for whom Woolf's polemics have indeed assumed scriptural status. Perhaps Woolf would have been gratified, but it seems unlikely. Only by a persuasive redefinition of politics, one that reduced it to "academic politics," could these works be so classified; and Woolf was not an academic, nor would she be one now. Woolf is no more a radical political theorist than Kafka is a heretical theologian. They are writers and have no other covenant. The pleasures they give are difficult pleasures, which cannot be reduced to categorical judgments. I am moved, even awed, by Kafka's aphoristic circlings of "the indestructible," yet it is the resistance of "the indestructible" to interpretation that becomes what needs to be interpreted. What most requires interpretation in *A Room of One's Own* are its "irreconcilable habits of thought," as John Burt put it back in 1982.

Burt showed that the book presents both a "feminist" central argument—the patriarchy exploits women economically and socially in order to bolster its inadequate self-esteem—and a Romantic underargument. The underargument gives us women not as looking glasses for male narcissism but (Woolf says) as "some renewal of creative power which it is in the gift only of the opposite sex to bestow." This gift has been lost, Woolf adds, but not because of the depredations of the patriarchy. The First World War is the villain, but what then has happened to the book's overt argument? Was the Victorian Period the bad old days or the good old days?

Burt's summary seems to me eminently just:

> The two arguments of *A Room of One's Own* are not reconcilable, and any attempt to reconcile them can be no more than an exercise in special pleading. *A Room of One's Own,* however, is not an argument but, as Woolf proclaims in its opening pages, a portrayal of how a mind attempts to come to terms with its world.

Woolf comes to terms only as Pater and Nietzsche did: the world is reconceived esthetically. If *A Room of One's Own* is characteristic of Woolf, and it is, then it is almost as much a prose poem as *The Waves,* and as much a Utopian fantasy as *Orlando.* To read it as "cultural criticism" or "political theory" is possible only for those who have dismissed esthetic concerns altogether, or who have reserved reading for pleasure (difficult pleasure) for another time and place, where the wars between women and men, and between competing social classes, races, and religions, have ceased. Woolf herself made no such renunciation; as a novelist and literary critic she nurtured her sensibility, which included a strong propensity for comedy. Even the tracts are deliberately very funny, and thereby still more effective as polemics. To be solemn about Woolf, to analyze her as a political theorist and cultural critic, is to be not at all Woolfian.

Clearly this is an odd time in literary studies: D. H. Lawrence actually was a rather weird political theorist in *The Crown* essays, in his Mexican novel *The Plumed Serpent,* and his Australian *Kangaroo,* another Fascist fiction. No one would wish to substitute the political Lawrence, or the somewhat more interesting cultural moralist Lawrence, for the novelist of *The Rainbow* and *Women in Love.* Yet Woolf is now more often discussed as the author of *A Room of One's Own* than as the novelist who wrote *Mrs. Dalloway* and *To the Lighthouse. Orlando*'s current fame has nearly everything to do with the hero-heroine's sexual metamorphosis and owes very little to what most matters in the book: comedy, characterization, and an intense love of the major eras of English literature. I cannot think of another strong novelist who centers everything upon her extraordinary love of reading as Woolf does.

Her religion (no lesser word would be apt) was Paterian estheticism: the worship of art. As a belated acolyte of that waning faith, I am necessarily devoted to Woolf's fiction and criticism, and I therefore want to take up arms against her feminist followers, because I think they have mistaken their prophet. She would have had them battle for their rights, certainly, but hardly by devaluating the esthetic in their unholy alliance with academic pseudo-Marxists, French mock philosophers, and multicultural opponents of all intellectual standards whatsoever. By a room of one's own, she did not mean an academic department of one's own, but rather a context in which they could emulate her by writing fiction worthy of Sterne and Austen, and criticism commensurate

with that of Hazlitt and Pater. Woolf, the lover of the prose of Sir Thomas Browne, would have suffered acutely confronting the manifestos of those who assert that they write and teach in her name. Herself the last of the high esthetes, she has been swallowed up by remorseless Puritans, for whom the beautiful in literature is only another version of the cosmetics industry.

Of Shelley, whose spirit haunts her works, particularly in *The Waves,* Woolf observed that "his fight, valiant though it is, seems to be with monsters who are a little out of date and therefore slightly ridiculous." That seems true of Woolf's fight also: where are those Edwardian and Georgian patriarchs against whom she battled? Approaching millennium, we have been abandoned by the monsters of the patriarchy, though feminist critics labor at conjuring them up. Yet Shelley's greatness, as Woolf rightly saw, prevailed as "a state of being." The lyrical novelist, like the lyrical poet, abides now as the re-imaginer of certain extraordinary moments of being: "a space of pure calm, of intense and windless serenity."

Woolf's quest to reach that space was more Paterian than Shelleyan, if only because the erotic element in it was so much reduced. The image of heterosexual union never abandoned Shelley, though it turned demonic in his death poem, the ironically entitled *Triumph of Life.* Woolf is Paterian or belated Romantic, with the erotic drive largely translated into a sublimating estheticism. Her feminism once again cannot be distinguished from her estheticism; perhaps we should learn to speak of her "contemplative feminism," really a metaphorical stance. The freedom she seeks is both visionary and pragmatic and depends upon an idealized Bloomsbury, hardly translatable into contemporary American terms.

The Penguin American edition in which I first read *Orlando,* in the autumn of 1946, begins its back cover by saying, "No writer was ever born into a more felicitous environment." Woolf, like her feminist followers, would not have agreed with that judgment, but it possesses considerable truth nevertheless. It did not retard her development to have John Ruskin, Thomas Hardy, George Meredith, and Robert Louis Stevenson trooping through her father's house, or to count the Darwins and Stracheys among her relatives. And though her polemics urge otherwise, the intricately organized Virginia Stephen would have broken down even more often and thoroughly at Cambridge or Oxford, nor would she have received there the literary education provided for her by her father's library and by tutors as capable as Walter Pater's sister.

Her father, Leslie Stephen, was not the patriarchal ogre portrayed by her resentment, though one would not know this by reading many of our current feminist scholars. I am aware that they follow Woolf herself, for whom her father was a selfish and lonely egotist who could not surmount his own consciousness of failure as a philosopher. Her Leslie Stephen is the Mr. Ramsay of **To the Lighthouse,** a last Victorian who is more of a grandfather than a father to his children. But Leslie Stephen's particular difference from his daughter centers upon her estheticism and his empiricism and moralism, indeed his violent repudiation of the esthetic stance, including a virulent hatred for its great champion, Pater.

In reaction to her father, Woolf's estheticism and feminism (again, to call it that) were so fused that they could never again be pulled apart. Probably an ironic perspective is best these days in contemplating how Woolf's disciples have converted her purely literary culture into a political *Kulturkampf.* This transformation cannot work, because Woolf's most authentic prophecy was unwilled by her. No other twentieth-century person of letters shows us so clearly that our culture is doomed to remain a literary one in the absence of any ideology that has not been discredited. Religion, science, philosophy, politics, social movements: are these live birds in our hands or dead, stuffed birds on the shelf? When our conceptual modes abandon us, we return to literature, where cognition, perception, and sensation cannot be wholly disentangled. The flight from the esthetic is another symptom of our society's unconscious but purposeful forgetting of its dilemma, its slide toward another Theological Age. Whatever Woolf may have repressed at one time or another, it was never her esthetic sensibility.

That books are necessarily about other books and can represent experience only by first treating it as yet another book, is a limited but real truth. Certain works lift the limitation entirely: *Don Quixote* is one, and Woolf's **Orlando** another. The Don and Orlando are great readers, and only as such are surrogates for those obsessive readers, Cervantes and Woolf. In life history, Orlando is modeled upon Vita Sackville-West, with whom Woolf was, for a time, in love. But Sackville-West was a great gardener, a bad writer, and not exactly a reader of genius, as Woolf was. As aristocrat, as lover, even as writer, Orlando is Vita and not Virginia. It is as a critical consciousness, encountering English literature from Shakespeare to Thomas Hardy, that Orlando is the uncommon common reader, the author of his/her book.

All novels since *Don Quixote* rewrite Cervantes' universal masterwork, even when they are quite unaware of it. I cannot recall Woolf mentioning Cervantes anywhere, but that scarcely matters: Orlando is Quixotic, and so was Woolf. The comparison to *Don Quixote* is hardly fair to **Orlando**; a novel far more ambitious than, and as well-executed as, Woolf's playful love letter to Sackville-West would also be destroyed by the comparison. The Don lends himself endlessly to meditation, like Falstaff; Orlando certainly does not. But it helps to set Woolf against Cervantes in order to see that both books belong to Huizinga's order of play. The ironies of **Orlando** are Quixotic: they ensue from the critique that organized playfulness makes of both societal and natural reality. "Organized playfulness" in Woolf and Cervantes, in Orlando and the Don, is another name for the art of reading well, or in Woolf's case for "feminism," if you must have it so. Orlando is a man, or rather a youth, who suddenly becomes a woman. He is also an Elizabethan aristocrat who, with no more fuss made about it than about his sexual change, is pragmatically immortal. Orlando is sixteen when we meet him, thirty-six when we leave her, but those twenty years of literary biography span more than three centuries of literary history. The order of play, while it prevails, triumphs over time, and in Woolf's **Orlando** it persists without travail, which may be one reason why the book's one flaw is its too-happy conclusion.

Love, in **Orlando,** is always the love of reading, even when it is disguised as the love for a woman or for a man. The boy Orlando is the girl Virginia when he is represented in his primary role, as a reader:

> The taste for books was an early one. As a child he was sometimes found at midnight by a page still reading. They took his taper away and he bred glow-worms to serve his purpose. They took the glow-worms away, and he almost burnt the house down with a tinder. To put it in a nutshell, leaving the novelist to smooth out the crumpled silk and all its implications, he was a nobleman afflicted with a love of literature.

Orlando, like Woolf (and quite unlike Vita Sackville-West), is one of those people who substitute a phantom for an erotic reality. His/her two grand passions, for the improbable Russian princess, Sasha, and for the even more absurd sea captain, Marmaduke Bonthrop Shelmerdine, can best be regarded as solipsistic projections: there is really only one character in *Orlando*. Virginia Woolf's love of reading was both her authentic erotic drive and her secular theology. Nothing in *Orlando,* beautiful as the book is, equals the concluding paragraph of "How Should One Read a Book," the final essay in *The Second Common Reader*:

> Yet who reads to bring about an end however desirable? Are there not some pursuits that we practise because they are good in themselves, and some pleasures that are final? And is not this among them? I have sometimes dreamt, at least, that when the Day of Judgment dawns and the great conquerors and lawyers and statesmen come to receive their rewards—their crowns, their laurels, their names carved indelibly upon imperishable marble—the Almighty will turn to Peter and will say, not without a certain envy when He sees us coming with our books under our arms, "Look, these need no reward. We have nothing to give them here. They have loved reading."

Those first three sentences have been my credo ever since I read them in my childhood, and I urge them now upon myself, and all who still can rally to them. They do not preclude reading to obtain power, over oneself or over others, but only through a pleasure that is final, a difficult and authentic pleasure. Woolf's innocence, like Blake's, is an organized innocence, and her sense of reading is not the innocent myth of reading but the disinterestedness that Shakespeare teaches his deeper readers, Woolf included. Heaven, in Woolf's parables, bestows no reward to equal the blessedness of the common reader, or what Dr. Johnson called the common sense of readers. There is at last no other test for the canonical than the Shakespearean supreme pleasure of disinterestedness, the stance of Hamlet in act 5 and of Shakespeare himself in the most exalted moments of his sonnets.

Woolf has finer works than *Orlando,* but none more central to her than this erotic hymn to the pleasure of disinterested reading. The fable of dual sexuality is an intrinsic strand in that pleasure, whether in Woolf or in Shakespeare, or in Woolf's critical father, Walter Pater. Sexual anxiety blocks the deep pleasure of reading, and for Woolf, even in her love for Sackville-West, sexual anxiety was never far away. One senses that for Woolf, as for Walt Whitman, the homoerotic, though the natural mode, was largely impeded by solipsistic intensity. Woolf might have said with Whitman, "To touch my person to someone else's is about as much as I can stand." We don't believe in Orlando's raptures, whether with Sasha or with the sea captain, but we are persuaded by his/her passion for Shakespeare, Alexander Pope, and the possibil-

ity of a new literary work. *Orlando* may indeed be the longest love letter ever penned, but it is written by Woolf to herself. Implicitly, the book celebrates Woolf's preternatural strength as a reader and a writer. A healthy self-esteem, well earned by Woolf, finds its accurate release in this most exuberant of her novels.

Is Orlando a snob? In current parlance, that would be a "cultural elitist," but Woolf herself has a candid essay, "Am I a Snob?" that she read to the Memoir Club, a Bloomsbury gathering, in 1920. Its self-mockery clears away the charge, while containing a fine phrase characterizing the Stephens: "an intellectual family, very nobly born in a bookish sense." Orlando's family is certainly not intellectual, but there can be few descriptions of Orlando so clarifying as "very nobly born in a bookish sense." The bookish sense is the book; no one need look for an underplot in *Orlando*; there is no mother-daughter relationship hidden in this spoof of a story. Nor does Orlando love reading differently after he becomes a woman. It is the female Orlando whose estheticism becomes wonderfully aggressive and post-Christian:

> The poet's then is the highest office of all, she continued. His words reached where others fall short. A silly song of Shakespeare's has done more for the poor and the wicked than all the preachers and philanthropists in the world.

Disputable as that last sentence must be, Woolf stands behind it, in passion as well as humorously. What if we rewrite it slightly so as to fit our present moment: A silly song of Shakespeare's has done more for the poor and the wicked than all the Marxists and feminists in the world.

Orlando is not a polemic but a celebration that cultural decline has made into an elegy. It is a defense of poetry, "half laughing, half serious," as Woolf remarked in her diary. The joke that goes on too long is its own genre, which has never had a master to rival Cervantes—not even Sterne, who is an authentic presence in Woolf's novels. Don Quixote is far vaster than Orlando, yet even the Don cannot run away from Cervantes, as Falstaff perhaps got away from Shakespeare, and as Orlando, except for the book's weak conclusion, pulls away from Woolf. Neither Vita nor Virginia, Orlando becomes the personification of the esthetic stance, of what it means for the reader to be in love with literature. Soon such a passion may seem quaint or archaic, and *Orlando* will survive as its monument, a survival Woolf intended: "Indeed it is a difficult business—this time-keeping; nothing more quickly disorders it than contact with any of the arts; and it may have been her love of poetry that was to blame for making Orlando lose her shopping list."

Timekeeping, as in Sterne, is antithetical to the imagination, and we are not expected to ask, at the book's conclusion: Can Orlando ever die? In this mockery of a book, this holiday from reality, everything is shamanistic, and the central consciousness exemplifies a poetry without death. But what can that be? The novel astutely defines poetry as a voice answering a voice, but Woolf avoids emphasizing that the second voice is the voice of the dead. Determined for once to indulge herself as a writer, Woolf removes every possibility of anxiety from her story. Yet she does not know how there can be poetry without anxiety, nor do we. Shakespeare is a presence throughout **Orlando,** and we wonder how he can be there without introducing something problematic into the novel, something that must be resisted as an authority, since every kind of authority except the literary variety is put into question or mocked in the course of the book. Woolf's anxiety about Shakespeare's poetic authority is subtly handled in **Between the Acts** but evaded in **Orlando.** Yet the evasiveness belongs to what I have called the novel's shamanism; it works, as nearly everything does in this testament to the religion of poetry, to the exaltation of sensation and perception over everything else.

* * *

The idiosyncratic in Woolf, the enduring strangeness of her best fiction, is yet another instance of this surprisingly most canonical of all literary qualities. Orlando is unlike Woolf in supposedly transcending the quest for literary glory, but a holiday is a holiday, and Woolf was unrelenting in her quest to join herself to Sterne and to Hazlitt, to Austen and to the hidden paradigm, Pater. Her estheticism is her center, figured most richly in **A Room of One's Own** as a Shakespearean intimation that the art itself is nature: "Nature, in her most irrational mood, has traced in invisible ink on the walls of the mind a premonition which these great artists confirm; a sketch which only needs to be held to the fire of genius to become visible."

Personality, for Woolf as for Pater, is the highest fusion of art and nature and far exceeds society as the governing determination of the writer's life and work. At the conclusion of **To the Lighthouse,** the painter Lily Briscoe, Woolf's surrogate, looks at her canvas, finds it blurred, and "With a sudden intensity, as if she saw it clear for a second,

she drew a line there, in the centre. It was done, it was finished. Yes, she thought, laying down her brush in extreme fatigue, I have had my vision."

Perhaps a time yet will come when we will all find our current political stances archaic and superseded, and when Woolf's vision will be apprehended as what it most centrally was: the ecstasy of the privileged moment. How odd it would seem now if we spoke of "the politics of Walter Pater." It will seem odd then to speak of the politics, rather than the literary agon, of Virginia Woolf.

TITLE COMMENTARY

A Room of One's Own

ELLEN BAYUK ROSENMAN (ESSAY DATE 1995)

SOURCE: Rosenman, Ellen Bayuk. "Difficulties and Contradictions: The Blind Spots of *A Room of One's Own.*" In *"A Room of One's Own": Women Writers and the Politics of Creativity,* pp. 103-16. New York: Twayne, 1995.

In the following essay, Rosenman explicates inconsistencies in Woolf's thought at key points in A Room of One's Own, *suggesting that some of the central issues raised by the essay remain disputed.*

Thus far I have been taking **A Room of One's Own** at its word, explicating its intentions and presenting it as a coherent, persuasive whole. But the essay does present the reader with certain difficulties. At key points Woolf's thought is in conflict with itself, revealing ambivalence about some of the essay's central issues. It is no insult to suggest that some of the essay's issues remain unresolved or in dispute. To begin with, it is arguably the first feminist literary history, and we could hardly expect it to reflect the feminist thinking that would come after it. While what is often called the second wave of modern feminism, begun in the early 1970s, rescued the essay from obscurity, it has also brought new considerations to bear that Woolf's essay, not surprisingly, did not anticipate. Moreover, many of these issues are thorny ones. The idea of androgyny, for instance, has undergone considerable revision in the last 30 years, going in and out of fashion. The gaps between second-wave feminism and Woolf's essay, along with fluctations in recent feminist thinking, confirm her notion that intellectual and artistic labors are culturally conditioned and historically specific; they change over time as their contexts change. Finally, *A Room of One's Own* is one of Woolf's first political arguments. She is still in the process of working out and working through difficult issues. It makes sense to regard *A Room of One's Own* as a transitional work in which Woolf begins to divest herself of cultural beliefs about the transcendence of art—traces of which still color her thinking.

The most dramatic problem presented by *A Room of One's Own* is this: despite Woolf's insistence on a gender-specific tradition, she undercuts that notion in several ways. Two comments are widely quoted. One is about Mary Carmichael: "She wrote as a woman, but as a woman who has forgotten that she is a woman, so that her pages were full of that curious sexual quality which comes only when sex is unconscious of itself" (93). What can Woolf mean by this? Why is the path to womanhood unconscious of gender? This is an odd assertion in an argument that takes gender identity so seriously and sees its characteristics as socially constructed. Does Woolf assume that there is an innate femininity lodged in the unconscious that can only be retrieved through forgetfulness? We might wonder, too, what value her own book would have according to this quotation. So much of its purpose is to clarify women's consciousness of their sex and to undo repression. Should the woman writer then forget what she has learned, hoping that her unconscious has somehow assimilated this knowledge and will give it back to her in a more artistic form, without her being aware of it? My questions are meant to suggest how difficult it is to reconcile this passage with the very conscious emphasis on gender in Woolf's essay. Surely no one would imagine that *A Room of One's Own* was written by someone who had forgotten she was a woman.

A second, similar passage occurs toward the end of the essay, its importance underlined by the fact that it is the "very first sentence" that the narrator plans to write on the subject "Women and Fiction": "It is fatal for a woman to lay the least stress on any grievance; to plead even with justice any cause; in any way to speak consciously as a woman. And fatal is no figure of speech; for anything written with that conscious bias is doomed to death" (104). Once again the writer is advised to be unconscious, although perhaps in a more narrow way. In this sentence, to speak consciously as a woman is to express a grievance. Perhaps we can interpret this as a rejection of polemic: Woolf does not want women writers to make speeches in their novels. But her essay often demonstrates the difficulty of *not* laying stress on

a grievance and the unhealthy role of repression in maintaining equanimity.

We recall that the narrator avoids a sense of grievance at Oxbridge by internalizing injunctions against women's presence: having been banished from the grass and the library, she has "no wish" to enter the chapel (8). But this lack of desire is a dead end: she has simply acquiesced to patriarchal prohibitions—an act that would hardly free her to write without being conscious of her sex. Throughout much of *A Room of One's Own*, to be a woman is to be aggrieved, and with good reason. How do we judge the works of the women writers Woolf discusses, almost all of whom express anger at their plight? Are they all "doomed to death," unable to "grow in the minds of others" (104), as Woolf claims? Has only Jane Austen survived?

When Woolf introduces "conscious bias" into the passage she further complicates the issue. These terms are not equal; there is a slippage between consciousness of a particular identity, grievance "with justice," and bias. Gender identity, with its distinctive perspective, has degenerated into a distorted perception. Ironically, in this passage Woolf seems guilty of the same kind of misreading that patriarchy has always given women, as when the redoubtable Desmond MacCarthy calls Rebecca West "that arrant feminist" for saying that men are snobs—which Woolf calmly characterizes as "a possibly true if uncomplimentary statement about the other sex" (35). In this kind of misreading, women's protests against male authority are conveniently dismissed as hysterical, distorted, dogmatic, and self-serving. Women's focus on their own experience, including their grievances, is a kind of special pleading, while men's protests against women, in contrast, take on the status of fact. Having deconstructed the notion of objectivity in the British Museum chapter, Woolf seems to reintroduce it in this passage as an appropriate criterion for women's writing.

From these passages it seems clear that Woolf cannot completely divest herself of a belief in the value of transcendence in art even in the face of her more sustained gender-specific and materialist assumptions. In part, Woolf's aesthetic tastes underwrote this contradictory belief. In the essay **"Modern Fiction"** she praises the Russian writers as "spiritualists" rather than "materialists" (the label she gave her antagonist Arnold Bennett), because they capture "life or spirit, truth or reality" rather than focusing on the physical and historical details of their stories and characters.[1] According to Woolf, spiritualists reject the depiction of the lives of people as they are embedded in a particular society and focus instead on more abstract philosophical questions: Does life have meaning? What makes us human? Of what does spiritual life consist? In the essay Woolf imagines a kind of primordial state of consciousness that is articulated into lived experience: "The mind receives a myriad of impressions—trivial, fantastic, evanescent, or engraved with the sharpness of steel. From all sides they come, an incessant shower of innumerable atoms; and as they fall, . . . they shape themselves into the life of Monday or Tuesday" (154).

As a novelist, particularly in the period before the publication of *A Room of One's Own,* Woolf obviously attempts to capture the shower of atoms and lets the life of Monday or Tuesday recede into the background—or, rather, she shows the process by which they shape themselves into the particularities of time, place, and individual experience. Woolf's love of the Russian novelists and her own philosophy as expressed here derive from a search for what transcends the here and now.

This viewpoint is clearly at odds with a focus on anything as specific as gender identity as historically constituted. The desire for transcendence runs as an undercurrent throughout *A Room of One's Own.* In her ideal representations of creativity, Woolf frequently uses metaphors of light. When she describes the inspirational effects of the Oxbridge meal, I have said that these metaphors point back to embodied experience. Elsewhere, however, their intangibility suggests a desire to escape from material life. Shakespeare, the ideal artist, is "incandescent" (56); his mind has consumed all impediments to a kind of perfect impersonality, much like that which T. S. Eliot describes in "Tradition and the Individual Talent." The "fire of genius" and the "inner light" that produce and discern great art are also part of the vocabulary of disembodied creativity (72).

Woolf likens the works of "these great artists" to messages written in invisible ink that become clear when held to the light. Somehow they contain what every reader has "felt and known and desired" (72). In place of a distinctive perspective Woolf posits a universal wisdom; in place of the broken sentence and sequence of Mary Carmichael's novel she envisions a kind of ur-truth that is perfectly, wonderfully, and almost mystically intelligible because it is, in some sense, already known, as if it were part of the human genetic code. The narrator's struggles with Mary's novel, her groping attempts to decide whether the novel is original or merely clumsy, drop out of sight. One might argue that Mary's novel has not attained the ideal of great art, otherwise it, too, would evoke this magical response, but Woolf works with an entirely different set of assumptions in these two versions of reading.

The invisibility of the ink suggests the degree to which Woolf's ideal leans toward a disembodied, ahistorical, transcendent version of art, represented as a private, esoteric transaction between writer and reader. On the other hand,

Mary Carmichael's authorship, figured in the female rider taking a fence in a crowd of patriarchs, is thoroughly grounded in gender, history, the body, and society. It is not that Mary Carmichael's novel is not as good; it is that Woolf has changed the rules. Thinking of Milton's bogey and of Charles Lamb's incredulity that *Lycidas* was a product of fallible human effort rather than divine inspiration, one wonders whether even the greatest author can blot a line in invisible ink and still work his magic.

With these considerations in mind, it is interesting to return to one example of distorted women's writing—Charlotte Brontë's *Jane Eyre*—because the issue of anger presents another conflict between Woolf's transcendent and materialist beliefs. The narrator criticizes Brontë for allowing her anger to show; because of this slip, her novel is not the incandescent work it ought to be. We might question, however, whether this criticism is too simple, for the narrator's own anger was an important source of insight for her in the British Museum. While Woolf's disappointment with Brontë seems genuine, we should also be alert to the possibility of reading these awkward breaks in a different way. Rather than being only technical flaws, perhaps they are also gateways to a distinctively female point of view. The narrator complains about the "jerk" in the novel when Jane delivers an extended speech about women's need for freedom and hears the laugh that she thinks is the servant Grace Poole's but really belongs to Rochester's mad wife, Bertha, whom he has imprisoned in his house (69). The narrator says that "the continuity is disturbed" by this "awkward break"; Jane's speech has run away with Brontë because it expresses her own grievance about her narrow life, and she must wrest her narrative back on track (69). In constructing this passage Woolf assumes that there is no connection between Jane's speech and the laugh, but, even granting room for the possibility of different interpretations, we might still suggest that Woolf has missed the point of the passage.

In fact, as Sandra Gilbert and Susan Gubar (1979, 349) have argued, the juxtaposition of Jane's speech and Bertha's laugh is thematically crucial; it contrasts the young girl's articulate but naive dreams of freedom with the sardonic and inarticulate yet powerful comment by the incarcerated mad wife, whose place Jane will shortly be asked to take when Rochester proposes. Brontë's "jerk" sharpens the irony of their relationship as both foils and doubles of each other. *Jane Eyre* is very much a cover story, like *A Room of One's Own*, encoding subversive messages about patriarchy and marriage in the figure of the mad wife. It is perhaps unfair to expect Woolf to deliver a particular interpretation of a novel, but it is certainly ironic that Woolf proves her own point with a critical lapse: she has missed the significance of the passage in *Jane Eyre* precisely because Brontë has disturbed the continuity or, to use Woolf's expression, has broken the sequence. Perhaps Woolf was distracted by the vexing issue of anger that the passage from *Jane Eyre* clearly represents, both in Jane's resentment and Bertha's madness. In any case, her insistence on an art free from grievance has led her to misread a now-classic example of women's writing as technically flawed rather than formally and ideologically meaningful.

Woolf's treatment of *Jane Eyre* obliquely and perhaps inadvertently suggests this. Woolf quotes Jane's angry speech at such length that its point commands our attention; in a sense, Woolf turns the stage over to Jane's anger even though she criticizes it. As Mary Jacobus says, this passage "opens up a rift in her own [Woolf's] seamless web. What she herself cannot say without a loss of calmness (rage has been banned in the interests of literature) is uttered instead by another woman writer. The overflow in *Jane Eyre* washes into *A Room of One's Own.*"[2] Jacobus implies that Woolf's ambivalence about female anger acts itself out in this passage: She displays Jane's outburst as a covert way of expressing the resentments of the female writer without leaving herself open to charges of personal grievance. As is often the case in this essay, it is difficult to reduce Woolf's "real" point of view to a single attitude. The essay suggests both that Brontë's anger disfigures her writing and that anger is a legitimate, essential source of female self-expression.

This conflict was very much on Woolf's mind as she wrote the essay. On the one hand, writing *A Room of One's Own* was therapeutic for her: "I seem able to write criticism fearlessly. Because of a R. of ones Own I said suddenly to myself last night" (*Diary*, 4: 25). This comment implies that Woolf does not need to disguise her opinions or her emotions. At the same time, the multilayered, allusive narrative also protected Woolf from sensitive material. In a letter to a close friend she writes, "I'm so glad you thought it good tempered—my blood is apt to boil on this one subject . . . and I didn't want it to" (*Letters*, 4: 106). She worried that "if I had said 'Look here, I am uneducated because my brothers used all the family funds'—which is a fact—'Well,' they'd have said, 'she has an axe to grind.'"[3] Woolf explained that she "forced myself to keep my own figure fictitious, legendary," to avoid the charge of personal grievance.[4] Woolf's ceremony of investiture is not entirely symbolic; as a woman writer she shares the conflicts of her narrator.

While Woolf may have legitimate reason to fear expressing anger, her desire to mask her boiling blood beneath a good-tempered facade smacks of the advice of the Angel in the House. The essay's ambiguous use of anger as the source of both artistic blemishes and political insight reflects Woolf's ambivalence about her uncensored self-expression. While Woolf's "I" at the end of the essay has presumably worked through all the issues of the preceding pages, the issue of anger and writing remained unresolved for Virginia Woolf herself. Her sophisticated narrative succeeds perhaps too well in pulling its punches, as contemporary reviews that praise its charm and lightness suggest. Woolf encodes her own anger so completely that it almost disappears, fictionalized and absorbed into the narrator. *A Room of One's Own* can be seen as Woolf's own cover story, distancing her from dangerous material and deflecting her uneasiness as a politicized woman writer into a series of stories about dead and imaginary writers. Given Woolf's fame as a writer, we might regard this phenomenon as a testimony to the power of her insights. If a writer of her stature fears exposure, how might lesser writers feel?

Probably the most controversial aspect of *A Room of One's Own* is its treatment of androgyny—a subject related to the tension between the materialist and transcendent threads in Woolf's argument. Woolf describes an androgynous mind that is more complete and resourceful than a purely masculine or feminine one. While the biological sex determines the dominant gender of the mind, the mind ideally consists of male and female halves. Woolf does not trace out her idea systematically, so it is difficult to tell exactly what she has in mind. Given the unflattering portrait of the masculine mind in her discussion of Kipling, we might wonder what would happen when it meets with its feminine counterpart. Will the mind then be composed of masculinity plus femininity—two self-contained entities that will interact productively with each other? How would such opposites interact except in conflict? Or would each gender dilute the other, so that rather than have "the Flag" on one side of the mind and "Anon" on the other, the androgyne would speak with an assertive but flexible, empathic voice. The generality of Woolf's vi-

sion has left the essay subject to reevaluation according to changing perceptions of androgyny. Whether her vision perpetuates the reified gender categories of masculine and feminine or attempts to create a new identity has been at issue since the second wave of feminism recovered the essay in the first place.

Whether the essay is conservative or radical in its formulation of androgyny, the very presence of the idea runs counter to much of Woolf's argument. Having spent so much time and effort constructing a distinctively female style, self, and tradition, she seems to demote such achievements as provisional and imperfect when she promotes a selfhood that goes "beyond" female identity, which is subsumed in the androgynous ideal. Woolf's notion of a single-sex artistic creation as "a horrid little abortion," like her comment that gender consciousness is fatal, flies in the face of her valorization of women's writing (103). One wonders whether Jane Austen, that exemplary inventor of the female sentence, would pass the test of androgyny. Like the passage about the fatality of sex-consciousness, this one is hyperbolic enough to raise a question in the reader's mind about what is at stake. Woolf's strong language seems designed, perhaps unconsciously, to compromise her feminist leanings, to dilute her emphasis on the particularities of gender and creativity. Although the placement of her comments on androgyny toward the end of the book suggests that it represents the culmination of her thinking, it deflects her emphasis on women into a different argument altogether.

Woolf's treatment of androgyny raises other questions as well. In its emphasis on mental faculties, it also erases the body. It disconnects the "nerves that feed the brain" and the gendered body from the imagination, now composed of abstract properties that enter into a mysterious communion (78). Even Judith Shakespeare, prisoner of her body in life, undergoes a sublimation in death, when she is transmuted into a mystical body that women writers bring into being with their achievements. Both Judith Shakespeare's corporeal body and the actual bodies of future women writers disappear beneath the symbolic weight of such a mystical incarnation. It is as if this is the only resolution Woolf can find to the female body's vulnerability, despite her insistence that it forms the foundation of women's authorship. Because of the cultural meanings that are deeply inscribed within it, the body remains an ambiguous source of inspiration. Woolf must insist on its reality, both to retrieve women from

Victorian stereotypes of purity and to undo women's oppression. At the same time, however, the body remains haunted by disability and danger, and Woolf longs to escape from its complications. The book's final image, of the woman writer putting on and taking off the body of Judith Shakespeare, figures the essay's vacillation between embodiment and transcendence.

Woolf's construction of androgyny also has the disquieting effect of exalting heterosexual relations. A surprising vision inaugurates the section: a man and a woman enter a taxicab together, prompting the narrator to observe, "One has a profound, if irrational, instinct in favour of the theory that the union of man and woman makes for the greatest satisfaction, the most complete happiness" (98). However one might feel about this instinct in one's own life, it is difficult to reconcile with the unions of men and women that appear in the essay: authoritarian fathers and rebellious daughters; cavalier theater managers and their pregnant, despairing mistresses; selfish kings and their discarded—if not beheaded—wives. The language of the androgyny passage relies heavily on metaphors of sexuality, childbirth, and marriage—hardly instances of female happiness throughout the essay. In the face of the image that comes to the narrator's mind in the previous chapter—that of a middle-aged woman and her elderly mother—it is disappointingly conventional in terms of both narrative and politics. We are back to "boy meets girl." The image is also conventional in relation to the subtext of lesbianism. One wonders how Woolf's writing of *Orlando,* inspired by her lover Vita Sackville-West, or the writing she did with Sackville-West's advice and encouragement could find a place in this theory of creativity.

Above the conflicts and inequities of the real world, the androgynous mind withdraws to "celebrate its nuptials in darkness" (104). Woolf imagines this mental life as magically exempt from patriarchy, a consummation of the taxicab scene and the narrator's belief that, despite its part in the oppression of women, heterosexuality is best after all. Perhaps, like the mystical body of Judith Shakespeare, these nighttime nuptials represent an attempted resolution as well as a contradiction, transposing heterosexuality into an abstract and imaginative power in order to rescue it from its dangerous, even fatal, consequences for women. It may also be exactly what Woolf says it is: "a profound if irrational" investment in the

very social structures she sets out to criticize, reminding us how difficult it is to think of one's self out of one's culture.

Critics have raised two other significant objections to *A Room of One's Own,* both of which reflect changing ideas in contemporary literary criticism. First, it has been argued that Woolf's depiction of a female literary tradition is inaccurate and incomplete. No one could fault Woolf for not knowing about women authors and varieties of female experience that were unknown in her age, of course. The problem is that Woolf's essay has been so influential that it has shaped modern accounts of women's writing even in the face of contradictory evidence. Woolf tells a story of women's literature that consists of little but silence and suffering through the Renaissance; that barely begins until the eighteenth century, with Aphra Behn; and that posits an evolution in women's writing that depends in part on very specific criteria, such as commercial publication, the use of particular genres such as the novel, and public success.

According to Margaret Ezell, these assumptions are difficult to maintain in the light of modern scholarship.[5] For one thing, efforts to recover women writers before the eighteenth century have succeeded beyond Woolf's imagination, although contemporary collections such as *The Norton Anthology of Literature by Women* continue to regard earlier periods as relative wastelands of women's literature.[6] For another, Ezell argues, earlier women writers were prolific practitioners of forms such as religious essays, advice books, and prophetic writings, along with the diaries and letters that Woolf acknowledges, and that these forms had more prestige in their era than in ours. Imposing twentieth-century notions of which genres "count" is anachronistic. And even if these kinds of writing never enjoyed the status of the epic poem, we might still question the wisdom of applying a traditional hierarchy of importance to women's writing given Woolf's emphasis on difference. To judge it by the same standards is to misread it.

Woolf's essays on traditionally "minor" women authors as well as *A Room of One's Own* betray an allegiance to conventional standards, even as they set out to revise them. Woolf's ambivalence about figures such as the Duchess of Newcastle or Lady Winchilsea suggests that, while she wishes to acknowledge female achievement wherever it appears, she remains uneasy about promoting work that has traditionally been considered second-rate. As one critic says, "Woolf's own excavations [of forgotten women writers] were marked by a cultural wariness of and palpable disdain for 'minor' literary achievements."[7]

Moreover, Ezell, argues, many women writers of the Renaissance wrote poetry for circulation among a coterie of intellectuals and not for publication as we know it, just as their male counterparts did. In such circles manuscripts, not publications, are the index of achievement. Because Woolf focused on writing as a means of economic empowerment, she may have been less open to the value of other, less professionalized contexts for writing. She may also have underestimated the extent to which these women participated in literary culture. Judith Shakespeare may not be entirely representative of women writers in the Renaissance, isolated and silenced. Ironically, according to Ezell, because *A Room of One's Own* has achieved such fame, it has carried more authority than it deserves in shaping our modern understanding of women's writing in the past.

Finally, and extremely important, is the critique that women of color have made of Woolf. Woolf's inspiring model of a coherent, collective female voice, symbolized by Judith Shakespeare, has also effaced difference. Once again the point is not to blame Woolf for her failure to anticipate changes in modern feminist criticism but to note the ways in which the blind spots of this influential essay have moved others to continue its project of re-vision. Woolf herself may have been a powerful foremother for some writers, but her economic, class, and racial privilege make her a problematic ancestor for writers of different backgrounds. Woolf's critique of Empire has not erased all traces of racism, for example. When she praises women for not wishing to make an Englishwoman out of a "very fine negress," she implies that her reader is white and the Negress remains other—perhaps already commodified by the adjective "fine," often applied to the accoutrements of expensive living, such as fine wine and fine china.[8] While Woolf's woman writer might not want to colonize the black woman, neither does she identify with her. The flexible selfhood of women writers does not, apparently, extend to other races.

The African-American writer Alice Walker, author of *The Color Purple,* addresses this difficulty in her famous essay "In Search of Our Mothers' Gardens." In many ways Walker's essay deliberately parallels Woolf's. Walker also seeks female creativity in unusual places in order to connect her artistic aspirations with the past. Like Woolf, Walker reevaluates forgotten women, including

her own mother, whose gardens were the envy of everyone who saw them. Walker quotes *A Room of One's Own* directly, showing her sense of inheritance from Woolf as a woman writer and historian of creativity. At the same time, however, she revises Woolf's text by inserting her own race-specific additions. Considering the case of Phillis Wheatley, the eighteenth-century African-American poet, she writes,

> Virginia Woolf wrote further, speaking of course not of our Phillis, that "any woman born with a great gift in the sixteenth century [insert "eighteenth-century," insert "black woman," insert "born or made a slave"] would certainly have gone crazed. . . . For it needs little skill and psychology to be sure that a highly gifted girl who had tried to use her gift for poetry would have been so thwarted and hindered by contrary instincts [add "chains, guns, the lash, ownership of one's body by someone else, submission to an alien religion"], that she must have lost her health and sanity to a certainty."[9]

With these insertions, Walker tells the story of the African-American woman writer, whose experience in slavery intensifies and alters the dynamics of oppression and repression that Woolf describes. There will be both common ground and divergence in the experiences of black and white women writers. Woolf argues that male standards have masqueraded as universal ones and that they leave out the story of women writers. Walker says that the standards of white women have masqueraded as universal ones for women, absorbing or marginalizing the works of African-American women just as British patriarchy silences women. Ironically, we find Virginia Woolf in the position of Arthur Quiller-Couch, arguing for an expanded understanding of the material conditions of creativity but leaving out a significant set of voices and experiences because of her own blind spot.

Thus while Woolf's essay has been deeply influential and is frequently cited as a classic text of feminist thought, it continues to inspire discussion and controversy. The essay's fame makes it worth fighting over, and with. It remains a text to be reckoned with, whatever its contradictions and blind spots. In many ways *A Room of One's Own* has set the agenda for modern feminist criticism. Therefore it is continually renewed, not by some mystical force that annoints masterpieces but by the sustained interest its historical significance provokes for women, and men, who enter the conversation from their own points of view and social positions.

Notes

1. "Modern Fiction," in *The Common Reader* (1925; New York: Harcourt, Brace, Jovanovich, 1953), 153; hereafter cited in text.

2. Mary Jacobus, *Reading Women: Essays in Feminist Criticism* (New York: Columbia University Press, 1986), 35.

3. Christopher St. John, *Ethyl Smyth* (London: Longmans Green, 1959), 229, 230; quoted in Jane Marcus, *Art and Anger: Reading Like a Woman* (Columbus: Ohio State University Press, 1988), 112-13.

4. Jane Marcus, "'No More Horses,'" in *Art and Anger*, 113.

5. Margaret J. M. Ezell, "The Myth of Judith Shakespeare: Creating the Canon of Women's Literature," *New Literary History: A Journal of Theory and Interpretation* 21 (1990): 579-92.

6. *The Norton Anthology of Literature by Women: The Tradition in English*, ed. Sandra Gilbert and Susan Gubar (New York: W. W. Norton, 1985).

7. Bradford K. Mudge, "Burning Down the House: Sara Coleridge, Virginia Woolf, and the Politics of Literary Revision," *Tulsa Studies in Women's Literature* 5 (1986): 231.

8. Elizabeth Abel, "Matrilineage and the Racial 'Other': Woolf and Her Literary Daughters of the Second Wave," paper read at the Third Annual Virginia Woolf Conference, Jefferson City, Mo., 13 June 1993.

9. Alice Walker, "In Search of Our Mothers' Gardens," in *In Search of Our Mothers' Gardens* (New York: Harcourt, Brace, Jovanovich, 1983), 235; my ellipses.

FURTHER READING

Bibliographies

Kirkpatrick, B. J. *A Bibliography of Virginia Woolf, 4th Edition.* Oxford: Clarendon Press, 1997, 472 p.

Updates the 1967 edition, reflecting the release of numerous diaries, drafts, and papers after the death of Leonard Woolf in 1969.

Majumdar, Robin. *Virginia Woolf: An Annotated Bibliography of Criticism.* New York: Garland, 1976, 118 p.

Comprehensive guide to Woolfian criticism, including books, articles, essays, and chapters on Woolf, introductions and prefaces to her works, memoirs and obituaries, correspondence, reviews of Woolf's works, miscellaneous references to Woolf in general studies, and additional bibliographical sources.

Biographies

Bell, Quentin. *Virginia Woolf: A Biography.* London: Hogarth Press, 1972, 314 p.

Recalls Woolf's life from the perspective of her nephew, whom some critics have considered biased against Woolf in deference to her sister, Bell's mother.

Black, Naomi. "Virginia Woolf and the Women's Movement." In *Virginia Woolf: A Feminist Slant*, edited by Jane Marcus, pp. 180-97. Lincoln: University of Nebraska Press, 1983.

Focuses on the significance of Three Guineas *to the evolution of Woolf's feminist writings and her participation in the women's movement.*

Caws, Mary Ann. *Virginia Woolf.* London: Penguin, 2001, 136 p.

Biography of Woolf.

DeSalvo, Louise. *Virginia Woolf : The Impact of Childhood Sexual Abuse on Her Life and Work.* Boston: Beacon Press, 1989, 372 p.

Biographical study of Woolf's early life and analysis of her career.

Gordon, Lyndall. *Virginia Woolf, A Writer's Life.* New York: Norton, 1984, 341 p.

Provides interpretations of early life experiences shaping Woolf's writing career.

Gorsky, Susan Rubinow. *Virginia Woolf: Revised Edition.* Boston: Twayne, 1989, 150 p.

Studies Woolf's life and work in light of post-1979 scholarship and additional volumes of previously unpublished diaries, letters, fiction, and essays written by Woolf.

Leaska, Mitchell. *Granite and Rainbow: The Hidden Life of Virginia Woolf.* New York: Farrar, Straus, Giroux, 1998, 513 p.

Studies Woolf's life.

Lee, Hermione. *Virginia Woolf.* London: Chatto & Windus, 1996, 892 p.

A highly praised biography examining details of Woolf's life and career often overlooked in other biographies.

Marder, Herbert. *The Measure of Life: Virginia Woolf's Last Years.* Ithaca, N.Y.: Cornell University Press, 2000, 418 p.

Biographical examination of Woolf's later years.

Reid, Panthea. *Art and Affection : A Life of Virginia Woolf.* New York: Oxford University Press, 1996, 570 p.

Highly regarded biography of Woolf examining her early life experiences, and providing psychological grounding for her artistic choices in her work.

Criticism

Allan, Tuzyline Jita. "*Mrs. Dalloway*: A Study of Woolf's Social Ambivalence." In *Womanist and Feminist Aesthetics: A Comparative Review*, pp. 19-44. Athens: Ohio University Press, 1995.

Examines Mrs. Dalloway *in terms of a dialectic between condemnation of and support for institutions of patriarchal domination that informs Woolf's feminist ideals on one hand and her upper-class literary and material privileges on the other.*

Blain, Virginia. "Narrative Voice and the Female Perspective in Virginia Woolf's Early Novels." In *Virginia Woolf: New Critical Essays*, edited by Patricia Clements and Isobel Grundy, pp. 115-36. London: Vision Press, 1983.

Explores the "intellectually unashamed female perspective" of Woolf's early fiction, concentrating on stylistic devices and narrative techniques in terms of gender differences.

Bowlby, Rachel. "'We're Getting There': Woolf, Trains and the Destinations of Feminist Criticism." In *Feminist Destinations and Further Essays on Virginia Woolf*, pp. 3-15. Edinburgh: Edinburgh University Press, 1997.

An essay originally published in 1988 relating the overt concerns with representation and sexual difference in "Mr. Bennett and Mrs. Brown" to the principal issues of contemporary feminist criticism.

Goldman, Jane. *The Feminist Aesthetics of Virginia Woolf: Modernism, Post-Impressionism and the Politics of the Visual.* Cambridge: Cambridge University Press, 1998, 243 p.

Discusses the feminist implications of the aesthetics informing Woolf's writing career with respect to the influences of suffrage art and the English Post-Impressionist movement.

Harrison, Suzan. *Eudora Welty and Virginia Woolf: Gender, Genre, and Influence.* Baton Rouge: Louisiana State University Press, 1997, 158 p.

Compares the symbols, motifs, themes, and narrative strategies of American novelist Eudora Welty with those of Woolf.

Jackson, Bev. "'A Vicious and Corrupt Word': Feminism and Virginia Woolf." *Dutch Quarterly Review of Anglo-American Letters* 17, no. 4 (1987): 249-61.

Summarizes conflicting views of Woolf's critique of the word "feminist" in Three Guineas *in terms of contemporary feminist literary theories and practices.*

Jacobus, Mary. "Reading Woman (Reading)." In *Reading Woman: Essays in Feminist Criticism*, pp. 3-24. New York, N.Y.: Columbia University Press, 1986.

Discussion of feminist literary interpretation as it relates to Woolf's Orlando.

Little, Judy. "Virginia Woolf: Myth and Manner in the Early Novels" and "The Politics of Holiday: Woolf's Later Novels." In *Comedy and the Woman Writer: Woolf, Spark, and Feminism*, pp. 22-65, 66-98. Lincoln: University of Nebraska Press, 1983.

Investigates the subversive nature of the comic imagery in Woolf's novels, contrasting their narrative function with that of traditional comic forms.

Marcus, Jane. "Thinking Back through Our Mothers." In *Art & Anger: Reading Like A Woman*, pp. 73-100. Columbus: Ohio State University Press, 1988.

Surveys Woolf's oeuvre within the context of female artistic and socialist predecessors, paying particular attention to their influence upon the feminist concerns of "A Society," A Room of One's Own, *and* Three Guineas.

Maze, John R. "*Mrs. Dalloway*—A Questionable Sanity." In *Virginia Woolf: Feminism, Creativity, and the Unconscious*, pp. 61-84. Westport, Conn.: Greenwood Press, 1997.

Compares and contrasts the characterizations of Clarissa Dalloway and Septimus Smith in Mrs. Dalloway *with respect to conventional distinctions between sanity and insanity.*

Muller, Herbert J. "Virginia Woolf, and Feminine Fiction." In *Critical Essays on Virginia Woolf*, edited by Morris Beja, pp. 29-37. Boston: G. K. Hall, 1985.

Originally published in 1937, an essay evaluating the strengths and weaknesses of Woolf's literary methods and materials, leading to an overall assessment of "feminine fiction."

Olano, Pamela J. "'Women Alone Stir My Imagination': Intertextual Eroticism in the Friendships/Relationships Created by Virginia Woolf." In *Communication and Women's Friendships: Parallels and Intersections in Literature and Life*, edited by Janet Doubler Ward and JoAnna Stephens Mink, pp. 45-63. Bowling Green, Ohio: Bowling Green State University Popular Press, 1993.

Discusses Woolf's perception of sexual differences between genders and the centrality of female companionship in her life.

Ratcliffe, Krista. "Minting the Fourth Guinea: Virginia Woolf." In *Anglo-American Feminist Challenges to the Rhetorical Traditions*, pp. 32-64. Carbondale: Southern Illinois University Press, 1996.

Speculates on Woolf's contributions to rhetorical history, theory, and practice by examining her critiques of women, language, and culture as well as her own writing strategies.

Rigney, Barbara Hill. "Objects of Vision: Women as Art in the Novels of Virginia Woolf." In *Critical Essays on Virginia Woolf*, edited by Morris Beja, pp. 239-47. Boston: G. K. Hall, 1985.

Analyzes the formation of the subjectivities and identities of various female characters in Woolf's fiction in terms of traditionally male definitions of beauty.

OTHER SOURCES FROM GALE:

Additional coverage of Woolf's life and career is contained in the following sources published by the Gale Group: *Authors and Artists for Young Adults*, Vol. 44; *Beacham's Encyclopedia of Popular Fiction: Biography and Resources*, Vol. 3; *British Writers*, Vol. 7; *British Writers: The Classics*, Vol. 2; *British Writers Retrospective Supplement*, Vol. 1; *Concise Dictionary of British Literary Biography, 1914-1945*; *Contemporary Authors*, Vols. 104, 130; *Contemporary Authors New Revision Series*, Vol. 64; *Dictionary of Literary Biography*, Vols. 36, 100, 162; *Dictionary of Literary Biography Documentary Series*, Vol. 10; *DISCovering Authors*; *DISCovering Authors: British Edition*; *DISCovering Authors: Canadian Edition*; *DISCovering Authors Modules: Most-studied, Novelists*; *DISCovering Authors 3.0*; *Encyclopedia of World Literature in the 20th Century*, Ed. 3; *Exploring Short Stories*; *Feminist Writers*; *Literary Movements for Students*, Vol. 2; *Literature and Its Times*, Vol. 3; *Literature and Its Times Supplement*, Ed. 1; *Literature Resource Center*; *Major 20th-Century Writers*, Eds. 1, 2; *Nonfiction Classics for Students*, Vol. 2; *Novels for Students*, Vols. 8, 12; *Reference Guide to English Literature*, Ed. 2; *Reference Guide to Short Fiction*, Ed. 2; *Short Stories for Students*, Vols. 4, 12; *Short Story Criticism*, Vol. 7; *Twayne's English Authors*; *Twentieth-Century Literary Criticism*, Vols. 1, 5, 20, 43, 56, 101, 123, 128; *World Literature and Its Times*, Vol. 4; and *World Literature Criticism*.

INDEXES

The main reference

Austen, Jane 1775-1817 **1**: 122, 125, 220; **2**: 104, 196, **333-384**

lists the featured author's entry in volumes 1, 2, 3, 5, or 6 of Feminism in Literature; *it also lists commentary on the featured author in other volumes of the set, which include topics associated with* Feminism in Literature. *Page references to substantial discussions of the author appear in boldface.*

The cross-references

See also AAYA 19; BRW 4; BRWC 1; BRWR 2; BYA 3; CD-BLB 1789-1832; DA; DA3; DAB; DAC; DAM MST, NOV; DLB 116; EXPN; LAIT 2; LATS 1; LMFS 1; NCLC 1, 13, 19, 33, 51, 81, 95, 119; NFS 1, 14, 18; TEA; WLC; WLIT 3; WYAS 1

list entries on the author in the following Gale biographical and literary sources:

AAL: Asian American Literature

AAYA: Authors & Artists for Young Adults

AFAW: African American Writers

AFW: African Writers

AITN: Authors in the News

AMW: American Writers

AMWR: American Writers Retrospective Supplement

AMWS: American Writers Supplement

ANW: American Nature Writers

AW: Ancient Writers

BEST: Bestsellers (quarterly, citations appear as Year: Issue number)

BG: The Beat Generation: A Gale Critical Companion

BLC: Black Literature Criticism

BLCS: Black Literature Criticism Supplement

BPFB: Beacham's Encyclopedia of Popular Fiction: Biography and Resources

BRW: British Writers

BRWS: British Writers Supplement

BW: Black Writers

BYA: Beacham's Guide to Literature for Young Adults

CA: Contemporary Authors

CAAS: Contemporary Authors Autobiography Series

CABS: Contemporary Authors Bibliographical Series

CAD: Contemporary American Dramatists

CANR: Contemporary Authors New Revision Series

CAP: Contemporary Authors Permanent Series

CBD: Contemporary British Dramatists

CCA: Contemporary Canadian Authors

CD: Contemporary Dramatists

CDALB: Concise Dictionary of American Literary Biography

CDALBS: Concise Dictionary of American Literary Biography Supplement

CDBLB: Concise Dictionary of British Literary Biography

CLC: Contemporary Literary Criticism

CLR: Children's Literature Review

CMLC: Classical and Medieval Literature Criticism

CMW: St. James Guide to Crime & Mystery Writers

CN: Contemporary Novelists

CP: Contemporary Poets

CPW: Contemporary Popular Writers

CSW: Contemporary Southern Writers

CWD: Contemporary Women Dramatists

CWP: Contemporary Women Poets

CWRI: St. James Guide to Children's Writers

CWW: Contemporary World Writers

DA: DISCovering Authors

DA3: DISCovering Authors 3.0

DAB: DISCovering Authors: British Edition

DAC: DISCovering Authors: Canadian Edition

DAM: DISCovering Authors: Modules

DRAM: Dramatists Module; *MST:* Most-Studied Authors Module;

MULT: Multicultural Authors Module; *NOV:* Novelists Module;

POET: Poets Module; *POP:* Popular Fiction and Genre Authors Module

DC: Drama Criticism

DFS: Drama for Students

DLB: Dictionary of Literary Biography

DLBD: Dictionary of Literary Biography Documentary Series

DLBY: Dictionary of Literary Biography Yearbook

DNFS: Literature of Developing Nations for Students

EFS: Epics for Students

EXPN: Exploring Novels

EXPP: Exploring Poetry

EXPS: Exploring Short Stories

EW: European Writers

FANT: St. James Guide to Fantasy Writers

FW: Feminist Writers

GFL: Guide to French Literature, Beginnings to 1789, 1798 to the Present

GLL: Gay and Lesbian Literature

HGG: St. James Guide to Horror, Ghost & Gothic Writers

HLC: Hispanic Literature Criticism

HLCS: Hispanic Literature Criticism Supplement

HR: Harlem Renaissance: A Gale Critical Companion

HW: Hispanic Writers

IDFW: International Dictionary of Films and Filmmakers: Writers and Production Artists

IDTP: International Dictionary of Theatre: Playwrights

LAIT: Literature and Its Times

LAW: Latin American Writers

JRDA: Junior DISCovering Authors

LC: Literature Criticism from 1400 to 1800

MAICYA: Major Authors and Illustrators for Children and Young Adults

MAICYA: Major Authors and Illustrators for Children and Young Adults Supplement

MAWW: Modern American Women Writers

MJW: Modern Japanese Writers

MTCW: Major 20th-Century Writers

NCFS: Nonfiction Classics for Students

NCLC: Nineteenth-Century Literature Criticism

NFS: Novels for Students

NNAL: Native North American Literature

PAB: Poets: American and British

PC: Poetry Criticism

PFS: Poetry for Students

RGAL: Reference Guide to American Literature

RGEL: Reference Guide to English Literature

RGSF: Reference Guide to Short Fiction

RGWL: Reference Guide to World Literature

RHW: Twentieth-Century Romance and Historical Writers

SAAS: Something about the Author Autobiography Series

SATA: Something about the Author

SFW: St. James Guide to Science Fiction Writers

SSC: Short Story Criticism

SSFS: Short Stories for Students

TCLC: Twentieth-Century Literary Criticism

TCWW: Twentieth-Century Western Writers

WCH: Writers for Children

WLC: World Literature Criticism, 1500 to the Present

WLCS: World Literature Criticism Supplement

WLIT: World Literature and Its Times

WP: World Poets

YABC: Yesterday's Authors of Books for Children

YAW: St. James Guide to Young Adult Writers

The Author Index lists all of the authors featured in the Feminism in Literature set. It includes references to the main author entries in volumes 1, 2, 3, 5, and 6; it also lists commentary on the featured author in other author entries and in other volumes of the set, which include topics associated with Feminism in Literature. Page references to author entries appear in boldface. The Author Index also includes birth and death dates, cross references between pseudonyms or name variants and actual names, and cross references to other Gale series in which the authors have appeared. A complete list of these sources is found facing the first page of the Author Index.

A

Akhmatova, Anna 1888-1966 **5: 1–38**
See also CA 19-20; 25-28R; CANR 35; CAP 1; CLC 11, 25, 64, 126; DA3; DAM POET; DLB 295; EW 10; EWL 3; MTCW 1, 2; PC 2, 55; RGWL 2, 3

Alcott, Louisa May 1832-1888 **2: 78, 147, 297–332**
See also AAYA 20; AMWS 1; BPFB 1; BYA 2; CDALB 1865-1917; CLR 1, 38; DA; DA3; DAB; DAC; DAM MST, NOV; DLB 1, 42, 79, 223, 239, 242; DLBD 14; FW; JRDA; LAIT 2; MAICYA 1, 2; NCLC 6, 58, 83; NFS 12; RGAL 4; SATA 100; SSC 27; TUS; WCH; WLCWYA; YABC 1; YAW

Allende, Isabel 1942- **5: 39–64**
See also AAYA 18; CA 125; 130; CANR 51, 74, 129; CDWLB 3; CLC 39, 57, 97, 170; CWW 2; DA3; DAM MULT, NOV; DLB 145; DNFS 1; EWL 3; FW; HLC 1; HW 1, 2; INT CA-130; LAIT 5; LAWS 1; LMFS 2; MTCW 1, 2; NCFS 1; NFS 6, 18; RGSF 2; RGWL 3; SSC 65; SSFS 11, 16; WLCS; WLIT 1

Angelou, Maya 1928- **5: 65–92**
See also AAYA 7, 20; AMWS 4; BLC 1; BPFB 1; BW 2, 3; BYA 2; CA 65-68; CANR 19, 42, 65, 111; CDALBS; CLC 12, 35, 64, 77, 155; CLR 53; CP 7; CPW; CSW; CWP; DA; DA3; DAB; DAC; DAM MST, MULT, POET, POP; DLB 38; EWL 3; EXPN; EXPP; LAIT 4; MAICYA 2; MAICYAS 1; MAWW; MTCW 1, 2; NCFS 2; NFS 2; PC 32; PFS 2, 3; RGAL 4; SATA 49, 136; WLCS; WYA; YAW

Atwood, Margaret (Eleanor) 1939- **5: 93–124**
See also AAYA 12, 47; AMWS 13; BEST 89:2; BPFB 1; CA 49-52; CANR 3, 24, 33, 59, 95; CLC 2, 3, 4, 8, 13, 15, 25, 44, 84, 135; CN 7; CP 7; CPW; CWP; DA; DA3; DAB; DAC; DAM MST, NOV, POET; DLB 53, 251; EWL 3; EXPN; FW; INT CANR-24; LAIT 5; MTCW 1, 2; NFS 4, 12, 13, 14; PC 8; PFS 7; RGSF 2; SATA 50; SSC 2, 46; SSFS 3, 13; TWA; WLC; WWE 1; YAW

Austen, Jane 1775-1817 **1: 122, 125, 220; 2: 104, 196, 333–384**
See also AAYA 19; BRW 4; BRWC 1; BRWR 2; BYA 3; CD-BLB 1789-1832; DA; DA3; DAB; DAC; DAM MST, NOV; DLB 116; EXPN; LAIT 2; LATS 1; LMFS 1; NCLC 1, 13, 19, 33, 51, 81, 95, 119; NFS 1, 14, 18; TEA; WLC; WLIT 3; WYAS 1

B

Beauvoir, Simone (Lucie Ernestine Marie Bertrand) de 1908-1986 **5: 125–174**
See also BPFB 1; CA 9-12R; 118; CANR 28, 61; CLC 1, 2, 4, 8,

The Title Index alphabetically lists the titles of works written by the authors featured in volumes 1, 2, 3, 5, and 6 of Feminism in Literature *and provides page numbers or page ranges where commentary on these titles can be found. English translations of foreign titles and variations of titles are cross referenced to the title under which a work was originally published. Titles of novels, dramas, nonfiction books, and poetry, short story, or essay collections are printed in italics; individual poems, short stories, and essays are printed in body type within quotation marks; page references to illustrations appear in italic.*

A

Abahn Sabana David (Duras) **5:** 368

"The Abortion" (Sexton) **6:** 352, 365

The Absentee (Edgeworth) **3:** 99, 110–111, 125

Ada (Stein) **6:** 406

Adam Bede (Eliot) **3:** 130–132, *158*

"The Addict" (Sexton) **6:** 352

"Address: First Women's Rights Convention" (Stanton) **3:** 428–430

"Address to the Atheist" (Wheatley) **1:** 477

"An Address to the Deist" (Wheatley) **1:** 519

Adieux: A Farewell to Sartre (Beauvoir)
    See *Le céremonie des adieus: Suivi de entretiens avac Jean-Paul Sartre*

"Advancing Luna—and Ida B. Wells" (Walker) **6:** 475–476, 480–481

"African Images" (Walker) **6:** 473

"After Death" (Rossetti) **3:** 276, 282–288

The Age of Innocence (Wharton) **6:** 495–497, 506–507, 509, *520*

Agnes of Sorrento (Stowe) **3:** 456–457

Alexander's Bridge (Cather) **5:** 213–215, 247

Alias Grace (Atwood) **5:** 101–103, 105–107

"Alicia and I Talking on Edna's Steps" (Cisneros) **5:** 272

"Alicia Who Sees Mice" (Cisneros) **5:** 272

"All God's Children Need Radios" (Sexton) **6:** 353–357

All God's Children Need Traveling Shoes (Angelou) **5:** 66–76

All My Pretty Ones (Sexton) **6:** 352, 365, 367, 369, 370

"All My Pretty Ones" (Sexton) **6:** 352, 368

All Said and Done (Beauvoir)
    See *Tout compte fait*

"A Allegory on Wimmen's Rights" (Holley) (sidebar) **3:** 212

De l'Allemagne (de Staël) **3:** 405–406, 423; **4:** 403–404

"Am I a Snob?" (Woolf) **6:** 567

L'amant (Duras) **3:** 362; **5:** 359–360, 364–366, 375

L'amante anglaise (Duras) **5:** 368

"Amaranth" (H. D.) **1:** 438; **5:** 336–339

"Amé, Amo, Amaré" (Cisneros) **5:** 266

"America" (Angelou) **5:** 66

American Appetites (Oates) **6:** 275–277, 279

"Amnesiac" (Plath) **6:** 312

André (Sand) **3:** 312

"The Angel at the Grave" (Wharton) **6:** 507

"Angel of Beach Houses and Picnics" (Sexton) **6:** 384

"Angel of Fire and Genitals" (Sexton) **6:** 384

"Angels of the Love Affair" (Sexton) **6:** 383–384

"Anguiano Religious Articles Rosaries Statues . . ." (Cisneros) **5:** 258

"Anna Who Was Mad" (Sexton) **6:** 364

Anne Sexton: A Self-Portrait in Letters (Sexton) **6:** 377

X

Y

The Subject Index includes the authors and titles that appear in the Author Index and the Title Index as well as the names of other authors and figures that are discussed in the Feminism in Literature *set. The Subject Index also lists literary terms and topics covered in the criticism, as well as in sidebars. The index provides page numbers or page ranges where subjects are discussed and is fully cross referenced. Page references to significant discussions of authors, titles, or subjects appear in boldface; page references to illustrations appear in italic.*

A

SUBJECT INDEX

secularism in 3: 437
society reflected in literature 2: 116–119
women Renaissance playwrights 1: 202–218
women writers in 18th century 1: 112–132
women writers in 19th century 2: 99–109
World War II and women writers 4: 261–270
English, Deirdre 2: 67–71; 5: 522
The English Woman's Journal (sidebar) 3: 294
Engraving 4: 87–88
Enlightenment 1: 524–525; 2: 40–42, 63
"Ennui" (Edgeworth) 3: 94, 99, 107–110
Ensler, Eve 4: 458–459
Enstad, Nan 4: 94–117
"Entering the Literary Market" (Mermin) 2: 129–140
Entre l'écriture (Cixous) 5: 286
"Envy" (H. D.) 5: 336–339
Ephron, Nora (sidebar) 6: 75
"Epigram" (H. D.) 5: 313
"An Epilogue To Mary, Queen of Scots" (Montagu) 1: 403–404
Epistemology of the Closet (Sedgwick) 4: 532–533
"An Epistle from a Lady in England, to a Gentleman at Avignon" (Tickell) 1: 401–402
"Epistle from Arthur Grey, the Footman after his Condemnation for attempting a Rape" (Montagu) 1: 403, 404
"Epistle from Mrs. Y[onge] to her Husband" (Montagu) 1: 396–397
The Epistle of Othea to Hector (Christine). *See L'epistre d'Othéa*
"An Epistle to Lord B—t" (Montagu) 1: 403–404
L'Epistre au dieu d'amours (Christine) 1: 282, 283, 288; (sidebar) 1: 290; 1: 293–296
Epistre de la prison de vie humaine (Christine) 1: 282, 283
L'epistre d'Othéa (Christine) 1: 282, 304
"Epitaph for the Race of Man" (Millay) 6: 180
Equal pay 4: 5–7, 50, 366–367
See also Wages and salaries
Equal Rights Amendment (ERA) 4: 408–411
abortion and 4: 418–419
in Alaska 4: 423
American Equal Rights Association 2: 249–250
athletics legislation and 4: 420
child custody legislation and 4: 420
in Colorado 4: 423

conflict in 1920s 4: 224–231
Eastman, Crystal 4: 18–19
feminist opposition to 4: 387–388
Fourteenth Amendment and 4: 417, 418
in Hawaii 4: 423
in Illinois 4: 419–421
inception 4: 18–19
labor unions and 4: 226–230
male criminal behavior and 4: 420–421
march on Washington, D.C. 4: *373*
marriage legislation and 4: 420
in Maryland 4: 423
in Massachusetts 4: 423
in Montana 4: 423
National Organization for Women 4: 410–411
National Women's Party 4: 18–19, 52, 224–230
in New Hampshire 4: 423
in New Mexico 4: 423–424
opposition to 4: 408, 418–422
in Pennsylvania 4: 424
race issue and 4: 18–19
ratification of, state-by-state 4: 417–425
in Utah 4: 421–422
in Virginia 4: 422–423
in Washington 4: 424
in Wyoming 4: 424
Equality. *See* Feminism, equality of the sexes
Equality League of Self-Supporting Women 4: 206–207, 206–211
ERA. *See* Equal Rights Amendment
ER-America 4: 409–410
Erdrich, Louise 5: *433*, 433–467
motherhood 5: 434–436
mythology (sidebar) 5: 452
National Book Critics Circle Award 5: 433
principal works 5: 434
sexuality in fiction 5: 445–449
transformational power of female characters 5: 443–449
women's relationships 5: 436–443
Erdrich, Louise on 5: 434–436
Erkkila, Betsy 1: 482–493, 494–495; 3: 65
"Eros" (H. D.) 1: 438; 5: 336–339
Eroticism
Bataille, G. 5: 408
Beauvoir, Simone de 5: 150–155
Broumas, Olga 4: 516–517
Chopin, Kate 3: 11–12
Stein, Gertrude 6: 400–401
in Victorian era 3: 11–12
See also Sexuality

"Der Essay als Form" (Adorno) 5: 296–297
Essay on Irish Bulls (Edgeworth) 3: 100–101, 104–106, 107, 111–112
An Essay on Mind, with Other Poems (Browning, E.) 2: 467
Essay on Slavery and Abolitionism (Stowe) 3: 475
"An Essay on the Noble Science of Self-Justification" (Edgeworth) 3: 94, 117
L'Eté 80 (Duras) 5: 384, 386
"The 'Eternal Eve' and 'The Newly Born Woman': Voices, Performance, and Marianne Moore's 'Marriage'" (Henderson) 6: 224–231
Ethan Frome (Wharton) 6: 495–497, 506–507; (sidebar) 6: 527
domesticity in 6: 525–528
gender roles in 6: 527–528
narrative voice in 6: 526
New England regionalism and 6: 522–528
The Ethics of Ambiguity (Beauvoir). *See Pour une morale de l'ambiguïté*
"Ethnic and Gender Identity in Zora Neal Hurston's *Their Eyes Were Watching God*" (Meisenhelder) 6: 102–107
Europe, suffrage movement in 2: 283–285; 4: 149–158
See also specific European countries
"Eurydice" (H. D.) 5: 327
Eva Luna (Allende) 5: 40, 44, 46, 48–55
Evans, Mary Ann. *See* Eliot, George
Evans, Richard 4: 148
Eve (biblical character) 1: 58–59
Evelina; or, A Young Lady's Entrance into the World (Burney, F.) 2: 503–505, 508–509, *517*
matriarchal power in 2: 516–526
naming as motif 2: 527–537
patriarchal power in 2: 511–526
"Even now that Care" (Sidney, M.) 1: 155–156
Evening (Akhmatova). *See Vecher*
"An Evening Praier" (Wheathill) 1: 105
"Every Morning" (Walker) 6: 473
"Everyday Use" (Walker) 6: 470, 482–488
Eviction protests 4: 43–44
Evolution, in Victorian era 2: 414–415
Excerpt from an untitled, unpublished essay (Browning, E.) (sidebar) 2: 477
Execution of Justice (Mann) 4: 480

GWATHMEY, GWENDOLYN B.

Gwathmey, Gwendolyn B. **3:** 208–218

"Gwendolyn Brooks" (Mullaney) (sidebar) **5:** 188

H

H. D. **3:** *313;* **4:** 287, 291–293; **5:** **313–357**
  Aldington, Richard and **5:** 334–335, 337, 339
  autobiographies **5:** 315–317, 329–330, 348–356
  Award of Merit Medal **5:** 314
  Bryher and **5:** 337
  compared to Dickinson, Emily **5:** 355
  in *Contemporary Literature* **5:** 319–322
  critical neglect of **5:** 317–333
  Durand, Lionel and **5:** 324–325
  feminist theory and (sidebar) **5:** 335
  Freud, Sigmund and **5:** 319–320
  Heydt, Erich and **5:** 349
  Imagism **5:** 313–314, 318, 328, 342
  lesbianism **5:** 337
  Levertov, Denise and **5:** 329
  male literary criticism of **5:** 317–326
  masochism **4:** 291–294
  mythology and **5:** 322–323, 327, 330–332, 347–356
  penis envy and **5:** 320, 323
  Pound, Ezra and **5:** 313, 318, 328, 349, 351
  principal works **5:** 315
  psychoanalysis and **5:** 314, 319–321
  Sappho and (sidebar) **1:** 433; **1:** 436–439; **5:** 334–341

"H. D. and Sappho: 'A Precious Inch of Palimpsest'" (Rohrbach) **5:** 334–342
"H. D. and the 'Blameless Physician'" (Holland) **5:** 319–321
"H. D. and the Poetics of 'Spiritual Realism'" (Riddel) **5:** 319–321
Hacker, Marilyn **6:** 185
Hagen, Lyman B. **5:** 87–91
Haggard, H. Rider **3:** 9
Hagiography **1:** 304–307
Hagood, Margaret Jarman **3:** 32–33
Haight, Amanda (sidebar) **5:** 23
"Hairs" (Cisneros) **5:** 258
Hakluyt, Richard **6:** 553–554

Halifax, George Savile, Marquis of **1:** 108–109, 141–142
Halkett, Anne **1:** 230
Hall, James **2:** 161
Hallett, Judith P. **1:** 44–48
Hamelton, Mary **2:** 10
Hamilton, Catherine J. **2:** 181
Hamilton, Cecily **4:** 137–138, 140
Hammett, Dashiell **6:** 63–64
Hammon, Jupiter (sidebar) **1:** 510
A Handfull of Holesome (though Homelie) Hearbs" (Wheathill) **1:** 104–108
The Handmaid's Tale (Atwood) **5:** 93–94, 101, 105–107, 108
Haney-Peritz, Janice **5:** 515
Hankins, Liz Porter (sidebar) **6:** 381
Hansberry, Lorraine **6:** *1,* **1–30**
  chronology of life **6:** 8–9
  Du Bois, W. E. B. and **6:** 15–16
  feminist movement and **6:** 10–14
  Nemiroff, Robert and **6:** 1, 2, 9
  New York Drama Critics Circle Award **6:** 1, 2, 8–9
  political activism of **6:** 11–14
  principal works **6:** 3
  on race issue **6:** 11–13
  radicalism and **6:** 11
  social change and **6:** 12–14
  socialism and **6:** 13
  Theatre of the Absurd **6:** 9–10
Hanson, Elizabeth **1:** 257–261
Happersett, Minor v. (1875) **2:** 246–247
"Happy Women" (Alcott) (sidebar) **2:** 310
Hardy, Thomas **2:** 132–133
Harlem **4:** 31–32
Harlem Renaissance **4:** 30–32
  African American playwrights **4:** 331–337
  women writers **4:** 248–251
  See also names of writers
Harmonium (H. D.) **5:** 327
Harper, Frances Ellen Watkins (sidebar) **2:** 13
  American Woman Suffrage Association and **2:** 268–269
  on slavery **2:** 49–50
  on suffrage **2:** 251
  themes in poetry **2:** 143–146
  on women in politics **2:** 12–15
Harper, Ida Husted **4:** 129
Harper's Bazaar **4:** 125
The Harp-Weaver and Other Poems (Millay) **6:** 179–180, 189, 192–193
"Harriet Beecher Stowe's Christian Feminism in *The Minister's Wooing:* A Precedent for Emily Dickinson" (Ramirez) **3:** 480–490

"Harriet Beecher Stowe's Interest in Sojourner Truth, Black Feminist" (Lebeden) (sidebar) **3:** 466
"Harriet Jacobs' *Incidents in the Life of a Slave Girl:* The Re-Definition of the Slave Narrative Genre" (Braxton) **3:** 224–228
Harris, Susan K. **2:** 120–129; **3:** 487
Harris v. McRae (1976) **4:** 419
Harrison, Jane **6:** 332
Hatton, Bessie **4:** 137–138
Haunted (Oates) **6:** 268
"The Haunted Chamber" (Chopin) **3:** 6–7
The Haunted Marsh (Sand). *See La mare au diable*
Hause, Steven C. **2:** 50–53
Hawaii **4:** 423
Haworth Village **2:** *417*
Hawthorne, Nathaniel **4:** 339; **5:** 514–515
Haywood, Eliza **1:** 120, 126
Hazards of Helen (Edison Company) **4:** 112–114
He and She (Crothers) **4:** 305–306, 320–322
"He fumbles at your Soul" (Dickinson) **3:** 54, 73
"He Wrote the History Book" (Moore) **6:** 212
Head above Water (Emecheta) **5:** 418
Head, Bessie **6:** *31,* **31–61**
  apartheid **6:** 31–32, 50
  autobiographies **6:** 32
  "great man" and **6:** 55–56
  patriarchy **6:** 53–55
  presence of evil (sidebar) **6:** 37
  principal works **6:** 32
  on South African feminism **6:** 38–59
  storytelling **6:** 51–53
  on women writers (sidebar) **6:** 49
Healey, Dorothy Ray **4:** 45
Heape, Walter **4:** 76, 80
Heard, Josephine **2:** 144, 145, 146
"The Heart Knoweth its Own Bitterness" (Rossetti) **3:** 295
The Heart of a Woman (Angelou) **5:** 66, 67–76, 83–91
Heartbreak (Dworkin) **5:** 406
"Heat" (H. D.) **5:** 317, 319
The Heat of the Day (Bowen) **4:** 279
"Heaven is not Closed" (Head) **6:** 52
Heaven Realiz'd (Davy) **1:** 253
"Heavy Women" (Plath) **6:** 310
Hecate **3:** 85–89
Hedges, Elaine **5:** 512
Hedrick, Joan D. **3:** 482–483, 487

SUBJECT INDEX

SUBJECT INDEX

SUBJECT INDEX

For Reference

Not to be taken from this room